Must
Grumble

Mustn't Grumble

The Autobiography

TERRY WOGAN

© Terry Wogan 2006

The right of Terry Wogan to be identified as the
author of this work has been asserted by him in accordance
with the Copyright, Designs and Patents Act 1988.

First published in hardback in Great Britain in 2006 by
Orion Books
an imprint of the Orion Publishing Group Ltd
Orion House, 5 Upper St Martin's Lane,
London WC2H 9EA

1 3 5 7 9 10 8 6 4 2

A CIP catalogue record for this book is available
from the British Library.

ISBN-13: 978 0 75287 438 8 (Hardback)
ISBN-10: 0 75287 438 1 (Hardback)
ISBN-13: 978 0 75287 615 3 (Export Trade Paperback)
ISBN-10: 0 75287 615 5 (Export Trade Paperback)

Typeset by Input Data Services Ltd, Frome

Printed in Great Britain by Clays Ltd, St Ives plc

The Orion Publishing Group's policy is to use papers that are
natural, renewable and recyclable and made from wood grown in sustainable
forests. The logging and manufacturing processes are expected to conform
to the environmental regulations of the country of origin.

Every effort has been made to fulfil requirements with regard to
reproducing copyright material. The author and publisher will
be glad to rectify any omissions at the earliest opportunity.

www.orionbooks.co.uk

For my son, Mark, and Luigi Bonomi, without whose drive and enthusiasm I might have spent most of the year just lying about enjoying myself . . . For my ever expanding family: Alan, Katherine, Henry, Susan, Kate, Freddie and the Queen of my heart, Helen, without whom none of it would be worth a tinker's curse . . .

Acknowledgements

Thanks will never be enough for the irreplaceable Jo Gurnett, the wonderful Amanda Harris and all at Orion, my dear friend Paul Walters, the 'team', Deadly, Boggy and Fran, Alan Boyd, Lesley Douglas and all the great people with whom it's been such a pleasure to work on the Coffin-Dodgers network, BBC Radio 2. Would that I could mention my loyal TOGs by name, but all I know is their pseudonyms; they're my joy, my constant friends and inspiration. I know that they won't mind if I single out the brilliant Mick Sturbs, whose inspired 'Janet and John' tales regularly reduce million to tears and mild hysteria, and have been instrumental in raising almost a million pounds for *Children in Need*.

Contents

Mustn't
Grumble

Prologue

This finely honed little tome, through which you are thumbing before returning it, unbought, to the bookstore shelf, is by way of what they call in Dublin a 'follier-uppier' to my last oeuvre, *Is It Me?* That went surprisingly well, except with a little old man in Belfast. I'd gone there, in the grand tradition of bookselling, as part of a tour of the UK, hawking my little book shamelessly from Reading to Cambridge, from Norwich to Bristol, from Bath to Belfast. Jolly crowds greeted me everywhere, some even bought the book. A man in Reading rushed to my side in the bookstore there, and asked me fervently to sign his prayerbook. I did so, with an even-handed flourish. He looked a little puzzled, smiling wanly as he left. The sales assistant was most sympathetic: 'He thought you were Terry Waite,' she explained.

For reasons that now escape me, unless it was the usual one of a boys' night out, two of my underlings from *Wake Up to Wogan*, an obscure radio show that need not detain us here, accompanied me to Northern Ireland for the book tour. Paul Walters, my producer, otherwise known as Dr Wallington P. de Wynter Courtney Claibourne Magillicuddy Walters, or, for short, 'Doctor Wally', was one, and hanging on, like grim death, to our coat tails, Alan Dedicoat, otherwise known as Deadly

Alancoat, the Wealdstone Weather-Boy, the Voice of the Balls, or, to keep it short, 'Deadly', was the other.

Naturally, Deadly was not allowed to travel with us across the Irish Sea, but magically materialised at our hotel outside Belfast. Walters and I had made the mistake of travelling with him once before, on British Midland. Appropriately enough, the Voice of the Balls was seated on the other side of the blue curtain which, in all aeroplanes, separates the well-to-do from the riff-raff. As Paul and I toasted each other in lukewarm champagne, on the other side of the curtain the unfortunates were being doled out dishwater and rolls wrapped in clingfilm. Deadly made the mistake of thinking the customer might choose the filling in his stale roll. 'Ham?' he mildly inquired. 'Have you got ham?' The impertinence of the request struck the ancient stewardess dumb, but when she found her voice, the whole plane heard it: ''Am?!'' she shrieked. ''Am? There's no 'am 'ere! That's on the other side of the curtain! There's cheese or tuna, which d'ya want? 'Am! Honestly, some people . . .'

The great Michael Devine had come up from Dublin to drive us around Belfast. Michael Devine is one of those rare beings, who, quietly and without fuss, can do anything, make all your dreams come true. This is a quiet-spoken, gentle Dublin man, who looks after all the celebrities and stars who come to Ireland. Julia Roberts stays in his little house in the Dublin suburbs when she craves anonymity. A few years ago when Julia wanted to be alone, Michael borrowed The Edge's (of U2) house on the banks of Lough Corrib in Galway, and looked after the superstar there. Julia gave him her apartment in New York when Ireland were playing in the World Cup in the Big Apple. When Julia got married a year or so ago, she flew Michael and his family to the

West Coast to attend the joyous nuptials. And guess who, *in loco parentis*, gave away the biggest female film star in the world? A Dublin taxi driver named Michael Devine. Whenever Ireland won the Eurovision, which it seemed to do every second year in the nineties, I'd get in touch with the great Michael. He catered for our every whim in Dublin, but his tour de force was the Big Night. Up to our hotel would roar a full police escort. Into Michael's limos we'd get and off we'd go, at breakneck speed, to the Point, where the Contest was being staged. Through the narrow streets and backroads of Dublin we'd scream, ignoring red lights and roundabouts, pedestrians, cyclists and other road-users, as first one and then another police motorcyclist roared ahead of us to hold back the traffic. You can keep your roller coaster and your Wall of Death – these were white-knuckle rides I will never forget. At the end of it, we were deposited at the front door of the Point, and Michael slipped the sergeant-in-charge a handful of crisp oncers. 'Right, lads,' said Michael, 'off you go to the Park.' And off the bikes would roar to the residence of the President of Ireland. I often wonder if she knew that we had first use of her escort. . .

As we travelled from one book-signing to another, Michael tried to explain the intricacies of Northern Ireland to the eejits from England.

'This is green,' he would say, 'a Republican, Nationalist area.'

'How do you know?' asked Deadly.

'You just do,' explained Michael, 'and this is an Orange street.'

'How do you know?'

Michael gave a sigh: 'You just do. A couple of streets over there, it's all Black.'

'Ah,' said Doctor Wally, 'like Brixton, in London.'

'No,' said Michael Devine, struggling to keep a pitying look off his face, 'Black Protestants.'

The Doctor and Deadly fell silent.

'That's a Catholic dog,' I said.

'How do you know?'

'I know from the look of it . . .'

It's very difficult to explain the religious differences that separate Northern Ireland to a secular Englishman, but trying to explain that you can tell a Nationalist from a Unionist, a Catholic from a Protestant just by looking at them is impossible. An Irish person, whether of Northerly or Southerly persuasion, knows immediately what you're talking about. My wife thought *I* was a Protestant when we first met. I had the look of one, she said. To think that that foolishness still prevails in certain parts of these islands makes you want to weep . . . And if you can't tell them apart by their looks, you can tell by their names, or how they spell them. Don't ask . . .

After two years without any contact with her family or friends, a young Irish girl returns home.

'B'jesus yer safe!' says her father. 'Thank the Lord – we were worried sick! Why didn't you contact us?! Why didn't you let us know you were OK? The last two years have been a nightmare.'

'Sit down, Da. There's something I have to tell you.'

He sits down and she continues, 'Da, I've become a prostitute.'

'You WHAT?! How could you?! How dare you . . .'

'Da, don't . . .'

'Whaddaymean, DON'T? I'll give you DON'T! What reaction did you expect?! And what are you doing here anyway?'

'I came here today to make amends. I have the deeds for me Ma to sign for a £450,000 detached property in County Cork; I've booked you both on a "round the world" cruise for six weeks whilst the removal men take all yer stuff from here and move it to the new place – I've even arranged for a private designer to come and talk to me Ma about how she wants it fitted out; I've bought a horse each for the two bairns and have paid for their tuition fees at the fancy girls' school in Dublin – only the best for me little sisters! And I've got me brother his very own pub in Templegate – he can run it as his own and get out of that rough Tinker-owned Clover place down the road – he can make his fortune. And for you, Da, just for you; here are the keys for the E-type Jaguar you always wanted . . .'

'What is it you said you'd become?'

'A prostitute, Da!'

'Oh that's fine – I thought you said a Protestant. Come and give your auld Da a hug!'

The funniest Eurovision incidents always happened in Ireland: hardly surprising in view of the ever-cheery nature of the inhabitants of my native place. Ronan Keating was one of the presenters about five years ago. He was, even then, a huge international star, as the lead singer of Boyzone, and certainly Ireland's most famous export and probably the best-known face in the country. After the show, we all repaired to a huge barn of a place in the University College Dublin grounds, for the usual, terrible, overcrowded, anti-climactic post-Eurovision party. Loyally enough, Ronan himself turned up. He didn't get in though. The woman on the door turned him away because he didn't have an invitation with him . . . It was the Irish, not the Australians who invented the 'tall poppy' syndrome. 'Sure, I knew his oul' fella.' Actually, I didn't, but my dear brother Brian knew Ronan Keating as a lad; his family lived nearby. In view of Brian's two stunning daughters, it's no surprise that Ronan and the local Lotharios hung around my brother's household quite a bit. Ronan always wanted to sing, to be a pop star, and one evening Brian offered him a word of good advice: 'Now listen, Ronan. Give up all this old pop-singing nonsense; it'll get you nowhere. Concentrate on your studies. Do your exams, and make something of yourself.' We fast-forwarded some years, and my brother and his old jalopy are held up in traffic near his home. A limousine with blacked-out windows slows down opposite Brian's car. The window slips noiselessly down, and Ronan Keating looks out: 'Ah, there you are, Mr Wogan! How're ya?' The brother winds down his creaky window: 'Ronan!' says Brian. 'Well – was I not right?' . . .

Michael decanted us at a bookshop where I was to sign a couple of hundred of my books, but it wasn't to be a public appearance, as I had already flung myself at the unfortunate denizens of Belfast at a public meeting the night before, and another bookstore that morning. Publishers get their money's worth. As I sat in a corner of the store, signing away good-oh, with the beginnings of repetitive strain injury nagging at my shoulder, a little man materialised at my side. He was about seventy, neatly dressed in quiet sports coat, slacks and suede shoes, and appropriately hatted. He had an umbrella over his arm, always a wise move in Ireland. He leaned over me. I smiled encouragingly.

'You're a lickspittle,' he said. No, he snarled it.

I watched him as he walked to the door, his every fibre quivering with rage. He turned.

'*A lickspittle!*' he shouted.

He exited, and walked off down the street, a nicely dressed, respectable, harmless old man. And one with 'hatred' in his heart. For me.

OK, I'm not Saint Anthony, and I understand that as soon as you stick your head above the parapet, somebody's going to want to knock your block off. Dislike I understand. The more some like what you do, on television or radio, the more will find you a pain in the proverbial. But *hatred*? Splenetic, fierce loathing? And 'lickspittle'? Old-fashioned, Edwardian, a preacher's curse. Only in Norn Iron. No. My mother was born there, in a British Army barracks. I love the place, as I love my Dublin, my Limerick. Some of my funniest correspondents to the Radio 2 morning extravaganza write to me from Ulster. 'The Crooked Man of Old Bangor Town', or as we know him 'Crooky'.

> *Spring has sprung, the week's begun*
> *Ready to be filled with Godfrey fun.*
> *Your other listener can fear no harm*
> *When surrounded by her bouncy charm.*
> *Since May's well out without a doubt*
> *She'll be casting many a fleecy clout.*
> *And make us privy to home-life facts*
> *Delighting chaps in dirty macs.*
> *With charming anecdotal quips*
> *About her bathroom and its drips.*
> *Tilers, plumbers, painters too*
> *She'll eagerly discuss with me and you.*
> *But since she acts so prim and proper*
> *Nobody's got the heart to stop her.*

Mustn't Grumble

For ever since the Beeb began
No totty's been toppier than our dear Fran.

Whether they love me, I would not presume to conjecture. As long as I keep to myself in Britain, I'm OK. The Irish, like the Scots, have always preferred 'the King across the water' . . .

1

I knew him when he was a young fella

⁓

'Let the tap run.' Nellie Nolan's watchword. My mother always had to leave the kitchen, in case one of the two Nellies would catch her smiling. The other Nellie was her eldest sister, whose misanthropic view of life my mother always found ridiculous and, usually, hilarious. As soon as we were out of earshot, my mother would explode into laughter.

'"Let the tap run, Nell." She says it every time she's offered a glass of water! Does she think everybody's an eejit except herself?'

In Ireland, in those days, everybody let the tap run before they had a glass of water. The popular notion was that it got the lead out. These days, it's a slang term for getting a move on, but in the hungry forties in Ireland, there wasn't a lot of trust in public utilities. There was the Gas Board, the Electricity Board, the Water Board, the Turf Board. Nothing to do with racing – for 'turf', read 'peat'. All of them had Gaelic names, and you couldn't get a job in any of them unless you were educated by the Christian Brothers and had had the native tongue beaten into you until you were senseless. For countless years, life in Ireland was hoisted on the ridiculous petard of an archaic language that nobody loved, and nobody, apart from a few native-speakers and those my mother called 'blood to the beak', craw-thumping politicians, ever spoke. Only those who love it speak it now; it's not a political football any more. Every so often, a Northern Irish Republican will drag the old language out to show that he's more Irish than the other side, but otherwise, certainly as far as the urban Southern Irish are concerned, Gaelic is with O'Donovan Rossa, in the grave.

I slipped into a calumny there, as far as the Irish are concerned: 'Southern' Ireland. Try saying that in Davy Byrnes or Nearys in Dublin, and you'll soon get your head bitten off. 'Eire' is another word that might get you into trouble, particularly if, like most English people, you pronounce it 'Ire', as in 'anger'. It'll certainly provoke that. For the 'Southern' Irish, their country is called 'Ireland', or, at a push, 'the Republic'. The vexatious bit on the top right-hand corner is termed 'Northern Ireland'. Recently, at a rather snobby do in London, an elegant woman with a slight Northern Irish twang asked where I came from, in 'Southern' Ireland. 'Limerick,' I said, 'in Ireland.' I'd been away too long and forgotten the old sensitivities, the real prejudice, and, yes, hatred, that bubbles just below the surface of the sad old problem. The lady bristled: 'Ireland? It's got at least four names!' I could have riposted that Northern Ireland has got at least four as well – Six Counties, Ulster, Northern and Great Britain – but, like most good comebacks, I didn't think of it in time, and anyway, the conversation had frozen over.

Nellie Nolan, a formidable battleship of a woman, never without a hat, was the bosom friend of my Auntie Nellie, who was in charge of curtains in Clerys: at the time, the only department store worthy of the name in Dublin. Clery, they used to say, was the original family name of Desirée Clary, who gave Napoleon all that trouble. That's the kind of thing they say in Ireland, and if you're a big enough eejit to believe it, then fair enoughski. The two Nellies, invariably clad in black, went everywhere together. These days, people would look knowingly at the two of them and speculate about the true nature of their friendship. Sorry and all that, but homosexuality did not exist in Ireland in the forties. Nor the fifties or sixties. There was no such thing. I never came across it once, in the classroom, in the showers, in the rugby scrum. I certainly never met it while clerking in the bank. I have a vague recollection of a priest grabbing me by the arm and telling me that I was his favourite, but the clearer memory is of the same priest trying to knock my hand off with a leather strap. One of my classmates once said to me: 'I love you in the manner of Gide,' but he laughed as he said it, and his nose was running at the time . . .

My dear Auntie May had a special friend as well, Enda Fitzgerald. Enda is one of those Irish names that can work for a man as well as a woman. I think Saint Enda was a man; perhaps there was a doubt about his sexual orientation, but probably not, for the reasons stated earlier. It was Bertie Wooster who said to his man, upon hearing the name of a newly christened child: 'There's some raw work done at the baptismal font, Jeeves.' Nowhere more so than in Ireland. Obscure saints come into their own: I know somebody saddled with the handle 'Berchmanns'. How do you fancy Fursey? Setanta? Oisin? Cornelius? There are families who zealously name their infants after foreign saints – Majella, Attracta – and at least one I know who named their four babies after the Portuguese children who claimed to witness the miracle at Fatima. The least dangerous of those was Carmencita. The baby in question went on to become the mayor of Dublin. Perhaps it's not a bad idea to give your child an extra hurdle to overcome. Now that I think of it, Terry swings both ways as well. Let's not even go there . . .

Auntie May and Enda, or Auntie Enda as I called her, were the antithesis of the two Nellies. They loved a laugh, and they smoked like chimneys. Together or apart they were two of a kind: loving, warm, and, like my mother, deeply committed to having a good jeer at anybody and everybody. Instead of coming to the church and the reception on the day Helen and I got married, Auntie Enda stayed in the little house in Drumcondra to look after my frail granny, Muds. We stopped, on our way from the church, to see them both. It was one of the last times I saw my Granny alive. And one of the last times I saw Auntie Enda. Auntie Enda's marriage came as a bolt from the blue. I thought she and Auntie May would soldier on together for ever. I've got a picture of Enda's wedding, sent to me by her niece. Have a look at it. The gang's all there. The two Nellies are on the left.

When he was on holidays, Michael Wogan wore a beret. When he was cycling back and forward, up and down the Ennis Road, back and forward over Sarsfield Bridge and round the back of O'Connell Street by the Franciscan church, to and from Leverette & Frye, victualler to the gentry, the horse-people, the remittance men and the middle-class wives of solicitors and dentists ('A half a pound of ham, Mr Wogan, that'll do us for the weekend'), the Da wore a cap. A beret, in the streets of Limerick, was an invitation to the abuse of corner-boys and the sniggering of bank clerks, cattle jobbers and other lousers.

Just to stop some well-meaning editor from sticking his or her quill in here, the word is 'louser' not 'loser', 'losser', 'tosser' or any other word with which the Anglo-Saxon ear may be more familiar. A 'louser' is essentially a Dublin form of expression, beloved of my father, to describe a ne'er-do-well, a sneak, a rotter. Politicians were lousers to a man, as were most policemen, a fair few priests, and anyone else who did not come up to my father's exacting moral standards. The kindest man who ever walked, he could forgive cheating, stealing, lying and, probably, manslaughter, but not if it became a habit. The curse of the Irish – legendary small-mindedness, craw-thumping, back-biting and downright treachery, were all the mark of the 'rotten louser' in my Da's book. He wasn't a great judge of character, and got let down more than once by people he had liked, and promoted; like the rest of us, he liked people who appeared to like him. I rarely give advice to my children, mainly because they are adults now and have more sense than me, but if there is a sage word left in my locker, it would be: 'Those who flatter you are not necessarily your friends, and those who give it to you straight, like it or not, are not necessarily your enemies.'

Anyway, Michael Wogan's beret. It was a brave and strange choice for such a conventional man in the strait-laced Ireland of the forties and fifties, where any deviation from the norm was looked upon as a sin, against either the faith, de Valera, or Holy Mother Ireland herself. The beret, like the cigar, the bow tie or any drink other than a pint of Guinness, was foreign, pretentious, an attempt to rise above your appointed station in life. Bettering yourself was not regarded as a virtue in the Ireland of my youth. Knowing your place was. And staying in it, that was the main thing. A beret would be regarded as a shout for notice, the last thing any self-respecting person would want. The greatest sin was vanity, in the absence of sex, which was, indeed, itself conspicuous by its absence, at least as far as Irish newspapers and the radio were concerned. Occasionally, an English Sunday newspaper would sneak in under the razor wire of censorship, and the scandalised talk in the snugs and parlours of Limerick would be of vicars and scout masters and London's naughty Square Mile. 'Never happen here, in Holy Catholic Ireland . . .'

Sex only reared its ugly head once a year in my home town, when Redemptorist preachers took over certain churches for a week to breathe fire and brimstone, promising eternal damnation in the fires of hell for even the most trivial of offences. You were toast for thousands of years for a venial sin such as lying or bad language; anything more serious – for instance, one of the seven 'deadly' sins: pride, covetousness, lust, anger, gluttony, envy or sloth – and you were a goner for all eternity: 'Think of it: when you burn your finger on the stove – that would not be a millionth part of the eternal agony you would suffer, every single second of every single day of eternity in the fires of hell!' This for eating too much, or fancying one of the girls from Laurel Hill convent. And people believed it. Some people still do. I wonder if the preacher from hell believed it himself? My father certainly didn't, and my mother's sense of humour wouldn't allow her to, either. There was always an element of schism and doubt in the Wogan household. Blind faith, and an unquestioning belief in the rantings of an apparently deranged priest, were just not a factor of everyday life in 18 Elm Park, Limerick.

So was my father's beret a cry for attention, a still, small shout of 'me, me, me'? No, the beret simply meant 'holiday'. He went to work in a cap, to Mass in a hat, and to the various seaside resorts we went to on family holidays in a beret. It was probably the only beret in Ireland. I never saw anyone else sporting one. Berets don't suit the Irish, and my father was no exception. He never looked right in it; it needed to be pulled forward and tilted at a rakish angle. His was pushed too far back on his head and gave him a boiled-egg look, particularly when he'd caught the sun. The beret is the least attractive head-covering known to man. Even the French have trouble with it. You never saw Maurice Chevalier or Charles Boyer in a beret, did you? And Gerard Depardieu? Don't make me laugh. Even in France nobody under eighty wears a beret, and even then I'm sure it's only worn by one of those little old actors employed by the French government to walk up and down the streets of deserted French towns with a baguette under their arm to give the illusion that there are actually people living there. They don't fool me – there's nobody at home in rural France. Those shutters never open, it's all a film set, and all those agricultural subsidies are being trousered by the boys in the sharp suits in the Elysée Palace. Isn't it extraordinary how we of the Outer Islands jeer Johnny Foreigner, and the French in particular? And at the same time live there in our hundreds of thousands, and flee there in our millions every summer?

My father, who had never been further afield than the Isle of Man, once visited France on a wine-tasting trip. This was after his brains and hard work had promoted him to the heady heights of general manager of Leverette & Frye, which subsequently became the Peter Dominic chain of wine shops, and a director of the distinguished wine and spirits merchants, Gilbeys. Loudenne was their Chateau on the Gironde, near Bordeaux, and the visit one of the highlights of the Da's life. On his return he talked about it incessantly, until the penny finally dropped that all this talk of fine food and delicious sauces was getting on my mother's nerves, a woman with no patience for cooking, whose idea of a sauce was either something you poured from a bottle, or a cube of something or other that you crumbled into hot water. What really got up my mother's nose, however, was 'the woman'. A paragon, apparently; a woman of surpassing beauty and charm, as skilled at the skillet as she was at the decanter, and whose sparkling repartee kept the entire company in fits. A passing reference to this combination of Joan of Arc and Catherine Deneuve might just have passed muster, but my dad was an innocent in the ways of women, and went on and on as the frost that was setting over our house threatened to become a glacier.

Mr Michael Thomas was not wise in the ways of women, but then, who is? Recently, when introducing the topic of 'Womanly Wiles: How to Combat Them Before Finally Giving In', on my admittedly too self-consciously intellectual radio programme, someone asked how best to counter the perennial feminine query: 'Does My Bum Look Big in This?'. Forty years of marriage had prepared me for just such a question. There is only one answer: 'No', delivered à la de Gaulle – resoundingly, positively, without a scintilla of doubt. Anything else – an aversion of the eyes, a flicker of the lids, a moistening of the lips, or, worst of all, a nanosecond's hesitation before replying – can only end in an inquisition to rival Torquemada at his best, inevitably ending with an exasperated 'I don't know why I bother!', a brisk turn of the heel, and the slamming of several doors. I received enough material from my listeners on this vital question to fill a slim volume. Indeed, I toyed with the idea of a thesis. Imagine me, with a doctorate!

Actually, you can. A couple of years ago, Professor Kevin Ryan astounded me with a letter, inviting me to accept an Honorary Doctorate of Letters at the University of Limerick. Would I? I'd have swum the Shannon for it. Those who followed my last adventure into autobiography will know that I had already swum in the Shannon at Corbally, where my great hero, Gordon Wood, had taught me to swim. In all truth, he wasn't much of a teacher, thinking that everyone was, like himself, built like Johnny Weissmuller and a natural athlete, so all a poor, half-grown, measly muscled young limb like myself would have to do would be to fling myself into the freezing river and thrash about like a young Mark Spitz. Gordon saved me from drowning several times; it was the least he could do, since he'd thrown me in in the first place.

When I think of how my two boys, Alan and Mark, learned to swim: underwater, in the Hilton hotel pool in Nicosia, Cyprus. The water warm, the teacher gentle and encouraging. And now I suppose you expect me to tell you that they grew up soft and unable to do more than paddle about in the shallow end, along the timeworn lines of, 'They don't know they're born,' and, 'It never did me any harm.' Well, they may not, and it didn't, but they're both better swimmers than me. Mark was the Maidenhead and District Champion. It must be said that neither could match my leg-thrash, but I could only keep that up for fifty metres. I'm much the same on a tennis court – you ask Dr Bev Daily, who used to play with me before our legs and backs gave out. Mind you, he'll claim the same electric pace over ten metres as I have myself, being also Celtic-bodied, with short legs and long trunk – a mesomorph from the Principality. The original Wogans came from there as well, which probably accounts for my thirty-inch inner leg and short arms. Incidentally, I find it reprehensible that jacket- and shirtmakers make their stuff with arms long enough for simians. How many gentlemen do we see these days with their knuckles brushing the ground? French rugby players excepted, of course . . .

Ah, rugby. I played the great game from the time I was eight when I moved to the gentle ministrations of the holy Jesuit Fathers at Crescent College. Crescent was a famous rugby school in Limerick, the very heartland, the soul, of Irish rugby. Everybody in Limerick who could raise a fist played rugby. Dockers, solicitors, doctors, cement factory and mill-workers, corner-boys, shopkeepers and small sons of grocery-store managers. Limerick was more like a Welsh town, where the only class that mattered was what you showed on the rugby field. Thomond Park, Limerick, was where I saw the Springboks play, the 'Afrikaanse' men as I heard them call themselves. I always loved language, and that one word has stayed with me, like 'appelkose', which the Da used to sell in his extraordinary Fortnum & Mason-type emporium on O'Connell Street, Limerick. He pronounced it 'appelkosay', but why wouldn't he? Lychees were always 'Lichees' to him. Later, when he retired, he would cross the road to the pub on Ballymun Avenue, Dublin, and order a 'Kronenburge'. Nobody corrects your pronunciation in Dublin; it's considered bad manners, and it is. Someone once corrected me on my pronunciation of 'salade niçoise', and I've never forgiven them. Here's another word to the wise: don't be a smart-ass if you know something; keep it to yourself. Wait until people ask you for your opinion.

A national newspaper once complimented me on my cleverness in not allowing people to know how clever I really was. Cracked it! I've fooled 'em by giving the impression of being more clever than I really am. I'm a product of an Irish education, a butterfly brain. I can trot out small bursts of Greek, Latin, Gaelic, German, Spanish and French without being fluent in any of them. I know the first couple of lines of any classic poem you care to name, and can throw in the telling Shakespearean quote whether called for or not. I know a lot of words, I find it easy to speak and write (although as you plough through this, you could easily point out that it's not that easy to read . . .). Maybe that *is* a definition of cleverness, but I don't think any of my teachers at the Salesian Convent or the Jesuits of Belvedere and Crescent Colleges would agree. A little above average, I think they'd say, and, mercifully, there's none of them alive to say more.

Cleverness comes in many forms, and is often confused with intelligence, but it's not the same thing. The former US President, Bill Clinton, an Oxford Scholar, is undoubtedly clever, but his social intelligence is that of a caveman. And for all his cleverness, history will show Ronald Reagan, forever lampooned here as a moronic B-movie actor, to have been the better president. I never met Ron, although I interviewed the elfin Nancy, but I saw Bill Clinton once, in a West End theatre. He was in a box beside the stalls, and the Americans in the audience spotted him early. At the interval, they swarmed around his box, mostly women, it must be said, simpering and squealing like teenagers. How is it that men who treat women badly seem to attract them like flies to a honey-pot? Anyway, the normally sedate interval became a maelstrom of female excitement, an American woman beside me returning to her seat, flushed: 'I got it! Bill Clinton's autograph! Imagine! Wow!' and other expressions of high transatlantic delight. All around me, the British remained motionless, scarcely deigning to look in the direction of Bill's box. I thought I caught the censorious clicking of a tongue . . . Maybe I'm being a bit hard on Clinton; I'm sure he could interact socially with the best of them. Charm, you could call it – I'm sure he has that in spades. So had dear old Ron. What Bill really lacked was sexual intelligence. His brains had a habit of drifting southwards in the presence of anything in a skirt.

I came to women late myself. Everybody did in my gang in Limerick, but I think I was particularly backward. The table football crowd that I mixed with in my early teens just didn't see girls. They weren't there. They didn't play our games, go to school with us, or talk about the same things. What did we talk about? I'm racking my brains here, and it's not all due to my admittedly declining powers, but I can't remember anything. I know we talked about football, about school, about our friends and foes, about films – but never about books, politics, the radio (I was an avid listener to the BBC Light Programme; they listened to Irish Radio, because their parents did). There was no television. What would today's teens talk about if there was no television? The one topic that I'm quite certain never came up was sex. We weren't shy or afraid of it, we just knew nothing about it. You'd be a long time waiting for the Jesuits to instruct us in it, and our parents had yet to come up with the goods.

As it turned out, mine never did, apart from a passing reference by my father to a 'secret sin' that flew in the face of God and His Holy Mother, and could leave a person mentally impaired. He probably felt he should say something in view of the fact that my bed sheets were standing up of their own accord every morning. We boys, lads, growing young men, never talked about it. There were the precocious ones, who talked in innuendos, and made sniggering references that I pretended to understand. I got the general gist, of course, but it never occurred to me that I would meet, talk and generally socialise with a girl on a one-to-one basis. My friend Billy came to his senses early, probably because he had a sister. I've always felt that fellows with sisters were that important step ahead. Sisters have friends, you see. Now that I think of it, I hadn't enough friends who had sisters – it obviously stunted my growth.

Billy was one of the few. His sister Mary was very pretty, and I think her mother thought that Mary and I might be friends, but Mary wasn't really interested in boys, and the whole business was over my head. Billy started to slip away from our little coterie. I saw him cycling into town early one evening. 'I'm going to the pictures,' he said with a knowing grin as he whizzed by. We remained fast friends, and still never talked about sex, nor bandied women's names about, but I knew who he was going to the pictures with. Not that I could understand why . . . Then Billy began to smoke. James didn't, and John didn't, and I didn't, but Billy had a wild streak. Cigarettes and women – the rocky road to hell. Billy began to affect an American twang, and then, one day, he took me aside to tell me he'd changed his name. 'Ned,' he said. 'That's what they call me now.' He'd never liked 'Billy' very much, and he had my sympathy; I'd never liked 'Terry'. He felt he had a right to call himself Ned – it was his name, Edmond, but it was also his father's, and his mother had called him by his second name, William, 'Billy', to avoid confusion.

Precisely the same thing as had happened as soon as Rose Wogan had got her firstborn home to 18 Elm Park. Michael's my name, but it was also my father's, so my second, Terence, became my real name, 'Terry'. I don't mind it now, but I'm still not crazy about it. It's always seemed on the effeminate side to me, and as soon as I got over here, it became 'Tel', which is even worse. I suppose if I'd stuck with Michael, it would be Mickey or 'Mick' by now, so I must be grateful for small mercies. Tom Lynch, the uncrowned king of Ireland's storytellers (which is saying something in a country where nobody shuts up), hates being called 'Tommy', but, like all of us, he has been called worse. As a young man with an uncontrollable mop of hair, he took to pulling on one of his sister's hairnets before he retired to his trundle bed of an evening, in an effort to look less like a hedgehog the following morning. His friends called round, his mother showed them up to his bedroom, and from then on he was known as 'Rosebud'. Tom Lynch's marvellous stories of his family life are something that he can tell much better than I can, but I've always been affected by his recounting of the evening he opened his front door to drink in the last of the setting sun over Dublin docks, and let rip with the ripe, resounding fart that he had been building nicely to all night. Even as he did, he heard the muffled groan of his sister, who had been kissing her boyfriend a fond goodnight on the other side of the door . . .

Many a casual liaison was cemented in the doorways of

Ireland. Where else were you going to get a 'coort'? That's the Irish version of 'court' – when couples started going out together on a regular basis, they were said to be 'coorting'. This could take the form of long walks together down dusty boreens, just holding hands, meeting every weekend at the 'ballrooms of romance', and cycling the ten miles home abreast or being asked round to the girlfriend's house for tea on a Sunday. This happened to me when I started coorting Helen, and it came as a particularly nasty shock when, after a tasty dish of rashers and egg and homemade cake to follow, we all went down on our knees for the family rosary, something that never happened in our house. Luckily, Helen's father, Tim, was a quick man with the responses, so we didn't dwell over the sorrowful mysteries, but I got to my feet shaken.

Then came an even more severe jar: the dreaded sing-song. Why the Irish feel that they have to burst into song and ruin a decent meal, or a reflective pint of stout, has always been a mystery to me. Nobody ever burst into song in my house, or they'd be looked on as a complete eejit. You can't walk into a pub in Ireland without some gobdaws launching into 'The Fields of Athenry' at the slightest gap in the conversation. The next thing, someone produces a banjo from their vest pocket, out comes a tin whistle, then a bodhran, and the whole evening's banjaxed. I think it's something the Irish feel they have to do, that somehow they're letting down those who fought and died for the Ould Country if they don't intone a dirge. It's called the 'craic', a word that fills me with horror. I'm an effete, urban Irishman. If anybody starts playing a banjo or an accordion around me or my family, we throw a couple of coppers in his hat. Unfortunately, good Dublin bourgeois common sense has long since gone out the window. They're all at it, even the 'new' Irish, the multimillionaire big players who seem to be coming out of the country on a production line. A wealthy young Englishwoman told me of how she abhors that frightening moment after dinner in an Irish house in Barbados, when the host says, 'Now then, Cosima, you'll give us a song.' And it's not as if anyone enjoys it. Take a look around the next time you're caught in the pub and they strike up 'The Irish Rover'. Unless he's past caring and inoculated by the demon drink, the soloist is performing self-consciously, as if his mother has forced him to do it. Everybody else is looking at everybody else and smiling rictus-like, desperately pretending to be having a good time, and wishing the row would stop and they could go back to their pint and a good old chinwag. It never does, of course, and in the end, with the drink dulling their wits and their inhibitions stunned, everybody joins in, and they stagger off home in the wee small hours thinking that they've had a good time. It's happened to me, and every time it does, I can't believe it . . .

I couldn't believe it when it happened in Helen's house, that first time. 'Helen will give us a song,' commanded her mother Ellie. I've always put Ellie together with my beloved granny, Muds, as the gentlest, sweetest-natured people I've ever met. Along with the present Mrs Wogan, of course. (That was a close one.) Beneath the almost angelic face and soft voice, though, Ellie had steel. She had to – Tim Joyce, at his worst, was a bully and a tyrant. (At his best, which he was during the long years of Ellie's illness, he was a saint, considerate, caring and loving. A man who had for years required his soup to be cooled on the window sill at one o'clock on the dot, back rashers only, and the skin to be taken from his chicken, became a cook, housekeeper and nurse without a murmur . . .) So, Helen obliged with a song, 'My Love is Like a Red, Red Rose'. Everybody seemed to enjoy it, but they weren't fooling me. I knew what was going on in their heads: exactly what was panicking me: 'Whose turn is it next? What the hell am I going to sing? I don't know the words to anything.' The fear that stalks the family sing-song: nobody knows the words. You think you know them as you sing along with the radio, but on your own, you're dead after the first couple of lines. My good friend and radio producer Paul Walters has twelve guitars, and a long nail on one of his thumbs for playing them, which he does in public only under threat of death, or at a Christmas carol concert. I've been there, when he's played for people who want a good old singalong knees-up.

'Play "The House of the Rising Sun"!'

'*There is a house in New Orleans, they call the Rising Sun — and it's been the ruin of many a poor boy, and Lord, I think I'm one . . . The . . . I . . . My . . .* I don't know any more . . . What about "Cathy's Clown"? Oh, no, I don't know that, either . . .'

And so the long night wears on. At least the Irish can finish a song, if they're still standing. Or maybe they only think they can. My reaction to the threat of being called upon to sing of a Sunday evening in Helen Joyce's front room in Rathmines, Dublin, was the coward's way out: I hid. Behind the sofa. I made myself invisible. I can do that. You have to, if you're shy, or have a low threshold of embarrassment. I can 'slip away' — ask Helen or any of my friends.

My mother always said, in later years, that I was a 'strange' child. Having dutifully played with my little friends in Elm Park, I would come through our front gate, closing it firmly behind

25

me in case any of them would follow. The child is father to the man. I've been like that all my life. They say that to travel is more important than to arrive, but for me, knowing when to leave is more important than either. And sooner, rather than later. I'll sneak away from anything – receptions, cocktail parties, weddings, dinners, even grand dos at Buck House. I've been privileged to attend there more than once at Her Majesty's request, but I feel that once I've bowed and exchanged a word or two of airy badinage with Their Majesties, they wouldn't be too distraught if they didn't see me again that evening; or possibly ever . . . So I sidle away through the madding crowd, and I'm tucked up in my bed while the marble halls are still echoing to their chatter.

A year or so ago, the Queen and Prince Philip hosted a grand levee at the Palace to celebrate the music industry's contribution to the public purse, and British life in general. I got there early and was given a special badge, then ushered through one great room after another, hung with magnificent paintings and imposs-ible chandeliers. Gilt was everywhere, on the walls, the ceilings, the chairs. It was overwhelming, and there I was, the boy from Limerick, alone in this grand room, awaiting the arrival of the Queen of England. What would Michael and Rose Wogan have said? Or Auntie May, Muds or Great-Aunt Maggie? Or all those teachers who thought I was OK, but would never amount to much? All those years in short trousers, on the crossbar of my father's bike, playing table football with myself on the floor of the front room in Elm Park – were they all leading up to this?

Then the other rooms started to fill up, but only one or two joined me in what I was beginning to think was my own personal salon. Shirley Bassey, Vera Lynn, Tim Rice, Tessa Jowell, Phil

Collins. In another room, Brian May from Queen and Eric Clapton were just a couple of the great names of British music who hadn't made the final cut. We lined up, Shirley Bassey knocking over an occasional table in her nervousness, and Her Majesty and Prince Philip entered, all welcoming smiles. They moved slowly down the line, exchanging pleasantries. When the Queen came to me, she told me what a wonderful musical afternoon she'd enjoyed, listening to the music of, among others, Katie Melua. She complimented me on my discovery of such a bright talent. I blushed modestly, but didn't have time to tell Her Majesty that the discovery was my producer Paul Walters', not mine, because with that charming smile of hers she had moved on to exchange airy badinage with the next in line, Phil Collins. Prince Philip asked me how I kept up my incessant babble every morning on the radio, and I said I was just babbling to myself, which seemed to satisfy him, and he followed the Queen, who by now was making her way to the door and the next bunch of hobbledehoys and ne'er-do-wells.

As she did so, Phil Collins whistled the five notes from *Close Encounters of the Third Kind*.

The Queen turned, still smiling, but puzzled.

'What was that?' she inquired.

Collins was speechless.

'He was calling ET, Ma'am,' I said, even as I said it wishing I'd kept my mouth shut.

'Ah,' said the Queen, nodding understandingly. They'd obviously warned her about the kinds of idiots she'd be meeting that evening.

As the door closed, Phil Collins turned to me, whining piteously. 'Why did I do that? What came over me?'

'The Royal Effect,' I answered sagely. 'You say the first thing that comes into your head, and you carry the memory of your foolishness with you to the grave.'

Then I slipped away into the night, as swiftly as I had come.

Speaking of Her Majesty, many years ago, when the world was young, a doddering old geezer would wheel his mobile commode into my radio studio and, unbidden, rattle off, in a wheezy baritone, the supposed highlights of his programme, which used to follow mine, like a wounded snake. Every week, I would cling to the forlorn hope that his wheels would come off, or the monkey-gland injections fail, but then came the dreadful news: in a moment of weakness, the Queen had given the old bloke a gong! I knew then that there'd be no getting rid of him, and in fact I was the first to crack, running off in desperation to television for nine years. And you'll never believe it, but he was still there when I came back . . .

On the day after Jimbo got his gong, he walked in virtually unaided, wheezing away, and pointed to the medal swinging against his chicken chest.

'It's the OBE!' he chortled, going into another paroxysm.

'Congratulations, Jimbo,' I snarled through gritted teeth.

'Yes, and do you know what she told me?'

'If you mean our beloved Queen . . .'

'Yes, she said she listens to our little chinwag, what about that?'

'Well,' I replied, with a hint of petulance, 'why didn't I get a gong as well?'

'Har-har,' he chuckled, bringing on another fit of coughing. 'Har! She says it's the part of *my* programme she enjoys best, har-har . . .'

How I didn't spit live on the air, I'll never know. The listeners, of course, who never knew any better, were impressed, and one old soldier who claimed to be a contemporary of Jimbo wrote in praise, 'Jimmy Young did sterling work in the war, and us chaps home from the Veldt on leave liked nothing better than to take a popsy to the old Alhambra in Leicester Square to see the old boy perform. His rendition of "The Boers Have Got My Daddy" will live long in the memory . . .'

It's but a hazy recollection, but I think it was dear Jim who gave me a piece of advice, shortly after he realised that I was not there solely as his warm-up man:

'Always remember, lad, don't bleed in front of the men.'

They don't make 'em like that any more.

2

I must be talking to myself . . .

~⚬~

Jimmy Young went on to get a knighthood, and then left us all in the lurch in what can only be described as a marked manner. It was sad that a great broadcaster, held in affection and respect by millions of his daily listeners, and widely respected, too, as a first-class political interviewer, particularly by Margaret Thatcher, should leave the BBC, to whom he had given such service, under a cloud. Jimmy was never an easy man. He had fought his way up the bill in variety in the forties and fifties, became one of the biggest names in British popular music with huge hits such as 'The Man from Laramie', and then, when pop music changed the Hit Parade, carved another career for himself as a disc jockey, presenter and, finally, an interviewer that every politician wanted to talk to. He'd come up the hard way, and was ever fierce in his defence of himself and his radio show. That show was everything to Jim. He lived it; his whole life revolved around it. Although his programme didn't start until midday, he would be in at half-eight in the morning, checking the papers, reading the research, formulating the questions for the interviews. With my incapacity for any kind of preparation or rehearsal, it made me tired just to look at him. Even his relationship with, and subsequent marriage to, his delightful and supportive Alisha didn't soften his commitment to his beloved show. But, as everybody in radio and television knows, what we do is not permanent and pensionable. We know it, but we don't believe it, and Jimmy Young was no exception.

I've always said that I hope I'll have enough sense to get off the beach before the tide comes in, but mark well that word 'hope'. Will I be able to walk away when my time has come? How will I know when my time has come? As I've said elsewhere, one of my defining virtues, or perhaps vices, is to leave; and sooner, rather than later. I walked away from *Come Dancing* in the early seventies (hard to believe that Bruce Forsyth would revitalise his career by walking back into the ballroom in his early seventies). I gave *Blankety Blank* the elbow when I felt the public had had enough (Les Dawson proved me wrong). *Auntie's Bloomers* had run its course when I took a powder (Lily Savage and Anne Robinson continued to flog the dead horse for several more years), but I didn't listen to my instinct for escape with *Wogan*, and was persuaded to continue with it for at least two years longer than I should have. You remember they were building that village, Eldorado, in Spain and needed to drag me out until it was finished.

Nobody was brave or honest enough to tell me, of course, which is exactly what happened to Jimmy Young. Them upstairs had made their decision to say goodbye to him long before they told him. He was in his eighties, he didn't fit with the new image of Radio 2, which was aiming for a younger market to take up the slack left by the continuing failure of Radio 1. Nobody explained it to Jim, nobody took him out to lunch to break it to him gently. Not, in fairness, that you could break that kind of thing gently to Jim, who was spiky, defensive, resistant to any change. Still, he did deserve better than the unholy mess that marked his departure. I think the suits were hoping that he'd just disappear without them saying anything. It remains one of the greatest faults of BBC management: nobody ever says anything to your face. Confrontation is a dirty word, much better to send a memo. The one for the chop is expected to read the signs, interpret the body language, read between the lines, then do the decent thing and fall on his sword.

Michael Aspel tells a poignant story about being wined and dined, flattered and cajoled, and then, after an excellent meal, convinced that all was well and that his contract was being renewed for another two years. Actually, he was being fired. Exceptions prove the rule, naturally, and the BBC exception was Alistair Milne, who'd come up through the ranks as an outstanding producer, full of brains and ability, to the heady heights of Director-General. This was a man who fired from the hip, exemplified by his dismissal of a Managing Director of Television. They'd spent the day together delightfully, at a shooting party. Several brace of game bird were in the boot, and, suffused in the warm glow induced by good claret and game pie, they sat together companionably in the back of their BBC car.

'A good day,' remarked Alistair.

'Wonderful,' agreed his managing director.

There was a pause, then Milne spoke again.

'Oh, by the way, boy. You're fired. Clear your desk by midday tomorrow.'

It may not be coincidental that Alistair Milne is the only Director-General of the BBC in living memory not to be ennobled . . .

Jimmy Young's and my morning exchanges became part of the warp and weft of our listeners' daily lives; as a lady from Benfleet, Joan Wells, put it, 'Whoever it was, was right, in saying the JY interlude is the best part of your show, but then it's also the best part of Jim's.' Dammit, Jimbo and I made the cover of the *Radio Times* on the strength of it, the ultimate accolade. Actually, the more important accolades are those that come unbidden from the likes of the aforementioned St Joan:

> *In the rarefied air of the BBC*
> *Two minds magnificent meet and mingle*
> *And the brilliant flashes of repartee*
> *Are sufficient to make one's toenails tingle.*
> *The shafts of conversational wit .*
> *The serendipitous well-turned phrase*
> *Illumine the world of the listening TWIT,*
> *And set his questioning mind ablaze.*

There's more in that vein, but I've never encouraged flattery nor sycophancy, believing that when friends communicate, it's usually on a level of gentle persiflage. Which is why I'm the subject of dog's abuse from my listeners, particularly when I appear on television: 'My old granddad recognised that suit you wore last night, it was his demob one, which Oxfam took away in pity in 1950. He says he left half-a-crown in the pocket. Hand it over.' And that's a particularly gentle example of what I've put up with over the long, weary years.

I don't know why it struck me that the Radio 1 jocks were doing it wrong when I arrived to relieve Jimmy Young in late 1969. All I could hear was people reading cards and letters in praise of themselves: 'Dear Tony, Dave, Pete, Rosko, we think your programme is fab!' Nearly forty years on, I still hear far too much of it: 'Keep up the good work.' 'We love your programme.' Sorry, but it's sickening. If they're heaping praise on your unworthy head, blush modestly by all means, but keep it to yourself.

Radio presenters get the mail they encourage; they get what they deserve. For all those years, the people who write to me know what I want to hear, and it's not gratitude nor platitude. I'm looking for wit, originality, a keen eye for the ridiculous, lateral thinking, a laugh at life. Ever since I took over the afternoon Radio 1 and 2 joint show in 1972, my listeners have obliged. As I've often said, without them and their marvellous letters I'd have sat there, mumchance, in front of the microphone for years on end. Nowadays, we rejoice in the flights of fancy of Mick Sturbs, Willie Gofar, Edina Cloud and the thousands of others who write under an assumed name, some of them blatant in their attempts to trip up an honest broadcaster about his daily toil: a Miss Tickles, first name Tess; the Bushes, Tudor and Anita; a Mr Hucker, first name Rudolph; Mr Peacock, first name Drew; and a charmer who claimed to live in 2 Effin Close, Far Corfe, Dorset. In olden times, in the seventies and early eighties, people were decent and unsuspecting enough to sign their real name, but the tone was always, as it has remained, the same – foolish but fun.

Lately, that fine upstanding young limb of a broadcaster, Richard Allinson, reminded me of how his mother had rejoiced in the late seventies to the daily reports of the man who took his budgie for a walk in Birmingham. Luckily his doings are recounted in an earlier tome of mine, *The Day Job*. Apparently, our man would stroll along every day as far as the Robin Hood roundabout, and stand there letting his feathered friend breathe in the health-giving fumes, causing many a dented bumper to the unsuspecting passing motorist. Denizens of Solihull and Hale Green wrote in their hundreds to tell me that they'd met the man who took his budgie for a walk, and not to make fun of him because he was a nice little man and they didn't want him upset. 'Anyway,' said one, 'we need something around here to make us famous. We do not have a park, a swimming bath, a nursery school, a place where you can get a cup of tea, or a Sainsbury's' . . . Many claimed to know who he was: a man from Wolverhampton thought that he might be his Uncle Andy, whom he had carelessly mislaid at the Spaghetti Junction Lupin Festival. Another identified him as Jim Smith, then manager of Birmingham City, claiming that the supporters had given Jim the bird, and that it was an albatross, not a budgie, and that he was doomed to stop one in three to tell his sad tale . . .

Then, from Wales, the Celtic fringe lifted, and another one made his escape, this time from Swansea. 'Taking a budgie for a walk is nothing, look you. I knew a man once who took his goldfish for a walk. It took years of training, starting by taking the fish out of the water for a few seconds, and gradually increasing the time. While this was going on, the water in the tank was gradually reduced, until the fish became totally "oxygenised". After all this effort, tragedy. One day, while they were crossing a bridge, the fish slipped its lead, fell into the river below, and was drowned.' You could see that coming, but there was no avoiding it. That's often the case, but half the fun is in the terrible inevitability of the punchline.

We've often whiled away the idle hour with punchlines alone: 'Don't push me past me mother's'; 'No, not a twelve-inch pianist', 'How much?' (the dreaded Preston joke). A day doesn't go by without recycling, 'Are you a doctor, then?' 'No, I never really bothered.' (Antony Aloysius St John Hancock), or the perennial, politically incorrect, 'Waiter, this chicken is rubbery.' 'Oh, thank you velly much.' Daily radio is about familiarity, repetition and even predictability. For instance, the only possible reaction to a good ol' country song is, 'Ee-hah, dang ma britches,' or, 'Set a spell and let your saddle cool.' A romantic ballad requires a simple postscript, such as, 'I am promised to another, you hussy.' A tear-jerker may be pre-empted by, 'Here's one to wring the withers,' and followed by, 'It's hard to beat a good laugh.' 'Give the woman in the bed more porther' is still acceptable after a burst of hooligan music, and anything vaguely Mexican or Latino must of necessity have 'Arriba, arriba, andale' as a postscript. These traditions have been handed down through the ages of *Wake Up to Wogan*, and it's much too late to change them now. Anyway, I can't think of anything new.

Nothing dates like humour, but although the names of my listeners have changed, the quality of their contributions seems permanent. Or maybe that's because we share the same sense of humour. Back in the seventies a man called Pat Carr of Norwich used to write to me, and his flights of fancy could only be compared to the magnificent Milligan. A report had come through of a Channel swimmer (why does nobody do that any more?) who, on landing at Dover, claimed to have slept part of the way from Cap Gris Nez. I cast some doubt on this, feeling that sleeping while swimming was a sovereign way to sink to the bottom like a stone. Carr wrote:

> Following the news of this fellow swimming the Channel while asleep, I decided to be the first person to swim the Channel while tied to a lamppost in Birmingham. Sadly, due to the swarms of greenfly sticking to the margarine covering my body, I was arrested on the M6 as a sexual pervert. This was a fatal blow to my chances, and I've had to postpone my attempt. Please send best wishes to my wife who is waiting for me in Calais with the key to the chains, and say 'Hurry home.'

Plus ça change. A couple of years ago, inflamed by the efforts of Richard Branson, my friend Willie Gofar attempted a solo balloon flight around the world from Peterborough. He was hampered by wishing to go home every night for his tea, requiring the balloon to be tethered to a convenient lamppost every evening at dusk, and further held back by having to keep one foot on the ground, in the interests of safety.

Anybody listening to *Wake Up to Wogan* in 1993, when I began my second incarnation as a daily radio presenter, would have been listening to an entirely different type of show than what passes for entertainment between 7.30 and 9.30 a.m. on Radio 2 these days. The content now is entirely different. The music has changed, to cater for a newer, younger, bigger audience. And it's not just me chunter any more; I can hardly get a word in edgeways for Doctor Wally's petulant mumbling, the Voice of the Balls' vibrant intonation, John Marsh's curmudgeonly moaning, and Fran Godfrey's incessant chirruping, 'Me, me, me.' What's really interesting is that nobody's noticed. The show is constantly changing, while remaining the same.

I've never believed in standing still; my whole professional career has been one of change, and, if you like, risk-taking. I left Ireland in 1969, having established myself there on radio and television, for a thirteen-week contract with BBC Radio. On the strength of that, I moved my little family of wife and son from the comfort of a charming bungalow overlooking Dublin Bay to a nondescript rented house miles from London. That Helen never complained is something I will never forget. The new BBC job didn't pay as much as I was making in Ireland, so I reversed what I had been doing between 1967 and 1969, and in 1970 started commuting the other way, from London to Dublin, to record the commercial radio shows I was still doing in Ireland. It never occurred to me that the BBC might not renew my contract, and I might have to crawl back to Ireland under cover of darkness. I'm not all that sure I'd take the same risk now . . .

The essence of any daily show, but particularly one in the sensitive early-morning hours, is, as I've said, familiarity. One of the reasons for my show's popularity is the fact that the public have been listening to me, man and boy, granny and grandchild, since Mafeking was relieved. I receive letters on a daily basis from fathers and mothers who tell me that they are now forcing their children to listen to me, just as their parents did. I know I should find that heartening, but somehow . . .

I've always maintained that you can't contrive at change. I'm still there, clinging to the wreckage, but I've learned from experience that the very idea that you think a cracker, the one that will run and run, is the one that dies without a murmur, while Paul Walters remarking that he had a special affection for rhubarb, and tinned, at that, produced an enormous listener reaction (punchline: 'We put custard on ours') that is revived every year by the Wakefield Rhubarb Festival. You can force rhubarb, but you can't force change on the listeners, you can only respond to their whims, their changing moods. You can suggest, even point, but you must let them lead the way. Nobody knows better than Paul and me the ever changing face of Britain, the new directions taken by public opinion. We'd have to be pretty thick not to know the way things are going, and what the public wants, with up to six hundred emails on our computer overnight, and another couple of hundred in the course of the programme.

The biggest factor in the show's changing face has been the email. In my previous incarnation on the Radio 2 morning show, 7.30 to 10, with added Jimmy Young from 1972 to 1984, all my incoming mail was by card or letter. I would initiate a topic, and it would take at least three or four days before I got a response. Or a listener would come up with a blinding notion, but again it would be several days before the rest of the gang caught the ball and ran with it. It was fine while the show was trundling on, but as you can imagine, there was something of a hiatus when I took a holiday. When I reinstated the whole rotten business in 1993, I asked for faxes, to get a more instant response, but within a year or so the email had taken over. Many of my listeners actually bought computers so that they could communicate with the programme on an instant basis. It is marvellous to have a reaction to the previous day awaiting you in the morning, and even better to have yourself shouted down within minutes of opening your mouth.

Dear Sir,

On the 50th anniversary of the famous *Waiting for Godot*, I, literary impresario Winston Flange, have managed to unearth this early 1st draft of the famous play by Samuel Buckett:

WAITING FOR WOGAN

VLADIMIR: Is he going to say something significant soon?

ESTRAGON: Who?

VLADIMIR: Wogan – I've been listening for weeks but nothing ever happens.

ESTRAGON: Yes, it's ridiculous – the whole show is completely meaningless.

VLADIMIR: Shall we switch off then?

(*They do not move. Silence.*)

ESTRAGON: There's nothing else to do. We'd better carry on listening.

And there the manuscript breaks off.

> *I remember way back around '78*
> *We tuned in to Radio 2*
> *To find Terry Wogan was 'Fighting the Flab'*
> *Though his waistline mysteriously grew.*

41

Our Terry went on to host Children in Need
And a chat show that ran on the telly,
It was usually all right but one terrible night
Anne Bancroft reduced him to jelly.

They made him a knight in 2005
For his services and his quips,
With his thick Irish brogue, this old Limerick rogue
Is now more English than fish and chips.

So here's to our Terry, the Master of TOGs,
Here's to him wherever he roams,
He's the king of the wits (with a silent T)
And the thinking man's Eamonn Holmes!

W.B. Yeast

Things were slower in days of yore, but my listener was just as sharp. The topics that exercised them are lost in the mists of time, but I can easily recall taking a deal of unfair comment on my interpretation of the Cornish Floral Dance. To refresh your jaded memory, an instrumental version of that grand old tune became a surprise hit in the mid-seventies by the Brighouse and Rastrick Brass Band, or as they were known to my crowd, the Faggots and Gastric. I started to intone along with the crowd-pleaser, remembering my father's relentless outpouring of the same thing every evening as he shaved.

Eventually, a chap called Mike Redway, who should have known better, produced my vocal version, and it, in turn, became a hit. The glow of pardonable pride that I feel when remembering this grand achievement is vitiated by the hurtful remarks I endure with strong resolve to this very day. While joining a long queue to enter Turkey for the Eurovision Song Contest the other year, out of the blue a voice with a distinct Cornish burr said, 'We'll never forgive you for what you did to the Floral Dance.' 'And the rest of the world will never forgive you for your damned pasties,' I retorted, and as Wodehouse put it, I meant it to wound. For heaven's sake, Cornwall, get over it! I suppose that I should be inured to it, for God knows I had my share of contumely at the time:

> *I thought I heard the curious tone*
> *Of Terry Wogan on the gramophone,*
> *Grunting here and groaning there,*
> *Devoid of timing, tone and flair,*
> *Trying to make the most of his chance*
> *With his hideous attempt at the Floral Dance*

As I've said before, I'm supposed to have no feelings.

Back then we spent some time on Knickers of World War Two, with particular reference to Messerschmitts, which came down without a fight; *Dallas*, and the endless machinations of J.R. and the Ewing family, whose fabulous wealth only afforded them one phone, wire coathangers and a small space in front of the garage where they held weddings and parties. 'Who killed J.R.?' took years off my life. Those who nowadays think that Dirty Den returning from the dead is a big deal should have been around when Bobby Ewing got out of the shower and it turned out that everything we'd been watching for the past six months had been a figment of his imagination . . .

Listeners liked word-play in those olden times. Paul McCartney's 'Mull of Kintyre' became 'Muck in the Byre', 'Mulligan's Tyres'. Kenny Rogers's 'Lucille' – '*You picked a fine time to leave me Lucille, with four hungry children and a crop in the field*' – provoked the unusual reaction that it was no wonder the woman left, with four hundred children and a croc in the field. Nana Mouskouri became Nana Moussaka, Shirley Bassey, Burly Chassis. And at Wimbledon, there was an American tennis player of pleasing and reputed playboy tendencies (it's all become a bit serious and intense these days) who rejoiced in the name of Vitas Gerulaitis. Now, what could you do with a name like that? Plenty, if you're one of mine:

Oh Vitas Gerulaitis
All in shining whites
With your shorts all nice and tightus
I could really fancy you
Oh Vitas Gerulaitis
I won't put up a fightus
Come round and have a bitus
And a mug of Aqua Vitus
And I'll get nicely Titus
Andronicus with you . . .

As I've said before, if you were paying attention, times change but some things remain the same: the weather and its ways has been a constant source of inspiration and vexation to the thinking listener. Sometime in the very early eighties, a misguided fan of our feathered friends remarked that, apart from a man's best friend being his duck, these gifted birds repaid observation in the matter of weather forecasting. Naturally, there was a comeback:

> *If your duck goes ballroom dancing*
> *Swallows you will soon be glancing*
> *But if your duck throws off his sequins*
> *A freak frost will do your beans in.*

And,

> *If your duck do bite you twice*
> *'Tis certain that there will be ice.*
> *If your duck stamp on your toe*
> *You can expect a fall of snow.*
> *If your duck do kick your nethers*
> *You probably won't care what the weathers.*

That was from someone who claimed to be named Bill Waddell, probably the first example of the use of the pseudonym on my show. I'll get *Time Team* on to it. Come on, Carenza . . .

All these talented contributors thought of themselves as TWITS, the forerunners of my beloved TOGs. Incidentally, it's indicative of Radio 2's ever growing new audience that I'm continually being asked, 'What's a TOG?' You young limb, a TOG is a Terry's Old Geezer or Gal. Don't ask me again, or I'll set your granny on you. A simple example of Togdom will suffice for now:

The clock radio came to life at 7.30 after a long weekend. Ah well! Back to work.

Leaping out of bed, I decided not to wake her majesty: let her have a lie in, she deserves it.

I hurriedly dressed, had a quick bowl of cornflakes, made the tea and toast, and just as the 8 o'clock (Dance with me) pips were sounding, I took a cup of tea in for her.

'Here you are my dear, a nice cup of tea to wake you up. I'm just off before the traffic gets too bad.'

She yawned and sleepily sat up. 'Thank you. It's a long time since you brought me tea in the morning.'

'Yes, well, can't stop, see you at dinner time.'

I was outside heading for the car when she opened the bedroom window. 'Where are you going?' she called.

'To work of course.' I could see what she was thinking – it was a Bank Holiday weekend, and she was still half asleep. She thought it was Monday but in fact the Bank Holiday was yesterday. 'Wake up, it's Tuesday today. Just listen to the radio and you'll see. Wogan's back,' I yelled.

I turned away with a wave, and as I opened the car door she shouted, 'But you don't go to work any more, you retired two years ago.'

Francis Frogbound

The TWITS were the Terry Wogan Is Tops Society, and, like TOGs, they seemed to evolve spontaneously, a Big Bang of Broadcasting. One minute they weren't there, the next they were all over the shop when I'd open a supermarket, wearing their TWITS T-shirts with my fizzog all over them. Unlike TOGs, who have a national convention every year and regional get-togethers whenever their trained senses tell them, the TWITS claimed to hold their AGM in a phone box somewhere in Wigan. Like TOGs, they had their own secret handshake and sign, and may well have carried something for taking the stones out of horses' hooves. But where the TOGs have been content to increase and multiply 'neath one proud banner with a single device, the TWITS lost control from an early stage. I regret that I didn't impose some sort of structure, a coven, even a committee, for it all got out of hand. Breakaway groups proliferated, TWIRL (Terry Wogan Is Really Lovely), TWADDLE (Terry Wogan And Daffy Duck Look Effeminate), TWINKLETOES (Terry Wogan Is Not Kinky Like Everyone Thinks Or Everyone Says). Then it got really personal: WIDOW (Wogan Is a Dreadful Old Woman) and WOGANS (Workshy, Overpaid, Grouser And Naggers Society). In the end, they all passed as the idle wind when I folded my tent and made my weary way to television. I like to think that somewhere, a small group of the intelligentsia still meet under the forbidden sign of IDIOTS (I Drool Incessantly Over Terry Society).

Of all the topics I've introduced to my demented pack, none have produced, before or since, such a reaction as my light-hearted comment on motorway cones. I lightly touched on the fact that although mile after mile of motorway lane was 'coned off', nary a soul was to be seen working on the other side of the little red and white blighters. The British public fell on the cones like ravening wolves. They sent me photographs of ones about their evil work — encircling holes in the road and telegraph poles, hijacking lorries, intimidating police cars. Everyone had a tale of cone horror, but of course, being TWITS, sanity broke through, and a young lady from Penarth produced a fragrant nosegay of children's rhymes:

> *Terry, Terry, quite contrary,*
> *How do the motorways grow?*
> *With tarmac grey*
> *And men who play*
> *With pretty cones all in a row.*

> *Oh where oh where have the workmen gone?*
> *Oh where oh where can they be?*
> *With a cone put here and a cone put there*
> *They must have gone to their tea.*

> *Pat-a-cone, pat-a-cone motorwayman,*
> *Close me a lane as fast as you can.*
> *Stop it and block it, and mark it with glee,*
> *Put out your cones, and go home to your tea.*

I still have people reminding me of the Days of the Cone – it seemed to leave an indelible mark on the unfortunate motorist's psyche. Of course, worse things have happened since, such as congestion charging and bus lanes, but the cones are still with us, miles and miles of them, without even a man leaning on a shovel on the other side.

A couple of years ago, in a rush of blood to the head, the Highways Agency put up signs here and there on motorways and A-roads. 'Cones Hotline' was the bold message, with a phone number the exasperated traveller might ring if it all got too much for him. It was too good an opportunity to miss, even for the beleaguered British motorist, bowed down by fuel prices, road taxes that didn't pay for roads, speed cameras and traffic jams. At last, an opportunity to let fly and tell them, whoever they were, where to get off . . . After a year, the Highways Agency withdrew the 'Cones Hotline'. It wasn't the success they had been hoping for, they said. Ninety-five per cent of the complaints they got were wrong. And did you know that the man who was responsible for the bus lane on the M4 (you know the one, it's on the outside lane, and has never seen a bus. Motorbikes and taxis, yes) was awarded an OBE for his fine work?

I suppose that I could go on jumping up and down in the same old rut about motorways, cones and the sad lot of the nation's abused majority, the motorists, but I suppose I've become infected by the classic phlegmatism of the British, and can't be bothered banging on, when I know that neither the Highways Authority nor the Government give a rattling damn, because they know that the 'silent majority' are not called that for nothing. It's minorities that change the world; if you belong to a minority, you're on the pig's back, as the Granny used to say. Look at the money that's spent on Radio 3 . . .

3

On the other hand, talk is cheap

⁓

In 1982 Michael Parkinson left his comfy chair as chat show host to the nation with the BBC, and joined David Frost, Robert Kee, Anna Ford and Angela Rippon, the Famous Five, in their ill-starred adventure into breakfast television. The BBC countered with their old reliable, Frank Bough, and Selina Scott, whom they had pinched from ITN. The Famous Five foundered, not because of Bough's cardigans, nor brisk professional style, but because of the sensational Scott, who always looked as if she had just fallen off the chaise longue after a night to remember. Nobody, before or since, has brought such languid sex appeal to early morning television. Thank goodness, otherwise I wouldn't have given you odds on the well-being of early-morning radio in Britain. Mercifully, Selina seemed to disappear into the mist. The thinking viewer still misses her of a morn, I'll be bound . . .

It is extraordinary how breakfast television has failed to make any real impact. Whenever I go to the States, and wake up of an early morn to my sunny-side-up with crispy Canadian bacon and coffee that tastes of nothing, I turn on the television, not the radio. Maybe that's because I'm in a hotel bedroom, but it's due, at least in part, to the way they do it in America. The mood is light, the presenters attractive, the pace smart, and it's all done with professional ease. There's none of the self-consciousness, the uncomfortable lack of rapport, of the British breakfast sofa. I suppose this criticism could be levelled more at GMTV than the BBC, but the Corporation's idea of breakfast news is flawed, in its turn, by not being quite sure whether it's supposed to be light-hearted or serious. So the attractive presenters are caught between two stools, and the interaction between them in the lighter moments seems forced, rather like John Humphrys' desperate attempts at badinage on Radio 4's *Today*.

Everything today is about image, not substance, and it was Tony Blair and new Labour's realisation, and masterly exploitation, of this fact that brought them to power and has kept them there. If any endeavour should realise this, it's television and radio. Yet how often do we see, on television news, reporters who look like unmade beds? Unattractive, badly dressed, unkempt reporters are a distraction, just as bad as the stumbling verbal incompetence we hear far too often from contributors to radio news. Ums and aahs, monotonous untutored tones, and even lisps. It reminds me of the little fellow I met, years ago, in Henry Street, Dublin.

'Hello, Sean,' says I.

'Hello yourthelf,' he said.

'Where are you off to?' I inquired.

'I'm off to the radio thathion,' he said, 'to do an audithion to be a newthreader.'

'Good man,' I said, 'good luck.'

'Ah thure, luck won't come intho it. I should geth ith, eathy.'

Some weeks later, I met him again.

'Ah there, Sean,' I asked, 'did you get the job?'

He looked a little downcast. 'Didn't geth ith,' he answered, 'too thmall' . . .

When I joined Radio Eireann, we had a month of training, every day of the week, in how to speak on the radio: intonation, pronunciation, inflection, emphasis and expression. And after all that, I was the only one who got a job at £17 3s 4d a week, rising by annual increments of pitiable amounts. I was poor, but I was a trained broadcaster. I'm sure that they used to do it that way in the BBC, but I'm equally sure they don't do it that way now. Journalism has become more important than presentation, and that's the wrong way round, lads – ask Tony Blair . . . On *Sky News*, I watched a reporter from the Fox Network in America deliver from a hurricane-lashed location a perfect interpretation of what was going on around her – no hesitation, no stumbling, no verbal crutches, no looking down at the script. It was straight-forward, succinct, without acting or affectation. Oh, and she was young and beautiful. That was the reason the Fox Network picked her, then they checked out her brains and journalistic ability, and found that they excelled even her beauty. Please don't tell me that British universities are not churning out just such young women and men in their thousands from media studies courses every year. So who's picking television news-hounds who look like bag ladies and tramps? Don't tell me that it can't be easy to look your best if you're 'embedded'. Or on a rain-lashed promontory in Caithness. What's the cameraman there for, if not to tell you that your hair is sticking up at the back, your nose is running, your anorak is cheap and nasty, and you look like the wrath of God?

So Parky left the chat show (or 'prat show', as it's called in Holland) leaving the unfortunate viewing public to darkness, and to me. The Saturday night talk spot was mine, the producer Marcus Plantin, whom I'd worked with first when he was assisting the great (in every sense of the word) Stewart Morris, and with whom I soldiered through the muck and bullets of *Blankety Blank*. Though the memories are hazy, I think I enjoyed it, and the critics and reviewers were kind. Robin Day came on as a guest, and was his usual blustering self, but told me how much better I was than Michael Parkinson. I put the blessed Parky's name in full there, just to show that we're pals, and I know his first name. One of the more hurtful, yet perceptive, letters I received lately was one that pointed out the oddity that those whom the British public revere and love are known universally by their first names: Cilla, Elton, Ant and Dec, John, George, Paul and Ringo. Those in the public eye that they hold in little regard, not to mention disgust, they know by their surnames: Hitler, Crippen, Chirac, every prime minister and football manager since Churchill and Ramsey, Mussolini, de Gaulle and, dammit, Wogan. And – sorry, Mike – Parkinson!

Robin Day's compliment wasn't worth tuppence, as I found out a couple of years later when, in a fit of pique over his wages from the BBC for politically pontificating, he fulminated like a gas boiler when some minion wound him up by telling him how much *I* was earning with my far less important, and even trivial, chattering. Robin, who rightly saw himself as the British political inquisitor par excellence, had earlier become as a coiled spring when he heard what his equivalent on US television, Dan Rather, was trousering. Robin could not contain himself, bursting into print and dragging my name all over the papers with him. At the time I was on holiday with the family, and when I returned, Michael Grade (the head honcho for one brief shining hour, before he left in a marked manner when he found that John Birt had the power to second-guess him), insisted that Day should come on *Wogan* so that we could have a proper dust-up for the public's delectation.

I didn't like the idea, and I was right. The late lamented Sir Robin had spent most of his life bullying, blustering and shouting opponents down, and I was no match for him. When the show was over, he was sweetness and light itself, introducing me to his son. Light entertainment always pays more than news-based shows; bigger audiences will always bring higher rewards. They should have paid the old curmudgeon more – he was an actor, an entertainer to his fingertips. He would be pleased, and probably jealous, that his tradition of dogged, aggressive hectoring of the great and the good is being carried on today by John Humphrys and Jeremy Paxman, two right Dobermanns, their bite as bad as their bark, and socially two of the most civilised, urbane gentlemen you could meet.

Elsewhere, I've said that chat show hosts are never remembered by their triumphs, but by their disasters. After eight to nine years of relentless chatter, live, three nights a week at peak time, all *Wogan* will ever be remembered for will be George Best, drunk as a skunk. Possibly Anne Bancroft, for her dumb act.

The producer of *Wogan*, my friend the late, and sadly missed,

Peter Estall, kept a record of my infamous interview with Anne Bancroft. A model of its kind, it should be preserved in a vault in the deepest recesses of the Haunted Doughnut, to be brought out only when some presenter who has enjoyed success on a gardening programme or a 'reality' show thinks that the time is ripe for a chat show. I began the Nightmare of Shepherds Bush by asking the lady about her meeting with royalty at her film premiere the night before:

WOGAN: Did you get to exchange words with any members of royalty?

BANCROFT: I did.

WOGAN: Didn't speak until you were spoken to, I hope?

BANCROFT: I don't remember.

WOGAN: I had the pleasure of interviewing your husband, Mel Brooks, about four years ago. He told me that I had to talk to you.

BANCROFT: Why?

WOGAN: Because he said that you're his inspiration.

BANCROFT: That's not true.

WOGAN: Is he a help to you?

BANCROFT: No. We barely see each other, to tell you the truth.

WOGAN: That's not good, is it?

BANCROFT: Well, yes it is.

WOGAN: In your new film *84 Charing Cross Road* you swap letters with Anthony Hopkins, but you don't meet him. He's in London and you're in New York. You acted separately – how did you do that?

BANCROFT: What do you mean, how?

WOGAN: It must be difficult.

BANCROFT: It's a lot easier than this.

WOGAN: Didn't Mel Brooks give you *84 Charing Cross Road* as a birthday present?

BANCROFT: That's a pack of lies.

WOGAN: Why do you hate this kind of interview so much? Is it me?

BANCROFT: Probably.

WOGAN: Do you do this kind of thing in the States?

BANCROFT: No.

WOGAN: Are you glad you did this?

BANCROFT: No.

WOGAN: Thank you, Anne Bancroft . . .

And Michael Parkinson thinks he had a hard time with Meg Ryan . . .

Over the years I've tried to excuse her extraordinary, unprofessional behaviour, but I'm not going to bother any more, having read what her husband, Mel Brooks, had to say about it. He said that she was furious that we had used a sexy still from *The Graduate* to spice up the programme. Since the movie was about the seduction of a young man by an older woman, and Bancroft spent much of it in bra and pants in the bedroom, I think I'll pass on that excuse, and put it down charitably to a bad day at the office for a fine actress.

Paradoxically, I've always felt that the best, most spontaneous interview I ever conducted was with the brilliant Mel Brooks on my old Saturday night show. It was verbal ping-pong, and I loved it, although it's probably true that the public's enjoyment of something is in inverse proportion to the presenter's. So what I'll be remembered for will be Georgie and Annie. Parkinson will never escape the memory of that blasted Emu, the late Russell Harty for Grace Jones's slap in the face, Richard Whiteley (I miss him yet) for the ferret attached to his finger. My own personal favourite is not a disaster at all, but a *Tomorrow's World* piece in black and white, by Raymond Baxter. A new and exciting invention that would revolutionise the music world, he proclaimed – the compact disc! And its greatest asset was its durability: he threw it on the ground, he smeared jam on it, he had a tractor roll over it, and still it played! Several centuries on, I play compact discs every day on the radio, and know from sad experience that if you as much as graze the surface with a fingermark, the damned thing won't play . . .

The Saturday evening Wogan show had its frissons too: I mind well Raquel Welch getting into a right two-and-eight about something. I've a vague recollection that she wanted to be taken seriously, not all that easy in view of her previous form in a fur bikini in some prehistoric romp. I do recall her telling me that she was married to a renaissance man. She and Leonardo da Vinci parted soon afterwards . . . And I will always remember the pleased expression on the face of Chevy Chase, then a big American comedian turned movie star. Whenever I asked him a question, he would smile benevolently and wink roguishly at the studio audience, but not a word came from his lips. Obviously that was enough to reduce American audiences to helpless hilarity, but our lot were bemused. I think he may well have thought he had delivered himself of a blinder, it just didn't get past his teeth. Another of that ilk was the great rock and roll pianist hell-raiser, Jerry Lee Lewis. He, too, gave me the silent treatment, while leaving me with the indelible impression, by his merry smile, that he thought that he had delivered a lightning riposte.

The mildest question would set certain people off in a strop. Neil Kinnock threw a wobbly for no particular reason that I could discover on the Saturday night show, Michael Heseltine stormed off after a *Wogan*, letting the producer have a mouthful as he went his patrician way. Heseltine always bore himself like a patrician, although didn't some Tory grandee dismiss him because 'he had to buy his own furniture'? Vanessa Redgrave, unsurprisingly, just got up in the middle of a show and left. Bored, I suppose. Some I would have preferred to leave or not turn up, if it was their intention to sit there like stuffed dummies. I'm bound to say this only happened occasionally, and usually with American film stars whose eyes had already glazed over in make-up. I never decided whether this was preferable to American film stars on whom whatever they were taking had the opposite effect. There are few things more disconcerting than an interviewee doing handsprings in the middle of a conversation.

Then, in 1988 began my great American adventure. A charming Californian named David Simon, who was minding Mickey's interests for Walt Disney in Britain, rang me up and asked me to lunch. He said that he'd been watching *Wogan*, and thought that I'd be the very man to do a similar thing for Walt and his boys in the States. Calming my natural excitement at the prospect of breaking through in the Mother of All Televisions, I agreed to talk about it. And talk about it we certainly did: high-flying executives rushed to my side from Burbank, Hollywood, and we talked the talk, while they indulged themselves in what is known in the States as 'fine dining', followed by port, cognac and cigars. Eventually, the vexed subject of money came up, and there seemed to be plenty on offer, with a five-year contract and ten per cent of the net profit. This latter incentive didn't seem to me all that rosy, not having come up the Shannon on the last lily, and knowing that these endeavours usually show a net loss for the taxman, after the tea ladies, grips and best boys have been paid. A small percentage of the gross would suit me better, I said, and we agreed to talk further when I visited the States later that year.

As luck, and the late Peter Estall, my producer, would have it, we were already scheduled for a whole week of *Wogan in Hollywood*. Off we popped to sunny Sunset Boulevard, bringing Helen, and Jo Gurnett, my friend and manager, in case there was any chance of fisticuffs. It was idyllic. I lounged about the pool of the St James Hotel, high in the Hollywood hills, looking down on the smog-enshrouded city of Los Angeles. Then, of an early evening, to the television studios, where before a studio audience who hadn't the smallest notion who the guy with the funny accent was, I recorded two shows a night. An American audience would applaud a fly crawling up the wall if instructed, but such was the strength of the line-up of guests, they didn't need the likes of some Limey to keep their hands warm. Bob Hope, Cyd Charisse, James Caan, the Golden Girls, Dom de Luise, denizens of *Dallas* and *Dynasty*, Harrison Ford made it worth the trip in terms of star names, although Harrison Ford, charming man that he is, delivered most of his replies from behind his hand, being one of the shyest people that I've ever interviewed. Not a fault that you could ever level at Bob Hope, who insisted on whatever he was selling being mentioned in the first ten seconds, and when we'd finished the recording, took over the studio to record a charity appeal, a deal he'd cut as a condition to doing the show. No flies on Bob.

The television shows went well, the Disney people came to

watch, we went out to dinner to bond. It was pleasant enough, but noticeable that the same executives who had indulged them-selves in the port, cognac and cigars in London were remarkable for their abstemiousness on their home turf, in front of their colleagues. Eight of us round the table, sharing the bottle of wine . . . It might have stayed that way if Jo Gurnett hadn't said in a loud voice, 'I suppose a second bottle of wine is out of the question?' Mind you, it's true to say that they don't give it a lash in LA in the same wholehearted manner that we're used to when pulling on the old nosebag. Helen and Jo went out to lunch there, and when the wine captain ('I'm only doing this while waiting to produce my own movie, which is in development') asked them their desire in the way of booze, Helen said, 'We'll have a bottle of Chardonnay'.

The honest fellow nearly passed away. 'A bottle?'

'A bottle,' replied herself, calmly, 'chilled as you like.'

Helen swears that the entire kitchen staff came to gape at the two hussies as the news spread around the restaurant like wild-fire. The outrage continued when the two ladies then ordered a hearty meal, instead of a green salad and omelette made only with the white of egg.

It all came to a head over brunch in the Beverly Hills Hotel. Helen and I made our way through the tasteful grounds, over a little bridge that spanned a charming small lake, on which swam a stately swan. An overdressed flunky led us to the table where the Disney folk were sitting. One of them said, 'Did you see the swan?' and Helen and I knew from that moment that the Great American Dream was never to be. We didn't tell them that swans were pretty familiar to us, or that waiters in epaulettes and brocade didn't impress. Instead, we ordered a Kir Royale each, which was our mistake, because the drink on the set brunch was a Mimosa. Our hosts, recovering from the body-blow to their expenses nicely, began to tell me of their plans for me: 'Let me just run this by you . . .' Helen says it's the only time in all the years she's had to sit around a table with me that I appeared to be getting smaller. I felt it myself – a terrible, heavy weight of stultifying boredom dragging me beneath the table. Eventually the painful ordeal looked like coming to an end, when the waiter ('I'm not really a waiter, I'm just doing this while an idea I have in development comes through') asked our preference for coffee or tea. Somebody said, 'I'll have a decaffeinated camomile tea,' and Helen and I were on the next plane out of there.

The previous American outing with the *Wogan* crew had been a couple of years earlier, when *Dynasty* ('Dienasty', or even 'Dysentery', to my discerning listener) was pulling in the viewers. *Dynasty* had followed *Dallas* as a homely, ongoing tale of another family of American folk, as rich as Croesus, and lords of all they surveyed in Denver, Colorado. Their palatial home was much grander than Southfork, with sweeping staircases, marble halls and candlelit dinners. The Carringtons never left their orange juice and scrambled eggs behind at breakfast, they power-breakfasted in the corridors, or dining rooms, of power. Nobody ever held a wedding or a party in the drive in front of the garage, like those honky Ewings. They had a chauffeur as well, who, if I remember, put himself about a bit among the female members of the Carrington clan. Otherwise, the show was a carbon copy of *Dallas*. Same treachery, backstabbing, family feuds. People were shafted in every sense of the word, right, left and centre in every episode. The characters were

identical to the Ewings and their acolytes, as well. There was
Blake Carrington, a steely-haired mixture of Daddy Ewing and
J.R., Lucy the Poison Dwarf had her equivalent, various sons,
relatives and lovers circled the action, the only difference being
a lack of ten-gallon hats. Sue Ellen and Pammy were the
undoubted forerunners of Linda Evans and Joan Collins, who
were ever at each other's throats, and who invented 'bling'
before Posh Spice could pout. To watch those two ladies at it
hammer and tongs, all cleavage, shoulder pads and skintight
dresses with no visible panty-line, was a weekly treat, and
although it never achieved quite the dizzy heights of *Dallas* at its
peak, *Dynasty* was not so dusty.

The main reason for the similarity of the two shows, apart
from the obvious television rule of beating a good idea to death,
was that they were both the brainchild and creature of the
producer Aaron Spelling. Aaron was a crowd-pleaser whom the
success of *Dallas* had put right at the top of the Hollywood food
chain, and a firm believer in the philosophy of 'If You've Got It
Flaunt It'. Every year, he would bring down thousands of tons
of snow from the mountains to carpet his lawns in seasonal style
for Christmas, and every Christmas morning hide little trinkets
in the snow, like Cartier watches and Tiffany bracelets, for his
children to find. He even had his entire house lifted and moved
around, so that it would catch the sun in the morning. 'What a
man!' I hear you cry. Well, yes, unless you were relying on him
and his production team to deliver on their promises.

Dinner with the Carringtons was the big idea cooked up by my
feisty producer, Frances Whittaker – a Christmas special, with
the entire Carrington gang gathered round the festive board,
exchanging airy badinage with me over the drumsticks, sprouts

and stuffing. Helen and I stayed in the eccentric Chateau Marmont Hotel along with Kevin Lygo (then a humble researcher, now Director of Programmes at Channel 4, and I'm sure, destined for even greater things), Jon Plowman (producer, who went on to trail clouds of glory with *Absolutely Fabulous*) and the redoubtable Frances, who never left her room or put down the phone for the entire stay, desperately trying to piece together the shards of a good idea smashed to smithereens by people who, having promised the earth and dragged us all the way to the West Coast of America, couldn't, or couldn't be bothered, delivering. We got bits and pieces, chats in various locations with the main players; I walked down the staircase of the Carrington mansion. It was OK when it was all edited together – just a series of interviews interwoven – but it was a far cry from the advertised *Christmas with the Carringtons*, and there wasn't much festive cheer when it transmitted. The press lies in wait for those whom they think have had an easy ride, and this was their chance. They panned the thing, and I hate to say it, but they were right. Old Aaron Spelling hasn't exactly set the world alight since then. The curse of the Wogans . . .

The late Peter Estall simply loved the States. Any excuse and my *Wogan* producer, who took over after Frances Whittaker had left for pastures new in 1990, was off to LA and the Big Apple. He decided that we should cover the opening in New York of an exciting new restaurant, Planet Hollywood. A poor enough excuse for a trip across the Pond, but this restaurant had Sylvester Stallone, Arnold Schwarzenegger and Bruce Willis as its investors, and they were turning up to add to the glitter, glamour and publicity of the big night.

It had been a rush to get the restaurant up and running for

the opening gala, but with typical American get-up-and-go, there it was, ablaze with lights, Hollywood memorabilia, stars, wannabes, hamburgers and fries. And, mercy me, unlike the unfortunate *Dynasty* debacle, the three major backers were there, and willing to sit down together and talk with me like regular guys. At the time, these were the three most macho, hottest males on the planet, so it was a scoop. Except that I never liked interviewing anyone away from our little grey home in the West, the Shepherds Bush Empire theatre. I missed the audience and their feedback, but mainly the fact that it wasn't 'live'. A talk show is a little thing, cheap television for the audience that it delivers. Apart from the famous faces, surely its only real attraction is the frisson of fear, the thrill of the unexpected when things go wrong, personalities clash or someone or other throws a hissy fit. Talk shows should be unpolished, unedited, with their shirt tails hanging out. I've been on talk shows where deeply uninteresting guests have been allowed to maunder on for thirty minutes or more, in the desperate hope of getting at least five minutes of interesting chat. 'Live' keeps everyone on their toes, but mainly the host . . .

So, the Three Big Bears of the Silver Screen came in to Planet Hollywood and chatted freely, but the most interesting part was before the interview started, when Sly and Arnie engaged in a spirited discussion on how to maximise their pecs.

The sad fact about talk shows is that some of the people who come on them have nothing to say. They'll talk about their movie, their book, their music, but beyond that, zip. Why should they divulge anything about the things we'd really like to know about: their personal lives, beliefs, convictions, relationships, politics? A Paxman, a Humphrys, a dear old Day might bully and incite them to indiscretion, but it wouldn't be much of a series after the word got out to the other stars, their managers and publicity people. After about six weeks, mine host with the incisive questions would be talking to himself. Mrs Merton had a burst of chat show notoriety in the nineties, but in the end ran out of people willing to be the butt of her tart tongue, particularly as it was impossible to have a go back at an ostensibly kindly, old, grey-haired lady. It was a brilliant concept of Caroline Aherne's, but I'm sure that she knew that it wasn't built to last. Alan Yentob plucked Clive Anderson out of his comfortable niche on Channel 4 and tried to make him a major chat show host on a big boy's channel, BBC 1. But what works for a niche audience doesn't necessarily play for the majority, a lesson the BBC has been slow to learn. The energy and obvious talent of Johnnie Vaughan has yet to find a suitable vehicle on BBC, and, at least at the time of writing, Graham Norton, another lured from his wildly successful minority slot by the promise of mass popularity, appears to be still in search of the Grail.

These are all talented people who've enjoyed great success in a narrow context, and talent's not so thick on the ground that you can blame a Head of Light Entertainment or a Controller of Programmes for trying them on a bigger stage. It just doesn't appear to work too often. Except in the case of the brilliant Jonathan Ross, who seems to have made his brand of bad language, doubtful jokes and generally offensive behaviour acceptable to the public at large. Why? Because they can see beyond the Big Act. The same public that hangs on every episode of *EastEnders*, and loves *I'm a Celebrity, Get Me Out of Here!*, is perceptive enough to recognise the qualities it admires in its presenters in Jonathan: humour, wit, warmth and, behind all the fast talk, a man whose family is more important than anything else.

If you're going to make it big on the box, you need a Mr or Ms Big rooting for you. You can have all the talent in the world, and a diligent agent knocking on every door on your behalf, but if someone up there in the corridors of power doesn't take a smack to you, you could be hawking yourself around for ever. I've always said that anybody in our game who fancies that their success is due to their good looks and talent is due for a big fall. Luck – that's what really counts, and anybody who forgets it is a fool.

I have been inordinately lucky with the people who've found something in me that was worth a shot: my wife, of course, without whom it wouldn't have happened (and even if it had, it wouldn't have been any good without her anyway); Denis Meehan, who took me from behind a bank teller's counter in Dublin and stuck me in front of a microphone; Mark White, who rewound a back-to-front tape from some unknown gobdaw in Ireland, and gave him a show on the BBC Light Programme; Barrie Edgar, who persisted with me on *Come Dancing*, even though I didn't smoke a pipe like Peter West and himself; Jimmy Gilbert, who saw something in *A Song for Europe* that was enough for him to give me *Blankety Blank*; Bill Cotton, who thought I was good enough for Saturday nights, and then three nights a week. Michael Parkinson might never have returned to the glories of his BBC chat if it hadn't been for Peter Salmon, newly appointed Controller and a big fan of Mike's. Peter was keen enough on Gaby Roslin, too, to give her her own show, but, at least as far as Noel Edmonds was concerned, Salmon was his nemesis. Which is the other side of the coin: if somebody up there *doesn't* like you, it doesn't matter what the public think, you're for the outer darkness.

A few years ago, two young producers, Angela Ferreira and Paul Smith, had the bright idea of exploiting the popularity of *Wake Up to Wogan* on the radio by making it into a daily mid-morning television show, *Wogan's Web*. Like the radio show, the idea was to keep it loose and fun, with my producer, Paul Walters, collating the emails live on the air, and generally putting himself about in a friendly, handsome manner. He bought a half-dozen new shirts on the strength of it. We had a team of Old Gals answering the phones, marshalled by a young lady so pretty she had to be known as 'Bag of Spanners'. The Voice of the Balls weighed in fruitily, there were guests, contributors, and it was fun. The cameraman, the sound guys, the crew all loved it. So did the public – it grabbed thirty per cent of the audience almost from the start. Not that it got much past the start. After a couple of weeks of success and public approval, it got reduced to three mornings, and then two, and then – zero. You see, a new Head of Daytime had taken over, and she wanted the slot for her friend and new discovery, Vanessa Feltz. The Feltz show didn't last long either, but they didn't ask *Wogan's Web* back. They tell me that the lady who made the decision has never forgiven me for her mistake . . .

When David Liddiment, trailing clouds of glory from Granada TV, took over as Controller of BBC 1, he immediately commissioned a series called *Wogan's Ireland*, which I think you will have read enough of in my first mighty work of auto-biography, *Is It Me?*. If, like many a discerning reader, you missed that, don't trouble yourself. *Wogan's Ireland* never set the turf ablaze, but it was a pleasant enough meander round the Four

Green Fields. I wonder if that poor man who went around County Cavan in his car every night, painting yellow circles around the potholes that are such a feature of that fine county, is still at it, still being arrested for his pains, and still being ignored by the County Council? Liddiment was quite keen to bring me back on a more regular basis on BBC Television, but somebody was standing in the way. This was hinted to me more than once by various producers, but the somebody was all sweetness and light whenever our paths crossed. David Liddiment arranged dinners and lunches between myself and the somebody, and pleasant social occasions they were, with nobody saying anything of any consequence whatsoever. Nothing came of them, David eventually moved elsewhere in television, and, when last I looked, was the Director of the National Theatre. The somebody was still there in the upper reaches of the BBC when last I looked there, a great survivor cast in Teflon.

Maybe my suspicions had no grounds, but after all these years in the business, I cleave to Thoreau's maxim: 'Some circumstantial evidence can be very strong, particularly when you find a trout in the milk . . .'

4

The moving target

I'm proud of *Wogan*. We did it live, at peak viewing time, for three nights every week for almost nine years, with viewing audiences that they'd die for, these days.

Never mind that it was the agents, managers and their clients, the stars, who dictated terms, which is why we were forced to fly to Cannes for Madonna, Nashville for Dolly Parton and the other junkets I've described, as well as the dreaded satellite interchanges. Most of the time, it really worked. I'd say three nights a week of star-studded chatter would be impossible to sustain in the new millennium, and a nightly show, such as Jay Leno conducts on US television from Hollywood, well-nigh impossible in Britain. The growth of the *Entertainment Tonight*-type show and promotional interviews which are shown on satellite and cable television around the world would seem to have devalued the whole concept of the 'star' interview. It will go on as long as there are movies, plays and books to be sold, but hardly more than once a week as far as British television is concerned.

The beauty of radio is that you can interview who you like, when you like and where you like, and nobody's going to know the difference. You can be halfway up Croagh Patrick on your annual pilgrimage, or potholing in the Pitcairn Islands, but nobody's expecting a picture. You may sound like you're trapped inside a corrugated iron biscuit box, but the listener makes allowance, even if the engineer in London is biting lumps out of his control desk. I've come through loud and clear myself from many a foreign field: in the seventies, Radio 2 was overly keen on the 'outside broadcast', and I found myself at half-past seven on a Bank Holiday morning, microphone in hand, by a deserted funfair on the promenade at Great Yarmouth. It hadn't occurred to my producer, Derek Mills, that the thing didn't open until 10 a.m., coincidentally just when my programme finished. It's not easy talking to yourself on a deserted promenade with only the screaming of the gulls and the crashing of the waves on the shingles for company.

It happened again when we visited Jersey, probably to cover the Battle of the Flowers (you've got to hand it to Radio 2 – a parade of flowers and floats, in sound only. Lord Reith must have been saluting in his grave). My job was to kick the day off – and so I did, once again to the sound of seagulls and surf, on a deserted beach. For reasons that escape me, Aubrey Singer, then Managing Director of BBC Radio, and David Hatch, Controller of Radio 2, accompanied the good Derek Mills and myself to Jersey, and before I started my monologue to the lonely sea and the sky, we all breakfasted together. Dear Derek Mills is no longer with us, but David Hatch still reminds me of the poignant moment when Aubrey said to Derek, 'Pass the honey, will you?'

Derek did as he was bid, with an ingratiating smile.

Aubrey Singer hardly looked up from his toast. 'This is marmalade,' he barked. 'You're fired.'

For a couple of terrible moments, we all watched the colour drain from my producer's face. The Managing Director buttered his toast, looked up slowly, and, upon seeing Derek's stricken look, burst into laughter. It took me the whole day to persuade Derek that it was just old Aubrey's waggish way, and he didn't mean it . . .

I mind well when the bold Aubrey, having been promoted from MD Radio to MD Television, held a celebratory dinner at Broadcasting House. The table undulated like a snake, so that nobody would feel that they were below the salt. Many were the heads of departments who rose to their feet, extolling Singer's Herculean efforts on behalf of radio, and I particularly remember the Head of Radio Drama, Ronnie Mason's, impassioned plea: 'Don't forget about us, Aubrey! Don't forget us!' Aubrey Singer smiled enigmatically, delivered himself of some encouraging words, and the following day moved his desk across London to the Television Centre and forgot about radio. It's understandable, but BBC Radio and BBC Television have never really got on. The radio thinks of itself as the senior service, the bearer of the flame, the upholder of the principles of public service broadcasting, and television is simply not aware of radio's existence. Radio people are dismissive of their counterparts on BBC Television as overpaid and shallow, and the people in White City couldn't care less because they know that television is for the up-and-coming, and radio's for the been-and-gone . . .

I could never understand why we took off on those radio away-days. It seemed to me that by leaving the studio and wandering off into the wide blue yonder, we were leaving our audience behind, abandoning the warmth and familiarity of our, and their, daily routine, and substituting something alien. No letters or faxes, none of the usual contumely and badinage, just seagulls, the sea and bad-tempered holidaymakers who had been dragged to the beach at all hours of the morning by their children. Derek Mills maintained stoutly that it was good for the network, giving us a presence and a sense of our reality to the listeners we met, and talked to, as we made our way around Britain's holiday resorts. It also enabled him to curry favour with old and young alike by giving away Radio 2 pens. We're not talking bagfuls here: Derek was a BBC man of the old school – good husbandry was the watchword. The pens were eked out, almost grudgingly, one at a time, to local dignitaries, or members of the public who had spoken nicely into the microphone. They were BBC pens, and Derek guarded them like his own. Meanwhile, the beat went on: we saw Bridlington and were suitably braced, Mousehole, and Penzance, where the largest pasty in all Christendom fell to the floor and covered the outside broadcast van and all its inhabitants from head to toe in potatoes, turnips and mince . . . And then we went to Singapore.

What the justification was for Derek and me to hop aboard Concorde for its inaugural flight to Singapore, I'm not sure, but I put aside my reservations about outside broadcasts and off we went into the ionosphere. I reported into various programmes as we made our supersonic flight halfway round the world in about six hours. I reported from Dubai ('It's hot here, Jimmy, I can tell you. No, I can't see any camels. I'm in the airport lounge.

Fancy any duty-free perfume?'), then, next stop Singapore. We had three hours there before Concorde turned around and went home. I reported from Singapore ('It's hot here, John, I can tell you. No, I can't tell you about the market in Bugis Street. I'm lying down in my hotel room'). Fifteen minutes at the Shangri-La Hotel, quick cocktail round the pool, back to the airport. I noticed that the side of the plane bearing the logo 'Singapore Airlines' was gleaming. The other side, which said 'British Airways', was still dusty from its outward journey. Some hours later, back in Blighty, I made my final report. ('Well, no, I didn't see much. You can't with Concorde, it's too quick.')

In the early eighties a fresh-faced young limb of a producer called Paul Walters took my helm, and we've been firm friends ever since. He's been producing *Wake Up to Wogan* for over ten years now, and is proving impossible to dislodge. In those early days he was bearded like the pard, but otherwise he was the same laconic, languid, charming eejit that he is today. He likes to get out and about in God's green air when he gets the chance, as well. He accompanies Ken Bruce and me to all the Eurovision Song Contests, and we've blazed a trail to Nashville, British Columbia, Crewe and an oil platform in the North Sea. That was the first trip we took together, out there in the Forties field. I bedded down for the night in one of the oil-workers' bunks, and even as I rose for my early-morning show he got into the bed after his night shift. It made for a fascinating programme, but it wasn't until last year, when he was the worse for drink, that Walters admitted to me that *he* didn't have a hot-bunk turnover on the oil platform all those years ago. He, being the producer, and me a mere hobbledehoy, the oil company had given him a cabin of his own . . . (And this a good ten years after

I had fought my groundbreaking battle to travel first class on British Rail to *Come Dancing* locations. Hitherto, the producer travelled first class, the talent only travelling second class because the railway had abandoned third class. Now that I think of it, I always got the bedroom at the back on all those trips . . .)

Paul Walters has laboured under many a pseudonym since he started to work (work? what am I saying?) with me. He quickly became known as 'Pauly', and then Poorly, the sickly producer, and nowadays the TOGs call him everything from Phil to Reg to Eric. He answers to all, like one of Pavlov's dogs, and particularly to Doctor Wallington De Wynter Magillicuddy Walters, although, as he readily admits, he's not a *real* doctor ('Never really bothered'). As you may be aware, if you're a regular listener, I'm a doctor myself, having been awarded an honorary doctorate by the splendid University that graces my home town of Limerick. Dr Wally and I greet each other civilly in the studio as medical men might in the operating theatre each morning.

'Morning, doctor.'

'Morning, doctor.'

A brief roundelay of well-worn medical badinage ensues.

'Pop up on the couch'

'This may smart.'

'Leave your clothes over there beside mine.'

And, 'Oh, doctor, what are you going to do with that?'

'I'm going to open a window . . .' and we're ready to begin another day of unrestrained, unrehearsed, unprofessional, unbelievable numptyness.

The boy Walters and I and other members of our team have flung our nets far and wide, from Nashville to Crewe, taking in

British Columbia on the way. Twice to Nashville, actually, for the Country Music Association Awards. Nashville – the buckle on the Bible Belt – has got a church on every corner, miraculous guitar-players in every bar, and the best spare ribs you ever did eat in the South Street Rib Shack. And I was cream-crackered from the moment I arrived until the moment we left. The six-hour time difference meant that I started my live show at 1.30 in the morning, so the day's routine went as follows: breakfast at ten, then a gentle stroll down Music Row, with a seemingly endless stream of great musicians and singers in every bar, all of them playing for beer and a sandwich, and waiting for their Big Break. Then lunch, and a recorded interview with stars who beat the huge odds and made the breakthrough: Reba MacIntyre, Chely Wright, Faith Hill. For it's the Nashville women who've really made it big, beyond the narrow confines of what used to be called 'country and western', over the last few years. Rafts of female songwriter singers have broken the cowboy hat 'n' boots tradition of the Grand Ol' Opry, and had hits that 'cross-over' from country to pop. Emmylou Harris, Mary Chapin Carpenter, Nanci Griffith, Shawn Colvin, Gretchen Peters, Beth Nielsen Chapman, the list goes on and on. The men, on the other hand, seem stuck in the cowboy rut, unable to break free from their grass roots. Only Kenny Rogers can get away with appearing on the Grand Ol' Opry without a ten-gallon hat, but then he's one of the few males to have cracked the 'cross-over'.

Anyway, to return to the good ol' Nashville routine, after lunch and whatever, Pauly and I would return to our hotel, the Renaissance. We pronounced it in the European manner, Ren-ay-sance, and could never get a taxi driver to take us there.

'Ren-ay-sance? Never heard of it.'

'But it's a big hotel, right in the centre of town.'

'Nah.'

'Here, I'll spell it for you.'

'Oh! You mean the Ren-a-sense!' . . .

A little nap in the boudoir, and then down to the hotel's music lounge, where one evening two women and a piano were making the worst racket I've ever heard in my life. They were so off-key, we thought that they must be doing it for a joke, but nobody was laughing. Apart from Pauly and me, who couldn't stay away. Tuneless and toneless, the pair sang and played their hearts out, pausing only when some tone-deaf drunk pressed money into their hands. It was extraordinary to behold, in a town bursting with musical talent breaking its heart to be heard. Off we would pop, spirits restored, and when not putting ourselves outside most of a large pig, we would have one of those combinations so beloved of Americans, like surf and turf, or steak and spaghetti. Then, bursting at the seams, back to the hotel, and bed, for a couple of hours, before tottering to the feet again to make our way to the radio studio for the 1.30 a.m. start. I loved it, but it was a killer. Still, it was worth it for the fried green tomatoes, the off-key women, the guitar-pickin', and the rising country star who sat down beside me in a Nashville restaurant.

'Hey!' he said, sociably. 'So where are you guys from?'

'Well, we're from BBC London, but I'm from Ireland originally.'

'Ireland, huh? That's kinda like Scotland, isn't it?'

The record company executive next to me consoled me.

'Don't worry. I was at a meeting recently, and my American boss was looking in a puzzled manner at a map of Europe. He eventually turned from the map with a hopeless sigh, and said,

'I don't get it. I can't find Japan anywhere there.'

I'm not sure what took Radio 2 to Crewe, but it wasn't to tour the Rolls-Royce factory. I found myself in the signalman's box of the great railway marshalling yard, straining for two hours of entertaining chat as the trains came and went. Members of the public turned up too, thank goodness, but I particularly remember a very well-dressed, youngish, attractive couple who had also been in the hotel's dining room the night before. We exchanged some airy banter, and they went on their way. A week later, a very charming letter arrived from the husband, who asked if Paul and I might meet him and his wife for breakfast when they were next in London. The letter was so well written, and they seemed such charming people, that we felt that we could meet them. And so we did, in a hotel near Broadcasting House, and they were fine, smartly dressed, causing no embarrassment, apart from the man's excessive enthusiasm for the radio show, and for me. Then, as the weeks and months went by, the letters came with increasing frequency, at first good-humoured, and even witty, then slowly drifting into maudlin obsession. I'm sure the poor young wife knew nothing of it, but in long, tortured letters the man told me of his fixation on me, how he thought of me as not just a friend, but his father. Naturally we were very worried by these sad outpourings, but at a loss to know what to do. Replying to the letters, we knew, would certainly make things worse. Then, out of the blue, the tabloids reported the sad story of a man who had got into trouble for persecuting and stalking Ulrika Jonsson. The papers published his picture. It was our man. He had committed suicide . . .

Like everybody who sticks their nose in front of a television camera or a microphone, I've had my share of overenthusiastic fans. They mean no harm, and must always be treated with good manners. No sensible person can have any truck with 'stars' who are uncivil and downright rude to the very people who have put them where they are. Sometimes, the public themselves can be downright rude: 'Here, sign this piece of paper. I can't stand you myself, it's for my wife . . .' It's hard, but the only answer is a smile. Obsession is something else, and has always made me uneasy. For a long time, a young woman would be waiting for me in all weathers as I left the studio in the morning. We'd exchange a few words; that's all she seemed to need. Then, one weekend, I saw her ride by my house. She had joined a stables nearby to be near me. As suddenly as she had appeared, she was no longer there every morning. Her letters had told me that she was a medical student, but they, too, stopped abruptly. A couple of years ago she wrote to me again, this time a sensible, cheery letter, the sort you'd expect to get from a doctor. You shouldn't believe *Green Wing*.

Every year, wee Pauly and I put ourselves forward as prizes – if you like, booby-prizes – on the *Children in Need* Auction for Things that Money Can't Buy, on Radio 2. I know that you'll find it astonishing, but people are prepared to spend good money to be in our doubtful company. Fifteen thousand pounds to play golf with us at Mid-Herts and Doonbeg, ten quid to have lunch with two sad old geezers at the Ivy, and a lot more to accompany our heroes to Sheeprock Lodge at Penticton in British Columbia, Canada. Four good people paid through the nose to join the two of us, with the bonus of Deadly, the Voice of the Balls, to bring added value and lick everybody's plate. Helen came with me, and we all went up and down the snowy mountains on sno-cats, which were so frightening no one felt the cold, and lifts on which it was cold enough to make your hair stand on end. Somewhere in this mighty tome, as you riffle through it in the bookshop without the slightest intention of buying, you'll find a picture of Pauly shortly after he was lifted, rigid, from the ski-lift . . . Penticton was starkly beautiful, a true winterscape, and a skiers' paradise. Well, a serious skiers' paradise. No crowds, but no social life; great runs, but no smart little restaurants on the slopes. Just a hut that served onion soup so hot that you simply gave up trying to break through its molten cheese crust. There was food, of course, at ground level, and Pauly had the buzzard balls. Even with his cast-iron digestion they did him in, but not before he displayed an aptitude for the ancient Canadian sport of 'naggling'. I know, it sounds like something Kenneth Williams, as Rambling Sid Rumpo, would do in *Round the Horne*, but all it involved was ramming a stick into a hole in the middle of a revolving wheel, or something. A child could do it, and Pauly did. He boasts about it frequently, and only a reference to buzzard balls quietens him . . .

The strange thing about the majestic forest that covered the foothills of the mountain was the lack of wildlife. Few birds, and no animals. The area was full of native Americans, or as the vigilantly politically correct Canadians call them, the First Nation. Canadians tiptoe around the First Nation, whether from guilt over ancient wrongs, or to show how much more enlightened they are than their American neighbours over the border. They filled a lake with fish in order to provide the local First Nation with both a pastime and a source of food. The First Nation hired a boat and some dragnets, and cleared the lake of all fish in a couple of days. I think I know where all the wildlife went . . .

We went on to see Vancouver, surely one of the most beautifully situated cities in the world, all shimmering water and bobbing boats. It reminded me of Limerick with scenery; it rains a lot in Vancouver. On the way home on the plane, I passed Pauly half a sleeping tablet. He went out like a light in the middle of a sentence. And this is the man who claims that he bummed around Europe with a guitar, a beard and an Afghan coat in a permanent fog of wacky-baccy. I don't think so . . .

I'd been to Canada a couple of times before Paul and I made the long haul to British Columbia, once at the behest of Bob Burrowes, then the Head of BBC Radio Sport, to drink in the heady atmosphere of Montreal prior to leading the radio coverage of the Olympics there. You need more than a couple of days to get more than a fleeting impression, and all I really remember were the flights out and back. I flew out in the company of Mary Peters, a great Olympic champion, but like myself, sturdily made. We were like a pair of sardines, well to the back of the plane. It might have been painful if it hadn't been for Mary's company. A great athlete, but an even greater person – ever smiling, ever optimistic, Northern Ireland's greatest ambassador, her life given over to the service of her beloved people. If anybody ever deserved to fly first class through life, she does, but it's your BBC and they husband your resources like misers. Unless, of course, you're a very senior executive, or a star they desperately want to sign up for television. Then, the sky's the limit, even if they don't know what to do with the star after they've paid a fortune for him.

Mary and I travelled steerage, but on the way back, Bob Burrowes pulled a few strings and I left Montreal in the first-class cabin for New York. My first time in first class, and I can remember it clearly, thirty years on. The scrambled-egg breakfast, the beef carved from the trolley, the champagne, the wines. I've been lucky enough to turn left at the top of the steps many times since, but nothing has ever come close to my feeling of luxury and well-being on that first first-class flight. It explains why I have no patience with people who fall asleep the minute they park themselves in the premier cabin. They're showing off; it's inverted snobbery: 'Oh, I travel this way all the time . . .' Let me never get so blasé. Another glass of champagne, please, and, yes, I'll have breakfast, lunch, dinner, two movies and all the fine wines you can throw at me. I've paid plenty for it, and I'm going to enjoy it. I'll sleep when I get there, and don't make it too quick . . . (I just love flying – airports I hate. Who could love them? Crowded, stressful, customer unfriendly, where you never see a smiling face. People worried, late, delayed, drained, every single passenger wondering whether any trip or holiday is worth so much mental and physical strain.)

I also went to Edmonton, on the Alberta plains, with my old pal Derek Mills – once again a fleeting glance – preparatory to presenting the Commonwealth Games for Radio Sport. This time we went first class through the kindness of Air Canada, but I have no recollection of scrambled eggs. Edmonton rears out of the landscape like Dallas from the Texan prairie, and still seemed a little raw and unfinished when I was there; I'm sure it's a polished, sophisticated metropolis now. Then, it seemed as if all the beggars and drunks on the street were native Americans, while the well-to-do queued for discos and clubs at 4.30 in the afternoon with dinner at six, and everybody in bed by ten.

I've no more recollection of the Games themselves than I have of the Montreal Olympics, although I recollect that they bankrupted Montreal. Let's hope London 2012 will be a financial, as well as a sporting, success. The Los Angeles Olympics, in 1984, which I covered from an outside broadcast van in a Hollywood back-lot, was the first Olympic Games of the modern era to show a profit. Some twenty-two years on, I can remember nearly everything about those Games: Carl Lewis, Seb Coe, Steve Ovett. The stadium where all the track and field events were held was smack in the poorest part of the city, yet as we passed through the ghetto, on all sides we were greeted with smiles and friendly greetings. As far as I know, no one got robbed, mugged or otherwise dumped on for the entire two weeks of the Games. Hard to reconcile with the subsequent race riots, burnings and the shootings and murders that we hear about, on an almost daily basis, from the City of Angels.

A wonderful woman, now sadly passed on, Julie Lewis, bid a hatful in the Radio 2 auction for Things that Money Can't Buy to witness the cutting-down of the Trafalgar Square Christmas tree in a Norwegian forest, and, once more, there were our two favourite funsters cheering on the sidelines. We all had a marvellous time: sleigh-rides in the snow, decimating whole herds of reindeer at the dining table, and stumbling about Oslo in the gloom. Or maybe that should be gloaming; it's a weird sensation to exit your hotel at eleven in the morning in a kind of oyster light. As you wander about, you expect it to brighten up at any moment. You go in for lunch, and when you come out at three in the afternoon, darkness has fallen. The Norwegians are a remarkably cheery folk, considering . . .

A week later, we joined Julie Lewis for the raising of 'our' Christmas tree in Trafalgar Square. Julie must have enjoyed it, because the following year she bid even more money, and we all went off to Norway again. To hell and back. Hell was chilly, but a jolly outing, with our friends the reindeer playing their full part again at dinner. Scandinavian meals have a quaint formality: your tongue would be hanging out for a drink, but not a drop is offered until the food is served. Then you can't get at the food, because they're up on their feet, downing the akavit with every speech of welcome. When they ran out of people to make speeches, they went out into the streets and dragged in passers-by to say a few words. Then came the lutefisk, a delicacy peculiar to those born north of the Skaggerak. It's a simple enough recipe: you bury a fish in the ground, and when it is sufficiently rotten, you dig it up. Then you eat it. And Pauly thought he'd gone a bridge too far with the buzzard balls . . . Choirs sang for us, and children danced, and we vowed to return, even if hell froze over.

It was raining when we flew into Aberdeen for the Tall Ships Race, but nothing could detract from the sight of those magnificent craft, assembled from all over the world. The towering masts with their huge sails were impressive enough, but the sight of young sailors clambering all over the dizzy riggings was even more remarkable, particularly for someone who can't climb more than three rungs of a ladder without being paralysed with fear. I'm not prone to vertigo, I've never felt the urge to fling myself off heights; I'm just a chicken when it comes to climbing. All vestiges of self-confidence disappear as soon as my feet are off the ground. As a young man, I've embarrassed myself time out of number, transfixed by terror while climbing rocks no more than six feet off a sandy beach. We visited many of the tall ships – smoked salmon, soda bread and whiskey on the Irish ship contrasted with the more meagre fare of the Russian vessel.

Vodka aplenty, but we'd already heard that food was in short supply, and the other nationalities were donating their 'past use-by-date' foodstuffs to the starving Russians. There was a remarkable spirit of camaraderie among the crews; mostly young volunteers. A well-spoken lady said to me, 'Isn't it marvellous to see these young people all mixing together? Boys from the inner city mixing with chaps from the public schools – those poor boys must be learning so much.' It struck me that the public-school boys might be learning a great deal more from the streetwise kids.

Last year, Pauly Walters and I went to the Granite City of Aberdeen again, as part of a grand week of BBC Radio 2 entertainment. The mighty network staged concerts all over town, featuring major artistes. Ken Bruce, Mark Radcliffe, Bob Harris, Richard Allinson all displayed their wares to the general delight of the eager population. I was the only disappointment.

It all started well enough at a civic reception, where councillors and dignitaries of the town warmly welcomed Radio 2 and myself, the veteran broadcaster, and flagship show presenter of the network. I'll let you into a secret that only eight and a half million regular listeners know: this 'veteran' thing is beginning to get on my nerves. I'm always surprised at the age I am, and I'd appreciate it if people would show a bit of manners; everybody knows 'veteran' is a euphemism for 'ancient', 'decrepit' and 'past it'. Whatever happened to 'distinguished', or even 'mature'? Sir David Frost says that age is only important if you're a cheese, but that hardly carries any weight since he's the same age as me. Yes, I know he looks a lot older, but he doesn't take care of himself like I do, with my racing-snake figure and complementary six-pack. I'll admit that I owe much of that to my highly strung temperament and the constant state of nervous tension that causes me to literally burn off the calories, even when I'm just sitting there. I am constantly being exhorted by my colleagues and friends to 'eat more!' I urge them to calm themselves: 'I eat every bit as much as you, but the weight just won't stay on,' I explain. It's breeding; the Duke of Devonshire hadn't a pick on him . . .

Anyway, back in Aberdeen, all was sweetness and light. I had a decent piece of halibut and a tasty viognier for dinner, and slept like a baby. The following morning, we arrived to present the morning show at BBC Scotland's studios, coinciding with the arrival of a mountain of foodstuffs. Pauly, Deadly, Boggy and I make no pretension to be anything other than rugged, no-nonsense trenchermen. Fran Godfrey's a more delicate flower, so we usually eat her share of the available provender as well. Rare indeed is the week that the show is not victualled from some food source eager for a mention. We've eaten full Christmas dinners, right down to the stuffing and sprouts, at eight o'clock in the morning. Many's the full English breakfast and Ulster fry that gets put away between music and emails, not to mention snorker and bacon butties, Krispy Kremes, Danish pastries and the good old muffin. Pauly and I have shared a curry at quarter past eight in the morning, and been the better for it. People think that you can't eat and broadcast at the same time. Pshaw! All right, I may sound a little indistinct and muffled from time to time, but my listeners understand that blood-sugar levels must be maintained, and the inner man sustained, if high broadcasting standards are not to drop.

There were hampers-full of good things to welcome us to

the studio at Aberdeen: doughnuts aplenty, bacon baps and a great big box of the local delicacy, the Rowie, or Buttery, if you're from Inverness. Aberdonian listeners had been singing the praises of this 'Rowie' for weeks in advance of my arrival there. I was not to miss it, it was the very food of the gods. In far-flung corners of the globe, expats cried themselves to sleep every night for want of a Rowie. I had a box of forty to choose from, so picking a hearty-looking specimen at random, I took a manly chunk . . .

I'll never understand local fascination and delight in their own peculiar little specialities. You'll hear Londoners raving over pie and mash with liquor. If you haven't tried it – don't, it's disgusting. Ditto jellied eels. Irish stew is not something you should ever risk in Ireland, the Pekinese can't do duck, and no one in Kiev should be let near a chicken.

So it is with the Rowie of old Aberdeen – a sort of lardy-cake, with so much salt that it felt like a mouthful of the North Sea. With all my years as a 'veteran' broadcaster, I should have known better than to say so over the airwaves. The good burghers of Aberdeen were aghast, and those who didn't fall into a dead faint at my heretical words were whipped up into a frenzy by the local newspapers. Even the Scottish nationals got in on the act, their headlines expressing shock and horror at my 'outburst', as they put it. An enterprising baker leapt on the band-Wogan and produced a variation on the theme, calling it a 'Wowie'. Alex Salmond, leader of the Scottish National Party, sprang to the inedible thing's defence, just a tad inaccurately: 'Terry Wogan's a judge at the Eurovision, so he can't be much of a judge of the Rowie'. Back to the old drawing board, Alex. I was lucky to get out of town before it all really hit the fan, but naturally, it brought out the worst in a poetic TOG:

The Man Who Put the 'Row' into 'Rowie'
(It's like a Bateman cartoon – you really couldn't make it up . . .)

Noo – dinny think I'm bein' pushy,
but Jings! Ye've caused an awfy stooshie!
It seems that, while in Aiberdeen
you passed remarks on their cuisine?

'This morning rowie tastes like seaweed!'
was not construed as praise indeed –
the comment caused them much distress,
and outrage in the national press!

Nae wonder then, you fled the place
sae quickly, tryin' tae leave wi' grace
ere champions of the salty buttery
could offer you assault and battery . . .

But dinny panic! Mustn't grumble!
You needny grovel or be humble –
for you, as for the Granite City,
there's nae such thing as bad publicity!

Sally Forth

Doonbeg Golf Club, where Pauly and I played on behalf of
Children in Need, is on the Wild West Atlantic coast of Clare,
and the brainchild of an American, the owner of Kiawah Island

Golf Club on the East Coast of the States, facing the Atlantic. He wanted it both ways, you might say. Doonbeg has joined the ranks of the great golf clubs that line Ireland's Atlantic coast: Ballybunion, Tralee, Waterville – and, just up the road from Doonbeg, Lahinch. I'm privileged to be a member of both of the latter. Lahinch is the elder by many years, founded by the British garrison in Limerick in the nineteenth century. It's a mighty course, and I have suffered there, usually in the company of my great friends the Clancy clan. The wind blows in off the huge beach with such force that on one occasion when the late, great Michael Clancy sought to take his car out of the garage, a passing zephyr lifted the garage door from its hinges and carried it fifty yards down the road.

I haven't played Lahinch for years, but I visited there last year while I was staying in Doonbeg. Nothing has really changed; the main street with the church at the top, the bar that my family's dear friend, the late Gordon Wood, once owned, still there. The shops and the restaurants look a little brighter, but it was raining the day I went, and I'd only gone anyway because I couldn't face another round at Doonbeg in a force ten gale.

I'd a hangover as well; that's the trouble with Ireland, you can't just go out for a meal and a quiet drink and be back in your little bed in the arms of Morpheus by ten o'clock. In total contrast to Scandinavians, the Irish insist on getting themselves and everybody else stocious with drink before they even see the menu, and long after any sensible nation would have called a halt and staggered off into the night, they're still at it. Only in Ireland is the pint of stout regarded as a digestif, and on this particular occasion it was followed by a variety of drinks that seemed to be in celebration of the European Community: Irish coffee, followed by sambuca, then Cointreau with ice. I swear I saw Peter Houlihan, my convivial host, with a balloon glass of crème de menthe frappé.

Things have changed in Ireland, and not just the stuff they're drinking. The Irish *Wirtschaftswunder*, the Celtic Tiger, has transformed the countryside. When I first went to golf at Lahinch, the houses were few and far between. Deserted cottages dotted the stony hillsides, and the houses that were there were grey and spoke sadly of the region's, and indeed the country's, poverty. Now, on all sides, the houses proliferate and assault the eye with a mad variety of colour. Just as the Irish have changed the colour of their drinks, they've brightened the landscape with rainbow-coloured houses: peppermint-pink bungalows, scarlet cottages, custard-yellow mansions, developments in every pastel shade from primrose to sky-blue. It's as if the Irish want to trumpet their success from their rooftops, and who could begrudge them after so many barren years of hunger, deprivation and emigration? The houses and the drinks have changed colour — the people remain the same: welcoming, funny, generous and with no idea when it's time to go home . . .

No matter what the colour of the houses, or the innate vivacity of their inhabitants, a wet day in Lahinch is not conducive to gaiety, and I remembered when Helen and I had stayed there with Michael and Kathleen Clancy. Devout Catholics, they brought us to Mass with them on Sunday. It was raining, and I can smell the inside of that church to this day. It was like being smothered with a very old wet sock. I didn't chance the church the last time I was in Lahinch. Not only good memories should be treasured, or at least preserved.

Peter Houlihan, a man whose ebullient, cheery nature

embodies the spirit of the new Ireland, asked me to join the advisory board of the Doonbeg Golf Club, and I did so like a shot before wiser counsels at the club prevailed. It's rare enough that I'm asked for my advice on anything, least of all by those who know me. Luckily, there are other, shrewder heads on the board, and I agree with them.

When I go there, I stay with Tony and Maeve at their bed and breakfast, Links Lodge. The bed and breakfast phenomenon broke out in Ireland about twenty years ago and swept through the countryside like a bush fire. There are thousands of them, and the full Irish breakfast rules OK. Bacon, eggs, sausages, mushrooms, toast. A heart attack on a plate. There's black and white pudding as well, and fried bread if you really want to go down with all guns blazing. The healthy option is always proffered – orange juice, fresh fruit, cereals, skimmed milk. It's just that you'd better follow it with the Full Irish, otherwise your hostess is going to be very offended . . .

You'd need plenty of ballast if you're thinking of playing Doonbeg. When the weather's bad at Lahinch, the goats shelter in the lee of the clubhouse, and even the pluckiest all-weather masochist knows better than to venture abroad on the links. There are no animal weathervanes at Doonbeg, unless you count a few head of cattle several fields away. Of course, it's a well-known fact that if the cattle are lying down in the grass, it means rain. If they're standing up, it's going to get heavier.

There are creatures that play a major role at Doonbeg, however. Snails. Unfortunately for Greg Norman, the course designer, this particular corner of the Four Green Fields of Ireland is the habitat of a rare breed of snail. As soon as the golf course was proposed, every environmentalist and tree-hugging mollusc-lover in the country rallied to the snails' defence. Mr Norman was very lucky to get his course built at all, and only after he guaranteed to protect the snails' environment by cordoning off hundreds of acres. The snails were fenced in, although how you can prevent a snail no bigger than your little fingernail from sneaking out when the mood takes him, I don't know. I suppose the fencing is more to keep the golfers out than the snails in, and if you hit an errant ball into the snail reservation, don't go climbing in after it. With your golfers' feet, you'll wipe out thousands of the little blighters. Paul Walters, who would eat a baby's bottom through a wickerwork chair, wondered if they might be tasty, but you'd need many hundreds to make a decent sandwich, and you'd be better off waiting until you get back to the clubhouse for a hamburger.

Hamburgers are big in Doonbeg, because it has many American members. They fly in for the weekend to Shannon, stay at Dromoland Castle, and take a helicopter to the course. These are real golf-lovers, giving up a couple of weekend rounds on a sunny, easygoing American course to get sand-blasted and blown to kingdom come, with every chance of killing whole families of rare snails with a careless shot . . .

The sand dunes of Clare were the site of our Wogan family picnics. We didn't have a car; dammit, we didn't have a phone, and television had barely been invented. We had a wireless, thank goodness, that helped to mould me into the eejit I am today. Not having a car was a drawback, although I don't remember any of our neighbours in Elm Park, Ennis Road, Limerick, having one, either. When I last looked in at the little avenue of semi-detached houses where I was born and reared, the cars were bumper to bumper for its entire length, which could only have been a couple of hundred yards, from the Ennis Road to the Union Wall. It seemed miles long when I was a lad. The Union Wall was too tall and pebble-dashed, even for somebody who could climb, and nobody bothered to put up a ladder because we knew what was on the other side: the workhouse.

Yes, in 1940s Ireland, a workhouse in the Dickensian tradition, for the homeless, penniless and destitute. I think I went inside once, but I can't be sure if I didn't dream or imagine it. There were other places in Limerick that disturbed me as a boy: the Blue School, from which issued the occasional small crocodile of pale little children. I didn't know whether they were orphans, abandoned or illegitimate, but they weren't like us. There was something sad about them, something pitiful. I can remember worrying about them, but none of my pals knew anything, nor did my parents. Maybe they did, but in those days, there were lots of things a growing boy would be better off not knowing. The memory of those children remains with me, evoking the sadness I used to feel when queuing with my Auntie May for an evening of cine-variety at the Theatre Royal, Dublin, and being unable to enjoy it because we'd encountered a poor, ragged creature who begged us for a penny. The compassion of childhood – just a memory, never as intensely felt again.

I suppose the Wogans could have been more mobile if we could have got my mother up on a bike, but Rose Wogan had a highly developed sense of her own dignity, and felt that the bicycle was for people in trousers. Also, it got her husband and two sons out of her way, at least for Sunday afternoon, when my father would take us fishing, my little brother Brian perched on Dad's crossbar, and me with my own trusty two-wheeler. Then, people we knew started to have motor cars, and our weekends changed. Gordon Wood, by then, I'm sure, only in his very early twenties, started to enjoy the same success in insurance as he did on the rugby field, and bought a car. A foolish extravagance, my father thought, but accepted Gordon's offer of a trip to the seaside. Almost every weekend of summer, it seemed, we'd picnic in the sand hills on the Atlantic coast of Clare. Miles of sandy beach, deserted, from where Michael Wogan and Gordon could hurl their fishing lines into the breakers, while we dashed up and down the dunes and Rose doled out the tea and sandwiches. I've never been able to resist a sandwich since, and I've been left with a lifelong passion for corned beef. Gordon Wood, a magnificent athlete, would put down his rod and hurl himself into the surf, thrashing through the waves like a dolphin. 'Wood versus the Atlantic!' my father, who couldn't swim a stroke, would shout in admiration. Gordon Wood, who gave up his weekends just to bring a family to the sea, went on to play for Garryowen, Ireland and the British and Irish Lions. His son, Keith, did the same, and became Ireland's most charismatic captain, an icon, a national hero. I'm as proud to call him friend as my father was of his father. The wheel turns full circle, and here I am playing golf in the very sand dunes where I tumbled as a boy . . .

Our friends, the Kneafseys, had a car as well, and two families would pack into that for carefree, sunny days by the sea. I hate to drag up the old cliché, but how was it that those days by the shores of Clare were invariably lit by the sun, and nowadays, whenever I go to the same place, I'm Big Chief Rain-in-the-Face? Jack Kneafsey was a bit of an entrepreneur, and had the bright idea of importing an exciting new Japanese product into Ireland. 'Aji-no-moto' I distinctly remember it was called, an additive to bring zest and flavour to even the simplest of meals. My mother sprinkled it over everything, untested, unproven. It could have killed us, for all she knew. With the wisdom of the passing years and a thousand Chinese takeaways, I know now that it was monosodium glutamate, but it could have been arsenic. That was the way it was, then – suck it and see. If some food fell off the kitchen table when you were eating, your mother would pick it up off the floor, wipe it in her apron, and stick it back in your mouth. Nobody bothered doctors with minor ailments, your father would lance that boil, your mother slap a red-hot bread poultice on that wounded knee. I've even seen an aunt take a razor blade to a cyst. Dr Collis Browne's Chlorodyne cured coughs, fevers and probably malaria, having as one of its ingredients morphine. They gave it to children as well; I remember a not unpleasant feeling of drowsiness. People on the verge of mental breakdown were given a 'nerve tonic'. Still, we mustn't scoff – look at the people today who swear by 'rescue remedies': herbal concoctions with that extra, vital ingredient that really does the rescuing, alcohol . . .

When I was a growing lad, the demon drink was Ireland's equivalent of the Great Satan. A curse upon the land, and railed at from the pulpit almost as much as sex. The lot of the Irish working man was pretty desperate, and there is consolation in drink and oblivion. Drink and its consequences were adding to the poverty and plight of families. Frank McCourt's great book, *Angela's Ashes*, paints the picture in harsh colours that the people of Limerick thought unfair, but his story was not, I think, exceptional. Stark poverty and squalor were endemic in the Ireland I grew up in, from the 1930s to the 1970s. A few hundred yards from Dublin's main O'Connell Street were slums comparable only to Delhi and Calcutta. It lifts my heart, every time I return, to see the new prosperity and the end of the grinding suffering that was the lot of the Irish for too many years.

Early in the twentieth century, a certain Father Matthew started a campaign to try and wean the Irish drinker away from his mother's milk. The abstinence movement took on, and its members became known as 'pioneers'. Pioneers wore a little enamel pin, white, with an image of the Sacred Heart, on their lapels. There was a time when it became a mark of respectability, of the upright citizen. For that reason, the badge seemed more popular with the aspirant bourgeoisie than those lower down the ladder at whom it was really aimed. The drink problem was not that of the Irish middle class; they were too busy scrimping and saving to waste money on drink. I never saw my father drink more than a half-pint of stout in the early Limerick days, and I certainly never saw him drunk! My mother never touched a drop, but she had a sweet tooth and would prefer a lemonade anyway.

The Pioneers got you early, and it would be the independent soul indeed who wouldn't denounce the Devil, with all his words and pomps and his right-hand man, the Drink. There wasn't a single boy in my class in the Crescent, Limerick, who didn't enrol. I wore the badge for a few years, but I'd abandoned it long before I had my first drink, a glass of cider when I was seventeen, on a rugby tour in Scotland. In common with every other well-brought-up child in the land, Helen was a Pioneer too, although one of the great sadnesses in her life was being rejected as a Child of Mary at fifteen, when she was caught smoking. We now know that fags will kill you, but nobody knew that then, so why it was such a terrible sin to have a quick puff is hard to fathom, unless you were brought up in Holy Catholic Ireland, where everything was a sin, particularly if you were only fifteen. It's a wonder Helen wasn't excommunicated. She clung to her faith, and when she left school, joined the Pioneer Musical and Dramatic Society. At the time, you couldn't throw a stone in a country road in Ireland without hitting a member of an amateur dramatic society. Helen, who has a lovely voice to go with the rest of her, played principal boy in panto. There's a picture of her in full fig somewhere, but she wouldn't let you see it, even if we could find it . . . I myself, having starred in school productions of Gilbert and Sullivan, went on to join the Rathmines and Rathgar Musical Society, but that's another story, and you've heard it before.

The R and R, for that was how they were known to the cognoscenti and music lovers, were unashamedly the cream of the crop when it came to Dublin's – nay, Ireland's – amateur musical scene. As usual, there were far more women applicants for a place in the back row of the chorus, which explains how the likes of me passed the audition. The thing about the R and R was that they didn't give their all in some dingy old temperance hall, but on stage at Dublin's premier variety theatre, a grand old music hall, the Gaiety Theatre. The Gaiety was where Ireland's greatest comic actor, the legendary Jimmy O'Dea, most often trod the boards in variety and pantomime along with the almost equally legendary Maureen Potter, and a very small sidekick, Mickser Reid. Whenever this winning team took to the stage, it was a full house. Television came a little late to Ireland to catch them at their peak, and on the odd occasion when they did appear on the box, it didn't really work. They were theatricals; television was too small for them. I often think that's why so many British actors don't measure up to their American and Australian counterparts in television comedy or drama series. Their expressions, their gestures, their delivery are too big. Too much RADA, LAMDA and Rep, love. Watch somebody like Anthony LaPaglia in the American series *Without a Trace*, or William Shatner in *Boston Legal*. They mutter, they pause, they scarcely move. It's television acting, acting in close-up, in a whisper. Very few British actors can bring themselves to do it. Laurence Olivier, the greatest stage and Shakespearean actor of his generation, was, at least in my humble, pure ham on film. There are still actors like him, and you can see them on television most weeks exaggerating, gesticulating, projecting, still trying to reach the back row of the stalls . . .

The legendary Bourke family ran the Gaiety Theatre, and they were larger than life, and any mere actor. The two brothers, Rick and Lorcan, had a flair for showmanship, and the tales of their doings and sayings are still told with relish in Nearys, McDaids, Davy Byrnes and other Dublin watering holes.

Rick's retort, when asked if a certain popular artist would fill the place: 'Rubber walls. We'll need rubber walls'.

Lorcan's impassioned appeal to a Variety Club of Ireland lunch, on behalf of the blind: 'I know what a tragedy blindness can be. Haven't I two blind children myself?'

Afterwards, a friend who knew the family took him aside and said: 'But, Lorcan, your children aren't blind!'

'I know,' said Lorcan, 'I got carried away.'

When Lorcan Bourke was Deputy Lord Mayor of Dublin, he welcomed Sir John Barbirolli and the Hallé Orchestra to the facility with the ringing welcome, 'And a hearty *ceadmile failte* to Sir John Barolli and his band!'

Then there was a reception for Senator Edward Kennedy at the Mansion House, Dublin. Lorcan, all bonhomie, engaging the senator in fine-sounding talk: 'How honoured we are tonight, Edward, may I call you Edward? Good man, to have you and your lovely wife–'

A small man tugs at Lorcan's sleeve and whispers in his ear.

'No!' says our hero, turning once again to his new American friend. 'And further, Senator, Edward, I know that I speak on behalf . . .'

The little man interrupts again, whispering in Lorcan's ear.

'No, I said!' this time with anger bubbling up, which he controls as he turns again to his distinguished visitor '. . . of the plain people of Ireland in whose place I stand today, to welcome you and yours to our little island–'

Another tug at his sleeve, another plaintive whisper. It's one whisper too many. Lorcan Bourke loses it.

'Listen!' he shouts, 'I've told you before! There's no f-in' stout!'

5

The Togmeister of Eurovision

〜⌢〜

In 1971, I returned to the Gaiety Theatre, Dublin, not to relive my triumphs in *The Gondoliers*, *Naughty Marietta*, *Bitter Sweet* or *Love from Judy*, but as the BBC commentator for the Eurovision Song Contest, my very first. Who would have thought that I'd still be at it thirty-five years later? Extraordinary to think too, that this little variety theatre, which could seat no more than, say, a thousand people for a Jimmy O'Dea panto, staged the Eurosong. When you remember the 35,000 that packed a football stadium in Copenhagen a few years ago, it's hard to imagine the tiny scale of Dublin, 1971. There can only have been five hundred people in the audience, to accommodate all the cameras and sound crews; the commentators were at the back of the gods, and the presenters did it all from a box overlooking the stage. There could only have been fifteen countries taking part, in contrast to the twenty-four who contested the final in Kiev, Ukraine, in 2005. And, of course, the twenty countries who took part in the semi-final, two days earlier.

I'm still astounded by the number of people who, after all these years, still ask me if I enjoy doing the Eurovision Song Contest. I'm fed up asking them to complete the question, 'Has ... Pope ... balcony?', or 'Does ... bear ... in the woods?' Thirty-five years on, would I still be doing something that I didn't like? I've always loved the Eurovision, through the long weary years of critics and reviewers who missed the point and lambasted it for its silliness and lack of musical content, through the opposition of those at the BBC (at least one of whom is still clinging to the wreckage) who can't tell the difference between popular and trendy. I even love the travesty of a contest that it has become ever since they threw it open to phone voting, and the arrival of the former members of the Union of Soviet Socialist Republics.

In 1999, to avoid what the European Broadcasting Union (EBU) saw as elements of national prejudice and the settling of old scores ruining the Contest, the voting was taken out of the hands of national juries and handed over to the plain, honest straight-voting people of Europe. It immediately became apparent that they were even more biased than the juries against their neighbours and historical enemies.

We got used to it. Every commentator worthy of his microphone could predict each country's voting on the basis of their political and national bias. I knew that the UK was going to find it very hard to win the Eurovision ever again – Europe didn't like us, we'd been too big for our boots for too long. And, of course, Britain had made the crucial error of saving Europe in World War Two. The British will never be forgiven for that . . .

Over the past six years, however, it has become even more obvious that not only will the UK find it impossible to win the Song Contest, so will every country in Western Europe. The West won the Cold War, but it lost the Eurovision in the process . . .

The Eurothing of 2006 was held in Athens, Greece, since they won the title in Kiev the previous year. Ukraine, Turkey, Latvia, Estonia, Denmark were the previous five winning countries, three of them from the former Soviet bloc, which came as no surprise to even the casual observer of how the influx of the 'new' countries, from the Baltic and the Balkans, has changed the voting pattern. We'd got used to the petty national prejudices of Western Europe, but the bloc voting of the founder members of the Warsaw Pact, and those who had suffered in the shadow of the Russian Bear, caught us on the hop. Suddenly, whole regions were voting for each other, and unashamedly at that: 'And we have great pleasure in awarding twelve points to our dear neighbours . . .' The Balkans voted for the Balkans, the Baltics for the Baltics. It didn't matter about the song – keep your allies sweet.

The result depended on which group had the most representatives in the final. Denmark just sneaked in before the new order took over, but the next two winners, Estonia and Latvia, kept it in the Baltic. It's a hangover, I suppose, from the bad old days when these countries were part of an oppressive dictatorship that allowed no room for individual expression, and, indeed, only allowed voting if it was for the ruling party. All of these newly independent countries are reaching for democracy, but old habits die hard, and it will take a few years yet before they extend the democratic principle to voting for songs from countries that they had been brought up to regard as enemies for at least a half a century.

It's not without its own significance that the four countries that brought up the rear in the 2005 Song Contest were France, Germany, Spain and the UK, incidentally the four major financial contributors to the Eurovision. It helps that, because of these hefty contributions, none of the Big Four may be relegated to suffer the indignity of having to requalify in the semi-final round, a fate meted out in 2005 to Ireland, of all countries – the nation that has won the Song Contest more than any other. Mind you, the Irish entry was a far cry from their halcyon days of the nineties, when Ireland seemed to win at will. Then, they were meticulous in their song selection, picking the winner of their national contest on exactly the principles of the Eurovision itself, with regional juries. The Song Contest changed its method, Ireland changed theirs, and haven't come close to winning since then.

The UK's failure to trouble the judges has been just as abject since Katrina and the Waves won in 1996. It has to be accepted that no country is going to vote for the UK out of sympathy, or love, any more than they'll vote for any of the other 'big countries', but that doesn't explain, or excuse, Britain's shocking recent record.

'But,' I hear you cry, 'surely if there's one thing in which Britain leads the world, it's popular music?'

Calm yourselves, *mes braves*. First of all, the Eurovision Song Contest is not about popular music as we know it, but as Europe knows it. And not even Western Europe, but beyond the Danube to the very foothills of the Urals and the shores of the Bosphorus. In the not-so-good-old days, it was bad enough having to cope with the French idea of pop music (Plastic Bertrand, Johnny Hallyday) or the German (Lilo Wanders, Oompah and heavy-handed attempts at 'camp'), the Spanish (frills, flamenco and flounce), the Icelandic (blonds and black leather) or the Portuguese (sun, sea and sad sailors), but at least we knew where we stood. Well, you never quite knew with the Italians. I mind well when the contest was staged in Rome, and everybody — delegates, musicians, singers and commentators — were lumped together in a Holiday Inn-type establishment well outside the Eternal City, with a view of motorway flyovers. It might just as well have been Slough, even down to the Italian waiters. We were all bussed to the location, the Italian film studios, Cinecitta. There, we drank in the glory of the setting for the Contest. The set seemed to be constructed of rusty tin-plate, but when I pointed this out, I was reassured, 'No, on camera it will look like marble.' On the big night, it looked just like rusted tin-plate. Not to put a tooth in it, the Italians couldn't have cared less.

We had a couple of marvellous evenings in the trats of Rome, but the Contest itself looked as if it was thrown together. We queued up in our DJs in the soft Italian rain, knowing that it was going to be a shambles. So it was, but the repercussions were surprising: delegates and commentators sitting in their soaked finery vowed never to get dressed up again, and the Eurovision ceased to be a 'black tie' event. More importantly, the extraordinary performance of the male Italian presenter seemed to breathe new life into the Contest itself. He missed his cues, he interrupted, and he argued with the referee, the God-like Frank Naef, on the scoring. I personally think that he was auditioning for the Commedia dell'Arte, but the man's buffoonery seemed to strike a responsive chord, at least with the viewers at home. It was as if the shades had fallen from their eyes, and they realised that the Eurovision Song Contest was not at all what it proclaimed itself to be, but an evening of unexpected delight where you never knew what was coming next, but whatever it was, you weren't going to sleep through it. You might leave it in disdain, you might wince, you might laugh, you might even throw things at the television in anger, but you couldn't ignore it.

For a couple of years preceding the Rome event, it seemed to me that the BBC, or at least my *bête noire*, the one who could never distinguish the popular from the fashionable, was blowing cold on the Eurosong. It wasn't broken, but in the time-honoured tradition, they were of a mind to break it. Rome's popularity put paid to that, and it's true to say that the Contest has never looked back since then. The Italians themselves, however, took umbrage, and stalked from the stage in a marked manner. I don't know why; some say it was wounded pride, others that Rai, the Italian national television service, didn't want to spend the money. I favour the theory that Italy sees itself as the pre-eminent European musical nation – after all, it invented the first Song Contest, the San Remo Song Festival, and it just got fed up being an also-ran to what it considered less musical nations. If the bloc-voting of the new countries in the Contest continues, I wouldn't be at all surprised if one of the other Western countries, and possibly even one of the Big Four, took a powder.

Anybody who takes even a passing interest, and it's probably wise to take no more than that, will know that the Eurovision is an impossible dream, a fantasy that works for the wrong reasons.

How can anybody reared on the shores of the Caspian, or in the shadows of the Carpathians, possibly share the same musical traditions or taste as someone from the banks of the Seine or the foothills of the Alps? As the Contest has grown to include much of Eastern Europe, so the musical divisions have become more marked. In the old days, whined the Ancient Commentator, there was an orchestra on stage, and each country provided its own conductor. I miss those conductors – they were always good for a laugh. The Contest sorely misses the orchestra, which ensured that every performance was entirely 'live', in the musical sense. Nowadays, the backing track is all over us like a cheap suit.

Indeed, it was the sad mistiming of her vocals against the backing track that caused poor Jemma Abbey of Jemini to earn Royaume Uni the shame of last place, and '*nil points*', a few years ago. Then, just as we were beginning to grin and bear it, along came the drum-machine. And a drum-machine with a difference: a drum-machine that brings with it a whiff of the mystic East, a breath of the souk. It brought success to Turkey, and every other country jumped smartly on the bandwagon, even those who should have known better, including the UK. In 2005, we went for it with a song so full of Eastern promise that it wouldn't have been out of place in the old bazaar in Cairo. Much good it did us; we brought up the rear, again.

There doesn't seem to be a solution to the UK's decline in the Contest, but then, it's not that unusual; Italy have gone, Ireland have faded, Monaco's disappeared along with Luxembourg. Maybe they'll come back, and so may we, but it'll have to be a blockbuster of a song. So many people ask me, 'With all our song-writing talent, why can't we come up with the goods?' Well, you can't expect Elton John, Tim Rice, James Blunt, KT Tunstall or their ilk to come out fighting for Britain. What if they lose? And as we've established beyond reasonable doubt, there's no guarantee that even the most copper-bottomed sure-fire hit in the British charts is going to mean a light in Moldova. Speaking of which former Soviet Republic, it made the final in 2005, much to the distress of the French TV commentator, who said to me after the Contest, 'You know, for one awful moment I thought Moldova was going to win! Do you know where it is? Can you imagine? No hotels, no restaurants!' We were in Kiev, in the Ukraine, at the time, and a sympathetic shiver ran through me. (Incidentally, why is it that the signature dish of every city, or country, is always so much better elsewhere? As I've said before, Chicken Kiev, in its city of origin, is terrible. The duck I had in Peking was the worst I've ever had anywhere, I've been disappointed by salade niçoise in Nice, Chianti in Chianti, and Irish stew in Ireland – but that could have been my mother, and I'll give them this: only the Irish can make proper Irish coffee . . .)

Usually, my manager, Jo Gurnett, comes along for the ride to the Eurovision, and Helen comes, too, to drink in the delights of places you'd never think of visiting for pleasure: Lausanne, Oslo, Bergen, Malmo, Tallinn, Riga, Kiev. Actually, neither Helen nor Jo came to Kiev – the memory of the Orange Revolution was but a few months old, and we'd heard rumours: accommodation was so scarce that the local authorities were pitching several thousand tents on an island in the river to cater for the anticipated rush of thousands of Eurosong-mad spectators with nowhere to rest their weary heads. As it turned out, there wasn't a tent to be seen and the local population's attitude to the

Great Event seemed at best half-hearted. There was no evidence whatsoever of teeming multitudes rushing westwards from the Urals, or northwards from the Black Sea. Hotel and guest rooms were freely available, although 'freely' is the wrong word, since they were being charged at five times the normal rate. The oldest trick in the book had backfired on Kiev's hotels and guest houses: when the rest of Europe heard that rooms were scarce, they didn't rush to pay extra – they just didn't bother to come.

I didn't think that Kiev would have much to offer Jo and Helen, two of the most feared shoppers in Europe, and, stap me vitals, I was right. The gateway of the former satellite states to Mother Russia, one of the great cities of the Union, Kiev has broad, treelined boulevards, the better, one felt, to facilitate the swift movement of troops and armour than the indolent stroller or the carefree passer-by. Not many shoppers, not many shops; underground malls, full of cheap goods, although there was a Bentley/Rolls-Royce dealership with the up-and-coming oligarch in mind. A great covered market took a whole block in the very centre of the city. Fruit, vegetables, and, everywhere, caviar. Oscietra, sevruga, beluga, in every size of tin. And the prices? Let me at it! In case your wandering ways ever take you to Kiev, a word: taste it before you buy it. The stuff I tasted was fine, the rest was like tiny rubber balls. If they don't open the tin, save your money for vodka. Although I'll have a taste of that too, first, if they let you open the bottle.

'Not coming with your wife? Ha! Careful!' they admonished. 'The most beautiful women in Europe are Ukrainian!'

A quick survey of the boulevards and the hotel lounge, which appeared to be heaving with the aforementioned loveliest women in Europe, confirmed the well-worn phrase of beauty being 'in the eye of the beholder'. On every side were skintight jeans, six-inch heels and peroxide hair. It's extraordinary, the notions that smaller, or more remote, countries have about themselves. My own country, Ireland, cannot be excluded from those others with delusions of grandeur. 'The loveliest scenery in the world,' is a boast you will frequently hear from Irish people who have never put a foot outside their country. My daughter, visiting Buenos Aires, was confidently informed that 'the best pizzas in the world' came from Argentina. My son, in Australia, was told in no uncertain terms that Australian Rules Football was 'the greatest game in the world'. Nobody else in the world plays it, but when in Sydney . . .

Speaking of small countries, Denmark, and Copenhagen in particular, was a delightful setting for the Song Contest. We ate herring by the waterside, drank our share of schnapps, and admired the *real* contenders for the title of 'the most beautiful women in Europe'. A supermodel on every corner, a Hollywood starlet on every bicycle. Denmark had won the year before with two old geezers in knitted pullovers, whose plaintive dirge was in such marked contrast to the yelling and jumping about that had gone before that every right-thinking citizen in Europe who wanted a bit of peace had voted for them.

The Danes, who fancy themselves as the entrepreneurs of Scandinavia, and think Swedes and Norwegians dull dogs, held the Eurovision in a football stadium. Thirty-five thousand people, which put Stockholm's fifteen thousand firmly in their place, vodka-sellers in every aisle, and a stage so far away that the commentators might as well have stayed at home. No matter, the atmosphere was jolly, the crowd's spirits well boosted by the passing vodka shots.

Up came the Euro-anthem, on came the presenters. It must have seemed like a good idea at the time to have the two unfortunates deliver their links in rhyming couplets, but for this commentator, at least, the quaint conceit quickly lost its charm and descended into farce. Not by any means unusual, and always welcome to the eager observer stuck for something to say. So I said, 'It's Doctor Death, and the Tooth Fairy,' struck by his cadaverous appearance and her resemblance to Rebecca of Sunnybrook Farm. They continued with their ridiculous couplets, I with my cheery ribbing . . .

The following morning I rose to my herring and croissant to find myself reviled as Denmark's Public Enemy Number One. European television is no great shakes, and Danish TV no exception, so half the population watched the Song Contest on BBC Prime TV. Obviously, they did so wishing to hear only good things about their staging of the Eurovision, and were none too pleased at my cavalier attitude. Not to put too fine a point on it, their newspapers were spitting blood. My comments were taken as a slap in the face to the Danes, nay, to all that was best in Danish life. You see, not only do small countries have delusions about themselves, they also have inferiority complexes. The Danes, like the Irish, and indeed the Australians, want to hear you speak well of them. The first question you will be asked upon arrival is, 'And what do you think of our beautiful country?' To which there is only one answer, and it had better not be in the negative. The Danes took my gentle banter as a foul slur on their fine country, and I had to be smuggled down the Skaggerak in a herring boat. Nor have they forgotten. I rarely meet a Dane, but on the odd occasion since then that I have, they pin me to the wall. 'You don't think much of Denmark, then?' A weak smile, and I'm off. My ancestors had the same trouble with berserkers . . .

Eurovision Song Contest presenters are always good for a jeer – wasn't I one myself, along with Ulrika Jonsson, in Birmingham, the year following Katrina and the Waves' 'Love Shine a Light' winning for the UK? An evening to remember, with me making announcements in French and English, then tearing around the back to the commentary position, and back out front again for the next link. I'll swear that I passed some cutting comments on myself, but you'll have to ask Ulrika – the whole evening was a blur for me. Only one thing moved slowly – the winner, Dana International. The usual form, when the winning song and singer is announced is, after the shrieking and hysteria have died to a dull roar, is for the winner to briskly make their way to the stage, take the Grand Prix, then go straight into a reprise of their winning effort. Dana International was nowhere to be seen. The cheering waned, Ulrika looked at me, I looked at Ulrika, we both looked at the camera, mouthed banalities, and fell silent. It was as long a few minutes as I've spent in broadcasting, with four hundred million people all over the world hanging on my silence.

Then Ulrika broke the spell with a fit of girlish giggles: 'She's here!'

Where had she been? Changing her dress. How I restrained myself from slapping her senseless, I'll never know . . . However, next year, in Jerusalem, fate took a hand, and Dana International got her comeuppance. As last year's winner, Dana International was to present the award to the winning singer. On she teetered in her twelve-inch heels, and, as she handed over the trophy, staggered and fell over. Thinking the worst, six members of

Mossad immediately flung themselves on top of her. The Gods of the Eurovision are not mocked . . .

When Ulrika and I presented the Contest, it was in the usual manner such things are done on British TV. Two pals together, some good-natured joshing, with never, ever, a hint of a flirtatious glance nor sexual frisson. As far as Europe is concerned, though, put a man and a woman on the stage together and it's Nelson Eddy and Jeanette MacDonald time. She flutters her eyelashes, he winks in a manly way, and within minutes they're all over each other like a rash. They hug, they hold hands, they look into each other's eyes as they speak. And how they speak. The lady in Kiev in 2005 had a voice like a plaster torn from a hairy leg, but was severely upstaged by the two guest presenters, Ukraine's most famous sons, the Klitchko Brothers. Who? you may ask; as indeed did all of Europe. Heavyweight boxers is the answer. Their job was to bang a gong, which might have worked if it had been one of the J. Arthur Rank variety, requiring a show of strength, and, perhaps, a glistening pec or two. The gong was of the small Chinese type, and nobody even removed a jacket.

I don't always keep a record of the places I've been lucky enough to visit through the auspices of the blessed Eurosong, but here's just a little taste of the capital of Estonia, which we all loved so much, I wrote this paean of prose in my diary:

For three lovely days in Tallinn, the sun shines. Way up north, on the toe of the Baltic, with nothing between us and the Urals, the temperature is in the seventies, the skies are clear. The weather forecast on the BBC World Service shows

wind and rain all over the Mediterranean. Don't you love it
when it's raining on everybody but yourself? And don't you
hate it when you return home from holiday and everybody
tells you how good the weather's been at home?

There are only 1,300,000 people in Estonia, with approximately a quarter of them living in Tallinn. Apart from trees,
and the Baltic lapping up against their shoes, these people have
no mineral nor natural resources, no industry. They've been
bullied, occupied and oppressed for centuries, most recently
by Nazi Germany and Soviet Russia. They've only been independent for eleven years, yet Tallinn is bursting with life,
commerce, new building and optimism. I know that I'll never
make an economist, but I don't get it. Why is Estonia on the
up and up, when its neighbours, Latvia, Lithuania, and even
Russia, are in the doldrums? It's not that the people are particularly sparkling. They're civil enough, but, in the shops and
on the street, unresponsive, unsmiling, the old Soviet Bloc
mentality still hanging on in there.

Tallinn has become a big tourist town, almost overnight. It
has almost replaced Dublin as the Mecca of the stag weekend
for the British. It's the girls. And the drink. What are stag
weekends for? The young ladies are beautiful and leggy, but
just a little too old-fashioned: skintight jeans and stiletto heels.
The beer flows from early morn, and is for nothing. Everywhere you look, Irish pubs. The kind of Irish pubs that you'd
never find in Ireland, and that the Irish themselves would never
be caught dead in, but that's true the world over. Apart from
the staggers, every weekend half the drinking population of
Helsinki, Finland hops on the ferry and spends the weekend
stocious in Estonia's capital. A pint is about five quid in

Helsinki ... The food's cheap and good, as well, although there doesn't appear to be any particular Estonian delicacy. The universal chip seems to play a major role, but there's a disappointing lack of indigenous fare. We've eaten rotten fish in Norway, reindeer in Sweden, but what of the local dish of the day in this little corner of the Baltic? No elf, no eagle, no creatures of the forest floor. Still, the barbecued chicken isn't bad ...

Tallinn itself, apart from the historic old town with its cobbles and thirteenth-century town hall, is a sprawling mess of old Eastern Bloc housing and most of it in poor repair – the living conditions are pretty terrible. But then, who are we to criticise? I've seen worse in Dublin, in London's East End, in Glasgow, in the North East ... These people are famously undemonstrative, untactile, yet everywhere you sense forward movement, strength, determination. These people are going to make their independence count. And they see the Eurovision Song Contest as a major step forward.

This Eurosong is the most important event in Estonia's brief independent history: a chance to let the world know of its existence, a window of opportunity to showcase itself. The atmosphere in the Saku Suurhall on the big night is electric with excitement, the decibel level bouncing off the roof. It stays up for the whole evening, the noisiest, most exhilarating Song Contest evening since the Irish staged 'Riverdance' at the Point, Dublin, six years ago. It ends up a ding-dong struggle between Latvia and Malta, right down to the wire. Actually it seemed more exciting than it really was. Neck and neck for most of the evening, Malta's chance had gone by the time the last two countries announced their votes. Latvia and Lithuania were never going to help Malta; Latvia for obvious reasons, and Lithuania because they're Latvia's next-door neighbours. I know that each country's votes are supposed to be counted and locked away until the moment of announcement, but all of us who have been around the block with Eurovision for a few years know that this splendid idealistic concept doesn't always work. Certain countries have been known to be economical with the concept in moments of high drama, or when they want to get their own back on some country that's given them a lousy '*nul points*'. Latvia gave Malta just enough points to bring the two countries level with each other, knowing full well that their next-door neighbour would give them the full '*douze points*'. So it goes; so it went.

Kiev is not yet, I would judge, a tourist destination, unlike Tallinn or Riga, who have come out of their starting blocks under the Russian Bear's shadow like sprinters after capitalist gold, yet Kiev is a lot easier to get into than to get out of. We arrived as VIPs with an amount of gratifying fussing, while at the same time being frisked and patted in a rough, but essentially friendly manner. The Contest itself went well, I think, although I can remember no more about it than any other. Only the occasion itself counts for a Eurovision; trying to recall the song or the singer the following day is futile. A few minutes' confusion in the hotel, where the porters had lost our bags, and then Kevin Bishop, Head of Delegation, or 'GB One' as he likes to be known, pushed us into a car for the airport. Unfortunately, he neglected to tell the driver to drop us off at departures, and the

The only wedding photo you'll ever see to feature a dustbin, 1945. That's Auntie Kitty who's the bridesmaid, a laughing Michael and Rose Wogan right at the back, and me, doing my Toulouse-Lautrec impersonation in front.

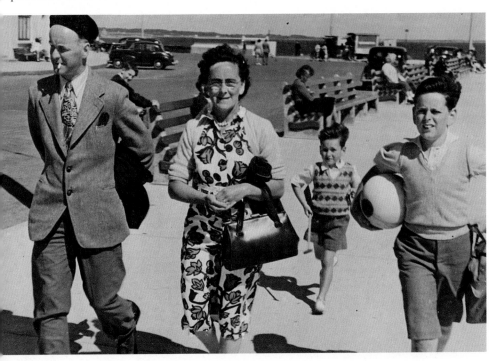

Michael T., Rose, the Brother and Big Ears in 1950. It must be summer holidays, the Da is wearing a beret …

'Auntie' Enda's wedding day. The gang's all here: the two Nellies, Great-Aunt Mag, Muds the Granny, the Ma, the Da, the Brud, Aunties May, Kitty and Dinah. I won the prize for the most teeth.

Michael and Rose at the peak of their form in 1952. The photo was taken at the opening of Peter Dominic, Grafton St, Dublin – the very premises where they first met ...

Michael T. Wogan and the dreaded beret strike again. Is that me or Bugs Bunny behind him?

THE BARON DE WOGAN.

After the defeat of the Jacobites, members of the Wogan family became soldiers of fortune in France. They didn't do too badly for themselves although obviously the thrifty family tradition of knitting your own clothes dies hard.

THE BARON DE WOGAN AT THE WAR-POST.

For some reason, the good Baron de Wogan took to the Americas, little knowing that his moustaches would infuriate the natives …

Card Times

MAGPIE PUBLICATIONS
70 Winifred Lane,
Aughton, Ormskirk,
Lancashire, L39 5DL
Tel : 01695 423470

21·1·99

Dear Sir Terry de Wogan,

As editor of Card Times, top magazine for the cigarette card collector, I believe I have come across evidence of one of your ancestors. The Carreras card attached, from their 1934 Believe It Or Not series, tells of one **Tanneguy de Wogan** of Paris who **'travelled 2,500 miles in a paper boat'**! Apparently no other materials were used in its manufacture but compressed paper.

The only thing which puzzles me - he must have been a pretty bad navigator to miss England on his way over from Ireland, to finish up in paris. No wonder he travelled 2,500 miles. He probably went via the Pentland Firth.

Anyway, hope you like it. All felicitations.

David Stuckey

David Stuckey : Editor, Card Times

2,500 MILES IN A PAPER BOAT

Presented to Princess Margaret in 1975, I apologise for my shirt which has just exploded, a button narrowly missing the Princess but causing a nasty flesh wound to a commissionaire standing fifty yards away ...

A proud moment for a local lad, as the University of Limerick confers me with an honorary degree. They let me keep the hat and coat. I wear them at the weekends ...

The chap in front gets a gong, backs off, white with fright. This is it. Remember to bow…

The newest Knight of the British Empire, **Sir Terry Wogan**, relives his moment of glory

The thing is, nobody really cares. All they want to know is "What did she say to you?" After a hundred such queries it's hard not to answer: "Hello mush, here's your gong. Now clear off – don't want to be late for lunch…"

My loyal listeners (and Her Majesty's loyal subjects) were all concerned for my well-being at the hands of the sword-wielding monarch. One offered to tape back my ears, lest the cold steel leave a lobe on the Palace carpet, while another suggested a small but serviceable device not unlike a stair-lift that would help me off my knees.

After my dangerous moment with the blade was shown on television, a worried mother wanted to know how the Queen gets all that swordplay past Health and Safety, when it's too dangerous for her own children to play conkers? This perceptive viewer also noticed that Dr Brian May of Queen (the pop group – do keep up) who was receiving a CBE for playing his guitar on the roof of the Palace in the biting wind, had blagged a Bushy as a souvenir and wanted to know if I'd managed to nick anything, such as a bottle of Blue Nun, or a couple of teaspoons.

First of all, that's Brian's hair, and second, there was no strong drink. There wasn't any tea, not to mind spoons… No time, you see. Three hundred spectators to be corralled into the Ballroom, and 110 nervous wrecks to be rehearsed in the protocol of investiture. You think you can just walk out there, exchange the airy banter with Herself, trouser the gong, and off to the bar? There's no such thing as a free lunch (although, having been up since all hours of the morning, I could

Sir Terry at the Palace 'They are very jolly when they rehearse you… but it makes you even more sick with worry'

rehearsal room at the Palace is a definite step-up in class. Huge, vaulted, hung with drapes and grand portraits, chandeliers, and a generous daubing of gold leaf, it is well calculated to reduce even the most confident and self-regarding of worthy recipients to apprehensive shivers. In case you've forgotten who you are, this will get you

All those equerries, commanders and colonels haven't gone to all this trouble for some hobbledehoy to swan in as if he owned the place

have done with a sustaining sausage-roll or two) and there are no free rides at the Palace.

All those Beefeaters with their halberds, Gurkhas, chamberlains, equerries, commanders and colonels, Hussars in highly-polished boots, haven't gone to all this trouble for some hobbledehoy to swan in and out as if he owned the place, even if he has got into a frock coat and a top hat. Then there's the Orchestra of the Welsh Guards, running the gamut from Sinatra to Bach, who haven't come all the way from the Valleys for their own amusement. Although the pianist did seem to have a mind of his own.

If you're used to draughty, empty rooms in North Acton, or some

back on the straight and narrow. A charming military man, in blinding boots and spurs, about seven feet tall, takes us through the routine. Come to the entrance; wait. When the shaking figure in front of you moves on towards Her Majesty, step forward a few wobbly paces and stand by the equerry. Chap in front gets a gong, backs off, white with fright. The man calls out your name.

This is it, forward a couple of paces, then turn to face the Queen; bow the head, not the body, kneel on the cushion, head up. Down comes the sword. Up you get, while they hand Her Maj the doings on a cushion. She hands them over. You speak when you're spoken to – not before. She's

One of the greatest, proudest moments of my life. Sir Terry Wogan KBE and Lady Wogan on the day Her Majesty dubbed me Knight at Buckingham Palace, 2005.

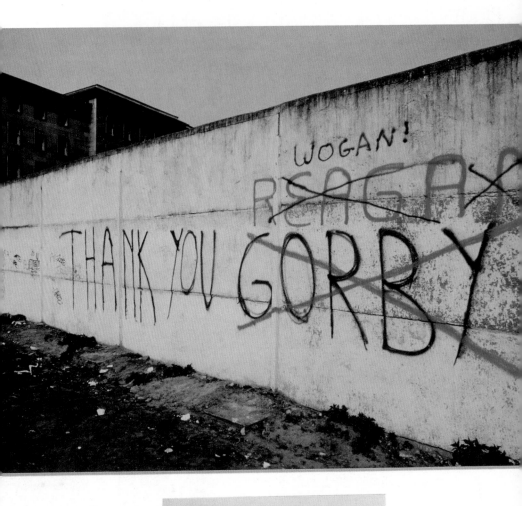

THE BERLIN WALL
APRIL 1990

I may not leave behind me 'footprints in the sands of time' but I made the Berlin Wall before they tore it down.

fellow set us down at the VIP entrance. They welcomed us in and left us.

We stood there, Paul Walters, Ken Bruce and I, for some time, tickets and passports in hands, before we realised that we could be there until hell froze over. It's all very well being a sophisticated polyglot, but not much good if you haven't got a word of Russian. I stopped a member of the ground staff and pressed our tickets and passports into her hand. She smiled, took them in a purposeful manner, and disappeared.

Time passed.

Paul went into another room, and there they were – tickets and passports, on a counter, abandoned. Now we're panicking. We may never see home and Mother again. Do they still have gulags?

Some shouting and sign language later, it turns out that we have no business to be in the VIP room, because British Airways have no agreement with the Kiev Airport Authority. I point out that we didn't want to be in the blasted VIP room in the first place, how do we get out? Not without paying . . . I hand over seventy-five quid; now we can enjoy the luxurious surroundings and someone may try to get us on our plane. Upstairs to the bar. Vodka and tonics; it looks as if we're going to make that run for freedom. The barmaid comes out to the lounge. I've got to pay for the vodka and tonics. But I've just paid seventy-five quid . . . Never mind. You're not in the pay of the Danes, are you? . . .

Having survived the worst excesses of the Eurovision, including Death by Drums and the Incredible Shrieking Woman, it came as something of a body-blow to find myself all over the papers a couple of days later, portrayed as a lickspittle strikebreaker: BBC staff were protesting about severe cuts in personnel. It's hard enough to pass a picket that includes friends and colleagues without the implication of being a traitor. Look, I crossed the line because I'm a freelance radio and television presenter who would otherwise have been in breach of contract. Then, to add insult to injury, some eejit in the *Daily Mail* writes, while trying to make a case against the BBC and its profligacy, on the subject of the Eurovision: 'Terry Wogan, and his enormous retinue of support staff.' That'll be my radio producer and my television producer, then. If the BBC wastes money, it's not on the likes of me. With eight million listeners every morning, five mornings a week, my programme commands the BBC's biggest audience, on radio or television. Two and a half people work on the programme: a producer, a part-time assistant and me. The producer also makes the coffee. I wash up. Some retinue.

At the beginning of March 2006, Natasha Kaplinsky and I presented *Making Your Mind Up*, another futile attempt to pick a song – any song – that would proudly fly the flag for the UK at the Eurovision Song Contest. The year before, the show had excited a deal of popular interest because of the performance of Katie Price, aka Jordan, who delivered herself of a lively routine while barely togged out in a pink rubber number, which did nothing to hide the fact that she was six months pregnant. It got a lot of votes – old Jordan can certainly pull in the punters – but the winner was Javine, wearing even less and bouncing merrily to a ditty that owed more to the mystic East than her home turf. As I've said earlier, the rhythms of the souk are all-pervading of late at the Eurothrash, but it availed Javine and the UK little as she trotted in with eighteen points, in twenty-second place.

Criticism, as ever, was rife: why had we tried to ape the music of another culture? Since when had belly-dancing been a British pastime? The ghosts of Lulu, Sandie Shaw and Cliff Richard were freely invoked (a little strange in Cliff's case, since he came second. Never mind, everybody here thinks he won). Jordan fulminated mightily at her loss, and in her highly successful book, *A Whole New World*, she says that appearing on *Making Your Mind Up* was the biggest mistake of her life. Which, when you think of what she's got up to so far, is saying something. I can't see it myself; winning or losing on that show makes not the slightest difference to a career. If you lose, at least six million people have seen you strut your stuff, which, in the case of most of the performers, is five million, nine hundred and ninety-nine thousand more than have ever seen you before. If you're a winner, three hundred million people all over the world will see you on the Eurovision. But even if you win that, they'll have forgotten you, and the song, ten minutes after the show is over . . .

The winner in 2006, picked as they only can be by the great British public, with no regard for what they're picking, or why, was a rap number called 'Teenage Life' by a gentleman called 'Daz'. 'Teenage Life', as the music-lover will know, featured the rapper with schoolgirls. One of our panel of judges, Kelly Osbourne, thought it was 'pervy', but it provoked an avalanche of mail that was greater even than Jordan's pink rubber pregnancy.

A must-win selection! Were those girls from Farnborough Hill Convent? Brought back tears to my eyes as a boy attending the

Salesian College, riding on the bus between Camberley and Farnborough – without the courage to chat the girls up . . .

From Dame Ariadne Ledinispensil, Headmistress of the Cheltenham School for Young Ladies of Athletic Prowess, Halifax:

Recently I agreed to let several of my girls act as supporting dancers to one of the acts on your show. So far, none have returned to the school, and I am somewhat concerned as they are a shy and retiring group . . .

Chuffer Dandridge, the old Shakespearean actor-manager who is permanently resting, and who enlivens most of our mornings with salty tales of life in the fit-ups, loved it all:

You and Natasha were wonderful on Saturday! Which one was which? She's a smasher! So 'Grange Hill, the Musical' won, eh? That's what comes of giving people with mobile phones a text vote, without including an IQ test! Well, look on the bright side, at least the UK won't have to host the Eurovision next year. And by the way, what was the story with Jonathan Ross's new hairstyle? Is he starring as Moe in a *Three Stooges* remake?

Admittedly, Jonathan did look as if he was addressing us through a hedge, but it was the insanely lovely Natasha Kaplinsky that got as big a reaction as the winning song:

Shouldn't Saturday's programme have carried a health
warning for those of a weak disposition? My dear husband
had to go for a lie-down after spotting where Miss Ker-
plunkski was hiding her ample supply of marbles. Just when
he returned with his magnifying glass (for his newspaper, he
claimed) he was taken all funny again by the sight of those
schoolgirls, and a chap who seemed to be trying to hail a
taxi . . .

That judges for *Making Your Mind Up* were Bruno Tonioli,
Fearne Cotton, Jonathan Ross and Kelly Osbourne tells you
how seriously you should be taking the thing. I'm convinced
Bruno's real name is Mick O'Shaughnessy, from Cork, but his
cool-Italian routine works a treat, Jonathan is always good for
an outrageous remark, and Fearne and Kelly were charming,
while confessing that they didn't know what they were doing
there. Not their kind of music. But it's nobody's kind of music,
except that of the audience in the studio, camp to a man, and
loving it.

The column I write weekly for the *Sunday Telegraph* has a
Friday deadline, but I knew that they'd want a deeply reflective
thought-piece on the 2006 Eurosong Contest, so I wrote this a
couple of days before the event:

Kalimera! You find me in Athens, the Edinburgh of the South,
for the umpteenth running of the Eurovision Song Handicap.
By the time you read this, the tumult and the shouting will
have abated, the winning song been awarded the Grand Prix,

and already been forgotten. I'll bet you can't even remember which country won . . .

I'd hardly be sticking my neck out, writing this before the event, if I predicted that the emerging nations of the former Soviet bloc will dominate the contest by the simple ploy of voting for each other, as was their enforced habit while festering under the Kremlin's shadow. I'll be amazed if Belarus gives anything other than '*douze points*' to Russia; the Big Bear is on their doorstep. The jolly exchange of full marks between Cyprus and Greece is as old as the Odyssey; the Scandinavians will vote for each other, Iceland and Denmark will cement their ancient ties, and nobody will vote for us. France won't give us a saucisson, and although the UK will award marks to Ireland, I'll eat the Blarney Stone if Ireland have given anything to Royaume Uni. The UK is there to pay for the thing, pretend we think it's all a bit of nonsense, and we wouldn't want to win anyway. Germany will get the usual votes from Turkey, because the Turkish *gastarbeiten* in Germany will have monopolised the phones and awarded top marks to their homeland . . .

On the basis of the previews, I know that I will find you sated this morning by a musical macédoine the likes of which even fifty years of this grand farrago will not have prepared you for: Germans in Stetsons, Finns like a cross between Klingons and Orcs, Icelanders phoning God, Latvians a cappella, Disco, Twist, Rock 'n' Roll, Torch songs, the now inevitable breath of the souk, choreography straight out of the sixties, bongos, banjos, musical saws, and I'll swear I saw somebody try to get a tune out of a sheep's stomach . . .

I have high hopes of the presenters, and look to them to flirt heavily, and possibly sing to each other, rather in the manner of the unforgettable Estonian presenters, who bellowed into each other's faces at a distance of six inches. She was an opera singer, and he was the country's leading Shakespearean actor, who also played accordion in a folk band. And you ask me why I love the Eurovision?

As it turned out, I wasn't a million miles off the mark as far as the scoring was concerned, but then, you don't have to be Nostradamus in this game. Andorra gave '*douze points*' to Spain, which caused nobody a sharp intake of breath. Cyprus, of course, did the right thing to Greece, but I was wrong about Ireland, who donated eight big ones to the UK's entry, Daz Sampson.

Finland carried off the Grand Prix with a Gothic hard rock horror show, featuring a lead singer with wings and what looked like the worst case of broken veins ever seen on television. My TOGs, TYGs (Terry's Young Geezers) and assembled Euro-fanatics reacted in their thousands with predictable panache and vigour:

To: Terry Wogan
From: Stars in their Eyes

Strewth, Terry! I nearly choked on my Sanatogen. Did you see all that hideous gothic make-up and that lumpy, scary clothing? Anyway, enough about you. What about those Finnish blokes...?
  Stars in their Eyes

To: Terry Wogan
From: Elaine Cohen-Dorf

Congratulations to the BBC for their acquisition of *Stars in Their Eyes*, which I watched on Saturday evening (admittedly with the sound turned down so as not to frighten the budgie). I particularly liked the one where Old Mother Riley emerged from the piano. Bet Lynch seemed to have spent a lot of time at the tattoo parlour since leaving the Street, but I couldn't work out how the football hooligans dressed for their court appearance had got on to the show. The best part was the Finnish.

    Elaine Cohen-Dorf

One of my regular correspondents, the resting actor-manager, Chuffer Dandridge weighed in with a theatrical word or two.

To: Terry Wogan
From: Chuffer Dandridge

Does 'Amazing' mean something different in Greek?

    What Ho Me Old Voice in the Wilderness.

    Well, wasn't the Eurovision ... amazing? Wasn't the female presenter ... amazing? Did she know any more adjectives other than ... amazing? But she was right! I haven't seen a show like that since a cabaret in pre-war Berlin, where I was naked, painted in zebra stripes and sitting bareback on a horse ... and I was in the audience! I must say Moldova was robbed! They had three changes of costume and a rapper on a scooter.

I've been in three-act plays with less going on! Latvia sang a cappella and brought their own cyberman! Too scary. And poor old Daz Sampson didn't win. The rest of Europe obviously don't find chav culture as amusing as we do! But the winners were appropriately named – Lordi! Because that's what I said when I saw them perform and again when they won! Nice to know the Eurovision has a 'Best Make-Up' category. You always suspected it wasn't about the song, didn't you? It means next year we'll be inundated with fire-eaters, tightrope contortionists and people juggling accordions! The gimmick's the thing! And did you notice the deliberate error in the interval act? How could you have a celebration of songs from *Grease* without anything by John Travolta and Olivia Newton-John?

I must congratulate you on your stoical reserve throughout the show. You were . . . amazing! Well done, you were so entertaining you should have won! Less said about the voting the better. I'm beginning to think it's strategic. Say nothing!

Cheery Pip.

Chuffer Dandridge

P.S.: I think you've found your next holiday stand-in in that chap who read out the Netherlands vote. He's a raw talent, isn't he?

The British public will never grasp with what pride other countries regard a Eurosong win.

To: Terry Wogan
From: Asa Sandberg

Good morning, Terry!

Are you back from Athens yet? Just wanted to write in because I'm a Finn and am sitting here beaming with a glorious grin, since Finland went home with the win.

It's amazing, isn't it?

In my almost forty years on this planet (the last eleven in sunny Morecambe) it had never entered my head that Finland stood a chance in the Eurovision Song Contest.

And here we are. Finland's small ethnic sub species 'The Lordis', who until a few decades ago lived in caves in the far north of the country and hunted polar bears with their bare hands. Flushing the meat down with raw vodka has done it!

It is amazing! Maybe now this tiny ethnic group will be allowed into the Finnish school system. And by the way, all you TOGs out there, Finland is not situated close to Switzerland and we are not that close to China either. The capital of the country is Helsinki and I'm sure the Hartwall Arena in the capital will give everybody a great spectacle next May.

And Terry, Helsinki normally has very warm and sunny days in May.

I'm sure you'll find that amazing!

Asa Sandberg

The 'amazing' reference is to the show's Greco-American co-presenter, a feisty baggage named Maria, whom I had pegged as a loose cannon from the first rehearsal; and so, mercifully, she proved. She found everything 'amazing', and said so at least twenty times, on one occasion four times in the same sentence. She was supported in this by the UK's spokeswoman, Fearne Cotton, who also found the whole business 'amazing'. 'Amazing' was the word for it, but a thesaurus wouldn't have come amiss for a few alternative epithets.

The Greeks had been waiting to strut their stuff again after the triumph of the Olympic Games, and the opening sequence was the most stunning I've seen in thirty-five years. 'Terry's Chocolate Orange', with gold-painted nymphs, cherubs and possibly dryads clinging to its sides, swung over the 18,500 raving flag-wavers in the Olympic indoor arena, while dolphins frolicked on the stage, and a very loud soprano sang a hymn to life. I was expecting the presenters to swim on, but they flew in from the rafters on kirby-wires. A far cry from the Gaiety Theatre Dublin, 1971.

The interval took us through four thousand years of Greek music, starting with Aristophanes' 'Frogs' and 'Birds', and ending up with a giant 'Zorba's Dance' to a bouzouki. 'Riverdance' it wasn't. Still, it didn't detract from what, to my rheumy old eye, was the best staged and produced Eurovision ever. It reflected the confidence that has pervaded Greece since the country staged the Olympic Games with such panache and success a couple of years ago. Athens is a city transformed – a new airport, new motorways, by-passes, flyovers, tunnels, trams, a magnificent Olympic stadium. It made for a wonderful trip, particularly the sunny day we went to Glyfada, thirty minutes from the city by the shining Aegean, and ate fresh fish by a beautiful beach, while sirens and naiads frolicked in the waves . . . Roll on Helsinki! Anyone know the Finnish for 'amazing!'?

I used to joke that the good old Song Contest would be my pension; that it would eventually grow into a massive creature like the World Cup, with preliminary rounds, first rounds proper, then quarter-finals and semi-finals before exploding into a Grand Finale. It would take all year, and involve some lucky commentator in endless foreign travel, staying in luxurious hotels and eating for Britain. How we chuckled at such a preposterous prospect. Nobody's laughing now, as the monster swells before our very eyes. A couple of years ago, the EBU, reflecting, they said, the growth of the European Union and the ever increasing number of countries wishing to join what they obviously saw as the gravy-train, decided to expand the remit of the Song Contest. 'Everybody In!' was the cry, and so they came, from the Adriatic to the Black Sea, from the Urals to the very shores of Asia – Albania, Macedonia, Moldova, Slovenia – and surely only a matter of time before Azerbaijan, Uzbekistan, and with a little tolerance, Outer Mongolia, join the merry throng. The more the merrier? Not for this curmudgeonly commentator. As I've said earlier, the influx of countries, new to our decadent democratic Western ways, have cocked the Contest up. It'll never be the same again, but hey! Let's go with the flow. I just think it's all going to be a bit too much for the British viewer, an over-egging of what is already a very rich pudding. The semi-final, or qualifying round, with which the Song Contest has been saddled for the past three years is simply, as they say in Ireland, going to the fair with the story. The Eurovision stands alone, straddling the world of television like a colossus. The last thing it needs is another contest in the same week, with twenty-four more countries taking part, ten of whom hope to qualify for the Grand Prix on the Saturday. It's overkill and it diminishes the Contest itself. The British viewing public will end up not watching either, if we show both. Which is why it's a mistake for BBC 3 to have jumped on the bandwagon and transmitted the semi-final. BBC 3's coverage of the Big One scarcely adds to the gaiety of nations, either. Camping up the Eurovision Song Contest is leaning on an open door. If you leave it alone, it sends itself up – let's not beat the thing to death.

6

They can't all love you

⟿

I see no reason why, if the Middle East and Asia are to be welcomed into Europe, Australia cannot be invited to participate. The great majority of the Lucky Country are of British and Irish stock, and the Eurovision has a sturdy following there, and increasingly includes immigrants from Europe who desperately miss their yearly Festival of Fine Music. Also, they like *me*! A couple of years ago, the Australians sent their own commentator to cover the show, an unfortunate named Des Morgan. Obviously, old Des didn't quite cut the mustard: 'When will SBS realise that the reason for the popularity of the Song Contest is Terry Wogan's brilliantly humorous and politically insightful commentary?' That was a shrewd observer from Murrumbeena. Ferntree Gully, Wantirna and Princes Hill all wanted to be associated with the remarks of the last speaker.

I could be big in Australia, given half a chance. However, it appears that I'm the only person in British showbiz for whom there is no demand Down Under. When I last heard, Max Bygraves is still touring there, and Val Doonican continues to knock 'em dead. I shouldn't be surprised if the Krankies go down a storm in Alice Springs. Yet, for me, the call of the distant didgeridoo never comes . . . Still, who needs to swim in a sea full of killer sharks and box jellyfish, or scour the dunny for a deadly red-back spider before you sit down?

People are forever asking, 'Why do you do the Eurovision Song Contest?', as if it were somehow beneath me; then, in the same breath, 'And you still do the early morning radio?' as if I'm somehow desperate for work and will get up at all hours just to get my face in front of a microphone. I gave up explaining years ago that I do the Eurothingy because I love it, and it loves me, and ditto the early morning radio. I used to take people aside, in the same way as I once saw Sir Clement Freud do to explain why he didn't give autographs, and try to make it clear to them that in my sad old game, popular broadcasting, popularity is what counts. The Song Contest is one of the high spots of the viewing year, with eleven million viewers watching and cringing long past their bedtime. If it didn't get the audience, it would have been consigned to the waste bin long ago, and me with it. Forget *Wogan*, *Blankety Blank*, *Auntie's Bloomers*, *Points of View* and the hundred and one other flawed epics with which I've been associated, the Eurovision Song Contest is *the* television show by which the public identify me, more so even than *Children in Need*. It's probably something to do with the fact that they don't have to look at me . . . which is undoubtedly at least one of the major reasons for the success of *Wake Up to Wogan*.

For the benefit of those who don't watch the Eurovision, and who can't be bothered to listen to a lot of ould talk on the radio, the reason I get up at half-past five every morning, eschewing the full Irish breakfast in favour of a mango (eaten, of course, while standing naked in the sink, otherwise every stitch of clothing is covered in juice) and a cup of instant coffee, is not *just* because I love the fun and frolic, the jolly bonhomie of my underlings, the rebuilding of the studio after Johnnie Walker has dismantled it the evening before, the muffins from catering, of which I never get a taste, since the producer seems to think they belong to him, and distributes to passing females in a desperate attempt to curry favour; nor even the delights of sitting in the traditional traffic jam that is the Marylebone Road. No, if you're still with me, I'm doing the blasted thing because if you're a presenter on a 'popular' radio station, breakfast-time is the only game in town. It's where the audience is. Mercifully, whether it's because most people don't have a TV in the kitchen, or because British breakfast television is either tedious or terrible, upon rising from their trundle beds the public reach for the radio. Every radio station in Britain's biggest audience show is their 'breakfast' programme. If the breakfast show is a bust, there goes the network. Radio 1's steep decline over the past few years can be directly attributed to its unfortunate choice of early morning presenters. (As I write, Chris Moyles seems to have halted the fall, but from where he started, the only way was up.)

Any presenter worth their salt should want the network's flagship programme; why else are you in the game, if not to be the biggest and the best? I didn't join up to be an also-ran, and when the day arrives when they take away my locker-key, don't look for me on the graveyard shift or a Christmas Special. I'm where I've always wanted to be, just as with 'Hospitals' Requests' on Irish radio all those years ago – where the audience is.

My fellow early-morning men and women tend to sniff a bit when my dear little show is referred to as 'breakfast-time'. Most of those other hobbledehoys have been moiling and toiling long before I rear my ugly head. God knows what time Chris Moyles gets up, but then he always looks like he's never been to bed, anyway. Many of these unfortunates start as early as six o'clock in the morning, and often gabble wearily on until ten. When I returned to BBC Radio 2 for my second incarnation in 1993, my start time was 7 a.m. Whether I'd still be doing the thing if this madness had persisted is doubtful, but luckily the then Controller of Radio 2, Frances Line, and her cohort, David Vercoe, who had never really wanted me back in the first place, decided to start Sarah Kennedy at 6 a.m. and extend her to 7.30 a.m.

This was to be the thin end of the wedge for me – I could eventually be eased out and the network returned to the form that everybody knew and loved with, say, Derek Jameson returning, and lots more organ music and songs from the shows. Unfortunately for everybody, instead of withering on the vine, *Wake Up to Wogan* prospered. There was no getting rid of me. Obviously, if the programme were to be extended by a half, or even a full, hour, then the listening figures would be even better. But I'm content – all right, pleased with myself – that each successive year shows a bigger audience for Radio 2 and my show.

When I took over again in 1993, I'm quoted somewhere as saying that if I could add a half-million to the audience, I'd consider it a job well done. The journalist expressed considerable doubt: hadn't I just been 'axed' from the television – would the public bother to listen to old washed-up Wogan? It was a valid point, but I hope he was still around in 2001 when the penny really dropped for the print media. If I may trouble you with a modest quote from the *Daily Telegraph* editors five years ago:

> The supposed king of the media, television, has suffered a body-blow: for the second time in a year it has emerged that average daily radio listening has exceeded the number of hours the nation spends watching television. And the most popular presenter is neither young, nor married to a pop star. Radio 2 has drawn in a million new listeners for the real master of the airwaves – Terry Wogan.

And so it has gone, year on year. In 2001 the listening audience was over five million; as I write, it's over eight million. By January 2005, the *Daily Express* was calling me the 'most popular man in Britain'. And you and I and everybody else with even a tittle of wit will know that as soon as there's even a suggestion of a slippage, they'll be on to me like a pack of ravening wolves: 'Is Wogan finished?', 'Woe-begone Wogan' – we could all write the headlines now. It's happened before, and they were wrong. Next time, they might be right, but when, and if, I quit, it'll be my decision. And you can tell 'em I told you so . . .

All that kind of stuff, while burnishing the ego to a high-gloss finish, should never be taken seriously. The media are obsessed with themselves. Journalists read every newspaper, editors every other editorial, the print watches the television, the television laps up every word in print. Everything in the media, for those intimately involved, assumes a far greater importance than it does for the man in the street. Piers Morgan, former editor of the *Mirror*, turned television presenter, is rarely out of the newspapers. A passing foreigner might imagine him a major media figure, yet I would suggest that, to the great mass of the public, he, and his name, are completely unknown. Rageh Omaar, dubbed 'the Scud Stud', following his TV reports on the Iraq war, was lionised in the press. Hundreds of thousands of pounds changed hands for his war diaries in advance of their publication. The British book-buying public, being unfamiliar with the name, ignored the book . . .

Hard to believe that they would also ignore Greg Dyke's book of dirty doings at the BBC. After all, the papers and the TV had been full of it for weeks. Once more, a large advance was repaid by public indifference. Jon Snow, who takes both himself and his news very seriously, had a similar chastening experience. Meanwhile, Jordan, who is famous for an enhanced embonpoint and reality television, has had two books ghosted for her that sold like hot-cakes. People decide for themselves who, and what, is important, worth watching or reading about. And it's been my experience that the media are always behind the public when it comes to knowing what's popular. Not that anybody is as popular as they think they are. For most people, you're just a face or a voice that's vaguely familiar. They think they've met you somewhere, at a party or in a pub. Only recently I went into a post office. The man selling me the stamps smiled, then turned to his workmate.

'Look who it is!' he said, obviously hoping that his partner would know who it was.

'Yes!' the other man smiled, completely in the dark.

I thanked them civilly and went downstairs to the card department.

'Hello,' said the man at the counter, smiling vaguely. He called to his wife: 'Come, look who's here!'

Out she came, smiling brightly. 'What are *you* doing here?' she asked.

'Buying cards,' I replied brightly.

'Oh, good,' she said, and retired.

As I was looking at the cards, a voice behind me said, 'We don't see much of you these days.'

My smile was becoming a real effort.

'I'm still on the radio and television.'

A puzzled look:

'Oh, really? What do you do now?'

Don't talk to me about eight and a half million listeners. There are fifty-two million others out there who couldn't care less . . .

It's undeniably flattering when people say, 'You're not going to retire, are you? What'll we do when you're gone?' Listen to whoever takes my place, is the answer. It's only about being there. When you're gone, you're gone. Nobody on radio and television leaves footprints on the sands of time. It's debatable whether any 'great' man or woman does, outside of the history books. How often does Alexander the Great crop up in conversation these days? People for whom I've been a steady drone in the background of their lives from child to adult may miss the familiarity of my voice for a week or two, at most, then it's onwards and upwards with the next incumbent. Film stars survive their movies repeated again and again, their charisma, star quality undimmed by time, but television and radio is a much more mundane business. The public become familiar with you, you share their sitting rooms, kitchens and bedrooms. If you're any good, you might even become their friend; but it's distance that lends enchantment to the view. Film stars are unreachable, an impossible dream; television and radio personalities are a face or a voice in the corner, forgotten long before they're gone. Still, Tom Cruise never got a letter like this from a lady in Cirencester to the *Telegraph*:

Sir, I note that Terry Wogan's popularity continues to increase. I believe the Government should try to analyse why its citizens are tuning to him in their droves. I believe they are driven by a variety of factors, including: bill demands from electricity companies which have already been notified by phone, fax and letter that no money is due; the requirement that empty paint tins and empty Cornflake packets be disposed of in separate bins; advice from the Food Standards Agency that floors that are going to come into contact with food should be kept clean. In my youth, I used to watch *Star Trek*, and hoped that humans would learn to embrace the ideals of the Federation, who had done away with greed, and respected diversity. Instead, it appears we more closely resemble an outpost threatened by assimilation into the Borg. The inhabitants of the outpost know that their only champion is Terry Wogan.

I'm sure I could add to that those whose bins remain

unemptied because they're not full enough; the lonely travellers, sitting, even as we speak, in a newly built bus shelter in a Midlands town which is not on any bus route; and the many thousands, nay millions, of people of a certain age who are deprived of nourishment by their bumptious offspring who demand that all foodstuffs past their 'use by' date are thrown out. I am ready to serve. I await the call . . .

And just in case you think it's all braggadocio, let me assure you that the title 'Ireland's Greatest Living Entertainer' rests lightly on my shoulders. You're not dealing with hobbledehoy rubbish here. It was a glittering evening in Dublin in 2005, when Gay Byrne, a little-known, elderly Irish television presenter, handed me the award, cursing and swearing like a sailor under his breath. It came as a shock and a delight that my own people had not forgotten me, thirty-odd years after I took the immigrant ship and arrived barefoot and in rags at the door of the BBC. The commissionaire told me to be on my way in the kind of language that's all too familiar these days, particularly on the Jonathan Ross show, but I survived, striking up a warm friendship with Lord Jimmy Young, as he then was, by dint of plying him with drink and licking his boots. There was never anything remotely sexual between us, which is a disappointment to the publisher, and means that you're never going to read racy excerpts from this in your favourite red-top. Other people with whom I've never had sex are Joanna Lumley, Sophia Loren and Sir Sean Connery. As for the drugs, the closest I've come is Dr Collis Browne's Chlorodyne. They took it away some time ago, and I shall miss that floating feeling.

The Irish award left me with a warm glow, which was immediately vitiated by the, as ever, begrudging tributes of my listener, who wrote that there was no need for me to get all hoity-toity, Iceland was a tiny country with only 300,000 inhabitants, most of whom were too cold to care about anything, and anyway, he had voted for Björk. Another go-be-the-wall wondered if my new status in Iceland meant that I would meet and greet the customers as they entered the supermarket? It was ever thus . . .

Nothing I've done, nor ever will do, on television or radio, gives me more pride than *Children in Need*. It's a classic example of a show that only the public love, for the critics have always looked upon it with a rheumy eye. It reminds me of the critical reaction to the Eurovision Song Contest, right up until the nineties, when the penny finally dropped for the hacks, and they realised that criticising the Song Contest for its lack of intrinsic merit was not only flying in the face of public opinion, but completely missing the point. It took them about thirty years to cop on, and with *Children in Need* merely in its twenty-sixth year, it'll be a couple of years yet before they realise that they've yet again been barking up the wrong tree!

Children in Need raised over £34 million last year, its greatest total to date, and the gross amount contributed by the public over twenty-six years is close to £400 million, every penny of which goes straight to the children. All costs are paid from interest earned on the capital, something no other charity can claim. That's why it's become Britain's most popular, and Pudsey Bear the country's best-loved icon. Through the seven hours of the telethon, the viewing figures rarely flag, while the public in their millions make their contributions, big and small. It's family viewing, not cutting-edge, nor trendy. It's not smart, it's not stand-up, it's not 'yoof'. (That's *Comic Relief*, and magnificent that is, for catering for its audience and raising millions for the world's starving.) It's a critic's job to carp and cavil – he's being paid for his subjective opinion, and the more pungently he puts it, the more attention he attracts. But where do you leave a twerp in *The Times*, who wrote in 2005: 'November is short of ersatz national days, except for the annual BBC *Children in Need* atrocity, an event better calculated than any other to make me contemplate self-harm.' Don't contemplate it, chum, do it. Start with your heart, if you can find it.

How in heaven's name can anybody be so crass? There are innumerable other channels this moron could watch on the night with a light heart and no compulsion for self-abuse. Nobody's forced to watch *Children in Need*, but millions do from choice, and, unbelievably, they seem to enjoy it in their simple, unsophisticated way. I've been privileged to be a trustee of the charity for some years, and it's been a chastening experience. It's the trustees' responsibility to distribute the immense amount of money raised, but if all the worthy applications for help were to be satisfied, we'd need at least five times the money raised in 2004. To be a trustee is to have a heart-rending education in the seemingly innumerable ways in which children may be deprived, abused, ill-treated; but worst of all are the diseases and afflictions, most of which I'd never heard of, that make life almost impossible for these children and their families. I say 'almost', because these children and their families do not countenance impossibility – they struggle; they do not yield to what those of us who are more fortunate with the health of our children would deem insurmountable odds. All over this country there are hundreds of small charities formed by the parents of children with rare, unheard-of diseases and conditions. They can't afford publicity, and since the disease only affects the lives of a tiny minority, they're ignored by the media. These are the people and the children that I'm most proud to be helping. There is no glow of pride, however, for we can never do enough. For all that the public contribute more and more money every year, the mountain of need grows higher and higher.

Not that that is going to stop the thousands of good people who want to help. No day goes by that I don't receive news of a school, a council, a golf club or just a good-natured group of friends who have rallied round to raise money for *Children in Need*.

Contributions come pouring in all year for *Children in Need*. It's significant that whatever is raised on the Big Night in November is inevitably doubled by the time the grand total for the year is announced – witness 2004, the record year: £17 million on telethon night, over £34 million as a total figure. The build-up starts in earnest in October, when the fun packs are announced; they're free to whoever wants to help, full to bursting of ideas, suggestions and fun ways in which individuals and groups can raise money and have a laugh into the bargain. The TOGs start to flog their calendar, which raised £80,000 the last time I looked; then there's the special TOGs Pudsey T-shirt, which went flying off the shelves as soon as I mentioned it. Photographic sessions (pretty rough work, with Natasha Kaplinsky and Fearne Cotton, but it's all for the kiddies), TV and newspaper interviews, recordings for every BBC local radio station. Local radio is a great supporter now, a far cry from the early days, when some stations looked upon the Appeal as unwanted interference from Big Brother at White City.

As I've said elsewhere, although *Children in Need* night got off to a great start in 1980, it wasn't with the wholehearted support of the BBC. Recently, Sir Bill Cotton, who was Managing Director of Television at the time, told me that the Director-General, Alaistair Milne, didn't like the idea at all when it was first mooted. Many producers resented having their programmes interrupted, and I suspect the general view was that it was worth giving the thing a try, but perhaps not quite what the BBC should be doing. Ridiculous in retrospect, it was a view that quite a few mandarins and apparatchiks on the upper floors of Television Centre held for many years.

Indeed, it hasn't been entirely stamped out yet. We seem to get a great deal more support from some ITV programmes than we ever do from some of our own. *Coronation Street* and *Emmerdale* have been particularly helpful, and at a considerable cost of money and time, have produced features that have been among the highlights of the night. *Children in Need* might have poodled about indefinitely after its tentative beginnings, scratching around and pleading for support from BBC programme-makers, if Michael Grade, then Director of Programmes, hadn't given everybody a kick in the pants five years in and told the laggards and the begrudgers to get their fingers out and support what, even then, was manifestly the most important, and, as far as the Corporation was concerned, the most cohesive, programme that the BBC produced every year. Hard to believe that it's still not trendy enough for some, who seem to think that *Comic Relief* will carry more kudos, even if it's only on every second year.

And why anybody – producer, presenter, comic or actor – would imagine that helping one should preclude you from

143

helping the other can only be guessed at. *The Royal Variety Performance*, which, every year, alternates between the BBC and ITV, in 2005 was ITV's baby. Anybody who appeared on it was excluded from helping us out on 18 November. Now, whether this exclusivity was at the behest of ITV or the BBC, I neither know nor care. But in the name of all that's holy, who gives a rattling damn whether a star who graces the boards for Her Majesty turns up the following week on *Children in Need?* Appearing on the television is what these people do for a living, quite often more than once a week. Who is it hurting, that they should do both shows? Don't tell me that the Queen cares . . .

Not that we've ever had any support from Buck House or elsewhere in the realms of royalty for our appeal. It does seem a little strange that one of the country's major charities, and probably its best-loved, which raises millions every year for the common good, our most precious resource, our children, never gets a word of praise, nor even a passing glance, from the monarchy. Princess Anne rallied round one year, I remember, to help Riding for the Disabled, but apart from that gracious gesture, from the Palace has only come a great silence. Every year I ask Nick Vaughan-Barrett, our Executive Producer, and also the BBC's man at the Palace, whether we may expect, if not an appearance, any sort of endorsement. As ever, there are only two alternatives: either he's not asking, or they're saying 'no'. Which latter, frankly, I find impossible to believe, don't you? Tony Blair helped last year by holding a tea in Downing Street, which was much appreciated, but Margaret Thatcher actually appeared on the programme when she was Prime Minister. It didn't seem to affect her, electorally . . .

Nor will it do any harm to Mr Blair. In 2005 he shone in a

send-up of himself by Jon Culshaw, who does a frighteningly good Tony B. Culshaw doesn't do a bad Terry W., either, and remains the only impressionist who doesn't make me sound like the late, lamented Eamonn Andrews.

In a wildly misguided effort to whip up uncontrollable waves of enthusiasm for the 2005 Children in Need Appeal, it was thought a superwheeze to have me make an even bigger eejit of myself than usual and star in the 'commercial'. Break-dancing. Naturally, I leapt at the chance. The Wogans have always been big in Terpsichore. I only gave up ballet because I grew too tall, so boogeying, twisting, rocking 'n' rolling, and, lately, break-dancing was the only way to go, bro'. I spent a day strutting my stuff in front of an appreciative crowd of fellow ravers, and when it hit the screen, people couldn't believe it. The main reason they couldn't believe it was because, just before the 'commercial' was transmitted, the *Radio Times* blew the whole thing out of the water in a revealing double-page spread of 'how it was done'. Computer wizardry and photographic chicanery, apparently. I retired, exhausted and not a little hurt. Wilting Baz, who thinks he's Lewis Carroll, showed no mercy:

Wilting Poem

'You are old father Wogan,' the young man said,
'And your hair is fast turning to grey
'And yet you continue to spin on your head
'Tell me, how do you do it that way?'

'In my youth,' said Sir Wogan, 'I'd dance and I'd sing
'And spin till I'm all of a tizzy,

'But now that I'm old, I'm not quite so bold,
'And watching it makes me feel dizzy.'

'You are old,' said the youth, 'and to tell you the truth
'You just shouldn't be spinning like that
'If you do it again, try protecting your brain
'And spin on your head in a hat.'

'In my youth,' said Sir Terry, 'I used to be merry
'And dance every night until three.
'But now that I'm old, the truth must be told.
'The one who is dancing's . . .not me!'

Wilting (with apologies to Lewis Carroll)

I'm supposed to have no feelings, of course . . .

Everybody played a blinder again in 2005, and the grand total on the night broke the record yet again, comfortably over £17 million. If it's anything like previous years, we should double that – I predict another record-breaking total. Certainly, we broke all records with Radio 2's contribution of £1,066,000. It was presented on the big night of Friday, 18 November by the extraordinary Osbournes, Sharon and Kelly, who both pledged £10,000 each as they handed over the cheque.

In the four days, Monday to Thursday, in the run-up to *Children in Need* night on the Friday, my Auction for Things that Money Can't Buy on Radio 2 raised £440,000. My early training in the Royal Bank of Ireland, Cattle Market branch, Philsborough, Dublin, enables me to calculate that that's £110,000 a day. And that's from five past eight to quarter to nine in the morning. When I came back from the wilderness of *Wogan* on TV in 1993, all the Radio 2 presenters participated in the auction, and for the first few years after my return to the stained carpets of Broadcasting House, I joined in. In a good year, we barely raised £30,000 between us. For the past ten years, they've left it to me. Well, me and Paul Viney, gentleman auctioneer, who abandons his lucrative wheeling and dealing in antiques to join me with his mighty gavel, and spur the bidding listener on with word and gesture. Paul gives his time freely and generously, like thousands of unsung heroes up and down the country.

In the Auction for Things That Money Can't Buy, the bidders give freely of their hard-earned cash ever more generously with every passing year. In the first year that Viney and I ran solo with the auction, I'm sure we made less than £40,000. In 2004, it was £300,000, and we thought that simply couldn't be topped. But with Mark Hill pulling some extraordinary strokes, the items on offer have got better, more extravagantly unattainable every year. And it's marvellous to get feedback from the successful bidders. Mary and Alex Seldon paid plenty for a trip to Ascension Island, and Mary wrote to tell me all about their time at this unique outpost of one of the last British territories. The island dentist, scoutmaster, hotel operator and much more, Johnny Hobson, catered for their every whim, from green turtles to land crabs to feral sheep. They had tea at the administrator's residence, and the RAF flew them there and back from Brize Norton.

The Young family outbid all comers for a day on the set of *Doctor Who* in Wales, and were enthralled, not only by the day's shooting, but by the kindness of everybody on the set, from director to stuntman, from clapper-boy to Billie Piper. The great

Doctor himself, David Tennant, came in on his day off to greet the Youngs. It was the same on the set of *The Archers* at the BBC studios in the Mailbox, Birmingham. It was a rest day, but they turned up. David Hunt had paid handsomely for his wife Christine, an avid *Archers* fan, to play a part in a special scene of the story of everyday country folk. And despite the fact that I stuck my nose in, Christine Hunt repaid her husband's faith (and money) and played a blinder. I transmitted the scene on my morning show to loud applause from all lovers of finely wrought radio drama. Mind you, they weren't dealing with some johnny-come-lately in my case. I'd been to Ambridge before, when declaring the then new Country Club open. Dame Judi Dench turned up as well, in the role of Pru, gamekeeper Tom Forrest's wife, who had never opened her mouth previously. She never spoke again either, a cruel blow to a great actress. At least I got asked back, even if it was in the guise of charity.

Talking of work for charity, any praise would be too faint for Helen Bach and Norm, also far-famed as the Bushes, Anita and Tudor, of Exotic Films Ltd, the makers of doubtful movies for the discerning gentleman, starring the TOGs' favourite sex symbol and stud-muffin, John 'Boggy' Marsh, as freely discussed elsewhere in this motley tome. Helen and Norm, who found romance at a TOGs convention, traipse up and down the country, begging and cajoling the great and the good, the famous and the infamous to pose with Pudsey for the TOGs calendar. A loyal band is ever at their side – Edina Cloud, Dora Jarr, Cocktail Clare, Mick Sturbs, Antonious the Anonymous and the Willowy Iris. It's thanks to their charm and dogged persistence that the calendar roused £120,000 for *Children in Need* last year. And it's not just persuading people to put their famous faces beside a one-eyed teddy-bear – Helen, Norm and the geezers and gals design the thing, get the sponsors, persuade W.H. Smith to sell it. Not only that, they package and post thousands of calendars to those who order by post or internet. And just as not a penny donated to *Children in Need* is spent on anybody but the children, so every penny spent by these good people comes out of their own pockets as they travel the country.

This year, they haven't left it at that: Pauly Walters and I had been talking for some time about putting the 'Janet and John' stories on CD and selling them for *Children in Need*. John, a BBC engineer also known to those who love him best as 'Mad Dog', put together a series of the charming kiddies' tales, and with the cooperation of 'Punxsutawney' Phil Hughes, and the gracious blessing of Dame Lesley Douglas, finest BBC Controller of this or any other century, the CD became a reality, with sleeve notes from myself, Pauly and the hero himself, John Marsh. Pauly has even thrown in a few arpeggios on the guitar to further lull the innocent. Guess who is collating, posting and packaging? Helen Bach and Norm. I mentioned the website at the beginning of April – by the middle of the month, they'd sold £12,000 worth. Hang on, it's the middle of June, and they're past 60,000! That should be £600,000 for *Children in Need*, but of course VAT has to take $17\frac{1}{2}$ per cent – thanks, Gordon.

As a postscript, Helen and Norm had John and Janet Marsh cavort on the back of the TOGs calendar with a cool ad for Exotic Films Ltd (with the discerning gentleman in mind . . .). You'd be surprised at the number of people who wanted to know where they could be bought . . .

On the Friday before the Big Night in 2005, we launched what was hoped would be a major money-spinner for *Children in Need — The Great Big Bid.* Like many television ideas, this seemed a good one until it made the studio floor, where it smartly, no, slowly, fell apart. A slow death over five hours of recording, it made a limp show even when edited to less than an hour for Sunday night viewing. The idea was Lorraine Heggessey's, and before she left the BBC for pastures new, she handed it over to Tiger Aspect, a highly successful and respected independent production company. We had a jolly lunch together and several meetings, and all seemed set fair to get the Appeal off to a multimillion-pound start in 2005.

Unfortunately, no one spotted the fatal flaw in the idea: a studio full of multimillionaires bidding for exotically desirable lots was entirely against the spirit of *Children in Need*, which has always had its core support from the common people. I've called it the 'Widows-Mite' Charity for years, and although the big battalions of the banks and supermarkets contribute mightily, it's the ordinary people's efforts that give real worth to the charity. Every day, for weeks, they write to tell me of their efforts to help. A mother speaks of her two sons, aged twelve and ten, who swam over three miles between them and raised over £500; a child of five has a sale at her garden gate of her unwanted toys, and raises £10; I play a record in the Music Marathon on Radio 2 for £50, and the next one for 50p; a children's therapist who has ME and has been unable to work for a year holds a forty-eight-hour sponsored silence and raises £80 . . .

The Great Big Bid for Millionaires sits uncomfortably in this context, and we should have known that from the start. Still, we did raise £400,000 on the night, but the four nightly shows that followed only added £350,000, despite the valiant efforts of Eamonn Holmes. So, back to the drawing board for 2006 . . .

The Big Night itself of 2005 was thought by many whose opinions I respect to be the best yet. Certainly it got off to a roaring start, with an early appearance by Madonna, and the hectic pace was sustained through the evening, as were the viewing figures – over eleven million at the peak, and handing out a sound hiding to all comers, including *Coronation Street*. Gaby Roslin having decided that, after ten years of propping an old geezer up, enough was enough, I was joined on stage by Natasha Kaplinsky and Fearne Cotton. You wouldn't expect me to say anything against them, nor will I, even if I could, but Natasha is beautiful, cool and charming, and Fearne, whom my son Mark recommended for this, having seen her on *Live 8*, was all gamine warmth, and perfect for 'live' television. If ever a girl has got a future, it's Fearne – just so long as hanging around the likes of me is not the kiss of death. Will they risk it again this year? Will we top the 2005 total? Every year we make a rod for our own backs by going for more and more, but win or lose, I'm not giving up. Will someone please tell me when it's time to go – because I'll never do it of my own accord.

When I left Radio 2 at the end of 1984, it was to the sound of weeping, wailing and gnashing of teeth, at least according to the national press. 'How will we wake up without Wogan?' bemoaned one headline. 'Mornings won't sound the same, now that Wogan's jacked it in,' as another put it, less felicitously. It went on: 'Wogan can be excruciating at times, but you can't help liking the feller'. The *Daily Mail* had me saying, 'It's time I gave listeners' ears a rest. The days of the huge mass radio audience are over. Since breakfast TV started, I've lost between a quarter- and a half-million listeners . . .' Which just goes to show that I know no more about this great imponderable business than anyone else.

It's extraordinary how we latch on to trends and extrapolate them into far-fetched predictions for the future that inevitably turn out to be 'pants'. When television really got going in the sixties the wise pundit sounded the death knell for radio. At the turn of the new millennium, the audience for radio began to outnumber that of television, and by now, there's a considerable amount of blue water between them. Television was to be the death of magazines; currently you can hardly keep up with the number of new titles on the market. Books were going to be banjaxed by the box; the reverse is true. In America *The Oprah Winfrey Show* has boosted book sales by millions, and, shrewd enough to jump on the bandwagon, over here Richard and Judy have done the similar decent thing by the written word.

On the day after my final radio show on Friday, 28 December 1984, the *Daily Mail*, in a centre spread, splashed: 'Wogan – The secret of the magic that has left our mornings'. It went on, 'After 13 years, breakfast time will never be quite the same again. It's the end of more than a decade of unique broadcasting.' The writer, after several thousand words of unstinting praise, went further: 'On television, his future arena, he is emerging as a nigh-perfect people's surrogate. He doesn't smarm like Parkinson, he could never be as irritating as Harty.' Once again, prediction bites the dust. Six years later, according to the same worthy publication, when it came to smarm and irritation I was in a class of my own, with added smirk. It was the *Guardian*, in a long editorial, that delivered the ultimate imprimatur, with a headline, 'The end of good morning'. Written a couple of months before my departure for pastures new, it went on, alarmingly: 'The impending demise of the Terry Wogan morning show on Radio 2 gets more and more like Marie Lloyd's final tour every day, each show heaping fresh wreaths of fragrant national epitaphs upon a particularly ebullient corpse . . . The fact that he has turned up at all has continually verged on the miraculous. How could one frail figure cram so much quiz show and chat show and disc jockey and Eurovision into a working day? Devoted listeners over the twelve years have long awaited the moment when the gags and banter ran dry. He couldn't, surely, keep rabbiting on, for ever?'

You see: another prediction gone West.

I remember Jimmy Moir, then the Head of Light Entertainment, Television, saying that the *Guardian* editorial was the greatest tribute to a presenter he'd ever read. This is the same Jimbo who got the elbow from BBC TV about the same time as I got shafted by *Eldorado*, one of the very few soap operas to have failed. *Neighbours*, *Home and Away* and even more mindsapping daily serials survive, why not *Eldorado*? I'm convinced that if they'd persisted with it, it would be now enjoying the same success as, say, *Emmerdale*. Not up there with *Corrie* or *Enders*, but pulling in an audience far bigger than anything that's replaced it. Would *Wogan*? I doubt it, in the deadly time slot in which my chat show was placed. Dear Bill Cotton, who was the begetter of the show, is still convinced that had it been scheduled as a late-evening show, like every other talk show on either side of the Atlantic, *Wogan* would be still there, chatting endlessly on, like a Letterman or a Leno. It's hard to imagine, and I'm bound to say that I'm glad it isn't.

The 'axeing', as the press had it, of *Wogan* in 1992 was the best thing that could have happened, in retrospect. At the time, of course, it didn't seem much of a boon. BBC TV gave me dinner and a specially bound book. Jonathan Powell, then Controller of BBC 1, thanked me for taking the blow so gamely, and promised me more television work. Indeed, the press, who, as ever, had a keen eye for a man down, saw another chance to resume the kicking. The BBC apparently was paying not one, but two executives an enormous amount of money to find a programme, any old programme, for 'Worn-out Wogan'. Somehow, I doubt it, but we did end up with *Friday Night with Wogan*, which had an interesting format that included Danny Baker and Frank Skinner, and might have succeeded if anybody had cared, but as far as some people were concerned, I was a busted flush, and after a season or two the show was suddenly not there any more.

The 'axeing' of *Wogan*, however, again turned out to be a blessing in disguise. Again, not one that Mystic Meg would have predicted. David Hatch, who'd always been a fan as well as a friend since the days when we'd worked together on *Late Night Extra* in the sixties, and was now Managing Director of Radio, suggested to Frances Line, the Controller, that I be brought back to breakfast on Radio 2. David Hatch was not a man whose suggestions were to be trifled with, and in 1993 our hero was back. 'Terry Wogan gives Radio 2 another spin'; 'Tired Terry is Back'; 'Air I Go Again' the headlines trumpeted. The critics were welcoming: 'Welcome back to the breakfast bunker, weird and wonderful Wogan'; 'Return of the Prodigal Wogan'. Inevitably, comparisons were drawn: 'The television Wogan is wooden, cumbersome, awkward. The radio one is a cascade of quirky verbal felicities, meaningful pauses and throwaway wit . . .' 'His television show was sunk by his lack of interest in his guests; incuriosity killed the chat. Now the only person he has to talk to is himself.' If ever there was praising with faint damns.

Frances Line's doubts about the wisdom of returning a ghost to his haunts was endorsed by at least one columnist: 'Hitler's invasion of Russia, Kennedy's visit to Dallas and Wogan's Return to Radio 2, all have one thing in common – they were mistakes.' How do you like that? And he wasn't alone. The *Daily Mirror* of August 1993 reported: 'Pensioner Gwyn Shaw wanted to listen to the radio while she had a hip operation. But she switched off when she could only get Terry Wogan.' It seemed as if my return was being received with the enthusiasm of one hand clapping, and the listening figures were no improvement on the previous incumbent, Brian Hayes, so, more in hope than in anger, the BBC launched a series of newspaper ads. At first, these didn't seem to be having the required effect: 'As a licence holder, I am incensed at the vast sums of money the BBC must be paying out for full-page newspaper adverts promoting Terry Wogan's early-morning radio show. If he can't pull listeners without this expensive plugging then it is high time he was pensioned off.' The expensive plugging worked, thank goodness, because, despite the earlier publicity, a large section of the potential listening audience were not aware that I had returned to the old homestead. Figures started to move upwards in a marked manner and have been doing so ever since, leaving the show at the present time with nearly eight times the audience when I took over . . .

By 1995, there were still those to whom I was anathema: 'I fully agree with readers who complained about Terry Wogan; they endorse the feelings of many thousands of others. Wogan must go.' 'I'm glad somebody else as well as me is fed up with

Terry Wogan's stupid banter.' 'I wonder how many people can stand listening to Terry Wogan's idiotic burbling?' All of these from the *Birmingham Evening Mail*. I think we can safely say that the Letters editor wasn't a fan. And thank heavens for him. It is a vital lesson for everybody who sticks their head above the parapet in showbiz, theatre, radio, television, politics, football and any allied trade, to learn: that for every person who worships the ground you walk on, there'll be another who can't abide you. And another, representing the great majority, who couldn't care less one way or the other . . . Then, just when you think 'they're all agin me', a heartening word from about the same time in the *Daily Express*: 'BBC Radio 2 is spending a small fortune on newspaper ads – *Wake Up to Wogan*, The rest of the day can only get better. A woman I met last week takes that quite literally. She told me that she had been suffering from depression following a serious operation. "Honestly," she said, "if it wasn't for Wogan, I don't know what I would do. I switch him on for therapy. They'll be prescribing him on the NHS next."' There was even a cartoon to go with it, by Hector Breeze; it's in this mighty tome somewhere . . .

7

Can you hear me, Mother?

⌒

Two years on from my reincarnation on Radio 2, things were looking up sufficiently for Frances Line to invite me to deliver the Radio 2 Lecture. This misguided venture had started in 1992, when Richard Stilgoe gave a talk on 'Popular Culture: The Endangered Oxymoron'. I titled mine 'Radio Two – The Slumbering Giant Awakes', and on 4 April 1995 delivered it to a select audience in the Council Chamber, Broadcasting House. The marvellous Duke Hussey, the beloved Chairman of the BBC, was there, the Managing Director who had lately taken over from David Hatch, controllers of programmes, heads of departments and producers, among them Paul Walters, who had just rejoined me as producer of *Wake Up to Wogan*. He told me that for the first couple of minutes, the Managing Director was laughing along with the best of them, but slowly, inexorably, the laughter stopped, and the smile was like a rictus on her lips. All around, taking their cue, senior management shuffled uneasily, while dear old Dukie chortled throughout, along with most of the creative people.

The gist of what I had to say was against the Birtian ethos of the day, but I don't think that, these days, many would disagree.

I started with a couple of illustrations of what my listeners enjoyed in the way of music:

K-Tel, in association with Paltry Productions, are proud to present:
The Greatest TOGs Album in the World — Never!
Come with us as we shuffle down memory lane to enjoy some Toggie tunes of yesteryear. Give your hearing aid a treat with much-loved favourite melodies, such as:

Waking Up Is Hard to Do
Zimmer Holiday
It's My Cardy, and I'll Cry if I Want to
Do You Know Where I'm Going to?
Hit Me with Your Walking Stick
Wake Me Up Before my Cocoa
Dewdrops Keep Falling Off My Nose

This limited edition offer is not available in the shops, so order now to ensure disappointment. Send cheques, postal orders, pension books, Green Shield stamps to:
Tel & Wally Enterprises
Box 222
Cayman Islands.

Followed by how to identify them:

Good morning, Terry and Pauly,
I thought that I would like to check with you if I yet qualify as a TOG under the following conditions:

You're asleep, but others worry that you're dead.
You can live without sex but not without glasses.
You are proud of your lawn mower.
You constantly talk about the price of petrol.
You enjoy hearing about other people's operations.
People call at 9 p.m. and ask, 'Did I wake you?'
You have a dream about prunes.
The end of your tie doesn't come anywhere near the top of your pants.
You get into a heated argument about pension plans.

Then I turned on the assembled crowd:

And where does *that* leave the distinguished audience gathered here in the gloom tonight?
Apart, of course, from the majority – a clique, paid by myself at considerable expense to laugh hysterically and applaud enthusiastically at appropriate moments. I can only assume that they're saving themselves for a big finish . . . Don't forget, I have all your names and these cheques are post dated . . .
But to return to the rest of this audience: some of the

best and brightest of the BBC are gathered here: managing directors, controllers, executives, producers. The very people who *appoint* the megalomaniacs! These people who even now are feigning indifference, or trying to hide under their chairs, are the ones who decide what you're listening to, when you listen to it and who you're listening to. 'But these people can't be mad also,' I hear you cry. These are people in charge of the greatest broadcasting organisation that the world has ever known. They must perforce be of high intellect and the product of rigorous training, who, by an almost savage process of elimination and cull, are finally selected as being qualified to decide to what and to whom the Great British Public may listen. Well, that's as maybe, but I'm here to tell you that they know nothing. *Nada.* Worse than that, *nobody* knows anything. Oh, you can train technicians, sound engineers, camera crew, floor managers, directors, lighting men, scene shifters and even producers, but if any one of them ever comes up to you and tells you that they know the secret of *popular* success, have them gently taken away to the nearest Home For the Bewildered. Or Channel Five, whichever is the nearest . . .

You see, this is not brain surgery – this is the radio. Like television or theatre and the movies, nobody knows what's going to work until they've tried it. Oh, you can do sequels, of course, but eventually it's one Bond too many, or a Die Hard too far, and even Arnold Schwarzenegger has been known to fall on his gluteus maximus. You see, there's no master plan, no previous form, no breeding data, no formula, no recipe for success. You can put all the correct ingredients together: Ace producer/director/scriptwriters, with a proven record of success, the most popular artists or presenters in the country, throw all the money in the world at it, and still come up with zip. The entire length and breadth of this fair land there is only one person who can make a popular programme, or, more correctly, make a programme *popular*. It's you. Yes, you. Half listening while you're waiting for the kettle to boil or the phone to ring or the lights to change. You, gentle listener, you decide with a careless flick of the button whether we succeed or fail. And by the time you've decided, it's too late for us. Which is why we're out there with charts and graphs, projections and questionnaires trying to find out what you think before you've even thought it. I'm not big on all this focus group, survey and poll stuff – as Messers Gallup and Mori will readily agree, there's a hell of a difference between what people tell you and what they actually believe. Most people tell pollsters and researchers what they think is *expected* of them, not what they're *really* going to do. It also depends on how you ask the questions. I could produce charts and figures within a week that would prove convincingly that what the Radio 2 listener *really* wanted to hear was a diet of brass band music and religion:

'Hello, I bet you like brass bands, don't you?'

'Well yes, actually, I *do*.'

'Do you like listening to brass band music on radio?'

'Yes, I *do*.'

'Do you think there's *enough* brass band music on the radio?'

'Well no, actually, I *don't* . . .'

'Would you like to hear *more* brass band music on Radio 2?'

'Yes, you know, I think I would . . .'

'Do you believe in God?'

'Yes!'

'Do you think there's a place for religion on radio?'

'Yes! Why not?'

'Would you listen to religious programmes on Radio 2?'

'Certainly.'

'Do you think a half an hour's programme every day would be too much for people?'

'Certainly not! We're a Christian country, aren't we?'

Or – on a more mundane level, I think of the man who compliments his wife at dinner:

'Do you know, dear, this cabbage is wonderful!'

'Oh, do you like it?'

'It's delicious!'

Six months later, at dinner, he complains:

'Oh no! Not cabbage *again*?'

'But you said you *liked* it . . .'

As any well-worn politician will tell you, the only poll worth its while is the 'exit' poll, when they come out of the booth and tell you how they voted. As I've said earlier, nobody knows *anything*, and nobody can *predict* a thing in this business, until the fat lady sings . . .

Not just because people tell you one thing in public, and in the privacy of their homes do something completely different; not just because the whole business of radio listening is entirely subjective. We talk of a radio audience as if it were a group, as if it moved in blocks. There are millions of people out there – but they're all *individuals*. When people are listening to the radio, a ripple of laughter does not run around the stalls. Nobody chortles in Chorleywood because somebody chuckled in Cleckheaton. Every single radio listener makes up their own mind. My postbag over the years is full to bursting of letters from loyal lady listeners whose husbands leave the room in a marked manner whenever they turn me on. And vice versa.

Radio is the most individual, the most personal medium. Which is why it's a terrible mistake for broadcasters to categorise their listeners. 'Radio 2 is for the fifties and over' ignores the basic precept of radio listening. It's *personal*. What pleases one fifty-year old won't please another, but may delight a forty-year old. Many of my listeners are in their twenties and thirties. I tell 'em to get lost, of course, but they won't go away. When you say 'Radio 2 is for the fifty-year old and over', what you *really* mean is this network is for the 'old geezer', and as a fifty-six-year old, I resent that. It's politically incorrect for a start – it's *ageist*!

So, I take it, when you claim to broadcast to fifty-year olds and over, you mean you're going to play music to suit that age group. Music from fifty to fade-out. I've news for you – it's impossible. Because every day, hundreds, perhaps thousands, of people become 'new' fifty-year olds. Because in five years' time a couple of million forty-five-year olds will be fifty and a similar number of fifty-year olds will be fifty-five; and believe me, their tastes in popular music will not be the same. Not to even mention the disparity of taste between the new intake and those at the other end of the spectrum who were seventy and are now seventy-five . . .

I'm sorry – you cannot lump your grown-up listeners into age groups. God Almighty Himself could not devise a music policy to satisfy a national age group as broad as fifty to Curtain Time. And a *computer* certainly can't . . .

Luckily for Radio 2, you don't *have* to . . .

Because, and let me break this to you gently – Radio 2 is *not* a music network. It never has been. The vast majority of the people who listen to Radio 2 – that is, the people who tune in every weekday from, say, seven in the morning until seven in the evening, the most loyal, the most consistent group of any in the country – do *not* listen for the music. I realise this will cause confusion, nay, panic, among songwriters, musicians, producers, middle management and even, mayhap, a frisson at controller level. Perhaps I should nail this thesis to the door of Western House.

Radio 2 weekdays is a 'personality' network.

People don't listen to Sarah Kennedy, Jimmy Young or even *me* for the *music*. They listen because they've become attached to the person presenting the programme – and, because of the personal, very intimate nature of the radio, far more deeply attached than they would ever become to any presenter on television. An indication of this is the listeners' need to fax, to email, to write to their radio favourite to contribute, to establish a dialogue. I've often said that I can present a television show to eighteen million viewers and not receive a letter from one of them. I do a radio show for five and a half million, and get three hundred letters, emails, faxes and cards a day. So . . . where does the music come in? The music only matters when it's wrong. When it jars, when it's inappropriate, when it sits uneasily with the personality of the presenter.

Radio 2 music should be selected to complement the personality of the presenter and the content of the programme. My programme differs from Sarah Kennedy's as much as hers differs from Jimmy Young's, and Jimmy's from Ken Bruce's.

Self-evidently the music should reflect that difference. Radio 2 music is the mortar between the bricks we make . . . or drop. It should be as different as the personalities who present it, and reflect these personalities.

A draconian music 'policy' is a mistake for a national radio station. Opt for a specific type of music, and you are opting for a 'niche' audience. Now a 'niche' audience is fine for a commercial radio station that doesn't want to compete in the mass marketplace and attract advertisers to its specific audience. It's fine for Channel 4. Radio 3 is another good example. But 'niche', by definition, means small – a little corner of the market.

No national, popular radio network should be looking for a 'niche'. Least of all BBC Radio networks funded by the public. If each BBC network seeks its own 'niche', trust me, each BBC network will end up in its own little corner, and the whole mass of the middle ground, the popular audience, will be swallowed up by commercial independent radio. And then, how will anybody justify a licence fee for BBC national radio?

I believe in Corinthian Casual broadcasting. Strolling out at Wembley to play the Arsenal in the cup final with hands in the pockets of our baggy shorts, having nonchalantly flicked away a careless cigarette . . . Lord Burghley training for the Olympic high hurdles with a glass of champagne balanced on each obstacle . . . C.B. Fry and the crown of Albania . . . Broadcasting without the strain showing, broadcasting without effort, without tedious training, without mind-numbing, spontaneity-killing rehearsal. Broadcasting without a safety net! Broadcasting that relies on wit, intelligence, but, most of all, on talent. Broadcasters that can do it without thinking about it too much. Broadcasters that can open the microphone without a thought in their heads, and rely on whatever it was that put them there in the first place to get them through this time . . .

Let me have presenters about me that rely on their own invention, rather than newspaper cuttings; that don't have to write it down before they say it; that don't have to fill up their air time with phone calls from the obsessed and deranged. Let me have ad-libbers, the ones who make it up as they go along. The finely chased, minutely sculpted, meticulously delivered prose is fine if you're Alistair Cooke, but has it got warmth, has it got heart, passion? Popular radio should be peopled by risk-takers, arm-chancers – stone-brave broadcasters who teeter on the tight-rope but never quite fall over.

It's not about research and figures and futures and focus groups, memos and papers and polling; and worrying yourself sick whether you're super-serving the bourgeoisie and under-cutting the ethnic minorities. It's not about planning – you can't work it out by logarithms and graphs. It's about what comes out the other side of the microphone or the camera, and that's about talent and instinct and creativity and spontaneity – all the very antithesis of planning and polling.

The problem is, the BBC's never been very good with the Talent. And I don't mean the normal producer/performer jealousy. With some honourable exceptions, the attitude of BBC senior people to the poor old hobbledehoys who actually keep them in their jobs has been, to put it at best, supercilious. 'Who does he think he is?' 'He'll come crawling back.' 'Nobody is bigger than the BBC.' These are the historic watch-words, the leitmotifs of the Reiths, the Sloans, the Wyndham

Goldies. Sentiments that ring around upper corridors of BH to this day.

'I see Wogan's put on another half-million listeners according to the latest Rajar figures.'

'Yes, but that's due to the weather, and our insistence on a clear Greenwich Time Signal at 8 o'clock . . . anyway, don't tell him, he'll be unbearable . . .'

'Yes, bit too big for his boots as it is.'

'Absolutely. *And* he's talking far too much anyway. He'll need to speed up his links if we're going to get that five-minute social action piece in every morning at quarter past eight . . .'

The message still hasn't got through – indeed the forest appears to be growing ever fainter through the hectares of trees that are needed to produce the miles of BBC papers and the morass of meetings: *this is a broadcasting organisation.* Its most important asset is its presenters, performers, producers, directors – its programme people. Is it really necessary to say that if you don't value your programme people, if you don't encourage them, cherish them, and continually challenge them, then you've missed the point – lost the plot. The BBC produces television and radio programmes. That's it. That's what it does. That's what it has done incomparably better than any other broadcasting organisation since the whole rigmarole began. The BBC has been, and remains, the benchmark by which all other radio and television, both national and international, is judged. Its loss to the British public, and the world, would be incalculable, and unthinkable. Its slow erosion would be indecent. As it was in the beginning, so it will be, for ever and ever. But only if you damn the torpedos, keep the faith – and for heaven's sake – trust the talent.

It's a measure of how 'those who must be obeyed' took the lecture that no tapes were issued to the critics for review, and the Radio 2 Lecture was never broadcast again in the land.

From the late seventies until the early nineties, the British press and I had what could only be described as a love affair. The 'Wonder of Wogan' was, by all accounts, a delight to eye and ear. Tabloids had 'Wogan Weeks', broadsheets extolled my virtues in long-winded articles on 'turning non-stop trivia into an art'. It seemed that *Blankety Blank* would have been irredeemable rubbish in lesser hands, but by dint of coruscating wit and ineffable charm, I had turned the dross into gold. Series such as *You Must Be Joking*, and *What's On Wogan*, although not much cop, never got the kicking they deserved, because of my ongoing honeymoon with press and public. *Wogan's Guide to the BBC* in 1982 was received with the kind of plaudits normally reserved for classical music programmes, ballet or David Attenborough – 'as hilarious and entertaining a programme as you're likely to see all year'; 'the temptation to snap Auntie Beeb's garters is irresistible, and Wogan and his producer had a go at both legs. The twang of elastic was exhilarating'. The awards came thick and fast – *TV Times* Personality of the Year for ten years running; Best-Dressed Man in Britain; Variety Club Showbusiness and Radio Personality; Television and Radio Industries Club Radio and Television Personality on seven occasions; then, to put the tin hat on it, 'Terry Wogan's named today as the all-time favourite man on television'. Clint Eastwood was second . . .

In view of the barrage of contumely that came my way as *Wogan* petered out, it's instructive to dip lightly into the earlier reviews of the chat show: 'A spectacular success'; 'easily the best chat show'; and so on, enough to turn a chap's head. Compare and contrast that with the dog's abuse of the final year, when 'boring' was the least offensive epithet. I was self-obsessed, I smirked, and where I used to twinkle charmingly, I now smarmed oleaginously. 'Woebegone' took over from 'Wonderful', executives publicly questioned the wisdom of persisting with 'cheap' shows such as *Wogan*. 'Wogan is past his sell-by date,' a BBC insider said, 'he's a quintessentially seventies figure' . . .

(Ah, 'sell-by' dates. Terry's Old Geezers and Gals have a thing about them, and even more about 'use-by' dates. They pay no attention to them; in fact my mailbag is full to bursting with tales of young limbs returning home for the weekend and throwing out perfectly good food from their parents' larders and fridges, on the grounds that the stuff is past its 'use-by' date. Those of us well-weathered by the passing years, and wise to the ways of commercialism, take these arbitrary dates with the pinch of salt we're not supposed to have any more, and providing the foodstuff smells all right and has no furry growths we'll dive in. Even the furry growth may be scraped off if the larder has been left bare by the over-cautious young . . . Maybe that 'BBC insider' – a famous euphemism for when the reporter can't get a quote from anybody – was right about my 'sell-by' date, but I'm ignoring my 'use-by'; I'm showing very little signs of fungus, and my loved ones tell me that my smell is hardly noticeable.)

I wouldn't remember a damned thing about my television

and radio past if it wasn't for newspaper cuttings, and sifting through the tonnes of printed matter that has accumulated in sideboards, drawers and files has been no labour of love. How many supermarkets, dress shops, fêtes, fairs and charities have I opened; how many public appearances, concerts, corporate events; how many film premieres, opening nights, record receptions and glitzy parties have I attended? And how many of them do I remember? The fading pictures in the yellowing cuttings stir no memories, apart from vague recollections of openings that went too well, in terms of public attendance, and too badly when the impatient crowd came through the plate-glass windows. But then, I used to find it difficult on *Wogan* to remember who I had chatted to a couple of days previously. I suppose it's my attitude: I've never put any great stock on what I do for a living; it's just what I do, and I know that I'm lucky to be doing it, although any self-respecting young person would have thrown me out of the larder years ago.

I sometimes wonder, but not for long, what I would have done if Radio Eireann hadn't beckoned to me. Probably stayed in the bank and moved up steadily by annual increments through the ranks, even to the dizzy heights of manager. I'd be long-since retired by now, probably with a part-time job looking after some convent's financial affairs a couple of mornings a week. I'd be playing a lot more golf, of course, and probably bridge. I might occasionally think, with a twinge of regret, of what I might have been, had I been brave, nay, reckless enough to leave my permanent pensionable position with the bank to chance my arm at the radio. I'd be happy because, luckily, that's my nature, and anyway I could never possibly imagine the good fortune that would have come my way. Would I have married Helen? I doubt it. A mere bank clerk would never have the gumption to approach such a beautiful creature. Would I have married and had a family? Probably, but I can't envisage any state of wedded bliss approximating the sheer joy that Helen and our children bring me. Life turns on an instant, and everything changes on a single throw; if I hadn't answered that ad in the Irish paper for radio announcers; if I'd been sensible and accepted that I didn't have the qualifications required; if I hadn't lied about a dentist's appointment, or the bank manager had refused to give me time off and I hadn't attended the audition; if RTE hadn't given me the job; if Mark White had thrown my back-to-front tape into the wastepaper basket when I applied to the BBC . . . So many lucky breaks – and if only one had failed, a different life. And people think that I'm being falsely modest when I put it down to luck!

8

A citizen of no mean city

~~~~~~~~~

In late 2000, the first, and some would hope, last, volume of this mighty autobiography was published to universal acclaim.

'Love the book! Great stuff! I've been reading it for two weeks now and I'm still only on page 49. It's the funny bits that keep slowing me down. As soon as I start slapping my thighs, crying with laughter and rolling about on the floor, what happens? Yes! The bookshop's security chap marches up, grabs the book off me, sticks it back on the shelf, and turfs me out . . .'

I've never read *Is It Me?*. Why would I? I wrote the thing. It's the same reason I never watch myself on the television, nor listen to myself on the radio. As I've said before, I'm easily embarrassed, particularly by myself. Having been brought up in a culture of repression of virtually every natural instinct, if I listened to, or watched, myself, I'd never be able to bring myself to do either again. It's 'showing-off', and so's this book. I'm often accused by discerning critics of false modesty, of self-denigration that is merely a front for a rampant ego. Maybe they're right, maybe there's a touch of Nietzsche lurking behind the façade, but I'm inclined to think that it's a bit simpler than that. I'm just getting my retaliation in first, in the best Munster rugby tradition. I'm apologising before anybody accuses me of anything, particularly self-regard, cockiness, or vaunting ambition. I was brought up not to rock the boat, to be one of the crowd; and there's no 'i' in 'team'.

We were a conventional lot, we lads of Crescent College, Limerick. No arts and crafts, no drama and culture. Lots of cinemas in the town, but I'm damned if I can remember a theatre. If there was, I certainly never went to one. There were the 'fit-ups' – the travelling players who toured Ireland with their repertory of Shakespeare, Yeats and Synge. Their caravan must have rested in Limerick every year, but it was only the inside of circus tents that I ever saw. 'Fossett's' and 'Duffy's' turned up in a field off the Ennis Road on a biannual basis, and were required viewing for any young fellow who wanted to be part of what the in-crowd were watching. Look, this was long before television, and the radio was something for grown-ups. (I was the only one of my age group who listened to the wireless.) There weren't too many people with whom I could have a literary discussion on the merits of *Just William* or *Billy Bunter*, either.

Young and all as I was, I knew a terrible circus when I saw one: tacky costumes, scruffy people, poor sad animals. 'Stand well back there, and let the lady see the monkey!' Mind you, I had the advantage over my schoolmates – I'd been to a proper zoo, Dublin Zoo, with my Auntie May. I knew what well fed, cared-for wild animals were supposed to look like, even if they were behind bars. The touring circuses were cheap and nasty, and I've never been to a circus since, although I knew Billy Smart personally . . . And clowns? I wouldn't thank you for a clown, while I'm sure the art and practice of clowning is steeped in history. They just don't make me laugh, any more than a jester hitting the king over the head with a pig's bladder would provoke a smile.

Humour dates, even the knockabout stuff – except, of course, at the Eurovision Song Contest. I mind well one such in the seventies, where the organising country (it had to be somewhere in Europe, the only place where they still had circuses, even in the seventies), decided that a capital turn for the interval would be a clown act. And guess who was doing the commentary for BBC Radio? Ten minutes of silence to fill. It doesn't sound much, but trust me, it's a lifetime in front of a microphone when all you have to describe is a crowd of capering eejits in baggy trousers, huge feet and red noses falling over each other. There are probably still circuses in Europe, just as there are still mime acts. Sorry again – I'm sure it goes all the way past the Commedia dell'Arte – but mime also leaves me cold. Only the French could think that Marcel Marceau was hilarious. What's all that about, pressing against an invisible pane of glass or walking into an imaginary gale? And if you really want to know, even as a boy I thought Charlie Chaplin was as funny as the plague; and now you're going to agree with me and say, 'Ah, yes – but Buster Keaton?' Sorry. If it comes to that, Oliver Hardy was funny, Stan Laurel wasn't, and the Marx Brothers were awful, apart from Groucho. See? I'm a curmudgeon when it comes to knockabout. I blame the circus; send out the clowns . . .

Somebody in Limerick who did go to see the 'fit-up' touring players was a young man a few years older than me named Dickie Harris. Dickie was something of a hero to little lads like me – a fine rugby player, good at tennis and, by Limerick and Crescent College standards, a bit of a wild card. Even in his late teens Dickie Harris was a recognised character in our town, and, surprisingly in a parochial setting in which individuality was generally regarded as the mark of Cain, he was well loved. Then he ran away to join, not the circus, but the strolling players, the hobbledehoys. In a very few years he had made his mark on the London stage, married a titled lady and changed up from Dickie to Richard. I met him in London in the mid-seventies, a big Hollywood star by then, but still the wild, mercurial big boy that I remembered from Limerick and Kilkee. He kept the table entertained with his memories of youth: stealing an extra drop of cordial when Mrs Hough, the little woman who kept a shop near the Pollock Holes in Kilkee, was pretending she wasn't looking; mad priests; the savage nature of Limerick rugby and its noble camaraderie. That nobility, that Corinthian attitude, combined with fierce aggression, still characterises Limerick rugby and its people. The rest of Ireland calls it 'Stab City' because of a reputation for gang violence, but anybody who has ever seen a rugby match at Thomond Park, Limerick, will tell you that it is the last bastion of the true spirit of fair play and sportsmanship. Let the crowds in the Stade de France whistle and jeer when opposing sides enter the arena; in Thomond Park, they are applauded on and off the field. Let them hoot and holler in Melbourne, Jo'burg and Auckland when an opponent runs up to take a penalty kick; in Limerick, there's silence . . .

Richard Harris loved his Munster rugby, and dragged Peter O'Toole along with him to cheer them on. 'Hellraisers' is the well-worn phrase, probably more true of their youthful days together, making their breakthroughs in the West End. I meet Peter O'Toole every year at the *Oldie* magazine's prize-winners' lunch, and a cheerier chap would be hard to meet. If 'raising hell' is falling about with laughter, then he's the real deal. Spike Milligan was another who frequented the 'Oldie of the Year' lunches when he was still with us. More of a laughter-maker than a laugher, you never knew quite where you were with Spike, but he too, like O'Toole and Harris, was a rugby player from way-back-when. On the wing for London-Irish actually, my own rugby club. I never had the pleasure of seeing Spike scamper down the wing, but I'd give anything to have seen it. 'Like a startled deer' was how an older member described it to me.

Limerick rugby has produced more than its share of char-acters, many of them swapping the jerseys of young Munster, Shannon or Garryowen for the green of Ireland – 'Musty' Clifford, Gordon Wood, his son Keith, Tony Ward, Anthony Foley, Clohessy the 'Claw'. Such is the enduring reputation in a hard town for its hardest man that the 'Claw' is reputed to be the only man in Limerick who can leave his car door unlocked. Gordon Wood used to recall his fellow Garryowen men with great humour – in particular a nuggety front-row who had lost most of his front teeth, and, since he was playing rugby every week, saw no sense in replacing them only to have them knocked out again the following week. After a game in Dublin against the rather more patrician Trinity College team, the little fellow was placed at the dinner table beside the Provost of Trinity, a Protestant clergyman. The meal progressed in a rather more stately fashion than the boys from Garryowen were used to, until the coffee and cakes. Then, our toothless hero, having hurled a huge lump of cake through the yawning gap where his teeth should have been, turned triumphantly to the provost. 'Aha!' he shouted, 'you has me with the mate, Father – but I has you with the buns!'

He would have had no idea that there was such a thing as a Protestant clergyman – anyone with a collar was a Roman priest. Limerick was a *very* Catholic town, not just priest-ridden, but under the thumb of the lay organisation, 'The Arch Confraternity' as it was known. This unelected body held itself responsible for the morals and behaviour of the town's citizens, and was the power behind the throne of the mayor and councillors. That power was never more ardent than in the mid-forties, when Shannon Airport had become the most important international airport in the western hemisphere, a staging post between America and newly liberated Europe. Limerick, the closest big town to the airport, had what a friend of mine from Mayo used to call a 'bozana'. Americans came and lived in our midst, chewing gum, drinking Coke, eating chocolate that tasted like chocolate. They threw parties, which my mother and father attended. Extraordinarily, for a town that had been wrapped up in itself for hundreds of years, these parties had people of all nationalities: the displaced, the fleeting, the conquerors, the conquered. Feelings sometimes ran high in the aftermath of a terrible war, and my mother told us of an occasion when the party was at its height, with music and dancing. A striking blonde, who had been a dancer, was asked for a solo performance. 'I vill dance for you,' she announced proudly, 'as I danced for my Führer.' Skin and hair flew in all directions. 'It was such a good party, too,' said my mother.

There was a thriving black market. Men would hop on a plane in Shannon with a side of ham and return from Stuttgart with a bag of Leica cameras. Limerick was alive with foreigners, with money to spend. Inevitably, this was brought to the attention of certain entrepreneurial elements in Dublin, and pretty soon the trains from there were disgorging a disproportionate number of young ladies. These fun-loving girls and, indeed, some right old boilers were, within the hour, on the arms of the aforementioned well-heeled foreigners, parading up and down O'Connell Street as if they owned the place. The Arch Confraternity knew its duty, both to God and the moral well-being of innocent Irish men and women. Swiftly and silently the fallen women were 'disappeared', never to be heard of again in the City of the Broken Treaty. The foreigners were allowed to stay; they had the money, if not always the affection of the locals. At another dinner, my father observed another one of the town's timeless characters, Steve Coughlan, who was the mayor at the time. An American made the mistake of asking the mayor's lady to dance. But this was Limerick, not Massachusetts, and Steve the mayor was across the table like an avenging angel, his hands around the unfortunate's throat. Another party gone West. 'I didn't mind,' said my mother, 'they were a boring crowd . . .'

In case you need it, I've included photographic evidence – proof, if proof were needed – that all those aunties, great-aunts and grannies were not figments of my over-wrought imagination. There's one of the wedding of Auntie Enda, who wasn't my aunt at all, but beloved Auntie May's best friend, who shared her love of laughter and of fags, and who I thought would remain May's spinster-chum for the duration. The fellow with the rictus grin in the front is the groom, having separated Enda, on the left of the picture, from May, on the right. The little chaps are the brother, Brian, on the left, whose angelic looks belied his nature, and a young shaver on the right, who, although he has the ears, is no relation of mine. Seated on the right are the angelic Muds, and my mother, Rose. See the identical set of their heads, and smiles, and then look over Muds's right shoulder at her youngest daughter, Dinah. Exactly the same slight inclination to the right, exactly the same smile.

The eejit with his mouth open and a headful of buck-teeth behind Muds (the Granny) is our hero, and directly behind him, his Da, Michael Thomas Wogan, victualler of O'Connell Street, Limerick. Auntie Dinah's clinging on to Uncle Eddie Cunningham. They're recently wed as you can see from the excessive body contact. Beside Eddie is his sister in a pork-pie hat, and, slightly overshadowed, as she was all her life by her sisters, Auntie Kitty. A further couple of heads to the left and there's Great-Aunt Mag, Muds's sister, proprietor of 207 Clonliffe Road, and, typically, with her head inclining in the opposite direction to the rest of her family. The smile's there, though, and one that shouldn't be discounted; this was not a woman to waste a smile. On her right, and far left, the two Nellies: the taller, Nellie Nolan, the smaller, my Auntie Nellie. Looking at myself and the brother, I would say the date is around 1949–50, and that's 207 Clonliffe Road in the background, although why

Wogan has lost his other listener. Please check down the sides of your armchairs.

Amnesia victim fears he could be Wogan's other listener.

Security firm loses Wogan's other listener.

Wogan's other listener believed to have gone abroad.

Wogan's other listener spotted by Elvis.

Wogan's other listener. Revealed.

First, we got them looking.
Now, we've got them listening

B B C   R A D I O   T W O

Created by Arc Advertising · February - March 1994

Some call 'em 'the crew', others 'the team'. To me, they are the underlings — Pauly, Deadly, Boggy and Fran. (© *BBC Photo Library*)

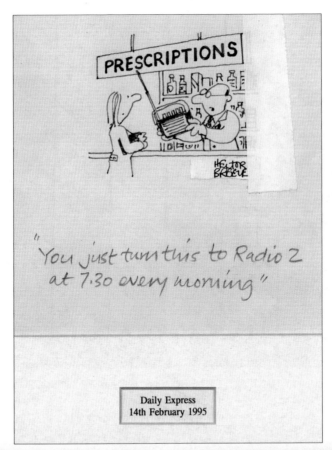

"You just turn this to Radio 2 at 7.30 every morning"

Daily Express
14th February 1995

Edward Scissorhands lives. Paul Walters frightens the elks on Sheeprock Mountain, British Columbia, 2001. Later that day he was downed by a buzzard ball.

Her Majesty the Queen touring BBC Broadcasting House on her 80th Birthday, 2006. It was shortly after this that John Humphrys (on my left) put a damper on the happy day by asking Her Majesty if she was aware that she shared her birthday with Fidel Castro. (© *Rex Features*)

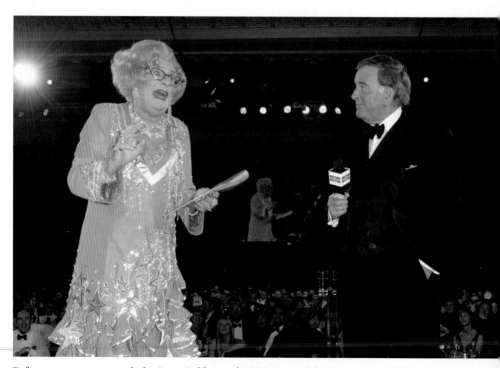

Before presenting me with the Sony Gold Award 2006, Dame Edna Everage extolled my virtues in a charming poem. Here you see us, both close to tears. (© *Rex Features*)

NOW: Liam Neeson flew over especially from New York to talk, little expecting me to do my 'stuffed dummy' impression. (*UK TV Gold*)

NOW: Jerry Hall – she must have a painting in the attic … (*UK TV Gold*)

THEN: A relaxed moment in a seedy alleyway off Shepherd's Bush, London. (© *Mirrorpix*)

NOW: David Icke – 20 years on. Still crazy after these years … (*UK TV Gold*)

NOW: Cilla Black claims I relaunched her career in the early eighties. Strange … to many others, I'm known as the kiss of death. (*UK TV Gold*)

Eurovision 2006 – and another British hopeful prepares to bite the dust. (© *BBC Photo Library*)

Lordi – Finnish winners of the 2006 Eurovision Song Contest. If you think they look odd, you should see them without their make-up. (© *Rex Features*)

...earne Cotton, Natasha ...aplinsky and A. N. Other. ...hortly after this I broke into a ...reak dance that stunned the ...ation. (© *BBC Photo Library*)

The NEW Wogan – Pink Socks at Karate. (© *BBC Photo Library*)

The present Lady Wogan and myself, at one of the very few grand occasions to which I'm invited these days. (© *Rex Features*)

It's not only the listeners he sends to sleep … (© *Mirrorpix*)

Auntie Enda should get married from my Granny's house, I don't know.

It may not look much to you, but I thought 207 Clonliffe Road, Drumcondra, Dublin, was huge. And so it was, compared to 18 Elm Park, Limerick. An entrance hall with a large grandfather clock, and a living room to the right, with a large fireplace, a cabinet for the best china, and, against the opposite wall, a piano that nobody in the family could play. At least two wedding receptions were held in this cluttered room, including Michael and Rose Wogan's. Next on the right was the dining room, with a big circular table in the middle that was exclusively used for playing cards at Christmas. All the dining was done in the kitchen. The room had two armchairs on either side of the fireplace, Auntie May and the usual packet of Player's in one, and Muds in the other, under a picture of the Sacred Heart of Jesus, whose eyes followed you around the room, like all good pictures. The kitchen was down a small flight of stairs, and a longer flight took you upstairs to the bedrooms.

My brother Brian, who has been an invaluable aid to these recollections, tells me that in a desk on the second landing were bound copies of minutes of the first Daíl, or Irish Parliament, and all my Grandad's military medals, including those of the Boer War. On leaving Clonliffe Road, Auntie Nellie dumped them all, including some incriminating pictures of herself and Nellie Nolan enjoying the attentions of some SS Officers in a Hofbrauhaus in Berlin, *circa* 1938. While not exactly blaming Nellie for the outbreak of hostilities, my father, with whom she shared a mutual distrust, always felt that things might have been different if Nellie hadn't made her fateful visit to the Third Reich. The 'Magpie', he called her, and although in retrospect it was a touch unfair to the woman, much of what she touched turned to dust. She always overcooked the Christmas turkey, for instance, which infuriated the Da, who wanted to cook it himself, and there was a major falling-out one Christmas when she cooked somebody else's ham, rather than the one my father had lugged up all the way on the train from Limerick. When Nellie would bid at cards, my father would always say, 'Dearly bought, Nell,' which infuriated her.

My brother, the fairest of men, put no store by my father's estimation of Nellie as the harbinger of doom until one night, during severe flooding which had banjaxed the bus services, when Auntie Nellie's taxi had broken down, he offered her a lift home, and, halfway there, watched the front wheel of his car, having inexplicably taken on a life of its own as he slowed for traffic lights, roll past his car window. In view of my brother's own record, I'm not entirely sure that this incident can be laid at the Magpie's door. This, let us not forget, is the same Brian Wogan who, in a moment of boyish high spirits, tried to push his ageing granny down the stairs, having a little earlier failed in a game attempt to set the house ablaze by lighting matches under the curtains . . .

Talking of Auntie Nellie consorting with the enemy reminds me that Auntie Enda (friend of May's, no relation) was one of the very few people living in neutral Ireland at the time to have suffered the parlous dangers of World War Two. She was buried in the wreckage of her house on Dublin's North Strand for forty-eight hours, after the Germans made their one and only bombing raid on Dublin, mistaking the fair city for Belfast a fair bit up the road in Northern Ireland, which, as a part of the United Kingdom, was a legitimate target. Enda had all our sympathy. If it had happened to Nellie, of course, no one would have been surprised.

Let it not be thought, however, that the Byrne sisters knew nothing of war and its dangers: on the morning of the Easter Rising in 1916, my mother, who was six, and another sister, probably Kitty, were staying with their Auntie Maggie (my Great-Aunt Mag) in her house in Rutland Street, Dublin. When the shooting started and news of the doomed revolution reached Mag, she immediately decided that the safest place for the two little girls would be back with their mother and sergeant major father in the British Army barracks at Beggars Bush on the other side of the Liffey, miles away. She crossed twenty blockades with the children, and it took nearly twelve dangerous hours, through a city full of snipers and trigger-happy soldiers. Rose never forgot the sight of a sniper falling from a roof-top on to the pavement close to her. They made the safety of the barracks, and then Mag turned again for home, through the bullets and the shelling. It took her twenty-four hours . . .

Although my Grandad's Boer War medals are no longer with us, my brother still has the bronze medal that my mother won for Irish dancing at a *Feis Ceoil*, a major competition. Although the children of a British Army soldier, no one questioned the right of my mother and her sisters to call themselves Irish; but things could have been very different for Brian and myself, according to Rose. Warmed by a nice cream sherry, she would tell the tale of a Christmas at the barracks, the commanding officer and his lady dispensing good cheer to the men and their families under the Christmas tree. Rose, a pretty little handful, asked to touch the angel on the top of the tree, and the commanding officer lifted her up to do so. He took an immediate shine to her, and as he and his wife had no children, asked Granny and Grandad if they might adopt Rose. Although money was scarce and they had five mouths to feed, they turned the offer down. As Brian says, that's how we were both lucky enough to miss Singapore, Aden/Burma and who knows what other theatres of war.

Another wedding photo, this time from the early forties and something of a collector's piece. How often do you see a dustbin in a wedding photograph? The happy couple centre-stage are Michael Nolan and Patricia Nevin, and it was sent to me out of the blue by their son-in-law Eugene Shannon. The scene is Rutland Street, North Dublin, where my mother's family lived before moving to Clonliffe Road, Drumcondra. Way up at the top right-hand corner are Michael T. and Rose Wogan, both looking younger than I ever remember them, my mother with a careless arm over some gay blade's shoulder, and a girlish attitude that was never captured in any photograph before or since. Yer man with the tie in front is already displaying the ears that were to become such a major feature of British life and a source of merry ribaldry to so many, but at least he's kept his mouth shut and spared us the buck-teeth. Dublin hadn't changed much in fifty years, and this photo could have been taken in O'Casey's or Joyce's time. The faces, the suits, the hairstyles, the attitudes epitomise a city that was still a village, and would remain so for at least another twenty-five years.

The bridesmaid is Auntie Kitty, always the odd-one-out of the Byrne sisters. It's interesting, at least to me, that there's no sign of Nellie, May or Dinah, or, if it comes to that, Auntie Mag. After all, she owned the house in Rutland Street in which Granny, Grandad and their girls lived after Grandad left the

British Army. Kitty had followed her Auntie Maggie into the French-polishing game, but Brian and I grew up thinking of her as somehow different from her sisters. We learned that by observing how the others treated her: not as an equal, but someone to be nurtured and treated with a kindness and gentility that they never displayed to each other. All of the Byrne girls had sharp wit and tongues to match, but Kitty was never part of the general banter. My brother Brian, whom she particularly loved, remembers her as kind, strange, childish – always the one to join in our games while the others sat about chattering like jackdaws. He remembers the crushing nature of her embrace – she was always the most affectionate and tactile of the family – and my own children remember the horror of her enthusiastic, hairy kisses. My brother can keep a small crowd entertained for some time by recounting the tale of the naked fear that showed on my face when, during *This Is Your Life*, in the seventies, he whispered to me, 'Kitty's on next' . . .

The innocent, gentle Kitty might have strolled through life under the strong, protective wings of her family had she not been hit by a car while on a pedestrian crossing on the main Drumcondra road. She barely survived, and after a considerable time in hospital received a ludicrous sum by way of com- pensation, which, nonetheless, enabled the remaining sisters to move to more manageable accommodations in Iveragh Road, Whitehall. They were north-side Dubliners through and through; the south side of the Liffey was another country. It was ever thus, and still remains, in the city that was so lately a village.

The terrible accident had its effect on Auntie Kitty. From being the quiet, uncomplaining, cheerful and gentle soul, over- night she became, at least according to Nellie, who had taken charge, as she always did of everything, being the elder sister, 'difficult'. Timid Kitty demanded her place in the pecking order from the bed she rarely left. Brian remembers the little lady that thought the sun shone from his every pore disagreeing vehemently with everything he said in her later years. She took on the mantle of the invalid, and with strong, reliable Nellie doing everything for her, she remained in bed. And that's my last memory of dear, sweet Kitty: propped up in bed, the pretty, round smiling face now aged and a little drawn, and over the coverlet the French-polisher's delicate hands now milk-white, their perfect nails painted a bright crimson . . .

Next we have Michael T. and Rose Wogan, otherwise known as the Ma and Da, pictured in their prime – well, certainly the best time of their lives, at the opening of the flagship store of the Peter Dominic wine shop chain, on Grafton Street, Dublin, about 1952, I'd say. The Da was general manager of Peter Dominic, and had masterminded the conversion of the Leverette & Frye chain of grocery stores into wine shops. Not bad for a young fellow who had run away from home at fourteen years of age after a fight with his father over the old fellow's mistreatment of the Da's adored mother. He used to say that he was 'apprenticed' to a grocer's in Bray, Co. Wicklow, but I'm sure he just got a job and a roof over his head by dint of living in the cellars by the wine vats. He learned his trade there, and although the very name 'Bray' was anathema to him for the rest of his life, he learned enough to get a job behind the counter of the finest grocery store in Dublin, Leverette & Frye, Grafton Street. Which is where you find him and the woman he loved all his life in this picture where the wheel has come full circle. For it was in that very shop that he met Rose, who worked in the cash office. Shortly after their marriage, in 1936, he took her to Limerick, where he had been made manager of the branch. Nineteen years later they were back in Dublin with two sons, and Michael T. was the general manager. And so we find them ten years on, plump, successful, healthy and happy. When people compliment me on my career, I always think of my father. Compared with his extraordinary rise, I'm only in the ha'penny place . . .

A man called Frank Dolan, who knows a thing or two and writes an erudite column in the *Irish Post*, a distinguished publication that keeps the Irish in Britain up to date on Hibernian happenings in perfidious Albion, put it forcibly in 1997: 'What I object to about Terry Wogan's inclusion in the New Year's Honours List is the modesty of the thing – only an OBE, for God's sake! An OBE is the most lowly national or international honour ever bestowed on the noble Wogan family. Previous Wogans have been recipients of Europe's most splendid honours – from France, Spain, Italy, and, indeed, Britain . . .'

Up to then, I'd been beside myself that Her Majesty had graciously bestowed an Honorary OBE on my unworthy head. Because it was honorary, I didn't have the pleasure of a visit to Buck House, and the privilege of some light banter with the monarch as she pinned the medal to my heaving breast. Chris Smith, then the Minister for Culture, handed me the gong with grace and charm before an audience of friends, colleagues and family in the old council chambers of Broadcasting House, 'neath the portraits of various Director-Generals. (The very spot where Paul Walters sent an entire tray of chipolatas flying, most of them over the forbidding countenance of Lord Reith, who was minding his own business over the fireplace. But that was another do, another story . . . Suffice it to say that Walters' career never really recovered. You can make a mess of a programme, and turn up drunk as often as you like, but throwing snorkers around the Council Chamber gets you noticed. You won't get fired, of course – nobody does, in the BBC – but a little black mark goes on your file. Responsible employer that it is, the BBC keeps a file on all its employees. They're usually dragged out as a source of sneering merriment on retirement. They can also be a revelatory source: the late Charles McClelland, when he was Controller of Programmes, Radio 2 (he had come from the BBC's Middle Eastern Service, not an easy leap to make), told me that while idly flipping through the file of his Head of Music Programmes before an annual interview, he'd come across the fellow's startling promotion through the ranks of the British Army. He'd joined the BBC after National Service as an acting corporal; twenty-five years on, he'd been promoted to major, according to his latest file. He'd been upgrading himself at every annual interview, as he went along.

Anyway, back among the branches of the Wogan family tree, the bold Dolan went on to say that, in the beginning, the Wogans were Welsh 'Gwgan', meaning a frown, or a scowl. Here he was not telling me anything I didn't know, because hardly had Helen, myself and two-year-old Alan arrived by steam packet from across the Irish Sea, but a large scroll arrived at our simple bothy – from whom or where I have no record – which spilled the beans on what it called 'the Wogan Pedigree'. Now, you know me: plain-spoken, honest yeoman broadcaster, no airs or graces, call a spade something else, no need for any great fuss or palaver, up off your knees, for goodness' sake – yet when your family tree kicks off with 'Cradog of the Strong Grin, Lord of Gloucester, Knight of the Dolorous Tower and the Round Table', there is a tendency to lift the chin, straighten the back, and look down the nose at the passing peasantry.

Old 'Gwgan' makes his appearance midway through the eleventh century, trading up, by marrying the daughter of the Lord of Wiston in Pembrokeshire. Suddenly, there are Wogans everywhere – Sir Walter Wogan, then Sir Mathew, then several Sir Johns, one of whom became Sir John Wogan of Picton Castle, and another who, in 1295, became the Lord Chief Justice of Ireland and founder of the Wogan chapel in St David's Cathedral. The early fifteenth century has a Sir David and a Sir Henry, but by the close we're back into the Johns again. The female name that is most prominent is Katherine – which is why we called our daughter by that name. I suppose we should have called our second son John, but certainly not after the Thomas Wogan who, in 1646, was one of the judges who signed the death warrant of King Charles I. Mind you, there was a Sir John who got beheaded at Pontefract in 1483.

The founder of the Irish branch was, apparently, another Thomas, in the early fifteenth century. Now, distinguished and all as the Welsh line is, it can't hold a candle to the swashbuckling Irish Wogans. They fought for James Stuart at the Battle of the Boyne, at Aughrim, and, paradoxically, at the last heroic stand in Limerick. After that, in 1691, the Wogans joined the Wild Geese, soldiers of fortune, fighting in the pay of France, or Austria, for generations. The brothers Charles and Nicholas took part in the Jacobite insurrection of 1715; Charles was captured, escaped and rejoined the Irish Brigade in France. Three years later, James III, still aspiring to be King of England, asked Wogan to find him a wife, from among the Catholic royal families of Europe.

The dashing Charles came up with Maria Clementina Sobieski, granddaughter of the King of Poland, who had saved Western Europe from the Turks. All he had to do was get the lady to Rome. Unfortunately, the English, hearing of the plan, imprisoned the princess in Innsbruck Castle. With three members of his Irish Brigade, one of whom Peter O'Toole claims was an ancestor of his, the gallant Wogan breached the battlements and carried off the princess, over the Austrian mountains and beset by danger at every turn, to her wedding with James III in Rome. After a decent interval she delivered the Old Pretender a son, Charles, better known to history as Bonnie Prince Charlie.

By then, Charles Wogan was a chevalier de France, a senator of Rome and a hereditary baron of England. However, disappointed with the Stuarts and their lost cause, he fought for the Spanish king and became a brigadier general, and then governor of La Mancha. Charles Wogan died in Barcelona in 1754. His younger brother, Nicholas, however, was with Bonnie Prince Charlie in Scotland in 1745, limping back to France the following year after the disaster of Culloden. The French made him a chevalier as well, and he died in Paris in 1770. The proud tradition was carried on by a nephew, Francis, who joined the Irish Brigade and, like old Gwgan long ago, married well, into the aristocratic du Chastel family. His last direct descendant, Baron Tanneguy de Wogan, died in Paris in 1906. Charles Wogan's portrait hangs in the National Gallery, Dublin, and his brother Nicholas's in Malahide Castle, Co. Dublin.

Some years ago, somebody sent me two pictures of yet

another fearless adventuring Wogan. I don't know where he got the outfit, or why the Injuns tied him to a totem pole. I don't even know what a Wogan is doing in America in the eighteenth century, but I know that the chevaliers would be proud of him . . . And have a look at this:

Dear Sir Terry de Wogan

As editor of *Card Times*, top magazine for the cigarette card collector, I believe I have come across evidence of one of your ancestors. The Carreras card attached, from their 1934 Believe It Or Not series, tells of one **Tanneguy de Wogan** of Paris who '**travelled 2,500 miles in a paper boat**'! Apparently no other materials were used in its manufacture but compressed paper.

The only thing which puzzles me – he must have been a pretty bad navigator to miss England on his way over from Ireland, to finish up in Paris. No wonder he travelled 2,500 miles. He probably went via the Pentland Firth.

Anyway, hope you like it. All felicitations.

David Stuckey:

Editor, *Card Times*

I hope that the old ancestors might be happy, too, and even Frank Dolan satisfied, that in June of 2005 Her Majesty the Queen appointed me an Honorary Knight Commander of the Most Excellent Order of the British Empire, in recognition of my services to broadcasting. I was even more honoured when, in November 2005, Her Majesty appointed me an Additional Knight Commander, allowing me the title of Sir Michael Terence Wogan, KBE, and Helen, Lady Wogan. Whatever Charles and

Nicholas might have thought, Michael and Rose Wogan would have been mightily pleased, although my father would have been slightly puzzled, as he always was, by my success. Helen's mother would have been thrilled for her, and the old Tim Joyce, her blustering dad, would have pretended that he'd hardly noticed, but would have spent the rest of his life boasting about it to his cronies in the pub.

The family, my friends and the public were enthusiastic and generous in their praise when the news broke on the morning of Saturday, 11 June. We were in Fowey, Cornwall, with our friends the Smiths, Temporals, Hugheses and Saads, to celebrate the wedding of Kits and Hacker Browning's lovely daughter Grace, Helen's godchild. Of course Helen and the family had known about the honour for weeks, but you're not supposed to tell anybody until the Honours List is published. On Friday night we all had dinner together, eagerly anticipating the wedding. The following morning, Helen and I were woken by the phone and a tirade of abuse from Michael and Lorna Smith, who wanted to know what kind of friends we thought we were, keeping a secret like that to ourselves. The sun shone, the wedding went beautifully, and the bride looked gorgeous, just as her mother had done all those years ago in Dublin . . .

Unusually, the press were as kind as the public. David Jason had also received a knighthood, and as his most famous role was as 'Del Boy' in *Only Fools and Horses*, the headlines were, almost inevitably, 'Arise, Sir Del and Sir Tel!' A wonderful editorial in the *Daily Telegraph* enthused: 'Tony Blair has frequently been accused of abusing the honours system . . . today we acquit him on all counts . . . we rejoice at Wogan's knighthood. When that voice is on the radio, as mellifluous and soothing as the shipping forecast, we know that the world can't be all bad. If anyone deserves an honour, he does . . .'

So on Tuesday, 6 December 2005, I presented my radio show like Alvar Liddell in the 1930s, in full fig, frock-coat and all. Sarah Sands, the then editor of the *Sunday Telegraph*, asked me to relive my moment of glory for her paper. My recollection of the day, written while it was still fresh in my memory is in the picture section, take a look.

And by the way, Her Majesty didn't say, 'Arise, Sir Terry'. She never does, which will come as a blow to whoever it was who brought out a book to exploit my Great Day, in time to catch the Christmas rush, in October 2005. They called this cheap bit of opportunism *Arise, Sir Terry*, and got it on the bookshelves without so much as a 'by your leave' from me. I've never read it, and I don't know anybody else who has, either. So let's hope that this tacky bit of cut-and-paste hackery has sunk without trace.

Many years ago, an Irish journalist, Gus Smith, wrote an unauthorised biography, and at the time I was furious and ready to drag old Gus before the courts for invasion of privacy, exploitation of my good name and anything else an 'Injury Lawyer for You' could throw at him. Then I met Eamonn Andrews at a drinks party, and the wise man set me right: the names of people in the public eye are in the public domain. It's one of the so-called 'prices of fame'. If your name's up there in lights, anybody unscrupulous enough knows that the law is not going to bother its bewigged head if they use said name for their own fell purposes, as long as they stay just the right side of the law. Some smart alec tried it on once for Virgin, when they were trying to break into the lucrative London–Dublin flight market.

Something along the lines of 'Getaway from Wogan to Dublin'. I confess that I had a humour bypass and rang Sir Richard Branson, who gave the ad the sharp elbow.

It *is* a bit much to see somebody trying to make money out of your name without asking permission or, indeed, offering to cross your palm with silver, but as dear Eamonn said, it's not worth the hassle. You just have to ignore it – paying attention, jumping up and down, is playing into the exploiter's hands. And as for going to court; my great friend, the distinguished solicitor, the late Sir David Napley, told me never to do it. No matter how watertight your case, no matter how much you know yourself to be in the right, warned Sir David, don't take it before a judge and jury. This former president of the Law Society, one of the most respected solicitors of his generation, said that you could never tell which way a jury, and even more so, a judge, was going to jump. Cases are not always won on rights or wrongs – all too often they are lost on the personal prejudices or the minor likes and dislikes of jurors and judges.

So what are you supposed to do if some fly-by-night is bruiting your name abroad? Starve them of the oxygen of publicity. Don't comment, don't react, rise above it. It worked with *Arise, Sir Terry*, and also in 2005 when Chris Moyles started a campaign on BBC Radio 1 to 'Stop Wogan'. The idea was to convince the younger radio listeners to wrest control of the family wireless, or car radio, from their parents and tune in at breakfast-time to 'Moylesy', rather than me. Like any good tabloid, the *Sun* jumped at the idea of a 'Battle of the Networks', and, even better, a personal ding-dong between Chris and me. Banners, posters, badges were printed and sent all over the country. I even saw the legend 'Stop Wogan' written in the dirt on the back of a filthy van. The great campaign lasted about a week because I refused to rise to the bait, apart from commenting that things must be more desperate at Radio 1 than we had suspected. It withered and died, and culminated in ultimate shame for old 'Moylesy' when his supporter, the *Sun* newspaper, held a poll to find out which of us was the more popular, and I won, by a large margin. Recently, they backed the boy once more, on *Celebrity X-Factor*. Wrong again.

The knighthood was welcomed by all and sundry, at least by all whose opinions mattered to me. I replied to everyone who had been kind and gracious enough to write to congratulate me. I've kept all their letters, including one from Mary McAleese, the President of Ireland. My knighthood was first promulgated as an honorary one because I am a citizen of the Republic of Ireland. An honorary knighthood is a very great honour indeed, and rarer than the usual knights bachelor award, but it was suggested to me that I might be entitled to a 'regular' knighthood, and the right to call myself 'Sir' and Helen 'Lady', because, having been born in Ireland while the country was still part of the British Commonwealth, I was entitled to dual citizenship, both British and Irish. I made inquiries, and then an application, and in no time the Foreign and Commonwealth Office wrote to confirm that Her Majesty was pleased to make me an Additional Knight Commander to add to my honorary title. In the end, I've got two gongs for the price of one: Sir Terry Wogan, KBE. You can call me Terry (even better, 'lucky' . . .).

Somebody sent me a cutting from an Irish newspaper – one owned, interestingly enough, by my fellow Belvederian and dual Brit/Irish citizen, Sir Tony O'Reilly – which said: 'There will be those who argue because Ireland was occupied by England,

and because our ancestors fought a long and bloody war to win our independence, it must therefore be a shameful and treasonable offence against our ancestors if an Irish citizen accepts an honour from the Queen of England.' The final few words put the tin hat on the begrudgery: 'It is acceptable, such people argue, to accept honours from foreign powers, not just ones we were at war with'. So no Englishman has the right to accept the légion d'honneur from France because of the Hundred Years War? No Spaniard the right to accept an English award because of the Peninsular War, no German the right to accept any award from anyone, because of World Wars One and Two? As I've remarked elsewhere in this homely tome, my own ancestors gave their all in the fight for Irish freedom, and at least two of them were knighted. To hell with small-minded begrudgers; I'm proud to join my knightly Irish ancestors.

9

Trying not to count my chickens

⌒

The last couple of years have been pretty damned good in the way of what an old Radio Eireann favourite of mine, Seán Bunny, used to call 'prizes'. Not Seán Bunny himself, of course, because he was merely a figment of his author's imagination. It was his author, who, when recounting the little chap's weekly adventures on the radio, had trouble with her 'Rs', so Seán used to 'wun' rather than 'run' and 'pwesent his pwizes rather than . . .' Well, you know.

Deadly Alancoat and Pauly Walters were immediately taken with Seán Bunny, just as they were intrigued by Curly Wee and Gussie Goose, more cartoon figures from my innocent youth. Poor souls, they'd been brought up on a meagre diet of Rupert Bear and some early Noddy. But there are no 'prizes' on *Wake Up to Wogan*, and it's a sore point. All over the country, on a thousand ramshackle commercial radio stations, prizes are scattered daily like confetti. Free skiing holidays, a lifetime's supply of snorkers, sports cars, private jets, and £10,000 a week for the rest of your life are offered, if you'll only listen to Capital, Kiss, Kerrang! and a million others.

They don't get it. There are no incentives to listen to me, and precious few to listen to anyone else on Radio 2. So why do millions do it? Why, as the redoubtable Catherine Tate might say, 'ain't they bovvered' by the promise of untold wealth and luxury? Because until some commercial radio station can put together a combination of presenters and music to rival Radio 2, 'we ain't bovvered'. In twenty years of independent radio, run, presumably, by smart people with sharp commercial brains, the penny still hasn't dropped. It's not about giveaways, television commercials, or the 'right' music. It's about getting some decent presenters with whom the daily listening public can identify. Forget doctrinaire playlists, mid-week chart positions and the other false gods of popular music; identify the real music that your core audience want to hear, blend it in so it sits easily with your presenters, and you have half a chance.

This is not the USA. British and American radio grew up with more than just the Atlantic between them – the habits of listening are poles apart. In America, radio sprang into the air unrestricted; overnight there were a million stations clamouring for attention. Little towns would have ten, twenty stations, the bigger cities, hundreds. They still do. There just weren't enough presenters who could put two words together to go around. There still aren't. So Americans sped around the dial until they found the kind of music they could listen to, and there they stayed. If you go to America today, you'll find yourself doing the same thing.

In Britain, under the severe presbyterian mantle of Reith, radio grew up in a straitjacket; well, a dinner jacket, anyway. It wasn't until the sixties, and the pirates offshore, that anybody had a choice of listening to anything other than the BBC. Yes, there was Radio Luxembourg, but it never worried the establishment, although it must be said that present-day commercial radio could learn a thing or two from old '208'. They got the music right, and the presenters – Jimmy Young, Pete Murray, Keith Fordyce, Barry Alldis – or their equivalents today, if you could find them, would certainly challenge Radio 2. The rascally radio pirates got it right as well, and in the space of a couple of years, Tony Blackburn, John Peel, Ed Stewart, Johnnie Walker, Pete Brady, Emperor Rosko and many others were household names. The habit of listening to people first, of identifying with the presenter, had become ingrained in the British listening public through the years of BBC dominance of the airwaves, and that's the way it is to this day.

. And just as the listening habits of Americans and ourselves differ, so, as far as presenters are concerned, radio and television are poles apart. You can be a star overnight on television; on radio it takes longer. It takes years. Years for the listening public to grow to know and warm to you. The idea that you can take a shining star from television and turn him overnight into a radio broadcaster is beyond foolishness. I think we're at the core of why commercial radio is finding it so difficult to compete with BBC Radio: it just doesn't have the time, the patience or the money to nurture a promising presenter over, not weeks, not months, but years. I came to the BBC from Ireland entirely unknown, they gave me a daily radio show because they thought I had potential, they let me grow into it, and my faithful listeners grow with me. After a couple of years, people began to recognise me, although there's still a hard core who believe that I am Eamonn Andrews and Val Doonican's love child. I grew, and brought an audience with me. That's the only way to success on the radio. It takes time and faith, and until commercial radio can find those two qualities, they'll struggle for a loyal audience.

In January 2002, Charlotte Green of Radios 4 and 2, and I graced the cover of the *Radio Times* (other listings magazines are available, as if you cared . . .). We had been selected by several thousand discerning, possibly cloth-eared, listeners as the most attractive voices on the radio. It scarcely came as a surprise to the bold Charlotte or myself, since we'd had our photo taken for the cover a couple of weeks before. You always take your life in your hands when you submit to a photograph for half the world to sneer at, but after a sneaky glance, I thought mine was OK, until Paul Walters said it made me look like Jack Nicholson in *The Shining*.

I got off lightly. A fragrant nosegay from my diary of April of that year:

12 April 2002
The *Sun* has a picture of David Beckham's foot on its front page. It asks all its loyal readers to place their hands on the picture, and pray. Pray for Beckham's foot and England, for how can we win the World Cup without him?

And just in case we think we're in the final throes of tabloid populist insanity, GMTV's *Breakfast Show* has Uri Geller on board, asking every one of their loyal viewers to do the same thing, like a spoon. It was an Argie that did it while playing in the vital Europeans Champions League tie between Manchester United and Deportivo La Coruna. It's not without its own significance that England and Argentina are drawn together in the same first round of the World Cup. It's a plot. The Argies have hated us since Sir Alf Ramsey called them 'animals' in 1966; never mind the Falklands . . .

Becks is England's hero, ever since he saved the country's football bacon with a last-minute goal against Greece in the World Cup preliminaries. They've forgotten the last World Cup, when, with a typical display of petulance, dear old Becks got himself sent off, and England were knocked out. Guess who were the opponents? Who else but those dastardly Argies? Beckham was reviled and cursed the length and breadth of this sceptred isle, booed every time he touched the ball. For months he and Posh were subjected to disgraceful abuse. Now, all that matters is Becks' foot. A less secular society would be rubbing relics and sprinkling holy water . . .

My listeners' sense of irony and the rightness of things do not desert them: 'All is not lost. Put him in goal. They'll never get the ball past his crutches.'

13 April 2002
Poor old Beckham; the cynics are up and running: a TOG in a dog collar, Father Gerard Quigley of Bury St Edmunds:

As you may have seen in a national newspaper, the *Sun*, has asked us all to place a hand on a picture of David Beckham's injured foot and pray for it to heal quickly.

Anxious to do my bit for good old England, I purchased a copy of said newspaper, placed my hand on the picture and prayed thus: 'Please restore this broken appendage to David's body in time for the World Cup game.'

You can imagine my alarm when I looked down and saw to my horror that I had actually placed my hand on a picture of page three of said publication, which showed a picture of a well-endowed lady in the Bristol area.

Whoops!!! OK, well, if it works . . . they will go well with the sarong.

And a Carl Ott, from Solihull:

On Saturday we were in Solihull town centre when we came upon a young lad dressed in Man U strip. He was bouncing a ball pretty competently and I asked him who he wanted to be. He answered, 'I want to be just like David Beckham.'

So I gave him a swift kick on the ankle and walked on. I still cannot understand his mother's protests or his ear-splitting screams.

Is it me?

Is there anybody out there with even the dregs of human kindness?

With the World Cup 2006, history repeats itself – only now it's Rooney's foot. The curse of the metatarsal strikes again.

In January 2004, one of the proudest moments of my life was when I was to be conferred with an honorary Doctorate of Letters by the University of Limerick. It was on that happy weekend in my hometown, too, that my daughter Katherine and her delightful husband, Henry Cripps, announced that she was pregnant. 'He shoots, he scores!' as my son Alan put it; it could have been more elegantly expressed, but it summed up our joy. Freddie Cripps emerged into the welcoming arms of his family in October of the same year, turning the most beautiful girl in Ireland, whom I'd married it seemed like only a couple of years before, into a granny, and someone who'd never had a proper, grown-up job into a grandfather. It's strange, but I have only the most fleeting of memories of my children as babies, so little Fred is an all-new, constant source of wonder and love. Gimme more! . . .

Limerick University is relatively new, certainly when compared to Trinity, Dublin, founded by Elizabeth I, but the Irish have always made education a priority, and Limerick has already built a huge reputation in the groves of academe. Professor Kevin Ryan delivered my citation, a paean of praise which I received blushing hotly and sweating lightly under my robes and quaint bonnet. The President, Professor Roger Downer, conferred the doctorate, and we all repaired for a reviving drop. There was a dinner in the evening at the university, to which the family were invited, and it was typical of my brother Brian and his Pauline to come all the way from Dublin. The other doctorates were awarded to Mary Davis, who had masterminded the Special Olympics in Ireland in 2003, and the ever youthful and still dazzling author, Edna O'Brien. It was Edna who said: 'Ireland has always been a woman, a cave, a cow, a Rosaleen, a sow, a bride, a harlot, and, of course, the gaunt Hag of Beara.' She doesn't spare the horses, Edna, but they love her for her eloquence and fearlessness.

As ever, when you return to the places of your youth, everything that seemed so big now seems small, and Limerick itself, like all Irish towns since the Celtic Tiger emerged from the bog, has expanded, grown so that its outskirts are unrecognisable. Some things remain: the Treaty Stone, in memory of a great siege that ended in my ancestors fleeing to serve a foreign king, King John's Castle, the mighty Shannon, the Da's shop . . .

In September 2005, an old friend from the ill-fated Century Radio days in Ireland, Enda Marren, rang me from Dublin to tell me that I had won the award as 'Ireland's Greatest Living Entertainer', the presentation to be made on a live RTE television show. I'm not big on showbiz, radio or television awards; I've had more than my share, and doubt whether I was worthy of most of them. I presented the Variety Club awards for years on BBC TV, with voiceovers by my pal, Ray Moore, and every few years they'd give me one to keep me from feeling left out of it. I must have presented it for the best part of ten years, and then Ken Griffin retired, a new producer came in, and I was out. And following the well-worn BBC principle, the new guy broke the mould, and the show. From prime-time weekday, it was relegated to early afternoon Sunday. It has been replaced in the schedules by the Comedy Awards, a scary evening, particularly if Johnny Vegas is around, and brilliantly compèred by Jonathan Ross. And then, of course, there is the BAFTAs. I presented the BAFTAs once, with my friend Stewart Morris producing and directing. I've never been invited to another one, not to mind winning a BAFTA. It hardly hurts at all . . . Anyway, I've got roomfuls of Carl Alan Awards from the palmy days of *Come Dancing* and other ballroom extravaganzas to make up for it. I even had my picture taken at some Lyceum or other with Princess Margaret, as you can see in the picture section.

The Princess and I were no strangers; low down on the royal totem pole, she got stuck with more than her share of award ceremonies, and since for much of the seventies and eighties I was either winning or presenting, we shared many a prawn cocktail and breast of chicken. She liked to light up early on these occasions, and many's the time we'd rise to our feet, at her behest, for the royal toast, just after the prawn in Marie Rose. She tended to ignore women, when she wasn't frightening them to death with a basilisk stare. I remember the formidable Joan Collins being intimidated and whispering to me, 'She doesn't like me, you know.' I had to reassure Joan that looking the way she did, she had no chance with Princess Margaret. At a Radio Industries Club Awards do, Margaret ran through the award-winners with me during lunch. She hadn't a clue who anybody was, and those whose names she recognised were dismissed with a scornful click of the tongue. I met her again, many years later, at Sunday lunch with the Marchioness of Reading. Princess Margaret had invited herself to drinks after church, and we engaged in airy banter. Distracted, I turned away for a moment, and when I turned back the Princess had disappeared.

No sign of her – and then I looked down. There she was, on her knees, tidying Margot Reading's grate . . .

So off I went across to Dublin, and there, in a great barracks of a hotel, thousands were assembled in their finery for dinner and live television awards. On came Gay Byrne, the doyen of Irish Radio and TV, and on they came, the award-winners of the year, each one more remarkable than the next for outstanding achievement in every field of Irish life. By the time they got to me, 'The Greatest Living Entertainer', I was looking for somewhere to hide. A film of tributes had been assembled, many and warm-hearted from my BBC radio and television friends, and a couple from Ireland that majored on amused puzzlement, which came as no surprise as I had been greeted at the door of the hotel by an Irish newspaper reporter who, in place of congratulation, asked me how I felt about those who thought I shouldn't be getting the award. Later, I learned that an entire radio show on RTE had been given over to blunt discussion on my right to call myself an Irishman, not to mind an entertainer. And people still ask me if I'd fancy going back to Irish radio and television . . .

Actually, I'd gone back to Dublin a little earlier in the year to take part in a tribute by the music industry to an old pal, Ireland's premier radio disc jockey, Larry Gogan. Larry has always been that *rara avis* among presenters of all races: modest, unbegrudging, happy with his own success and that of others. So it was no hardship to join him and his family in another huge barn of a hotel, and lead the cheering for a good man. Apart from that, the remarkable aspect of the evening was that, smartly after the tribute, and with the coffee still as lukewarm as when it had arrived, the great dining hall was almost entirely empty.

Nobody had said goodnight, but we did, with a plane to catch the following morning. As we exited into the soft Irish rain, we saw where the missing hundreds had gone: every one of them, in the car park, in the rain, sucking desperately on a cigarette. No smoking anywhere indoors in Ireland. It's working. Everybody's outdoors.

I've been pretty begrudging myself about the annual award-fest for radio, the 'Sonys', which might be regarded as ungrateful, in view of the fact that I've won a few in my time. And it's got nothing to do with the debacle of the one I was awarded a couple of years ago. Rising gracefully from the Radio 2 table, I received the award and prepared to deliver a succinct homily to the assembled throng, by now well sauced, if not well fed. Why can no supposedly five-star hotel in London deliver a decent meal to more than twenty people? Anyway, as I launched into my address, up on stage came a large, overdressed woman who proceeded to follow me around, as I dodged about, trying to avoid her and say my few well-chosen words at the same time. It was an unequal contest; I cut it short and got off before she laid a glove on me. She wandered about for a while longer before the ever alert security led her gently to her table, where she sat down again on the dessert which had decorated her backside throughout the spectacle. No hard feelings; it could happen at any award ceremony, where people are so bored by endless presentations and speeches that they find consolation in drink.

Despite my pleading, Radio 2 submits my name and show every year for a Sony Award. I don't like it because, in my view, these awards are not presented on merit, but rather on a rotational basis – Buggins' turn, as they say. Come second this year? You'll be OK next year. Your radio station got nothing last year? Don't go away . . .

My main objection, until a couple of years ago, was that local radio, with its lesser resources, was pitched up against the might of the BBC networks. It was an unequal contest. The Sonys should be about rewarding the talents and efforts of local radio, both BBC and independent. Let the big boys play on their own and pick on somebody their own size.

I'm sure it seems like biting the hand that feeds me, criticising the Sony Awards, in view of the fact that this year they presented me with the ultimate accolade, the Gold Award; and because, in fairness, they have made considerable efforts to make the awards more inclusive: there are now gongs for the stations that, because of their size or geographical location, have only small audiences. These are the very heart and soul of radio, and to see the enthusiasm and the elation of the winners lifts the heart. It was these sentiments that were in my mind when I drafted my speech of acceptance for my Gold Award for Achievement:

Here I stand, a shining example of the old showbiz maxim: if you hang around long enough, they're bound to give you something. Mind you, this honour, combined with the knighthood, makes me wonder if the powers-that-be are not trying to tell me something as well . . .

But radio takes time. Television is the medium of the quick fix, radio is for the long run. You can walk through the doors of the Big Brother House completely unknown and, a week later, be one of the best-known faces in the country. Of course, it involves being interviewed by Davina McCall, but that's a small enough price to pay for fame and fortune. You can't do that on radio; it doesn't take days or weeks, it takes years. Years to build a relationship of trust and affection.

I came over here from Ireland in late 1969, unsung and unknown. The British public had never heard of me, yet the BBC, or specifically, Mark White, Assistant Head of Gramophone Programmes, gave me a daily show on Radios 1 and 2. Could that happen today? I don't think so. You see, radio has become infected with the television culture of instant fame, instant success. Give that television star a radio show! And it'll work for a few weeks of public curiosity, but unless that person has the necessary ingredients of voice, warmth, wit, intelligence and ability to identify and relate to his audience, in the long run, they're doomed to failure.

The success of Radio 2 is built on the familiarity, the very predictability of its presenters. They know us, we know them. And I hate to say this to the advocates of playlists, but my friend Paul Walters – sadly not with us tonight and sorely missed, and indisputably the finest music programmer in popular radio – has always said: 'The music is only important when it's wrong.' This is not the USA. Popular radio success, indeed all radio success, is built on presenters. Even classical music radio needs people with whom their public can identify. This is how the British public grew up with radio, and how it will always be.

So, forget the instant fix; it's not going to work in the long run that successful radio requires. Go out and find the voices and the personalities that are making radio work all over this country. Listen to local radio, commercial and BBC. Try hospital radio. They're out there, the ones with the gift. Find them, give them their own shows, have faith in them, and your judgement. And give them time. Time. Radio takes time. And mine is up . . .

Thank you, you do me great honour . . .

I like to think that it would have gone down well, if I had ever had the chance to deliver it. However, once again I was sandbagged by a woman. Not a tipsy woman who had sat in her dessert, and not really a woman, but Dame Edna Everage. The grande dame of the Antipodes made her entrance from the very top of the sweeping staircase that leads into the great ballroom of Grosvenor House. Acknowledging every hurrah, and pausing freely to bow and graciously smile, she made her regal way to the stage. It was like the arrival of the Queen of Sheba, and took about twenty minutes. Once on stage, the Dame was once again accorded her due accolade of praise, and milked it like a good 'un, with many a barbed quip. This took another two minutes, before she was kind enough to mention my name. I rose, and so, it must be said in due modesty, did the crowd. It hardly helped quell the apprehension gnawing at my very vitals at the prospect of having to follow one of the world's funniest acts. Things didn't get any better. As I arrived on stage, the Dame announced that she would read a poem that she had written in tribute to me. It was funny, witty, clever, and took another ten minutes while I hung about trying not to look like a lemon in front of thousands of my fellow broadcasters.

So I didn't deliver my speech, and I can't repeat what I actually said, but it was the kind of situation for which only forty years of experience can prepare you. I do remember saying that I wanted to share the award with dear Paul Walters, sadly not with us as he fights a grievous illness with courage and humour, and it was gratifying to hear the loud applause for a great producer and a lovely man. They stood up again when I left, but maybe it was because it was the final award and they were getting up to go anyway . . .

Naturally, my listeners were sparing with their enthusiasm in response to my triumph:

To: Terry Wogan
From: Ellie

Dear Terry *et al*,

Surely 'outstanding achievement' suggests that there is still some achievement outstanding? It's celebrating the fact that you still haven't managed to do anything really impressive.

Just a thought,

Ellie

P.S. Is it wrong that I'm 22 and listen to the show? Love the show. x

Don't ask how this slipped under the wire – I only encourage abuse.

To: Terry Wogan
From: Liz

Dear Terry

Congrats on the latest award. Could this be linked to your

return from the recent hols, the outstanding achievement being that you turned up for work?

Liz (forever youngish)

That's more like it.

And this manages to combine both praise and blame, compliment and brick bat . . .

To: Terry Wogan
From: Katie Mallet

Dear Terry,

Congratulations for whatever.
Sir Terry's got a gold award,
But can't tell why he's got it,
Perhaps he knew, but like a Tog
Immediately forgot it,
But I can tell you what it's for –
For simply being there,
As like a warming duvet
He comforts us on air.
His voice wraps all around us,
And though it's getting old
It manages to stop us
Becoming tired and cold.
Byeeee.

Katie Mallett

There are far too many 'awards', and as a consequence they lack credibility. Who decides the winner? A panel? Who picked them? Are they entirely independent and unbiased in their judgements? In your dreams. Was it the public? Who counts the votes? Are there impartial observers to make sure it's all above board? Come on . . . As long as everybody knows that it's just a bit of fun, and the results are tomorrow's fish-and-chips wrapper, fine and dandy. But spare me the 'awards' that are based on the arbitrary, subjective opinions of a 'panel of judges'. You're not talking to a know-all know-nothing here; I've sat on panels, I've judged. All right, they've been beauty contests, but the same rules apply when you've got more than one judge: everybody thinks a different girl is the most beautiful, so the contestant that most of the judges thought was third best, wins. Eye of the beholder. As William Goldman said about Hollywood, and anybody who knows anything about radio, television and the theatre knows all too well, 'Nobody knows anything.' I always thought the emphasis was on 'anything', but my friend, the extremely bright producer Tom Webber, maintains it's on 'knows'. Either way, never a truer few words were spoken.

Of course, the public are even more quirky in their judgement of winners and losers, than panels of experts, juries and the Lords of Appeal. Just look at the bummer that they regularly select to represent the United Kingdom at the Eurovision Song Contest. I'm the spokesman, the cheerleader who's supposed to 'big-up' our song's chances, but every year at the end of *Making Your Mind Up*, the cold fingers of reality clutch at my vitals, and I know that the Great British Public has voted in their thousands yet again for some repetitive, imitative tosh that will rightly be dismissed out of hand by the discerning music-lovers of Moldova and the former Yugoslav Republic of Macedonia. Admittedly it's no easy task to pick something even remotely musical from the six songs preselected by the dead hand of another panel of 'experts', but at times it does seem that there are darker forces at work. Or at least a bloody-minded public resolve to have it their way.

Years ago, that fine singer, Michael Ball, put his tonsils on the block, where no other of his musical standing and ability was prepared to chance their reputation, by agreeing to sing the regulatory six songs for Europe and bellow the winner for Britain at the final, in Malmo. It's not without its own significance that no artist of Michael's stature has risked their neck for the old country since. As befits the Broadway and West End star that he has become, Ball gave his all to every last note of every one of the six contenders. But Stewart Morris, the producer, and the acknowledged maestro of musical television, knew the song that was going to win the UK the Eurovision. Paul Walters, no sluggard at picking a winner himself, agreed. As ever, my opinion counted for nothing, but I echoed the choice of the two great men. We were long overdue a win at the Eurosong, and this was the one – and, just as importantly, we had the singer to do it.

The trouble was, could the public be trusted to pick what was clearly the best song?

Despite decades of exposure to the Eurovision, watching little girls on stools singing to a guitar, or grey-beards from Denmark, or a couple of geezers round a piano from Ireland all win the thing, the British public still thinks a Eurosong is 'Puppet on a Boom Bang Making Its Mind Up'. Stewart Morris was worried; there was a headbanger in Michael Ball's six that they might go for. He tried to get me to praise it with faint damns, to emphasise that what we were looking for, the one that would knock 'em dead in Malmo, was a romantic ballad. We were whistling into the wind. Unerringly, the great British public voted with their feet, the ones that they could thump up and down on the floor. We took the 'Boom-Bang-a-Puppet' to the Eurovision final and came second. I swear that with a lesser singer than Michael Ball we would have brought up the rear.

Music is a matter of taste, subjective; so it's possible that our views on what song should win might be interpreted as elitist, and we've no guarantee that our choice would have won anyway, and we must bow to public opinion. Although . . . Is it only me, or has anyone else noticed a certain mischievous note that has crept into public voting since the growth of the 'reality' show? Time and again, on *Celebrity Big Brother, I'm a Celebrity, Get Me Out of Here!, Strictly Come Dancing, Just the Two of Us*, the meritorious, the intelligent, the sympathetic, the decent get turfed out by the public in favour of the coward, the whinger, the bully and the downright disgusting. And, of course, the mediocre, whom they inevitably pick as the winner. These pro- grammes are a slap in the face for anybody who thinks that they can define public taste. They are also a hard lesson to those television executives who imagine that they know about popu- larity – who the public likes, and who they don't.

It was particularly instructive to watch the first run of *Just the Two of Us*, in which, inexplicably, some established television presenters linked up with established pop singers for a vocal version of *Strictly Come Dancing*. As with that, so with the singing contest: it didn't matter what the judges said, it didn't matter whether they could sing, the public voted for the personality they *liked*. Or, in at least one case, for somebody without a note in her head, just for the hell of it. The old saw that 'nobody ever got poor by underestimating the public's taste' might possibly be true if you're running a supermarket, but if you want to do anything on television or radio, you'd better keep an eye and an ear out for the wit, the sense of the ridiculous and the subversive humour just below the surface that characterises the British public.

Éamon de Valera, like all great Irish leaders a hero to some, a villain to others, used to say: 'Whenever I want to know what the Irish people want, I look into my own heart,' condemning at least a couple of generations to his vision of Sinn Féin (ourselves alone), a ridiculous fairyland of whitewashed cottages, turf fires, comely maidens dancing at crossroads and relentless piety. People like me, with a daily audience of millions, thousands of whom communicate with me every week, must constantly be on our guard against falling into the trap of thinking that a passing glance at our own prejudices will give an insight into the public's frame of mind.

For reasons that escape me now, in 2002 I kept a diary. (Prince Charles kept a 'journal', which we all were privy to this year; what's the difference?) No more than the present tome, it's unremarkable stuff, but a salutary lesson in never trying to second-guess the public:

30 March 2002
Easter. Flowers, a card and an Easter egg from Patisserie Valerie on Marylebone High Street for Helen. Alan comes to play golf at Stoke Poges. Katherine and her boyfriend, Henry – and the almost human Spike – will be here at Hitcham Close tomorrow, and Mark and his partner Susan,

with eccentric schnauzer, Pop – will keep me company on Easter Monday, while Helen and Alan play Mixed Gruesomes at Stoke. That's OK – Mark's cooking.

As we watch a movie on Saturday evening, up flashes a message that the Queen Mother has passed away. Television and radio clear the decks for the obituary tributes that they have been planning, rewriting and rehearsing for forty years. Trouble is, the event still seems to have taken them all by surprise. Sky Television's reporter is a stumbling embarrassment; we switch to the voice of the nation, the BBC. It swiftly becomes apparent that handling an on-the-spot crisis which requires quick thinking and spontaneous responses is not Peter Sissons' forte. It's a hesitant coverage, with a lot of 'filling' from reporters. The woman reporting from outside Windsor Castle promises to talk with members of the public, who are flocking to the environs to pay their respects. Sissons returns to her after a few minutes, but she's alone. The mourning public are there, claims the reporter, but are being held back by police. Even as she speaks, a couple of passers-by stroll by the camera. It's obvious that there's nobody there, apart from a couple of tourists . . .

2 April 2002

The newspapers, the rabidly anti-BBC *Daily Mail* in particular, are having a field day. Prince Charles has pointedly recorded his tribute to his beloved grandmother with ITV, snubbing the BBC. This is grist to the *Mail*, and all of the rest of the print media, who would love to kick television and radio, and the BBC in particular, to death. It appears that the Prince and his mother, the Queen, have been deeply offended by the BBC's coverage of the Queen Mother's death. (Not true – it was just ITV's turn.) They apparently echo the *Daily Mail's* view that her sad passing was not accorded sufficient time or dignity. The last straw appears to have been Peter Sissons' choice of tie colour: red. He says he was told not to wear black. Hanging, drawing and quartering is not good enough for him. Let him rot in the Tower! Lorraine Heggessey, Controller of BBC1, had better reserve a place on the nearest tumbril while she's at it – it was her decision to return to normal programming after two hours. And while the print media foam at the mouth, it appears that there were 100 phone calls of complaint to BBC TV about their coverage of events. And 700 more complaining that the evening schedule of programmes had been changed . . .

The newspapers have been preparing for years: the tributes to the Queen Mother, the special editions, with their photographs of the lady from her birth, the nostalgic supplements of the last 100 years, all will go on for some days yet, right up to the final tribute of her funeral. So, who's got it right, the papers or Lorraine Heggessey? There is a great sadness, I sense, at the passing of a great queen; nobody in British life was held in greater affection or esteem. But it's nothing like the outpouring of real grief that I remember gripping the nation at Diana's sudden tragic death. We still have to wait for the funeral, but I will be surprised if the Queen Mother's cortège brings weeping crowds to the streets in their thousands, as did Princess Diana's.

Some time ago, I was told that the Queen Mother had planned the route that her funeral would take. She had one unshakeable proviso: 'The procession must not pass that *awful* man's store . . .'

9 *April 2002*

Well, I was wrong, and so was everybody else who thought the nation largely unaffected by the old queen's death. Hundreds of thousands queued for hours to view her catafalque, a million lined the streets to mark her final passing. And it wasn't middle-class, middle England either. It was young and old, black and white, every stratum of society. And they cried: not the hysterical grief accorded Diana, Princess of Wales; more a genteel, discreet, British sobbing. The funeral was a magnificent spectacle, staged with extraordinary precision and discipline – and yet moving, particularly when the plaintive pipes rent the air. The Queen had asked that it be as much a celebration of her mother's life as a lament for her death, but there weren't many smiles. Prince Charles has taken his grandmother's death badly; nine days on he still looks on the point of bursting into tears.

Charles wears his emotions on his sleeve – the British expect imperturbability, if not stoicism, from their once and future King. Charles expresses his emotions and opinions freely: politics, architecture, farming, the environment. Nobody has elected him to speak on their behalf, and he has no qualifications, but he expects to be listened to. He wants to be one of us, but as the first among equals. His problem, and indeed that of his siblings, is that nobody has ever disagreed with him. Surrounded, as he has been all his life by sycophants and courtiers, who has ever sayed him nay? Whether he will ever mount the throne is doubtful; his mother looks as if she could outlive *her* mother, and it would be a brave prime minister who agreed to her abdication. It would be a shame if Charles doesn't accede; he is intelligent, concerned deeply with the country and its people and, in his Duchess, has a warm and supportive partner.

10

Home and away

�artwork⟩

In the early eighties, our friends Derrick and Mina Russell
invited us down to stay in the house they'd just bought on
Villamartin Golf Course, near Torrevieja, south of Alicante
on the Costa Blanca of Spain. I've always loved the sun, and it
was typical of Helen, who has always sheltered from it, that
she was as enthusiastic as I was about the place. North of Alicante
was Benidorm: 'English tea served here', 'full English breakfasts', real ale, Irish pubs, discos, all the cheap vodka and Spanish
brandy you could drink, and, day and night, all the charm of an
English country town on a Saturday night: lads and ladettes,
drunk, doped and disorderly. I'd spent a holiday there myself in
the sixties with my friend Mick Heary. And yes, the drink was
cheap and plentiful, and we had plenty of it. And yes, we slept
off our hangovers on the beach and boogied until dawn – but
then the place had a charm, a still-Spanish innocence about it,

enforced by Franco's Guardia Civil, who had a short way with anything or anybody who seemed to be undermining all that was best in Spanish life.

South of Alicante in 1983 were miles of deserted beaches, undeveloped land given over to agriculture, the kind of Spain that I remembered from twenty years before – small towns, a gentle, unhurried way of life, and, even better, in Villamartin, an empty golf course. A friendly clubhouse, a few villas on the first fairway, just turn up, pay a pittance of a green fee, and play. Within a year we had bought a place overlooking the sea, with a garden, a pool and a maid, Josefa, who took at least three years to get over the loss of the previous owners, a Spanish doctor and his family from Murcia, the main city of the region. We had a gardener, Bartolo, full of charm, who never lifted a finger in the garden until he heard on the grapevine that we were coming over, then he'd put in a team to cut the grass, trim the hedges and clean the pool. And every time he'd have an excuse for the reasons why the fruit trees had perished and the flowers had died. It was the wind from the sea, the red dust from Africa, and in no way due to the fact that the trees and the plants had not seen a drop of water since we were last there.

Our friends, the Clancys, also bought a place in Villamartin, and they were followed by many of their friends from Lahinch, Co. Clare. In a very short time, Villamartin became Lahinch-by-the-Mediterranean. Our children loved it, and because Cabo Roig, where we lived, was almost entirely populated by Spanish families swapping the intense heat of inland Murcia for cooler sea breezes, they soon picked up a working knowledge of colloquial Spanish. Later on, Alan taught English in Murcia, and Katherine's university degree is in Hispanic Studies. She spent a year in Complutense University in Madrid, which knocked all the regional dialect out of her, and she still looks down from her dizzy Castilian heights on the rest of us and our rough country Spanish. Mind you, my grasp of the language was, at best, tenuous. I'm a mimic, another way of saying I've a 'good ear' for languages. It's why I'm doing the job I'm in. I'd never have passed that audition all those years ago at Radio Eireann if I hadn't been able to fake the Gaelic, French, Italian and German. Spanish I learned by a process of osmosis – all my verbs were in the infinitive, with scant regard for tense, all my nouns were singular, and careless of gender. I didn't know much, but what I knew I could pronounce correctly, and the Spanish will tolerate a lot from a foreigner who tries to speak their language.

As the children grew older, so our little deserted corner of Spain began to grow up too; almost overnight there were bars and discos, and they became creatures of the night, sleeping during the sunlit days to the annoyance of their parents. A story as old as time . . .

As the years went by, Josefa, our maid, began to warm to us. We learned to pay her a little more than she expected, and *olé!* she began to display her skill with skillet and pan. I never order paella or tortilla now, not since Josefa. She would spend a whole day cosseting the paella pan, clicking her tongue at what she saw as the inordinate amount of chicken we asked her to put in it. She grew to love our children, and when Alan was teaching in Murcia and living at the weekends in Cabo Roig, she would invite him to join her family for dinner in her little house in San Miguel de Salinas.

The changes came gradually, and then with almost breakneck speed. We first began to notice the developments on the hitherto deserted fields between Alicante airport and Torrevieja. Every couple of months, new apartment blocks, rows of villas of every colour, shape and size; Torrevieja, a charming coastal town with a pretty marina, where you could stroll and take a dry sherry with your tapas, became a forest of cranes. The traffic became so bad they built a bypass, and the jerry-built little houses and ugly apartments staggered along beside the road. Villamartin Golf Club acquired a new owner and what seemed like a thousand back-to-back villas. In a year, the course was crowded every day. The owner of our little promontory, Cabo Roig, sold much of the land to a developer with the usual results – houses and apartments squeezed into every available space.

Still, for a couple of years, we were happy enough – we could sit in our garden, surrounded by hedges and trees, and ignore the changing face of our Spain. Then our trees and hedges began to die, and when we began to taste the salt in our showers and swimming pool, we understood why: in order to keep up the water pressure to cope with the enormous increase in demand, the local council had hit upon a cunning plan – they had introduced sea water into the domestic pipes . . . Now, the flowers and fruit trees had no chance, and the grass was going the way of the trees and hedges. Then an empty building on the cliffs just in front of our house, a former jail which had been deserted for years, became a barracks for the Spanish equivalent of the Special Boat Squadron. *Apocalypse Now* came to Cabo Roig. I remember sitting in our garden with our friends, Hacker and Kits, watching the military helicopters whirr deafeningly overhead while their occupants abseiled into the sea. A noise matched only by the din of the rough soldiery every evening. Only the Spanish would carry out dangerous military operations in a residential area, yards off a marina and beach crowded with holidaymakers . . .

It was time to go, and not only because the area was going to hell in a handcart. Our young people had outgrown the urge for all-night bars and music and were seeking more mature pleasures. I love the Spanish, for all their lack of civic pride, their carelessness, the corruption that was endemic, at least when I was there. For all their foolish pride, they're a friendly, warm, hospitable people. The entire Spanish coastline, from Barcelona to Cadiz, has become a monument to greed, but the cities and towns of the interior retain the dignity and splendour of the old Spain. Burgos, where they carve the lamb with a spoon, Zaragoza, where the morcilla, the black pudding, is 'historic', to plagiarise another man who loves his food . . .

We put the house in Cabo Roig on the market with the same agent who had sold it to us twelve years earlier, and in a remarkably short time he sold it to a Dutchman who didn't seem to care about salt in his water, houses all over his golf course, and soldiers in his back yard. We'll never go back – we probably wouldn't recognise the place anyway – but there will always be memories: the *gambas rojas*, the huge grilled prawns, in a little restaurant named 'Moderno' in a village called San Javier which had a lemon-coloured church; 'Moderno' was always deserted when we ate there, only when we were leaving, at about eleven o'clock, would the locals begin to drift in. That's another thing I admire about the Spanish: their digestion. They don't eat breakfast, have a sandwich or a cake at about eleven in the morning, lunch at three in the afternoon, and, at least in Madrid, dinner at anything up to one o'clock the following morning.

I bought a boat in Spain – always a mistake. Little boats are like lawnmowers: no matter how much care you take when you're putting them away in the winter, they never start in the spring. Still, when we did manage to get the thing going, it was fun to chug around to deserted bays. Then, one hot day, as we lolled about, once again with Hacker and Kits Browning, the damn boat inexplicably stalled and stopped dead. There was nothing for it but for the ladies to stay aboard while Kits and I waded through the shallows up into a little place where we hailed a taxi, whose driver obviously didn't mind his back seat being covered in sand and sea water. Back we went to Cabo Roig marina, where everybody was out to lunch. We waited impatiently, ever conscious of our wives slowly sizzling to a frazzle in an open boat in the Spanish sun. Eventually the boat men turned up, and we set out in one of theirs for our becalmed craft, with two ladies done to a turn.

You hardly need me to tell you what happened when we got there. The Spanish boatman stepped aboard, fixed the key on to a lock from which it had slipped, turned the key, and started the boat. They had explained this 'dead man's lock' thing, or whatever it was called, when I'd bought the boat, but I'd forgotten. The boatman looked at me pityingly, and I'd rather draw a veil over the comments of my wife and friends. I sold the boat shortly afterwards; I was never so glad to get rid of anything. Have I mentioned to you already about me and inanimate objects? We're incompatible . . .

For the next year or so, Helen and I took our holidays elsewhere. We went for a golfing holiday, to the marvellous Boulders Resort, near Phoenix, Arizona, where they clean your clubs before every round and remember your name. The *casitas*, little pueblo-type cottages, are delightful, unobtrusively scattered in the *arroyos* of this green oasis in the middle of a desert. If only some Spanish developers had taken a look at this before they did their worst . . . The food was delicious, the room service impeccable, and every morning, as you drew the blinds and stepped out on to the little patio, a wildlife experience: quail, wild boar, coyote, deer, chipmunks, strolling by as if they owned the place, even stopping graciously to taste a little of our breakfast. And that's the only cavil I have about the place – breakfast. Not just Boulders' breakfasts, American breakfasts in general. The coffee tastes of nothing, you eat bacon with your fingers, grits are an inedible mystery, the sausages are an insult to a proud tradition, there's fruit all over the plate, and are they really expecting you to pour that maple syrup over everything? OK, I *do* like that Canadian bacon you eat with your fingers . . .

When the children were young, we took many a holiday in the States – to Florida, where they lost our luggage, Key Biscayne, and then, in a big old air-conditioned gas-guzzler, across the State, to Walt Disney World in Orlando. As we trundled along, suddenly a sunny day went dark. I pulled in off the highway to find the air alive with insects, and the entire car covered in the little blighters. The windscreen wipers couldn't cope, and we limped slowly into a nearby garage. The air was still thick with these creatures, their millions blotting out the sun. I asked the attendant hosing down every car that came in the reason for this biblical plague. 'It's the love bug,' he said. 'Every year, 'bout this time, those good ol' boys get to matin', and they just don't care who knows it.' The clouds of love soon passed, but long after we've forgotten Walt Disney World and its delights, my family will remember those gallant bugs, giving their all for love, even as they crashed to oblivion on our windscreen.

Another year, we all went to the West Coast, to San Francisco, where we stayed in a hotel on the Embarcadero. The same hotel where Mel Brooks shot his movie about fear of heights, *High Anxiety*. He'd picked his location well: the hotel had a dizzyingly high glass dome above the atrium lobby, from where a glass-walled lift whizzed you vertiginously to the bedrooms. Ours was on the twentieth floor. In *High Anxiety*, Mel Brooks can be seen gibbering with fear in that self-same elevator, and then edging his way to his room facing the wall, with his back to the huge drop to the atrium floor. For Mel Brooks, read Helen Wogan, whose fear of heights easily matched that of the movie's character. A little later, we moved to the second floor and took the stairs to our room . . .

From 'Frisco we took the Pacific Highway to Pebble Beach, then on to Lake Tahoe and, finally, Yosemite National Park. Helen and I often wonder how we did all this with a car full of children and not a care in the world. And then we burst into our Maurice Chevalier/Hermione Gingold duet: 'Ah yes – I remember it well . . .' Ah, me lost youth . . .

The wilderness is all the Americans have in the way of ancient history, and they attempt to preserve it in quaint ways: my children were incensed to discover that there were no radios nor television in the hotel. The scenery and the wildlife dissolved the disappointment soon enough, and we went riding on cow-ponies, the one and only time I've ever been on a horse in my life. Why do people always imagine that, if you're Irish, you have a natural affinity with horse flesh? They've seen *The Commitments*, with the kids keeping the horses on the waste ground outside the terrible Dublin Ballymun flats now flattened, thank the Lord and they've been to Cheltenham, with the Irish being more Irish than they'd ever dare to be back home, but when I was growing up in Limerick, close to some of the greatest horse-rearing country in the world, nobody I knew had ever been on a horse, nor wanted to. Anyway, this little ol' cow-pony trotted, cantered and walked just as if I was in charge. Somebody helped me off the critter and I walked away like John Wayne; I know now why he walked like that . . .

While we were in Yosemite, it was Katherine's fifth birthday. We'd got all her cards and presents, but for some reason, which in retrospect seems a cruel joke to play on a little girl, we pretended we'd forgotten. Nobody mentioned the birthday all day, and the poor girl became more and more silent. We'd booked a table on the terrace for dinner, and, on cue, in came the waiters with a huge cake, ablaze with candles, singing 'Happy Birthday to You'. I can still see her face – the surprise, the joy and the tears of happiness. We fed some of the birthday cake to the racoons, and although I've had more than my share of happy memories, that was an evening that I can conjure up without even closing my eyes. Looking back, I see that I have bored you with this story before, and indeed there may be one or two more in this sturdy tome, but as you get older, most memories fade – only the very special ones remain, and they're the ones that old geezers tell again and again . . .

People often ask if we've kept a home in Ireland, and the answer is no. We spent four idyllic years in our little bungalow on Killiney Hill, Co. Dublin. It was where our first son, Alan, was born, and we've only happy memories of the place, but we had to sell it to buy our first home in Britain. So having sold our hacienda in Spain, we thought it mightn't be a bad idea to refresh our Irish roots, and Helen and I flew into Cork, and then on to

Kenmare. It's a lovely town, its shops and houses every colour of the rainbow, every second one a pub or a restaurant, and the location of, at least in my opinion, the two best hotels in Ireland, Sheen Falls Lodge, and the Park. Just outside town is the Ring of Kerry Golf Club, which surely can challenge any in the world for the sheer beauty of its location. Look across the still waters of the broad Kenmare River estuary to the blue hills of Gougane Beara, with the Atlantic beyond, and even a three-putt won't take the beatific grin off your face.

On Helen and I went to Waterville, another great golf club, where, if the wind is up, you can hit the best drive of your life and the ball will still come back to your feet. Then to Killarney, still beautiful in its lakes and mountains, for all the tacky commercialism of the town itself, and Tralee, where I introduced the first 'Rose of Tralee' International Beauty Contest all those years ago. It's still going. Irish Television gives it prime-time coverage every year, in the face of accordionists from Kerry, nose-flutes from Paraguay and banjos from Mississippi. No swimsuits, of course – this is County Kerry, not Las Vegas, Nevada.

We crossed the Shannon and stayed at Ashford Castle, a former pile of the Guinness family (the riches an ould pint of stout can bring . . .) and sailed across Lough Corrib into Joyce country, so called because every second person there bore that name in a previous century, and not in honour of the birth there of Helen's father, Tim Joyce, although he stoutly declared it so, and indeed would fight any man who denied it. Up to Westport and more golf, this time in the shadow of Croagh Patrick, Ireland's penitential mountain, up which thousands climb, some in bare feet, for all sorts of reasons apart from the glory of God and to pay for their sins. They do it for special intentions: the health of a loved one, the birth of a child, the passing of an exam.

There's another pilgrimage in Ireland, Lough Derg, where, again, thousands flock every year for their own reasons. Three days and nights of prayer, privation and starvation on an island in the middle of a lake. Some of the most unlikely people I know have 'done' Lough Derg: rascals, rogues, lechers. And Helen Wogan, just to tip the balance in favour of the good guys. She said that the pepper in hot water that they give you at the end of the ordeal was the finest dish she's ever tasted. Faith . . . it's a gift.

We flew back from Shannon with our hearts full of Ireland, but somehow we never pursued the idea of having a place there again. I suppose it's because the months we'd enjoy most in Ireland are the times we enjoy best in Britain. Although Ireland, its people and their attitudes are different, we needed a more marked contrast in life and culture. And then, one Sunday, I found it: an article on south-west France, the old Gascony. It talked of tranquillity, rolling hills, sunflowers, vineyards and space, lots of space. In an unprecedented move, at least for me, I followed it up, and in July 1996 we travelled to the capital of the department of Gers, the lovely town of Auch, with its magnificent cathedral. We were ready to stay there and look around the region, but the agent, an Englishman named Ian Purslow, persuaded us to try instead a bed and breakfast, a *chambre d'hôte* that he knew, deep in the heart of the countryside. A lovely house, in a beautiful park of magnificent trees, with vineyards on all sides, and a church.

The hosts, a charming English couple, Jean and John, had not only refurbished, but rebuilt the little chateau, restoring the plumbing, the heating, the electricity, and had built a lovely swimming pool in their spare moments. Then, after a delicious *déjeuner sur l'herbe*, they told us that they were returning to England, to be closer to their first grandchild, and the house was for sale. We looked at other places; indeed, we returned later that year to look at some more, but it was no contest. I knew I would never have the time, or the patience, to restore an old ruin of a farmhouse, or rebuild a crumbling chateau, and this place had everything in working order.

Helen and I flew into Toulouse, just after that Christmas, for our first stay in our very own French chateau. It was snowing, hard. After a perilous drive, we arrived in six inches of snow to our freezing French dream, which looked like turning into a nightmare, with no heating and a sudden plunge into utter darkness as we attempted to plug in an electric heater and fused every light in the place. That first night in our new home, lit by candles and sleeping under six layers of blankets, is another memory that I'll carry with me to the grave. The following day, I found the fuses, a helpful farmer brought us the necessities on a tractor, and ten years on, although we had our doubts on that first night, Helen and I don't regret a thing.

The Gers retains its languid, unspoiled beauty, the people are courteous and friendly, the sunflowers bloom, the vineyards march in their precise lines up and over the gentle hills. The fruit, the vegetables, even the fish, from the Atlantic, an hour and a half away, are a world away from the supermarkets of Britain. The Gers is famous for the heartiness of its cuisine, although I'm bound to say that if you're not a fan of our feathered friend, the duck, you might go hungry. Foie, confit, magret, aiguillettes, rillets, gesiers – that one small bird could do so much. The French get their money's worth out of the duck. For instance, last year we went with friends to one of the innumerable fêtes that every French village and hamlet throws every year. This was 'Demoiselles' night – melon, duck, cheese, dessert, wine and armagnac, ten euro per person. The 'demoiselles' were the carcasses of duck, after all the aforementioned delights had been taken away. No prizes for finding any meat on them, but there should have been. Still, everybody chewed and gnawed, the bones went into huge bags, and, given the thriftiness of the French, were probably recycled for pebble-dashing. Next year we'll go to the same village for the 'Escargot' festival. Just so long as they don't take the snails out beforehand and expect us to eat the shells . . .

A couple of years ago, a native of the south-west of France, having given the vin du pays a severe thrashing the night before, clambered unsteadily into his Deux Chevaux to go and collect his morning baguette at the boulangerie. Some time later his little car was found wrapped around one of those magnificent trees that line, so graciously, the little roads of France. The car was a write-off, and so, unfortunately, was he. The driver was subsequently found to have the alcohol from the night before still lapping up against his back teeth. Not to put too fine a point on it, the poor fellow was still drunk when he left the road and hit the tree. The car/tree confrontation is one that is not that unusual on the bosky routes of France. A local deputy, however, came up with a solution: cut the trees down. If the tree hadn't been there, he shrewdly reasoned, the car could have continued its erratic way until coming to a halt in a field of waving corn, or a vineyard, with little chance of loss of life. It's a tribute to the French way of life that when I last looked, this solution to drunk driving was still being considered by the local department. Can't a man have a drink without some blasted tree leaping out on the road to kill him?

What put me in mind of this was a conversation with a television cameraman who told me that he had just completed a film on a new Swedish invention, a collapsible lamppost which not only caves in when hit by a car but, by some Nordic trickery, also slows the careering vehicle down. 'Splendid!' I hear you cry, 'let's hear it, for the clever, caring Swedes.' Not everybody feels that way, least of all in Sweden, where there have been protests that the invention interferes with the inalienable right of every Swede to commit suicide when the mood takes him. Lampposts and trees – they'll be the death of us all . . .

2003 was a great year for the Wogans: two weddings, no funerals; although the present Lady Wogan might have been excused for buckling under the strain of organising a summer wedding in the Gers, and a winter one in Bucks.

Mark, our second son, and Susan Acteson, his beautiful fiancée, decided that they wanted to be married from our house in France. It was all the vindication we ever needed for buying the place. There was much to be done, most of it from a distance, but Helen Wogan had the energy and determination of ten. She visited traiteurs and restaurants before selecting someone who would cater for the reception, which was going to be held in the garden for about 150 people. Then there was the marquee and the band for dancing, and the string quartet for the church, hotel rooms to be reserved in every surrounding town and village, and, finally, the church itself. It's a beautiful little church, at the top of our parc, but it hadn't been used for years.

We asked the parish priest, Abbé Commenge, for help. He's everybody's idea of a French priest – rotund, apple-cheeked and kindly. And without a word of English. It was to be an ecumenical service, Susan being Church of England, and Mark, Catholic. I doubt if we'd have got to first base without the help of our great and good friend Father Brian D'Arcy, but after a lot of toing and froing, bishops on both sides of the Channel were placated. It was then that Abbé Commenge came into his own. Although he was committed to another wedding on the same day, he arranged for the reconsecration of the church. Not only that, but the local commune refurbished, restored and repainted the little church, just for our wedding, without being asked, and without payment. It's a constant source of pride and joy that it has been revived as a place of worship, and Mass is once again celebrated regularly there.

Susan and her family arrived a couple of days before the Big One, and stayed with our friends Nicky and Michael just up the little road. Mark and Alan arrived a couple of days early too, having driven my car, the bridal limousine, all the way from home. Abbé Commenge came to dinner, with the con-celebrants, my two friends from *Pause for Thought*, Father Brian D'Arcy and Canon Roger Royle. The guests rang to confirm their arrival from every *relais, ferme d'auberge, chambre d'hôte* and hotel in the region.

As the sun rose on the morning of the wedding, we knew it was going to be a hot one. The guests began to arrive, reflecting the glorious summer day, the ladies all glamour, hats and dresses of every hue, the men in their lightweight suits and panama hats. Monsieur Bousigon, a neighbour and the sexton, rang the bell and everybody made their way through the parc to the church. It looked like a painting from a time long gone, as they strolled, all finery and elegance, through the trees in the sunlight. It was a beautiful ceremony, with Brian and Roger speaking both truly and wittily; the quartet played and the church was full of flowers and candles and goodwill to all men. And 150 people all crammed into a space designed for half that number.

Outside, the temperature climbed to 103 degrees; inside – well, how half the congregation didn't expire on their little wooden seats I'll never know. I suppose that it's a sadness, but Mark and Susan's wedding day is destined to be remembered not for its charm, its gaiety, or even the beauty of the bride but the heat that had every lady fanning herself with a hymn sheet and every man's shirt stuck to his back. Water, not champagne or wine, was the drink of choice; indeed, there was enough champagne and wine left over to more than cater for the thirst of the 220 guests at Katherine's wedding the following December.

Despite the heat, only the parfait melted, and the reception was all fun and laughter and the occasional tear, just as it should be. The heat of the day blended into the warmth of the evening, the live band struck up, the dancing began, Susan and Mark sang to each other, and their perfect day drew to a close as they set off for their hotel and their honeymoon down the Pacific Highway that Mark had never forgotten from that family holiday years ago. The following day, we held a lunch in the marquee for all the guests, a buffet, and Monsieur Bousigon, who had been so instrumental, with his wife, in preparing the church, instructed everybody in the arcane art of sucking armagnac through a sugar cube. And, hallelujah!, it rained. It's the only time I've ever heard an Anglo-Irish crowd applaud the rain. More speeches, more laughter, more of whatever you're having yourself; and then it was time for the panama hats and the summer dresses to depart, leaving Helen and me with the happiest memories of one of the happiest days of our life.

My beautiful daughter, Katherine Helen Bernadette Wogan, had always dreamed of a winter wedding, and on 6 December 2003 her dream came true. She has never really been that enthused over the 'Bernadette', claiming that her mother chose it for her confirmation name without consultation, at a time when Katherine was too young to put up much of an argument. It's certainly not something you could accuse Katherine of in maturity. This is a modern young woman with a mind of her own, a forceful way with words, and a short-arm left cross of which Sir Henry Cooper would not have been ashamed. In this, she is not unlike her mother, who can also punch her weight. (Incidentally, Mark Wogan's confirmation name should not go unremarked; as his brother Alan reminded us at Mark and Susan's wedding, my eleven-year-old second son insisted on 'Mark' for his third Christian name. Mark Paul Mark Wogan – those who know and love him were not surprised.)

Mark and Susan's French country wedding took some organising, particularly as it was being done from a distance, but in retrospect it was a languid *déjeuner sur l'herbe* compared with Katherine's. Again, it was to be an ecumenical wedding, her fiancé, Henry Cripps, being Church of England and Katherine, a Catholic. This time, the nuptials were to be celebrated in the Church of England by our local vicar, the Revd Alan Dibden, with my redoubtable old chum, Father Brian D'Arcy, keeping a close eye on any loose Reformist talk or heretical tendency.

Katherine and I arrived by vintage Rolls, entering the beautiful Church of St Nicholas Taplow, aglow with candles and the warmth of family and friends. Creamy white roses were everywhere, trailing over the pews with ivy and lilies, but my daughter and I were just concentrating on making it to the altar rails without breaking down. We nearly did it, too, until we both caught sight of the groom, dear Henry, his chin quivering, his eyes full of tears. Katherine nearly fainted at the altar rails, just as her mother had done in Rathmines Church, Dublin, a lifetime before. They signed the register to a lovely choral arrangement of Elgar's 'Nimrod', and the bride and groom exited, all tears forgotten, with smiles and laughter, to 'Adeste Fideles'.

Thanks to our friends from the north, Mahoods, the marquee that covered the terrace and lawn was truly a winter wonderland. Christmas trees from Henry's parents' land, with a dusting of fake snow and twinkling with pea-lights; great pots of white-painted twigs; the theme of white roses with amaryllis carried through to every table; glass panels on both sides looking out on to trees and bushes of the garden covered with lights. And the pièce de résistance: the vaulted room of the marquee covered in black cloth with a thousand little stars shining through. In the course of my speech, with which I will not trouble you, I made passing reference to the Mahood's enormous structure, saying that, along with the Great Wall of China, it was probably the only other man-made object that could be seen from the moon. They called it 'Terry's Tent'. We went north for the food as well, and Heathcotes did us proud, right down to mini fish and chips and hamburgers in the wee small hours. However, the one thing everybody who was there seems to remember, just as they remember the heat of Mark and Susan's great day, was the *coup de théâtre*, as the curtain behind the top table was drawn back to reveal the dance floor and Jamie Cullum with an eight-piece band.

Henry and Katherine took the floor to 'More', and the hooley was off and running. They boogied to the fish and chips and far beyond; Henry and Katherine left, trailing laughter and tears, a friend caught her bouquet, and married herself, this year. Helen Wogan breathed a sigh of sadness and satisfaction – nothing would ever be quite the same again. The little Wogan family was growing bigger, and better, and now there's Freddie, our only grandchild to date . . .

On the other side of the Irish Sea, the other branch of the family was set to spread its wings as well. In 2004, my brother Brian's daughter Jane kept the Wogan wedding ball in the air by marrying a New Yorker, Richie Notar, in Portofino, in a beautiful monastery overlooking the Gulf of Genoa and the spectacular Ligurian coast. We stayed in Santa Margarita in the kind of charming little hotel that only Italy can provide, a simple room with a little balcony overlooking palm trees and the sea, where we ate warm croissants and drank good coffee, and dreamed of being young again . . .

The night before the wedding, everybody gathered in a quay-side restaurant, a get-together to bind the two families and their friends. The priest who was celebrating the marriage, a Jesuit from Rome, came too. With his guitar. Useless for me to protest that one of the reasons I left old Ireland was to get away from singing priests. The warm Italian night air was pierced by Elvis

Presley favourites, and every rock 'n' roll rabble-rouser from the long-dead past.

The trouble about singing priests is the same problem we have with the Royal Family: nobody ever tells them to shut up. Everybody applauds and sings along because it's a priest with a guitar. He's never been told that he's rubbish, and so he infests every social gathering to which he's invited, in the mistaken notion that he can not only play the guitar, but sing as well. He came to the wedding reception, of course, and I was relieved that there was no sign of the dreaded guitar. Silly me – he had it under the table all the while. He did requests in between the courses. Richie and Jane have since had a little daughter, and Richie said that on first sight, she had little piggy eyes like her grandfather, my brother Brian. She'll be lucky – Brian has the light, bright blue eyes of our father, Michael T. Little Freddie Cripps, Katherine and Henry's son, has Helen's father's magnificent head of auburn hair. So it goes on, the only immortality . . .

11

Where do we go from here?

〜♦〜

Over the past couple of years, television shows have come and gone. *Children in Need* and the Eurovision are hardy annuals, and I count myself very fortunate to be associated with both of them. Along with my radio show, it's more than enough to keep me going; I'm not exactly looking for work. I've very few ambitions left for radio or television; looking back, it's hard to believe how much I've done, how far I've come since that first evening in the old Henry Street studios of Radio Eireann in Dublin, and the cattle market report, my first broadcast.

With the seemingly ever increasing success of *Wake Up to Wogan* on the radio, it has occurred to some BBC Television executives that possibly I may still have something to offer. Whenever I meet one or more of them socially, it's the same old song: 'We really *must* find something for you on television . . .'

I've heard it so often I could put it to music. They never follow through, of course; if anything happens, it'll be an accident. Most of what happens on television is an accident. Sometimes it's fatal, and less frequently you walk away unscathed, with a BAFTA. Bruce Forsyth's reincarnation on *Strictly Come Dancing* is entirely due to a young producer who, pretty unfamiliar with the great man's work, saw him play a blinder on *Have I Got News For You*, and, bingo!, the old boy's back in town. Who could have predicted that ballroom dancing would make a comeback? There are people on the sixth floor of Television Centre who still don't believe it. But what have we always said? Right. In this business, nobody knows anything . . .

As far as I'm concerned, BBC TV can't think outside the box, so it's *Making Your Mind Up*, selecting the UK's entry for the Eurovision, or a cheap and cheerful pull-through of the Song Contest's sillier moments. *Auntie's Bloomers*, of course, could have turned me into a fatter, smaller version of Denis Norden if I hadn't walked away. Then there's *Points of View* – always a joy to do, but shunted around the Sunday evening schedules like the stopgap they obviously think it is. If you can find it, even the duration varies – and they don't show it during the peak viewing months of autumn and winter. Obviously they're not really interested in viewers' opinions, otherwise the programme would be given the status and time it deserves. As I know from my radio show, the public love to comment on what they see on the box, but ten minutes on a Sunday evening in the summer is hardly throwing open the network for viewers' opinions.

However, the world of television no longer revolves solely around the BBC, and a couple of years ago Chris Evans, just returned from his two-year sabbatical and newly wed to the delightful Billie Piper, sold my friend Kevin Lygo, at that time Head of Everything on Channel Five, now just Five, on the idea of Gaby Roslin and me presenting a daily morning magazine show. It seemed a good idea at the time – and Chris is one of the great salesmen of our time, so I bought into it. The trouble was, Kevin Lygo bought out, just before the thing started, so we lost our most important supporter. He headed off into the sunlit uplands of Channel 4, Ant and Dec, Davina McCall and *Big Brother*. I should have seen the writing on the wall then, remembering what had happened to *Wogan's Web*, when its most important mentor, BBC Head of Daytime, moved on just before the series started.

The Terry and Gaby Show came live from County Hall, London, with marvellous views of the Thames and the Mother of Parliaments, but no clear view of what it was or who it was aimed at. Gaby ratcheted up her bubbly personality several notches, and never really lost her conviction that we were trying to appeal to the readers of *Heat*, or those viewers who had made her into a star, with Chris, on *The Big Breakfast*. Although we'd worked together amicably and successfully on *Children in Need* for ten years, we never really gelled on *Terry and Gaby*. I should have been able to carry my radio audience with me, but after a couple of weeks they stopped writing about the show; they had lost interest. It was too noisy, too frantic for them, and it wasn't me. Not that it wasn't a cheery, lively little show, but it needed much more publicity than Five was prepared to pay for, and, rather like the apathy shown by listeners on my return to radio, you can't get an audience if they don't know you're there.

Despite the fact that I was convinced that we were screaming into the wind, directing our efforts in entirely the wrong direction, it was one of the happiest shows I've ever done. I will always remember Danny Baker saying, at the little party we held when Five pulled the plug, that all the young floor managers, researchers, production assistants and runners should treasure the memory of *Terry and Gaby*, because nothing they would ever do in the future on television would ever give them so much fun again.

Lack of publicity was not a mistake UKTV Gold made with *Wogan – Now and Then*. They covered any available site with huge posters of our hero as he was and as he is. It's not the most salubrious sight at quarter to seven on a Monday morning as you're bowling down the A40 into London, to be confronted with, not one, but two large pictures of yourself, the one rosy-cheeked and fulsomely sideburned, and the other a raddled shadow of his former self. And it wasn't only on the roadways of Britain that people's sensibilities were assailed; posters were all over London's underground as well.

To see yourself as others see you is bad enough. To see yourself as they saw you twenty years ago . . . You'll see the word 'legend' freely bantered about here. I'm sure that it's meant in a complimentary way but you and I know very well that 'legend', like 'icon' and 'veteran', is merely a euphemism for 'past it', 'over the hill', and 'forgotten but not gone'. My radio listeners were on to it, like ravening wolves: 'Those posters on the Underground are a jolly good idea – they keep people away from the edge of the platform.' 'I thought ventriloquism was dead and buried – which one of you is Archie Andrews?' They speculated cruelly on the name and very nature of the programme. 'What's it called – "*Wogan, Never Again?*" "*Not Again?*" "*Here and There?*" "*Over and Out?*"'

Whatever about the programme, the posters paid off, and after the first week of the show, UKTV Gold were taking full-page ads in *Broadcast* to boast of an unprecedented (for satellite programmes) audience of 1,700,000 viewers. I was surprised, delighted and not a little flattered that major stars were prepared to rake over the coals that were twenty years cold, but they came, and happily. We interspersed the retrospective with names that I hadn't had the pleasure of interviewing before, like Jordan, Ricky Tomlinson, Simon Cowell, but it was a real pleasure to see again Rory Bremner, Nigel Havers, Christopher Lee, Eric Sykes and all the old Wogan riff-raff; and David Icke, no longer a gentle soul convinced that he was descended from the God-head, that wearing turquoise was the way to salvation, and that we were all doomed, but now a ranting demagogue convinced that we were all manipulated sheep, and, of course, all doomed ... The production team and the crew made this another show that was a pleasure: relaxed and fun.

At the time of writing, I don't know how many more *Now and Thens* are in the locker, but I suspect that whatever their success, there must be a limit to the number of stars who want to see themselves as they were, apart from the considerable number who have fallen off the perch in the intervening years. The general consensus was that *Wogan – Now and Then* was a good thing, and I'll take that, because you're never going to do better. The begrudgers we have always with us, whether it be through misanthropy, jealousy, sheer bloody-mindedness or downright nastiness; you have to learn to accept the knocks, however mean-spirited or unnecessarily vitriolic. It would be a queer career indeed if you didn't sometimes deserve them. As I've said before, the wounds could be fatally deep if you don't understand that for every one who listens and watches with pleasure, there's another who loathes the very ground you walk on, and others – the vast majority of the population – who couldn't care less, and who think, whenever they bother, that if you're not Michael Aspel, you could well be Tony Blackburn.

This is one up on that fine body of men, the security guards at BBC Television Centre. They don't know who anybody is. All they know is that it's their job to keep you out. Nowadays, their ignorance can be excused by the fact that many seem to have only lately arrived in Britain, and could hardly be expected to know who the Prime Minister is, not to mind the Director-General or some fly-by-night hobbledehoy. The result is a daily traffic jam on Wood Lane as the queue of lorries, vans and cars passes excruciatingly slowly through the one narrow entrance gate. It's a good job nothing is 'live' any more on BBC TV; there'd be a lot of missed deadlines. It's not new of course, it was ever thus. Jobsworths will be jobsworths, and who do you think *you* are, anyway? I've been called 'Logan?' a lot lately, but even when I was 'Wogan', I had to endure my share of 'Who? Why?' and 'Just a minute while I ring reception and see if they know anything about you'. I mind well the occasion when dear old Kenny Everett was kept waiting so long that he turned his car around and went home. An hour later, blind panic in the studio at the non-appearance of the star: 'The audience is in, we start in ten minutes, where is he?' 'He's at home, says he thought you didn't want him today . . .'

The best BBC executives of my generation, David Hatch, Bill Cotton Jnr, Michael Grade, Mark White, all understood that any radio or television service is only as good as the people who make the programme. Hundreds of other things are important too –

budgetary control, administrating buildings, human resources, compliance; the list grows every year in the BBC – but what really matters, or should, in any broadcasting organisation, and certainly in the world's greatest, is what happens at the sharp end; the tiny bit of the iceberg that is audible and visible to the outside world, the reason for the whole huge edifice's existence: the programmes. Without good people to make and present these programmes, the new Broadcasting House, the White City Broadcast and Media Centres, and all the security men and project managers in the world are as chaff in the wind. Everything a broadcasting organisation does must be directed towards its end product. However, in one as big as the BBC, this simple truth can be easily forgotten. We have a 'talent' department, of course, but I wouldn't know where to find it. I've certainly never met anybody from it, nor, indeed, anybody in or out of the business who knows anything about its function. Perhaps it *is* mysteriously discovering and nurturing the writers, producers, directors, actors and presenters of tomorrow, but could somebody possibly open the door an inch or two so that we might get a glimpse of the burgeoning 'talent'?

I've recounted already the early days, when the talent was expected to travel third class while the producer went first. That attitude had to change, as ITV, commercial radio and satellite broadcasting took to the airwaves, but there is still detectable in the BBC a certain mindset: 'Stars may come, and stars may go, but we'll still be here . . . Nobody is bigger than the BBC . . .' The old mantra misses the point. Stars *are* the BBC. Without popular actors, presenters and newsreaders, nobody's going to watch or listen, and you can't keep asking for a licence fee from a public that isn't interested. But old habits die hard; only lately has it occurred to somebody that you can't ask anybody to sit all day in a tiny dressing room with tacky curtains and stains all over the carpet. For twenty years of *Children in Need*, I spent ten hours in just such a room, and if I didn't like it, well, nobody else was complaining, were they? Things have improved, mainly because independent production companies are using the BBC's facilities, and won't accept the old BBC 'they should be grateful they're here' mentality. My recent experiences of working with independents show them to be worlds ahead of the BBC in people skills. Everybody is looked after, and while nobody believes that every whim should be catered for, a bouquet of flowers or a scented candle are the little touches that help the performer to a better frame of mind, and bring them back for more. It all comes down to commercial reality: independent production companies live or die by success or failure; the BBC will carry on. Which is where we came in . . .

Putting complacent attitudes aside, nobody with any regard for broadcasting standards in this country would wish it other-wise. It is the independence of the BBC, the licence fee that frees it from the yoke of commercialism, that sustains it as the greatest broadcasting organisation in the world. As Michael Grade said when running Channel 4, it's the BBC that keeps all the rest decent. The BBC is the keeper of the flame, the guardian of standards, and if ever a misguided government or deluded population decide to dispense with the licence fee, television and radio in this country will go to hell in a handcart. CBC in Canada, ABC in Australia, both built in the proud image of the BBC, are now mere shadows, like PBS in the States: barely alive on handouts and charity.

All of which does little to alleviate the impatience that can be provoked by the BBC's cheese-paring. For the past two years, at the request of the Managing Director of Radio, Jenny Abramsky, I have presented the Corporation's own award ceremony, in which the unsung heroes are properly lauded – cameramen, engineers, producers, directors, sound men, the people who actually make the programmes – while the likes of me get the applause. It's an honour and a privilege to host the evening, and I gladly do it for nothing, apart from a hotel bed, because the do has a tendency to run on a bit. What does tend to niggle, just a tad, is that the bed is *all* I get from the BBC. Breakfast I have to buy myself . . . Incidentally, the awards so proudly received by the unsung heroes are old slates from the original Broadcasting House roof. With the BBC, sometimes you don't know whether to laugh or cry . . .

12

TOGs! Can't live with 'em . . . Can't live without 'em

~~~

I've never encouraged common sense, fair comment or reality on the old show, and as nobody ever writes in under their real name, for fear of being laughed at in the street, it's only fitting that none of the contributors to *Wake Up to Wogan* are known by their own names either. There's Deadly Alancoat, the Voice of the Balls, the Wealdstone Wonderboy. Boggy Marsh, Masked Star of Films for Discerning Gentlemen, Shed-dweller and Organist. Frank Godfrey, Traffic Totty and Mimi (Me, Me, Me, Me, Me . . .). People sometimes misguidedly refer to these underlings as my 'team'. Nothing could be further from the truth. It's everybody for themselves, and watch your back. They jostle, shriek and elbow for the microphone, so that the simple and retiring star of the show can hardly get a word in edgeways. Occasionally, I admonish them gently.

'Whose show *is* this, anyway?'

'We give up,' they chortle. 'Whose is it?'

'Mine,' I softly remind them. '*Wake Up to Wogan.*'

'Oh,' the bitter ingrates riposte, 'we thought it was, *Wake Up Wogan*, or *Wake Up with Wogan*, 7 to 9, *Monday to Saturday, BBC Light Programme.*'

It's my own fault. In my usual selfless way, I've encouraged them, and I've bred monsters: the Voice of the Balls, Deadly, is so named because, in his relentless pursuit of the almighty dollar, he intones the numbers on the National Lottery. He claims to live in faded decency in Harrow, but everybody knows that he lives above a hairdressing salon in Wealdstone, on the wrong side of the Hill, albeit with a splendid view of the automatic bollards that are Wealdstone's finest feature. He plays a full, if somewhat seedy, part in the town's activities.

What follows is only a fragrant nosegay of the rafts of denigratory letters aimed squarely at the vitals of the 'Voice of the Balls'. It makes not the slightest bit of difference – it's the original brass monkey:

Deadly has been at it again.

He was at a bus stop in Wealdstone yesterday when an elderly lady asked him when is the number 44 due. Quick as a flash Deadly said it last appeared two Wednesdays ago. Then something about it had made 48 appearances in the last few weeks. The lady was totally confused and hailed a taxi.

Perhaps you could have a quiet word.

Many thanks,

Paul Valter

Actually, he has no idea when any ball made its first or last appearance. He makes it all up, and who's going to know any different?

Mr Dedicoat,

As you will be aware, this weekend sees the opening of the brand new Wealdstone Ornithology Centre, the Wealdstone 'Bird-a-Rama', and we need a well-known local to perform the opening ceremony. Even though you are currently rated as an 'E'-list celebrity, you are the best we could come up with.

Please be aware that Mrs Betty Bickerdike's synchronised ferret jugglers will be performing and we would prefer not to have a repeat of their last performance involving you, the cactus and the balloon full of liquidised black pudding, which caused such mayhem in the park. Mrs Bickerdike is making her first appearance since that unfortunate incident, now that her hair has grown back.

Apparently your mate Eric Walters has offered to give us a slide show – he says he has several hundred slides of birds, gathered over the years by use of a camera with a very long lens. I never knew that there was such wildlife in and around the Harpenden Nurses' Accommodation.

Please bring your other friends: the Irishman who hasn't a clue where he is and the grumpy little yellow chap, but not the posh lady who attended the band concert in the park last week and terrified the young conductor by offering him lessons in how to use his baton. Out-of-date scotch eggs and buckets of Pinot Grigio will be available to you and your guests.

Shona Mercy,
Wealdstone Development Council

We are delighted that your North London announcer has reduced the number of references to Pinot Grigio in his ramblings. (It is well established that Dedicoat has a marked tendency to a certain variety of Italian plonk. Place a vat of it before him, with a side of ham, and apart from the slurping, gargling and munching, a blessed silence will reign.) It had been having a serious impact on our otherwise successful marketing efforts to create an aspirational image for this beverage.

I think it is fair to say that Alan Dedicoat was to Pinot Grigio as Lorraine Chase was to Campari.

By way of thanks, a mixed case of Black Tower, Blue Nun and Mateus Rosé is winging its way to the Wealdstone Wineorama where he should be able to collect it this evening, with our compliments.

Neil Woodcock

The oaf's insistent denial of his Wealdstone birthright fools nobody . . .

There was a young man from Wealdstone
So handsome and so tall
He lived above the fish shop
Right next to the marble hall
His only claim to fame was
He could whistle like a sparrow
And say 'I'm not from Wealdstone
I really come from Harrow'
Be not ashamed young Deadly
To tell whate'er is true

TOGs! Can't live with 'em . . . Can't live without 'em

> *The good folks up in Harrow*
> *Wouldn't have the likes of you!*

Wilting Baz

'Wilting Baz' is also known as 'Baz of Wilts', a relentless sales-man, who also applies his marketing skills to selling the TOGs calendar and helps to raise a ton of money for *Children in Need*. He sometimes turns up in the morning with a box of biscuits. I never give any to Deadly . . .

From: Radio Licensing Officer — Wealdstone District

Dear Mr Dedicoat,

We are delighted to inform you that we have approved your application to run 'Wealdstone FM', your planned new 'cutting-edge' radio station for the Wealdstone and Northolt area.

We were impressed with your experience – the list of top people who have worked under you reads like a *Who's Who* of recent broadcasting, and we particularly liked the testimony from Phil Walters, who we know used to work with the Irish chap in your Radio 2 department. His eulogy about your broadcasting talents was particularly impressive, although we were surprised that he had signed it in purple crayon, and we were also confused by the Pinner postmark, as we thought he lived in Harpenden.

We like your ideas for the station – the idea that the presenters should inter-act with the newsreaders sounds par-ticularly interesting. We have heard Terry Wogan try the idea without much success, but we feel that freed from his petty restrictions you may well make it work.

Nora Treadwell sounds like a splendid choice for the breakfast show DJ, and we look forward to visiting her Tan and Touch-Up Emporium, and using the special vouchers that you sent us here on the licensing committee.

We have one reservation – you are not able to scramble the signal to avoid the 'riff raff from Harrow on the Hill' listening to the show. You will have to include something for everybody, even them. Try and be all-inclusive.

Good luck, and thanks for the wine.

Infamy! Infamy! . . . but you know the rest! The honest listener is not gulled by false bonhomie. He knows well the treachery and back-stabbing that is such an attractive part of everyday life at the BBC.

From: Harrow & Wealdstone Home for Fallen Women
Good Morning, Mr Wogan, (then there's the moral decay . . .)

We have recently had a sudden upsurge of young women whose lives have been sullied by the activities of a certain Algernon Beddicoat, whom we understand is known to you.

The sad story is always the same, in that they are approached by Beddicoat, who informs them that he holds an important position in the entertainment world. Furthermore having guided your career from that of a humble bank clerk, to the eminent role you now play in the BBC.

With promises of fame and fortune he lures these poor unfortunates into letting him have his way with them, then discards them. Perhaps you could use your influence to dissuade him from such behaviour in the future as our resources are now stretched to the limit. Thank you.

Thomas Bikersdike
Proprietor

One foolish day, Deadlyballs made passing mention of one of the great glories of his environs, the Northolt Swimerama. After a few weeks of this kind of thing, he wished he hadn't . . .

Dear Mr Dedicoat,

The plans you submitted for the redevelopment of the Wealdstone Swimerama have been rejected by the planning committee. Some of the proposed shops are a little suspect to say the least.

Religious Books – Psalmarama
Italian Delicatessen – Palmarama
Security Specialist – Alarmarama
Bondage Equipment – Harmarama
Meditation Suite – Calmarama
Ointment Specialist – Balmarama

We would also like to point out that the suggestion from your associate of Neicearama is out of the question. I trust you will resubmit your revised proposal. Otherwise we will have no alternative but to grant the application sent to us by Miss Godfrey to establish a number of units devoted to tradesmen to be called FRANS HAREEMARAMA.

John Brown

From: Dickie Mountshaft
Proprietor
The Wealdstone Stainerama
Belvoir Cuttings
Wealdstone

Dear Mr Dedicoat,

I refer to the garment you left with us, wrapped in plain Brown Paper, with a request that it be cleaned using our 'Bespoke Service for Discreet and Discerning Gentlemen'.

I have to advise that the garment is now ready for collection. However, I would make the following observations:

1. The stain on the 'seat' of the garment has not been totally removed despite our best efforts.
2. The codpiece has suffered a degree of shrinkage; however, I am assured by my Manageress, Mrs Betty Bickerdyke, that it should pose no problems for a gentleman of your dimensions.
3. We would recommend that if the garment is to be worn again only cotton undergarments are used as man-made fabrics may cause a static charge to develop leading to spontaneous combustion.

Thank you for your custom and *I do hope that my West End Agent, Andy Nutherthing, duly delivered the provinder for your personal consumption.*
D. Mountshaft

All pretty distasteful, but as Paul Walters always says: 'I only print 'em'. And as I always say: 'I only read 'em . . .'

Dear Mr Dedicoat,

Here at the Wealdstone Development Corporation, we appreciate your continued efforts to find a suitable venture for the Northolt Swimarama site, as it gives us all a good laugh when you send us another suggestion.

We are not dismissing out of hand your idea for a 'super-pub' on the site, as we understand that such establishments are catching on nowadays and there could well be a local demand. However, some of your plans may prove somewhat fruitless.

We do not think that you will stop binge-drinking by setting a minimum age of 40. As you yourself well know from experience, you older types can put it away better than most. You will just have to have a good team of cleaners.

We also think you may be confusing two different sets of legislation and directives. You appear to have applied for a 24-hour smoking licence, whilst banning drinking throughout the premises as you will be serving food. You may get an interesting set of customers this way, but we do not think you will have much chance of making any money.

Finally we are also unhappy about your co-licensee, Ms Nora Treadwell. We have already had several problems with Ms Treadwell and her 'Tan and Touch-uparama' in the High Street. She is continually trying to claim her seedy premises serve a long-felt need for the gentlemen of the area, and the fact that you are her most regular client does not sit well with your application. However, if you can arrange a discount for council staff, we may be able to consider this more favourably. See what you can do.

The Wealdstone Weather-Boy claims to hail from Hollywood, but it's the one in Birmingham, not LA. He has a full England cap for eating, but is fastidious in his gourmandising; at dinners in our mutual golf club, Mid-Herts, he will allow no plate to return to the kitchen until it is licked clean. By him. I have feasted on balti with the ne'er-do-well in his native purlieus, the Midlands, where he walked out of the restaurant on the grounds that the balti was served on a table with plates, forks, spoons and napkins. The Voice insists that the true balti connoisseur sits on the pavement, while the dish is hurled at him from the door of the restaurant. As you have read, Deadly has been refused ham on a British Midland flight, and has never forgotten the slight. Frankly, I feel that he showed more front than was wholesome to demand meat while travelling steerage.

If only the whole rotten business would stop with Dedicote, but there's more – and it gets worse. Best avert your eyes . . .

Boggy Marsh is a failed television cameraman and Radio 4 announcer with something of a reputation as a Lothario, based on a tissue of lies and an overwrought imagination. However, there's one born every minute, or two, if you count Tudor and Anita Bush, producers of Exotic Films Ltd. They've made him the star of their doubtful celluloid romps:

Dear Terry,

Good morning. We were disappointed last weekend that we couldn't film our latest production for the discerning gentleman, it was going to be a remake of the classic Hitchcock thriller *The Birds* only none of the birds in our film would have been crows, because John had informed us he had a prior engagement playing your quaint English game, cricket. Well that got me thinking and we have scrapped the idea of doing *The Birds* in favour of a new production based on cricket entitled *Legs Eleven*. This will star our hero as a classic all-rounder and a succession of beauties taking to the field with him, all of them game, to say the least. John tells us he's the finest long leg in the business, although some of the girls seemed to think he'd be better at short leg! We've brought in a demon bowler from the Swedish ladies' cricket team and she'll deliver a couple of bouncers that'll have him reeling. Mind you her googly is pretty stunning too. Our hero will, of course, bowl a maiden over, well quite a few maidens actually as he delivers a series of spinners before taking up his bat and practising a few strokes at the bowler's end. Seems there could be a few innings in this one.

Best wishes,

Anita Bush

Lead Actress

Exotic Films Ltd

Frankly, it sounded like a celluloid winner to me. I can't imagine what some people got so upset about. Boggy was all eagerness to play his part. Up for it, you might say . . .

Hollywood's a far cry indeed from the pretty town of Uckfield, which Boggy calls home. Actually, his home is not strictly his home, as he spends most of his conscious hours in his shed, with his collection of magazines and buckets of his home-made wine. In moments of quiet recollection, he resembles nobody so much as Vincent Price in the role of Dr Phibes, the insane organist. I wonder if you are familiar with the old Victorian crowd-pleaser, 'Seated one day at the organ, I was weary and ill at ease, and my fingers wandered idly, over the noisy keys'? It ends with, 'I struck one chord of

music, like the sound of a great amen . . .' And that's the way
Boggy plays the organ. For keeps. It's not just his organ-
playing, Bogs brings out the worst in people – witness those
appalling Bushes – but also, it must be said, the best. Mick
Sturbs, an ungainly fellow with a strange way with words,
writes regularly with homespun tales of Janet and Boggy (let's
call him John, for that is his real name). The Janet and John
stories have become a watchword among my listeners, for
their simplicity, homespun charm, and truly disgusting double-
entendres.

Janet and John go to the horticultural show

Today, Janet and John are going to the horticultural show.
Horticultural is a big word, isn't it?

Do you know what it means? Horticulture is all about
growing things. John knows how to grow things.

Clever John.

Janet goes to talk to Mrs Harrison from the college. John
sees Mrs Norris.

'Hello, Mrs Norris,' says John. 'What a nice display,' says
John. 'I can't grow fruit as I have a lot of trouble keeping the
birds off my plums.'

John's friend Reg knows a song about that.

John says, 'Are those conference pears?'

'Yes,' says Mrs Norris. 'My Charlie grows these. You can
feel that they're a bit firm for eating just now, but they would
be nice cooked. Would you like some?'

Kind Mrs Norris.

'Thank you,' says John, 'I'll have them tonight.'

Do you like pears? John does.

Then John sees Mrs Waller.

'Hello, Mr Marsh,' says Mrs Waller. 'Are you not exhibiting? Your rocket was the talk of the village last year!'

'No,' says John. See John blush. Paint John's face red.

Mrs Waller says, 'I have something for you to try, Mr Marsh, it's okra with thyme. Call in on the way home and I'll let you have the recipe, or if you fancy a snack now, I think I have some lettuce here.'

John says, 'Thank you, Mrs Waller, but I don't want to spoil my dinner.'

Sensible John.

John sees Janet coming back. Janet has bought some new shears.

'Have you been a good boy?' says Janet.

'Yes, of course,' says John. 'I saw Mrs Norris. I told her I was looking for a nice firm pear, so she let me try her Charlie's. Then I saw Mrs Waller. She told me I could have wild thyme if I popped in later, or if I couldn't wait, she'd lettuce behind the stall.'

See Janet get out the shears.

Can you hit twenty miles an hour in two seconds? John can.

Poor John.

Little old ladies constantly approach me to tell me how much they enjoy 'Janet and John'. I can't believe that they get all the double meanings. Don't tell me Britain's grannies are going to the dogs – we're all doomed.

Janet and John go to the garden centre

Today, Janet and John are going to the garden centre. Janet wants to buy a climber to cover up one of John's sheds.

(Janet says that John's sheds are an eyesore.)

See Janet looking at all the flowers. Do you like flowers? Janet does.

John is looking at the garden ornaments.

John is laughing at how funny the big concrete gnomes look with their round bellies and white beards.

John is watching the workmen make the gnomes. See the men tip concrete into the moulds.

See the workmen point at John and laugh. Poor John.

John sees Mrs Perkins from the Co-op.

'Hello, Mrs Perkins,' says John.

'Hello, Mr Marsh,' says Mrs Perkins.

What fun!

Mrs Perkins says, 'I am looking for a nice *Thymus serpyllum* for my window-box, and I wanted to find something to perk up the privet in my front garden. It is very dull in the winter, and I can't seem to find anything here that suits dry soil. I was wondering if I could have a cutting from your *Clematis vitalba*?'

'Of course,' says John. 'I will see if I can find you one.'

Kind John.

Do you know what clematis is? John does. John has lots of helpful books in his shed.

John says, 'Janet is looking for a climber.'

Mrs Perkins says, 'You ought to try *ipomoea purpurea*. My Doug has a nice reliable one at the back of the woodshed. Get Janet to pop round to see if she wants a cutting.'

'Thank you,' says John.

John walks around looking at the flowers until he sees Janet.

'Hello, John,' says Janet. 'Who was that lady I saw you talking to?'

See the warning signs.

John says, 'That was Mrs Perkins from the Co-op. She was after a wild thyme, and asked if she could have a bit of my Old Man's Beard in her front hedge. She said that in exchange, Mr Perkins has a purple Morning Glory that you could look at behind the woodshed.'

See Janet push John into one of the big tubs of concrete. Do you think John looks like a garden ornament? Janet does. See Janet waiting for the concrete to set.

Poor John.

The 'Janet and John' epics are the work of a TOG, a brilliantly witty man who has given me permission to include them in this poor effort. I'm sure that he'd prefer to be known by his *nom de grâce*, Mick Sturbs. It was Mick who set up the TOGs website, it's Mick who provides us with our weekly horoscopes, under the pseudonym of Xavier Mousepractise. If he ever gives up, I'm banjaxed . . .

Janet and John go to the seaside

Today, Janet and John are going to the seaside. John is very excited. John likes the seaside.

Janet is making bloater-paste sandwiches. John does not like bloater-paste.

Do you know what dry-heaves are? John does.

Soon it is time for Janet and John to catch the bus at the

end of the lane. Janet gives John a barley-sugar twist to suck. Janet has to wipe John's beard with a wet hankie. See John wriggle.

When they arrive at the seaside, Janet gives John his bucket and spade, his sandwiches, and some money to spend on the pier.

Janet says, 'I am going to the Bingo now. I will see you by the candy-floss stall in an hour. If you've been a good boy, you can have some candy-floss.'

Do you like candy-floss? John does.

John skips down to the pier. John likes the pier. See John throw his sandwiches to the seagulls.

John goes to the shellfish stall and buys some winkles. John likes shellfish.

John sees Mrs Bickerdyke. 'Hello, Mrs Bickerdyke,' says John.

'Eh-up Fluffywhiskers,' says Mrs Bickerdyke. Mrs Bickerdyke is from Yorkshire – see Jeremy Clarkson.

'What are you doing here?' says John.

Mrs Bickerdyke says, 'I came down for the American ice-cream tasting, they are trying out some new flavours. Are those winkles any good? I bet they aren't as good as they are down in Devon. They do them hot from the pan with cider vinegar down there. I'll be having some of those next week when I go on holiday. Now I can't stand here listening to you all day, I'm going to pop me flip-flops on and take t'whippet for a walk on the beach.'

Do you know how to get a word in edgeways? John doesn't.

John walks down to the beach and makes a big sandcastle.

Soon it is time to go back and meet Janet.

See John cross the road and stand by the candy-floss stall. Janet sees John.

'Hello, John,' says Janet. 'What have you been doing?'

'Well,' says John, 'I walked down to the pier to look at the stalls and I saw Mrs Bickerdyke. Mrs Bickerdyke had just spent all afternoon tasting Ben and Jerry's. Next week she is going to Devon to get some hot winkles in cider. Then she got her flip-flops out and said it was time to let her whippet out on the beach . . . Can I have some candy-floss now?'

See Janet push John's head into the candy-floss machine and switch it on.

See John go pink and fluffy.

Poor John.

'Winkles in cider' . . . truly, a gem in the diadem. Sturbs, we bow before you . . .

John learns how to be a journalist

John is not a journalist. John reads the news. Journalists make it up.

John is on a conversion course.

Do you know what a conversion course is?

A conversion course is something you do when you want to be taken seriously. John is not taken seriously. People point and laugh. Poor John.

For his homework, John has to have dinner and some wine in a restaurant, and then write all about it.

If he writes a nice story, he will get six gold stars. Lucky John.

John's friend Alan knows all about food and wine. Paint Alan's nose red.

Alan suggests a nice restaurant near Waterloo Bridge.

John looks worried.

'What's the matter, John?' says Alan.

John says, 'I have to take someone with me, but I don't know who to ask.'

See John blub.

'There, there,' says Alan. 'I will ask Amanda on reception. I've heard that she will do anything for a nice meal.'

Kind Alan.

John and Amanda go to the restaurant. Do you think Oxo is a funny name for a restaurant?

John is very excited. John likes his food. Amanda is a bit nervous as the restaurant is on the 8th floor and she is afraid of heights. While they wait to be served John gets Amanda some wine and she soon feels better.

Soon the waiter arrives with the food. John gobbles down his dinner. See Amanda picking bits of food out of her hair.

Soon it is time to go. Amanda does not have enough money to pay for both meals so John makes up the difference. Do you know what a hairy old skinflint is? Amanda does.

When John gets home, Janet asks what he did at work today.

'Today I was behaving like a journalist. I gave our receptionist a treat. Alan said he wanted Amanda Ryder on the desk in reception because she would do anyone a favour. We went to a very nice place to eat. But Amanda needed a few drinks because she'd never been taken up the Oxo Tower before and was a bit nervous. Afterwards she said that she would suggest it to her boyfriend.

Can you hit a moving target with a four-slice toaster? Janet can. See Janet chase John.

Run, John, run.

Let's leave it at the Oxo Tower, shall we? Here is another Musketeer – one who attracts an entirely different audience – mostly naked under a dirty raincoat.

Frank Godfrey, or Fran, as she prefers to be known, plays Tinkerbell to my Peter Pan and Pauly Walters' Smee. An elfin creature with a pleasing lilt to her voice and a tinkling laugh that would test the patience of a saint, she disturbs the early-morning placidity of otherwise sensible grown men who regularly demean themselves for her favours. She's a baggage and a tease, perpetuating the fairy tale that she is but an innocent convent girl, while in reality she spits like a sailor and swears like a trooper. And still they fawn upon her:

Ode to a Tasty Chick
by W. McGonagall
(Voted most promising poet, Brit Awards 1988)

> *Of those who toil at the BBC*
> *There's only one who'll do for me.*
> *Although I've only heard her voice,*
> *I think she must look rather noice.*
> *She reads the news with such aplomb,*
> *I'd really like to take her homb.*
> *Oh Fran! Oh Fran! Will you be mine?*
> *The thought of you drives me insine.*

And though I'm just a humble oik,
I'd even let you ride my boik.
But Fran if you resist my charms,
I'll run away and eat some warms.

It's a foul and contemptible calumny, but Fran brings it on herself. An excessive eagerness to please creates an impression of an 'easy woman'. Nothing could be further from the truth – unless of course, you're male. And have a pulse . . .

Dear Terry,
So no one is too old for Fran?

Come on you wizened suitors
With wrinkles like a prune
And backs bent like a hoop as
You try to make her swoon,
For Franny's made it very clear
To get her bosom heaving
With lust or love, she will not sneer
At anyone who's breathing.
So come with your decrepit charms
Though with a frame or trolley,
She'll welcome you with open arms
And especially those with lolly.

Or maybe I do her a disservice, and she's just got a fetish for high-waist trousers and enlarged prostate problems.

Byeeee (hope this keeps till tomorrow)
Katie Mallett

Grown men build their fantasies around Fran Godfrey. I'm sure it does them good – the woman's a broadcasting enema!

A Friday Ode to Fran . . . (Hic!)

Dear Sir Terry, Fran and The Team,
  An ode to Fran!!

  There was a time not long ago
  When Fran was young and bright,
  She'd set off every evening
  down the pub to spend the night.
  'I'll 'ave a foaming pint, my dear,' the punters often call.
  'Comin' right up, I've got one 'ere, the froth is nice and tall!'
  'My goodness, that's my Guinness . . . cor blimey what a caper,
  With so much foam I'll 'ave to ask for chopped nuts and a wafer!'
  And while our Fran was serving in a blouse of rough delight,
  The chaps all stood there leering, saying, 'What you doing tonight?'
  'Oh no, Sir . . .' said the young maid . . . 'I'm a good girl and must go home to my Mum!'
  'Well, 'fore you leave then come round 'ere and let us pinch yer bum!'

271

Now Fran was sorely tempted but knew that it was wrong,
Besides she'd told the Sister that she gone to sing a song.
Her mission was to make those men see the error of their ways;
It did seem rather strange that she'd been there for forty days.
'Young Frances, please come to my room and tell me what goes on,
I thought by now you'd have a convert keen to join our throng.
But ev'ry night you come back here with glassy eyes and money,
And will you stop from saying to the porter, "Hello Honey"!'
Yours as ever,

Info for Fran

Morning Tel,

Welcome backome. I have news for Fran should she ever consider cosmetic surgery:

A doctor at the University of Cosmetic Surgery has developed a breast implant with electronic music incorporated into the implant.

When asked why the doctor developed this, he replied, 'All these years women complain about men staring at their breasts and not listening to them.'

Fran will be the first to tell you that men always look her straight in the eye.

DAFTA in May

> *Not everyone can have a BAFTA —*
> *some are winners, some are duds —*
> *but here's a babe who'd win a DAFTA . . .*
> *Fran! and both her Darling Buds . . .*
>
> Byron Bonniebanks

Don't mention the BAFTA around me . . . There's Noel 'Tidybeard' Edmonds, a scant ten minutes back on the box, and he picks up a nomination. How long have I been haunting the thing? Never mind troubling the judge – I don't even trouble the starter . . .

Fran's lavish penthouse, within shrieking distance of the BBC, has been the scene of many an unsavoury tale: honest artisans imprisoned for weeks in the cupboard under her stairs, lured there on the pretext of some urgent plumbing, grouting or rendering; electricians' apprentices, sturdy lads as they enter Fran's portals, shattered husks as they emerge days later.

It's hard to credit, but each post brings the plaintive cry from newborn listeners, 'In God's holy name, what are you on about? What's a TOG?' Or, 'TOGs sound good to me – how do I join?' Or, 'I'm only sixteen, can I be a TOG?' (always answered by the traditional mantra, 'Clear off, you young limb!'). *Oldie* magazine, that splendid source of consolation for those well stricken in years, but still fondly deluding themselves that there is 'snap in their celery', asked me to define the glorious state of Togdom. I could scarce say than nay:

What is . . . a TOG?

For once, Chambers, Webster's and Oxford dictionaries are of one mind.

> TOGs: Terry's Old Geezers/Gals; listeners to *Wake Up to Wogan*, 7.30 a.m. to 9.30 a.m., Monday to Friday, BBC Radio 2. Thought to be in direct line of descent from the TWITS (Terry Wogan Is Tops Society), a movement which enjoyed 'a far, fierce hour and sweet' and burned out just as quickly. Rather like Wogan himself . . .

Like the aforementioned once-proud broadcaster, TOGs are well stricken in years, while remaining about twenty-five years of age on the inside. They have a fierce resentment of anybody younger than themselves: 'They don't know they're born!', and are loath indeed to allow them into their purlieus. 'Clear off, you young limb!', is the rallying cry.

TOGs usually come in flat caps, Volvos and the centre lane of the motorway at 60 m.p.h. ('I'm within my rights; 50 m.p.h. on the inside, 70 on the outside and 60 in the middle . . .'). They have a secret sign, known only to those who see it flashed, rather like some Bat Signal, on the radio every morning.

There is an even more secret Grand Master, or TOG-MEISTER, sign always exchanged under cover of darkness, or the snug of a seedy pub near Broadcasting House, which is known only to Wogan himself, the ailing producer, Pauly Walters, and the Duke of Kent.

TOGs may also be recognised by their use of such arcane

phrases as, 'Is it *me?*' or, 'I never saw a bar of chocolate until I was fourteen,' or, 'What am I doing, standing here in front of an open fridge with a torch in my hand?'

Many thousands of TOGs car stickers have been sent to eager applicants, who, once they receive them, get cold feet and hide them in the back of an upstairs drawer. Those brave enough to flaunt the sticker in the back windows of their Reliant Robin or Morris Mini-Traveller pay a terrible price, not only in loss of face among nearest, dearest and the rest of the population, but in the trade-in value: the thing is impossible to remove.

The TOGs sweater, which, like the car sticker, is rarer than hen's teeth, bears the legend: 'Do I come here often?' – a tried and trusted TOG chat-up line. There was a strong groundswell of opinion to have 'I stop for no particular reason' on the back, but it soon petered out.

Currently a movement is gathering strength to have the logos changed to 'It's never *your* fault' on the front and 'Mustn't grumble' on the back. It will come to nothing. They'll forget about it if you don't pay any attention. This condition is known to TOGs as a *'senior moment'*, a euphemism culled from America, to indicate a temporary loss of all marbles in anyone over fifty . . .

As is the current practice within the BBC itself, TOGs feel a deep-seated need to form themselves into groups, clusters or tribes. Witness this letter from a well set-up woman from Norfolk:

We decided to start our own local branch of TOGs and the very first meeting took place last week. The session started with a game, to break the ice, of 'I-Spy'. This proved to be a mistake because most of the members had forgotten to bring their glasses. Undeterred, we decided to be more daring – the men then threw their false teeth into the middle of the carpet and the ladies had to pick a denture and pair off with its owner! They then adjourned to other rooms to discuss their operations. We ended with a raffle, first prize of which was a knitted pension-book cover . . .

But I see that you are all eagerness: 'How do I become a TOG?' Be of good cheer. You're in. Welcome to the club . . .

Lately, a television ad gave poor old sods a glimmer of hope:

Shakespeare, as ever, got there first, but a current television ad identifies the 'Seven Stages of Ageing', espousing a miracle cream that will arrest the march of time. It has given at least one old geezer heart. After one application:

1. He may walk around a shoe shop without exclaiming, 'Ooh, they look comfy' at every pair of slippers.
2. He will stop saying 'It's bitterly cold' every time the wind changes.
3. Will not go 'Aahhh' after a first sip from a cup of tea . . .
4. . . . Nor 'Aahhh' every time he sits down.
5. He will desist from muttering 'Never did me any harm' when there's a debate on the smacking of children.
6. When anyone mentions the price of a Mars bar, he will refrain from crying out in anguish: 'That's *nine* shillings! I remember when they were threepence.'

7. And finally . . . On hearing something from today's pop charts, will not moan 'They all sound the same to me', mainly because not only is he beginning to look like his father, he's beginning to sound like him . . .

The rash of reality continues unabated on television. The keen observer will notice that what started as fly-on-the-wall voyeurism of ordinary people in *Big Brother* has been taken over by 'celebrities' who flaunt themselves before us in a variety of guises: in the jungle, in the ballroom, on the ice, on the farm, on the island – the more bizarre, the merrier. These excesses bring a daily response from my over-alert listeners. A couple of the less lunatic:

To: Terry Wogan

From: Len Horridge

Yo!! Clooney Boy!!

Hey, my creative juices have been flowing and I've just come up with a brilliantly fresh and novel idea for BBC1's evening schedules.

The programme is tentatively called **Celebrity Couples Strictly Horse Jumping and Singing on Ice in a Jungle**. Sounds like a winner already, eh?

The premise is this: celebrity couples (i.e. people you've never heard of) sing their favourite songs whilst riding on a horse and jumping over smaller celebrities who are strapped to the floor in seventies-style comedy outfits.

The winners will be the couple who stay on the horse the

longest, who sing the longest and who have hit and injured the most celebrity jumps in comedy outfits.

Oh, and don't worry about the *ice* bit. The horses are actually pantomime horses with minor radio celebrities at either end, and no animals will be injured during the making of this extravaganza.

A ratings winner, I feel.

How do you fancy co-hosting with me in a red dress?

Len Horridge

To: Terry Wogan

From: Nodding John

I have it! The key to wealth. I knew if I waited long enough I'd have an idea that would make me millions: **Newsreaders on Ice**.

Every night ten newsreaders (Deadly could take part?) start off each reading news stories whilst dancing around on ice. Every five minutes we vote someone off. You could host and on the panel could be Bruno Raviolli *et al.*

The last newsreader left gets to read the 'And finally' item.

Is it a winner or what?

If not, **Big Brother Darts** – viewers get to watch darts players twenty-four hours a day locked in a house – Sid Waddell commentates.

I am on a roll now . . .

Name:

Nodding John

TOGs! Can't live with 'em . . . Can't live without 'em

To: Terry Wogan
From: Bill Shakespear

Great idea for a new reality show:

Fat Celebrity Camp on Ice Looking 10 Years Younger Because of What They Eat and How They Dress. We the public will love this as it combines six shows in one and will allow the BBC time to make much more innovative programmes such as **What's Happening at the Bottom of My Garden?**, or **Does My Ceiling Need Another Coat of Paint?**

Name:

Bill Shakespear

If you can keep your shed when all about you
    Is rising damp and condensation,
If you can read the travel as if it's true,
    Reporting three car shunts with no hesitation,
If you can play the great Widor Toccata
    Yet never make it to the end,
And people say your wife's a martyr
    'Cause your recitals drive her round the bend;

If your perfect diction never falters
    And you've a mighty organ at your fingertips,
If you can meet with Wogan and Pauly Walters
    And get those two impostors to sort their pips,
If you can fill the unforgiving minute
    When the headlines don't go quite to plan,

Then take my heart – for you'll surely win it
And – which is more – I bet *you* don't need Viagra to prove
you are a man!

Having perused the 'Are you a TOG' section of the website
the memsahib and myself decided to put together a list of
pointers to help decide if one is a Christmas TOG.

1. The fruitcake aunt/embarrassing uncle that every family
   suffers at Christmas stares back at you out of the bathroom
   mirror.
2. You remark (to a younger relative) on the decrepit appearance of an ageing celebrity before remembering that they
   were four years below you at school.
3. You wrap this year's presents in wrapping paper that you
   salvaged from last year's presents.
4. You go to a Christmas party and find more people that you
   want to slap than cuddle.
5. The knitted sweater you receive for Christmas that looks
   as if it was modelled on a deformed gibbon turns out to be
   deceptively form-fitting.
6. You see a scantily clad member of the opposite sex and
   your first three thoughts are:
   - They look cold!
   - They need feeding up!
   - Their mother needs a good slapping for allowing them
   out dressed like that.
7. You remember mince pies/drinks being bigger.
8. You insist on everyone gathering around the TV for the
   Queen's speech and no one can hear it over your snores.

9. Whilst being fitted for the trousers of a Santa suit your tailor asks if 'Sir' hangs 'to the left or the right?', and you answer, 'Just make them baggier at the knees!'

The annual firework display on *Wake Up to Wogan* is the highpoint of the year for many a discerning listener, and certainly the only radio firework display anywhere in the world. Furthermore, through the miracle of the internet, it is experienced all over the known world. Letters from Canada, the American west coast, China, and New Zealand bear witness to the unmatched colour, sparkle and excitement of this, the world's greatest firework display: a constant riot of every colour in the spectrum that goes on for two whole hours. A treat for adults or kiddies alike, and particularly for animal lovers. For there are *no* bangs, explosions or any upsetting loud noises to disturb the little ones, or their pets.

Dear Terry,
Fireworks on the Radio
   Could you please move over a little bit because I can't see the fireworks! Or am I going blind? If there are enough sausages, do you think I could have one, please.

There will always be the whingers, of course . . .

Terry,
   Who lit that last rocket?????
   Although it looked beautiful, the damn stick came down in my garden and skewered the cat.
   Please, please be more careful.

How heart-warming, the unsolicited testimonial . . .

To: Terry Wogan
From: Elizabeth

What a wonderful firework display this morning – colours, and such a variety! In fact my egg got cold because I was enjoying them so much – this year I got the distance from the wireless exactly right and could enjoy the colours to the full.

And because they were silent, my cat enjoyed them too – in fact she was jumping up to try and catch the sparks and colours as they flew about. Luckily we were in the kitchen so there was no chance of the carpet catching fire.

The only problem was I didn't get my sparkler and we all know you can't enjoy a firework display without a sparkler! As you couldn't get it to me on time, I would be happy to get a TOGs sweatshirt instead (extra large size)?

Elizabeth

(Love the show – best antidote to 'road rage' I know!!)

No matter how hard you try . . .

Very clever!

You've set off every smoke detector in the house and we don't have a TV licence should the detector vans come round.

Anyway, I'm not really keen on bright colours so perhaps next year you could send up a nicely camouflaged 'Sky Blue' rocket for people like me.

Ta muchly!

Katherine Weal

We even lay on the culinary delights that are part and parcel of every display – snorkers; hotdogs, roast potatoes – virtually.

Greetings, snorkermeister.

What a wonderful display!

I am finishing off the last of the pumpkin soup for breakfast whilst delighting in the sensory extravaganza. Unfortunately t'other half is in the bath and has missed the first half-hour of the masterpiece. Any chance of some edited highlights?

Can I have a hot dog, please, with onions and mustard, but no bread because I have developed a wheat allergy.

Thank you.

Des Parrot-Measures

Feed my lambs, feed my sheep. What more can I give? How far can I go? Watch this space . . .

Epilogue

So, that's the height of it. Whether it's the end of the beginning or the beginning of the end, I hope it's too soon to say. And I'm certainly not going to say that this is as far as I go. That wise man Eamonn Andrews always said to me that the three vital factors in getting the elbow were: 1. The public get tired of you; 2. You get tired of doing it; and 3. Your employer gets tired of you. Of these, he said, by far the most important was the third factor.

So far nobody in authority has suggested I fling myself off Beachy Head. Equally, my audiences for radio and television seem to be growing rather than diminishing, and I'll never get tired of talking to myself and my listener. Why else would a man of my declining years get out of bed at 5.30 on a dark and dreary January morning? I've always said that it's important, unlike Canute, to get off the beach before the tide comes in. I've seen too many once great broadcasters cling to the wreckage long after the ship has gone down. They don't know it, and nobody will tell them, but the edge has gone – no more than a half-beat, the blink of an eye . . .

There's a time to live and a time to die, but in my business, the most important of all is the time to say goodbye. I hope that

I can recognise it when it comes around, and greet it as a friend. And if I don't, keep your opinions to yourself; I'll go when I'm ready.

Index

287

Index

65–6, 153–5, 169, 246–9;
patronage and influence in, 67–9;
star interviews, 71–2; and
popularity, 135–8, 158–68, 247;
critics, 140–1; and publishing,
151–2; soap operas, 153; niche,
165; satellite, 247; public-
service, 248; *see also* radio;
television
Brooks, Mel, 56–7, 228
Browning, Grace, 192
Browning, Hacker and Kits, 192,
224, 226
Bruce, Ken, 75, 86, 117, 164
Buenos Aires, 110
Burghley, Lord, 165
Burgos, 225
Burma, 184
Burrowes, Bob, 82
Bury St Edmunds, 201
Bygraves, Max, 132
Byrne, Dinah, 180, 184
Byrne, Gay, 139, 206
Byrne, Kitty, 180, 184–6
Byrne, May, 11–12, 26, 94, 175,
180–2, 184
Byrne, Muds, 12, 24, 26, 180–1
Byrne, Nellie, 9, 11–12, 180–6

Caan, James, 60
Cabo Roig, 222–6
Caithness, 54
Calcutta, 97
Canada, 248, 281; Wogan in, 80–3
Cannes, 71
Carpenter, Mary Chapin, 77
Carr, Pat, 37–8

Carroll, Lewis, 145–6
cartoons, 197
CBC, 248
Celebrity Big Brother, 215
Celebrity X-Factor, 195
Century Radio, 204
Channel 4, 64, 66, 165, 243, 248
Channel Five, 160, 243–4
Chaplin, Charlie, 175
Chapman, Beth Nielsen, 77
Charisse, Cyd, 60
Charles I, King, 189
Charles, Prince, 217–20
Chase, Chevy, 58
Cheltenham, 228
Chevalier, Maurice, 15, 228
Chianti, 108
Chicken Kiev, 88, 108
Children in Need, 42, 80, 89, 132,
140–51, 241, 243, 248, 255
Children of Mary, 97
China, 126, 281
Chirac, Jacques, 54
Christian Brothers, 10
Churchill, Winston, 54
cigarettes, 97, 180, 207
circuses, 174–6
Cirencester, 138
Clancy, Kathleen, 91
Clancy, Michael, 90–1
Clapton, Eric, 27
Clarkson, Jeremy, 266
Clary, Desirée, 11
Clifford, 'Musty', 177
Clinton, Bill, 19–20
Clohessy, Peter, 177
clowns, 175–6

Index

Index

293

ed
ds,
el.

ur
ts
d,
experience and a passion for travel.

**Rely on Thomas Cook as your
travelling companion on your next trip
and benefit from our unique heritage.**

Thomas Cook **rail** guides

EUROPE BY RAIL
YOUR GUIDE TO EXPLORING EUROPE ON A BUDGET

Edited by Tim Locke

Published by Thomas Cook Publishing
A division of Thomas Cook Tour Operations Limited
Company registration No. 3772199 England
The Thomas Cook Business Park, 9 Coningsby Road
Peterborough PE3 8SB, United Kingdom

Telephone: +44 (0) 1733 416477
Email: books@thomascook.com
www.thomascookpublishing.com

Route maps: Pixel Cartography and Studio 183
Europe map and city maps prepared by
  Lovell Johns Ltd, Witney, Oxfordshire
Country maps prepared by Polly Senior

ISBN 978-1-84848-314-9

Project Editor: Kelly Anne Pipes
Production/DTP Editor: Steven Collins
Cover design and layout: Thomas Cook Publishing

Printed and bound in India by Replika Press

Rail information checked
by the compilers of the
Thomas Cook European Rail Timetable:
Brendan Fox (Editor), John Potter,
Reuben Turner, David Turpie and
Chris Woodcock

Produced by The Content Works Ltd
Aston Court, Kingsmead Business Park,
Frederick Place, High Wycombe,
Bucks HP11 1LA
www.thecontentworks.com

Editorial management: Lisa Plumridge
Production: Alison Rayner
Proofreaders: Lesley McCave
& Linda Bass

SEND US YOUR FEEDBACK

We are always striving to make this guide as useful, interesting and up-to-date as possible. So whether you like a particular feature, have a criticism to make or simply want to share updated information, we'd love to hear from you. We would also like to hear your experiences of travelling by rail in Europe.

If we incorporate your suggestion in the next edition, or if we publish your experience, we'll send you a copy of the book free of charge. Write to the Project Editor, Europe by Rail, Thomas Cook Publishing, Coningsby Road, Peterborough PE3 8SB, or email: books@thomascook.com

Alternatively return the form at the back of the book.

COMMENTS FROM READERS ON PREVIOUS EDITIONS

'All the information needed to plan a trip.'
Victoria Homer, Whitley Bay, Tyne and Wear

'Value for money, packed full of essential information.'
Ruth Bale, Leicestershire

'First-class tips, and hints very useful. I doubt if you could improve on it.'
June Taylor, Colne, Lancashire

'Detailed Inter-Railer's guide, good value.'
Tadhg Ryan, Tipperary

'Very clear and detailed route explanations.'
Emma Turner, Edinburgh

'Easy to follow, lots of helpful tips.'
Jon Brown, Telford, Shropshire

'It's the best around – gives you all the help you need without the waffle you get with other guides.'
Keith Saunders, Boston, Lincolnshire

'Crammed with information, accurate, easy to read and use.'
Jean-Pierre Confesson, Audes, France

AND THE REVIEWERS:

'The indispensable Inter-railer's guide to budget Europe.'
Wanderlust

'Essential reading – a mine of vital up-to-date information.'
Mail on Sunday

ESSENTIALS

General information for travellers about each of the European countries covered in this book is set out in an Essentials section at the start of each country's introduction. As well as information on climate, currency, public holidays, tourist information and other essential facts for travellers, each Essentials section also gives general notes on rail travel in the country concerned, the validity of international and regional rail passes (see p27) on the country's rail network and any special passes valid in the country. The following abbreviations are used in those notes:

IR	InterRail Pass
EP	Eurail Pass
Aus	Australia
Can	Canada
Ire	Republic of Ireland
SA	South Africa
NZ	New Zealand
UK	United Kingdom
USA	United States of America

Exchange rates of the national currency against the Euro, Pound Sterling and US Dollar are also noted in the Essentials sections, as an approximate guide. They were compiled in autumn 2009 but of course can fluctuate. More up-to-date guides to exchange rates are to be found in the latest monthly edition of the *Thomas Cook European Rail Timetable*.

COVER PHOTOGRAPHY

© J. Clarke/Getty Images

THE AUTHORS AND UPDATERS OF THE CURRENT EDITION

Tim Locke is an editor and guidebook writer who has journeyed over much of Europe including backpacking over the Alps and cycling in France. As well as being a trained walks leader he has written and contributed to many walking and general guides to Britain, as well as guides to New England and Thailand. He dedicates this guide to Ronald Locke (1921–1999) who enthused him with his passion for rail travel and discovering new places.

USA-born **Roger Norum** studied literature and sociology in Norway and Finland and now speaks enough Danish, Norwegian, Swedish and Finnish to fool locals into thinking he is from Albania. He teaches weekend travel writing and photography courses with Creative Escapes.

Nicky Gardner and **Susanne Kries** are Berlin-based writers and joint editors of *hidden europe* magazine. Both women are keen explorers of Europe's unsung corners, and take their time en route to catch the flavour of local communities. They like nothing better than a good night train journey. Both are much indebted to Als and Greg for keeping them on the ball about nocturnal happenings in towns and cities across Europe.

Lisa Gerard-Sharp is a London-based language expert turned travel journalist, feature-writer and author who has lived in Paris, Brussels, Tuscany and Rome, where she worked as a television producer for temperamental, Fellini-esque Romans. Currently UK correspondent to Italian *Vogue* and Italy winter sports editor for the *Good Ski Guide*, Lisa contributes to numerous publications, including *The Times*, and is the Italy specialist for *Insight Guides*.

Neil Taylor first visited the Baltics in 1992 and got immediately hooked. He now has a flat in Tallinn and spends about three months of each year either leading groups or exploring nooks and crannies for his next Bradt guidebook to the area.

Paul Murphy made his first European 'Grand Tour' at the age of 12 and ever since then wanted to write so badly. Now he does! A full-time travel writer for nearly 20 years Paul has over 40 travel guidebooks to his name and contributes regularly to the travel press and travel websites. He lives in Surrey with his rabbit (plus wife and children). His website is www.paulwmurphy.co.uk.

British-born Neville Walker studied geography at Cambridge University before training as a journalist. He speaks German, French and Spanish (though not usually at the same time) and lives in London and Austria.

After editing school textbooks for a while, **Lindsay Hunt** ran away to Spain for a belated gap year, and discovered a lasting love of travel. She now writes guidebooks and magazine articles for a variety of publishers, and heads for pastures new whenever the chance arises.

Jane Foster lives in Split on the Dalmatian coast, where she works as a freelance travel writer. She contributes to a number of British and American publications and websites, concentrating primarily on Croatia, Slovenia and Italy.

Gorana Nad-Conlan was born in Zagreb in Croatia, and studied aeronautical technology and journalism. Married and now based in London, she provides language services to prisons, courts, mental health and travel industry, amongst others.

Robin McKelvie is a travel writer and photographer, as well as a seven-time Inter-railer. He is also a contributing editor of *International Railway Traveler* in the US, and has published Insight and Berlitz guides to Croatia and a Bradt guide to Slovenia.

Thanks to all the following for their painstaking efforts in checking phone numbers, Tourist Office details, and all the other on-the-spot information packed into these pages: David Cawley, Aude Pasquier, Nadia Feddo, Carrie-Marie Bratley, Alison Thomas, Tim Skelton, Mike & Bettina Lock, Sonia Marotta, Kimberley Hundborg, Inga Govasli Nilsen, Veera Julkunen, Maria Lundqvist, Riina Sepp, Oleg Polikarpov, Martins Zaprauskis, Saulina Kochanskaite, Zuzanna Ananiew, Kristina Konikova, Polia Mihaylova, Petra Hajnal, Craig Turp and Balaban Cerit.

CONTENTS

INTRODUCTION

'Ever since childhood ... I have seldom heard a train go by and not wished I was on it. Those whistles sing bewitchment: railways are irresistible bazaars, snaking along perfectly level no matter what the landscape, improving your mood with speed, and never upsetting your drink. The train can reassure you in awful places – a far cry from the anxious sweats of doom aeroplanes inspire, or the nauseating gas-sickness of the long-distance bus, or the paralysis that afflicts the car passenger. If a train is large and comfortable you don't even need a destination; a corner seat is enough, and you can be one of those travellers who stay in motion, straddling the tracks, and never arrive or feel they ought to.'

Paul Theroux, *The Great Railway Bazaar* (1975, published by Penguin Books)

That canniest of travel writers, Paul Theroux, got it pretty much spot on. Trains simply leave other modes of long-distance transport way behind when it comes to searching for the perfect travel experience. You can watch the world go by from the window, meet other travellers, snooze, picnic, read or chat. Once you've got the hang of the ins and outs of the rail network trains are a lot less hassle than driving, far pleasanter than taking a bus, and there's little carbon footprint, certainly compared with going by plane. Often they get you right into city centres – where driving can be a nightmare – right where you want to be. And usefully the cheap hotel area in much of Europe often happens to be right next to the main station itself. The whole of Europe links up with an astonishingly dense rail network that would take a lifetime to explore.

I first got the InterRail/Eurail bug when a 19-year-old student. It's an exciting but also quite a daunting feeling: you buy this ticket, and the whole of Europe is yours.

For a glorious month, the train was my way of life: I was glued to the constantly changing views outside. Europe was more startlingly varied than I could ever have believed.

The main problem was information: there wasn't a guidebook like this in those days, and it wasn't that easy to work out where to go. I ended up sleeping in a field one night because that promising-sounding seaside town in former Yugoslavia turned out to have no accommodation whatsoever. And I had the nagging feeling I was missing out; as my homeward-bound night train glided through stations whose names promised so much – among them Venice, Verona, Arles and Orange – I realised how much there was to come back and see. And somewhere to the north there were some amazing mountain rail routes through the Alps – but where exactly?

What I've sought to do in this book is to help you make the choices. It's all too easy to fall in the trap of trying to do too much. Then eventually Europe becomes one confused blur of cathedrals, railway stations and youth hostels. Instead, well it might have been nicer to have mixed things up more – a few great cities, some smaller towns, and maybe the chance to relax on a beach or hike into the mountains.

Over the past few years, the InterRail/Eurail system has changed, and it's been simplified into a straight choice between an all-Europe pass, and a pass for one country (or, in the case of Eurail, a group of countries) only; you can also choose how many days you travel within a given time period. This may signal a change in style for many rail travellers. The temptation of constantly pushing on and sleeping in trains may be replaced by a tendency to slow down and explore individual countries. This book is arranged by country, so it's easy to focus on one before moving on.

And since the first edition of this guide came out back in 1999, eastern Europe has opened up appreciably. A lot of it is now in the European Union, and countries such as the Czech Republic, the Baltic States and Poland are much easier to make your way around. They're also extremely good value, and if you're just confining your rail trip out that way you would probably do best to buy train tickets as you go and not bother with a rail pass. Budget flights from the UK make much of it very inexpensive to get to.

Another possible change in emphasis is how we get to continental Europe. The murmurings of unease about plane travel and carbon footprints, and the appreciable hassle of airport security and the tedium of lengthy journeys to distant airports and endless waiting around have recently got just that bit louder. Travelling by train to Europe from the UK is getting much more feasible: the new high-speed link by Eurostar from St Pancras has shaved half an hour or so off the journey time, and reasonably priced tickets to anywhere in Belgium, or connections down into France, make western Europe at least a lot more accessible from London by train than it was.

Travel by train almost anywhere across this continent and you can be struck by the way it changes from one region to the next – architecture, people, language, culture, food, drink and landscapes – from the baroque cities of eastern and northern Europe to the rugged, parched sierras of inland Spain, or from the wildflower-speckled meadows of the Pyrenees to the astonishing ancient ruins of Greece and Italy.

With all this in mind I have arranged the bulk of this book into rail tours that really take in the cream, and with the expert help of the European Rail Timetable team at Thomas Cook have worked out the logistics of rail travel – connections, where to go next, how long trips take, and so on. So those great trans-Alpine routes are in the book, together with the amazing trips up through Scandinavia and up to the Arctic Circle. I've also pieced together routes that are memorable for their cultural attractions, and for their sheer contrasts. No other guidebook to Europe has ever been published in this rail tour format; to avoid overwhelming you with information and ensure that the book is reasonably portable, I've endeavoured to keep descriptions concise.

Do buy the latest *Thomas Cook European Rail Timetable* (published monthly). This masterpiece of compression gives all the main rail routes in Europe, and lots of minor ones. It also has rail maps for each country, showing corresponding table numbers for each route. Also useful is the *Thomas Cook Rail Map of Europe*, which highlights scenic routes and shows Europe all in one go – handy for planning trips across borders.

Have a great trip.

Tim Locke

Route Map

Featured routes with page numbers ──(178)──

Long distance routes

Other main lines

London

Cherbourg

Calais

Ostend

247

AMSTERDAM

254

HAMBURG

Cologne

Aachen

288

288

Hanno

298

BRUSSELS

247

90

83

Luxembourg

96

PARIS

90

Strasbourg

96

Tours

Konstanz

309

96

83

105

Berne

352

ZURICH

362

Poschia

Clermont
Ferrand

Lausanne

352

344

Santiago de
Compostela

Bordeaux

Lyon

Geneva

MILAN

429

198

Biarritz

113

134

105

Avignon

Ver

190

San
Sebastián

Toulouse

134

Bologna

419

Salamanca

113

Nîmes

Ventimiglia

186

138

Béziers

113

Menton

42

176

Marseille

123

Pisa

LISBON

MADRID

CORSICA

BARCELONA

142

176

176

Seville

Valencia

BALEARICS

SARDINIA

Cádiz

208

Granada

161

143

Málaga

MOROCCO

142

ROUTE MAP

START/FINISH POINT

SCENIC RAIL ROUTES SHADED IN GREY

STOPS ON ROUTE

RAIL ROUTE

START/FINISH POINT

ROUTE DETAIL		
Helsinki–Oulu		ETT table 794
Type	Frequency	Journey Time
Train	7–8 daily	6 hrs 29 mins
	2–4 nightly	9 hrs 3 mins
Helsinki–Parikkala		ETT table 797
Type	Frequency	Journey Time
Train	4–5 daily	3 hrs 30 mins

▲

ROUTE DETAIL

Helsinki–Oulu:
direct journey details
Helsinki–Parikkala:
point to point details

Mode of travel, typical journey time,
frequency of service and *ETT* table
numbers are given.

KEY TO ICONS	
	Telephone
	Rail Stations
	Public Transport
	Ferry Services
	Airports
i	Information
	Accommodation
	Food and Drink

Europe by Rail aims to inform and inspire you, and it's arranged unlike any other travel book. So we begin with a few words of explanation on how to find your way around it.

The opening chapter is on **Getting to Europe from Britain**. This begins with a look at how you can use cheap flights to get you to the part of Europe you want to visit. We've listed the main airlines and where they fly, organised country by country, in alphabetical order of country. Then there's a brief summary of crossing by ferry and by Channel Tunnel. After that, **Rail Travel in Europe** summarises pretty much everything about types of trains, overnight trains, on-board facilities, rail passes – those covering the whole of Europe or several countries as well as ones that just give you travel over one country. There's a two-page table showing direct rail connections and journey times for day and night trains between major cities. We also dip briefly into travel by bus or car.

Traveller's Guide to Europe has an A to Z of handy information, such as internet access, visas, sales tax, student and youth travel, mobile phones and a list of what to take with you.

After that comes the **main part of the book**, which is divided into countries, beginning with the United Kingdom (included just as a starting point: so it's a short description of London and doesn't include other places), and spreading across Europe in a geographical sequence, moving on to France, Spain and Portugal, Benelux (the term for Belgium, the Netherlands and Luxembourg), Germany, Switzerland, Austria, Italy, Croatia and Slovenia, Scandinavia (Denmark, Finland, Norway and Sweden), the Baltic States, Poland, the Czech Republic and Slovakia, and finally Southeast Europe. Each country section has an opening introduction, with an overview of accommodation and food and drink, as well as an **Essentials** box listing embassies, opening hours and other general bits of information.

Within each **country section,** you'll find one or more city chapters – focusing on the major city or cities within that country. After the **introduction** there follows a section on public transport, with information on Metro and bus systems, types of tickets, taxis and any general hints. The **accommodation** listings are aimed at budget travellers, so we include predominantly hostels, inexpensive hotels and pensions and campsites – with the emphasis on location (central or near the rail station), though we do have some more moderately priced places that are particularly welcoming. **Food and drink** highlights general areas to head for (and avoid) if you want a meal or a drink, as well as local specialities and street markets. The **highlights** section covers the best of that city – museums, walks, viewpoints, parks, free attractions and monuments: it's only a selection to give you an idea what to prioritise if time's limited. We don't include opening times (which you can invariably find out on the web or at Tourist Offices, and which in any case have a nasty habit of changing from one year to the next), though if an attraction involves a hefty traipse to reach and is closed on (say) Monday then we say so. We also give a rundown of **night-time and events**, as well as **shopping**. Finally, we may mention one or two **side trips** that you can take from that city – places not featured elsewhere in the book but easily reached by bus, ferry or train.

After the city chapter(s) come the **Rail Tours**. These are routes from one place to another that are specially recommended (mostly by rail, though in a few cases we've included ferries and buses too). The route map immediately precedes the pages you are currently reading. You'll see on the **route map** that all the routes join up, so you can use part or all of a route to devise your own variants, such as routes across two or more countries. Rail tours begin with a map with the main route picked out in black and other railways in grey. This is accompanied by a box giving **route detail** – the frequency of train services and the journey time. You'll also see the **ETT table number** – ETT stands for the **Thomas Cook European Rail Timetable.** This is the invaluable timetable for rail services across Europe: like this guide, it's divided into countries or groups of countries, and has rail maps with the timetable by each part of the route so you can find the right timetable easily. You will see ETT table numbers throughout this book, but note that they do change when services are altered. Don't forget also to check station timetables as you travel, as the ETT has insufficient space to show every local rail service.

Rail tours have selections of **places** worth stopping off for. The information for these places is less detailed than for the city chapters, but covers tourist information, where to stay, and a pithy description of what the city, town or village is about. Throughout the text, there are **Where next?** boxes – with suggestions of other journeys to make, or ways of linking up to other rail tours in the book.

To help you get your bearings, there are street maps for many city centres throughout the book. **Accommodation price bands** reflect relative costs within a country (not given for hostels and campsites, which all fall into the € band):

€	budget
€€	moderate
€€€	expensive

TOP WEBSITES FOR RAIL TRAVELLERS

www.bahn.de: the German railways' website, with a very handy journey planner for anywhere in Europe – it doesn't have to be a route through Germany, and there's an English-language button. Simple to use, and usually quick and accurate. It gives timings, platform numbers, connections and some fares.

www.seat61.com: the most comprehensive European rail travel resource you'll find, this has details of passes and general information on rail travel in Europe, web links, booking services, and a guide to rail travel in each European country.

GETTING TO EUROPE FROM BRITAIN

FLYING   You can save a lot of time by using budget flights to get you into continental Europe, and by booking in advance you can take advantage of incredibly inexpensive deals, especially if you're flexible about where you travel to. In this section, we show you some of the main starting points, as well as a lot of ones that sound like they're in the middle of nowhere – certainly nowhere near the places they're named after – but can turn out to be really useful in getting you to worthwhile parts of the continent. So there's no need to feel you have to start and return from a major city like Paris or Rome: it might save megabucks to go to some obscure airport and return from somewhere else. Don't get seduced too much by low-looking prices. Some budget flights start late at night or early in the morning, so you may have to doss down in the airport overnight, or splash out on an expensive hotel or taxi fare. Stansted Airport, where many of them go from, is not that near London (actually nearer Cambridge) and you can be in for an expensive train fare at peak time before you've reached the airport. Check out www.whichbudget.com – a useful directory of many budget flights. There are quite a few websites comparing flight deals, such as www.travelsupermarket.com, www.skyscanner.net and www.cheapflights.co.uk, but note that few comparison sites show Ryanair fares, and the 'hidden extras' which can vary enormously between companies may not be included. Possibly the main disadvantage to starting your trip by air is the limit on the amount of baggage you can take.

MAJOR BUDGET AIRLINES   Ryanair, easyJet and Flybe are among the biggest no-frills airlines. You don't get free meals or drinks on board (and note that prices quoted may not include taxes and various other add-ons, such as charges for hold baggage and even for paying by credit card). No-frills flights are ticketless – you need to keep a note of your booking number as you aren't issued with a ticket. It's worth emailing yourself a note of this so you can retrieve it later on should you lose the crucial bit of paper you've written or printed it on. Watch out for new requirements and charges when booking with any of the budget airlines, as they are continually streamlining their procedures. For Ryanair, for example, you now need to check in online (from 21 days to up to four hours before departure) and print your own boarding pass to bring with you: don't leave this until you get to the airport, as you might not find an internet connection or printer, and there's a whopping charge (£40 at the time of writing) if you miss the four-hour deadline.

Ryanair (www.ryanair.com) London Stansted is the main UK airport; also large number of flights from regional airports, and numerous continental airports to other cities in Europe.

easyJet (www.easyjet.com) Bristol, Liverpool, London Luton, and London Gatwick are the main departure airports; Belfast, Edinburgh, Glasgow, London Stansted, Manchester and Newcastle have quite a few flights; flights to Geneva from Bournemouth and Birmingham. Flights to London Gatwick and/or London Luton from Aberdeen and Inverness.

Flybe (www.flybe.com) Useful if you're starting outside London: the main gateway airports are Southampton, Manchester, Exeter and Birmingham; also many other regional ones in UK, Isle of Man and Dublin with flights to their main airports. Flights to western Europe and Croatia.

bmibaby (www.bmibaby.com) Flights to Europe are mainly from Birmingham, Cardiff, Manchester and Nottingham East Midlands. Mostly goes to Mediterranean destinations.

British Airways (www.ba.com) Deals are often as cheap, sometimes cheaper, though it's not a no-frills operator as such.

Other airlines Don't confine your searches to the big boys – smaller operators may have better deals, such as airBaltic (www.airbaltic.com) for the Baltic States and elsewhere, Blue Air (www.blueair-web.com) for Romania and Greece, Centralwings (www.centralwings.com) for Poland, Cimber Sterling (www.cimber.dk) for various points in Europe from Denmark, My Air (www.myair.com) from Venice and Milan particularly, and SmartWings (www.smartwings.net), based in Prague, Helvetic (www.helvetic.com), based in Zürich. Other low cost airlines include: jet2.com, germanwings.com, airberlin.com and tuifly.com), all based in Germany; wizzair.com goes to Poland and eastern Europe.

COUNTRY BY COUNTRY   In this section, we concentrate on the two major budget airlines, and where they go in Europe, and indicate them as E=easyJet and R=Ryanair. Many of these places are featured on the rail tours in this book; for those that aren't we explain below how they connect to our rail tours. We list the main destinations in 2010 but it's worth browsing the airlines' websites to see what's new. Note that some airports are not that close to the places mentioned; check the airlines' websites for transport connections. ETT refers to the table number in the Thomas Cook European Rail Timetable. Timings given are approximate, and are from the rail station nearest the airport (for details of buses from the airports, see the airlines' websites). For some countries we've also outlined recommended international routes that cross several frontiers. Each of them would make a superb holiday in itself. All the main places of interest and many of the lines travelled are covered in this book.

Austria
Graz (R), in the southeastern corner of the country, is near the borders with Slovenia and Hungary. Direct services to Vienna (2 hrs 30 mins, ETT 980), through Slovenia and Maribor to Zagreb (4 hrs, ETT 1315), and you can travel into the Styrian Alps to Salzburg (4 hrs, ETT 975), where you can join the featured Innsbruck–Vienna rail tour. The most scenic areas are to the west and south, and Graz itself is a lively city to hang out in for a while. **Innsbruck** (E, R), **Vienna** (E, R) and **Linz** (R) are also on the Innsbruck–Vienna rail tour. **Salzburg** (R) is on the Salzburg–Rijeka–Osijek route (see pp380–382, 464). **Klagenfurt** (R) is handy for some beautiful areas of the Alps, and is close to the Slovenia border; from there you can reach Graz in just over 2 hrs 30 mins (ETT 980, also 980a for an express bus link 2 hrs), or head via Villach to Salzburg (3 hrs

Getting to Europe from Britain

20 mins; ETT 970). Vienna and Innsbruck are other good starting points. **Recommended international route**: Vienna–Bratislava–Poprad-Tatry–Kraków–Warsaw (ETT 996, 1180, 1182, 1078, 1065). An eastern tour through Slovakia and Poland, from the poignantly beautiful capital cities of Vienna and Bratislava. The route then heads through the hilly backwaters of Slovakia and rounds the Tatra Mountains to reach Kraków, Poland's best-preserved large city. From there, divert into the mountain resort of Zakopane, the Royal Salt Mines or to the grim Holocaust memorial that is Auschwitz before continuing to Warsaw.

Belgium
Brussels (R) is the only city to fly to in Belgium by no-frills operators; you may think it's hardly worth flying such a short distance from Britain, but there are Ryanair flights direct from there to various cities, including Rome, Stockholm and Venice. Note that Ryanair flights go to Charleroi, some way from Brussels itself. Brussels is featured on the rail tour from Ostend to Luxembourg, which links with Strasbourg and Berne from Luxembourg. **Recommended international route:** Brussels–Antwerp–The Hague–Amsterdam–Hamburg–Lübeck–Copenhagen (ETT 15, 22, 50). First stop, Antwerp, as good-looking as Bruges, but less dominated by tourists. The Hague and Amsterdam are two Dutch highlights, with plenty of smaller places such as Haarlem and Leiden also worth stopovers. After Hamburg and the old Hanseatic city of Lübeck, either take the direct train to Copenhagen, which goes aboard the train-ferry for the 45-minute crossing to Denmark, or take the long way round via Odense. You can also begin from London, via the Channel Tunnel to Brussels (ETT 12).

Bulgaria
Sofia (E) is on the Athens–Plovdiv tour.

Croatia
Dubrovnik (E), **Osijek** (R) and **Split** (E) feature in our rail and bus tours leading into Austria and Slovenia. Other options on the coast are **Pula** (R; rail and bus connections to **Rijeka** and **Ljubljana**) and **Zadar** (R; trains to Split, changing at Knin, ETT 1330).

Czech Republic
Brno (R), 3 hrs from Prague, is on the Prague–Bratislava–Poprad-Tatry rail tour. **Prague** (E, R) has its own chapter in this book. **Recommended international route:** Prague–Munich–Zürich–Milan–Nice–Marseille–Barcelona–Madrid–Lisbon (ETT 57, 75, 82, 90, 355, 657, 650, 48). An epic trip from the Czech Republic, through Bavaria and the Alps, across southern France to Perpignan, and over the eastern end of the Pyrenees to Barcelona, crossing Spain and Portugal to end near Europe's southwestern corner.

Denmark
Aarhus (R), Denmark's second city, is on the Copenhagen–Gothenburg route, in the middle of Denmark and 3 hrs 40 mins from **Copenhagen** (E). **Esbjerg** (R) is 1 hr 30 mins from Odense, ETT 705) and 3 hrs 10 mins from Copenhagen (ETT 700, 705). **Billund** (R) is home to Legoland and has buses from the airport to Aarhus.

Getting to Europe from Britain

Recommended international route: Copenhagen–Odense–Aarhus–Gothenburg–Oslo–Bergen (ETT 700, 701, 2320, 770, 780). From the Danish capital you head through some of the liveliest towns in Denmark, and after the Swedish cultural gem of Gothenburg, the scenery steps up a gear beyond the Norwegian capital, Oslo. The finale to Bergen and the fjords rates as one of the great train rides of the world.

Estonia
Tallinn (E), is covered on the rail and bus tour from Vilnius to St Petersburg.

Finland
As well as **Helsinki** (E) itself, **Tampere (Tammerfors)** (R) is on the Stockholm–Oulu–Helsinki rail tour, and is a useful starting point for southern Finland, with trains to Helsinki taking 1 hr 45 mins (ETT 790). **Recommended international route:** Helsinki–Tallinn–Riga–Vilnius–Warsaw–Poznan–Berlin (ETT 2410, 1800, 1040, 93, 1005, 1001, 56). From the Finnish capital you cross by ferry to Estonia (where you can divert to St Petersburg; visa required), and head by train and bus through the other Baltic states of Latvia and Lithuania. Then cross Poland to end at the German capital.

France
Basel–Mulhouse (E), **Béziers** (R), **Biarritz** (R), **Bordeaux** (E), **Brest–Brittany** (R), **Brittany–Dinard** (R; buses to St Malo take 25 mins), **Carcassonne** (R), **La Rochelle–Rochefort** (E, R), **Lille** (R), **Limoges** (R), **Lourdes** (R), **Lyon** (E), **Marseille** (E, R), **Montpellier** (E, R), **Nantes** (E, R), **Nice** (E,R), **Nîmes** (R), **Paris** (E, R; R flies to Paris-Beauvais), **Pau–Pyrenees** (R), **Perpignan** (R), **Poitiers** (R), **Toulon–St Tropez** (R), **Toulouse** (E) and **Tours** (R) are all covered in the France section (pp65–143). Those not included are **Angouleme** (R), (45 mins from Poitiers, ETT 300), **Bergerac** (R; 1 hr 20 mins from Bordeaux, ETT 349), **Grenoble** (E, R; numerous routes into the French Alps; 2 hrs to Geneva via Aix les Bains, ETT 364; 1 hr 30 mins to Lyon, ETT 343) and **Rodez** (R; 2hrs 20 mins from Toulouse via Albi, or 1 hr 25 mins to Millau, ETT 323). **Recommended international routes:** Paris–Bordeaux–Burgos–Madrid–Granada (ETT 46, 300, 305, 689, 661) heads down via the castles of the Loire and the unique Futuroscope theme park near Poitiers to France's southwestern corner and into Spain's Basque country, past the cathedral at Burgos and the Spanish capital to end in the heart of Andalucía, with its amazing Moorish monuments such as the Alhambra as reminders that Africa is not far away. Paris–Milan–Florence–Rome (ETT 44, 620) offers four strongly contrasting cities, with a magnificent scenic experience through the Swiss Alps, via Lausanne and Brig, to Milan, followed by a journey through Tuscany to the Italian capital. Lyon–Zürich–Innsbruck–Salzburg (ETT 345, 500, 86, 951) crosses the Alps from west to east, passing Geneva and Berne (both of which are handily placed if you want to detour into the Swiss Alps – Interlaken and Kandersteg are great places to head for), then through to Salzburg, city of Mozart and *The Sound of Music*. From there you can divert to the mountains of the Salzkammergut, where Hallstatt is a lovely lakeside town to find yourself in for a few days.

Germany
Berlin (E, R – to Schönefeld, which has its own station, and a direct link to Potsdam),

Getting to Europe from Britain

Bremen (R), **Cologne–Bonn** (E), **Düsseldorf** (E), **Düsseldorf–Weeze** (R; note this airport is near Kleve, Nijmegen and Arnhem and is very near the Netherlands), **Frankfurt–Hahn** (R; 1hr 45 mins by bus to Frankfurt), also **Hamburg** (E), **Hamburg–Lübeck** (R; nearer Lübeck than Hamburg), **Karlsruhe–Baden** (R), **Leipzig–Altenburg** (R), **Munich** (E) and **Stuttgart** (F) are all covered in the Germany section. **Friedrichshafen** (R) is on Lake Constance (Bodensee), 20 mins to Lindau, ETT 933 and 1 hr 10 mins to Ulm ETT 933; **Dortmund** (E) is 1 hr 15 mins to Cologne or 45 mins to Düsseldorf, ETT 800; **Memmingen** (R) is 30 mins to Ulm, ETT 935. **Recommended international route:** Berlin–Dresden–Prague–Vienna (ETT tables 60, 840, 1100, 1150). From Berlin, one of Europe's most vibrant cities, through the resurrected city of Dresden in former East Germany, to Prague and Vienna, two wonderfully unspoilt old capitals.

Greece

The capital, **Athens** (E), has its own chapter, and is the southern end of the rail tour from Plovdiv (Bulgaria) via Thessaloniki (E). **Recommended international route:** Athens–Sofia–Plovdiv–Veliko Târnovo–Bucharest–Braşov–Budapest (ETT 1400, 1560, 1520, 1525, 1500, 1600, 60). An epic and demanding trip from the southeastern corner of Europe through some untouched old towns and remote landscapes in Greece, Bulgaria and Romania, this includes Transylvania (Braşov is in Dracula country). Start with a leisurely exploration of Classical Greece, from Delphi to Athens – ideal for lazy excursions to islands for those cultured out.

Hungary

Budapest (E, R) is covered on p622, and is featured on the rail tour from Bratislava (Slovakia) to Istanbul (Turkey), p635. There are also plentiful rail links to eastern and central Europe, including Vienna and Prague. **Balaton** airport (R) has bus links to Budapest (3 hrs 10 mins) to connect with flights, but unless you want to relax around the nicely laid-back Lake Balaton region it's not that useful. **Recommended international route:** Budapest–Zagreb–Ljubljana–Trieste–Venice (ETT 1340, 1300, 1305, 605, 89). From the Hungarian capital of Budapest, the train skirts the shores of Lake Balaton, you reach Zagreb, the Croatian capital, and from Ljubljana there's access to Slovenia's Alps at Bled. There's the chance to visit two of Europe's most spectacular caverns, near Postojna and Trieste. Trieste, at the head of the Adriatic, is more Austrian than Italian. Not far away, Venice – with its art and canals – could hardly be more different.

Italy

Bologna (R), **Florence–Pisa** (actually in Pisa; E, R), **Genoa** (R), **Milan** (E, R), **Naples** (E), **Rome** (E, R), **Trieste** (R), **Turin** (E, R), **Venice–Treviso** (E, R) and **Verona–Brescia** (R) are covered in the section on Italy. Bologna, Milan, Venice, Pisa, Trieste, Turin (featured as a side trip from Milan; Genoa is also easily reachable from Milan by train in approximately 2 hrs) and Verona are useful airports on our featured rail tours in northern Italy, and it's easy to travel into the Alps and into Austria, along the Italian Riviera towards France too. Rome is as central as you can get, while Naples is close to the ruined Roman cities of Pompeii and Herculaneum, as well as the Amalfi coast and the island of Capri. **Palermo** (E, R), **Trapani** (R) and **Catania** (E) are on Sicily, while

Alghero–Sardinia (R), **Olbia** (E) and **Cagliari** (E, R) are on Sardinia: both islands have enough for at least a week's exploration, though they're a long way from anywhere else. **Lamezia** (E, R), in southern Italy, is on the Rome–Naples–Palermo rail tour on p445, between Naples and Messina. **Ancona** (R) is 2 hrs 30 mins to Bologna or 4 hrs 15 mins to Milan, ETT 630, 3 hrs 15 mins to Rome, ETT 625, via Foligno, where you can change to trains for Assisi and Perugia, ETT 615. **Bari** (E, R) is 4–6 hrs to Rome, changing at Foggia (but there are several through services), ETT 631, 626. **Brindisi** (E, R) as Bari, above, to which it takes 1 hr–1 hr 30 mins, ETT 631. **Cuneo** (R) is 2 hrs from Ventimiglia, ETT 581. **Parma** (R) is 50 mins to Bologna, ETT 620. **Pescara** (R) is 3 hrs 45 mins to Rome, ETT 624. **Rimini** (R) is 1 hr–1 hr 30 mins to Bologna, ETT 630 and 1 hr to Ravenna, ETT 621. **Recommended international route:** Venice–Bologna–Pisa–Nice–Marseille–Paris–London (ETT 10, 350, 360, 580, 610, 613, 620). From the canals of Venice you pass through the historic cities of northern Italy, the chic resorts of the Italian and French rivieras and the Provençal cities of Avignon and Arles.

Latvia

The Latvian capital, **Riga** (E, R), is on the featured rail and bus tour through the Baltic States (Vilnius–Tallinn–St Petersburg) on p553.

Lithuania

The pre-war capital, **Kaunas** (R), is featured as a side trip from Vilnius on the rail and bus tour through the Baltic States (Vilnius–Tallinn–St Petersburg).

Netherlands

Amsterdam (E) is covered in its own chapter and features in a circular rail tour taking in Gouda and Rotterdam (p254). **Maastricht** (R), in the southern corner of the country, is on the Ostend–Luxembourg tour. **Eindhoven** (R) is 1 hr 20 mins to Amsterdam, ETT 470 or 1 hr 10 mins to Rotterdam, ETT 472.

Norway

Oslo (R, Oslo–Torp) features on three rail tours on pp512–527 through Norway, Sweden and Denmark. **Haugesund** (R) has no rail connections but is 2 hrs 50 mins by ferry to Bergen, ETT 2240. **Recommended international route:** Oslo–Trondheim–Bodø–Luleå–Oulu–Tampere–Helsinki (ETT 785, 787, 759, 769, 794, 790). Venture to the very north of Europe: the Arctic Circle, Lapland and the midnight sun in the far reaches of Scandinavia. Seek out the Munch paintings in Oslo to put you in the Nordic mood, and beyond Trondheim aim to stop off at Bodø, a boat's ride from the improbably jagged mountains of the idyllic Lofoten Islands. In summer, bus services head even further north towards the spectacularly remote town of Hammerfest, ETT 789. Carry on into Finland, through the second city of Tampere and the stylish capital, Helsinki.

Poland

Kraków (E, R) and **Poznan** (R) are on the Poznan–Zakopane rail tour. **Bydgoszcz** (R) is 1 hr to Torun, 2hrs 15 mins to Poznan or 4 hrs to Warsaw, ETT 1020; **Gdansk** (R) is 4 hrs 20 mins to Warsaw, ETT 1030; **Lodz** (R) is 1 hr 30 mins to Warsaw, ETT 1090;

Getting to Europe from Britain

Rzeszów (R) is 2 hrs 15 mins to Kraków, ETT 1075; **Katowice** (R) is 1 hr 40 mins to Kraków, ETT 1075; **Szczecin** (R) is 2 hrs 40 mins to Poznan, ETT 1010; **Wroclaw** (R) is 2 hrs 20 mins to Poznan, ETT 1070 and 4 hrs 30 mins to Kraków, ETT 1075.

Portugal
Lisbon (E), has its own chapter and is the starting point for rail tours to Barcelona via Madrid and Santiago via **Porto** (E, R). **Faro** (E, R), in the Algarve, is remotely located in the southeastern corner of the country (3 hrs 40 mins to Lisbon, ETT 697).

Slovakia
The capital, **Bratislava** (R), is on the Prague–Poprad-Tatry rail tour.

Slovenia
Ljubljana (E), is on the Ljubljana–Split–Dubrovnik rail and ferry tour.

Spain
Almeria (E, R), **Asturias** (E), **Barcelona** (E), **Bilbao** (E), **Girona–Barcelona** (R), **Granada** (R), **Madrid** (E), **Málaga** (E, R), **Reus–Salou** (R), **Santander–Bilbao** (R), **Santiago de Compostela** (R), **Seville** (R), **Valencia** (E, R) and **Zaragoza** (R) are all covered in rail tours or city sections of our Spain section. **Palma** (E) is on Majorca; **Mahon (Maó)** (E) is on Menorca, with ferries to Palma and Barcelona (ETT 2510), and you can also fly to **Ibiza** (E). **Alicante (Alacant)** (E, R) and **Murcia** (E, R), in southeast Spain, are not very well located for starting a rail trip across the country (1 hr 30 mins to Valencia from Alicante, or 3 hrs 45 mins from Murcia, ETT 672; 3 hrs 45 mins Alicante to Madrid, ETT 668). **Jérez** (R) is useful for western Andalucía (45 mins to Cádiz or 1 hr 10 mins to Seville, ETT 671). **Valladolid** (R), while not that exciting a city in itself, is handy for much of northern and western Spain (1 hr 10 mins to Avila, 1 hr 25 mins to Burgos, 2 hr 30 mins to Madrid, 1 hr 40 mins to Salamanca, ETT 689; 1 hr 50 mins to León, ETT 681).

Sweden
Stockholm (E, R), described in its own chapter, is on two rail tours from Copenhagen and Helsinki. **Gothenburg** (R), is on two rail tours into Denmark and Sweden. **Recommended international route**: Stockholm–Copenhagen–Hamburg–Würzburg–Munich–Verona–Venice (ETT 730, 50, 900, 70, 595, 600); Europe in all its moods, from the watery northern beauty of Stockholm, Copenhagen and Hamburg, through the heart of Bavaria, through the Alps, to sunny northern Italy, the Roman amphitheatre at Verona and the canals of Venice.

Switzerland
Geneva (E), **Zürich** (E), **Basel** (R) and **Basel–Mulhouse** (E) – the airport is just in France – all have excellent rail services.

Turkey
Turkey's great western city, **Istanbul** (E), is described in its own chapter and is on the Bratislava–Bucharest–Istanbul rail tour.

Getting to Europe from Britain

SURFACE CROSSINGS FERRIES

Some rail passes such as InterRail have discounts for ferry travel, and if you have the time it's a nice way to arrive, with mostly good connections from nearby rail stations at each end. If you're a foot passenger, you are unlikely to need to book, though on some night services you might be excluded, so it's worth checking first. Services for the summer season are given below (a rough guide only; subject to alteration). There are up-to-date details in the shipping section in the *Thomas Cook European Rail Timetable*. Useful websites include www.ferrybooker.com and www.directferries.co.uk.

Dover to Boulogne (fast ferry), LD Lines. **Dover to Calais**, P&O Ferries, Sea France. **Dover to Dunkirk**, Norfolkline. **Harwich to Esbjerg**, DFDS Seaways. **Harwich to Hook of Holland** (fast ferry), Stena Line. **Hull to Rotterdam Europoort** and **Zeebrugge**, P&O Ferries. **Newcastle to Amsterdam (Ijmuiden)**, DFDS Seaways. **Newhaven to Dieppe**, Transmanche Ferries. **Plymouth to Roscoff** and **Santander**, Brittany Ferries. **Poole to Cherbourg** (fast ferry and ship), Brittany Ferries. **Poole to St Malo**, Condor Ferries. **Portsmouth to Bilbao**, P&O Ferries. **Portsmouth to Cherbourg** (fast ferry and ship), Brittany Ferries, Condor Ferries. **Portsmouth to Le Havre**, LD Lines. **Portsmouth to Ouistreham (Caen)** (fast ferry and ship), Brittany Ferries. **Portsmouth to Santander and St Malo**, Brittany Ferries. **Ramsgate to Boulogne**, Euroferries. **Rosyth to Zeebrugge**, Norfolkline. **Weymouth to St Malo**, Condor Ferries.

Brittany Ferries 0871 244 0744, www.brittanyferries.co.uk
Condor Ferries 01202 207216, www.condorferries.co.uk
DFDS Seaways 0871 522 9955, www.dfds.co.uk
Euroferries 0844 414 5355, www.euroferries.co.uk
LD Lines 0844 576 8836, www.ldlines.co.uk
Norfolkline 0844 847 5042, www.norfolkline.com
P&O Ferries 08716 645 645, www.poferries.com
Sea France 0871 423 7119, www.seafrance.com
Stena Line 08705 707070, www.stenaline.co.uk
Transmanche Ferries 0800 917 1201, www.transmancheferries.co.uk

THE CHANNEL TUNNEL

Rail passes don't include travel on **Eurostar** trains through the Channel Tunnel (although passholders do get a discount) but from time to time Eurostar sell bargain tickets and you can get good deals by buying tickets in advance. Eurostar gets you effortlessly from London's new terminal at London St Pancras via Ebbsfleet (Kent) and, for some trains, Ashford International, to Paris Gare du Nord or Brussels Midi) and, unlike the plane, right into the city centres; journey times are are just over 2 hrs. Eurostar also serves Lille-Europe, with useful connections to elsewhere in France and adjacent countries, and in summer there are some direct services to Avignon in southern France. There is an automated check-in system at all Eurostar terminals, and passengers can check in up to 30 mins before departure, clearing customs and immigration before boarding. Eurostar bookings: 08705 186 186 (www.eurostar.com). Note that the **Eurotunnel** shuttle service from Folkestone to Calais transports cars and buses only (four times per hour, taking 35 mins; 08705 35 35 35, www.eurotunnel.com).

RAIL TRAVEL IN EUROPE

This chapter provides general information about train travel in Europe, followed by alternative transport options. Information about rail travel for individual countries is given in their Essentials sections.

TICKETS It's generally safest to buy your ticket before travelling (from a station or travel agent) as passengers found without tickets can face heavy penalties or criminal prosecution; however, if boarding at a station that has no ticket office or machine, pay on the train. Always ask about discounts (e.g. for travel outside the rush hour and at weekends) before you buy a ticket. Most countries have discounts for children; the age limits vary from country to country, but commonly children under 4 travel free and those under 12 at half price.

ADVANCE RESERVATIONS There's no firm rule as to whether it's worth reserving (and it isn't always possible to do so anyway); some trains never get busy (especially many leisurely back-country routes), while others (such as some InterCity expresses) are packed in high season and around public holidays, and you could spend hours standing in a crowded corridor. In some cases, you may be refused permission to board at all if there are no seats available. There's normally a small fee for reservations. If you are travelling during the busy summer period and have no reservation, board your train as early as possible. Some of the major express trains (usually marked in timetables by an 'R' in a box) are restricted to passengers with reservations, and you can usually make a reservation about two months in advance. You should book if you want sleeping accommodation, though you can chance your luck and just turn up in the hope that a couchette will be available; in this case pay the supplement to the attendant.

SUPPLEMENTS If you are travelling with certain types of rail pass you'll be exempt from many routine surcharges made on express trains, but sometimes you'll have to pay a little more (so always travel with some local currency); ask if you're uncertain – there may be a surcharge-free slower service. Some special high-speed services (such as the French TGV, the Swedish X2000, Eurostar Italia, Eurostar trains and Spanish AVE services) invariably require a supplement. Holders of a first-class Eurail Pass can use most of the special services without paying extra, but even they should check its validity if they want to use certain types of high-speed train or branded overnight trains – for example, Trenhotel (Spain) or City Night Line. The fee for reserving seats is normally included in the supplementary payments for faster trains. Sleeping accommodation (see p26) always attracts charges. Sort out the extras before you start your journey. You may be able to pay the supplements on the train, but it almost always costs more than doing so in advance.

TYPES OF TRAIN Many of the best daytime international trains are branded **EuroCity** (EC) and most have names. To qualify, trains have to be fast and offer a certain standard of service, such as food and drink during the journey. **Eurostar** trains are the only trains in operation through the Channel Tunnel between Britain and France, apart from the Eurotunnel shuttle trains carrying vehicles and their passengers from one side of the tunnel to the other. Many **overnight trains**, particularly in Western

Europe, are progressively being upgraded with refurbished or new coaches, often with air-conditioning, and extras such as evening drinks and breakfast may be available. Many carry brand names such as EuroNight (EN), Lunéa (France) or City Night Line (Germany). Passes may not be valid, although pass-holders will usually be eligible for a discount. The **IC** or **InterCity** label is applied by many countries to the fast long-distance trains, although there are slight variations in what they provide. The **ICE (InterCity Express)** designation is applied to the latest high-speed trains in Germany. **Inter-regional express** services, which make more stops than InterCity trains, go under a number of classifications, such as IR in Switzerland (where it's short for InterRegio). Each country has its own way of distinguishing faster trains from local or stopping trains – further details are given in the *Thomas Cook European Rail Timetable*. Most longer-distance trains in Europe offer both first- and second-class travel, but second class is the norm for local stopping services. Where overnight trains offer seating accommodation, this is usually second class only. As a rule in Western Europe, second class is perfectly adequate for all but the most ardent comfort-seeker. A few Eastern European services still leave a lot to be desired, but as tickets are relatively cheap it's worth paying the extra to upgrade to first class.

FINDING YOUR TRAIN Larger stations have potential for confusion. Look for the electronic departure boards or large paper timetables (often yellow for departures and white for arrivals) that list the routes, the times of departure and arrival, and the relevant platforms; double-check footnotes and symbols – that seemingly ideal train may in fact turn out to run only on a handful of dates. In some stations, the platforms are also labelled with details of regular trains or the next departure and may even give the location of specific carriages and the facilities on board. If you have a reservation, board your allocated carriage (they are all numbered, usually by the entrance). Look for destination boards or displays on each carriage: even if you've found the right platform you might end up in the wrong place. Make sure you board in the right place: some long platforms serve more than one train at a time, and quite a few trains split en route, with only some carriages going the full distance. First-class coaches usually have a yellow stripe above the windows and large number '1's on the side of the coach, on the door or on the windows. A sign near the compartment door often gives seat numbers and sometimes indicates which are reserved. In open carriages (without compartments) seats are usually numbered individually (on the back or on the luggage rack) and reserved seats may have labels attached to their headrests (or the luggage racks). In some countries, however, reserved seats are not marked – so be prepared to move if someone who has booked boards the train. Very few trains in Europe now have provision for smokers.

OVERNIGHT TRAINS A night on the train, being rocked to sleep, soothed by the clatter of the wheels, is not to be missed. Sleeping cars can cost about the same as a hotel but have the advantage of covering large distances as you rest and you won't waste precious time in transit. Couchettes are more crowded bunk-type arrangements, but are reasonably comfortable and inexpensive. You can save quite a bit of money if you are prepared to curl up on the ordinary seats (don't do this too often without a break, however, or you will end up exhausted; the chatter of other passengers and regular checks to make sure you still have all your bags can lead to a disturbed night). Take earplugs and possibly an eyemask, and, as there are often no refreshment facilities, plenty of water and a supply of food. In Eastern Europe, you may be woken for Customs and Immigration checks, which can involve a search of luggage or the compartment/berth. Within Western Europe, it's unlikely you'll notice the borders, even if you're awake. If you have a rail pass and the night train is due to reach your next destination too early in the morning, consider booking to a town an hour or so further along the line; you can then get some extra sleep and backtrack to your intended destination (assuming there's a suitable early train back).

SLEEPING ACCOMMODATION **Sleeping cars** have bedroom-style compartments with limited washing facilities (usually just a washbasin) and full bedding. WCs are located at the end of the coach. En suite facilities are sometimes available at extra cost. An attendant travels with each car, or pair of cars, and there are sometimes facilities for drinks and/or breakfast – but be prepared to pay extra. First-class sleeping compartments usually have one or two berths, while second-class compartments have two or three. However, there are some special sleeping cars (described as 'T2' in schedules) that have only one berth in first class and two in second class. An exception is Spain: their T2 cars are first class and their Talgo trains have four berths in second class. Compartments are allocated to a single sex and unaccompanied children are placed in female compartments. In Estonia, Latvia and Lithuania berths are allocated on a first-come, first-served basis without regard to sex. Claim your berth within 15 minutes of boarding the train or it may be reallocated. **Couchettes** are more basic – and much cheaper. They consist of simple bunk beds with a sheet, blanket and pillow. They are converted from the ordinary seats at night and there are usually four berths in first class and six in second class, with washing facilities and WCs at the end of each coach. Males and females are booked into the same compartment and are expected to sleep in their daytime clothes. In a few cases (notably France and Italy), overnight trains also have airline-style reclining seats, which are allocated automatically when you make a seat reservation. These are sometimes free if you have a rail pass. Attendants will often keep your ticket overnight, and return it prior to your stop. They will also give you an alarm call if you tell them you are leaving the train before the final destination – specify the stop rather than the time, so you can sleep longer if the train runs late. If you want to go to sleep before other passengers have arrived, switch on their berth lights and switch off the main overhead light. Before boarding, sort out the things you will need for the night and put them somewhere easily accessible (preferably in a small separate bag), as busy compartments don't allow much room for searching through luggage. Sleepers and couchettes can usually be reserved up to three months in advance; early booking is recommended as space is limited. If you don't have a booking, it's still worth asking the conductor once you are on board. Keep some local currency handy to pay him/her.

WASHING Showers are generally restricted to a few luxury-class compartments (notably Gran Clase cars on the overnight Spanish Talgos; Intercity Natt cars in Sweden; and City Night Line trains in Germany/Austria/Switzerland). A few large rail stations have showers for public use.

EATING Facilities for buying food and eating on board trains varies widely between different countries and different types of train. Full meals served in a restaurant car (sometimes at set meal times) can be found on some long-distance services, and on certain trains you may be able to have a meal served at your seat (generally only in first class; your ticket may include the cost of the meal). Increasingly common are bistro cars serving a limited range of hot food – you normally order at a counter before taking a seat. Buffet cars selling snacks and drinks are also commonplace; there may be limited seating or you can take your purchases back to your seat. Also widespread are trolleys which are wheeled through the train, whilst others may have vending machines. Timetables and departure boards often indicate the type of catering provided, although it may not be available throughout the journey. Of course there may be no facilities at all for buying food or drink, so even if money is no object it is always wise to carry some water and food of your own. Don't leave the train to buy food unless you are sure you have enough time (and the correct currency); long stops at borders are no longer commonplace.

BAGGAGE Lockers are invaluable if you want to look around a place without carrying heavy baggage, and most stations (and other transport hubs) have them; sometimes it's cheaper to use a manned left-luggage office (which will be subject to opening hours). The initial payment generally covers 24 hours, but many lockers allow you to prepay for up to 72 hours. For longer periods you will normally need to find a left-luggage office. The newest lockers have display panels and are automatic: rather than a key, you get a code number which is used to release the door on your return. Baggage trolleys (where available) are usually free, but often supermarket-style: you need a coin to release them, returned when you take them back to a stand.

THROUGH TRAINS The grid overleaf indicates the availability of direct trains between selected major European cities. Standard services are shown in most cases (certain rail pass holders may be required to pay a small supplement). High-speed trains and overnight 'Hotel' trains (with premium fares or a higher supplement) are only shown where there is no alternative through service. Direct day trains are indicated by a typical journey time in the unshaded section of the grid. Overnight through services are shown in the shaded section. Full details of these services, together with a multitude of other journey possibilities, can be found in the *Thomas Cook European Rail Timetable*.

RAIL PASSES Passes for travel within a specific country are detailed within the Essentials panel of each country's chapter in this book. Rail passes represent excellent value for train travellers and, if you are taking a number of journeys, usually allow you to make substantial savings over point-to-point tickets. Passes may cover most of the continent, a regional group of countries or individual countries. You should get details of any extras when you buy the pass. A feature on rail passes appears in the summer and winter seasonal editions, and the May regular edition, of the *Thomas Cook European Rail Timetable*.

Rail Travel in Europe

	Amsterdam	Athens	Barcelona	Belgrade	Berlin	Bratislava	Brussels	Bucharest	Budapest	Cologne	Copenhagen	Florence	Frankfurt	Hamburg	Istanbul	Lisbon	Ljubljana
Amsterdam					✓						✓						
Athens																	
Barcelona																	
Belgrade								✓	✓						✓		✓
Berlin	6h20									✓							
Bratislava				9h15					✓								
Brussels	1h54																
Bucharest						18h02			✓						✓		
Budapest				7h26	11h57	2h42		14h42									
Cologne	2h34*				4h22		1h47				✓						
Copenhagen					6h45								✓				
Florence																	
Frankfurt	3h56				4h12		3h12*			1h12*				✓			
Hamburg					1h40		11h20		14h00	4h04	4h31		3h36				
Istanbul																	
Lisbon																	
Ljubljana				8h51					9h30								
London							2h01*										
Madrid			2h38*														
Milan												3h36‡					
Munich				16h20	5h52				7h24	4h42		8h21	3h45	5h40			6h27
Nice																	
Oslo																	
Paris	3h19*						1h22*			3h15*			3h50				
Prague					5h00	4h10			7h00					7h01			
Rome												2h05‡					
Sofia				8h30				11h00									
Stockholm											5h09*						
Thessaloniki		5h00															
Venice												3h04‡					
Vienna				9h21		1h10			2h50	9h35			7h00	11h45			6h17
Warsaw					5h51												
Zagreb				6h26					6h20								2h15
Zürich							8h20			6h05			4h08	7h34			

3h30	Daily day train(s) with typical journey time. A supplement may be payable for certain journeys.
*	High-speed train (supplement payable with certain rail passes). Shown only when there is no alternative.
‡	Faster and more frequent Eurostar Italia services operate (supplement payable)
§	Faster ICE services operate (supplement payable)

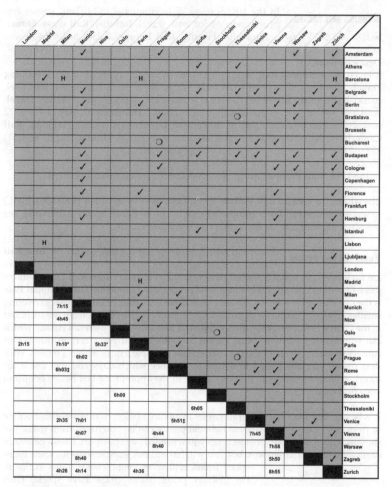

	London	Madrid	Milan	Munich	Nice	Oslo	Paris	Prague	Rome	Sofia	Stockholm	Thessaloniki	Venice	Vienna	Warsaw	Zagreb	Zürich
Amsterdam				✓				✓							✓		✓
Athens										✓		✓					
Barcelona	✓	H					H										H
Belgrade				✓						✓		✓	✓	✓		✓	✓
Berlin				✓				✓						✓	✓		✓
Bratislava								✓				O		✓			
Brussels																	
Bucharest								O		✓		✓	✓	✓			
Budapest				✓				✓		✓		✓	✓		✓		✓
Cologne				✓									✓	✓			✓
Copenhagen				✓													
Florence				✓			✓							✓			
Frankfurt								✓									
Hamburg				✓										✓			✓
Istanbul										✓		✓					
Lisbon		H															
Ljubljana				✓													✓
London																	
Madrid							H										
Milan							✓							✓			
Munich			7h15				✓	✓					✓	✓		✓	
Nice			4h45				✓										
Oslo											O						
Paris	2h15		7h10*	5h33*				✓					✓				
Prague			6h02							O			✓	✓	✓		✓
Rome			6h03‡										✓	✓			✓
Sofia												✓		✓			
Stockholm						6h00											
Thessaloniki										6h05							
Venice			2h35	7h01			5h51‡							✓		✓	
Vienna				4h07				4h44					7h45		✓		✓
Warsaw								8h40						7h58			
Zagreb			8h40											5h50			✓
Zurich			4h26	4h14			4h36							8h55			

✓ Daily overnight train in both directions.

O Overnight train in both directions (does not run daily and may be seasonal).

H Quality overnight hotel train with premium fares. Shown only when there is no alternative through train.

Rail Travel in Europe

BOOKING RAIL PASSES
In the UK: Sources of international rail tickets, passes and information about rail travel include: **Rail Pass Direct**, ☎0870 084 1413 (www.railpassdirect.co.uk). **Rail Europe**, ☎0844 848 4064 (www.raileurope.co.uk), also at Britain Visitor Centre, 1 Regent Street, London SW1Y 4LR. **Deutsche Bahn UK** (German Railways), ☎0871 880 8066 (8p per min) (www.deutsche-bahn.co.uk). **European Rail**, ☎(020) 7619 1083 (www.europeanrail.co.uk). **Ffestiniog Travel**, Minffordd, Gwynedd LL48 6LD, Wales, ☎(01766) 772050 (www.festtravel.co.uk). **RailChoice**, ☎0870 165 7300 (www.railchoice.co.uk). **Stephen Walker Travel**, ☎(01205) 310000 (www.stephenwalkertravel.co.uk). **Trainseurope**, ☎0871 700 7722 (www.trainseurope.co.uk) also at St Pancras International station, London. **Rail Canterbury**, ☎(01227) 450088 (www.rail-canterbury.co.uk). **Ultima Travel**, ☎(0151) 339 6171.

In the USA: Rail Europe Group, ☎1-800-622-8600 (www.raileurope.com).

Elsewhere: To contact Rail Europe in Canada, ☎1-800-361-7245 (1-800-361-RAIL) (www.raileurope.ca). For a comprehensive list of all Eurail agents worldwide, see www.eurailgroup.com, or book direct on www.eurail.com.

EUROPEAN RAIL PASSES
European residents of any age are able to buy the **InterRail Global Pass**, which covers most of Europe. Although there are no longer any zonal InterRail passes, you can also buy **InterRail One Country** passes for most countries. For those resident outside Europe the **Eurail Global Pass** is the one that covers the widest area, plus there is a range of Eurail passes covering smaller groups of countries or just a single country (some of which are not included in the Global Pass). Several national railways also offer their own rail passes, which can sometimes be better value. Passes are either valid for a certain number of consecutive days, or are of the flexi variety, for example 5 days within a month. With flexi passes you don't need to decide in advance which days you will use it for travel, as long as you write that day's date in the appropriate box before boarding your first train.

It is best to buy InterRail or Eurail passes in advance before you leave, either online or from one of their agents. Some national passes can be purchased from major rail stations when you arrive. In most cases you will need your passport. Passes generally cover all national rail services, but you will have to pay supplements for some high-speed trains, and most long-distance trains in Spain. On globally priced trains (these have special fares which include the seat reservation fee or sleeping accommodation) a special pass-holder fare is generally available if you have a valid pass covering the appropriate countries – examples include Eurostar, Thalys, and most international trains to and from France. On night trains you always pay extra for couchette (i.e. bunk) and sleeper berths, and some high-quality night trains are globally priced, so you pay

Note Prices quoted in this chapter were correct at time of going to press. However, rail pass prices are liable to fluctuate so check prices with the organisations listed.

a special fare. The *Thomas Cook European Rail Timetable* will tell you if it is compulsory to reserve a particular train in advance or whether you can just hop on, although at busy times you may wish to reserve a seat anyway.

Lines which are not part of the national network or which are operated by private companies may be included in the pass, but sometimes you get a discount or it may not be valid at all. This sort of information is generally included with your pass, or you can check it out on-line when planning your trip. There may also be bonuses on your pass such as discounts on ferry crossings or river cruises, and maybe even hotels, bike hire and museums, so it's worth reading the small print! Another point to note with flexi passes is that a direct overnight train leaving after 1900 hrs normally only requires the following day to be used as a travel day.

CHILDREN

Although there are exceptions, the norm is for children aged 4–11 to pay approximately 50% of the adult fare and for children under 4 to travel free – but babies are not entitled to a seat in crowded trains. Children's fares can vary from country to country, anywhere between 4–6 and 11–17.

The principal types of pass are described below:

INTERRAIL GLOBAL PASS

You are eligible to buy an InterRail pass if you are a national of a European country with a valid passport, or have been resident in Europe for more than six months. The InterRail Global Pass is valid for unlimited travel on the national railways of 30 European countries, namely Austria, Belgium, Bosnia-Herzegovina, Bulgaria, Croatia, Czech Republic, Denmark, Finland, France, Germany, Great Britain, Greece, Hungary, Republic of Ireland, Italy, Luxembourg, FYR Macedonia, Montenegro, the Netherlands, Norway, Poland, Portugal, Romania, Serbia, Slovakia, Slovenia, Spain, Sweden, Switzerland and Turkey, also on ferry services between Italy and Greece operated by Attica (i.e. SuperFast Ferries and Blue Star Ferries). Passes are not valid in the purchaser's country of residence (in some cases you can get a discount on a return ticket to the border, though this does not apply in Great Britain). Passes valid in Ireland are now also valid in Northern Ireland.

There are five different periods of validity to choose from, including a new 15 day pass. Prices are in euros. The two flexi passes are: any 5 days within 10 days (adult 1st/2nd class €374/249, youth 2nd class €159) and any 10 days within 22 days (adult 1st/2nd class €539/359, youth 2nd class €239). The other options are for consecutive days: 15 days (€599/399/279), 22 days (€704/469/309) or 1 month (€899/599/399). From January 1st 2010 there is a new Senior (60+) pass valid for all options and available in 1st or 2nd class, giving a 10% reduction on the adult fare.

Youth prices are available to those aged 25 or under on the first day for which the pass is valid. Child fares for ages 4 to 11 are available at approximately half the price of the adult pass. For the latest fares and details of supplements and bonuses see the official InterRail website www.interrailnet.com.

Rail Travel in Europe

INTERRAIL ONE COUNTRY PASS A **One Country Pass** is available for travel in any one of the participating countries listed on p31, with the exception of Bosnia-Herzegovina or Montenegro. It is not available for travel in the purchaser's country of residence. Note that Benelux (Belgium, Luxembourg and the Netherlands) counts as one country. There are two passes for Greece – the **Greece Plus** variant includes ferry services between Italy and Greece operated by Attica (i.e. SuperFast Ferries and Blue Star Ferries).

These are flexi passes, valid for 3, 4, 6 or 8 days within 1 month. Prices shown are for adult 1st class, adult 2nd class and youth (under 26) respectively, and are in euros. Eligibility, supplements and discounts are as for the InterRail Global Pass.

Price Level 1 – France, Germany, Great Britain: 3 days €291/194/126, 4 days €314/209/136, 6 days €404/269/175, 8 days €449/299/194. Price Level 2 – Austria, Norway (2nd class only), Spain, Sweden: 3 days €258/172/112, 4 days €287/191/124, 6 days €378/252/164, 8 days €436/290/189. Price Level 3 – Benelux, Denmark, Finland, Greece Plus, Italy, Ireland, Switzerland: 3 days €168/112/73, 4 days €209/139/90, 6 days €284/189/123, 8 days €344/229/149. Price Level 4 – Croatia, Czech Republic, Greece, Hungary, Poland, Portugal, Romania: 3 days €106/71/46, 4 days €134/89/58, 6 days €179/119/77, 8 days €209/139/90. Price Level 5 – Bulgaria, FYR Macedonia, Serbia, Slovakia, Slovenia, Turkey: 3 days €75/50/33, 4 days €104/69/45, 6 days €149/99/64, 8 days €179/119/77.

EURAIL GLOBAL PASS The various types of Eurail pass can be purchased by anyone resident outside Europe (but excluding residents of Russia and CIS or Turkey). The Eurail Global Pass is valid for unlimited travel on the national railways of 21 European countries, namely Austria, Belgium, Croatia, Czech Republic, Denmark, Finland, France, Germany, Greece, Hungary, Ireland (including Northern Ireland), Italy, Luxembourg, the Netherlands, Norway, Portugal, Romania, Slovenia, Spain, Sweden and Switzerland. Note that additional countries participate in the Eurail Select Pass, Eurail Regional Pass and Eurail One Country Pass schemes (see opposite).

Adult Eurail Global Passes are valid for first-class travel (naturally you can also travel in second class), whereas the under-26 Youth version is for 2nd class travel only. Versions are available for both consecutive days and flexi travel: fifteen days: adult $799, youth $519. Twenty-one days: adult $1039, youth $669. One month: adult $1289, youth $839. Two months: adult $1819, youth $1185. Three months: adult $2245, youth $1459. Ten days within two months: adult $945, youth $615. Fifteen days within two months: adult $1239, youth $805.

Children aged 4–11 pay half fare, and children under 4 travel free (except if a reservation for a separate seat or bed is required). Two or more people travelling together are eligible for the Saver rate, giving a reduction of 15% on the adult fare (there is no youth Saver, children aged 4–11 in the group pay half the Saver rate). For latest fares and details of supplements and bonuses see the Eurail website www.eurail.com (details of overseas agents are on www.eurailgroup.com).

EURAIL SELECT PASS For those visiting a smaller area of Europe, the **Eurail Select Pass** allows unlimited travel in 3, 4 or 5 adjoining countries selected from the following (note that some countries are grouped together and count as one): Austria; Bulgaria/Montenegro/Serbia; Benelux (Belgium/Netherlands/Luxembourg); Croatia/Slovenia; Denmark; Finland; France; Germany; Greece; Hungary; Republic of Ireland; Italy; Norway; Portugal; Romania; Spain; Sweden; Switzerland.

Adjoining means linked by a direct train (not through another country) or shipping line included in the Eurail scheme; for example Italy's links include Spain and Greece, and France can be linked with Ireland. The Select Pass is available for 5, 6, 8 or 10 travel days within a two-month period (the 5-country pass is also available for 15 days). The 5-day adult pass costs $505/565/625 for 3/4/5 countries respectively; 6 days costs $559/619/679, 8 days $665/725/785, 10 days $769/825/885, and the 5-country 15-day pass costs $1039 USD. The Saver pass for two or more people travelling together gives 15% reduction. The Youth (under 26) pass is priced at 65% of the adult price and children aged 4-11 travel at half the adult fare. As with the Gobal Pass, the adult version gives 1st-class travel, the youth version 2nd-class.

EURAIL REGIONAL PASS A **Eurail Regional Pass** allows unlimited travel in two European countries (or country combinations) as listed below. Conditions vary but all are available for 5, 6, 8 or 10 days within two months, and some also for 4, 7 or 9 days (Portugal-Spain also for 3 days). All are available in adult and saver 1st class versions (most also in 2nd class), and there is a youth 2nd class version for all except Portugal-Spain. Passes should be obtained before travelling to Europe, but certain passes are also for sale in the countries where the pass is valid (but not to European residents). For current prices see www.eurail.com and for further information see www.eurailtravel.com.

Regions available: Austria-Croatia/Slovenia, Austria-Czech Republic, Austria-Germany, Austria-Hungary, Austria-Switzerland, Benelux (Belgium, Netherlands, Luxembourg), Benelux-France, Benelux-Germany, Croatia/Slovenia-Hungary, Czech Republic-Germany, Denmark-Germany, Denmark-Sweden, Finland-Sweden, France-Germany, France-Italy, France-Spain, France-Switzerland, Germany-Poland, Germany-Switzerland, Greece-Italy, Hungary-Romania, Italy-Spain, Norway-Sweden, Portugal-Spain, Scandinavia (Denmark, Finland, Norway, Sweden).

Sample adult prices: France-Spain 4 days 1st/2nd class $409/355, 10 days 1st/2nd class $689/605; Hungary-Romania 5/10 days 1st class $275/409.

EURAIL ONE COUNTRY PASS A **Eurail One Country Pass** (previously called Eurail National Pass) allows unlimited travel in a single European country selected from the following: Austria, Bulgaria, Croatia, Czech Republic, Denmark, Finland, Greece, Hungary, Republic of Ireland, Italy, Norway, Poland, Portugal, Romania, Slovenia, Spain, Sweden. Each pass has its own

Rail Travel in Europe

characteristics regarding class of travel, number of travel days, and availability of saver, youth and child versions. A few also have discounts for seniors. For prices see www.eurail.com and for further information see www.eurailtravel.com. Sample adult prices: Spain 3–10 days $299–609 1st class, $239–$489 2nd class; Czech Republic 3–8days $169–395 1st class, $125–295 2nd class.

BALKAN FLEXIPASS   Gives unlimited 1st class travel in Bulgaria, Greece, FYR Macedonia, Montenegro, Romania, Serbia and Turkey for any 5, 10 or 15 days in one month. Available in the countries above (but not for residents of those countries), also in the USA (e.g. Rail Europe). Typical US prices: adults $256/447/539, youth (12–25) $153/268/324, senior (60+) $206/359/433. Children half adult fare. Supplements payable for IC trains. A 2nd class version appears to be available if purchased in the countries where it is valid.

BENELUX PASS   Unlimited rail travel throughout Belgium, Luxembourg, Netherlands for any 5 days in a month. Available in UK (e.g. International Rail) and USA, and from stations in Belgium and Luxembourg, but not the Netherlands. 1st class £202, 2nd class £128, under 26 (2nd class) £92. Not valid on Thalys.

EUROPEAN EAST PASS   Available to non-European residents; offers unlimited rail travel throughout Austria, Czech Republic, Hungary, Poland and Slovakia for any 5 days within a month. 1st class $299, 2nd class $209 (up to 5 extra days $36/28 per day). Children aged 4–11 half price. Discounts available on river cruises, steam trips in Hungary, Children's Railway, etc.

OTHER PASSES   Day tickets covering more than one country include the **Euregio Bodensee Tageskarte** (border region of Austria, Germany and Switzerland bordering Lake Constance), and **Saar–Lor–Lux** (Saturday or Sunday in Luxembourg, Saarbrücken area of Germany, and Lorraine area of France). Other passes covering a single country or a region of that country are shown later in the relevant Essentials panel for each country.

ALTERNATIVES TO RAIL   **BUSES**   To most people, buses simply aren't as much fun as trains for exploring Europe. However, in parts of southern Europe (such as Spain, Portugal and Greece) the bus may be a convenient add-on – making life easier where the train journeys are rather convoluted, or getting you to places the trains simply don't run. Local bus stations are often at or near rail stations, and you can usually buy tickets from the driver. For bargain-price long-distance express coach travel to over 40 cities across most of Europe, contact **Eurolines**, ☎0871 781 8181 (www.eurolines.co.uk). They also offer 15- and 30-day passes offering unlimited travel and you can make bookings for the next stage of your journey online as you go.

FLYING   If time is short, you might prefer flying within Europe and focusing on one or two countries. London's Stansted, Luton and Gatwick airports (each quite a way out of the centre) are the main departure points for budget and charter airlines, with plenty of inexpensive flights on offer. Increasingly, budget airlines such as easyJet and Ryanair are also running routes from the regional English, Scottish and Irish airports. For details of budget flights to Continental Europe from Britain, see pp16–23.

CARS You may get the best deals for car hire by booking from Britain (it pays to shop around).

Holiday Autos, ☎0870 400 0099 (www.holidayautos.co.uk) and **carhire3000**, ☎0800 358 7707 (www.carhire3000.com), often have good deals, and easyJet run a bargain car rental agency with online bookings (www.easycar.com). Other web-based operators include www.autosabroad.com, www.carhire4less.com and www.novacarhire.com. Check you're insured if the car gets damaged (read the small print for huge excess charges – you may have to pay considerably extra up front if you want to avoid the risk), and inspect the vehicle thoroughly before you drive off; some Mediterranean resorts have a notorious reputation for dodgy vehicles. The same goes for motorbikes (some hirers won't give you any insurance cover at all). Driving laws, standards and styles vary greatly within Europe.

WALKING Many of the rail journeys in this book traverse superlatively alluring scenery. If you want to immerse yourself in it, there's no better way than walking, be it a couple of hours round a lake or a fully kitted-out mountain trek.

Paths: The availability of walks varies hugely across the continent. In some countries, particularly Germany, Switzerland and Austria, walking is super-organised, with paths very clearly marked; conversely, in parts of southern Europe, including Greece and much of Spain, you've got to know what you're doing, as the mapping can be pretty useless and the paths can be hard to follow. France is covered by a dense network of Sentiers de Grande Randonnée (GRs) – long-distance paths – each with a number (such as GR10). A great thing about Alpine and other ski areas is that in summer many lifts stay open for walkers, cutting out steep ascents and descents and whisking you straight up to the sunny higher paths. These often have surprisingly level and easy options for the less intrepid, as well as being starting points for the high passes. There will usually be a few cosy cafés or mountain huts within walking distance.

When to go: In mountain areas such as the Alps and the Pyrenees you're more or less restricted to going between June and August as the weather can get wintry outside that time (which does mean some areas get pretty crowded). The famous Alpine meadows give glorious displays of wild flowers before the grass is cut for hay in early to mid-July.

Accommodation: Don't assume you can necessarily camp anywhere in mountain areas. The major mountain areas are dotted with manned huts that provide dormitory accommodation and food. The huts are marked on maps and there's often a small discount if you are a member of the National Hut Association. At peak times you should book ahead – contact the National Hut Association for the respective country (there is no umbrella organisation).

CYCLING If you want to get to the parts of Europe trains don't reach, a bicycle may be your answer, taking you via quiet roads and tracks into the heart of the country. Consider whether it's worth taking a bicycle with you or hiring once you're there. If you simply want to do a day ride from time to time, hiring can save you hassle, where it's available. Another option is to have a folding bike or dismantle your bike so that you can carry it in a bike bag as ordinary luggage.

Taking your bike abroad: You can still take bikes for free on many trains in Britain, though some routes require an advance reservation (generally £3), and bikes are barred from certain rush-hour services. On many ferries you can take the bike free as a foot passenger (but check with the ferry company first). For inland destinations in France and beyond you generally need to send a bike ahead separately as unaccompanied baggage and hope that your machine is there when you arrive. You can now book your bicycle onto Eurostar between London and Paris or Brussels, for a £20 charge (advance booking, subject to space being available). For other destinations, Eurostar guarantees that bicycles and other baggage sent ahead will arrive within 24 hours. Folding and dismantled bikes in bike bags no larger than a suitcase can be taken on Eurostar as normal baggage.

European Bike Express, ☎(01439) 422111 (www.bike-express.co.uk), operates cycle-carrying buses that head down from northern England to Dover, and into Europe by four routes into southwest France, Spain, the Mediterranean coast and the French Alps. You can join or leave at numerous points; you can also travel on one route and cycle across to meet the returning bus on another. Fares in 2010 are £214–234 return, £129 single.

Budget and charter airlines generally charge for carrying cycles, while many scheduled carriers don't. Flying can be the quickest and easiest way of reaching an inland starting point, but some baggage handlers aren't that careful with bikes; it's probably safest to wrap your machine in heavy duty plastic so that they can see what it is, and have it well insured. You may need to take off the pedals, turn the handlebars and let air out of the tyres, so make sure you have the right tools and a pump to put your bike back into a rideable state when you arrive. Get a detailed map of the airport area before you go: cycling out of a major European airport can be a nerve-wracking affair. Look for cycle paths and small back routes, or try to get your bike on a local train or bus to escape the congestion.

Transporting a bike: You can usually travel with your bike on local train services; you may need to buy a separate ticket for it. Typically on long-distance routes there are only occasional trains with luggage vans, often indicated on the timetable by a bicycle symbol. You can travel with your bike on these services, but may have to send it separately as registered luggage at other times. Long-distance buses, particularly in Southern Europe, will often take bikes for a small fee if they have a baggage compartment underneath. For further information about cycling matters (including taking bikes on ferries, European trains and planes, and routes abroad), join the **Cyclists' Touring Club (CTC)**, ☎0844 736 8450 (www.ctc.org.uk). Membership entitles you to fact sheets and online access to a range of information useful for planning a cycling trip abroad.

Hiring a bike: In France and many parts of northern Europe, cycles can easily be hired at major stations and bike shops. To check about availability of cycle hire, try emailing the Tourist Office for the area you want to see (we give websites for most of the towns and cities in this book, under Tourist Offices). Try asking for a discount if you want the bike for a week or so. In Paris the pioneering **Vélib** scheme (www.en.velib.paris.fr) has thousands of virtually free bikes for hire from points throughout the city: subscribe online or from service points at stations and elsewhere.

Where to cycle: Dutch, Belgian, German and Scandinavian towns and cities are usually well set up with cycle paths that link to the railway stations, and many other urban areas are investing in traffic calming and cycle-friendliness. Much of rural Europe has a good network of back roads ideal for cycling, which you can pick up by taking a local train to a country station. They go through the centres of historic towns which main routes pass by: find them with the help of a large-scale map. Belgium, the Netherlands, Denmark and Sweden have much flat country and are rarely too hot for cycling in summer. France has something for everyone: deep countryside and a spectacular coast in Brittany, sleepy villages and long but well-graded climbs and descents in the Alps and Pyrenees following Tour de France routes. Facilities are less developed in southern and eastern Europe but cycling is becoming more popular. In Spain, wearing a cycle helmet and reflective vest is compulsory in theory, but reportedly patchily enforced – with exemptions for long climbs and hot weather.

TRAVELLER'S GUIDE TO EUROPE

This chapter is full of helpful tips for anyone planning to travel around Europe. For information covering specific countries, see individual countries' Essentials sections.

ACCOMMODATION Compared to the UK, accommodation almost anywhere in continental Europe seems pretty good value, and generally prices get lower the further east and south you go. It's worth checking out that where you plan to stop doesn't have some major event that fills every available room in the city. In many European countries, you tend to pay by the room, so it can be much better value if you share. The quality of cheaper hotels in Eastern Europe may be less than inspiring and you could do better with a private room. This can be a good, in-expensive and friendly option (local Tourist Offices often have lists), and enterprising owners are increasingly setting up their own English-language websites), but you may be expected to stay for more than one night. Local Tourist Offices are almost always your best starting point if you haven't pre-booked. If they don't handle bookings themselves (there's usually a small charge), they will re-direct you to someone who does and/or supply you with the information to do it yourself – tell them your price horizons. If you just want to turn up and look around for somewhere to stay, a very useful rule is to remember that the cheapest places are often nearest the rail station. If you're concerned about noise, ask to look at the room first, and request a room at the back if it fronts a busy road. **Hostels** are a good bet if you're travelling solo or just want to cut down on costs. There's an ever-increasing supply of privately run backpackers' hostels across the continent, many with private rooms though in some cases you have to share with others in dormitories. Quite a lot of hostels have internet access, often for free. The 5000 or so 'official' youth hostels are part of Hostelling International: you can join through the youth hostel organisation in your own country before you travel, or you can buy an international membership on arrival at a hostel in Europe, or pay a small supplement. There's no age limit to joining, though some countries have rules giving preference to younger people (for example in Bavaria, southern Germany, priority is for under-26s). Accommodation varies from dormitories to single, twin or family rooms. Many offer inexpensive meals and many have self-catering and/or laundry facilities. All HI hostels and hostelling organisations are listed on www.hihostels.com. You can book some of the bigger hostels online through the website. Some hostels are open 24 hours, but most have curfews and lock-out times, and reception's hours are usually limited – check what they are and advise them if you are arriving out of hours. Reservation is advisable – especially in summer, when many hostels fill well in advance and even those with space are likely to limit your stay to three nights if you just turn up without booking. For listings of private and HI hostels, see www.hostels.com, www.hostelbookers.com, www.backpackglobe.com, www.hostelseurope.com and www.backpackeurope.com. **Camping** is obviously the cheapest accommodation if you're prepared to carry the equipment. There are campsites right across Europe, from basic (just toilets and showers) to luxury family-oriented sites with dining rooms, swimming pools and complexes of permanent tents. The drawback is that sites are often miles from city centres. Most Tourist Offices can provide a directory for their country. Or check out locations and costs of a wide range of sites through www.eurocampings.co.uk.

BORDERS Land borders between the EU (European Union) countries are virtually non-existent and it's only if you arrive/leave by air or sea that you're likely to encounter any formalities. Once you're within the EU's boundaries, there are no routine border controls between the 25 countries party to the Schengen Agreement (Austria, Belgium, Czech Republic, Denmark, Estonia, Finland, France, Germany, Greece, Hungary, Iceland, Italy, Latvia, Lithuania, Luxembourg, Malta, the Netherlands, Norway, Poland, Portugal, Slovakia, Slovenia, Spain, Sweden and Switzerland) but there are checks on entering the UK and Ireland. Some former Eastern bloc countries, however, still go through the full routine and you should be prepared for delays when crossing between East and West.

CHILDREN Most children find train travel a great novelty and thoroughly enjoy themselves. However, they can get bored on long journeys. Most tourist destinations in Europe are reasonably well adapted for children and babysitters are not hard to find (ask at the local Tourist Office); some southern European countries, such as Spain and Italy, are particularly child-friendly. Many hotels offer family rooms or provide a cot in a normal double. Many sights and forms of transport accept babies for free, and children under 12 for half price. For useful background reading try Brigitte Barta's *Travel with Children* (Lonely Planet) or www.travelforkids.com.

CLIMATE The climate in Europe is affected by three main factors: latitude (Scandinavia is colder than Spain); altitude (the Alps are colder than Belgium); and distance from the sea (the Central European countries, such as the Czech Republic, can suffer surprisingly harsh winters and unexpectedly hot summers). That said, most of Europe has a pretty gentle climate compared to many other regions of the world. Rain is common throughout the year, except along some stretches of the Mediterranean. The summer heat rarely exceeds 30°C/86°F, except in the far south (the Mediterranean area), where it can be agonisingly hot (occasionally even 40°C/104°F) in high summer. Winter tends to be grey and wet, with temperatures hovering around -5/+5°C and relatively little snow, except in Scandinavia, the high mountains and parts of central Europe. In the far north, midsummer is the best time to travel, to take advantage of the ultra-long days. Almost everywhere else, May and September are the best months, and have the added advantage of avoiding school holiday crowds. A useful website is www.weatheronline.co.uk.

CONSULAR SERVICES/EMBASSIES Most embassies/consulates/high commissions will lend a helping hand if their nationals have real problems – and charge a small fee for any services rendered. Help should be available if: your passport is stolen (or a travel document that will get you home); there's a death or serious accident (advice on procedures, next of kin notified – probably also sympathetic help); you go to jail – don't expect sympathy, nor direct intervention, but they will explain your rights and tell you how to get a lawyer. Should something happen to make the area dangerous (an act of God, local rebellion, etc), contact your embassy to register your presence and ask for advice. In case of real financial trouble, embassies may agree to make a small loan or contact next of kin with a request for help, but they do not look kindly on people who have simply overspent. Don't expect them to act as surrogate travel agents, banks, interpreters, etc. If your own country has no representation, get advice from one with which it has ties, e.g. Commonwealth citizens can try the British Embassy.

CURRENCY The Euro (€) is the currency of Austria, Belgium, Cyprus, Finland, France, Germany, Greece, the Republic of Ireland, Italy, Luxembourg, Malta, the Netherlands, Portugal, Slovakia, Slovenia and Spain; notes and coins issued by each country can be spent in any of the other Euro countries. The Euro is also legal tender in Andorra, Kosovo, Monaco, Montenegro, San Marino and the Vatican City. Most European countries place no limit on the import/export of currencies. However, Russia and Belarus state that the amount taken out must not exceed the amount taken in, so always declare large amounts of cash on arrival. Carry **credit or debit cards** (which can be used in cash machines; credit cards usually charge per transaction made, both types of card charge interest from the time you make the withdrawal) and **traveller's cheques** (usually best in the local currency; if you're travelling through several countries, cheques in sterling or US dollars will probably do fine; keep the counterfoil separate from the cheques, as you can be reimbursed if you lose the cheques; record which cheques you have cashed). Note that, unlike in the US, you can't commonly spend travellers' cheques like bank notes in ordinary shops and restaurants, but need to change them into cash at a bank first. Though it's obviously risky to carry wads of notes, you should always try to obtain some **local currency** before you enter a new country. If you are unable to do so and arrive outside banking hours, the best bet (albeit an expensive option) is to ask the receptionist at a big hotel to change some for you. Try to always carry one or two coins of each denomination for use in station lockers, WCs etc. In border towns and on cross-border transport, you can almost always use either of the relevant currencies (a good way to dispose of excess coins), but you generally pay less if you choose the one in which prices are marked. A useful online currency converter is www.oanda.com.

CUSTOMS Importing narcotics and offensive weapons is banned throughout Europe, and pornography is banned in many countries. Never carry luggage across borders for other people. If you have to take a prescribed drug on a regular basis, carry a doctor's letter to prove it's legitimate. There are often restrictions on the import and export of plants and fresh foodstuffs (particularly meat and meat products), as well as certain souvenirs (such as those made of tortoiseshell) and you might be asked to abandon them at borders.

EU customs allowances: Whether within or outside the European Union, the principle is that goods taken across borders should be for your own use (including gifts), not for re-sale. EU member states (Austria, Belgium, Bulgaria, Czech Republic, Denmark, Estonia, Finland, France, Germany, Greece, Hungary, the Republic of Ireland, Italy, Latvia, Lithuania, Luxembourg, Malta, the Netherlands, Poland, Portugal, Romania, Slovakia, Slovenia, Spain, Sweden), with the exemption of Cyprus, have a common tobacco, alcohol and perfume basic allowance which applies to anyone aged 17 or over. There are no restrictions between the EU countries for goods bought in ordinary shops and including local taxes, but you may be questioned if you have amounts exceeding the following: 3,200 cigarettes (but only 200 from Bulgaria, Romania, Estonia and Lithuania), 200 cigars, 400 cigarillos and 3 kg tobacco plus 90 litres wine (maximum 60 litres sparkling), plus 10 litres alcohol over 22% volume (e.g. most spirits), plus 20 litres alcohol under 22% volume (e.g. port and sherry), plus 110 litres beer. The duty-free allowances for goods bought outside the EU are much more restricted: 200 cigarettes or 50 cigars or 100 cigarillos or 250 g tobacco, plus 4 litres still table wine, plus 1 litre spirits or 2 litres sparkling or fortified wine, plus 60 ml perfume, plus £340 worth of all other goods including gifts and souvenirs. The tobacco and alcohol allowances do not apply to under-17s. Some EU countries have more generous tobacco allowances for non-Europeans arriving from outside Europe – check with the duty-free shop or your carrier. **Allowances for those returning home:** Australia: goods to the value of Aust$900 (half for those under 18) plus 250 cigarettes or 250 g tobacco/cigars and 2.25 litres alcohol. Canada: 50 cigars and 200 cigarettes and 200 g tobacco plus 1.14 litre alcohol, or 1.5 litre wine or 24 x 355 ml bottles/tins beer, as well as goods not exceeding a total value of Can$750. New Zealand: goods to the value of NZ$700. Anyone over 17 may also take 200 cigarettes or 250 g tobacco or 50 cigars or a combination of tobacco products not exceeding 250 g in all plus 4.5 litres of beer or wine and 1.125 litres spirits. South Africa: goods to a total value of 3000 Rand. Those aged 18 or more are allowed 200 cigarettes and 50 cigars and 250 g tobacco plus 2 litres wine and 1 litre spirits plus 50 ml perfume and 250 ml toilet water. Republic of Ireland and UK: standard EU regulations apply (see above). USA: goods to the value of US$800 as long as you have been out of the country for at least 48 hrs and only use your allowance once every 30 days. Anyone over 21 is also allowed 1 litre alcohol plus 50 (non-Cuban) cigars or 200 cigarettes or a reasonable quantity of tobacco.

DISABILITIES, TRAVELLERS WITH Usually only the more modern trains and more upmarket hotels cater for travellers with disabilities, who need to reserve and ensure there is someone on hand to help. The amount of advance warning required for trains varies; Austrian State Railways ask for three days' notice, while the ever-efficient Swiss need only one day. In many European stations the platforms are quite low and passengers have to climb steep steps to board trains. Once aboard, only the more modern carriages provide space for a wheelchair; otherwise, space will be provided in the baggage car. Express services, such as the French TGV and the Spanish AVE, have good facilities, while some Scandinavian trains have adapted hydraulic lifts, accessible toilets and spacious compartments. Some national rail offices and Tourist Offices have leaflets about rail travel for the disabled. A few national networks offer discount passes for the disabled. The best routes to travel include the main lines in Scandinavia, Switzerland, Germany, the Netherlands and France. The worst facilities are in Turkey, Spain, Hungary, Greece, Bulgaria, the Czech Republic and Slovakia. UK information: RADAR, Unit 12, City Forum, 250 City Road, London EC1V 8AF; ☎(020) 7250 3222 (www.radar.org.uk) can help with information on rail stations, airports, seaports and other transport matters across Europe concerning travellers with disabilities. US information: SATH (Society for Accessible Travel and Hospitality), 347 5th Avenue, Suite 605, New York NY 10016; ☎(212) 447 7284; www.sath.org. Australia: National Disability Service (NDS), 33 Thessiger Court, Deakin, ACT 2605, ☎(02) 6283 3200, www.nds.org.au.

DISCOUNTS In many countries reductions are available on public transport and on entrance fees for senior citizens, students and the young. Carry proof of your status, e.g. an official document that shows your age or an International Student Identity Card (ISIC; see p45) from your student union or travel agents such as STA. Some destinations offer (for a small fee) a book of discount vouchers covering anything from museums to restaurants.

DRIVING If you want to hire a motor vehicle while you are away, check requirements with the AA/RAC, or your own national motoring organisation, well before you leave, so that you have time to get any necessary documentation and additional insurance cover. To hire a vehicle (except a moped), you usually have to be over 21, with two years' driving experience. In most European countries your national licence is valid for up to six months, but you may need a translation as well and it can be easier to get an international licence.

ELECTRICITY With a few exceptions (notably the UK, which uses 230/240V), the European countries use 220V. The shape of plugs varies and, if you are taking any sort of electrical gadget, you should take a travel adaptor (easily purchased at airports or electrical shops). For details on which plug for which country, see www.kropla.com.

HEALTH There are no compulsory **vaccination** requirements. However, it is always advisable to keep your tetanus protection up to date and vaccination against typhoid and hepatitis A is also a good idea. You must be able to produce a certificate against yellow fever if you have been in a yellow fever endemic zone in the six days before entering Europe. **Health insurance** is strongly advised, especially if you are a non-EU citizen or are visiting non-EU countries. EU citizens should get a European Health Insurance Card or EHIC (available free from post offices or online through www.ehic.org.uk) which gives you free medical cover in other EU countries, though it will not cover costs such as mountain rescue and repatriation. Note that this has replaced the old E111. It's worth visiting a **pharmacy** before consulting a doctor: European pharmacists tend to be well trained and may well save you medical bills. Although most of Europe is temperate, there is a definite risk of **sunburn** in the south and in high mountain areas. Heat exhaustion is another hazard of travelling at hot times of the year, so don't overdo it and keep taking in plenty of fluids. If you use them, bring condoms with you if travelling to remoter parts and Catholic countries. **Animal hazards:** the risk of rabies or snake bites is very small, but be wary of stray and wild animals, and carry a stick to ward off dogs if you're walking in the countryside. Lyme disease – caught from ticks in undergrowth – is present in Central European forests (long trousers and long-sleeved shirts are a useful method of avoidance); symptoms are similar to arthritis and if they show up within three months of possible exposure ask your doctor for a blood test – early treatment is nearly always effective. **Tap water:** Most tap water in Europe is safe. Boil or sterilise all tap water (including the water you use to brush your teeth) if you think there may be cause for concern – or use only bottled water if you really want to be sure.

Traveller's Guide to Europe

HITCHHIKING AND LIFT SHARING Hitching, which used to be fun and a good way to meet local people is now often thought to be too risky, and isn't advisable for lone women. In rural areas used to hikers, you may well get a lift if you look harmless enough, but don't rely on it. There are signs of a revival though: the website www.bugeurope.com has some useful hints, and some cities and big events such as music festivals have internet-based lift share schemes to match up drivers and passengers. See also www.liftshare.com and www.freewheelers.com.

INSURANCE Take out travel insurance that covers your health as well as your belongings. It should also give cancellation cover and include an emergency flight home if something goes really wrong. If you are likely to do something that might be classified as risky (e.g. ski, drive a moped, dive), make sure your policy does not exclude that risk. Annual travel insurance policies are often good value if you're planning more than one trip a year.

INTERNET ACCESS Finding a place to go online isn't much of a problem nowadays, unless you're really off the beaten track. At many hostels, there's internet access – often cheap or even free – and in most towns and cities there are internet cafés and sometimes internet points at rail stations, airports and other strategic points. Check before you leave that you have a webmail account that you can log into remotely (and obviously don't forget your user name and password – or change them to something memorable): it's easy to set up a free internet-accessible account via providers such as www.hotmail.com, but if you already have an internet service provider it's likely there's a way to pick up mail away from your own computer via their website. An increasing number of city centres and other places such as airports also have wireless networks.

LANGUAGE You can pretty much rely on English in much of Scandinavia, the Netherlands and tourist hot spots such as Prague, the Spanish costas and many Greek resorts. But you'll need at least to attempt to speak other languages if you're venturing further around Europe. Along with their series of phrase guides covering eleven individual European languages, Thomas Cook publish two phrase-books (both £5.99) with over 300 phrases, each translated and with phonetic spellings: the *European Phrasebook* covers French, German, Italian, Spanish, Portuguese, Polish, Czech, Hungarian, Romanian, Bulgarian, Greek and Turkish; the *Eastern European Phrasebook* features Bulgarian, Croatian, Czech, Estonian, Hungarian, Latvian, Lithuanian, Polish, Romanian, Russian, Slovenian and Ukrainian; for details see www.thomascookpublishing.com and select 'travel essentials'. Check out www.bbc.co.uk/languages for all sorts of exercises, tutorials and MP3 downloads. Keep a pen and paper handy at all times so you can ask people to write down such figures as times and prices, and so you can write down words if others can't understand your pronunciation.

PASSPORTS AND VISAS Ensure that your identity document is valid well beyond the end of your stay. EU citizens can travel to other EU countries with a National Identity Card instead of a full passport. Those who aren't citizens of Western Europe, Australia, Canada, New Zealand, South Africa or the USA should check about visas with the relevant embassies. Otherwise, consult the Essentials panels of each country chapter for visa regulations (bear in mind these can change overnight; always check before going), and allow plenty of time to obtain them. Agencies can speed up the process, but you'll have to pay for the privilege. Generally speaking, Australians, Canadians and citizens of New Zealand need visas for some Eastern European countries, while UK and US residents only need visas for certain former Soviet states such as Belarus, Moldova and Russia (but not Ukraine at time of writing), plus Turkey (where you pay for visas at the point of entry). Anyone planning to stay more than 90 days in any single country may need a visa. Some countries will refuse entry if you don't have an onward/return ticket and enough money to cover the cost of expenses during your stay. A credit card is a practical way of avoiding precise cash requirements.

SALES TAX Value Added Tax (known as VAT in the UK) is automatically added to most goods in Western European countries. The level is usually 10–20%. In most countries (except Greece), non-residents can reclaim the tax on major spending; each country sets a different minimum. The refund is also intended to apply to only one article, but if you buy several things in the same shop on the same day, the authorities seldom argue. Ask the shop assistant to fill in a tax refund form for you. Show the form, the receipt and the goods to customs on leaving the country and they will give you an official export certificate. This can sometimes be exchanged on the spot (necessary in Scandinavia); alternatively, post the certificate back to the shop (within a month) and they should send the refund.

SECURITY Things can certainly go wrong for any traveller, but don't get paranoid: Europe's still generally safe and fear of crime should not spoil your trip. Travel insurance softens the blow if you have possessions stolen (in which case be sure to get the required paperwork from the police as proof for your claim). You can cut the chances of being ripped off by carrying valuables in a money belt or in a pouch concealed under your shirt, and by being extra-vigilant at cash machines (ATMs) and with bags at stations and airports.

SINGLE TRAVELLERS It can be an expensive business travelling solo in Europe, as accommodation is often priced per room regardless of how many people are sleeping in it – or at best you might be paying about three-quarters the cost of a double. Then there are the other hassles – looking after your belongings, personal safety and (for some) loneliness. Staying at hostels gets round some of these problems, though the basic comforts most offer will not be to everyone's taste. We have, however, had a complaint from one senior traveller that she wasn't admitted to HI hostels in some parts of Europe, on grounds (apparently) of age, despite holding an Irish youth hostelling card. Some women travelling on their own might also feel more comfortable wearing a 'wedding' ring and carrying a photo of someone purporting to be their husband or boyfriend.

SMOKING Many public places ban smoking and, even where it is allowed, there may be a special area for smokers. In some countries, such as France, Italy and Spain, prohibitions are often ignored by locals, but if in doubt ask before lighting up.

STUDENT AND YOUTH TRAVEL If you are a full-time student, under 26, or a teacher of any age, you can buy a card entitling you to a range of discounts on accommodation, museums, theatres, transport etc, with wide-ranging benefits offered in 'gateway cities' (which include Amsterdam, Athens, Barcelona, Berlin, Edinburgh, Frankfurt, Glasgow, Liverpool, London, Madrid, Manchester, Munich, Paris, Prague and Rome); it also gives access to a 24-hour helpline. Details can be found at www.isic.org. Allow time before leaving home to get one, as you will need to show documents and have a passport-sized photograph. In the UK, the International Students' Identity Card (ISIC), the International Youth Travel Card (IYTC – for under-26s) and the International Teacher Identity Card (ITIC) cost £9 (similar prices in other countries), and are available from the UK issuer www.isiccard.com, by phone ☎(0871) 230 0040 or from branches of STA Travel. There's a £2 handling fee for postal applications.

TELEPHONES AND MOBILE PHONES (CELLPHONES) You'll be able to use your **mobile (cell) phone** anywhere with a signal in Europe if it's enabled for 'roaming' (ask your network provider before you go if you're not sure), but this can be expensive and you may be charged to receive as well as make calls. Using texts (SMS) is the cheapest way of staying in touch. If you'll be making a lot of calls in one country it may be worth buying a local pre-pay SIM card for your phone while you're there. The UK ISIC card deal (see above) includes a roaming SIM card which you can pre-pay. Since 2009, charges for international mobile calls, texts and internet access have been capped across the EU, with a text costing a maximum of about 10p (plus tax), and a voice call about 45p a minute to make and 20p a minute to receive, but this may not apply if your phone company is outside the EU. For details on mobile phone systems and which phone adaptors are required in different countries, see www.kropla.com. **Payphones** are common in European towns and everywhere is on direct-dial. Increasingly, payphones take pre-paid cards (commonly available from newsstands, local shops and cafés) rather than coins: you may be able to use your credit card too. The student travel website www.isic.org has details on the ISIConnect Phonecard, which also has voicemail and text messaging services. You can pick up messages via phones or the website, and can keep travel document numbers encrypted on the 'online travel safe'. Avoid phones in hotel rooms: they invariably cost exorbitantly.

TIME ZONES United Kingdom, Ireland and Portugal: Greenwich Mean Time in winter, and GMT+1 hr in summer. GMT+1 hr in winter, GMT+2 hrs in summer: Austria, Belgium, Croatia, the Czech Republic, Denmark, France, Germany, Hungary, Italy, Luxembourg, the Netherlands, Norway, Poland, Slovakia, Slovenia, Spain, Sweden and Switzerland. GMT+2 hrs in winter, GMT+3 hrs in summer: Bulgaria, Estonia, Finland, Greece, Latvia, Lithuania, Romania and Turkey. Clocks change on the last weekend of March and October.

Traveller's Guide to Europe

WHAT TO TAKE   Backpack and day sack; sort your luggage into see-through polythene bags and take plastic bags for dirty clothes, etc, and elastic bands for sealing them. If travelling with a friend, divide all your possessions between two items of luggage, so that if one goes missing you both have enough to get by on. You cannot take sharp objects, like nail scissors, or liquids, gels, aerosols and pastes, such as drinks, toothpaste or sun cream, in hand luggage on planes. You can take only very limited quantities of liquids, etc, in containers no larger than 100ml, and they all have to fit into a small (20cm by 20cm) transparent resealable plastic bag you show at the baggage check – anything else gets confiscated. However, you can buy as much liquid as you like at the airport shops once you go through the check, providing you don't exceed your airline's hand baggage allowance.

Clothing: Lightweight clothing, preferably that doesn't need ironing; smart casual clothes for evening wear, at least three sets of underwear, swimsuit, sun hat, garments to cover bare arms and legs (essential in some churches/temples; women may need headscarves); non-slip footwear. All-purpose hiking boots are useful for big walks around cities – or rubber sandals with chunky soles, good when it's hot; flip flops for the shower, etc.

First aid/medical: Insect repellent and antihistamine cream, sun-screen cream, after-sun lotion, something for headaches and tummy troubles, prescription medicines, antiseptic spray or cream, medicated wet-wipes, plasters for blisters, bandage, contraceptives and tampons (especially if visiting Eastern Europe, where they can be difficult to get). Spare spectacles/contact lenses and a copy of your prescription. Take a European Health Insurance Card (EHIC) if you are from the EU and travelling in EU countries (see Health, p42, and Insurance, p43).

Documents: Passport, tickets (or printouts of flight times and booking reference numbers if you're using a ticketless airline), photocopies of passport/visas (helps if you lose the passport itself) and travel insurance, traveller's cheques counterfoil, passport photos, student card, the numbers of your credit cards and where to phone if you lose them.

Other items: A couple of lightweight towels, lightweight sleeping bag (optional), sheet liner (for hostelling), inflatable travel pillow, earplugs, eyemask, small bar of soap (hotels in Germany and Austria, for example, tend not to supply soap), water-bottle, pocket knife, torch (flashlight), sewing kit, padlock and chain (for anchoring luggage), safety matches, mug and basic cutlery, toothbrush, shampoo (can also be used for washing clothes), string (for a washing line), travel adapter, universal bath plug, MP3 player, sunglasses, noise-reducing headphones (which make air and train travel much more peaceful; you don't even have to be plugged into music, as the white noise eliminates the low-frequency roar), alarm clock, notepad and pen, pocket calculator (to convert money),'mobile phone and charger, a contact list of important phone numbers/addresses/email addresses (it's worth emailing this to yourself too), a money-belt and a good book/game (for long journeys).

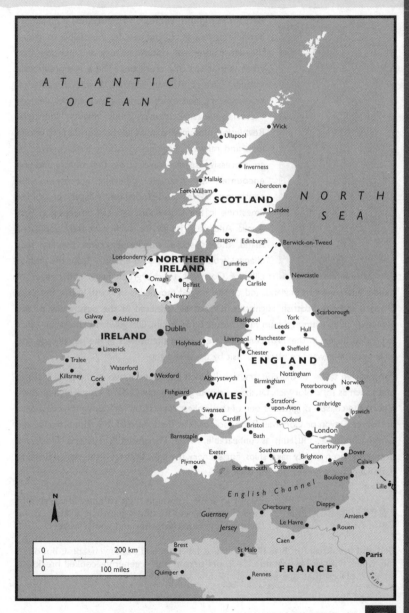

ATLANTIC
OCEAN

Wick
Ullapool

Inverness

Mallaig
Aberdeen
Fort William
SCOTLAND
NORTH
Dundee
SEA

Glasgow   Edinburgh   Berwick-on-Tweed

Londonderry   NORTHERN   Dumfries
IRELAND   Newcastle
Omagh   Belfast   Carlisle
Sligo   Newry

Galway   Athlone   Scarborough
Blackpool   York
IRELAND   Leeds   Hull
Dublin   Liverpool   Manchester
Limerick   Holyhead   Chester   Sheffield
ENGLAND
Tralee   Nottingham
Killarney   Cork   Waterford   Wexford   Aberystwyth   Birmingham   Peterborough   Norwich
Fishguard   WALES   Stratford-   Cambridge
upon-Avon   Ipswich
Swansea   Oxford
Cardiff   Bristol   London
Barnstaple   Bath
Canterbury   Dover
Exeter   Southampton   Brighton   Rye   Calais
Plymouth   Bournemouth   Portsmouth   Boulogne
Lille

English Channel
Cherbourg   Dieppe
Guernsey   Amiens
Jersey   Le Havre   Rouen
Caen
Brest   St Malo   FRANCE
Quimper   Rennes   Paris
Seine

N

0   200 km
0   100 miles

United Kingdom

Britain (England, Wales and Scotland) is an almost bewildering mix of old and new. It's impossible to ignore the dense layers of culture, history and heritage that greet you at virtually every turn. There are prehistoric standing stones, Roman remains, medieval cathedral cities, literary landscapes, maritime mementoes, demure Victorian seaside resorts and mighty Industrial Revolution monuments such as the world's first textile mills and railways. Regional variations have survived to an impressive degree: travel across the country and you encounter, for example, different accents in the southwest, Wales and Yorkshire, villages of golden limestone in the Cotswolds, and half-timbering in East Anglia. And, surprisingly for such a densely populated island, there's some wonderfully rural scenery that changes from one valley to the next – from the granite cliffs of Cornwall, to the green fields and hedges of middle and southern England, and to the rugged mountains of north Wales, the Lake District and the Scottish Highlands. It's not all fossilised in the past: many of the industrial cities – among them Manchester, Birmingham, Glasgow and Liverpool – that expanded hugely in the 19th century have revived themselves in the last decade and have become rewarding places to visit by day and night.

For a varied taster of the country, visit London plus one or two of the great historic cities such as York, Norwich, Durham, Edinburgh, Glasgow, Oxford, Cambridge or Bath. Get to the coast – Brighton is one of the liveliest resorts, or walk along the coast path in Dorset, Devon or Cornwall. For a look back at the Industrial Revolution, Ironbridge Gorge Industrial Museum is unbeatable, while Portsmouth's Historic Dockyard preserves three mighty naval ships. For scenery, the Lake District is the star of Britain's national parks, a great place for walking.

ACCOMMODATION

Except in some resorts in high summer, there should rarely be a problem finding somewhere to stay. At the cheapest level are **campsites** and **youth hostels**.

Bed and breakfast (or 'B & B') is the next level up, and not the cheapest, but often fair value, with prices around £15–30 per person plus a generous cooked breakfast: smaller places that are effectively a few spare rooms in someone's home or

ESSENTIALS

Population 61.4m **Capital** London **Time Zone** Winter GMT, summer GMT+1.

CLIMATE

Cool, wet winters, mild spring and autumn, winter can be more extreme. Wetter in the west. Aug and Bank Holiday weekends busiest in tourist areas.

CURRENCY

Pounds Sterling (£). $1 = £0.61; €1 = £0.87.

EMBASSIES AND CONSULATES IN LONDON

Aus: Australia House, Strand, WC2B 4LA, ☎(020) 7379 4334. **Can**: 1 Grosvenor Sq., W1K 4AB, ☎(020) 7258 6600. **Ire**: 17 Grosvenor Pl., SW1X 7HR, ☎(020) 7235 2171. **NZ**: New Zealand House, 80 Haymarket, SW1Y 4TQ, ☎(020) 7930 8422. **SA**: South Africa House, Trafalgar Sq., WC2N 5DP, ☎(020) 7451 7299. **USA**: 24 Grosvenor Sq., W1A 1AE, ☎(020) 7499 9000.

LANGUAGE

English, plus, in a very small way, Welsh and Gaelic.

OPENING HOURS

Banks: Mon–Fri 0930–1530. Some open Sat morning. **Shops**: Mon–Sat 0900–1730. Many supermarkets and some small shops open longer, plus Sun. **Museums**: usually Mon–Sat 0900/1000–1730/1800, half-day Sun.

POST OFFICES

Usually Mon–Fri 0930–1730, Sat 0930–1300; stamps sold in newsagents, etc.

PUBLIC HOLIDAYS

England and Wales: 1 Jan; Good Fri; Easter Mon; May Day (first Mon May); Spring Bank Holiday (last Mon May); Summer Bank Holiday (last Mon Aug); 25, 26 Dec. Variations in Scotland and Northern Ireland.

PUBLIC TRANSPORT

Inter-city buses are cheaper, but slower, than trains. Main operator: **National Express** (www.nationalexpress.com). Alternatively, try **megabus** (www.megabus.com) for low cost national travel. Most town networks are good, but rural services patchy. National enquiry service: **Traveline** ☎0871 200 2233 (10p per minute plus 6p to connect) (www.traveline.org) covers most of the country.

RAIL PASSES

IR (see p27). **All-Line Rover**: unlimited travel on most National Rail services: 7 days £650/430 (1st/2nd class), 14 days £990/650 (1st/2nd class). **Freedom of Scotland Travelpass**: valid on all rail services within Scotland and to Berwick and Carlisle in England. Also valid on all Caledonian McBrayne ferries, and on many bus services. Holders are entitled to a 10% discount on Caledonian Sleeper services. 4 out of 8 days £111; 8 out of 15 days £148 (not valid before 0915 Mon–Fri). **Freedom of Wales Flexi Pass**: allows 4 days travel in an 8-day period and bus travel for all 8 days. Also valid on the Ffestiniog and Welsh Highland (Caernarfon) Railways, and offers discounted travel on many other tourist and heritage railways. 4 out of 8 days £74.00 (not valid before 0915 Mon–Fri). A 34% discount on the price of the passes above is available to holders of Senior/ Disabled/16–25 Railcards (note that 16–25 Railcards are **not** entitled to a discount on First Class All Line Rovers). **BritRail** (non-UK residents only), can only be bought before arriving in Britain. Available in 'consecutive day' and 'flexipass' versions (prices shown are for the 'flexipass'). **BritRail Pass:** valid on all National Rail services in England, Scotland and Wales. 3/4/8/15 days within 2 months: 1st class $375/465/679/1025, standard class $255/315/459/689. **BritRail England Pass:** valid on National Rail services within England only. 3/4/8/15 days within 2 months: 1st class $305/379/549/819, standard class $205/255/369/549. **BritRail All Britain + Ireland Pass:** valid on all National Rail services in England, Scotland and Wales, and on all rail services in Northern Ireland and the Republic of Ireland. 5/10 days within 1 month only: 1st class $699/1245, standard class $469/839.

Other 2-month passes are available covering London and southeast England, and central Scotland. For full details of all passes and to order, visit www.britrail.com

RAIL TRAVEL

Website: www.nationalrail.co.uk. Passenger services run by private sector companies; booking office staff will give cheapest fare if asked. National enquiry number ☎0845 748 4950. Fast trains, comfortable and frequent; 1st and standard class. Other long, medium and short-distance regional services, often standard class only. Refreshments usually available on trains that have 1st class. Sleepers: cabins are two-berth or (higher charge) single. Reservation (essential for sleepers) available for most long-distance services and is normally free of charge. Travel between Sat morning and Sun afternoon is often interrupted by engineering works when buses may replace trains. Online booking up to 3 days before departure, and timetable information: www.thetrainline.com. For Northern Ireland see www.translink.co.uk.

TELEPHONES

Pay phones take coins; many take credit or debit cards. Dial in: ☎+44; omit initial 0 from code. Outgoing: ☎00 + country code. Emergency services: ☎999 or 112.

TIPPING

Tip 10% in restaurants, but not in pubs, self-service restaurants or bars; there is no need to tip in restaurants where the service is included (this is becoming increasingly common). Tip taxis (10%) hailed in the street, but you do not need to tip minicab drivers (where you order a cab by phone and agree a price).

TOURIST INFORMATION

Websites: www.visitbritain.com, www.enjoyengland.com, www.visitscotland.com, www.visitwales.co.uk, www.discovernorthernireland.com. Britain and London Visitor Centre, 1 Regent St, London SW1Y 4XT. ☎0870 156 6366 (London info only). Local tourist offices in most towns.

VISAS

Visas not needed by EU citizens, or by tourists from Australia, Canada, New Zealand, South Africa and USA.

farmhouse are often the most comfortable and friendly. **Tourist Information Centres** can usually book in the area, sometimes for a small deposit that is refunded when you pay your bill. Alternatively, in tourist areas it's usually easy to find places to stay just by strolling likely-looking streets. Some pubs have inexpensive accommodation, though they can be noisy.

Large **hotels** are generally expensive. There's a wide choice of country house-style hotels in historic buildings, often in remote locations. **VisitBritain, AA (Automobile Association)** and other organisations each publish guides with different rating systems. There's a very extensive network of youth hostels (www.yha.org.uk; beds £10–25).

FOOD AND DRINK

These days, British cuisine is no longer a contradiction in terms. The notion of cooking as a creative pastime rather than a chore has entered the country's consciousness, and now the top chefs are philosopher-kings who advise the government on matters of nutrition. Eating out has progressed immeasurably in the last 20 years, with an explosion in variety and quality, with international, specialised ethnic (particularly **Italian, Hong Kong Chinese, Indian** and **Thai**), **whole food/vegetarian** and **fast food** available in most medium-sized and larger towns. Famously British, **fish and chips** are still going strong, and traditionally features deep-fried battered haddock or cod with thickly sliced chips (fries). If you want to start your day with an inexpensive meal that could easily see you through until dinner, seek out the **Full English** breakfast (often available in B&Bs), a cornucopia of carbs and calories that consists of bread, eggs, sausages, bacon, mushrooms and tomatoes – all fried. Do be aware, though, that this dish is known informally as the 'heart attack on a plate', and, delicious as it is, you would be hard pressed to find a doctor who would recommend it as a dietary staple. **Pub food** is generally the best-value sit-down fare, though some of it is pre-cooked and frozen by distributors and bought in by the pubs.

Britain's food profile has always been notable for its wide regional variations; as you travel around, you'll have the opportunity of sampling such delicacies as **Lancashire hotpot, Yorkshire pudding** and **Cornish pasties**, as well as no fewer than 700 different types of cheese. If you're in London and feeling adventurous, you might head to the East End and try **jellied eels**.

Great Britain's most traditional drink is **tea** (taken with milk, and often with sugar, too), though the various types of American-style coffee are becoming the daytime beverage of choice of busy professional types. When it comes to down-time drinking, the UK has a well-established tradition of alcohol consumption. Naturally conditioned brown 'real ale' is served in pubs from long wooden handpumps that sit on the counter, or is dispensed direct from the barrel. It's slightly less chilled than pasteurised beer or lager; it varies greatly in taste and character, and there's an increasing amount of choice. 'Bitter' is the most popular of these brown beers. Cider is an alcoholic apple drink, stronger than beer and occasionally available in 'real' draught form, which can be sweet or acidically dry. All come in either pint or half pint measures.

Wherever you are in the country, you won't have to look far to find a pub. Many are now open all day, and Britain's fondness for pub culture has survived the ban on smoking in public areas. (If you want to smoke, you are now legally required to go outside, but fear not: you won't be alone out there.)

Britons' predilections for eating well and being in the proximity of a supply of alcohol have been most harmoniously synthesised in the phenomenon of the **gastropub**, which was invented in London in 1991. The standard of the fare in these establishments is much higher than that of traditional pub grub, and can actually be very good value.

UNITED KINGDOM: LONDON

Its gateway airports and rail links to the Continent, reinforced by the direct **Eurostar** services through the Channel Tunnel to Paris and Brussels, make **London** a natural starting point for overseas visitors embarking on a rail tour of Europe. Though it can't compete in terms of sustained physical beauty with, say, Paris or Rome, London is undoubtedly one of the world's great cities – with a huge number of indoor attractions, concerts and theatres. It's an expensive place to stay, but this can be offset by visiting the many free museums and exploring on foot. There's an excellent range of possible day trips by rail, some of which are listed here.

> **AREAS FOR WALKING**
> include St James's/ Westminster, the Inns of Court/City, the South Bank, Hampstead, Richmond and the Regent's Canal between Camden and Little Venice.
>
> Central London is pretty safe (although be wary of thieves in crowded places). Women on their own should avoid the King's Cross area.

ARRIVAL AND DEPARTURE

There are 16 main-line rail stations (all linked by Underground trains) in Central London. The most important are **Victoria** (trains to Gatwick and the south coast); **Waterloo** (southwest, including Portsmouth for ferries to France and Spain; London Visitor Centre tourist office); **Liverpool Street** (eastern England, including services to Harwich for ferries to the Netherlands and Scandinavia; see p23); **King's Cross** (northeast and Scotland); **Euston** (West Midlands, northwest and Scotland); **Paddington** (west and Wales); and **St Pancras** (Eurostar services to Europe, plus Sheffield and East Midlands). For information about trains to Continental Europe, consult the *Thomas Cook European Rail Timetable* or contact **Rail Europe**, ☎0844 848 4064 (www.raileurope.co.uk), or any other ticket agent handling Continental rail.

Buses: Victoria Coach Station, 164 Buckingham Palace Rd, is the main London terminal for long-distance buses; the main operator is **National Express**, ☎0871 781 8181 (or book online at www.nationalexpress.com); tourist and other passes available.

✈ **Heathrow Airport**, ☎0844 335 1801, is 24 km west of Central London. The **Piccadilly Line** underground (journey time 1hr) serves all five terminals. The **Heathrow Express** is more expensive, but takes 15–20 mins to reach Paddington and runs every 15 mins. **Heathrow Connect**, also to Paddington, is cheaper but slower, taking 25 mins. A **taxi** to the centre costs about £40–70, cheaper if you share. The **tourist information desk** at Heathrow is located by the Underground station for Terminals 1, 2 and 3, and at Terminal 5.

Gatwick Airport, ☎0844 335 1802, is 45 km south of London. **Gatwick Express** trains run non-stop up to every 15 mins (rail passes not valid), from London Victoria, taking 30 mins (Express class £16.90, 1st class £24.50); other trains (not called Gatwick Express) are slower but cheaper. National Express buses run up to every 30 mins from Victoria Coach Station taking 1 hr 25 mins. Taxis cost £80–100 to Central London. There's **tourist information** on the arrivals concourse of the South Terminal.

TOURIST OFFICES

The main Tourist Office is the **Britain and London Visitor Centre**, 1 Lower Regent St, near Piccadilly Circus (personal callers only; Underground: **Piccadilly Circus**); www.visitbritain.com. It provides comprehensive multilingual information; has a hotel booking service for the whole of the UK; can book guided tours, shows and events; and sells transport passes. The **London Visitor Centre**, at Waterloo Station can also help (personal callers only). Otherwise contact **Visit London**, ☎0870 156 6366 (calls charged at 60p per minute); www.visitlondon.com.

Other international airports are: **Stansted** (trains to London Liverpool Street station take 45 mins, £18 one way), **City** (Docklands Light Railway to Bank, takes 22 mins) and **Luton** (shuttle bus to Luton Airport Parkway rail station for services to London St Pancras or King's Cross Thameslink).

PUBLIC TRANSPORT

Travel during rush hour (primarily Mon–Fri 0800–0930 and 1700–1900) is no fun at all. Free bus and Underground maps and other information about Transport for London (TfL), including tickets, are available in most Underground stations (24-hour enquiry line: ☎(020) 7222 1234) www.tfl.gov.uk. Travel Information centres are located at key points including Victoria train and coach station, Piccadilly Circus and Heathrow Airport underground stations. As for street maps, the *A–Z Map of London* covers the central area, while the full *London A–Z* or *Nicholson Street Guides* include the whole city and its suburbs.

UNDERGROUND TRAINS London Underground ('the Tube'), the world's oldest and deepest **metro** (subway), is extensive, efficient and often quickest way to get around, but can be impossibly crowded during rush hours. Most lines operate Mon–Sat 0500–0030, Sun 0730–2330. Smoking is forbidden everywhere in the system. Each line is colour-coded and named. Indicators on the platforms and the front of the trains show the destination. Keep your ticket handy: there are occasional inspections and are inserted into the turnstiles at the beginning and end of your journey.

BUSES London's bright red double-decker buses have become a tourist attraction in their own right, although the traditional Routemaster buses have been replaced by modern low-floor buses (there is still a limited service on the central sections of routes 9 and 15). The roads are often congested and travel can be slow, but some routes (e.g. 🚌 9/11/12/15/88) are excellent for sightseeing and the view from the top deck is always great. Most services run 0500–0030, with many routes now operating 24-hr services. Keep your ticket until you reach your destination as there are random checks. Buses sometimes cover only part of the route, so check the final destination display on the front or back. There are bus stops every few hundred metres, showing the relevant bus numbers.

TAXIS The famous 'black cabs' may be painted in other colours, but their shape remains distinctive. Fares are metered and not cheap; there are extra (metered) charges for baggage, for more than one passenger, and for travelling in the evening (after 2000) or at weekends; drivers expect a tip of 10% of the fare (but you don't need to tip minicabs that you order by phone). There are taxi ranks at key positions, but you can also hail them in the street. When a taxi is available, the roof-light at the front is on.

REQUEST STOPS

The red signs are request stops and the buses halt at them only if you signal: by raising your arm if you are at a stop or ringing the bell (once only) if you are on board.

United Kingdom

London Travelcards

Worth buying if you're making more than two trips in a day, these give unlimited travel on all London's public transport except Airport Expresses and give a 33% discount on river services. Costs for one day: zones 1 and 2 (£5.60 off-peak, £7.20 peak) cover all you're likely to need in Central London, while zones 1–6 (£7.50 off-peak, £14.80 peak) cover all the suburbs (and Heathrow Airport). There is also the London Visitor's Travelcard (essentially the same) for overseas visitors purchasing a card before arriving in London; there are agents in most countries. The Oyster Card is useful if you want a good-value (it offers big reductions on normal fares), pay-as-you-travel option: you pay a £3 refundable deposit for the card which you top up with amounts of your choosing.

Tickets

The minimum single fare for a journey on **London Underground**, **Overground** and **Docklands Light Railway** if paid by cash is £4 within zones 1–6. If you are not travelling through zone 1 (Central London), the minimum fare is £3.20. If you use an Oyster Card this cost falls, although the exact amount depends on how many zones you travel through; an Oyster single between two stations in zone 1 is £1.60 at all times. An off-peak Oyster single between zones 1 and 6 is £2.20.

On **buses**, the cash single fare is £2, whilst with an Oyster is £1.

If you are travelling around London a lot during one day then an off-peak Day Travelcard (valid after 0930) may offer you the best value for money. Both cash and Oyster versions are available. For full information about the different fare options available go to www.tfl.gov.uk and click the 'tickets' link.

ACCOMMODATION

London has an enormous range of accommodation, from world-renowned hotels with sky-high prices to bed and breakfast establishments. Among the best value for **cheap accommodation** are the seven **Hostelling International youth hostels** in London (www.yha.org.uk). Useful private hostels include **Piccadilly Backpackers Hostel**, 12 Sherwood Street, W1F 7BR, ☎(020) 7434 9009, (www.piccadillyhotel.net), handily placed near Piccadilly Circus, and **St Christopher's Inns**, ☎(020) 7407 1856 (www.st-christophers.co.uk), a small chain of well-located private hostels, with meals, internet access and laundry facilities, with locations in Camden (48–50 Camden High Street, NW1); Borough High Street, SE1, on the South Bank near London Bridge (three hostels); plus (out of the centre) Greenwich and Shepherd's Bush. The **Paddington**, **Victoria** and **Earls Court** areas, in particular, have a good range of **bed and breakfasts** at around £30 per person. In the northwest suburbs by Hendon Central tube station (20 mins to central London) is **London Backpackers**, 1st Floor, Queens Parade, Queens Road, Hendon, NW4 3NS, ☎(020) 8203 1319 (www.ukhostels.com). **Visit London** ☎0845 644 3010 (local-rate call; daily) will take hotel bookings by phone (£5 booking fee) or via their website: www.visitlondon.com if you have a debit or credit card (no booking fee). The London School of Economics, ☎(020) 7955 7575 (www.lsevacations.co.uk) lets out rooms in centrally located student halls of residence in Bloomsbury, Clerkenwell, Covent Garden and the South Bank during

Easter, summer and Christmas holidays, and you don't have to be a student to stay there; triples, twins and singles are available. Singles are from £33, twins from £45 (more expensive with bathroom), with breakfast; you can prepare your own food in the kitchens. **Happy Homes** 📞(020) 7352 5121 (www.happy-homes.com) is an agency that places tourists into private family homestays (Central and southwest London) from £25 per person per night.

FOOD AND DRINK

London is a superb hunting ground for food, with restaurants of every conceivable type, from traditional British to those of countries few could pinpoint on a map. The cost is equally varied: from fast-food chains, where you can get something filling for about £4, to places that will easily set you back £100 for a couple of courses plus drinks. The **Covent Garden** and **Soho** districts (there's an endless choice of **Chinese** places in the Gerrard St/Wardour St area of **Soho**) offer the best array of West End restaurants. The **Queensway**, **Victoria**, **Leicester Sq.**, **Panton St** and **Earls Court** areas are very lively, especially in the evenings, with innumerable **cheap eateries** of all types, including some of the eat-your-fill variety. **Italian**, **Chinese**, **Indian**, **Greek** and **Turkish restaurants** are common and many are excellent, with a wide range of cheap dishes on offer. Many do **takeaways** and there are still plenty of **fish and chip shops**. Food in **pubs and wine bars** is usually good value though pubs in the centre are often unpleasantly crowded. For upmarket food shopping, visit **Fortnum & Mason**, Piccadilly, and the Food Hall in **Harrods**, Knightsbridge. Alternatively visit **Borough Market** on the South Bank for more down to earth prices but equally tasty fare, www.boroughmarket.org.uk. There are **pubs** on virtually every street, including **historic inns** reputed to have been frequented by everyone from Ben Jonson to Charles Dickens.

HIGHLIGHTS

You can take in a lot of the most famous landmarks in a couple of days. From **Big Ben** (Underground: **Westminster**), the famous Gothic clock tower of the **Houses of Parliament** (where you can hear parliamentary debate if you're prepared to queue), there's a great walk over **Westminster Bridge**, after which you turn left along the **Thames Embankment**, enjoying river views from the **South Bank**, where you'll see the transition from the **West End** to the **City**, with domed **St Paul's Cathedral** rising spectacularly; on the South Bank are the **London Eye**, the **Millennium Bridge** and the thatched **Shakespeare's Globe Theatre**, a faithful 1990s replica of the place where many of Shakespeare's plays were performed in his lifetime. Around **London Bridge** there are some atmospheric (converted) Victorian warehouses, with high catwalks; then comes **Tower Bridge**, the best known Thames span, which is still raised to allow tall ships through; cross to the north bank here to the **Tower of London**, one of Britain's best-preserved Norman castles, where many famous and notorious prisoners of the Crown met a grisly end. It's home to the Crown Jewels and is guarded by Beefeaters in Tudor-era uniform.

United Kingdom

In the other direction from Big Ben you can delve into the best of the **West End**. In **Parliament Square** is **Westminster Abbey**, crammed with memorials and famed as the crowning place of British monarchs. Along Whitehall, with its limestone-fronted government buildings, the **Banqueting House** is a remnant of the otherwise vanished **Palace of Whitehall**, and the breastplated Horse Guards keep watch in Horse Guards Parade. **Trafalgar Square** is London's big set piece, with **Nelson's Column** flanked by a quartet of lions and looked over by **St Martin's-in-the-Fields Church** and the **National Gallery**. From the **Admiralty Arch** runs The Mall, a Parisian boulevard lined by Regency terraces on one side and the greenery of **St James's Park** (a lovely spot with a lake and bandstand) on the other; at the end is **Buckingham Palace** (the Queen's main residence), rather cold and austere (its state rooms are open Aug–Sept: you can also visit the Queen's Gallery and Royal Mews collection of state coaches). Victoria Street is home to the 19th-century **Westminster (Catholic) Cathedral** with its cavernous interior. A lift whisks you up the tower for fine views of London.

The **City of London** (the east part of the centre) houses such venerable and ancient City institutions such as the **Guildhall**, the **Inns of Court** (the heart of legal London) and the **Bank of England**. The 17th-century architect Sir Christopher Wren built numerous City churches, most famously **St Paul's Cathedral**, with its **Whispering Gallery** providing remarkable acoustics. Buildings to look out for near Fenchurch St include **Leadenhall Market** (exuberantly Victorian) and the **Lloyd's Building** (provocatively high-tech).

MUSEUMS AND GALLERIES Of the countless art galleries, three are outstanding – and admission is free, except for special exhibitions. **The National Gallery**, Trafalgar Sq., displays 12th–19th-century art, with a superb cross-section of Impressionists and post-Impressionists (try to catch one of the free gallery tours). **Tate Britain** (incorporating the **Clore Gallery**), Millbank (Underground: **Westminster/Pimlico**) is another free gallery, with some excellent Turners among its all-British collection. On the South Bank, not far from the London Eye (a huge ferris wheel with great views) and the Millennium Footbridge, is the wonderful **Tate Modern**, a hulking former power station filled with modern art. The **Cabinet War Rooms** offer an intriguing insight into bunker life during the Second World War for Churchill and his government (Underground: **Westminster**). The **British Museum**, Great Russell St (Underground: **Russell Sq.**), is a treasure trove (entrance free); it's daunting in scale – many come in just to see the **Elgin Marbles** (originally the frieze of the **Parthenon** in Athens) and the ancient Egyptian section. The **Museum of London**, London Wall (Underground: **Barbican/St Paul's/Moorgate**), offers a beautifully displayed history of the city with an excellent Roman section and a reconstruction of a Victorian street of shops (entrance free). Most visitors enjoy **London's Transport Museum**, Covent Garden (admission £10). The free **Imperial War Museum** (Underground: **Lambeth North**) looks at modern warfare since 1914, with lots on social history and how wars affect our lives – so you don't need to be turned on by guns to get a lot out of a visit; there are brilliant re-creations of a blitzed London street and a First World War trench, and often highly worthwhile temporary exhibitions. Clustered together (Underground: **South Kensington**) are three other truly great museums (entrance free). The kid-friendly **Science Museum**, Exhibition Rd, has an array of hands-on exhibits demonstrating all things scientific. The adjacent **Natural History Museum** has many interactive exhibits, and there's a wonderful section on dinosaurs. Across the road is the **Victoria and Albert Museum**, Cromwell Rd, a vast treasure house of arts and crafts. For something less genteel, **The London Dungeon** offers all kinds of heart-stopping moments in its spooky and chilling underground labyrinths (Underground: **London Bridge**).

OUT OF THE CENTRE A distinguishing feature of the suburbs are the old villages incorporated into the cityscape but still with attractive old centres. Along the Thames to the west there are delightful riverside walks from **Richmond** (Underground: **Richmond**) and up to **Richmond Park**, a huge deer park; within reach are Chiswick Mall, just west of **Hammersmith Bridge** and with several old waterside pubs and imposing Georgian houses, and **Kew Gardens (Royal Botanic Gardens)** (Underground: **Kew Gardens**), one of the greatest plant collections in the world. A bit further out is Henry VIII's superb **Hampton Court Palace** (famous for its maze) and **Windsor Castle** (still a royal residence, but parts of it are open); both are accessible by suburban train from **Waterloo** station – these and Kew Gardens can be reached by boat. East from the centre, **Greenwich** was once the hub of nautical Britain and is still the definitive Meridian, or 0 degrees longitude. In **Greenwich Park** and towards the river are the **National Maritime Museum**, **Old Royal Naval College**, **Royal Observatory**, and the refurbished **Queen's House** (free entrance to all these). From Greenwich a slightly creepy tiled foot tunnel (free) under the Thames leads to Island Gardens station on the elevated **Docklands Light Railway**, which gives a futuristic ride north from here, past **Canary Wharf** (London's tallest building) in the heart of redeveloped Docklands to **West India Quay**, where you can carry on to **Tower Gateway** near the **Tower of London** to finish a memorable day at Tower Bridge.

SHOPPING

The West End is full of famous shopping areas. For serious shopping, including many department stores, try **Oxford St** and **Regent St** (home to **Hamleys** toy shop). For designer clothes and upmarket window shopping, try Bond St, South Molton St, Beauchamp Place and Brompton Rd (home of **Harrods**; Underground: **Knightsbridge**). For **books**: Charing Cross Rd. For **trendy boutiques**: Covent Garden and Kings Rd (Chelsea). For **electronic goods**: Tottenham Court Rd. **London-related souvenirs** don't extend much beyond ephemeral tat; a better bet are items on sale at museum shops such as the **Museum of London**, **British Museum**, **National Gallery** and **London's Transport Museum**. Some of London's **street markets** are tourist attractions in themselves. Among the best are **Portobello Rd** (Underground: **Ladbroke Grove** or **Notting Hill Gate**), Mon–Sat (best Sat morning; antiques and junk) and **Camden Lock**, all week, but best on Sun, with antiques and crafts (Underground: **Chalk Farm**): you can tie a visit in with a walk westwards along the Regent's Canal, passing **Regent's Park**, the Zoo and leading to a pretty canal basin at **Little Venice**. For sheer East-End atmosphere seek out **Brick Lane** on a Sun morning (much better than the touristy **Petticoat Lane** nearby), with some real bargains among piles of cheap junk (Underground: **Whitechapel/Aldgate East**).

United Kingdom

NIGHT-TIME AND EVENTS

There are several publications listing London's entertainments, of which the best are the weekly magazine *Time Out*, the daily *Evening Standard* and the free *TNT Magazine* (help yourself from special stands in central areas).

CLUBS, DISCOS, PUBS Almost everything is on offer in terms of nightlife, including **casinos, jazz clubs, discos, straight and gay clubs** and **pub entertainment**. Most clubs offer one-night membership at the door and often have a dress code, which might be a jacket and tie or could just depend on whether you look trendy enough. Jeans and trainers are usually out. The larger **rock venues** (such as the **London Apollo** in **Hammersmith** and the **O2 Arena**) are all a little way from the centre, as are many of the **pubs with live entertainment**.

THEATRE, CINEMA AND MUSIC London is one of the world's greatest centres of theatre and music. In addition to the **National Theatre** and the **Barbican**, the London home of the **Royal Shakespeare Company**, there are about 50 theatres in central London. West End theatre tickets are expensive, but there is a **half-price ticket booth**, Leicester Sq. (the south side), for same-day performances. To book ahead, go to the theatre itself – most agents charge a hefty fee. Seats for big musicals are hard to come by, but it's worth queuing for returns.

There's a wide range of classical music, from free lunchtime performances in churches to major symphonies in famous venues. **The Proms** are a huge summer-long festival of concerts held at the **Royal Albert Hall**, with the cheapest tickets sold on the day to 'Promenaders' who stand at floor level; the flag-waving 'Last Night' is massively popular. Other major classical music venues are the **Barbican Hall** and the **Royal Festival Hall**. The latter, part of the **South Bank Centre** (Underground: **Embankment**, then walk over Hungerford Bridge) is a stylish 1950s hall where there's lots going on in the daytime in the way of free foyer concerts, jazz and exhibitions, and there's an inexpensive self-service restaurant downstairs. The cheapest tickets for concerts are in the 'choir' behind the orchestra, where the sound's a bit distorted but you are really close to the musicians.

Also on the South Bank are the **National Theatre**, **BFI (British Film Institute)** (where you can get temporary membership if you just want to see one film) and the **BFI London IMAX Cinema**, boasting a gigantic screen (Britain's largest). For mainstream cinema, the **Odeon Leicester Square** is the venue for recent releases, British and world premieres. It's also well worth catching a play at **Shakespeare's Globe Theatre**, where it's very cheap to get a ticket for standing space (or 'groundling').

EVENTS It's not difficult to see British pageantry if you time your visit to coincide with one of the many traditional annual events. These include **Trooping the Colour** (second Sat June), the **State Opening of Parliament** (early Nov) and the **Lord Mayor's Show** (second Sat Nov). Other free spectacles include: the **Flora London Marathon** (Apr: the world's largest, truly international); the **University**

Boat Race (Sat near Easter: a traditional contest between Oxford and Cambridge Universities); and the **Notting Hill Carnival** (which takes over a wide area for three days over the Summer Bank Holiday weekend in late Aug – the largest of its type in Europe, noisy and fun, but don't take any valuables).

DAY TRIPS FROM LONDON

For public transport in Britain, browse www.travelline.co.uk or ☎0871 200 2233; for train times and journey planning see www.nationalrail.co.uk ☎0845 748 4950.

BATH (1 hr 25 mins from **Paddington**; ETT table 130): A fine Georgian town, at the height of fashion in the 18th and early 19th centuries, began life as a Roman spa, and the original **Roman Baths** are impressively intact next to the 18th-century **Pump Room**, where you can sip tea to the accompaniment of chamber music or even take to the soothing waters; adjacent **Bath Abbey** was known as the 'Lantern of the West' for its display of stained glass. Among some of the masterpieces of Georgian town planning are the **Royal Crescent** (No.1 is open as a museum house) and **The Circus**, built like much of the rest in mellow Bath stone. Pick of the museums are the **Museum of Costume** at the **Assembly Rooms**, the **Building of Bath Museum** (explaining how John Wood transformed the city), the **Museum of Bath at Work**, and the **Jane Austen Centre** which reveals how living in the city influenced her literature. There are **river cruises** from Pulteney Bridge. ⓘTourist Office: ☎0906 711 2000 (UK only, calls charged at 50p/minute) or +44 (0)844 847 5257 (overseas callers only) (www.visitbath.co.uk).

BRIGHTON (55 mins from **Victoria**; ETT table 102): Over the past few years, Brighton has developed quite a reputation for its cool living and nightlife and is a particular magnet for the gay and lesbian community as well as one of the best places to go to experience the traditional English seaside resort. George IV made sea-bathing fashionable when he erected his **Royal Pavilion**, an Indian fantasy Regency mansion sprouting domes and minarets, as astonishing inside as out. This is also home to the impressive **Brighton Museum & Art Gallery**. Virtually contemporary are the imposing stucco crescents and terraces lining the seafront; below are numerous booths offering palm-reading and tattooing, and two 19th-century piers – **Brighton Pier**, very much alive with tacky amusements, and the wrecked **West Pier**, about to crumble into the sea. The maze-like old fishing quarter, now full of eateries, boutiques and antique shops, is known as the **Lanes** – not to be confused with the **North Laine**, a line of pedestrianised shopping streets at the heart of trendy, alternative Brighton. You can return to London by way of **Lewes**, a handsome and surprisingly untouristy town on a ridge between the chalky **South Downs**, with views of the rooftops and coast from its **Norman castle**, and lots of second-hand bookshops and ancient alleys (known as 'twittens'). ⓘTourist Office: ☎0906 711 2255 (calls charged at 50p/minute, UK only; www.visitbrighton.com).

CAMBRIDGE (55 mins; quickest service from **King's Cross**; ETT tables 186/187): Along with Oxford, one of Britain's two oldest universities, its architecturally-rich college style variations scattered around the city combine a cloistered tranquillity

United Kingdom

with some lovely walks along the river (popular for punting – an ancient boating tradition). Many colleges charge for entry and some close to the public in term time, with the chapel at **King's** (a superb example of Perpendicular Gothic) and the main courtyard and library at **Trinity** among the obvious highlights. The **Fitzwilliam Museum** (free) is a magnificent general museum with some choice art collections. The station is a 15–20 min walk, but there are frequent bus services from Victoria Coach Station in London getting you closer to the centre. [*i*]Tourist Office: ☎0906 586 2526 (calls charged at 60p/minute), from overseas: +44 (0)1223 464732; www.visitcambridge.org).

CANTERBURY (1 hr 25 mins from **Victoria**; ETT tables 100/101): Seat of the head of the Church of England, **Canterbury** has some gems, notably the **cathedral** (with medieval stained glass, Norman crypt and cloister) and its precincts, which miraculously escaped wartime bombing that obliterated part of the centre (unimaginatively rebuilt) but left some old streets intact. You can walk around the remaining city walls past whirling traffic, and pass under the medieval **Christ Church and Westgate**; one of the former pilgrims' hostels, **Poor Priests' Hospital** now houses a good museum covering the city's heritage. Also worthy of time is **Canterbury Tales**, an interactive museum recreating medieval life during Chaucer's life, and **St Augustine's Church**, the oldest church in England, having been in use since the 6th century. [*i*]Tourist Office: ☎(01227) 378100 (www.canterbury.co.uk).

DORSET COAST Designated a UNESCO World Heritage Site as one of the most geologically varied places in the world, the coast of the county of Dorset extends from the edge of Bournemouth to beyond Lyme Regis – there's no other stretch of coast this close to London that's as wild or remote as this. The seclusion and otherworldliness is further enhanced by the gorgeously golden-coloured stone-built villages inland. A coastal footpath takes in Dorset's entire length – it has some of the toughest walking in southern England, with severe gradients in places, but really helps you appreciate how the landscape varies from one moment to the next. ETT table 110 gives some options from London Waterloo to Bournemouth (1 hr 45 min), Wareham or Weymouth; it's an area worth spending a bit of time in, so is more suited to short breaks than day trips from London. **Bournemouth** is a large, modern resort with decent sandy beaches, and a bus from the station to Sandbanks gets you on to a ferry across Poole Harbour. On the other side, it's a different world – with heathland and huge beaches as you round **Studland** and descend from chalky cliffs to **Swanage**. Here, a steam railway (www.swanagerailway.co.uk) leads out to **Corfe Castle** – a jagged ruin in a village of the same name, and there's easy access by bus from Corfe or Swanage to Wareham. Further along the coast, **Lulworth Cove** is a massive scoop in the wild coastline (the area east of here is used by the army, but open in holiday periods and at weekends), and beyond are the natural arch of **Durdle Door**, and the amiable resorts of **Weymouth** and **Lyme Regis**.

DOVER (79–81 mins from London St Pancras by "Javelin" service; 1 hr 45 mins from London Charing Cross; 25 mins from Canterbury East; ETT tables 100/101): The main channel port, Dover was sadly clobbered by both wartime bombing and subsequent town planners. However, it does have a tremendous setting, with sheer precipices (the famous 'white cliffs') giving great coastal walks in either direction (to

Folkestone or Deal; both have rail services to Dover), and looking across the Channel to France. **Dover Castle** is one of the best-preserved Norman keeps in the country and you can visit the miles of secret tunnels that in World War II housed the HQ for the Dunkirk evacuation and a military hospital; the site also includes a Roman lighthouse and a Saxon church. _i_ Tourist Office: ☎(01304) 205108 (www.whitecliffscountry.org.uk).

EASTBOURNE (1 hr 30 mins from Victoria; ETT table 102): Very different from nearby Brighton, **Eastbourne** is a sedate, peaceful resort, with spacious rows of stucco-fronted hotels along the front, and a bandstand in earshot of the ornate pier. Despite its serene demeanour, sporty activities feature large here, with rollerblading along the promenade, professional women's tennis in the week before the Wimbledon tournament in summer, and paragliding from the nearby South Downs and cliffs. Eastbourne marks the eastern end of the South Downs Way, a long-distance path from Winchester, which ends here in spectacular fashion on the dizzying sheer chalk clifftops of the **Seven Sisters** – a rollercoaster of seven dips and rises – and finally **Beachy Head**, above Eastbourne's western fringes. If you don't fancy the fairly arduous hike up, there are buses from the pier to Beachy Head and the Seven Sisters Country Park, and in summer you can take a boat cruise towards the Seven Sisters. You can also head further east by train to **Hastings**, a slightly run-down seaside town with tremendous atmosphere: beyond a shingle beach of fishing boats, and strange tall wooden sheds erected for storing nets, is the huddled Old Town, with an appealing warren of stepped alleys and narrow lanes lined with timber-framed and beach-cobbled cottages, and there are two cliff railways – one going up towards the scant remains of a Norman castle, the other to a bracing cliff top where a path leads over wild sandstone cliff tops towards Fairlight Glen. The famous Battle of Hastings in 1066 didn't actually take place here but at the small town of Battle (a short train ride away), where **Battle Abbey** marks the final stand of English king, Harold, against William the Conqueror's invading forces. There's an absorbing trail around the battlefield site, and a good museum about the last foreign victory on British soil and one of the pivotal points of British history.

OXFORD (1 hr from Paddington; ETT tables 137/138): In many ways Oxford is similar to Cambridge, with a river to explore and many ancient colleges with pretty gardens. It's virtually all built in honey-coloured Cotswold stone. Of the colleges, **Christ Church** and **Magdalen** are among the finest. If time is short, one of the daily guided walking tours is the best way to get the most from a visit. Seek out the free **Ashmolean Museum**, with a superb collection of art and artefacts. The station is a 15–20 min walk, but there are frequent bus services from Victoria Coach Station in London to the heart of the city. _i_ Tourist Office: ☎(01865) 252200 (www.visitoxford.org).

PORTSMOUTH 1 hr 32 mins from **Waterloo**; ETT table 108): This is the hub of Britain's navy, but for visitors, the bulk of interest is in the **Historic Dockyard** (www.historicdockyard.co.uk), where three historic craft are on show. HMS _Victory_, the flagship of Nelson, whose defeat of the Franco-Spanish fleet at the Battle of Trafalgar in 1805 raised him to hero status, has naval staff on hand fleshing out the details of the horrendously cramped and disease-ridden conditions on board, and also point out the spot where Nelson died in battle. HMS _Warrior_, when launched in 1860, was the most powerful naval ship in the world, and has been marvellously restored to what she was. By complete contrast, the *Mary Rose* is a spectral wreck – a warship of the time of Henry VIII and which sank in the harbour in 1545: preserved in silt for centuries until being raised in 1982, It's the only vessel of its era and type on view anywhere in the world. You can pay individually to see each exhibit, or get an all-inclusive ticket (though you would need a very full day to see everything here) – there's also the outstanding **Royal Naval Museum**, and Action Stations gives you a vivid idea of life in the present-day Navy. Unmissable on the waterfront, the 170 m **Spinnaker Tower** (www.spinnakertower.co.uk) offers three viewing platforms, a harbour history presentation and café serving snacks by day and bottled beer come sundown.

RYE (1 hr 45 mins from **London Bridge**; change at **Ashford**; ETT table 105): One of the Cinque Ports, which in medieval times supplied men and ships to defend the coast and received special privileges, **Rye** has survived as one of the best-preserved small towns in England, though the sea that brought fame and fortune has receded. The town is full of quaint alleys and cobbled lanes, Mermaid Street being the best known. Take the train one stop to **Winchelsea** – another lapsed port, laid out as a medieval town but now a handsome, French-looking hilltop village. To the east of the county is **Camber Sands**, made popular by its 11km of fine sandy beach, protected dunes and the varied flora and fauna they protect. *i* Tourist Office: ☎(01797) 229049 (www.visitrye.co.uk).

STRATFORD-UPON-AVON (2 hrs 20 mins from **Marylebone** station; ETT table 140): famous as Shakespeare's birthplace, the main places connected with the Bard are **Shakespeare's Birthplace** (within a small timber-framed house), **Anne Hathaway's Cottage** (the thatched cottage of his wife, located 1.7 km from the centre of town), **Mary Arden's House** (his mother's childhood home) and the **Royal Shakespeare Theatre** (productions by the Royal Shakespeare Company). Shakespeare aside, it's an agreeable town but extremely touristy, and if you're not into literary pilgrimage you might want to give it a miss. *i* Tourist Office: ☎0870 160 7930 (national rate call; www.shakespeare-country.co.uk). Try the nearby university and medieval castle city of **Warwick** (www.warwick-uk.co.uk) as a quieter alternative.

YORK (2 hrs from **King's Cross**; ETT table 180): Without doubt, the most satisfying British medieval city, encircled by impressively preserved walls (with extensive walks along the top of them), and graced with the magnificent **York Minster** (Britain's largest medieval cathedral, renowned for the quality of its stained glass, roof-top views and undercroft). Close by **Clifford's Tower** (a 14th-century castle) is the **York Castle Museum**, with a reconstructed street of shops among its excellent displays of social history, while **JORVIK** is a remarkable time journey back to 10th-century York. Foremost among the rest of an excellent set of museums is the free **National Railway Museum**. The centre is enjoyably traffic free, and full of buskers and street life; the **Shambles**, with its jettied, overhanging houses, and the **Merchant Adventurers' Hall** are among the best medieval timber-frame survivals. Just 20 minutes away is the magnificent stately pile and estate of **Castle Howard** (www.castlehoward.co.uk) – a full day is needed to do this vast private home justice. *i* Tourist Office: ☎(01904) 550099 (www.visityork.org).

France

Many people holiday nowhere else but France. It has more culture and heritage, scenery and architecture than you can experience in a lifetime, plus food and wine that at its best verges on the sublime. To top that, **Paris** is arguably the world's most romantic capital, featuring as backdrop and inspiration for a thousand films and novels.

In the northwest, **Normandy** is a bucolic scene of half-timbered farms and graceful old manor houses, while Celtic **Brittany** has the best coastal scenery on France's Atlantic seaboard, studded with fishing villages, megalithic sites and idyllic sandy bays. Vast war cemeteries and towns reconstructed after massive bombing are sobering reminders of the toll inflicted by two World Wars on this part of France. Inland lies the **Loire Valley**, remarkable for its châteaux that span the ages from feudal times. Despite its impressive medieval architecture, including some superb cathedrals, much of inland northern France is fairly humdrum scenically, consisting of uneventful farmland, and long straight roads. It is in the **Massif Central**, the volcanic upland covering much of southern central France, that the scenery becomes wilder. Heading south through western France, you reach the vineyards of Bordeaux and the gentle hills of the **Dordogne**, studded with prehistoric remains and pretty (if sometimes over-discovered) villages. Along the Spanish border stretch the Pyrenees, a spectacular region for walks and wildlife. Between the Massif Central and the Alps, **Provence** is France at its most Mediterranean, with red tiled roofs, Roman remains, vineyards, olives and cypress trees shimmering in fierce summer sun. The **Riviera coast** is renowned for its glamorous beach resorts. North of the Alps, **Burgundy** and German-influenced **Alsace** offer wine-tasting, rural touring and gastronomic delights.

> Trains are fast, comfortable and usually reliable. The French are proud of the **TGV** *(Train à Grande Vitesse)*, among the fastest in the world, with speeds of up to 320 km/h. Most of the scenic routes are in the south – in the **Massif Central**, through the **Pyrenees**, in **Provence** and through the **Alps**.

Essentials

Population 64.3m **Capital** Paris (divided into *arrondissements* numbered 1 to 20; 1st or *1er*, 2nd or *2e*, etc.) **Time Zone** Winter GMT+1, summer GMT+2.

Climate

Cool–cold winters, mild–hot summers; south coast best Oct–Mar, Alps and Pyrenees, June and early July. Paris best spring and autumn.

Currency

Euro (€). 1 Euro = 100 cents = £0.89 = $1.46.

Customs allowances

Standard EU regulations apply (see pp40–1).

Embassies and consulates in Paris

Aus: 4 r. Jean Rey, 15e, ☎01 40 59 33 00. **Can**: 35 av. Montaigne, 8e, ☎01 44 43 29 00. **Ire**: 12 av. Foch, 16e, ☎01 44 17 67 00. **NZ**: 7 ter r. L-da-Vinci, 16e, ☎01 45 01 43 43. **SA**: 59 quai d'Orsay, 7e, ☎01 53 59 23 23. **UK**: 35 r. Fbg-St. Honoré, 8e, ☎01 44 51 31 00. **USA**: 2 av. Gabriel, 8e, ☎01 43 12 22 22.

Language

French; many people can speak some English, particularly in Paris.

Opening hours

Paris and major towns: shops, banks and post offices generally open 0900/1000–1700/1900 Mon–Fri, plus often Sat am/all day. Small shops can be open Sun am but closed Mon. Provinces: weekly closing is mostly Sun pm/all day and Mon; both shops and services generally close 1200–1430; services may have restricted opening times. Most super-/hypermarkets open to 2100/2200. Museums: (mostly) 0900–1700, closing Mon and/or Tues; longer hours in summer; often free or discount rate on Sun. Restaurants serve 1200–1400 and 1900–2100 at least. Public holidays: services closed, food shops open am in general, check times with individual museums and tourist sights.

Post offices

Called *La Poste*. Letter boxes are small, wall- or pedestal-mounted, and yellow. The basic rate postage stamp (*timbre*) can also be bought from *Tabacs* or *Cafés-Tabacs*.

Public holidays

1 Jan; Easter Mon; 1, 8 May; Ascension Day; Whit Sun–Mon; 14 July; 15 Aug; 1, 11 Nov; 25 Dec. If on Tues or Thur, many places also close Mon or Fri.

Public transport

The Metro systems in Paris and several other major cities are clean, efficient and relatively cheap. For urban and peri-urban transport, *carnets* (multiple-ticket packs) are cheaper than individual tickets. Some city transport passes combine discount entries to certain tourist attractions. Bus and train timetables are available from bus and train stations and Tourist Offices; usually free. Always ask if your rail pass is valid on local transport. Bus services may be infrequent after 2030 and on Sun. Rural areas are often poorly served. Licensed taxis (avoid others) are metered; white roof-lights when free; surcharges for luggage, extra passengers and journeys beyond the centre.

Rail passes

IR, EP valid (see pp27–34). Stamp all tickets (except InterRail) in orange machines (*composteurs*) on platform. Two fare periods: blue (quiet) and white (peak). France Railpass is only available to non-European residents, valid for 3–9 days within one month; discounts available for tourist railways, ferries, some museums. Adult 3 days $293/250, 1st/2nd class plus $45/37 per day; Youth (12–25) $217/186 plus $33/28 per day; Senior (60+, 1st class only) $268 for 3 days plus $40 per day. 15% discount for 2–5 people travelling together. Allows special Passholder fare on Eurostar, Thalys, Artesia, TGV, Téoz. Regional tickets: several regions have rover tickets on local TER trains at weekends/public holidays; some are summer only. Carte 12–25 and Carte Sénior: for 12–25 (€49) and over 60 (€56), valid 1 year and give at least 25% discount (up to 50% for journeys purchased in advance). Paris Visite includes entry to 20 attractions, fares according to zone. Mobilis gives 1 day on Paris transport but excludes airports.

RAIL TRAVEL

Société Nationale des Chemins de fer Français (SNCF) (www.sncf.com), ☎3635 (premium rate, in French), followed by 1 for traffic status, 2 for timetables, 3 for reservations and tickets, 4 for other services. Excellent network from Paris to major cities with *TGV* trains using dedicated high-speed lines (up to 320 km/h on the *Est Europé*en line to eastern France) as well as conventional track. However, some cross-country journeys can be slow and infrequent. Trains can get very full at peak times, so to avoid having to spend the journey standing, book a seat. Prior reservation is compulsory on TGV high-speed trains and the charge is included in the ticket price; rail pass holders will have to pay at least the reservation fee. Tickets can cost more at busy times (known as 'white' periods). Long distance trains on several non-TGV routes are branded *Corail Téoz* using refurbished rolling stock – reservation is compulsory. Reservation is also compulsory on all overnight trains: most convey couchettes and reclining seats only (sleeping cars are only conveyed on international trains). A certain number of couchette compartments are reserved for women only or those with small children; otherwise, couchette accommodation is mixed. There is a minimal bar/trolley service on most long-distance trains. Larger stations sometimes have pay-showers.

TELEPHONES

Phone boxes: most have instructions in English. Many post offices have metered phones: pay when you've finished. Restaurants etc have (more expensive) pay phones; avoid calling from hotel rooms. Different denomination phonecards (*télécartes*) on sale in post offices, some tobacconists and certain Tourist Offices; few phones still accept coins; some do credit cards. Dial in: ☎+33 and knock off the initial zero from telephone number. Outgoing: ☎00 + country code: Police: ☎17. Fire: ☎18. Ambulance: ☎15. Emergency from a mobile phone: ☎112. Mobile phone rental: try www.cellhire.com (free incoming calls) or www.cellularabroad.com.

TIPPING

Not necessary to tip in bars or cafés although it is common practice to round up the price. In restaurants there is no obligation to tip, but if you wish to do so leave €1–2.

TOURIST INFORMATION

Website: www.franceguide.com (French only). Try also www.france-voyage.com/en, in English, with photos and maps, plus hotel, restaurant and camping suggestions. At a new destination call at the local Tourist Office: look for *Syndicat d'Initiative* or *Office de Tourisme*; staff generally speak English. Opening times seasonal. Many sell passes for local tourist sights or services and can organise accommodation (for a fee).

VISAS

Visas needed by South Africans; but for others, only for stays of over 90 days (subject to change, so enquire before travelling).

ACCOMMODATION

HOTELS If you're staying at hotels, it's much cheaper if you share rather than go single, as prices are often quoted per room. Half-board (i.e. breakfast and evening meal included) can be excellent value in smaller towns and villages. As elsewhere in Europe, budget hotels are often clustered near stations. In summer, it is advisable to book ahead in larger towns and resort areas. *Offices de Tourisme* or *Syndicats d'Initiative* (Tourist Offices) usually provide free lists of local accommodation alternatives, and may also offer a booking service for a small charge. **Gîtes de France** produces catalogues of B&Bs, *gîtes d'étape*, farm accommodation and holiday house rentals for each *département*, available from certain retail outlets or **Maison des Gîtes de France et du Tourisme Vert**, 56 r. St-Lazare, 75439 Paris; ☎01 49 70 75 75 (www.gites-de-france.com). Accommodation tax (around €1/person/day) may be charged in addition to the price. Hotels are graded from 1 (basic) to 5 (luxury) stars. Paris is much more expensive than the rest of France: whereas a comfortable double room in the provinces might cost €35–50; in Paris you could expect to pay €80. Hotels in large towns and popular tourist areas are predictably more expensive too, but it might be worth trying to bargain: owners are often ready to drop their prices if demand is low. Breakfast in hotels is generally continental (coffee, bread/croissants and jam) and hardly ever included in quoted rates. It's cheaper to have breakfast in a local café.

Price codes for France: € – In Paris, starting price for a double €50; elsewhere €30. €€ – In Paris, doubles start at €75; elsewhere €50. €€€ – In Paris, doubles €100–130; elsewhere over €75.

CHAMBRES D'HÔTE *Chambres d'Hôte* are the French equivalent of bed-and-breakfast. Rooms can be found in all kinds of private homes, from simple farms to luxurious châteaux, but the price always includes breakfast, and a *table d'hôte* (evening meal) is often available by arrangement. A useful travelling companion is the detailed Thomas Cook *Bed & Breakfast France* (£14.99 plus p&p), available from **Thomas Cook Publishing**, Coningsby Road, Peterborough PE3 8SB, United Kingdom; ☎(01733) 416477, online at www.thomascookpublishing.com and in bookshops.

GÎTES D'ÉTAPE These are rural hostels, usually with private rooms as well as dormitories, and are mainly used by groups. It is advisable to book.

YOUTH HOSTELS Most **Auberges de Jeunesse** belong to the Hostelling International (HI) organisation, **Fédération Unie des Auberges de Jeunesse** (FUAJ), ☎(33) 1 44 89 87 27 (www.fuaj.org). Their prices (including linen) range from €12.60 to €16.80 (€13.50–17.80 including breakfast), in Strasbourg €19.70–20 (including breakfast) and in Paris €21–23 (including breakfast). They all have kitchen facilities and some serve meals. If you don't have the HI card, you will have to buy a €2.90 *timbre* 'Welcome Stamp' before you can book a room. Many close late Dec–early Jan, or from Oct–March if there are two hostels in the same town. Also HI-affiliated but with fewer hostels is **Ligue Francaise pour les Auberges de Jeunesse** (LFAJ), 67 r. Vergniaud, 75013 Paris; ☎(33) 1 44 16 78 78, (www.auberges-de-jeunesse.com).

France

CAMPING This is a national obsession, and there are hundreds of campsites all across France. 1- or 2-star *Camping Municipal* are basic but cheap. High-grade sites (4- and 5-star) provide entertainment and facilities such as watersports. Predictably, sites in popular areas can get very crowded in high season. Comprehensive camping guides are published by **Michelin** and the **Fédération Française de Camping et de Caravaning**, 78 r. de Rivoli, 75004 Paris; ☎(33) 1 42 72 84 08 (www.ffcc.fr). The *Accueil à la Ferme* brochure, available from Tourist Offices, lists farms with serviced campsites.

REFUGE HUTS In mountain areas, a chain of refuge huts is run by **Club Alpin Français** d'Île-de-France, 12 r. Boissonade, 75014 Paris ☎(33) 1 42 18 20 00 (www.clubalpin-idf.com).

FOOD AND DRINK France's gastronomic reputation often lives up to its promise, providing you're prepared to look beyond mere tourist fodder such as *steak frites* (steak and chips). The regional variations are vast, and exploring them is all part of the French experience. In general, northwest France tends towards butter-based cooking, with meat and cream much in evidence, while the south is influenced by Mediterranean ingredients such as olive oil, fish, wine and herbs; in mountainous areas the cuisine is more rustic, based on home-cured hams and cheeses. In restaurants, eating *à la carte* can be expensive, but the *menu* (set menu, of which there may be several) or the *plat du jour* (dish of the day), is often superb value, especially at lunch time. Strictly **vegetarian** restaurants are rare, but just about anywhere can rustle up a salad, an omelette or a meat-free tart, and many offer far more imaginative fare. Coffees and beers can be surprisingly expensive: **wine** is generally cheaper and usually drinkable – order a *pichet* of house red (*rouge*), white (*blanc*) or rosé. If you ask for *café*, you'll get a small black coffee; coffee with milk is *café crème*. Ask for *un grand crème* if you want a large one. You need to specify *thé au lait* (tea with milk) or *thé citron* (tea with a slice of lemon), or your tea will be served black. Herbal teas, especially *tilleul* (lime-flower) and *verveine* (verbena) are widely available. *Thé à la menthe* (mint tea) is generally the sweet Arab speciality. **Beer** is mostly yellow, cold, French and fizzy, though gourmet and foreign beers are popular. *Une pression* or *demi* is draught beer, better value than bottled. Northern France has the best selection of beers. France has many speciality **liqueurs** and **apéritifs**, but these can be expensive, as can mixed drinks. *Baguettes* (french bread sticks) with a variety of fillings from cafés and stalls are cheap – as are *crêpes* and *galettes* (sweet and savoury pancakes). Morning markets are excellent for stocking up on picnic items. Buy provisions before noon as shops can be closed for hours at lunchtime.

Paris has always held great allure – it's been a byword for style, glamour and romance since railway tourism began and the British started to go there for weekends in the 19th century. Everyone is familiar with the city through films, photographs and paintings. Café accordion songs celebrate everything from its bridges to its womenfolk. In the 19th century Baron Haussmann transformed the city for Napoleon III, sweeping away many of its crowded slum *quartiers* and replacing them with treelined **boulevards** too wide to barricade. Today, these stately avenues of elegantly matching, shuttered buildings and imposing **monuments** form the framework of much of modern Paris. The city is divided into 20 numbered *arrondissements*, or districts, which spiral from the centre in a clockwise pattern as far as the orbital ring road (Boulevard Périphérique). The Louvre area is referred to as the first (1er), the Opera district is the second (2e), and so on.

The geometrical layout and long vistas make it fairly easy to get your bearings on the western side of the city. If you stand amid the nonstop whirl of traffic at the **Arc de Triomphe**, you can look right along the ruler-straight Grand Axe, or main axis. To the west looms the huge archway heralding the modern business sector of **La Défense**. In the other direction you look past the obelisk in the **Place de la Concorde** through the **Jardin des Tuileries**, where old ladies toss crumbs to plump pigeons, to the glass pyramid at the entrance of the **Louvre**, one of the world's biggest and best art museums.

Paris is now very much a city for young people. Students traditionally hang out in the **Latin Quarter** on the Left Bank, so-called because studies at the Sorbonne were originally in Latin. The once seedy area around **Bastille** has shaken off its revolutionary past to become one of the city's trendiest nightspots with a multitude of bars and restaurants. Older quarters such as **Le Marais** and Montmartre remain warrens of picturesque old streets. Parisian night views (from a riverboat, the top of the **Eiffel Tower** or the steps in front of **Sacré-Coeur**) are part of the experience too. In the peak holiday month of August, Parisians desert their city en masse, leaving it strangely quiet.

ARRIVAL AND DEPARTURE

⊞ There are six main rail stations in Paris, all with tourist information and some with left luggage. Each has its own Métro stop; all except Montparnasse and Gare de l'Est are also served by express RER trains. For SNCF schedule information for the whole country call ☎36 35 (premium rate; in French) or visit www.sncf.com. **Paris-Nord (Gare du Nord)**: for Belgium, the Netherlands, Cologne and the UK (via Eurostar or Boulogne/Calais ferries). **Paris-Est (Gare de l'Est)**: northeast France, Luxembourg, Germany, Austria and Switzerland. **Gare St-Lazare**: Normandy. **Gare Montparnasse**: Brittany, Versailles, Chartres and TGV services to the southwest. **Gare d'Austerlitz**: Loire Valley, south and southwest France and Spain. **Gare de Lyon**: southeastern

France

France, the Auvergne, Provence, the Alps and Italy. Night trains to the south leave from **Gare d'Austerlitz**, to Italy from **Bercy**. Travellers by TGV trains through France may not need to pass through Paris; there's a bypass line calling at Roissy-Charles-de-Gaulle airport.

✈ **Roissy-Charles-de-Gaulle** (CDG) is 27 km northeast of the city: flight times, ☎39 50 (from abroad, +33 1 70 36 39 50; www.adp.fr); three main terminals, bureaux de change, cashpoints, tourist information and hotel booking desk. Links to the city. **RER B** ☎32 46, premium rate; (www.ratp.fr) to Gare du Nord and on to Châtelet-Les Halles, 0456–2356, every 10 or 15 mins, taking about 35 mins to/from Châtelet-Les Halles, fare €8.50; **Roissybus** (☎32 46; premium-rate; www.ratp.fr) to rue Scribe near L'Opéra 0600–2300 every 15–20 mins, taking 45 mins (15 mins more if the traffic is heavy), fare €9.10. **Air France coaches** (☎0892 35 08 20, premium-rate; www.cars-airfrance.com) to the Arc de Triomphe (1 avenue Carnot) and Porte Maillot (1 blvd Gouvion-St-Cyr), 0545–2300 every 30 mins, taking 35–50 mins, fare €15 (return €24), and to Gare de Lyon and Gare Montparnasse 0700–2100 every 30 mins, taking 45–60 mins, fare €16.50 (return €27). **Noctilien night bus** (☎32 46, from abroad +33 8 92 69 32 46, premium rate; www.ratp.fr). Night buses N140 and N143 to Gare du Nord and on to Gare de l'Est every hour or half-hour 2400–0430, between the last train in the evening and the first train in the morning. From either station you will find connections to other night buses. Fares vary. A taxi to the centre (40 mins–2 hours) should cost around €50.

TOURIST INFORMATION

Paris Convention and Visitors Bureau, ☎0892 68 30 00 (premium-rate number; 24-hr recorded information in English and French); www.parisinfo.com. Covers **Paris** and the surrounding **Île-de-France**, a booking service for **excursions**, a France-wide **hotel reservation** desk, desks for **SNCF** and **Disneyland Paris**. **Main Office**: 25 rue des Pyramides, other offices at **Gare de Lyon**, **Gare du Nord**, **Gare de l'Est**, the **Louvre Clemenceau** (av. des Champs-Élysées/av. Marigny), **Anvers** (median strip, opposite 72 blvd Rochechouart), **Montmartre** (21 pl. du Tertre) and **Paris Expo** (Porte de Versailles).

Orly is 14 km south; information service, ☎39 50 (from abroad, +33 1 70 36 39 50, premium rate, 24-hr; www.adp.fr); two terminals (Sud and Ouest), each with a tourist information booth and bureau de change. **Orlyrail** (shuttle bus then RER line C) to Gare d'Austerlitz, 0530–2330 every 20 mins, taking 50 mins, fare €6.20; **Orlyval (shuttle train)**; ☎32 46, premium rate; (www.orlyval.com) connecting with RER B at Antony, 0600–2308, every 4–7 mins, taking 8 mins, then RER B, taking 25 mins, fare €9.85. **RATP Orlybus** (☎0892 68 77 14, premium rate; www.ratp.fr) to Denfert-Rochereau Métro station, 0600–2320 and back to the airport 0535–2305, (one more hour service on Sat, Sun & holidays) every 15–20 mins, taking 30 mins, fare €6.40; **Air France coaches** (☎0892 35 08 20; premium rate; www.cars-airfrance.com) to Gare Montparnasse, Aérogare des Invalides and Place Charles de Gaulle-Etoile 0600–2300 (2330 from Orly) daily, every 30 mins, fare €11.50 (return €18.50). If you arrive late, night buses 31/131 going to Gare de Lyon should help, leaving every hour from about 0100 to 0400. A budget option from Orly-South is ☐ 285 going to Métro station Villejuif-Louis Aragon (line 7) or ☐ 185 going to Métro station Porte de Choisy (line 7), both stations located in the southeast, every 7 to 30 mins. Fare €3.70, then you'll have to use a new Métro ticket (the transfer is only possible to another bus). A **taxi** to the centre (20–40 mins) should cost around €35–45 (not recommended at rush hours).

PUBLIC TRANSPORT

You can see Paris on foot, but it's worth taking advantage of the efficient and well co-ordinated public transport system, made up of the **Métro** (subway) and **buses of RATP** (*Régie Autonome des Transport Parisiens*) and **RER** (*Réseau Express Régional*) **trains**.

Free **maps** of the networks are available from Métro and bus stations (plus many hotels and big stores): the *Petit Plan de Paris* covers the centre; the *Grand Plan de Paris* is more extensive.

MÉTRO The impressive Métro system runs every few mins 0530–0030 (0530–0130 on Fridays and Saturdays). Lines are coded by colour and number and named after their final destination. A recent addition is the driverless Météor line 14 linking St-Lazare station with the new National Library via Gare de Lyon. Maps of the whole system are at all stations and signs on platforms indicate connecting lines (*correspondances*). To reach the platform, slot your ticket into an automatic barrier, then retrieve it.

RER TRAINS This system, running 0530–0030 (0530–0130 on Fridays and Saturdays), consists of five rail lines (A, B, C, D and E), which are basically **express services** between the city and the suburbs. They form a cross through Paris and have a few central stops. The numbers following the letters (usually in the suburbs) indicate a branch from the main line. Not all trains stop at every station, so check the sign on the platform before boarding. There are **computerised route-finders** at the RER stations. These give you alternative ways to reach your destination – on foot, as well as by public transport.

BUSES RATP have 28 information offices throughout Paris (located inside main Métro or RER stations) and an **information line** (in French), manned 0700–2100, 0900–1715 weekends (automatic service 24 hours) ☎32 46 (premium-rate); information in English at www.ratp.fr. Bus stops show the numbers of the routes using them and display route maps. On some there are on-board announcements of the next stop. **Tickets** and **Carte Orange** must be validated when you board, but other **passes** are just shown to the driver. Most buses run 0630–2030, but some lines continue until 0030. Services on Sundays and bank holidays (*jours fériés*) are infrequent.

Night buses (*Noctilien*) run 0030–0530 and have 35 routes throughout the Île-de-France. Good bus routes for **seeing the city** are 🚌 24/63/67/69.

TICKETS

The same tickets (known as **t+**) are used for the Métro and RER (one journey per ticket) and for buses and trams throughout Paris (good for 90 minutes from first boarding; several transfers allowed). They cost €1.60 each, or €11.60 for a booklet of ten (probably the best value for a short stay), and are available from ticket machines as well as Métro and RER ticket offices. Bus drivers also sell tickets, but these are valid for one journey only (€1.70). Passes are sold at airports, stations, Tourist Offices and some tobacconists (*tabacs*). The **Mobilis** pass gives one day unlimited city travel covering zones 1 and 2 up to zones 1 to 8, but excludes the airports (€5.90). On weekends and holidays, under 26s can buy a **Ticket Jeunes Week-end** (€3.30 zones 1–3 to €8.20 zones 1–6). The **Paris Visite** pass for zones 1–3 or 1–6 is valid for one, two, three or five consecutive days; it also gives discounts at some tourist attractions (from €8.80 one day zones 1–3 to €48.40 five days zones 1–6). You can also get a **Navigo Découverte pass** with a **Carte Orange** (weekly or monthly pass; passport photo needed). The **weekly** (*Carte Hebdomadaire*) runs Mon–Sun
cont. p74.

France

(price depends on the number of zones, from €17.20). The **monthly** (*Carte Mensuelle*) is valid from the first day of the month (price depends on the number of zones, from €56.60). **Imagine R**, a yearly pass (barring July–Aug), allows student-card holders under 26 to travel in zones 1–2, 1–3, 1–4, 1–5, 1–6, 1–7 or 1–8 but only at weekends, public holidays and short school holidays.

TAXIS Flagging them down in the street is rarely successful. **Licensed taxis** have roof lights; white indicates that the taxi is free, orange means it is occupied. **Fares** are determined by three time zones and a host of extras, but they are regulated. Rates increase 1900–0600. Major companies include **Alpha**, ☎01 45 85 85 85, **Taxis Bleus**, ☎0891 70 10 10, **G7**, ☎01 47 39 47 39. **Avoid unofficial taxis**. **Tips** are expected (say 10%).

ACCOMMODATION

Despite Paris's huge number of tourist beds, finding accommodation can be a problem at busy periods (usually May, June, Sept and Oct). Bureaux d'Accueil at the main Tourist Office and main-line stations offer a **room-finding service** for hostels or hotels and there are automated room-finding machines at airports.

Cheaper accommodation is getting harder to find anywhere near the city centre, and if you're on a tight budget, you may have to stay a bit further afield, for instance in Bastille or République (11e), Montparnasse (14e) or Montmartre (9e and 18e). There's plenty of cheap accommodation around the Gare du Nord (10e), though it's a somewhat sleazy area. The Quartier Latin (5e) and St-Germain-des-Prés (6e), on the Left Bank, have some delightful medium-priced hotels. The fashionable Marais (3e and 4e) tends to be pricey now, but still has the odd gem here and there, like the **Hôtel du Septième Art**, 20 r. St-Paul, 4e, ☎01 44 54 85 00 (www.paris-hotel-7art.com), €€€, with a black-and-white movie theme and a lively bar (Métro: Châtelet/Les Halles). Another very central budget option is **Hôtel Tiquetonne**, 6 r. Tiquetonne, 2e, ☎01 42 36 94 58, €, near Les Halles (Métro: Étienne Marcel).

The most coveted and atmospheric parts of the city for accommodation are the islands in the Seine. There's just one hotel on the Île de la Cité in the heart of Paris, and amazingly, it's a budget option: **Hôtel Henri IV**, 25 pl. Dauphine, 1e, ☎01 43 54 44 53, €, (Métro: Pont Neuf/Cité). It's basic, but the location is unbeatable. Île St-Louis has more choice of accommodation, but hotels here are expensive.

Out in Clichy, the **Hôtel Eldorado** is a trendy find at 18 r. Dames, 17e, ☎01 45 22 35 21 (www.eldoradohotel.fr), €€, (Métro: Place de Clichy). In Grands Boulevards, the **Hôtel Chopin**, 46 impasse Jouffroy, 9e (entrance 10 bd Montmartre), ☎01 47 70 58 10 (www.hotelbretonnerie.com), €€, (Richelieu Drouot) is a friendly place in a glazed 19th-century shopping arcade. **Regyn's Montmartre**, 18 pl. Abbesses, 18e, ☎01 42 54 45 21 (www.regynsmontmartre.com), €€, is a Montmartre favourite (Métro: Abbesses). The **Hôtel Langlois**, 63 r. St-Lazare, 9e, ☎01 48 74 78 24 (www.hotel-langlois.com), €€€, (Métro: Trinité-d'Estienne d'Orves), is a lovely place full of character and well worth the price-tag. **The Hôtel Garden Saint Martin**, 35 r. Yves Toudic, 10e, ☎01 42 40 17 72 (www.hotel-parisgardensaintmartin.com), €€, is a modest but charming find in an interesting area of cafés and shops (Métro: République).

On the Left Bank, the welcoming **Familia Hôtel**, 11 r. des Ecoles, 5e 📞01 43 54 55 27 (www.hotel-paris-familia.com), €€€, has glimpses of Notre Dame (Métro: Cardinal Lemoine or Jussieu). The **Hôtel de Nesle**, in St-Germain, 7 r. de Nesle, 6e, 📞01 43 54 62 41 (www.hoteldenesleparis.com), €€, has a garden and loads of relaxing charm, every room with a different style and furniture (Métro: Odéon).

HI youth hostels: **Le d'Artagnan**, 80 r. Vitruve, 20e, 📞01 40 32 34 56 (paris.le-dartagnan@ fuaj.org; Métro: Porte-de-Bagnolet); **Cité des Sciences**, 24 r. des Sept Arpents, le Pré-St-Gervais, 19e, 📞01 48 43 24 11 (ajprestgervais@wanadoo.fr; Métro: Hoche, Porte de Pantin); **Jules Ferry**, 8 blvd Jules Ferry, 11e, 📞01 43 57 55 60 (www.hihostel.com; Métro: République); **Léo Lagrange**, 107 r. Martre, 92110 Clichy, 📞01 41 27 26 90 (paris. clichy@fuaj.org; Métro: Mairie de Clichy); **BVJ Louvre**, 20 r. Jean-Jacques Rousseau, 📞01 53 00 90 90 (bvj@wanadoo.fr; Métro; Louvre Rivoli Palais Royal). **Non-HI youth hostels**: **MIJE–Maison Internationale de la Jeunesse et des Étudiants**, 📞01 42 74 23 45 (www.mije.com; Métro: St Paul) has three hostels in lovely historic buildings (singles, doubles, triples and dorms; no age limit, no credit cards) in the nicely central and characterful old Marais district (most hotels hereabouts have gone upmarket, so this is a relative bargain): **Fourcy**, 6 r. de Fourcy, and **Fauconnier**, 11 r. du Fauconnier, are located in 17th-century aristocratic townhouses and **Maubisson**, 12 r. des Barres, is a converted convent. Near the Gare de Lyon, the **Blue Planet hostel**, 5 r. Hector Malot, 📞01 43 42 06 18 (www.hostelblueplanet.com; Métro: Gare de Lyon), has dorm beds for €25 including breakfast, and is open 24 hrs. Another similarly priced hostel is the **3 Ducks Hostel**, 6 pl. Etienne Pernet, 📞01 48 42 04 05 (www.3ducks.fr; Métro: Commerce), next to the Eiffel Tower. **The Woodstock Hostel**, 48 r. Rodier, 9e, 📞01 48 78 87 76 (www.woodstock.fr; Métro: Anvers), has young, friendly staff and is a 10-min walk from Gare du Nord (dorms €19–25 including breakfast).

Easily the most central **campsite** is **Camping du Bois de Boulogne**, 2, allée du Bord-de-l'Eau, 16e, 📞01 45 24 30 00, www.campingparis.fr (Métro: Porte Maillot). Next to the Seine and very popular, so book well in advance.

FOOD AND DRINK

Paris is still a great place to eat, with many fabulous restaurants, both French and exotic, at relatively cheap prices. Cafés and bars are the cheapest, brasseries slightly more expensive. The closer to the bar you stand, the less you pay. Self-service restaurants are usually fine, if a little institutional, and a snack at a crêperie will keep hunger at bay. Set lunches tend to be much better value than the evening equivalents. A trip to a *boulangerie* or market and an hour's picnic in the **Tuileries** gardens of the **Palais Royal** make a lovely way to lunch. Try the organic produce market, blvd Raspail, on Sun morning (Métro: Rennes). Alternatively, treat yourself to tea and a pâtisserie at one of the *salons de thé*. A favourite is **Le Loir dans la Théière**, 3 r. des Rosiers (Métro: St Paul).

France

For evening meals, study the set menus outside most restaurants; these often provide a reasonable choice at affordable prices. The **Bastille area**, the **Latin Quarter**, **Marais**, **Montmartre** and **Montparnasse** are good areas for cheap eating and multi-ethnic cuisine, especially Greek, North African, East European and Vietnamese. For kosher food, try r. des Rosiers and r. Xavier Privas. Vegetarian food is now much easier to find in Paris with bio (organic) cafés, soup shops and veggie restaurants springing up all over the city. The weekly listings magazine, *Pariscope*, provides a guide to Paris restaurants. If you fancy eating alfresco, make an early evening visit to r. Mouffetard (Métro: Monge/Censier Daubeton) or r. de Buci (Métro: St-Germain-des-Prés/Mabillon), where a range of mouth-watering ready-made delicacies is on offer in local *traiteurs*.

HIGHLIGHTS

Apart from the free museums belonging to the Paris City Council, almost all visitor attractions in Paris charge entrance fees, and these can be quite steep. However, the majority of national museums and monuments are free to under 18s and to all on the first Sun of the month. *Paris Visite* gives discounts on some major attractions. Much more comprehensive are the *Paris City Passport* (€5), which lasts a calendar year and gives 10 to 50 per cent discounted admission to 33 sites, and Paris Museum Pass, which offers entrance (without waiting to buy your ticket) and reductions to over 60 museums and monuments in and around Paris for two, four or six consecutive days (€32/€48/€64); available from participating museums and monuments, Tourist Offices, principal Métro and RER stations, FNAC ticket counters and Batobus stops. Most monuments (with the notable exceptions of the Eiffel Tower, the Musée d'Orsay and Les Invalides) are on the **Right Bank**, while the islands in the middle of the River Seine are the oldest part of the city and offer some of its best historic buildings. The **Left Bank** was traditionally popular with artists and the Bohemian crowd but is now primarily residential.

THE ISLANDS (LES ÎLES)   Take time out to wander round the largely 17th-century Île St-Louis, and stop off at the the major sights on **Île de la Cité**, which is linked to it by a footbridge (Métro: Cité). The great cathedral towers and 13-tonne bell stand of **Notre Dame**, built between 1163 and 1345, make it one of the world's finest examples of Gothic architecture. Tiny **Sainte-Chapelle** (in the courtyard of the Palais de Justice) has a magnificent set of stained-glass windows – on a sunny day, it's like standing in a kaleidoscope. The **Conciergerie**, once a prison for those awaiting the guillotine (most notably, Marie-Antoinette), is also worth a look.

THE RIGHT BANK (LA RIVE DROITE)   Just over the bridge from the islands, the Hôtel de Ville marks the start of the **Marais**, filled with well-restored streets and squares. Make a point of seeing the beautiful Renaissance pl. des Vosges; the Maison Victor Hugo, where the novelist resided, occupies a corner building. The best of the Marais museums are the **Musée Carnavalet**, 23 r. de Sévigné, 3e (closed Mon, permanent exhibitions free), an exhibition on the history of Paris housed in two historic mansions, and the **Musée Picasso**, 5 r. de Thorigny, 3e (unfortunately, closed until 2012), a fine collection of the artist's work and artefacts, ordered chronologically (Métro for both: St-Paul/Chemin Vert).

Just outside the area is the unmistakable **Centre Pompidou** (also known as Beaubourg; Wed–Mon 1100–2100, closed Tues; free first Sun of month and daily for under 26s), pl. Georges-Pompidou (Métro: Hotel-de-Ville), a high-tech glass-and-metal building with ducts and pipes of varying colours stuck to the outside. The escalator snaking up the exterior gives a great city view. Inside, the **Musée National d'Art Moderne** (closed Tues) houses one of Europe's greatest collections of modern art. Outside, street performers congregate near the humorously eccentric fountains by the modern Swiss sculptor Tinguely.

Back beside the river, the **Louvre** (Métro: Palais-Royal; enter via Métro to avoid long queues; Thurs and Sat–Mon 0900–1800, Wed and Fri 0900–2200; closed Tues) is one of the world's greatest art museums. Housed in a former palace, it's a sightseeing marathon, with miles of corridors. Its most famous exhibits, the **Mona Lisa** (*La Joconde* in French) and the **Vénus de Milo**, are always surrounded by vast crowds. I M Pei's startling glass pyramid has marked the entrance since 1989. West of the Louvre, the formal **Jardins des Tuileries**, designed by the royal gardener, Le Nôtre, in 1649, lead along the river to the pl. de la Concorde. At the far end the **Musée du Jeu de Paume**, 1 pl. de la Concorde (Métro: Concorde/Tuileries; open daily except Mon), hosts changing exhibitions of photography and video, while the **Musée de l'Orangerie**, pl. du Carrousel (closed Tues, free 1st Sun of the month), is devoted to the Impressionists and post-Impressionists, notably Renoir, Matisse and Picasso – it was created largely as a showplace for eight of Monet's large water-lily paintings, which have two oval rooms to themselves.

From pl. de la Concorde the av. des Champs-Élysées leads up towards the **Arc de Triomphe**, pl. du Géneral-de-Gaulle (Métro: Charles de Gaulle-Étoile); open 1000–2300 Apr–Sept; 1000–2230 Oct–Mar, free for European Citizens under 26, dedicated to all French armies and the resting place of the Unknown Soldier. A climb to the top reveals the 12 boulevards fanning out from the arch in a star-like formation.

The **Paris sewer tour** (Musée des Égouts de Paris), opposite 93 Quai d'Orsay (Métro: Alma-Marceau), open Sat–Wed 1100–1700 (1600, Oct–Apr), closed two weeks mid–Jan, is a trip with a difference, taking you deep into the bowels of the city and the world's first underground sewer system.

THE LEFT BANK (LA RIVE GAUCHE)

Visiting the **Eiffel Tower** can involve a lengthy queue (taking the stairs to the second level reduces the wait and the cost). All but the incurably height-phobic should clock this astonishing monument once in a lifetime. It's located at Champ de Mars (Métro: Bir-Hakeim; open 0930–2300, 0900–2400 mid-June–Aug). There's an interesting exhibition on the tower's construction and history on the first level, and, of course, unrivalled views over Paris on a clear day from the top. Afterwards, head towards the magnificent 17th-century Hotel des Invalides (Métro: La Tour-Maubourg/Varenne), to see Napoleon's tomb

TOURS

Paris Vision, 214 r. de Rivoli, ☎01 42 60 30 01, offer **recorded commentary multilingual bus tours** of all the main sights in about two hours. **Paris à vélo, c'est sympa!**, 22 r. Alphonse Baudin, ☎01 48 87 60 01, offer **cycling tours** of Paris and also rent scooters and tandems. Most of the **boat companies** operate half-hourly departures with multilingual commentaries, and some offer evening **dinner cruises**. The glass-topped **Bateaux-Mouches** have frequent departures from Pont de l'Alma, ☎01 42 25 96 10. Other companies include **Vedettes de Paris**, ☎01 44 18 19 50, from Port de Suffren, and **Bateaux Parisiens**, ☎0825 01 01 01 (premium rate), from Port de la Bourdonnais. Buy a ticket before boarding. The **Batobus**, ☎0825 05 01 01 (premium rate), is a water-bus (without commentary) every 15–30 mins, 1000–1900 (late Mar–May and Oct), 1000–2130 (June–Sept) and 1030–1630 (Nov–early Jan), stopping at the Eiffel Tower, Musée d'Orsay, St-Germain-des-Prés, Notre-Dame, Jardin des Plantes, Hôtel de Ville, the Louvre and Champs-Élysées. You can get a day-ticket, 2-day ticket or 5-day, even a 1-year pass. (€12–55).

and the **Musée de l'Armée** (Army Museum). Nearby is the **Musée National Rodin**, 77 r. de Varenne (Métro: Varenne), a magnificent house and garden full of the sculptor's works including *The Kiss* and *The Thinker*, open daily 1000–1800 (1700 winter).

On the river bank, the **Musée d'Orsay**, 1 r. de la Légion d'Honneur (formerly r. de Bellechasse), 7e (Métro: Solférino), open Tues, Wed, Fri–Sun 0930–1800, Thurs 0930–2145; closed Mon; free for under 26s), is a converted railway station housing a spectacular collection of 19th- and early 20th-century art, including famous works by Renoir, Degas, Monet, Manet, Van Gogh and Delacroix.

Beyond this are the narrow medieval streets of the Latin Quarter, home of the **Sorbonne University** and two great parks: **Jardin du Luxembourg**, r. de Vaugirard, and **Jardin des Plantes**, pl. Valhubert. Between them is the **Panthéon**, pl. du Panthéon, France's hall of fame for the great and the glorious (1000–1830, 1815 in winter). **Musée du Moyen-Âge**, 6 pl. Paul-Painlevé (Métro: Cluny-La Sorbonne/ St Michel/Odéon), in a 16th-century monastery, contains a huge and splendid collection of medieval works of art and tapestries, the most famous of which is the *Lady and the Unicorn* (closed Tues).

FURTHER OUT North of the river, **Montmartre** offers the most accessible views of the city. Topping the hill are the overblown white cupolas of the basilica of Sacré-Coeur, built at the turn of the 20th century (0600–2300), while portrait artists await custom at their easels in the nearby pl. du Tertre. The area is besieged by tourists and touts, yet its charm still outweighs the kitsch.

On the northeastern edge of the city, **Parc de la Villette** (Metro: Porte de la Villette) is home to the vast **Cité des Sciences et de l'Industrie**, a state-of-the-art science museum (Tues–Sat 1000–1800, Sun 1000–1900, closed Mon) both in its architecture and in its contents; and the polished-steel sphere of **La Géode**, containing a hemispheric screen for IMAX films. Parc de la Villette can be reached by canal: boats leave Jaurès Métro station every 30 mins 1100–1800.

On the western side of Paris, the **Bois de Boulogne** (Métro: Porte-Maillot) is a huge Sunday strolling ground, fun for people-watching, and looking at some of the most elegant of the city's suburbs; after dark it's a very different place – notorious for its transvestite nightlife and not very safe. Nearby is the **Musée Marmottan Monet** (2 r. Louis-Boilly; Métro: La Muette; 1000–1800 (2100 Tue), closed Mon), housing a choice collection of Monet paintings, including several water-lily canvases and scenes of the garden at Giverny.

Towards the eastern edge of the city, the **Cimetière du Père Lachaise** (Métro: Père Lachaise) is the most aristocratic of cemeteries, a fantastically atmospheric place both for the quality of the monuments and the fame of its permanent residents (who include Bizet, Chopin, Oscar Wilde, Edith Piaf, Balzac, Corot and Jim Morrison).

NIGHT-TIME AND EVENTS

Weekly listings are published on Wednesdays in *Pariscope* (€0.40) and *L'Officiel des spectacles* (€0.35), on sale at newsagents. **Half-price theatre tickets** can be purchased for same-day performances from the kiosks opposite 15 pl. de la Madeleine (Métro: Madeleine) and espl. de la Tour, 14e (Métro: Montparnasse-Bienvenüe). Both open Tues–Sat 1230–1945 and Sun 1230–1545; credit cards not accepted. **Online booking** is available through www.francebillet.com.

Paris is famous for its elaborate and risqué cabaret, notably **Bal du Moulin Rouge**, 82 blvd de Clichy, the **Lido de Paris**, 116 bis av. des Champs-Élysées, and **Crazy Horse**, 12 av. George V. The best and most Parisian is **Le Paradis Latin** (28 r. du Cardinal Lemoine). Be warned – these shows are exorbitantly expensive.

There are regular seasons of both ballet and opera at **Opéra Bastille**, pl. de la Bastille, **Palais Garnier**, 8 pl. de l'Opéra (which sells cheap stand-by tickets on the day of the performance; special tariff for under 26s), and **Opéra-Comique**, pl. Boieldieu. There are also numerous concerts, held everywhere from purpose-built auditoria to museums, with a variety of free performances in several churches (including Notre Dame).

Other live music (especially rock) is also easy to find, and there's no shortage of discos. For listings, take a look at *Pariscope* or *LYLO* (free booklet published every two weeks, available in some bars). At cinemas, there are often discounts on Sun morning. VO (*Version Originale*) means the film is in the original language, while VF (*Version Française*) means it's been dubbed.

The most famous annual celebration is **Bastille Day** (13–14 July), when fireworks and parades mark the anniversary of the storming of the city prison in 1789. Other major events include **Mardi Gras** (Feb); **May Day workers' marches** (1 May); the **French Open Tennis Championships** (late May – early June); **Paris Cinéma** film festival (late June–early July); the final stage of the **Tour de France** cycle race along the Champs Élysées (last or second to last Sun in July); and **Paris Autumn Festival** (mid-Sept–Dec).

France

SHOPPING

You can buy anything in Paris – but at a price. For designer style, head for r. du Faubourg St-Honoré, av. Montaigne and r. de Rivoli. More reasonable prices can be tracked down at **Les Halles** (popular and trendy), **St-Germain-des-Prés** (boutique/brand fashions) and the r. de Rennes. The most famous department stores are **Galeries Lafayette**, 40 blvd Haussmann, **Printemps**, 64 blvd Haussmann, and, on the Left Bank, **Le Bon Marché**, 24 r. de Sèvres. **Markets** are big business in Paris, and the Tourist Office produces a free list. Quayside stalls sell flowers and books on Sunday mornings near Île St-Louis. The best-known flea-market is **St-Ouen**, av. de la Porte de Clignancourt (Métro: Porte de Clignancourt), held Sat–Mon 1000–1800 (www.parispuces.com), which consists of 16 separate markets, including **Jules-Vallès** (curios, lace and postcards), **Marché Serpette** (products from the 1900s–1930s) and **Marché Malik** (second-hand clothes and records). Bargains are hard to find. Free first Sun of the month, Oct–Mar.

SIDE TRIPS FROM PARIS

VERSAILLES (RER line C5 to Versailles-Rive Gauche, then walk through the town.) Versailles (www.chateauversailles.fr) was the pride and joy of Louis XIV, the long-reigning 'Sun King' who in 1668 transformed his father's hunting lodge to this stupendous palace. Most famous of all are the dazzling Galerie des Glaces (Hall of Mirrors) and the Petit Trianon and Grand Trianon – two elegant pavilions built for the king's mistresses – where the doomed Marie-Antoinette used to play at peasant life before the Revolution. Crowded at the height of summer, but the huge grounds, with their statuary, topiary and water parterres, are always rewarding. Gardens open daily, châteaux open daily except Mon, 0900–1830, Nov–Mar 0900–1730.

FONTAINEBLEAU (Rail from Gare de Lyon to Fontainebleau-Avon, then bus A or B) Fontainebleau (www.musee-chateau-fontainebleau.fr) is another famous royal palace to the south of the city. The massive and beautiful château restored to Renaissance splendour by François I in the 16th century is the main draw, but so too is the surrounding hunting forest, now a favourite retreat at weekends for picnics, walks and outdoor pursuits. Open Wed–Mon 0930–1800; Oct–May 0930–1700 (gardens open daily); free 1st Sun of month.

WHERE NEXT FROM PARIS?

Gare de Lyon is the Parisian station for the southeast and is served by the high-speed TGV trains. These trains get you down to southern France in 3–4 hrs (5½ to Nice), with services to Lyon, Avignon, Marseille, Nice, Aix-en-Provence, Perpignan, Béziers, Montpellier and elsewhere.

ROUTE DETAIL

Calais–Boulogne ETT table 261

Type	Frequency	Typical journey time
Train	Every 1–2 hrs	30–40 mins

Boulogne–Amiens ETT table 260

Type	Frequency	Typical journey time
Train	Every 1–2 hrs	1 hr 30 mins

Amiens–Paris (Nord) ETT table 260

Type	Frequency	Typical journey time
Train	Every 1–2 hrs	1 hr 15 mins

Paris (Austerlitz)–Orléans (Les Aubrais) ETT 294

Type	Frequency	Typical journey time
Train	Every 1–1½ hrs	1 hr

Orléans (Les Aubrais)–Limoges ETT 310

Type	Frequency	Typical journey time
Train	10–12 daily	1 hr 50 mins

Limoges–Cahors ETT table 310

Type	Frequency	Typical journey time
Train	8–9 daily	2 hrs 20 mins

Cahors–Toulouse ETT table 310

Type	Frequency	Typical journey time
Train	8–10 daily	1 hr 10 mins

KEY JOURNEYS

Calais–Paris ETT tables 260, 265

Type	Frequency	Typical journey time
Train	5–6 daily	2 hrs–3 hrs 30 mins

Paris–Toulouse ETT tables 300, 310

Type	Frequency	Typical journey time
Train	6–7 daily	5 hrs 15 mins–6 hrs 45 mins

Notes

Calais to Toulouse: change trains in Paris. The fastest (TGV) trains between Paris and Toulouse travel via Bordeaux. A shuttle train connects main line Les Aubrais–Orléans station to the town of Orléans.

France

This grand north-south cross-section of France begins from the Channel ports of **Calais** and **Boulogne** and heads through the flat arable lands of the north that witnessed some of the fiercest fighting of World War I. **Amiens** is a good centre for seeking out the battlefields and memorials of the era. Allow plenty of time for crossing Paris by Métro. **Orléans** is worth a stay, with its cathedral and history of Joan of Arc. The porcelain-making town of **Limoges** gives scope for branching into the more out-of-the-way uplands of the Massif Central; meanwhile the main route continues into the Dordogne, a rural region much visited for its prehistoric sites and unspoilt old towns, castles and villages. **Cahors** has a strong southern flavour, while **Toulouse** is a big, demanding city and **Albi** a rewarding detour.

CALAIS

Just under 40 km from the English coast at Dover, this busy cross-channel port gets brisk trade from English day trippers stocking up at local hypermarkets, including the mammoth **Cité Europe** mall near the Channel Tunnel loading area, west of town (on regular bus routes from the centre of town). But there's a more authentically French feel about the shops and restaurants along the main road from the port, especially on market day in pl. d'Armes (Wed/Sat) or blvd Lafayette (Thur/Sat). Rodin's famous statue of the **Six Burghers of Calais** stands in front of the Flemish-style **Hôtel de Ville** (town hall), commemorating the English capture of the town in 1347. Opposite, in the Parc St-Pierre, is the **Musée de la Guerre**, devoted to a more recent conflict – World War II – and originally used as a bunker by German forces. The **Musée de la Dentelle et de la Mode** (recently opened in a 19th-century lace factory on r. Sambor) celebrates a local industry.

🚆 **Calais-Ville**, the main station, is almost opposite the Hôtel de Ville (town hall). The other station, **Calais-Fréthun**, near the mouth of the Channel Tunnel, is about 8 km from Calais and serves the Eurostar (London–Paris).

🚢 Both ferry companies run buses between **Calais-Ville** station and the docks to connect with sailings.

INFORMATION

P&O (Dover)
☎0825 12 01 56
(☎0871 664 5645
from UK),
www.poferries.com

SeaFrance
☎03 21 17 70 26,
www.seafrance.com

ℹ️ **Tourist Office**: 12 blvd Clemenceau; ☎03 21 96 62 40 (www.calais-coteopale.com).

🏨 Plenty of hotels around r. Royale, such as the friendly, family-run **Hôtel du Beffroi**, 8 r. André Gerschell, just off place d'Armes. **Hostel** (**HI**): **Centre Européen de Séjour**, av. du Maréchal de Lattre de Tassigny, ☎03 21 34 70 20, (www.auberge-jeunesse-calais.com), 1 km from rail station. Out at the Cité Europe are three well-managed chain hotels, **Etap**, **Ibis** and **Suite-Hotel** (all adjacent). Etap is cheapest, €; Suite-Hotel very stylish and comfortable, €€€ (www.accor.com).

BOULOGNE-SUR-MER

After wartime damage, most of Boulogne-sur-Mer's Basse Ville (lower town) is unremarkable, though the vast port area is a constant hive of activity. One of the town's major attractions is **Nausicaá** (www.nausicaa.fr), a huge and entertaining (if expensive) aquarium on the seafront at blvd Sainte-Beuve. But the best thing to do in Boulogne-sur-Mer is to head straight up the Grande Rue towards the Ville Haute (upper town), tantalisingly visible from the lower town within its well-preserved 13th-century ramparts. A walk around the city walls immediately transports you into medieval France, and provides fine views of the harbour. Besides the moated Château (containing a history museum), the main sights are the 19th-century Basilique Notre-Dame with its landmark Italianate dome, and the ancient Hôtel de Ville on a charming cobbled square.

Boulogne-Ville, 1 km south of the centre; all buses stopping here go to the centre.

i **Tourist Office**: Parvis de Nausicaá, ☎03 21 10 88 10 (www.tourisme-boulognesurmer.com). From the station, take blvd Daunou to the port and keep following the port around to the fish stalls: the Tourist Office is opposite. There's an additional bureau in summer at Porte des Dunes.

Boulogne-sur-Mer has good-value hotels right in the heart of town. Try the reasonably priced, very central, 2-star **Hôtel de Londres**, 22 pl. de France, ☎03 21 31 35 63 (www.hotel delondres.net), €€. There's a pleasant waterfront **Ibis** hotel handy for the station, 11 blvd Diderot, ☎03 21 30 12 40 and another up in the Ville Haute, r. Porte Neuve, ☎03 21 31 21 01 (www. ibishotel.com), €€. **Youth hostel (HI)**: pl. Rouget de Lisle, ☎03 21 99 15 30 (boulogne-sur-mer@fuaj.org) is 100 m from the station.

AMIENS

Two world wars did great damage to what was a major industrial centre, sparing only the **Cathédrale Notre-Dame d'Amiens**, Europe's largest and arguably France's purest example of Gothic architecture. The west doorway lingers in the memory, a 'book in stone' featuring the famed *Beau Dieu* portal. Sympathetically restored to their original character, the winding streets of the **St-Leu** district, straddling the Somme just north of the cathedral, date from medieval times. In summer, take a boat trip on the tiny canals criss-crossing the 'Hortillonnages' (market gardens), just beyond the cathedral. Sci-fi author Jules Verne spent his last years in Amiens. You can visit his house (2 r. Charles-Dubois), and his grave in the Cimetière de la Madeleine (r. Saint-Maurice), where he appears to be pushing up his own tombstone.

The main station, easily spotted near the austere post-war Tour Perret, lies about 500m southeast of the cathedral. Turn right on blvd d'Alsace Lorraine and then second left on r. Gloriette. Certain buses are allowed into the pedestrianised centre, but it is usually much faster to walk – and certainly the best way to explore.

i **Tourist Office**: 6 bis r. Dusevel, ☎03 22 71 60 50 (www.amiens-tourisme.com).

France

Trains from **Calais** arrive at **Paris Nord** station. Ask at Information (*Renseignements/Accueil*) which station your connection leaves from, and allow 1 hr to cross Paris via the Métro.

PARIS

See p71.

ORLÉANS

Strategically sited in the middle of France, Orléans has been attacked since Roman times. Its older quarter, containing several Renaissance mansions, has been restored since World War II. Today Orléans makes much of its associations with **Jeanne d'Arc** (Joan of Arc, the Maid of Orléans), who saved the town from the English in 1429. Her statue takes pride of place in the spacious pl. du Martroi, and the nearby **Maison de Jeanne d'Arc**, pl. du Général de Gaulle, is a reconstruction of her lodgings with a museum recounting her life and the events of 1429. The annual **Fête de Jeanne d'Arc** (Apr 29, May 1 and 7–8) features a living 'Jeanne' riding through the streets.

The impressive **Cathédrale Sainte-Croix** (Holy Cross Cathedral) commemorates Jeanne in its 19th-century stained-glass windows. Guided tours of the roof include a panoramic city view.

🚆 **Gare d'Orléans** is on the northern edge of the centre, right by the **pl. d'Arc** shopping complex; r. de la République runs straight ahead to pl. du Martroi, in the heart of town. Gare d'Orléans is actually on a short spur, just off the main rail line, and through-services stop only at nearby **Fleury-les-Aubrais-Orléans** station. A train shuttle service (*navette*) linking the two stations connects with every through-train; there is also a tram service.

🚌 r. M-Proust, ☎02 38 53 94 75, a block from Gare d'Orléans (connected by a covered passage).

ℹ️ **Tourist Office:** 2 pl. de l'Étape; ☎02 38 24 05 05 (www.tourisme-orleans.com).

🏨 The streets around r. du Fg-Bannier and pl. Gambetta have some inexpensive hotels, such as the 2-star **Hôtel Le Saint-Aignan**, 3 pl. Gambetta, ☎02 38 53 15 35, (www.hotel-saintaignan.fr), €€. The central **Le Brin de Zinc**, 62 r. Saint Catherine, ☎02 38 53 38 77, has a restaurant, €. **Youth Hostel (HI):** **CRJS Stade Omnisports**, 7 av. Beaumarchais, ☎02 38 53 60 06 (auberge.crjs45@wanadoo.fr); 🚌 20 to Recherche Scientifique or tram to L'Indien.

WHERE NEXT FROM ORLÉANS?

*Take the train down to Tours (p102; journey time 1 hr, frequent services, ETT table 296) to pick up the Paris–Bordeaux line. Stop off at **Blois**, with its superb château where the Duc de Guise and his brother were murdered on the orders of Henri III in 1588, and then visit the 440-room Château de Chambord nearby.*

LIMOGES

Capital of the Limousin region, Limoges is a large industrial city, renowned for its high-quality enamel and ornate porcelain. Its delightful medieval centre is a web of dark, narrow streets filled with half-timbered houses, small boutiques and antique and china shops. Surrounded by well-maintained botanic gardens and overlooking the River Vienne is the Gothic **Cathédrale de St-Étienne** (St Stephen's). The nearby bishop's palace contains some fine collections of porcelain and enamel (place de la Cathédrale – admission free), though it scarcely matches the magnificent array of porcelain and faïence on show at the **Musée Adrien-Dubouché**, pl. Winston-Churchill (closed Tues and at lunchtime), with over 12,000 pieces. For more on the porcelain industry, take a tour of the **Bernardaud factory**, 1 km north of town (27 av. Albert Thomas, ☎05 55 10 55 91; closed Sun; book ahead). Limoges was a centre of the Resistance during WWII. The **Musée de la Résistance et de la Déportation** traces some of the Resistance operations (r. Règle, Jardin de l'Évêché; closed Tue off-season; free admission).

Gare des Bénédictins, 500 m northeast of the Old Town (a wonderful example of Art Deco). Walk straight along av. du Gén. de Gaulle, across pl. Jourdan and into blvd de Fleurus – or take 🚌 8/10 to pl. Jourdan.

i **Tourist Office**: 12 blvd de Fleurus, ☎05 55 34 46 87 (www.tourismelimoges.com).

🛏 Cheap accommodation near the train station; try **Familia**, 18 r. du Gén. Bessol, ☎05 55 77 51 40 (www.hotelfamilia.fr), €€. **Hôtel de la Paix**, 25 pl. Jourdan, ☎05 55 34 36 00, €–€€, is quiet and within walking distance of the station and town centre, and hosts a phonograph museum for the curious.

🍽 Well-priced ethnic restaurants and student bars crowd the southern end of r. Charles Michels. Le Bistro d'Olivier at the **Halles Centrales** (covered market) does cheap, hearty lunches. Alternatively, stock up at the market, open daily until 1300.

> ### WHERE NEXT FROM LIMOGES?
>
> *Trains head east to Clermont-Ferrand (ETT table 326) with optional detour to Le Mont-Dore; see p136.*

CAHORS

An important Roman base on the tortuously winding River Lot, Cahors is famed for its red wine, which at its best rivals the vintages of Bordeaux. Its major monument, frequently depicted on wine labels, is the 14th-century **Pont Valentré**, west of the centre (reached via the r. du Président Wilson) a six-arched fortified bridge with three towers. Gallo-Roman remains dot the town, and medieval houses are grouped around the cathedral.

France

[RAIL] A 10-min walk west of the centre: leave pl. Jouinot-Gambetta by av. J-Jaurès (to the right) and turn left on r. du Président Wilson. At blvd Gambetta, turn right and then right again onto pl. F-Mitterrand for the **Tourist Office**.

i **Tourist Office**: pl. F-Mitterrand, ☎05 65 53 20 65 (www.mairie-cahors.fr, www.quercy.net).

[HOTEL] For a special treat, the **Grand Hôtel Terminus** is a beautifully restored station hotel dating from the 1920s, 5 av. Charles de Freycinet, ☎05 65 53 32 00, www.balandre.com, €€. **Hôtel de la Paix**, 30 pl. St-Maurice, ☎05 65 35 03 40 (www.hoteldelapaixcahors.com), €, and the 8-room **Hôtel La Bourse**, 7 pl. Claude Rousseau, ☎/fax 05 65 35 17 78, €, are both on small squares in the old centre. **Hostel (HI)**: 20 r. Frédéric Suisse, ☎05 65 35 64 71 (fjt46@wanadoo.fr); former convent, 500 m from the station.

[TO] At night, head out to one of the cafes and restaurants on blvd Léon Gambetta or parallel street rue Nationale.

WHERE NEXT FROM CAHORS?

*SNCF buses heading east from Cahors snake along one of the most beautifully sinuous sections of the Lot Valley to **Figeac**, a likeable old town that makes a pleasant base for a day or two. The bus passes through Conduché, from where it's a walk of just over 5 km past Cabrerets to **La Grotte du Pech-Merle**. This cave is one of Europe's great underground sights, not only for its stalactites and stalagmites, but also for its Stone Age art, including paintings of horses and bison, ochre-outlined 'signatures' of human hands, and fossilised footprints of a man and a child. Also on the way are **Saint-Cirq-Lapopie** and **Cajarc**, quaint medieval villages well worth visiting.*

*On the rail line north from Figeac to Brive la Gaillarde, **Rocamadour** is the stunningly situated village (4 km from Rocamadour station) set on narrow ledges of a cliff face, where the famous Black Virgin has drawn pilgrims since the 12th century. The village actually looks more impressive from a distance. Wall-to-wall kitsch shops pander to the tourists and the devout who pack its main street for much of the year.*

TOULOUSE

Now a lively university city and cultural centre, the capital of the Midi region is one of France's largest cities, not consistently attractive but with a wealth of medieval religious art. The pinky-red brick of many of the grandiose town houses has earned the city the epithet of the Ville Rose.

The centre is walkable, but there is also a bus service and two-line Métro (and a one-line tram to be opened in 2010), run by **Tisséo** ☎05 61 41 70 70 (www.tisseo.fr). Tickets cover both the bus and Métro, the best value being the *carnet* (pack) of ten, available from ticket booths or the main office: buses only sell single tickets. Also consider the *Tribu* pass (for one to six people travelling together).

Many of the main attractions are in the Old Town, centred on **pl. du Capitole**, dominated by the 18th-century **Le Capitole** (town hall). The superb **Basilique St-Sernin** is the sole survivor of an 11th-century Benedictine monastery established to assist pilgrims en route to Santiago de Compostela (see p205). The **Musée des Augustins** has an exceptional show of medieval sculptures rescued from long-gone city churches (open Wed to 2100).

[RAIL] **Toulouse–Gare Matabiau**, northeast of the city; a 15–20-min walk from pl. du Capitole – or take the Métro (the station stop is **Marengo–SNCF**). The railway station has showers.

i **Tourist Office**: Donjon du Capitole, Square Charles de Gaulle, ☎05 61 11 02 22 (www.toulouse-tourisme.com).

🛏 Budget places can be found in the centre, around pl. Wilson (r. St-Antoine) and pl. du Capitole (r. du Taur and r. de Romiguières). There are cheap hotels around the station, but the area is best avoided. **Anatole France**, 46 pl. Anatole France, ☎05 61 23 19 96, €, is right in the centre of town.
Youth hostel (HI): **Résidence de Jolimont**, 2 av. Yves Brunaud, ☎05 34 30 42 80 (foyerjolimont@wanadoo.fr); 500 m from rail station, **Campsites**: all four are on the outskirts of the town, but accessible by bus (information from the Tourist Office).

🍴 Try **Casa Manolo**, 24 rue des Trois Piliers, open daily, a bodega with plenty of Spanish food, tapas and salads and marinated rums. There's also live salsa, zouk and Latin bands with dancing. In summer, treat yourself to a home-made ice cream from **Ô Sorbet D'Amour**, 28 rue Montardy.

LA CITÉ DE L'ESPACE
La Cité de l'Espace
(Space City), av. Jean Gonord, ☎0820 37 72 23 (premium rate) (www.cite-espace.com), lies east of **Toulouse** in a large park. There are space themed exhibitions, a planetarium and the rocket *Ariane 5*. Open daily 0930–1700 (1800 or 1900 in high season), except Mon (Sept–Dec) and early Jan–early Feb. Get there by Métro line A to Jolimont (Sun, to Marengo/SNCF), then 🚌 37.

WHERE NEXT FROM TOULOUSE?

Albi (about an hour from Toulouse; ETT table 323), another city of pink-red brick, has one of the strangest cathedrals in Christendom: from outside it resembles a fortress (erected by crusading bishops in the wake of their systematic slaughter of the peaceable Cathar sect in the 14th century), its interior completely covered with murals, including a depiction of Heaven and Hell intended to strike terror and unswerving faith into the hearts of the congregation. It's a scene that was familiar to Henri Toulouse-Lautrec, the city's best-known son, many of whose most famous works are displayed in the adjacent Musée Toulouse-Lautrec. He emerged as one of the great portrait artists; he chose to depict prostitutes for the reason that brothels gave him a unique opportunity to observe women at their most unaffected and unposed. For an explanation of the major pictures, rent the multilingual audio tour.

Alternatively join the **Biarritz–Marseille** route (see p113) or continue from Toulouse over the Pyrenees on the **Toulouse–Barcelona** route (see p138).

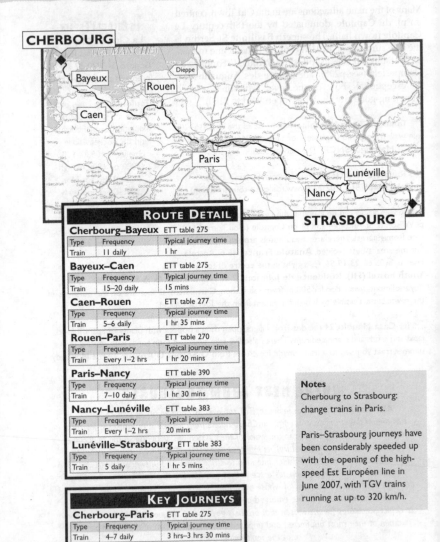

CHERBOURG

STRASBOURG

ROUTE DETAIL

Cherbourg–Bayeux   ETT table 275

Type	Frequency	Typical journey time
Train	11 daily	1 hr

Bayeux–Caen   ETT table 275

Type	Frequency	Typical journey time
Train	15–20 daily	15 mins

Caen–Rouen   ETT table 277

Type	Frequency	Typical journey time
Train	5–6 daily	1 hr 35 mins

Rouen–Paris   ETT table 270

Type	Frequency	Typical journey time
Train	Every 1–2 hrs	1 hr 20 mins

Paris–Nancy   ETT table 390

Type	Frequency	Typical journey time
Train	7–10 daily	1 hr 30 mins

Nancy–Lunéville   ETT table 383

Type	Frequency	Typical journey time
Train	Every 1–2 hrs	20 mins

Lunéville–Strasbourg   ETT table 383

Type	Frequency	Typical journey time
Train	5 daily	1 hr 5 mins

KEY JOURNEYS

Cherbourg–Paris   ETT table 275

Type	Frequency	Typical journey time
Train	4–7 daily	3 hrs–3 hrs 30 mins

Paris–Strasbourg   ETT table 390

Type	Frequency	Typical journey time
Train	15–17 daily	2 hrs 20 mins

Notes

Cherbourg to Strasbourg: change trains in Paris.

Paris–Strasbourg journeys have been considerably speeded up with the opening of the high-speed Est Européen line in June 2007, with TGV trains running at up to 320 km/h.

RAIL TOUR: CHERBOURG – PARIS – STRASBOURG

The prelude to Paris is a trip through **Normandy** (*Normandie*), named after the invading Norsemen who settled in the Seine Valley in the Dark Ages. To the north are some of the most attractive chalklands of the region, dotted with gracious manors and half-timbered farmhouses and culminating in great white cliffs around **Dieppe**. It was on the beaches of Normandy that the Allied invasion began in June 1944; many larger towns were badly bombed and have been reconstructed. East of Paris the route crosses the **Champagne** region, Épernay being the winemaking headquarters (you can tour champagne cellars by underground train and often enjoy free samples). Next is **Nancy**, with its monumental architecture, the star of Lorraine, a region separated by the Vosges hills from Alsace, where the architecture, dialect and place names are distinctly Germanic. On the French side of the Rhineland plain, **Strasbourg** leads you into Germany. The new TGV line gives much quicker access to eastern France.

CHERBOURG

Essentially a commercial and military port, Cherbourg played a key role in the Battle of Normandy. It was liberated by American troops three weeks after the landings on Utah beach and used as a deep-water port. Hilltop **Fort du Roule**, overlooking the town and port, contains a museum commemorating the Allied liberation of Cherbourg and the Cotentin peninsula. A worthwhile recent attraction is the Cité de la Mer, housed in the former transatlantic ferry terminal, a grand Art Deco building. Its exhibits cover the theme of underwater exploration, and include Europe's largest aquarium plus a decommissioned nuclear submarine.

🚈 Pl. Jean Jaurès, at the south end of Bassin du Commerce (harbour). The Gare-Maritime (ferry port) is northeast of the town centre; a shuttle bus runs between the two.

DAY TRIP FROM CHERBOURG

A bus service (the bus station is opposite the rail station) heads down the Cotentin peninsula to the hilltop town of **Coutances**, via the villages of Martinvast and medieval Bricquebec, whose ancient fortress has a mighty keep housing a tiny museum.

⛴ There are cross-channel ferry services to the UK: Poole (ETT table 2145), Portsmouth (table 2160), also to Rosslare in Ireland (table 2010).

ℹ️ **Tourist Office:** 2 quai Alexandre III, ☎02 33 93 52 02 (www.ot-cherbourg-cotentin.fr). On the far side of Bassin du Commerce, between the lifting bridge and r. Maréchal Foch. An office also opens at the Gare-Maritime on ferry arrivals and departures, ☎02 33 44 39 92.

🏨 The area north of the Tourist Office offers some cheap lodging options. Try the **Hôtel de la Renaissance**, 4 r. de l'Église, ☎02 33 43 23 90, €€, with views of the sea; the **Régence**, 42 quai de Caligny, ☎02 33 43 05 16 (www.laregence.com, €€–€€€). Just off the main square, the **Croix de Malte** is a modernised option, 5 r. des Halles, ☎02 33 43 19 16 (www.hotelcroixmalte.com), €€. **Hostel (HI)**: 55 r. de l'Abbaye, ☎02 33 78 15 15 (cherbourg@fuaj.org), 3 km from the station by 🚌 3 to 'Chantier'.

🍴 Lots of glass-fronted restaurants line the quayside road; there are cheaper options in the streets behind, where vestiges of the Old Town survive around pl. Centrale.

DAY TRIP FROM BAYEUX

Low tide at **Arromanches** (about 10 km from Bayeux, 🚌 75), reveals the remains of Mulberry Harbour – the artificial port and floating landing-stage for transporting troops and vehicles from the UK during D-Day operations.

Visit the **Musée du Débarquement** for a comprehensive panorama of the events leading up to and during D-Day.

WHERE NEXT FROM BAYEUX?

A neat way of avoiding Paris is by changing at Caen for trains to Le Mans and Tours (ETT tables 275 and 271), both on the Paris–Bordeaux route.

BAYEUX

The first town liberated by the Allies after World War II, Bayeux escaped any damage to its fine medieval centre, dominated by the spires of the magnificent **Cathédrale Notre-Dame**.

The world-famous **Bayeux tapestry** is a 70 m length of embroidered linen illustrating the Norman Conquest of England. (It is thought to have been commissioned soon after the Battle of Hastings by the Bishop of Bayeux from an Anglo-Saxon workshop run by monks.) Despite the passage of time, the colours are bright and the design is amazingly detailed. The historical explanations, film shows and displays in the **Centre Guillaume-le-Conquérant**, where it is housed, rue Nesmond, interpret the scenes very thoroughly, but it is worth hiring a multi-lingual audio-guide as you walk round.

The **Musée Mémorial de la Bataille de Normandie**, blvd Fabian Ware, is one of the best museums in the area covering the Normandy campaign (open daily).

🚉 pl. de la Gare, a 10–15 min walk southeast of the centre; turn left on blvd Sadi Carnot, bearing right until it becomes r. Larcher. Continue to r. St-Martin on the left: the Tourist Office is on the right. There are also buses into the centre from the bus station right by the train station.

ℹ️ **Tourist Office:** pont St-Jean, ☎02 31 51 28 28, (www.bessin-normandie.fr).

🏠 The **Reine Mathilde** has simple rooms over a popular brasserie, 23 rue Larcher, ☎02 31 92 08 13 (www.hotel-reinemathilde.com), €€, while the **Hôtel d'Argouges**, 21 r. St-Patrice, ☎02 31 92 88 86 (www.ohotellerie.com/dargouges), €€–€€€, is an upmarket option in an 18th-century building. The **Youth hostel (HI):** 39 r. Général de Dais, ☎02 31 92 15 22 (www.bayeux-familyhome.com) doubles as a popular guesthouse.

ROUEN

DIEPPE

Dieppe, reached in just over an hour from Rouen by train (ETT table 270a) and with ferries to Newhaven in England, is an attractive coastal town, with a flint-and-sandstone château perched on the lofty white cliffs rising high above the shingle beach. The museum inside contains a fascinating collection of ivory artefacts carved by seafarers. The harbour is a lively area, lined with seafood restaurants. In the streets behind, a spectacular Saturday market (Pl. Nationale/ Grande Rue/r. St Jacques) draws crowds from far and wide. **Tourist Office**, Pont Jehan Ango, ☎02 32 14 40 60 (www.dieppetourisme.com). Accommodation includes **Au Grand Duquesne**, 15 pl. St Jacques, ☎02 32 14 61 10 (http://augrand duquesne.free.fr), €€, right by the market. **Youth hostel**: 48 r. Louis Fromager, ☎02 35 84 85 73 (dieppe@fuaj.org) 3 km from rail station; 🚌 2 to Château Michel (open May–Sept).

Your first stop in Rouen should be the **Cathédrale Notre-Dame**, the subject of a series of Monet's paintings. An example of his work showing the west front can be seen at the attractively restored **Musée des Beaux Arts**, pl. Verdrel (closed Tues; free under 26s). A good-value joint ticket gives admission to two other Rouen museums.

The Old City centre, restored after war damage, has many colourful half-timbered buildings. On the main street, r. du Gros Horloge, a 16th-century gatehouse supports an ancient clock, with a single hand. At the end of the road, in pl. du Vieux Marché, a 20-m cross by the church marks the spot where Joan of Arc was burned at the stake in 1431.

La Tour Jeanne d'Arc, r. du Donjon (closed Tues), is the only remaining tower of the castle where Joan of Arc was imprisoned just before her execution.

🚉 r. Jeanne d'Arc, 1 km north of the centre. Either walk down into town (10–15 mins) or take the Métro. The centre is pedestrianised, and all the main sights lie within walking distance of each other, so there's little point in buying a bus and Métro day-pass.

ℹ️ **Tourist Office:** 25 pl. de la Cathédrale, ☎02 32 08 32 40 (www.rouentourisme.com; accueil@rouentourisme.com), right in front of the cathedral.

🏨 There are many affordable hotels in town, most in the north, but also in the Old City. Try **Le Bristol**, 46 r. aux Juifs, ☎02 35 71 54 21, €€, by the cathedral; or **Hôtel des Carmes**, 33 pl. des Carmes, ☎02 35 71 92 31 (www.hoteldescarmes.com), €€. In a cobbled street, the **Hôtel de la Cathédrale** is a real charmer, 12 r. St Romain, ☎02 35 71 57 95 (www.hotel-de-la-cathedrale.fr), €€–€€€.

Trains from Cherbourg/Rouen arrive at **Paris St-Lazare** station, while trains for the Strasbourg direction leave from **Paris-Est** station. Allow 1 hr to cross Paris via the Métro (lines 3 and 7, changing at Opéra) or use the RER line E from Haussmann St-Lazare to Magenta, close to **Paris-Est**.

France

PARIS

See p71.

NANCY

The historical capital of Lorraine is a stylish town, surprisingly little known for its architectural treasures. Its three main squares combine to create one of France's great masterpieces of town planning, commissioned by the Polish-born Duke of Lorraine, Stanislas Leszczynski, in the 18th century. Cream stone, ornate gateways and stately arches characterise the neoclassical **place Stanislas**, its entire south side taken up by the palatial Hôtel de Ville (town hall). Behind is the pl. d'Alliance, and to the north, through the Arc de Triomphe, the 15th-century pl. de la Carrière. In the early 1900s Art Nouveau made its mark on Nancy. Visit the **Musée de l'École de Nancy**, 36–38 r. du Sergent Blandan (closed Mon–Tues; ▤ 123 to Painlevé or Thermal) for fine examples of the style.

▥ Pl. Thiers; a 10-min walk from the town centre along r. Stanislas.

ℹ️ **Tourist Office:** pl. Stanislas, ☎03 83 35 22 41 (www.ot-nancy.fr). A couple of inclusive tourist passes give discounts on local museums and transport. Pick up a walking tour leaflet to see some of the best Art Nouveau buildings in town.

🛏 If you fancy staying in an official historic monument, the 4-star **Grand Hôtel de la Reine**, 2 pl. Stanislas, ☎03 83 35 03 01(www.hoteldelareine.com), €€€, fits the bill, but the **Hôtel de Guise**, 18 r. Guise, ☎03 83 32 24 68 (www.hoteldeguise.com), €€–€€€, or **Les Portes d'Or**, 21 rue Stanislas, ☎03 83 35 42 34 (www.hotel-lesportesdor.com), €€, are more affordable. **Youth hostel**: 15th-century **Château de Rémicourt**, 149 r. de Vandoeuvre, Villers-lès-Nancy, ☎03 83 27 73 67, 4 km west of Nancy station (▤ 126/134/135 or tram line 1). Close by is **Camping Campéole**, av. P-Muller, Villers-lès-Nancy, ☎03 83 27 18 28 (www.camping-brabois.com), open Apr–Oct; ▤ 122/125 from the station to Camping.

🔟 Try pl. Stanislas and r. des Maréchaux for smart cafés and late-night bars: *macarons* (almond biscuits) and *babas aux rhum* (rum cakes) are local specialities.

LUNÉVILLE

Lunéville's chief glory is its massive 18th-century **château**, built by Duke Leopold of Lorraine in imitation of Versailles and graced with magnificent gardens, but its collections were destroyed by fire in 2003. However, some temporary exhibitions are held (free entry) and the Tourist Office is located within the château. The church of **St-Jacques**, pl. St-Rémy, has a unique baroque organ with no visible pipes.

🚆 A 15-min walk from the centre.

ℹ️ **Tourist Office:** Aile Sud du Château, ☎03 83 74 06 55 (www.ot-lunevillois.com).

🏨 **Hôtel du Commerce**, 93 r. d'Alsace, ☎03 83 73 04 17 (www.hotelducommerce-luneville.com), €, or **Hôtel des Pages**, 5 quai des Petits-Bosquets, ☎03 83 74 11 42, €€, opposite the château.

STRASBOURG

The old capital of Alsace, once a mere fishing village, has grown into a most attractive city, successfully combining old with new, business with tourism. It's best known today as the seat of the European Parliament, housed in an imposing new building on the city outskirts. The prettiest bit of town is **Petite-France**, a former tanning and milling quarter, where 16th- and 17th-century houses crowd around narrow alleys and streams. The river is spanned by the picturesque **Ponts Couverts**, a trio of medieval covered bridges with square towers. The **Cathédrale Notre-Dame**, built over three centuries, is a Gothic triumph, with a carved west front. Highlights include the 13th-century **Pilier des Anges** (Angels' Pillar) and the 19th-century **Horloge Astronomique** (Astronomical Clock), which strikes noon at 1230 each day. The tower, a 330-step climb, provides a marvellous city view.

🚆 Pl. de la Gare: 10-min walk to the centre (which is on an island in the River Ill) straight along r. du Maire Kuss or by tram (direction Illkirch).

ℹ️ **Tourist Office:** 17 pl. de la Cathédrale, ☎03 88 52 28 28 (www.ot-strasbourg.fr), with a branch at pl. de la Gare (same tel. no.). The Tourist Offices sell a good-value 3-day **Strasbourg Pass**, which covers admission to one museum, the cathedral tower, the Astronomical Clock in the cathedral, a boat trip, use of a bicycle and half-price tours.

🏨 There's a good choice of hotels in every grade, including a clutch in the wide semicircle of buildings around pl. de la Gare. More reasonable and in the old centre by the cathedral is **Hotel Patricia**, 1A r. du Puits, ☎03 88 32 14 60 (www.hotelpatricia.fr), €€. **Youth hostel (HI): René Cassin**, 9 r. de l'Auberge de Jeunesse, ☎03 88 30 26 46 (www.hihostels.com), 1 km from the station (🚌 2: Auberge de Jeunesse), and there's a campsite next door; **2 Rives Parc du Rhin**, r. des Cavaliers, ☎03 88 45 54 20 (strasbourg.2 rivers@fuaj.org); 4 km from the station (🚌 2/21 to Parc du Rhin, closed Nov–early Jan).

🍴 There are plenty of cafés and *winstubs* (traditional Alsatian restaurants) near the cathedral, on r. des Tonneliers and in the Petite France quarter.

WHERE NEXT FROM STRASBOURG?

Continue east over the border into Germany, to Offenburg or Baden-Baden (ETT table 912) on the Munich–Konstanz route (p309). You can also continue through Alsace to enter Switzerland at Basel (p348) on the Lausanne–Milan route.

ROUTE DETAIL

Paris (Montparnasse)–Chartres ETT 278

Type	Frequency	Typical journey time
Train	Every hr	1 hr 5 mins

Chartres–Le Mans ETT table 278

Type	Frequency	Typical journey time
Train	10 daily	1 hr 25 mins

Le Mans–Rennes ETT table 280

Type	Frequency	Typical journey time
TGV	10 daily	1 hr 15 mins

Rennes–Brest ETT table 284

Type	Frequency	Typical journey time
Train	12 daily	2 hrs 30 mins

Brest–Quimper ETT table 286

Type	Frequency	Typical journey time
Train	7 daily	1 hr 10 mins

Quimper–Vannes ETT table 285

Type	Frequency	Typical journey time
Train	11 daily	1 hr 15 mins

Vannes–Nantes ETT table 285

Type	Frequency	Typical journey time
Train	6 daily	1 hr 20 mins

Nantes–Angers ETT table 289

Type	Frequency	Typical journey time
Train	Every hr	45 mins

Angers–Tours ETT table 289

Type	Frequency	Typical journey time
Train	9 daily	1 hr

Tours–Poitiers ETT table 300

Type	Frequency	Typical journey time
Train	12 daily	1 hr 5 mins

Poitiers–Bordeaux ETT table 300

Type	Frequency	Typical journey time
Train	Every 1–2 hrs	1 hr 45 mins

KEY JOURNEYS

Paris–Brest ETT table 284

Type	Frequency	Typical journey time
Train	4–7 daily	4 hrs 30 mins

Paris–Nantes ETT table 280

Type	Frequency	Typical journey time
Train	Every hr	2 hrs 15 mins

Nantes–Bordeaux ETT table 292

Type	Frequency	Typical journey time
Train	4–5 daily	4 hrs

Paris (Montparnasse)–Bordeaux ETT 300

Type	Frequency	Typical journey time
TGV	Every 1–2 hrs	3 hrs

Notes

For TGV trains, you need to make advance
seat reservations and pay a supplement.
More services are available between Vannes
and Nantes by changing trains at Redon.
Tours–Poitiers: the through-line station in
Tours is St Pierre des Corps.

Above: Buckingham Palace, London (Graeme Purdy/iStockphoto)   Below: St Paul's Cathedral, London (Paul Preacher)

Left: Sacré-Coeur, Paris (Alison Rayner)

Above: Bordeaux region, France (Christian Bauer)
Below: Corsica (Christophe Libert/SXC.hu)

Above left: **Barcelona** (Oxana Morozova/BigStockPhoto)

Above right: **Madrid** (Jaume Felipe/Fotolia)
Below: **Ronda, Spain** (Fonin/Dreamstime)

RAIL TOUR: PARIS – TOURS – BORDEAUX

Western France offers a heady mix of wine and brandy, cathedrals, châteaux, long beaches and rocky coastlines. Beyond **Chartres** you enter **Brittany** (*Bretagne*), where regional identity is still strongly emphasised in the Breton language (similar to Welsh), the cuisine (crêpes and cider) and summer festivals in which villagers don traditional costumes. The three peninsulas on Brittany's west coast make up **Finistère** (Finis Terrae, the end of the earth), buffeted by the Atlantic, and littered with shipwrecks. Only the fickle climate might dampen your enthusiasm for a seaside holiday among these distinctive fishing towns and superb beaches. Just to the east, **Roscoff** is an attractive Channel port with services to Plymouth (England). At **Nantes** the route joins the Loire, famous for its châteaux and wines. Further south lie the ancient university city of Poitiers, the high-profile theme park called Futuroscope, Angoulême (at the eastern end of the cognac region), and **Bordeaux**, capital of one of the world's greatest wine-producing areas. It's feasible to shorten the route by omitting the Loire and heading directly down from Nantes to Bordeaux via **La Rochelle**.

PARIS

See p71.

CHARTRES

One of France's greatest Gothic buildings is the **Cathédrale Notre-Dame**, which replaced an earlier building destroyed by fire in 1194. It's known especially for the quality and brilliance of its 13th-century stained glass, dazzling even on the dullest of days, and the wealth of carved stone, notably around the west doorways.

Nothing else in Chartres matches the splendours of its cathedral, but several other churches deserve a look, and the rest of the town is an enjoyable place with winding streets and a pleasant Old-Town area by the **Eure**, with good views of the cathedral.

🚃 Pl. Pierre Sémard. Follow the signs to the cathedral to reach the centre.

ℹ️ **Tourist Office**: pl. de la Cathédrale, 📞02 37 18 26 26 (www.chartres-tourisme.com).

🏠 **Le Grand Monarque** is a safe and comfortable bet in a historic building with a bistro, 22 pl. Epars, 📞02 39 80 15 15, www.bw-grand-monarque.com, €€€. Cheaper options include eight-room **Chêne Fleuri**, 14 r. de la Porte Morard, 📞02 37 35 25 70, €, with its two restaurants, log fire and shady patio by the Eure River; or closer to the station is the 2-star **Jehan de Beauce**, 19 av. Jehan de Beauce, 📞02 37 21 01 41 (www.jehandebeauce.fr), €€. **Hostel (non HI)**: 23 av. Neigre, 📞02 37 34 27 64 (www.auberge-jeunesse-chartres.com), 🚌 minibus service from near the Tourist Office.

France

RENNES

Brittany's commercial and administrative capital lacks the obvious appeal of the coast, but is worth at least a day trip. On Saturday mornings a colourful market takes over the place des Lices in the Old Town (stock up on Breton food specialities) and in early July, the **Festival des Tombées de la Nuit** (Festival of Nightfall, www.lestombeesdelanuit.com) draws the crowds with street theatre, music and costumed folk events. Following a huge fire in 1720, Rennes was largely rebuilt in stone, but some of its stripy half-timbered houses survive.

The 17th-century **Parlement de Bretagne** was one of the few major structures to survive the first fire, but was less lucky when another fire broke out in 1994. After painstaking restoration, it is now open again (guided tours can be arranged through the Tourist Office). The **Musée des Beaux Arts**, 20 quai Émile Zola, houses a collection of French art from the 14th century onwards. The **Musée de Bretagne**, in a shiny new complex called the Champs Libres, 10 cours des Alliés, gives an excellent multimedia introduction to Brittany's history. There's also a science centre and planetarium (closed Mon).

🚂 Pl. de la Gare. About a 15 min walk southeast of the centre or take the Métro (VAL).

ℹ️ **Tourist Office**: 11 r. St Yves, ☎02 99 67 11 11 (www.tourisme-rennes.com).

🏨 The easiest place to find hotels is near the station, such as the **Hôtel de Nemours,** 5 r. de Nemours, ☎02 99 78 26 26, €€, but there are one or two places in the Old Town, such as the excellent **Hôtel des Lices,** 7 pl. des Lices, ☎02 99 79 14 81; www.hotel-des-lices.com, €€, or the tiny **Rocher de Cancale**, 10 r. St Michel, ☎02 99 79 20 83, €. **Youth hostel (HI)**: 10–12 Canal St-Martin, ☎02 99 33 22 33 (rennes@fuaj.org) 2 km from the station (🚌 18 to Auberge de Jeunesse or, faster, the Métro to pl. Sainte-Anne, then walk along r. de St-Malo). **Campsite**: **Camping Municipal des Gayeulles**, r. du Professeur M-Audin, ☎02 99 36 91 22 (Métro to République, then 🚌 3 to Gayeulles-piscine).

🍴 Pl. des Lices following through r. St Michel right to r. St Melaine; and r. St Georges and r. du Chapitre, are packed with a variety of multi-cultural restaurants.

SIDE TRIPS FROM RENNES Regular buses link Rennes with many other Breton towns. The long-distance bus station is at blvd Solférino (near the station). Trains run from Rennes to St-Malo (every 1–2 hrs, journey time 50–60 mins; ETT table 281) and then on to Dol, where you can change for Dinan.

The romantically named **Côte d'Emeraude** (Emerald Coast) and **Côte de Granit Rose** (Coast of Pink Granite) are fringed with rugged cliffs and unspoilt sandy beaches, interspersed with sheltered fishing ports, many doubling as resorts.

St-Malo's walled town, guarding the mouth of the Rance estuary, has been carefully restored since wartime destruction. This lively ferry port makes an enjoyable base for exploring the coastline by bus. **Tourist Office**: Esplanade St-Vincent, ☎0825 13 52 00 (premium rate) (www.saint-malo-tourisme.com). ▣ **Hôtel Quic en Groigne**, 8 r. d'Estrées, ☎02 99 20 22 20 (www.quic-en-groigne.com), €€–€€€, has small but pretty rooms within the Old Town walls; or if you want to be right opposite the beach try **Les Charmettes**, 64 blvd Hébert, ☎02 99 56 07 31 (www.hotel-les-charmettes.com), €€–€€€. **Youth hostel (HI)**: **Centre Patrick Varangot**, 37 av. du R P Umbricht, ☎02 99 40 29 80 (www.centrevarangot.com), 1.5 km from the station (▣ 2/5). Buses and ferries connect St-Malo with **Dinard**, a glamorous resort of early 20th-century turreted villas with several lovely beaches.

East of St-Malo, the astonishing fortified abbey of **Le Mont St-Michel** perches on its craggy island – a must-see attraction, despite hordes of visitors; walk around the abbey, the village and the ramparts for sweeping views of the surrounding bay. The nearest rail station is at Pontorson, 9 km away, but regular bus lines run from St-Malo and Rennes (ETT table 264), as well as an irregular service from St-Malo.

Inland, **Dol-de-Bretagne** has a fine Gothic cathedral and arcaded medieval houses. Just outside the town at **Champ-dolent** (2 km S off D795 – freely accessible) one of Brittany's finest menhirs (prehistoric standing stones) reaches a height of 9 m. **Dinan**, upstream in the Rance Valley, is a gorgeous fortified town with a 16th-century castle, a Romano-Gothic basilica and cobbled streets of timbered 15th-century houses.

QUIMPER

Quimper is the most important town in southwestern Finistère. The Gothic Cathédrale St-Corentin features a strangely off-centre nave. Close by are the **Musée Breton** (closed Mon except June–Sept) and the outstanding **Musée des Beaux-Arts** (closed Tue except July–Aug), both of which capture the spirit of Brittany.

Along the riverside in Locmaria, the **Musée de la Faïence** (www.quimper-faiences .com; temporarily closed) has an excellent collection of traditional Quimper pottery; the factory next door (H B Henriot) offers tours.

▨ Av. de la Gare: east of town, a 15-min walk to the centre; turn right along av. de la Gare, cross the River Odet and turn left. The Tourist Office is on the same side of the river at the foot of a hill called Mont Frugy.

ⓘ **Tourist Office**: pl. de la Résistance, ☎02 98 53 04 05 (www.quimper-tourisme.com).

▣ Sadly, Quimper is short on accommodation, and there's nothing cheap in the Old Town. Budget hotels by the station include **TGV**, 4 r. Concarneau, ☎02 98 90 54 00 (www.hoteltgv.com), €, and **Le Derby**, 13 av. de la Gare, ☎02 98 52 06 91 (www.hotel-le-derby.fr), €, and **Le Pascal**, 19 av. de la Gare ☎02 98 90 00 81, €€. **Youth hostel (HI)**: 6 av. des Oiseaux, ☎02 98 64 97 97 (quimper@fuaj.org), 3 km from the station (▣ 1 to Chaptal); Apr–Sept.

France

SIDE TRIPS FROM QUIMPER
Douarnenez (30 mins northwest by CAT bus) is a working fishing port with lots of activity to watch on the harbour and quays. The major sight is **Le Port-Musée**, where you can explore a variety of vessels and watch demonstrations of skills such as boat-building and rope-making. The **Crozon peninsula**, further north, is also reachable by bus (plan an overnight stop). At the tip of the peninsula (forming part of the **Parc Naturel Régional d'Armorique**), **Camaret** is a small resort and lobster fishing port; a jetty leads to a quaint 17th-century tower built by the military architect Vauban. Boat trips downriver from Quimper lead to the popular beach resort of Benodet, from where other boats go to the **Îles de Glénan** (the path round the isle of St Nicolas makes a pleasant walk) – or to **Concarneau**, a busy fishing port with a medieval *ville close* (walled island town).

VANNES

At the head of the island-strewn Golfe du Morbihan, Vannes makes a handy base for boat trips and for exploring southeastern Brittany. Its quaint walled town is a delight to explore. Near the **Cathédrale St-Pierre**, the ancient covered market of **La Cohue** has been restored, as an art and exhibition gallery. Behind the cathedral, you can walk along the foot of the old ramparts, past some well-preserved 19th-century wash-houses. Buy a picnic in the market on place des Lices, or at a lovely bakery in the square called La Huche à Pains, and enjoy it in the stream-side gardens.

[RAIL] A good distance northeast of the centre: turn right onto av. Favrel et Lincy and left along av. Victor Hugo. Continue straight ahead for the old centre and the port.

[*i*] **Tourist Office:** 1 r. Thiers, ☎0825 13 56 10 (www.tourisme-vannes.com), near the port.

[🏨] The town gets crowded in season, and hotels are often booked up. On the harbour front is **Le Marina**, 4 pl. Gambetta, ☎02 97 47 22 81 (www.hotellemarina.fr), €€.

SIDE TRIPS FROM VANNES
Carnac (southwest of Vannes and reachable by bus) is a major resort, with numerous campsites and caravan parks and a long beach. In the area are some 5000 menhirs (prehistoric standing stones). The most famous formation is the **Alignements du Ménec**, probably dating from 3000BC and consisting of over 1000 megaliths stretching for more than 1 km. They are now fenced off to prevent erosion; guided visits in high season; off-season you can visit at your own pace. An informative museum explains what is known about these mysterious structures, and displays finds from the sites. Nearby **Locmariaquer** has yet more ancient monuments.

Several companies offer boat tours and ferry services around the Morbihan coast and its many islands – you can reach the various departure points by bus. **Belle-Île** (reached from Quiberon, south of Carnac) is the largest of Brittany's off-shore islands. It has a fine citadel, superb coastal scenery and beaches, good walking and picturesque villages.

Within the Golfe du Morbihan is the **Île de Gavrinis**, which has an impressive decorated tomb beneath a grassy cairn. It can be reached by a boat (in season) from Larmor-Baden (southwest of Vannes).

ANGERS

This attractive wine-producing town stands amid black schist and slate quarries. It is dominated by the massive striped walls of the 13th-century **Château d'Angers**, whose 17 towers now reach only half of their original height. The moat has been converted into formal gardens. Inside is a series of great 14th-century tapestries known as the *Tenture de l'Apocalypse* (the Apocalypse of St John), executed in graphic detail. The nearby **Cathédrale St-Maurice** has a medieval façade and Gothic vaulting over an unusually wide nave, lighted by stained glass. Across the river, the **Hôpital St-Jean** contains another spectacular tapestry, the 20th-century *Chant du Monde* (inspired by the Apocalypse) by Jean Lurçat. As well as wine, Angers produces the liqueur Cointreau (guided visits from the distillery museum on blvd des Bretonnières).

🚉 About a 10-min walk south of the centre – or 🚌 1.

ℹ️ **Tourist Office**: 7–9 pl. Kennedy, ☎02 41 23 50 00 (www.angersloiretourisme.com).

🏨 The **Hôtel du Mail**, 8–10 r. Ursules, ☎02 41 25 05 25 (www.hotel-du-mail.com), €€–€€€, is a quiet 17th-century mansion, or try the conveniently located **Hôtel des Lices**, 25 rue des Lices, ☎02 41 87 44 10, €–€€.

SIDE TRIPS FROM ANGERS   Infrequent trains run from Angers (taking 20–25 mins; ETT table 289) to the town of **Saumur**, with its famous cavalry riding school (the Cadre Noir). The 14th-century château has a fascinating history: originally a fortress for Louis I, it became a country residence for the Dukes of Anjou, then a state prison, and it now houses two museums. There are tours in English in summer. Vineyards surround the town, and mushrooms are grown in the caves that riddle the local hills, making good use of by-products from the riding school.

Most of the châteaux in the 1000-km-long Loire Valley were originally medieval fortresses converted into luxurious country residences by 16th-century nobles. Some lie on bus routes or within range of railway stations (rail services may be erratic – the Saumur–Tours line provides the best access), but to visit others you really need a car – or if you're energetic, a bike, which you can take on most of the trains to cover longer distances.

South of Angers (Anjou 🚌 9), the **Chateau de Brissac** is the Loire's tallest chateau, lavishly decorated inside. **Villandry** is famous for its magnificent terraced gardens, with formal box-hedged beds. The fortress-like **Langeais** and the more graceful **Montsoreau** and **Montreuil-Bellay** can be reached by bus from Saumur.

France

TOURS

Tours has a long and venerable history, and is home to one of the most prestigious universities in France. Today, it is the largest city on the Loire, restored to its stately former glory after damage during World War II. The classical architecture of pl. Jean Jaurès provides a focal point. The flamboyant Gothic-style **Cathédrale St-Gatien** has some wonderful 13th-century stained glass, while the **Cloître de la Psalette**, to one side, has 13th- and 14th-century frescos. The 17th-century Archbishop's Palace contains the **Musée des Beaux-Arts**. In the evening, head for the heart of the Old Town, around the pl. Plumereau, which offers an excellent selection of inexpensive bars and restaurants, many occupying the carefully restored half-timbered houses that line this maze of mostly pedestrianised narrow streets. Walk east to r. Colbert if you want an even greater choice. The botanic gardens on blvd Tonnelle are an enticing place for a quiet stroll.

▨ Pl. du Maréchal Leclerc. Near the *Mairie* (town hall) in the city centre.

i **Tourist Office**: 78–82 r. Bernard Palissy (opposite the train station), ☎02 47 70 37 37 (www.ligeris.com).

🏨 There are some cheap hotels around the station and the cathedral. The **Val de Loire**, 33 blvd Heurteloup, ☎02 47 05 37 86, €, and the **Hôtel du Cygne**, 6 r. Cygne, ☎02 47 66 66 41 (www.hotel-cygne-tours.com), €€, are cheap and charming. Central, 2-star **Hotel Mirabeau**, 89 bis blvd Heurteloup, ☎02 47 95 24 60 (www.hotel-mirabeau.fr), €€, has a garden, perfect for alfresco breakfasts. **Youth hostel (HI)**: 5 r. Bretonneau, ☎02 47 37 81 58 (tours@fuaj.org); 1 km from station; 🚌 4 to Vieux Tours.

SIDE TRIPS FROM TOURS At the heart of château country, Tours is an excellent base for exploring the tributary valleys of the Loire, Loir, Cher and Indre. Here lie the famous castles of **Amboise**, **Azay-le-Rideau**, **Chambord**, **Chenonceaux**, **Chinon**, **Loches** and **Blois**. Most are some distance apart, as well as from Tours, so take one of the many chartered bus trips or a regular bus line (info at the Tourist Office).

FUTUROSCOPE

This massive lakeside theme park 7 km north of Poitiers is dedicated to the moving image, and has more than anyone could possibly see in a day. The spectacular cinematic experiences (some of which have height and/or health restrictions) – involve liquid crystal glasses, gigantic screens and the most technologically advanced digital imaging processes. Admission rates are seasonal but the best option is a Séjour Liberté 2-day pass (from €94), including on-site budget accommodation with breakfast (booking agency, ☎05 49 49 11 12). There are dozens of hotels in the local area. From Poitiers station, Vitalis 🚌 9 and 🚌 E serve the park from the rail station called Parc des Loisirs. The TGV station for Futuroscope has direct trains to Paris (about 1 hr 30 mins): www.futuroscope.com.

POITIERS

For many visitors, Poitiers is simply the nearest place to **Futuroscope**, but the city has one of France's oldest universities and also lays claim to an impressive array of churches. Not for nothing is it known as the city of a hundred bell towers. The oldest, founded in 356, is the **Baptistère Saint-Jean**, r. Jean-Jaurès. Nearby is the 12th- to 13th-century **Cathédrale Saint-Pierre**, r. de la Cathédrale, squat from outside, but inside, the nave soars to lovely 13th-century stained glass. Behind the cathedral is the **Église Ste-Radegonde**, r. Sainte-Croix, founded in the 6th century. It has fine Romanesque and Gothic additions and alterations. On summer evenings the façade of **Notre-Dame-la-Grande** is spotlit, recreating its colourful medieval appearance. Poitiers has a number of Renaissance and 18th-century buildings, as well as some high-tech modern civic architecture. One of Poitiers' best secular buildings is the 13th-century **Salle des Pas Perdus** inside the Palais de Justice.

🚆 Blvd du Grand Cerf, about a 15-min walk from the centre; there is a pedestrian overpass shortcut.

ℹ️ **Tourist Office**: 45 pl. Charles de Gaulle, ☎05 49 41 21 24 (www.ot-poitiers.fr). The free city map shows various self-guided walks.

🏨 Plenty of hotels both around Futuroscope and in the town, but not easy to find budget beds. Try the **Hôtel Central**, 35 pl. du Maréchal Leclerc, ☎05 49 01 79 79 (www.centralhotel86.com), €. **Youth hostel (HI)**: 1 allée Roger Tagault, ☎05 49 30 09 70 (poitiers@fuaj.org); 🚌 7 to Cap Sud.

🍽️ Restaurants on r. Carnot have regional specialities but tend to be expensive; the squares pl. de Maréchal Leclerc and pl. de Gaulle have a wider choice. The Poitiers region is noted for its goats' cheese.

DAY TRIP FROM POITIERS   Poitiers has a train service to the historic port of **La Rochelle** (ETT table 300), a popular sailing centre; it's elegant and striking, built in bright limestone, with gracious old squares, a fine town hall and arcaded Renaissance houses. Life focuses on the old harbour, which has some excellent fish restaurants. Two medieval towers preside over the harbour entrance, once linked by a protective chain. La Rochelle is a springboard for boat trips and island visits, notably to the **Ile de Ré**, connected to the town by a 3 km toll bridge, offering beaches (some are naturist ones) and quiet picnic spots. It's reachable by bus, but best explored by bike.

BORDEAUX

Set on the **Garonne River** just before it joins the Dordogne and Gironde, Bordeaux is a busy, working city with an 18th-century core of monumental splendour surrounded by industrial gloom. A massive recent revitalisation programme has restored the handsome old centre and made it accessible to pedestrians. Above all, the city is the commercial heart of one of the world's greatest wine-growing areas, surrounded by revered appellations such as **Saint-Emilion**, **Graves**, **Médoc** and **Sauternes**. The **Maison du Vin de Bordeaux**, opposite the main Tourist Office, arranges courses, tours and tastings, 1 cours du XXX Juillet, ☎05 56 00 22 85 (http://ecole.vins-bordeaux.fr).

Most of Bordeaux's main sights lie within easy walking distance, but a high-tech tram network is now in place. Best of the city's historic buildings include the majestic neoclassical **Grand Théâtre** (guided tours 1400 daily), on pl. de la Comédie, **Musée National des Douanes**, housed in the 18th-century Customs House, and the elegant (private) **Hôtel de la Bourse**. Around the **Cathédrale St-André** are the superb 18th-century **Hôtel de Ville**, the **Musée des Beaux-Arts**, 20 cours d'Albret (nicely varied collection) and the **Musée des Arts Décoratifs**, 39 r. Bouffard (furniture, silver, pottery, etc). Most of Bordeaux's museums are free of charge.

🚉 **Gare St-Jean**, r. Charles Domercq. About 2 km from the south of the centre (tram line C runs from Quinconces to the station).

✈ **Bordeaux-Mérignac**, 12 km from the city, ☎05 56 34 50 50 (www.bordeaux.aeroport.fr). There are buses (Jet'Bus) every 45 mins to Gare St-Jean.

ℹ **Tourist Office**: 12 cours du XXX Juillet, ☎05 56 00 66 00 (www.bordeaux-tourisme.com), with an annexe at the station and one at the airport.

🏨 Many of the cheapest hotels, scattered around the grimy docks and the red-light district immediately around the railway station, can be a bit seedy. Nearer the centre, r. Huguerie is a good place to look for budget accommodation. Try the **Hôtel Touring**, 16 r. Huguerie, ☎05 56 81 56 73 (www.hoteltouring.fr), €€, or **Le Choiseul**, 13 r. Huguerie, ☎05 56 52 71 24 (www.hotelchoiseul.com), €€. **Hostel** (non-HI): 22 cours Barbey, ☎05 56 33 00 70 (www.auberges-jeunesse-bordeaux.com), €.

🍴 The quartier Saint-Pierre is a bustling district filled with small boutiques and cafés, and pl. du Parlement is a good place to look for restaurants. Look out for *guingettes* (waterfront seafood stalls) along the quai des Chartrons.

DAY TRIPS FROM BORDEAUX

Probably the main reason for coming to Bordeaux is to visit the great wineries spread out through the surrounding countryside. There are bus tours (ask at the Tourist Office), but also a local rail line to **Pointe-de-Grave** (ETT table 307), whose stations include such redolent names as **Château Margaux** and **Pauillac** (for **Château Mouton-Rothschild** and **Château Lafitte**). There are also services to **La Rochelle** (ETT table 292; takes 2 hrs 30 mins).

WHERE NEXT FROM BORDEAUX?

*Carry on to **Biarritz** to join the **Biarritz–Marseille** route (p113).*
*Alternatively carry on south over the Spanish border to **Seville** (p217).*

ROUTE DETAIL

Paris (Lyon)–Dijon — ETT table 370

Type	Frequency	Typical journey time
Train	Every 1–2 hrs	1 hr 40 mins

Dijon–Beaune — ETT table 373

Type	Frequency	Typical journey time
Train	Every hr	20 mins

Beaune–Lyon — ETT table 373

Type	Frequency	Typical journey time
Train	Every 2 hrs	2 hrs

Lyon–Orange — ETT table 351

Type	Frequency	Typical journey time
Train	7–10 daily	2 hrs

Orange–Avignon — ETT table 351

Type	Frequency	Typical journey time
Train	Every 1–2 hrs	1 hr 15 mins

Avignon–Marseille — ETT tables 350, 351

Type	Frequency	Typical journey time
Train	Every 1–2 hrs	1 hr 20 mins

KEY JOURNEYS

Paris–Lyon — ETT table 340

Type	Frequency	Typical journey time
Train	Every hr	2 hrs

Lyon–Marseille — ETT table 350

Type	Frequency	Typical journey time
Train	Every 1–2 hrs	1 hr 45 mins

Paris–Marseille — ETT table 350

Type	Frequency	Typical journey time
Train	Every hr	3 hrs 10 mins

Notes

High-speed TGV trains operate between Avignon TGV station (13-min bus ride from centre) and Marseille every 1–2 hrs, journey 30 mins.

France

The prime interest of this trip is in its southern sections. Paris to Dijon passes uneventfully, though **Dijon**, at the heart of the wine region of **Bourgogne** (Burgundy), is appealing enough for a break of journey. Further south beyond the captivating town of Beaune, **Mâcon** is at the hub of more vineyards, with the classy whites of the Mâconnais to the west and the light reds of Beaujolais to the south. **Lyon**, France's third city after Paris and Marseille, is often missed by tourists but has a surprising Renaissance quarter, superb food and some evocative Roman remains; from there you can strike out east into the Savoie Alps into Switzerland via some of the highest and most spectacular railways in Europe, or cross the Italian border and carry on via Turin to Milan.

Meanwhile the main route continues into **Provence**, unmistakably Mediterranean in character, and harbouring the great Roman remains at **Orange** and the lively, arty city of **Avignon**, with its vast Papal Palace and famously incomplete bridge.

To continue south, travel on to **Tarascon** to join the Biarritz–Marseille route (see p113). The high-speed TGV gives easy access from Paris, Lyon and Avignon to **Marseille** itself.

PARIS

See p71.

MUSTARD AND CASSIS

Besides the fine wines of Burgundy, Dijon is famed for *moutarde* (mustard) and *crème de cassis*, the sweet blackcurrant liqueur that's often mixed with dry white wine to make kir – a good way to cheer up an indifferent bottle.

DIJON

Dijon's grandest building is the massive **Palais des Ducs et des États de Bourgogne**, best viewed from the pl. de la Libération. This imposing structure, built to demonstrate the vast wealth of the Dukes of Burgundy, now serves as the town hall and houses the **Musée des Beaux-Arts** (closed Tues, free entry), a rich ensemble of painting, sculpture and tapestries. Don't miss the marvellously carved, gold-encrusted tombs in the **Salle des Gardes** (guards-room). Dijon's partly pedestrianised city centre is dotted with attractive squares and historic buildings. R. Verrerie has many half-timbered houses featuring ornate woodcarvings (some are now antique shops). Pl. de la Libération contains an elegant crescent of *hôtels particuliers* (17th-century mansions). There are more behind the palace, especially in r. des Forges, a former haunt of jewellers and goldsmiths. The 13th-century Gothic **Église de Notre Dame**, in r. de la Chouette, has a façade adorned with three tiers of arches. Look out for the lucky chouette (owl) on a corner buttress. Overhead, life-size figures on the 14th-century **Horloge de Jacquemart** (Jacquemart's clock) spring into action every quarter-hour. Beneath the **Cathédrale de St-Bénigne** is a fine Romanesque crypt. Many **museums** are free to students, and there's also a tourist pass giving reduced rates.

🚆 Cours de la Gare, 5 mins west of the centre. The station is at the end of av. Maréchal-Foch.

✈ **Aéroport de Dijon Bourgogne**, ☎03 80 67 67 67 (www.dijon.aeroport.fr), 6 km south of Dijon.

ℹ️ **Tourist Offices**: 34 r. des Forges, ☎0892 70 05 58 (premium rate), (www.dijon-tourism.com), and Pl. Darcy (same tel. no.). A suggested walking tour covering all the main sites is available.

🏨 The lowest-priced hotels (mainly 2-star) tend to be in the Old Town; try the **Hôtel du Palais**, 23 r. Palais, ☎03 80 67 16 26 (www.hoteldupalais-dijon.com), €€, the charming **Hostellerie 'le Sauvage'**, 64 r. Monge ☎03 80 41 31 21 (www.hotellesauvage.com), €€, a former staging inn, or **Le Jacquemart**, 32 r. Verrerie, ☎03 80 60 09 60 (www.hotel-lejacquemart.fr), €€. If you feel like sleeping in Napoleonic style go for the 4-star **Hostellerie du Chapeau Rouge**, 5 r. Michelet, ☎03 80 50 88 88 (www.chapeau-rouge.fr), €€€, built for the Emperor himself. **Hostels** (non HI): **Centre de Rencontres Internationales**, 1 blvd Champollion, ☎03 80 72 95 20 (www.cri-dijon.com), quite a way from the centre (🚌 7 then 4, or 🚌 3 but you'll have to walk a little; or night 🚌 A). **Campsite: Camping Municipal du Lac Kir**, 3 blvd Chanoine Kir, ☎ 03 80 43 54 72 (www.camping-dijon.com), by a lake about 1 km from the centre (🚌 12 to CHS La Chartreuse; closed mid-Oct–March.).

🍽 There are lots of lively pizzerias and foreign restaurants, many with outside tables in summer, in the streets around pl. Emile Zola. This is also the home of *bœuf bourguignon* and *coq au vin* – well worth trying here.

WHERE NEXT FROM DIJON?

Three trains a day run to Nancy (taking 2 hrs 20 mins; ETT table 379), to join the Cherbourg–Strasbourg route (p90).

*En route you can change at Culmont for **Troyes** (1 hr 30 mins, ETT table 380), a captivating half-timbered town in the heart of Aube-en-Champagne; highlights include the cathedral and a wonderful modern art museum, but much of the pleasure is just strolling around and peeking into alleyways and courtyards. From Troyes you can continue westwards to Paris.*

BEAUNE

Beaune is a charming old town of cobbled streets and fine mansions. The magnificent **Hôtel-Dieu**, r. de l'Hôtel-Dieu, with its flamboyant patterned roof of colourful geometric tiles, was originally built in the 15th century as a hospital for the sick and needy. Inside, don't miss the 15th-century *Polyptych of the Last Judgement*, showing sinners tumbling to an unpleasant fate. This building is the centre of the prestigious **Côtes de Beaune** and **Côtes de Nuit** wine trade; the Tourist Office lists local caves (wine cellars) that offer tastings (*dégustations*). The old ducal palace houses a museum dedicated to the subject: **Musée du Vin**, r. d'Enfer (closed Tue Dec–March).

🚉 Av. du 8 Septembre. East of town, just outside the old walls.

France

LYON

This big metropolis (population 1.5 million) at the junction of the Saône and the Rhône has a lovely old centre, with a hive of charming streets and some truly amazing restaurants; it's rated as one of France's gastronomic high-points, and as you might expect from a major university city, there's plenty going on. The two rivers divide the city into three parts. On the west bank of the Saône is **Vieux Lyon**, the Renaissance quarter, while on the east bank of the Rhône is the modern business sector, with its high-rise offices and apartment blocks. In between the rivers lies the partly-pedestrianised city centre, dating largely from the 17th and 18th centuries. It runs from pl. Bellecour, where the Tourist Office stands, north to the old silk quarter of **La Croix-Rousse**.

Lyon is famous for its *traboules* – covered passageways between streets that once served as shortcuts for the silk traders and protected their precious cargoes from the weather. Most *traboules* are in **Vieux Lyon** and **La Croix-Rousse**. Lyon's best museums are the **Musée des Beaux Arts** on pl. des Terreaux (closed Tues) and the **Musée des Tissus et des Arts Décoratifs** (closed Mon), 34 r. de la Charité, recounting the history of the textile industry in Lyon. Old silk looms are still in use at **Maison des Canuts**, 10–12 r. d'Ivry, (closed Mon, Sun). Just across Pont Galliéni over the Rhône from Perrache station is the poignant **Centre d'Histoire de la Résistance et de la Déportation**, 14 av. Berthelot (closed Mon, Tues).

Julius Caesar founded the Roman town of Lugdunum, on the hillside of Fourvière above Vieux Lyon. Take the funicular railway from near the cathedral up to the **Basilique Notre-Dame-de-Fourvière** for spectacular city views. Then walk down to the **Musée Gallo-Romain de Fourvière**, 17 r. Cléberg (closed Mon), which has mosaics, coins and jewels: the neighbouring **Théâtre Romain**, r. de l'Antiquaille, is the oldest Roman amphitheatre in France. Take the other *funiculaire* back down to the riverside.

PÉROUGES

Pérouges, 35 km east of Lyon, is a medieval hill-top village with cobbled streets and 15th-century houses which served as a backdrop for the movie *The Three Musketeers*. In the main square is the Tree of Liberty, planted in 1792 to commemorate the Revolution. Approx. 12 trains a day, fewer at weekends, taking 40 mins; trains stop at Meximieux-Pérouges, about 2 km away.

🚆 There are two main line stations; many trains stop at both. **Lyon-Perrache**, pl. Carnot, is the more central. It provides left-luggage facilities, 0615–2300, showers, money exchange offices, a restaurant and bar. For the Tourist Office, cross pl. Carnot, then follow r. Victor Hugo to pl. Bellecour (15 mins). **Lyon-Part-Dieu** (mainly TGVs) is on the east bank of the Rhône and serves the business district. It has similar facilities to Perrache.

✈ **Aéroport de Lyon-Saint Exupéry**: 32 km east of Lyon,

Rail Tour: Paris – Lyon – Marseille

☎0826 80 08 26 (www.lyon.aeroport.fr). Buses every 20 mins (0600–2320) between the airport and Perrache rail station (via Part-Dieu rail station); takes 50 mins.

ℹ️ **Tourist Offices:** pl. Bellecour, ☎04 72 77 69 69 (www.lyon-france.com) (Métro: Bellecour). Additional branch in summer at av. Adolphe Max in Vieux Lyon.

🏨 There is a huge choice of hotels in every category and finding a room should not be difficult even at the height of summer. Try around the stations or in the Presqu'île quarter, north and south of the Tourist Office. **Hôtel Bayard**, 23 pl. Bellecour, ☎04 78 37 39 64 (www.hotelbayard.fr), €€, or the **Iris**, 36 r. de l'Arbre Sec, ☎04 78 39 93 80 (www.hoteliris.fr), €, are good value. **Youth hostels** (HI): 41–45 montée du Chemin Neuf, ☎04 78 15 05 50 (lyon@fuaj.org), ideally located in the old quarter and with local character (Métro: Saint Jean then funicular or 🚌 28 from Part-Dieu rail station, 🚌 31 from Perrache to Vieux Lyon quarter, then the funicular to Les Minimes). Also (non-HI): **Foyer Majo Moulin à Vent**, 164 r. Challemel-Lacour, ☎04 72 78 03 03 (🚌 12 to Moulin à Vent or 🚌 32 to Challemel-Lacour). **Campsite: Camping International de Lyon**, Porte de Lyon, 10 km northwest, ☎04 78 35 64 55 (www.camping-lyon.com); (🚌 89 from Gare de Vaise to Porte de Lyon).

🍽️ Lyon is renowned for its cuisine and boasts some of the best restaurants in France, serving fantastic food but often with prices to match. More traditional restaurants are known as *bouchons*, mainly found in Presqu'île, the area to the north of the Tourist Office, and Vieux Lyon, where simple, and often very good-value, meals are served. The name *bouchon* dates from the time when inn keepers used to a hang a handful of straw outside so that travellers knew they could eat and drink there while their horses were being rubbed down (*bouchonner*). Lyon has many specialities: *tablier de sapeur* are slices of tripe fried in breadcrumbs; *andouillette*, tripe sausages cooked in white or red wine; and

---

PUBLIC TRANSPORT IN LYON

Buses, funiculars, tramways and subway trains (Métro) are run by **TCL** (*Transports en Commun Lyonnais*). Get the map (*plan du réseau*) from the Tourist Office or any TCL branch; For information, ☎8082 04 27 00 00 (http://tcl.canaltp.fr). The Métro is modern, clean and safe. Four lines, A, B, C and D, criss-cross the city. It operates 0500–2400. The two *Funiculaires* (funicular trains) depart every 10 mins until 2200 (2400 for the Fourvière line) from Vieux Lyon Métro station to either the hill-top Basilique or the Roman ruins. Buses cover every corner of Lyon, generally 0500–2100. Two tram lines T1 and T2, both run through Perrache station, and T3 from Lyon-Part-Dieu (T1 links the two stations).

NIGHT-TIME IN LYON

The weekly *Lyon Poche* lists the week's events (www.lyonpoche.com, not in English). The best areas for clubbing are near the Hôtel de Ville and quai Pierre Scize. The 1200-seat Lyon Opera House on pl. de la Comédie is a surprising mix of 18th- and 20th-century architecture, with 18 storeys inside, and a glass cupola that glows red as it fills up with people. Lyon is the birthplace of Guignol, the original 'Punch and Judy'. Shows for kids and adults alike are on either at the Théâtre le Guignol de Lyon, 2 r. Louis Carrand in Vieux Lyon, ☎04 78 28 92 57, or in the open air in the Parc de la Tête d'Or.

France

quenelles de brochet, poached pike fish balls. Lyon has some wonderful street **markets**. There are food markets every day except Mon at **Les Halles** and **La Croix-Rousse**. On Sun mornings don't miss the art and craft market, **Marché de la Création**, on the riverside by the cathedral in Vieux Lyon; and on the opposite bank, the *bouquinistes* stalls (old cards, maps and books) at quai de la Pêcherie (Saturdays too).

WHERE NEXT FROM LYON?

Lyon is handily placed for exploring the Alps by rail. For a superb route into Switzerland, either to Geneva (p359) or to Martigny, go via Culoz, Aix-les Bains, Annecy and La Roche sur Foron, where you can either continue to Geneva or take the route via Chamonix-Mont Blanc to Martigny. There's also a (less interesting) direct line from Lyon to Geneva (ETT table 345; takes 2 hrs).

Culoz *is a gateway for the **Marais de Lavours**, a national park noted for its marshland habitats, while beyond the well-heeled lakeside spa of **Aix-les-Bains** (where excursion boats cross Lac du Bourget to the mystical monastery of L'Abbaye d'Hautecombe) is **Annecy**, an (upmarket) lakeside resort in the heart of the Savoie Alps. If you continue to Martigny, you switch to a metre-gauge line and climb into the mountains, with the option of a side-trip on the **Tramway du Mont Blanc** (ETT table 397) from St-Gervais-le-Fayet to (summer only) the Nid d'Aigle (2386 m – and a 15-min stroll from the Bionnassay Glacier). Chamonix is placed beneath snow-capped Mt Blanc, the highest peak in the Alps; the **Montenvers rack railway** (ETT table 397) climbs 5 km to 1913 m, looking over the Mer de Glace, France's biggest glacier, which you can actually enter by way of a tunnel to visit the ice grotto. A great way of venturing into Italy is by travelling to Turin via Chambéry, Modane and through the 12.8-km **Fréjus tunnel** and past the Italian ski resort of Bardonecchia.*

ORANGE

This northern gateway to Provence had a population of some 80,000 in Roman times and several sites from the period are still in existence. The **Arc de Triomphe** is the third largest Roman arch to have survived, and was originally in fact a gate to the ancient walled city. Dating from about 25 BC, it is a majestic three-arched structure lavishly decorated with reliefs depicting battles, naval and military trophies and prisoners, honouring the victories of Augustus and the setting up of *Arausio* (Orange) as a colony. Orange's most famous sight is its **Roman theatre**, dating from the 1st century AD and with the best preserved back wall in the Roman Empire, standing 37 m tall, a magnificent setting for the town's song and opera festival in summer. A museum (open daily) opposite the amphitheatre has some unique local Roman finds as well as some intriguingly incongruous scenes of British life painted by the Welsh artist Frank Brangwyn; some 800 of his paintings having been donated to the town. In the evening, walk around place Sylvain or place de la République for a drink or a dinner.

RAIL Av. F. Mistral, 1.5 km east of the centre; the main Tourist Office is across town, follow av. F Mistral right, cross pl. de la République to r. St-Martin and straight on (15 mins).

i **Tourist Office:** 5 cours Aristide Briand, ☎04 90 34 70 88 (www.otorange.fr). Another branch on pl. des Frères Mounet (open July–Aug only).

🛏 **Hôtel St Jean,** I cours Pourtoules, ☎04 90 51 15 16 (www.hotelsaint-jean.com), €€; the lobby is actually a cave. At the station, **Hôtel de Provence,** 60 av. Frédéric Mistral, ☎04 90 34 00 23, €€, has a little swimming pool.

AVIGNON

In 1305, troubles in Rome caused the pope to move his power base to Avignon. Wealth flowed into the town – and remained after the papacy moved back to Rome 70 years later. The city walls, built to protect the papal assets, still surround the city and enclose just about everything worth seeing here. Jutting from the northwestern section is **Pont St-Bénezet**, the unfinished bridge famed in song (*Sur le pont d'Avignon*), inevitably a tourist trap (admission payable), but now with a museum and a restored rampart walk leading up to the **Rocher des Doms** garden with its great views over both the bridge and the nearby town of Villeneuve-lès-Avignon. Take the steps from the gardens down to the Romanesque cathedral, **Notre-Dame-des-Doms**, dating from the 12th century and containing the tombs of Pope John XXII and Pope Benedict XII. Adjacent is the most photographed sight in the city, the huge **Palais des Papes** (**Papal Palace**), boasting a 45-metre-long banqueting hall where cardinals would meet to elect a new Pope. In appearance it's more like a fortress than a palace and is still the most prominent landmark in the city. Its bleak walls are etched with arches and openings, and topped with castellations and a pair of pointy towers. You can wander by yourself or take a 90-minute guided tour in English. The popes acquired the dignified **Petit Palais** in 1335, and a couple of centuries later it was adapted into a sumptuous residence for Cardinal Giulio della Rovere, the future Pope Julius II, who took a lively interest in the arts; he began the collection of Renaissance treasures that has now made the building into an art museum (closed Tues). Contemporary art is to be found at the **Collection Lambert** (5 r. Violette; closed Mon), while several private mansions have **art collections** open to the public.

In the middle of the Rhône lies **Île de la Barthelasse**, a favourite picnic island, with its own summer swimming pool. Also try people-watching at **Place de l'Horloge**, popular for its street entertainment and outdoor cafés.

LE FESTIVAL D'AVIGNON

For three weeks in July, Avignon hosts one of Europe's largest drama festivals (www.festival-avignon.com). Soak up the ambience and see theatrical events of all dimensions, or watch the events themselves, held outdoors or in venues running from the majestic Palais des Papes to quaint courtyards to barn-like warehouses.

France

RAIL Avignon-Centre, just outside Porte de la République gateway in the city walls: head through this gateway and straight along cours J Jaurès for the centre. Shuttle buses (ETT table 350a) from this station link up to Avignon-TGV station, 5 km to the south.

i **Tourist Office:** 41 cours J Jaurès, ☎04 32 74 32 74 (www.avignon-tourisme.com). Another branch at Pont St-Bénezet (mid-Mar–Oct only).

🛏 During the drama festival in July (see box p111) everywhere gets completely booked up and you'd do better to stay at Tarascon or elsewhere, and travel in. At other times, from Avignon-Centre head through the gateway into the Old Town, where you'll find a large number of reasonably priced pensions and hotels in the backstreets a few minutes away: try the **Innova**, 100 rue Joseph Vernet ☎04 90 82 54 10 (www.hotel-innova.fr), €€. To step back to the future – just for a look as it's extremely expensive – visit **Cloître St Louis**, 20 r. du Portail Boquier, ☎04 90 27 55 55 (www.cloitre-saint-louis.com), €€€, a unique 4-star hotel. An oasis of calm just off Avignon's main street, it combines tradition and modernity; the old part is housed in original 16th-century cloisters and the new wing was designed by Jean Nouvel. The restaurant, overlooking the impressive courtyard, is particularly stunning in the evening when the cloisters are illuminated. **Hôtel Central**, ☎04 90 86 07 81 (www.avignon-central-hotel.com), €€, is true to its name, with a lovely, Provence-style garden. 31 r de la République. **Hostels** (non-HI): **Auberge Bagatelle**, Île de la Barthelasse, ☎04 90 86 30 39 (www.campingbagatelle.com) (🚌 10/11 from the post office opposite Avignon-Centre rail station to Barthelasse on the bridge); also has all-year 3-star camping facilities. The **Centre de Rencontres Internationales YMCA** is over the Rhône, in Villeneuve-lès-Avignon, 7 bis chemin de la Justice, ☎04 90 25 46 20 (www.ymca-avignon.com); 🚌 10 from the post office opposite Avignon-Centre station to Monteau. **Campsites:** several on Île de la Barthelasse. Try 4-star **Camping du Pont d'Avignon**, ☎04 90 80 63 50 (www.camping-avignon.com); 🚌 10/11, as for Auberge Bagatelle (open late Mar–late Oct); or 2-star **Camping les Deux Rhônes**, ☎04 90 85 49 70 (www.camping2rhone.com) 🚌 20 from Porte de l'Oulle; infrequent; open all year. Both have pools.

MARSEILLE

See p120, and the following two rail tours for suggestions of where to go next.

ROUTE DETAIL

Biarritz–Pau — ETT table 325

Type	Frequency	Typical journey time
Train	7 daily	1 hr 45 mins

Pau–Lourdes — ETT tables 305, 325

Type	Frequency	Typical journey time
Train	Every 2 hrs	30 mins

Lourdes–Toulouse — ETT table 325

Type	Frequency	Typical journey time
Train	9 daily	2 hr 10 mins

Toulouse–Carcassonne — ETT table 321

Type	Frequency	Typical journey time
Train	Every 2 hrs	50 mins

Carcassonne–Narbonne — ETT table 321

Type	Frequency	Typical journey time
Train	Every 2 hrs	30 mins

Narbonne–Béziers — ETT table 355

Type	Frequency	Typical journey time
Train	Every 1–2 hrs	15 mins

Béziers–Montpellier — ETT table 355

Type	Frequency	Typical journey time
Train	Every hour	45 mins

Montpellier–Nîmes — ETT table 355

Type	Frequency	Typical journey time
Train	Every hr	30 mins

Nîmes–Arles — ETT table 355

Type	Frequency	Typical journey time
Train	8 daily	25 mins

Arles–Marseille — ETT tables 351, 355

Type	Frequency	Typical journey time
Train	Every hr	50 mins

KEY JOURNEYS

Biarritz–Toulouse — ETT table 325

Type	Frequency	Typical journey time
Train	3 daily	4–5 hrs

Toulouse–Marseille — ETT table 355

Type	Frequency	Typical journey time
Train	8–9 daily	4 hrs

Toulouse–Nîmes — ETT table 355

Type	Frequency	Typical journey time
Train	7–8 daily	2 hrs 45 mins

France

From the Atlantic coast at **Biarritz**, the route edges along the plain to the vast mountain backdrops of the northern Pyrenees. The journey visits **Lourdes**, with its bizarre yet moving non-stop pilgrimage scene, **Carcassonne** and its massive fortifications, and the lively university town of **Montpellier**. **Nîmes** and **Arles** are two of the great Roman sites of the Midi, and the finale, **Marseille**, is a big, bustling port, stronger in atmosphere than in sights. If you have time, stop off en route at **Tarascon** to admire the Château du Roi René, gloriously seated on the Rhône and impressively intact despite the heavy bombing of the surrounding town during World War II. You can lengthen and vary the journey by diverting onto the Béziers–Nîmes route (p134), heading up to Clermont-Ferrand before returning south through the Allier gorge.

BIARRITZ

The smart set have been coming to Biarritz since the splendid beaches and mild climate were 'discovered' in the mid-19th century by such visitors as Napoleon III and Queen Victoria. Although less grand now, it is still essentially a fairly upmarket coastal resort with a string of good sandy beaches, great surfing and a casino.

[RAIL] Gare de Biarritz-La Négresse, 3 km from the centre, along a winding road: about a 40-min walk. Left-luggage facilities open daily 0900–1200 and 1415–1800. Take 🚌 2 for a 20-min ride to the town hall – 🚌 9 (replaced in summer by the 'Plages' route) also goes there, but via a longer route.

✈ Aéroport International de Biarritz-Anglet-Bayonne, ☎05 59 43 83 83 (www.biarritz.aeroport.fr), 3 km from town; 🚌 6 costs just over €1 from town centre (also links the airport to Bayonne).

ℹ Tourist Office: 1 sq. d'Ixelles, Javalquinto, ☎05 59 22 37 10 (www.biarritz.fr). Free maps and information on the Basque region. Branches open July–Aug at the station and at pl. Clemenceau.

🏨 Hôtel Argi Eder, 13 rue Peyroloubilh, ☎05 59 24 22 53 (www.hotel-argieder.fr), with its traditional Basque façade, is ideally located (closed mid-Dec–mid-Jan), €€. **Hostel** (HI): 8 r. Chiquito de Cambo, ☎05 59 41 76 00 (biarritz@fuaj.org), 0.8 km from rail station, 🚌 2/9.

PAU

This elegantly prosperous town is perched on a south-facing cliff above its river, enjoying panoramic views of the snow-capped **Pyrenees**. Pau has strong links with the British, who adored its favourable climate and flocked here in droves in the 19th century, bringing their much-loved pastimes (golf, rugby, steeplechasing and a casino) with them. Pau's attractions are easily walkable and a free map is available from the

Tourist Office. Its **château** (reached via r. Henri IV from the pl. Royale, or by a free lift from pl. de la Monnaie) was the birthplace of the charismatic French monarch, Henri IV, and contains some of his personal possessions, as well as fine **Gobelin** tapestries and the **Musée Béarnais** (the provincial museum). Soak up more history at the **Musée Bernadotte**, 8 r. Tran, the birthplace of one of Napoleon's marshals, whose descendants are today's Swedish royal family.

Av. Gaston Lacoste. On the southern edge of town. It's a tough 15-min uphill walk to the centre, but the funicular railway opposite the station will take you to pl. Royale for free. It operates every 3 mins, Mon–Sat 0645–1210, 1235–1910 and 1935–2140; Sun 1330–1910 and 1935–2050.

i **Tourist Office**: Hôtel de Ville, pl. Royale, ☎05 59 27 27 08 (www.pau-pyrenees.com).

Youth hostel (HI): **Logis Gaston Marsan**, **Base de Plein Air**, chemin de Saligue, ☎05 59 35 09 99 (auberge.de.jeunesse@habitat-jeunes-pau-asso.fr), out of town (2 km SE of Pau station near Gelos; ☒ 1 to Gelos or ☒ 7 to Hounau). **Le Postillon**, 10 cours Camou, ☎05 59 72 83 00 (www.hotel-le-postillon.fr), €€, or **Hôtel Central**, 15, r. Léon Daran, ☎05 59 27 72 75 (www.hotelcentralpau.com), €€, are fine value.

LOURDES

The mountainous riverside setting of this famous pilgrimage centre is undeniably beautiful. Lourdes swarms with visitors (over six million a year), and every other building in town is a shop overflowing with kitsch religious souvenirs. For all that, a visit here is an unforgettable and sometimes moving experience even for the faithless. It all began in 1858, when the 14-year-old Bernadette Soubirous experienced visions of the Virgin Mary in a local grotto. A spring appeared, and word spread that its waters had miraculous curative powers. Today, water from the spring supplies local baths and drinking fountains. The 19 baths (rebuilt in 1955) are open to sick and healthy alike and hundreds of people plunge into them daily, many in search of cures for intractable ailments. Key locations associated with Bernadette can be visited in the town, including **Boly Mill**, where she was born, and the *cachot* (dungeon), where she lived during the time of the apparitions. Obtain a free map from the Forum information centre, **St Joseph's Gate**, off pl. Mgr Laurence. Bus excursions tour the surrounding area, including the **Parc National des Pyrénées**, which follows the Franco-Spanish border for 100 km; and the **Grottes de Bétharram**, vast underground caverns full of limestone formations.

Av. de la Gare. A 10-min walk northeast of the centre. ☒ 1 goes to the centre and the Grotto. To reach the Tourist Office, turn right out of the station down av. de la Gare, and then left at the end along chaussée Maransin to pl. Peyramale.

i **Tourist Office:** pl. Peyramale, ☎05 62 42 77 40 (www.lourdes-infotourisme.com).

Paris aside, Lourdes has more hotels than anywhere else in France, including a huge number of budget and moderate establishments close to the station and around the castle. The Tourist

France

Office has a list of all types of accommodation. Try the **Hôtel de l'Europe Lourdes**, 38 av. Peyramale, ☎05 62 94 01 50 (www.lourdes-hotel-europe.fr), €€; or the **Hôtel Concorde**, 7 r. du Calvaire, ☎05 62 94 05 18 (www.concordelourdes.com), €€, for moderate lodging (both open Mid-Apr–late Oct only). **Hostel** accommodation for 18–30 year olds (**non-HI**) can be found at **Village des Jeunes**, av. Mgr Rodhain, ☎05 62 42 79 95 (village.jeunes@lourdes-france.com); Easter–Nov 1. There are 13 **campsites**, including two along the rte de la Forêt: **Camping du Loup**, ☎05 62 94 23 60 (www.camping-du-loup-lourdes.com; open Apr–mid-Oct), and **Camping de la Forêt**, ☎05 62 94 04 38 (open Apr–Oct).

TOULOUSE	CARCASSONNE

See p88.

From the 13th century, Carcassonne was the greatest stronghold of the Cathars, a Christian sect ruthlessly annihilated by crusaders sent out on the orders of Rome. The great **fortress** held out for only a month, but the structure survived for long afterwards, until being pillaged for building materials. Most of what you now see was restored in the 19th century by the architect Viollet-le-Duc. Today there are two distinct towns. On one side of the River Aude is the Ville Basse (Lower Town), which although modern and grid-like, dates from the 13th century. The more impressive **Cité** perches on a crag on the other bank of the river and is entered by two gates – Porte d'Aude and Porte Narbonnaise. If you are walking up from Ville Basse, look for the footpath beside St-Gimer, which leads to the 12th-century Château Comtal (Counts' Castle, guided tour only).

▆ Behind Jardin André Chénier, in the Ville Basse, on the north bank of the Canal du Midi. It's a long walk to La Cité – about 30 mins and the last part uphill; cross the bridge and head straight on r. G-Clemenceau. Turn left onto r. de la Liberté and then right along blvd Jean Jaurès. At sq. Gambetta, take r. du Port-Vieux and cross the old bridge, from where La Cité is signposted. ▆ 4 goes from the station to sq. Gambetta, then change and take ▆ 2 to just outside the walls of La Cité.

✚ 5 km from town (www.carcassonne.aeroport.fr); Agglo'bus ▆ 7 (3–8 services daily scheduled for each flight) to rail station and hotels.

i **Tourist Offices**: In the Ville Basse – 28 r. de Verdun, ☎04 68 10 24 30 (www.carcassonne.org). In La Cité – **Tour Narbonnaise**, ☎04 68 10 24 36 (all year). Also at Port du Canal du Midi, ☎04 68 25 94 81 (Apr–Oct only).

▤ The most picturesque area to stay is in the Cité but hotels can be extremely expensive. Best to find a hotel in the Ville Basse and 'commute': a couple of cheap options are **Hôtel Astoria**, 18 r. Tourtel, ☎04 68 25 31 38 (www.astoriacarcassonne.com), €, and **Hôtel de la Bastide**, r. de la Liberté, ☎04 68 71 96 89, €. **Youth hostel** (**HI**): r. du Vicomte Trencavel, ☎04 68 25 23 16 (carcassone@fuaj.org), though is in La Cité, 2.5 km from the rail station, ▆ 2/4 to station 'Centre-Ville' (closed Christmas–Jan). **Camping: Camping de la Cité**, rte de St-Hilaire, ☎04 68 25 11 77 (www.camping-lacite.com), across the Aude, ask Tourist Office for bus routes (open mid-Mar–mid-Oct).

NARBONNE

A fine Midi town, lapped by vineyards and good beaches, Narbonne's most striking building is the magnificent Gothic **Cathédrale St-Juste-et-St-Sauveur**. It has some lovely stained glass and the views make it worth climbing the towers. Together with the adjacent **Palais des Archevêques** (Archbishops' Palace) this forms a remarkable group of civil, military and religious buildings. Flanked by medieval towers, the **Passage de l'Ancre** is a cobbled, L-shaped way between the cathedral and the old and new palaces; the new palace contains archaeological and art museums. Below ground is **L'Horreum**, 16 r. Rouget-de-l'Isle, a well-preserved Roman granary.

WHERE NEXT FROM NARBONNE?

Trains to Perpignan take 50 minutes and run every 1–2 hrs (ETT table 355); from there you can join the Toulouse–Barcelona route (p138).

🚆 A 10-min walk northeast of the centre: turn right along blvd F Mistral to the river, and left along r. J Jaurès.

ℹ️ **Tourist Office**: r. Jean Jaurès, in a 16th-century mill, ☎04 68 65 15 60 (www.mairie.narbonne.fr), is near the cathedral. Pick up a copy of the free *Escapades en Pays Narbonnais*.

🏨 Close to the station is the charming **Hôtel Le Régent**, 15 rue Suffren & 50 rue Mosaïque, ☎04 68 32 02 41 (www.leregentnarbonne.com), with a terrace and a small garden, €–€€. Another budget option close to the station is the **Wills Hotel**, 23 av. Pierre Sémard, ☎04 68 90 44 50 (www.willshotel-narbonne.com), €–€€.

DAY TRIP FROM BÉZIERS

West of town, the **Canal du Midi** leads from the Mediterranean to the Atlantic and there are day cruises through the locks and vineyards, while buses serve the long, sandy beaches not far from town.

BÉZIERS

Vineyards spread from the outskirts of Béziers at the heart of the Languedoc wine country. Rising from the Pont-Vieux over the River Orb, the Old Town climbs to the 13th-century Gothic **Cathédrale de St-Nazaire**, which replaced an earlier cathedral burned down with 7000 citizens locked inside during the Albigensian Crusade (1209). **Musée du Biterrois** has more cheerful exhibits on wine and local history.

🚆 For the centre of town, head straight up through the charming Plateau des Poètes. This is a lovely 19th-century park with statues and a dripping grotto topped by Atlas standing on two horses. When you reach the top, head along Allée Paul Ricquet, marked by an avenue of limes; the Old Town lies ahead and to the left.

ℹ️ **Tourist Office**: Palais des Congrès, 29 av. St-Saëns, ☎04 67 76 84 00 (www.beziers-tourisme.fr). Details of local wine festivals are available here. There's an additional branch at Place Lavabre, r. du 4 septembre, ☎04 67 36 06 27.

France

📧 There are hotels near the station, but it's more fun to stay in the centre of town. The budget hotel here is the recently renovated **Cécil**, 5 pl. J Jaurès, 📞04 67 28 48 55 (www.hotelcecil beziers.com), €. For more comfort, try the **Angleterre**, 22 pl. J Jaurès, 📞04 67 28 48 42, €€.

MONTPELLIER

High-tech, young and trendy, Montpellier's main attraction is that it's simply fun to spend time in. As a university town, with 55,000 students to feed, Montpellier abounds with inexpensive eating places, bars and hotels. The **Vieille Ville** (Old Town) mixes cobbled streets with many 17th- and 18th-century mansions. To the west, the **Promenade de Peyrou** leads to an impressive clump of monumental sculpture, consisting of a triumphal arch, a hexagonal water tower and an equestrian statue of Louis XIV. Northwards lies the **Jardin des Plantes**, France's oldest botanic garden. For paintings, head to the newly restored **Musée Fabre**, in a townhouse (closed Mon).

🚆 Gare St-Roch, a 5-min walk southeast of the Tourist Office (or take tram 1).

ℹ️ **Tourist Office**: 30 allée J de Lattre de Tassigny, espl. Comédie, 📞04 67 60 60 60 (www.ot-montpellier.fr).

📧 For a hotel in the historic centre, try **Hôtel du Palais**, 3 r. du Palais des Guilhem, 📞04 67 60 47 38 (www.hoteldupalais-montpellier.fr), €. **Youth hostel (H1)**: r. des Écoles Laïques, 📞04 67 60 32 22 (montpellier@fuaj.org); 1 km from the station (🚌 to Mosson, stop Louis Blanc).

NÎMES

Nîmes has become a household word, though many wearers of its most famous product may not realise where the name comes from. The cloth known as **serge de Nîmes**, manufactured here from the 18th century onwards, became shortened to denim. It achieved lasting mass-market popularity when Levi Strauss began importing it in the 1860s to turn into hard-wearing clothes for Californian gold-miners. But the history of Nîmes stretches back much further than its textile heyday, and several superb Roman buildings survive from classical times. **Les Arènes**, 📞04 66 21 82 56, seating 23,000 in 34 elliptical tiers, is said to be the best preserved Roman amphitheatre in the world, and still stages concerts, theatrical events and bullfights (open daily). **Maison Carrée**, a well-preserved 1st-century temple, is now an exhibition centre (open daily). Next door is the futuristic **Carré d'Art**, a contemporary art gallery designed by Norman Foster (closed Mon). To the west, the 18th-century **Jardin de la Fontaine** (Garden of the Fountain), off av. J Jaurès, features a romantic Temple of Diana.

PONT DU GARD

The **Pont du Gard** is a spectacular Roman aqueduct 48 m above the Gard River (at a popular swimming spot), accessible by bus eight times a day from Nîmes. The site attracts two million visitors a year. Water was brought to the aqueduct from **Uzès**, a medieval village centred on a formidable castle, where today waxworks and holographic ghosts entertain visitors.

🚃 Blvd Talabot, a 10-min walk southeast of the centre: head down av. Feuchères to espl. C de-Gaulle, then along blvd Victor Hugo.

ℹ️ **Tourist Office:** 6 r. Auguste, 📞04 66 58 38 00 (www.ot.nimes.fr).

🏨 For budget hotels, try blvd des Arènes, or around blvd Amiral Courbet such as **Hotel Terminus Audrans**, 23 av. Feuchères, 📞04 66 29 20 14, (www.hotel-terminus-nimes.com), €–€€. The **Kyriad**, 10 r. Roussy, 📞04 66 76 16 20 (www.kyriad.fr), is a useful mid-range choice, €€–€€€. Or try the more expensive **Hôtel Majestic**, 10 r. Pradier, 📞04 66 29 24 14 (www.hotel-majestic-nimes.com), €€€. **Youth hostel (HI)**: 257 Chemin de l'Auberge de Jeunesse, 📞04 66 68 03 20 (nimes@fuaj.org), is about 4 km from the station, 🚌 line i; 400 m uphill walk from bus stop to hostel. **Campsite: Camping Domaine de la Bastide**, rte de Générac, 📞04 66 62 05 82 (www.camping-nimes.com), 5 km to the south; cheap (🚌 D: La Bastide direction).

ARLES

Ancient Rome meets Van Gogh and black bulls in Arles, the spiritual heart of Provence and a great place to relax and absorb history. Most major sights and museums are tucked into the sleepy old town and are easily accessible on foot. Arles is one of the best-preserved Roman towns in the world. **Les Arènes** is a mini Colosseum, less intact than the Roman amphitheatre at Nîmes but still used for bullfights (Easter–Sept; closed Nov–Feb). Summer theatrical productions are still staged at the **Théâtre Antique** (closed Nov–Feb). Elsewhere in town are the 4th-century **Thermes** (baths), r. du Grand Prieuré, of the otherwise vanished palace of Emperor Constantine and the seating and columns of the **Théâtre Antique**. Built next to a Roman racetrack, the modern **Musée de l'Arles et de la Provence Antique** has some superb Roman sarcophagi, mosaics and statuary (open daily). Art buffs should seek out the **Musée Réattu**, 10 r. du Grand Prieuré, which houses a collection of Picasso sketches, the **Espace Van Gogh**, an exhibition centre within the former hospital where the artist was treated after chopping off his ear, and **Alyscamps** (Elysian Fields), an ancient burial ground painted by Van Gogh and Gauguin. Unfortunately none of Van Gogh's works are still in the town, but the Tourist Office runs Van Gogh tours to some of the places that inspired his paintings. The **Cathédrale St-Trophime** has a west front regarded as one of the pinnacles of Provençal medieval stonework, depicting the damned descending naked into the flames of Hell while the Heaven-bound and robed saved people smirk self-righteously. The airy cloisters blend Gothic and Romanesque styles. Arles parties through the summer: mid-July, the *Les Suds à Arles* (www.suds-arles.com) fills the streets with music of the south. In mid-Aug, the *Festival Musique et Paix* celebrates gypsy music and way of life.

🚃 Av. P Talabot. A few blocks north of Les Arènes: walk down av. P Talabot and along r. Laclavière.

ℹ️ **Tourist Office**: blvd des Lices (🚌 4 from rail station), 📞04 90 18 41 20, (www.tourisme. ville-arles.fr). Accommodation service. Differently themed walking tours and self-guided tours use symbols embedded in the pavement. The *Petit Train d'Arles* (a road train) departs every day

France

from Easter–Oct between 1000 and 1900 for a tour (with commentary) of the historic centre (about 40 mins), ☎04 93 41 31 09.

🛏 For budget hotels look around pl. du Forum and pl. Voltaire (also good for cafés and restaurants). Two elegant upmarket hotels are **Jules César**, 9 blvd des Lices, ☎04 90 52 52 52, (www.hotel-julescesar.fr), €€€, and **Hotel d'Arlatan**, 26 r. du Sauvage, ☎04 90 93 56 66 (www.hotel-arlatan.fr), €€€. **Hôtel Gauguin**, 5 pl. Voltaire, ☎04 90 96 14 35, fax 04 90 18 98 87, €€, is one of the better moderate places. **Youth hostel (HI)**: 20 av. Maréchal Foch, ☎04 90 96 18 25 (arles@fuaj.org), is 1.8 km southeast of town, a 15-min walk from town centre or 🚌 3: Clémenceau, then 🚌 2: Maréchal Foch; open early Feb–mid-Dec. **Camping**: **Camping-City**, 67 rte de Crau, ☎04 90 93 08 86 (www.camping-city.com); open Apr–Sept, or **Les Rosiers**, Pont de Crau, ☎04 90 96 02 12 (www.arles-camping-club.com).

SIDE TRIP TO THE CAMARGUE
Hourly buses run between Arles and **Stes-Maries-de-la-Mer**, on the coast. This is the site of an annual gypsy pilgrimage in late May and the main base for the **Camargue**. The Camargue is now a nature reserve, an area of marshland and rice fields where semi-wild white horses and black bulls roam free and lagoons are often pink with flamingos in summer. Horseback is the best way to get around; the **Stes-Maries Tourist Office**, 5 av. Van Gogh, ☎04 90 97 82 55 (www.saintesmaries.com), can supply a list of some 30 farms with horses for hire. Cycling is the best alternative: bikes can be hired either from Stes-Maries or from Arles (the Tourist Office, train station, or **Le Vélociste**, route d'Arles, pl. Mireille, ☎04 90 97 83 26).

MARSEILLE

This earthy Mediterranean city is hectically vibrant, with a great music scene and superb fish-based cuisine. The busiest port in France, it's a melting pot of French and North African cultures. Marseille's grubby, rough-and-ready character appeals to some, while others will want to move on swiftly – though watch this space, because big regeneration schemes are changing the city, especially in the northern dock areas. There's a good Métro and bus system (regular buses stop running at 2100) and two new tram lines.

Full of small restaurants and street cafés, the **Vieux Port** (Old Port) is the hub of Marseille life and is guarded by the forts of St Jean and St Nicholas on

---

MARSEILLE'S MUSEUMS

The streets of Le Panier lead up to the **Vieille Charité**, 2 r. de la Vieille Charité, an erstwhile workhouse now housing two museums covering African, Oceanian and American Indian art and Mediterranean archaeology (closed Mon). Also try **Musée Cantini**, 19 r. Grignan, ☎04 91 54 77 75 (Métro: Estrangin Préfecture), which houses a considerable collection of modern art (closed Mon). For a more contemporary slant, visit **La Friche La Belle de Mai**, 41 r. Jobin, ☎04 95 04 95 04 (www. lafriche.org), a hip multidisciplinary arts centre in a converted tobacco factory in the north of the city (open daily).

GETTING AROUND MARSEILLE

The central (Vieux Port) area is walkable. Elsewhere, use the Métro and buses, both run by **RTM** (*Réseau de Transport Marseillais*). Plan du Réseau (from the Tourist Office and RTM kiosks) covers the routes: the map looks complicated but the system is easy to use. After 2100 the normal bus routes are replaced by a 10-route evening network called Fluobus, centred on Canebière (Bourse). Most of the city centre is safe but avoid wandering too far off the main streets at night particularly in the 6th *arrondissement* and around St Charles.

either side of its entrance. From the **quai des Belges**, the main boulevard of **La Canebière** extends back into the city. Across the port from the steep narrow streets of Le Panier – the oldest part of Marseille – rises **Notre-Dame-de-la-Garde**, an impressive 19th-century basilica that is Marseille's most distinctive landmark (take 🚌 60 or the tourist train – it's a steep uphill climb otherwise). The golden Virgin atop the church watches over all sailors and travellers; the interior is full of paintings and mementos of the disasters the Virgin is supposed to have protected people from. In Dumas' novel of the same name the Count of Monte Cristo was imprisoned in **Chateau d'If** on one of the little **Îles de Frioul** just outside the harbour; it can be visited by boat. Contact Frioul If express, 1, quai des Belges, ☎04 91 46 54 65 (www.frioul-if-express.com). Marseille also has some good beaches south of the Vieux Port.

🚉 **Gare St-Charles**, pl. Victor Hugo, is the main station, 20-min walk northeast of the **Vieux Port** (Old Port): head down the steps and straight along blvd d'Athènes and blvd Dugommier to La Canebière, then turn right; or Métro direction La Timone, station Vieux Port – Hôtel de Ville. Facilities include left luggage; open daily 0815–2100. **SOS Voyageurs**, ☎04 91 62 12 80.

🚢 For information on ferries to Corsica, Sardinia and North Africa, contact **SNCM**, 61 blvd des Dames, ☎3620 (+33 825 88 80 88 from abroad) (www.sncm.fr). The ferry terminal (Gare Maritime) is north of the Old Port; follow r. de la République.

✈ **Marseille–Provence Aéroport**, ☎04 42 14 14 14 (www.mrsairport.com); at Marignane, 25 km northwest. (Terminal 1 handles international flights.) An airport bus runs between the airport and St Charles railway station every 20 mins, taking 25 mins.

ℹ **Tourist Office:** 4 La Canebière, ☎04 91 13 89 00 (www.marseille-tourisme.com). Student and youth information: **Centre Régional Information Jeunesse (CRIJ)**: 96 La Canebière, ☎04 91 24 33 50 (www.crijpa.com). Various walking tours in English and other languages are available; check the tourist information website for the month's programme or book in advance at the Tourist Information Office.

🏨 The Tourist Office has a free accommodation booking service. For cheap, functional and tranquil hotels, try around allées L Gambetta or south of the Vieux Port and Préfecture, but tread cautiously in the still rather dodgy streets southwest of the station (roughly the area bordered by blvd d'Athènes, blvd Charles Nédélec, cours Belsunce and La Canebière). One option in this area is **Hôtel Vertigo**, 42 rue des Petites Maries, ☎04 91 91 07 11 (www.hotelvertigo.fr), €€; with trendy doubles and inexpensive hostel rooms. **Hôtel St Louis**, 2 r. des Récolettes,

France

☎04 91 54 02 74 (www.hotel-st-louis.com), €€, is off La Canebière, inexpensive and air-conditioned. Nearer to the port, rooms tend to be pricier, though the **ETAP Vieux Port**, 46 r. Sainte, ☎0892 68 05 82 (www.etaphotel.com), €–€€, is a good budget option a block from the harbour. **Youth hostels (HI)**: **Château de Bois Luzy**, Allée des Primevères, ☎04 91 49 06 18 (www.fuaj.org/aj/marseille), Métro to Chartreux, then ⊟ 6 to Richard Py; **Bonneveine**, imp. du Dr Bonfils, beginning at 47 av. Joseph Vidal, ☎04 91 17 63 30 (marseille-bonneveine@fuaj.org), is 5 km south in a residential district near the beaches; take Métro 2 to rond-point du Prado then ⊟ 44 to Bonnefon; closed mid-Dec–mid-Jan.

TO The harbour and the streets leading from it are lined with North African and fish restaurants: **Cours Julien** is good for trendier, international fare, and more elegant restaurants are found along **corniche J F Kennedy**. Specialities include *bouillabaisse*; the authentic version of this fish stew contains rascasse, an ugly Mediterranean species, and is served with potatoes and croutons.

SIDE TRIP TO AIX-EN-PROVENCE Aix-en-Provence, the capital of Provence, and 30–40 mins from Marseille by train (ETT table 362), is a charming university town. **Cours Mirabeau**, flanked by plane trees and dotted with ancient fountains, forms the southern boundary of **Vieil Aix**, whose markets are among the most colourful in Provence. To the south is the **Quartier Mazarin**, a grid of tranquil streets with elegant 17th-century houses. The **Cathédrale St-Sauveur** is an architectural mishmash, but has lovely Romanesque cloisters. Aix was the birth-place of Cézanne and inspired some of his work, although he despised the town, which ridiculed him and his art. Later it came to its senses and his studio, **Atelier Cézanne**, has been lovingly preserved (open daily). Using studs embedded in the pavement and a tourist guide you can follow the main stages of Cézanne's life. Aix is also renowned for its **thermal springs**; ☎04 42 23 81 82. The **station** is 5 mins south of the centre: take av. Victor Hugo to La Rotonde; the **Tourist Office** is on the left, at 2 pl. du Général-de-Gaulle, ☎04 42 16 11 61 (www.aixenprovencetourism .com). The TGV station (with direct trains to Paris) is 9 km west of the town.

WHERE NEXT FROM MARSEILLE?

Marseille is a major rail junction, from which run some of the most scenic lines in France. In addition to exploring the Marseille–Menton route (p123) and perhaps continuing from Menton over the Italian border, you can take the slow train to Paris via the Allier gorge.

Béziers–Nîmes (p134). The line through Aix-en-Provence continues round the hills of the **Lubéron** *(the subject of Peter Mayle's book* A Year in Provence*), and then through increasingly dramatic limestone scenery as you enter the foothills of the Alps.*

Beyond **Gap***, you're really into the Alps proper; you can continue on to* **Briançon** *(ETT table 362), a major centre for the mountains. Alternatively, stop at* **Montdauphin-Guillestre** *(between Gap and Briançon); from here there are connecting minibuses to the* **Parc Régional de Queyras***, one of the most rural parts of the French Alps. Good bases are St-Véran (Europe's highest permanently inhabited village) and Ceillac.*

RAIL TOUR: MARSEILLE – NICE – MENTON

KEY JOURNEYS

Marseille–Nice
ETT table 360

Type	Frequency	Typical journey time
Train	Every 1–2 hrs	2 hrs 30 mins – 2 hrs 45 mins

Nice–Milan
ETT table 90

Type	Frequency	Typical journey time
Train	3 daily	4 hrs 45 mins

ROUTE DETAIL

Marseille–Cassis
ETT table 360

Type	Frequency	Typical journey time
Train	Every 1–2 hrs	25 mins

Cassis–Toulon
ETT table 360

Type	Frequency	Typical journey time
Train	1–2 hrs	35 mins

Toulon–St-Raphaël
ETT table 360

Type	Frequency	Typical journey time
Train	12 daily	1 hr

St-Raphaël–Cannes
ETT table 361

Type	Frequency	Typical journey time
Train	Every hr	22 mins

Cannes–Antibes
ETT table 361

Type	Frequency	Typical journey time
Train	1–2 every hr	12 mins

Antibes–Nice
ETT table 361

Type	Frequency	Typical journey time
Train	1–2 every hr	15–25 mins

Nice–Villefranche-sur-Mer
ETT table 361

Type	Frequency	Typical journey time
Train	1–2 every hr	8 mins

Villefranche-sur-Mer–Eze
ETT table 361

Type	Frequency	Typical journey time
Train	1–2 every hr	7 mins

Eze–Monaco (Monte Carlo)
ETT 361

Type	Frequency	Typical journey time
Train	1–2 every hr	8 mins

Monaco (Monte Carlo)–Menton
ETT table 361

Type	Frequency	Typical journey time
Train	1–2 every hr	10 mins

France

This stretch of coast, the **Côte d'Azur**, became the haunt of British aristocrats in the 19th century, heralding its new status as a sophisticated playground for the famous, beautiful or just plain rich. Grand hotels and casinos sprung up to cater for their tastes, and although parts have declined into untidy sprawls there's still an enticing mix of ostentatious villas, pretty waterside towns and fine beaches. **Cannes** (marking the westward bounds of the glamorous Riviera) and **Juan-les-Pins** are hot spots for nightlife, while **Nice** is large, cosmopolitan and backpacker-friendly and tiny, independent **Monaco** is super-compressed and super-rich. Inland the land rises abruptly and you're into a different world, of rugged mountains and ancient perched villages; much of it is difficult to reach without a car.

MARSEILLE

See p120.

CASSIS

Centred around a pretty fishing harbour ringed with restaurants and making an easy day trip from Marseille via bus or train, Cassis makes a handy base for seeing the spectacular *calanques*, rocky inlets that cut into the limestone cliffs. Coastal walks (including the long-distance path GR98 west to Cap Croisette) offer stunning views.

🚆 3.5 km from the town centre, on foot or by taxi (there is a bus per hour from the station). Go along av. des Albizzi to av. Auguste Favier then av. Augustin Isnard, which leads into town.

ℹ️ **Tourist Office**: Oustau Calendal, quai des Moulins, ☎0892 25 98 92 (premium rate) (www.ot-cassis.fr). Cassis has a Spartan, eco-friendly youth hostel (HI): **La Fontasse**, ☎04 42 01 02 72 (www.fuaj.org/aj/cassis), in stunning wild landscape west of the town (closed Jan–Mar). No bus takes you there – it's about one hour by foot through the first *calanque*, then up a footpath on the hill. Otherwise there are some charming 1- or 2-star hotels in town.

FRÉJUS AND ST-RAPHAËL

The ancient Roman port of **Fréjus** and the modern beach resort of **St-Raphaël** fuse to form one urban area, though each has its own identity, its own station and Tourist Office. St-Raphaël is the upmarket end and the main transport hub, with spacious beaches and a tiny Old Quarter. Fréjus-Plage is a strip of bars, restaurants and a giant marina lying between the sea and Fréjus town. Fréjus' Roman port was created by Julius Caesar in 49 BC and there are quite a few Roman remains scattered around the town. The **amphitheatre**, Arènes, r. Henri-Vadon, is still used for bullfights and rock concerts. **Fréjus Cathedral**, pl. Formigé, was Provence's first Gothic church, and has beautiful cloisters (entry charge). West of town, the **Aqualand** water park and **Base Nature** activity area offer scope for fun in the sun.

🚆 **Gare de St-Raphaël** is central: for the sea, head down r. Jules Barbier to Promenade de la Libération.

🚌 **St-Raphaël bus station**: behind the rail station, av. Victor Hugo, ☎04 94 83 87 63.

ℹ️ **Tourist Offices**: **St-Raphaël**, quai Albert 1er, ☎04 94 19 52 52 (www.saint-raphael.com), opposite the station. **Fréjus-Ville**, 325 r. J Jaurès, ☎04 94 51 83 83 (www.frejus.fr), dispenses a guide to the (widespread) Roman sites.

🏠 **Youth hostel (HI)**: chemin du Counillier, ☎04 94 53 18 75, fax 04 94 53 25 86 (frejus-st-raphael@fuaj.org; Mar–mid-Nov), in a large park 1.5 km from Fréjus town along the RN7 road towards Cannes (by foot as there are only two buses a day). **Campsites: Parc Camping Agay Soleil**, 1152 blvd de la Plage, Agay, ☎04 94 82 00 79 (www.agaysoleil.com), open Apr–Oct; **Camping de Saint Aygulf Plage**, 270 av. Salvarelli, ☎04 94 17 62 49 (www.camping-cote-azur.com), is 4 km from Fréjus station (🚌 9 from St-Raphaël bus station to St-Aygulf), 100 m from the sea, open early Apr–late Oct.

SIDE TRIPS FROM ST-RAPHAËL   **Hyères** makes a pleasant excursion from St-Raphaël via Toulon; this charming old town, with a hilly medieval core set back from the sea, first attracted winter visitors in the late 19th century: Tolstoy, Queen Victoria and Robert Louis Stevenson enjoyed its mild climate.

From Hyères you can catch a ferry to offshore islands – **Île de Porquerolles** (20 mins), **Île de Port-Cros** (1 hr) and **Île du Levant** (1 hr 30 mins) – which offer some of the most beautiful beaches in the Mediterranean. Take a bus from the town to the port at La Tour Fondue for the ferry to Île de Porquerolles (21 ferries a day in summer, six a day off season); ferry information: ☎04 94 58 21 81 or 04 94 58 95 14), Port la Gavine for Port-Cros and Île du Levant, ☎04 94 57 44 07 (five ferries per day in summer, three every other day off season). **Hyères Tourist Office**: 3 av. Ambroise Thomas, ☎04 94 01 84 50 (www.ot-hyeres.fr). Note that **Île du Levant** is a naturist island.

St-Tropez, a famously chic resort accessible by Suma bus (8–12 a day from St-Raphaël, ETT table 358), can be difficult to reach in hellish summer traffic (take the boat from Ste-Maxime instead) and it's grossly overpriced, but it does have a party atmosphere and a superb art gallery, the **Musée de l'Annonciade**, on the port (closed Tue). The best way to get around the town and the pretty surrounding area is to cycle; you can hire bikes or mopeds locally. There are two small beaches in town. Further out is **Pampelonne**, a 5-km stretch of sand that draws most of the glamour crowds and is credited with starting the fashion for topless bathing. **Tourist Office**: quai Jean-Jaurès, ☎0892 68 48 28 premium number) (www.ot-saint-tropez.com).

CANNES

Cannes lives up to the Riviera's reputation as an overpriced, overcrowded fleshpot, but it's possible to enjoy it without spending a fortune. Looking good, spending money and sleeping little is the Cannes style, yet there's free fun to be had on the sandy beaches west of the port. Orientation is easy: the town stretches around the **Baie de Lérins**, the promenade is **La Croisette**. Everything is within walking distance and virtually all the

France

cultural activities (including the film festival) centre on the hideous concrete **Palais des Festivals**.

Cannes' nightlife can be fun. Twinned with Beverly Hills, it's surprisingly welcoming to those without MGM contracts or family jewels, especially if they wander away from La Croisette to the small winding streets and hidden squares inland: try **r. Jean-Macé** and **r. Félix Faure** for some reasonably priced bars. Cannes specialises in reflected glamour. Begin at the **Palais des Festivals**, built in 1982 and christened 'the bunker'. During the film festival the limos glide up here, disgorging world-famous faces (and many not so familiar), while the world of cinema pats itself on the back.

There are few specific sights, but try climbing r. St-Antoine to the hill of Le Suquet, the oldest quarter. The **Musée de la Castre**, housed in the old citadel here, displays antiquities from around the world and gives a history of the town (closed Mon off season).

🚉 250 m from the sea and the Palais des Festivals: head straight (south) down r. des Serbes.

ℹ️ **Tourist Offices**: Palais des Festivals, 1 blvd de la Croisette, ☎04 92 99 84 22 or 04 93 39 24 53 (www.cannes.fr). Also at the station (1 pl. de la Gare) and 1 av. P Sémard.

🏨 Some of the most exclusive hotels in the world overlook the Croisette. Try the streets leading from the station towards the seafront for more reasonably priced rooms: r. des Serbes, r. de la République or r. du Maréchal Joffre. Advance reservations recommended; during the festival rooms in Cannes are a highly prized commodity often booked from year to year. For celebrity spotting try the **Carlton InterContinental**, 58 blvd Croisette, ☎04 93 06 40 06 (www.ichotelsgroup.com), or the **Martinez**, 73 La Croisette, ☎04 92 98 73 00 (www.hotel-martinez.com), both €€€. If your budget won't stretch this far try the **Atlantis**, 4 r. du 24 Août, ☎04 93 39 18 72, (www.cannes-hotel-atlantis.com), €€, or the **Claremont Hotel**, 13 r. du 24 Août, ☎04 93 38 36 73, €€. Otherwise, there's one hostel in Cannes (non HI): **Auberge le Chalit**, 27 av. Maréchal Gallieni ☎04 93 99 22 11, €. **Camping**: **Cannes La Bocca** (reached by train from Cannes), Parc

---

EVENTS IN CANNES

With towns all along the coast competing for custom, Cannes keeps ahead of the game by organising an ever-increasing number of special events: barely a week goes by without some kind of conference or festival – concerts, jazz and blues galas, even chess tournaments. 'The' event, of course, is the prestigious **Cannes Film Festival**, which takes place in mid- to late May. Public tickets for films outside the main competition are sold daily from a special office next to the Tourist Office.

DAY TRIP FROM CANNES

Off Cannes, the **Îles de Lérins** are an antidote to chic. **Île de Ste-Marguerite** is the larger of the two, and boasts the better beaches. At the north end, Fort Ste-Marguerite is an impressively stark fortress commissioned by Richelieu and enlarged by Vauban in 1712, and the legendary home of the mythical Man in the Iron Mask, made famous by the author Alexandre Dumas. There are daily ferry departures from the quai Laubeuf (close to rue du Port) operated by Trans Côte d'Azur (☎04 92 98 71 30) and other companies like Planaria (☎04 92 98 71 38).

Rail Tour: Marseille – Nice – Menton

DAY TRIPS FROM ANTIBES

Juan-les-Pins, the playground of the coast, is where the Côte d'Azur's summer season was invented in 1921; it has sandy beaches (many are private, but there is still some public space), bars, discos and in July, the Riviera's most renowned jazz festival, Jazz à Juan. Accessible by train or bus from Antibes – of which it is a suburb – it is a pleasant place to while away a few days. Just inland, to the west of Juan-les-Pins and reachable by bus, **Vallauris**, meaning 'Valley of Gold', is pottery capital of the Riviera, famous for ceramics since 1500. Picasso came here in 1946 (to make pots) and was commissioned to paint a huge fresco, *War and Peace*, in a chapel which has become the small **Musée National Picasso La Guerre et la Paix**, pl. de la Libération (closed Tues).

Bellevue, 67 av. M Chevalier, ☎04 93 47 28 97 (www.parc bellevue.com); is convenient for the wide sandy beaches to the west of the town but not really for the centre (🚌 2), open Apr–Sept.

ANTIBES

The biggest boats in the northern Med may moor here, but the likeable old town of Antibes is a pretty unpretentious place, with a relaxed atmosphere and a lively bar and restaurant scene. Take a walk along the port, and don't miss the **Musée Picasso**, looking over the sea from its home in the **Château Grimaldi**, pl. Marijol. Picasso worked here in 1946 and this excellent museum displays some of his most entertaining creations from that period (closed Mon).

🚊 For the centre, head down av. Robert Soleau to pl. de Gaulle. From here blvd Albert 1er leads to the sea.

ℹ️ **Tourist Office:** 11 pl. du Gén-de-Gaulle, ☎04 97 23 11 11 (www.antibesjuanlespins.com). There is a branch at 55 blvd Charles Guillaumont, ☎04 97 23 11 10. Free maps and accommodation information. Guided tours, ☎04 97 23 11 25, Thur–Sat at 1000 (90 mins; reservation only).

NICE

Nice has been the undisputed Queen of the Riviera ever since the 19th century British elite began to grace the elegant seafront **Promenade des Anglais**, created by them as somewhere to take their afternoon strolls and named in their honour. Here are hotels such as the **Negresco**, still as luxurious and imposing as ever, and not excessively expensive for a snack or a drink to sample how the other half lives. Standing apart from the *belle époque* hotels and villas, **Vieux Nice** (the Old Town) is the

NICE'S BEACHES

The beaches of Nice are pebbly, but this does not deter sun-worshippers from crowding onto the Baie des Anges, below the Promenade des Anglais. Whilst private beach clubs cover some of the central section, charging heftily for a day's hire of lounger and umbrella, most of the long beach is free. For less hectic sunbathing, seek out the long beach between Cagnes-sur-Mer and Antibes to the west.

However, the prettiest beaches are to the east, at Villefranche (young, lively crowd), Beaulieu (elderly and sedate) and St-Jean Cap Ferrat (well-heeled and laid-back).

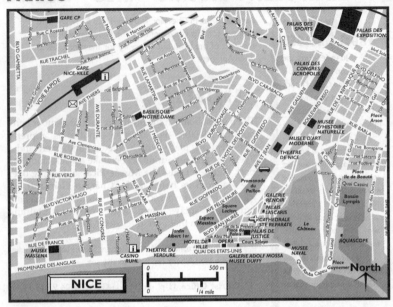

NICE

true heart of the city, and seems more Italian than French (which it was until 1860). It has wonderful outdoor markets, countless cafés and restaurants, and many of Nice's liveliest bars and discos.

Nice boasts some of the best museums in France. Most open 1000–1800 and close Tues and most are easily accessible by local bus. Best of the bunch is the **Musée Matisse**, 164 av. des Arènes de Cimiez (www.musee-matisse-nice.org), wonderfully set in a 17th-century villa amongst the Roman ruins of Cimiez. It houses Matisse's personal collection of paintings (🚌 15/17/20/22/25 from pl. Masséna; closed Tues). Next door **Musée et Site Archéologiques de Nice Cimiez**, 160 av. des Arènes de Cimiez (www.musee-archeologique-nice.org), exhibits the copious finds dug up while excavating the Roman arenas in Cimiez (🚌 15/17/20/22/25 to Arènes; closed Tues). Matisse and fellow artist Raoul Dufy are buried in the nearby Couvent des Frères Mineurs. Also in Cimiez, the **Musée Marc Chagall**, av. du Dr Ménard, is a graceful temple to Chagall's genius – beautifully lit to display his huge biblical canvases (🚌 22; closed Tues), €9.50.

In the centre of town, the **Musée d'Art Moderne et d'Art Contemporain**, Promenade des Arts, is unmistakable: a

> **FRENCH RIVIERA PASS**
>
> The French Riviera Pass (www.frenchrivierapass.com) gives free access to several museums, churches and galleries in Nice, Antibes, Juan-les-Pins, Biot, Cagnes-sur-mer, Eze and Monaco, €24 for one day, €54 for three days. Passes can be purchased from museums or the Tourist Office.

white marble cliff rising above the street, and filled with striking pop art (🚇 3/4/6/7/9/10/16/17; closed Mon, free entrance). Further out of town, the **Musée Départemental des Arts Asiatiques**, 405 Promenade des Anglais, is an exquisite modern structure in a parkland setting; tea ceremonies are regularly held here (closed Tues).

🚆 **Nice-Ville**, av. Thiers. Information Office. Frequent services to all resorts along the Côte d'Azur. Left luggage 0800–2100; baths and showers 0800–1900 in the basement. For the town centre, turn left from station to av. Jean Médecin, the main thoroughfare, right down to pl. Masséna (300 m), right again to the sea, a 15-min walk.

🚢 **SNCM**, quai du Commerce (on the east side of the port), ☎32 60 then say SNCM (premium rate). Regular crossings to Corsica.

✈ **Nice-Côte d'Azur**: Promenade des Anglais, 7 km west of the city. Information: ☎0820 42 33 33 (premium rate) (www.nice.aeroport.fr). Airport buses (🚌 98) run along Promenade des Anglais to the Gare Routière (bus station) every 20 mins (0600–2350) and route 99 to the Gare SNCF (rail station) every 30 mins (0735–2100); also 🚌 23 to the rail station every 20 mins (0600–2050).

ⓘ **Tourist Offices**: 5 Promenade des Anglais, ☎0892 70 74 07 (premium rate); www.nicetourism.com. Also av. Thiers (at the rail station), and Airport, Terminal 1. **Post Office**: 23 av. Thiers. Open 0800–1900, 0800–1200 Sat.

🏨 For the budget conscious, good-value accommodation is available near the station – r. de Suisse, av. Durante, r. Pertinax. The **HI youth hostels** are **Les Camélias**, 3 r. Spitalieri, ☎04 93 62 15 54 (www.fuaj.org/nice-les-camelias), 500 m from the rail station, and **Mont-Boron**, Route Forestière du Mont Alban, ☎04 93 89 23 64 (www.fuaj.org/nice-mont-boron); 4 km from the station (tram to Cathédrale-Vieille-Ville, then 🚌 14 to Auberge), open June–Sept. Non-HI hostels: **Relais International de la Jeunesse de Clairvallon**, 26 av. de Scudéri, ☎04 93 81 27 63, is up in Cimiez, north of the centre (🚌 15/22, stop at Scudéri), located in a park with a pool. **Backpackers Hostel Chez Patrick**, 32 r. Pertinax, ☎04 93 80 30 72 (www.chezpatrick .com), €€, is 5 mins from the rail station, while **Villa Saint-Exupéry**, 22 av. Gravier, ☎0800 30 74 09 (free call from

GETTING AROUND NICE

The Old Town quarter is manageable on foot, but to get between the various museums and sights requires transport. Bus services are good, most radiating from pl. Masséna. **Bus and Tram Information**: Agence Masséna, 3 pl. Masséna, ☎0810 06 10 06 (local rate), www.lignedazur.com. Renting a car or motorbike is a popular option, but the traffic is hectic and parking difficult. Rent motorbikes from **Nicea**, 12 r. de Belgique, near the station, ☎04 93 82 42 71. **Taxis** (☎04 93 13 78 78 or 04 93 88 25 82) are expensive.

WHERE TO SHOP

Vieux Nice with its outdoor markets and small shops is a good place to start: head for the pedestrian area around r. Massena. **Cours Saleya** is the main market place – there is a colourful flower market here every day except Mon when an antique and flea market replaces it. All the big department stores line av. Jean Médecin, while luxury goods and designer boutiques are on r. Paradis and r. Alphonse-Karr.

France

France) (www.vsaint.com), €, is some distance north of the centre but has excellent facilities (tram to Comte de Falicon, then they can pick you up if called in advance). The nearest **campsite** is **Camping Terry**, 768 rte de Grenoble, St-Isidore, 📱04 93 08 11 58 (🚌 59 from Nice gare routière to La Manda).

🍴 Something of a culinary paradise, Nice is influenced by its neighbour – Italy, and by the Mediterranean. The city has many specialities. *Pissaladière* is a Niçois onion tart, garnished with anchovies and olives; *socca*, a traditional lunchtime snack of flat bread made from crushed chickpeas, served hot; and of course *salade niçoise*. Vieux Nice (the Old Town) is best for eating out – particularly the warren of streets running north from Cours Saleya and the cathedral. North of the Old Town, pl. Garibaldi boasts the best shellfish.

NIGHT-TIME Nice is the cultural and social capital of the South of France, offering a choice of opera, concerts and plays. **FNAC (Fédération Nationale d'Achats des Cadres)** in the Nice Étoile shopping mall, 44–46 av. Jean Médecin, supplies tickets, 📱0825 02 00 20 premium rate; 📱0892 68 36 22 for bookings). In summer, Nice grinds on long after midnight, thanks to its many Irish-style pubs and live music venues, though younger visitors often gravitate to the beach. For many it is enough simply to stroll along the Promenade des Anglais or sit on the Cours Saleya and watch the world go by.

DAY TRIPS FROM NICE Auguste Renoir spent the last years of his life in **Cagnes-sur-Mer**, buying an isolated house overlooking the sea. These days engulfed in urban sprawl, the house is nevertheless preserved as the **Musée Renoir**, chemin les Colettes, (closed Tues and 1200–1400), with rooms as he kept them until his death in 1919 (from the rail station, take the bus to Béal-Les-Colettes). In the beautiful old village above the modern town, the medieval citadel is now a museum: Château-Musée Grimaldi, Montée de la Bourgade, Haut-de-Cagnes, (closed Tues). You can take a free bus up to the citadel from the main bus station in Cagnes-sur-Mer. There is an hourly bus (🚌 400) from Nice to **St-Paul-de-Vence**, a picturesque village which houses one of the most interesting modern art museums in France, the **Fondation Maeght** (www.fondation-maeght.com; open daily), built by the Maeght family, friends of Matisse. The lovely garden is a sculpture park designed by Miró. **Vence**, 3 km further up the valley, is another delightful little town. Here Matisse was nursed by local nuns and repaid them by designing a simple yet breathtakingly beautiful chapel – that he considered his masterpiece – **La Chapelle du Rosaire**, av. Henri Matisse (open Mon, Wed, Sat 1400–1730, Tues and Thurs 1000–1130, closed Fri and Sun). A mosaic by Chagall enlivens the Romanesque church. The old perfume town of **Grasse** is an hour or so by train from Nice. Here you can visit perfume factories and see the villa of the painter Fragonard (www.fragonard.com; open daily), complete with cartoon frescos and a collection of paintings, or shop and idle in the pl. aux Aires farmers' market and flower stalls.

WHERE NEXT FROM NICE?

A superb route through the Alps to Lyon can be taken via the CP private narrow-gauge line to Digne-les-Bains (ETT table 359); see Where Next From Lyon? on p110.
Nice is also served by international trains to Milan (ETT table 90).

VILLEFRANCHE-SUR-MER

The incredibly steep little resort of precariously tall ochre houses has one of the deepest ports on the coast, so it's a major stop for cruise ships and also has the liveliest beach in the region. From Villefranche beach you can walk up to St-Jean Cap-Ferrat, a peninsula with gorgeous beaches plus some of the world's most expensive – and closely guarded – properties. The port is tranquil and lined with restaurants, many of them not excessively expensive. If you make it to **St-Jean Cap-Ferrat**, don't miss the **Villa Ephrussi** (www.villa-ephrussi.com; open daily). Once owned by Béatrice de Rothschild, the house is a visual delight, but the exotica-filled gardens are stunning, with views down to Villefranche and Beaulieu.

LA TURBIE

La Turbie, just above Monaco, is accessible from Monaco by 🚌 114, or 🚌 6 from Gare routière de Nice, (five–six times a day, but not Sun or Sat afternoon) – or a steep bicycle ride. The culminating point of the Roman road *Via Aurelia*, and marking the boundary between Italy and Gaul, La Turbie is renowned for the restored remnants of a huge statuesque tower of 6 BC known as the Trophée des Alpes (in Latin: *Tropaea Augusti*). The only other Roman monument of its kind is in Romania. During the 13th century it was converted into a fortress, but was later blown up. Closed Mon.

🚇 Access platform 2 to promenade des Marinières, turn right and follow signs to Vieille Ville (uphill).

ℹ️ **Tourist Office**: Jardins François Binon, ☎04 93 01 73 68 (www.villefranche-sur-mer.com).

BEAULIEU-SUR-MER

'Beautiful place' (the name was bestowed by Napoleon) is a tranquil spot full of affluent retired people, and palms flourish profusely in its mild climate. Don't miss the **Villa Kérylos** (www.villa-kerylos.com; open daily) – built by two archaeologists at the turn of the 20th century, this is a faithful replication of a 5th-century BC Athenian home, complete with furnishings.

🚇 A few mins' walk north of the centre.

ℹ️ **Tourist Office**: pl. G Clémenceau, ☎04 93 01 02 21 (www.ot-beaulieu-sur-mer.fr).

🏨 There's a decent range of 1- and 2-star hotels at the back of the town; the waterfront is much pricier. **La Réserve de Beaulieu**, 5 blvd du M-Leclerc, ☎04 93 01 00 01 (www.reservebeaulieu.com) €€€, is distinctly select.

EZE

The perched village of Eze (as opposed to the sea-level Eze-sur-Mer) is a stiff climb from the station. It's inevitably a tourist trap, but you're rewarded by arguably the best views on the Riviera; cacti flourish in the botanic gardens.

France

i **Tourist Office**: pl. du Gén. de Gaulle, Eze, ☎04 93 41 26 00
(www.eze-riviera.com). Summer branch: Ave de la Liberté,
Eze-sur-Mer, ☎04 93 01 52 00 (May–Oct only).

MONACO (MONTE-CARLO)

Covering just a couple of square km, this tiny
principality has been a sovereign state ruled since 1308
by the Grimaldis, a family of Genoese descent. Later it
grew rich on gambling and banking, and now high-
rises crowd round the harbour, some built on man-
made platforms that extend into the sea. Whatever the
geographical and aesthetic limitations of the place, its
curiosity value is undeniable.

Old Monaco is the extra-touristy part, with its narrow
streets, the much-restored **Grimaldi Palace**, and the
19th-century **Cathédrale de Monaco**, containing the
tombs of the royals, including Princess Grace. In av.
St-Martin is the stimulating **Musée Océanographique**,
in the basement of which is one of the world's great
aquariums, developed by Jacques Cousteau (open
daily). Monte-Carlo is the swanky part, with its palatial
hotels, luxury shops and the unmissable, world-
famous **Casino**. To the west, a pretty coastal path
meanders into France from the modern marina district
of Fontvieille to Cap d'Ail and, just beyond it, the
lovely, unspoilt beach of **Plage Mala**.

The **Monte-Carlo Rally** (Jan) includes exciting stages
in the hills behind Monaco, while the second week in
May is a good time to avoid the town unless you are
interested in watching the **Grand Prix** – which takes
over the city streets.

RAIL Av. Prince Pierre: head straight down past pl. d'Armes
to the port (with the palace off to the right), then turn left
for the Tourist Office and casino (500 m); or take 🚌 4.

i **Tourist Office**: 2A blvd des Moulins, Monte-Carlo.
☎(00 377) 92 16 61 16 or (00 377) 16 61 66
(www.monaco-tourisme.com).

CASINOS IN MONACO

Monaco is synonymous
with gambling and there
are several casinos,
but you must be
over 21 (they check).
Granddaddy of them all
is the most famous
casino in the world, the
Casino de Paris, pl. du
Casino, which is worth
a look for the interior
gilt alone. You can play
the slot machines at the
entrance, but to get any
further you'll have to pay
just for the pleasure of
walking into the
hallowed gaming rooms
– and smart dress is
required. The adjoining
Café de Paris has no
entrance fee, but it's
definitely less classy.

LONG-DISTANCE WALKS IN THE CÔTE D'AZUR

From Menton you can
venture into the **Parc
National du Mercantour**,
in the French Alps, by
following the waymarked
long-distance path GR52.
Another route, GR51
(forking from GR52 north
of Menton), heads west
parallel to the coast and
over wild, broken country.
Both paths require good
levels of fitness.

🛏 Budget accommodation is scarce – the youth hostel was demolished recently – but there are a few more moderate hotels within reach of the station. Otherwise, walk uphill from Monte-Carlo into the French settlement of Beausoleil, where there's a scattering of budget places. **Hôtel de France**, 64 r. de la Turbie, ☎(00 377) 93 30 24 64 (www.monte-carlo.mc/france), is relatively cheap, €€. The cheapest available is **Hôtel le Versailles**, 4 av. Prince-Pierre, ☎(00 377) 93 50 79 34, from €100–120 for a double. In Beausoleil, **Hôtel Villa Boeri**, 29 blvd du Général Leclerc, ☎04 93 78 38 10 (www.hotelboeri.com) is relatively inexpensive, €€–€€€.

🍴 Eating out in Monaco ranges from simple bistros and pizzerias – Italian food is often the cheapest – to some of the most decadent restaurants in the world. Expect to pay big money in any of the restaurants around the casino. There are also a number of takeaway establishments, particularly around La Place d'Armes from which you can sample typical snacks such as *socca* and *tourte*.

MENTON

Looking into Italy, Menton is a retirement town of ample Italianate charm, endowed with long stony beaches and full of lemon, orange and olive trees. Wander around the hilly Old Town, constructed by the Grimaldis in the 15th century. The baroque **Église St-Michel** (St Michael's), built in 1640, is an attractive structure. To the west, **Palais Carnolès** and its gardens, 3 av. de la Madone, was the summer residence of the princes of Monaco and now houses an interesting art collection (mainly Impressionists and modern; closed Tue and 1200–1400, free entry). **Musée Jean-Cocteau**, Bastion du Vieux-Port, 111 quai Napoléon-III (closed Tues) was established by Cocteau himself and contains many of his works. In summer, the short curve of beach between the port and marina is lined with beach bars, some of them quite trendy.

🚉 Pl. de la Gare. West of the centre. For the sea (about 300 m), head down av. Edouard VII or r. Morgan.

ℹ️ **Tourist Office**: inside Palais de l'Europe, 8 av. Boyer, ☎04 92 41 76 76 (www.villedementon.com). Turn left from the station for about 100 m, then right.

🛏 Plenty of undistinguished 1- and 2-star places in the town centre. Rather better (and more expensive) is the 3-star **Hôtel Chambord**, 6 av. Boyer, ☎04 93 35 94 19 (www.hotel-chambord.com), €€€, with spacious rooms (closed last two weeks of Nov). **Youth hostel (HI)**: Plateau St-Michel, ☎04 93 35 93 14 (www.fuaj.org/menton); 1.5km from the station, 🚌 6 to Camping St-Michel, ☎04 93 35 81 23 (closed mid-Oct–mid-Feb);); there's also a campsite here (same tel. no.).

WHERE NEXT FROM MENTON?

Continue to Ventimiglia in Italy (ETT table 360) and join the **Ventimiglia–Pisa** *route (p419).*

ROUTE DETAIL

Béziers–Millau ETT table 332

Type	Frequency	Typical journey time
Train	2–4 daily	1 hr 50 mins

Millau–Clermont-Ferrand ETT table 332

Type	Frequency	Typical journey time
Train	1–2 daily	5 hrs

Clermont-Ferrand–St-Georges-d'Aurac ETT table 333

Type	Frequency	Typical journey time
Train	1–4 daily	1 hr 20 mins

St-Georges-d'Aurac–Le-Puy-en-Velay ETT table 333

Type	Frequency	Typical journey time
Train	1–4 daily	50 mins

Le-Puy-en-Velay–Nîmes ETT table 333/334

Type	Frequency	Typical journey time
Train	2–4 daily	6–7 hrs

Notes

Infrequent services may mean that getting back to the main line out of Le-Puy-en-Velay involves returning to Brioude before heading south. Alternatively, there are a few buses from Le-Puy-en-Velay to Langeac but connections are poor.

KEY JOURNEYS

Béziers–Clermont-Ferrand ETT table 332

Type	Frequency	Typical journey time
Train	1 daily	7 hrs

Clermont-Ferrand–Nîmes ETT table 334

Type	Frequency	Typical journey time
Train	3 daily	5 hrs 40 mins

Rural France doesn't come any better than this, as the train slices through the heart of the **Massif Central**, the vast upland area of extinct volcanoes in central southern France. The one drawback is the infrequency of services, so you would need several days to explore the area thoroughly – but the views from the window are reason enough to make the trip. On the northern leg towards Clermont-Ferrand you encounter the limestone heights of the Cévennes, a region of remote plateaux cut by huge gorges. Though we haven't described them here, the intervening towns of **Marvejols** and **St-Flour** are both characterful and well off the tourist circuit. Marvejols has a lively Saturday market and medieval buildings; St-Flour has an extraordinary high town perched on volcanic crags (a good 20-min walk up from the station, where most of the hotels cluster) with a cathedral built of lava rocks that resemble breeze blocks. There's accessible hiking west of Clermont-Ferrand where you can base yourself at **Le Mont-Dore** for a few days in the dramatic peaks of the Monts Dore. From Clermont, the route leads back south, through **Issoire** and **Brioude**, both of which have magnificent Romanesque churches. The city of **Le-Puy-en-Velay** is off the main route, but well worth a stopover. South of Langeac you travel through the spectacular **Allier Gorge** amid the wild, volcanic scenery of the Auvergne. It's not a wealthy area, and some of the medieval red-roofed villages look distinctly depopulated.

BÉZIERS

See p117.

MILLAU

Prettily situated at a confluence of valleys, this town is a good base for the Cévennes, one of the most ruggedly remote parts of the Massif Central uplands. The historic centre is quietly attractive and almost traffic-free, with a spectacularly tall **belfry** (open mid-June–mid-Sept), the delightful arcaded **Place Foch**, and a **museum** chronicling Millau's former glove industry (closed Sun and 1200–1400 off-season). Within the Parc de la Victoire is the **Jardin des Causses**, with flora typical of the neighbouring limestone plateaux. A 3-km walk on the far bank of the Tarn leads to **la Graufesenque**, a 1st-century AD Gallo-Roman settlement with a kiln site where vast quantities of pottery have been unearthed, and are now on display in the museum. However, Millau's main claim to fame since Dec 2004 has been the **Viaduc de Millau**, the world's tallest vehicular bridge, crossing the Tarn gorge. This engineering miracle can be visited by open-top bus tour (details and booking from the Tourist Office).

Much of the area is hard to explore without your own transport, so hire a car to visit stunning geological formations such as the impressive limestone gorges of the Tarn and the Jonte, the show cave of Aven Armand and the Chaos de Montpellier-le-Vieux.

France

One word of warning, though: these sites get pretty packed in high summer, and you may do better to arm yourself with a detailed map and explore the top of the virtually empty windswept Causses (plateaux) above. For the very fit, hire a bike (from **Cycl' Espace Orts**, 21 blvd de l'Ayrolle, ☎05 65 61 14 29) or take the long-distance marked walking paths GR62, GR71c or GR 71d, to get up there. There are excursion buses (July and Aug) to the cheese-making village of Roquefort, to surrounding Knight Templar villages and to the Tarn Gorge, plus regular buses to Montpellier, Rodez and St-Affrique.

📶 A 10-min walk from the centre: walk along av. A Merle, turn right at the T-junction.

ℹ️ **Tourist information**: 1 pl. du Beffroi (by the big belfry), ☎05 65 60 02 42 (www.ot-millau.fr).

🏨 Hotels: nothing really in the historic core, but cheap and central is **Hôtel du Commerce**, 8 pl. du Mandourous, ☎05 65 60 00 56, €; or central and with a pool is **Cévénol Hôtel**, 115 r. du Rajol, ☎05 65 60 74 44 (www.cevenol-hotel.fr) €€€. **Hostel (non-HI)**: **Sud Aveyron Accueil**, 26 r. Lucien Costes, ☎05 65 61 27 74, fax 05 65 61 90 58, 800 m from the station (🚌 1 to Cardabelles).

CLERMONT-FERRAND

Clermont, centre of the French rubber industry, and birthplace of Michelin tyres, is built of a dark volcanic stone, and is not exactly picturesque. But the centre has an absorbing maze of little lanes and alleys, dominated by the hilltop Gothic **cathedral**. The building to seek out is the 11th-century church of **Notre-Dame-du-Port**, 5, r. Saint-Laurent, one of France's greatest examples of the local Romanesque style, displaying some wonderful stone carving inside and out.

📶 **Station**: 1 km east of the old centre: turn left to pl. de l'Esplanade and take either av. de la Grande Bretagne or av. Carnot.

WHERE NEXT FROM CLERMONT-FERRAND?

*To venture into the mountains, take the train southwest to **Le Mont-Dore** (ETT table 326). This pretty spa and ski resort is ideally placed for walks into the Monts Dore, a volcanic mountain range laced with 650 km of marked paths, including long-distance Chemins de Grande Randonnée – or GRs. For example from Mont-Dore you can head up to the 1373-m summit of Roc de Cuzeau via the GR4, then hike along the ridge to the Puy de Sancy (1885 m) before taking the GR30 back down to Mont Dore. It's quite tough walking, with appreciable slopes and (if you're lucky) far-ranging views. **Tourist Office**: av. de la Libération, ☎04 73 65 20 21 (www.mont-dore.com). **Hostel (HI)**: Le Grand Volcan, Rte de Sancy, ☎04 73 65 03 53 (closed Nov). Trains continue west to join the **Calais–Toulouse route** (p83) at either **Brive-la-Gaillarde** (a scenic route skirting the Plateau des Millevaches, one of the major watersheds of France) or **Limoges**.*

🛈 **Tourist Office**: pl. de la Victoire, 📞04 73 98 65 00 (www.clermont-fd.com).

🏨 Most hotels are uninspiring, but by lively pl. Jaude is **Hôtel Foch**, 22 r. Maréchal Foch, 📞04 73 93 48 40 (www.hotel-foch-clermont.com), €€. A budget option close to the station is **Foyer Le Phare**, 7 av. de l'Union Soviétique, 📞04 73 92 46 40 (http://pagesperso-orange.fr/lephare/fr_index.htm), €. **Hostel (non-HI): Corum Saint Jean** 17 r. Gaultier-de-Biauzat, 📞04 73 31 57 00 (www.corumsaintjean.fr), 🚌 3 to 1er mai, then tram A to Hôtel de Ville, or 15 mins by foot.

ST-GEORGES-D'AURAC

Change here for the connecting train to Le-Puy-en-Velay. Other ways of getting to Le Puy include the SNCF bus from Langeac (the next stop on the main line).

LE-PUY-EN-VELAY

With its cathedral, monumental statue and ancient chapel each capping a volcanic hill Le Puy is an enticing city with a memorable skyline; inevitably it's hard work to explore. On Rocher Corneille (Crow Rock) is the bizarre 19th-century red statue of **Notre-Dame-de-France** (Our Lady of France), a colossal 110-tonne figure fashioned from 213 melted-down cannons from the battle of Sebastopol. Walk up the internal staircase for stunning views over the town. The 11th-century chapel of **St-Michel d'Aiguilhe** can be reached by climbing 268 steps. The vast black-and-white striped **cathedral**, one of the great pilgrimage churches of France and reached by 134 steps from rue des Tables, has a lovely cloister and a carved grand entrance; its famous dark cedar Black Madonna on the high altar is a 19th-century copy of a figure reputedly brought back from the Crusades and burnt during the French Revolution.

Traditional lace-making is still a local industry and **Le Centre d'Enseignement de la Dentelle au Fuseau**, 38–42 r. Raphaël (closed Sat and Sun and 1200–1330), has an exhibition and demonstration room. Bobbin lace-work from the 16th–20th centuries is on display at the **Musée Crozatier**, Jardin Henri-Vinay (closed Tue and 1200–1400 and Nov–Dec).

🚃 A 15-min from the centre; turn left from station, follow av. Charles Dupuy.

🛈 **Tourist Office**: 2 pl. du Clauzel, 📞04 71 09 38 41 (www.ot-lepuyenvelay.fr). Summer branch at pl. du Breuil (Municipal Theatre du Puy).

🏨 **Hostel (HI): Centre Pierre Cardinal**, 9 r. Jules Vallès, 📞04 71 05 52 40, 500 m (all uphill!) from the station (call ahead if you're planning to go there during a weekend).

NÎMES

See p118.

ROUTE DETAIL

Toulouse–Foix
ETT table 312

Type	Frequency	Typical journey time
Train	8–10 daily	1 hr 10 mins

Foix–Villefranche
ETT tables 312, 354

Type	Frequency	Typical journey time
Train	3–4 daily	2 hrs 30 mins–4 hrs 30 mins

Villefranche–Perpignan
ETT table 354

Type	Frequency	Typical journey time
Train	5–6 daily	50 mins

Perpignan–Collioure
ETT table 355

Type	Frequency	Typical journey time
Train	11–13 daily	25 mins

Collioure–Figueres
ETT tables 355, 657

Type	Frequency	Typical journey time
Train	6 daily	1 hr 40 mins

Figueres–Girona
ETT table 657

Type	Frequency	Typical journey time
Train	Every hr	30 mins

Girona–Barcelona
ETT table 657

Type	Frequency	Typical journey time
Train	Every hr	1 hr 20 mins

KEY JOURNEYS

Toulouse–Perpignan (change at Narbonne)
ETT tables 321, 355

Type	Frequency	Typical journey time
Train	10–12 daily	2 hrs 30 mins–3 hrs

Perpignan–Barcelona
ETT table 49

Type	Frequency	Typical journey time
Train	2 daily	3 hrs

Toulouse–Latour-de-Carol
ETT table 312

Type	Frequency	Typical journey time
Train	4–5 daily	2 hrs 45 mins

Latour-de-Carol–Barcelona
ETT table 656

Type	Frequency	Typical journey time
Train	5 daily	3 hrs 15 mins

Notes

Toulouse to Barcelona: for fastest journey change trains at Narbonne. Collioure to Figueres: change trains at the border. Toulouse or Foix to Villefranche: change trains at Latour-de-Carol.

RAIL TOUR: TOULOUSE – PERPIGNAN – BARCELONA

The **Pyrenees** mountain chain is one of the world's most emphatic national boundaries, a great wall of snow-capped peaks separating France from Spain. Virtually any route over it is a thrilling encounter: here the journey rises up to **Latour-de-Carol** at 1250 m before either running straight south to Barcelona (sit on the right-hand side of the train for the best views), or twisting and turning down the mountains in the scenic narrow-gauge Petit Train Jaune (Little Yellow Train), which twists and turns its way through the mountains to **Villefranche-de-Conflent**, with the great summit of Canigou rising to the south. From **Perpignan** you are firmly in Catalunya (Catalonia), a distinctive region that strongly holds on to its regional identity. Beyond **Collioure**, the route heads close to the Mediterranean and into Spain, where the rugged coast of the Costa Brava (reached by bus from **Gerona** or **Figueres**) has been much developed for the package holiday industry, but has some pleasantly tranquil coves. **Barcelona** is covered on p153.

TOULOUSE

See p88.

FOIX

This almost perfect looking medieval town stands just south of the Plantaurel hills at the meeting of two rivers, with the three towers of its castle dominating the scene from a lofty crag. About 6 km northwest, take a boat-trip (1 hr 30 mins) on the Labouiche, Europe's longest navigable underground river, and some 15 km south there are superb caves: admire 12,000-year-old cave paintings at the **Grotte de Niaux** (☎05 61 05 88 37, www.niaux.net; booking compulsory) and majestic stalactites and stalagmites in the **Grotte de Lombrives** (www.grotte-lombrives.fr).

🚆 10 mins northeast of town: follow the Ariège River and cross the bridge to the centre.

ℹ️ **Tourist Office**: 29 r. Delcassé, ☎05 61 65 12 12, www.ot-foix.fr.

🏨 The charming 2-star **Hôtel du Lac**, ☎05 61 65 17 17 (www.hotel-lac-foix.federal-hotel.com), €€€, by the lakeside, can be reached by bus from the centre. There is also camping year round at Camping du Lac. **Hostel (non-HI)**: **Foyer Léo Lagrange**, 16 r. Noël Peyrevidal, ☎05 61 65 09 04 (www.leolagrange-foix.com), is conveniently situated in the town centre.

VILLEFRANCHE-DE-CONFLENT

The tiny fortified village of Villefranche is riddled with narrow streets and seems almost to have been transported from the Middle Ages. It is dominated by the enormous 17th-century **Fort Liberia**: walk up to it (open all year) along the original soldiers' path (30 mins), coming back down via the 734 steps of the underground staircase that leads directly to Pont St-Pierre, the medieval village bridge. For the less athletic, there is a minibus from the Porte de France gateway.

🚆 Villefranche-Vernet-les-Bains, 3 km from the village.

France

i **Tourist Office**: pl. de l'Église, ☎04 68 96 22 96.

PERPIGNAN

Unmistakably Spanish in character though unfortunately overrun in summer, Perpignan was formerly the mainland capital of Majorca and is now a vibrant, large city at the heart of French Catalonia. Catalan is spoken hereabouts, and the *sardane*, Catalonia's national dance, is performed to music a couple of times a week in summer in the 14th-century pl. de la Loge, Perpignan's main square and still the hub of the city's life. A 15th-century fortified gatehouse, **Le Castillet**, quai Sadi-Carnot, houses Casa Pairal (a museum of local folk traditions; closed Tue), while the **Cathédrale St-Jean**, pl. Gambetta, is Gothically grand. The imposing Citadelle, to the south, guards the 13th-century **Palais des Rois de Majorque** (Palace of the Kings of Majorca).

🚉 R. Courteline, 600 m from the centre: walk straight along av. Gén. de Gaulle to pl. Catalogne, and continue ahead to the centre; or take 🚌 1/20.

🚌 **Bus station**: av. du Gén. Leclerc, ☎04 68 61 01 13. There are regular services to the nearby beaches, especially in summer. 🚌 City bus 1 also goes to Canet beach.

i **Tourist Office**: pl. Armand Lanoux, at the Congress Centre (Palais des Congrès), ☎04 68 66 30 30, fax 04 68 66 30 26 (www.perpignantourisme.com); a 30-min walk from the station.

🏨 Lots of 1- and 2-star establishments along and off av. Gén. de Gaulle (leading from the station to the town centre). Actually on pl. de la Loge, **Hôtel de la Loge**, 1 r. Fabriques d'en Nabot, ☎04 68 34 41 02 (www.hoteldelaloge.fr), €€, is central. Or else, try the **Hôtel Victoria**, 57 av. du Maréchal Joffre, ☎04 68 61 17 17 (www.hotel-victoria-perpignan.com), €€. **Hostel (HI)**: Parc de la Pépinière, av. de la Grande-Bretagne, ☎04 68 34 63 32 (perpignan@fuaj.org), 600 m from the station (Mar–mid-Nov).

COLLIOURE

Easily visited as a day trip from Perpignan, this is the most picturesque of the local ex-fishing villages, on a knob of land between two bays, and overlooked by a 13th-century château. Matisse, Braque, Dufy and Picasso discovered Collioure, and artists still set up their easels here. The domed church steeple looks distinctly Arabic.

🚉 300 m west of the centre, ☎04 68 82 05 89.

i **Tourist Office**: pl. du 18 Juin, ☎04 68 82 15 47 (www.collioure.com).

🏨 **Hôtel Madeloc**, r. Romain Rolland, ☎04 68 82 07 56 (www.madeloc.com), €€€, has a pool in a garden setting, but is pricey (as are other options). Open Apr–Oct.

Rail Tour: Toulouse – Perpignan – Barcelona

FIGUERES (FIGUERAS), SPAIN

The much-visited **Teatre-Museu Dalí** (www.salvador-dali.org; open daily except Mon, Oct–May) is the only real attraction, honouring the town's most famous son. Whether you consider Dalí a genius or a madman (or both), the museum is likely to confirm your views of the Surrealist artist. Appropriately enough, it's a bizarre building, parts of which Dalí designed himself (including his own grave), a terracotta edifice sporting giant sculpted eggs.

[RAIL] Plaça de la Estació. Central. Luggage lockers and cash machine.

[i] **Tourist Office**: Plaça del Sol s/n, [☎]972 50 31 55 (www.figueresciutat.com). There are also visitor information points beside the bus station across the Plaza from the train station, and in Plaça Gala i Salvador Dalí, near the entrance to the Teatre-Museu Dalí.

GIRONA (GERONA), SPAIN

The medieval Old Town stands on the east side of the River Onyar, connected by the Pont de Pedra to a prosperous new city in the west. From the bridge you can see the **Cases de l'Onyar** – a line of picturesque houses overhanging the river. In the heart of the labyrinthine Old Town is the superlative Gothic **cathedral**. Inside is the largest single-naved vault ever constructed. Buy a ticket for entry to the Romanesque cloister and the museum within the chapterhouse, containing the 15th-century **Tapis de la Creació** (Tapestry of the Creation). Also seek out the **Banys Arabs** (Arab Baths), Romanesque with Moorish touches and dating from the 13th century. **Museu d'Art**, housed in a splendid Renaissance bishop's palace, displays paintings and carvings from the Romanesque period to the 20th century. In the narrow streets of **El Call** (old Jewish quarter) is the **Bonastruc Sa Porta Centre**, which contains a Museum of Jewish Culture. The 11th- to 12th-century Benedictine **Monastery Sant Pere de Galligants** now houses the archaeological museum.

[RAIL] In the new town; a 10-min walk from the river and Pont de Pedra.

[✈] **Aeroport de Girona Costa Brava** [☎]972 18 66 00 (www.aena.es). Buses connect with Ryanair and Thomsonfly flights: Girona (journey time 20 mins) and Barcelona (70 mins).

[🚌] Bus station: adjoins the railway station.

[i] **Tourist Offices**: Rambla de la Llibertat 1, [☎]972 22 65 75 (www.ajuntament.gi/turisme), by the river, on the east bank.

[🏨] Try around the cathedral, or head for Plaça de la Constitució. **Youth hostel (HI): Cerverí de Girona**, Carrer dels Ciutadans 9, [☎]972 21 80 03 (www.xanascat.cat).

BARCELONA

See p153.

Morocco, Corsica and Sardinia

The possibilities for lingering in the far south of Europe are endless.
Here's a quick guide to three further and very contrasting areas
you may want to head for by ferry or by air.

Morocco

You can actually see Morocco from parts of southern Spain, but it's an incredibly
different world from Europe – a melting pot of French colonialism, Berber culture,
Roman remains, atmospheric street markets (souks), huge snow-capped mountains and
northern African desert. **Costs** are about half of those in Spain and **public transport** is
good, with a network of very reasonable trains and excellent buses, though you would
be wise to stick to air-conditioned services in the hot season. Some buses even
penetrate the desert. For train times see the *Thomas Cook Overseas Timetable*. Citizens
of the EU, USA, Canada, Australia, New Zealand and many other countries don't need
a **visa. Algeciras**, the main Spanish port for Morocco, is served by express trains
from Madrid and local trains from Granada, and by buses from Cádiz, Tarifa and Málaga.

Most visitors start from Ceuta (Sebta), Melilla or Tánger (Tangiers). **Tánger** is much
more lively, with bustling markets, and an interesting, though shabby, old quarter (medina)
just above the port. If you only want to take in one Moroccan city, make it **Fes**,
the former capital, with a huge and remarkably timeless medina, beautiful palaces
and two hilltop castles (borj). From Fes you can visit the country's finest
Roman remains out of town at **Volubis**.

Marrakech is Morocco's major southern city: it has city walls and pink-hued
buildings. For sightseeing, try the Saadian Tombs and the Koutoubia Minaret, or soak
up the atmosphere at the Djemaa el Fna, a vast space crammed with tribespeople.

The downside of being a tourist in Morocco is the amount of **hassle** you
can get from touts, carpet sellers and (not always official) guides. People do get
ripped off, lone women may find themselves as an unwanted centre of attention,
and such activities as haggling can test one's patience. However, many travellers find
the locals extremely friendly and welcoming.

For more information see www.tourism-in-morocco.com or www.visitmorroco.com.

Corsica

Scheduled and budget airlines go to Corsica and you can choose **flights**, with CCM,
Air France, easyJet (there is a Paris–Bastia air link) or Ryanair (Figari–Milano),
or a long **ferry** journey from France, or from Sardinia – Bonifacio is a 1 hr trip
from Santa Teresa di Gallura in Sardinia, and other ferries connect Marseille,

Nice and Toulon (from France), Genova, Savona and Livorno (from Italy) with various ports on Corsica. **Prices** on this large Mediterranean French island are higher than in the rest of France, and rail passes aren't valid on trains. All that might sound a compelling reason for giving Corsica a miss, but it does have a largely unspoilt coastline with fishing villages and a wonderfully rugged and mountainous interior, crossed by the ultra-tough footpath, the GR20. For getting around, there's a limited **rail network** (ETT table 369), leading from the northern port of Bastia to Ajaccio on the west coast, and Calvi in the northwest; **buses** work pretty well and cover a much larger area. The best **beaches** are in the southeast, around Rondinara, Santa Giulia, Palombaggia and Pinarellu.

Bastia has an interesting Old Port area and citadel, with fishing boats in the harbour and washing-lines strung over dark, shuttered alleys; there's plenty of accommodation between the rail station and the port along av. du Maréchal Sebastiani. Inland and on the railway, **Corte** makes a good base for walking. Within the compact old centre of **Ajaccio** is the birthplace museum of Napoleon Bonaparte, while the Fesch Museum has the island's premier art collection (closed until at least June 2010). **Bonifacio** is a gorgeous place to arrive at by sea, as it clings close to a spur above the harbour. The maze of alleys contains lots of restaurants and hotels. The massive 16th-century Genoese Gate with its drawbridge and moat opens on to the medieval Rue Longue, where the house of Napoleon Bonaparte's ancestor stands.

For information on the island in general see www.visit-corsica.com, and for Corsica Regional Park visit www.parc-naturel-corse.com.

SARDINIA

This Mediterranean island belongs to Italy and lies between Corsica to the north and the African coast to the south; Palau has **ferries** to Corsica and mainland Italy (Napoli), and Cagliari serves Trapani in Sicily. There are **budget flights** run by Ryanair to Alghero and easyJet to Olbia and Cagliari. It's not as sensationally mountainous as Corsica, but it's very pleasantly relaxed and there is plenty for a week or two.

The largest and most modern-looking city on the island, **Cagliari**, was much rebuilt following wartime bomb damage, but there's a compact Old City inside the imposing 13th-century walls, with a warren of brick-paved lanes and two Pisan towers, Nuraghi artefacts in the National Archaeology Museum (closed Mon) and a Roman amphitheatre. As the capital of Sardinia, Cagliari offers the greatest opportunity to sample the fine cuisine and wines specific to the island.

Sardinia's second city, **Sassari**, is a busy commercial, administrative and university town. You can experience real Sardinian life here in the knot of medieval streets before taking the train on to **Alghero**, a bustling and unsophisticated west-coast seaside resort.

SPAIN AND PORTUGAL

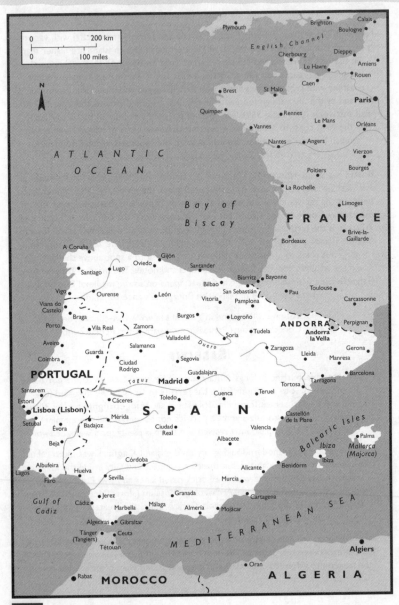

0   200 km

0   100 miles

N

A T L A N T I C
O C E A N

*Bay of
Biscay*

Plymouth
English Channel
Brighton
Calais
Boulogne
Cherbourg
Dieppe
Le Havre
Amiens
Rouen
Caen
Brest
St Malo
Paris
Quimper
Rennes
Le Mans
Orléans
Vannes
Nantes
Angers
Vierzon
Bourges
Poitiers
La Rochelle
Limoges

F R A N C E

Bordeaux
Brive-la-
Gaillarde

A Coruña
Santiago
Lugo
Oviedo
Gijón
Santander
Bilbao
Biarritz
Bayonne
San Sebastián
Pau
Toulouse
Vigo
Ourense
León
Vitoria
Pamplona
Carcassonne
Viana do
Castelo
Braga
Vila Real
Zamora
Burgos
Logroño
Soria
Tudela
ANDORRA
**Andorra
la Vella**
Perpignan
Porto
Aveiro
Guarda
Salamanca
Valladolid
Duero
Zaragoza
Lleida
Gerona
Manresa
Coimbra
Segovia
Ciudad
Rodrigo
Guadalajara
Tortosa
Tarragona
Barcelona
PORTUGAL
Tagus
Madrid
Santarem
Cáceres
Toledo
Cuenca
Teruel
Estoril
Lisboa (Lisbon)
Mérida
S P A I N
Castellón
de la Plana
Balearic Isles
Setubal
Évora
Badajoz
Valencia
Palma
Beja
Ciudad
Real
Albacete
Ibiza
*Mallorca
(Majorca)*
Albufeira
Córdoba
Alicante
Benidorm
Ibiza
Lagos
Huelva
Sevilla
Murcia
Faro
Granada
*Gulf of
Cadiz*
Cádiz
Jerez
Marbella
Málaga
Almería
Mojácar
Cartagena
Algeciras
Gibraltar
M E D I T E R R A N E A N   S E A
Tánger
(Tangiers)
Ceuta
Tétouan
Algiers
Rabat
MOROCCO
Oran
A L G E R I A

144 **Spain and Portugal**

Inexpensive to travel in and blessed with a warm climate, **Spain** is astonishingly varied, ranging from the fashion-conscious sophistication and pulsing atmospheres of Madrid and Barcelona to rural scenes that look as if they might belong to another continent, or even another century. It's not consistently beautiful – views from the train might take in ugly high-rise developments or monotonous cereal plains, while on much of the coast are concrete resorts that sprang up in the 1950s and 1960s to provide cheap holidays. But the classic Spanish elements are there too: parched landscapes dotted with cypresses and cacti, backed by rugged sierras; lines of poplars receding to hazy horizons, and red-roofed fortified towns clustered round castles. Some scenes are peculiarly regional: the luxuriant greenness of Galicia; the snowy pinnacles of the Picos de Europa; the canyon-like badlands of Aragon on the southern fringes of the Pyrenees.

Although bordered by Spain, **Portugal** contrasts strongly with its Iberian neighbour, with a different language and customs; indeed, for centuries the two countries were at war. Portugal once prospered as a great maritime power and ruled a far-flung empire across Africa, the Far East and South America. For some 500 years the Arabs held sway over the country, and part of their legacy is Moorish-style buildings with low domes and flat roofs. In other areas, the architecture is uniquely Portuguese; in Lisbon, and elsewhere, you'll come across the Manueline style, a flamboyant transition between Gothic and Renaissance with maritime influences and motifs (knotted ropes, sails, anchors and so on) inspired by the Age of Discoveries in the 15th and 16th centuries. By contrast with the sunbaked plains of Iberia, northern landscapes of rolling hills dotted with orange, lemon and olive groves look positively lush. Inland rises a chain of lowish mountains, dotted with ancient fortified towns. Away from the touristy Algarve, there are many places awaiting discovery, and the landscape is amazingly untouched – you'll still see peasants leading donkeys and find communities rich in rural customs. Low prices make it tempting to linger and distances are relatively small.

In Spain you must reserve and pay a reservation fee for all trains that have a train category shown in the timing columns of the *Thomas Cook European Rail Timetable* (AVE, Talgo, Arco, etc), even if you have a rail pass. You also have to reserve for AP and IC trains in Portugal.

Spain and Portugal

SPAIN

ACCOMMODATION

There's generally no problem finding somewhere to stay, outside major festivals and other peak periods; however, some large cities (notably Madrid and Barcelona) can be problematic, with virtually everywhere booked up by 0900; accordingly, book ahead, for example through the **Hostelling International Booking Network** (**IBN**), www.hihostals.com.

BUDGET ACCOMMODATION

By strolling around, you'll often find budget places congregated near the station and around the main square. Thanks to a useful hierarchy imposed by regional tourist authorities, accommodation is graded according to facilities. The cheapest option are *albergues juveniles* (youth hostels). Then there are the basic **boarding houses**, known variously as *Fondas* (look for plaques marked F), *Pensiones* (P), *Posadas, Ventas* and *Casas de Huéspedes*; then come *Hostales* (HS) and *Hostales Residencias* (HR); generally higher in the pecking order are *hoteles* (H), ranging from 1 to 5 stars. Note that there can be an overlap between different types of accommodation, e.g. the best *Hostales Residencias* are often more expensive than the low-grade (1- to 2-star) hotels. If there is also an 'R' on the plaque, do not expect a full dining service.

HISTORIC ACCOMMODATION

There's also scope for staying in a number of castles, old monasteries and other historic buildings, converted to government-run hotels called *Paradores*; these tend to be more expensive. Central booking service for *paradores* throughout the whole country: ☎90 254 79 79 (www.parador.es).

PRIVATE HOMES

Private homes that offer rooms are known as *Casas Particulares*. They seldom have much in the way of facilities, but are usually centrally located and almost invariably very cheap. *Casas rurales* are farmhouses and *Refugios* are mountain huts.

Tourist Offices will give you information about accommodation, and, in some instances may provide hotel booking services. In major cities, there are often hotel booking agencies at the airports and railway stations. Prices away from major resorts start at about €30 for a double room (€25 for a single). Double rooms usually have twin beds, so ask for *una cama matrimonial* if you want a double bed. By law, places that officially provide accommodation must place a notice (updated annually) in every bedroom stating the maximum amount payable for that room. The price includes all taxes and service charges (but seldom breakfast), and you should pay no more than the stated amount (which is for the room, not per person). When paying for your room, it is a good idea to keep a copy of the quoted price or a copy of the accommodation guide handy as some places may put the prices up for tourists. All hotels and hostels are listed in the *Guía de Hoteles*, an annual publication available from Tourist Offices.

ESSENTIALS (SPAIN)

Population 46.5m **Capital** Madrid **Time Zone** Winter GMT+1, summer GMT+2.

CLIMATE

Very hot, dry, long summers – uncomfortable in inland cities such as Seville and Madrid, idyllically warm on the coast. Spring and autumn usually pleasantly warm. During winter, cool in Madrid, snow on the mountains but very mild in the south.

CURRENCY

Euro (€). 1 Euro = 100 cents = £0.89 = $1.46.

EMBASSIES AND CONSULATES IN MADRID

Aus: Torre Espacio, Paseo de la Castellana 259D (24th floor), ☎91 353 66 00. **Can:** C. Núñez de Balboa 35, ☎91 423 32 50. **Ire:** Paseo de la Castellana, ☎91 436 40 93. **NZ:** C. Pinar, 7 (3rd Floor), ☎91 523 02 26. **SA:** C. Claudio Coello 91, ☎91 436 37 80. **UK:** Torre Espacio, Paseo de la Castellana 259D, ☎91 714 63 00. **USA:** C. Serrano 75, ☎91 587 22 00.

LANGUAGE

Castilian Spanish most widely spoken. Three other official languages: Catalan, spoken in the east; Galego, spoken in Galicia (northwest), and Euskera, common in the Basque country, Navarra, even across the Pyrenees into France. English is fairly widely spoken in tourist areas. In Spanish listings 'CH' comes at the end of the 'C' section, 'LL' at the end of the 'L' section, Ñ after N.

OPENING HOURS

Banks: Mon–Thur 0930–1630; Fri 0830–1400; Sat 0830–1300 (winter); Mon–Fri 0830–1400 (summer). **Shops:** Mon–Sat 0930/1000–1400 and 1700–2000/2030; major stores do not close for lunch, food shops often open Sun. **Museums:** vary; mostly open 0900/1000, close any time from 1400 to 2030. Few open Mon and some also close (or open half day) Sun. Expect to find most places closed 1300–1500/1600, especially in the south.

POST OFFICES

Most *correos* open 0800–1400 and 1700–1930. Larger ones offer poste restante (*lista de correos*). Stamps (*sellos*) also sold at tobacconists (*estancos*). Post boxes: overseas mail in slot marked *extranjero*. Postal system is very slow.

PUBLIC HOLIDAYS

1, 6 Jan; several days at Easter; 1 May; 25 July; 15 Aug; 12 Oct; 1 Nov; 6, 8 Dec and several days at Christmas. Each region has at least four more public holidays, usually local saints' days.

PUBLIC TRANSPORT

Numerous regional bus companies (*empresas*) provide fairly comprehensive, cheap (if confusing) service. City buses and the Metro system in large cities like Madrid, Barcelona, Seville and Valencia are both very efficient.

RAIL PASSES

IR, EP valid (see pp27–34). Fares based upon date and time of travel. Eurail Spain pass: for non-European residents, 3–10 days unlimited travel within 2-month period; 3 days $275 (1st class), $219 (2nd class) – add approx $40 1st class/$30–35 2nd class for each extra day; supplement on AVE/Talgo 200 and Trenhotel trains.

Spain and Portugal

RAIL TRAVEL

Website: www.renfe.es. ☎90 224 02 02; international: ☎90 224 34 02; FEVE: ☎90 210 08 18; AVE: ☎91 506 63 29; Grandes Líneas: ☎90 210 52 05; international: ☎93 490 11 22. The national railway company is RENFE. Website: www.renfe.es. ☎90 224 02 02 (information, reservation), ☎90 224 34 02 (international). Of several narrow-gauge railway companies the largest is FEVE (website: www.feve.es), which operates a 1250-km network, chiefly in the northern coastal provinces. RENFE's passenger operations are divided into Alta Velocidad/Larga Distancia (High Speed/ Long Distance) and Cercanías y Media Distancia (Suburban and Medium Distance). An extensive high-speed network is currently under construction and Spain has some of Europe's fastest and most reliable rail services (you get your money back if your train arrives more than five minutes late on the Madrid – Seville line, for instance) though journeys can be very slow on the as yet unimproved lines (great for sightseeing, though!). You must reserve a seat before travelling on all but suburban trains plus some other local services – on all those trains, in fact, for which a train category is indicated in the *Thomas Cook European Rail Timetable*. The train categories are many and include: AVE, Alvia, Altaria, Avant (all of these are high-speed trains, some of which can change gauge and run on both the new and old networks), Arco, Euromed and Talgo. Second class is called Turista and first class Preferente. AVE also has a 'super-first class' called Club. Night trains are classified Estrella and Trenhotel (train-hotel), the latter, pricier option offering sleeping compartments with en-suite shower and WC.

TELEPHONES

At least one Telefónica office (the former state telephone company) in every large town: use a booth to make a call and pay the clerk afterwards. Public telephone booths (*teléfono público* or *locutorio*) usually have English instructions. Accept credit cards, money or *Teletarjeta* (phonecard – sold in tobacconists, post offices, some shops). Pay phones in bars are usually more expensive. Dial in: ☎+34. Outgoing: ☎00. Police: ☎091 everywhere. Fire: ☎080 in most towns, can vary. General emergency number: ☎112. Area code must be used even when phoning from inside that area.

TIPPING

Not necessary to tip in bars and taxis; tipping is more common in restaurants. If you want to tip for good service, add around 5–10%.

TOURIST INFORMATION

Websites: www.spain.info.com, www.okspain.org. *Oficinas de Turismo* (Tourist Offices) can provide maps and information on accommodation and sightseeing, and generally have English-speaking staff. Regional offices stock information on the whole region, municipal offices cover only that city; larger towns have both types of office.

TYPICAL COSTS

Accommodation varies considerably, but as a rough guide: in a hostel: €9–15; in a pension €17–25. Beer in a bar €1.30–3; coffee: €0.90–2. Basic meal: €8–16 (*menú del día*). Internet access/hour: €2–4.50.

VISAS

Visas not needed by citizens of Australia, Canada, EU, New Zealand, USA for visits of up to 90 days. Non-EU citizens must hold onward or return tickets plus a minimum of £25 (sterling) per day of their intended stay, or a minimum of €300.

YOUTH HOSTELS There are dozens of HI youth hostels around the country, and some universities offer accommodation in student dormitories (*Colegios Mayores* or *Residencias*) when students are not in residence. Prices are around €12.50–20. Head office: Red Española de Albergues Juveniles, C. Castello 24, 28001 Madrid, ☎ (34) 91 522 70 07 (www.reaj.com).

CAMPING There are over 500 **campsites** (some open all year, others just in summer); the Spanish Tourist Office issues a list of the approved ones (*Guía de Campings*), which are classified as luxury, first, second and third class. You can camp 'rough' in most suitable places, but not on tourist beaches. Book locally or through the **Federación Española de Empresarios de Campings**, C. Valderribas 48, 28007 Madrid, ☎ (34) 91 448 12 34 (www.fedcamping.com).

FOOD AND DRINK The locals take a light breakfast: coffee or hot chocolate with rolls or a *pan con tomate* (toasted bread rubbed with a ripe tomato, and sometimes garlic, and then drizzled with olive oil) or perhaps *churros* (deep-fried fritters dipped in hot chocolate). The main meal is **lunch** (1330–1500 – nearer 1500 on Sunday). Dinner is a little lighter, but can still consist of three courses, and is eaten later, around 2200 in the towns, but much earlier in resorts. Restaurants are open only for lunch and dinner, so go to *cafeterías* (usually open 0800–midnight) for breakfast and light meals/snacks. *Platos combinados* and *menú del día* are both good value. If you want an inexpensive light meal, ask for *raciones*, a larger portion of *tapas* (little more than nibbles, intended as aperitifs). The best-known Spanish dish is *paella*, which originated in Alicante (near Valencia); it is at its best when made to order – which takes about half an hour. Another famous dish is *gazpacho* (chilled tomato soup), which originated in Andalucía and is found mainly in the south.

Choose your drinking place according to what you want to consume. For **beer**, you need a bar or *cervecería*, for wine a *taberna* or *bodega*. For **cider** (in the north), you need a *sidrería*. The custom is to pay for all your drinks at the end of the evening, although this is changing in some resort areas, and in busy popular places you may well be asked to pay after each drink. Many drinking places also sell food, either tapas or basic snacks, or they might have a separate dining room (*comedor*) at the rear where you can get a full meal. A more formal restaurant is usually denoted by the title *restaurante* or *mesón*. Water is generally safe to drink, but if in doubt (for example on outside taps) check for a 'potable' (drinking) notice. Mineral water is available everywhere. Coffee tends to be strong, and usually good. There are some excellent wines (notably, though by no means exclusively, from the Rioja and Ribera de Duero regions) and Jerez is, of course, the home of sherry. Sangría is a summer favourite based on red wine and orange juice. San Miguel is the most famous Spanish lager brand but other, better beers are available, from Spain and all over the continent. ¡Salud!

Spain and Portugal

PORTUGAL

ACCOMMODATION

A good bet in most places is to find a room (*quartos* or *dormidas*) in a private house, or in a pension (*pensão* – more of a business than a house, and graded from 1 to 3 stars). Other inexpensive places are boarding houses (*hospedarias/casas de hóspedes*) and 1-star hotels.

INFORMATION

Tourist Offices have details of many places to stay, and can make bookings.

YOUTH HOSTELS

Hostels are mostly open 24 hrs and cost €9–16, including bed linen and breakfast; for details, contact **Movijovem** (www.pousadasjuventude.pt).

CAMPING

For **campsites**, contact the **Federação de Campismo e Montanhismo de Portugal (Portuguese Camping and Caravan Association)** (www.fcmportugal.com).

POUSADAS

Advance reservations are essential. For information or to make a reservation, contact **Pousadas de Portugal** (www.pousadas.pt).

Pousadas are state-run establishments in four categories. Some are converted national historic monuments (Pousadas Históricas, Historic Pousadas); those in historic buildings but which incorporate stylish new renovations are the Pousadas Históricas Design (Historic Design Pousadas). The Pousadas Charme (Charm Pousadas) are unusual and romantic, while the Pousadas Natureza (Nature Pousadas) are in remote locations. More information from www.pousadas.pt.

FOOD AND DRINK

The Portuguese pattern of eating is to have a fairly frugal breakfast and two big main meals: **lunch** (1200–1500) and **dinner** (1930–2230). Places that have evening entertainment may stay open until around midnight and, if so, tend to offer a late supper. The **cafés** and **pastry shops** usually stay open all day.

Eating is not expensive but, if your budget is strained, go for the meal of the day, *prato do día* or *menú*. Eating is taken seriously, the cuisine flavoured with herbs rather than spices and rather heavy on olive oil. There is lots of delicious seafood, such as grilled sardines and several varieties of *caldeirada* (fish stew). Other local dishes are *bacalhau* (dried salted cod in various guises) and *leitão* (roasted suckling pig). The most popular pudding is a sweet egg custard.

Portugal is, of course, the home of **port**, but there are also several excellent (and often inexpensive) wines, such as the *vinho verde* 'green' wines and the rich reds of the Dão and Bairrada regions. Do not be surprised if you are charged for pre-dinner bread, olives or other nibbles that are brought to your table unordered. If you don't want them, say so.

ESSENTIALS (PORTUGAL)

Population 10.6m **Capital** Lisbon (Lisboa) **Time Zone** Winter GMT, summer GMT+1.

CLIMATE

Hotter and drier as you go south; southern inland parts very hot in summer; spring and autumn milder, but wetter. Mountains are very cold in winter.

CURRENCY

Euro (€). I Euro = 100 cents = £0.89 = $1.46.

EMBASSIES AND CONSULATES IN LISBON

Aus: 2nd Floor, Avenida da Liberdade 200, ☎213 101 500. **Can:** 3rd Floor, Avenida da Liberdade 198–200, ☎213 164 600. **Ire:** R. da Imprensa à Estrela 1–4, ☎213 929 440. **NZ** (Consulate): Rua do Pèriquito, Lote A-13, Quinta da Bicuda, Cascais, ☎213 705 779. **SA:** Avenida Luis Bivar 10 A, ☎213 192 200. **UK:** Rua S. Bernado 33, ☎213 924 000. **USA:** Avenida das Forças Armadas, ☎217 273 300.

LANGUAGE

Portuguese; English, French, German in some tourist areas. Older people often speak French as second language, young people Spanish and/or English.

OPENING HOURS

Banks: Mon–Fri 0830–1445/1500. **Shops:** Mon–Fri 0900/1000–1300 and 1500–1900, Sat 0900–1300. City shopping centres often daily 1000–2300 or later. **Museums:** Tues–Sun 1000–1700/1800; some close for lunch and some are free on Sun. Palaces and castles usually close on Wed.

POST OFFICES

Correio indicates both post boxes and post offices. Most post offices open Mon–Fri 0900–1800, Sat 0900–1300; smaller ones close for lunch and Sat. Most large post offices have poste restante. Stamps (*selos*) on sale at places with a sign depicting a red horse or a white circle on green background.

PUBLIC HOLIDAYS

1 Jan; National Carnival – end Feb/beginning March; Shrove Tues; Good Fri; 25 Apr; 1 May; 10 June; Corpus Christi; 15 Aug; 5 Oct; 1 Nov; 1, 8, 25 Dec. Many local saints' holidays.

PUBLIC TRANSPORT

Usually buy long-distance bus tickets before boarding. Bus stops: *paragem;* extend your arm to stop a bus. Taxis: black with green roofs or beige; illuminated signs; cheap, metered in cities, elsewhere fares negotiable; drivers may ask you to pay for their return journey; surcharges for luggage over 30 kg and night travel; 10% tip. City transport: can buy single tickets as you board, but books of tickets or passes are cheaper; on boarding, insert 1–3 tickets (according to length of journey) in the machine behind driver.

Spain and Portugal

RAIL PASSES

IR, EP valid (see pp27–34). Heavy fines if you board train without ticket bought in advance. Intra-Rail are zonal passes (4 zones) for ages 12–30, 3 days (Fri–Sun) €55; 10 days (starting Mon–Thurs) €185. Reduced to €49/159 with a youth card. Includes nights at youth hostels.

RAIL TRAVEL

Website: www.cp.pt. National rail company: Comboios de Portugal (CP); cheap and generally punctual; 1st/2nd class on long-distance. Fastest trains are IC and AP (Alfa Pendular), modern, fast; supplement payable; buffet car; seat reservation compulsory. CP information line ☎808 208 208. Lockers in most stations.

TIPPING

Not necessary in hotels; customary to round up taxi fares and bills in cafés/bars, though not essential. Tip 10% in restaurants.

TELEPHONES

Phonecards (from post offices and some tobacconists), plus coin-operated and (erratic) credit card phones. Surcharge for phones in hotels, etc. International calls best made at post offices; pay after the call. Dial in: ☎+351. Outgoing: ☎00. Directory Enquiries: ☎118. International directory enquiries: ☎117. Emergency services: ☎112. Area codes are built into the numbers; simply dial.

TOURIST INFORMATION

Websites: www.portugalinsite.com, www.portugal.org. Multilingual telephone information service for tourists, based in Lisbon, ☎0800 296 296. The police (dark blue uniforms in towns, brown in rural areas) wear red arm bands if they are bilingual.

TYPICAL COSTS

Hostel (HI) accommodation €9–16 for a dormitory bed, €9–21.50 for a bed in a twin-bed room; cheaper hotels around €35 for a double room. You can eat well in a snack bar for €8–11 and on a tourist menu in a restaurant for around €12; espresso coffee (bica) in a café €0.50–0.60, for a coffee with milk (galão) €0.70–1.20; 0.5 litre beer in a bar €1–1.50 (draught beer is cheapest). Internet cafés charge around €5 per hour. Entrance to a museum €2–5, theatre €10–30, cinema around €5.50, concert €25–75 and a bullfight €15–75.

VISAS

Not required by citizens of Australia, Canada, the EU, New Zealand or USA. Citizens of South Africa must obtain visas before travelling.

It may officially only be Spain's second city (after Madrid), but Barcelona is the capital of Catalonia, with a real sense of regional pride, energy and style, and during the last decade or so has become one of Europe's most visited cities; give it at least a couple of days of your time. The city is home to many remarkable organic-looking Modernist (Spanish Art Nouveau) buildings by Antoni Gaudí and his contemporaries, and some wonderful specialist galleries displaying works by Spanish masters such as Picasso and Miró.

Barcelona is pretty spread out with lots of wide busy roads and apart from the old **Gothic Quarter** (the Barri Gòtic) and around the **Ramblas**, it's best to use the Metro or the Bus Turístic for getting about.

As a result of hosting the Olympic Games in 1992, the Catalan capital was transformed by an imaginative large-scale urban renewal programme which has given it a cosmopolitan, prosperous, even glamorous air. Ever since, tourism has arrived here in a very big way, and in summer the whole place can seem oppressively crowded, especially around major attractions such as the **Sagrada Família**.

Another unappealing aspect of the city is its petty crime rate. In particular, beware of bag-snatchers at night in the Barri Gòtic and the Ramblas.

ARRIVAL AND DEPARTURE

🚉 There are two main stations: the central **Estació de França**, Avda Marquès de l'Argentera, ☎90 224 02 02 (Metro: Barceloneta), for most regional trains and certain long-distance national and international services; and **Estació de Sants**, Plaça dels Països Catalans, about 3.5 km from the old town (Metro: Sants-Estació), for suburban, regional and international trains as well as those to the airport.

🚌 **Estació de Autobuses Barcelona Nord**: Carrer d'Alí Bei 80, ☎90 226 06 06 (www.barcelonanord.com; Metro: Arc de Triomf). **Estació de Sants**: Plaça dels Països Catalans, ☎93 490 40 00 (www.eurolines.es; Metro: Estació de Sants).

⛴ From the port, ferries leave for the Balearics and the Italian ports of Civitavecchia and Livorno. For details, contact **Trasmediterránea**, ☎90 245 46 45 (www.trasmediterranea.com).

✈ **Aeroport del Prat** is 12 km southwest of the city. It has four terminals. Airport information: ☎91 393 60 00 (www.aena.es). RENFE trains run every 30 mins, between about 0600 and 2230, to and from Estació de Sants (journey time: 22 mins) and Estació Plaça de Catalunya (27 mins). For Ryanair and Thompson flights, see **Girona** (p141). The **Aerobús** bus service runs every 6–15 minutes (0530–0015 from Plaça Catalunya; 0600–0100 from airport). Additional stops are shown on the city map available from Tourist Offices. For information: ☎93 415 60 20. Official city map online at www.bcn.cat/guia.

Spain and Portugal

TOURS

From the quay below the Columbus monument, at Plaça del Portal de la Pau, **Las Golondrinas** (pleasure boats) ferry visitors around the harbour or across to the Olympic Port. Round trips last 30 mins or 2 hrs.

INFORMATION

For **city information** ☎ 93 285 38 34 (www.bcn.cat; www.barcelonaturisme.com; www.barcelonaconnect.com). City tourist information centres at: Plaça de Catalunya 17 (underground, opposite the El Corte Inglés department store); City Hall, Carrer Ciutat 2; Estació de Sants (Sants Station). **Regional tourist information** for Catalunya and the rest of Spain: at the airport; at Palau Robert, Passeig de Gràcia 107, ☎ 93 238 80 91/2/3. The city information line, ☎ 010, usually has some English-speaking operators. Also from late June to late Sept at Plaça de la Sagrada Família. The Tourist Office also runs street information services during summer. Look for staff in red and white uniforms, with the standard 'i' symbol on their shirt sleeves. There is a tourist information centre for cultural events and activities only, at Las Ramblas 99, ☎ 93 316 10 00.

The main youth information office: **Centre d'Informació i Assessorament per a Joves**, is at Carrer Oleguer 6–8, 08001 Barcelona, ☎ 93 442 29 39 (www.bcn.es/ciaj). It gives information and assistance on cultural, sports and leisure facilities in the city. **Oficina de Turisme Juvenil**, Carrer Calàbria 147, ☎ 93 483 83 41 (www.tujuca.com), gives advice on the best travel prices and issues IYHF and ISIC cards, amongst other services. The **Barcelona Card** gives free public transport travel and discounted and free admission to attractions (2–5 days, €26–42).

Over 500 spaces now have municipal Wi-Fi access of up to 200 kbps including civic centres, libraries, sports centres, cultural centres, the airport, municipal markets and museums. **Internet access: Verdi Click**, Carrer Verdi 9, Gràcia, ☎ 93 415 88 39 (Metro 3, Fontana) or **Abre Barcelona**, Carrer Aribau 308, ☎ 93 202 02 74, www.abrebarcelona.com (FGC Muntaner or Sant Gervasi).

PUBLIC TRANSPORT

METRO The **Metro Service** is fast and clean. It has seven colour-coded lines. Trains are designated by the name of the last stop. The **Ferrocarrils de la Generalitat de Catalunya**, a local train service run by the Catalan State, serves fewer places in the centre, but can take you out into the suburbs and beyond. The same tickets are valid on Metro and Generalitat lines and there is a flat rate for all journeys, regardless of distance or location, as long as you stay within the city limits. You have to pay again if you transfer between the two lines. The Metro runs Mon–Thur, Sun & holidays 0500–2400, Fri 0500–0200, Sat 24 hrs. The Metro also runs non-stop overnight between 31 Dec/1 Jan, 23/24 June, 14/15 Aug and 23/24 Sept.

PASSES

The T10 pass is valid for 10 journeys by Metro, Ferrocarrils de la Generalitat de Catalunya, bus or RENFE regional trains. Price depends which of the six zones you travel in. The T-Dia ticket gives unlimited travel on public transport for a day. Tickets are also available for 2, 3, 4, 5 or 6 days.

TOURIST BUS The **Bus Turístic** (tourist bus) runs every day 0900–2000 Apr–Oct (approx every 6–10 mins) and until 1900 Nov–Mar (approx every 30 mins). The **Bus Turístic de Nit** (night bus) runs 2130 Fri–Sun, May–Sept. Pick up a map and guide, which outlines the monuments and sights, buy a ticket on-board, or in advance from the Tourist Office. The routes start from Plaça de Catalunya, though to avoid the queues you might do better to walk on to the next stop and then start from there. You can hop on and off as many times as you please.

TAXIS Yellow and black cabs can be hailed in the streets. Make sure you have change as drivers do not have to change anything larger than a €20 note. **Radio Taxi**, ☎93 303 30 33, **Fono-Taxi**, ☎93 300 11 00. For a firm specialising in disabled access and adapted taxis call **Taxi Amic**, ☎93 420 80 88 (advance booking required).

FURTHER INFORMATION

Barcelona Hotel Association
(www.barcelonahotels.es)
Youth Hostels
(www.tujuca.com)
Associació de Campings de Barcelona
(www.campingsbcn.com)

ACCOMMODATION

Barcelona has as wide a range of hotels as any major European city, but prices are pretty high compared to the rest of Spain; rates vary throughout the year, with high summer generally the peak time – when it's worth reserving well in advance or arriving early in the day as demand is high. The main area for inexpensive accommodation is around the Ramblas, particularly on the east side around Carrer Ferran (take the Metro to Liceu) and the Raval. *Pensiones* (basic rooms) are graded 1- or 2-stars (generally €40–60 for a double with shared facilities).

In this area is the **Hostal Albergue Fernando**, Carrer Ferran 31, ☎93 301 79 93 (www.hfernando.com), a popular backpackers' haunt with dorms (with and without private bathrooms) and private rooms (mostly en suite). Just off this street is the quiet **Hostal Levante**, Baixada de Sant Miquel 2, ☎93 317 95 65 (www.hostallevante.com) with singles, doubles and triples (with or without bathroom). For style on a budget, try the **Sol y K Guesthouse**, C. Cervantes 2 2–1, ☎93 318 81 48 (www.solyk.com), in the Gothic Quarter; the more luxurious **Gat Xino**, C. Hospital 149–55, ☎93 324 88 33 (www.gataccommodation.com), in the Raval, and nearby sister hostel, **Gat Raval**, Carrer Joquin Costa 44, 1º, ☎93 481 66 70; or the **Hostal Goya**, C. Pau Claris 1, ☎93 302 25 65 (www.hostalgoya.com), in the Eixample, which is kitted out in slick coffees and creams, as smart as a good hotel. Just 300 metres off Plaza de Catalunya is **Hostal Girona**, C. Girona 24, 1º 1ª, ☎93 265 02 59 (www.hostalgirona.com), a charming stylish place where you are greeted with local antiques, chandeliers and Moorish rugs. All the bedrooms feature similar rustic furniture and fittings. The funky **Equity Point** chain (www.equity-point.com) is a boon for backpackers with three excellent locations: Centric Point (Passeig de Gràcia 33, ☎93 215 65 38), Gothic Point (Carrer Vigatans 5, ☎93 268 78 08) and Sea Point (Plaça del Mar 1–4, ☎93 224 70 75), all with doubles and dorms, mostly en suite.

Over a dozen **student halls of residence** become hostels for young people in summer. For details, contact a youth information centre (Oficina de Turisme Juvenil; see p154). There are also three **HI youth hostels** (reservation recommended; www.tujuca.com).

The most central is **Barcelona Ramblas**, Carrer del Hospital 63, ☎93 412 40 69 (www.center-ramblas.com; Metro: Liceu); others are **Pere Tarrés**, C. Numància 149–151, ☎93 410 23 09 (www.peretarres.org/alberg; Metro: Mariá Cristina, 1.3 km) and **Mare de Déu de Montserrat**, Passeig Mare de Déu del Coll 41–51, ☎93 210 51 51 (www.tujuca.com; Metro: Vallcarca). There are also several private hostels, such as **Kabul**, Plaça Reial 17, ☎93 318 51 90 (www.kabul.es), for the very sociable who don't mind noise and bustle, in the Gothic Quarter (Metro: Liceu), and **Itaca**, Carrer Ripoll 21, ☎93 301 97 51 (www.itacahostel.com), with dorms only. **Paraiso Travellers Hostel**, Ronda de Sant Pau 55–57, ☎93 329 93 78, (www.paraisohostel.com). Two and four-bed dorms, private twins and doubles. Another useful place is **Backpackers BCN**, Carrer Diputació 323, Principal 1A, ☎93 488 02 80 and also at Carrer Casanova 52, ☎93 566 67 25 (www.backpackersbcn.com), with doubles and 4-bed dorms. **Campsites**: there are 12 within easy reach of Barcelona. **Camping Tres Estrellas**, Carretera de Castelldefels C-31, km 13,2, ☎93 633 06 37 (www.camping3estrellas.com). Can be reached by the ☒94/95 from Plaça d'Espanya or Plaça de Catalunya. **La Ballena Alegre**, Autovía de Castelldefels, ☎90 251 05 20 (www.ballena-alegre.es) has bungalows as well as tent pitches. In the opposite direction, up the coast, try **Camping Masnou**, Carretera N2, km 633, Carrer Camil Fabra 33. It is located near the Masnou train station (RENFE Line 1 from Plaça de Catalunya and Sants Estació). For more details, call the **Associació de Campings de Barcelona**, ☎93 412 59 55 (www.campingsbarcelona.com).

FOOD AND DRINK

Catalan cooking derives from peasant fare, with grilled meats and casseroles alongside Spanish staples such as paella, serrano ham, salt cod and dozens of tapas dishes. *Crema catalana* is a delicious local dessert, like egg custard with caramelised sugar on top. Catalunya is also famous for its champagne-style sparkling wine, cava – the speciality of establishments known as *Xampanyeries*.

In general, modern, upmarket and avant garde establishments are to be found in the Eixample, while the Raval specialises in economic Asian restaurants and curry

DAY TRIP FROM BARCELONA

The most dramatic way to reach **Montserrat Monastery** (www.montserratvisita.com) is by train and cable car. Trains depart from under the Plaça d'Espanya, and connect at Montserrat Aeri with a cable car (leaves every 15 mins). Go to the next stop, Monistrol de Montserrat, to take the rack-and-pinion railway (the Cremallera) up the mountain, or take one of the regular buses that leave from the Plaça de la Universitat. Don't miss the the 12th-century statue of the Virgin of Montserrat, housed in the cavernous basilica, or the attached museum with its many acclaimed artworks. Note that the church gets very crowded when the celebrated boys' choir, the *Escolania*, sings mass (every day except Saturday) at 1300. Even at the busiest times it's easy to lose the crowds by taking a walk amid the formidable crags of the Montserrat ('serrated mountain'). Funiculars climb rapidly to lofty hermitages and offer sublime views. From these points you can explore further afield or hike back down to the monastery.

Spain and Portugal

For Free

Basílica de Santa Maria del Mar

Parc de la Ciutadella

Park Güell

La Seu Cathedral

CaixaForum

Temple Romá d'Augusti

Palau Güell

houses. The Gothic Quarter has food of all stripes, from dark old tascas to funky fusion start-up restaurants run on a shoestring. Local wines are widely on offer everywhere at a very reasonable price. For seafood specialities, try Barceloneta, the old fishermen's neighbourhood. Away from the Old Town, the Olympic Village is packed with modern bars and restaurants. The *Guía del Ocio*, published weekly, and *Time Out Barcelona* have good coverage of restaurants and are available from most newsstands. Off Las Ramblas is **La Boqueria** covered market, with an excellent selection of fruit, vegetables and meats.

HIGHLIGHTS

Museums are closed on Mon.

Art goes hand in hand with architecture in Barcelona. In this deeply style-conscious city, there is always a brave juxtaposition of old and new. Further-flung sights can easily be reached using the efficient Metro.

Best seen on foot, the **Barri Gòtic** is an enchanting, if disorienting, Gothic quarter inhabited from Roman times. A web of tiny, dark streets radiates from **La Seu Cathedral**, a magnificent Gothic edifice, started in 1298 but only finished in 1892. The small Romanesque chapel of **Santa Llúcia** opens off the cathedral cloister, which encloses a lush central garden with palm trees, ducks and magnolias; on Sun mornings, the *sardana*, the Catalan 'national' dance, is performed in the square outside the cathedral. Nearby, in **La Ribera**, is the 14th-century **Basílica de Santa Maria del Mar**, regarded as one of the finest examples of Catalan Gothic.

Barcelona is famed for its Modernist architecture; the most startling and innovative is located around the Passeig de Gràcia, the so-called **Quadrat d'Or** (Golden Square) in the **Eixample**. At the fore was Antoni Gaudí (1852–1926), who used the city as his canvas, leaving such extraordinary, swirling masterpieces as the wave-like **Casa Milà** (Passeig de Gràcia) – also known as **La Pedrera**. It's worth buying the ticket to both parts of the building. Tour the apartment, set up as it might have looked in Gaudí's time with the latest kitchen equipment, electric light fittings and Modernist furniture. Then visit the adjacent **Espai Gaudí**, a wonderful brick-vaulted attic housing an exhibition with models and photos of the architect's other works; a staircase gives access to the roof, whose twisted chimneys and weird ducts provide great photo opportunities. The **Casa Batlló** (Passeig de Gràcia) is also known as 'The House of Bones' for its fairytale façade, which is said to symbolise the story of St George and the Dragon. The undulating roof

Camp Nou

This vast 100,000-seater stadium is home to FC Barcelona, one of Spain's most successful soccer teams, whose arch rivals are Real Madrid. Fans unable to go to a match can visit the club museum and souvenir shop (Metro: María Cristina).

is the dragon's scaly back and the 'bones' of its victims support the curvaceous windows. Inside, the ceilings look like ice cream. Gaudí's most famous building, however, is the **Sagrada Família**, the astonishing expiatory temple to which he dedicated the last 43 years of his life, but which remains as yet unfinished with its ever-present cranes. The Sagrada Família is a synthesis of all Gaudí's architectural styles, and incorporates complex religious symbolism and visual representations of the mysteries of faith. Since Gaudí's death in 1926, work has continued on the building, but progress has been slow and hampered by controversy. If you have a head for heights you can climb the winding 400-step staircases of the spires (of which a couple have lifts), rising to over 100 m; for an idea of what the final structure should look like, visit the

AQUARIUM AND ZOO

Barcelona has two notable wildlife collections: the **Aquarium** (www.aquariumbcn.com), on the harbour, where a moving walkway conveys you through a tunnel of tropical and Mediterranean marine life; and the **Parc Zoològic**, Parc de la Ciutadella (www.zoobarcelona.com), Spain's foremost zoo.

cathedral museum in the crypt. The Quadrat d'Or isn't all Gaudí, however: for instance, on the same block as the Casa Batlló are works by two other Modernista design giants: Puig i Cadafalch's **Casa Amatller** and Domenèch i Montaner's **Casa Lleó Morera**.

Follow the Ruta del Modernisme (www.rutadelmodernisme.com) to see more works by other Modernista architects. There is a museum dedicated to the Catalan master, the **Casa-Museu Gaudí**, in the **Park Güell**, an area he designed as part of an eccentric residential garden city. Inside the park, a flight of steps, guarded by a brightly coloured salamander, lead up to a large pavilion supported by over 80 columns – the original marketplace of the development. Above the pavilion, a colourful mosaic bench curves its way around the perimeter of an open terrace, from which there are superb views over the city.

Another classic panorama of Barcelona is from **Montjuïc Castle**, which is reached by cable car from Avda Miramar in **Parc de Montjuïc**. You can reach the cable car station by funicular railway from Avinguda del Parallel (Metro: Parallel), and there's also a cable car to **Montjuïc** from the harbour. Near here is the **Olympic Stadium**, while just across the hillside is the **Poble Espanyol** (Spanish Village), a Disneyesque attraction with convincing replicas of both typical regional styles of architecture and famous Spanish buildings and monuments and plenty of shopping opportunities. The **Picasso Museum**, Carrer de Montcada, is housed in five Gothic palaces on a narrow atmospheric street. The collection is largely made up of the artist's early work, but includes *Las Meninas*, a series of paintings inspired by Velázquez.

In Montjuïc, modern art lovers should beat a path to the **Fundació Joan Miró**, which features paintings, sculptures, ceramics and tapestries by Miró, one of Catalonia's cultural giants. Within a short walk, the **Museo Nacional d'Art de Catalunya** brings together a thousand years of Catalan art under one roof. The highlight is a superb collection of Romanesque art housed in the **Palau Nacional**, a former exhibition hall of the 1929 Universal Exhibition. Another acclaimed modern Catalan artist, Antoni Tàpies, is given place of honour in a Modernist building housing the **Fundació Tàpies**, C. Aragó 255 in the Eixample (closed for renovation until 2010).

Spain and Portugal

Barcelona's most famous street, the **Ramblas** is a tree-lined avenue full of hawkers, tourists, human statues and strolling locals. Just off it is the beautiful **Plaça Reial**, whose fancy lampposts were Gaudí's first commission in the city. At the sea end, the **Monument a Colom** is a monumental column to Columbus, which you can climb up for the view (it gets extremely busy). Here you're overlooking the revamped harbour, known as **Port Vell**, with its **Aquarium**, the **Maremàgnum** shopping and leisure centre, **IMAX** cinema and the **Rambla de Mar**, a wavy walkway over the water.

Beyond this is the excellent city beach, some 7 km of imported golden sands, jam-packed in the summer months with tourists and some of Barcelona's beautiful people – though serious sunseekers and hedonists head down the road to **Sitges**, which is to Barcelona what Brighton is to London.

SHOPPING

Barcelona is one of the great European centres of fashion and design. For international names in fashion and homeware, the main shopping streets are **Portal de l'Àngel**, **Passeig de Gràcia**, **Rambla de Catalunya** and the central section of **Avinguda Diagonal**. Wandering off these promedades and into the tiny back streets brings a rewarding plethora of outlets: the Ribera has boutiques with vanguard street fashion, the Gothic Quarter is full of tiny old shops specialising in anything from espadrilles to sausages while the Raval and Gràcia are a little edgier with plenty of underground record shops and boho jewellery stores. Barcelona's most prestigious shopping centre, the **L'Illa Diagonal**, is housed in an attractive white building designed by prizewinning architect Rafael Moneo.

NIGHT-TIME AND EVENTS

Barcelona offers a superb range of bars and clubs, catering for all tastes; busiest nights are Thur–Sat. Clubbing can be expensive, but admission usually includes a drink. It depends on where you go, though: plenty of *bars musicals* (late-night bars that play music and don't close until 0300) don't charge. The *Guía del Ocio* has comprehensive listings of what's on. The **Eixample**, has most of the swanky clubs, while the **Gothic Quarter** and **El Raval** are more alternative. One of the world's most extraordinary concert halls, the tiled **Palau de la Música Catalana** is an astonishing Modernist building with a huge stained-glass dome, designed by Montaner and finished in 1908; tours are available, or attend a concert.

WHERE NEXT FROM BARCELONA?

There are international services to Paris, Zurich, Montpellier, Geneva and Milan. Cross Spain to Vigo (ETT tables 681, 682) on the west coast, or escape to Majorca (or one of the other Balearic islands) by ferry. Palma (ETT table 2510; quickest crossing 6 hrs 30 mins), is a buzzing little city with great beaches close by (see opposite page).

Nearly every district in Barcelona and every village and town has its own *festa*, or festival. The main ones in Barcelona are:

- **Festes de la Mercè**: week of 24th September. The city's big annual party– parades, free concerts and fire runs.
- **Festa Major de Gràcia**: third week in Aug. Decorated streets and hundreds of free activities.
- **Festes de Sarrià i de Les Corts**: 1st Sun of Oct.
- **Revetlla de Sant Joan**: Night of 23rd June – Summer Solstice, culminating in all-night fireworks on the beach.

MAJORCA (MALLORCA)/BALEARICS

Reached by ferry from Barcelona (ETT table 2510), this perennially popular island is the largest and most varied in the Balearic group. While Majorca is massively touristy, it has some surprisingly beautiful scenery and unspoilt villages, particularly in the rugged northern mountains. The island capital, **Palma**, is at the hub of a bay that has been densely developed, but the compact old city is a gem and includes the splendid Gothic cathedral, the Moorish palace and Arab baths. There's no shortage of excellent sandy **beaches** around Palma and the other resorts though in summer many get impossibly crowded. The big resorts around Palma Bay are the best places for raucous **nightlife**, though Palma itself has much classier nightspots.

Narrow-gauge **railway lines** link Palma to Sa Pobla (57 mins, trains hourly), Manacor (66 mins, trains hourly) and Sóller (55 mins, up to 7 trains a day); trains leave from the two stations in Plaça d'Espanya – the trip to the old fishing village of Port de Sóller is recommended. **Buses** serve all the main towns and many villages; timetables from the tourist information kiosk on Plaça d'Espanya. Bono Bus travel cards give freedom of travel on city buses in Palma. **Boat trips** offer one of the most pleasant ways of seeing Majorca. A popular cruise heads around the northwest coast from Port de Sóller to Sa Calobra; for information contact Barcos Azules, ☎97 163 01 70. There's plenty of sightseeing elsewhere on the island, including some fine **caves** on the east coast; the caves of Drach feature musicians performing on an underground lake. A must-see is the beautiful 14th-century **Monastery of Valldemossa** where Chopin and George Sand spent a winter.

The majority of **accommodation** is in the form of large hotels built for the package industry, although Palma does have a number of inexpensive *hostales*, a growing number of characterful converted properties (most of which are relatively expensive), and two youth hostels – near Palma and outside Alcudia. You can also stay in monasteries inexpensively. The Palma **Tourist Offices** are at Parc de ses Estacions building, Plaça d'Espanya, and Plaça de la Reina 2; ☎90 210 23 65 (www.palmademallorca.es; www.illesbalears.es).

Ferries also serve the other Balearic islands. **Ibiza** is a brash nightlife haunt. **Menorca** is much more low-key, and popular with families and older tourists; seek out the island's intriguing Bronze Age sites. Tiny **Formentera** is comparatively undeveloped, with hostel accommodation in La Savina; Playa Illetas and Playa Levante are among the best beaches.

CITIES: MADRID

Chosen by Philip II in 1561 to avoid inflaming regional jealousies, the Spanish capital lies right in the geographical centre of Spain; indeed, the Puerta del Sol is the point from which all distances in the country were traditionally measured. Beyond the compact old quarter, most of it looks 19th-century or later, the grand boulevards punctuated with triumphal arches and lavish fountains; elsewhere, there's pretty much relentless high-rise, most of it fairly drab. Architecturally, it must be admitted, the city dwindles into insignificance besides the likes of Barcelona or Seville. What **Madrid** does score for, however, is its street- and nightlife, with the smart, fun-loving Madrileños taking their evening *paseo* along **Calle del Carmen** and **Calle de Preciados**; thereafter the city keeps going late into the night.

Sightseeing is dominated by the **Prado**, one of the world's great art galleries, needing a couple of days to do it justice; the **Royal Palace** is similarly daunting in size, while the **Parque del Retiro** makes a handy escape from the hectic whirl of the city. Meanwhile, the almost equally unmissable **Centro de Arte Reina Sofía** boasts a choice selection of 20th-century Spanish art and is a bit more manageable than the Prado.

With so many railways fanning out from Madrid, the city makes a good base for trips to such places as Toledo (p181), El Escorial (p188) and Segovia (p186).

ARRIVAL AND DEPARTURE

▦ **Puerta de Atocha Station**, Glorieta del Emperador Carlos V (Metro: Atocha RENFE), just south of the city centre, is Madrid's most prestigious station and the terminal for high-speed trains to the south (Córdoba, Málaga, Algeciras, Seville, Huelva and Cádiz) and northeast (Pamplona, Logroño, Zaragoza and Barcelona) as well as for trains to Algeciras. The magnificent original 19th-century building now shelters tropical gardens.

Alongside Puerta de Atocha is the smaller through station of **Atocha Cercanías**, which as well as serving surburban trains (*trenes de cercanías*), also sees calls by a number of long-distance trains connecting the north and south of the country via Madrid and regional services to Cáceres and Badajoz.

Most trains to the northwest and north of Spain, and Valencia, (and to France via Irún/Hendaye and the overnight train to Lisbon), however, start and finish their journeys at Madrid's other main station, **Chamartín**, Calle Agustín de Foxá (Metro: Chamartín), in the suburbs, 8 km north of the centre.

The lines between Atocha and Chamartín run in a tunnel beneath the city, with intermediate stations, served by surburban trains, at **Recoletos**, Paseo de Recoletos 4 (near Plaza de Colón, Metro: Colón); and **Nuevos Ministerios** (on the corner of Calle Raimundo Fernández Villaverde and Paseo de la Castellana; Metro: Nuevos Ministerios). The Metro station adjoining Nuevos Ministerios has check-in desks for a number of the airlines operating from Madrid Barajas Airport, to which it is connected by line 8. Two further *cercanías* stations in central Madrid are **Príncipe Pío** (Metro: Norte) in Paseo de la Florida (corner of Cuesta de San Vicente) and **Sol**, Puerta del Sol (Metro: Sol).

RAIL INFORMATION

The main **RENFE office** is at C. Alcalá 44. For general RENFE information: ☎90 224 02 02 (www.renfe.es).

TOURIST INFORMATION

Websites: www.turismomadrid.es www.munimadrid.es.

Main tourist office: C. del Duque de Medinaceli 2, ☎914 29 49 51 (closed Sun). There are also branches in Plaza Mayor, Atocha station and the airport. In summer, there are temporary tourist stands around the city (general tourist information: ☎902 10 00 07).

Museum card: *Paseo de Arte* voucher costs €17.60 and gives discounted entry to the three main art museums. Free Wi-Fi and/or internet cafés can be found at: **El Corte Inglés**, C. de la Princesa 41, **FNAC**, C. Preciados 28 (Metro: Callao or Sol); **Café Faborit**, C. Alcalá 21, www.faborit.com (Metro: Sevilla or Sol).

✈ **Madrid Barajas Airport**, ☎90 240 47 04 (www.aena.es), is 12 km northeast of town. There is a Tourist Office in the international arrivals hall. **Metro** line 8 connects the airport to **Nuevos Ministerios** (20 mins), for train connections to Chamartín and Atocha (6–8 mins) or line 10 to **Alonso Martínez**. A **bus** (🚌 200) operates every 10–20 mins between the airport and La Avenida de América Metro interchange. The journey takes about 30 mins.

PUBLIC TRANSPORT

METRO With services every 5 mins (0600–0200) and colour-coded lines marked according to the destination, the Metro (subway) is easy to use. Free maps are available from ticket offices, Tourist Offices and many hotels. Single tickets cost €1 (pay on entry; valid until you leave the system) (www.metromadrid.es).

BUSES The EMT city bus system is comprehensive, efficient and the same price as the Metro, but not as easy to master. Single-ride tickets cost €1 (pay on boarding). You can get a map of the whole system (*Plano de los Transportes*) from Tourist Offices, bookshops and the EMT booths on Plaza de la Cibeles or Plaza del Callao.

There are also route plans on the bus stops (*paradas*). The regular city buses mostly operate 0600–2400 (there are a few night services from Puerta del Sol and Plaza de Cibeles, with stops marked 'N', which run every 30 mins to 0200 and then every hour until 0600, but late at night it's safer to use taxis). All long-distance buses use the state-of-the-art terminal at Méndez Alvaro (Metro: Méndez Alvaro). This has good facilities, including hot showers.

METROBÚS TICKETS

Costing just €7.40 and valid for 10 trips on the Metro or EMT buses, a **Metrobús ticket** represents a considerable saving for those spending more than a a day or two in the city. Alternatively, the **Abono Turístico** gives unlimited travel for 1, 2, 3, 5 or 7 days.

TAXIS An inexpensive way of getting around late at night; ☎91 405 55 00 or 91 547 82 00, or 91 547 85 00. At the airport you can buy pre-paid taxi vouchers, guaranteeing fixed taxi fares.

ACCOMMODATION

If you don't mind sharing a bathroom, you can get a big choice of accommodation offering doubles for under €30. Your best bet may be to take the Metro to Sol and then head southeast towards the Plaza de Santa Ana, where there are a number of pleasant streets that are close to the action but less seedy and noisy than the other large accommodation area just north of Sol.

On the Plaza Santa Ana is the mildly eccentric **Hostal Delvi**, Plaza Santa Ana 15, 3rd floor, ☎91 522 59 98 (www.hostaldelvi.com; Metro: Sol), with doubles at €42. Close by is the bright and colourful **Hostal Alaska**, C. Espoz y Mina 7, 4th floor, ☎91 522 41 51 (www.hostalalaska.com; Metro: Sol), with doubles from €52. **Hostal Cervelo**, C. Atocha 43, ☎91 429 95 94 (www.hostalcervelo.com, Metro: Sol), also has doubles from €52 and the small, family-run **Hostal Armesto**, C. San Agustín 6, 1st floor, ☎91 429 90 31 (www.hostalarmesto.com; Metro: Antón Martín), charges €50 for doubles. A more luxurious 3-star hostel here is **Hostal Lisboa**, C. Ventura de la Vega 17, ☎91 429 46 76 (www.hostallisboa.com; Metro: Sol or Sevilla), with doubles €50.

For cheap places around Sol itself, try the ever popular **Hostal Triana**, C. Salud 13, 1st floor, ☎91 532 68 12 (www.hostaltriana.com; Metro: Gran Vía), with doubles from €53, or for 1-star hotel comfort right next to Sol, try **Hotel Europa**, C. Carmen 4, ☎91 521 29 00 (www.hoteleuropa.es; Metro: Sol), with doubles from €92. **Hostal La Perla Asturiana**, Plaza Santa Cruz 3, ☎91 366 46 00, www.perlaasturiana.com; Metro: Sol), is cheaper (doubles from €42) and has private bathrooms; cheaper still is the **Hostal A Nebrija**, Gran Vía 67, 8th floor, ☎91 547 73 19 (www.spaindreams .com; Metro: Plaza de España or Santo Domingo), with doubles at a rock bottom €36.

Nearby, Calle Arenal is virtually lined with reasonably priced accommodation. Just behind the Congreso de los Diputados **Hostal Mirentxu**, C. Zorilla 7, 3rd floor, ☎91 429 18 14 (www.hostalmirentxu.es; Metro: Sol), within a stone's throw of Puerta del Sol is cheap (doubles from €40) and clean. Or try **Hostal Persal**, Plaza del Ángel 12, ☎91 369 46 43 (www.hostalpersal.com; Metro: Sol), situated in a 1870s building by the tapas-laden Plaza Santa Ana; doubles from €81. Just across the street you'll find the **Hostal Plaza D'Ort**, Plaza del Ángel 13, ☎91 429 90 41 (www.plazadort.com; Metro: Sol), small, family-run and very friendly with doubles from €48.

To the east of Puerta del Sol, good deals can be found on Carrera de San Jerónimo and its side streets. The Gran Vía is a hectic and noisy thoroughfare with a not unjustifiable reputation for prostitution; however, together with side streets such as Calle de Fuencarral, the area offers plenty of accommodation. Calle de la Montera runs from Gran Vía to Sol. Although fairly seedy, it has a number of acceptable lodgings. There's also cheap accommodation around Atocha station, but it's a rather creepy area at night.

Youth hostels (HI): **Santa Cruz de Marcenado**, C. Santa Cruz de Marcenado 28, ☎91 547 45 32 (www.hihostels.com; Metro: Argüelles), gets heavily booked; dorm bed from €8.50 including breakfast. **San Férmin**, Avda de los Fueros 36, ☎91 792 08 97

Spain and Portugal

(www.san-fermin.org; Metro: San Fermín), offers dorm beds from €12 including breakfast and sheets. **Richard Schirrmann**, Casa de Campo, ☎91 463 56 99 (www.madrid.org/inforjoven; Metro: Lago), is a long way out of the centre but very cheap with dorm beds from €7.80. Among a great number of private hostels (online booking for a selection at www.hostels.com) are **Hostal Metropol**, C. Montera 47, 1st floor, ☎93 231 20 45 (www.equity-point.com; Metro: Gran Vía), with 180 beds in 65 rooms, beds from €21–35 (ask about special offers); **Cat's Hostel**, C. Cañizares 6, ☎91 369 28 07 (www.catshostel.com; Metro: Anton Martin or Tirso de Molina), with its own bar/disco, and dorms for 4–14 people (from €12 per bed); and **Los Amigos Backpackers' Hostel**, Campomanes 6, 4th floor, ☎91 559 24 72 (www.losamigoshostel.com; Metro: Ópera, Santo Domingo or Callao), with 4–12 person dorms, beds from €19 including breakfast, in a quiet back street, but very central.

Campsites: both are out of town, but are self-contained. **Camping Madrid** is 11 km from town on the N1 to Burgos, exit 10 (Metro: Plaza de Castilla, then ▣ 151 to Iglesia de los Dominicos). **Camping Osuna**, ☎91 741 05 10, is on the Ajalvir–Vicálvaro road (Metro: Canillejas, then ▣ 105 to Avda Logroño). **Camping Alpha**, ☎91 695 80 69 (www.campingalpha.com) is 12 km to the south from Madrid on the N-IV to Andalucia, exit 13 (Metro: Getafe Central or ▣ 447).

FOOD AND DRINK

Madrid offers a full range of regional dishes from all over Spain; for local fare look for Castilian-style roasts and stews, tripe in spicy sauce (*callos a la madrileña*) and *cocido* (often served on Tues) – a satisfying concoction – part soup, part meat and veg, cooked in a broth, and often served as two or three separate courses. Restaurants don't really get going until well after 2200, late even by Spanish standards. The old town, southwest of Plaza Mayor, is full of 'typical' Spanish bars and restaurants built in cellars and stone-walled caves, where *Madrileños* tend to head for after the evening *paseo* (stroll). However, as with the tapas bars surrounding Plaza Mayor, some of these tend to be touristy and overpriced.

A better area is around Plaza de Santa Ana: Calles Echegaray, Ventura de la Vega and Manuel Fernández González all host a number of quality budget restaurants, and Plaza de Santa Ana itself is great for tapas. Pork lovers can't leave Madrid without visiting the **Museo del Jamón**. A restaurant, not a museum, its walls are covered in huge slabs of meat, and diners can feast on Iberian ham in any conceivable shape or form. There are several branches throughout the city, including Gran Vía 72 and Calle Atocha 54.

HIGHLIGHTS

Madrid's major sights occupy a relatively compact area, stretching from the Palacio Real to the west, to the Prado and the Parque del Retiro to the east. This historic core is pleasant and compact enough for walking, taking just half an hour or so to cross.

Plaza Mayor (Metro: Sol) is a stately square surrounded by neoclassical buildings dating from the 17th century, where such dubious entertainments as bullfighting and the Inquisition's *autos-da-fé* were staged. Today's pleasures are more civilised: you can sit at a pavement café, admire the equestrian statue of King Philip III and watch the world go by. The old **Habsburg** area, southwest of Plaza Mayor, is the most attractive in Madrid.

The **Parque del Retiro** (Metro: Retiro/Atocha) is a park that was laid out in the 17th century as the grounds of Felipe IV's palace; it's a cooling retreat from the summer heat of the city, with wooded corners, formal avenues, brilliant flowers and a large boating lake. Adjoining it is the **Jardín Botánico** (Metro: Atocha), with three separate terraces, some of which feature vegetables as well as shrubs, herbs and flowers, including many exotic species.

Bear in mind that practically all museums close all day on Mon, except the **Centro de Arte Reina Sofía**, closed Tues (www.museoreinasofia.es), and the **Palacio Real** (www.patrimonionacional.es) open daily, unless there's a special event. The **Museo del Prado** (www.museodelprado.es; Metro: Atocha/Banco de España) is one of the world's greatest art galleries, free on Sun; closed Mon. Many of its paintings were collected by Spanish monarchs between the 16th and 18th centuries. Today there are individual sections devoted to Goya, Velázquez, Murillo, Zurbarán and El Greco.

Picasso's masterpiece *Guernica* – showing the misery of a small Basque town bombed by the Germans during the Spanish Civil War – hangs in the art museum **Centro de Arte Reina Sofía** (free Sat after 1430 and Sun; Metro: Atocha), also home to a fabulous collection of 20th-century Spanish works, including paintings by Miró and Dalí. The **Museo Arqueológico Nacional** (http://man.mcu.es; closed Mon, Sun afternoon; Metro: Serrano or Colón) contains a major collection of artefacts from all over Spain, including stone-carved Iberian mother-goddesses from the 4th century BC.

The late-Renaissance **Palacio Real** (Metro: Ópera; free on Wed), or Royal Palace, is a vast 18th-century Italianate pile, with colonnaded arches and some 2800 rooms; the Spanish Royal Family now live in Zarzuela Palace outside the city. The state rooms were decorated in the 18th and 19th centuries and are full of priceless treasures: Tiepolo frescos, magnificent tapestries, glittering chandeliers, silverware, and works by a variety of famous artists – rather swamped by their surroundings. Other highlights are the king's over-the-top dressing room, an 18th-century pharmacy, and a huge hall lined by prancing horses. It can be a bit overwhelming, but the adjacent free **Jardines de Sabatini** make a relaxing escape, with views over the mountains. Just opposite the palace is **Plaza de Oriente**, a small garden adorned with over 40 statues of Spanish royalty. For something distinctly different, visit the small **Convento de la Encarnación** (closed Mon and Fri & Sun afternoon; Metro: Santo Domingo or Ópera), with its astonishing collection of relics.

The 16th-century **Convento de las Descalzas Reales** (Metro: Sol) was a convent for noblewomen and was handsomely endowed by their families. Now it houses a closed order, but parts are open: it has a superb collection of religious art (fittingly displayed in a series of shrines) and a magnificent set of tapestries with Rubens' designs.

Spain and Portugal

The **Museo Thyssen-Bornemisza** (www.museothyssen.org, closed Mon; Metro: Banco de España) is, with the Prado and the Reina Sofía, part of Madrid's Golden Triangle of outstanding museums. After lending the city his priceless 800-piece art collection for a limited period in 1992, Baron Thyssen decided it should be on permanent view and sold it to the nation; it represents a chronology of Western art, from the Italian primitives and medieval Germans to 20th-century Pop Art.

SHOPPING

Chueca is the neighbourhod for streetwear and club fashion boutiques, particularly Calle Fuencarral and Calle Almirante (known locally as 'fashion street'). For cheap high-street chains such as Mango and Zara, hit Gran Vía. Foodstuffs, including wine, hams, sausages, cheese and olive oil, are good value and high quality, and there are some splendid food shops in Old Madrid. Two venerable old foodie emporia to look for are **La Duquesita**, C. Fernando VI 2 (closed Mon; Metro: Alonso Martínez), for those with a sweet tooth try the *turrón* (almond nougat), and **González**, C. León 12 (Metro: Antón Martín), going since 1931 and now a classy deli with Spanish charcuterie, cheeses and wines. **El Rastro** (Metro: La Latina) is a huge flea market (beware of pickpockets) that is something of a Sunday-morning institution. Go early; it's crowded by midday and begins to pack up around 1400. Around **Plaza Mayor** is a huddle of craft shops selling fans, ceramics, lace and leather. The square itself hosts a collectors' market (coins, stamps, books, etc) on Sunday mornings. A secondhand bookmarket, Cuesta de Claudio Moyano (Metro: Atocha), is held when the weather's fine; Sunday is the main day.

NIGHT-TIME

Madrid has a pulsating nightlife, centred on its numerous restaurants, bars and dance venues. Live music can easily be found. At weekends, many bars stay open until 0300 and some close much later than that. Discos tend to have a cover charge, but bars with dance floors don't. The **Malasaña** area (Metro: Bilbao/Tribunal) is good for music and bars, and is mainly popular with a younger crowd. It centres on Plaza Dos de Mayo, Calle de Velarde and Calle de Ruíz. Although flamenco guitar playing, dancing and singing belong to Andalucía, Madrid is said to have the best performers around, though some of it is aimed at tourists, with prices to match. **Huertas** (Metro: Antón Martín) is the area around Plaza de Santa Ana and has a huge variety of bars that stay open pretty much through the night. **Paseo del Prado** (Metro: Atocha/Banco de España) is rather more upmarket, with smart and expensive café-bars. **Chueca** has a lively gay scene, particularly along Calle de Pelayo.

The *Guía del Ocio* (www.guiadelocio.com) is a weekly Spanish-language publication with listings of what's on in Madrid; it is sold at newsstands. Useful free handouts from Tourist Offices and hotels include the English-language *In Madrid* (www.in-madrid.com) and *Madrid Connect* (www.madridconnect.com).

The Portuguese capital lies on seven low hills at the estuary of the River Tagus (Tejo). A massive earthquake in 1755 destroyed most of the city, but spared the Alfama quarter – a flower-bedecked labyrinth of cobbled alleys and balconied whitewashed houses – and, remarkably, the ancient 18-km-long aqueduct. The rest of Lisbon was redesigned on a grid system and rebuilt on a grand scale, with classical squares and wide esplanades paved with mosaics. It's a relatively small capital by European standards, but you need at least two to three days to explore it. Lisbon has an excellent range of day trips by rail, notably to the historic cities of **Évora** and **Óbidos**, and the palaces at **Sintra**.

ARRIVAL AND DEPARTURE

For general rail enquiries, ☎808 208 208 (www.cp.pt). **Santa Apolónia Station**, on the banks of the Tagus near Alfama, is the main station, handling all international trains and those to east and north Portugal; accommodation desk, luggage lockers. All trains to and from Santa Apolónia also call at the **Gare Intermodal do Oriente**, where there is an interchange with the Metro system. From Oriente take the Metro (changing at Alameda) to Rossio or Baixa-Chiado, the main areas for accommodation. **Rossio station** is the terminal for the line to Sintra. **Cais do Sodré station** doubles as the quay for the Tagus ferries and as the station handling the local coastal services. **Terreiro do Paço station** is the terminal for the ferries across the Tagus to **Barreiro**, although it is no longer necessary to cross the river for trains to southern Portugal as fast trains now leave from Oriente. The 30-min ferry crossing costs about €1.75 single and there are sailings every 30 mins (frequent service in the rush hours).

Express **bus services** to the Algarve and Porto are run by **Renex**, ☎218 874 871, departing from Arco do Cego and Oriente. **Terminal Rodoviario do Arco do Cego**, Av. Duque De Avila 12. **Taxis**: Inexpensive, ☎217 932 756 or 218 155 061.

Portela de Sacavém Airport, ☎218 956 836 (www.ana.pt) is 7 km north of the city, with no train link; Tourist Office. 🚌 5/22/44/45 go to the centre, or take the Aerobus (every 20 mins; daily 0745–2045; buy tickets from driver; tickets valid for any bus, tram or funicular that day), which stops at various points in the city, including Cais do Sodré station and Restauradores.

INFORMATION

Tourist Offices: the main Tourist Office is in **Lisboa Welcome Center**, Praça de Comércio Loja 1 ☎210 312 810 (www.askmelisboa.com or www.visitlisboa.com). **Branches:** Rua do Arsenal 25, ☎218 450 660; Palácio Foz, Praça dos Restauradores, ☎213 463 314; Estação Santa Apólonia, ☎218 821 606; **Kiosks:** C. Augusta, ☎213 259 131; Monasterio de los Jerónimos, Belém, ☎213 658 435. Two of the best cyber-cafés (with free internet) are **Mar Adentro Café**, Rua do Alecrim 35, ☎213 469 158 (Metro: Baixo Chiado or Cais do Sodré), open 1000–2300 Mon–Sat,

Spain and Portugal

and **BossNet Café**, Av. Almirante Reis 158 (Metro: Arroios or Alameda), open 1000–2400. Most hotels have internet and computers.

PUBLIC TRANSPORT

Public transport in Lisbon is cheap, efficient and varied, consisting of buses, trams, the Metro and funiculars (*elevadores*) between different levels of the city. Make a point of getting a walking map of the labyrinthine Alfama district.

METRO AND TRAMS

The **Metro** is fast, frequent... and cool! **Trams**: still an integral part of the city and easy to use. Carris offer tram and bus tours: a slow and picturesque way to see the city. Tours leave from Praça do Comércio and cost more for the tram (€17) than for the bus (€14); you can hop on and off the bus as you like, but have to stay on the tram for the whole trip. Buy tickets from the driver.

For intensive sightseeing, the **Lisboacard** (valid for one, two or three days) gives unrestricted Metro access and free travel on most buses, trams, funiculars and lifts, as well as free entry to 25 museums and monuments and discounts of up to 50% at other places of interest. Available from **The Lisboa Welcome Center**, Praça de Comércio Loja 1 ☎210 312 810 (www.askmelisboa.com). If you're only visiting a couple of sights a day, it probably isn't worth it.

TICKETS

Train: available from travel agencies or principal stations.
Buses and trams: tickets for single trips on buses and trams operated by Carris cost €1.40 on board, €0.81 if you use a stored value smartcard (available from Carris kiosks and Metro stations for €0.50). With the *7 Colinas* or *Viva Viagem* smartcards you can also get a one-day network ticket (bus/tram/Metro) for €3.70.

ACCOMMODATION

Accommodation is scarcest and priciest at Easter and in summer; out of season you may be able to find a room for around €30–35, but around €40–50 at busier times. The website www.insidelisbon.com has a good selection of cheaper pensions. The vast majority of cheap places are in the centre of town, on and around Avda Liberdade or the Baixa. In the latter, head for the three squares Praça da Figueira, Praça dos Restauradores and Praça Dom Pedro IV. Reasonable no-frills places are **Pensão Ibérica**, Praça da Figueira 10, ☎218 865 781, €€; **Pensão Residencial Praça da Figueira**, Travessa Nova de São Domingos 9, ☎213 424 323 (www.pensaopracadafigueira.com), €€, with internet and laundry, plus a range of rooms; and **Pensão Beira Minho**, Praça da Figueira 6, ☎213 461 846, €€. If these are full, try the choice on Avda Almirante Reis (to the east). The perenially popular **Duas Nações Residence**, Rua da Vitória 41, ☎213 460 710 (www.duasnacoes.com), €€, is very good value, with breakfast and TV; one month advance booking is generally recommended but you might try your luck and just turn up.

Heading a short way north from Rossio, turn left just after the Elevador Glória: there are a number of possibilities in the backstreets here. The attractive and excellent value **Nova Avenida**, Rua de Santo António de Glória 87, ☎213 423 689, €€, is friendly and quiet; English is spoken. Just around the corner, is **Residencial Milanesa**, Rua da Alegria 25, ☎213 426 456 (€20–25 per person). Or try the charming **Residencial Alegria**, Praça da Alegria 25, ☎213 220 670 (www.alegrianet.com).

Youth hostels (HI): Rua Andrade Corvo 46, ☎213 532 696 (lisboa@movijovem.pt; Metro: Picoas); be careful with your belongings here, as there have been thefts from rooms. There are dorms as well as private rooms with own bathrooms at **Pensão Beira-Mar**, a '*hostal* backpacker's place' at Largo Terrerio do Trigo 16, ☎218 869 933, €, in Alfama, near the waterfront and only a 10-min walk from Santa Apolónia station; laundry, internet, kitchen facilities, sea views, free transport to beach and nightlife.

Campsites: **Parque da Câmara Municipal de Monsanto Lisboa Camping**, Estrada da Circunvalação (on the road to Benfica), ☎217 623 100 (www.lisboacamping.com), is very pleasant and 4-star amenities include a pool (🚌 43 from Rossio to Parque Monsanto Florestal); **Clube de Campismo de Lisboa**, Costa da Caparica, ☎212 900 100 (www.cclisboa.com) is 5 km out of town, with a beach (🚌 from Praça de Espanha Metro station).

FOOD AND DRINK

Lisbon's restaurants are inexpensive and offer a wide choice. The increasingly hip **Bairro Alto** area is frequented by locals and particularly good value, as are the restaurants in **Alfama**. **Baixa** is aimed at tourists and more expensive, but still worthwhile. If you're really into cheap eats, there are food stalls in the market behind Cais do Sodré station. Students can also use the *cantinas* on the university campus.

HIGHLIGHTS

Obtainable from Tourist Offices, the free magazine *Follow Me Lisboa* is useful for opening times and events. Lisbon is a wonderful place for exploring on foot, enjoying the many views and riding the old wooden trams. **Tram 28** is a great introduction to the city (beware pickpockets), and can be picked up from Martim Moniz (on the east side of the square); it squeals its way along a tortuous, hilly route, beneath the Castelo de São Jorge and above the cathedral in the Alfama district. Also ride an *ascensor* (funicular); the much-photographed **Ascensor Glória** is really just a steep tram ride up to the Bairro Alto district, while the **Elevador Santa Justa** is an amazing 19th-century wooden lift within a startlingly odd iron tower – spiral steps lead from the upper exit to a viewing platform. For the best views of the waterfront ride the **ferry** to Barreiro and back.

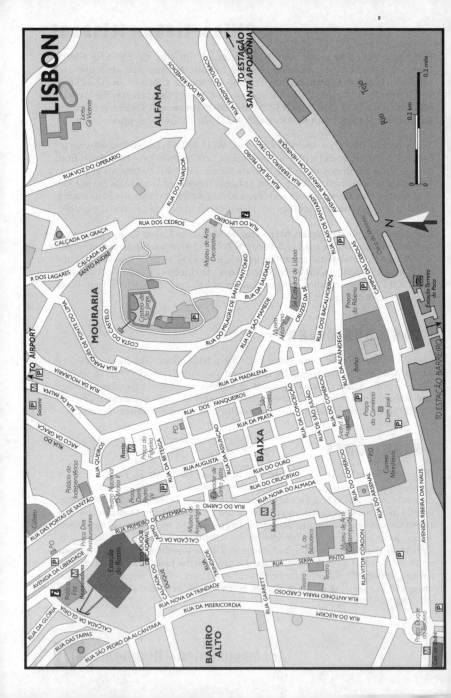

The **Alfama** (Metro: Rossio) is the old Moorish quarter, little changed since the 12th century, with winding cobbled streets overhung with washing lines and flanked by whitewashed houses, and leading to lots of dead ends. One of the few areas to survive the earthquake of 1755, it's a marvellous place to explore on foot. The medieval **Castelo de São Jorge** (🚌 37 from Praça da Figueira) has ten towers linked by massive battlements and stands on one of the seven hills, giving superb views over the city. A royal residence for four centuries, later it served as a prison and houses the **Olissiponia Museum**, covering the history of Lisbon. The **Sé Patriarcal** (Cathedral), Largo da Sé, was once a fortress. It contains some notable 14th-century tombs, a magnificent Romanesque screen and a fine collection of religious art, and exquisite cloisters.

> Most attractions are closed all day Mon and Tues morning, but are free on Sun morning.

> The **Torre de Belém**, with its lace-like loggia, is an exquisite example of Manueline architecture. This tower was built during 1512–21 to protect the harbour entrance, and the fifth floor has a great view across the estuary. The tower was restored in 1845 and is furnished in period style.

Adjoining the **Museu de Arte Sacra** is the **Church of São Roque**, with its marvellous 18th-century chapel dedicated to St John the Baptist, which was constructed in Rome, then shipped in its entirety to Lisbon.

The **Parque Eduardo VII** (Metro: Parque/Rotunda) is a landscaped park with a lake, a good view of lower Lisbon and some attractive tropical plants in its greenhouses.

The **Mosteiro dos Jerónimos** (Jerónimos Monastery; tram E15) began life as a chapel for Henry the Navigator's seamen. Vasco da Gama was royally received in the chapel when he returned from his triumphant voyages. The present building was designed by Boytac, the best of the Manueline architects, and construction began in 1502; its magnificent south door is often cited as the finest example of the style. Unfortunately, as Portugal's greatest church building it does get absolutely packed with tourists. Nearby is Lisbon's excellent **Design Museum** (www.ccb.pt).

Lisbon's foremost museum, with a delightful park, is the **Calouste Gulbenkian Museum** (Metro: Praça de Espanha), housing the private collection of oil magnate Calouste Gulbenkian, with a superlative and all-embracing collection of art and applied art – from all ages and parts of the world, from Ancient Egypt to the French Impressionists. Next door is the **Centro de Arte Moderna Calouste Gulbenkian**, with exhibits by 20th-century Portuguese painters and sculptors. The **Museu Nacional de Arte Antiga** in Rua das Janelas Verdes is home to a 15th-century polyptych, which is a masterpiece of Portuguese art. Other exhibits include tapestries, ceramics, ancient sculptures and oriental rugs. The **Museu Nacional do Azulejo** (National Painted Tile Museum), Rua da Madre de Deus 4, is in a 16th-century convent that was badly damaged in the 1755 earthquake, but restored in the original Manueline style. The cloister survived and the *azulejos* (decorative tiles) include a huge depiction of Lisbon before the earthquake.

Spain and Portugal

There are **beaches** west of the city centre. Take a train to Carcavelos or Estoril from Cais do Sodré Metro station.

SHOPPING

The **Baixa** and **Chiado** districts are good for shopping of all kinds, while Rua do Ouro is a centre for jewellery. The neo-modern **Amoreiras** shopping centre on Avenida Engenheiro Duarte Pacheco is a huge complex with over 300 shops. The Colombo Centre (🚇 Estação Colégio Militar) is said to be the largest mall on the Iberian peninsula. There's a dawn fish and flower market daily opposite **Cais do Sodré** station. **Feira da Ladra** flea market takes place in the Campo de Santa Clara on Tues and Sat.

NIGHT-TIME

There are many bars, discos and nightclubs, the streets around Rua Diário de Noticias (in the **Bairro Alto**) being a particularly lively area. Lisbon also has a lot of bars that feature *fado* singing (a uniquely Portuguese melancholy chant) and guitar playing. The best places are in the **Bairro Alto**; there may be an entrance fee or cover charge. Performances usually begin around 2200 and it's quite common for them to continue until 0230 or later.

SIDE TRIPS FROM LISBON

ÓBIDOS   An enchanting medieval walled town (formerly a coastal settlement, but the sea has receded 10 km) and designated a national monument, Óbidos has winding streets and small whitewashed houses, their balconies brimming with flowers. The many places of interest include the 12th–13th-century **castle** (now a hotel), the 15th–18th-century **Church of the Misericórdia**, the Renaissance **Church of Santa Maria** and the 18th-century **town gate**. There are trains from Mira Sintra-Meleças, with suburban connections from Lisbon; the journey takes about 2 hrs. **Tourist Office**: Rua Porta da Vila 2, ☎262 959 231 (www.cm-obidos.pt). **Accommodation: Hospedaria Louro de Louro & Marques Lda**, Rua Antiga E Real 2, A-da-Gorda, Santa Maria, ☎262 955 100 (www.hospedarialouro.com), €€.

QUELUZ AND SINTRA   The trains to Queluz continue to Sintra (the full journey takes 45 mins; four trains an hour; ETT table 699), so both can be visited in a one-day trip. **Queluz** is the home of an exquisite small, pink rococo palace (closed Tues; www.ippar.pt) that was inspired by Versailles, built in the 18th century for Dom Pedro III. It became the summer residence of the Bragança kings; the interior and the formal gardens have scarcely changed since.

Sintra (Tourist Office: Praça da República 23, ☎219 231 157 (www.cm-sintra.pt), with a branch at the station; the station is a 15-min walk from town – turn left, then left at the junction by the turreted town hall) is a small town built up against the luxuriantly vegetated granite upland of the Serra de Sintra. In town is the **Palácio Real** (closed Wed; www.ippar.pt), the royal summer palace – a mixture of architectural styles and with two remarkable conical chimneys. From here take ▧ 434 up to the architecturally eccentric **Pena Palace** (closed Mon), a hotchpotch of mock medievalism, porcelain pillars, Arabic motifs and baroque flourishes. It's more fun to walk up (ask the Tourist Office to mark up a map with the path for you) – this takes about an hour: turn uphill by the sign for the Tourist Office as you enter the town, follow the road past the Pensão Bristol, take the first right (marked by 'no entry' roadsigns), then turn left, up past a church, and right 50 m later on Rampa do Castelo; this becomes a path, and after a turnstile fork left at a mini castellated tower; to the right here you'll reach the rest of the **Moorish Castle**, with tremendous views from the restored ramparts. There are several places to stay in Sintra: cheapies include **Chalet Relogio**, ☎219 241 550 (www.chaletrelogio.com), €, and **Pensão Nova Sintra**, Santa Eufemia, S. Pedro de Sintra, ☎219 230 220 (www.novasintra.com), €€; the **Two Squared – Rei de Copas Hostel** is located directly above Sintra's train station at Rua Joao de Deus 70, ☎967 143 37 (reidecopashostel@gmail.com), €. From Sintra, you can take the bus (hourly services; a day pass lets you get on and off any bus in the area) to **Cabo de Roca**, the westernmost point on mainland Europe, with stunning clifftop views.

ÉVORA This is a stupendous walled city southeast of Lisbon (train from Lisbon Oriente three times daily; ETT table 698; 2 hrs). It's best known for the 2nd-century AD **Templo Romano** (Roman Temple; its Corinthian columns standing to their original height) in the square in front of the magnificent 12th–13th-century façade of the cathedral, while the cathedral museum's collection of sacred art is noted for its 13th-century ivory statue of the Virgin of Paradise. The **Museu de Évora** houses an all-embracing collection of art from Roman to modern times. Other highlights include the **Paço dos Duques de Cadaval** (Palace of the Dukes of Cadaval) and the **Igreja de São João Evangelista** (Church of St John the Evangelist), with its splendid painted *azulejo* tiles. **Tourist Office**: Praça do Giraldo 73, ☎266 777 071 (www.cm-evora.pt). The lovely, family-run **Pensão Policarpo**, Rua da Freiria de Baixo 16, ☎266 702 424 (www.pensaopolicarpo.com), nestles within a 16th century building, €€.

THE ALGARVE The Algarve (Portugal's southwest coast) is served by trains to **Lagos**, **Albufeira** and **Faro** (ETT table 697), plus a good bus network. The area is renowned for the quality of its beaches, as well as its sports facilities and nightlife, but some of the resorts are hideously overdeveloped; June and Sept are less busy than July and Aug, and the climate's more bearable. Some places, such as **Carvoeiro**, **Luz** and **Ferragudo**, have kept their old fishing village character, while **Albufeira** and **Lagos** are busy nightspots. There are fine coastal walks from **Lagos** to **Salema** and from **Carvoeiro** to **Armação de Pêra**. **Faro**, the capital of the Algarve, has an international airport (5 km west of **Faro**; ▧ 14/16, www.ana.pt). There is a Tourist Office in Faro airport, by the arrivals section, ☎289 818 582 (turismo.aeroporto@rtalgarve.pt), as well as a main tourism bureau in the city centre (**Entidade Região de Turismo do Algarve (ERTA)**, Avenida 5 de Outubro 18, ☎289 800 400). For other Algarve Tourist Offices see www.visitalgarve.pt.

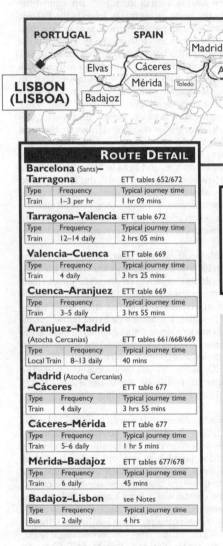

PORTUGAL   SPAIN   Madrid   Zaragoza   **BARCELONA**

Elvas   Cáceres   Aranjuez   Tarragona

LISBON (LISBOA)   Mérida   Toledo

Badajoz   Cuenca

Valencia

ROUTE DETAIL

Barcelona (Sants)– Tarragona
ETT tables 652/672

Type	Frequency	Typical journey time
Train	1–3 per hr	1 hr 09 mins

Tarragona–Valencia
ETT table 672

Type	Frequency	Typical journey time
Train	12–14 daily	2 hrs 05 mins

Valencia–Cuenca
ETT table 669

Type	Frequency	Typical journey time
Train	4 daily	3 hrs 25 mins

Cuenca–Aranjuez
ETT table 669

Type	Frequency	Typical journey time
Train	3–5 daily	3 hrs 55 mins

Aranjuez–Madrid
(Atocha Cercanías)   ETT tables 661/668/669

Type	Frequency	Typical journey time
Local Train	8–13 daily	40 mins

Madrid (Atocha Cercanías) –Cáceres
ETT table 677

Type	Frequency	Typical journey time
Train	4 daily	3 hrs 55 mins

Cáceres–Mérida
ETT table 677

Type	Frequency	Typical journey time
Train	5–6 daily	1 hr 5 mins

Mérida–Badajoz
ETT tables 677/678

Type	Frequency	Typical journey time
Train	6 daily	45 mins

Badajoz–Lisbon
see Notes

Type	Frequency	Typical journey time
Bus	2 daily	4 hrs

KEY JOURNEYS

Barcelona–Madrid
ETT table 650

Type	Frequency	Typical journey time
Train	15–27 daily	2 hrs 57 mins (day)
	1 daily	9 hrs (night)

Madrid–Lisbon
ETT table 45

Type	Frequency	Typical journey time
Train	1 daily	9 hrs 33 mins (night)

Notes

Most trains in Spain need advance reservations.

Those wishing to complete (most of) the Badajoz to Lisbon route by rail should note that the cross-border line from Badajoz to Elvas (20 km west of Badajoz) has no passenger service, requiring the use of a bus or taxi for this section. There is a daily rail connection from Elvas to Lisbon taking 4 hrs 40 mins (with a change of trains at Entroncamento).

Barcelona to Lisbon: change trains at Madrid.

Badajoz to Lisbon: take the bus to Elvas (5 daily Mon–Fri; journey time 30 mins) then train (change trains at Entroncamento).

Remember Spain's time is 1 hr ahead of Portugal's.

RAIL TOUR: BARCELONA – MADRID – LISBON

This trip across central Spain and Portugal links the three largest cities on the Iberian peninsula – **Barcelona** (p153), **Madrid** (p162), and **Lisbon** (p169). From the heart of Catalan-speaking Spain you head along the Costa Dorada – not Spain's most beautiful stretch of coast, but endowed with impressive Roman remains at **Tarragona** (where you can opt to head inland direct to Madrid via **Zaragoza**). Further down at the centre of the orange-and-vegetable-growing Levante region is **Valencia** – big but with a lively historic core. Beyond the wine-making town of **Requena**, with its Moorish castle, extend the excitingly rugged sierras of the northeast corner of New Castile, where you encounter **Cuenca**, with its precariously perched houses beside a precipice. **Madrid** and **Toledo** give good reason for lingering in the very centre of Spain. Extremadura (meaning 'the land beyond the Duero') is the name given to west central Spain, a deeply rural region of vast rolling sierras, forests and landscapes rich in wildlife; there are also some deeply atmospheric settlements virtually untouched by the passage of time, notably **Cáceres** and **Trujillo** – a beautiful little time capsule – and the Roman remains at **Mérida**. Over the border into Portugal, **Abrantes** provides a base for visiting **Marvão**, an enchanting hilltop town in the wild Alentejo region.

BARCELONA   TARRAGONA

See p153.

A great place to stay for a night or two, Tarragona has an ancient walled town above the modern settlement, and enjoys a glorious cliff-top position above a long golden beach, a rich heritage of Roman sites – including the remains of temples, a substantial **amphitheatre** and the Roman forum, which now abuts modern housing. There is also a necropolis, where early Christians were buried, and a very well-preserved aqueduct a couple of miles out of town. Along the foot of the 3rd-century BC Roman walls extends the **Passeig Arqueológic**, an archaeological walkway. Catalonia's foremost collection of Roman sculptures, temple friezes, bronzes and mosaics is housed in the **Museu Arqueológic**, Plaça del Rei, while the neighbouring *Pretori*, a Roman palace, contains the **Museu de la Romanitat**, with historical displays ranging from Roman to medieval finds. **La Seu** (the cathedral), one of the finest churches in the region, exemplifies the transition from Romanesque to Gothic.

Passeig de Espanya. Taxis and 🚌 2/24 take you into the old town. It's a 10-min walk uphill to the old centre: take C. d'Orosi opposite, uphill; go right at the junction with C. d'Apodaca, and carry on up to the main street (Rambla Nova); the Tourist Office is left and immediately left again, while the old town lies ahead.

DAY TRIP FROM TARRAGONA

Port Aventura is Spain's best adventure theme park (mid-Mar–early Jan). There are at least 12 trains a day from Tarragona, taking about 10 mins. For further details ☎ 90 220 22 20 (www.portaventura.es).

Spain and Portugal

🏨 The best budget bets are in Pl. de la Font, a pleasant traffic-free square in the old town (also some good places to eat); here are two clean, adequate pensions – for sea views, try **Hostal Mediterrani**, Carrer Orosi 10, ☎97 724 93 53 (wwwhostalmediterrani.com), right by the station (doubles from €45), and **Hotel Noria**, Plaça del Font 53, ☎97 723 87 17 (www.booking.com; €48 double). The **HI hostel** is at C. Lluís Companys 5, ☎97 724 01 95 (www.tujuca.com). Also good is the **Hostal Forum**, Pl. de la Font 37, ☎97 724 01 95 (www.hihostels.com; €43 double).

ℹ️ **Tourist Office**: **(Regional)** Carrer Fortuny 4, ☎97 723 34 15 (www.tarragonaturisme.es). **(Municipal)** Carrer Major 39, ☎97 725 07 95 (near the cathedral). Below the main town.

SIDE TRIP TO ZARAGOZA   Zaragoza (ETT tables 650/651 and 652) is on the direct line from Barcelona to Madrid (it is 1 hr 20 mins from Tarragona to Zaragoza; reservations needed). Although flanked by immense tower blocks and traffic-ridden *paseos*, the old town reveals a lively, historic centre. The station (where you can pick up a city map) is 3 km out; to avoid the 25-min walk, take 🚌 22 into the centre.

There are two cathedrals: **La Seo** is Romanesque and Gothic, and contains fine Flemish tapestries and a Gothic reredos; more famous is the mosque-like 18th-century **Basílica de Nuestra Señora del Pilar**, with its domes of coloured tiles, named after the pillar bearing a tiny, much-venerated statue of the Virgin within the church (where the Virgin Mary is said to have descended from heaven in a vision of St James in AD 40). You get a good view from the tower (reached by lift, then stairs). The **Plaza del Pilar** features an interesting water monument of South America: stand at the closest point of the pool to the Basilica, crouch down, and you will see a clear outline of the continent. The **Museo Camón Aznar**, C. Espoz y Mina 23 (closed Mon), has a fine art collection assembled by a devotee of Goya. Zaragoza's most impressive sight, the **Aljafería**, is a stunning Moorish fortress-palace just outside the city centre; look out for the ornate stucco oratory in the northern portico. Tours also take in the Gothic quarters added by Fernando and Isabel.

A modern attraction is the theme park **Parque Zaragoza** (www.atraczara.com), 1 km north from the station on Duque Alba. Open Mar–Oct, there are ferris wheels, rollercoasters and houses of horror.

The **Tourist Office** is on Plaza del Pilar (☎90 214 20 08 (www.zaragoza.es), and offers guided walking and bus tours. The **Hotel Las Torres**, Pl. del Pilar 11, ☎97 639 42 50 (www.hotellastorres.com; €€), gets a superb view of the Basilica. Alternatively, try the **Hostal Milmarcos**, C. Madre Sacramento 40, ☎97 628 46 18 (www.infohostal.com), €, or the **Hostal Zaragoza**, C. Predicadores 70, ☎97 628 20 43 (www.zaragozahostel .com) where mixed dorms sleep 4–10, €.

VALENCIA

Spain's third city, known as the home of paella, is a large and mostly faceless modern metropolis, but at its heart there's a bustling atmospheric old town with two medieval

ORXATA

In summer, many cafés and bars in Valencia offer *orxata*, a sweet milky drink made from *chufas*, or earth almonds, traditionally eaten with bread sticks (either chewy, sweet *fartons*, or more brittle *rosquilletas*). The place to drink it is the **Orxateria Santa Catalina**, in the Plaça de la Reina.

gateways (**Torres de Serranos** and **Torres de Quart**), pleasant squares, characterful run-down backstreets, crumbly baroque mansions and a handful of other historic landmarks. There's a sizeable student population and the nightlife is good.

Santiago Calatrava's stunning **City of Arts and Sciences** ☎ 90 210 00 31 (www.cac.es), has become the city's top attraction and a symbol of the 'new' Valencia. It's a gleaming, white, futuristic entertainment complex which encompasses an excellent hands-on science museum, a vast aquarium, an arts centre and a planetarium. The port and beach area were dramatically revamped for the 2007 America's Cup and Valencia is fast becoming one of the Med's most fashionable hot-spots.

The old town, which contains the main sights, is easily covered on foot. EMT buses operate throughout the city; most can be boarded in Plaça de l'Ajuntament (tickets from *tabacos* and kiosks), a traffic-ridden triangle overlooked by the copper-domed town hall. Two towers preside over the Plaça de la Reina: the baroque spire of **Santa Catalina** and the **Miguelete**, which is the bell tower of the cathedral; climb the spiral staircase to the top for a good view. Valencia's key building is its **Cathedral**, a mixture of styles ranging from Romanesque to baroque. A 1st-century agate chalice adorned with gold and pearls is said to be the Holy Grail and is displayed behind the altar in a side chapel.

The city's finest building is the Gothic **Llotja de la Seda**, Plaça del Mercat, a legacy of the heady days of the 15th-century silk trade, while the nearby **Mercat Central** is a vast Art Nouveau market hall. The **Palau del Marques de Dos Aigües** is a baroque pile with an eye-catching alabaster doorway and home to the **Museu Nacional de Ceràmica** (National Ceramics Museum; closed Sun and Mon), its displays ranging from ancient Greek vases to 20th-century creations by the likes of Picasso.

[RAIL] The main station is **Estació del Nord**, with its magnificent Art Nouveau entrance hall, centrally located (Metro: Xàtiva; [bus] 5/8/10/11/14/19; lockers), 10 mins by rail from **Cabanyal** station ([bus] 81), which serves the ferries.

i **Tourist Offices: Regional**: C. de la Pau 48, ☎ 96 398 64 22 (www.comunitatvalenciana.com) and at Estació del Nord. **Municipal**: Pl. de la Reina 19, ☎ 96 315 39 31, Plaça de l'Ajuntament 1, ☎ 96 351 04 17, and Avda de Catalunya (www.turisvalencia.com).

LAS FALLAS IN VALENCIA

Las Fallas, a week-long festival in mid-March, centres on a competition to produce the best *falla* – a huge character made of papier-mâché. Entries are paraded through the streets and (on the last night) ritually burned, to the accompaniment of a huge firework display.

Spain and Portugal

🏨 Good budget areas are around Pl. de l' Ajuntament and Pl. del Mercat. The **Hotel Venecia**, C. en Llop 5, ☎ 96 352 42 67 (www.hotelvenecia.com) is an excellent value 2-star hotel next to the Town Hall (doubles from €61). The **Antigua Morellana**, C. En Bou 2, ☎ 96 391 57 73 (www.hostelam.com), is friendly and well located (doubles from €55). **Youth hostels (HI): Alberg Ciutat de Valencia**, Balmes 17, ☎ 96 392 51 00 (www.alberguedevalencia.com), 1 km from station (dorm beds from €12 plus ensuite doubles). **Hôme** have two funky, friendly hostels in the old town: the **Backpackers Hostal**, Plaza Vicente Iborra, ☎ 96 391 37 97 (www.home backpackershostal.com), with dorm bunks from €12, and the **Youth Hostal**, C. la Lonja 4, ☎ 96 391 62 29 (www.homeyouthhostal.com), with beds from €19. The most convenient **campsite** is **Devesa Gardens**, Carretera d'el Saler km13, ☎ 96 161 11 36 (www.devesagardens.com)
🚌 El Saler to Valencia Centre, every 30 mins.

CUENCA

For sheer physical drama, with its extraordinary position over two river gorges, Cuenca is a spectacular place to wander around with a camera. Finely carved wooden balconies, armorial bearings, impressive doorways and breathtaking views are keynotes. Especially striking are the **Casas Colgadas**, the 13th-century tiered houses that hang over a sheer chasm and form the city's emblem. Level ground is in pretty short supply, a notable exception being the arcaded **Plaza Mayor**, flanked by the cathedral, which dates from the 12th century. It's more refined inside than its unfinished exterior suggests, and houses an absorbing treasury with paintings by El Greco. The best museums are the **Diocesan Museum** and the **Museo de Arte Abstracto**, the latter within one of the hanging houses and displaying Spanish abstract art. An iron footbridge in one of the gorges provides a much-photographed view of the hanging houses. Don't miss the very top of the town either: keep going right up, through an old gateway, for breathtaking views from the crags over the whole town.

🚉 C. Mariano Catalina, 10. It is a hard climb from the station to the old town and most prefer to take 🚌 1. The walk takes 20–25 mins: take the street diagonally left from the station, past a sign for Hostal Cortes in Ramón y Cajal.

ℹ️ **Tourist Office**: C. Alfonso VIII 2, ☎ 96 924 10 51 (www.cuenca.org or www.jccm.es).

🏨 Several cheap places are found between the station and the old town, including **Hotel Francabel**, Avenida de Castilla la Mancha 7, ☎ 96 922 62 22 (www.hotelfrancabel.es), with doubles from €50. A few doors up is the comfortable **Hostal Cortés**, Ramón y Cajal 49, ☎ 96 922 04 00 (www.hostalcortes.com; doubles €45). A nicely placed pension (with a lovely restaurant) below the old town is **Posada Tintes**, C. de los Tintes 7, ☎ 96 921 23 98 (posadatintes@latinmail.com), doubles from €35. There are two pensions at the top of the old town (served by 🚌 1): **La Tabanqueta**, Plaza del Trabuco 13, ☎ 96 921 12 90, €€, dramatically perched by the edge of the gorge. For a real splurge, try the **Parador de Cuenca**, Convento de San Pablo, Subida a San Pablo, ☎ 96 923 23 20 (www.parador.es), in a renovated convent and across a footbridge from the old town. For a treat in the old town, stay at the beautiful **Posada San José**, Julián Romero 4, ☎96 921 13 00 (www.posadasanjose.com), with doubles from €40–85.

🍴 Meaty variations occur on Cuenca's menus, most famously *morteruelo*, a spicy dish combining a multitude of meats, including game, chicken, pig's lard, cured ham and grated pig's liver, with the odd walnut thrown in for good measure. Something of an acquired taste, *zarajos* is roasted lamb's intestines, one of a number of local concoctions that are rolled on vine leaves, while *ajoarriero* is a more generally palatable dish of cod, eggs, parsley and potato; trout and crayfish are also on offer. *Resolí* is a liqueur made of orange peel, cinnamon and coffee.

ARANJUEZ

On the south bank of the Tagus, Aranjuez is famous for its spectacular **Royal Palace** and gardens (www.patrimonionacional.es, closed Mon, gardens open daily; free for EU passport holders on Wed), the inspiration for the world-famous Concierto de Aranjuez, or Rodrigo's Guitar Concerto. The structure dates from the 18th century and is a succession of opulently furnished rooms with marble mosaics, crystal chandeliers and ornate clocks. In the gardens are the **Casa del Labrador** (literally 'Farmer's Cottage', but more like the Petit Trianon at Versailles) and the **Casa de Marinos**, housing royal barges.

🚆 1 km outside town and 10-min walk from the palace. As you exit the station, take the road to the right and then turn left at the end.

ℹ️ **Tourist Office:** Plaza de San Antonio 9, ☎91 891 04 27 (www.aranjuez.es).

MADRID

See p162.

TOLEDO

A sense of history permeates every street of this famous walled city, perched on a hill and with the Río Tajo (River Tagus) forming a natural moat on three sides. Over the centuries Christian, Moorish and Jewish cultures have each left their mark on Toledo, which was a source of inspiration to El Greco, who lived and worked here for nearly 40 years. Although possible as a day trip (only half an hour from Madrid), it's highly recommended that you stay longer. Only the sheer number of tourists detracts from the atmosphere.

The station, not big but a spectacular gem, boasts colourful tiles, chandeliers, stained glass, Moorish windows and Art Nouveau signs, and is a sign of things to come. Cross the Tagus and you soon reach the **Alcázar** (old fortress; closed until further notice for major renovation). Home to a military museum and on a site that's been fortified from Roman times, it has been repeatedly rebuilt, most recently following its near-total destruction in the Spanish Civil War. Another of the city's most famous sights, the **Museo de Santa Cruz**, is located in the beautifully restored Renaissance hospice (Calle Miguel de Cervantes 3, ☎92 522 14 02, free, closed Sun afternoons). It has temporary art exhibits by local artists along with displays on fine arts (including El Greco's *Assumption of the Virgin*), archaeology and industrial arts.

The city's pride and joy is its heavily buttressed cathedral. Contructed over some 250 years, it's one of the wonders of Spain for its stained glass, for the sculpture in the choir, for the tombs within its chapels, and for its works of art, notably the **Transparente** – an extravagant baroque creation of paintings and marble sculptures which catches the light in a most dramatic way. In the Sacristy hang paintings by El Greco, Van Dyck, Goya and Velázquez; in the treasury is a huge 16th-century monstrance of solid gold and silver which is paraded through the town during the **Corpus Christi celebrations** (May/June), on a route decked with awnings, embroidered shawls, flags, lanterns and tapestries. In the old **Jewish quarter** to the south are the two spectacular surviving synagogues. **El Tránsito** is a 14th-century Mudéjar edifice with a ceiling of carved cedarwood, now home to the **Museo Sefardí**, a museum about Jewish culture. The 12th-century synagogue of **Santa María la Blanca** is very different: its conversion into a Christian church did not affect the basic layout of the interior, with five aisles separated by horseshoe arches and supported by pillars with unusual capitals and stone carvings.

The **Iglesia de San Tomé** (Church of St Thomas), dates from the 14th century and houses El Greco's famous masterpiece *The Burial of Count Orgaz*. The **Museo de El Greco** nearby is closed for long-term restoration.

Apart from Corpus Christi (see above) other **processions** take place in Holy Week. On 1 May is a pilgrimage to the shrine of the Virgen del Valle, while the Festival of the Patroness in mid-Aug features sports, bullfights and shows.

RAIL Paseo de la Rosa, just east of the centre (🚌 5/6 to the Plaza de Zocodover). It's more pleasant to take the 20-min walk in; cross the main road from the station, turn right and immediately fork left on a quiet road with no-entry road signs, then cross the 10th-century bridge known as the Puente de Alcántara, with the classic view of the town, and take the road rising opposite into town.

i **Tourist Offices**: the main office is at Puerta de Bisagra, ☎ 92 522 08 43 (www.toledo.es, www.toledo-turismo.es). There is a branch in the town hall opposite the cathedral.

🏠 It can be difficult to find somewhere to stay for summer weekends. The best cheap lodgings are in the old town (try around C. de Juan Labrador or C. de Descalzos), such as **Hotel Maravilla**, Plaza Barrio Rey 9, ☎ 92 522 33 04, (www.hotelmaravilla.com; doubles €50); **La Belviseña**, Cuesta del Can 5, ☎ 92 522 00 67, with doubles €20; **Hostal Descalzos**, C. Descalzos 30, ☎ 92 522 28 88 (www.hostaldescalzos.com), a lovely inn with great views over the city from the patio jacuzzi (doubles from €45); and the **Hostal Centro**, C. Nueva 13, Plaza de Zocodover, ☎ 92 525 70 91 (www.hostalcentro.com), doubles €50. There is a **youth hostel (HI)** on the outskirts of town in a medieval castle (near the station), the **Albergue Juvenil**, Castillo San Servando, ☎ 92 522 45 54 (www.reaj.com). The university sometimes has rooms available. **Campsites**: **Circo Romano**, Avda Carlos III 19, ☎ 92 522 04 42, reasonably comfortable and only a 10-min walk from Puerta de Bisagra; and **El Greco**, ☎ 92 522 00 90, which has much better facilities, but is 1.5 km out of town, on Ctra. Toledo-Puebla de Montalbán (🚌 7 from Plaza de Zocodover).

The street Calle de Barrio Rey has a good range of inexpensive places to eat. Shops sell locally produced marzipan (*mazapán*).

CÁCERES

Not a lot of visitors make it out to this golden-stone World Heritage Site, though the storks do in incredible numbers – they have built nests on every conceivable perch. Its old centre has bags of charm, and is almost totally unspoilt. In medieval times it prospered as a free trade town, and was largely rebuilt in the 15th and 16th centuries; thereafter, it fell into decline and very little was added, hence the time-warp quality. Ancient city walls surround a largely intact old town, with its Jewish quarter and numerous gargoyle-embellished palaces, displaying the heraldic shields of the status-conscious families who built them; the place particularly comes into its own after dark, when it's dramatically floodlit. The obvious starting point is the cobbled, partially arcaded Plaza Mayor, from which the gateway of 1726, known as the **Arco de la Estrella** (Arch of the Star), leads into the compact old town (easily explored on foot). You immediately reach the Plaza de Santa María, abutted by the **Concatedral de Santa María** (with an interesting cedarwood retable), the **Palacio Episcopal**, and the **Casa de los Golfines de Abajo** (one of the two mansions of the Golfine family).

The **Palacio de Carvajal**, with its Moorish tower, houses the tourism and craft council, but you can visit the chapel and the first floor gallery (decorated in 19th-century style). On the top of the town's hill, the **Church of San Mateo** has a fine array of nobles' tombs, while the nearby **Casa de las Cigüeñas** (House of the Storks) was the only noble's house exempted from a royal decree and allowed to keep its fortifications. Home to a small provincial museum, the **Casa de las Veletas** (House of the Weathervanes) stands on the foundations of a Moorish citadel and contains an *Almohade* water cistern (*aljibe*), with a vaulted ceiling supported by horseshoe arches.

Avda Alemania. **Bus Station**: Carretera de Merida. The bus and train stations are together, about 3 km from the centre. 1 goes to Plaza Obispo Galarza, near the Plaza Mayor. From the station, cross the green footbridge over the road, then turn left 100 m for the bus stop (or walk up from here); a taxi to Plaza Mayor will cost about €5. Luggage lockers.

i **Tourist Office**: Plaza Mayor, 92 701 08 34 (www.turismoextremadura.com).

There's a good choice of hotels; the best area for both staying and eating cheaply is in the vicinity of Plaza Mayor. For a complete list of Cáceres' budget accommodation, see www.caceresjoven.com. Cheapies (€ to €€) include **Hostal Al-Qazeres**, Camino Llano 34, 92 722 70 00 (www.alqazeres.com), doubles €40; **Albergue Turístico Las Veletas**, C. Margallo 36, 92 721 12 10, dorm beds from €17; **Pensión Carretero**, Plaza Mayor 22, 92 724 74 82, doubles €25; and **Hotel Castilla**, C. Ríos Verdes 3, 92 724 44 04, doubles €50, central and reasonably quiet (take the turning between the two main restaurants in Plaza Mayor and turn right).

Spain and Portugal

SIDE TRIP FROM CÁCERES TO TRUJILLO Trujillo (47 km east of Cáceres; reached by bus; journey 40 mins), overlooked by a 10th-century Moorish castle, was built largely from the proceeds of the Peruvian conquests and known as the 'Cradle of the Conquistadores'. From the bus station, a 15-min walk uphill leads to the **Plaza Mayor**, built on two different levels, connected by steps, and lined with once-magnificent palace-mansions, arcades and whitewashed houses. It is dominated in one corner by the **Iglesia de San Martín**, at the foot of which stands a bronze statue of conquistador Francisco Pizarro (who conquered the Inca empire in Peru), mounted and in full regalia. The **Palacio de los Marqueses de la Conquista** was built by Hernando Pizarro (the elaborate window grilles and corner balcony are particularly attractive), and there are many other 16th- and 17th-century seigneurial mansions with lavish armorial bearings. From Plaza Mayor, C. de Ballesteros leads up to the old walls, in which there is a gateway to the 13th-century Romanesque-Gothic church of **Santa María la Mayor**, which contains Roman sarcophagi as well as the tombs of Pizarro and other Spanish heroes, and a winged retable by Fernando Gallego. A short distance away is the **Casa-Museo de Pizarro**, with a reconstruction of the 15th-century house of a *hidalgo* (nobleman) and an exhibition of the life of Pizarro.

Tourist Office: Plaza Mayor, ☎92 732 26 77 (www.trujillo.es). **Accommodation**: **Alojamientos Plaza Mayor**, Plaza Mayor 6, ☎92 732 23 13 (www.trujilloplazamayor.com), doubles €40; **Hostal Nuria**, Plaza Mayor 38, ☎92 732 09 07, doubles €45; **Hostal Trujillo**, Francisco Pizarro 4, ☎92 732 22 74 (www.hostaltrujillo.com), doubles €50.

MÉRIDA

Around 25 BC Mérida was one of the wealthiest and most important centres in Roman Spain. Today it's unremarkable at first sight, but look around and you'll find an impressive array of Roman monuments (open daily) that fully deserve a day's visit. Head for the theatres, the Casa del Mitreo and the Roman bridge, and look in at the museum. It's worth buying the €5 ticket (www.mcu.es) covering all the sites apart from the Roman Museum: you can get this from any site. Free attractions include the Roman bridge, the Forum Portico and the Temple of Diana. As you arrive by train from Cáceres, the appreciable remains of the Roman **aqueduct** are visible immediately on the left (north) side. Most points of interest lie to the south of the station, however. On José Ramon Melida, where you'll find a number of shops selling replica Roman artefacts, including some quite convincing pots and oil lamps at reasonable prices. By the Tourist Office is the entrance to the 14,000-seater **Anfiteatro** (amphitheatre), used by the Romans for 'entertainments' such as gladiatorial combat, and the acoustically perfect **Teatro** (theatre), still used for theatrical events, its magnificent collonades rising two storeys and enclosing the back of the stage. In the adjacent **Casa del Anfiteatro** (House of the Amphitheatre) look out for the mosaic depicting three men treading grapes. The nearby **Museo Nacional de Arte Romano** deserves a couple of hours, with exhibits ranged on three floors, and including some superb items such as a vast mosaic of a boar hunt and a statue of Chronos trapped by a snake. Close to the bullring (some things haven't changed that much since the days of amphitheatres) the **Casa del Mitreo** is a Roman house with a celebrated cosmological mosaic. Carry on past the **Alcazaba** – successively a Roman, Visigothic and Moorish fort – to the much-renewed **Roman bridge** over the Río Guadiana, 792 m long and with 60 arches, within sight of the handsomely sleek modern concrete road bridge to the north. Behind the main street, the **Temple of Diana** retains full-height columns. Near the station, the **Basílica de Santa Eulalia** is built over the remains of a 5th-century church constructed during the reign of Emperor Constantine; there's a museum and you can walk into the underground archaeological excavations.

🚉 In the centre of town.

ℹ️ **Tourist Office**: C. Santa Eulalia 64, ☎92 433 07 22 (www.merida.es). Pick up a map and a free guide to the sights of Mérida here.

🏨 There's not a huge amount of budget accommodation in the town centre; good bets are **Hostal El Alfarero**, C. Sagasta 40, ☎92 430 31 83 (www.hostalelalfarero.com), doubles €45, and **Hostal Nueva España**, Avda Extremadura 6, ☎92 431 33 56, doubles €42 (between the station and Pza España).

ABRANTES, PORTUGAL

Sited high above the Tagus, the small hillside town of Abrantes originally defended the old Portuguese province of Beirã. Above the town, approached through a maze of flower-bedecked alleys, are the remains of a castle of uncertain, pre-12th-century origins, rebuilt by King Denis in the 14th century. The keep has been partially restored and is now a belvedere offering panoramic views of the town, the Tagus Valley and the mountains. The 13th-century **Church of Santa Maria do Castelo** (in the castle grounds) was restored in the 15th century and houses a museum containing Gothic works of art and *azulejos* (decorative blue and yellow tiles), and is also home to a trio of superb tombs of the Counts of Abrantes (the *Almeidas*).

🚉 4 km south of the town centre; 🚌 3/4/5 run from the station car park every 30 mins.

ℹ️ **Tourist Office**: Largo 1° de Maio, ☎241 362 555 (www.cm-abrantes.pt; www.turismo.cm-abrantes.pt). Turn left out of the small street at the station. Cross the bridge over the Tagus, follow the road round, then take the turning on your left-hand side and continue up the winding steep hill, past the hospital, to Abrantes; the Tourist Office is near the town's market and car park.

🏨 **Pensão Alianca**, Largo do Chafariz 50, ☎241 362 348, €; **Casa de Hospedes Central**, Praça Raimundo Soares 15, ☎241 362 422, €; **Pensão Vera Cruz**, Avda Dr Augusto Silva Martins, Rossio ao Sul do Tejo, ☎241 333 250, €. **Youth hostel (HI):** Avda Eng Avelino, Amaro da Costa, ☎241 379 210 (abrantes@movijovem.pt).

🍴 Budget places are around O Pelicano, Rúa Nossa Senhora de Conceição and Praça Raimundo Soares (pleasant for sitting outside one of the cafés by the fountains).

LISBON

See p169.

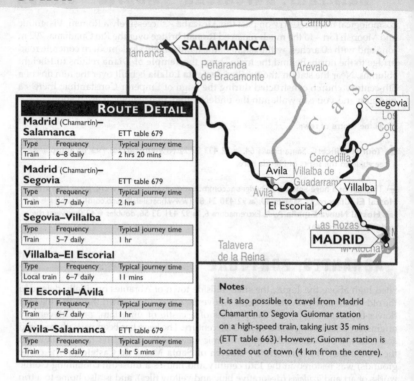

ROUTE DETAIL

Madrid (Chamartín)– Salamanca
ETT table 679

Type	Frequency	Typical journey time
Train	6–8 daily	2 hrs 20 mins

Madrid (Chamartín)– Segovia
ETT table 679

Type	Frequency	Typical journey time
Train	5–7 daily	2 hrs

Segovia–Villalba

Type	Frequency	Typical journey time
Train	5–7 daily	1 hr

Villalba–El Escorial

Type	Frequency	Typical journey time
Local train	6–7 daily	11 mins

El Escorial–Ávila

Type	Frequency	Typical journey time
Train	6–7 daily	1 hr

Ávila–Salamanca
ETT table 679

Type	Frequency	Typical journey time
Train	7–8 daily	1 hr 5 mins

Notes

It is also possible to travel from Madrid Chamartín to Segovia Guiomar station on a high-speed train, taking just 35 mins (ETT table 663). However, Guiomar station is located out of town (4 km from the centre).

From **Madrid** an incongruously suburban-looking train climbs onto the **Sierra de Guadarrama** to **Segovia**, one of the most exciting places in Spain. At Segovia station there is no hint of the nearby old city, but it soon comes into view after a short bus journey. From here, retrace the route over the Sierra to the junction at Villalba de Guadarrama (or else take the bus from Segovia to Salamanca), and change trains, soon passing close to the vast complex of **El Escorial**, seen on the right-hand side of the train. Beyond the walled pilgrimage town of **Ávila** lies **Salamanca**, an elegant old university city built in a gorgeous yellow stone. Rail routes from there include west to Portugal and north to Zamora and Burgos.

MADRID

See p162.

SEGOVIA

This romantic walled hilltop city has a tremendous situation, perched above the **Río Eresma** and looking out to the heights of the Sierra de Guadarrama. The **cathedral**, which towers majestically above the rest of the town, dates from the 16th century and was the last Gothic church to be built in Spain. It's huge inside; one side chapel has great metal dragons supporting censers each side of a ceramic altar. Segovia also has a fine clutch of smaller medieval churches, notably **San Esteban**, with its 12th-century tower, **La Trinidad**, an exceptional Romanesque church; **Vera Cruz** (closed Mon and lunchtime), a remarkably interesting Templar church with a 12-sided nave and 15th-century murals (outside the city walls); and the **Convent of S. Antonio de Real**, noted for its 15th-century portal and painted wooden Calvary of the Flemish school.

Heading down towards the gorge that cuts around the town, you reach the **Alcázar** (castle), an amazing pile bristling with spiky towers. A massive fire in 1862 destroyed much of it, and most of what you see today is architectural bravado dating from the 1882 restoration. Fake it may be, but it does make an entertaining visit, with quaintly undersize suits of armour dotted around the rooms, and dizzying views from the tower. It's also worth following the riverside path from just below the Alcázar – a delightful semi-rural walk with views up to the old town.

Believed to have been built by Augustus, the **aqueduct** is one of Spain's most magnificent Roman monuments, with 165 arches spanning 813 m. It was constructed without mortar – each granite block has a groove whereby the Roman machinery lifted it into place – and although partly repaired in the 15th century is still intact. The Plaza del Azoguejo, where the aqueduct is a double-decker construction, is the main viewing point, though it's fun to follow the structure as it runs along more obscure streets, where the arches get increasingly wonky and amateurish.

🚉 The railway station is in the new town; take 🚌 3 (it's much too far to walk) to the Plaza Mayor in the old town, or get off just outside the walls. The **bus station** is a 15-min walk from the centre, or you can take the bus.

ℹ️ **Tourist Office**: Plaza Mayor 10, ☎92 146 03 34 (www.turismodesegovia.com, www.segovia.es). Another Tourist Office is at Plaza del Azoguejo (by the aqueduct).

🛏️ Stay in the old town. **Hostal El Hidalgo**, José Canalejas 3–5, ☎92 146 35 29 (www.el-hidalgo.com), doubles from €37, has a pleasantly old-fashioned restaurant. Slightly cheaper are the **Pensión El Gato**, Plaza Salvador 10, ☎92 142 32 44 (right by the aqueduct; doubles €40); **Hostal Juan Bravo**, C. Juan Bravo 12, ☎92 146 34 13 (very central; doubles without bath €35, with bath €40); and **Hostal Taray**, Plaza San Facundo 1, ☎92 146 30 41 (www.hostaltaray.com; very central; doubles €37. Splurge a little at the **Hotel Las Sirenas**, C. Juan Bravo 30, ☎92 146 26 63, (www.hotelsirenas.com) with doubles for €75. **Youth hostel (HI)**: **Albergue Juvenil Emperador Teodosio**, Paseo Conde de Sepúlveda s/n, ☎92 144 11 11 (www.reaj.com), dorm beds from €8.50; open July–mid-Sept only.

🍴 Reasonable bars, cafés and restaurants in and around Plaza Mayor, the attractive central square of the old town.

Spain

EL ESCORIAL

Although it's some way from the station, you can easily see this vast grey palace and monastery, set beneath a hillside, from the railway. El Escorial is a magnificent 16th-century complex that includes a monastery, where the kings of Spain are buried, and a library with nearly 3000 5th–18th-century documents. Many notable works of art are on display in the complex, some forming an intrinsic part of the décor. The **palace** is of particular interest. Closed Mon; free on Wed for EU nationals only.

For something verging on the bizarre, **El Valle de los Caídos** (the Valley of the Fallen; regular buses from El Escorial) is a huge kitsch Fascist memorial to Civil War casualties. Built by Franco in the 1950s using political dissidents as slave labour, it's the largest cross in the world (492 ft high), placed above a cave church.

▨ About 2 km from town, uphill, so it's better to take a local shuttle bus to the centre.

ℹ️ **Tourist Office**: C. Grimaldi 2, ☎91 890 53 13 (www.sanlorenzoturismo.org).

▨ **Hostal El Retiro**, C. Ausencia 17, ☎91 890 09 46, doubles €40, is central; a 15-min walk from the palace and monastery. A bit pricier (doubles from €51) is the **Hostal Cristina**, Calvario (nr Juan de Toledo), ☎91 890 19 61 (www.hostalcristina.es), with a restaurant and garden.

ÁVILA

The highest city in Spain, Ávila is encircled by **medieval walls** in such a perfect state of preservation that the whole place looks like a cardboard model from a distance. Much of the walled town is surprisingly neglected and underpopulated, though it's obviously the most atmospheric area to stay in. Throughout Spain and beyond pilgrims are drawn to Ávila, indelibly associated with its native mystic and reformer Santa Teresa de Jesús (now the city's patron saint), canonised in 1622. Apart from the **walls** (part of which you can walk along the top of), Ávila's main attractions are the **cathedral**, the **Monastery of Santo Tomás**, the **Basilica of San Vincente** and a number of other buildings associated with Santa Teresa. The **cathedral** and **Basilica de San Vincente** each deserve a visit, while **El Real Monasterio de Santo Tomás** is a real time-warp of a monastery, which became the summer palace of Ferdinand and Isabella. There are three cloisters, in different styles, containing gardens graced with a romantic, overgrown air of repose; the monastic church has the tomb of Torquemada, the infamously nasty grand inquisitor.

▨ Avda de José Antonio; luggage lockers. (The bus and rail stations are 2 km out. 🚌 1/3/LP run from Avda de José Antonio – opposite the rail station – to the centre.)

ℹ️ **Tourist Office** (provincial): C. San Segundo 17, ☎92 021 13 87 (www.avilaturismo.com, www.avila.es). A visitor's reception centre (municipal) is on Avenida Madrid 39, ☎92 022 59 79.

⌨ Cheap options within the old city walls include the **Hostal Don Diego**, C. Marqués de Canales y Chozas 5, ☎92 025 54 75 (doubles €40); **Hostal Cara Felipe**, Plaza del Mercado Chico 1, ☎92 021 39 24 (doubles €38 without bath, €45 with bath); **Hotel Arco San Vicente**, C. López Núñez 6, ☎92 022 24 98 (www.arcosvicente.com; doubles €60). **Youth hostel (HI)**: **Albergue Juvenil de Profesor Arturo Duperier**, Av de la Juventud, ☎92 022 17 16 (www.jcyl.es; dorm beds from €8.15), July–mid-Sept.

SALAMANCA

Salamanca is beautifully built in yellow stone and home to one of Spain's oldest universities. Virtually throughout the year there's a generous offering of concerts, exhibitions and other cultural events, many of them free.

Echoing to hundreds of footsteps, the Plaza Mayor is one of Spain's finest squares, a strikingly unified example of the baroque style. Walk south from here, past the **Casa de las Conchas** (House of Shells), a 15th-century mansion named after the carved shells embellishing its exterior, the motif of the Santiago pilgrimage. Dating from 1243, the main part of the **university** (at the south end of Rúa Mayor) is the country's prime instance of the Plateresque style, seen on the ornamental façade, with its carvings of floral themes, royal heraldry, children, women and beasts. Inside you can look around the cloister, off which lie some of the oldest rooms, giving an idea of the university in medieval times, notably a dimly lit lecture hall austerely furnished with narrow, backless benches, and with a pulpit for the lecturer; the temptation to nod off must have been great. The benches were installed in the 18th century – before that, students had to sit on the floor (richer ones employed servants to sit on the floor beforehand and warm up their spaces).

The two cathedrals stand side by side – the **Romanesque Catedral Vieja** (Old Cathedral), with wonderful frescos, cloisters and a 15th-century retable, and the **Catedral Nueva** (New Cathedral), displaying ornate relief carvings in the so-called churrigueresque style. Nearby, the **Convento de San Esteban** (Monastery of St Stephen) is highly atmospheric. Just below the cathedrals, the **Casa Lis** (www.museocasalis.org) is a striking modernist edifice of glass and filigree ironwork, restored and now home to the city's collection of Art Nouveau, Art Deco and (for some reason) dolls. From here, you can walk down to the river and the 26-arch **Puente Romano**; the 15 arches on the city side are Roman.

🚉 Paseo de la Estación. Luggage lockers; shopping and entertainment centre. Central. 🚌 1/1B.

ⓘ **Tourist Office** (provincial): Casa de las Conchas, Rúa Mayor 70, ☎92 326 85 71 (municipal): Plaza Mayor 14, ☎92 321 83 42 (www.salamanca.es).

⌨ Accommodation is plentiful; head for the Plaza Mayor, around which numerous pensions are signposted at the foot of staircases. The **youth hostel (HI)** is at C. Escoto 13–15, ☎ 92 326 91 41 (www.alberguesalamanca.com; dorm beds €13), 1 km from the rail station. **Campsite: Regio**, carretera Salamanca-Madrid km. 4, ☎92 313 88 88 (www.campingregio.com), 4 km from the city centre, buses every 30 mins.

ROUTE DETAIL

Lisbon (Sta Apolónia)–
Coimbra (B) — ETT table 690

Type	Frequency	Typical journey time
Train	16–18 daily	2 hrs 10 mins

Coimbra (B)–
Oporto (Campanha) — ETT table 690

Type	Frequency	Typical journey time
Train	17–19 daily	1 hr 10 mins

Oporto (Campanha)–
Viana do Castelo — ETT table 696

Type	Frequency	Typical journey time
Train	4–6 daily	1 hr 35 mins

**Viana do Castelo–
Valença** — ETT table 696

Type	Frequency	Typical journey time
Train	7–10 daily	1 hr

Valença–Tui — ETT table 696

Type	Frequency	Typical journey time
Train	2 daily	7 mins

Tui–Vigo — ETT table 696

Type	Frequency	Typical journey time
Train	2 daily	39 mins

Vigo–Pontevedra — ETT table 680

Type	Frequency	Typical journey time
Train	14–21 daily	25 mins

**Pontevedra–Santiago
de Compostela** — ETT table 680

Type	Frequency	Typical journey time
Train	12–16 daily	1 hr 5 mins

KEY JOURNEY

Lisbon–Oporto — ETT table 690

Type	Frequency	Typical journey time
Train	13–16 daily	3 hrs 10 mins

Notes

Lisbon to Santiago: change trains at Oporto and Vigo. Fast trains call at Coimbra B station: a frequent rail shuttle connects to Coimbra station a few mins later. Additional trains available Oporto–Viana do Castelo by changing at Nine.

SANTIAGO DE COMPOSTELA

Vigo
Pontevedra
Viana do Castelo
Tui
Valença
Braga
Guimarães
Oporto (Porto)

PORTUGAL

Coimbra

Óbidos
Tomar
SPAIN

Sintra

LISBON (LISBOA)

Évora

Extremadura

From the Portuguese capital the route heads north through a series of photogenic towns such as the old university town of **Coimbra**, the port-producing city of **Oporto** and the delightful coastal resort of Viana do Castelo, lying close

Remember Portugal's time zone is 1 hr behind Spain's.

to sweeping golden beaches. You can add on **Tomar** (to visit the fortified Convent of Christ, one of the architectural pearls of Portugal; see below) by changing at Lamarosa. From **Oporto** it's worth spending a few days exploring the scenic and deeply rural Douro Valley. Between **Valença** and **Tui** you cross the border into Spain, and enter **Galicia**, with its wild coastal inlets known as the Rías Baixas; the journey ends in the breathtaking pilgrimage city of **Santiago**.

LISBON

See p169.

TOMAR

Hourly trains from Lisbon serve Tomar (journey time 2 hrs, ETT table 699); these go via Entroncamento, itself halfway between Lisbon and Coimbra – so if you're heading north you can detour to Tomar, then retrace to Entroncamento, where you change for Coimbra.

On a wooded hill above the old town of cobbled streets is the 12th-century castle and subsequent monastery of the Order of the Knights Templar (see p192), the **Convento de Cristo** (open daily). The structure was erected in 1160 for the master of the Knights Templar (responsible for keeping open pilgrim routes to the Holy Land during the Crusades), but from the 1320s became the seat of the royally created Order of the Knights of Christ. Highlights include the Templars' Rotunda (the round chancel), modelled on the Holy Sepulchre in Jerusalem, and the magnificent Manueline-style window between the west end of the nave and Santa Barbara cloister. The window combines every maritime and nautical motif known to the Manueline style: ropes, shells, coral, fishing floats, seaweed, even an anchor chain. The Convento parking terrace overlooks **Nossa Senhora da Conceição**, perhaps Portugal's finest early-Renaissance church. While the outside is plain, the beautifully proportioned interior has finely carved Corinthian columns and faces with acanthus-leaf beards flanking the sanctuary arch. Other sights in the old town are the **Igreja de São João Baptista**, with two fine Manueline doorways and a richly carved altar covered in gold, and the 15th-century **Sinagoga**, housing the **Museu Luso-Hebraico**, a museum of Portuguese Judaism (open daily, admission free).

▣ Located just south of the centre; hourly trains to Lisbon (ETT table 699).

ℹ **Tourist Office:** Av. Dr Cândido Madureira, ☎249 322 427 (www.rttemplarios.pt, in Portuguese).

Spain and Portugal

COIMBRA

Coimbra was a centre of the Portuguese Renaissance and is the seat of one of the oldest universities in the world. Set on a hillside above the River Mondego, the town is packed with medieval character; in term-time it has a lively, youthful air. Coimbra has its own version of the *fado*, a melancholy, monotonous and sentimental chant originally sung by sailors in the 18th century.

BOAT TRIPS

Start from **Parque Doctor Manuel Braga** (trips take 1 hr, not Mon) ☎ 239 433 770 (www.basofias.com).

Although founded in 1290, the old university building is baroque, with a magnificent library resplendent in painted ceilings and gilded wood; you can also visit the grand **Graduates' Hall** and a small museum of sacred art.

The 12th-century **Sé Velha** (cathedral) is a striking Romanesque building with a fine altarpiece and Gothic cloisters, while the **Monastery of Santa Cruz** contains a 16th-century Manueline cloister, an elaborately carved stone pulpit and the tombs of the first two kings of Portugal.

Machado de Castro Museum, a choice display of medieval and Renaissance art, is housed in a former palace; access to the old Roman forum underneath the building.

RAIL **Coimbra**, ☎ 808 208 208 (www.cp.pt), a 10-min walk from centre or 🚌 1/7/11/24. **Coimbra B**, 3 km northwest of town, handles long-distance trains, including those from Lisbon; 🚌 5/33. Frequent trains between Coimbra and Coimbra B. For luggage lockers go to the Café Internacional. For the town centre, follow the road along by the river and fork left by the Tourist Office.

ℹ️ **Tourist Office**: (regional) Largo da Portagem, ☎239 488 120, (municipal) Edifício da Biblioteca Geral da Universidade de Coimbra (University Library building), Praça da Porta Férrea, ☎239 859 884 (www.cm-coimbra.pt). Or see website www.tourism-centro.pt.

🛏️ Several cheap places near Coimbra, such as **Pensão Atlântico**, Rua Sargento Mor 42, ☎239 826 496, €. **Youth hostel (HI)**: Rua Doutor Henriques Seco 14, ☎239 822 955, (coimbra@moijovem.pt), 🚌 6/7/29 from Largo da Portagem. **Campsite**: the municipal-run campsite offers excellent, modern facilities and is open 24 hours all year round. Rua da Escola – Alto Areeiro, Stº António dos Olivais, ☎239 086 902 (www.campingcoimbra.com, www.cacampings.com), 🚌 38 from Largo da Portagem.

🍽️ Plenty of centrally placed cheap eateries, for example in the University Gardens and in Beco do Forno and Rua dos Gatos (alleyways between Largo da Portagem and Rua do Soto).

OPORTO (PORTO)

Portugal's seductive second city, spectacularly sited on the steep banks of the River Douro near its mouth, gives its name to the fortified wine the English-speaking world knows as port (fortuitously invented by two Englishmen who used brandy in an attempt to preserve Portuguese wine). See www.portoturismo.pt.

Get your bearings by climbing the **Torre dos Clérigos**, Oporto's symbol, an 18th-century granite bell tower that gives a magnificent view. Below, the characterfully shabby old town, with its pastel shades and changes in level, is strongly atmospheric, notably in the **Ribeira** riverside area. The **Soares dos Reis Museum** (closed Mon), housed in the Carrancas Palace, is acclaimed for its collection of the decorative arts, including Portuguese faïence.

PORT TRIVIA

Port wine production is full of mystique. Snippets of information you may pick up on a tour of one of the port lodges include:

- The Portuguese don't actually drink much port themselves: Brits, Americans, Canadians, French and Italians are much keener.
- All ports are blends of different wines, and can be from different years. Vintage reserves are blends of wines from the same year.
- The brandy used is French, and some barrels end up in Scotch whisky distilleries.
- It takes 200 years to grow vines to a suitable height.

For an astonishing temple to money-making, take the guided tour of the **Palácio da Bolsa** (former Stock Exchange, now headquarters of the Chamber of Commerce, www.palaciodabolsa.pt), rather grey and boring-looking from outside but revealing a lavish interior which includes the Arabian Hall, a 19th-century gilded evocation of the Alhambra in Granada (see p213). The nearby **Church of Santa Clara** is a fine example of the Manueline style and with a dazzling baroque interior.

The vineyards themselves are a long way upriver in the magnificently scenic **Douro Valley**, but most of the port is aged in the numerous **port lodges** in the district of **Vila Nova de Gaia**, linked to the city centre by the double-decker coathanger-shaped Dom Luis I Bridge; walk over the top level for dizzying views. The lodges offer **free tours** with tastings (Sandeman and Offley charge admission) and booking is not generally necessary; Taylor's gives an authoritative tour of their 300-year-old lodges; don't miss the fabulous views from their terrace. Barros are particularly generous with the tastings. Moored on the river, small barrel-laden sailing craft (*barcos rabelos*), last used in 1967, serve as a reminder of how the young ports used to be brought downriver from the vineyards. Oporto's port days are probably limited: operations may all move upriver over the next couple of decades.

In 2005 Porto gained a new concert hall, the **Casa da Música**, a stunning design remarkable for its use of interior space. To the west of the town, amidst magnificent gardens, is the **Fundação de Serralves**, an Art Deco mansion with a fine collection of modern art.

🚉 **Campanhã**, Rua da Estação, near the southeast edge of town, serves Lisbon trains (🚌 35 to centre); luggage lockers and cash machine. **São Bento**, near Praça da Liberdade, much more central (wonderful tiling makes it a sight in itself), handles local/regional services. Frequent connections between the stations, taking 10 mins. Leave **São Bento** station and turn right up Praça da Liberdade then go left to Avda dos Aliados; Tourist Office is on your left, towards the top of this large square.

✈ **Francisco Sá Carneiro**, 🖀 229 432 400 (🚌 nos 87/120/601 or Aero Bus from Avenida dos Aliados or take the Metro); Tourist Office (www.ana-aeroportos.pt).

ℹ **Tourist Offices**: (national) Praça Dom João I, 🖀 222 057 514; (municipal) Rua Clube dos Fenianos 25, 🖀 223 393 470, (Riverside) Rua do Infante D. Henrique 63, 🖀 222 060 412, (Cathedral – Sé – Casa da Câmara) Terreiro da Sé, 🖀 223 325 174 (www.portoturismo.pt). The free city map shows five **walking tours**: Medieval, Baroque, *Azulejos* (tiles), Neoclassical, and the Garrett Tour.

🚌 **Day passes** (€5) – cheaper than four separate fares – and **3-day passes** (€11) cover all transport and are sold at STCP kiosks. Diana run hop-on-hop-off **bus tours** (buy ticket on board). The **Museu Carro Eléctrico** is a vintage tram that tours the city from near the Church of São Francisco. If using the Metro, buy a rechargeable 'Andante' card.

⚓ 50-min **boat trips** depart from Cais da Estiva (Ribeira) and near the Sandeman port lodge and tour the river.

🏨 For cheap lodgings, try the central area around Avda dos Aliados. Avoid the dockside Ribeira. A friendly place with a variety of rooms from budget singles and quads to more comfortable doubles with private bathrooms is the **Pensão Residencial Duas Nações**, Praça G G Fernandes 59, 🖀/fax 222 081 616 (www.duasnacoes.com), €–€€. Other places close by are the **Pensão Residencial Portuguesa**, Travessa Colonel Pacheco 11, 🖀 222 004 174 (www.residencialportuguesa .com), €; **Pensão Estoril**, Rua de Cedofeita 193, 🖀 222 002 751 (www.pensaoestoril.com), €–€€;

and **Pensão França**, Praça Gomes Teixeira 7, ☎222 002 791, €. **Youth hostel (HI)**: Rua Paulo de Gama 551, ☎226 177 257 (porto@movijovem.pt); a long way west by the mouth of the Douro, with beaches and a supermarket nearby; ☐ 35/37 from the city centre. **Campsites**: in Angeiras, around 20 km from Porto, is **Campsite Orbitur**, Rua de Angeiras, Lavra, ☎229 270 571 (www.obitur.com); two in Vila Nova de Gaia (**Camping de Salgueiros**, ☎227 810 500, and **Camping Marisol**, ☎227 135 942).

SIDE TRIPS FROM OPORTO   Allocate time to explore the mountain-backed **Douro Valley** east of Oporto (ETT table 694), with its many vineyards as well as some enchanting places accessible by train. **Amarante**, memorably placed by the River Tâmega, has photogenic houses of wooden balconies and iron grilles, and a monastic church with gilded baroque woodwork. **Vila Real**, placed on Corgo gorge, has a host of 16th–18th-century patricians' houses.

Northeast of Oporto, **Guimarães** (ETT table 695a) was once the Portuguese capital and contains a rewarding medieval core within its industrial outskirts; **Paço dos Duques** (still used as the president's residence) includes a town museum, and there's a fine wooden ceiling within the Banqueting Hall.

Braga (Tourist Office: Avda da Liberdade 1, ☎253 262 550, www.cm-braga.pt), the nation's religious capital, has more than 300 churches as well as Portugal's oldest cathedral; it's the site of massive celebrations in Holy Week, and 5 km east is the pilgrimage site of **Bom Jesus do Monte**, with a 116-m climb up the monumental 'Staircase of the Five Senses' to its Chapel of Miracles and massive reliquary. Trains from Oporto to Braga run approximately hourly (ETT table 695); there are also direct trains and buses from Lisbon.

VIANA DO CASTELO

This old fortress town doubles as the Costa Verde's most pleasant resort, with the beach on one side of the River Lima and the charming little town (noted for its Renaissance and Manueline architecture, which appeared when trade began with the great Hanseatic cities of northern Europe) on the other. It's also a centre of Portuguese folklore and famous for its handicrafts.

With the exception of **Santa Luzia** on the top of the **Monte de Santa Luzia** (accessible by funicular from Avda 25 de Abril; excellent view), interesting sights are walkable. The central square, **Praça da República**, has a 16th-century fountain that has been copied all over the region. Some choice examples of *azulejos* (tiles) can be seen in **Misericórdia Church** and the **Municipal Museum** (also showing glazed earthenware and furniture; closed Mon). Viana do Castelo's **Romaria** (in Aug) is the biggest festival in the country.

There are several spectacular sandy beaches accessible by train within half an hour, on the line to **Valença**.

Spain and Portugal

▨ Avda dos Combatentes near the town centre.

ℹ **Tourist Office**: Praça da Erva, ☎258 822 620 (www.rtam.pt, www.cm-viana-castelo.pt).

🛏 Pensions are easy to find, but not that cheap; rooms in private houses are often a better bet. **Youth hostels (HI)**: The modern **Viana do Castelo**, Rua de Limia, ☎258 800 260 (vianacastelo@movijovem.pt) and **Gil Eannes Ship**, Doca Comercial, ☎258 821 582 (www.pousadasjuventude.pt), former hospital ship for cod fishermen and city landmark, now a floating hostel with 55 beds.

VALENÇA

Unsightly modern sprawl has marred the approaches to this ancient town by the Minho River, but it still has its fortress-within-a-fortress guarding the border with Spain. Much survives of the 17th–18th-century walls and there are narrow old streets of white houses.

▨ On the east side of the new town.

ℹ For information call provincial office of **Rías Baixas** (Pontevedra) ☎98 684 26 90.

TUI, SPAIN

A bridge connects this tiered Spanish town to Portugal. Tui has grown around the lichen-encrusted **Cathedral of Santa Maria**. This impressive, austere Romanesque and Gothic building has a 13th-century cloister, carved choir stalls, an ornate 14th-century porch and fine Gothic sepulchres. Visit the churches of **San Bartolomé** and **San Telmo** if time permits.

▨ Central.

ℹ **Tourist Office**: C. Colón, ☎98 660 17 89.

🛏 **San Telmo**, Avenida de la Concordia 84, ☎98 660 30 11 (doubles from €35); **Generosa**, Calvo Sotelo 37, ☎98 660 00 55 (doubles from €25).

VIGO

Spain's major fishing port lies on a beautiful sheltered bay. It's a clamorous, busy place built of grey granite, not immediately attractive except in the old, sloping quarter near the seafront. Castro Castle, the ruined fort on a hill just above, provides a fine view. There are **beaches** and an **open-air pool** 2 km west at **Samil** (🚌 L15/L16/L27/LN). The wonderfully unspoilt **Islas Cíes** archipelago, reached by ferry from Vigo from mid-June to mid-Sept, is the main reason for stopping here. Designated a national park, the islands have white sands and rugged hilltops, with enough trails to provide a day's walking on the main two isles (which are joined together by a sandbank). The third island is a bird sanctuary and is not open to visitors. Book ahead (☎98 643 83 58) to camp in summer. For ferry information ☎98 622 52 72; visitors are limited to 2000 per day, so go early in the day if you haven't reserved.

🚉 Plaza de la Estación. Station information counter has free city maps (10 mins from the quays/ Tourist Office: turn right out of the station, along C. Alfonso XIII). Lockers and cash machine.

ⓘ **Tourist Office**: Plaza de Rey, ☎96 681 01 99 (www.turismodevigo.org); regional Tourist Office at C. Cánovas de Castillo 22, ☎98 643 05 77.

🏨 **Residencia Casais**, C. Lepanto 16, ☎88 611 29 56 (www.hostalcasais.com), doubles €35. **Hotel Atlántico Vigo**, Avenida García Barbón 35, ☎98 622 05 30 (www.hotelatlanticovigo.com), doubles €57. **Hotel Arias**, C. Lepanto 6, ☎98 622 34 03, (www.hotelarias.com), doubles from €30. **Youth hostel (HI): Residencia Juvenil Altamar**, C. Cesáreo González 4, ☎98 629 08 08 (www.xunta.es), 3 km from the rail station, dorm beds from €7.50; open July & Aug.

PONTEVEDRA

This typical old Galician town on the River Pontevedra began life as a port, but its importance dwindled as the old harbour silted up. Although surrounded by a new city, the compact old town is pretty much intact, with parts of the original walls still visible around a maze of cobbled streets, arcaded squares with carved stone crosses and low houses with flower-filled balconies. **La Peregrina**, an unusual chapel in the shape of a scallop shell, is situated by the partly arcaded main square, Plaza de la Ferrería, on the boundary between the old and new towns. The Gothic façade of the **Convent of San Francisco** looks onto the Herrería. **Iglesia de Santa María la Mayor** has an impressive Plateresque façade, which is floodlit at night. The 13th-century Gothic **Convent of Santo Domingo** by the **Jardines de Vincenti** is now in ruins but still evokes a certain splendour. It forms part of the **Provincial Museum**, other sections of which are at Plaza de la Leña.

🚉 Plaza Calvo Sotelo, about 1 km from the centre; lockers.

ⓘ **Tourist Office**: C. Gutiérrez Mellado 1B, ☎98 685 08 14 (www.turgalicia.es).

🏨 Budget accommodation is limited; there are some *fondas* and *pensiones* near C. de la Peregrina and Plaza de Galicia; try **Vedra Hotel**, Rua Profesor Filgueira Valverde 10, ☎98 686 95 50 (www. vedrahotel.es), doubles from €58. Others include **Casa Maruja**, Avda Santa Maria 12, ☎98 685 49 01 (doubles €30), and **Hostal La Paloma**, Rúa da Pomba 11, ☎98 684 42 10 (doubles €37).

SANTIAGO DE COMPOSTELA

See p205.

SPAIN

ROUTE DETAIL

San Sebastián–Vitoria ETT table 689

Type	Frequency	Typical journey time
Train	7–8 daily	1 hr 45 mins

Vitoria–Burgos ETT table 689

Type	Frequency	Typical journey time
Train	7–8 daily	1 hr 25 mins

Burgos–León ETT table 681

Type	Frequency	Typical journey time
Train	4 daily	1 hr 55 mins

León–Astorga ETT table 682

Type	Frequency	Typical journey time
Train	5–8 daily	30 mins

Astorga–Santiago de Compostela ETT tables 680, 682

Type	Frequency	Typical journey time
Train	1 daily	5 hrs 25 mins

Notes

Reservations are needed on most services in Spain. For Madrid and Seville, change at Burgos.

KEY JOURNEYS

San Sebastián–Burgos ETT table 689

Type	Frequency	Typical journey time
Train	5 daily	3 hrs 5 mins

Burgos–Bilbao ETT table 689

Type	Frequency	Typical journey time
Train	4–5 daily	3 hrs 10 mins

If it were ever possible to make a pilgrimage by rail, this is it, for **Santiago de Compostela** (or just plain Santiago to most) has been the objective for millions of pilgrims over many centuries, walking the routes from France and across northern Spain that have come to be known as the 'Camino de Santiago'. San Sebastián stands on the coast beneath the green, rainy foothills of the Pyrenees in the Basque province, known to the assertively independent Basque people as *Euskadi*. Never conquered either by the Romans or the Moors, the Basques suffered appalling repression during the Franco period and their language, one of Europe's oldest, was banned. This area has a reputation for the best cuisine in Spain.

Burgos and **León**, both with superlative cathedrals, lie in the great *meseta* (high plain) of Castilla y León (formerly known as Old Castile). To the north rise the Picos de Europa, not that well served by public transport, but offering some of the best mountain scenery in the country. By contrast, Galicia, comprising Spain's northwest corner, is lushly verdant and intricately hilly, with a complicated coastline buffeted by Atlantic gusts and characterised by fjord-like scenery.

SAN SEBASTIÁN (DONOSTIA)

Known as Donostia to the Basques, San Sebastián is now an elegant resort, with tamarisks gracing the promenade that runs along a crescent-shaped bay. Formerly a whaling and deep-sea fishing port doubling as a stopover for pilgrims en route to Santiago de Compostela (p205), San Sebastián really came into its own in the mid-19th century, when someone recommended sea-bathing as a cure for Queen Isabel II's herpes. She arrived, along with a great retinue, and San Sebastián became fashionable.

Take time to wander the streets of the 'old' town, or *parte vieja*, nestled at the foot of Monte Urgull. Although mainly rebuilt in the 19th century, it retains a characterful maze of small streets, tiny darkened shops and bars, arcaded plazas like the **Plaza de la Constitución**, which used to serve as a bullring, and churches such as the beautiful baroque **Basílica of Santa María del Coro**. Fishing is still much in evidence, with the daily catch on show on stalls in the fish market.

The **Museum of San Telmo** occupies a former Dominican monastery, with archaeological displays in the cloister and a changing exhibition in the church. At the far end of the quay are the **Naval Museum** and the renovated **Aquarium**.

For superb views, climb **Monte Urgull** itself, topped by a much-rebuilt fort (the **Castillo de la Mota**). Standing proudly near the top of the hill is the statue of the **Sagrado Corazón de Jesús**, which watches over the city.

Spain

🚆 **RENFE: Estación del Norte**, Paseo de Francia. Cross the ornate María-Cristina Bridge, turn right, and it is a few mins' walk through the 19th-century area to the Old Town. **Euskí Tren: Estación de Amara**, Plaza de Easo. Beware of being hounded by unregistered hotel owners who group outside the station. Luggage lockers.

ℹ️ **Tourist Offices**: The municipal and regional Tourist Offices have joined forces in a huge tourist information complex on the main pedestrian promenade, Alameda de Boulevard 8, ☎ 94 302 31 50 (www.sansebastian.turismo.com).

🏠 For budget accommodation head for the Old Town: hidden amongst the narrow streets are many *pensiones*. Try **Pensión Amaiur**, C. 31 de Agosto, ☎ 94 342 96 54 (www.pensionamaiur.com), which offers spotless, comfortable rooms and a friendly welcome, or the newly refurbished **Adore Plaza**, Plaza de la Constitución 6, ☎ 94 342 22 70 (www.adoreplaza.com), doubles from €45. Rooms can be difficult to find during July and Aug. **Youth hostels (HI): Albergue La Sirena**, Paseo de Igueldo 25, ☎ 94 331 02 68 (www.donostiaalbergues.org), 3 km to station, 🚌 5/6/15/16/ 22/24/25/27; **Albergue Ulia**, Paseo de Ulia 297, ☎ 94 348 34 80 (www.donostiaalbergues.org), 5 km from city centre. There is a **campsite**, **Camping Igueldo**, on the fringes of the city at Pueblo de Igueldo, ☎ 94 321 45 02 (www.campingigueldo.com), 🚌 16 from Alameda del Boulevard.

🍴 San Sebastián has a reputation for gourmet cuisine; there are many superb backstreet tapas bars – monkfish kebabs, stuffed peppers and wild mushroom vol-au-vents may be on offer. There are two excellent markets: **La Bretxa**, on Alameda del Boulevard, and **San Martin**, near the cathedral on C. Loiola. For the best small **restaurants**, try the Old Town and the fishing harbour at the north end of Playa de la Concha.

SIDE TRIPS TO BILBAO AND SANTANDER

These trips can be done by narrow-gauge railway (Euskí Tren) or bus from San Sebastián (ETT tables 686, 688; alternatively there are trains from Zaragoza and Madrid/ Ávila/Burgos, all via Miranda de Ebro; ETT tables 653, 689).

Bilbao, a sprawling industrial port, has been put firmly on the tourist map since 1997 with the opening of the **Museo Guggenheim Bilbao**, ☎ 94 435 90 80 (www. guggenheim-bilbao.es), Tues–Sun, 1000–2000, open daily in July–Aug. This stunning modern art gallery has changing exhibitions of part of the collections of the fabulously wealthy New York art collector Solomon R Guggenheim. It's one of the most talked-about examples of architecture that came out of the late 20th century, and its titanium-clad geometry looks different according to where you approach it from. Elsewhere the **Museo de Belles Artes** in Doña Casilda Iturriza Park surveys early Spanish art up to the 17th century, and has collections of Basque, Dutch/Flemish and contemporary works. Bilbao's old town, on the right bank of the river and beneath the hillside, is pleasant for strolling around. **Tourist Office**: Plaza Ensanche 11, ☎ 94 479 57 60 (www.bilbao.net/bilbaoturismo). The **HI hostel** is at Carretera Basurto-Kastrexana 70, ☎ 94 427 00 54 (www.albergue.bilbao.net), dorm beds from €14.45; take 🚌 58 from the rail station. Buses run from the **airport** to the city centre (C. Sendeja) every 20 mins.

Santander is an elegant, cosmopolitan resort and university town set in a beautiful bay and endowed with fine sandy beaches. The town is quite modern, having been destroyed in 1941 not by bombing but by a tornado. There are up to four buses a day to **Potes**, on the edge of the **Picos de Europa** mountains (see p204). Trains from Santander to Torrelevega connect with frequent buses to the touristy town of **Santillana del Mar** (not actually by the sea, despite its name); from there it's a 20-minute walk to the **Caves of Altamira**, one of the greatest Stone Age painted caves anywhere. Alas, they're not open (because of the damage visitors' breath causes), but an exact replica is alongside, by an excellent museum (closed Sat) and a natural cavern. **Comillas** (six buses a day from Santander) is a great little seaside resort, with an idyllic beach, plus an Old Town where the moneyed classes of Madrid and Barcelona built villas, some in the Modernist tradition of Gaudí. **Santander Tourist Office**: (regional) C. Hernán Cortés 4, Mercado del Este, ☎94 231 07 08, (www.turismodecantabria.com); (municipal) Jardines de Pereda, ☎94 220 30 00. A centrally located backpackers' hostel (non HI) is **Albergue El Albaicín**, C. Francisco Palazuelos 21, ☎94 221 77 53; dorms and doubles, open July-mid Sept.

VITORIA (GASTEIZ)

Vitoria, capital of the Basque country and known to the Basques as Gasteiz, is surprisingly little visited. Known for making playing cards and chocolate truffles, it also has considerable charm. Within ugly outskirts, the almost perfectly preserved medieval hill town focuses on handsomely arcaded squares; at the centre of **Plaza de la Virgen Blanca**, a monument commemorates a nearby battle of 1813 in which Napoleon's army was defeated by the Duke of Wellington. From here you can explore a tangled web of narrow streets, filled with inexpensive eateries as well as several fine churches and Renaissance palaces. Look out for the **Church of San Miguel**, beside the steps at the top of the large and open Plaza de la Virgen Blanca, and the 16th-century **Palacio de Escoriaza-Esquibel**, with its fine Plateresque-style patio. The **Catedral de Santa María** is currently closed for renovations until further notice (tours are available if you want to see how the restoration is progressing); its unfinished 20th-century replacement, the huge neo-Gothic **Cathedral of María Inmaculada** (open 1100–1400), stands amid parkland in the flat new town. From here you can stroll C. Correría, where a mansion houses the **Museo de Bellas Artes** (Museum of Fine Art), containing works by Picasso and Miró.

🚉 Off the C. Eduardo Dato, about four blocks from the cathedral and Tourist Office.

ℹ️ **Tourist Office**: Plaza General Loma, ☎94 516 15 98 (www.vitoria-gasteiz.org/turismo).

🏠 **Carlos Abaitua Aterpetxea**, Escultor Isaac Diez ☎ 94 514 81 00, dorm beds from €13.90.

Spain

BURGOS

In medieval times Burgos grew rich on the wool trade, and in the 11th century the city became the capital of Christian Spain as well as home of Rodrigo Díaz de Vivar, better known as El Cid, the romantic mercenary. During the Civil War in the 1930s, it again rose to fame as the Nationalist headquarters. It was here that Franco formed his Falangist government and (18 months later) declared a ceasefire that ended the war. Burgos has now grown into a large and busy modern city, but its heart is the atmospheric Old Town around the ruined castle (itself of little interest apart from the views from it). The grand entrance to old Burgos is formed by the **Arco de Santa María**, a fortified 14th-century gateway, altered and decorated in 1536 to pacify Charles V, depicting his figure and those of the founder (Diego Porcelos) and El Cid (whose equestrian statue stands near the **Puente de San Pablo**). From here, it's a short walk to the bulk of the main attractions, eating places and hotels. Foremost is the **cathedral**, consecrated in 1260 but not completed until the 18th century, making it the third largest cathedral in Spain (after Toledo and Seville), and also probably the richest. Amidst the splendour of the 19 chapels and 38 altars, positively dripping in gold leaf, is El Cid's unobtrusive tomb and a grotesquely real-looking crucifix, made in the 13th century with human hair, fingernails and a body of buffalo hide. Evening sees everyone promenade along the **Paseo del Espolón**, graced with fountains and statues and stretching along the river, with cafés and restaurants making the most of the atmosphere.

WHERE NEXT FROM BURGOS?

*One train a day makes the 4-hr 30-min journey from Burgos southwards to Madrid (ETT table 689), a beautiful route over the **Sierra de Guadarrama**, rising to over 1400 m. Alternatively, services to Salamanca (2 hrs 35 mins; ETT table 689) join the **Madrid–Salamanca** route (p186).*

*En route you can change at Medina del Campo for **Zamora** (ETT table 680): it's refreshingly untouristy, with an old centre, a sublime cathedral noted for its Black Tapestries (made in Flanders in the 15th century, depicting scenes of the Trojan War and Hannibal's battles) and a clutch of Romanesque churches in and around Plaza Viriato. By Plaza Mayor is **Hostal La Reina** (C. La Reina 1, ☎ 98 053 39 39, doubles €29–35), a pleasant and inexpensive place to stay. A couple of blocks north of the rail station is the bus station, with hourly direct services to Salamanca (www.ayto-zamora.org).*

Outside the Old Town, the 16th-century **Casa de Miranda** houses one of Spain's best archaeological museums, exhibiting finds from the Roman city of Clunia. The collection The collection moved to the glossy, high-tech Museum of Evolution in early 2010. Two of Spain's most interesting monasteries are on the town's outskirts: the Cistercian convent of **Las Huelgas**, of the once powerful abbesses of Huelgas (closed Mon; free Wed), and **La Cartuja de Miraflores** (free, open daily), reached through a shady park, and full of art, including the carved tomb of Juan II and Isabel of Portugal, four years in the making, and a lifelike wooden statue of St Bruno.

🚆 About 1 km southwest of the cathedral on the far side of the Arlanzón River. 🚌 3/5/7.

ℹ️ **Tourist Office**: Pza San Rey Fernando, ☎94 728 88 74 (www.aytoburgos.es). (regional) Plaza Alonso Martínez, ☎94 720 31 25 (www.jcyl.es).

🏠 **Youth hostel (HI)**: **Gil de Siloe**, Avda General Vigón, ☎94 722 02 77 (gildesiloe-ij@jycl.es), beginning July–mid-Sept only; 2.5 km from station. **HS Hilton**, Vitoria 165, ☎94 722 51 16; a reasonable, recently renovated *hostal* (although not very central), doubles €35; absolutely nothing to do with the Hilton chain.

LEÓN

Nestling between the Bernesga and Torio rivers and surrounded by the rolling plains of the *meseta*, León was founded by the Romans (the *Legio Septimo,* or Seventh Legion, gave its name to the city), and over the years was ruled by Visigoths, Moors and Christians. In 1188, Alfonso IX summoned his first Cortes (parliament) here – one of the earliest democratic governments in Europe – but the court moved away permanently in the 13th century, and León became little more than a trading centre until 1978, when it was made the capital of the province of León. Today it's thriving once again. The major monuments are within easy walking distance of each other in the old city.

Of all the city's buildings, the most spectacular from the outside is the 16th-century, Plateresque-style **Hostal de San Marcos** (now an upmarket *parador*, or state-run hotel), which was founded by Ferdinand and Isabella, the Catholic monarchs, as a pilgrim hostel and was later rebuilt as the headquarters for the Knights of Santiago. What is left of the old city is still bounded by fragments of the 14th-century city walls, which followed the line of the original Roman (and medieval) fortifications. Thirty-one of the original 80 bastions are still standing, and are best seen around the cathedral and the **Royal Basilica of St Isidore**. Much influenced by the cathedrals of France, the **cathedral** has some of the very finest medieval stained glass in Europe (even rivalling Chartres in brilliance), with 125 windows dappling the interior with coloured light. Meanwhile, the Royal Basílica possesses a magnificent Romanesque pantheon, where some 20 monarchs are laid to rest.

🚆 **RENFE: El Norte**, C. Astorga, on the west bank of the river. **FEVE**: Avda del Padre Isla 48, near the Basilica de San Isidoro. Luggage lockers.

ℹ️ **Tourist Office**: Palacio de los Guzmanes, C. Cid 1, ☎98 723 70 82 (www.leon.es); next to the cathedral (turn right out of the station to reach it).

🏠 The city has a wide range of hotels and guesthouses, ranging downwards from the ultra luxurious **San Marcos** (see above), Plaza San Marcos 7, ☎98 723 73 00 (www.parador.es). The Tourist Office has a list of places to stay. A good area to find budget accommodation is on and around Avda de Roma and Avda de Ordoño II. Budget places include **Pensión Avenida**, Avda de Palencia 4, 3rd floor, ☎98 722 37 63, double (shared bathroom) €28, in a pleasant 1920s building.

Spain

Youth hostels (HI): **Albergue Unamuno**, San Pelayo 15, ☎98 723 30 10 (July–Sept; albergue@unamuno.es); **Residencia Juvenil Infanta Doña Sancha**, C. Correndera 2, ☎98 720 34 14, July–mid-Sept; **Consejo de Europa**, Paseo del Parque 2, ☎98 720 02 06, July–mid-Sept; **Albergue La Estación Pedrún**, C. Campos Góticos, ☎98 708 18 32 (alberguedeleon@hotmail.com), open all year.

SIDE TRIP TO THE PICOS DE EUROPA   From León you can head north by bus (to **Posada de Valdeón** via **Riaño**; other approaches include from Santander to Potes and Fuente Dé; services are infrequent and you should check with Tourist Offices what's running) into the high mountains of the **Picos de Europa**, a stunning (often snow-capped) cave-riddled karst limestone wilderness that still shelters a few wolves and bears. **Potes** has a good choice of accommodation, restaurants and campsites, jeep excursions into the Picos plus three buses a day to **Fuente Dé** for the **cable car** (where you can walk 4 km to the Hotel Refugio de Áliva, then down to Espinama, for the same bus back to Potes; but expect long queues for the cable car in summer).

Said to have been the first sign of European land seen by sailors returning from the New World, the peaks rise almost vertically from the Bay of Biscay and offer magnificent views and walking, notably through gorges (such as the **Cares Gorge**). The scope for longer hut-to-hut walks is more limited, unless you're extremely fit and experienced in mountain walking; the area isn't huge (roughly 40 km across) but it's very easy to get lost in if you stray from the waymarked paths, and there are numerous sink holes and other hazards. Unreliable weather is a further drawback: for much of the time the peaks are swathed in mist. Summer is obviously the time to go, though rooms get heavily booked up from late July to the end of Aug.

ASTORGA

Described by the Roman historian Pliny in the 1st century AD as a 'magnificent city', this is now a small, gracefully decaying country town, capital of the bleak moorland region of La Maragatería.

Sections of the 6-m Roman walls survive around the Old Town. Towering over it all, the 15th–17th-century **cathedral** displays an intriguing hotchpotch of late Gothic, Renaissance, baroque and Plateresque styles, with motley towers, one grey and the other pink (there wasn't enough stone to complete it all in the same material). It's a frequent visit for pilgrims on their way to Santiago; next door, the flamboyant **Palacio Episcopal** (Episcopal Palace), designed by Gaudí in 1889, now houses the **Museo de los Caminos** (Museum of the Pilgrims' Way). Smaller buildings of interest centre on the **Plaza Mayor**.

🚉 Plaza de la Estación, about 1 km east of the town centre. Lockers.

ⓘ **Tourist Office**: Plaza Eduardo Castro 5, ☎98 761 82 22 (www.ayuntamientodeastorga.com). From the station head straight on up Pedro de Castro, across to Enfermeras, then right through Plaza Obispo Alcolea and up Los Sitios. The Tourist Office is on your left near the Episcopal Palace.

GETTING AROUND SANTIAGO

The Old City is tiny and everything of interest is easily accessible on foot. A tourist train tours the sights of interest, leaving C. San Francisco every 20 mins (July and Aug only).

Budget options include **Delfín**, Carretera Madrid-Coruña 417, ☎ 98 760 24 14, doubles €40 (quite far from the centre); **Pensión Garcia**, Bajada del Postigo 3, ☎ 98 761 60 46, doubles (shared bathroom) €30; and **La Ruta Leonesa**, Carretera de León 82, ☎ 98 761 50 37, doubles €30.

SANTIAGO DE COMPOSTELA

A magnet for millions of pilgrims for the last thousand years, Santiago de Compostela hit the big time when the tomb of St James (*Sant' Iago*, Spain's patron saint) was discovered in AD 813, supposedly by a shepherd who was guided to the site by a star. Destroyed in 997 by the Moors, the town was rebuilt during the 11th century and began its golden age. In the 12th century, the Pope declared it a Holy City: for Catholics, only Jerusalem and Rome share this honour. The newer sections of the city do not have a great deal of charm, but the Old Town (contained within the medieval walls) is one of the most beautiful urban landscapes in Europe. It's not entirely given over to the pilgrimage, endowed as it is with a theatre, a concert hall and plenty of bars and clubs offering dancing and late-night drinking. Around the Old Town, free entertainment in the form of music and singing is provided by *tunas* – groups of buskers dressed in medieval clothes. Souvenir shops do a roaring trade.

The 12th-century Colegiata de Santa María del Sar, about 2 km from the Old Town, has a beautiful Romanesque cloister with wild flowers sprouting from its crumbling stone walls; the pillars inside the church lean at such precarious angles that it's a wonder the building still stands. Alameda is a delightful park, with shady walkways, ancient oak trees and superb views of the cathedral and the surrounding countryside.

The Old Town contains a host of fine churches and monasteries as well as notable secular buildings tucked down the narrow side streets. The **cathedral** (started in 1075) is the obvious centre of attention. Its existing 18th-century baroque façade covers the original 12th-century façade, the *Pórtico de la Gloria* by Maestro Mateo, said to be the greatest single surviving work of Romanesque art in the world, with 200 exceptionally imaginative and detailed sculptures. To celebrate their arrival in the Holy City, pilgrims traditionally touch the base of the **Jesse tree** on the central column, accordingly known as the 'Pilgrim Pillar', and deeply worn down by millions of fingers over the centuries. On the other side of the pillar, facing the altar, is a figure of the sculptor Mateo, popularly known as the 'Saint of bumps on the head', as people knock heads with him in the belief that his talent is

ATLAS THE BALL BOY
In the **Praza do Toral**, a little statue of **Atlas** stands on top of one of the buildings. Legend has it that if any female student in Santiago is still a virgin at graduation time, Atlas will drop his ball!

contagious. Pilgrims mark the end of their journey by climbing up behind the shiny statue of St James and kissing the scallop shell (the symbol of the pilgrimage) on the back of his gown. The interior is dominated by a silver Mexican altar and a dazzling 17th-century baroque altarpiece. The **museum** contains a valuable collection of tapestries, including a series based on cartoons by Goya, manuscripts from the *Codex Calixtus* and a huge silver *botafumeiro* (incense burner) that is spectacularly swung through the transept on special occasions, with eight men clinging to it.

Four plazas surround the cathedral, each architectural gems in themselves. On the largest, the pigeon-populated Plaza del Obradoiro, stand the impressive **Hostal de los Reyes Católicos** (the former hospital for pilgrims, now a *parador*) and the classical **Pazo de Raxoi** of 1772 (now the town hall).

Along one side of Plaza de Quintana is the austere façade of the **Monasterio de San Paio de Antelares**. Entrance to the church and the monastery's **Museum of Sacred Art** are via the steps at one end of the square. Another landmark is the 16th-century **Monastery of San Martín Pinario** (whose monks used to give new clothes to pilgrims who looked worse for wear after their journey), though the interior is no longer open to the public.

THE FEAST OF ST JAMES IN SANTIAGO

The city's main fiesta, the feast of **St James**, takes place in the three weeks leading up to 25 July. The entertainment becomes ever more riotous until the eve of the feast itself, which begins with a massive firework display in the Plaza do Obradoiro. The following day the statue of St James is processed through the streets in a haze of incense, followed by *gigantes*, vast masked figures representing the Christians and Moors.

Rúa do Hórreo, 1 km south of the old city. C2 goes into the centre, but it's quicker to walk. Luggage lockers, accommodation service and cash machine.

10 km from the centre, 98 154 75 01; takes 30 mins.

Bus station: **Estación Central de Autobuses**, Plaza Camilo Díaz Baliño, 30-min walk from the Old Town; 10 runs every 20 mins from Plaza de Galicia. There is a good local bus system and route plans are posted at most stops.

Taxis: There are taxi ranks at the bus and train stations; 98 158 24 50 or 98 159 84 88.

i **Tourist Offices:** (regional) Rúa do Vilar 30, 98 158 40 81 (www.turgalicia.com); (municipal) Rúa do Vilar 63, 98 155 51 29 (www.santiagoturismo.com). From the station turn right along Avenida de Lugo then left up Rúa do Hórreo, to Plaza de Galicia.

During the three weeks leading up to the feast of St James on 25 July, the town is absolutely packed and you should book well in advance. Accommodation ranges from the 5-star **Hostal de**

los Reyes Católicos, Plaza do Obradoiro 1, ☎98 158 22 00 (www.parador.es), €€€, a magnificent 16th-century pilgrim hostel built by Ferdinand and Isabella, to an array of small, relatively inexpensive guesthouses in both the old and new parts of the city. For budget accommodation in the Old Town, try around Rúa do Vilar and Rúa Raiña. **Hospedaje Ramos**, Rúa Raiña 18, 2nd floor, ☎98 158 18 59, doubles €36, is very central, with small, basic rooms. Other good-value places are **Hospedaje Sofia**, Rúa del Cardenal Payá 16, ☎98 158 51 50, doubles €33; **Hostal Pazo de Agra**, Rúa da Caldeirería 37, ☎98 158 35 17 (www.hostalpazodeagra.com), doubles €40; **Hospedaje San Jaime**, Rúa do Vilar 12, 2nd floor, ☎98 158 31 34, doubles €25; **Pensión Bandeira**, Rúa Santiago de Chile 15, 2nd floor, ☎98 159 63 93 (www.pensionbandeira.com), doubles €38; **Hostal Fornos**, Rúa Hórreo 7, ☎98 158 51 30 (www.fornossantiago.com), doubles from €39. Rúa de Montero Ríos (just outside the Old Town) has a number of reasonably priced hostels. **Youth hostel (HI):** Carretera de Santiago Aeropuerto km 3, ☎98 155 89 42, towards the airport, is part of the Monte do Gozo complex (see below), and not ideally located.

There are three large **campsites** outside the city. **Cancelas**, Rúa do 25 de Xullo 35, ☎98 158 02 66 (www.campingascancelas.com), is the best option, being only 2 km from the centre (🚌 6 from Plaza de Galicia). **Campsites: Monte do Gozo**, Carretera del Aeropuerto km 3, ☎98 155 89 42 (www.montedogozo.com), 3 km from centre of Santiago, 🚌 7/UN (note this site is more of a holiday complex and residencia with bungalows; camping July & Aug only); **Punta Batuda**, Playa de Ornanda-Gaviotas, Porto do Son (30 km from Santiago), ☎98 176 65 42 (www.puntabatuda.com), 🚌 Santiago-Noia, every 30 mins.

🍴 There are plenty of **budget restaurants** around the Old Town, especially on the streets leading south from the cathedral. Slightly further out of town, the Plaza Roxa area, near the university, is very cheap.

Side Trip to A Coruña

A Coruña (frequent rail services, taking about 1 hr 5 mins) is a large maritime city, with its old town on an isthmus between the beach and the harbour. The town's main attractions (after its beaches) are the **Castelo de San Antón**, which now houses an Archaeology Museum, and the **Torre de Hércules**, a 2nd-century Roman lighthouse, restored in the 18th century and still in use today, standing at the extreme north of the isthmus. There are also a number of fine churches and gardens. Contemporary attractions include Domus, or Museum of Man, designed by Arata Isozahi, with lots of touchy-feely exhibits, and, just around the headland, the Aquarium, with a huge subterranean tank and outdoor seal pool.

The rail station is a 45-min walk from the centre; 🚌 5 goes to the **Tourist Office:** Plaza de María Pita 6, ☎98 192 30 93 and Plaza de Orense, ☎98 118 43 40 (www.coruna.es). Budget accommodation includes **Hostal Mara**, Rúa Galera 49, ☎98 122 18 01 (www.hostalmara.com), doubles from €38; **Carbonara**, Rúa Nueva 16, ☎98 122 52 51 (www.hostalcarbonara.com), doubles €36; and **Roma**, Rúa Nueva 3, ☎98 122 80 75 (www.pension roma.com), doubles from €42; July to Sept only.

WHERE NEXT FROM SANTIAGO?

*Carry on to **Lisbon** by taking the **Lisbon–Santiago** route in reverse (p190).*

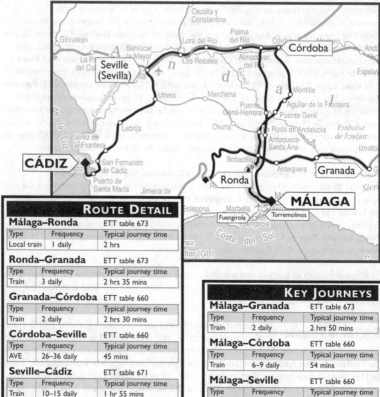

ROUTE DETAIL

Málaga–Ronda — ETT table 673

Type	Frequency	Typical journey time
Local train	1 daily	2 hrs

Ronda–Granada — ETT table 673

Type	Frequency	Typical journey time
Train	3 daily	2 hrs 35 mins

Granada–Córdoba — ETT table 660

Type	Frequency	Typical journey time
Train	2 daily	2 hrs 30 mins

Córdoba–Seville — ETT table 660

Type	Frequency	Typical journey time
AVE	26–36 daily	45 mins

Seville–Cádiz — ETT table 671

Type	Frequency	Typical journey time
Train	10–15 daily	1 hr 55 mins

KEY JOURNEYS

Málaga–Granada — ETT table 673

Type	Frequency	Typical journey time
Train	2 daily	2 hrs 50 mins

Málaga–Córdoba — ETT table 660

Type	Frequency	Typical journey time
Train	6–9 daily	54 mins

Málaga–Seville — ETT table 660

Type	Frequency	Typical journey time
Train	4–6 daily	1 hr 55 mins

Málaga–Algeciras — ETT tables 671, 673

Type	Frequency	Typical journey time
Train	3 daily	4 hrs 15 mins

Algeciras–Tangier — ETT table 2502

Type	Frequency	Typical journey time
Ship	up to 4 daily	2 hrs 30 mins
Hydrofoil	up to 4 daily	1 hr 20 mins

Notes

AVE high-speed trains run Madrid–Córdoba–Sevilla and Málaga on dedicated high-speed lines. Special fares apply and reservations are compulsory.

Málaga to Ronda: change at Bobadilla on most services. Málaga to Granada: change at Bobadilla. Málaga to Algeciras: change at Bobadilla.

Andalucía (Andalusia) conjures up the classic images of Spain – with great parched plains dotted with cypresses and groves of olive trees, backdrops of rugged sierras, flamenco music, lively fiestas and timeless hilltop castles. The Moors left evidence of their occupation in the form of spectacular monuments such as the Alhambra in **Granada** and the Mezquita in **Córdoba**, and there's also a very rich Catholic heritage.

Sit on the left-hand side of the train as you leave the port of **Málaga**, for the views soon become stupendous as you snake along the Garganta del Chorro, a huge chasm 180 m deep, only visible from the train.

The scenery is less special after the little rail junction of Bobadilla, but westwards lies **Ronda**, one of the most spectacular of the aptly named *Pueblos Blancos* ('white towns') of Andalucía, perched improbably above a precipice. There's more of the same at **Arcos de la Frontera**, reachable by bus from Ronda and Cádiz. **Antequera** merits a stop for its remarkable prehistoric dolmens, but top of most travellers' must-see lists is Granada. From there, you could take a bus up to **Capileira**, the highest village in the Sierra Nevada range, and look down on Granada. Cádiz is an atmospheric old port, but much of the rest of the coast, at least along the built-up Costa del Sol, is a mess.

For further information check out the websites www.andalucia.com and www.andalucia.org.

A visit to the region can tie in with a ferry trip to Morocco (p142).

MÁLAGA

The fourth largest city in Spain and a busy working port, Málaga is also the communications centre for the holiday coasts on either side. At first sight it isn't pretty, with high-rise modern apartment blocks built up close together within close range of a dismal-looking canalised river. But the centre is a hundred times more cheerful and resolutely Spanish in character, with a tree-lined main boulevard, dark back alleys, an atmospheric covered market and traditional shops and bars where Spanish (not holidaymakers' English!) is very much the first language. Restaurants are relatively inexpensive and lively, and the city has a real sense of place far removed from the tourist excesses of much of the rest of the Costa del Sol.

THEATRE IN THE OPEN

At **Paseo del Parque** there is an open-air theatre, which sometimes stages free productions in summer (ask at the Tourist Office for details).

Málaga's past is most evident in the area near the port. The long, shady walks of Paseo del Parque are overlooked by the **Alcazaba** (🚍 35 from Paseo del Parque), a fort built by the Moors on Roman foundations; it has the character of the Alhambra in Granada, albeit on a smaller scale, and the views extend over the city to the coast. Its neighbour, the **Gibralfaro** castle (separate entrance), is of Phoenician origin, reconstructed later by the Moors, and offers even better views.

Just off the Paseo is the **Cathedral**, set in a secluded square and built between the 16th and 18th centuries. Close by, in Calle San Agustín, is the city's star attraction, the **Museo Picasso** (www.museopicassomalaga.org), where you can admire over 150 of the master's works in a 16th-century palace. Picasso was born in Málaga in 1881 and you can visit his birthplace, now the **Museo Casa Natal**, on the Plaza de la Merced (www.fundacionpicasso.es) with works of art and personal effects. **Plaza de la Merced** is the city's liveliest and most attractive square with several good bars and restaurants. Fans of contemporary art might also like to visit the **Centro de Arte Contemporáneo** (www.cacmálaga.org) on Calle Alemania. It has a small permanent collection of art and is highly regarded for the quality of its temporary exhibitions.

Málaga buzzes after dark, with most action around the Plaza de la Merced and Plaza Uncibay. Serious clubbers tend to converge at **Roof** (Jardines del Puerto, Puerto Banús), and many a decent band graces the stage of **ZZ Pub** (C. Tejón y Rodriguez). **O'Neill's Irish Pub** (C. Luis de Velázquez 3) always promises the sort of knees-up that makes Brits feel at home, but for a slightly quieter, more traditional drink seek out **El Pimpi** (C. Granada 62) and look out for the signed barrels by the Picasso family in this warrenlike bodega. At **Vista Andalucía** (Av. de los Guindos) you'll see authentic – as opposed to plastic, for-the-tourists – flamenco, and if you'd like some live music to go with that, head for **El Jardín** (1 C. Cañón). You can blend into the student crowd any night at **Weekend** (Plaza de la Merced 14), a great place to kick back and relax. If you packed your tux or Dior gown, you could always James Bond it at the **Fortuna Nightclub** (Benalmádena Costa), which has its own casino and cabaret dancers. They'll have been expecting you. The flares-and-miniskirt retro brigade will love the classics that belt through the woofers at **Disco Inferno** (Muelle de Rivera Local 7-9, Puerto Banús). If you're not in town for long, you'll find the best encapsulation of the local night-time vibe at **Olivia Valere** (Ctra de Istan), which has the lot (dance floor, restaurant, chill-out zone) and is amazingly good value if you're trying to be thrifty. In summer and at the weekends and holidays there is also a lively young beach nightlife scene at **Malagueta** (the city's beach front) and **Pedregalejo**, a short bus ride along the coast.

Explanada de la Estación (luggage lockers and accommodation services; for currency exchange go to the nearby bus station), a 20–30-min walk from the centre of town. 3 goes to Alameda Principal and Paseo del Parque near the centre. Local trains for the coastal resorts leave from here as well (at a different level), and this line is also served by another more centrally located station, Centro Alameda.

8 km from the city, 95 204 88 04/90 240 47 04. There is a Tourist Office in the main hall. Trains to Málaga run every 30 mins, taking about 10 mins. There is also a bus every 20 mins (19), which stops near the Ayuntamiento (City Hall) and takes 20–25 mins.

i **Tourist Offices**: (municipal) Casa del Jardinero–Park, Avda. Cervantes 1, ☎ 95 213 47 30, (www.malagaturismo.com); branch at Paseo de los Tilos 21, plus information vans stationed throughout the city; (regional) Pasaje de Chinitas 4, ☎ 95 221 34 45, fax 95 222 94 21. There is a small municipal office in the bus station, Paseo de los Tilos.

🛏 There is a good choice of hotels, including a small *parador* set in the gardens of the Gibralfaro castle (🚌 35 from Paseo del Parque) above the town. Budget accommodation is functional, but lacking in any obvious regional charm. Good areas for cheap lodgings are around the Plaza de la Constitución (northwest of the cathedral) and immediately off either side of the Alameda Principal (although the south side is less salubrious). In high season, central Málaga is lively at night (all night); the only solution is to ask for a room away from the street, or buy earplugs. **Hostal Domus**, C. Juan Valera 20, ☎ 95 229 71 64 (www.hostaldomus.com), doubles €42, is friendly and central. **Hostal Juanita**, C. Alarcón Luján 8, ☎ 95 221 35 86 (www.hostaljuanita.es), doubles from €36. South of Alameda Principal, and slightly more expensive, are **Picasso's Corner**, C. San Juan de Letrán 9, ☎ 95 221 22 87 (www.picassoscorner.com), a backpackers' hostel with mixed dorms (€18) and doubles (€40), and in the centre of town **Hotel Alameda**, C. Casas de Campos 3, ☎ 95 222 20 99, €. **Youth hostel (HI): Albergue Juvenil de Málaga**, Plaza Pío XII 6, ☎ 95 230 81 70 (www.inturjoven.com), (🚌 18), also has camping in summer. **Campsite**: the nearest is 12 km away in **Torremolinos**, Carretera Cádiz-Barcelona Km 228, ☎ 95 238 26 02, reached by 🚌 Málaga–Benalmádena or train.

🍽 There are several good **restaurants** around the cathedral, especially along C. Cañón. Seafood and *gazpacho* are good bets. **Paseo Marítimo** and the seafront in Pedregalejo are the best areas for seafood restaurants. Málaga gives its name to an inexpensive sweet fortified red wine. Convent *dulces* are cakes made by nuns throughout Andalucía: in the morning nuns of **Santa Clara** at C. Cister 11 (just east of the cathedral) sell these.

SIDE TRIPS TO THE COSTA DEL SOL

A frequent train service runs west from Málaga (Centro–Alameda and RENFE stations) along the **Costa del Sol**, connecting it to the airport and the busy resorts of Torremolinos, Benalmádena and Fuengirola. **Torremolinos** is a tacky, exuberant, concrete high-rise resort, with a plethora of discos, fish and chip shops and bars, much of it run by a huge expat population. The western part of the resort is more attractive, frequented by Spanish holidaymakers. There are abundant beach facilities along the expansive stretch of grey sands. To the east, **Fuengirola** is another sun and sand haunt, slightly calmer than Torremolinos, but equally ugly. **Marbella**, with its many beaches, charming Old Town and glitzy Puerto Banús marina, is further but a more attractive option in every way. You can go by train from Málaga airport to Fuengirola, then take a bus to Marbella. Alternatively there's a direct bus to Marbella from Málaga airport.

Another popular excursion is by boat (75 mins) to **Benalmádena Costa** (alternatively you could catch the C1 train to Benalmádena). This smart marina resort has bars, restaurants and family attractions. Benalmádena 'Pueblo', the original village 5 km inland, is a charming if somewhat stage-managed traditional whitewashed village.

Spain

Málaga is also at the centre of a bus network reaching out to many smaller resorts. Eastwards, it is possible to reach Nerja and other assorted seaside towns all the way to Almería. **Nerja** is a relatively peaceful resort, built around an old town that still feels distinctly Spanish, about 50 km from Málaga. Buses run approximately every hour, the journey taking 1 hr 30 mins. It is noted for its panoramic views of the coast, especially from the promenade known as the **Balcón de Europa**. Just east of the town is the **Cuevas de Nerja**, a series of large caverns full of breathtaking rock formations (**Tourist Office:** C. Carmen 1, ☎ 95 252 15 31; www.nerja.org).

RONDA

Ronda is a small town of pre-Roman origin set in the rugged Serranía de Ronda, split in two by a dizzying gorge, with white houses clinging to the rim, and spanned in quite spectacular fashion by an 18th-century bridge known as the **Puente Nuevo**. The view from the bridge is hair-raising, even more so when you learn that it was from here in 1936, during the Civil War, that 512 prisoners of the Republicans were hurled to their deaths, an incident adapted by Ernest Hemingway in *For Whom the Bell Tolls*. It was in Ronda that Pedro Romero invented the modern style of bullfighting – on foot rather than from horseback – and his father is said to have invented the red rag that provokes the bull! Near the bullring is the **Alameda**, a public garden beside the gorge, enjoying breathtaking views of the surrounding area, with olive groves stretching into the hilly distance.

DAY TRIP FROM RONDA

Setenil, reached by a handful of buses per day from Ronda, is a picturesque village crammed into a gorge with houses built into overhanging rock ledges. Take a picnic and enjoy it on the hillside above. Other tourists are unlikely to be much in evidence.

On the other side of the bridge is the old Moorish quarter, with the attractive **Casa del Rey Moro** (House of the Moorish King), an early 18th-century mansion. You can visit the gardens, designed in 1912, and the mines, which provided Ronda with water as early as the 14th century. A path from this side of the bridge leads into the gorge for another interesting view, though the whiff of sewage can be a turn-off. The *Baños Árabes* (Arab Baths) near **Puente San Miguel** were constructed in the late 13th and early 14th centuries and are thought to be the best-preserved baths on the Iberian peninsula. Entry is free. Ronda is at its most charming during one of the many fiestas that occur throughout the year.

🚆 10–15-min walk to centre. Luggage lockers and accommodation service.

ℹ️ **Tourist Office**: (municipal) Plaza de Blas Infante, ☎ 95 218 71 19 (www.turismoderonda.es); (regional) Plaza de España 1, ☎ 95 287 12 72 (www.turismoderonda.es).

🏨 You'll pass plenty of inexpensive places as you walk in from the station. Options include **Hostal San Francisco**, C. María Cabrera 18, ☎ 95 287 32 99, doubles from €50; **Hostal**

Virgen del Rocio, C. Nueva 18, ☎95 287 74 25, doubles €40; and **Hostal Biarritz**, C. Almendra 7 (C. Cristo), ☎95 287 29 10, doubles €25.

GRANADA

Founded, according to legend, by a daughter of either Noah or Hercules, what is not in doubt is that in 1492 Granada was the last of the great Moorish cities to succumb to Ferdinand and Isabella's ferocious Christian Reconquest. The main reason for visiting is to see its fabulous fortress-palace, the **Alhambra**, resplendent on its lush hilltop. If you don't fancy the pleasant but often hot walk uphill from town catch a bus from Plaza Nueva (every 12 mins).

Most of the exterior of the Alhambra (see box) dates from rebuilding in the 13th–14th centuries and is reasonably simple, giving no hint of the decoration inside (www.alhambradegranada.org). There are three principal sets of buildings: the **Alcazaba** (Fortress), the **Alcázar** (Palace), and the **Generalife** (Summer Palace and Gardens), with a combined entrance fee. The number of visitors to some areas of the Alhambra is now being limited to 8000 per day with timed tickets, so it is advisable to arrive in the morning (or reserve your tickets in advance at any branch of La Caixa bank, through any of their yellow Servicaixa machines, or through www. alhambra-tickets.es) if you don't want to face a very long wait to get in. The Generalife shelters a stunning garden with patios and running water; the Moors used their irrigational expertise to divert the River Darro to supply the pools and fountains. The main Christian edifice in the complex is the 16th-century **Palace of Charles V**, which houses the **Museum of Fine Arts** and the **National Museum of Hispano-Islamic Art**. Sat evenings see a parade of newly-married couples being photographed beside the ramparts.

> ## HIGHLIGHTS OF THE ALHAMBRA
> The **Alcazaba** was predominantly used as a military outpost and is the oldest part of the present site. Its **Torre de la Vela** (watchtower), from where the Catholic flag was hoisted in 1492, commands panoramic views of Granada and the Sierra Nevada. The **Alcázar** was the main palace. Richly decorated and stunningly beautiful, with brilliant use of light and space, it was largely built in the 14th century. Of particular note are: the **Mexuar** (council chamber); the **Patio de los Arrayanes**, with an incredible honeycomb cupola made up of thousands of small cells; and the **Patio de los Leones**, so-named for the famous Lions fountain. The **Sala de Embajadores** is the largest and most sumptuous room, its walls covered with inscriptions from the Koran, ornamental motifs, and brilliantly glazed tiles that glint in the sunlight.

In the city below the Alhambra, the **Capilla Real** (Royal Chapel) deserves a visit for the tombs of the Catholic monarchs, Ferdinand and Isabella, and their daughter and her husband; displayed in the Sacristy are some notable paintings from the private collection of Queen Isabella. Next door, the Cathedral was completed in the early 18th century, and boasts a gloomily impressive classical grandeur.

Spain

The **Albaicín** quarter, on the hill opposite the Alhambra, out from the hectic whirl of the city centre, retains some Moorish atmosphere and is a rewarding and tranquil place for a stroll in its maze of stepped alleys; beware of bag-snatchers here. Seek out Calle Calderería Nueva/Calle Calderería Vieja, a narrow street with Moroccan teashops and eateries. Nearby, on the edge of town, are the gypsy cave-dwellings of Sacromonte (buses from Generalife or Plaza Nueva; every 15 mins); note that the gypsy entertainment evenings are a renowned tourist trap. The city has a great flamenco tradition, though, upheld in establishments such as **Peña de la Platería** (Placeta de Toqueros 7, ☎95 821 06 50) in the Albaicín. For general nightlife and lively bars try C. Pedro Antonio de Alarcón, west of the old centre, where Granada's students hang out.

> **BEING PAMPERED IN GRANADA**
> If you're willing to splash out for the experience, **Al Andalus Baths**, C. Santa Ana 16, ☎95 822 99 78 (www.hammamspain.com), provide the chance to bathe in therapeutic waters for 2 hrs in Alhambra-like surroundings; massages are on offer for a very reasonable price.

🚉 Avda de los Andaluces. Lockers. No currency exchange or showers, but you can get information on accommodation. **Viajes Ronda,** ☎95 826 65 15, Camino de Ronda 63, can provide cheap young-persons' rail passes. 🚌 30 leads from the Plaza Nueva to the Alhambra. From the station it's a 20-min walk to the centre or take 🚌 4/6/11. Walk straight out of the station and up Avda de los Andaluces. Turn right onto Avda de la Constitución, which becomes Gran Vía de Colón. Turn off by Reyes Católicos on your right; at Plaza del Carmen follow Calle Mariana Pineda behind Reyes Católicos. The **Tourist Office** is by the cathedral. 🚌 3/4/6/9 go to the Gran Vía and the centre from the main road up the hill from the station; they run every 20 mins.

✈ 17 km from Granada on Ctra de Málaga, ☎95 824 52 00. Only 9 buses a day to the airport (bus info at ☎95 849 01 64).

ℹ️ **Tourist Offices**: (municipal) C. Santa Ana 4, ☎95 822 59 90 (www.granadatur.com); (Regional) Plaza Mariana Pineda 10, ☎95 824 71 28 (www.turismodegranada.org or www.andalucia.org), (closed Sun and after 2pm on Sat). The Bono Turístico city pass costs €22.50, including numerous sights (among them the Alhambra) and 9 bus rides.

🏠 Budget accommodation is plentiful, especially off Plaza Nueva, Plaza de la Trinidad, Gran Vía de Colón and on the streets north of Plaza Mariana Pineda. Cuesta de Gomérez leads directly up to the Alhambra and is lined with hostals. **Hostal Arteaga**, C. Arteaga 3, ☎95 820 88 41, is friendly young hostal with funky rooms, just off the Gran Vía (€48 doubles), and nearby is **Britz**, Cuesta de Gomérez 1, ☎ 95 822 36 52 (www.lisboaweb.com),

GUADIX

Guadix (east of Granada) is an old walled town with a sandstone cathedral, and remarkable for its cave district, the **Barrio Santiago**. Around 10,000 cave dwellings, most with mod cons, have been cut into the pyramids of red rock. Some inhabitants will show you their homes, often for an exorbitant fee; you can find some deserted caves, and there's a museum near San Miguel Church. Frequent buses run from Granada to the town centre and there's a less frequent train service (the station is some way out). The journey by bus or by train takes about 1 hr 15 mins.

SIDE TRIPS
FROM GRANADA

The rail connections from Granada to Córdoba are not that good (though there is a direct bus taking 4 hrs, 3 services a day) and you could instead opt to take the train to **Linares-Baeza**, for the connecting bus to **Baeza** (ETT table 661), which has a sleepy charm in its Renaissance squares and palaces; from there you can take a bus on to **Úbeda**, a stunning Renaissance town, linked by bus to Córdoba and Seville. You can also head on by train from Linares-Baeza through spectacular desert to **Almería**, a landscape that's been used as a location for 'Spaghetti Westerns'.

Buses from Granada zigzag up onto the **Sierra Nevada**, the great mountain mass that looms over the city. A good place to stay here is **Capileira**, the highest village in the range. There are several places to stay among its whitewashed houses, and it boasts spectacular views. Walking here can be fun; try following the many irrigation channels built by the Moors, but be careful not to get too close to the mountain edge.

€34–44, with several rooms overlooking the Plaza Nueva. Popular backpacker hostals include **Oasis**, Placeta Correo Viejo 3, ☎ 95 821 58 48 (www.oasisgranada.com) with dorm beds from €18. Next to the Cathedral and the Capilla Real is the **Hotel Carlos V**, Plaza de los Campos 4, ☎ 95 822 15 87 (www.hotelcarlosvgranada.com), doubles €79. At the top end of the scale, the *parador* is located in the former convent **Parador de San Francisco**, Real de la Alhambra, ☎ 95 822 14 40, (www.parador.es), €€€, in the Alhambra complex. Enjoying the same magical location is the small but comfortable (and much cheaper) 1-star **Hotel América Granada**, Real de la Alhambra 53, ☎ 95 822 74 71 (www.hotelamericagranada.com), doubles €115. **Youth hostel: (non HI) Albergue Juvenil de Granada**, Avenida Ramón y Cajal 2, ☎ 95 800 29 00 (www.reaj.com, www.inturjoven.com), dorm beds from €14, ▦ 11 from the station – camping is also available. **Campsite: Sierra Nevada**, Avda de Madrid 107, ☎ 95 815 00 62 (www.campingsierranevada.com), is very central and not too far from the bus station. They also have a two-star motel with doubles from €59.50; ▦ 3 from Acera de Darro. **Granada campsite**, Cerro de la Cruz, Peligrosi (www.camping granada.es), ☎ 95 834 05 48, ▦ to Peligros every 20 mins (3 km away).

▣ Plaza Nueva and the streets around it are where the locals eat: not always cheap, but fair value. A glass of Arabian tea in one of the *teterias* (tea shops) on Calderería Nueva will invoke the Moorish spirit.

CÓRDOBA

The main attraction of this former capital of the Moorish caliphate is undoubtedly the **Mezquita**, the grandest and most beautiful mosque ever built in Spain. Córdoba has a really strong atmosphere of the past, with one of the largest medieval townscapes in Europe, and certainly the biggest in Spain, offering a harmonious blend of Christian, Jewish and Moorish architecture. There's a distinctly Moorish character, with a labyrinth of whitewashed alleys and gorgeous patios, as well as a fascinating Jewish quarter.

The huge Mezquita (it's free to attend Mass in the cathedral section of the building) was founded in

CÓRDOBA'S MUSEUMS

The grisly **Museo de Arte Taurino** on Plaza de Maimónides is devoted to bullfighting. The **Museo Arqueológico**, Plaza de Jerónimo Páez, is housed in a 16th-century mansion with visible Roman foundations. The **Museo Torre de la Calahorra** chronicles the Muslim occupation of Córdoba from the 9th to the 13th centuries. Recorded information is given to you through headphones (various languages available) as you enter each room.

WALKING TOUR OF CÓRDOBA

This walk encompasses the main attractions of Córdoba in a couple of hours. Begin at the Plaza del Potro, see the fountain, the **Museo de Bellas Artes** and the inn, **La Posada del Potro**, where Cervantes is thought to have stayed. Walk down Paseo de la Ribera, along the banks of the *Río Guadalquivir*. Turn right down Cano Quebrado to take in Córdoba's most famous sight, the **Mezquita**. Carry on along to the riverside Ronda de Isasa; on reaching an Arab waterwheel on your left, with the **Alcázar** off to your right, go down Santa Teresa de Jornet. Go back onto Ronda de Isasa/ Avenida del Alcázar and continue alongside the river. Turn left onto Puente San Rafael, cross the bridge, and turn left to head back in the direction you just came, but on the opposite side of the river. Call at the **Museo Torre de la Calahorra** and afterwards cross Puente Romano and continue straight ahead into the little shops and inexpensive cafés of the **Judería**.

the 8th century by Caliph Abd al Rahman I and was enlarged over the next 200 years. At the foot of the bell tower, the delicately carved **Puerta del Perdón** leads through the massive outer walls to the **Patio de los Naranjos** (Courtyard of the Orange Trees), a courtyard with fountains for ritual cleansing. Inside the mosque, the fantastic forest of 850 pillars, joined by two-tiered Moorish arches in stripes of red brick and white stone, extends over a vast area. The pillars are not identical: materials include alabaster, marble, jasper, onyx, granite and wood; some are smooth, others have ribs or spirals; most are Roman in origin and were shipped in from places as far apart as France and North Africa, then cut to size. The capitals are equally varied. After the Moors departed, the Christians added the cathedral within the complex, incongruous but stunning, and blocking out the light that was an integral part of the design. The Third Mihrab once housed the original copy of the Koran. Unlike the other two, it survived Christian vandalism and its walls are covered in mosaics of varied colours and friezes of texts from the Koran. Its unusual off-centre position in the *qibla* (the south-facing holy wall) is the result of the final enlargement of the mosque in the 10th century, which, because of the proximity of the river in the south and the palace in the west, had to be made on the east side.

The **Puente Romano** is a bridge of mainly Moorish construction, but the arches have Roman foundations. Downstream are the remains of an Arab waterwheel, which originally transported water to the grounds of the Alcázar. The **Torre de la Calahorra** (on the other side of the river) is a high-tech museum with a model of the Mezquita as it was before the Christians got to work on it.

Rail Tour: Málaga – Granada – Cádiz

The **Alcázar de los Reyes Católicos**, on the north bank, retains the original Moorish terraced gardens and pools. In August, these stay open until midnight, perfect for an evening stroll. Less gloriously, this was the headquarters of the Spanish Inquisition for over three centuries.

The **Judería** is the old Jewish quarter, a maze of lanes surrounding a tiny synagogue in C. Judíos. Open doorways provide tantalising glimpses of chequered courtyards filled with flowers; to get a better look visit the town in May, when the **Festival de los Patios** (a 'best-kept patio' competition) takes place.

Glorieta de las Tres Culturas. Tourist Office and taxis at the station. 1 km north of the main area of interest; 20–30 mins on foot, or take 🚌 3 (every 15 mins). Luggage lockers and cash machine.

i **Tourist Offices**: (provincial) C. Torrijos 10 (Palacio de Congresos y Exposiciones), ☎95 735 51 79 (www.andalucia.org); (municipal) C. Rey Heredia 22, ☎95 720 17 74 (www.turismodecordoba.org). There are three further information points: opposite the Alcázar, in the train station, and at Plaza de las Tendillas. The provincial information office is easy to find: it's right next to the Mezquita.

🛏 Cheap places are near the station, in and around the Judería (Jewish Quarter) and off Plaza de las Tendillas. Plaza de la Corredera, although cheap, is a less savoury area. Calle Rey Heredia has lots of cheap accommodation (the street changes name five times), including the **Hostal Triunfo**, C. Corregidor Luis de la Cerda 79, ☎95 749 84 84, (www.hostaltriunfo.com), doubles from €58, which is a clean and light 2-star hostal near the Mezquita. **Bagdad Backpackers Hostel**, Fernández Ruano 11, ☎95 720 28 54 (www.sensesandcolours.com), has a beautiful central courtyard (dorm beds from €14, en suite doubles from €40). **Hostal Luis de Góngora**, Horno de la Trinidad 7, ☎95 729 53 99, fax 95 729 55 99, doubles from €45, is lacking in traditional charm, but is clean, quiet and comfortable. Other budget options include: **Pensión Los Arcos**, C. Romero Barros 14, ☎95 748 56 43 (www.pensionlosarcos.com), doubles from €45; **Hostal Lineros 38**, C. Lineros 38, ☎95 748 25 17 (www.hostallineros38.com), doubles from €48; **Maestre**, C. Romero Barros 4–6, ☎95 747 14 10 (www.hotelmaestre.com), which is a hotel, hostal and apartments; and **Hostal Ronda**, Avenida de las Ollerías 45, ☎95 748 02 50, doubles around €40. **Youth hostel (HI)**: **Albergue de Córdoba**, Pl. de Judá Leví, ☎95 735 50 40 (www.inturjoven.com), dorm beds €18–24, located in the Jewish quarter, very near the Mezquita, and a **campsite**, **El Brillante**, at Avda del Brillante 50, ☎95 740 38 36 (www.campingelbrillante.com) (🚌 10/11 from Avda de Cervantes).

🍴 There are a number of restaurants around the Judería. Budget eateries can be found along C. Doctor Fleming or in the Judería.

SEVILLE (SEVILLA)

Of all the Andalucian cities, Seville has the most to see. The capital of Andalucía, it's a romantic, theatrical place, with a captivating park, a gigantic cathedral and two very important fiestas, the **April Feria** and the processions of **Holy Week**. Columbus sailed from Seville to discover the New World, and *Don Giovanni*, *Carmen*, *The Barber of Seville* and *The Marriage of Figaro* were all set here. The downside is the high level of petty crime: be on the alert for bag-snatchers and pickpockets, and never leave anything of value in your hotel room or your car.

The prime sights are in a very small area, but the secondary ones are quite widespread. All but the keenest walkers will probably want to hop on a bus or two along the way. Most places of interest are in the Barrio de Santa Cruz. A pleasant place for a stroll, it lives up to the idealised image of Spain; white and yellow houses with flower-bedecked balconies and romantic patios. The focal point is the **Giralda**, a minaret that has towered over the old city since the 12th century and which now serves as belfry to the cathedral. Built by the Almohad rulers 50 years before Ferdinand and Isabella's Christian Reconquest, it consists of a series of gentle ramps designed for horsemen to ride up; it's in excellent condition and worth climbing for the views.

The **cathedral** is the largest Gothic structure in the world, simply groaning with gold leaf. The **Capilla Mayor** has a vast gilded retable, which took 82 years to complete. The **Sacristía Mayor** houses the treasury and **Sacristía de los Cálices** contains Murillos and a Goya. A huge memorial honours Christopher Columbus (who may or may not be buried here!) while outside is the pretty **Patio de los Naranjos** (orange-tree courtyard).

The **Alcázar** (closed Mon, www.patronato-alcazar sevilla.es) was inspired by the Alhambra of Granada (see p213), but has been marred by later additions. Within is the **Salón de Embajadores**, where Columbus was received by Ferdinand and Isabella on his return from the Americas, and there are also shady, inter-connected gardens separated by arched Moorish walls. The neighbouring **Casa Lonja** contains a collection of documents relating to the discovery of the Americas.

There's more 16th-century history captured in the relatively unvisited but very atmospheric **Casa de Pilatos** on Pl. Pilatos (a 5–10-minute walk from the cathedral). It is a wonderful confection of Mudéjar, Gothic and Plateresque styles and takes its name from

DAY TRIP FROM SEVILLE

Itálica (closed Mon; free to EU nationals) is a substantial excavated Roman town at **Santiponce**, about 9 km from Seville, with remains of streets, baths and mosaics. The 25,000-seater amphitheatre is particularly interesting. Itálica was first founded by Publius Cornelius Scipio, and it was thought to be the home of Trajan and Hadrian in the 2nd century AD. Buses leave Pza de Armas every 30 mins and cost €1.

TOURS OF SEVILLE

Bus tours depart every 45 mins touring the Plaza de España, Torre del Oro, Monasterio de la Cartuja and Isla Mágica (www.islamagica.es). The tours run from 1000–1900. Tickets are a little expensive but they are valid all day and you can get on and off as you please.

Take a **boat tour** along the Río Guadalquivir to see the sights of Seville. They embark at 1100, 1200, then every 30 mins until 2200; ☎ 95 456 16 92 (www.crucerostorredeloro.com). City tours by **horse-drawn trap** leave from outside the cathedral.

the unlikely story that it is a replica of Pontius Pilate's house in Jerusalem. There are gorgeous courtyards, and rooms, plus fine paintings by Spanish masters including Goya.

Hospital de la Caridad, C. Temprado, was commissioned by a reformed rake, reputed to have been the real-life inspiration for Don Juan. The church contains several works by Valdés Leal, depicting death in ghoulishly disturbing ways; there are also paintings by Murillo.

Nowadays, the 18th-century *Fábrica de Tabacos* (on C. de San Fernando south of the Alcázar) houses parts of the university, but it was once a tobacco factory, employing over 10,000 women (supposedly including Bizet's gypsy beauty, Carmen). Southeast of the factory is **María Luisa Park**, a delightful mixture of wilderness areas and formal gardens laid out for a trade fair in 1929 and shaded by trees from Latin America. It contains the **Plaza de España**, which was the central pavilion (now municipal offices, but on an incredible scale and with some eye-catching ceramics), and Plaza de América, a peaceful place that is home to the **Archaeological Museum**, containing a famously rich Roman section (closed Mon; free for EU citizens). The Latin American countries that exhibited at the fair each built a pavilion in their own national style, most of which survive.

The **Museo de Bellas Artes** (closed Mon, free for EU nationals), Pl. del Museo (between Santa Cruz and Cartuja), has a collection of 13th–20th-century Spanish paintings, second only to that in the Prado in Madrid. The decorative **Maestranza** (bullring), near the river, dates from the 18th century. Fights are held every Thur Mar–Oct, but there's also a worthwhile museum here so you can get a peek of the structure inside. A short way along the river bank is the 13th-century **Torre del Oro** (Golden Tower), named after the gold-coloured tiles that once covered its twelve sides. It now contains a small **naval museum** (free to EU citizens on Tues). **Cartuja Park** (across the river from the Old Town) was the site of Expo 92 and part of the site is home to the Isla Mágica funfair (www.islamagica.es). The fleamarket, **Alameda de Hércules**, held Thurs, is usually entertaining. On Thurs, **El Jueves antique market** is held in La Feria.

Spain

RAIL **Estación Santa Justa**, Avda Kansas City; 15-min walk from the centre. 🚌 27 goes from the station to Plaza de la Encarnación; 🚌 70 goes to Plaza de España. Tourist Office and taxis. Luggage lockers; the locker area is open 0600–2400. Currency exchange, cash machines and tourist information booth.

🚌 There are two bus stations: **Prado de San Sebastián**, Plaza Prado de San Sebastián, 📞 95 441 71 11, is mainly for buses to Andalucía; Plaza de Armas, Avda Cristo de la Expiración, 📞 95 490 80 40, is for buses elsewhere.

City buses: C1 and C2 are circular routes around the town. Many buses pass through Plaza de la Encarnación, Plaza Nueva and Avda de la Constitución. If you're making more than four trips, buy a **Bonobús** ticket €6, valid for ten journeys.

Taxis: There's a rank on Plaza Nueva. To order a taxi 📞 66 384 22 59 or 95 458 00 00.

✈ **San Pablo Airport**, 12 km east of town, 📞 95 444 90 00; tourist information desk, 📞 95 478 20 35. Trains to Seville take 15 mins; taxis cost about €18. Express buses take 30 mins to the centre.

i **Tourist Offices**: (regional) Avda de la Constitución 21B, 📞 95 478 75 78 (www.andalucia.org); (municipal): Plaza de San Francisco 19, Edificio Laredo, 📞 95 459 52 88, (www.turismosevilla.org). **Centro de Información de Sevilla**, Plaza de la Concórdia, 📞 91 490 52 67. There are also tourist information booths in strategic locations, including the station.

🏨 During Holy Week and the April Fair accommodation is very difficult to obtain, and must be prebooked. On the whole, staying in Seville tends to be expensive. For the least pricy lodgings, try the **Barrio Santa Cruz**: C. Archeros, the streets around Plaza Nueva (C. Marqués de Paradas or C. Gravina), or down towards the river. Also in Santa Cruz is **Hostal Sierpes**, C. Corral del Ry 22, 📞 95 422 49 48 (www.hsierpes.com), doubles from €72. **Hostal Arias**, C. Mariana Pineda 9, 📞 95 421 83 89 (www.hostalarias.com), doubles from €40, is small and plain but located right next to the Alcázar. **Hostal Aguilas**, C. Aguilas 15, 📞 95 421 31 77, doubles from €40, has clean rooms. **Pensión Alcázar**, C. Dean Miranda 12, 📞 95 422 84 57, (www.pensionalcazar.com), all rooms en suite with doubles from €55, is right next to the Alcázar wall. **Hotel Simón** (1-star), García de Vinuesa 19, 📞 95 422 66 60 (www.hotelsimonsevilla.com), doubles from €50, is in a former 18th-century mansion. **Youth hostel (HI): Albergue Juvenil de Sevilla**, C. Isaac Peral 2, 📞 95 505 65 00 (www.inturjoven.com), dorm beds from €18, 🚌 6/34; located 2 km from station. All the **campsites** are about 12 km out of town. Campsites include **Dos Hermanas**: **Club de Campo**, Avda de la Libertad 13, 📞 95 472 02 50 (open all year), and **Camping Villsom**, Ctra Seville-Cádiz km 554.8, 📞 95 472 08 28 (www.guiacampingfecc.com/sevilla/villsom), buses from Prado de San Sebastián every 30–45 mins.

TO Seville is probably the best place to sample such typical Andalusian dishes as *gazpacho* (chilled tomato and pepper soup) and *pescaito frito* (deep-fried fish). Eating out can be expensive, but there are a few places with excellent menus for reasonable prices. The liveliest bars and restaurants, frequented by students, are in Barrio Santa Cruz. Perennially popular is the Plaza Alfalfa, with a wide choice of bustling bars and nightspots. For a meal with a view, try restaurants on the other side of the river by the Puente de San Telmo. Buying your own food is a cheap option and to be recommended if you go to the **Mercado del Arenal**, C. Arenal and C. Pastor, the town's largest market.

CÁDIZ

Like Venice, that other once-great naval city, Cádiz is approached by a causeway and all but surrounded by water. Its tight grid of streets, squares and crumbly ochre buildings exudes an atmosphere of gentle decay, but it's all the better for that, and really comes into its own during the huge **carnival** in Feb (one of the best in Spain) and in the evening, when the promenaders come out and the bars open. Colourful tiling is a feature of the pavements, parks and even the **Catedral Nueva** (New Cathedral), which was rebuilt, like much of the rest, in the city's 18th-century heyday. However its origins go back to 1100 BC when it was founded by the Phoenicians; the port was of vital importance at the time of the conquest of the Americas (which was why Sir Francis Drake attacked it). You can get a panoramic view of it all from **Torre Tavira**, both from the top of the tower and in the camera obscura below, via a mirror and lens on the roof.

The **Museo Histórico Municipal** contains an 18th-century ivory and mahogany scale model of Cádiz, while **Museo de Cádiz** has an eclectic display of exhibits from sarcophagi to paintings by Murillo, Van Dyck and Rubens. The chapel of the **Hospital de Mujeres** houses El Greco's *St Francis in Ecstasy* and **Oratorio de la Santa Ceura** has, among other works, three Goya frescos.

🚆 The **main station** is at Plaza de Sevilla.

ℹ️ **Tourist Office**: (municipal) Paseo d Canalejas, ☎ 95 624 10 01 (www.sevilla.org); (regional) Avenida Ramón de Carranza, ☎ 95 620 31 91 (www.andalucia.org).

🏨 **España**, Marqués de Cádiz 9, ☎ 95 628 55 00, doubles from €40, (open Mar–Oct); **Hostal Canalejas**, C. Cristóbal Colón 5, ☎ 95 626 41 13 (www.hostalcanalejas.com), doubles from €57, is very central; or **Hostal San Francisco**, C. San Francisco 12, ☎ 95 622 18 42, (www.ampar hostales.es), doubles from €52, which is a step away from all the main sights.

JEREZ DE LA FRONTERA

Just before you reach Cádiz on the train from Seville you pass through the station for Jerez. This town has given its name to sherry and the bodegas are the town's main attraction; it's also home to Spanish brandy. Here you will find such familiar names as Harvey, González Byass and Domecq. Most bodegas offer tours (of varying prices; reservations necessary for some; many close in Aug) that finish with a tasting for a small fee. Sherry also appears in the local cuisine; kidneys in sherry sauce is a speciality. The other big attraction in town is the **Real Escuela Andaluza de Arte Ecuestre** (Royal Andalucian School of Equestrian Art). It's pricey but if you enjoy dancing horses being put through their paces you'll love it. If not, stick to the sherry tasting. The Old Town (to the west) is just about worth a visit.

BELGIUM, THE NETHERLANDS & LUXEMBOURG

No one would have a holiday for the scenery alone in the so-called **Low Countries**, which, for the most part, live up to their name. There are some really impressive cities, most memorably the likes of **Amsterdam** and **Bruges**, and the remarkably dense rail network gets you around very well. There are moments of pleasant dune-backed **coast**, mostly in the Netherlands, but much of the most satisfying landscapes are in the hills of the **Ardennes** of Belgium and Luxembourg. **Cycling** is a national passion in the Netherlands and parts of Belgium, with an excellent network of cycle routes making it a feasible way to get around the cities and to tour larger areas. You can hire a bike at many stations. There are well-signposted long-distance bike routes across all three countries – local Tourist Offices usually have a good supply of cycle maps.

BELGIUM

Belgium has found it hard to shake off a reputation for dullness. Certainly the coast – almost entirely built up – is undistinguished to the point of blandness, but elsewhere there are handsome brick-built cities with a great sense of history. **Bruges** is the most attractive of all, a canal-laced city dubbed the 'Venice of the North', graced with fine old merchants' houses. There's more fine waterside architecture and a notable cathedral at **Ghent**, while **Antwerp** is a lively cultural city with a medieval printing works. **Brussels**, the capital, has a magnificent central square as well as some surprises – including some of the best Art Nouveau buildings to be found in Europe.

For a country small in size and population, Belgium has a surprisingly diverse mix of **people** and **languages**. There are cultural as well as linguistic differences between the Flemish, who mostly live in the wealthier northern towns, and the poorer French-speaking parts of the country in the south. Bureaucracy, signposts and life in general are complicated by the need to produce all information in at least two languages (Dutch and French). In the northern towns of Flanders, the Flemish often prefer to be addressed in English rather than French.

ACCOMMODATION

The Benelux countries have similar hotel-rating systems, which issue one to five stars. In line with most international rating systems, one star may entail little

ESSENTIALS (BELGIUM)

Population 10m **Capital** Brussels (Bruxelles, Brussel) **Time Zone** Winter GMT+1, summer GMT+2.

CLIMATE

Rain prevalent at any time; warm summers, cold winters (often with snow).

CURRENCY

Euro (€). 1 Euro = 100 cents = £0.89 = $1.46. £1 = €1.13; $1 = €0.68.

EMBASSIES AND CONSULATES IN BRUSSELS

Aus: r. Guimardstraat 6, ☎02 286 05 00. **Can**: av. de Tervuren 2, ☎02 741 06 11. **Ire**: r. Wiertz 50, ☎02 235 66 76. **NZ**: sq. de Meeus 1, 7F, ☎02 512 10 40. **SA**: r. Montoyer 19, ☎02 285 44 53. **UK**: r. d'Arlon 85, ☎02 287 62 48. **USA**: blvd du Régent 27, ☎02 508 21 11.

LANGUAGE

Dutch (north), **French** (south) and **German** (east). Many speak both French and Dutch, plus often English and/or German.

OPENING HOURS

Some establishments close 1200–1400. **Banks**: Mon–Fri 0900–1600. **Shops**: Mon–Sat 0900/1000–1800/1900 (often later Fri). **Museums**: vary, but most open six days a week: 1000–1700 (usually Tues–Sun, Wed–Mon or Thur–Tues).

POST OFFICES

(*Postes/Posterijen/De Post*) open Mon–Fri 0900–1700 (very few open Sat morning). Stamps also sold in newsagents.

PUBLIC HOLIDAYS

1 Jan; Easter Mon; 1 May; Ascension Day; Whit Mon; 21 July; 15 Aug; 1, 11 Nov; 25 Dec. Transport and places that open usually keep Sun times.

PUBLIC TRANSPORT

National bus companies: De Lijn (Flanders), TEC (Wallonia, i.e. the French areas), and STIB (Brussels); few long-distance buses. Buses, trams and Metros: board at any door with ticket or buy ticket from driver. Fares depend on length of journeys, but are cheaper if bought before boarding. Tram and bus stops: red and white signs (all request stop – raise your hand). Taxis seldom stop in the street, so find a rank or phone; double rates outside city limits.

RAIL PASSES

IR, EP, Benelux Pass valid (see pp27–34). Go Pass (under 26) and Rail Pass (over 26) for 10 single journeys within a year: Go Pass €50 2nd class, Rail Pass €73/112 (2nd/1st class).

RAIL TRAVEL

Website: www.b-rail.be. SNCB (in French) or NMBS (in Dutch). Rail information offices: 'B' in an oval logo. Seat reservations available for international journeys only. Refreshments not always available. Some platforms serve more than one train at a time; check carefully. Left luggage and cycle hire at many stations. Timetables usually in two sets: Mon–Fri and weekends/holidays.

TELEPHONES

Most international calls cheaper Mon–Sat 2000–0800, all day Sun. Dial in: ☎+32; omit the initial 0 from the area code. Outgoing: ☎00 + country code. Police: ☎101. Fire/ambulance: ☎100. Note that you need to dial the area code (e.g. 02 for Brussels) even when calling from within that area.

TIPPING

Tipping in cafés, bars, restaurants and taxis not generally the norm, as service is supposed to be included in the price. Becoming expected in places where staff are used to receiving people from the international community (who often leave generous tips): 10 to 15%. Tip hairwashers in salons and delivery men €2.50–4, and cloakroom attendants €1.25–2.50. The toilet attendant's fee is usually a prominently displayed fixed price (€0.20–0.50), not a tip.

TOURIST INFORMATION	Websites: www.belgium-tourism.net (Wallonia and Brussels), www.visitflanders.com (Flanders). *Office du Tourisme* in French, *Toerisme* in Dutch and *Verkehrsamt* in German. Most have English-speaking staff and free English-language literature, but charge for walking itineraries and good street maps. Opening hours, especially in small places and off-season, are flexible.
TYPICAL COSTS	The cheapest hotels start at €35 for a single and €60 for a double. The categories represent; €: up to €79 per night, €€: between €80–130 and finally €€€: rooms upwards of €130 per night. The € rooms listed in the Benelux section of this guide refer to suites or private apartments. Most listings are in the € category, and some are very good deals indeed. A night in a hostel will generally run from €15–25. A cup of coffee will set you back about €1.50 and €10–15 will get you a decent meal. A 'half' (0.5 litre) beer will cost around €3.50. Internet cafés charge €1–2 per hour, sometimes more for non-members.
VISAS	Same requirements as The Netherlands (see p228).

more than a bed and a washstand in the room (although breakfast is often included), while five stars will ensure every luxury imaginable.

HOTELS Hotels tend to be pricey. Tourist Offices charge a deposit for booking hotels (which is then deducted from your bill), and can often offer reduced rates. They sometimes agree to check availability of other accommodation. In summer, accommodation of all kinds can be hard to find and it's sensible to book, especially in Bruges and on the coast.

HOSTELS Hostelling organisations: **Vlaamse Jeugdherbergen**, ☎(32)(3) 232 72 18 (www.vjh.be); Les Auberges de Jeunesse, ☎(32)(2) 219 56 76, (www.laj.be).

CAMPING Rough camping is not permitted, but some farmers may give you permission to use their land. A leaflet covering officially rated campsites should be available from your nearest Belgian Tourist Office.

FOOD AND DRINK Most restaurants have good-value fixed-price menus (*plat du jour*, *tourist menu*, *dagschotel*). There's a wide variation in prices; establishments in the main squares can charge two or three times as much as similar places in nearby streets. Try **waffles** (*wafels / gaufres*) and sweet or savoury **pancakes** (*crêpes*), **mussels** (*moules*) and freshly baked pastries. The most common snacks are *frieten / frites* (french fries with mayonnaise or other sauce) and (delicious) ice cream. Sweets are ubiquitous, notably **nougat** and the deservedly famous **chocolates**, but be warned: the ones containing cream have a very short shelf-life. Belgium produces literally hundreds of beers (both dark and light); **wheat beer** (*blanche*) comes with a slice of lemon in it in the summer.

Benelux

THE NETHERLANDS

Canals and 17th- and 18th-century gabled buildings are abiding memories of a visit to The Netherlands, whose numerous historic towns and cities have a strikingly uniform appearance. In between, the bulb fields and windmills lend the Dutch farmland a distinctive character. **Amsterdam**, laid-back and bustling at the same time, justifiably draws most visitors, and even the red-light area has become a tourist attraction. Elsewhere, **Delft**, **Haarlem**, **Leiden**, **Maastricht** and **Utrecht** are among many places with pretty centres, while **Rotterdam** has striking modern architecture. Cheese addicts should head for **Gouda**, **Edam** and **Alkmaar**. The inexpensive **Museum Card** gives you admission to 400 museums for a whole year across the entire country.

INFORMATION

HOTELS
Netherlands Reservation Centre (NRC),
☎(31) (299) 689 144
(www.hotelres.nl).

HOSTELS
Stayokay:
☎(31) (10) 264 6064
(www.stayokay.com).

BED AND BREAKFAST
Bed & Breakfast Holland,
☎(31) (20) 615 7527
(www.bbholland.com).
Holiday Link
☎(31) (50) 313 2424
(www.holidaylink.com).

ACCOMMODATION

Standards are high; lower prices reflect limited facilities rather than poor quality. Room rates start around €70 for a double, but most cost more. Booking is advisable. **Stayokay** youth hostels are around €16–24 (€2.50 discount for HI members), and private hostel dorms start from around €20.

HOTELS Tourist Offices (VVV) have listings of bed and breakfast accommodation in their area, where it exists, or you can book nationwide through **Bed & Breakfast Holland**. **Holiday Link** offers a similar service, and has a guide.

FOOD AND DRINK

Dutch cuisine is mainly simple and substantial: fish or meat, potatoes and vegetables. Many Indonesian restaurants offer spicy food and in cities a good variety of international cuisine is available. Most cheaper eating joints stay open all day. Some restaurants in smaller places take last orders by 2130 or 2200. Look for boards saying *dagschotel* (a very economical 'special'). 'Brown cafés' (traditional pubs) also serve good-value food. **Mensas** are subsidised student canteens in university towns; very cheap and not restricted to students, but open only during term-time.

Specialities include apple pie (heavy on cinnamon and sultanas), herring marinated in brine, smoked eels (somewhat pricey), *poffertjes* (tiny puff-pancakes with icing sugar) and *pannekoeken* (pancakes: try bacon with syrup). Street stalls for snacks abound, options invariably including *frites/patates* (a cross between french fries and

ESSENTIALS (THE NETHERLANDS)

Population 16.5m **Administrative Capital** Amsterdam **Legislative Capital** The Hague (Den Haag) **Time Zone** Winter GMT+1, summer GMT+2.

CLIMATE

Can be cold in winter; rain prevalent all year. Many attractions close Oct–Easter. Apr–May is tulip season, and the country gets very crowded. June–Sept can be pleasantly warm and the main cities are busy.

CURRENCY

Euro (€). 1 Euro = 100 cents = £0.89 = $1.46.

EMBASSIES AND CONSULATES IN THE HAGUE/AMSTERDAM

Aus: Carnegielaan 4, The Hague, ☎(070) 310 8200. **Can**: Sophialaan 7, The Hague, ☎(070) 311 1600. **Ire**: dr. Kuyperstr. 9, The Hague, ☎(070) 363 0993. **NZ**: Eisenhowerlaan 77N, The Hague, ☎(070) 346 9324. **SA**: Wassenaarseweg 40, The Hague, ☎(070) 392 4501. **UK**: Lange Voorhout 10, The Hague, ☎(070) 427 0427 (consulate in Amsterdam ☎(020) 676 4343). **USA**: Lange Voorhout 102, The Hague, ☎(070) 310 2209 (consulate in Amsterdam ☎(020) 575 5309).

LANGUAGE

Dutch; English widely spoken.

OPENING HOURS

Banks: Mon–Fri 0900–1600/1700 (later Thur or Fri). **Shops**: Mon–Fri 0900/0930–1730/1800 (until 2100 Thur or Fri), Sat 0900/0930–1600/1700. Many close Mon morning. **Museums**: vary, but usually Mon–Sun 1000–1700 (some close Mon). In winter many have shorter hours.

POST OFFICES

Logo is 'TNT post' (orange on white). Most open Mon–Fri 0830–1700 and some Sat 0830–1200. Stamps also sold in many postcard shops. Post international mail in left slot of mailbox, marked *overige* (other) *postcodes*.

PUBLIC HOLIDAYS

1 Jan; Good Fri; Easter Sun–Mon; 30 Apr; 5 May; Ascension Day; Whit Sun–Mon; 25, 26 Dec. Note that although Good Friday is a 'holiday' in The Netherlands, no one gets a day off and nothing closes (apart from some banks). The same is largely true of 5 May.

PUBLIC TRANSPORT

Centralised (premium rate) number for all rail and bus enquiries (computerised, fast and accurate): national, ☎0900 9292 (www.9292ov.nl). Taxis must be boarded at ranks or ordered by phone as they seldom stop in the street. In many cities (not Amsterdam), shared Treintaxis have ranks at stations and yellow roof signs (€4.60 for anywhere within city limits; tickets from rail ticket offices). *Strippenkaarten* (from stations, city transport offices, post offices, supermarkets and VVVs) are strip tickets valid nationwide on Metros, buses, trams and some trains (2nd class) within city limits; zones apply; validate on boarding; valid 1 hr; change of transport allowed. *Strippenkaarten* will eventually be replaced by a new electronic ticketing system, the *OV-Chipkaart* (similar to the Oyster Card used in London). This is currently being phased in across the country, and by 2012 will be used for all public transport, including trains. Once it is fully in place, *strippenkaarten* and normal NS railway tickets will cease to be issued. For more information, see www.ov-chipkaart.nl.

RAIL PASSES	IR, EP, Benelux Pass valid (see pp27–34). Day rover (*Dagkaart*) €74.80/44 (1st/2nd); add €5.50 for *OV Dagkaart* including bus/tram/Metro. *Zomertoer*: 1 day's unlimited 1st class travel, 1 July–early-Sept, €39.50 for 2 people. **I amsterdam Card** offers 1/2/3 days' (€38/48/58) public transport around Amsterdam, excluding trains, plus various attractions.
RAIL TRAVEL	Website: www.ns.nl. Most services are run by the national rail company: **Nederlandse Spoorwegen** (NS), though private operators run the services on some regional lines (through ticketing is available). Intercity (IC) trains provide the fastest connections, while slower, all-station trains (stoptreinen) are officially called Sprinters. Tickets are sold from vending machines, which accept Maestro debit cards or, in most cases, coins (but not credit cards, except at Schiphol Airport). The largest stations have ticket offices and medium-sized stations have shops which also sell tickets, though tickets obtained from machines are 50 cents cheaper. Over the next few years, normal rail tickets will be phased out and replaced by a new electronic ticketing system, the *OV-Chipkaart* (see Public Transport, p227).
TELEPHONES	Phone booths are green and found outside railway stations, but are becoming increasingly rare with the advent of mobile phones. Most take credit cards. International calls cheapest Mon–Fri evenings and all day Sat, Sun. Most information lines are premium-rate. Dial in: ☎+31, and omit initial 0 from area code. Outgoing: ☎00 + country code. Operator: ☎118. International directory: ☎0900 8418. National directory ☎0900 8008. Emergency services: ☎112.
TIPPING	Service charges are included, but it is customary to round off the bill in restaurants to a convenient figure. If paying by credit card, pay the exact amount on the card and leave a few coins.
TOURIST INFORMATION	Website: www.holland.com. Tourist bureaux are VVV (*Vereniging voor Vreemdelingenverkeer*): signs show a triangle with three Vs. All open at least Mon–Fri 0900–1700, Sat 1000–1200. Museumjaarkaart (€35, aged under 25 €15, from VVV and participating museums) is valid for one year; free entry to most museums; CJP (Cultureel Jongeren Paspoort), for those under 26.
TYPICAL COSTS	Similar to Belgium (see p225).
VISAS	Visas are necessary for citizens of South Africa, but not for those of Australia, Canada, the EU, New Zealand or USA.

British chips) with mayonnaise or other sauces. In **Limburg**, try the regional *zuurvlees*, a slightly sour meat dish. Automats (also at stations) sell heated croquettes, the *bami* and *nasi* varieties being spicy. Excellent coffee and hot chocolate are available everywhere, often topped with whipped cream – *slagroom*. Tea is hot water with a choice of teabags – ask if you want milk. Dutch beer is topped by two fingers of froth. Most local liqueurs are excellent. The main spirit is *jenever*, a strong, slightly oily gin made from juniper berries.

LUXEMBOURG

The Grand Duchy of Luxembourg covers some pretty terrain for hiking, with river valleys, forests and hills. Its eponymous capital has a dramatic and picturesque setting, straddling two gorges.

ACCOMMODATION

The national Tourist Office has free brochures featuring hotels (of all grades, plus restaurants), holiday apartments, farm holidays and camping in the Grand Duchy, plus a bed and breakfast booklet that covers all three Benelux countries.

HOSTELS

There are 11 youth hostels. The price of bed and breakfast includes linen and varies from 'standard' category to the slightly pricier 'comfort' category. Extra charges: €2.50 per person (double room) and €12 per person (single room). Non-members pay a €3 supplement.

INFORMATION

HOSTELS

Youth Hostelling organisation: **Centrale des Auberges de Jeunesse Luxembourgeoises**, ☎(352) 26 27 66 40 (www.youthhostels.lu).

FOOD AND DRINK

Cuisine has been pithily described as 'French quality, German quantity', but eating out is pricey. Keep costs down by making lunch your main meal and looking out for special deals: **plat du jour** (single course) or **menu** (two–three courses).

Local specialities include: Ardennes ham, *treipen* (black pudding), *quenelles* (calf's liver dumplings), *thüringer* (standard local sausage), *gromperekichelcher* (fried potato patties) and (in Sept) *quetschentaart* (a flan featuring dark, violet plums).

ESSENTIALS (LUXEMBOURG)

	Population 0.5m **Capital** Luxembourg (Ville de Luxembourg) **Time Zone** Winter GMT+1, summer GMT+2.
CLIMATE	Similar to Belgium (see p224).
CURRENCY	**Euro** (€). 1 Euro = 100 cents = £0.89 = $1.46.
EMBASSIES IN LUXEMBOURG	**UK**: 14 Blvd Joseph II, ☎22 98 64. **USA**: 22 Blvd Emmanuel-Servais, ☎46 01 23.
LANGUAGE	**Lëtzebuergesch, French** and **German** are the three joint national tongues. Most people also speak at least some English.
OPENING HOURS	Many establishments take long lunch breaks. **Banks**: usually Mon–Fri 0830–1200 and 1400–1630 or later. **Shops**: Mon 1300/1400–1800; Tues–Sat 0800/0900–1800. **Museums**: most open six days a week (usually Tues–Sun).

POST OFFICES	Usually open Mon–Fri 0800–1200 and 1400–1700.
PUBLIC HOLIDAYS	1 Jan; Feb (Carnival); Easter Mon; 1 May; Ascension; Whit Mon; 23 June; 15 Aug; early Sept (Luxembourg City Fête); 1 Nov; 25, 26 Dec. When holidays fall on Sun, the Mon usually becomes a holiday, but only twice in one year.
PUBLIC TRANSPORT	Good bus network between most towns. Taxis are not allowed to pick up passengers in the street; head for a rank in the city of Luxembourg. Taxis elsewhere are more scarce, but the towns are generally small and the distances short.
RAIL PASSES	IR, EP, Benelux Pass valid (see pp27–34). Billet Réseau: day card €4; unlimited 2nd-class travel on all public transport; *carnet* of 5 day cards costs €16; from CFL offices. Luxembourg Card (available Easter to October): unlimited transport on all trains and buses, free entry to more than 50 attractions within the Duchy of Luxembourg; 1 day (€10), 2 days within 2 weeks (€17), 3 days (€24); family pass for 2–5 people (maximum of 3 adults) at twice one person rate; available from Tourist Offices, hotels, youth hostels, campsites, stations etc.
RAIL TRAVEL	Website: www.cfl.lu. Rail services converge on Luxembourg City. National rail company: CFL, also runs long-distance buses; these and city buses covered by multi-ride passes. Stations: most are small, few facilities.
TELEPHONES	Dial in: ☎+352. Outgoing: ☎00 + country code. There are no area codes in Luxembourg. Police: ☎113. Emergency services (fire and ambulance): ☎112.
TIPPING	In restaurants, cafés and bars service charge is usually included, round up to nearest €1. Taxi drivers €2–5; porters €1–2; hairdressers €2; cloakroom attendants €0.50; toilet attendants €0.25.
TOURIST INFORMATION	**Luxembourg City Tourist Office**, 30 Place Guillaume, PO Box 181, L-2011 Luxembourg, ☎22 28 09 (www.lcto.lu). The national Tourist Office has a branch located in the main hall of Luxembourg City railway station, ☎42 82 82 20 (www.ont.lu).
TYPICAL COSTS	Similar to Belgium (see p225).
VISAS	Visas are not needed by citizens of Australia, Canada, EU, New Zealand or the USA. South Africans do need visas.

The Dutch say that they earn their money in Rotterdam, talk about it in The Hague and spend it in Amsterdam. Romantic and laid-back, **Amsterdam** combines tree-lined canals, bicycles and elegant gabled brick houses, with a vibrant, emphatically youthful streetlife. In summer it's full of tourists, while in winter it's often shivery and shrouded in fog, its visitors huddled in the famous 'brown cafés' over coffee and apple cake. In the 'Golden Age' of the revolutionary Dutch republic (the 17th century) Amsterdam was second only to London and Paris in importance – and assumed its present cobweb-like shape with the building of three new canals. Allow a couple of days for casual exploration, plus plenty of time to visit the marvellously varied museums and galleries around the city, and to take in a canal cruise.

The city centre is wonderful for walking (especially along the canals), though you would do best to concentrate on one area at a time and use trams to cross the city. VVV, the Amsterdam Tourist Board, suggests walking routes, which are well signposted and colour-coordinated by city maps at strategic points. Amsterdam's layout can be confusing; bear in mind that *gracht* means 'canal' and that the centre follows the horseshoe shape dictated by the ring canals. The **Singel** canal confines the old centre, with the red-light district around the handsome **Oude Kerk** (Old Church), and the **Royal Palace** at the Dam. Seek out the **Keizersgracht**, the **Herengracht** and the houseboats along the **Prinsengracht**, and explore the **Jordaan**, an enticing area of quirky shops, bars and restaurants that lies to the west of the ring canals. At night Amsterdam can be magical (get hold of an entertainments listing, as there's lots going on). The canals seem to come alive, with the largest lit by twinkling lights and the glow from windows.

ARRIVAL AND DEPARTURE

[RAIL] **Centraal** (www.ns.nl) is the terminal for all the city's trains and a 5-min walk north of Dam (the central area); beware of opportunistic thieves that hang around there. There's a manned left-luggage facility, as well as lockers, but the baggage area is closed 0100–0500.

✈ **Amsterdam Airport Schiphol** ☎ (020) 601 2182 (www.schiphol.com) is about 14 km southwest of town. Transfers by train to/from Centraal are the cheapest: every 10 mins 0600–2400 (hourly 2400–0600); journey time 20 mins. Connections are also available to the south of the city to RAI and Zuid/WTC.

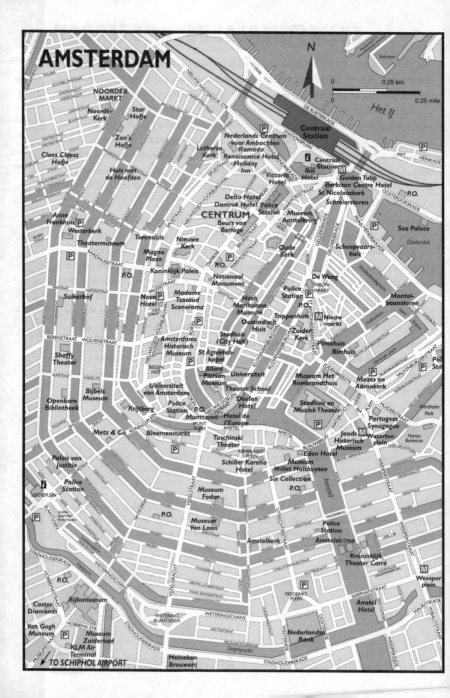

TOURIST OFFICE

Amsterdam Tourism & Convention Board, Stationsplein 10 (immediately opposite Centraal, in a wooden building just beyond the tram terminal), ☎0900 400 40 40 (www.iamsterdam.com); invariably very busy; computerised system for last-minute availability of rooms nationwide.

There's a booth in Centraal (in the international area, platform 2B), and branches at Leidseplein (corner of Leidsestraat), and Amsterdam Airport Schiphol (arrival hall 2) ☎(020) 551 2525, www.amsterdamtourist.nl).

INFORMATION

Amsterdam is something of a cyberpunk mecca and is chock full of internet cafés with impressive hacker-sounding names such as **The Mad Processor** (www.madprocessor.nl), and many (obviously) hold gaming competitions well into the night. Be aware that many of these internet cafés are 'smoking'.

INTERNET ACCESS Typical costs are €1–2 per hour, though some charge more for non-members. **Underworld**, Voetboogstraat 7 (www.underworld-amsterdam.page.tl), runs a more grown-up operation than most; find them just off the big shopping street Kalverstraat.

PUBLIC TRANSPORT

MAPS The free *Around Amsterdam: visitor's guide by public transport* shows how to use the city transport and how to reach the highlights; for details buy the *Public Transport Map*. Most tourist literature includes a small map of central Amsterdam.

TICKETS GVB (Amsterdam's public transport company: a few doors from VVV and easily identified by the large yellow signs in the windows) has a whole range. Worthwhile are day tickets (€7.00) and the *nationale strippenkaart* (with 15 or 45 strips), which is also sold at post offices, rail stations, supermarkets and VVV. VVV also sells day tickets, and combination passes (transport and attractions). Paying on board a tram/bus is expensive, so buy your ticket in advance. Each journey requires one strip plus a strip for each zone you travel in; so if you travel in the centre of town, leave one strip blank and stamp the second; for two zones, leave two strips blank and stamp the third. The ticket lasts one hour, with as many changes of tram or bus as you like. For transport information ☎0900 9292 (premium rate), Mon–Fri 0600–2400, Sat–Sun 0700–2400. The **I amsterdam** card (1, 2 or 3 days; €38/48/58; www.iamsterdamcard.com) covers public transport fares (not airport services or trains), free admission to most museums and a 25% discount for restaurants and attractions. The Amsterdam Dagkaart gives 24, 48 or 72 hours' travel on public transport. The *strippenkaart* system is gradually being replaced by the *OV-Chipkaart* electronic ticketing system (see p227).

METRO Primarily for commuters; few central stops.

TRAMS The most efficient method of travel in the centre; the network is extensive and services frequent and fast from early morning to midnight. The main terminal is just in front of Centraal. Pressure on the lowest step keeps the door open.

BUSES These begin/end just around the canal in front of Centraal (on the left side as you leave the station), but not all from the same terminal. They are less frequent than trams, but go further afield; limited night services (indicated by black square on bus stops).

The Netherlands

TAXIS Tip only for good service – maximum 10%. Taxis cannot be hailed: go to a rank. Main ranks are at Centraal, Dam, Rembrandtplein and Leidseplein, ☎0900 0724 (premium rate) or (020) 677 7777.

BICYCLES This can be a quick and fun way of getting around – but only if you know what you are doing! Amsterdam is a city of experienced cyclists and if you hire a bike you'll be expected to slip in seamlessly alongside them. Many riders are fast and some are plain reckless (pedestrians beware too). A few other things to note: tram tracks and special traffic lights for trams and bikes; riding on the right-hand side of the road; the brakes on some Dutch bikes are operated by back-pedalling; bike theft is notorious in the city so even if you park for only a minute or two, lock it to an immovable object! Bike paths are either separate or marked on the road, in red, or with lines. A way of breaking into Amsterdam cycling gently is to join a group such as Mike's Bike Tours, 134 Kerkstraat, ☎(020) 622 7970 (www.mikesbiketoursamsterdam.com). Hire shops require a deposit of around €50 (typical hire rates are €8.50 per day) and include **Bike City**, Bloemgracht 68–70, ☎(020) 626 3721 (www.bikecity.nl) (just west of Anne Frank's House, open daily), and **MacBike** (three locations, including Centraal Station); ☎(020) 620 0985 (www.macbike.nl), open daily.

ACCOMMODATION

It is best to reserve, particularly in the peak season through **Amsterdam Tourism & Convention Board Reservation Department**, ☎0900 400 4040 (premium-rate call), (www.amsterdamtourist.nl); open Mon–Fri 0900–1700. If all else fails consider commuting from Zandvoort or Haarlem but you may feel left out at night! You may encounter **accommodation touts** at Centraal station: bear in mind they are illegal.

Cheap 2-star options are **Agora**, Singel 462, ☎(020) 627 2200 (www.hotelagora.nl), €€, and **Acro**, Jan Luijkenstr. 44, ☎(020) 662 5538 (www.acro-hotel.nl), €€, while two good budget (1-star) establishments are **Museumzicht**, Jan Luykenstraat 22, ☎(020) 671 2954 (www.hotelmuseumzicht.nl); and **Pax**, Raadhuisstr. 37b, ☎/fax (020) 624 9735, €. The Raadhuisstraat and Damrak areas have a plethora of cheap hotels. If you're looking for somewhere different (though still cheap), at the heart of the action (deep within the red-light district) and you're pretty broad-minded, try the **Winston Hotel**, Warmoestraat 129, ☎(020) 623 1380 (www.winston.nl), €€. The arty rooms' décor range from minimalist to fetishist, and there's a buzzing club and bar next door.

Hostels: Highly recommended are the two **Flying Pig Hostels** (www.flyingpig.nl) in Centrum. These are friendly and secure; cheap bars, free internet and email, kitchens and breakfast: The larger **Downtown Hostel**, ☎(020) 420 6822 (downtown@flyingpig.nl), €, is well-placed, only 500 m from Centraal; **Uptown Hostel**, ☎(020) 400 4187 (uptown@ flyingpig.nl), €, is by Vondelpark (tram 1/2/5). Dorm accommodation is a good bet. There are three **HI youth hostels**, two in Centrum: **Vondelpark**, ☎(020) 589 8996 (www. stayokay.com/vondelpark; tram 1/2/5: Leidseplein); **Stadsdoelen**, ☎(020) 624 6832 (www.stayokay.com/stadsdoelen); tram 4/9/16/24/25: Muntplein), €, while **Zeeburg**, Timorplein 21, ☎(020) 551 3190 (www.stayokay.com/zeeburg), is 15 mins by tram east of Centrum. Two other large, popular private hostels are **Hans Brinker Budget**, ☎(020) 622 0687 (www.hans-brinker.com), €, Amsterdam's biggest hostel, with lots of singles, doubles and dorms (definitely not quiet); and **Youth Hostel Meetingpoint**, ☎(020) 627 7499 (www.hostel-meetingpoint.nl), €, a 2-min walk from Centraal. **The Bulldog Hotel**, ☎(020) 620 3822 (www.bulldoghotel.com) has beds from €27 and private apartments up to €255; on the quiet side of the red-light district. If you're planning your trip on a wing and a prayer, extra encouragement is at hand in the form of the Christian-run **Shelter Jordan Hostel**, ☎(020) 624 4717 and **Shelter City Hostel**, ☎(020) 625 3230 (www.shelter.nl), €.

Campsites: Camping Vliegenbos, Meeuwenlaan 138, ☎(020) 636 8855 (www.vliegenbos.com) (10 mins from Centraal on 🚌 32), open Apr–Sept. **Camping Zeeburg**, Zuider IJdijk 20, ☎(020) 694 4430 (www.campingzeeburg.nl), is on an island next to the A10 ringway; also has cabins; tram 14 from Dam to Flevopark (go past the swimming pool and over the bridge).

FOOD AND DRINK

Amsterdam is a good place to eat, with restaurants to suit every budget and a wide choice of international cuisine (especially Indonesian), though Dutch cuisine itself is not widely available (apart from pancakes). Restaurants may offer set menus, especially at lunch-time, which can be good value for money. Note that many restaurants close fairly early. There's a concentration of eating places around the **Leidseplein**, though this isn't the best place in terms of quality, and is frequented by some of Amsterdam's rowdier visitors.

Cheap food is easy to find, even in Centrum: the international fast-food chains are well represented, and there are plenty of other takeaways. A better bet may be to drop into a bar or café frequented by locals and try the bar snacks.

'Coffee Shops' legally sell marijuana; see The Fringe section on the following page. The tobacco smoking ban applies here, too, though so either smoke pure cannabis or use the partitioned or outdoor areas.

CANAL TRIPS

The canals are an integral part of Amsterdam and provide an excellent way to appreciate the city: **boat trips** can be very cheap and have multi-lingual commentaries. Most people embark at Centraal, but you can board at any stop; there are quays in each area of interest – get tickets at any quay where Rondvaart/Rederij boats are moored. The **Museumlijn** (Museum Line) (Prins Hendrikkade) every 30 mins (45 mins in winter), 1000–1730, with five intermediate stops convenient for 17 museums; day ticket (€20) includes several discounts; boats are turquoise and the stops have turquoise signs. **Canal Buses** (Weteringschans 26, ☎(020) 623 9886; www.canal.nl) operate daily 0945–1920 (every 30–45 mins) and issue day tickets (€20; valid 24 hours), allowing you to get on or off as often as you like at the 14 stops along three different routes. There are regular (free) **ferries** across the River IJ, linking Centrum with northern Amsterdam: departures from de Ruijterkade (behind Centraal). For individual exploration, you can hire **Canal Bikes** (contact details as for Canal Buses), pedal-boats for two to four people (from Leidseplein, Leidsestraat, the Rijksmuseum and Westerkerk).

DAY TRIPS FROM AMSTERDAM

Amsterdamse Bos, Amstelveenseweg 264 (🚌 170/172, www.amsterdamsebos.nl), on the southern fringe of the city, is an 80-hectare park, pleasant for swimming, rowing, canoeing, cycling and walking (200 km of tracks). **Enkhuizen** (www.enkhuizen.nl, 1 hour by train) was cut off from the sea when the Zuider Zee was dammed to create Lake IJsselmeer. The boat for the **Zuiderzee Museum** leaves from behind the station, and the ticket includes both the boat and museum. The indoor section, Binnenmuseum, contains traditional costumes and fishing craft, while the open-air section, Buitenmuseum, consists of whole streets rescued from fishing villages. You can enter any house with an open door and ask questions if you find someone at home.

If you want to buy your own groceries there's a good **Albert Heijn** supermarket on the corner of Singel and Koningsplein (nicely situated for picnics next to the floating flower market). For a sit-down meal at a reasonable price, try one of the many traditional 'brown cafés'. Around **Spui** it's mega touristy; there are better places in backstreets and along the quieter canals, while the areas near **Nieuwmarkt**, **Dam** and **De Pijp** (especially along Albert Cuypstr.) are the best for Eastern cuisine. Amsterdam has two *mensas* (student canteens): **Atrium** and **Agora**.

HIGHLIGHTS

Amsterdam has nearly 200 museums and art galleries. If you only have time for three, see the **Rijksmuseum**, the **Van Gogh Museum** and the **Anne Frank House**. Elsewhere there's torture, spectacles, coffee and tea, chess, trams, sex, pipes, pianolas, the Bible, cats, the Dutch Resistance and much, much more!

Cities: Amsterdam

THE CENTRE: DAM
From Centraal, Damrak leads directly to **Dam**, site of the original dam, with its distinctive **war memorial**. **Koninklijk Paleis** (the Royal Palace) dominates the square. The interior reflects the glory of the Golden Age and much Empire furniture remains from the time of Louis Bonaparte. The palace reopened in 2009 after four years of extensive renovation work.

Of more interest, next door, is the Gothic **Nieuwe Kerk** (New Church), used for important exhibitions and state functions: the investiture of the Dutch rulers has taken place here since 1814. Also in Dam is **Madame Tussaud's Amsterdam** (Dam 20), where audio-animation techniques bring some 130 waxworks to life for the delight of groups of teenagers.

WEST OF DAM
The **Anne Frank House**, Prinsengracht 267, www.annefrank.org (boat: Prinsengracht; tram 13/14/17: Westermarkt), is where two Jewish families hid from the Nazis for two years. They were betrayed in 1944 and only the father survived the concentration camps. Thirteen-year-old Anne recorded the family's ordeal in a moving diary that was discovered after the war and has subsequently been published worldwide. The house has been restored and the tour captures vividly what life must have been like in these cramped secret quarters. Don't be put off by the modern façade, which houses a study centre. Once you are inside, the house has been meticulously restored, and is exactly as it was in Anne's day; to avoid a long wait to get in, book on the internet.

A few yards away is the 17th-century **Westerkerk**, the largest Protestant church in the country, topped by the gold crown of the Austrian emperor Maximilian. The tower (Amsterdam's highest at 85 m) gives one of the few bird's-eye views of the city; informative guided tours take you up past the intricate belfry workings.

THE OLD CITY: EAST OF DAMRAK
Across the canal from Centraal is **Sint Nicolaaskerk**, with its dome featuring a cross donated by the prostitutes of the area. The red-light district (*De Walletjes* – Little Walls) covers (roughly) the area between Warmoesstr. and Gelderskade.

SOUTH OF DAM
The most notable museum here is the **Amsterdams Historisch Museum**, Kalverstr. 92 (www.ahm.nl; boat: Herengracht; tram 1/2/4/5/9/14/16/24/25: Spui), where you can not only view, but also try your hand at, bell-ringing. Turn right as you leave and signs lead to the **Begijnhof**, with its old almshouses (once home to pious upper-class women) and chapel surrounding a peaceful square and 15th-century church.

The fragrant **floating flower market**, Singel (between Muntplein and Koningsplein), takes place Mon–Sat 0900–1730, some stalls also open Sun 1100–1730. The backs of the stalls are on barges, but the fronts are squarely on terra firma. This is a good place to buy your proverbial 'tulips from Amsterdam'.

The Netherlands

Herengracht was the city's grandest canal and one stretch (between Vijzelstr. and Leidsestr.) is known as the 'Golden Bend'. This typifies the old architecture, when buildings were tall and thin (to minimise taxes based on width) and had protruding gables, which are still used today to winch up furniture too big for the narrow staircases.

THE MUSEUM QUARTER The allure of this district, southwest of the centre, has been temporarily lessened by the closure for renovation of two of its three big names – the **Rijksmuseum** (www.rijksmuseum.nl) displays the masterpieces from the world-class collection – including works by Vermeer, Rembrandt and Hals – in the Philips Wing while the rest of the museum is being refurbished (not expected to reopen in full until 2012 or 2013).

The **Stedelijk Museum** of modern art is closed until at least mid-2010, but has a temporary home in the port area. In the meantime, the Museum Quarter is still well worth visiting for the **Van Gogh Museum**, Paulus Potterstraat 7 (www.vangogh museum.nl; tram 2/3/5/12: van Baerlestraat) with some 200 paintings and 600 drawings spanning the artist's entire career, and Van Gogh's own collection of superb Japanese prints. The neighbouring **Vondelpark** is fun in summer; when the sun shines it's overrun with theatre, music and street artists, and has some pleasantly laid-back open-air cafés.

THE JEWISH QUARTER Lying southeast of Dam (Metro: Waterlooplein; boat: Musiektheater), this was the heart of a Jewish settlement which flourished for more than 300 years and formed 10% of the population until being almost annihilated by the Nazis. The **Joods Historich Museum** (Jewish Historical Museum), Nieuwe Amstelstraat 3–5 (www.jhm.nl; tram 9/14), celebrates this community, and its collection of art, documents and antiques has recently been greatly expanded by the gift of two important private family collections. The **Rembrandthuis**, Jodenbreestraat 4 (same trams) was Rembrandt's home from 1639 to 1659 and contains many of his engravings, drawings and personal possessions. At weekends and in summer there are often long queues for entrance. Across the Oudeschans canal is the splendid spire of the **Zuiderkerk** (South Church), which you can climb.

THE PORT The **Nederlands Scheepvaartmuseum**, Kattenburgerplein 1 (www.scheep vaartmuseum.nl; boat: Oosterdok; 🚌 22/28: Kattenburgerplein) is an exceptionally rich maritime museum with particular emphasis on the adventures of the VOC – the buccaneering Dutch East India Company, the world's most powerful trading organisation during the 17th and 18th centuries. The museum is housed in a 17th-century arsenal, and features complete vessels, the most spectacular of which is a convincing 18th-century East Indiaman replica, *The Amsterdam*. Normally you can watch costumed personnel performing shipboard duties, though occasionally it sails away to duties elsewhere.

There's also lots to take in at the ethnographical **Tropenmuseum**, Linnaeusstr. 2 (www.tropenmuseum.nl; tram 9/14: Mauritskade), which pulls no punches with re-created Indian slums, Middle Eastern bazaars, South American rainforests and much more – all with appropriate background music and exotic ethnic food in its fine restaurant.

SHOPPING

Leidsestraat, Kalverstraat, Nieuwendijk, Damrak and Rokin are the main shopping streets. For fun shopping, explore the small specialist shops in the alleys linking the main canals, especially in the area between Leidsegracht and Raadhuisstraat. The whole **Jordaan** area is scattered with second-hand shops and boutiques that offer the creations of young designers. For antiques and art, look around the Spiegelkwartier. Amsterdam's great stores are the enormous **De Bijenkorf**, Damrak and **Magna Plaza**, Nieuwezijds Voorburgwal. Most shops in the centre are open on Sunday.

The general market, **Albert Cuypmarkt**, Albert Cuypstr., is the largest in the country, held Mon–Sat 0900–1800 (tram 6/20/24/25). The **flea market**, Waterlooplein (next to the **Muziektheater**), takes place Mon–Fri 0900–1730, Sat 0830–1730; tram 1/2/5/13/14).

NIGHT-TIME AND EVENTS

The English-language magazine *Time Out Amsterdam* (published monthly), has extensive listings of events and useful addresses. You can buy it from newsagents and bookshops. **Amsterdams Uit Bureau (AUB)**, Leidseplein 26, ☎(020) 795 9950 (www.uitburo.nl), distributes information about the city's entertainments. AUB and VVV make bookings, but there is a charge.

The city's nightlife is both varied and affordable, with bars, live music, cinemas and classical concerts. Lively areas include **Leidseplein**, **Rembrandtplein** and **Nieuwezijds Voorburgwal**. The **Jordaan** area is less hectic, and pleasant for a quiet evening. Live music (including jazz and dance) can be heard at **Paradiso**, Weteringschans 6–8, ☎(020) 626 4521 (www.paradiso.nl). This is the place where the big-name rock acts do the now-compulsory smaller gig. **De Melkweg** (The Milky Way), Lijnbaansgracht 234A, ☎(020) 531 8181 (www.melkweg.nl) is particularly good for jazz and attracts some seriously stylish dudes – but you won't be turned away if your threads are a little more lived in. **Studio 80**, Rembrandtplein 17, ☎(020) 521 8333 (www.studio-80.nl), is conveniently located in the heart of the nightlife district, and has a reputation as the city's most cutting-edge and underground techno club. **Escape**, Rembrandtplein 11, ☎(020) 622 1111 (www.escape.nl), is a club where you can lose yourself in the crowd, and the classic dance anthems are banged out with no fuss and lots of decibels. That said, the city's loudest beats emerge from **Jimmy Woo**, Leidedwarsstraat 18,

The Netherlands

☎(020) 626 3150 (www.jimmywoo.nl), Amsterdam's hip hop city central. One of the hottest joints in town is **Panama**, Oostelijke Handelskade 4, ☎(020) 311 8686 (www.panama.nl), enjoys a growing reputation on the global club scene, and attracts top drawer DJs and artists. Should you feel the urge to groove soulfully, look no further than **Soul Kitchen**, Amstelstraat 32, ☎(020) 620 2333, where big dollops of hot, buttered soul and disco are served up to a reach-out-and-touch-me crowd. You can't really say you clubbed in Amsterdam – though of course you may not want to – unless you've thrown a few shapes in **Club More Amor**, Rosengracht 133, ☎(020) 624 2330 (www.clubmoreamor.nl). Being foreign and, therefore, cool will certainly help you gain admission to this beautiful people's posing-palace.

A fantastic bar in which to refuel historically is **Proeflokaal Wynand Fockink**, Pijlsteeg 31, ☎(020) 639 2695 (www.wynand-fockink.nl). This intimate little venue – it's a great place to take a new acquaintance – has been here since 1685. Somewhere you can really chill out (and in your travelling clobber, too) is **Lime**, Zeedjik 104, ☎(020) 639 3020. This is a boozeria that typifies the relaxed side of the city, and it does many a nifty little cocktail at a reasonable price. Genre-crossing **Nachttheater Sugar Factory**, Lijnbaansgracht 238, ☎(020) 626 5006 (www.sugarfactory.nl) is amazing: in the early part of the evening, when it features theatrical performances, poetry recitals, debates and what you might call the more pensive forms of expression. Then, at around midnight, it transforms into a heaving club, and things become decidedly more tribal.

Major venues for classical music and opera are the **Muziektheater** (www.het muziektheater.nl) at Waterlooplein and the **Concertgebouw** on Museumplein (which has free lunchtime concerts on Wednesday). Foreign movies are invariably subtitled, so there's a good choice of showings in English. There is a concentration of cinemas around the Leidseplein. Two spectacular Art Deco picture palaces are **Tuschinski** near the Rembrandtplein (screen 1 is the most impressive) and **The Movies** on the Haarlemmerstraat near the Jordaan.

Amsterdam has several water-related events and music festivals each year. The major arts event is the **Holland Festival** (June), which covers all the performing arts.

Above: Lisbon (Luis Elvas/Fotolia)

Below: Oporto, Portugal (Rene Drouyer/BigStockPhoto)

Left: **Lisse, Netherlands** (Regien Paassen/Dreamstime)

Above: **Bruges, Belgium** (Jean-Jacques Cordier/Fotolia)
Below: **Luxembourg** (Jean-Claude Berens/SXC.hu)

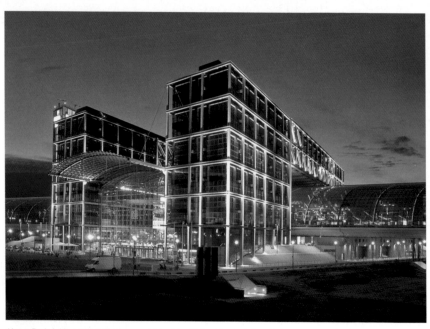

Above: Berlin's Hauptbahnhof, Germany (Holger Mette/BigStockPhoto)   Below: Freiburg countryside, Germany (Alison Rayner)

BELGIUM: BRUSSELS (BRUXELLES, BRUSSEL)

Headquarters of the EU and NATO, Brussels is an exceptionally cosmopolitan city, as well as home to a sizeable number of immigrants from around the Mediterranean. Though it's not the most glamorous or romantic of European capitals – its two most famous monuments are a statue of a urinating boy (the Manneken Pis) and an outsized 1950s atomic model (the Atomium) – it has some great art galleries, abundant greenery, a majestic central square and many excellent restaurants. There's also a wealth of Art Nouveau architecture, which, for the most part, you have to look at from the outside. Streets to head for include the Square Ambiorix and Square Marie-Louise (both just north of Schuman station) and avenue Louise, with several houses by the great Victor Horta.

Brussels is well placed for journeys by rail into the Netherlands, Germany, France and the UK, and the most interesting Belgian cities are accessible by day trip. The city is officially bilingual and there's often little similarity between the two versions of street names (e.g. French *Arts-Loi* is Dutch *Kunst-Wet*); this chapter uses the French ones.

ARRIVAL AND DEPARTURE

🚆 Virtually all long-distance trains stop at both **Midi** and **Nord** (change at Rogier from Metro No. 2 or at De Brouckère from No. 1), but many omit **Centrale** (Metro No. 1: Centrale, 5-min walk from Grand-Place). The facilities at all three include baggage lockers, eating places and newsagents that sell English papers.

Midi/Zuid (Metro No. 2) is the terminal for Eurostar services from London (fastest journey: 1hr 51 mins) and the Thalys train from Paris (1 hr 25 mins), although it's in an area best avoided at night; train information office ☎(02) 528 28 28 (daily 0700–2130; www.sncb.be or www.b-rail.be) with a Tourist Information desk (daily 0800–2000, except Fri to 2100 in summer; Mon–Thur 0800–1700, Fri 0800–2000, Sat 0900–1800, Sun 0900–1400 in winter); Midi/Zuid has good facilities for tourists but Centrale has fewer facilities for waiting passengers.

✈ **Brussels International Airport**, ☎(02) 753 77 53 (www.brusselsairport.be), at Zaventem is 14 km northeast of the centre; exchange offices and two Tourist Information desks: Brussels International–Tourism (daily 0800–2100) and Office de Promotion du Tourisme Wallonie–Bruxelles (Mon–Fri 0600–2200, Sat–Sun 0800–2100). An express rail link operates from soon after 0500 until around 2330 (four times an hour to all three main stations; journey time 20mins; fare €3). A taxi should cost just under €35.

INFORMATION

The *Brussels Guide & Map* (€3) is the most comprehensive tourist booklet available from the Tourist Office and bookshops. The English-language weekly *The Bulletin* has a useful 'What's On' supplement.

Belgium

Tourist Office

**Brussels International –
Tourism & Congress
(BI-TC)**, Hôtel de Ville,
Grand-Place, ☎ (02) 513 89 40
(www.brusselsinternational.be).
If you make a hotel booking
you will get free city and
transport maps. Better is
the **Belgian Tourist
Information Centre**:
r. du Marché-aux-Herbes 63,
☎ (02) 504 03 90,
(www.belgique-tourisme.be);
the **Brussels Card** covers
public transport and admission
to 30 museums for €20
(24 hours), €28 (48 hours)
and €33 (72 hours).

INTERNET ACCESS Brussels being the international place that it is, you're never far from an internet café or Wi-Fi point. Internet cafés offer excellent value for money too, at only €1–2 per hour. A good address is Dotspot, rue du Lombard 83, www.dotspot.be, conveniently located close to the Tourist Office Brussels International – Tourism & Congress (see left) on Grand-Place.

PUBLIC TRANSPORT

The city centre is smaller than it looks on maps and walking is the best way to get around, though it can be confusing initially. Away from the centre, the Metro and bus network is efficiently run.

MAPS Free route maps from STIB/MIVB kiosks, Metro stations and Tourist Offices. De Rouck maps are sold at newsagents.

TICKETS Individual tickets (€1.70, €2 if bought on board) can be purchased from bus drivers or in Metro stations, and multi-ride tickets from STIB/MIVB kiosks, Tourist Offices, Metro stations and some newsagents; 5-trip tickets are sold (€7.30) and 10-trip tickets (€12.30). The 1-day travelcard (€4.50) gives unlimited travel on all city transport (covers two people at weekends). Stamp your ticket in the machine by the Metro entrance or on board buses before travelling.

METRO Primarily for commuters, the Metro has few central stops. The terms 'tram' and 'Metro' are interchangeable here – of the six lines, 1, 2, 5 & 6 are metros; 3 & 4 are trams that run underground. Metro stations are indicated by a square white 'M' on a blue background. *Loket/guichet* booths for tickets are in all stations and the trams run 0530–0030. The system is comprehensive, efficient and easy to use: study the map before setting out. Lines are identified by number and colour (nos. 1/purple, 3/green, 4/pink and 5/yellow are central). Routes of the relevant line are shown on all platforms and trams, and every platform has a city map with the Metro system superimposed. Doors close automatically (don't use them after the warning buzzer sounds), but you have to open them yourself: by pressing a thin strip by the door. Smoking is prohibited throughout the system. Watch the escalators: they're pressure-activated, which is pretty smart until you miss the sign and try to walk up the down one. Trams are a great way to see the city too and the system is easy to use.

BUSES Buses also have a comprehensive network (approximately 0530–0030), and there's a very limited night service. If stops show *sur demande*, raise your hand to the driver as the vehicle approaches. If you want to get off, ring the bell.

TAXIS Ranks are strategically positioned at all the stations and main squares. Tips aren't expected but small change is always welcome.

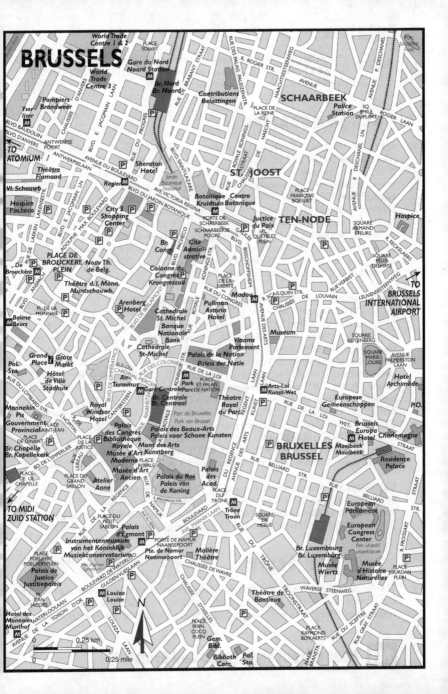

Belgium

The streets are a bit busy generally, but there's scope for cycling. Bikes can be hired from **La Maison des Cyclistes**, r. de Londres 15, ☎(02) 502 73 55 (€3/hr or €12/day); Metro: Trône. For **cycle tours** see www.provelo.be.

ACCOMMODATION

There's a fair choice of hotels in every grade, including plenty of budget establishments in the **Ixelles** and **pl. Ste-Catherine** areas, plus several hostels (HI and otherwise) and a number of bed and breakfasts. Nevertheless, advance booking is recommended – and essential in peak periods. Near Grand-Place is **Floris Arlequin Grand'Place**, 17–19 r. de la Fourche, ☎(02) 514 16 15 (www.florishotels.com), €€, offers cheaper weekend rates, and is reasonably priced and pleasant. At the bottom of the hotel price range are (all 1-star) **La Tasse d'Argent**, 48 r. du Congrès, ☎ (02) 218 83 75, € (Metro: Madou), **La Vieille Lanterne**, 29 r. des Grands Carmes, ☎(02) 512 74 94 (www.lavieillelanterne.be), €, a six-bedroomed hotel near the Manneken Pis (Metro: Gare Centrale) and **Saint Michel**, 15 Grand-Place ☎(02) 511 09 56 (www.hotelsaint michel.be), €€ (Metro: Gare Centrale).

Youth hostels: **Auberge de Jeunesse Jacques Brel (HI)**, r. de la Sablonnière 30, ☎(02) 218 01 87 (www.laj.be), € (Metro No. 2: Madou, direction Simonis, i.e. away from the centre). A sign in the ticket hall indicates the exit: leave by the right-hand stairs and continue straight along the road to the second turning left. One of the cheapest and most pleasant places, within walking distance from Nord and Centrale stations, is the **Sleep Well Youth Hotel (non-HI)**, r. du Damier 23, ☎(02) 218 50 50 (www.sleepwell.be), €. **Jeugdherberg Bruegel (HI)**, r. du St-Esprit 2, ☎(02) 511 04 36 (www.vjh.be), is 300 m from Centrale (behind Notre-Dame-de-la-Chapelle) and very modern. **Auberge de Jeunesse Génération Europe (HI)**, r. de l'Eléphant 4, ☎(02) 410 38 58 (www.laj.be), €, 2 km from Centrale (Metro: Comte de Flandre – 500 m). **CHAB–Centre Vincent van Gogh (non-HI)**, r. Traversière 8, ☎(02) 217 01 58 (www. chab.be), €, is the oldest youth hostel in Brussels and has the largest capacity, with dorm beds from €18, twins €26, singles €33. The **2Go4 Quality Hostel** is a fun hostel in downtown Brussels, blvd Emile Jacqmain 99, ☎(02) 219 3019 (www.2Go4.be), €.

Campsites: the nearest official campsite is **Camping Beersel**, Steenweg, op Ukkel 75, el 1650 Beersel, ☎(02) 331 05 61 (www.beersel.be), 9 km to the south (tram 55: Uccle). Another is **Bruxelles Europe A Ciel Ouvert**, Espace international, Chaussée de Wavre 205, ☎(02) 640 79 67, fax (02) 648 24 53 (tents only, open July and Aug only).

FOOD AND DRINK

The Belgians enjoy eating and there's a huge choice of restaurants serving excellent food, but prices tend to be high and it's advisable to book for the more upmarket restaurants. Many bars sell food and give better value than the restaurants. In the area surrounding Grand-Place you can find every imaginable type of eating place, including fast-food chains. Av. de la Couronne, especially around Ixelles cemetery and Chaussée de Wavre, offers several inexpensive establishments. One of the many bars is **La Fleur en Papier Doré**, r. des Alexiens 53–55, once a favourite of the artist Magritte. **Wittamer** (www.wittamer.com) is a renowned patisserie and tea room in pl. du Grand Sablon. There are up to 200 varieties of beer available in some bars – for something local ask for *gueuze* or *kriek*. At the extreme end of the scale, **Delirium Café**, Impasse de la Fidélité 4A, stocks an incredible 2010 different beers (in 2010), and an extra one is added each year.

HIGHLIGHTS

Grand-Place, with its ornate guildhouses, remains the heart of the city. The most imposing building is the Gothic **Hôtel de Ville** (Town Hall). The neighbouring brewers' house now contains the **Musée de la Brasserie** (Brewery Museum). Across the square, the **Maison du Roi** houses **Musée de la Ville**, covering the city's history (closed Mon). Don't miss the top floor: along with a selection of puppets is the extensive wardrobe of the **Manneken Pis**, the famous fountain (of a boy peeing) in r. de l'Étuve that was designed by Jérôme Duquesnoy in 1619. **Centre Anspach** stretches between blvd Anspach and pl. de la Monnaie. An escalator leads up from the shopping area to **Historium**, which consists of a series of wax tableaux depicting scenes from Roman times to the present. At opposite ends of Parc de Bruxelles are the **Palais de la Nation** (Belgian Parliament) and the **Palais Royal** (Royal Palace), open from late July (after the national day on 21 July) until the beginning of Sept (closed Mon) and full of rich decorations, including Goya tapestries. At the nearby **Musées Royaux des Beaux-Arts** (Royal Museums of Fine Arts), r. de la Régence 3, are two separate museums (closed Mon); don't expect to get round both sections in a day. The **Musée d'Art Moderne** has Dali's *Temptation of St Anthony*, and in 2009 a new wing opened with the world's largest collection of paintings by the Belgian surrealist Magritte (closed Mon). **Parc du Cinquantenaire** (Metro: Schuman/Merode) surrounds the Cinquantenaire, a monumental arch flanked by museums. The **Musée Royal de l'Armée et d'Histoire Militaire** (Royal Museum of the Army and Military History) has one of the world's best collections of vintage vehicles (closed Mon), while the **Musée Royaux d'Art et d'Histoire** (Royal Museum of Art and History; entrance on the far side) is a vast eclectic museum (closed Mon).

Housed in the magnificent Art Nouveau Magasin Old England, the **Musée des Instruments de Musique** has a collection of historical musical instruments from around the world, plus a superb roof-top café, r. Montagne de la Cour 2 (www.mim.fgov.be; closed Mon). Beer-lovers should visit the **Musée Bruxellois de la Gueuze**, r. Gheude 56, Anderlecht (a 10–15 min walk from Midi), a working brewery with tours that include a sampling (closed Sun). This is the only Brussels brewery producing beer by the traditional method of allowing fermentation using the natural yeasts present in the atmosphere.

Belgium

SOUTH OF THE CENTRE **Musée Victor Horta**, r. Américaine 26, Ixelles (tram 81/82/91/92), was once the home of the renowned Belgian architect, and the interior is typical of his flowing Art Nouveau style, notably the famous staircase (closed Mon). The **Belgian Centre for Comic Strip Art**, r. des Sables 20 (closed Mon), offers a different aspect of local culture, depicting the history of one of Belgium's more contemporary art forms in an Art Nouveau warehouse designed by Horta. The star is, of course, Hergé's Tintin. From Brussels, **Waterloo** battlesite is 30 mins by train, or 40 mins by bus from pl. Rouppe. Here, where Napoleon's forces were defeated in 1815, there's much more to see than at most battlegrounds, with an informative visitor centre, and two massive monuments: the grassy pyramid of the Butte du Lion memorial, and a Grand Panorama – a rotunda created in 1912 with battle scenes painted on its walls.

NORTH WEST OF THE CENTRE The 102-m-high **Atomium**, blvd du Centenaire (Metro 1/19/81: Heysel), is a gigantic model of an iron atom, built for the World Fair in 1958. Several modules are linked (escalators up, easy stairs down) to form a series of exhibits about the human body and medicine. Don't miss the view from the top module, to which there's a high-speed lift (keep the ticket to get into the museum).

SHOPPING

Much of the lace on offer is actually made in the Far East, so check that it's Belgian before buying. **Louise Verschueren** (www.belgian-lace.com) is a good local name to look out for. Of the many delicious chocolates, **Godiva** and **Leonidas** are popular. Around r. Neuve are many affordable shopping malls. **Galeries Royales St-Hubert** (off r. des Bouchers) is a vaulted arcade with lots of sculptures and a mixture of shops. Brussels has several markets. **Midi Market** (near Gare du Midi, Sun 0600–1300), resembles a North African *souk* and is the place for food and clothes bargains. There's a **flower market** in the Grand-Place, Tues–Sun 0800–1800, Mar–Oct.

NIGHT-TIME AND EVENTS

The Bulletin, a weekly English-language paper, has a comprehensive 'What's On' supplement, and the Tourist Office publishes free **Brussels Your Guide to the Night** plus a free list of musical performances that includes clubs and discos, jazz, opera, films, etc. Clustered around Fernand Cocq and the lower end of ch. d'Ixelles are lots of **bars** with music, many staying open until the early hours. The area around Grand-Place is lively at night. All major events centre on **Grand-Place**. These include several jazz festivals, **Ommegang** (a historical pageant, end June/early July) and the **Tapis de Fleurs** (mid-August biennial; even years), when the whole square is carpeted with flowers, and an ice-skating rink and Christmas market in December. The **National Holiday** (21 July) offers varied entertainments.

ROUTE DETAIL

Ostend–Bruges
ETT tables 400, 405

Type	Frequency	Typical journey time
Train	2 per hr	15 mins

Bruges–Ghent
ETT 400, 401

Type	Frequency	Typical journey time
Train	3 per hr	23 mins

Ghent–Antwerp
ETT table 406

Type	Frequency	Typical journey time
Train	2 per hr	49 mins

Antwerp–Brussels
ETT table 410

Type	Frequency	Typical journey time
Train	4 per hr	50 mins

Brussels–Liège
ETT tables 400, 401

Type	Frequency	Typical journey time
Train	2–3 per hr	1 hr 3 mins

Liège–Maastricht
ETT table 403

Type	Frequency	Typical journey time
Train	Every hr	29 mins

Maastricht–Namur
ETT tables 403, 435

Type	Frequency	Typical journey time
Train	Every hr	1 hr 20 mins

Namur–Luxembourg
ETT table 430

Type	Frequency	Typical journey time
Train	Every hr	2 hrs

KEY JOURNEYS

Ostend–Brussels
ETT table 400

Type	Frequency	Typical journey time
Train	Every hr	1 hr 12 mins

Brussels–Paris
ETT table 18

Type	Frequency	Typical journey time
Train	1–2 per hr	1 hr 22 mins

Brussels–Amsterdam
ETT table 18

Type	Frequency	Typical journey time
Train	1–2 per hr	2 hrs 44 mins

Brussels–Cologne
ETT table 20

Type	Frequency	Typical journey time
Train	Every 2 hrs	1 hr 57 mins

Note
Ostend to Luxembourg:
change trains at Brussels Midi.

Benelux

Not a hill in sight for most of the way, until you cross the hills of the Ardennes in southern Belgium and the Grand Duchy of Luxembourg, but there's plenty of man-made interest, notably the handsome cities of **Bruges**, **Ghent** and **Antwerp**, each boasting impressive legacies of medieval prosperity, and deserving at least a night's stay; Luxembourg itself has a remarkable natural site, perched on two deep gorges. A trip to **Maastricht** (just over the border in the Netherlands) is recommended. From the little capital of **Luxembourg** (Luxembourg City) it is only a short rail journey to the Roman town of **Trier** in Germany (p302) or southwards to **Metz** in France, where you can join the **Cherbourg–Strasbourg** route (p90).

OSTEND (OOSTENDE), BELGIUM

A fishing port, ferry port and seaside resort rolled into one, Ostend is not likely to detain you for long, but there are excellent seafood restaurants (oysters are a local speciality). The three-masted *Mercator*, a training vessel in authentic style, now houses a maritime museum, **Noordzeeaquarium** (on the front), which displays the flora and fauna of the North Sea. The studio where the Expressionist painter James Ensor worked has become a museum devoted to him (**James Ensorhuis**, Vlaanderenstraat 27, closed Tues), and many of his possessions are among the exhibits in **Museum voor Schone Kunsten** (Fine Arts Museum), Leopold de Waelplaats (closed Mon). **PMMK** (**Museum voor Moderne Kunst aan zee Oostende** (Modern Art Museum by the Sea Ostend), Romestraat 11, contains modern paintings and sculptures (closed Mon).

[RAIL] Adjacent to the port, a 20-min walk from the Tourist Office (or 🚌 5). Note: there are currently no foot passenger ferry services to Ostend.

[i] **Tourist Office**: Monacoplein 2, ☎(059) 70 11 99 (www.toerisme-oostende.be). Walk right from the station and along the seafront, then take the last turning left before the front curves. Sells the A–Z brochure and town map.

🏠 **Youth hostel (HI)**: **De Ploate**, Langestraat 82, ☎(059) 80 52 97 (www.vjh.be), 1 km from train and bus stations and ferry terminal.

BRUGES (BRUGGE), BELGIUM

A powerful trading city 500 years ago, Bruges became an economic backwater and the industrial age largely passed it by. Located in the heart of Flanders, it has survived as one of northern Europe's most impressive medieval cities and, despite the throngs of tourists, you still get the feeling of stepping back in time in its cobbled streets, although it's an expensive and affluent place and it's worth getting away from the crowded main squares into the quieter back streets. A boat trip on the extensive and pretty canal system is a good introduction to the town, with frequent departures from quays along **Dijver**, which, along with **Groene Rei** and **Rozenhoedkaai**, provide some of the vintage views of Bruges. After that, explore on foot – the Tourist Office has an English 'Walkman' guide. Most places of interest are in a small area around **Markt** and **Burg**, and much of it is tranquil and traffic-free. Seek out the windmills on the old city ramparts near **Kruispoort** (east of the centre).

Markt, Bruges' large, lively and impressive main square, is surrounded by guild buildings, many of which have been converted into restaurants and bars. All around are shops selling those world-famous Belgian chocolates and truffles. **Belfort**, an octagonal 88-m belfry and a useful landmark, is mainly 13th century, but the top storey was added in the 15th century. There are 366 steps to the top (closed Mon).

The Burg, the other main square, features monumental buildings, notably the **Heilige Bloed Basiliek** (Basilica of the Holy Blood), with an early 12th-century stone chapel below a 16th-century chapel (closed Mon afternoons, Oct–Mar). Other buildings around the square include the Renaissance **Civiele Griffie** (Recorder's House) and the neoclassical **Gerechtshof** (Court of Justice). The Gothic **Stadhuis** (Town Hall) has a magnificent hall with a vaulted ceiling and murals (closed Mon).

DAY TRIP FROM BRUGES

Quasimodo Tours, Leenhofweg 7 (www.quasimodo.be), runs an English-language day trip in a minibus, which includes **Damme**, two castles, **Zeebrugge** harbour, waffle sampling, a visit to Chocolate World and a guided tour of a chocolate factory and beer tasting. (departs Mon, Wed and Fri, Feb–Dec). They also run day trips to the Flanders Battlefields (departs Tue, Thur and Sun, Feb–Dec, and Wed, Fri and Sun (Apr–Oct). Departs Park Hotel ('t Zand) and picks up at various hotels (if you request this when booking).

BEGIJNHOF

A visit to Bruges would not be complete without a walk around the walled convent community of the Begijnhof. The houses where Beguine nuns lived are neatly arranged near the **Minnewater**, a tranquil, swan-populated lake whose name means 'Love Lake'.

Dijver is the central canal; Dijverstraat (scene of a weekend antiques and flea market) is home to several museums. **Groeningemuseum** (closed Mon) houses a fine collection of Flemish art from the 15th century to date, notably primitive and expressionist works. **Bruggemuseum-Gruuthuse** (closed Mon), on the same side of the street, was a 16th-century palace. **Arentshuis** is noted for its collection of lace (closed Mon). **Onze-Lieve Vrouwekerk** (Church of Our Lady), Mariastraat, has Belgium's second highest spire (122 m).

Among its treasures are a white marble Madonna and Child by Michelangelo. The nearby **Kathedraal St-Salvator** (St Saviour's Cathedral), Steenstraat, contains Gobelin tapestries, a rood-loft organ and a Louis XVI-style pulpit.

A 20-min walk southwest of the centre; buses stop in front (tickets and a free route map from the De Lijn kiosk). To the right as you leave the station is a branch of the Tourist Office.

i **Tourist Office**: (municipal): Concertgebouw (Concert Hall), 't Zand 34, and at

Benelux

the railway Station, ☎(050) 48 46 46, (www.brugge.be). (Provincial) (West Flanders): Koning Albert I-Laan 120, Sint-Michiels, ☎(050) 30 55 00 (www.westtoer.be).

🛏 Book ahead. **Youth hostel (HI)**: **Europa**, Baron Ruzettelaan 143, Assebroek, ☎(050) 35 26 79 (www.vjh.be), €, is about 1.5 km east of the station (2 km south of Markt; 🚌 2: Steenbruges). **Herdersbrug**, Louis Coiseaukaai 46, Dudzele, ☎(050) 59 93 21 (www.vjh.be), €, is about 5 km from the station (🚌 788: Brugges/Knokke or 🚌 2: Breskens). **Private hostels**: **Bauhaus**, Langestraat 133–137, ☎(050) 34 10 93 (www.bauhaus.be), €, 🚌 6/16: Kruispoort; **Snuffel Backpacker Hostel**, Ezelstraat 47–49, ☎(050) 33 31 33, (www.snuffel.be), €, characterful and central; **Lybeer Traveller's Hostel**, Korte Vuldersstr. 31, ☎(050) 33 43 55 (www.hostellybeer.com), a renovated Catholic rectory in Bruges' medieval city centre. **Campsite**: **Memling**, Veltemweg 109, (050) 35 58 45 (www.camping-memling.be), 3 km east of the station (🚌 11).

🍴 Bruges is a great place to eat, drink and enjoy the Belgian lifestyle. The main square has many inexpensive pavement restaurants serving mussels and chips, but there's more sophisticated fare on offer too, in the side streets and along the canals. There's no shortage of bars offering Belgian beers.

GHENT (GENT), BELGIUM

Ghent is a deeply Flemish town, steeped in culture, yet very lively during the university year. For ten days in July, **Gentse Feesten** (traditionally a holiday for factory workers) dominates the town, with lots of cheap food, high beer consumption and street entertainments, as well as a variety of more formal performances. The 12th–17th-century **guildhouses** along the **Graslei quay** and the old houses by the **Kraanlei quay** provide two of the city's classic views. There are summer boat trips on the River Leie, excursions including Bruges.

Sint-Baafskathedraal (St Bavo's Cathedral), resplendent with marble statuary and a baroque organ and pulpit, contains Van Eyck's multi-panelled masterpiece *The Adoration of the Mystic Lamb*, painted in 1432 and considered to be the most important work of church art in Belgium (entry fee); parts were repeatedly stolen through centuries of turbulence, and the Adam and Eve nude panels were at one stage replaced by bearskin-clad versions (since discarded, but on display), strangely reminiscent of the Flintstones. The Romanesque crypt contains medieval tombs, frescos and examples of local stonework. You can ascend the 90-m **Belfort** (belfry) by lift.

Gravensteen, Sint-Veerleplein, the 12th-century 'Castle of the Counts', has a museum that displays a selection of gruesome instruments of torture, with illustrations of how they were used. You can also walk round the ramparts and explore the castle grounds. Allow plenty of time for the fascinating **Het Huis van Alijn** (Alijn House), Kraanlei 65 (closed Mon), which spreads through three converted almshouses. It portrays the town's lifestyle at the beginning of the 20th century and is crammed with pleasingly unrelated everyday items – toys, flat irons, hats, etc.

🚆 **Gent-St-Pieters**: south of the centre (tram 1/10/11/12: Korenmarkt). De Lijn bus/tram information to the left as you exit.

$\boxed{i}$ **Tourist Offices**: (municipal): Botermarkt 17A (in the crypt of the Belfry), ☎(09) 266 56 60 (www.visitgent.be). (Provincial) (East Flanders): **Het Metselaarshuis**, St-Niklaasstraat 2, ☎(09) 269 26 00 (www.tov.be).

🖷 **Use-it Gent**, ☎(09) 324 39 06 (www.use-it.be) is an accommodation and information service for budget travellers. **Youth hostel (HI): De Draecke**, St-Widostraat 11, ☎(09) 233 70 50 (www.ghent-hostel.com), northwest of city centre and 3 km from the rail station; tram to Gravensteen, then 1.2-km walk northwest. **Campsite: Camping Blaarmeersen**, Zuiderlaan 12, ☎(09) 266 81 60 (www.gent.be/blaarmeersen); open Mar–mid-Oct.

ANTWERP (ANTWERPEN/ANVERS), BELGIUM

Belgium's second city, Antwerp has enough for at least a couple of days' sightseeing, including an extensive old Flemish quarter, plus views over the **River Schelde** (or Scheldt), on which boat tours are available.

The National Scheepvartmuseum (National Maritime Museum), previously located in the medieval **Steen** (Castle) which overlooks the River Schelde, is being re-housed – along with the Ethnographic Museum and other city collections – north of the historical centre in the new purpose-built **Museum aan de Stroom** (www.mas.be), scheduled to open in mid-2010. The **Diamantmuseum**, Koningin Astridplein 19–23 (walkable from Centraal station), covers all aspects of the diamond trade, one of the cornerstones of Antwerp's appreciable fortunes (closed Wed). Perhaps Antwerp's most astonishing survival is the unique **Plantin-Moretus Museum/Stedelijk Prentenkabinet**, Vrijdagmarkt 22-23 (closed Mon), a perfectly preserved 16th–18th-century printer's works and home built by the famous printer Plantin; don't spend too long on the first few rooms – the most interesting parts come later on. The **cathedral** is Belgium's largest (free multilingual tours; entrance on Handschoenmarkt), built 1352–1521. Its 123-m tower – Belgium's tallest – would have been one of a pair had the money not run out. Highlights here are four enormous masterpieces by Rubens and some recently revealed 15th-century frescos. Grote Markt is home to the 19th-century **Brabo Fountain** (which depicts the legend of the city's founding), elaborately gabled guildhouses and the Renaissance **Stadhuis** (Town Hall). Not far away is the **Vleeshuis** (Butchers' Hall), Vleeshouwersstr. 38/40 (closed Mon), now an applied arts museum with wood-carvings, antique china, old musical instruments and lots of ticking grandfather clocks. On Sunday mornings, **Vogelmarkt** (Bird Market), Oude Vaartplaats, sells birds – plus almost everything else. The **Openluchtmuseum voor Beeldhouwkunst** (Open-Air Sculpture Museum), Middelheimlaan 61 (🚌 18/17), is dotted with sculptures, notably by Rodin and Moore (closed Mon). All museums offer free admission on the last Wednesday of each month (except during temporary exhibitions).

🚆 **Antwerpen-Centraal**, 2 km east of the centre, linked by Metro-tram. The station has been completely redeveloped to accommodate the high-speed line to the Netherlands, opened in late 2009. De Lijn's office is in Centraal's Metro-tram stop, Diamant; you can get transport maps and tickets from them.

Benelux

ℹ️ **Tourist Office**: (municipal): Grote Markt 13–15, ☎(03) 232 01 03 (www.antwerpen.be). From Centraal, take Metro 2/15 to Groenplaats (direction: Linkeroever), near the cathedral. (Provincial): Koningin Elisabethlei 16, ☎(03) 240 63 73 (www.provant.be).

🏠 The Tourist Office gets good discounts. Some cheap places near Centraal (beware that some rent by the hour). **Abhostel**, Kattenberg 110 , ☎(04) 735 70166 (www.abhostel.com), is a super-friendly hostel run by a passionate backpacker; **Mabuhay**, Draakstr. 32, ☎(03) 290 88 15 (www.mabuhay.be), €, is an Asian-style gay-friendly Bed & Breakfast hotel in the hip Zurenborg area. **Guesthouse 26**, Pelgrimsstraat 26, ☎0497 428 369, fax: (03) 289 3994, is a small, friendly B&B just steps from the cathedral, €. **Youth hostel (HI)**: **Op Sinjoorke**, Eric Sasselaan 2, ☎(03) 238 02 73 (www.vjh.be); 0.5 km from south station, 🚌 2 to Bouwcentrum or 🚌 27.

BRUSSELS (BRUXELLES/BRUSSEL)

See p241.

LIÈGE (LUIK/LÜTTICH), BELGIUM

Change here for the detour to **Maastricht**. Liège is an industrial, sprawling city; the rail station is 2 km south of the centre.

MAASTRICHT, THE NETHERLANDS

Tucked into the southern, mildly hilly corner of the Netherlands, the provincial capital of Limburg and busy university town has a captivating atmosphere in its lively squares and precincts, in its distinctive stone houses and its ebullient February carnival. You can get a good view from the tower of **Sint Janskerk**, next to huge **Sint Servaasbasiliek** (see the 11th- and 12th-century crypts). The most atmospheric church is the elaborately decorated Romanesque **Onze-Lieve-Vrouwe Basiliek**, with a statue that is credited with miraculous powers. At **Museumkelder Derlon**, there are *in situ* remnants of Roman Maastricht, while centuries-old **fortifications** abound in and around the city, notably at **Fort Sint Pieter**. **St Pietersberg Caves** are the result of centuries of excavation of marl stone, which have left a labyrinth of more than 20,000 passages; you can visit two sections (daily guided tours in English in July and August). The rocket-shaped **Bonnefantenmuseum**, De Bosquetplein 7 (closed Mon), is a fascinating structure containing three distinct sections: sculpture and religious/magical artefacts, Old Masters and contemporary works.

🚉 A 10-min walk east of the centre.

ℹ️ **Tourist Office**: **VVV Tourist Office**, Kleine Staat 1, ☎(043) 325 21 21 (www.vvvmaastricht.nl).

🏠 Cheap options around the station and in the Markt area. **Youth hostel (HI)**: Stayokay Maastricht, Maasboulevard 101, ☎(043) 750 17 90 (www.stayokay.com). **Campsite**: **Camping Dousberg**, Dousbergweg 102, ☎(043) 43 21 71.

LUXEMBOURG (CITY)

One of Europe's smallest capitals, Luxembourg is a pleasant place in which to pass a day or two. The city was founded in Roman times and is dramatically sited on a gorge cut by the rivers **Alzette** and **Pétrusse**. It falls naturally into three sections: the **old centre** (north of the Pétrusse Valley and home to most of the sights); the **modern city** and **station** (south of the gorge); and **Grund** (the valley settlement), reachable by deep escalators or lift from the central part of town. Descending to the Grund ('the ground') is like entering a different, darker city, and it is this area that houses most of Luxembourg's racier nightlife. As well as the usual guided tours, there are circular self-guided walks (leaflets available from the Tourist Office) or take the **Pétrusse Express** (a misnomer: it's slow-moving; runs Mar–Oct) from pl. de la Constitution. The **Cathédrale Nôtre-Dame**, a 17th-century Jesuit church, contains the simple stone crypt that is the tomb of Duke John the Blind (King of Bohemia and Count of Luxembourg), backed by statues of mourners. Bronze lions flank a gate through which can be seen the burial chapel of the Grand-Ducal family. From pl. de la Constitution there is access to the **Pétrusse casemates**: the underground passages that formed part of the city's original defences (open Easter, Whitsun and school holidays). Tours take 45 mins and you need to be reasonably fit. If you're in doubt, opt for the similar casemates at **Rocher du Bock** (open Mar–Oct), which are easier. The entrance is on r. Sigefroi, the site where Count Siegfried built the **original fortress**, later expanded, especially by the French in the 17th century.

DAY TRIPS FROM LUXEMBOURG

About 25 mins by train north of the capital, Ettelbrück is the base for visiting (by bus) **Echternach**, a 7th-century Benedictine abbey founded by St Willibrord, an English missionary monk.

One wing of the basilica houses the **Musée de l'Abbaye** (open Easter–Oct), with its display of **illuminated manuscripts**, including Codex Aureus, the gospels decorated in gold and bound in a 10th-century gold cover encrusted with enamel and gems.

🚆 **Gare Centrale**, a 15-min walk south of the centre; showers.

ℹ️ **Tourist Office**: (city): pl. Guillaume II, ☎22 28 09, (www.lcto.lu) in the old town; (national): in the central station, ☎42 82 82-20 (www.ont.lu).

🏨 Most of the cheaper hotels are near the station. A good moderately priced (€–€€) option is the **Bristol**, 11 r. de Strasbourg, ☎48 58 29 (www.hotel-bristol.lu). Not cheap, but located right on Place d'Armes in the old centre is the 3-star **Hotel Français**, 14 pl. d'Armes, ☎47 45 34 (www.hotelfrancais.lu), €€–€€€. **Youth hostel (HI)**: 2 r. du Fort Olisy (3 km from the station), ☎22 68 89 20 (www.youthhostels.lu), €. 🚌 9: Vallée d'Alzette (150 m from the stop, down a steep hill, or call for shuttle pick-up (€2)). **Campsite: Camping Kockelscheuer**, Rte de Bettembourg 22, Kockelscheuer, ☎47 18 15 (www.camp-kockelscheuer.lu), is south of the centre, 4 km from Gare Centrale and 200 m from the 🚌 18 stop; open Mar–Oct.

🍽️ Avoid the tacky eateries near the station – there are much better mid-range ones in the old centre. Pl. d'Armes is full of cafés, with open-air entertainment on most summer evenings. There's a regular food market in pl. Guillaume II (Wed and Sat 0800–1200).

THE NETHERLANDS

Amsterdam–Haarlem ETT tables 450, 496

Type	Frequency	Typical journey time
Train	6 per hour	16 mins

Haarlem–Leiden ETT tables 450

Type	Frequency	Typical journey time
Train	4–6 per hour	19 mins

Leiden–The Hague ETT table 450

Type	Frequency	Typical journey time
Train	6 per hour	13 mins

The Hague–Delft ETT tables 450, 472

Type	Frequency	Typical journey time
Train	4 per hour	12 mins

Delft–Rotterdam ETT tables 450, 472

Type	Frequency	Typical journey time
Train	4–6 per hour	12 mins

Rotterdam–Gouda ETT tables 465, 481

Type	Frequency	Typical journey time
Train	6 per hour	20 mins

Gouda–Utrecht ETT table 481

Type	Frequency	Typical journey time
Train	8 per hour	20 mins

Utrecht–Arnhem ETT table 468

Type	Frequency	Typical journey time
Train	4 per hour	39 mins

Arnhem–Apeldoorn ETT tables 475, 498

Type	Frequency	Typical journey time
Train	2 per hour	50 mins

Apeldoorn–Amsterdam ETT table 480

Type	Frequency	Typical journey time
Train	2 per hour	1 hr 4 mins

Notes

Arnhem to Apeldoorn: change at Zutphen.

Apeldoorn to Amsterdam: change at Amersfoort on some services.

This is a circular tour of much of the best of the Netherlands, through such classic canal-laced towns as **Delft** and **Gouda** (famous for porcelain and cheese respectively), across the **Bulb District** between **Haarlem** (worth a stop for the Frans Hals Museum) and the university town of **Leiden**, and past **Arnhem**. The round trip offers an impressive show of past and present, with some remarkable modern architecture, magnificent art collections and such oddities as **Rotterdam**'s vertigo-inducing **Euromast**.

AMSTERDAM

See p231.

HAARLEM

The late Gothic **St Bavo/Grote-Kerk** (1370–1520), with its soaring 80-m wooden lantern tower, contains a notable 16th-century screen and the famous Christian Müller baroque pipe-organ (1738), on which both Handel and Mozart played; it's still used for regular concerts. The Antwerp-born painter Frans Hals is buried here. He spent most of his life in Haarlem, and much of his work is in the **Frans Hals Museum**, Groot Heiligland 62 (closed Mon); the highlight of the collection is a group of his paintings depicting militia companies. The Netherlands' oldest public museum, which first went on view in 1784, is the **Teylers Museum**, Spaarne 16, an entertaining miscellany of old scientific instruments, fossils, gemstones, coins and above all a fine display of drawings (by Raphael, Michelangelo, Rembrandt and others).

Corrie ten Boom Museum, Barteljorisstr. 19 (closed Sun & Mon), was founded by Willem ten Boom in 1837 as a clock shop; the family tradition of helping the needy extended to the Jews in World War II. The family were betrayed in 1944 and most perished in the camps, but the house is maintained as a monument to the family's courage and charity.

🚉 A 10-min walk north of the centre.

ℹ️ **Tourist Office**: Verwulft 11, ☎0900 616 1600 (premium rate), (www.vvvzk.nl).

🛏️ **Youth hostel (HI)**: Jan Gijzenpad 3, ☎(023) 537 3793 (www.stayokay.com/haarlem). Accommodation generally is limited; better choice in Zandvoort (see right).

DAY TRIP FROM HAARLEM

Zandvoort (10 mins by train and frequent buses in summer) is a busy beach resort (casino; sandy beaches including nudist beach 200 m from station) and has plenty of cheap pensions. Tourist Office: Bakkerstraat 2B, ☎(023) 571 7947 (www.vvvzk.nl).

The Netherlands

LEIDEN

Birthplace of Rembrandt, this delightful old university town has a medieval quarter, centred on the vast Pieterskerk, plenty of studenty haunts and some excellent museums, covering archaeology (**Rijksmuseum van Oudheden**, Rapenburg 28), local history and art (**De Lakenhal**, Oude Singel 28–32), changing exhibitions from around the world (**Voor Volkenkunde**, Steenstr. 1) and milling (within a windmill; **Molenmuseum de Valk**, Binnenvestgracht 1). In the **Boerhaave**, Lange St Agnietenstr. 10, is an anatomical theatre, complete with skeletons and displays of early medical paraphernalia. The university, founded in 1575, includes the world's oldest botanic gardens (**Hortus Botanicus**).

DAY TRIP FROM LEIDEN

Keukenhof Gardens (near Lisse; 🚌 54 in season from Leiden): the showcase of the Dutch bulb industry (late Mar–late May; best in April), noted for tulips, narcissi and hyacinths; take a picnic because the cafés are invariably overcrowded.

🚆 A 10-min walk northwest of the centre.

ℹ️ **Tourist Office**: Stationsweg 41, ☎(071) 516 6000 (www.vvvleiden.nl).

🏨 **Nieuw Minerva**, Boommarkt 23, ☎(071) 512 6358 (www.nieuwminerva.nl), €€. Stylish 3-star canalside hotel in town centre.

THE HAGUE (DEN HAAG, 'S-GRAVENHAGE)

GALLERIES

One of the great galleries of the world, the **Mauritshuis**, Korte Vijverberg 8 (tram/bus: see Binnenhof, right; closed Mon), is a Renaissance mansion on the famous Hofvijver (Courtpond), housing much of the royal collection, with paintings by the major Flemish masters, including Rembrandt and Vermeer. A few steps from the Mauritshuis is the **Escher in het Paleis** museum, Lange Voorhout 74, showcasing the work of Dutch graphic artist M C Escher. It includes a mind-bending multimedia exhibit which takes you inside some of his more impossible creations.

The administrative capital of the Netherlands is a pleasant town, spread over a wide area of parks and canals and centred around **Binnenhof**, the home of the **Dutch parliament** (guided tours; tram 1/2/3/6/8/9/10/16/17, 🚌 4/22). The 13th-century **Ridderzaal** (Knights' Hall) hosts official ceremonies.

Installed in a rotunda, the remarkable **Panorama Mesdag**, Zeestr. 65 (tram 10 – peak hours only – or 🚌 22/24; closed March), consists of a realistic circular view of the North Sea resort of **Scheveningen** painted by Hendrik Mesdag, his wife and some friends in 1881. The current equivalent might be the **Omniversum**, President Kennedylaan 5 (tram 17, 🚌 4 – or through the small garden to the rear of **Gemeentemuseum**), a stunning spectacle with a wrap-around movie screen that makes you feel like a participant in the action: English headphones are available.

Rail Tour: Amsterdam – Gouda – Amsterdam

Most of the city's palaces can be viewed only from the outside. An exception is the huge **Vredespaleis** (Peace Palace), Carnegieplein 2 (tram 1, 🚌 24), which houses the International Court of Justice and the Permanent Court of Arbitration; it is a strange architectural mishmash, with a display of items donated by world leaders. There are normally tours Mon–Sat 1100–1500 (advance booking only, ☎(070) 302 4242).

🚉 **Centraal (CS)** is a 5-min walk from the centre and serves most Dutch cities. Fast services for Amsterdam and Rotterdam use **HS** (Hollandse Spoor) station (1 km south). Centraal and HS are linked by frequent trains and by tram 10/17.

ℹ️ **Tourist Office**: Hofweg 1, ☎0900 340 3505 (premium rate), (www.denhaag.com). Buy a proper street map, as the free small ones are deceptive in scale.

🚌 There is an excellent bus and tram network.

🛏️ If money is a consideration, base yourself at Scheveningen or ask VVV about private rooms. One good bet is the **Youth hostel (HI)**: Scheepmakersstraat 27, ☎(070) 315 7888 (www.stayokay.com), €, a 5-min walk northeast of HS station.

DELFT

Long famed for Delftware porcelain and birthplace of the artist Vermeer, Delft is an elegant town with old merchants' houses lining the canal. It has a number of porcelain factories where you can watch the traditional processes in action; the oldest is **De Koninklijke Porceleyne Fles** (Rotterdamseweg 196; closed Sun, Nov–late Mar), but more central is **Aardewerk-atelier de Candelaer** (Kerkstr. 14).

Stedelijk Museum Het Prinsenhof (the Prince's Court), St Agathaplein 1, includes silverware, tapestries, paintings and Delftware. Across the road is **Nusantara Museum**, with a collection of art from the former Dutch East Indies.

Nieuwe Kerk (New Church) houses the huge black-and-white marble mausoleum of Prince William, and its 109-m spire provides great views.

A nice way to see Delft is by horse-drawn tram from Markt, or by canal cruise.

🚉 A 5-min walk south of the centre.

ℹ️ **Tourism Information Point**, Hippolytusbuurt 4, ☎(015) 215 4051 (www.delft.com).

The Netherlands

ROTTERDAM

The city was virtually flattened in World War II, but much of its modern architecture is strikingly innovative (**Lijnbaan** was the European pioneer of shopping precincts, for example). Situated at the delta of the rivers **Rhine**, **Maas** and **Waal**, **Europoort** is the world's largest container port; **harbour tours** operated by **Spido**, Willemsplein 85, ☎(010) 275 9988 (www.spido.nl) (Metro: Leuvehaven, tram 8/23/25); not running Mon–Wed, Nov–Mar.

The **Museum Boijmans Van Beuningen**, Museumpark 18/20, ☎(010) 441 9400 (Metro: Eendrachtsplein, tram 7; closed Mon), is massive and high quality, with applied and fine art (including clocks, lace and paintings by Dalí, Magritte, Rembrandt, Van Gogh and Bosch). **Maritiem Museum Rotterdam**, Leuvehaven 1, ☎(010) 413 2680 (Metro: Beurs, tram 8/23/25, ⊟ 32; closed Mon except July–Aug and school holidays), is the country's oldest and biggest maritime museum.

The 185-m **Euromast**, Parkhaven 20 (Metro: Dijkzigt, tram 7/20), towers over the trees in **Central Park**. This is the highest structure in the Netherlands. Even from the first platform you have panoramic views of the 37-km-long waterfront, but go right to the top on the **Space Adventure**, a simulated rocket flight: after blast-off you go into 'orbit' and have breathtaking views as the capsule ascends and revolves slowly to the top. **Abseiling** is possible May–Sept.

The most striking modern buildings are located on the south side of **Erasmusbridge** (Metro: Wilhelminaplein) and near Metro station Blaak, with its futuristic cube houses which are now home to the city's youth hostel (see below).

🚈 **Centraal**, on the northern edge of the centre (blue line Metro).

ℹ️ **Tourist Office**: Coolsingel 5 (5-min walk from Centraal; follow the signs), ☎0900 403 4065 (www.rotterdam.info). *R'uit* is a free monthly listing. VVV sells advantageous combination tickets (travel and attractions and reduction in restaurants).

🚌 **RET**: Coolsingel 141, ☎0900 92 92 (www.ret.nl). The Rotterdam Metro has fully embraced the new *OV-Chipkaart* electronic ticketing system (see Essentials, p227) and *strippenkaarten* are no longer valid (they can still be used on buses and trams, however). Metro stations are indicated by a large yellow M. Only two lines matter for the centre: blue (north–south) and red (east–west), intersecting at Beurs. Trams fill the gaps in the Metro; summer-service tourist tram 10 visits all the main places of interest. Buses are more useful away from the centre.

🛏️ Plenty of middle-range options. Cheap hotel areas: about 1 km southwest of CS (try Gravendijkwal and Heemraadsingel) and just north of CS (try Provenierssingel). **Youth hostel (HI): Stayokay Rotterdam**, Overblaak 85-87, ☎(010) 436 5763 (www.stayokay.com/rotterdam), €, (Metro: Blaak), is now spectacularly located inside the city's famous cube houses, created by Dutch architect Piet Blom in 1984. You can't miss them as you exit the Metro station. **Campsite: Stadscamping Rotterdam**, Kanaalweg 84, ☎(010) 415 3440 (www.stadscamping-rotterdam.nl), west of CS (⊟ 33), is open all year. Cheap dormitory accommodation (early June–late Aug) is at

Sleep-Inn SSR Rotterdam, Mauritsweg 29,
☎(010) 414 3256 (www.ssrr.nl/sleep-in),
a 5-min walk south of CS.

WHERE NEXT FROM ROTTERDAM?

*Head south to **Antwerp** (ETT table 450)
to join the **Ostend–Brussels** route.*

GOUDA

This quaint place exemplifies small-town Holland, with a ring of quiet canals around ancient buildings. The 15th-century **Stadhuis** (Town Hall) is the oldest Gothic municipal building in Holland, while **Sint Janskerk** (the Netherlands' longest church) is famed throughout the country for its 64 superb 16th-century stained-glass windows. The old **Waag** (weigh-house) in Marktplein (the market square) opens for trading on Thursday morning, 1000–around 1230 (mid-June–early Sept). Gouda cheese comes in several grades (the extra-mature is hard and deliciously strong), while syrup waffles (or *goudse*) are another speciality.

📠 A 10-min walk north of the centre.

i **Tourist Office**: Markt 27, ☎0900 468 3288 (www.vvvgouda.nl).

UTRECHT

Tree-lined canals encircle the old town at the heart of this sizeable city, not a major tourist destination but worth a brief visit. **Domtoren**, the 112-m cathedral tower (🚌 2/22, but the 10-min walk from CS takes less time), is the tallest in the Netherlands, and gives a marvellous view – if you can face 465 steps. Utrecht is the headquarters of Dutch Railways (NS), and home to the **Nederlands Spoorwegmuseum** (Rail Museum), Maliebaanstation 16, closed Mon, 🚌 11 or take the special train from Utrecht CS (only runs during school holidays). The highly entertaining **Nationaal Museum van Speelklok tot Pierement**, Steenweg 6 (10-min walk from Utrecht CS), covers mechanical musical instruments from music boxes to barrel-organs, with demonstrations given (closed Mon). To the east of the centre, the **Rietveld Schröderhuis**, Prins Hendriklaan 50a (closed Mon), dates from 1924 and represents one of the most radical architectural designs of its day, with an open plan divided by internal sliding doors, and ingenious use of light and space.

📠 **Centraal**: west of the centre, separated from the old quarter by the Hoog Catharijne indoor shopping centre. There are several outlying stations; don't get off until you reach Centraal.

i **Tourist Office: Utrecht City Centre**: Domplein 9, ☎0900 12 8732 (www.12utrecht.nl).

🛏 The **Hostel B&B**, Lucas Bolwerk 4, ☎06 5043 4884 (www.hostelutrecht.nl), part of a non-profit budget accommodation organisation; free internet access and lunch bag, TV in all rooms, 15 mins from rail station.

The Netherlands

ARNHEM

Attractions are scattered, but an excellent bus network makes reaching them easy.

Attractions include **Burgers' Zoo**, Antoon van Hooff-plein 1 (🚌 3, plus 🚌 13 in summer), a zoo with safari park, pride of place going to a giant greenhouse; and **Nederlands Openluchtmuseum**, Schelmseweg 89 (🚌 3, plus 🚌 13 in summer), an extensive and delightful open-air museum.

At **Osterbeek**, the **Airborne Museum**, Hartenstein, Utrechtseweg 232 (8 km west of the centre – 🚌 1), is devoted to Operation Market Garden, the Allied débâcle of Sept 1944 that was immortalised in the film *A Bridge Too Far*. You can find photographs, film footage, and weapons and equipment from both sides.

🚆 On the northwestern edge of town.

ℹ️ **Tourist Office**: Stationsplein 13, ☎0900 112 2344 (premium rate), (www.vvvarnhem.nl).

🏨 The 1-star **Hotel-Pension Parkzicht**, Apeldoornsestr. 16, ☎(026) 442 0698, €, is walkable from the station. A good budget place is the **Rembrandt**, Patersstr. 1–3, ☎(026) 442 0153 (in the city centre), (www.hotelrembrandtarnhem.nl), €.
Youth hostel (HI): Diepenbrocklaan 27, ☎(026) 442 0114 (www.stayokay.com/arnhem), 4 km north of the station (🚌 3 towards Alteveer: Ziekenhuis Rijnstaete). You'll see a sign with the HI logo; 30 m further on steps climb a forested hill to the hostel. Two **campsites**: **Camping Warnsborn**, Bakenbergseweg 257, ☎(026) 442 3469 (www.campingwarnsborn.nl), Apr–Oct (northwest of the centre, 🚌 2), and **De Hooge Veluwe**, Koningsweg 14, ☎(026) 443 2272 (www.dehoogeveluwe.nl), Apr–Oct, by the Hoenderloo entrance to the park (🚌 2 towards Schaarsbergen).

AMSTERDAM

See p231.

THE KRÖLLER-MÜLLER MUSEUM

De Hoge Veluwe National Park: to the northwest of Arnhem, this expanse encompasses dunes, fens, heath, forest and added attractions. The visitors' centre in the park houses **Museonder**, an underground museum devoted to every form of subterranean life; 🚌108 (from Ede/Wageningen and Apeldoorn or 🚌 105 from Arnhem, then change onto the 🚌 108 in Otterlo). Entrances: Otterlo (🚌 105 from Arnhem), Hoenderloo (🚌 108 from Apeldoorn or Ede-Wageningen) and Schaarsbergen (🚌 105 from Arnhem). Once at a gate, buy a map and borrow a white bicycle (free) as there's a lot of ground to cover. The **Kröller-Müller Museum**, Houtkampweg 6, (www. kmm.nl; closed Mon; a good 35-min walk from the Otterlo entrance, but 🚌 106 stops there, on its way between Otterlo and Hoenderloo), has one of Europe's best modern art collections, notably 278 paintings by Van Gogh (including *The Potato Eaters* and *Café Terrace at Night*), although only 50 or so are on show at any one time. The adjacent **Sculpture Garden** and **Sculpture Forest** contain works by Rodin, Epstein and Moore, plus Dubuffet's extraordinary *Jardin d'Email*.

Germany

Germany, bang in the middle of Europe, is hard to miss. Nor should anyone wish to: from the heathlands of the north to the Alpine peaks of the south, there is scenery galore. There are idyllic offshore islands and sandy beaches on both the North Sea and the Baltic coasts, great tracts of lakes and forests, especially in the northeast, and three of Europe's great rivers: the Rhine, the Danube and the Elbe.

The cultural and historical landscape of Germany is just as inviting. The country bristles with World Heritage Sites, with more entries on the official UNESCO list than any other European country bar Italy and Spain. There are magnificent cathedrals in **Cologne**, **Aachen**, **Speyer** and **Trier**; beautifully preserved old towns in **Lübeck**, **Goslar**, **Quedlinburg** and **Bamberg**; engaging forays into classicism at **Würzburg**, **Weimar** and **Potsdam**; and a galaxy of historic castles, most notably along the Rhine Valley between Bingen and Koblenz.

Of course, no country is uniformly beautiful, and Germany has its eyesores. Most cities endured an onslaught of bombing in World War II, and chaotic post-war redevelopment has made for some memorably awful cityscapes in the West. Things are scarcely better in the East, where the demise of the German Democratic Republic (GDR) left a legacy of dreary housing estates. Yet Germany still boasts five cities that rightly claim a place in the premier league of European tourism: **Berlin**, **Dresden**, **Munich**, **Cologne** and **Hamburg**. Berlin has, since the unification of the two German states in 1990, experienced a renaissance like no other European capital. Today, more than ever, it catches the very pulse of Europe. It combines a palpable sense of history with stylish chic and a vibrant club scene.

Germany is blessed with a superb public transport system, and its rail services are second to none. Expresses link major cities with timetables arranged to allow slick transfers. But the most modern lines, though fast, defy the cut and fold of the landscape, and you may not get to see a lot of the scenery. To really see Germany by train, you need to forsake the main ICE routes and resort to local services.

ESSENTIALS

Population 82m **Capital** Berlin **Time Zone** Winter GMT+1, summer GMT+2.

CLIMATE

Very variable! As you move east across Germany, the climate becomes markedly more continental than Britain. Summers become warmer and winters colder. The northeast is the sunniest part of the country. For snowy winters, look to Bavaria and the Black Forest. Note that winter snow can linger well into spring, especially at higher elevations.

CURRENCY

Euro (€). 1 Euro = 100 cents = £0.89 = $1.46. Credit cards are not accepted to anything like the same degree as in most other European countries.

EMBASSIES AND CONSULATES IN BERLIN

Aus: Wallstr. 76–79, ☎(030) 88 00 880. **Can:** IHZ Building, Friedrichstr.95, ☎(030) 203 120. **NZ:** Atrium, 4th Floor, Friedrichstr. 60, ☎(030) 206 210. **SA:** Tiergartenstr. 18, ☎(030) 220 730. **UK:** Wilhelmstr. 70, ☎(030) 204 570. **USA:** Pariser Platz 2, ☎(030) 830 50.

LANGUAGE

German. English and French widely spoken in the west, especially by young people, less so in the eastern side.

OPENING HOURS

Vary; rule of thumb: **Banks:** Mon–Fri 0830–1300 and 1430–1600 (until 1730 Thur). **Shops:** Mon–Fri 0900–1830 (large department stores may open 0830/0900–2000) and Sat 0900–1600. **Museums:** Tue–Sun 0900–1700 (until 2100 Thur).

POST OFFICES

Mon–Fri 0800–1800, Sat 0800–1200. Main post offices have poste restante (*Postlagernd*).

PUBLIC HOLIDAYS

1, 6* Jan; Good Fri; Easter Sun–Mon; 1 May, Ascension Day; Whit Mon; Corpus Christi*, 15 Aug*; 3 Oct; 1 Nov*; 24 Dec (afternoon); 25, 26 Dec. (*Catholic feasts, celebrated only in the south.)

PUBLIC TRANSPORT

Most large cities have U-Bahn (U) underground railway and S-Bahn (S) urban rail service. City travel passes cover both and other public transport, including ferries in some cities. International passes usually cover S-Bahn. Single fares are expensive; day card (*Tagesnetzkarte*) or multi-ride ticket (*Mehrfahrtenkarte*) pays its way if you take more than three rides.

RAIL PASSES

IR, EP valid (see pp27–34). More details on these and other discount tickets from **ServicePoint** at main stations (Hbf). **Schönes-Wochenende-Ticket:** one-day's travel at weekends on local trains (IRE/RE/RB/SB), 2nd class, €39 (€37 from ticket machines or internet) for 1–5 people; buy on the day. **Quer-durchs-Land-Ticket:** valid from 0900 Mon–Fri on all regional trains throughout Germany; €34 for 1 person plus up to 4 additional people for €5 each (must travel together at all times). **Regional tickets (Ländertickets):** one-day's unlimited travel after 0900 Mon–Fri and all day Sat or Sun; up to 5 people, areas: Schleswig-Holstein/Mecklenburg-Vorpommern/Hamburg (€30), Brandenburg (€27), Niedersachsen/Hamburg (€28), Sachsen/Sachsen-Anhalt/Thüringen (€25), Bavaria (€28), Baden-Württemberg (€28), Rheinland-Pfalz/Saarland (€27), Nordrheinwestfalen (€34),

Hessen (€30). All Ländertickets (except Brandenburg and Schleswig-Holstein) have a cheaper version for single travellers. All tickets cost €2 extra if bought from travel centres. **Bahncard**: 25% or 50% discount for one year, 2nd class, €52/206.

RAIL TRAVEL

Website: www.bahn.de. **Deutsche Bahn** (DB) ☎0180 599 6633 (premium rate) for timetable or fares information, also to purchase tickets and reservations. ☎0800 150 7090 (free automated service for timetables). Some services now privately operated. Discounts of 25% or 50% available on long-distance tickets if purchased at least 3 days in advance – 50%-discount tickets have restrictions. Long-distance trains: ICE (modern high-speed trains up to 186 mph/300 km/h), IC, EC, EN, CNL, D. Regional: IRE, RE, RB (modern and comfortable; these link with long-distance services). Frequent local S-Bahn services in major cities. ICE have special fares. Overnight services: seating and sleeping cars with up to three berths and/or couchettes with four or six berths. Seat reservations possible on long-distance trains. Most long-distance trains have refreshments. Stations: well staffed, often with left luggage, refreshments, bicycle hire. Main station is *Hauptbahnhof* (Hbf).

TELEPHONES

Kartentelefon boxes take only cards (buy almost anywhere). Dial in: ☎+49 and omit the initial 0 of the area code. Outgoing: ☎00 + country code (few exceptions, but kiosks give full information). Police: ☎110. Fire/ambulance: ☎112.

TIPPING

10% is usual, but for small items, just round up to the nearest 50 cents or whole euro (which may be less or a whole lot more than 10%).

TOURIST INFORMATION

Website: www.germany-tourism.de. Usually near station. English is widely spoken; English-language maps and leaflets available. Most offer room-finding service.

TYPICAL COSTS

Hostel dorm accommodation around €15 per bed, €15–25 per bed in a twin. Hotel twin rooms from €40 up (per room). Food prices vary greatly. For €10 you might feast in Berlin or Dresden, but still go hungry in Munich. 0.5 litre beer in a bar from €1.30 to €3. Around €2 for a coffee. Internet cafés charge about €4 per hour.

VISAS

EU National Identity Cards and ID cards acceptable for citizens of all EU countries and Switzerland. Visas not needed by citizens of Australia, Canada, New Zealand or the USA.

ACCOMMODATION You'll find a range of accommodation options at all price levels in Germany, but prices for rooms of comparable standards vary enormously across the country. Areas that were, until 1990, part of the GDR still offer the best value, and Berlin is noticeably cheaper than, say, Munich. Generally, you will find excellent accommodation deals in smaller communities, even in tourist areas, particularly if you can avoid the German school holidays. The holiday dates vary by Bundesland (State) but can be checked online at www.schulferien.org. Expect to pay peak prices if you coincide with major festivals (e.g. **Karneval** in the Rhineland or the **Oktoberfest** in Munich) or trade fairs. Consult the events calendar published on www.germany-tourism.de. Note that in major cities, including Berlin, there can be a shortage of budget beds during the summer peak period. All the more reason for taking in some of Germany's smaller towns.

PENSIONS *Pensionen* or *Fremdenheime* and **private rooms** *(Privatzimmer)* represent particularly good value: they're nearly always meticulously kept, and many of the family-run establishments in the country and in small towns are very welcoming and comfortable. You may be required to stay at least two nights at pensions. Less wonderful in general are city hotels, which frequently border on the characterless; the cheapest places tend to be clustered near main railway stations. *Zimmer frei* and *zu vermieten* (posted in a window) indicate availability, while *besetzt* means a place is full. You can usually book through **Tourist Offices** (many of which have lists of places to stay posted in their windows, often with an indication of which places have rooms free). Note that many establishments don't supply soap.

Be prepared to pay for pensions and private rooms in cash, as credit cards and cheques are seldom accepted by small establishments.

YOUTH HOSTELS There are around 600 *Jugendherbergen*, **Deutsches Jugendherbergswerk (DJH)** in Germany (mostly affiliated with **Hostelling International**). The average cost is €13.30 (extra charge for non-HI members). You should book well ahead in peak season (reductions under-27s and for those staying more than one night); self-catering is not usually available. Hostels have the emphasis firmly on youth (with an age limit of 26 in Bavaria, and preferential treatment given to under 27s elsewhere): they're often used by school parties. This has resulted in the introduction of a new category of accommodation, *Jugendgästehaus*, aimed more at young adults and mostly with two–four-bedded rooms, with the price including breakfast and bed linen. Most offer meals; self-catering is uncommon. There are discounts if you stay several nights. Bookings can be made by contacting **Deutsches Jugendherbergswerk (DJH)**, ☎(49) (5231) 9936-0, (www.jugendherberge.de).

CAMPING The cheapest form of accommodation is camping and site facilities are generally excellent, though few sites are conveniently close to stations. **Deutscher Camping-Club (DCC)** (www.camping-club.de), compiles an annual list of 1600 sites. The **German National Tourist Office (GNTO)** publishes a free list and

Germany

map showing more than 600 of the best sites nationwide. There are fewer sites in the east. Most sites open only Apr–Sept and it is advisable to book a few days in advance. A few are open all year and usually have space out of season.

FOOD AND DRINK

Germans tend to have biological clocks that run in advance of the rest of Europe. Families at home eat early, with supper often done and dusted by soon after six. But in restaurants, hotels and hostels expect breakfast from 0630 to 1000. Lunch is around 1200–1400 (from 1130 in rural areas) and dinner 1800–2030 (but much later in cities). Breakfast is often substantial (and usually included in the price of a room), consisting of a variety of bread, cheese and cold meats and possibly boiled eggs. Germans eat their main meal at midday, with a light supper (*Abendbrot*) in the early evening, but restaurants and pubs also offer light lunches and cooked evening meals. For lunch, the best value is the daily menu (*Tageskarte*); in the country there's often a snack menu (*Vesperkarten*) from mid-afternoon onwards.

Traditional German cuisine is widespread, both in towns and rural areas, and traditional recipes, which vary greatly by region, are produced with pride. Expect hearty fare, with large portions, and often good value. Look for home-made soups, high-quality meat, piquant marinated pot roasts (known as *Sauerbraten*) and creamy sauces. No further service charge is added, but waiting staff will expect a tip: 10% is normal.

For really cheap but generally appetising eats, there are roadside *Imbisse* (stalls) serving a variety of snacks, especially *Kartoffelsalat* (potato salad) and *Wurst* (sausage) in its numerous variations, plus fish in the north.

Local specialities include *Spätzle* in the southwest. These are home-made flour noodles, delicious in soup or with meat. Bavarian cooking is emphatically wholesome and peasanty, with *knödel* (dumplings) and sausages such as *Nürnberger Bratwurst* (a dark, grilled sausage) and *Münchner Weisswurst* (a white sausage eaten with sweet mustard) making frequent appearances on the menu. In Lower Saxony (around Hannover and Bremen), eel is popular, and there's a tasty local mutton known as *Heidschnucke*. In the north, during the soft-fruit season, look for *Rote Grütze*, a wonderful blend of vanilla cream and red fruits such as redcurrants and sour cherries – one of the best German desserts. Berlin is no gastronomic heaven, but can claim to have invented the currywurst and the döner kebab.

Berlin has re-invented itself since East and West Germany were united in 1990. The downbeat Bohemian life that was always a feature of old West Berlin has all but disappeared. The city centre (in what was East Berlin) has had a facelift and now oozes cosmopolitan chic. Yet Berlin remains very accessible; welcoming, easy to navigate, and often remarkably good value for money. You will find dazzling modern architecture, the best nightlife in Germany and attractive areas of forest and lakes – places to which Berliners escape on the long sunny days that are a feature of the Berlin summer.

The city comes with a few surprises. Not everyone drives a Mercedes! In fact, Berlin has high unemployment and suffers, like much of eastern Germany, from an outmoded industrial infrastructure that declines by the year. New knowledge-based industries are beginning to develop in the emerging fashionable areas in the east of the city (like **Prenzlauer Berg**), but the economy is sluggish and the city government is always pushed for cash.

Many parts of Berlin have a very Eastern European feel. They have more in common with Minsk than with Munich. New migrants from the east rub shoulders with an international crowd of young visitors and the city's long-standing Turkish minority. The old differences between East and West are difficult to detect on the ground, and there are few traces of the Wall that divided the city between 1961 and 1989. Yet, in the mindset of Berliners, there are still some attitudinal differences between the two halves of the city. The older generation of **Ossies** (i.e. those from the East) and **Wessies** have had very different life experiences. That sometimes finds expression, on both sides, in a nostalgia for the old days.

ARRIVAL AND DEPARTURE

🚂 Berlin's impressive new **Hauptbahnhof** (Hbf) is the city's main railway hub. This crystal cathedral was opened in May 2006, and ranks as a worthwhile sight in its own right. It offers a good range of passenger facilities, with shops and cafés that, unusually for Germany, are open seven days a week. There is a left-luggage office, a bank and a Deutsche Bahn travel centre where multilingual staff can assist with timetable queries and seat reservations. The downside is a perverse lack of toilets and public seating, and some famously slow lifts between the station's various levels. Note that the railway platforms are not all on the same level, so changing trains, particularly if you are unfamiliar with the station, might take a while. Avoid tight connections. The Hauptbahnhof is served by long-distance services, by regional trains and by S-Bahn services. Every long-distance train that serves the Hauptbahnhof also stops at one of the city's other main stations, but quite which one will depend on the route. It is worth checking carefully for you may find that one of the other stations is better placed for your accommodation. The other stations served by various long-distance services and night trains are **Ostbahnhof** (Ost), **Südkreuz** (marked as

Berlin Papestrasse on older maps), **Gesundbrunnen** and **Spandau**. Selected night trains and some regional trains also serve **Zoologischer Garten (Zoo)** or **Lichtenberg**. Ostbahnhof and Südkreuz have Deutsche Bahn travel centres, which are often less busy than that at Hauptbahnhof.

Certain long-distance trains continue to serve **Berlin Ostbahnhof**, situated in the east of the city. **Berlin Zoologischer Garten** (now served only by regional, S-Bahn and some overnight trains) lands you right in the centre of former West Berlin with Kurfürstendamm, one of the main shopping streets, just a two-minute walk away. Other centrally located stations (regional and S-Bahn trains only) include **Potsdamer Platz**, **Friedrichstrasse** and **Alexanderplatz**.

✈ 🖀 (0180) 500 0186; www.berlin-airport.de (all airports). The major budget airlines (easyJet, Germanwings, Ryanair) all jet into rapidly growing **Schönefeld Airport** (SXF), about 20 km southeast of the city centre (trains 0430–2300 to Zoo, Hbf and Ost stations; ETT table 847). The second airport is **Tegel** (TXL), about 12 km northwest of the city centre. It is served by most of the traditional airlines, among them Lufthansa, Air France and British Airways. The TXL bus connects Tegel Airport with Hauptbahnhof (20 mins), S-Bahn Unter den Linden (28 mins) and Alexanderplatz (35 mins). 🚌 109 and X9 take around 20 mins to Zoo, stopping on the way at U-Bahn Jakob-Kaiser-Platz (4 mins). Taxis to the centre cost around €16. The new **Berlin Brandenburg International** airport (BBI) is due to open in October 2011, replacing Schönefeld. Sadly, Tempelhof Airport, with its retro design dating from the Nazi period, closed in 2008.

🚌 **Long-distance buses**: These depart from the **ZOB (Central Bus Station)**, 🖀 (030) 301 0380 (bookings); (030) 302 5361 (information), www.zob-reisebuero.de. The ZOB is at Masurenallee 4–6, Charlottenburg, opposite the International Conference Centre (U-Bahn: Kaiserdamm; S-Bahn: Messe Nord/ICC). Buses run to all major German cities and selected resorts. Excellent international connections.

TOURIST OFFICES

Main administrative office:
Berlin Tourismus Marketing GmbH, Am Karlsbad 11, D-10785 Berlin; 🖀 (030) 250 025 (www.berlin-tourist-information.de).
BERLIN infostores, Europa-Center, Budapester Str. 45; 5 mins from Zoologischer Garten (Zoo) station (walk towards the Kaiser Wilhelm Memorial Church with its damaged spire), access only from Budapester Str.
Brandenburger Tor (Brandenburg Gate) Pariser Pl; 2 mins from Unter den Linden. **Fernsehturm** (TV Tower), Alexanderpl., Panoramastr. 1.

INFORMATION

Berlin Tourismus Marketing through its **BERLIN infostores** offer accommodation and ticket reservation services. From these offices you can pick up a copy of *Berlin City Map*, *Hotels und Pensionen* (Hotel Guide) and the quarterly *Das Berlin Magazin*, with information and listings in English.

Berlin has a number of internet cafés scattered across the city centre. There are also six easyInternetcafés, each with a large number of PCs. The central ones are located in the Sony Centre at Potsdamer Platz (open Sun–Thur 0700-2300, Fri-Sat 0700–2400), in Friedrichstrasse

Germany

station (open Mon–Fri 0630–2200, Sat 0700–2100, Sun 0800–2100), at Rathausstrasse 5 close to the Alexanderplatz and at Kurfürstendamm 224 (open 0630–0200).

PUBLIC TRANSPORT

Berlin's efficient public transport network combines buses, trams, underground and surface trains. Free maps showing public transport routes can be picked up from the Tourist Offices and hotel foyers. More comprehensive versions, some with street indexes, are available from newsagents. Train maps are easy to find, but for **bus maps** you must go to the **BVG Information Centre**, in a separate building outside Zoo station; here you can get the *Region Berlin Linienplan* (large) and free smaller transport maps. For timetable and ticket enquiries ☎(030) 19449 (daily 24 hrs or online at www.bvg.de).

TICKETS AND PASSES   Get **tickets** for buses, trains and trams from automatic machines on station platforms, from bus drivers or from ticket offices; validate your ticket by punching it on the special machine once on board or on the platform. A **short-distance ticket** is for a short trip on any bus, train or tram. A **single** allows travel on any bus, train or tram for a period of two hours. A **day ticket** and a **7-day ticket** is for travel on all public transport during that period. The **Berlin Welcome Card** allows you unlimited free use of public transport throughout the city and its suburbs for 48 or 72 hrs or 5 days (€16.50/€22/€29.50). The card also entitles you to up to 50 per cent reduction on city tours, museums, theatres and tourist attractions in Berlin and Potsdam for one adult and up to three children under 14 years. On sale at stations, bus ticket offices, hotels, Tourist Offices or online at www.berlin-welcomecard.de.

TAXIS   Taxis are plentiful, especially in the west, and relatively inexpensive; they can be flagged down on the street or from ranks at stations, the airport and other key points or by calling ☎0800 222 2255 (free call); www.cab24.de.

METRO   The 24 lines of the U-Bahn (underground) and S-Bahn (suburban surface trains) offer quick transport to most spots within the 40-km diameter of Berlin. The stations are recognised by the white 'U' on a blue square or white 'S' on a green circle and lines are colour-coded and numbered. Direction is indicated by the name of the final destination. Trains run 0500–0030 but 24 hrs at weekends, running at various intervals on all S-Bahn and U-Bahn lines (except the U4). A short new line (U55) linking the Hauptbahnhof with the Bundestag and Brandenburger Tor opened in August 2009.

BUSES   Buses are also a convenient way to see the city. A good sightseeing route is no. 100, which runs from Zoo station through the **Tiergarten**, the **Brandenburg Gate** and along **Unter den Linden**; pick up a free guide brochure to this route from the BVG information centre; route No. 200 is similar. Bus stops are indicated by a green 'H' on a yellow background. There are plenty of night bus services.

BOAT TRIPS   For daily (Mar–Oct) boat trips along the **River Spree** and **Landwehr Canal** contact **Reederei Bruno Winkler 349**, ☎(030) 349 9595 (www.reedereiwinkler.de).

ACCOMMODATION

Try to book in advance, as demand for accommodation often outstrips supply. The classiest (and most expensive) hotels are in the city centre, just east of the Brandenburg Gate and around Gendarmenmarkt. The centre of former West Berlin, especially around Zoo, Kurfürstendamm and Charlottenburg, is more mixed, with often heavy discounting of nominally high rack rates. For budget hotels and hostels, your best bet is in the eastern part of central Berlin (the Mitte district) – a trendy area, worth making for. Tourist Offices will make free reservations and give out accommodation lists. **Guest rooms** in private houses can be booked through **Bed & Breakfast in Berlin**, ☎(030) 250 025 (www.visitberlin.de).

Relatively inexpensive **hotels** (usually under €100 for a double room) include: **A&O Hotel**, with two branches, in Köpenicker Str. 127–129, Berlin–Mitte, ☎(030) 809 4752 00 (U-Bahn Heinrich-Heine-Strasse) and in Boxhagener Str. 73, Berlin–Friedrichshain (southeast of city centre), ☎(030) 809 4754 00 (S-Bahn Ostkreuz, bus 240 from Ostbahnhof); see www.aohostels.com for details; and **Ostel – GDR the Hostel**, Wriezener Karree 5, Berlin-Mitte, ☎(030) 2576 8660 (www.ostel.eu; a taste of old East Germany). Note that rates often plummet if you are able to book months in advance.

There are three **HI youth hostels** (www.hostel.de) in Berlin, all of which get heavily booked for much of the year. The most central is **JH Berlin International**, Kluckstr. 3, ☎(030) 747 6879 10, (jh-berlin@jugendherberge.de), 3 km from the centre, ▯ M29 to Gedenkstätte or U2 train to Kurfürstenstrasse. The others are **JH Berlin Ernst Reuter**, Hermsdorfer Damm 48, ☎(030) 404 1610 (jh-ernst-reuter@jugendherberge.de), 15 km from Zoo station (and the cheapest), ▯ 125 and **JGH Berlin am Wannsee**, Badeweg 1, Ecke Kronprinzessinnenweg, ☎(030) 803 2034 (jh-wannsee@jugendherberge.de), S-Bahn S1/S3/S7 to Nikolassee (500 m away), or ▯ 118 passes closer.

Private hostels and other budget accommodation: Jugendhotel Berlin City, Crellestr. 22, ☎(030) 7870 2130 (www.jugendhotel-berlin.de), U-Bahn: Kleistpark; **Hotel 4 Youth**, Schönhauser Allee 103, ☎(030) 446 7783 (www.hotel4youth.de), U-Bahn/S-Bahn: Schönhauser Allee; **Generator Hostel**, Storkower Str. 160, ☎(030) 417 2400 (www.generatorhostels.com); 904 beds, Germany's largest hostel; S-Bahn: Landsberger Allee; **Sunflower Hostel**, Helsingforser Str. 17, ☎(030) 4404 4250 (www.sunflower-hostel.de), S-Bahn: Warschauer Str; **Heart of Gold Hostel**, Johannisstr. 11, ☎(030) 2900 3300 (www.heartofgold-hostel.de); U-Bahn/S-Bahn: Friedrichstrasse; **Helter Skelter Hostel**, Kalkscheuenstr. 4–5, ☎(030) 2804 4997 (www.helterskelterhostel.de), U-Bahn/S-Bahn: Friedrichstrasse; **Circus Hostel**, Weinbergsweg 1A, ☎(030) 2839 1433 (www.circus-berlin.de), U-Bahn: Rosenthaler Platz; **Lette'm Sleep Hostel**, Lettestr. 7, ☎(030) 4473 3623 (www.backpackers.de), U-Bahn: U2 to Eberswalderstrasse. **Globetrotter Hostel Odyssee**, Grünberger Str. 23, ☎(030) 2900 0081 (www.globetrotterhostel.de), from Ostbahnhof ▯ 240.

Most **campsites** are out of town. One of the most central is **Campingplatz DCC Am Krossinsee**, Wernsdorfer Str. 38, Köpenick, ☎(030) 675 8687 (www.dccberlin.de), ▯ 733.

FOOD AND DRINK

A good place to start is in and around Hackescher Markt S-Bahn station, where you'll find a huge choice of outdoor and sit-in cafés. Head north into Oranienburger Str. for yet more. Don't discount the very heart of the city either. Business lunches at some of the chic looking restaurants on side streets off Gendarmenmarkt and Unter den Linden come for as little at €7 (exc. drinks).

In the west of the city, Ku'damm may seem reserved for German pensioners and tourists, but the side streets around Meinekestr. have a good range of brasseries and German pubs. For a treat, try the cakes at **coffee shops**, while for cheap food and a happy evening's drinking head for the *Kneipen* (pubs) around Prenzlauer Berg – particularly the side streets around Kollwitzpl. and in Kreuzberg.

HIGHLIGHTS

The city's main sights are clustered around **Unter den Linden**, the handsome boulevard that forms the principal east–west thoroughfare. It runs from the Brandenburg Gate to Alexanderplatz. West of the Brandenburg Gate, where the road is named Strasse des 17 Juni, that same lineal axis cuts through the **Tiergarten**, a huge area of parkland, en route to the old heart of West Berlin. That is the area around Kurfürstendamm and the Zoologischer Garten train station (usually just called Zoo). It no longer has the buzz so evident in the days of a divided Berlin, but there are some worthwhile sights.

TOURS

The **Original Berlin Walks** 📞 (030) 301 9194 (www.berlinwalks.com) run an excellent daily programme of walking tours with English-speaking guides (discount for under 26s and with Welcome Card), starting from the taxi rank at Zoo station and outside Häagen-Dazs, Hackescher Markt (no booking required).
The themes covered are Discover Berlin, Nightlife Berlin, Jewish Life in Berlin, Discover Potsdam, Infamous Third Reich Sites and the Sachsenhausen Concentration Camp.

A very useful eastwest railway line, conveniently elevated to afford excellent sightseeing, runs around the northern rim of the city centre. West from Hauptbahnhof it runs to Zoo and Charlottenburg, while eastbound it runs to Ostbahnhof via Friedrichstrasse and Alexanderplatz. Hop on any of the red Regionalbahn trains that travel this stretch and head for the upper deck for a good tour of the city. Bus routes 100 and 200 are also good for an introduction to the centre. Both run every ten minutes, seven days a week, and each route links Zoo station with Alexanderplatz via Tiergarten and Unter den Linden.

The two routes vary. Route 100 runs past the Reichstag and the presidential palace (Schloss Bellevue), while the 200 serves Potsdamer Platz and the embassy area on the south side of Tiergarten. Note that neither of these routes serves the Hauptbahnhof.

The Hauptbahnhof is a good starting point for a walking tour of the city. A new footbridge leads south over the River Spree, giving easy access to the **Reichstag**, the parliament building which reopened in 1999 after restoration. Today it houses the Bundestag, the Lower House of the German parliament. It's open to the public and you can climb to the top of the glass dome (free entry, open 0800–2400, last entry 2200) for superb views of the city.

MUSEUM PASS

A three-day Museum Pass, **SchauLUST MuseenBERLIN** (from main Tourist Offices, €19) is valid for over 70 of Berlin's museums and collections, including all national and state museums.

The **Brandenburger Tor** (Brandenburg Gate), just east of the Reichstag, is Berlin's most potent emblem. For years it was also a symbol of the Iron Curtain that divided Europe. The line of the Berlin Wall, which ran between the Reichstag (in the West) and the Brandenburg Gate (in the East), is marked by a double line of cobbled stones set into the pavement. Walking east from the Brandenburg Gate along Unter den Linden, you will pass Berlin's most celebrated hotel, the Adlon, and the monumental Russian embassy, both on the right. Just a stone's throw south of Unter den Linden lies **Gendarmenmarkt**, by far the most attractive square in Berlin. It boasts a matching pair of early 18th-century churches and the exuberant **Schauspielhaus**, built in 1821 to a design by Berlin's most famous architect, Karl Friedrich Schinkel.

Back on Unter den Linden, take a look at **Bebelplatz**, the elegant plaza that lies just west of the Staatsoper (State Opera House). In the very centre of Bebelplatz, set into the ground, is a powerful reminder of Germany's troubled history. The memorial marks the spot where the Nazis burned books from the adjacent library of the Humboldt University. Just south of Bebelplatz is the Catholic Cathedral, an interesting design with echoes of the Pantheon in Rome (free entry).

On the north side of Unter den Linden, moving further east, is the city's main Lutheran cathedral (the **Berliner Dom**) (not free). This area, known as the **Museumsinsel** (Museum Island), is home to Berlin's most prestigious museums, notably the **Pergamon Museum** (closed Mon), with its excellent collections of antiquities, especially the Hellenistic Pergamon Altar and the Babylonian Gate of Ishtar.

Other museums in the immediate vicinity are the **Museum of Everyday Life in DDR** (behind the Berliner Dom), the Old Museum, which hosts the Old National Gallery (closed Mon), and the German Historical Museum (closed Wed).

The conspicuous plot of empty land on the south side of Unter den Linden, opposite the Berliner Dom, is all that remains of the old East German Parliament building. Despite many local voices calling for its preservation, it was demolished in 2007. One block south of Unter den Linden is the Nikolaiviertel (Nikolai quarter), where a range of eateries cluster in the narrow streets around the Nikolaikirche. This twin-towered church is Berlin's oldest building. The Rotes Rathaus (Red Town Hall) is the dominant brick building just east of the Nikolaiviertel.

Unter den Linden then runs east to the shopping area at Alexanderplatz, where the **Fernsehturm** (TV Tower) is a Berlin icon. Open to the public, the tower is topped by a globe that houses a revolving restaurant and a viewing gallery.

Also within walking distance of Unter den Linden is the new Potsdamer Platz development. There, the Sony Centre houses a futuristic plaza with several coffee shops.

Further south is the **Martin Gropius Building**, now housing a variety of exhibitions (closed Tue), the **New National Gallery** (closed Mon) and the open-air **Topography of Terror** exhibition (free entry), which vividly documents Nazi repression. The exhibition site includes a stretch of the old Berlin Wall.

North from Unter den Linden, a footbridge over the Spree behind the Berliner Dom gives access to the **Hackescher Markt** area. Key sights here are the Hackescher Höfe shopping courtyards and the former Jewish heart of Berlin, centred on the Neue Synagoge on Oranienburger Strasse. The streets south of Koppenplatz once echoed to the sound of Yiddish and Hebrew, and still boast a number of memorials to the Jewish past.

Berlin's most celebrated modern museum is undoubtedly the **Jewish Museum** (Lindenstr 9–14). It is a 15-minute walk south of Gendarmenmarkt, but worth the hike. It evokes something of Jewish life in old Berlin, and chronicles the atrocities visited upon Germany's Jewish population. The building itself is as memorable as the superb exhibition.

The Wall exerts a magnetic pull on visitors, even if there is little left to see. Mühlenstrasse (on the north bank of the River Spree between Ostbahnhof and Warschauer Strasse) has the best remaining stretch (see www.eastsidegallery.com). North of the city centre at Bernauer Strasse 111 (S-Bahn: Nordbahnhof), there is an evocative wall memorial and good information. Another popular museum is the **Haus am Checkpoint Charlie** (www.mauermuseum.de), which, during the years of the Cold War, promoted its own particular (and pro-Western) perspective on events. It has not changed.

Further-flung sights include **Schloss Charlottenburg** (www.spsg.de; closed Mon; 10 mins from Zoo station on bus M48), Berlin's answer to Versailles, which boasts a fabulous collection of German Romantic art. Immediately opposite the Schloss, the **Berggruen Museum** has a small but exquisite collection of 20th-century art (especially strong on Picasso and Matisse; closed Mon). In the western suburb of Dahlem (20 mins from Zoo on Bus X10, alight at Königin-Luise Strasse), the **Alliierten Museum** gives a good account of life in a divided Berlin from the perspective of the Western Allies. The museum is at Clayallee 135 (free entry; closed Wed; see www.alliiertenmuseum.de).

The same story is presented from a very different perspective at the **Deutsch-Russisches Museum** in the eastern suburbs, just a 5-min walk from S-Bahn Karlshorst (see www.museum-karlshorst.de; closed Mon, free entry). The most impressive socialist relic is the memorial to Soviet war heroes at Treptow (S-Bahn: Treptower Park). For a taste of East Berlin, hop on the U5 to Frankfurter Tor, and walk west along Karl-Marx-Allee. You'll either love or hate this monumental display of Stalinist chic.

DAY TRIP TO POTSDAM   **Potsdam** is an eye-opening array of landscaped gardens and palaces, 30 km southwest of Berlin (Regional Express (RE), 24 mins from Hbf, also serves Ostbahnhof, Friedrichstr. and Zoo, every 30 mins, ETT table 839). The seat of the Hohenzollern kings in the late 17th century and now a UNESCO World Heritage Site, it is best known for the compact rococo **Sanssouci Palace** (1745–47) set in the huge Park Sanssouci. Arrive early to ensure a place on the guided tours. A leisurely walk through the park reveals the breathtaking **Chinese Tea House** (1754–57), the pagoda-like **Drachenhaus**, **Schloss Charlottenhof** and the so-called **Römische Bader** (Roman Baths).

SHOPPING

Berlin is a city for shoppers, with a price range to suit all pockets. In the Mitte district, the main shopping drag is Friedrichstrasse, particularly south of Unter den Linden around the Galeries Lafayette store. It tends towards the staid, but there are many big-name chains, and it's enlivened by the ultra-stylish Friedrichstrasse-Passagen. For something less conventional look to the Hackesche Höfe area (just north of S-Bahn Hackescher Markt), where boutiques and gift shops cluster around a series of interlinked courtyards.

In the west, the giant **KaDeWe** department store on Wittenbergplatz has long been a temple to consumerism. Walk west to Kürfurstendamm (always called Ku'Damm) for everything from clothes to jewellery with some of Berlin's best cake shops too! For more prosaic needs, try the **Arkaden** (The Arcades) at Potsdamer Platz.

The central food market is at **Winterfeldtplatz**, Schöneberg (Wed and Sat, 0800–1300; U-Bahn: Nollendorfplatz). Covered markets can be found on **Marheinekeplatz**, Kreuzberg; **Ackerstr.**, **Mitte** and **Arminiusstr.**, Tiergarten. On Sat and Sun, 1000–1700, the **Strasse des 17 Juni** is a long stretch of market stalls selling everything from antiques to CDs. Weekends see an antiques market at **Ostbahnhof**, while the **Turkish market** is Tue and Fri 1200–1830 at **Maybachufer** (U-Bahn: Kottbusser Tor).

NIGHT-TIME AND EVENTS

Berlin has long enjoyed a reputation for being a bit lively of an evening (think *Cabaret* and the Kit Kat Klub), and, over the past decade, the city has established itself as Europe's most happening capital. Hundreds of venues play host to world-class DJs and bands night after night. Club nights move from venue to venue on a nightly schedule; somewhere that hosts one of **Karrera Club**'s (www.karreraclub.de) massive indie gigs one night may be hosting one of the city's many gay or lesbian parties the next. The *Tip* and *Zitty* listing magazines are available from newsagents or online (www.berlinonline.de/tip; www.zitty.de; only in German).

Oraninenstrasse, Berlin-Kreuzberg (just south of city centre), is the heart of a lively club and bar scene, as is Oranienburgerstr. in northern Mitte. **Café Zapata** (Oranienburgerstr. 54, www.cafe-zapata.de) hosts an eclectic mix of artists playing world music in a chilled atmosphere. The ever-popular **Matrix** club (Warschauer Platz 18, Berlin-Friedrichshain; www.matrix-berlin.de; Mon–Sun) pulls in a young crowd with mainstream offerings of R'n'B, hip-hop, pop and techno. **Knaack Club** (Greifswalderstr. 224, Berlin-Prenzlauer Berg; www.knaack-berlin.de; Fri, Sat only) offers three floors of music, ranging from metal to karaoke. If you're feeling a bit Weimar Republic and fancy some decadence, the roguishly red décor of **Roter Salon an der Volksbühne** (Rosa-Luxemburg-Platz 2; www.rotersalon.de) will be right up your strasse, as will its constantly evolving menu of great nights.

Bands of every type play at the intimate **Kaffee Burger** (Torstrasse 60; www.kaffee burger.de), where, among the baby goths and emos you'll find many a geriatric hippy who thinks he might have roadied for Can. This is where you're most likely to hear purveyors of the now uber-trendy krautrock.

The city does a nice line in charismatic, low-rent dives that welcome the weary traveller, and one such is **Weinerei Café** (corner of Veteranenstrasse and Fehrbellinerstrasse). Here you flop out in a sort of living room and, for a couple of Euros, hire a wine glass, which you refill as many times as you wish and pay not a cent more. There's even a microwave, in case you want to heat up some food or steam your socks. A little posher, but still welcoming and good value is **Bergstüb'l** (Veteranenstr. 25), where, it is rumoured, David Bowie and Iggy Pop used to drink during their late-1970s sojourn. These days, it's the DJs who hold court and draw crowds here.

Berlin boasts a large number of cinemas, especially at Potsdamer Platz. Classical concerts are held at Philharmonie und Kammermusiksaal der Philharmonie, Herbert-von-Karajan Str. 1 (the home of the world-famous **Berlin Philharmonic**, for which tickets are extremely hard to get, www.berlin-philharmonic.com) and Konzerthaus Berlin, Gendarmenmarkt 2 (www.konzerthaus.de).

HAMBURG

Germany's largest seaport and the country's media capital, Hamburg is one of the most sophisticated and cosmopolitan German cities and is an invigorating place to visit – both as a stopping-off point on the way to Scandinavia and in its own right. Although comprehensively destroyed in turn by fire in 1842 and by World War II bombing, it has a special watery character of its own, with some enjoyable boat trips on offer in the Binnenalster and Aussenalster lakes and into the massive working port area. One of the main streets, the Jungfernstieg, resembles something of a seaside promenade, while six soaring green copper spires impose themselves on the skyline over the rebuilt historic centre, the numerous parks and the canals. Entertainment and nightlife ranges from the famously sleazy Reeperbahn to the musical offerings of the opera company and the city's resident orchestras.

Hamburg is Germany's largest city after Berlin, and also a federal state with its own parliament. The city's prominence as a port dates from the 12th century, with Hamburg becoming a member of the Hanseatic League in 1321, making it one of the most powerful and wealthy free cities in Europe.

Germany

The **Hamburg Card** can be bought from Tourist Offices and includes free travel on public transport, free or reduced admission to museums and sights, and reductions of up to 25% on sightseeing, lake and harbour tours. A **one-day card** (€8.50) and a **three-day card** (€18.90) are available, as well as a five-day card for €33.90.

TOURIST OFFICES

Main office: Steinstr. 7, 20095 Hamburg ☎(040) 3005 1300, (Mon–Sat 0900–1900 (www.hamburg-tourismus.de). Other Tourist Offices are at **Hauptbahnhof** (by the Kirchenallee main exit), and at the Port, between Piers 4 and 5 on the **St-Pauli-Landungsbrücken**, at the **airport** (terminal 4 arrivals), **train station** (Dag-Hammarskjöld-Pl) and at **Dammtor** ticket office. A **hotline** for hotel reservations and tickets operates daily throughout the year 0900–1900; ☎(040) 6899 9899 (www.hamburgtravel.de).

ARRIVAL AND DEPARTURE

🚆 The **Hauptbahnhof (Hbf)** handles most long-distance trains. It's huge, central and on the U-Bahn. It houses the main post office and a wonderfully cosmopolitan selection of eateries. The station's main exit is on Kirchenallee. **Altona**, in the west of the city, is the terminal for most trains serving **Schleswig-Holstein**. **Dammtor**, north of the centre, is mostly for convention traffic and is therefore unlikely to be of much interest to tourists.

✈ **Hamburg International Airport,** ☎(040) 50 750 (www.ham.airport.de), is 8 km from the town centre. Rapid-transit S-Bahn link S1 runs every ten minutes for most of the day and takes 25 minutes to and from Hamburg Hbf. The **Airport Express** bus to the Hauptbahnhof takes 25 mins. It runs every 20 mins, 0630–2250. In the opposite direction it runs 0530–2120. Ryanair use **Lübeck** airport (bus connects with flights; 75 mins to Hamburg or frequent local buses to Lübeck).

INFORMATION

Get the free *Map of Hamburg – Tips and Sights at a Glance*, also *St Pauli Tips from A–Z*, plus *Top Info* magazine, which includes a map of the city rail system, full details of Hamburg travel cards and an outline guide to the city's attractions from the **main Tourist Office**.

PUBLIC TRANSPORT

The main area of interest is small enough to be walkable. **HVV** (Hamburg Transit Authority) run efficient buses, U-Bahn (underground) and S-Bahn (urban trains), as well as a night bus service to most city districts. Enquiries: ☎(040) 19 449 (www.hvv.de).

ACCOMMODATION

Accommodation can be booked through the Tourist Office booking service: **Hamburg Travel**, Steinstrasse 7, ☎(040) 6899 9899 (www.hamburg-travel.de). **Rooms in private homes** can be booked through **Privatzimmervermittlung** 'Bed & Breakfast', Markusstr. 9, ☎(040) 491 5666 (www.bed-and-breakfast.de).

Cheaper **hotel-pensions** in the central area include: **Von Blumfeld**, Lange Reihe 54, ☎(040) 245 860 (www.pension-blumenfeld.de), €; **Galerie-Hotel Sarah Petersen**, Lange Reihe 50, ☎(040) 249 826 (www.ghsp.de), €€–€€€; **Schmidt**, Holzdamm 14, ☎(040) 280 2119 (www.pension-schmidt-hamburg.de), €€; **Rock'n'Roll Hotel Kogge**, Bernhard-Nocht-Strasse 59, ☎(040) 312 872 (www.kogge-hamburg.de), €; **Terminus am Hauptbahnhof**, Steindamm 5, ☎(040) 280 3144 (www.hotel-terminus-hamburg.de), €; **Annenhof**, Lange Reihe 23, ☎(040) 243 426 (www.hotelannenhof.de), €; **Kieler Hof**, Bremer Reihe 15, ☎(040) 243 024 (www.kieler-hof.de), €. Located by a park, **Europa Gästehaus**, Horner Landstr. 85, ☎(040) 659 0880 (www.europa-gaestehaus.de), is in the Horn district ((U-Bahn 2: Raues Haus). Also recommended are **Hotel Hamburg Novum**, Steindamm 29, ☎(040) 248 370 (www.novum-hotel.de), €, and, also in St Georg, the **Hotel Wedina**, Gurlittstr. 23, ☎(040) 280 8900 (www.wedina.de), €–€€.

The **HI youth hostels** are: **Jugendherberge Auf dem Stintfang**, Alfred-Wegener-Weg 5, ☎(040) 313 488 (www.djh-nordmark.de/jh/hamburg-stintfang), central (U/S-Bahn: Landungsbrücken); and **Jugendherberge Horner Rennbahn**, Rennbahnstr. 100, ☎(040) 651 1671 (www.djh-nordmark.de/jh/hamburg-horner-rennbahn), in the eastern suburbs (U-Bahn: Horner Rennbahn).

There are several non-HI hostels. **Junges Hotel (YMCA)**, Kurt-Schumacher-Allee 14, ☎(040) 419 230 (www.junges-hotel.de), is near the station; proceeds go to funding social projects in the city. **Schanzenstern**, Bartelsstr. 12, ☎(040) 439 8441 (www.schanzenstern.de), has dorms €19, singles €38.50, doubles €54–56 (S-Bahn 21/31 to Sternschanze). Its sister in Altona is **Schanzenstern Altona**, Kleine Rainstr. 24–26, ☎(040) 3991 9191 (www.schanzenstern-altona.de, dorms €19, singles €44, doubles €55–65). In the lively Schanzenviertel area is **Instant Sleep Backpacker Hostel** Max-Brauer-Allee 277, ☎(040) 4318 2310 (www.instantsleep.de), which has dorms from €16.50 (open 24 hrs).

FOOD AND DRINK

Hamburg's cosmopolitan nature is reflected in its restaurants, with some of the best fine dining in Germany. Seafood and fish are, of course, a speciality. Prices tend to reflect the areas in which they are located, but the places in **Rathausmarkt** are not exorbitant and it's a good place to watch the world go by. **Kirchenallee**, **Altona**, **Univiertel** and **Schanzenviertel** are cheap eating areas.

Germany

TOURS

The city is dominated by water and a boat trip is part of the experience. There are English-language harbour tours (lasting an hour) daily at 1200 Mar–Nov, departing from Pier 1; ☎(040) 3178 2231. Divided into the Binnen- (inner) and Aussen- (outer) alster, this 455-hectare stretch of water contributes to the city's relaxed, open-air ambience. The shortest Alster cruise takes about an hour, looping through the inner and outer lakes, but there are longer inland voyages like the 3-hour trip (late Apr–late Sept) to Bergedorf or the pretty summer twilight cruise through the backwater canals. For trips around the harbour, boats depart from Landungsbrücken (piers) 1–9, Deichstr., Binnenhafen and Vorsetzen daily every 30 mins 1000–1730 (Apr–Oct), and weekends hourly 1100–1530 (Nov–Mar); tickets from Tourist Offices.

The **Hummelbahn Tram** is a 1920s-style tram with multilingual guides that covers the major sights in 90 mins (daily, Apr–Sept); ☎(040) 792 8979. There are a number of walking tours in summer (ask at the Tourist Office for details). These feature the warehouse district, the St Pauli district and a tour of the city highlights.

HIGHLIGHTS

The oldest part of the city, which survived the great fire of 1842 and carpet bombing by the Allies in World War II, is around the harbour, where two **museum ships** are moored: the tall ship *Rickmer Rickmers* at **Pier 1** and the more modern *Cap San Diego* at the **Uberseebrücke**. **Speicherstadt**, just east of the docks, is a district of early 20th-century red-brick gabled warehouses, between Deichtorhallen and Baumwall. **Blankenese**, reached from St Pauli by ferry, has something of the character of a fishing village with its maze of alleys and steps.

The neo-Renaissance **Rathaus** (Town Hall), Marktpl. (U-Bahn: Rathaus), is a magnificent sandstone building constructed 1886–97. Some of its 647 rooms, which can be toured when government is not in session, are adorned with tapestries, chandeliers and paintings. Tours are conducted in English daily; for details ☎(040) 42831 2470. The **Rathaus Tower** is one of six towers dominating the city's skyline, the others belonging to churches, the most impressive of which is **St Michaelis**, Krayenkamp 4C (www.st-michaelis.de; U- or S-Bahn: Landungsbrücken), a 132-m high baroque structure with a crypt and a viewing level at 82 m, which gives panoramic views. This is the city's symbol and a trumpet solo is played from the tower every day.

Hamburg has a good range of museums, some of which are usually closed on Mon, with late night opening on Thur. Foremost is the **Kunsthalle**, Glockengiesserwall 1 (U- or S-Bahn: Hbf) with a superb international art collection that dates from the Gothic period to the present day (closed Mon). It includes a choice selection of German works, including the Grabow Altarpiece of 1379, its 24 panels constituting one of the greatest triumphs of the North German Primitive style. This is complemented by the modern works in the **Kunstverein**, Klosterwall 23 (www.kunstverein.de; U-Bahn: Steinstr.; closed Mon). **Museum für Kunst und Gewerbe**, Steintorpl. 1 (www.mkg-hamburg.de; U- or S-Bahn: Hbf), is the museum of arts and crafts with an excellent range of art from ancient Egypt,

Greece and Rome, along with medieval works, Art Nouveau and modern art (closed Mon). Elsewhere you can delve into the city's history at the **Museum für Hamburgische Geschichte**, Holstenwall 24 (www.hamburgmuseum.de; U-Bahn: St Pauli; closed Mon). Hamburg's tallest building, the 280-m **TV Tower**, Lagerstr. 2–8 (U-Bahn: Messehallen), has a viewing platform (presently closed for restoration) and a revolving restaurant. Just below is **Planten un Blomen** (U-Bahn: Stephanspl.; S-Bahn: Dammtor), the city's largest park, with a vast Japanese garden and illuminated fountain displays and concerts on summer nights (May–Sept).

SHOPPING

Rathausmarkt and Gänsemarkt is the **main shopping area**, easily covered on foot. Shops along Neuer Wall specialise in furniture and interiors, while the **Quartier Satin**, on the ABC-Strasse, is the place for designer names and antiques. **Colonnaden**, a delightful pedestrianised colonnade just off Jungfernstieg, has pavement cafés alongside designer shops, together with specialist tobacco, tea and coffee shops. Leading east from Rathausmarkt is the city's longest shopping street, the Mönckebergstr., a lively mix of small shops, cafés, noble restaurants and large department stores.

NIGHT-TIME AND EVENTS

Local nightlife is cosmopolitan, to say the least. In the **St Pauli** quarter, north of the Elbe riverfront, raunchy sex-show clubs tout their delights next to casinos, discos, tattoo parlours and some of Hamburg's best restaurants. The Reeperbahn, St Pauli's main drag, has been going strong for generations, though there is now an element of gentrification, with a growing number of bars popular with the bohemian and media set. The **DOM Amusement Fair** is open three times a year in the Heiligengeistfeld, from mid-Mar to mid-Apr, early July to late Aug, and early Nov to early Dec. **Nachtasyl**, Alstertor 1, ☎(040) 32 814 207 (www.thalia-theatre.de), Tues–Sat 1900–late, has a retro bar with regular concerts and discos. Directly opposite the Hauptbahnhof is **Nagel**, Kirchenallee 17, ☎(040) 24 71 21, (www.bodega-nagel.de), a pub serving potato-based fare with great draught beer. **The Cotton Club**, Alter Steinweg 10, ☎(040) 34 38 78 (www.cotton-club.org) has hosted jazz and blues for the past 50 years.

WHERE NEXT FROM HAMBURG?

Onward travel by train to **Denmark/Copenhagen** (ETT table 50; 4 hrs 30 mins; 4 trains daily) is popular. Trains have a small number of carriages and limited places so early booking is advisable, especially at weekends in the summer. The train spends about 30 minutes of the journey loaded on a ferry.

CITIES: MUNICH (MÜNCHEN)

Bavarians will often have you believe that Munich really should be the German capital; there's little love lost between Bavarians and their Prussian cousins in Berlin. And Munich does indeed have more to offer than many European capitals. Germany's third city is affluent, a stylish trendsetter and a centre for culture and industry. It comes with a price tag to match, but that's not to say that all visits to Munich need necessarily be expensive. The city is laid-back in a way that other German cities are not, and boasts a vibrant counter-culture that comes as a welcome respite from Bavarian formality.

ARRIVAL AND DEPARTURE

Münchin Hauptbahnhof (Hbf), Bahnhofpl. (about 1 km due west of Marienplatz in the city centre), is Munich's main railway station, and southern Germany's most important rail hub, with excellent day and night train connections via Austria into Italy, Slovenia, Croatia and Hungary. **Rail travel enquiries:** ☎0800 1507 090 (freephone).

Franz Josef Strauss Airport, 30 km northeast of Munich city centre, is a major intercontinental hub with two terminals served by over 60 airlines. Flight information: ☎(089) 9752 1313 (www.munich-airport.de). S-Bahn lines S1 and S8 run every 10 mins from the rail station via the Ostbahnhof and city centre to the airport; see ETT table 892 (if you're starting a rail trip from here, note that up to five people can travel anywhere in Bavaria in a day for the price of one ticket, €28 from ticket machines or purchased online, otherwise €30, including the airport S-Bahn station). For the city centre, get off at Marienpl. Journey time to the airport is 42 mins by S1 and 36 mins by S8. Buses also run every 20 mins 0520–1950 between the airport and the rail station; journey time about 45 mins.

TOURIST OFFICES

Administrative Office:
Fremdenverkehrsamt München, Sendlinger Str. 1, D-80313 München; ☎(089) 2339 6500, (www.muenchen-tourist.de).
Main Tourist Office: Bahnhofpl. 2, outside the main railway station. **Branch: City centre** in the **Rathaus**, Marienpl. 2. There is a central telephone number and fax number (as above for administrative office).

INFORMATION

The main Tourist Office offers an accommodation service, hotel listing, city map and theatre bookings.

PUBLIC TRANSPORT

The city centre, pedestrianised apart from trams and cycles, is easy to explore on foot, being only a 20-min walk across. For trips further afield, use the excellent public transport system of buses, trams and trains: **S-Bahn** (overground) and **U-Bahn** (underground). Nowhere is more than a few mins' walk from a stop or station; all transport runs 0430–0200.

The city also has an impressive 1100 km radius of cycle paths. Bicycle hire at **Tours & Bikes** (www.radiusmunich.com);

TICKETS

City transport tickets can be used on trains, buses or trams; they must be validated in the blue box the first time you board, or you are liable to be fined on the spot. Buy them at stations, newsagents, hotel desks and campsites (single and strip tickets can also be bought on board buses and trams). The price of a **single ticket** depends on the number of zones you'll be travelling: tickets for short trips, 1 zone, 2 zones, 3 zones, 4 zones or 5 zones are available. A **Streifen-karte** (a strip of 10 tickets) gives the best value if you're planning multiple journeys. A **Tageskarte** (day trip ticket that offers unlimited use of the system) for inner Munich can be bought in advance and validated when required. It runs from the time it isstamped until 0600 the following morning.

mid-Apr–mid-Oct at the rail station (platform 32); ☎(089) 596 113 (Apr–Oct). Daily walking tours (in English) start from the rail station (platform 32) at 1000. For a tour with a knowledgeable English-speaking guide, try one of **The Original Munich Walks**, ☎(089) 5502 9374 (www.munichwalks.com), or **Munich Walk Tours**, ☎(089) 2070 2736 (www.munichwalktours.de), which also covers Dachau, a brewery tour, a cycle tour and a Third Reich Tour.

Official taxis are cream-coloured, usually a Mercedes, and are plentiful and reliable; ☎(089) 21610 or (089) 19410.

ACCOMMODATION

Finding accommodation is rarely a problem except during the city's biggest tourist attractions, the annual Oktoberfest beer festival (mid-Sept–early Oct) and Fasching, the Bacchanalian carnival that precedes Ash Wednesday.

The biggest choice of **hotels** is around the rail station in streets like Schillerstr. and Senefelderstr.; it's a rather drab area but handy for the centre. Mid-range ones there include **Hotelissimo Haberstock**, Schillerstr. 4, ☎(089) 557 855 (www.hotelissimo.com), €, and **Leonardo Hotel München City Center**, Senefelderstr. 4, ☎(089) 551 540 (www.leonardo-hotels.com), €. Other moderately priced hotels include **A&O Hotel München** with two branches, one (with a hostel) at Arnulfstr. 102, ☎(089) 452 359 5800 (S-Bahn: Hackerbrücke), and the other Bayerst. 75, ☎(089) 452 357 5700 (close to Hauptbahnhof; www.aohostels.com); **Hotel Andi München City Center**, Landwehrstr. 33, ☎(089) 552 5560, €€€; and **Hotel Herzog**, Häberlstr. 9, ☎(089) 5999 3901 (www.hotel-herzog.de), €€.

Budget accommodation in Munich is in plentiful supply with several **youth hostels**, including **Jugendherberge München–Neuhausen (HI)**, Wendl-Dietrich-Str. 20, ☎(089) 131 156 (www.jugendherberge.de/jh/bayern/muenchen-city), with 351 beds for under-26s only (U-Bahn 1 to Rotkreuzpl.). A useful non-HI option open 24 hrs and just 50 m from the main station is **Euro Youth Hostel**, Senefelderstr. 5, ☎(089) 5990 8811 (www.euro-youth-hotel.de), with breakfast buffet; prices range from €12.50 for a dorm to €30–80 for a single; see also **4you München**, Hirtenstr. 18, ☎(089) 552 1660 (www.the4you.de): environmentally conscious hostel (close to Hauptbahnhof). For **other hostels** see *München Hotels*, available from the Tourist Office. There are also several hostels outside the city limits easily accessible by public transport.

The city's biggest **campsite** is **München–Thalkirchen**, Zentrallandstr. 49, ☎(089) 723 1707 (www.campingmuenchen.de), open mid-Mar–Oct (U-Bahn 3 to Thalkirchen). An interesting last resort in summer (July–Aug) is **Das Zelt** ('The Tent'), Kapuziner-hölzl, in den Kirschen 30, ☎(089) 141 4300 (www.the-tent.com), a marquee in the Botanischer Garten, where €9 gets you floor space. Facilities include washing machines, lockers and bicycle rental.

FOOD AND DRINK

Good eating areas include Schwabing, Gärtnerpl. and, across the River Isar, Haidhausen. An entertaining place for cheap snacks is the open-air **Viktualienmarkt**, a food market where a score of traditional taverns dispense beer, schnapps, sausage and soup – look out particularly for the tasty *Schwarzwaldschinken* (Black Forest smoked ham), black on the outside and red inside. The city's favourite titbit, particularly popular for mid-morning second breakfast washed down with beer, is the *Weisswurst*, a boiled white sausage flavoured with herbs and spices.

Munich is famous for its bread, but even more for its **beers**. The main varieties are *Helles* (normal), *Dunkeles* (dark) and the cloudy orange-coloured *Weissbier* made from wheat instead of hops. There are beer halls and gardens all over the city; the touristy **Hofbräuhaus**, am Platzl 9, is where Hitler launched the Nazi party in 1920. **Augustiner Gaststätten**, Neuhauserstr. 27 (www.augustiner-restaurant.com), is the home of Munich's oldest brewery. In traditional beer gardens, you can bring your own food. (Two useful bits of trivia: first, beer gardens always have chestnut trees, and are shown on maps by tree symbols; second, beer gardens have tables with and without tablecloths – you only get served at your table if it has a cloth.) The city's largest beer garden is by the Chinesischer Turm (Pagoda) in the Englischer Garten.

HIGHLIGHTS

At the hub of the pedestrianised city centre, the **Glockenspiel** (with its host of jousting knights, among others) of the clock of the **Neues Rathaus** (New Town Hall) performs (at 1100, 1200 and 1700) to the shoppers, buskers and sightseers on the Marienpl. (U and S-Bahn: Marienpl.), Munich's main square. Across Marienpl., the less prominent medieval **Altes Rathaus** (Old Town Hall) houses a small toy museum, while just west rise the twin onion domes of the 15th-century **Frauenkirche** (cathedral), Frauenpl. Facing the Altes Rathaus is **Alter Peter** (Old St Peter's church), which holds the strange skeleton of St Munditia, wearing a jewel-laden shroud and bearing a quill pen. From here, it's a short stroll north into Max-Josephpl., to the vast **Residenz** (U-Bahn: Odeonspl.), the baroque palace of Bavaria's Wittelsbach rulers, faithfully rebuilt after bomb damage. Oddly, some parts of the building are open in the morning and others in the afternoon. The highlights include the vaulted Antiquarium and the Schatzkammer (Treasury), with its dazzling collection of jewellery, gold and silver amassed by the Wittelsbachs. It's worth the separate charge to see the Cuvilliés Theater, a rococo gem that's still used for performances. A few steps further on is Odeonspl., Munich's stateliest streetscape, an admirable example of post-war reconstruction. Beside Odeonspl. are the manicured lawns and flowerbeds of the **Hofgarten** park.

To the northeast, the **Englischer Garten** (named because of its informal landscaping) is Europe's biggest city park, popular for the beer garden at its **Chinesischer Turm** (Pagoda) and the naturist meadow beside the **River Isar**. West of the city centre is **Schloss Nymphenburg** (U-Bahn: Rotkreuzpl., then tram 17), the summer palace of the Wittelsbachs. The highlight is its parkland, with lakes, varied gardens, pavilions and hunting lodges, including the **Magdelenklause**, a folly built in the form of a hermit's grotto.

The **Alte Pinakothek**, Barer-str. 27 (www.pinakothek.de; closed Mon; U-Bahn: Theresienstr.), is the place for Old Masters. It includes 65 paintings by Rubens, important Italian works and an unrivalled collection of great German masters. For something specially Bavarian, seek out the **Bayerisches Nationalmuseum**, Prinz-regentenstr. 3 (closed Mon, only €1 on Sun; 🚌 100 from Odeonspl.), with carvings by the medieval master Tilman Riemenschneider, and the world's largest collection of nativity tableaux in the basement. Or head for the **Lenbachhaus**, Luisenstr. 33 (www.lembachhaus.de; S-Bahn: Hauptbahnhof, closed Mon), for paintings by local artists and an outstanding collection of Expressionist works by Kandinsky and others of the 'Blauer Reiter' movement. Don't miss the **Jewish museum** on St Jakobs-Platz 16 next to the main synagogue (www.juedisches-museum.muenchen.de; U/S-Bahn: Marienplatz, closed Mon).

DACHAU – A HARROWING EXCURSION

The significance of the name will never fade. Dachau has a very attractive old centre, but visitors come to this town northwest of Munich for something else: Dachau was the Nazis' first concentration camp. The camp itself is now a memorial, known as the KZ Gedenkstätte (www.kz-gedenkstaette-dachau.de; closed Mon; free entry). It commemorates the 35,000 inmates, mostly Jews and political prisoners, who died there between 1933 and 1945. The museum has an excellent audiovisual presentation, in English at 1130 and 1530. (S-Bahn 2 from the rail station to Dachau; then 🚌 726 to the Memorial.)

SHOPPING

The main shopping area is the wide traffic-free roadway from Karlspl. to Marienpl., a mixture of department stores, supermarkets and fashion shops. For something more upmarket, the city's most elegant designer boutiques lie along Theatinerstr. and Maximilianstr. From late Nov to Christmas Eve, the **Christkindlmarkt** is held on Marienpl.

NIGHT-TIME AND EVENTS

On the bustling **Leopoldstr.** in the lively Schwabing district, students mix with young professionals in upmarket bars and pavement cafés. Most of the clubs in this area are centred around **Gärtnerplatz** and play mainstream pop and R'n'B for an older crowd – expect a hefty cover charge. More affordable are smaller venues such as **Babalu**, Leopoldstr 27 (www.popclub.info; U-Bahn: Giselastr.; Thur–Sat), playing indie, electro and punk. The cosy **Atomic Café** in the Old Town (Neuturmstr. 5; www.atomic.de; Tues–Sat), hosts big name indie bands and DJs, while the **Kultfabrik**, Grafinger str. 6 (www.kultfabrik.de), is an area of converted factories and warehouses near S/U-Bahn Ostbahnhof that now plays host to over 20 clubs, most of which are open till dawn every night. All tastes are catered for, with an emphasis on hip-hop, R'n'B and latino. Expect a cover charge of €5–10, but drinks tend to be cheap. Check out the free *In München* magazine for details of this and the city's other live venues, the Olympiapark and the Muffathalle.

The city also boasts a thriving jazz scene. Check out **Jazzclub Unterfahrt**, Einsteinstr. 42, (www.unterfahrt.de; U-Bahn: Max-Weber-Platz), or one of the many other jazz venues to be found in the Old Town. The monthly *Monatsprogramm* (in German) lists numerous events, from live music to art exhibitions. The English-language *Munich Found* contains up-to-date news on entertainment, restaurants and the like.

Europe's biggest festival of its kind, **Oktoberfest** is a massive indulgence in beer, with oompah bands, beer tents and parades. It lasts 18 days (mid-Sept–early Oct), with barbecued chicken the accompaniment to Bavarian band music, amusements and sideshows. It takes place in the Theresienwiese, southwest of the rail station (U-Bahn 4/5 to Theresienwiese).

WHERE NEXT FROM MUNICH?

*In addition to following the routes to **Berlin** (p267), **Verona** (p432) and **Frankfurt** (p303), you can take international trains to **Amsterdam** (ETT table 28), **Paris** (table 32), **Budapest** (table 32), **Bucharest** (tables 32/60), **Belgrade** via **Llubljana** and **Zagreb** (table 62), **Vienna** via **Salzburg** (table 890), **Rome** (table 70) and **Geneva** via **Zürich** (table 75).*

GERMANY

ROUTE DETAIL

Aachen–Cologne ETT tables 802/910
Type	Frequency	Typical journey time
Train	2–3 per hr	53 mins

Cologne–Düsseldorf ETT tables 800/802
Type	Frequency	Typical journey time
Train	4–5 per hr	22 mins

Düsseldorf–Hannover ETT tables 800/810
Type	Frequency	Typical journey time
Train	Every hr	2 hrs 33 mins

Hannover–Braunschweig ETT table 810
Type	Frequency	Typical journey time
Train	2 per hr	32 mins

Braunschweig–Magdeburg ETT table 810
Type	Frequency	Typical journey time
Train	Every hr	49 mins

Magdeburg–Berlin ETT table 839
Type	Frequency	Typical journey time
Train	Every hr	1 hr 42 mins

KEY JOURNEYS

Cologne–Berlin ETT tables 800/810
Type	Frequency	Typical journey time
Train	Every hr	4 hrs 20 mins

Cologne–Munich ETT tables 910/930
Type	Frequency	Typical journey time
Train	Every hr	4 hrs 36 mins

Cologne–Paris ETT table 20
Type	Frequency	Typical journey time
Train	Every 2 hrs	3 hrs 30 mins

Berlin–Warsaw ETT tables 56/1001
Type	Frequency	Typical journey time
Train	4 daily	5 hrs 51 mins

Berlin–Prague ETT table 60
Type	Frequency	Typical journey time
Train	6 daily	4 hrs 40 mins

RAIL TOUR: AACHEN – HANNOVER – BERLIN

You can speed from the Belgian border to Berlin on modern ICE trains in less than six hours. Or, take this tour, which stops off in some of Germany's most historic cities along the way. True, the route will win few prizes for scenery, traversing the largely monotonous North German Plain. But something of the soul of Germany lies in the great cathedral cities of Aachen and Cologne, and the tour covers a key transport axis. At Hannover, there is the option of heading north for Hamburg, Lübeck and Denmark, or of detouring south into the Harz Mountains, a beautiful area with two of Germany's best-preserved small towns, Goslar and Quedlinburg. The Harz area is served by a network of narrow gauge railway lines, most of which still regularly use steam engines.

AACHEN

Now important only as a frontier town close to where the borders of Belgium, the Netherlands and Germany converge, Aachen was already a great city more than 1000 years ago, when the Emperor Charlemagne the Great enjoyed the thermal springs and made it the capital of his empire. Charlemagne's octagonal chapel is now the heart of the **Dom** (cathedral; www.aachendom.de), built on the site of the imperial palace. Some of the original structure survives and his successors added many embellishments. Charlemagne's gilded tomb is here and you can see the imperial throne on a guided tour. The **Schatzkammer** (Treasury) is one of Europe's most dazzling, with such priceless objects as a gold bust of Charlemagne and a jewel-encrusted 10th-century cross. Statues of 50 Holy Roman Emperors adorn the façade of the 14th-century **Rathaus** (Town Hall). Other indoor sights are the **Ludwig Forum für Internationale Kunst** (Jülicher Str. 97–109, www.ludwigforum.de), with its excellent collection of **East European art** (closed Mon); the unique **International Press Museum** (Pontstr. 13, www.izm.de; Tues–Fri, free entry), which acts as the 'registry office' of the world's press, and the **Aachen Computer Museum** (Sommerfeldstr. 32; closed Thur–Mon; free), which charts the evolution from the earliest data processing to modern PCs. Nowadays, in a post-Schengen Europe free of border controls, Aachen thrives as the main city in the three-country Euregio district. You can visit the Dreiländerpunkt (three-country point) on the edge of town.

A spa town, Aachen also has several places to unwind in the thermal waters, including the **Carolus Thermen Bad Aachen**, Passstrasse 79, ☎(0241) 182 740, (www.carolus-therme.de) with prices €9.50–28.

📷 **Aachen Hbf**, Reumontstr. 1, about 1 km from the city centre.

ℹ️ **Tourist Office**: in the centre at Elisenbrunnen, Friedrich-Wilhelm-Pl., ☎(0241) 180 2960 (www.aachen-tourist.de). Hotel booking service, ☎(0241) 180 2950. Daily guided tours start here.

🏨 Medium-priced **hotels** include the two adjacent sister hotels **Am Bahnhof**, Bahnhofplatz 8, ☎(0241) 35 449 (www.hotel-ambahnhof.de), from €47 incl. breakfast buffet, and the pricier **Hotel Stadtnah**, Leydelstr. 2, ☎(0241) 4745 80 (www.hotelstadtnah.de) and the **Hotel Marx**, Hubertusstr. 33–35,

Germany

[phone](0241) 37541 (www.hotel-marx.de), €. The **HI youth hostel Euregionales Jugendgästehaus** is out of town at Maria-Theresia- Allee 260, [phone](0241) 711 010 (www.aachen.jugendherberge.de), [bus] 2 from Aachen Central station, direction Preuswald, stop Rhonheide. The nearest **campsite** is **Camping Hoeve de Gastmolen**, 7 km west of the centre at **Vaals** in the Netherlands, [phone](0031) (43) 306 5755 (www.gastmolen.nl); open mid-Mar–late Oct.

COLOGNE (KÖLN)

See p299.

Düsseldorf is the unlikely birthplace of **German Punk.** Along with Hamburg and Berlin, Düsseldorf nurtured the nascent punk culture, most notably at the **Ratinger Hof**, which has played host to a variety of big-name bands and remains an important music venue in the city's **Altstadt**.

DÜSSELDORF

Often derided as being no more than a banking and industrial city, Düsseldorf is now decidedly upmarket, its transition exemplified by the Königsallee (generally termed the 'Kö'), one of the most elegant shopping streets in Germany. The city has a substantial Japanese population, who seem to have learnt the art of drinking beer in the same quantities as German natives. Düsseldorf comes with a beer theme – try the local 'Alt'. Four modern monuments attest to the city's commercial success: the new **Stadttor**, the **Thyssen Skyscraper**, **Mannesmann Haus** and the **RhineTower**. Most of the areas of interest are along the Rhine, itself spanned by the graceful **Rhein-kniebrücke** (bridge) and with the **Rhine Tower** prominent on the skyline. Marked by the **Schlossturm**, all that remains of the original 14th-century castle, the **Altstadt** (Old Town), is small and walkable. Within it is **Flingerstr.**, a quaint pedestrianised shopping precinct, somewhat more affordable than Königsalle.

One of the most attractive corners is the **Marktpl.**, brimming over with outdoor cafés and restaurants. A pedestrian zone, Altstadt has more than 200 bars crammed into its busy streets and claims to be 'the longest bar in the world'. At Grabbepl. 5 is the **K20** (www.kunst sammlung.de; closed until summer 2010), a modern art museum with nearly 100 works by Paul Klee. Together with the **K21** at Ständehausstr. 1 it forms the state collection Art of the 20th and 21st Centuries.

The Romantic poet **Heinrich Heine** is Düsseldorf's most famous son, and his works are commemorated in the **Heinrich-Heine-Institut**, Bilkerstr. 12–14.

[rail] **Düsseldorf Hbf**, about 2 km from the east bank of the Rhine, near most places of interest.

[plane] 7 km from city; S-bahn S7 trains, every 20–30 mins. Ryanair fly to Niederrhein (70 mins by bus to main rail station).

[i] **Tourist Office**: Marktplatz 6, [phone](0211) 1720 2844 (www.duesseldorf-tourismus.de, opposite main rail station). Room booking service.

⌂ **Youth hostel (HI)**: Centrally located on Düsseldorferstr. 1, ☎(0211) 557 310 (www. duesseldorf.jugendherberge.de); 6 km from the station; 🚌 835/836. **Hotel Diana**, Jahnstr. 31, ☎(0211) 375 072 (www.hoteldiana.de), singles from €35, doubles from €55.

HANNOVER

A clutch of English kings hailed from Hannover (the first four King Georges). This quintessentially German city is gritty and industrial, but with a good array of historical buildings and some world-class landscape gardens. A fine route for first-time visitors is the '**Der Rote Faden**' ('the Red Thread'), a red line painted on the pavement that tracks a 4200-m (2 hr) path through the city centre and can be easily followed on foot; pick up a free map and explanatory leaflet from the Tourist Office. From the station, Bahnhofstr. leads to the Kröpcke piazza, in the heart of the largely reconstructed **Altstadt**; the **Kröpcke clock** is the most prominent rendezvous in town. For shopping, head for Georgstrasse, Galerie Luise and Kröpcke-Passage. The high-gabled, carefully restored **Altes Rathaus** is a splendid edifice with elaborate brickwork. Alongside is the **Marktkirche**, with 14th- to 15th-century stained glass and a bulky tower that is the city's emblem. Across town, over the Friedrichswall, is the high-domed **Neues Rathaus** located in a pleasant garden and reflected in a small lake. Next door, the **Kestner Museum**, Trammpl. 3 (www.kestner-museum.de), contains 'Hannover's most expensive head' (a 3000-year-old Egyptian bust). The wide-ranging **Landesmuseum**, Willy-Brandt-Allee 5 (www.landesmuseum-hannover.de), includes a fascinating archaeological section. The absolute must-see is the **Royal Herrenhäuser Gardens**, 10 mins from Kröpcke (U-Bahn: Herrenhäuser Gärten). It consists of four once-royal gardens, two of which are the English-style landscaped **Georgengarten** and the formal **Grosser Garten**, the scene of spectacular fountain displays in summer. Frequent musical and theatrical performances are staged in the palace and gardens.

Hannover's reputation as a business centre may deter younger travellers, but the city boasts a lively youth culture. For nightlife check out the **Kulturzentrum Faust** (www.faustev.de), a former factory building by the River Leine (U-Bahn: Glocksee). For cheap eats (daytime only) look for the **Markthalle** on Karmarschstrasse, which offers a range of ethnic cuisine plus the omnipresent *Wurst* and pizza.

🚊 **Hannover Hbf**, central location about 600m northeast of the Altstadt. A major hub, where the main west–east (Cologne to Berlin) and north–south (Hamburg to Munich) routes cross.

ℹ️ **Tourist Office**: Ernst-August-Pl. 8 (next to Hbf), ☎(0511) 1234 5111 (www.hannover-tourism.de).

⌂ The Tourist Office can make room reservations at all budget levels (no charge), ☎(0511) 1234 5555. Many conventions take place here, so cheap accommodation is hard to find, although prices drop further away from the centre. The **HI youth hostel** (reservations advisable) is at Ferdinand-Wilhelm-Fricke-Weg 1, ☎(0511) 1317 674 (www.djh-niedersachsen.de/jh/hannover); U-bahn: 3/7 to Fischerhof. Youth hostel-style accommodation at **Naturfreundehaus in**

Germany

der Eilenriede, Hermann-Bahlsen-Allee 8, ☎(0511) 691 493, (www.naturfreunde-hannover.de), Line 3 direction Lahe or Line 7, towards Fasanenkrug; bus stop Spannhagengarten. Head the same direction for **Hotel Formule I Hannover Ost Lahe**, Rendsburger Str. 28A, ☎(0511) 6166 9920 (15 km from city centre; U-Bahn 3 to Oldenburger Allee); part of the Accor hotel chain (www.accorhotels.com), rooms €31. Out of town but always great value.

SIDE TRIPS FROM HANNOVER **Celle** (41 km northeast of Hannover on the main rail route to Hamburg; hourly trains, 18–25 mins, ETT tables 902/903), overlooked by a magnificent 16th-century castle, rates among the best-preserved medieval towns in northern Germany. The **youth hostel (HI)** is at Weghausstr. 2, ☎(05141) 53208 (www.jugendherberge.de/jh/celle), while other room reservations can be made through the **Tourist Office**, Markt 14–16, ☎(05141) 1212 (www.region-celle.de).

WHERE NEXT FROM HANNOVER?

*You can join the **Hannover–Lübeck** route (p294) here. Express trains (ETT table 900, I per hr) from Hannover to **Munich** enable you to stop off at **Würzburg** and join the route to **Passau** (p308) or travel west via Frankfurt-am-Main to join the rail route down the **Rhine** via **Mainz** and **Koblenz**.*

BRAUNSCHWEIG

Change here for trains to Goslar (hourly trains, ETT table 859) and to Vienenburg for Wernigerode (tables 859, 860). There are also direct trains to these destinations from Hannover (ETT table 860).

GOSLAR

Goslar has a well-preserved medieval centre full of half-timbered houses. It gained its prosperity through silver and lead mining in the Middle Ages, and is now a UNESCO World Heritage Site. At its heart is the **Marktplatz**, presided over by the **Rathaus** and **Marktkirche**; on the 15th-century **Kaiserworth**, a statue of a boy on a gable illustrates the town's right to mint coinage by defecating a coin. Goslar is also the centre of the **Harz Mountains**. The highest peak, the Brocken, rises to 1142 m, and can be reached by train. The heart of the region is the **Hochharz National Park**, with a vast network of marked hiking trails. From Goslar, trains and buses connect east towards Wernigerode and Quedlinburg.

ⓘ **Tourist Office**: Markt 7, ☎(05321) 78060 (www.goslar.de).

🏠 **Youth hostel (HI)**: Rammelsberger Str. 25, ☎(05321) 22240 (www.djh-niedersachsen.de/jh/goslar), 4 km from the rail station; 5 mins from the centre is **Gästehaus Möller**, Schieferweg 6, ☎(05321) 23098, with singles from €22 and a noted buffet breakfast.

MAGDEBURG

If coming from the east, change here for Wernigerode and Quedlinburg via Halberstadt (ETT tables 862, 860).

WERNIGERODE AND QUEDLINBURG

Wernigerode is yet another historic half-timbered town, notable for what might well be the finest town hall (Rathaus) in all Germany. That, and the extravagant Schloss, justify a stop. The town is also the jumping-off point for the two-hour journey by steam train to the top of the Brocken. Further east is the most engaging small town in the region: **Quedlinburg** knocks spots off the Bavarian competition, and still seems undiscovered. It's a UNESCO World Heritage Site, and the ensemble of medieval buildings is remarkable. Trains run hourly to Magdeburg (ETT table 862), allowing you to join the main route eastwards towards Berlin.

i **Tourist Office**: In **Wernigerode**: Marktpl. 10, ☎(03943) 553 7835 (www.wernigerode-tourismus.de). In **Quedlinburg**: Marktpl. 2, ☎(03946) 905 625 (www.quedlinburg.de).

🛏 **Pensions** are the best bet for reasonably priced accommo-dation in Wernigerode, including **Pension Kristall**, Karl-Marx-Str. 12, Elbingerode, ☎(039454) 41235, (www.pensionkristall.de), €. **Youth hostel (HI)**: Am Eichberg 5, ☎(03943) 606 176 (www.jugendherberge.de/jh/quedlinburg). Quedlinburg's **youth hostel** is located at Neuendorf 28, ☎(03946) 811 703.

BERLIN

See p267.

THE HARZ MOUNTAIN RAILWAYS

Wernigerode is the northern terminus of Europe's most extensive narrow-gauge steam railway network. The **Harzer Schmalspurbahnen**: 140 km of scenic lines winding through the picturesque Harz Mountains. The longest section of the network is the **Harzquerbahn**, 61 km of track between Wernigerode and Nordhausen, traversed by three trains daily in summer, two in winter. Some are hauled by 1950s steam locomotives, but some older engines are used for special trips. The Harzquerbahn connects at Eisfelder Talmühle with the 60 km of the **Selketalbahn**, which runs through the scenic Selke Valley. A branch line, the **Brockenbahn**, reopened in 1992 for the first time since World War II, and connects with the Harzquerbahn at Drei-Annen-Hohne, from which it ascends 19 km to the exposed summit of the Brocken. Dress warmly! For timetables and fares, see the **Harzer Schmalspurbahnen** website (www.hsb-wr.de); see also ETT table 867. Rail passes are not accepted on these lines, although HSB has its own 3-day pass which is good value if you are lingering in the area.

ROUTE DETAIL

Hannover–Bremen ETT table 813

Type	Frequency	Typical journey time
Train	2 per hr	59 mins

Bremen–Hamburg ETT tables 800/801

Type	Frequency	Typical journey time
Train	2 per hr	55 mins

Hamburg–Lübeck ETT table 825

Type	Frequency	Typical journey time
Train	1–2 per hr	40 mins

KEY JOURNEYS

Hannover–Hamburg ETT tables 900/902

Type	Frequency	Typical journey time
Train	2–3 per hr	1 hr 15 mins

Hamburg–Berlin ETT table 840

Type	Frequency	Typical journey time
Train	Every hr	1 hr 40 mins

Hamburg–Copenhagen ETT table 50

Type	Frequency	Typical journey time
Train	4–6 daily	4 hrs 40 mins

Hannover, easily accessible from Amsterdam and on the **Aachen–Berlin** route (p288), is the starting point for a tour of three great cities that were members of the great 14th- to 16th-century trading association known as the Hanseatic League – **Bremen**, **Hamburg** (p277) and **Lübeck**. Beyond Lübeck you can continue by a train that boards a ferry for a memorable entry into Denmark.

BREMEN

Bremen is one of Germany's most remarkable maritime cities. It boasts rich Hanseatic connections, and traded on its links with the Americas. Bremen's wealth was based on trade in coffee and cotton and much of its 15th- and 16th-century structure survives – some of it quite Dutch-looking. Together with **Bremerhaven**, its outer harbour downstream towards the mouth of the Weser River, Bremen is one of the Länder (states) that make up Germany, continuing a proud tradition of self-government that dates back to the Middle Ages. The **Altstadt**, on the northeast bank of the river, is the main area of historical interest, boasting a wonderful selection of old buildings, many in a Dutch style. The wide Marktplatz is dominated by the **Rathaus**, a 15th-century structure overlaid with a Renaissance façade. It's worth joining a tour to see the splendid interior. In Marktplatz are two notable statues. One is a 15th-century, 10-m high sculpture of **Roland** (Charlemagne's nephew), which is a symbol of the town's independence; legend has it that Bremen will remain free as long as he is standing. The other (which is modern and much smaller) illustrates the Grimm Brothers' fairy-tale about the **Four Musicians of Bremen** – a donkey, a dog, a cat and a rooster.

The 11th-century twin-spired **St Petri Dom**, Sandstr. 10–12, is sombrely beautiful. In the **Bleikeller** (basement: open Easter–Oct) are some ghoulish corpses, believed to be of men who fell from the roof during construction, and preserved from decay by the lack of air. To the south side of Marktpl. is **Böttcherstrasse**, Bremen's most remarkable street. Dating from the 1920s, it's an eclectic mix of Jugendstil (Germany's version of Art Nouveau) and Art Deco. It houses craft workshops, restaurants, a casino and a musical clock that chimes every hour 1200–1800 (only at 1200, 1500 and 1800, Jan–Apr, but not in very cold weather). The **Schnoorviertel** area (between the Dom and the river) consists of well-preserved 16th–18th-century buildings, many of which are now **craft shops**. Just to the east is **Kunsthalle**, Am Wall 207 (www.kunsthalle-bremen.de; undergoing modernisation and closed until winter 2010/11), which has an eclectic collection of paintings and sculptures dating from the Renaissance to the present day.

Among other highlights are **Beck's Brewery** (English-language tours at 1400, Thur–Sat) and the fascinating excursion into the realms of science at the **Universum Science Center**, Wiener Str. 2 (www.universum-bremen.de).

RAIL **Bremen Hbf**, just north of the main area of interest.

Germany

i **Tourist Office**: Hauptbahnhof (main railway station), ☎(01805) 10 10 30 (€0.14 cents per minute) (www.bremen-tourism.de). Open Mon–Fri 0900–1900, Sat–Sun 0930–1800. Also at the junction of Obernstr. and Liebfrauenkirchhof (open Mon–Fri 0100–1800, Sat–Sun 0100–1600).

🛏 **Hotel Gästehaus Walter**, Buntentorsteinweg 86–88, ☎(0421) 525 950 (www.hotel-walter.de), €, has double rooms from around €60. The **Bremer Backpacker Hostel** is just 5 mins from Hbf at Emil-Waldmann-Str. 5–6, ☎(0421) 223 8057 (www.bremer-backpacker-hostel.de); dorms €18, single €29. The **HI youth hostel**, Kalkstr. 6, ☎(0421) 163 820 (www.jugendherberge.de/jh/bremen), is on the western side of Altstadt; 🚌 26 or tram 1/8 to Brill. **Campsite: Campingplatz am Stadtwaldsee**, Hochschulring 1, ☎(0421) 8410 748 (www.camping-stadtwaldsee.de).

With the exception of some museums, the places of interest cluster around Marktpl. The **ErlebnisCARD Bremen**, available for 1 day or 2 days (€8.90/10.90 one adult and two children, or a more expensive version for up to 5 persons €17.5/22), provides free bus travel as well as significant discounts on the city's attractions.

🅃🄾 **The Ratskeller** (in the Rathaus) has been a bar since the early 15th century and offers 600 different wines, although it is quite pricey. Cheap eating places can be found on and around Ostertorsteinweg. **Lift-Internet Café**, Weberstr. 18, ☎(0421) 77450 (www.liftcafe.de); 🚌 2/3/10/N12 to S-bahn stop Sielwall.

SIDE TRIPS FROM BREMEN   Located 110 km north of Bremen, **Cuxhaven** is Germany's favourite seaside health resort, with a long sandy beach and a small offshore island, **Neuwerk**, which you can visit at low tide by horse-drawn carriage. Trains from Bremen take 1 hr 30 mins (every 2 hrs, ETT table 815). En route you pass through **Bremerhaven**, and it is worth stopping here for the fine **Deutsches Schiffahrtsmuseum** (German Ship Museum; www.dsm.museum; see website for opening times), where exhibits include square-riggers and a U-boat. From Cuxhaven, ferries sail to the remote island of **Helgoland**, with pleasant walks above its red craggy cliffs – quite unusual in these parts. Once a British possession, it was swapped for (of all places) Zanzibar in 1890, and was nearly bombed to bits by RAF target practice in the immediate postwar years; it was reconstructed in 1952 and is now a busy little holiday resort. **Youth hostel: Haus der Jugend Helgoland**, Postfach 580, 27487 Helgoland, ☎(04725) 341 (www.jugendherberge.de/jh/helgoland); Apr–Oct. Germany's answer to Glastonbury, the huge **Hurricane festival**, takes place at Scheessel, just east of Bremen (direct train) in late June each year.

HAMBURG

See p277.

LÜBECK

If you only have time to visit one of the old Hanseatic towns, make it Lübeck, a city that's cut a dash in commerce, trade and the arts for seven centuries. The central area, on a moated island in a river, has been beautifully restored. Most places of interest are in the 12th-century Altstadt, the moated old city. Between this and the main station is Lübeck's emblem, the twin-towered **Holstentor**, which appears on the ubiquitous marzipan, the town's gastronomic speciality. It's a 15th-century structure, and now museum, that was one of the four city gates. Get your bearings by taking the lift up the 50-m spire of the Gothic **Petrikirche** (itself now an art gallery). Nearby, **Museum für Puppentheater**, Kleine Petersgrube 4–6 (www.tfm-luebeck.com), is devoted to theatrical puppets, while behind the handsome façades of Grosse Petersgrube is the **Music Academy**. Both places give regular public performances. The Marktplatz is dominated by the striking L-shaped 13th- to 16th-century **Rathaus**, typical of Lübeck's architectural style of alternating red unglazed and black glazed bricks, a style copied by the Dutch and more common in Holland. Opposite the east wing is **Niederegger Haus**, Breitestr., renowned for displays of **marzipan** (the town has been producing it since the Middle Ages and sells it in an endless number of varieties). Opposite the north wing is the 13th-century **Marienkirche**, a brick-built Gothic church with square towers that was the model for many in the area. It contains a magnificent gilded altarpiece dating from 1518. **Buddenbrookhaus**, the inspiration for Thomas Mann's Lübeck-based saga of the same name, is a museum at Mengstr. 4. To the south of Altstadt is the large brick-built **Dom**, which contains an allegorical triumphal arch and ornate rood screen. For a different perspective on Lübeck, consider a boat trip. Several companies offer short sightseeing canal trips, while others run from Lübeck Altstadt to nearby Travemünde, a small coastal resort with good beaches.

🚉 **Lübeck Hbf**, a 10-min walk west of Altstadt.

✈ **Flughafen-Lübeck**: ☎(0451) 583 010 (www.flughafen-luebeck.de). The local bus runs every 20 mins to Lübeck.

ℹ **Tourist Offices**: Holstentorpl. 1, ☎(0451) 889 9700 (www.luebeck-tourismus.de). There is also a branch at Berlingstr. 21 (inside Strandbahnhof).

🏨 There are several reasonably priced hotels around the station **(Hbf)**. Private rooms are also available, e.g. **Familie Zingel**, Vermehrenring 11A, ☎(0451) 625 029, (www.zimmer-luebeck.de), €, or **Frau Andresen**, G. Altefähre 17, ☎(0451) 930 8099, €. **Youth hostels (HI)**: Am Gertrudenkirchhof 4, ☎(0451) 33433 (jh-luebeck@djh.de, 🚌 1/3 from Hbf to Gustav-Radbruch-Pl.). There is a **Jugendgästehaus** at Mengstr. 33, ☎(0451) 702 0399 (jh-luebeck@djh.de). The YMCA (CVJM) runs a **Sleep-In**, Grosse Petersgrube 11, ☎(0451) 71920 (www.cvjm-luebeck.de).

WHERE NEXT FROM LÜBECK?

*Carry on northeast into **Denmark** (ETT tables 720, 825), crossing the border in style beyond Puttgarden, where the entire train is shipped onto the ferry; continue on to **Copenhagen** (p481).*

KEY JOURNEYS

Cologne–Frankfurt
(see **Notes**)   ETT tables 910, 912

Type	Frequency	Typical journey time
Train	2–3 per hr	1 hr 10 mins (high-speed line)

Frankfurt–Munich   ETT tables 920, 930

Type	Frequency	Typical journey time
Train	Every hr	3 hrs 10 mins

Notes

Choose your train carefully. Most ICEs heading out of Cologne towards Frankfurt-am-Main take a route to the east of the Rhine Valley. Ignore services that don't stop at Koblenz, as the finest of the classic Rhine gorge scenery lies immediately south.

ROUTE DETAIL

Cologne–Bonn   ETT tables 800, 802

Type	Frequency	Typical journey time
Train	4 per hr	20 mins

Bonn–Koblenz   ETT tables 800, 802

Type	Frequency	Typical journey time
Train	3–4 per hr	32 mins

Koblenz–Frankfurt   ETT tables 912, 914

Type	Frequency	Typical journey time
Train	1–2 per hr	1 hr 26 mins

Frankfurt–Würzburg   ETT table 920

Type	Frequency	Typical journey time
Train	1–2 per hr	1 hr 10 mins

Würzburg–Nuremberg   ETT tables 900, 920

Type	Frequency	Typical journey time
Train	2 per hr	54 mins

Nuremberg–Regensburg   ETT tables 920, 921

Type	Frequency	Typical journey time
Train	Every hr	51 mins

Regensburg–Passau   ETT tables 920, 921

Type	Frequency	Typical journey time
Train	Every hr	1 hr 2 mins

RAIL TOUR: COLOGNE – WÜRZBURG – PASSAU

Leaving **Cologne**, Germany's fourth city, the train takes you through **Bonn**, Beethoven's birthplace, and upstream via Koblenz to the **Rhine Valley**. This is one of Europe's classic rail journeys, with castles clinging to the slopes and a series of waterside towns and villages. **Trier**, with its astonishing Roman remains, makes an easy and worthwhile side trip from Koblenz. **Mainz** was where, in the 1450s, Gutenberg invented the first printing press with moveable type and has the outstanding Gutenberg Museum. Beyond **Mainz** the scene briefly becomes less appealing, taking in the high-rise commercial centre of **Frankfurt**. This route then enters **Bayern** (Bavaria) at **Aschaffenburg** and tracks southeast across Germany's largest state. Eastern Bavaria is a relatively little-visited area of Germany; **Passau** stands on a neck of land between two rivers, the **Ilz** and the **Danube**, and at the threshold of **Austria**.

COLOGNE (KÖLN)

During World War II, nine-tenths of what was Germany's largest Altstadt was flattened by bombing, and the quality of reconstruction has been patchy. But there's much to enjoy, in the cathedral, churches and museums, and Kölners themselves have an irresistible verve, exemplified in the city's Lent carnival. The twin spires of the **Dom** (**cathedral**), one of the world's greatest Gothic buildings, soar over the Rhineland capital, and greet the visitor arriving at the city's Hauptbahnhof. You can climb the tower for a splendid view of the city, the River Rhine and a largely industrial hinterland. Lively Cologne has a large Turkish minority. The city boasts excellent beer (look for the local Kölsch), and Germany's most famous Karneval (a few days of mayhem that reach their peak on Shrove Tuesday).

The city's Roman traces include remnants of the original 5th-century AD city wall. The superlative **Römisch-Germanisches Museum**, Roncallipl. 4, holds many of the finds of the ancient town, including an arched fortress gate and the famous Dionysus Mosaic. By the 13th century, Cologne was a thriving metropolis of 40,000 people, protected by Europe's longest city walls – a 6-km rampart pierced by 12 massive gates. Within the original city wall stand a dozen Romanesque churches, Germany's finest such architectural concentration. The most striking are Gross St Martin, overlooking the Rhine in the Altstadt, and St Aposteln. From 321 until 1424, the city was home to one of the most important Jewish communities in Germany. The remains of a 'mikvah' (a Jewish ritual bath) dating from 1170 are preserved under a glass pyramid in the middle of the square of the City Hall. Nearby, in Bischofsgartenstr., is

NIGHT-TIME

The **Kwartier Lateng** (Barbarossa Pl.), U-Bahn lines 12 and 16, and the **Südstadt** are where most of the student hangouts are, and these two areas are good places to start. The Altstadt has several good music venues. There are two good monthly listings mags: *Live!* (free) and *Kölner Illustrierte* (€1).

Germany

a modern complex incorporating the **Philharmonie Hall**, the **Agfa-Foto-Historama**, covering all things photographic and the **Museum Ludwig** (closed Mon), housing 20th-century works including Kirchner, Beckmann and Dix and an excellent collection of Pop Art (Warhol, Lichtenstein and more). The outstanding **Wallraf-Richartz-Museum**, with superb 14th- to 16th-century paintings by the Cologne school, is at Martinstr. 39 (www.museenkoeln.de), about a 10-min walk from the **Dom**.

Köln Hbf, centrally placed, right by the cathedral with a huge shopping centre, information desk, currency exchange and 24-hr service point; station closes 0100–0400; left luggage.

Flughafen Köln–Bonn, southeast of the city. **Information** (02203) 404 001 (www.koeln-bonn-airport.de). 170 connects the airport with the rail station in 20 mins, running every 15 mins 0700–2000 (every 30 mins 0530–0700 and 2000–2345). S-Bahn trains take 15 mins and run Mon–Fri every 20 mins and Sat–Sun every 30 mins (see ETT table 802).

i **Tourist Office**: Kardinal-Höffner Pl. 1, (0221) 221 30400 (www.koelntourismus.de) by the Dom. Also at Köln–Bonn airport.

Central rooms are almost always at a premium and the cheap hotels are very scattered. Book ahead. The **Tourist Office** can book hotels on the day or in advance (info@koelntourismus.de or online at www.koelntourismus.de). Cheaper options include: **Station Backpackers Hostel**, Marzellenstr. 44–56, (0221) 912 5301 (www.hostel-cologne.de), dorm from €17, free internet; **Brandenburger Hof**, Brandenburger Str. 2–4, (0221) 122 889 (www.brandenburgerhof.de), €; and **Hotel Berg**, Brandenburger Str. 6, (0221) 912 9162 (www.hotel-berg.com), 100 m from Hbf, €€. The more central of the two **HI hostels** is **Köln-Deutz**, Siegesstr. 5A, (0221) 814 711 (www.koeln-deutz.jugendherberge.de), a 15-min walk from the station, over the Hohenzollernbrücke, a couple of blocks south of Deutz station. The second hostel is at **Köln-Riehl**, An der Schanz 14, (0221) 767 081 (koeln-riehl@jugendherberge.de). The most accessible **campsite** is **Poll**, Weidenweg, (0221) 831 966, southeast of Altstadt (tram 16: Marienburg).

A typical Cologne dish is *Sauerbraten*, a 'sour roast', with beef soaked in vinegar and stewed, served with *Kartoffelklösse Schrägschrift* (potato dumplings) and apple sauce. The local sweet Rhine wine is *suuren Hungk* ('sour dog'), but local beer is just as popular. *Blootwoosch* (blood sausage) makes a snack served with mustard on a bread roll, known as 'Cologne caviar'. A dish that sounds like half a chicken (*Halve Huhn*) is actually just a cheese roll. Many local beer-pubs (*Brauhäuser*) offer good-value food.

The comprehensive public transport system includes U-Bahn (underground/subway), S-Bahn (surface suburban trains), trams and buses. **Day Tickets** are valid for up to five people.

KÖLN WELCOME CARD

The **Köln Welcome Card** (available from Tourist Offices and hotels) offers free public transport within Cologne and the region, up to 50% off admission to the city's museums and attractions, benefits on guided tours, theatre tickets, free drinks and more for 1, 2 or 3 days (€9/14/19). There is a Pink Welcome Card directed at gay and lesbian visitors, too.

BONN

With its palpable small town atmosphere, it's hard to believe that Bonn was still a capital city in the early 1990s. Packed with students, it's a lively stopover for a day or two. All the central areas are walkable, and the pubs near the river do a roaring trade at night and are crowded with young people and students. Deprived of its capital city status, Bonn now makes the most of its musical connections. Beethoven is the local big name. The **Geburtshaus** (birthplace), where he spent the first 22 years of his life, is at Bonngasse 20 and contains his instruments and a rather sad collection of ear trumpets as testament to his irreversible decline into total deafness. On the other side of the rail station, the **Rheinisches Landesmuseum**, Colmantstr. 14–16 (www.rlmb.lvr.de), has everything from old skulls to Celtic gold. The **Museumsmeile** (Museum Mile) is a complex outside the city centre, easily reached by Underground lines 16/63/66/67/68 (stop Heussallee/Museumsmeile) or 🚌 610/630 (stop Bundeskanzlerpl.). It includes (all closed Mon) **Museum Alexander Koenig** (Natural History Museum; www.zfmk.de), the **Kunst- und Ausstellungshalle** (for art exhibitions; www.kah-bonn.de), the **Kunstmuseum Bonn** (City Art Gallery; www.kunstmuseum-bonn.de), the **Deutsches Museum Bonn** (for German technology; www.deutsches-museum.de) and the **Haus der Geschichte**, Willy-Brandt-Allee 14 (www.hdg.de), a new high-tech museum on the history of Germany (free entry). To recover from all those museums, head for the Altstadt or Südstadt for beer aplenty. The **Brauhaus Bönnsch** (at Sterntorbrücke 4), is an excellent pub that brews a local beer called Bönnsch, with local food specialities to match.

🚆 **Bonn Hbf**, beside the bus terminal and right in the centre, near the pedestrian precinct.

ⓘ **Tourist Office**: Windeckstr.1/am Münsterpl., ☎(0228) 775 000 (www.bonn.de). There is a hotel booking service: ☎(0228) 910 4170 (www.bonn-region.de).

🏨 **Hotel Aigner**, Dorotheenstr. 12, ☎(0228) 604 060 (www.hotel-aigner.de), €; **Bergmann**, Kasernenstr. 13, ☎(0228) 633 891 (www.hotel-bergmann-bonn.de), €. Nearby Bad Godesberg can be cheaper: **Gästehaus Scholz**, Annettenstr. 16, ☎(0228) 379 363 (www.gaestehaus-scholz.com), €. **Youth hostel (HI)**: Haager Weg 42, ☎(0228) 289 970 (www.bonn.jugendherberge.de). **Campsite**: **Genienau**, Im Frankenkeller 49, ☎(0228) 344 949 is in Mehlem, part of Bad Godesberg.

KOBLENZ

Koblenz is a name intimately associated with travel: it was here that Karl Baedeker started publishing his famous guidebooks to Europe in 1823. The Mosel and Rhine rivers meet here at the **Deutsches Eck** (the German Corner), marked by a massive, heavy-handed monument to Kaiser Wilhelm I. The pleasant gardens that line the banks of both rivers combine to provide an attractive 8 km stroll.

Ehrenbreitstein (across the Rhine, ferries in summer) is dominated by an enormous fortress, the **Festung**. Its earliest fortifications date from the 12th century, but it grew to its present size during the 16th century. The **Sesselbahn** (cable car) operates Easter–end Oct. As well as providing a fantastic view, the fortress contains two regional museums and a youth hostel (see below). A big firework display (**Rhein in Flammen**) is staged here on the second Sat in Aug.

[RAIL] **Koblenz Hbf**, Bahnhofpl. 2. Southwest of the centre, 25-min walk downhill (or [bus] 1) to the riverside area from which cruises (*Rheinfähre*) depart.

i **Tourist Offices**: Bahnhofspl. 17 (opposite rail station), ☎(0261) 31304 (www.touristik-koblenz.de). It provides boat schedules and a city map that includes listings. There is another **Tourist Office** in the historical Rathaus (town hall), Jesuitenpl. 2.

🏨 **Hotel Jan van Werth**, v.-Werth-Str. 9, ☎(0261) 36500 (www.hoteljanvanwerth.de), €; **Hotel Grebel**, Planstr. 7–9, in the Güls district, ☎(0261) 42530 (www.hotel-grebel.de); take [bus] 355 from Hbf to Moselbrücke; and **Sessellift**, Obertal 22, ☎(0261) 73490 (www.hotel-sessellift.de), €, are reasonable. The **HI youth hostel** is housed in the **Festung** (see p301), ☎(0261) 972 870 (www.diejugendherbergen.de; closed till end 2010), and is popular, so book well ahead. The downside is that the ferry and chairlift both stop very early so, after taking a bus ([bus] 7/8/9/10) to Charlottenstr., you end the day with a long uphill climb. The **campsite** is at Lutzel, across the Mosel: **Campingplatz Rhein-Mosel**, Schartwiesenweg 6, ☎(0261) 82719 (www.camping-rhein-mosel.de). There's a ferry across during the day.

[TO] Some of the best food bargains are found by indulging in the *Stehcafés* (standing cafés) and *Biergartens* on the banks of the Rhine, just by the **Deutsches Eck**.

SIDE TRIP FROM KOBLENZ TO TRIER Worth the detour for its Roman and early Christian remains, Trier (ETT table 915; hourly rail services, taking 1 hr 25 mins) is Germany's oldest city, dating back to 16 BC. The rail trip from Koblenz to Trier gives good views of the beautiful Mosel Valley. The highlight in Trier is the **Porta Nigra** (Black Gate), one of the most impressive Roman structures north of the Alps. You can also see Emperor Constantine's throne room and part of a Roman street in the huge **Konstantin-Basilika**, Konstantinpl., part of the Imperial Palace, and the largest surviving single-hall structure of the ancient world. Backing onto it is the picture-perfect pink, white and gold rococo **Kurfürstliches Palais** in gardens with fountains (and a café). This area leads directly to the **Rheinisches Landesmuseum**, Weimarer Allee 1 (at the southern end of the pleasant and well-tended **Palastgarten**), which contains Roman remains (www.landesmuseum-trier.de). Close by are the **Kaiserthermen**, a huge complex of well-preserved imperial baths, and the **Amphitheatre** (c. AD 100), where crowds of up to 20,000 watched gladiatorial combat. Sedate Trier was the birthplace of Karl Marx, and dedicated politicos can visit the house where he was born at Brückenstr. 10 (closed Monday mornings). It houses an excellent exhibition on Marx's life and work. Trier's Renaissance **Marktplatz** is outstanding even by German standards. **Tourist Office**: Porta Nigra, ☎(0651) 978 080 (www.trier.de). **Youth hostel (HI)**: An der Jugendherberge 4, ☎(0651) 146 620 (trier@diejugendherbergen.de), 3 km southwest of the centre.

FRANKFURT-AM-MAIN

Frankfurt, the country's financial capital and major convention centre, has a brash Manhattan-style skyline. The city that is home to the European Central Bank and Germany's largest stock exchange doesn't rely on tourism, but the traffic-free boulevards with shops, parks and the leafy banks of the River Main, which flows through the centre, make Frankfurt surprisingly pleasant for strolling around. Affectionately known as the *gut Stubb* (front parlour), Roemerberg, a square of half-timbered and steeply gabled buildings, is at the heart of the Altstadt (Old Town). Along one side is the **Roemer**, the city's town hall, meticulously restored as it was in the Middle Ages. A short walk to the east leads to **Kaiserdom**, Domstr. (www.dom-frankfurt.de), the red-sandstone Gothic cathedral, with its dome and lantern tower, where emperors were crowned. Frankfurt was the birthplace of Germany's most famous writer, Goethe. The **Goethe Haus**, Grosser Hirschgraben 23 (www.goethehaus-frankfurt.de), is a careful post-war reconstruction of the house where he was born in 1749. It is furnished in period style and has a museum with manuscripts and documents next to it. The old **Sachsenhausen** district, reached by crossing the Alte Brücke (Old Bridge), has a village-like feel. Its little square and cobbled alleys of half-timbered houses survived World War II more or less intact. A recent addition to Frankfurt's famous zoo, **Zoologischer Garten**, Alfred-Brehm-pl. 16 (www.zoo-frankfurt.de; U-Bahn 6 to Zoo), which was founded in 1858, is the **Grzimek-Haus**, where nocturnal animals can be observed in daytime. To the north (U-Bahn 6/7 to Westend) are the botanic gardens, **Palmengarten**, Zeppelin allee, with lily ponds and conservatories of orchids and cacti. Twelve of the city's 40 museums are gathered on the south bank of the river along Schaumainkai, known as **Museumsufer** (Museum Bank).

🚉 **Hauptbahnhof** (Hbf), almost a city unto itself. Bustles day and night and has good cafés and shops. There's an airport-style lounge, with bar, armchairs and toys. The city centre is a 15-min walk straight ahead along Kaiserstr.

✈ **Flughafen Frankfurt-Main** (9 km southwest of the city) is central Europe's busiest airport. ☎(069) 6900 (www.frankfurt-airport.de). S-Bahn suburban trains (service S8) to Frankfurt Hbf, the city's main station, leave Frankfurt Flughafen Regionalbahnhof every 15 mins from 0430 to 0030; the journey takes 11 mins (ETT table 917a). Long-distance trains leave from Frankfurt Flughafen Fernbahnhof. Direct services are available to Cologne, Dortmund, Hamburg, Nuremberg, Stuttgart, Munich,

NIGHT-TIME AND EVENTS

For hints on happenings and clubs, look to the following listings magazines: *Prinz* (www.prinz.de), *Kultur News*, *Frizz* or *Strandgut* (www.strandgut.de). Kleine Bockenheimer Str. has a good jazz scene. Try the **Jazzkeller** (www.jazzkeller.com; from 2100, closed Mon). An evening 'must' is to wander over the Main bridges to **Sachsenhausen** to the many pubs where the local tipple, called Äppelwoi, is consumed in truly impressive quantities. There's an alternative scene in the city's Bockenheim district, where, particularly in Leiziger Str., you'll find a good choice of cheap cafés. Each year in mid-October, the city hosts the world's largest bookfair.

Germany

Freiburg and Basel. Note that Ryanair flies to the misleadingly named **Frankfurt Hahn** airport (www.flyhahn.com); buses connect with flights (journey 2 hrs, €12; to Cologne, 2 hr 15 mins, €15; and Heidelberg, 2 hr 20 mins, €18).

[i] **Tourist Office**: Frankfurter Hauptbahnhof (Hbf) station, ☎(069) 2123 8800 (www.frankfurt-tourismus.de). Hotel booking service: ☎(069) 2123 0808. Also a branch in the city centre at Römerberg 27.

🛏 No-frills pensions cluster around the rail station. Inexpensive accommodation includes one of Europe's biggest **youth hostels**, **Haus der Jugend (HI)**, by the river at Deutschherrnufer 12, ☎(069) 610 0150 (www.jugendherberge-frankfurt.de). Mid-range accommodation can be in short supply during the trade fairs. The **Frankfurt Hostel** is close to the Hbf at Kaiserstr. 74, ☎(069) 2475 130 (www.frankfurt-hostel.com), dorms from €18; **Pension Backer**, Mendelssohnstr. 92, ☎(069) 747 992 (U-Bahn: Westend-Süd), singles €25–30, doubles €40–50; **Campsite: City Camp Frankfurt**, An der Sandelmühle 35, in Heddernheim, ☎(069) 570 332 (www.city-camp-frankfurt.de), lines 1–3.

🍴 A range of cuisines are represented, and there's a plentiful choice of *Lokale* (taverns) serving local and regional treats like *Eisbein* (stewed pork knuckle), *Handkäse mit Musik* (sour cheese garnished with onions and caraway seeds) and *Sauerkraut*. Above all, of course, there's the original *frankfurter* – long, thin and tastiest eaten at a *Schnell Imbiss* (street stall) in a fresh roll. You'll find a good selection of restaurants along Fressgasse and the narrow streets running north. For the more informal *Lokale*, head south of the river to the **Sachsenhausen** district around Schweizerstr., or the cobbled Grosse Rittergasse and Kleine Rittergasse. Try the heady Äppelwoi cider and enjoy the local *Hochheimer* wine, from grapes grown in municipal vineyards.

GETTING AROUND FRANKFURT

Travel within Frankfurt is easy, with an efficient combination of S-Bahn (overground) and U-Bahn (underground) trains, trams and buses all run by **RMV**, the regional transport authority. Directions to the system, in six languages, including English, are on the blue automatic ticket machines at all bus stops, tram stops and stations. **Transport information**: ☎0180 235 1451. Buy **tickets** (valid for all RMV transportation) at newspaper booths and blue automat machines. If you are making more than two trips a day, it's worth buying a day pass. The **Frankfurt Card**, available from Tourist Offices for 24 hours (€8.70) or 48 hours (€12.50), gives unlimited travel on all public transport, including local and S-Bahn trains to the airport, as well as half-price admission to 20 museums, the botanic gardens and the zoo, 20% discount on river cruises, plus other benefits. To book a taxi, ☎230001, 250001, 230033 or 545011. A short city-centre ride costs about six times as much as a single RMV ticket. Bikes can be hired at the rail station.

WHERE NEXT FROM FRANKFURT?

*Frankfurt is a major international rail junction and has services to **Amsterdam** (ETT table 28), **Vienna** (table 28), **Paris** (table 30), **Prague** (table 30), **Berlin** (table 900 for onward connections to Poland) and **Strasbourg** (table 47 for onward night trains to the French Riviera and southwest France).*

WÜRZBURG

See p324.

NUREMBURG (NÜRNBERG)

The poet Longfellow has mixed feelings about Nuremberg, calling it 'a quaint old town of toil and traffic'. Nowadays the city of Lebkuchen (a speciality Advent gingerbread) and Bratwurst is most remembered for its Nazi associations. Hitler chose Nuremberg, one of the greatest historical cities in all Europe, to hold his mass rallies. Nuremburg has been trying to shake off the association ever since. Heading north from the station, you immediately enter the Old Town, which is surrounded by a 5-km **Stadtbefestigung** (city wall). Beyond the photogenic **Schöner Brunnen** (Beautiful Fountain), the spacious **Hauptmarkt** (market square) makes a perfect setting for one of Germany's liveliest Christmas markets. For a good view of the whole city, seek out the terraces of the **Kaiserburg** fortifications above the northwest corner of the Old Town. Below it nestles Nurembury's prettiest corner, including the gabled **Albrecht Dürerhaus**. Here the artist Dürer lived from 1509 until his death in 1528; it's furnished in period style and contains several of his woodcuts (closed Mon, except Dec). The **Germanisches Nationalmuseum**, Kartäusergasse 1 (www.gnm.de), founded in 1852, houses the country's largest collection of German art and culture (closed Mon, free entry Wed 1800–2100). Hitler's mass rallies were held in the vast **Reichsparteitagsgelände** (in the Luitpoldhain, in the southeastern suburbs), a huge area with a parade ground, stadium and the shell of a massive congress hall that was never completed. One of the remaining parts, the Zeppelin grandstand, Zeppelinstr. (S-Bahn: S2 to Frankenstadion), contains an exhibition called *Faszination und Gewalt* (Fascination and Violence). After World War II, the surviving Nazi leaders were put on trial in the city's court, Fürtherstr. 110, on the western outskirts (U-Bahn: U1 to Bärenschanze). The Tourist Office has a brochure on Nazi Nuremberg, and publishes a monthly listings guide, *Veranstaltungskalender* (€1).

🚉 **Nürnberg Hbf**, on the southern edge of the Old Town centre, a 5-min walk to Hauptmarkt via the underpass.

ℹ️ **Tourist Office**: Konigstr. 93 (opposite the railway station), ☎(0911) 23360 (www.tourismus.nuernberg.de). Also a branch at Hauptmarkt 18, ☎(0911) 233 6135. Hotel booking service.

🛏️ **Lette'mSleep**, Frauentormauer 42, ☎(0911) 992 8128 (www.backpackers.de); U-Bahn: Opernhaus, dorm from €16, doubles from €49; **Jugend-Hotel Nürnberg**, north of city centre, Rathsbergstrasse 300, ☎(0911) 521 6092 (www.nuernberg.jugendherberge.de), wheelchair accessible;

WHERE NEXT FROM NUREMBERG?

Join the **Munich–Berlin** route (p321) by taking the scenic line north via **Jena**; hourly fast trains from **Nuremberg** to **Berlin** via **Leipzig** (ETT table 851) and twice daily direct service to Prague (ETT table 57) and a new direct express bus service (six per day).

Germany

BAMBERG

From Nuremberg you can join the Munich–Berlin route (p321) by taking the scenic line north via Jena; see Where Next from Nuremberg?, p305. This route passes through **Bamberg**, arguably the most beautiful of all medieval Bavarian cities, itself a feasible day trip from Nuremberg, being only 45 mins away. The old centre, steeply placed above the River Regnitz, is crowned by a four-towered Romanesque-Gothic cathedral, known as the Kaiserdom and filled with wonderful sculpture – notably the Bamberger Reiter (Bamberg Knight) and the 16th-century tomb of Henry II and his queen by Tilman Riemenschneider. Houses sport all manner of façades, and the particularly striking Rathaus displays a strange blend of half-timbering and refined rococo. **Tourist Office**: Geyersworthstr. 3, ☎(0951) 2976 200 (www.bamberg.info); there's an **HI youth hostel** at Oberer Leinritt 70, ☎(0951) 56002 (jh-bamberg@stadt.bamberg.de).

Youth hostel (HI): Burg 2, ☎(0911) 230 9360 (jugendherberge-wolfsschlucht@dwbf.de); U-Bahn to Lorenzkirche (700 m) or tram 9 to Krelingstrasse and walk 500 m), wonderfully sited in the castle and for many travellers worth a visit in itself (age limit 26). **Campsite**: **Am Dutzendteich**, Hans Kalbstr. 56, ☎(0911) 981 2717 (www.knauscamp.de) (U-Bahn U6 and S-Bahn S6 to Frankenstadion).

⊤⊙ The Tiergartenpl. is a good place to go in the evenings, with music, night life and drinking. Don't forget to taste some *Lebkuchen* (spiced gingerbread), a local speciality that, though widely exported, still tastes best here. *Bratwurst* and cod typically appear on the menu in the city's restaurants.

REGENSBURG

Sitting at the confluence of the Regen and the Danube, Regensburg has leapt to prominence since its Old Town (Altstadt) was awarded UNESCO World Heritage status in 2006. With the knobbly twin towers of the grey stone **cathedral** dominant on the skyline, and a cheerful huddle of stone houses and red roofs, Regensburg boasts 1300 listed buildings of historical importance. It has preserved its medieval character particularly well. Pretty pastel plasterwork, in pinks, yellows and greens, and decorative towers on many of the former patrician houses in the narrow streets lend it a southern feel. Originally the city was divided into three areas where, respectively, the princes, churchmen and merchants lived. The town had strong trading links with Venice in the 13th century, when its merchants grew rich from the selling of silk, spices and slaves. They competed to have the biggest house (often incorporating its own chapel) in the style of an Italian fortified palace with the highest tower on top – these were never defensive, just status symbols. The most striking of the 20 surviving towers is the **Baumburger Turm**, Watmarkt, though the highest is the 9-storey **Goldener Turm**, Wahlenstr. Some of the chapels have been turned into restaurants but the tiny **Maria-Läng Kapelle**, Pfarrgasse, is still in use. **Domstadt**, the church area, centres on **Dom St Peter**, the magnificent Gothic

DAY TRIPS FROM REGENSBURG

In summer there are a variety of cruises on the Danube, departing from Steinerne Brücke. Destinations include **Walhalla**, where a 19th-century Grecian temple modelled on the Parthenon and filled with busts of German heroes gives a splendid view to reward the steep climb. The **Bayerischer Wald (Bavarian Forest)** is a traditional rural region encompassing wooded peaks, rivers and tiny villages with churches and ruined castles; there aren't a lot of highlights – the emphasis is on the simple life. An hourly bus service goes round the Bavarian Forest National Park and there are many marked trails (www.nationalpark-bayerischer-wald.de).

cathedral; started in the 13th century, its 105-m spires were completed six centuries later. It has fine stained glass, medieval and modern, and its own interior well. Look out for quirky details such as the tiny stone carvings of the devil and his grandmother just inside the main entrance – a warning to those stepping outside – and a laughing angel near the transept. The exterior of **Alte Kapelle**, Alte Kommarkt, belies the wealth of rococo decorations within, including a marble altar and superb frescos. The **Porta Praetoria** archway, Unter den Schwibbögen, is part of 2nd-century Roman defences. The southwestern part of town was formerly the monastic quarter and many of the old buildings survive. At the far end, the former Benedictine monastery of **St Emmeram** was once a great centre of learning. The 12th-century 14-arch **Steinerne Brücke** over the Danube gives the best view of the medieval spires, towers and battlements along the waterfront. **Schloss Thurn und Taxis**, Emmeramspl., consists of Benedictine buildings that were turned into luxurious residences in Napoleonic times. Hourly cruises around the city are available from Easter to the end of October with Regensburger Personenschifffahrt Klinger (www.schifffahrtklinger.de) (€7.50; €4.80 with student card).

🚉 **Regensburg Hbf**, a 10-min walk from the historic centre, or take 🚌 1/2/6.

ℹ️ **Tourist Office**: Altes Rathaus, Rathausplatz 4, ☎(0941) 507 4410 (www.regensburg.de). Accommodation booking service. Located in a 14th-century building.

🛏️ **Brook Lane Hostel**, centrally located, Obere Bachgasse 21, ☎(0941) 690 0966 (www.hostel-regensburg.de; dorms from €15, doubles €45); **Hotel Zum Fröhlichen Türken**, Fröhliche-Türken-str. 11, ☎(0941) 53651, fax (0941) 562 256 (www.hotel-zum-froehlichen-tuerken.de), €; and **Am Peterstor**, Fröhliche Türken-str. 12, ☎(0941) 54545 (www.hotel-am-peterstor.de), €–€€. **Youth hostel (HI)**: Wöhrdstr. 60, ☎(0941) 57402 (jhregensburg@djh-bayern.de), on an island in the Danube, 5-min walk from the centre (🚌 3/8/9 to Wöhrdstrasse). **Campsite: Azur-Camping**, Weinweg 40, ☎(0941) 270 025 (www.azur-camping.de/regensburg).

🍴 Regensburg hosts two annual beer festivals, one in May (Maidult) and one in late August (Herbstdult). With a high student population, there's a good choice of eateries in the city centre. The 850-year-old **Historische Wurstküche**, Weisse Lamm Gasse 3, by the Danube, is Germany's oldest sausage house and sells nothing else; note the flood-marks on the walls. **Alte Linde Biergarten**, Müllerstr. 1, on an island, is a lovely beer garden overlooking the Old Town.

Germany

PASSAU

'Living on three rivers' at the point where the Danube, Inn and Ilz come together, this captivating cathedral city on the Austrian border has plenty of scope for waterside walks and cruises on the Danube. With the exception of the **Veste Oberhaus**, a castle high on a hill across the Danube, everything of interest is within close range. The oldest part lies between the Danube and Inn; most of it postdates a major 17th-century fire and is an enjoyable jumble of colour-washed stone walls, assorted towers, and baroque, rococo and neoclassical styles. Like Regensburg, it's rather Italian in feel. The lofty **Stephansdom** (St Stephen's Cathedral) is home to the world's largest church organ (over 17,000 pipes); try to catch a concert (weekdays 1200–1230, Thur at 1930, no concerts on holidays, May–Oct). **Veste Oberhaus**, the former palace of the bishops, is on a peninsula between the Danube and the narrower River Ilz. It's a steep walk, but regular bus services run from the rail station and Rathauspl. The stronghold, which offers a view over the confluence of the rivers, now contains the museum of the history and art of Passau and its surroundings (54 rooms of artefacts spanning two millennia) as well as changing exhibitions (open early Apr–early Nov). Another, more accessible viewpoint is the **Fünfersteg** footbridge, looking over the Inn towards the **Innstadt** on the opposite bank. River ferries leave from the quayside, along Fritz-Schäffer-Promenade, in front of the Rathaus, and offer day and longer trips up and down the Danube.

[RAIL] **Passau Hbf**, west of the centre, a 10-min walk to the right along Bahnhofstr., or take [BUS] 7/8/9.

[i] **Tourist Offices**: Main office: Rathauspl. 3, [📞](0851) 955 980 (www.passau.de). Also a branch at Bahnhofstr. 28, opposite the rail station. Room reservation service.

[🛏] **Hotel Wienerwald**, adjacent to the restaurant in the Old Town, Klingergasse 17, [📞](0851) 33069 (www.hotel-wienerwald.de). The **Pension Rössner**, Bräugasse 19, [📞](0851) 931 350 (www.pension-roessner.de), €, is much more interestingly sited, near the confluence with a pleasant terrace facing the castle across the Danube. There are also cheaper **guesthouses** and **private rooms** available (see Tourist Office brochure). **Youth hostel (HI)**: Veste Oberhaus, Oberhaus 125, [📞](0851) 493 780, (jhpassau@djh-bayern.de), is in the castle across the Danube. Cross the bridge by the docks and be prepared for a steep climb, or take [BUS] 1/2/3/4 to the door. **Campsite**: **Campground Ilzstadt**, Halserstr. 34, [📞](0851) 41457, by the River Ilz ([BUS] 1/2/3/4).

[TO] Reasonably-priced restaurants spill out onto the promenades beside the Danube in summer, particularly around Rathauspl.

WHERE NEXT FROM PASSAU?

Continue into Austria from Passau to Linz (every 1–2 hours, taking 1 hr 15 mins; ETT table 950), joining the **Innsbruck–Vienna** *route on p377.*

ROUTE DETAIL

Munich–Augsburg ETT table 930

Type	Frequency	Typical journey time
Train	3–4 per hr	38 mins

Augsburg–Ulm ETT table 930

Type	Frequency	Typical journey time
Train	2–3 per hr	45 mins

Ulm–Stuttgart ETT table 930

Type	Frequency	Typical journey time
Train	3–4 per hr	55 mins

Stuttgart–Heidelberg ETT tables 924, 930

Type	Frequency	Typical journey time
Train	1 per hr	1 hr 55 mins
		(via Heilbronn)
Train	1–2 per hr	40 mins, direct

Heidelberg–Karlsruhe ETT tables 911/911a

Type	Frequency	Typical journey time
Train	1–2 per hr	30 mins

Karlsruhe–Baden-Baden ETT tables 912, 916

Type	Frequency	Typical journey time
Train	1–2 per hr	19 mins

Baden-Baden–Offenburg ETT tables 912, 916

Type	Frequency	Typical journey time
Train	Every hr	26 mins

Offenburg–Freiburg ETT table 912

Type	Frequency	Typical journey time
Train	2 per hr	30 mins

Offenburg–Triberg ETT table 916

Type	Frequency	Typical journey time
Train	Every hr	40 mins

Triberg–Konstanz ETT table 916

Type	Frequency	Typical journey time
Train	Every hr	1 hr 32 mins

KEY JOURNEYS

Konstanz–Heidelberg ETT tables 916/930/940

Type	Frequency	Typical journey time
Train	Every 2 hrs	3 hrs 40 mins
		(via Singen/Stuttgart)

Heidelberg–Munich ETT table 930

Type	Frequency	Typical journey time
Train	Every 1–2 hrs	3 hrs 4 mins

Germany

This tour takes in some of southern Germany's most spectacular rail routes. It is a tour for all seasons, and, if you have an affection for snow, would be as good in winter as in mid-summer. The highpoint is that stretch of railway that cuts through the **Schwarzwald** (Black Forest) leaving the Rhine Valley at Offenburg and running, via a tortuous series of hairpins and tunnels, over the hills to the **Bodensee** (Lake Constance) at the border with Austria and Switzerland. The prelude is no less distinguished, heading out from Munich to the beautifully sited old university town of **Heidelberg** via **Augsburg** (a starting point for visiting the amazing **Ludwig II castles** near Füssen) and **Ulm** – with its stupendously tall cathedral spire. **Stuttgart** has one of the world's greatest modern buildings in the Neue Staatsgalerie. You can shorten the route by going directly from Stuttgart to Konstanz, taking in the improbably perfect-looking hill town of **Rottweil**.

MUNICH (MÜNCHEN)

See p282.

AUGSBURG

Just a stone's throw from Munich, Augsburg nowadays is often overlooked. But there was a time when the city was respected as one of the largest and most influential centres in all Europe. Be it as a hub for finance and trade, in its social programmes to alleviate poverty or as a centre of Jewish life and culture, Augsburg towered above its rivals. The key to this was two families, the Welsers and the Fuggers who, in the early 16th century, dominated Augsburg life. Many pioneers in German industry and culture have Augsburg connections, among them Rudolf Diesel (he of the diesel engine!) and the playwright and poet Bertolt Brecht. The main sights are within walking distance of the central pedestrianised Rathauspl, with its distinctive onion-domed **Rathaus** (painstakingly rebuilt after World War II). There's a great view from the adjoining **Perlachturm** (70 m, open May–Oct), the tower of the **Peterskirche**, beside it. A short stroll east down narrow alleys and over three small canals leads to the **Fuggerei**, a pioneering 'village' that the Fugger brothers built in 1516 as accommodation for the poor, who were requested to pray for the Fuggers in lieu of paying rent. Augsburg's merchants lived in style in the stately mansions that still set the tone of Maximilianstr., where the **Schaezler Palace**, an 18th-century rococo edifice with a sumptuous banquet hall, now houses the state art gallery. There is a predictably imposing cathedral on the hilly north side of the city centre, and, just a stone's throw from the Hauptbahnhof (on Halderstr. 8), one of Germany's most remarkable synagogues.

▛ **Augsburg Hbf**, a wonderful building just a 10-min walk west of the city centre.

_i_ **Tourist Office**: Rathausplatz 1, ☎(0821) 502 0724 (www.augsburg-tourismus.de). Reservations for accommodation.

▤ An inexpensive option is **Pension Märkl**, Schillstr. 20, ☎(0821) 791 499 (www.pension-maerkl.de; bus 22 from Hbf to Fraunhoferstr.), singles from €23 incl. breakfast; a bit pricier is **Pension Herrenhäuser**, Georgenstr 6, ☎(0821) 346 3173 (www.pensionherrenhaeuser.online.de), €. **Youth hostel (HI)**: Unterer Graben 6, ☎(0821) 780 8890 (www.augsberg-judendherberge.de), tram 2 or ▤ 22 (both from rail station) to Stadtwerke. **Campsite: Campingplatz Augusta**, Mühlhauser Str. 54, ☎(0821) 707 575, 7 km from city centre (▤ 301/302/305 to Autobahnsee).

▯O There's no shortage of places to eat in the Old Town centre, mostly offering hearty local Swabian or Bavarian dishes. Plenty of jolly beer cellars too.

SIDE TRIPS TO THE ROYAL CASTLES Bavaria's most famous attractions are the Royal Castles – Neuschwanstein, Hohenschwangau and Linderhof – built at preposterous expense by King Ludwig II in the 19th century.

The easiest way of getting to Neuschwanstein and Hohenschwangau is to take the train to **Füssen**, an attractive old town beneath the mountains, served by trains from Augsburg (2 hrs, ETT table 935). There's an HI youth hostel in Mariahilferstr. 5, ☎(08362) 7754 (jhfuessen@djh-bayern.de). From Füssen, numerous buses make the short journey to the castles. For Linderhof, there are regular buses from **Oberammergau** (ETT tables 895, 897; reached from Munich via Murnau; hourly, 1 hr 45 mins), a touristy but attractive small Alpine town celebrated for its Passion Play and numerous painted houses; the play is performed only every ten years, but in the meantime you can visit the theatre and see the props and costumes. Alternatively you can go by **Europabus** (▤ 190), which follows the celebrated Romantic Road from Frankfurt to Füssen via Würzburg, Rothenburg, Dinkelsbühl, Nördlingen, Augsburg and several other historic towns (20% discount for holders of Eurail and German Rail passes; reservation strongly recommended, ☎(069) 790 3230 or (09851) 551 387 (www.romanticroadcoach.de); one bus daily, Apr–Oct, ETT table 927; you can join at a number of points).

Just over the road from Schwangau (and 4 km from Füssen), Hohenschwangau and Neuschwanstein are within walking distance of each other (involving a modest climb). Tudor-style **Hohenschwangau** (www.hohenschwangau.de), built in the early 19th century by Maximilian II, was an attempt to recreate the romantic past and was adorned with Wagnerian references by his son, King Ludwig II. Ludwig surpassed his father by building the fairy-tale neo-Gothic **Neuschwanstein** (www.neuschwanstein.de) on a rocky outcrop high above; it is best seen from the dizzying heights of the **Marienbrücke**, a bridge spanning a huge gorge. This most famous of his castles was never finished – hence the Throne Room without a throne, and doorways leading to suicidal drops.

The third castle, **Linderhof**, 20 km east, is a small French-style château, modelled on the

Germany

Petit Trianon at Versailles. The outstanding oddity is the king's dining table, engineered to be lowered to the kitchens and then raised again for him to dine entirely alone.

A fourth Ludwig castle is **Herrenchiemsee** on a wooded island on the Chiemsee southeast of Munich. Built in the style of Versailles near Paris, this building has a hall of mirrors but remains unfinished (train from Munich to Prien am Chiemsee, hourly, 1 hr, then ferry). He lived here for only a week, before being found mysteriously drowned.

ULM

This instantly appealing old town on the Danube has a quaint quarter known as **Fischer-und-Gerberviertel**, the old fishing and tanning district, with half-timbered houses and bars and cafés beside the Blau, a rushing tributary. Most places of interest are on the north bank of the Danube and the main attractions are easily walkable.

You can hardly fail to notice the soaring spire of the **Münster** (cathedral), all 161 m of it, the tallest such structure in the world. Dominating a huge traffic-free square, the cathedral represents Gothic architecture at its mightiest. Climb the 768 steps up the tower to survey the terrain, on a clear day, from the Black Forest to the Alps.

> Ulm was the birthplace of Einstein, marked by a memorial opposite the rail station. It was also the place where Albrecht Ludwig Berblinger, the 'Tailor of Ulm', made one of man's first attempts to fly. In 1811, he took off from the Adlerbastei (town wall), but didn't make it across the Danube.

Many buildings that were hit in a bombing raid of 1944 have been carefully restored, including the 14th-century **Rathaus** (Town Hall), Marktplatz, Neue Str., with its intricate astronomical clock. One notably fine Renaissance building houses the **Ulmer Museum**, Marktpl. 9 (www.museum.ulm.de), notable for its early Ulm paintings and an outstanding 20th-century collection. Towards the Danube, the **Metzgerturm** (Butchers' Tower), formerly a prison, is known as the leaning tower of Ulm (36 m high) as it's about 2 m off the vertical. Paths lead from it to a pleasant riverside walk dotted with sculptures or up onto a stretch of the Old City walls.

INTERNET ACCESS
Albert's Café,
Kornhauspl. 5; or for free at the public library, next to the Rathaus (town hall).

Ulm Hbf, a 5-min walk to the centre through pedestrian zone.

i **Tourist Office**: Stadthaus, Münsterpl. 50, ☎(0731) 161 2830 (www.tourismus.ulm.de). Free hotel booking service.

There are several reasonably priced central hotels, including **Gästehaus Heigeleshof**, Heigeleshof 3, ☎(0731) 602 6468 (www.statt-hotel.de), and the **Pension Jäger**, Söflinger Str. 210, ☎(0731) 389 643, €. **Youth hostel (HI)**: Grimmelfingerweg 45, ☎(0731) 384 455 (www.jugendherberge-ulm.de); 🚌 4 to Schulzentrum.

Rail Tour: Munich – Heidelberg – Konstanz

▣ The old fishermen's quarter near the Danube has a selection of restaurants in picturesque spots. The wood-panelled **Allgäuer Hof**, 'Ulm's First Pancake House', Fischergasse 12, ☎(0731) 67408 (www.erstes-ulmer-pfannkuchenhaus.de), features traditional pancakes on large platters, with a choice of over 40 toppings.

STUTTGART

Surrounded by green hills, the capital of Baden-Württemberg is best known as the home of the Daimler-Benz and Porsche motor factories. The traffic-free centre, radiating from the huge **Schlosspl.**, with its pavement cafés, buskers, fountains and gardens, is an inviting place to stroll. Along one side is the **Neues Schloss** (www. neues-schloss-stuttgart.de), the former palace of the Württemberg kings, now offices. The **Württembergisches Landesmuseum**, Schillerpl (www.landesmusum-stuttgart.de; closed Mon), occupies the Altes Schloss opposite, an imposing Renaissance palace. Its exhibits range from 19th-century crown jewels and Swabian sculptures to an intact Celtic grave and Renaissance clocks. The nearby **Stiftskirche**, extensively rebuilt over the centuries, has remarkable modern windows and Renaissance carvings of 11 of the rulers of Württemberg around the choir. Round the corner, the **Market Hall** groans with delicacies Mon–Fri from 0700-1830, and on Sat 0700–1600. A **flea market** is held on Karlspl. on Sat. The **Schlossgarten** park stretches all along the city centre as far as the River Neckar and then joins the Rosensteinpark, with the **Natural History Museum** (closed Mon) and the **Wilhelma**, a large zoological/botanic garden with about 9000 animals, buildings in Moorish style and a large lily pond.

The British architect James Stirling has firmly put the city on the map with his **Neue Staatsgalerie**, the post-modern wing of the **Staatsgalerie**, Konrad-Adenauer-Str. 30–32 (www.staatsgalerie.de; closed Mon), with its audacious use of materials. It's the setting for one of the world's largest Picasso collections, as well as a comprehensive survey of 20th-century art. The adjoining **Alte Staatsgalerie** (closed Mon) has earlier works, notably the superb *Herrenberg Altar* by Jorg Ratgeb.

Motor enthusiasts can head for the **Mercedes-Benz Museum**, Mercedes-str. 100, Bad Cannstatt (S1 to Gottlieb-Daimler Stadion), where 100 historic models are on show (closed Mon). Racing cars make up the bulk of the exhibits in the smaller **Porsche Museum**, Porscheplatz 1 (S6 to Neuwirts-haus), in the northern suburb of Zuffenhausen (closed Mon).

▣ **Stuttgart Hbf**, 5-min walk from the centre, along Schlosspl.

STUTTCARD AND VVS 3-TAGE TICKET

The **StuttCard** (valid 3 days; €9.70) allows free or reduced admission to nearly all state museums, reductions at other attractions including the zoo, planetarium, mineral baths, theatres and nightclubs, plus savings on city tours.

The **VVS 3-Tage Ticket** (€10.30) allows three consecutive days' travel on Stuttgart's public transport system (rapid-transit railway, city trains and buses). For the inner zone or entire Stuttgart region. Available on proof of hotel reservation only. The **StuttCard Plus** combines these two tickets and costs €20.

Germany

ⓘ **Tourist Office**: Directly on coming out from the rail station underpass, at Königstr. 1a, ☎(0711) 22280 (www.stuttgart-tourist.de). Free accommodation booking service. They also sell tickets, ☎(0711) 222 8233 (Mon–Fri 0830–1800).

🏠 **Alex 30 Hostel**, Alexanderstrasse 30, ☎(0711) 838 8950 (www.alex30-hostel.de); from Hbf U-Bahn 5/6/7/8/15 or S-Bahn 15 to Olgaeck; dorms from €22, internet café. **Jugendgästehaus Stuttgart**, Richard Wagner Str. 2, ☎(0711) 241 132 (www.hostel-stuttgart.de); tram 15 to Bubenbad. **Gästehaus Stuttgart**, Bottroperstr. 55, ☎(0711) 469 662 67 (www.gaestehausstuttgart.de), doubles €25 (from Hbf S1, S2 or S3 to Bad Cannstatt then from Wilhelmspl. 🚌 56 to Bottroperstr.). **Youth hostel (HI)**: Haussmannstr. 27, ☎(0711) 6647 470 (info@jugendherberge-stuttgart.de), a 15-min uphill walk from the rail station (🚌 42 or tram 15 to Eugenspl.). **Campsite**: **Campingplatz Cannstatter Wasen**, Mercedesstr. 40, ☎(0711) 556 696 (www.campingplatz.stuttgart.de) is beside the River Neckar (tram 1/2). Open all year.

SIDE TRIP FROM STUTTGART TO ROTTWEIL

From Stuttgart you can go south to Singen (1 hr 51 mins–2 hrs 22 mins; ETT table 940) and change trains there to Konstanz. This is a very pretty line through the **Neckar Valley**. On the way, **Rottweil** deserves a pause. It's a delightful little market town, squeezed on a spur of the Neckar between the Black Forest and the Schwäbische Alb (Swabian Jura), with tremendous views. Punctuated by the medieval Schwarzes Tor (Black Tower), the pedestrianised Hauptstrasse has a striking array of colourful Renaissance and baroque houses displaying a wealth of carvings and murals, and sprouting projecting oriel windows. The town is also the provenance of the ferocious Rottweiler dog, descended from Roman guard-dog stock and formerly used by local butchers to pull carts (hence the German name of *Metzgerhund* – butcher's dog). **Tourist Office**: Hauptstr. 21–23, ☎(0741) 494 280 (www.rottweil.de).

HEIDELBERG

Heidelberg's romantic setting, beneath wooded hills along the banks of the River Neckar and overlooked by castle ruins, makes it a magnet for tourists and movie-makers. Expect packed streets in the summer high season. The town has a long history and is home to Germany's oldest university, founded in 1386, but there's little that's ancient in the centre, as most of it was rebuilt in the 18th century following wholesale destruction by Louis XIV's troops in 1693.

The city's most famous sight is the part-ruined pink sandstone **castle**, high above the town. From its terraces, you get a beautiful view over the red rooftops and gently flowing river.

Many fine old mansions are scattered around the Old Town (*Altstadt*). The buildings around Marktpl. include the Renaissance **Haus zum Ritter** and the 14th-century **Heiliggeistkirche** (Church of the Holy Spirit). Universitätspl., which has the **Löwenbrunnen** (Lion Fountain) in the centre, is the location of both the 'old' and 'new' universities. Until 1914, students whose high spirits had got out of hand were

DAY TRIPS FROM HEIDELBERG

Summer **cruises** on the River Neckar depart from the quay by Stadthalle. Along the banks, half-timbered villages nestle in woods below old castles on rocky crags. Within a few minutes you reach **Neckargemünd** and then **Neckarsteinach**, which boasts four ruined castles.

Schwetzingen (frequent train service, change at Mannhein) is renowned for the 18th-century **Schwetzinger Palace**. The building itself is not vastly interesting, but its extensive gardens (at their colourful best in May) are an amazing rococo wonderland of statues, follies, mock ruins, tricks of perspective and fountains.

confined in the special students' prison round the corner in Augustinerstr. 2. Incarceration was regarded as an honour and self-portraits are common in the graffiti on the walls.

Across the river, over the Alte Brücke, the steep **Schlagenweg steps** zigzag up through orchards to the **Philosophenweg** (Philosophers' Path). This is a scenic lane across the hillside, so-called because the views inspired philosophical reflection.

🚆 **Heidelberg Hbf**, 10-min walk to the edge of the pedestrian district, or take 🚌 1/2; or 20 mins to the heart of the old Altstadt (or 🚌 33).

ℹ️ **Tourist Office**: Willi-Brandt-Pl. 1, directly in front of the rail station, ☎(06221) 19433 (www.heidelberg-marketing.de). Accommodation booking service. The **Heidelberg Card** is valid for city travel, castle admission and various discounts (for 1, 2 or 4 days, €12.50/17/22, including funicular ride to the Schloss). Guided walking tours of the Altstadt (Old Town) in English, Fri & Sat at 1030 (Apr–Oct) from Universitätspl. There are also themed guided tours, such as *Heidelberg in the Time of Romanticism*, or *Student Life in Heidelberg*: check with the Tourist Office for details.

🚌 A network of buses and trams serve the pedestrianised Altstadt, where a funicular ride saves the 300-step climb up to the Schloss. It's also possible to tour by bike; rentals available from **Eldorado**, Neckarstaden 52, ☎(06221) 654 4460 (www.eldorado-hd.de/bike-rental), particularly pleasant for exploring the banks of the Neckar.

🏨 Heidelberg is a prime tourist destination, so the later you book during the summer, the further from the centre you will find yourself. The **Goldener Hirsch**, Kleingemunder Str. 27, ☎(06221) 800 211, €, is away from the Altstadt, with simple rooms. **Pension Jeske** is located in the Old Town, Mittelbadgasse 2, ☎(06221) 23733 (www.pension-jeske-heidelberg.de); non-smoking, rooms from €25 excl. breakfast. **Youth hostel (HI)**: Tiergartenstr. 5, ☎(06221) 651 190 (www.jugendherberge-heidelberg.de); 🚌 32 from the station). **Campsite: Camping Heidelberg**, Schlierbacher Landstr. 151, ☎/fax (06221) 802 506 (🚌 35 from the station, 20 mins); open Apr–Oct.

Germany

🔲 The **Altstadt** is very touristy and its restaurants lively with a student atmosphere. Many spill out onto the traffic-free streets. This is also where most of the nightlife goes on. You are spoilt for choice along Heiliggeistr. and Untere-str. *Kneipen* (taverns) are an important part of Heidelberg life and in term-time they fill up with students. For details of what's on, look to the listings magazine *Heidelberg aktuell* (www.heidelberg-aktuell.de).

WHERE NEXT FROM HEIDELBERG?

Heidelberg is served by trains to **Frankfurt** *(55 mins, ETT table 911), where you can join the* **Cologne–Passau** *route (p298).*

KARLSRUHE

A major university city, Karlsruhe's most interesting sight is the huge **Schloss**, home of the Margraves and Grand Dukes of Baden until 1918. Built in 1715 by Margrave Karl Wilhelm, it's an enormous neoclassical pile with extensive formal gardens. From the tower, you see clearly how he designed the entire city to radiate out from it like a fan. Karlsruhe's grace derives from that ambitious urban plan.

Inside the Schloss, the wonderfully eclectic **Badisches Landesmuseum** (www.landes museum.de; closed Mon; free entry Fri 1400–1800) covers prehistory to the present day. The Orangerie merits a look for its 19th- and 20th-century European art. You'll need more time for the **Kunsthalle**, Hans-Thoma-Str. 2–6 (www.kunsthalle-karlsruhe.de; closed Mon), a wide-ranging collection from the 15th to 19th centuries and notable above all for its German primitives, among them Grünewald's astonishingly powerful *Crucifixion*; later German works include a fine set of paintings by the Black Forest artist Hans Thoma. **Marktplatz**, the enormous central square near the Schloss, is dominated by a pyramid of red sandstone, under which Karl Wilhelm is buried.

The **ZKM** (Zentrum fur Kunst und Medientechnologie Karlsruhe: Centre for Art and Media Technology), Lorenzstr. 19 (www.zkm.de), is an experience-oriented centre, media museum and interactive art gallery (tram 6 or 🚌 55 from the station). There's enough for a full day's visit (closed Mon–Tues).

Directly across from the rail station and right next to the Tourist Office is the **Stadtpark-Tiergarten**. The park is a very pleasant way to cross town (particularly handy for getting to the Schloss). There is a boating lake and in season, outdoor cafés and a blaze of flowers. For something less sedate, head for the pubs and clubs around Kaiserstr. For nightlife pointers try www.karlsruhe.eins.de.

🚈 **Karlsruhe Hbf**, a 25-min walk south of the centre (tram 3/4).

✈ **Karlsruhe Baden Airport** 📠(07229) 662 000 (www.baden-airpark.de), served by Ryanair flights, is actually nearer to Baden-Baden; regular buses to Karlsruhe and Baden-Baden.

i **Tourist Office**: Bahnhofpl. 6, ☎(0721) 3720 5383 (www.karlsruhe-tourism.de), opposite the rail station. Also at Weinbrennerhaus am Marktplatz. Free room-booking service. There are good bus and tram services. Rhine cruises operate Easter–Nov from the western edge of town.

🛏 **Pension Stadtmitte Garni**, Zähringer Str. 72, ☎(0721) 389 637 (www.pension-stadtmitte.de), €, and **Pension am Zoo**, Ettlinger Str. 33, ☎(0721) 33678 (www.pensionamzoo.de), €, both offer rooms from around €35–77 and €35–95 respectively. **Youth hostel (HI)**: Moltkestr. 24, ☎(0721) 28248 (www.jugendherberge-karlsruhe.de), west of Schlossgarten (tram 2 or 4 to Europaplatz).

BADEN-BADEN

The city is the European spa town par excellence. Almost oppressively elegant and full of visitors dripping with money, Baden-Baden is a throwback to an earlier age. But it has a compelling appeal, and nowhere else in Germany offers the same opportunities for people-watching (or even snaring a rich, aged spouse). The city has snob-appeal and everything is overdone, but it's all the more fabulous for that. You half expect to bump into the Russian tsar or a German countess as you stroll into the Casino. The town's opera house is the largest in Germany.

A long boulevard of plane trees and manicured parkland known as the **Lichtentaler Allee** is the resort's principal promenade. At the renovated Art Nouveau **Trinkhalle** (Pump Room), Kaiserallee 3 (www.in-der-trinkhalle.de), romantic murals depict the town's history as a spa; here you will find the Tourist Office and a bistro. There is a small well inside where you can try the saline waters.

Indulging in a spa treatment is a memorable experience that won't break the bank; at the historic **Friedrichsbad** (www.roemisch-irisches-bad.de) you get a 3-hour session (whirlpools, saunas, steam rooms and hot and cold baths), massages extra. It has a marvellous Romanisches-Irisches Bad (Roman-Irish Bath, which combines bathing in thermal spring water with exposing the body to warm dry air), nudity mandatory. Underneath the building you can see traces of the original Roman baths. The **Caracalla-Therme**, Römerpl. 1 (www.caracalla.de), is a complex with currents, whirlpools and hot and cold grottos; upstairs (nudity mandatory) has saunas, steam rooms and suntan areas. Inside, the huge pool is under a Roman-style dome and outside, both hot and cold pools are embellished by fountains. Take your own towel.

The Casino in the neoclassical **Kurhaus**, Kaiserallee 1, is Germany's oldest and biggest. Redecorated in French style in 1853, it is promoted as one of the world's most beautiful casinos. There are daily tours 0930–1200 (from 1000, Oct–Mar, no dress code). Gambling starts at 1400, strict dress code (jackets and ties available for hire); admission is €3 and the minimum bet is €2. Over 21s only.

🚉 Baden-Baden Station is at **Oos**, 12 km northwest of town; 🚌 201 runs every 10 mins 0500–2000, then every 20 mins until 2300.

Germany

i **Tourist Office**: **Trinkhalle** (Pump Room), Kaiserallee 3 (city centre); ☎(07221) 275 200 (www.baden-baden.de). Ticket service: ☎(07221) 275 233.

🛏 As the baths and casino attract many wealthy visitors, most hotels are glossy and expensive. Two cheaper options are **Hotel Deutscher Kaiser**, Lichtentaler Hauptstr. 35, ☎(07221) 72152, (www.hoteldk.de), €, (🚌 201 to Eckerlestr. from the rail station or town centre), and **Pension Löhr**, Adlerstr. 2, ☎(07221) 26204 (check in at Cafe Löhr, Lichtenstaler Str. 19). There are also **private rooms** available. **Youth hostel (HI)**: Hardbergstr. 34, ☎(07221) 52223 (www.jugendherberge-baden-baden.de), 🚌 201 to Grosse Dollenstr., then a 7-min walk. The closest **campsite** is at **Campingplatz Adam**, 77815 Bühl-Oberbruch, ☎(07223) 23194 (www.campingplatz-adam.de), approximately 12 km from Baden – the site also does bike rentals.

WHERE NEXT FROM BADEN-BADEN?

It is easy to get to ***Switzerland*** *or* ***France*** *from here, with regular trains to* ***Strasbourg*** *(direct trains 37 mins; most services require a train change at Offenburg and take approx 1 hr 10 mins) and trains every 2 hrs to* ***Basel*** *(1 hr 30 mins; ETT table 912), at the end of the* ***Cherbourg–Strasbourg*** *route across France (p90).*

OFFENBURG

Change here for trains to **Basel** (p348) via Freiburg.

FREIBURG

Placed at the western edge of the Black Forest, the city spreads around its Gothic cathedral. With most sights in the Altstadt (Old Town), it's very walkable so long as you don't fall into the numerous *Bächle* (gulleys) that run along the streets. This old drainage system was used as a fire precaution and for watering livestock and even now, particularly after a storm, the old gulleys still fill with water. Freiburg's famously easy-going atmosphere is immediately apparent; the university is very much the life and soul of the city. The university quarter, west of the Münsterplatz, is the area to head for to find student cafés and lively bars.

Topped by a 116-m spire, the red sandstone **Münster** (cathedral) has a Romanesque-Gothic interior illuminated by 13th- to 16th-century stained glass – many sections depicting the guilds who paid for them. From the tower, 331 steps up, you get a vertigo-inducing panorama.

On Münsterpl., the **Historisches Kaufhaus**, an arcaded merchants' hall, is flanked by two handsome baroque palaces, **Erzbischofliches Palais** and **Wentzingerhaus**. The latter was the house of the 18th-century artist Christian Wentzinger and is now a museum of the town's history. A short stroll away, Rathauspl. is notable for the **Neues Rathaus**. A bridge links **Altes** and **Neues Rathaus** (old and new town hall). The nearby red and gold **Haus zum Walfisch** (Franziskanerstr.) is a re-creation of the elegant house (bombed in World War II) where Erasmus lived for two years. The **Augustiner**, Am Augustinerpl. 1–3, the town's best museum, contains religious and folk art from the Upper Rhine area.

🚃 **Freiburg Hbf**, a good 10-min walk west of the centre.

ℹ️ **Tourist Office**: Rathausplatz 2–4, 📞(0761) 3881 880 (www.freiburg.de), two blocks down Eisenbahnstr. Free accommodation booking 📞(0761) 8858 1145 (info@freiburg-tourist.de).

🛏️ There are plenty of cheaper places (€–€€) to stay (and restaurants too) around the **Altstadt**, such as **Hotel Schemmer**, Eschholzstr. 63, 📞(0761) 207 490 (www.hotel-schemmer.de), €. Hostel accommodation is available at **Black Forest Hostel**, Kartäuserstr. 33, 📞(0761) 881 7870 (www.blackforest-hostel.de; take tram 1 to Oberlinden). **Youth hostel (HI)**: Kartäuserstr. 151, 📞(0761) 67656 (www.jugendherberge-freiburg.de), at the extreme east of town (tram 1 to Römerhof). **Campsite**: **Hirzberg**, Kartäuserstr. 99, 📞(0761) 35054 (www.freiburg-camping.de), near the youth hostel.

TRIBERG

Cuckoo-clock shops have arrived here with a vengeance, and there's a fabulous array of south German kitsch in Triberg. At the heart of the **Schwarzwald** (Black Forest) and known for the purity of its air, the touristy spa town has been a centre for cuckoo-clock making since 1824, when Josef Weisser started his business in the **Haus der 1000 Uhren** (House of a Thousand Clocks). The **Schwarzwaldmuseum** (www.schwarzwaldmuseum.com) is full of woodcarvings, some splendid local costumes and inevitably clocks. Apart from timepieces, **Triberg** is an appealing centre for walking; one walk is to the highest waterfall in Germany, which cascades down 163 m in seven stages and is floodlit at night.

🚃 1.5 km northeast of the town.

ℹ️ **Tourist Office**: At the **Kurhaus**, Wallfahrtstr. 4, 📞(07722) 866 490 (www.triberg.de). Accommodation reservation service.

🛏️ **Hotel Central**, Haupstr. 64, 📞(07722) 4360 (www.hotel-central-triberg.eu), €. **Youth hostel (HI)**: Rohrbacherstr. 35, 📞(07722) 4110 (www.jugendherberge-triberg.de).

KONSTANZ

The Swiss border cuts through the southern part of this town on the **Bodensee** (Lake Constance). Leafy gardens extend along the water's edge and there's a pleasant old quarter, **Niederburg**, where alleys wind between half-timbered buildings with decorated façades. The harbour is the departure point for lake cruises and ferries. At the mouth of the marina is the 9-m high Imperia, a controversial statue depicting a

Germany

courtesan holding the king in one hand (representing the state) and in the other, the pope (representing the church), thus questioning who has the real power. In the Marktstätte (Market Place), elaborate frescos on the Renaissance **Rathaus** depict the town's history, and children clamber on the bronze beasts of a decidedly jolly 19th-century fountain. Jan Hus was martyred here in 1415; the **Hus Museum**, Hussenstr. 64 (free, closed Mon) contains an exhibition about the life of this influential Czech reformer.

🚉 Between Bahnhofpl., the eastern boundary of Altstadt, and the **Bodensee** (Lake Constance).

ℹ️ **Tourist Office**: Bahnhofpl. 13, ☎(07531) 133 030 (www.konstanz.de/tourismus); includes accommodation service. Bicycles can be hired from **Kultur-Rädle Radverleih** which has its office at the station, ☎(07531) 27310 (www.kultur-raedle.de) **Pro Velo**, Konzilstr. 3, ☎(07531) 29329.

🏨 The centre of town is more expensive than the outlying villages, although there are some clean and affordable options, one being **Hotel Sonnenhof**, Otto-Raggenbass Str. 3, ☎(07531) 22257 (www.hotel-sonnenhof-konstanz.de), €. A cheaper alternative, situated close to Hbf, is **Pension Graf**, Wiesenstr. 2, ☎(07531) 128 6890 (pension.graf@t-online.de). In **Dingelsdorf**, 30 mins away on 🚌 4, is the **Gasthaus Seeschau**, Zur Schiffslände 11, ☎(07533) 5190 (www.gasthaus-seeschau.de), €, and **Gasthaus Pension Rose**, Wallhauserstr. 12, ☎(07533) 97000 (www.pension-rose.de), €; the last two have the cheapest rooms. **Private rooms** are available from about €32. **Youth hostel (HI)**: **Otto-Moericke-Turm**, Zur Allmannshöhe 16, ☎(07531) 32260 (www. jugendherberge-konstanz.de), 🚌 4 to Allmansdorf-Jugendherberge. **Campsite**: **Campingplatz Klausenhorn** Hornwiesenstr. 40–42, Dingelsdorf, ☎(07533) 6372 (www.konstanz.de/tourismus/ klausenhorn), open Apr–early Oct or **Campingplatz Litzelstetten-Mainau**, Grossherzog-Friedrichstr. 43, ☎(07531) 943 030, which is near the shore opposite Mainau island, open Easter–Sept.

AROUND THE BODENSEE (LAKE CONSTANCE)

The quay on the Bodensee (Lake Constance), behind the rail station, offers a wide choice of boat trips and cruises on the lake and the Rhine (into which it flows nearby). Most services are seasonal. The main operator is **Bodensee-Schiffsbetriebe**, Hafenstr. 6; ☎(07531) 364 0389 (www.bsb-online.com). **Lindau** (3 hrs 30 mins by ferry) has rail services to Ulm and Augsburg (ETT table 935). Other ferry destinations include **Meersburg**, an atmospheric hillside town with a picturesque *Markt* and old inhabited castle; **Unteruhldingen**, which has an open-air museum (with re-creations of neolithic dwellings) and a basilica that's fully worth the 20-min uphill walk; **Überlingen**, a strikingly attractive town with a Gothic **Münster** and a fine Moat Walk; and the island of **Reichenau**, which has three 9th-century monasteries, each surrounded by a village. Linked by a footbridge to the mainland, and reached by boat services from Konstanz, **Mainau** is a delightful 110-acre island, where a lushly colourful garden surrounds an inhabited baroque palace that was used by the Teutonic Knights for more than five centuries.

KEY JOURNEYS

Munich–Dresden

ETT tables 842, 851

Type	Frequency	Typical journey time
Train	Every hr	5 hrs 45 mins (change at Leipzig)

Munich–Weimar

ETT tables 850, 900

Type	Frequency	Typical journey time
Train	Every hr	4 hrs 30 mins (change at Fulda)

Weimar–Berlin

ETT table 850

Type	Frequency	Typical journey time
Train	Every 2 hrs	2 hrs 16 mins

Munich–Berlin

ETT table 851

Type	Frequency	Typical journey time
Train	Every hr	5 hrs 40 mins

ROUTE DETAIL

Munich–Eichstätt

ETT table 905

Type	Frequency	Typical journey time
Train	Every hr	1 hr 25 mins

Eichstätt–Steinach bei Rothenburg

ETT tables 905/905a

Type	Frequency	Typical journey time
Train	Every hr	1 hr 35 mins (change at Treuchtlingen)

Steinach bei Rothenburg–Würzburg

ETT table 905a

Type	Frequency	Typical journey time
Train	Every hr	45 mins

Würzburg–Fulda

ETT table 900

Type	Frequency	Typical journey time
Train	Every hr	30 mins

Fulda–Eisenach

ETT table 850

Type	Frequency	Typical journey time
Train	Every hr	50 mins

Eisenach–Gotha

ETT tables 849, 850

Type	Frequency	Typical journey time
Train	2 per hr	14 mins

Gotha–Erfurt

ETT tables 849, 850

Type	Frequency	Typical journey time
Train	2–3 per hr	19 mins

Erfurt–Weimar

ETT tables 849, 850, 858

Type	Frequency	Typical journey time
Train	3 per hr	15 mins

Weimar–Leipzig

ETT table 850

Type	Frequency	Typical journey time
Train	Every hr	52 mins

Leipzig–Dresden

ETT table 842

Type	Frequency	Typical journey time
Train	1–2 per hr	1 hr 15 mins

Dresden–Berlin

ETT table 840

Type	Frequency	Typical journey time
Train	Every 2 hrs	2 hrs 18 mins

Germany

This route does more than just link two important German cities: **Munich** and **Berlin**. It explores Germany's cultural heartland, taking in superb towns in northern Bavaria, and historical cities like **Weimar** and **Dresden**. If you are pushed for time, just choose one Bavarian stopover then head straight for eastern Germany. Cutting the corner from Würzburg on the direct route to Erfurt (ETT table 870) is one option. It won't save you a lot of time, but will give you a glimpse of the beautiful hill country of southern **Thuringia**. Forget any preconceptions you may have about the former German Democratic Republic. It isn't all run-down industry. Eastern Germany boasts some of Europe's most memorable cities.

EICHSTÄTT

For a great view of the town, make the steep but pretty 15-min climb from the station up a wooded hillside to the **Willibaldsburg**, a splendid white palace built between the 14th and 18th centuries. A recent addition to this is the **Hortus Eystettensis**, a garden based on the plants documented in the definitive 16th-century illustrated horticultural work. The Burg also houses the **Jura-Museum** of natural history, with a notable collection of fossils from the Altmühl Valley. The bustling market square consists of pretty gabled buildings, shops and pavement cafés, while nearby the **Residenzplatz** is a serene complex of pale green and white 18th-century mansions in a semicircle around the imposing **Residenz**, the former bishops' residence, which is now used by the town council as offices and reception rooms. The adjoining light and airy Gothic **Dom** (cathedral) is notable for its stained-glass windows by Hans Holbein and intricately carved 500-year-old Pappenheim altar.

Eichstätt Stadt is served by a shuttle train from **Eichstätt Bahnhof** on the main line, a 9-min journey. The Tourist Office is a 3-min walk over the bridge from the station.

i **Tourist Office**: Dompl. 8, ☎(08421) 600 1400 (www.eichstaett.info). Information on the **Naturpark Altmühltal**, the surrounding area, is at: Notre-Dame 1, ☎(08421) 98760 (www.naturpark-altmuehltal.de).

Spaces in guesthouses are easy to find. **Gasthof Goldener Adler**, Wesenstr. 76, ☎(08421) 4488 (www.gasthaus.heil@t-online.de), €; **Gasthof Ratskeller**, Kardinal-Preysing Pl. 8, ☎(08421) 901 258 (www.ratskeller-eichstaett.de), €, is slightly more expensive. **Private rooms** are also available (brochure at the Tourist Office). **Youth hostel (HI)**: Reichenaustr. 15, ☎(08421) 980 410 (jheichstaett@djh-bayern.de), 10 mins from the rail station (closed Dec–Jan).

STEINACH BEI ROTHENBURG

Change here for the 15-min train journey to **Rothenburg ob der Tauber** (ETT table 905a).

ROTHENBURG OB DER TAUBER

This little town may justify the title 'the Jewel of the Romantic Road' – the **Romantische Strasse** (ETT table 927 for Eurobus times; 20% discount for holders of Eurail passes and DB Railcard) being the best known of Germany's themed routes, running from Würzburg to Füssen. But Rothenburg comes with a warning: it is much beloved of American and Japanese tourists and can be impossibly packed with visitors in the high season. The town is situated on a rocky outcrop surrounded by medieval walls, its pastel-coloured steep-gabled houses – some half-timbered – are the stuff of picture-books, especially in summer, when window boxes trail with flowers.

> For Rothenburg nightlife try the **Bermuda Dreieck** ('Bermuda Triangle'), between Ansbach-, Adam- and Horberstrasse, with two discos, a cocktail bar and a couple of *Kneipen* (pubs).

As early as 1902, the local council, showing commendable foresight, imposed a preservation order, so physically not much has changed since the 15th century – if you ignore all the tourist shops, galleries, restaurants and crowds, which can dilute the atmosphere. One of the best walks is around the intact (and roofed) town walls, which are long enough for you to lose most of the hordes of visitors.

On **Marktplatz**, there is usually some entertainment, whether a musical concert or a theatrical performance. The glockenspiel on the 15th-century **Ratstrinkstube** (City Councillors' Tavern), now the Tourist Office, re-enacts on the hour (1100–1500 and 2000–2200) the historic scene in 1631, during the Thirty Years War, when Mayor Nusch rose to the challenge of knocking back a gallon of wine to save the town from destruction. The **Meistertrunk** festivities at Whitsun commemorate his feat. Climb the 200 steps (very steep and narrow at the top) onto the **Rathaus tower**'s roof for a dizzying view (Apr–Oct). Then walk down Schmiedgasse to the **Burggarten**; graced by a remarkable 15th-century backdrop of the town, these shaded gardens were the site of a castle destroyed in an earthquake in 1356. Well might you question why there is so much hype over Rothenburg. It's lovely, but no more so than dozens of other Bavarian communities: Feuchtwangen, Ansbach, Dinkelsbuhl and Eichstätt are examples.

The town centre is a 10-min walk straight ahead, then follow 'Stadtmitte' signs.

i **Tourist Office**: Marktpl. 2, ☎(09861) 404 800 (www.rothenburg.de); includes accommodation service. **Guided tours** in English at 1400 from Marktpl., Apr–Oct; evening tour at 2000 Apr–Dec.

There is plenty of choice, including **private houses**, both inside and outside the Old Town walls. These include **Hedwig Gärtner**, Krebengässchen 2, ☎(09861) 3248, € (non-smokers only). **Youth hostel (HI)**: **Rossmühle und Spitalhof**, Mühlacker 1, ☎(09861) 94160 (www.rothenburg.jugendherberge.de), located in a former horse mill in the Old Town. **Campsite: Tauber-Romantik Stadtteil Detwang**, Detwang 39, ☎(09861) 6191 (www.camping-tauberromantik.de), open Easter–Oct.

Germany

WÜRZBURG

Würzburg is a university town where in autumn the *Winzerfest*, a traditional annual harvest festival, celebrates the (justly famous) Franconian wines. The rebuilt domes, spires and red roofs are seen at their best from the terrace battlements of **Festung Marienberg**, an impressive white fortress on a wooded hill above the River Main. Converted to baroque style in the 17th century, little remains inside, though the **Mainfränkisches Museum** (www.mainfraenkisches-museum.de; closed Mon) displays a large collection of works by Franconian artists, including superb 16th-century woodcarvings by one of the city's most famous sons, Tilman Riemenschneider. The Festung is best reached by 🚌 9, a 10-min ride, otherwise it's a 40-min walk. The marketplace is notable for the **Marienkapelle**, a 14th-century church with more Riemenschneider carvings, and the richly decorated 18th-century **Falkenhaus**, which houses the Tourist Office. The town's main sight is the massive sandstone **Residenz**, Residenz-pl. Built as the new palace of the Prince-Bishops in the 18th century by Balthasar Neumann, it has been given World Heritage Site status. Statues line the roof façade, symbolising the church's wealth and power. The rooms are sumptuously decorated with frescos and sculptures by leading artists of their day, including the Venetian master Tiepolo (guided tours in English, daily at 1100 and 1500). Evening bevvies aplenty in and around Sanderstr., popular with students, and for clubs move on to the old harbour area.

INTERNET CAFÉS

Café Cairo, Burkardestr. 44 (near the youth hostel); **Café Franz**, Franz Ludwigstr. 6.

🚆 **Würzburg Hbf**, at the foot of vineyards on the northern edge of the town centre, a 15-min walk.

ℹ️ Tourist Offices: **Congress. Tourismus. Wirtschaft**, Am Congress Centrum, ☎(0931) 372 335 (www.wuerzburg.de). **Centre: Falkenhaus**, Markt ☎(0931) 372 398 (room reservation service).

🏨 There is no shortage of hotels in all categories. An inexpensive option close to the Hbf is **Babelfish Hostel**, Haugerring 2, ☎(0931) 304 0430 (www.babelfish-hostel.de; free internet access). Also moderately priced is **Pension Siegel**, Reisgrubengasse 7, ☎(0931) 52941 (www.pensionsiegel.com), €. **Youth hostel (HI)**: Fred-Joseph-Platz 2, ☎(0931) 42590 (www.wuerzburg.jugendherberge.de), on the bank of the Main, below Festung; tram to Löwenbrücke then 500 m walk. **Campsite: Kanu-Club**, Mergenheimer Str. 13b, ☎(0931) 72536 (cklingenmeier@web.de) (tram 3/5 to Judenbühlweg).

WHERE NEXT FROM WÜRZBURG?

Würzburg is on the *Cologne–Passau* route (p. 298).

FULDA

This Rhön city comes with a baroque theme, although the town goes back 1250 years. A modern fountain plays in the rose garden outside the twin-towered

Italianate 18th-century **Dom** (cathedral), where pilgrims come to see the revered tomb of St Boniface within the crypt; the dagger that killed him and the codex with which he tried to shield himself are exhibited in the crypt museum. It's worth taking a peek at the adjacent **Michaelkirche**, one of the oldest churches in Germany, which is reminiscent of an Arabic bath.

In the **Stadtschloss** (City Palace), the private apartments of the prince-abbots who once lived there are open to visitors and an impressive array of Fulda porcelain is on show.

Fulda is full of history but the modern town has a lively pulse too. For events listings, check out www.who-is-hot.de. Foodies should try the local Rhön region speciality, *Zwibbelploatz*, a tasty sort of onion pizza served with potato soup. It's the Fulda dish of choice on Fridays, when Catholic tradition prescribed a meat-free meal.

🚃 A 7-min walk from the centre.

i **Tourist Office**: Bonifatiuspl. I (in the Palais Buttlar), ☎(0661) 102 1813 (www.tourismus-fulda.de); arranges guided tours lasting I hour, Mon–Sat at 1130 and 1500, or tours lasting 2 hours, Fri/Sat/Sun at 1400.

🛏 Cheaper guesthouses near the station include **Pension Wenzel**, Heinrichstr. 38–40, ☎(0661) 75335 (www.hotel-pension-wenzel.de), €, and **Pension Hodes**, Peterstor 14, ☎(0661) 72862 (www.pension-hodes-fulda.de), €. **Youth hostel (HI)**: Schirrmannstr. 31, ☎(0661) 73389 (fulda@djh-hessen.de).

EISENACH

For a first taste of eastern Germany, Eisenach is a tad dour, but things are on the up with some of the city centre's fine old buildings now having a facelift. The real reason to visit is the splendid Wartburg, a medieval castle, on a hill on its southwest edge (12 mins by 🚌 10 from the rail station, and then 227 steps), the seat of the Landgraves of Thuringia. It dates from 1067 with many later additions, making an attractive complex where half-timbered buildings surround two courtyards. Wagner stayed there and used it as the setting for his opera *Tannhäuser*, and Martin Luther translated the New Testament into German there – in just 10 weeks – while being held in secret for his own protection in 1521–22 after being excommunicated.

The 15th-century **Lutherhaus**, Lutherpl., is where Martin Luther lodged as a boy; the present half-timbered structure encloses the original house. **Bachhaus**, Frauenplan 21, the former Bach family home is furnished in period style with documents and old musical instruments. A large statue of Bach stands just inside the big triple-galleried **St Georgenkirche**, Markt, where he was christened.

🚃 Turn right outside for the town centre, a 5-min walk.

Germany

Eisenach was where East Germany's second most famous car (after the notoriously unrobust Trabant), the **Wartburg**, was manufactured, until 1991 (www.wartburg-eisenach.de). The **Automobilbau-museum** (the Museum of Car Production), Friedrich-Naumann-str 10, ☎(03691) 77212 (closed Mon), commemorates 100 years of its production (together with the occasional BMW).

i **Tourist Office**: Markt 9, ☎(03691) 79230 (www.eisenach-tourist.de).

🖳 There is a reasonable selection of both *Pensionen* and *Gasthöfe* starting from about €25, such as **Gasthof am 'Storchenturm'**, Georgenstr. 43a, ☎(03691) 733 236 (www.gasthof-am-storchenturm.de), €, or **Pension St Peter**, Am Petersberg 7, ☎(0391) 872 830 (www.stpeter-eisenach.de), €. **Youth hostel (HI)**: **Artur Becker**, Mariental 24, ☎(03691) 743 259 (jh-eisenach@djh-thueringen.de; 🚊 3/10 to Liliengrund, 100 m), about 1 km from the city centre. **Campsite**: **Campingpark Eisenach**, Am Altenberger See 1, ☎(03691) 215 637 (www.campingpark-eisenach.de), some 10 km away, but is accessible by bus to Bad Liebenstein, from the bus station next to the rail station. It is on a lake in the Thuringian Forest.

GOTHA

This attractive little town, gateway to the Thüringer Wald (Thuringian Forest), was the home of the Saxe-Coburg-Gotha dynasty, ancestors of the British royal family. It's also known as the 'Residence City'– a label dating from the mid-17th century, when Duke Ernst I chose the duchy of Gotha as his residence.

The main **market square** is surrounded by immaculately restored and colourful Renaissance and half-timbered buildings, among them the 16th-century terracotta Rathaus. The plain white exterior of **Schloss Friedenstein**, on a hill overlooking the town centre, gives no hint of the ornate décor inside. Built by Duke Ernst I in 1634, after the Thirty Years War, it now houses the municipal museum. The **Ekhof-Theater** is Germany's oldest baroque theatre in its original state, and aptly hosts an annual summer baroque music festival.

DAY TRIP FROM GOTHA

Tram 4 (the **Thüringerwaldbahn**) from the rail station goes to **Tabarz** in the Thüringer Wald (Thuringian Forest), a 1-hr ride past **Marienglashöhle**, which has lovely crystalline caves. From Tabarz, a road-train called **Inselsberg Express** (daily 1000–1700, Easter–Oct) goes most of the way up **Grosser Inselsberg** (916 m).

🚋 At the southern end of town (tram 1/2/4 to the centre; alight at Huttenstr., then walk up Erfurterstr.).

i **Tourist Office**: Hauptmarkt 33, ☎(03621) 5078 5712 (www.gotha.de).

🖳 There are a good number of pensions and private rooms at inexpensive to reasonable prices as, for example, the centrally located **Pension Regina**, Schwabhäuser Str. 4,

☎(03621) 408 020 (www.pension-regina.de; pay on arrival – cash only), or the smaller **Pension am Schloss**, Bergallee 3a, ☎(03621) 853 206 (www.pas-gotha.de).

ERFURT

Sited on the River Gera, the Thuringian capital has shot to prominence as a tourist attraction, with its substantial variety of attractive old buildings from mills to monasteries, much spruced up since German reunification. A flight of 70 steps leads up to **Dom St Marien**, the hilltop Gothic cathedral beside the Dompl., a large market place and useful tram stop. An array of decorative buildings surround **Fischmarkt**. Markstr. leads off it to **Krämerbrücke**, a 14th-century river bridge lined with old houses and shops, best seen from the river itself. In the 15th century, Erfurt was noted for its altar pieces and a superb example can be seen in **Reglerkirche**, Bahnhofstr. To find out more on local traditions, visit the **Museum für Thüringer Volkskunde**, Juri-Gagarin-Ring 140a (closed Mon). For evenings, check out the Studentenclub Engelsburg, Allerheiligenstr. 20 (www.eburg.de) or the Museumskeller, Juri-Gagarin-Ring 140a (www.museumskeller.de).

▦ **Erfurt Hbf**, a 10-min walk along Bahnhofstr., or tram 3/4/5, to the centre.

✈ **Flughafen Erfurt** ☎(0361) 6560 (www.flughafen-erfurt.de), 6 km, city rail line No. 4 departs every 10 minutes.

i **Tourist Office**: Benediktspl. 1, ☎(0361) 664 0230 (www.erfurt-tourismus.de). Free accommodation booking service: ☎(0361) 664 0110. **ErfurtCard** (valid 2 days €12.90) provides free transport, a complimentary city tour and entry to city museums.

🛏 **Etap Hotel**, In den Weiden 11, ☎(0361) 423 2899 (www.etaphotel.com), €, offers relative simplicity. Smaller pensions include **Pension Reuss**, Spittelgartenstr. 15, ☎(0361) 731 0344 (www.pension-reuss.de), €. **Youth hostel (HI)**: Klingenstr. 4, ☎(0361) 562 6705 (jh-erfurt@djh-thueringen.de), tram 6 to Steigerstr.

WEIMAR

Smart shops, pavement cafés and a lively **Onion Fair**, which takes over the town for the second weekend in Oct, are outward signs of Weimar's vitality. But, famously, Weimar is steeped in German culture, having been the home of two of the country's greatest writers, Goethe and Schiller, as well as the composers Bach, Liszt and Richard Strauss, the painter Lucas Cranach and the philosopher Nietzsche. It was also where the ill-fated pre-Nazi Weimar Republic was founded. A replica 1925 bus, the **Belvedere Express** (www.belvedere-express.de), takes in the main sights (there are three stops). The entire town centre, with its wide tree-lined avenues, elegant squares and fine buildings, is designated a historical monument. After decades of neglect, extensive renovation for its role as European City of Culture in 1999 –

coinciding with the 250th anniversary of the birth of Goethe – has revived its gracious character. Architecture fans should not miss Weimar's Bauhaus connections. Look out the **Haus am Horn** (Am Horn 61), a Modernist prototype that stands out amid Weimar's baroque mansions.

The baroque mansion where Goethe lived, **Goethehaus**, Frauenplan 1 (closed Mon), displays furniture, personal belongings and a library of 5400 books. A stroll across the little River Ilm in the peaceful **Park an der Ilm** leads to the simple **Gartenhaus**, his first home in town and later his retreat. Goethe himself became a tourist attraction: people travelled from afar to glimpse the great man.

> The **Weimar card** gives three days' worth of free public transport and free or reduced admission to museums, exhibitions and performances at the German National Theatre and city guided tours all for €10.

In the **Marktplatz** a plaque marks the house in the south corner where Bach lived when he was leader of the court orchestra. The **Liszthaus** (closed Tues and Nov–Mar), on the town side of the park, is the beautifully maintained residence of the Austro-Hungarian composer Franz Liszt. He moved to Weimar in 1848 to direct the local orchestra and spend the last 17 summers of his life: his piano and numerous manuscripts are on display. Schiller spent the last three years of his life at **Schillerhaus**, Schillerstr., and his rooms are much as they were then (closed Tues). Statues of Schiller and Goethe stand in the nearby Theaterpl. outside the imposing **Deutsches National Theater**, where many of their plays were first performed. North of Weimar by 10 km is the memorial museum and site of **Buchenwald concentration camp**, a grim reminder of the horrors of the Nazi regime during World War II (closed Mon).

🚉 A 20-min walk north of the centre (🚌 1/7).

ℹ️ **Tourist Office**: At the **station**. Main office: Markt 10, ☎(03643) 7450 (www.weimar.de). Also at Friedensstr. 1. Can arrange hotel and private accommodation. City tours 1000 and 1400.

🏨 An inexpensive, out-of-the-ordinary guesthouse is the student-run **Hababusch Hostel** in the Old Town, Geleitstr. 4, ☎(03643) 850 737 (www.hababusch.de). **Zum Alten Gutshof**, Wohlsborner Str. 2, ☎(03643) 4587 5300 (www.zum-alten-gutshof.de), €, is one of the cheaper guesthouses in town (prices are lower at weekends). There are four **(HI) youth hostels** (www.djhthueringen.de), including **Germania**, Carl-August-Allee 13, ☎(03643) 850 490 (jh-germania@djh-thueringen.de), 2 mins from the station, and **Am Poseckschen Garten**, Humboldtstr. 17, ☎(03643) 850 792 (jh-posgarten@djh-thueringen.de), in the centre.

LEIPZIG

Leipzig has been a cultural centre for many centuries, famous particularly for its music: numerous great 19th-century works were premiered at the **Gewandhaus**. Augustus-pl., beside the broad ring road encircling the **Innenstadt**, makes a good starting point for a stroll around the pedestrianised centre, whose streets of long-neglected buildings and arcades are fast acquiring rows of smart shops, restaurants and offices – yet Leipzig retains some of the grace of an old European city.

In 1989, the mass demonstrations and candlelit vigils in **Nikolaikirche**, Nikolaistr., were the focus for the city's brave peaceful revolt against communism. The **Stasi 'Power and Banality' Museum**, Dittrichring 24, in the former Ministry of State Security, covers the years of communist oppression.

Marktplatz is the centre for many of Leipzig's outdoor activities, including free concerts and impromptu beer fests. The fine Renaissance **Altes Rathaus** has survived and now houses the **Stadtgeschichtliches Museum**, covering the city's history. From Leipzig a trip can be made to **Colditz**, an attractive little town dominated by its castle (youth hostel (HI): Schlossgasse 1, ☎ (034381) 45010; jhcolditz@djh.de) – made notorious as a prisoner-of-war camp in World War II.

Leipzig is second only to Vienna for its musical tradition, being the home of Bach, Mendelssohn and Schumann. The **Gewandhaus Orchestra, Opera House** and **Thomas-aner-chor** (St Thomas's Church Choir), which was conducted by Bach for 27 years, have a worldwide reputation. Performances of all kinds of music take place throughout the year.

🚉 On the edge of the Innenstadt (city centre), a 10-min walk to the middle. Known as the **Hauptbahnhof Promenaden Leipzig** and built in 1915, the station is an attraction in its own right, and is one of Europe's biggest and most impressive, recently refurbished and attired with a glossy shopping mall. Also part of the facelift is the magnificent *Deutsche Bahn* waiting room, complete with bar, stained-glass overhead ceiling and rich wooden interior.

✈ **Leipzig-Halle** ☎ (0341) 2240 (www.leipzig-halle-airport.de): trains every 30 mins (takes 14 mins to main station; ETT table 810).

ℹ️ **Tourist Office**: Richard-Wagner Str. 1, ☎ (0341) 710 4260 (www.ltm-leipzig.de). Just inside the Innenstadt, a 2-min walk from the rail station. Online free accommodation booking service (zimmer@ltm-leipzig.de), or phone ☎ (0341) 710 4255; no extra fee.

🚌 A good tram network from the rail station, but most things of interest are within the pedestrianised Innenstadt, encircled by a ring road. The **Leipzig Card**, including travel and museum discounts, is available for one or three days (€8.90/18.50).

🏨 **Central Globetrotter Hostel**, Kurt-Schumacher-Str. 41, ☎ (0341) 149 8960 (www.globetrotter-leipzig.de); close to station. Ask the Tourist Office for a list of local pensions; these include the **Herberge Zur Alten Bäckerei**, Zur Alten Bäckerei 12, ☎ (0341) 415 300. (www.herberge-zur-alten-baeckerei.de), €. **Youth hostel (HI)**: Volksgartenstr 24, ☎ (0341) 245 700 (www.leipzig.jugendherberge.de), tram 1 towards Schönefeld, alight Löbauerstrasse, then a 300m walk. **Hostel Sleepy Lion**, Käthe-Kollwitz-Str. 3, ☎ (0341) 993 9480 (www.hostel-leipzig.de): (**non HI**) clean, friendly, central, open 24 hrs and highly recommended; singles, doubles and dorms; bike

hire. **Campsite: Auensee Motel**, Gustav-Esche Str. 5, ☎(0341) 465 1600
(www.motelauensee.de).

🆃🅾 Restaurants crowd the pavements around Kleine Fleischergasse, such as **Zill's Tunnel**,
Barfüssgässchen 9, ☎(0341) 960 2078 (www.zillstunnel.de), a typical Saxon beerhouse serving
traditional dishes. Famed because Goethe featured it in *Faust*, having dined there as a student,
is the 16th-century wood-panelled **Auerbachs Keller** restaurant in the exclusive Mädler
shopping arcade off Grimmaische Str. 2–4, ☎(0341) 216 100 (www.auerbachs-keller-leipzig.de).
Lots of cafés crowd around the Marktpl., with music spouting out of most of them. **Spizz**
(www.spizz.org) does jazz nights, as well as an excellent breakfast.

DRESDEN

The capital of Saxony for four centuries, Dresden will long be remembered as one of
the great tragedies of World War II: on 13–14 February 1945, the city was carpet-
bombed by the Allies, and some 35,000 people died. But despite the devastation,
the city has risen from the ashes, and is once again a major cultural destination.
The baroque magnificence of the centre has been restored: the **Brühlsche Terrasse**
('Europe's Terrace'), a raised terrace by the banks of the Elbe, overlooks the
Stadtschloss (the tower of which gives another good view), and the spire of the
early 18th-century Catholic **Hofkirche** (Royal Cathedral). By the cathedral are the
Semper Opera House and the **Zwinger** (keep), a gracious complex of baroque
pavilions, fountains and statuary: it is free to walk around the grounds, though there
is a charge for admission to the Zwinger's world-famous museums (closed Mon).

One of the world's greatest art collections, the **Gemäldegalerie Alte Meister** (Old
Master Picture Gallery; closed Mon), houses, among others, Raphael's *Sistine
Madonna* with its immortal cherubs, and Dürer's *Picture of a Young Man*. The
Porzellansammlung (Picture Porcelain Collection; closed Mon) includes examples
from nearby Meissen. In the 16th-century **Albertinum** (Arsenal), the **Galerie Neue
Meister** (New Masters Gallery; closed Tues) is a superb modern collection, with
works by German Expressionists and French Impressionists. A particularly poignant
reminder of the war destruction is the Lutheran **Frauenkirche**, which the morning
after the bombing miraculously stood, but then abruptly collapsed. However, it has
been entirely rebuilt, and is now a symbol of the city's rebirth (open 1000–1200 and
1300–1800 Mon to Fri, restricted opening on Sat and Sun).

Out of the centre, Dresden is a mixed bag. The **River
Elbe** (which has a riverside cycle path as well as
steamer cruises) gives some gorgeous views of villas
perched on the hillside on the opposite bank, and
within moments of the centre you're virtually into
countryside as you head east. Further on, **Schloss
Pillnitz** was the only baroque building in Dresden to
have escaped bombing; entry is free. Cycle on a couple

> The excellent value 48-hr
> **Dresden-City-Card**, €21,
> allows free public transport,
> admission to ten main
> museums, reduced admission
> to nine other museums, plus
> reductions on city bus and
> walking tours.

of hours past the Königstein fortress into **Sächsige Schweitz** (Swiss Saxony), where huge sandstone outcrops tower above the river; many of them can be climbed by stairs; alternatively you can take the train to Kurort Rathen, cross the river by ferry and walk up the obvious summit. You can take river cruises or an S-Bahn train to the porcelain-making town of **Meissen** (Table 853a for river cruises or Table 857 for S-Bahn), which has a virtually pristine Altstadt (Old Town), and offers tours around the porcelain works. For chilling out, head for the laid-back area northeast of Albertplatz on the north side of the Elbe in the New Town (Neustadt). The university quarter south of the Hauptbahnhof is also worth a try. For listings, pick up *Frizz* and *Dresdner Kulturmagazin* (www.dresdner.nu).

Dresden Hbf: left luggage (Passage 4), exchange facilities, hotel information. Follow signs for Prager Str. – the Old Town is at the end of this street. **Neustadt station** is to the north.

i **Tourist Office**: Kulturpalast, Schlossstrasse 2, ☎(0351) 5016 0160 (www.dresden.de/tourism).

Hostels include **Rudi Arndt (HI)**, Hübnerstr. 11, ☎(0351) 471 0667 (www.jh-rudiarndt.de), and **Jugendgästehaus Dresden**, Maternistrasse 22, ☎(0351) 492 620 (jhdresden@djh.de), 800 m from the station, tram 7/10; and non-HI **Hostel Louise 20**, Louisenstr. 20, ☎(0351) 889 4894 (www.louise20.de), at the Neustadt, (tram 7/8 from the station); **Hostel Mondpalast**, Louisenstr. 77, ☎(0351) 563 4050 (www.mondpalast.de). Cheap, central **hotels** include the **Pension Am Dresdner Zoo**, Wiener Str. 107, ☎(0351) 471 1214 (www.pension-helth.de).

WHERE NEXT FROM DRESDEN?

*Trains to **Prague** (p587) take 2 hrs 15 mins for the 191 km journey; there are six services a day. ETT tables: 60, 1100. Dresden has excellent night train services, with direct trains to Budapest, Bratislava, Cologne, Munich, Vienna and Poprad Tatry (for the Tatra Mountains).*

*A must-see if you're Poland-bound is the border city of **Görlitz** (1 hr 20 mins from Dresden; hourly; ETT table 855; trains to Wroclaw on table 1085). Focus on the west bank to see one of the finest baroque town centres in Germany, with scarcely a window frame out of place in its cobbled streets. The town has many fine Jugendstil villas, one of which is now a **youth hostel (HI)**, at Goethestrasse 17, ☎(03581) 406 510 (www.jh-goerlitz.de), a 10-min walk from the station (but due to move in October 2010). En route to Görlitz from Dresden, the town of Bautzen has a super Altstadt, with a quirky cathedral. Half is Protestant, half Catholic! Bautzen is also a major centre of Upper Sorbian culture and language. Street signs are all bilingual.*

ROUTE DETAIL

Munich–Garmisch Partenkirchen
ETT table 895

Type	Frequency	Typical journey time
Train	Every hr	1 hr 23 mins

Garmisch Partenkirchen–Mittenwald
ETT table 895

Type	Frequency	Typical journey time
Train	Every hr	22 mins

Mittenwald–Innsbruck
ETT table 895

Type	Frequency	Typical journey time
Train	Every 2 hrs	56 mins

Innsbruck–Bolzano
ETT table 595

Type	Frequency	Typical journey time
Train	Every 2 hrs	2 hrs

Bolzano–Verona
ETT table 595

Type	Frequency	Typical journey time
Train	Every 1–2 hrs	1 hr 30 mins

KEY JOURNEYS

Munich–Innsbruck
ETT tables 895/951

Type	Frequency	Typical journey time
Train	7 daily via Garmisch, 8 daily via Kufstein	2 hrs 49 mins via Garmisch, 1 hr 50 mins via Kufstein

Innsbruck–Verona
ETT table 595

Type	Frequency	Typical journey time
Train	4 through trains daily	3 hrs 33 mins

Munich–Verona
ETT table 70

Type	Frequency	Typical journey time
Train	4 daily	5 hrs 30 mins

Munich–Salzburg
ETT table 890

Type	Frequency	Typical journey time
Train	1–2 per hr	1 hr 40 mins

RAIL TOUR: MUNICH – INNSBRUCK – VERONA

Despite its relatively short distance, this journey through **Germany**, **Austria** and **Italy** and across the **Alps** packs in astonishing variety. **Munich** and **Verona**, each worth at least a few days to explore, could hardly be more different, and the Alps change in character almost from one valley to the next.

MUNICH (MÜNCHEN)

See p282.

GARMISCH-PARTENKIRCHEN

Once two quiet Bavarian villages at the foot of the 2962-m **Zugspitze**, Germany's highest mountain, **Garmisch** and **Partenkirchen** were officially united to host the 1936 Winter Olympics. Though now separated only by the railway line, they retain individual personalities. **Partenkirchen** is more modern and upmarket while **Garmisch** has much more of a traditional Bavarian character – the most appealingly rustic part is around Frühlingstr.

Garmisch is Germany's most popular ski resort and has 52 lifts (13 open in summer), with downhill and cross-country skiing on offer. In summer, it's a centre for mountain walking, climbing and biking. The **Olympic Ice Stadium**, Olympiastr., built in 1936, stays open virtually year-round.

The **Zugspitzbahn** cog railway goes from beside the main rail station to a point near the summit of the Zugspitze, a 75-min journey. On the way, it stops at **Eibsee**, an idyllic mountain lake, where you can transfer to the **Eibseebahn** cable car (often appallingly crowded) to reach the summit; alternatively, take the easy 7-km path round the lake itself. Meanwhile, the train continues up through a winding 4.5-km tunnel to **Sonnalpin** (2600 m), from where the **Gletscherbahn** cable car goes the final stage to the summit. The views are impressively far-ranging in decent weather.

Several other summits around are accessible by chairlifts or cable cars from the town, giving plenty of scope for walks. These include **Eckbauer** (1238 m), from where you can follow a path down through the woods to the entrance to the **Partnachklamm**, one of the most dramatic of all Alpine gorges, and descend to the ski stadium.

🚉 Centrally located between Garmisch and Partenkirchen.

i **Tourist Office**: Richard-Strauss Plz. 2, ☎ (08821) 180 700 (www.gapa.de).

🏠 This is a popular ski resort, with plenty of rooms. Least expensive options are private rooms, such as **Huber Hildegard**, Schwalbenstr. 4, ☎ (08821) 3443, €, and **Hans Biehler**, Sonnenbergstr. 4 ☎ (08821) 73892, €. **Youth hostel (HI)**: Jochstr. 10, ☎ (08821) 967 050 (www.garmisch.jugendherberge.de), 4 km from town, in **Burgrain** (🚌 3/4/5). **Campsite**: **Campingplatz Zugspitze**, An der B23, ☎ (08821) 3180, west, near **Grainau** village.

🍽 Partenkirchen has plenty of typically Bavarian bar-restaurants.

MITTENWALD

Close to the Austrian border, **Mittenwald** is perhaps the most attractive town in the German Alps, with an abundance of character in its gabled, whitewashed houses, hung with green shutters and sporting creaky wooden balconies. Elaborate outside murals are another striking feature, but the town's main claim to fame is in its violins. Matthias Klotz (1653–1743), a pupil of the great Amati, began Mittenwald's tradition of high-quality violin-making that continues to this day.

🚉 5 mins east of the town centre.

ℹ️ **Tourist Office**: Dammkarstr. 3, ☎(08823) 33981, fax (08823) 2701 (www.mittenwald.de; touristinfo@marktmittenwald.de).

🏠 **Youth hostel (HI)**: Buckelwiesen 7, ☎(08823) 1701 (www.mittenwald.jugendherberge.de).

INNSBRUCK, AUSTRIA

See p378.

BOLZANO (BOZEN), ITALY

Although in Italy and with street names in Italian, **Bolzano** looks decidedly Austrian, with its pastel-coloured baroque arcades and Austrian menu items; for centuries Bolzano was in the possession of Austria. Set beneath Alpine slopes in a deep valley, it's handy for exploring the **Dolomites**. Piazza Walther is the focus of the town's outdoor life.

🚉 A 5-min walk from the town centre. Buses stop at an area by a small park, reached by crossing the main road outside the station and turning left.

ℹ️ **Tourist Office**: (municipal) Piazza Walther 8, ☎(0471) 307000 (www.bolzano-bozen.it).

🏠 Reasonable range, starting from moderately priced.

VERONA

See p432.

WHERE NEXT FROM BOLZANO?

*Buses from Bolzano climb eastward into the Dolomites for some of the most stunning scenery in the Alps. It's a virtually unbeatable region for walking, with paths to suit all abilities. A good centre to head for is **Ortisei** (St Ulrich in German), reached by direct bus twice daily from Bolzano. Famed for its woodcarving tradition, this pleasantly set small town at the meeting of valleys has plenty of accommodation and walkers are spoilt for choice. A cable car takes you onto the **Seiseralm**, said to be the largest of all Alpine pastures, and abundant in very easy strolls with strategically sited cafés.*

Switzerland

Even by European standards, Switzerland packs a lot into a small space, and, even with its admirable transport system, it can take a surprisingly long time to explore thoroughly, though it's predominantly scenery rather than sights that attracts the appreciable crowds. For once, reality lives up to the common preconception: the **Swiss Alps** have idyllically unspoilt Alpine pastures, grazed by bell-wearing cattle and backed with improbably perfect snow-topped pointy mountains, and the Swiss are still into traditions of the likes of alpenhorn-blowing, yodelling and folk music, as well as regional specialities, festivals (including classical music and jazz) and local pageantry. Costs can deter budget travellers from lingering, though it's not too bad if you use the hostels and mountain huts. Don't expect to find dazzling nightlife: a lot of it is decidedly peaceful after dark, although there's quite a bit happening in **Zürich**. Souvenir shopping can be rewarding, with numerous items special to certain areas, such as hand-woven linen, country crafts, painted pottery and woodcarving.

There are marked regional differences, and four separate languages. Although most of the population lives outside the Alps in cities such as **Geneva** and **Basel**, it is still easy to find pockets of rustic and architecturally varied picture-book charm, with quaint wooden chalets and traditional farmhouses scattered around the landscape (to a much greater extent than you'll find in neighbouring Austria). Some of the best areas to visit include the dramatic valley of the **Engadine** in such resorts as St Moritz, the majestic **Bernese Oberland** around Kandersteg and the side valleys of the **Valais** region (in the southwest).

Some of the most majestic scenery is in the **Bernese Oberland**, around the relaxed, provincial-feeling capital, **Berne**, and on the doorsteps of the pretty towns of **Interlaken** and **Grindelwald**. Less of a scenic jaw-dropper, central Switzerland does have some delicious lake scenery, notably around **Lake Lucerne** and **Lake Geneva** (Lac Léman). **Lugano**, in the south, is unmistakably Italian in feel.

ESSENTIALS

Population 7.7m **Capital** Berne (Bern) **Time Zone** Winter GMT+1, summer GMT+2.

CLIMATE

Rainfall spread throughout the year. May–Sept are best in the mountains. June or early July best for the wild flowers. Snow at high altitudes even in midsummer. Season in the lakes: Apr–Oct. July and Aug get very busy.

CURRENCY

Swiss Francs (S Fr.); £1 = S Fr.1.70; $1 = S Fr.1.03; €1 = S Fr.1.51.

EMBASSIES AND CONSULATES IN BERNE

Aus (Consulate): Chemins des Fins 2, Case Postale 172, 1211 Geneva 19, ☎(022) 799 91 00. **Can**: Kirchenfeldstr. 88, ☎(031) 357 32 00. **SA** (Consulate): Alpenstrasse 29, ☎(031) 350 13 13. **UK**: Thunstr. 50, ☎(031) 359 77 00. **USA**: Sulgeneckstrasse 19, ☎(031) 357 70 11.

LANGUAGE

German, French, Italian and **Romansch** are all official languages. Most Swiss people are at least bilingual. English is widespread.

OPENING HOURS

Banks: Mon–Fri 0800–1200 and 1400–1700. Money change desks in most rail stations, open longer hours. **Shops**: Mon–Fri 0800–1200 and 1330–1830, Sat 0800–1200 and 1330–1600. Many close Mon morning. In stations, shops open longer hours and on Sun. **Museums**: usually close Mon. Hours vary.

POST OFFICES

Usually Mon–Fri 0730–1200 and 1345–1830, Sat 0730–1100; longer in cities. Poste restante (*Postlagernd*) facilities available at most post offices.

PUBLIC HOLIDAYS

1–2 Jan; Good Fri; Easter Mon; Ascension Day; Whit Mon; 1 Aug; 25, 26 Dec. Also 1 May and Corpus Christi in some areas.

PUBLIC TRANSPORT

Swiss buses are famously punctual. Yellow postbuses stop at rail station; free timetables from post offices. Swiss Pass valid (see below), surcharge for some scenic routes. Best way to get around centres is on foot.

RAIL PASSES

IR, EP valid (see pp27–34). Swiss Pass: consecutive days on Swiss Railways, boats and most Alpine postbuses and city buses, plus discounts on mountain railways; 4, 8, 15, 22 days or 1 month (1st class S Fr.390/564/683/788/867; 2nd class S Fr.260/376/455/525/578); youth 16–26 deduct 25%. Swiss Flexi Pass: as above but valid 3, 4, 5 or 6 days within one month (1st class S Fr.374/453/524/596; 2nd class S Fr.249/302/349/397); no youth version. Both the Swiss Pass and the Swiss Flexi Pass offer a 15% discount when booking for two or more adults and provide

Switzerland

free entrance to 400 museums. Swiss Transfer Ticket: one month return from any airport/border station to any Swiss station (1st/2nd class S Fr.192/127); Swiss Card additionally offers half-fares for rest of month (1st/2nd class S Fr.255/182). There are several regional passes.

RAIL TRAVEL

Websites: www.sbb.ch. Principal rail carrier is Swiss Federal Railways; plus many small, private lines. Services are fast and punctual, trains spotlessly clean. Express trains stop only at major cities. *Regionalzüge*, slow local trains, stop more frequently on same routes. Some international trains have sleepers (three berths) and/or couchettes (up to six people). Sleepers can be booked up to three months in advance, couchettes/seats up to two months ahead. Reservations required on some sightseeing trains (e.g. Glacier Express and Bernina-Express). Information: ☎(081) 288 43 40, English-speaking operator. All main stations have information offices (and usually Tourist Offices), shopping and eating facilities. Provincial stations display train schedules. Cycle hire at most stations.

TELEPHONES

Swisscom offices sell phonecards (*taxcard*; also available from post offices, newsagents and most rail stations for S Fr.5/10/20/50). All operators speak English. Dial in: ☎+41; omit initial 0 from area code. Outgoing: ☎00 + country code. National enquiries: ☎111, international operator: ☎1141. Police: ☎117. Fire: ☎118. Ambulance: ☎144 (most areas).

TIPPING

Not necessary or expected in restaurants or taxis.

TOURIST INFORMATION

Website: www.myswitzerland.com. Tourist Offices in almost every town or village. The standard of information is excellent.

TYPICAL COSTS

Accommodation in a hostel: S Fr.18–33, in a pension: S Fr.45–70. Beer in a bar: S Fr.3.60–4.80; coffee: S Fr.2.50–3.50. Basic meal: S Fr.18–27. Internet access/hour: S Fr.1.50–3 (but often free).

VISAS

Valid passport required. Visas required for stays of more than three months. For shorter stays, visas not needed by citizens of the EU, Australia, countries of the American continents (except Belize, Dominican Republic, Haiti and Peru), Japan and New Zealand.

ACCOMMODATION

Swiss hotels have high standards but are expensive, and you'll be very lucky to get anything for less than S Fr.80 for a single or S Fr.125 for a double. In rural areas and Alpine resorts, it is often possible to get rooms in **private houses** (look for *Zimmer frei* signs posted in windows and gardens), but these are few and far between in cities. Budget travellers (unless they are camping) rely heavily on **youth hostels** – so book these as far ahead as possible. Every major town and major station has a **hotel-finding service**, sometimes free and seldom expensive. Prices vary widely according to season. **Switzerland Tourism (ST)** can provide information on accommodation, but does not make bookings.

YOUTH HOSTELS Rates (about S Fr.25–35 per night) include linen and breakfast (but excluding breakfast in group hostels). Self-caterers pay a small fee for use of fuel. Most hostels have family rooms. The hostelling headquarters is **Schweizer Jugendherbergen,** ☎(41) (1) 360 14 14 (www.youthhostel.ch).

BACKPACKERS' ACCOMMODATION Mountain backpackers can stay at **Swiss Alpine Club (SAC)** huts (**Schweizer Alpenclub,** Monbijoustr. 61, CH-3000 Berne 23, ☎(41) (31) 370 18 (www.sac-cas.ch); these are primarily climbing huts based at the start of climbing routes, but walkers are welcome. There are also (in more accessible locations) mountain inns known as *Berghotels* or *Auberges de Montagne,* with simple dormitory accommodation as well as private rooms ranging from basic to relatively luxurious.

CAMPING There are currently around 450 **campsites** in Switzerland (most open summer only). They are graded on a one- to five-star system. International *carnets* are required at many campsites. 'Rough' camping is not officially permitted, though it does happen. Guides are available from specialist bookshops or **Camping TCS** (Touring Club Schweiz), ☎(41) (22) 417 25 20 (www.tcs.ch) or **Verband Schweizerischer Campings,** ☎(41) (33) 823 35 23 (www.swisscamps.ch).

FOOD AND DRINK

Pork and veal are common menu items, but in the lake areas you'll also find fresh fish. Portions tend to be ample. Swiss cheese is often an ingredient in local dishes; the classic Swiss fondue, for instance, is bread dipped into a pot containing melted cheese, garlic, wine and kirsch. *Raclette,* a speciality of the canton of Valais, is simply melted cheese, served with boiled potatoes, gherkins and silverskin onions. The ubiquitous meal accompaniment in German-speaking areas is *Rösti,* fried potatoes and onions, while French Switzerland goes in for stronger tastes, such as smoked sausages. In the Grisons, *Bündnerfleisch* is a tasty raw smoked beef, sliced very thin. Swiss wines are also excellent and very difficult to get in other countries.

There is a wide range of food and places to eat. The cheapest are supermarket or department store cafeterias, such as those housed in the ubiquitous **Migros** outlets. Look out too for **EPA, Co-op** and, in Ticino, **Inova.** At lunchtime (and quite often in the evenings), most restaurants have a fixed-price dish-of-the-day menu (*Tagesteller, plat du jour, piatto del giorno*), which is good value. Tipping in Swiss restaurants is not the norm.

Virtually any list of the world's top ten rail journeys would include at least one trip in Switzerland. As well as the breathtakingly engineered routes over countless viaducts and through scores of tunnels, such as the **Glacier Express** from Zermatt to St Moritz, rack railways edge their way up improbable gradients to stunning viewpoints such as the **Jungfraujoch.**

CITES: ZÜRICH

Switzerland's largest city (though not its capital), publicised as the 'little big city', comes as a surprise. Despite a stern reputation as one of the world's major financial centres, it has a picturesque setting on the River Limmat beside Lake Zürich (Zürichsee), a mountain backdrop, immaculate quayside parks, smart shops, open-air cafés, chic shopping and ancient squares. With its sizeable immigrant population, the city wears a distinctly cosmopolitan air. The best view of the lake and city is from Quaibrücke, which crosses the Limmat where the lake flows into it.

ARRIVAL AND DEPARTURE

Zürich Hauptbahnhof (HB) is on the west side of River Limmat and leads out onto Bahnhofstr., the main shopping street.

Zürich Airport is 10 km northeast of the city centre; flight information ☎ 0900 300 313; general enquiries ☎ (043) 816 22 11 (www.zurich-airport.com). There are six to eight trains an hour from the rail station; journey time approximately 10 mins (ETT table 529).

TOURIST OFFICE

On the station concourse, Hauptbahnhof, ☎(044) 215 40 00, (www.zuerich.com). This efficient, well-stocked office sells a street map, provides a free accommodation service (☎(044) 215 40 40), and the monthly *Zürich City Guide*.

INFORMATION

INTERNET ACCESS Internet access in Switzerland is exemplary and almost ubiquitous. A variety of companies are providing a vast number of free access points throughout the city. Internet directories can be found at www.swisshotspots.ch and www.totalhotspots.com. **Starbucks** at Bahnhofstr. 39, Bleicherweg 30, Badenerstr. 21, Kreutzplatz 22, Limmatquai 4, Limmatquai 144, Rennweg 4 and Rindermarkt 1; **sunrise center**, Bahnhofsplatz 4; Club zum Rennweg, Fortunagasse 13; Webstubler, Allmendstr. 67; **Café Bar Canale Grande**, Limmatquai 118; **Café Casablanca**, Langstr. 62 (www.cafe-casablanca.ch).

PUBLIC TRANSPORT

🚋 The centre of Zürich is small enough to explore on foot. All buses and trams, run by **VBZ Züri-Linie**, ☎0848 988 988 (www.vbz.ch), leave the terminal outside the HB every 6–12 mins 0530–2400. Buy your ticket from machines at stops before boarding; 1 hr (city zone) costs S Fr.4 or 24 hrs S Fr.8. An all-zones day ticket valid after 0900 is available for S Fr.23. The Zürich Card covers public transport and visitor attractions (24 hrs S Fr.19, 72 hrs S Fr.38).

Taxis: ☎(044) 222 22 22 (Züri Taxi) or (044) 444 44 44 (Taxi 2000), or hail one in the street. **Bikes** can be loaned (free with a refundable S Fr.20 deposit) at the main rail station and, from May–Oct, at several other central locations including Enge, Oerlikon Swissotel, the Opera House and the Globus City department store (www.zuerirollt.ch).

ACCOMMODATION

The **Dakini's Bed & Breakfast**, Brauerstr. 87, ☎(044) 291 42 20 (www.dakini.ch), €/€€, is two apartment houses, including colour-coded rooms, and **ZicZac Rock-Hotel**, Marktgasse 17, ☎(044) 261 21 81 (www.ziczac.ch), €/€€, great atmosphere and value for money. The **St Josef**, Hirschengraben 64–68, ☎(044) 250 57 57 (www.st-josef.ch), €€, is between the rail station and university. **Hotel Biber/City Backpacker**, Niederdorfstr. 5, ☎(044) 251 90 15 (www.city-backpacker.ch), €, is in the lively Niederdorfer area and has dorms and private rooms.

The **(HI) youth hostel** is in Mutschellenstr. 114, ☎(043) 399 78 00 (www.youthhostel.ch/ zuerich), south of the city in Wollishofen (tram 7 to Morgental, then 5-min walk). Campers can try the **Campingplatz Zürich-Seebucht**, Seestr. 559, ☎(044) 482 16 12 (www.camping-zurich.ch), (🚌161/165 from Bürklipl.)

Switzerland

FOOD AND DRINK

Zürich has a large selection of restaurants of most nationalities, as well as its own local cuisine. Local specialities include *Kalbgeschnetzeltes* (veal in cream sauce) and the less expensive pork version, *Schweingeschnetzeltes*. There are numerous fast-food and conventional restaurants around the huge station complex. The largest selection of eating places is on or just off Niederdorfstr., the main nightlife area, which stretches for about 1 km on the east side of the river, a block back from it. Fierce competition keeps prices at a relatively reasonable level.

HIGHLIGHTS

On the west bank of the Limmat, just behind the station, is the **Schweizerisches Landesmuseum** (www.slmnet.ch) (Swiss National Museum; closed Mon), housed in a 19th-century mock castle, and giving an excellent cross-section of Swiss history. A stroll away, the city's highest spot, **Lindenhof**, is a wide terrace of lime trees with good views over the river. It's a favourite with chess players – three sets of giant pieces are for all to use. The nearby 13th-century **St Peterskirche** is remarkable for its 16th-century clock tower, the largest in Europe; each of the four faces is 8.7 m wide.

Near Münsterbrücke, the 13th-century **Fraumünster** has outstanding stained-glass windows by Chagall. Across the bridge, the twin towers of the Romanesque **Grossmünster** (Cathedral), offer great views from the top. It has stained glass by Giacometti and a statue of Charlemagne in the crypt. Nearby, **Wasserkirche** (Water Church), on Limmatquai, is attached to the 18th-century **Helmhaus**, cloth market hall, where contemporary art exhibitions are staged.

Other old **Zunfthäuser** (guild halls) line Limmatquai, some converted to restaurants. **Kunsthaus** (Fine Arts Museum), Heimpl. 1 (www.kunsthaus.ch), is Switzerland's premier art gallery (closed Mon) with works ranging from late Gothic to contemporary. On the east bank, in the heart of the **Niederdorf** area, stroll along the quiet Spiegelgasse to see the house where Lenin once lived (no. 14). On the east bank of the Zürichsee, the **Chinese Garden** is as exotic as it suggests. By tram 2 or 4, at Zollikerstr. 172, the **Sammlung Bührle** (Bührle Collection, www.buehrle.ch) is a treasure-trove of art displayed in the villa of the industrialist who collected it; Emil Bührle had a taste for Impressionist paintings, resulting in a rich show of works by Manet, Sisley and Van Gogh, as well as earlier masters such as Delacroix and Hals.

DAY TRIPS FROM ZÜRICH   **Lake Zurich** (Zürichsee) is the obvious starting point for short excursions, with cruises offered by Zürichsee-Schifffahrtsgesellschaft (there are also 1-hr trips along the River Limmat from outside the rail station by the Schweizerisches Landesmuseum). **Rapperswill**, a small town with a castle, is the prettiest place on the lake (boat or S-Bahn 5, 7, 15 and 55), and is famed for its roses.

For a high-level view from the city's own mountain, take the **Uetliberg Railway** (reached by S-Bahn 10 to Uetliberg) up to the 871-m summit of Uetliberg itself. There's a fine panorama of the Alps from the top, and you can walk a high-level path to Felsenegg (about 1 hr 30 mins), on a trail modelled somewhat unusually on the solar system. From Felsenegg a cable car takes you down to Adliswil for S-Bahn 4 back to Zurich. Just on the Swiss side of the German border are the 150-m wide and 23-m-high **Rhine Falls** – the dramatic start of the same Rhine that ends in the North Sea, having wound its way gently through the castles of middle Germany from Basel. After the 40-min ride to Schaffhausen (ETT table 940), you can then continue by train to the base of the falls themselves, a journey of only 3 mins (Apr–Oct). The walk down from **Schloss Laufen** (which is a youth hostel, ☎(052) 659 61 52 – re-opens spring 2010) skirts the water, leading to dramatic views. Halfway down, a tunnel opens out into the middle of the cascade, granting a spectacular, if damp, prospect. Continuing along the cliff and down to the water level, it's possible to take a boat trip to the tiny Swiss-flag adorned island in the middle of the stream (for boat information: **Rhyfall Mändli**, ☎(052) 672 48 11, www.maendli.ch).

SHOPPING

The main shopping street is Bahnhofstr. Look out particularly for **Franz Carl Weber** at No. 62 (www.fcw.ch), which sells toys of all sorts, including a big selection of model trains, and cuckoo clocks. **Sprüngli** is arguably the best *Konditorei* in town and sells superb chocolates, some not available outside Zürich. **Jelmoli Department Store**, just off Bahnhofstr., has the best selection and prices for Swiss souvenirs. Augustinergasse, off it, is charming and has buildings dating from the 14th century as well as several very smart boutiques.

NIGHT-TIME AND EVENTS

Zürich has plenty going on. In summer there are a number of outside bars, particularly by the lake. Around 500 venues stay open into the small hours at weekends, and cater for most tastes. There's no shortage of bars, clubs and street performers around **Niederdorfstrasse**, a lively, safe area, despite its reputation as the red-light district.

Zürich's acclaimed opera company performs at the **Opernhaus Zürich**, Falkenstr. 1, ☎(044) 268 64 00, www.opernhaus.ch; concerts are given at the **Tonhalle**, Claridenstr. 7, ☎(044) 206 34 34; www.tonhalle.ch. Mid-April sees the **Sechse-läuten**, or spring festival, when guild members celebrate the end of winter by parading in historic costumes before burning Böögg, a huge snowman, on a huge bonfire. In July there's the Zürich **Festspiele**, a three-week music festival. In August there is a **Street Parade** of young people and deafening music to celebrate love, peace and tolerance.

WHERE NEXT FROM ZÜRICH?

Two trains an hour to **Lucerne** *(50 mins; ETT table 555) join the* **Berne–Milan** *route (p362).*

SWITZERLAND

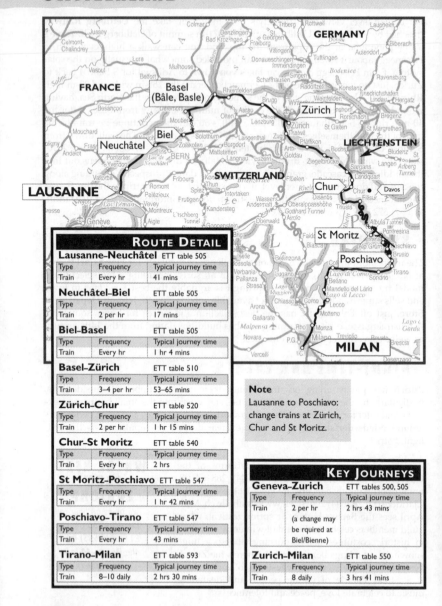

ROUTE DETAIL

Lausanne–Neuchâtel ETT table 505

Type	Frequency	Typical journey time
Train	Every hr	41 mins

Neuchâtel–Biel ETT table 505

Type	Frequency	Typical journey time
Train	2 per hr	17 mins

Biel–Basel ETT table 505

Type	Frequency	Typical journey time
Train	Every hr	1 hr 4 mins

Basel–Zürich ETT table 510

Type	Frequency	Typical journey time
Train	3–4 per hr	53–65 mins

Zürich–Chur ETT table 520

Type	Frequency	Typical journey time
Train	2 per hr	1 hr 15 mins

Chur–St Moritz ETT table 540

Type	Frequency	Typical journey time
Train	Every hr	2 hrs

St Moritz–Poschiavo ETT table 547

Type	Frequency	Typical journey time
Train	Every hr	1 hr 42 mins

Poschiavo–Tirano ETT table 547

Type	Frequency	Typical journey time
Train	Every hr	43 mins

Tirano–Milan ETT table 593

Type	Frequency	Typical journey time
Train	8–10 daily	2 hrs 30 mins

Note

Lausanne to Poschiavo:
change trains at Zürich,
Chur and St Moritz.

KEY JOURNEYS

Geneva–Zurich ETT tables 500, 505

Type	Frequency	Typical journey time
Train	2 per hr (a change may be rquired at Biel/Bienne)	2 hrs 43 mins

Zurich–Milan ETT table 550

Type	Frequency	Typical journey time
Train	8 daily	3 hrs 41 mins

RAIL TOUR: LAUSANNE – BASEL – MILAN

Vineyards cling to the hilly shores of **Lac de Neuchâtel**, where **Yverdon** and **Neuchâtel** are pleasantly set lakeside towns, and lake views are a feature from the right (south) side of the train as far as **Biel**. Beyond the watch-and-clock-making town of **Delmont**, the scenery is less remarkable between the cities of **Basel** and **Zürich**. Thereafter, things step up a couple of gears, with **Lake Zürich** and the **Walensee** immediately on the left, and beyond **Sargans** you pass within a stone's throw of the tiny prinicipality of **Liechtenstein**. **Chur** lies at the foot of an astonishing climb high up into the **Alps**, a section covered by the **Bernina Express** service (reservation compulsory and supplement payable), where the finely set resort of **St Moritz** is at the heart of the **Engadine**, the huge straight valley of the **Inn** that cuts across the **Grisons** (Grishun or Graubünden), Switzerland's canton in Romansch-speaking southeastern corner. **Poschiavo**, on the other hand, is distinctly Italian both in character and language, and from there you can cross into Italy via the **Bernina Pass**, along the shore of **Lake Lecco** to end at **Milan**.

LAUSANNE

Half Alpine and half Riviera, this university town, both a commercial centre and resort, has a hilly setting, with some of the best views from the cathedral and old town, perched 130 m above **Lake Geneva**. The steepness of the place is part of its appeal, and if you don't fancy the trudge up from the lakeshore suburb of **Ouchy**, with its grand hotels and large park, to the station and up to the old town, there's a useful Metro (actually a funicular) linking all three in a few minutes. The partly pedestrianised Old Town is small enough to be explored on foot.

The upper Metro terminal (Flon), **Pl. St-François**, just south of the main area of interest and dominated by the 15th-century steeple of the 13th–14th-century **Église St-François** (St Francis' Church). The **Cathédrale de Notre-Dame**, a 10-min walk up into the town, was consecrated in 1275. Italian, Flemish and French craftsmen all had a hand in its construction, and it is accepted as a perfect example of Gothic architecture. The night watch is still called from the steeple every hour from 2200 to 0200.

The **Musée Historique de Lausanne**, Pl. de la Cathédrale 4 (closed Mon except July and Aug), in the **Ancien-Evêché** (the bishops' palace until the early 15th century), exhibits a large-scale model of 17th-century Lausanne. Also by the cathedral is another fortified bishops' residence, the **Château St-Marie**, now the seat of the cantonal government (part open to the public). **Escaliers-du-Marché**, a wooden-roofed medieval staircase, links the cathedral square to **Pl. de la Palud**, an ancient square surrounded by old houses.

Switzerland

West of the cathedral, the Florentine-style **Palais de Rumine**, Pl. de la Riponne, was built by a Russian family at the turn of the last century. It now houses a number of museums. Take a 10-min walk northwest (or 🚌 2) to the **Collection de l'Art Brut**, Av. des Bergières 11 (www.artbrut.ch), housed in the **Château de Beaulieu**. This compelling post-war gallery was founded by a local collector, who sought the works of anyone who was not a trained or formal painter, from amateur dabblers to the criminally insane.

North of the centre is the **Fondation de l'Hermitage**, Rte du Signal 2 (www.fondation-hermitage.ch), an early 19th-century villa full of period fixtures and fittings, which hosts top-quality touring exhibitions of contemporary art. The view from the villa gardens, over the city and the lake to the Alps, is magnificent. For more lake views, take 🚌 16 to the **Forêt de Sauvabelin**, 150 m above the city centre. This 140-acre beech forest offers a choice of walking paths, a viewing tower and a deer reserve around a small lake.

The **quai de Belgique** is a shady, flower-lined, waterside promenade, looking towards the Savoy Alps. The 13th-century keep of **Château d'Ouchy** is now a hotel. Baron Pierre de Coubertin, founder of the modern Olympics in 1915, chose Lausanne as the headquarters of the International Olympic Committee. The unique **Musée Olympique**, quai d'Ouchy 1, is a large modern complex, cleverly designed to retain the natural beauty of its surrounding park. Boats can be hired near the 'cruise' pier.

🚃 Between the centre and Ouchy, connected by the Metro. Left luggage facilities and bike rental available.

ℹ️ **Tourist Office**: 2 av. de Rhodanie, ☎(021) 613 73 73 (www.lausanne-tourisme.ch). **Vaud Regional Tourist Office**: av. d'Ouchy 60, ☎(021) 613 26 26 (www.lake-geneva-region.ch). A walking tour (not always in English) of the old town leaves from the Town Hall at 1000 and 1500, Mon–Sat May–Sept.

🏠 There's plenty of budget accommodation. The **Pension Ada-Logements**, av. de Tivoli 60, €, is in the middle of town, not far from the station. **Lausanne Guest House & Backpacker**, Epinettes 4, ☎(021) 601 80 00. (www.lausanne-guesthouse.ch), €, has twins and dorms, all facing the lake; electric bike rental, internet. **Youth hostel (HI)**: Jeunotel, Chemin du Bois-de-Vaux 36, ☎(021) 626 02 22 (www.youthhostel.ch/lausanne), on the lakeside west of Ouchy, has 264 beds and offers simple modern rooms and dormitories (🚌 2 from Ouchy Metro station to Bois-de-Vaux then 5-min walk). **Campsite**: Camping de Vidy, Chemin du Camping 3, ☎(021) 622 50 00 (www.campinglausannevidy.ch).

NEUCHÂTEL

Set steeply beside the 38-km-long lake of the same name, **Neuchâtel** slopes down from its castle to its Old Town, and down to the busy quays. At the heart of the Old Town, itself characterised by Renaissance fountains and defensive towers, is **Place Pury**; markets are held in the adjacent **Place des Halles**. It's well worth the walk up to the top of town, past the **Tour des Prisons** (Prison Tower), used as a dungeon until 1848, for the views from the town's monumental set pieces: the imposing **Château**, built from the 12th to 16th centuries, now functions as the cantonal office; free guided tours take you within, though there's not much of historical interest inside nowadays. A walkway leads from there to the **Église Collégiale** (Collegiate Church), featuring a splendid 14th-century monument to the Counts of Neuchâtel (www.collegiale.ch). Museums include the **Musée d'Art et d'Histoire** (www.mahn.ch), boasting three 18th-century automata – a draughtsman, writer and musician – the latter representing a female harpsichordist.

🚆 I km north of the centre.

ℹ️ **Tourist Office**: Hôtel des Postes, ☎(032) 889 68 90 (www.neuchateltourisme.ch).

BIEL [BIENNE]

Beside **Lake Biel**, the busy clock-making town (home to Omega watches since 1879) is unique in Switzerland in that French and German share equal billing – you can even hear one person talking in French and the other answering in German; French speakers know it as Bienne. Its Old Town has a wealth of medieval architecture, with turrets and arcades characteristic of the Bernese style, and prettily painted wrought-iron signs. Some of the best of it is along Burggasse and the Ring, a fine old square with a 16th-century fountain in the middle.

🚆 **Hauptbahnhof**, town centre. The old town is a 10-min walk via Bahnhofstr. and Nidaugasse, while the lake is 5 mins away, behind the station via Badhausstr.

ℹ️ **Tourist Office**: Bahnhofpl. 12, ☎(032) 329 84 84 (www.biel-seeland.ch).

WHERE NEXT FROM NEUCHÂTEL?

Twice-hourly trains, taking 40 mins (ETT table 511), link Neuchâtel with **Berne**, *where you can join the* **Berne–Geneva** *(p352) or* **Berne–Milan** *(p362) routes.*

LAKE BIEL AND ST PETERSINSEL

Lake Biel (Bielersee or lac de Bienne) has a nearby beach, but its main attraction is **St Petersinsel** (St Peter's Island), a nature reserve reached by a 50-min boat trip from Schifflände, just west of Biel station. A monastery on the island has been converted into the **St Petersinsel Restaurant & Klosterhotel'**, ☎(032) 338 11 14 (www.st-petersinsel.ch); where in 1765 the Swiss-born French philosopher Jean-Jacques Rousseau spent a blissful time, which he recorded in his *Confessions* and in the *Reveries of the Solitary Walker*.

Switzerland

BASEL (BÂLE, BASLE)

Wedged into the corners of Switzerland, France and Germany, this big, working city (the second largest in the country after Zürich) has long been a crossroads for European culture, with many museums and other sights. If you are making day-trips to Basel it's worth considering the Basel Card. This gives free admission to museums, the zoo, sightseeing tours and ferries, plus discounts at shops, theatres, concerts, clubs, boat trips and taxis (S Fr.20 for 24 hrs, S Fr.27 for 48 hrs and S Fr.35 for 72 hrs). Visitors staying in a hotel or youth hostel receive a mobility ticket, which gives free bus and tram travel during your visit.

Of the six bridges across the River Rhine, **Mittlere Brücke** offers the best views. The medieval centre is on the south bank, in Grossbasel. Kleinbasel is the small modern area on the north bank. Admission to most museums generally costs around S Fr.7, with some, such as the **Basel Museum of Ancient Art** (www.antikenmuseum basel.ch) and the **Historisches Museum** (www.hmb.ch; closed Mon), offering free entry on the first Sun of the month.

Just south of the Rhine, Münsterpl. is dominated by the 12th-century red sandstone **Münster** (cathedral), which has decorative twin towers, a Romanesque portal surrounded by elegant carvings, and a rose window featuring the wheel of fortune. Housed within a Gothic church in Barfüsserpl., the **Historisches Museum** (closed Tues) has 13th–17th-century artefacts, including Luther's chalice; the 18th–19th-century sections of the collection are in the **Haus zum Kirschgarten**, Elisabethenstr. 27, about 300 m north of the SBB station.

TINGUELY IN BASEL

Tinguely is the Basel-born sculptor whose works typically resemble parodies of machines, manically juddering into action, seemingly against the odds. His **Fasnacht-Brunnen/ Tinguely-Brunnen**, Theaterpl., is an extraordinary fountain (1977) that looks like a watery scrapyard. A museum dedicated to Tinguely, the **Museum Jean Tinguely**, Paul Sacher-Anlage 1, (www.tinguely.ch), celebrates his life and work (closed Mon).

The one sight not to miss is the world-class **Kunstmuseum** (Fine Arts Museum; closed Mon; tram 2 from the SBB rail station), St-Alban-Graben 16 (www.kunst museumbasel.ch), in a building constructed in 1932–36 to house the art treasures the town had been accumulating since the 17th century, including important works by the 15th-century Basel master Konrad Witz, the world's largest collection of works by the Holbein family, and modern contributors such as Van Gogh, Picasso,

GETTING AROUND BASEL
Most of the old centre is pedestrianised. Elsewhere a frequent tram service is supplemented by buses. Information and tickets are available from machines at every stop.

Braque and Dalí. The permanent collection of the **Museum für Gegenwartskunst** (Museum of Contemporary Art, www.kunstmuseumbasel.ch), St-Alban-Rheinweg 60, includes pieces by Stella, Warhol and Beuys. The 16th-century **Rathaus** (Town Hall) has an ornate and very picturesque red façade that includes an enormous clock. It towers over Marktplatz, the long-standing heart of Basel. Of the two main surviving medieval city gates, **St-Alban-Tor**, St-Alban-Graben, takes second place to the splendid 14th-century **Spalentor**, Spalengraben. Near here, on Spalenvorstadt, is the pick of the town's older fountains, the **Holbeinbrunnen**, based partly on a Holbein drawing and a Dürer engraving. The **Zoologischer Garten**, Binningerstr. 40 (www.zoobasel.ch), west of the SBB station, has gained a reputation for breeding armoured rhinos, but is also known for its collections of pygmy hippos, gorillas and penguins.

🚆 Basel is a frontier town for both France and Germany. The main station, **Bahnhof SBB**, is a 10-min walk south of the city centre (5 mins on tram 1/8 from the terminus in front of the station), and handles Swiss and principal German services. Facilities include left luggage, bike rental, showers, a post office and a supermarket with extended opening hours. The **SNCF** station provides French services and boasts a large, suspended and animated Tinguely sculpture. Both stations evoke the heady old days of train travel, owing to the city's location at the 'Triangle' of Europe.

✈ 9 km, 18 mins by 🚌 50 (every 20–30 mins, or 30–60 mins at weekends) to rail station. www.euroairport.com.

i **Tourist Office**: Stadtcasino, Barfüsserplatz, ☎(061) 268 68 68 (www.basel.ch) and at the SBB rail station.

🏨 Moderate hotels in the old town include the **Rochat**, Petersgraben 23, ☎(061) 261 81 40 (www.hotelrochat.ch), €€, with doubles for S Fr.190. The **Haus zur Sonnenwende**, Eulerstrasse 27, ☎(061) 302 39 55 (www.haus-zur-sonnenwende.ch), €, and **Casa La Luz**, Kembserweg 8, ☎(061) 321 38 00 (www.bed-andbreakfast.ch), €, are central and easy on the wallet. The **HI youth hostel** (**Auberge de Jeunesse Bâle**, re-opens spring 2010) is at St Alban-Kirchrain 10, ☎(061) 272 05 72 (www.youthhostel.ch/basel), a 15-min walk from the SBB station or tram 2, then a 5-min walk. **Camping Waldhort**, Heideweg 16, Reinach, ☎(061) 711 64 29 (www.camping-waldhort.ch), is 20–30 mins south of the Bahnhof SBB rail station, via tram 11 to Landhof.

LIECHTENSTEIN

The Principality of **Liechtenstein**, independent since 1719, is a green, mountainous little country covering just 158 square km; the train passes very close to it at **Sargans**, from where buses go to the capital, **Vaduz** (Swiss Passes valid). Apart from giving the chance to pick up a passport stamp of an obscure country, there isn't much to attract visitors, though the **Kunstmuseum** (Museum of Fine Arts) (www.kunstmuseum.li) has some fine works (including a dazzling golden carriage) from the private collection of the Prince, who lives with his family in **Schloss Vaduz** (not open). Liechtenstein issues its own postage stamps, and philatelists may like to pay a visit to the **Briefmarkenmuseum** (Postage Stamp Museum).

Switzerland

ZÜRICH

See p340.

CHUR

A cathedral city as well as capital of the canton of Grisons (population 32,000), **Chur** (pronounced 'Koohr') has an appealing old town. Green and red footprints mark recommended walking tours of the town (details from Tourist Office). With a fair range of places to eat and stay, it makes a feasible stopover. Its Romanesque-Gothic cathedral, built 1150–1272, has a dark, impressive interior with an exceptional Gothic triptych of carved and gilded wood, made by Jakob Russ 1486–92. In Postpl. the **Kunstmuseum** (Museum of Fine Arts) has works by artists associated with Grisons (www.buendner-kunstmuseum.ch).

⊞ In the town centre; cycle hire and left-luggage facility.

ⓘ **Tourist Office**: Bahnhofplatz 3, ☎(081) 252 18 18 (www.churtourismus.ch).

SIDE TRIP FROM CHUR TO DAVOS From Chur, hourly narrow-gauge trains (1 hr 35 mins, ETT table 545) take you to Davos (two stations: Davos Dorf and Davos Platz, the latter being the main place for activity). Change trains at Landquart. Information on the ski resort is available from the **Tourist Office**: Talstrasse 41, ☎(081) 415 21 21 (www.davos.ch). **Davos** is the highest town in Europe (1560 m), and though it's rather dominated by modern purpose-built blocks and lacking in genuine Alpine atmosphere, it is an excellent centre for walking: a favourite easy excursion is to take the funicular up to the Alpine Garden at **Schatzalp**, where 800 plant species flourish. Schatzalp has a summer toboggan run and toboggans are for hire. Alternatively, take the cable car to **Jakobshorn** for superlative views along waymarked paths from the top. Forward trains from Davos complete a loop connecting at Filisur (25 mins, ETT table 545a) into the main Lausanne–Milan route. **Youthpalace Davos (HI)**, Horlaubenstrasse 27, ☎(081) 410 19 20 (www.youthhostel.ch/davos); open all year.

ST MORITZ

Even in the face of opposition from the likes of Zermatt and Davos, **St Moritz** still pretty much leads the way as a Swiss sports resort, with a breathtaking location and a sunshine record (322 sunny days a year) unrivalled elsewhere in the country.

St Moritz divides into **Dorf** (village) on the hill, and **Bad** (spa) 2 km downhill around the lake; in St Moritz-Dorf lie the main hotels, shops and museums (including the **Engadine Museum**, offering an absorbing look at the furniture and house interiors of the Engadine). The centre for downhill skiing is **Corviglia** (2486 m), but even if you're not skiing it's worth the 2-km funicular trip for the views and a glimpse of the 'beautiful people' at play. From there, take the cable car up to **Piz Nair** (3057 m) for a panorama of the Upper Engadine.

WHERE NEXT FROM ST MORITZ?

*Take the **Glacier Express** (see p357), one of the great scenic rail journeys of the Alps from **St Moritz** to **Zermatt** via **Andermatt** and **Brig** (ETT tables 540, 575, 579).*

🚉 Near the centre of the town.

ℹ️ **Tourist Office**: Via Maistra 12, ☎ (081) 837 33 33 (www.stmoritz.ch).

🏨 Accommodation and food are generally less expensive in St Moritz Bad than in St Moritz Dorf. **Youth hostel (HI)**: Via Surpunt 60, St Moritz Bad, ☎ (081) 833 39 69 (www.youthhostel.ch/st.moritz); postbus to Hotel Sonne then 5-min walk.

POSCHIAVO

Tucked just inside the Swiss-Italian border, **Poschiavo** is distinctly southern in appearance, with a lovely central piazza surrounded by dignified Italianate houses. A wander round town reveals the 17th-century **town hall**, the Lombardian-style Gothic **church of San Vittore** and the 17th–18th-century **church of Santa Maria Presentata**, with its glorious ceiling. Spanish settlers in the 19th century built colourful houses in the Spaniola quarter.

🚉 In the town centre.

ℹ️ **Tourist Office**: Via de la Stazion, ☎ (081) 844 05 71 (www.valposchiavo.ch).

MILAN (MILANO), ITALY

See p430.

ROUTE DETAIL

Berne–Interlaken (Ost) — ETT table 560

Type	Frequency	Typical journey time
Train	1–2 per hr	53 mins

Interlaken (Ost)–**Kandersteg** — ETT tables 560, 562

Type	Frequency	Typical journey time
Train	Every hr	1 hr 11–1hr 41 mins

Kandersteg–Brig — ETT table 562

Type	Frequency	Typical journey time
Train	Every hr	42 mins

Brig–Sion — ETT table 570

Type	Frequency	Typical journey time
Train	2 per hr	38 mins

Sion–Montreux — ETT table 570

Type	Frequency	Typical journey time
Train	2 per hr	41 mins

Montreux–Lausanne — ETT table 570

Type	Frequency	Typical journey time
Train	2 per hr	21 mins

Lausanne–Geneva — ETT tables 505, 570

Type	Frequency	Typical journey time
Train	5 per hr	33–51 mins

Notes

Interlaken to Brig: change trains at Spiez. Trains also run directly from Berne to Brig (see ETT table 560).

KEY JOURNEYS

Geneva–Milan — ETT table 570

Type	Frequency	Typical journey time
Train	5 daily	4 hrs 25 mins

Berne, the easy-going Swiss capital city, is the prelude to the dramatic heights of the Bernese Oberland, a long-established area for tourism, then continuing along the partly industrialised Rhône Valley to end along the vineyards above Lake Geneva. It's well worth exploring the side trips, such as the expensive but spectacular mountain railway from Interlaken up **Jungfraujoch**, Europe's highest railway station; or explore the paths around **Kandersteg**. At **Brig** you can leave the route and go eastwards on the spectacular **Alpine Express** route (which in its entirety is Zermatt to St Moritz; Eurail/Inter-rail not valid; for a taster go up the **Goms Valley**, with its quaint wooden villages, as far as Oberwald), or carry on and take the optional detour into **Zermatt**, a mountain resort near the Matterhorn. At **Martigny** choose between venturing into France and taking an exciting route past **Chamonix** and **Mont Blanc**, or passing Château Chillon beside **Lac Léman** (**Lake Geneva**), the largest of all the Swiss lakes.

BERNE (BERN)

One of Europe's more relaxed capitals and much less international than Zürich or Geneva, Berne is pleasant for wandering around, with its harmonious medieval houses of yellow sandstone, its irregular roofscape, its ancient arcaded streets that make up Europe's largest covered shopping promenade (all 6 km of it) and its numerous fountains. The Alps are often visible in the distance, though the immediate surroundings are unremarkable.

From the main station, the first of 11 monumental fountains is the **Pfeiferbrunnen**, on Spitalgasse, a flamboyant 16th-century creation with technicolour carvings and flowers around the base. Münsterpl. is home of the Gothic **Münster** (Cathedral, www.bernermuenster.ch). There's been a cathedral here since 1200, but the building you see today was begun in 1421 and completed in 1893 when the spire was added. It has a magnificent depiction of the Last Judgement above the main entrance, elaborate carvings on the pews and choir stalls, and superb 15th-century stained glass. The 100-m steeple (Switzerland's highest) provides a good view if you feel like climbing its 344 steps.

Berne was founded in 1191 by Berchtold V, Duke of Zähringen, who supposedly declared he would name his new city after the first creature he killed while hunting. The unfortunate victim, a bear, thus became the town's mascot.

Back on the main street (by now Gerechtigkeitsgasse), you pass Gerechtigkeitsbrunnen, where the blindfolded Goddess of Justice stands over the severed heads of historical figures. Cross the river by the 15th-century **Nydeggbrücke** and climb the hill facing you to look back on the picture-postcard view of the city.

The **Kunstmuseum** (Fine Arts Museum), Hodlerstr. 8–12 (www.kunstmuseumbern.ch; closed Mon) (near Lorrainebrücke, north of the station), has a fine display of works

Switzerland

by the Swiss artists Ferdinand Hodler and Paul Klee (of whom this is the world's largest collection). Look too for exhibits by such diverse artists as Fra Angelico, Matisse, Kandinsky, Cézanne and Picasso. The other major museums are around Helvetiapl., south of the River Aare, across the Kirchenfeldbrücke (tram 3/5). **Kunsthalle**, Helvetiapl. 1 (www.kunsthalle-bern.ch), hosts temporary exhibitions of contemporary art. Opposite, **Schweizerisches Alpines Museum** (www.alpinesmuseum.ch) contains an interesting assemblage of items connected with the history of mountaineering. Close by, the **Naturhistorische Museum**, Bernastr. 15 (www.nmbe.ch) features Barry, the St Bernard dog, that rescued over 40 people, as well as African animals and the inevitable bears. The apartment and **workplace of Albert Einstein**, a resident of Berne, is at Kramgasse 49.

ZYTGLOGGETURM CLOCK TOWER

The clock tower, which was the original western gate, was first built in the 12th century. In the 16th century, an astronomical clock was added on its Kramgasse face. At exactly 4 mins to each hour, a mechanical jester summons a lion, a rooster and a procession of bears.

🚆 **Hauptbahnhof (Hbf)** is at the western end of the old centre.

GETTING AROUND BERNE

Berne's main thoroughfare runs east–west through the town centre, linking the station and Nydeggbrücke, and changes name four times: Spitalgasse, Marktgasse, Kramgasse, Gerechtigkeitsgasse. Other than the museums, much of interest is on or just off this street. There's an excellent tram and bus network. 🚋 9A/15 and trolleybus 12 cover this street, as well as the Bärengraben, on the other side of the river. Departures from track 1 in the Vorpl. outside the station. The Tourist Office has details of city tours.

ℹ️ **Tourist Office**: Hauptbahnhof, ☎(031) 328 12 12 (www.berninfo.com). Its bilingual brochure *Bern Guide* contains plenty of useful information.

🏨 Cheap accommodation is not plentiful but at least most of it is quite central. In the thick of things is **Hotel Glocke Backpackers Bern**, Rathausgasse 75, ☎(031) 311 37 71 (www.bernbackpackers.ch), €. The 2-star **Arabelle**, Mittelstr. 6, ☎(031) 301 03 05 (www.arabelle.ch), €€, offers doubles with a shower for S Fr.130–224 (🚋 2, Mittelstr.). **Youth hostel (HI)**: Weiherg. 4, ☎(031) 326 11 11 (www.youthhostel.ch/berne), a 10-min walk from the rail station, just below Bundeshaus. **Campsites: Eichholz**, Strandweg 49, Wabern, ☎(031) 961 26 02 (www.campingeichholz.ch), 2 km southeast of centre (tram 9 to Wabern), Apr–Sept, also **camping and bungalows: Eymatt**, Wohlenstr. 62, Hinterkappelen, ☎(031) 901 10 07 (www.campingtcs.ch), 5 km northwest of the centre (Postbus to Eymatt from station).

🍽️ The area around Spitalgasse and Zeughausgasse is good for menu browsing. The best-value lunch is at the pleasant **EPA** department store at Marktgasse 24. On Gerechtigkeitsgasse, at No. 62, is the **Klötzlikeller**, Berne's oldest wine cellar (dating from 1635), serving meals (www.kloetzlikeller.ch). For a picnic with a view, cross the Nydeggbrücke to the lovely **Rose Garden**, or cross the Lorrainebrücke to the **Botanic Gardens**.

INTERLAKEN

This distinctly lively resort boomed in the 19th century when it became popular with British visitors as a base for exploring the mountains, and fanciful hotels sprang up along the Höheweg, the town's principal avenue (which links the two stations). It's still virtually unrivalled in the country as a centre for scenic excursions. You don't need transport for getting around town, but hiring a bike to explore the adjacent lakesides can be fun. Horse-drawn carriages (at a price) are available for hire outside both stations. From the Höheweg a wonderful, uninterrupted view extends across the undeveloped meadow where the original 12th-century monastic site of the town once stood, to Jungfrau (4158 m) and other peaks looming beyond – especially magnificent in the later afternoon Alpenglow.

One of the period pieces in town is the distinctive 19th-century **Kursaal** (Casino), which in addition to gambling (high rollers should note that the ceiling for bets is only S Fr.5) stages concerts and folklore evenings (www.casino-kursaal.ch). Across the River Aare is the old part of town known as **Unterseen**, with the oldest buildings in the region. Cross the bridge and walk along the river to **Marktplatz**, with its 17th-century town hall and palace, 14th-century church and **Touristik Museum** (charting the rise and rise of Interlaken's tourist industry).

Ostbahnhof is on Lake Brienz, a 10-min walk from the centre. **Westbahnhof**, by Lake Thun, is central. The two stations are 15 mins apart on foot, 4 mins by rail. It is the Ostbahnhof that connects with the railway to Jungfraujoch. From Berne, Westbahnhof is the first stop and the journey, by hourly trains, averages 50 mins – sit on the left as you head south.

i **Tourist Office**: Höheweg 37, (033) 826 53 00 (www.interlaken.ch).

There's no shortage of hotels, many catering largely for tour operators, but private rooms can be better value. **Backpackers Villa Sonnenhof**, Alpenstr. 16, (033) 826 71 71 (www.villa.ch), €–€€, has twins, triples, quads and dorms; internet facilities; online reservation; 10 mins from station or 2. Other reasonably priced hotels include **Arnold's Bed & Breakfast**, Parkstr. 3, (033) 823 64 21 (www.arnolds.ch), €€. **Youth hostel (HI):** Aareweg 21, am See, (033) 822 43 53 (www.youthhostel.ch/boenigen), a 20-min walk east from **Ostbahnhof**, in the village of **Bönigen** on Lake Brienz (1). There's also an excellent private **hostel**: **Balmer's Herberge**, Hauptstr. 23, (033) 822 19 61 (www.balmers.com), 15-min walk from both stations, in the suburb of **Matten** (5/15). Seven **campsites** are within easy walking distance, so ask the Tourist Office for details.

Interlaken doesn't offer a wide choice of interesting cheap eats, though there are the usual fast-food outlets. In the summer, spontaneous outdoor restaurants and grills sprout, offering cheaper fare. **Internet Café: Fun**, Hauptstr. 19, (033) 822 01 75 (www.funrental.ch).

DAY TRIPS FROM INTERLAKEN A highly popular excursion is the 2 hr 20-min journey – each way – to **Jungfraujoch**, the highest railway station in Europe at 3454 m. Services are at least hourly, and changes of train may be necessary

Switzerland

in **Lauterbrunnen** or **Grindelwald** and **Kleine Scheidegg**. The earlier you start, the better, to increase the chance of clear views. Ostbahnhof has weather reports. It's best to dedicate a whole day to the trip, if the weather warrants it, as stops can be made en route. This trip is undeniably breathtaking, but also very expensive (currently S Fr.181.80, passes not valid), although from November to April you can save around 15% by splashing out on a 'Good Morning Ticket' (valid on the 0705 train, for S Fr.157.80). From May to October you must start your descent from the Jungfraujoch by 1230. On a good day, you'll see the best of Switzerland, including phenomenal glaciers. The little rack-and-pinion railway then goes into the face of the Eiger, emerging from the long tunnel at the 3454-m summit. As well as the Jungfraujoch there are other, cheaper funicular rides up **Harder Kulm** (1320 m) and **Heimwehfluh** (669 m); both are close to town. A **boat or bus ride** will take you to the **Beatushöhlen** – dramatic cliff caves along the Thunersee. For the best views of **Interlaken** and the **lakes of Thun and Brienz**, from which the towns take their names, catch a train to **Wilderswil** for the rack railway to **Schynige Platte** (summer only, 52 mins, ETT table 564), its summit adorned with an Alpine garden. Beyond **Lauterbrunnen**, a bus ride to **Trummelbach waterfalls** (actually inside the mountain face) is a good afternoon's trip. The cliff steps are not for the infirm, though. Also from Lauterbrunnen, it's possible to take a cable car up to the revolving restaurant on the 2970 m **Schilthorn**.

Just outside Interlaken, with a free bus from Interlaken-Ost station, **Mystery Park** (open daily; www.mysterypark.ch) has been a massive crowd-puller since opening in 2003. Set up by Erich von Däniken (of *Chariots of the Gods* fame) it's a theme park with seven pavilions focusing on the mysteries of leylines, Mayan temples, alien contact and so on – fascinating or kitsch nonsense, according to your viewpoint, but carried off with verve.

KANDERSTEG

With its excellent train and bus links, and chairlifts up into the mountains, this large, old-fashioned village is perfectly sited for exploring the Bernese Oberland. Everything's geared to outdoor activities, with year-round walking trails and winter sports. Pick of the walks is up to the **Oeschinensee**, a stupendously sited mountain lake (walk up or take the chairlift), or take the Sunnbüel cable car and walk up to the Gemmi Pass. Other options include **Adelboden** (another pleasant old village, reached by train to Frutigen then bus; ETT table 562) or the deeply traditional villages of the **Lötschental** (train to Goppenstein for connecting postbus to Blatten, where you can walk down to the valley to another village such as Kippel and pick up the bus back).

🚉 A 3-min walk from the village centre.

ℹ️ **Tourist Office**: 3718 Kandersteg, 📞 (033) 675 80 80 (www.kandersteg.ch). From the station take the road into the village centre, turn left along main street; Tourist Office is on the right.

⊟ Wide choice in the village, with bed and breakfast from around S Fr.50. Cheaper places include the **Gemmi Lodge Backpackers**, ☎ (033) 675 85 85 (www.gemmi-lodge.com), €, with indoor pool and shuttle bus from the station, and **Erika**, ☎ (033) 675 11 37 (www.hotelerika.ch), €, owned by an Anglo-Swiss couple.

BRIG

The town stands at a major meeting of rail routes, where you can change for trains to Zermatt. Now home to municipal offices, the vast Italianate palace of **Stockalper Castle** is the largest private building ever erected in Switzerland. It was constructed in 1658–68 by Kaspar Stockalper, a merchant who made a fortune controlling the flow of goods between France, Lombardy and Switzerland.

🚉 Near the town centre.

ℹ️ **Tourist Office**: Bahnhofplatz 3, ☎ (027) 921 60 30 (www.brig-belalp.ch).

SIDE TRIP FROM BRIG TO ZERMATT Served by narrow-gauge railway (1 hr 20 mins from Brig, hourly; ETT table 576), **Zermatt** is a major ski centre and car-free. In summer it's a superb place for hiking. The little town's popularity largely rests on its proximity to the 4477-m **Matterhorn**, one of the best-known mountain profiles in the world, best appreciated by walking a little out of town. Zermatt is very touristy, but nothing (except the frequent clouds) can detract from the glory of its magnificent jagged peak. The **Gornergrat Mountain Railway** and a network of cable cars provide superb views of the whole area. The **Kleiner Matterhorn Cable Car** makes a three-stage ascent up to 3828 m, giving an extremely dramatic, and very different, view of the Matterhorn, as well as the Alpine range; Mont Blanc in France is prominent on a clear day. The journey to Zermatt is the westernmost stage of the famous **Glacier Express** route (see below: Where Next from Brig?). **Tourist Office**: Bahnhofpl., ☎ (027) 966 81 00 (www.zermatt.ch).

WHERE NEXT FROM BRIG?

*From Brig you can continue south through the **Simplon Tunnel** (one of the world's longest rail tunnels at 20 km) and into Italy, proceeding along the shores of **Lake Maggiore** (p366) to **Milan** (p430) (a 1 hr 50 mins–2 hr 15 mins trip – see ETT table 590).*

*One of the great scenic Alpine routes is east on the **Glacier Express** (narrow-gauge line) to **St Moritz**; the full Glacier Express route begins from Zermatt. There are some through services; for others change at **Andermatt** (takes 8–8 hrs 30 mins; ETT tables 575 and 576; reservations recommended). At St Moritz you can join the **Lausanne–Milan** route (p344). In its entirety, from Zermatt to St Moritz, the route crosses 291 bridges and passes through 91 tunnels and many hairpin bends.*

Switzerland

SION

Though the area's a bit marred by industrial development, the attractive old centre of Sion looks terrific from a distance, with two hills popping up beside it, both excellent viewpoints in themselves. One is crowned by the scant ruins of **Château Tourbillon**, the other by a strange fortified church called the **Basilique de Valère**. As capital of the Valais canton, the town has provincial **museums** covering fine arts, archaeology and natural history.

RAIL Near the town centre.

i **Tourist Office**: Pl de la Planta, ☎(027) 327 77 27 (www.siontourism.ch).

🏠 **Youth hostel: (HI)**, R. de l'Industrie 2, ☎(027) 323 74 70 (www.youthhostel.ch/sion), 350 m from the station. There is a riverside **campsite: Camping des Îles**, Route d'Aproz ☎(027) 346 43 47 (www.campingtcs.ch), 4 km west of the centre.

WHERE NEXT FROM SION?

*Cross into **France** in style by taking the route via Martigny, Chamonix–Mont Blanc and St Gervais, and re-entering **Switzerland** to end at **Geneva**, getting stunning mountain views most of the way. ETT tables 572, 365a and 365.*

*The **Mont Blanc Express** train grinds up an incredible one-in-five gradient to the French border village of **Vallorcine**; some trains run through, though others require a change here or at Le Châtelard Frontière. At **Chamonix Mont Blanc**, you have the option of taking the **Montenvers** rack railway up to Europe's biggest glacier (ETT table 397).*

MONTREUX

The best-preserved of the **Lake Geneva** resorts, Montreux is blessed with a mild climate, with palm trees, magnolias and cypresses along its 10-km waterside promenade – a lovely place for strolling. Smart hotels make the most of the views, while the rest of the town rises in tiers up the hillside. The effect is slightly spoiled by a garish casino.

RAIL In the centre of town.

i **Tourist Office**: r. du Théâtre 5, ☎(0848) 86 84 84 (www.montreux-vevey.com).

🏠 **Youth hostel (HI)**: Passage de l'Auberge 8, ☎(021) 963 49 34 (www.youthhostel.ch/montreux). Just 150 m from Territet rail station (2 km from Montreux station); 🚌 1 from Montreux's main station. Closed mid-Nov–mid-Feb.

DAY TRIPS FROM MONTREUX Take the narrow-gauge rack railway up to the 2042-m summit of **Rochers de la Naye** (55 mins, ETT table 569), or about a 3-hr walk. There are a couple of wonderfully sited restaurants at the top. Reached by No. 1 train or a pleasant walk of 3 km south from Montreux, **Château de Chillon** (www.chillon.ch) is an impressive and well-preserved medieval castle. Famously, the Reformationist Bonivard was chained to a pillar in the dungeon here for four years, an event immortalised in verse by Byron in *The Prisoner of Chillon*; the poem itself brought the castle to public notice, and it's become the most visited attraction in Switzerland.

LAUSANNE

See p345.

WHERE NEXT FROM MONTREUX?

An even more scenic option from the main route is to divert from Montreux to Zweisimmen, then to Spiez where you rejoin the main route (ETT tables 563, 566). This is truly one of Switzerland's great train rides; there are ordinary trains as well as Golden Pass observation trains.

GENEVA (GENÈVE, GENF)

With a dual role as a banking centre and a base for many international organisations, Geneva is a cosmopolitan, comfortably prosperous place, with promenades and parks beautifying the shores of **Lac Léman** (**Lake Geneva**). The River Rhône splits the city into two distinct sections, with the international area on the Rive Droite (right bank, to the north) and the compact old town on the Rive Gauche (left bank, to the south).

On Rive Droite (🚌 5/8/14/F/Z) is Pl. des Nations, near which most of the international organisations are grouped. The **Musée International de la Croix-Rouge**, av. de la Paix 17 (www.micr.org), is a stern building with high-tech exhibits tracing the history of the Red Cross and its Islamic offshoot, the Red Crescent. Profoundly moving, it covers natural disasters and man's inhumanity to man. Close by, the **Palais des Nations**, av. de la Paix 14, is home to the European headquarters of the United Nations, which replaced the League of Nations in 1945; there are guided tours. Between here and the lake is the lovely **Jardin Botanique**, a perfect place for a quiet stroll (once you're away from the main road) and featuring a rock garden, a deer and llama park and an aviary.

On Rive Gauche, south of the centre, the **Jardin Anglais**, on the waterfront, is famous for its **Horloge Fleurie** (floral clock), while the city's trade mark, the 140-m high fountain (**Jet d'Eau**), spouts from a nearby pier.

GETTING AROUND GENEVA

Geneva's sights are fairly scattered and a bit of route-planning is worthwhile. There is a good network of buses and one tram route. From May to Sept, **Compagnie Générale de Navigation sur le Lac Léman (CGN)** (ETT table 506) operate lake ferries from Quai du Mont-Blanc and Jardin Anglais, a 10-min walk straight ahead out of the station subway down R. des Alpes; ☎0848 81 18 48; www.cgn.ch. Tramway and little train tours through the city operate in season.

At the heart of the Old Town is the lively Place du Bourg-de-Four, Geneva's oldest square. Take rue de l'Hôtel de Ville to the 16th-century Hôtel de Ville (town hall), where the first Geneva Convention was signed in 1864. Adjacent is the former arsenal and the 12th-century **Maison Tavel**, Geneva's oldest house and now an evocative museum, with several period rooms and exhibits covering the 14th–19th centuries.

The original 12th–13th-century Gothic façade of the **Cathédrale de St-Pierre** has incongruous 18th-century additions. Most interior decorations were stripped out in the Reformation, but there are some frescos in the neo-Gothic Chapelle des Maccabées. Calvin preached here and his chair has been saved for posterity. The north tower, reached by a 157-step spiral staircase, offers a great view of the Old Town. Beneath the cathedral is the **Site Archéologique**, where catwalks allow you to see the result of extensive excavations, including a 4th-century baptistery and a 5th-century mosaic floor. Two blocks south, the vast marble **Musée d'Art et d'Histoire**, R. Charles-Galland 2 (www.ville-ge.ch/mah), has several rooms in period style, Hodler landscapes and the famous painting *The Fishing Miracle*, by Witz, which portrays Christ walking on the water – of Lake Geneva.

The 19th-century **Petit Palais**, Terrasse St-Victor 2, has an impressive array of modern art and includes works by Cézanne, Renoir and the Surrealists. Nearby, the **Collections Baur**, r. Munier-Romilly 8 (www.collections-baur.ch), contains some lovely Japanese and Chinese objets d'art, ranging from samurai swords to jade and delicate porcelain.

West of the cathedral, **Parc des Bastions** houses the university (founded by Calvin in 1559) and the vast **Monument de la Réformation** (erected in 1909), a 90-m-long wall featuring four central characters – Farel, Calvin, Bèze and Knox – each over 4.5 m high.

Gare de Cornavin is the main terminal, a 10-min walk north of the centre (🚌 5/8/9). **Gare Genève Eaux-Vives**, on the eastern edge of the city, is the terminal for SNCF trains from Annecy and St Gervais (30-min walk from Cornavin station or tram 16). **Metro Shopping**, a large complex that includes the *'Alimentation Automatique'*, is open Sun. The Aperto supermarket is open 0600–2200 every day.

✈ The airport has its own station (Genève Aéroport), with frequent trains into central Geneva taking 6 mins; services continue to all major cities in Switzerland.

i **Tourist Office**: r. du Mont-Blanc 18 (in main post office), ☎(022) 909 70 00 (www.geneve-tourisme.ch). Travellers' Information Office also at Gare de Cornavin, ☎(022) 732 00 90. For hotel reservations ☎(022) 909 70 20. *Genève Guide Pratique* and *Info-Jeunes* are free guides definitely worth picking up. *Genève Agenda* is the free weekly city entertainment guide.

There are numerous **internet cafés**, one in the main station, with prices typically around S Fr.5/hr. At **Laundrenet**, r. de la Servette 83, ☎(022) 734 83 83 (www.laundrenet.com), you can do your washing while you surf.

🏨 Most hotels are expensive, but there are plenty of hostels and private rooms. Ask at the Tourist Office for a copy of *Info-Jeunes*, which lists useful information. From 15 June to 15 Sept, the **CAR (Centre d'Accueil de Renseignements)**, located in a trailer in the pedestrian area opposite the station, offers accommodation booking and other advice to young people. There are a handful of hotels listed that are within walking distance of the centre, offering a room with shower from around S Fr.70, including **De la Cloche**, r. de la Cloche 6, ☎(022) 732 94 81 (www.geneva-hotel.ch/cloche), €. Just as cheap are the many university and religious institution lodgings on offer, including the **Cité Universitaire**, av. Miremont 46, ☎(022) 839 22 22, €, and during the summer holidays the **Residence Universitaire Internationale**, r. Rothschild 22, ☎(022) 716 02 02 (www.ruige.bizland.com). In addition there's the **Youth hostel (HI): Auberge de Jeunesse Genève**, r. Rothschild 30, ☎(022) 732 62 60 (www.genevahostel.ch), in the Paquis area close to the main rail station; the **City Hostel Geneva**, r. Ferrier 2, ☎(022) 901 15 00 (www.cityhostel.ch), is just around the corner. **Campsites: Camping Pointe-à-la-Bise**, Chemin de la Bise, Collonge-Bellerive, ☎(022) 752 12 96, fax (022) 752 37 67, open Apr–Oct, 7 km northeast, close to Lac Léman (🚍 E); **Camping d'Hermance**, r. du Nord 44, Hermance, ☎(022) 751 14 83, open Apr–Sept, 14 km northeast (🚍 E).

🍽 Because of its French influence and cosmopolitan nature, Geneva claims to be the culinary centre of Switzerland. The majority of places, however, cater for international business people. Good places to look for reasonably priced restaurants are on the r. de Lausanne (turn left out of Gare de Cornavin) and around place du Cirque (blvd Georges-Favon). Otherwise, try **Café du Centre**, place du Molard 5 (in the old town) or **Aux Halles en l'Ile**, place de l'Ile 1, where you can listen to jazz. Consult *Info-Jeunes* (see Accommodation above) for a list of university restaurants and for other cheap eats. **Parc des Bastions** is also great for picnics.

WHERE NEXT FROM GENEVA?

Trains cross the border to France, where you can take TGV services to **Paris** *and* **Mâcon** *(ETT table 341),* **Lyon** *(ETT table 345) and* **Marseille, Nice** *and* **Montpellier** *(ETT tables 350, 355, 360). Geneva to Paris takes 3 hrs 30 mins, Geneva to Lyon 1 hr 50 mins.*

Notes

Brunnen to Lugano requires a change at Bellinzona.

ROUTE DETAIL

Berne–Lucerne   ETT table 565

Type	Frequency	Typical journey time
Train	Every hr	1 hr

Lucerne–Brunnen   ETT table 550

Type	Frequency	Typical journey time
Train	Every 2 hrs	45 mins

Brunnen–Lugano   ETT table 550

Type	Frequency	Typical journey time
Train	Every hr	2 hrs 23 mins

Lugano–Milan   ETT table 550

Type	Frequency	Typical journey time
Train	11 daily	1 hr 2 mins – 1 hr 18 mins

KEY JOURNEYS

Berne–Milan   ETT table 560

Type	Frequency	Typical journey time
Train	3 daily	3 hrs

Lake Lucerne is the outstanding scenic feature of central Switzerland, an irregularly shaped body of water encompassed by flattish land around the dignified old resort of **Lucerne** itself, as well as picture-book snowy mountains dotted with wooden chalets to the south. Beyond the **Gothard Tunnel**, the landscape changes abruptly, as you enter the canton of **Ticino**, to an emerald-green valley dotted with rustic granite houses and tall campaniles as you head towards the Italian border. **Lugano** has the atmosphere of a smart Italian provincial town, and makes a good base for excursions.

BERNE (BERN)

See p353.

LUCERNE (LUZERN)

This resort straddles the River Reuss, itself crossed by quaintly roofed medieval footbridges, at the end of Lake Lucerne. Old-fashioned hotels attest to the town's long standing as a holiday place. There's a major music festival mid-Aug to Sept.

Old Lucerne is characterised by its many elaborately painted houses, its cobbled squares, its fountains, its Renaissance town hall by the Kornmarkt, and the two bridges over the Reuss. As you cross the 14th-century **Kapellbrücke**, a wooden-roofed footbridge that straggles crookedly over the river, you pass under a succession of 111 triangular-shaped paintings depicting local and national history. Halfway across, the bridge goes through a sturdy 13th-century octagonal **Water Tower**, which has undergone several changes of function over the centuries, including use as a prison. A little further down the river is the other medieval roofed bridge, the **Spreuerbrücke**, also lined with 17th-century paintings, in this case depicting the macabre Dance of Death. Near the south end of Kapellbrücke, the **Jesuit Church** is plain from the outside, but has a gorgeous pink-and-white baroque interior dating from 1677. **Nolliturm**, near the north end of Spreuerbrücke, is a fortified gate at one end of a well-preserved stretch of **Musegg Wall**, the old fortifications. You can follow this all the way (and climb three of its nine surviving towers) as it curves east to end just off Löwenpl.

The graceful twin-spired **Hofkirche** (Cathedral), off Schweizerhofquai, has an organ with 4950 pipes and a 10-ton bell. The city's mascot, the **Löwendenkmal** (Lion Memorial), Löwenstr., is a massive but movingly portrayed dying lion carved in the cliff-side, commemorating the Swiss Guards massacred at the Tuileries in Paris during the French Revolution. Nearby is the **Gletschergarten** (Glacier Garden), Denkmalstr. 4, a bed of smooth rocks pitted with holes, created by glacial erosion. There's an ingenious mirror-maze here too.

Switzerland

Anyone with an interest in transport in all its guises and vintages should make for the **Verkehrshaus** (Swiss Transport Museum), Lidostr. 5 (www.verkehrshaus.ch), 2 km east of town (near the campsite), reached by a pleasant lakeside walk (or 🚌 6/8); it's one of Europe's leading museums on the theme, with exhibits covering locos, vintage cycles, space rockets and more, plus an IMAX movie theatre (with a huge, almost vertigo-inducing screen), a 360-degree cinema.

🚆 On the south bank of the River Reuss, where it meets Lake Lucerne, a few mins' walk over the bridge to the old town. In the basement is the '24-hr shopping' automat, for emergency rations.

ℹ️ **Tourist Office**: Zentralstr. 5 (in station); ☎ (041) 227 17 17 (www.luzern.com). Also in the station basement. Accommodation booking service. The *Luzern City Guide* is free and full of useful information. Ask about the **LucerneCard**.

🛏️ Lucerne is a popular tourist destination, so advance booking is advisable for its limited range of cheap options, especially in summer; some of the 19th-century hotels surrounding the old town can be noisy. The **Tourist Hotel**, St Karliquai 12, ☎ (041) 410 24 74, €€ (www.touristhotel.ch), has singles from S Fr.85–105 and twins from S Fr.120–170. The **Pickwick**, Rathausquai 6, ☎ (041) 410 59 27 (www.hotel pickwick.ch), has singles for around S Fr.85–95 and twins for around S Fr.110–125. **Backpackers Lucerne**, Alpenquai 42, ☎ (041) 360 04 20 (www.backpackerslucerne.ch), €, offers student-style accommodation by the south shore of the lake (12-min walk from the station). **Youth hostel (HI)**: Am Rotsee, Sedelstr. 12, ☎ (041) 420 88 00 (www.youthhostel.ch/luzern), is situated by the lake northwest of town (🚌 18 to Jugendherberge or 🚌 19 to Gopplismoosweg). **Campsite**: **Camping International Lido**, Lidostr. 19; ☎ (041) 370 21 46 (luzern@camping-international.ch) (🚌 6/8/24 to Verkehrshaus), on the north shore of the lake.

🍽️ There are reasonably priced restaurants and cafés all round Lucerne's many squares and waterside promenades. The town's speciality is *Kügelipasteti*, a large meat and mushroom vol-au-vent covered in rich sauce.

DAY TRIPS FROM LUCERNE You can get to most of the settlements around Lake Lucerne, which covers 114 square km, by regular local boat services, as well as excursion cruises in summer;

contact **Schifffahrtgesellschaft Vierwaldstättersee**, Werftestr. 5, ☎(041) 367 67 67 (www.lakelucerne.ch), or book through the Tourist Office. These boats combine nicely with walks as well as rack railway and cable car trips. From **Alpnachstad** (reached by steamer), south of Lucerne, take the world's steepest rack railway (climbing a 48% gradient) up **Mt Pilatus** (2132 m). Supposedly haunted by the spirit of Pontius Pilate, the summit is also accessible by cable car from **Kriens** (🚋 1), on the southern outskirts of Lucerne – giving scope for a circular tour of the mountain. From Vitznau, on the eastern shore, Europe's oldest rack railway ascends **Mt Rigi** (1800 m), where the summit view from **Rigi-Kulm** at sunrise (including the Jungfrau and Titlis) has attracted generations of tourists, including Victor Hugo. There's also a cable car from the sunny waterside resort of **Weggis**; if you prefer to walk, there's a 4-hr route from Weggis, or you can take the cable car up from **Küssnacht** to within a 2-hr hike of the summit. At **Engelberg**, 16 km south of the lake and 1 hr from Lucerne by train (hourly; ETT table 552), the huge **Rotair**, the world's first rotating cable car, gives an unparalleled view of the permanently snow-capped **Mt Titlis** (3020 m).

BRUNNEN

You may like to pause here to enjoy the site, at the meeting of **lakes Uri** and **Lucerne**. The bustling resort is well set-up for most watersports, as well as walking on Lake Uri's shores. Brunnen can claim to be the cradle of the nation's history. Here the forest states of Unterwalden, Uri and Schwyz were sworn together as the Confederation in a declaration on 1 Aug 1291 in Rütli Meadow by the lake, an event immortalised in the legend of William Tell as told by Schiller in 1804; 1 Aug is Swiss National Day, celebrated nationwide with bonfires lit on high spots and the **Rütli Meadow** floodlit. The **Swiss Way** is a 35-km walkers' route round the lake, divided into 26 sections; each section represents a canton or half-canton, with the length of each determined by the proportionate populations of each canton.

🚉 Close to the town centre.

ℹ️ **Tourist Office**: Bahnhofstr. 15, ☎(041) 825 00 40 (www.brunnentourismus.ch).

LUGANO

Lugano, the largest town in the Italian-speaking canton of Ticino, is a handsome, sophisticated resort of Lombardic arcades and piazzas beside **Lake Lugano**. It climbs the hillside around a horseshoe bay surrounded by verdant mountains, so is an ideal base for walking as well as watersports. The lakeside promenade is a popular place to stroll or roller-blade in July and Aug, when vehicles are banned from it. At its eastern end is the **Parco Civico** (Municipal Park), the pleasant setting for summer concerts and graced with fountains, statues and trees. Swimmers can head for the lido (to the east of the river), with its pool and sandy beaches. Funiculars climb the two mountains guarding the bay: up **Monte Brè** (930 m) from **Cassarate** and up **San Salvatore** (912 m) from **Paradiso**, both 20-min walks from the centre or take 🚋 1.

THE ITALIAN LAKES

Locarno on **Lake Maggiore** is 1 hr 10 mins by train from Lugano (change at Bellinzona; ETT table 550). **Youth hostel (HI)**: via Varenna 18, ☎ (091) 756 15 00 (www.youthhostel.ch/locarno). From the town, the scenic **Centovalli** (Hundred Valleys) route runs to **Domodossola** in Italy (ETT table 528). The 53-km line clings to dramatic hillsides, soars across dozens of steep valleys (hence its name) over spectacular bridges and viaducts to **Santa Maria Maggiore**. Afterwards, continue exploring Switzerland via the major rail junction at **Brig**, 42 km north of Domodossola through the **Simplon Tunnel**. Northeast of Lugano, just beyond Gandria, is the Mediterranean-flavoured **Menaggio**. In Italy, this Lake Como town provides lovely views over the water. To get to the other bank, there are frequent trains from Lugano to Como (about 35 mins). Continuing on the Italian side, the train skirts the shore, providing views of Italian villages on both sides of the lake.

The arcaded Via Nassa is the main pedestrianised shopping street, where you can take your pick of such Swiss specialities as expensive wristwatches or chocolate in all its national varieties. There's more worthwhile art in **Thyssen-Bornemisza**, a collection of 19th- and 20th-century paintings and watercolours housed in the **Villa Favorita**, Riviera 14 (Fri–Sun, Easter–Oct), while the **Cantonal Art Museum**, Via Canova 10 (www.museo-cantonale-arte.ch), also has many 20th-century works.

🚉 At the top of the town. From it a funicular descends to the middle (otherwise a 6-min walk), halfway down to the lake.

ℹ️ **Tourist Office**: Palazzo Civico, Riva Albertolli, ☎ (091) 913 32 32 (www.lugano-tourism.ch); on the lakeside opposite the central landing stage. Accommodation booking service.

🛏 Try the **Rosa**, v. Landriani 2–4, ☎ (091) 922 92 86 (www.albergorosa.ch), S Fr.72–104 singles, S Fr.124–164 twins. **Youth hostel (HI)**: Lugano-Savosa, v. Cantonale 13, Savosa, ☎ (091) 966 27 28 (www.youthhostel.ch/lugano; 🚌 5 from station to Crocifisso then a 3-min walk). Generally, **Paradiso** (the southern part of Lugano) is slightly better value.

🍴 There are several restaurants along the lakeside, as well as around the main square, the Piazza Riforma.

MILAN (MILANO)

See p430.

WHERE NEXT?

See Milan (p430) for a selection of routes.

Austria

Sharing borders with Germany, Switzerland, Liechtenstein, Italy, the Czech Republic, Slovakia, Slovenia and Hungary, **Austria** feels very much at the centre of Europe. Its capital, **Vienna**, a stately affair of boulevards, parks and palaces, has a poignant air of once being at the centre of bigger things, but it is at the same time a lively, cosmopolitan city, unfairly hampered with a frumpy reputation. The rest of the country is quite different. **Salzburg**, the city indelibly associated with Mozart (though he hated the place), has bags of charm with its baroque squares. The Alps, which dominate the map of Austria, cover much of the country, and have enough diversity to make them well worth exploring, with gentler but extremely beautiful lakeland landscapes like the Salzkammergut interspersed with the taller peaks. Lush green Alpine meadows, steep-roofed chalets with heavy wooden balconies full of geraniums, and onion-domed churches are all typically Austrian.

Tyrol and **Vorarlberg**, in western Austria, include the country's highest mountains and are dramatic indeed, with villages to match; Vorarlberg is also a renowned centre for modern architecture. **Innsbruck** and **Kitzbühel** are among the larger places worth seeing. The **Salzkammergut** is the obvious upland region to venture into from Salzburg, where pleasant resorts lie scattered beside lakes under miniature limestone mountains. Further south are the lesser-known areas of **Carinthia**, with more lake resorts, and the peaks of **Styria**, not quite as breathtaking as the Tyrol but very fine in their own right.

ACCOMMODATION

Hotels are graded on the usual five-star system; even one-star establishments can be pricey, though standards of cleanliness and comfort are usually high even in the most Spartan places. *Gasthaus/Gasthof* indicates an **inn** and *Frühstückspension* a **bed and breakfast** place. The best value is usually a **private room** (look for signs or check with local tourist offices, who have lists), but many require stays of several nights and some charge extra for short stays. *Jugendherberge* is the word for a **youth hostel**; there are nearly 100, few of them are self-catering but most serve meals. They cost around €11.60–26. For details of hostels contact the **Österreichischer Jugendherbergsverband (ÖJHV)**, 📞(01) 533 5353 (www.oejhv.or.at), or **Österreichisches Jugendherbergs-werk (ÖJHW)**, 📞(01) 533 1833 (www.jungehotels.at). In summer, some universities let rooms.

ESSENTIALS

Population 8.0m **Capital** Vienna (Wien) **Time Zone** Winter GMT+1, summer GMT+2.

CLIMATE

Moderate Continental climate. Warm summer; high winter snowfall.

CURRENCY

Euro (€). 1 Euro = 100 cents = £0.89 = $1.46.

EMBASSIES AND CONSULATES IN VIENNA

Aus: Mattiellistr. 2–4, ☎(01) 506 740. **Ire**: Rotenturmstr. 16–18, ☎(01) 715 4246. **NZ**: Salesianerg. 15/3, ☎(01) 318 8505. **SA**: Sandg. 33, ☎(01) 320 6493. **UK**: Jaursg. 12, ☎(01) 716 130. **USA**: Boltzmanng. 16, ☎(01) 313 390.

LANGUAGE

German. English is widely spoken in tourist areas.

OPENING HOURS

Banks: mostly Mon, Tues, Wed, Fri 0800–1230 and 1330–1500, Thur 0800–1230 and 1330–1730. **Shops**: Mon–Fri 0800–1830 (some closing for a 1- or 2-hr lunch), Sat 0800–1700. **Museums**: check locally.

POST OFFICES

Indicated by golden horn symbol; all handle poste restante (postlagernde Briefe). Open mostly Mon–Fri 0800–1200 and 1400–1800. Main and station post offices in larger cities open 24 hrs. Stamps (Briefmarke) also sold at Tabak/Trafik shops.

PUBLIC HOLIDAYS

1, 6 Jan; Easter Mon; 1 May; Ascension Day; Whit Mon; Corpus Christi; 15 Aug; 26 Oct; 1 Nov; 8, 25, 26 Dec.

PUBLIC TRANSPORT

Long-distance: bus system run by Bahnbus and Postbus; usually based by rail stations/post offices. City transport: tickets cheaper from Tabak/Trafik booths; taxis: metered; extra charges for luggage (fixed charges in smaller towns).

RAIL PASSES

IR, EP, European East valid (see pp27–34). Einfach-Raus-Ticket: one-day's 2nd class travel on regional trains for groups of 2–5 people, €28 (not before 0900 Mon–Fri.) 1-Plus Ticket: 2–5 persons; journey over 101 km; 25–40% discount. Gruppenticket: six or more persons; discounts of 30–40%. Day tickets and 72-hr tickets in Vienna available.

RAIL TRAVEL

Website: www.oebb.at. Run by Österreichische Bundesbahnen (ÖBB). Mostly electrified; fast and reliable, with EC/IC trains every 1–2 hrs. Other fast trains: RJ (Railjet – Austrian high-speed train); ICE (German high-speed train); D (ordinary express train); REX (semi-fast regional train). Regional trains connect with fast services. Most overnight trains have sleeping cars (up to three berths) and couchettes (four/six berths), plus 2nd-class seats. Seat reservations available on long-distance trains. Most stations have left-luggage facilities.

TELEPHONES

Cheapest to phone long distance 2000–0600 and public holidays. Dial in: ☎+43 and omit the initial 0 of the area code. Outgoing: ☎00 + country code. International enquiries and operator: ☎11 88 77. National enquiries/operator: ☎1611. Police: ☎133. Fire: ☎122. Ambulance: ☎144.

TIPPING

Hotels, restaurants, cafés and bars: service charge of 10–15%, but tip of around 10% still expected. Taxis 10%.

Austria

TOURIST INFORMATION

Website: www.austria-tourism.at. Staff invariably speak some English. Opening times vary widely, particularly restricted at weekends in smaller places. Look for green 'i' sign; usually called a *Fremdenverkehrsbüro*.

TYPICAL COSTS

Accommodation: €15–22 in a hostel, €25–35 in a pension. Beer in a bar: €2.20–3.50; coffee: €2–4. Basic meal: €10–16. Internet access/hour: €1.50–3 (but often available free).

VISAS

An EU National Identity Card or passport is sufficient. Visas are not needed by citizens of Australia, Canada, New Zealand or the USA.

GUEST CARDS

Several resorts issue a guest card to visitors in higher quality accommodation. The cards entitle holders to anything from free escorted mountain hikes to discounts for ferries or museums. The cards are generally issued by *Gasthofs* or hotels.

Camping is popular and there are lots of sites, mostly very clean and well run, but pricey. Many sites are open summer only. In Alpine areas, there are also **refuge huts** – details from the local Tourist Office. For all accommodation it is advisable to book ahead for July, Aug, Christmas and Easter.

FOOD AND DRINK

Food tends towards the hearty, with wholesome soups and meat-dominated main courses (famously *Wiener Schnitzel* – a thin slice of veal or pork fried in egg and breadcrumbs), while *Goulasch* (of Hungarian origin) and dumplings are also prevalent. Cakes may be sinfully cream-laden, high in calories, but are rarely sickly; *Apfelstrudel* is the best option for those watching their waistlines. A filling snack, sold by most butchers, is *Wurstsemmel* – slices of sausage with a bread roll.

The Austrian pattern is: breakfast – which can be an elaborate affair, with hams, cheeses and boiled eggs as well as rolls and jam – lunch (1200–1400), coffee and cake (*Kaffee und Kuchen*) mid-afternoon, then dinner (1800–2200). Beer and wine are almost equally popular: Austrian *Märzenbier* is sweeter and darker than lager, but Austrian wine is good – notably Grüner Veltliner (a white wine), but increasingly the reds too – and there are numerous varieties of *Schnapps*. A service charge of 10–15% is included in restaurant bills. It is the custom to leave a further 10% if you're happy with the service.

Drinks in bars and clubs cost more than in places where food is served.

Not for nothing does Austria's capital regularly top surveys to find Europe's most livable city, for Vienna is an enviably civilised place, safe and manageable yet rarely dull. Long famous as one of the world's great music centres – the waltz was born here in 1820 and virtually every great musician of the classical period is linked with the city – these days it wears a more open, cosmopolitan and at times even trendy face than its slightly stuffy image would suggest. The grandiose reminders of the vanished Habsburg empire are everywhere, but often reworked in surprising and innovative ways – at street level Vienna may still be very historic, but look up and you'll often see a daring modern loft extension tagged onto some imperial edifice. Around 100 years ago Vienna became a leading architectural exponent of *Jugendstil* – the Austrian Art Nouveau – and gorgeous examples still dot the city. The *Aldstadt*, or historic core, is traffic-calmed if not entirely pedestrianised, with cobbled streets, old merchants' houses, spacious gardens and hundreds of atmospheric places to eat and drink, though some of the most charming – and least touristy – lie in the districts just beyond the ring. A visit to one of the classic **coffee houses** for coffee and home-made cake is *de rigueur*. Most sights are on or inside the famous **Ringstrasse**, which encircles the city centre. For architectural splendours of the late 19th century, take trams 1 or 2, passing the neo-Gothic **Rathaus** (City Hall), **Burgtheater**, **Parliament** and **Staatsoper**.

ARRIVAL AND DEPARTURE

🚆 Vienna has a new main station under construction on the site of the Südbahnhof. To be called **Hauptbahnhof**, it is due to open in 2012/13. In the meantime, trains to and from the south and east serve **Wien Meidling**, linked to the centre by frequent S-Bahn trains, whilst trains to Bratislava leave from temporary platforms called Südbahnhof (Ostbahn). The west, also Germany, Switzerland and Hungary, is served by the **Westbahnhof**, Europapl., whilst the area northwest of Vienna is served by **Franz-Josefs-Bahnhof**, Julius-Tandler-Pl. All stations are linked by tram or underground services and have good facilities. Information: ☎(01) 1717 (24 hrs)

✈ **Vienna International Airport** (www.viennaairport.com) is 19 km southeast of the city at Schwechat. Flight information, ☎(01) 7007 22233 (24 hrs). Express bus transfers (Vienna Airport Lines: ☎(01) 7007 32300) run from the airport to City Air Terminal (U-Bahn and S-Bahn station: Landstrasse/Wien Mitte) and back and to Westbahnhof and Südbahnhof every 30 mins 0500–2400 (journey time 20 mins). There are also S-Bahn trains to Wien Mitte. Vienna airport connections, ETT table 979. A non-stop City Airport Train (CAT) service runs to/from Wien Mitte every 30 mins (journey time 16 mins, ETT table 979).

INFORMATION

Pick up the free city map from the Tourist Office: **Vienna Tourist Board**, Albertinapl. (corner of

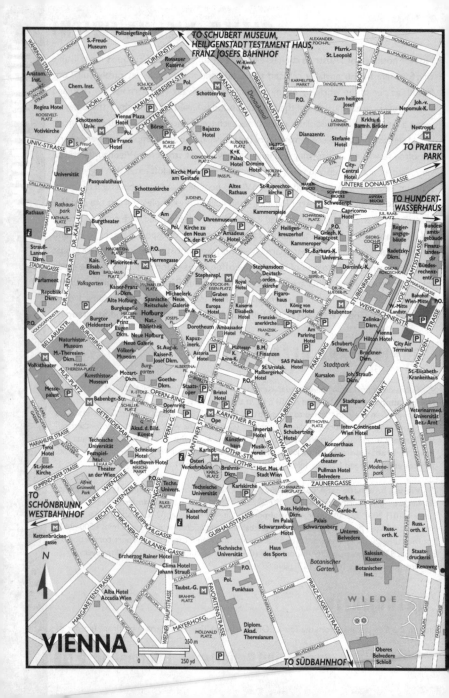

Maysedergasse), ☎(01) 24 555 (www.info.wien.at), the *Vienna Scene* for an overview of the city and the monthly *Programm*, which lists events for that month. Information and accommodation bureaux are also at Westbahnhof, Südbahnhof and Schwechat Airport. In addition, visit **wienXtra jugendinfo (youth information)**, Babenbergerstr. 1 (U2 Babenbergerstrasse and trams 1, 2, D); Mon–Sat 1200–1900, ☎(01) 1799 (www.wienxtra.at) for brochures *time4vienna* and *Camping & Youth Hostels* and information on the 'alternative' Vienna.

Finding **internet access** in Vienna poses no problem at all – over 120 free Wi-Fi hotspots across the city should do the trick: **Aera**, Gonzagagasse 11 (www.aera.at); **Pickwick's**, Marc-Aurel-Strasse 10 (www.pickwicks.at); **Café Prückel**, Stubenring 24 (www.prueckl.at) and **Wirtshaus Zum Leupold** (www.leupold.at) are just a few. The **central post office**, Fleischmarkt 19, has poste restante facilities (open 24 hrs) and money exchange. **To phone Vienna** from abroad, ☎00 (or 011 from the US or Canada) +43 (Austria) +1 (Vienna) + number; to phone the city from elsewhere in Austria: ☎01 + number.

PUBLIC TRANSPORT

The **U-Bahn** has five lines, 0500–2400. **Trams:** run on 33 radial routes as well as in both directions around the Ringstr., 0500–2400. **Buses:** include 22 night routes (0030–0430), marked by a green N symbol. **Taxis**: not cheap; hail one with a *'frei'* sign, or ☎(01) 31 300, (01) 40 100, (01) 60 160 or (01) 81 400. **Cycling**: fun, as the city is largely flat with many marked paths. The Tourist Office has a free booklet (*Tipps für Radfahrer*) with route maps. Hire bikes from stations: **Westbahnhof**, **Wien Nord** and **Südbahnhof**; discount with same-day rail ticket. **Pedal Power** deliver bikes to your hotel (Mar–Sept), ☎(01) 729 7234, www.pedalpower.at.

TICKETS

U-Bahn (underground trains), **S-Bahn** (suburban trains) inside city limits, **trams** and **buses** all use the same tickets, with transfers allowed. Single tickets, €1.80 or €2.20 if bought on board, are sold in blocks of four (under-sixs travel free, under-15s travel free on Sundays, public holidays and school holidays; photo ID required). You can get a 24-hour (€5.70) or 72-hour (€13.60) **rover ticket**; there are also 8-day **network tickets** (€28.80, which can be used by several people travelling together). Just before travelling, validate (time-stamp) the ticket. Another option is the **Wien-Karte** (Vienna Card €18.50, from hotels, Vienna Transport ticket offices and Tourist Offices), valid for 72 hrs' transport, plus four days' discounts on museums, sights, shops, restaurants, concert and theatre tickets and so on.

ACCOMMODATION

There are lots of options, and takers, so book ahead for May–Oct. Email hotel booking service: info@wien.info.at. Expect to pay €40–50 per person for a cheap hotel, including breakfast. Moderately priced hotels and guesthouses include **Pension Dr Geissler**, Postgasse 14, ☎(01) 533 2803 (www.hotelpension.at), €€; some cheaper rooms with shared facilities are available at the very central **Hotel Austria**, Am Fleischmarkt 20, ☎(01) 51 523 (www.hotelaustria-wien.at), €€. Southwest of the cathedral is **Pension Quisisana**, Windmühlgasse 6, ☎(01) 587 3341, (www.quisisana.at), €€. Close to the new

Austria

Museumsquartier, **Pension Wild**, Lange Gasse 10, ☎(01) 406 5174 (www.pension-wild.com), €€, has great rooms and is both backpacker- and gay-friendly.

Youth hostels (HI): **Jugendherberge Wien-Myrthengasse**, Myrthengasse 7, ☎(01) 523 6316 (www.jugendherberge.at), U6 to Burggasse or U3 to Neubaugasse; **Jugendgästehaus Wien-Brigittenau**, Friedrich-Engels-Pl. 24, ☎(01) 3328 2940 (jgh.1200wien@chello.at), north of centre, U6 to Handelskai, 500m; **Jugendgästehaus Hütteldorf-Hacking**, Schlossberggasse 8, ☎(01) 877 1501 (www.hostel.at/jgh), Hütteldorf U-Bahn station 500 m; **Hostel Schlossherberge**, Savoyenstr. 2, ☎(01) 481 0300 (www.hostel.at/shb), U3 to Ottakring then ☒ 46b/146b to Schlosshotel Wilhelminenberg. **Non-HI: Hostel Ruthensteiner**, Robert-Hamerlinggasse 24, ☎(01) 893 4202 (www.hostelruthensteiner.com); **Wombat's City Hostel**, Mariahilferstr. 137, ☎(01) 897 2336 (www.wombats.eu), near Westbahnhof. **Camping**: **Aktiv Camping Neue Donau**, Am Kleehäufel 119, ☎(01) 202 4010 (www.wiencamping.at) (early Apr–mid-Sept) is across the Danube Canal.

FOOD AND DRINK

Vienna has given the gastronomic world delicious *Wiener Schnitzel* (thin escalope of pork or veal in breadcrumbs), heavy *Kaiserschmarrn*, the dessert of emperors, and *Sachertorte*, a bitter chocolate cake. However, the café is the great Viennese culinary institution, open from breakfast until late serving everything from coffee to light meals and more substantial fare, typically with a heavily curtained door to keep out the winter chill and a selection of newspapers to read – the more intellectual the café, the better the selection. Authentic examples include the wonderfully shabby **Jelinek**, Otto Bauer Gasse 5, and the bustling **Hummel**, Josefstädterstr. 66. *Café Konditoreien* (cake shops/cafés) are temples to Austria's cake-making genius; **Demel**, Kohlmarkt 14. by the Hofburg is perhaps the most famous, though these days it's very touristy. In summer, the *Heurige* (wine taverns) of Grinzing (tram 38) on the city's northwestern fringe are tempting, while at any time of year the multicultural offerings of the Naschmarkt's food stalls offer superb picnic pickings. For late night cravings, *Würstelstände* (hot-dog stalls) are the best bet. Veggies will treasure **Maschu, Maschu**, Neubaugasse 20, for its excellent and filling falafel.

TOURS

Bus tours of the city are operated by several companies, including **Vienna Sightseeing Tours**, ☎(01) 7124 6830, (www.viennasightseeing.at), whose hop-on, hop-off multilingual service stops at 15 places of interest; half-hourly or hourly 1000–1700. For a 1 hr 15-min boat trip on the River Danube/Danube Canal, start from Schwedenpl. (May–Oct; **DDSG-Blue Danube**, ☎(01) 588 800 (www.ddsg-blue-danube.at).

HIGHLIGHTS

The Tourist Office runs specialist walking tours (on such themes as Art Nouveau and food and drink (www.wienguide.at); reduction for holders of Vienna Cards, but finding your own way around the compact city centre is easy.

An ornately carved spire soars over **Stephansdom** (St Stephen's Cathedral), U1/3 to Stephanspl., Austria's greatest Gothic building. Its colourful roof, tiled in jazzy stripes, is best seen floodlit at night. The magnificent 14th-century **Südturm** (South Tower), known locally as the *Steffl*, is climbed by 343 steps for a terrific city view, while a lift whisks you up the (considerably lower) North Tower, the **Pummerin**. Interior highlights include the Albertine Choir, the pulpit and organ loft by Anton Pilgrim, and the tomb of Friedrich III.

The **Hofburg**, the Habsburgs' winter residence until 1918, occupies a prime spot on the edge of the Ring overlooking formal gardens. It comprises 18 wings, 54 stairways and 2600 rooms, and now houses several museums. The **Imperial Apartments** have been preserved as they were in Emperor Franz Josef I's time, while the **Schatzkammer** (Treasury) displays the crown of the Holy Roman Empire.

The **Burgkapelle** is the chapel where the **Vienna Boys' Choir** sing Mass on Sun morning (Sept–June) at 0915 (charge for sitting, standing room free but you need to queue by 0830; bookings ☎(01) 533 9927), you must book weeks in advance or try for a last-minute ticket at the Burgkappelle box office. For afternoon concerts at the **Musikverein**, ☎(01) 505 8190 (tickets@musikverein.at).

> **SPANISH RIDING SCHOOL**
> The famous Lipizzaner horses perform on Sun and some Thurs, Fris and Sats (late Feb–June and late Aug–Oct and Dec; U1/3: Stephansplatz).
> **Tickets** can be bought from **Spanische Hofreitschule**, Hofburg, Michaelerplatz 1, A-1010 Vienna, ☎(01) 5339 0310, (www.srs.at). Or queue at the door (gate 2) of the **Redoute**, Josefspl., to see 'morning training' with music, usually Tues–Sat 1000–1200 (late-Feb–June and late Aug–Oct and Dec).

Vienna has roughly 100 museums (most open Tue–Sun, 1000–1800; some open late on Thur). The major gallery, the **Kunsthistorisches Museum** (Museum of Fine Arts), Maria-Theresien-Platz 1 (www.khm.at), is based on the Habsburgs' collection. Nearby is the impressive **Museumsquartier**, Museumsplatz 1 (www.museumsquartier.at), an imaginative conversion of the former imperial stables into a massive cultural complex, with two important museums of modern art, the **Leopold Museum** (www.leopoldmuseum.org) for classic modern Austrian and the **MMK** (Museum Moderner Kunst; www.mumok.at) for contemporary art. The courtyard is a favourite place for young people to hang out in fine weather. The superb 18th-century baroque **Belvedere Palace**, Prinz-Eugen-Str. 27 (www.belvedere.at), has two galleries and delightful gardens; its **Österreichische Galerie** (Austrian Gallery) contains works by Klimt, Schiele and 19th-century artists. One of the most enjoyable of Vienna's museums is the **Naturhistoriches Museum** (Natural History Museum), opposite the Kunsthistorisches Museum (www.nhm-wien.ac.at). The archaeology galleries have fascinating displays from prehistoric Hallstatt culture, including a saltminer's rucksack that looks as if it's still serviceable.

The **Sigmund Freud Museum**, Berggasse 19, (www.freud-museum.at; U2/U4 to Schottenring, trams D/36/38/40/41/42 to Schottentor), is where the great psychoanalyst lived and worked from 1891 until his expulsion by the Nazis in 1938.

Austria

A leaflet from the Tourist Office highlights interesting 20th-century architecture, including the anarchic **Hundertwasserhaus** (Lowengasse/Kegelgasse), named after the painter-architect who redesigned this municipal housing estate in 1985, transforming it into an astonishing riot of colours and textures. The **Secession**, Friedrichstr. 12 (www.secession.at), is a temple to the gorgeous Art Nouveau style that flourished in Vienna around 1900, with a frieze by Klimt. The legendary **Prater Park** (U1 to Praterstern, tram O/5) was originally the imperial hunting grounds. Riding the giant old ferris wheel (famously filmed in the movie *The Third Man*) provides a great view, but take care in the park at night. Vienna has several *Jugendstil* baths, such as **Amalienbad**, Reumannpl. 23 (baths, saunas, steam rooms, swimming pools). Further out, **Schloss Schönbrunn**, Schönbrunner Schlosstr. (www.schoenbrunn.at; U4 to Schönbrunn, trams 10/58/60), is the former Habsburg summer residence, with fabulously baroque decoration and extensive gardens (audio-guided tours €12.90).

SHOPPING

Kärntnerstr. is the busiest shopping street and, together with Graben, is the place to promenade. The nearby **Ringstrassen Galerien**, Kärtner Ring 5–7 (www.ringstrassen-galerien.at), is a smart modern mall, open until 1900 (1800 Sat). Department stores are in Mariahilferstr., outside the Ring leading to the Westbahnhof. Flea market: **Flohmarkt**, U4: Wienzeile/Kettenbrückengasse, by station, open Sat (except public holidays) 0630–1600.

To avoid high agency commissions, apply for tickets to **Österreichische Bundestheater**, A-1010 Wien, Hanuschgasse 3, ☎(01) 513 1513, www.bundestheater.at, at least three weeks in advance; standing tickets sold 1 hr before the performance.

NIGHT-TIME AND EVENTS

Programm (monthly), listing all entertainment except cinemas (see newspapers), is free from Tourist Offices. Festivals abound: the May–June festival features classical music and jazz, while the **Danube Island Festival** (June) is an open-air event with rock, pop and fireworks. In July–Aug, the **Mozart in Schönbrunn** festival features open-air concerts in front of the Roman ruins. In July–Aug, there's the free **Festival of Music Films**, shown on a giant screen in Rathauspl., which hosts a great **Christmas market** from mid-Nov to Christmas. For cheap drinks, the **'Bermuda Triangle'** (so called because people go into it and disappear) is an area of lively bars, discos and pubs around Ruprechtspl., particularly Judengasse and Sterngasse. The **Staatsoper** (Vienna State Opera), Opernring 2 (www.staatsoper.at), stages operas Sept–June. The **Volksoper**, Währingerstr. 78 (www.volksoper.at), offers operettas and musicals. The **Vienna Philharmonic Orchestra** can be heard in concerts at the **Musikverein**, Bösendorferstr. 12 (www.musikverein.at), and first-class musicians give concerts there and at the **Konzerthaus** (http://konzerthaus.at) throughout the year.

ROUTE DETAIL

Innsbruck–Kitzbühel ETT table 960

Type	Frequency	Typical journey time
Train	1–2 per hr	1 hr 20 mins

Kitzbühel–Salzburg ETT table 960

Type	Frequency	Typical journey time
Train	Every 1–2 hrs	2 hrs 31 mins

Salzburg–Linz ETT table 950

Type	Frequency	Typical journey time
Train	2 per hr	1 hr 18 mins

Linz–Vienna ETT table 950

Type	Frequency	Typical journey time
Train	2–3 per hr	1 hr 30 mins

KEY JOURNEYS

Zürich–Innsbruck ETT table 86

Type	Frequency	Typical journey time
Train	4 daily	3 hrs 26 mins

Innsbruck–Salzburg ETT table 951

Type	Frequency	Typical journey time
Train	Every 1–2 hrs	1 hr 50 mins

Salzburg–Vienna ETT table 950

Type	Frequency	Typical journey time
Train	2 per hr	2 hrs 39 mins

Austria

Austria's elongated shape permits few long journeys within its borders, but this is one well worth seeking out, making a trans-Alpine experience from the heart of the Tyrol to Salzburg, famed as Mozart's birthplace, before ending up at the Austrian capital (see p371). The most scenic route between Salzburg and Linz is via Bischofshofen and Selzthal (ETT tables 960, 975).

INNSBRUCK

The 800-year-old Tyrolean capital on the River Inn is a bustling, amiable city overlooked by the Karwendel mountains to the north and the Patscherkofel mountains to the south – making it an excellent base for walks and other activities in the Alps (guided hikes start daily June–Oct, meeting 0845 at the Congress Hall; free with Club Innsbruck Card, which you get when you stay overnight anywhere in Innsbruck – not to be confused with the Innsbruck Card). The Hungerburgbahn cog railway, which ascends from the Alpenzoo on the edge of the city on to the Hungerburg plateau – a superb place for walks and views – opened in 2007, following the earlier rebuild of the Nordkettenbahn, which takes visitors from the Congress Centre up onto the Hafelekar.

The **Altstadt** is dotted with 15th- and 16th-century buildings, many with elaborate stucco decorations and traditional convex windows to catch extra light on the narrow streets. Its most famous sight is the 15th-century **Goldenes Dachl**, Herzog-Friedrich-Str. 15 (www.goldenes-dachl.at), a roof of 2738 gilded copper tiles covering a balcony, which Emperor Maximilian I (the subject of an exhibition inside) added in 1500 to the **Neuhof**, the residence of the Tyrolean princes. The **Stadtturm** (City Tower) opposite the balcony offers views across the rooftops to the mountains. Nearby is the **Dom zu St Jakob**, a striking baroque cathedral.

The **Hofburg** (Imperial Palace), Rennweg (www.hofburg-innsbruck.at), has a sumptuous ballroom lined with portraits of Empress Maria Theresa's family, who also feature in 28 larger-than-life bronze statues on Emperor Maximilian's grand tomb in the 16th-century **Hofkirche**, the Court Church. Wander round the **Hofgarten** (Court Gardens). The neighbouring **Tiroler Volkskunst Museum** (www.tiroler-landesmuseum.at) concentrates on Tyrolean culture, displaying traditional costumes and wood-panelled rooms. The **Tiroler Ferdinandeum**, Museumstr. 15 (closed Mon), is more diverse, with beautiful stained glass, medieval altars and works by Cranach and Rembrandt.

INNSBRUCK CARD
All-inclusive **Innsbruck Card**, covering local transport (including some cable cars) and entrance to 36 museums and attractions plus reductions on tours and other attractions; valid 24, 48 or 72 hours (€25/30/35); from Tourist Offices, cable cars and museums. Children: 50% off.

📧 **Innsbruck Hbf**, left luggage, showers, tourist information. Walk down Salurner Str. and then right at the 1765 triumphal arch into Maria-Theresastr. (10 mins).

Rail Tour: Innsbruck – Salzburg – Vienna

✈ **Innsbruck Airport**, ☎ (0512) 225 250 (www.innsbruckairport.com), 4 km west of the city centre (🚌 F from the station).

ℹ️ **Tourist Office**: Burggraben 3, ☎ (0512) 59 850, edge of the Altstadt (www.innsbruck.info); branch at the station. Accommodation booking service; money exchange, concert tickets, ski/cable car passes and Innsbruck Cards.

🚌 24-hr ticket available for **tram**, **bus** and **trolley bus** system. Bikes can be hired from Inntour, Leopoldstrasse 4, ☎ (0512) 5817 4217 (www.inntour.at).

🏨 Budget rooms are scarce in June, when only three hostels are open, but 'summer hotels' usually open in university accommodation July and Aug. The family-run 4-star **Hotel Sailer**, Adamgasse 6–8, ☎ (0512) 5363 (www.sailer-innsbruck.at), €€, notable for its Tyrolean restaurant and décor, is handy for the station. Relatively central **HI youth hostels** are **Torsten-Arneus-Schwedenhaus**, Rennweg 17b, ☎ (0512) 585 814 (youthhostel@aufbauwerk.com), July–Aug only, and **Jugendherberge Innsbruck**, Reichenauer Str. 147, ☎ (0512) 346 179 (www.youth-hostel-innsbruck.at). **Glockenhaus**, Weiherburggasse 3, ☎ (0512) 2865 15 (www.hostelnikolaus.at), is also fairly central, though not HI. **Campsite**: **Camping Innsbruck Kranebitten**, Kranebitter Allee 214, ☎ (0512) 284 180 (www.campinginnsbruck.com), is west of town (🚌 O).

🍴 The **Altstadt** area is generally expensive. **Café-Konditorei Munding**, Kiebachgasse 16 (www.munding.at), is the oldest Tyrolean café and pastry-shop, and serves fabulous cakes. Try the studenty music bar **Zappa**, Rechengasse 5.

> ## WHERE NEXT FROM INNSBRUCK?
>
> Innsbruck *is on the* **Munich–Verona** *route. You can also continue west to* **Liechtenstein**, *then enter Switzerland at* **Sargans** *to join the* **Lausanne–Milan** *route (ETT table 951).*

KITZBÜHEL

With its mountain backdrop, this pleasant old town, with tree-lined streets of steeply gabled pastel-coloured buildings, is one of Austria's prettiest and largest ski resorts (though the snow's not that reliable; main season Christmas–Easter). The **Museum Kitzbühel**, Hinterstadt 32 (www.museum-kitzbuehel.at), occupies the town's oldest house and displays paintings by Alfons Walde (a contemporary of Klimt). Don't miss the **Kitzbüheler Hornbahn** cable car to the summit of the Horn; near the top, some 120 species of flowers bloom from May to October in an **Alpine Flower Garden**, 1880 m high (free guided tours 1100 and 1330, July and Aug). The ski élite arrive in January for the **Hahnenkamm Ski Competition**, a World Cup leg down one of the world's trickiest ski runs. At the top of the Hahnenkammlift, the **Bergbahn Museum** reveals the history of skiing in Kitzbühel since 1893 (free entry).

Austria

The Tourist Office organises free guided hiking and bike trips (register one day before). A 2.5-km walk leads to the **Schwarzsee**, a good bathing lake. In summer, hikers can buy lift passes valid for three days in a week or six in a ten-day period.

Kitzbühel Hbf, Bahnhofpl. 2. A 10-min walk to town centre; go straight across the River Ache, left along Achenpromenade, then follow signs right for centre. Bike hire at station: rates for 1, 3 or 7 days (reduction with rail ticket).

[i] **Tourist Office**: Hinterstadt 18, (05356) 777 (www.kitzbuehel.com), next to the **Rathaus** (town hall). Free accommodation service, free street and hiking maps.

Keep hold of **guest cards** from your accommodation, as these give discounts on lifts, cable cars, etc. The *Frühstückpensionen* (bed and breakfast) are cheap, such as **Pension Hörl**, Josef-Pirchl-Str. 60, (05356) 63 144 (pensionhoerlerika@aon.at), €. **Youth hostel (non HI)**: **Jugendhotel Noichl**, Wieseneggweg 3, (0664) 783 0457 (www.noichl.com). **Campsite**: **Bruggerhof**, Reitherstr. 24, Schwarzsee, (05356) 62 806 (www.bruggerhof-camping.at), near Schwarzsee station.

SALZBURG

Wonderfully sited between the Alps and the lakes of the Salzkammergut, Salzburg is renowned as Mozart's birthplace and is where *The Sound of Music* was filmed in 1964. Much of the city's appearance dates from the 17th century, when many of the old buildings were pulled down and others given a baroque makeover to create Italian-style squares with spectacular fountains. Salzburg's entire **Old City** (**Altstadt**) is designated a UNESCO World Heritage Site and much of it is sweetly beautiful, although some find it cloying, and the crowds can be oppressive. The compact centre is largely pedestrianised; the main shopping street is narrow Getreidegasse, bordered by elegant old houses, decorative wrought-iron signs and medieval arcades, which now house jewellery shops or boutiques. **Mozarts Geburtshaus**, No. 9, where the composer was born in 1756 and spent most of his first 17 years, is now a museum. In nearby Residenzpl. is the **Residenz** (hourly tours), the former Prince Archbishop's palace, built after the need for fortification had passed. Mozart conducted in its grand rooms. Opposite stands the Neue Residenz, home to the **Salzburg Museum** (www.salzburgmuseum.at). The **cathedral**, in adjacent Dompl., is considered the finest early baroque church north of the Alps.

On **Mönchsberg** (Monk's Mountain), high above the Altstadt, looms the formidable **Festung Hohensalzburg**, Mönchsberg 34 (www.hohensalzburg.com; entry fee), once the stronghold of the Archbishops of Salzburg. Built over six centuries, it's almost perfectly preserved, with medieval torture chambers, early Gothic state rooms, and a 200-pipe barrel organ that booms out once the 7th-century 35-bell carillon of the **Glockenspiel**, Mozartpl., has pealed (at 0700, 1100 and 1800). The castle can be reached on foot from Festungsgasse behind the cathedral, or by the **Festungsbahn**, Austria's oldest cable railway dating from 1892. Alternatively, the **Mönchsbergaufzug** (Mönchsberg Lift) operates from Gstättengasse 13 (by

DAY TRIPS FROM SALZBURG

Just south of town (5 km) is the ornate 17th-century **Schloss Hellbrunn**, www.hellbrunn.at (🚌 25 from station or Mirabellpl.). The gardens of this Italian-designed pleasure-palace are famous for their lovely sculptures and fountains, especially those that squirt unexpectedly from stone stools to surprise drunken guests (guided tours, Apr–Oct; evening tours, July–Aug).

Museumpl.) and takes you to the uncompromisingly minimalist contemporary art museum, the **Museum der Moderne**, from whose café terrace there are breathtaking views over the city. Across the river is **Schloss Mirabell**, Mirabellpl., built in the 17th century for Prince Archbishop Wolf Dietrich's mistress, Salome Alt, who bore him 15 or 16 children. It houses the **Marble Hall**, a magnificent venue for chamber music concerts. The garden is a tranquil oasis, one of the most instantly recognisable locations in *The Sound of Music*. Nearby is the Mozart-Wohnhaus, Makartpl. 8, where the Mozart family lived from 1773 to 1787.

🚃 **Salzburg Hbf**, Südtiroler Pl. 1, 20-min walk from the old centre (🚌 1/2/5/6/51 to Staatsbrücke, the main bridge). Tourist information, accommodation service, left luggage (by platforms 4 and 5, daily 0600–2200), money exchange, shops.

✈ **Salzburg Airport**, 4 km west of the city; ☎ (0662) 8580 (www.salzburg-airport.com), 🚌 2/8 every 15 mins connects station with airport; journey time about 25 mins. Taxis to the city centre: ☎ (0662) 8111.

ℹ️ **Tourist Offices**: Auerspergstr. 6, ☎ (0662) 889 870 (www.salzburg.info); accommodation service (fee). Branches at the **station** and Mozartplatz 5.

🏨 During festivals, it pays to book early as accommodation often gets very scarce. Cheaper options, near the rail station, include **Pension Sandwirt**, Lastenstr. 6a, ☎ (0662) 874 351 (sandwirtszg@aon.at), €€. Centrally located are **Junger Fuchs**, Linzergasse 54, ☎ (0662) 875 496 (www.pensionjungerfuchs.com), €, and **Schwarzes Rössl**, Priesterhausgasse 6, ☎ (0662) 874 426 (reservation@academiahotels.at), €€; summer only. **Youth hostels (HI)**: Aignerstr 34, ☎ (0662) 623 248 (www.lbsh-aigen.at), 🚌 7; Haunspergstr. 27, ☎ (0662) 875 030 (www.lbsh-haunspergstrasse.at), open July–late Aug only; 5-min walk from station; **Jugend und Familliengästehaus**, Josef-Preis-Allee 18, ☎ (0662) 842 670 (www.jufa.at); 🚌 5/25 to Justizgebäude. **Yo-Ho**, Paracelsusstr. 9, ☎ (0662) 879 649 (www.yoho.at) is a non-HI hostel a few minutes' walk from the station. **Campsites** include **Camping Nord-Sam**, Samstr. 22a, ☎ (0662) 660 494 (www.camping-nord-sam.com); open April–Sept (🚌 23).

🍽 **Café Tomaselli**, Alter Markt 9, is elegantly authentic. Also try the **Augustiner-Bräu** beer garden, Augustinerg. 4, where beer is brewed by the monastery.

Salzburg Card
Provides admission to most of Salzburg's attractions, free public transport and other discounts; valid 24, 36 or 72 hrs (peak season €24/32/37; off-peak €22/30/35).

SalzburgerLand Card
Free access to over 180 attractions in the region for six or 12 days (€43/52; www.salzburgerland card.com).

Bus and trolley tickets
From vending machines or tobacconists; more expensive from driver (punch ticket on boarding). Day passes also available.

Austria

NIGHT-TIME AND EVENTS   The big event is the **Salzburg Festival**, mid-July–late Aug. For major performances, tickets must be booked months ahead from **Kartenbüro der Salzburger Festspiele**, Herbert-von-Karajan-Pl. 11, Postfach 140, A-5010 Salzburg, ☎(0662) 8045 500 (www.salzburgfestival.at). Last-minute standing tickets sometimes available in the **Kleine Festspielhaus**. Events linked to the festival include an opening *Fackeltanz* (torch-dance) in the Residenzpl. (free) and performances of *Jedermann* ('Everyman'); standing tickets only sold at the Dompl. door 1 hr before start. Other events include **Mozart Week** in late Jan, a Nov **Jazz Festival** and an **Easter Music Festival**. In addition, there's always a concert on somewhere in the city. The **Salzburger Marionettentheater**, Schwarzstr. 24, ☎(0662) 872 4060, (www.marionetten.at), presents operas 'performed' convincingly by puppets that 'sing' to recordings.

WHERE NEXT FROM SALZBURG?

*Salzburg is ideally placed for exploring the **Salzkammergut**, an area of Alpine peaks and glimmering lakes. You get tremendous views of it by taking a circular rail tour southeast of Salzburg: go east on the main route from Salzburg (towards Linz), but change at Attnang-Puchheim for Stainach-Irdning, returning to Salzburg via Bischofshofen (ETT tables 950, 960, 961, 975). You can do the whole trip without stopping in under six hrs, but it's worth having a break along the way at Hallstatt (one stop north of Obertraun; Tourist Office: Seestr. 169, ☎(06134) 8208, www.hallstatt.net or www.dachstein-salzkammergut.at), from where a passenger ferry connects with the train and takes you across the Hallstätter See to Hallstatt itself. This is an enchanting lakeside village with plenty of inexpensive accommodation (including the characterfully old-fashioned Haus Sarstein, on the lake just to the right of the ferry; Gosaumühlstr. 83, ☎(06134) 8217, www.pension-sarstein.at.tf, €); walk uphill or take the cable car to the Salzberg salt mines, worked since prehistoric times and the oldest in the world to be still mined; there's often a queue to get in, but for your money you get a train ride into the mountain, two descents down wooden slides and a view of a beautiful, improbably clear underground lake.*

*From Salzburg you can also join the **Salzburg-Osijek** route (see p464).*

LINZ

Selected as European City of Culture 2009, Austria's industrial third city is gradually reinventing itself with ultra-modern museums and events, such as the annual classical *son et lumière* **Klangwolken**. **Ars Electronica Center**, Hauptstr 2 (www.aec.at; Tue, Wed, Fri 0900–1700, Thur 0900–2100, Sat & Sun 1000–1800), is Europe's only museum dedicated to virtual reality. Facing it across the river, the sleek **Lentos Kunstmuseum** (www.lentos.at; daily 1000–1800, Thursdays until 2100) glows with changing colour after dark. **Hauptplatz** blends colourful baroque and rococo façades around the baroque marble **Trinity column**. In 1938, Hitler – who grew up here – stood on the balcony of No. 1 (now the Tourist Office) to inform the Austrians that the

Nazis had annexed their country. The 17th-century **Alter Dom**, Domgasse, one of the city's two cathedrals, is simple outside, restrained baroque within. The other, the huge neo-Gothic **Neuer Dom**, Herrenstr., can hold 20,000 people. **Landhaus**, Promenade 24, is where the astronomer Johann Kepler developed the third law of planetary motion. Across the river, the **Pöstling-bergbahn**, the world's steepest rack railway, chugs from tram 3 terminus at Landgutstr. 19 to a fortress and pilgrimage church (every 30 mins Mon–Sat 0600–2200 Sun 0730–2200).

Linz09 Card (1 day €15, 3 days €25) gives unlimited travel within the city, free admission to all museums in Linz, a round trip on the *Pöstlingbergbahn* and various other discounts.

Linz Museum Card (€12) qualifies you to one visit to each of Linz's 12 museums.

🚉 Electronic information service, left-luggage lockers (24 hrs), shops. For the centre, take tram 3 to Hauptpl. (10 mins).

ℹ️ **Tourist Offices**: Hauptpl. 1, ☎ (0732) 7070 1777 (www.linz.at/tourismus).

🏨 **Goldenes Dachl**, Hafnerstr. 27, ☎/fax (0732) 775 897 (www.oberoesterreich.at/goldenes-dachl) is central and affordable; **Wilder Mann**, Goethestrasse 14, ☎ (0732) 656 078 (www.members.aon.at/wilder-mann) is reasonable and close to the station. **Youth hostel (HI)**: Stanglhofweg 3, ☎ (0732) 664 434 (www.jugendherbergsverband.at), 🚌 17/19/45 (to Goethekreuzung, then 7-min walk). The nearest **campsite** is **Campingplatz Pichlingersee**, Wiener Bundesstr. 937, ☎ (0732) 305 314 (www.camping-linz.at), trams 1/2 or 🚌 11/19/400.

DANUBE STEAMBOAT

Trips and cruises (Apr–Oct) are operated from the quay by **Donauschiffahrt Wurm & Köck**, Untere Donaulände 1, ☎ (0732) 783 607, www.donauschiffahrt.de.

🍴 The pedestrian zone around Hofgasse is busy at night and has plenty of reasonable eateries. **Klosterhof**, Landstr. 30 (www.klosterhof-linz.at), boasts Austria's biggest beer garden. Sample *Linzer Torte* (almond cake topped with redcurrant jam).

WHERE NEXT FROM LINZ?

*Join the **Cologne–Passau** route (p298) by taking the train over the German border to **Passau** (ETT table 950; 1 hr 15 mins).*

VIENNA (WIEN)

See p371.

ITALY

As the cornerstone of Western civilisation, **Italy** has been on the tourist trail since the days of the 18th-century 'Grand Tour'. But rather than recreate the Grand Tour yourself, select routes that appeal, whether for scenery or sights. For drama, the **Ligurian Coast** (Ventimiglia to Pisa line) whisks you along the coast to the cliff-hugging **Cinque Terre** villages. For arty sights and romantic scenery, the **Pisa** to **Orvieto** route is the finest introduction to the Tuscan and Umbrian landscape, which is dotted with hill-towns and scenery depicted by the Renaissance masters. The art and architecture of medieval **Siena** and Renaissance **Florence** are unmissable, but spare time for compelling but less-well known cities, such as **Lucca** and **Orvieto**. Lovers of lakes and mountains scenery can head to Lake Como and Lake Garda from Milan (leaving time to explore the lakes by ferry) or travel on to Trento and Bolzano for access (by bus) to the **Dolomites**, which are the only sites excluded from the rail network. Venice and Verona are two other 'places to see before you die', although Venetian cuisine can be uninspired and over-priced.

Heading down to **Rome, Naples** and **Sicily** is a journey back to classical times. Mix the passion and chaos of Rome and Naples with the classicism of **Herculaneum** and **Pompeii**. As for a beach break, the Neapolitan Riviera has great scenery around Sorrento and Amalfi, and small beaches, but beaches around Paestum, Sardinia and Elba are better still. Tuscan beaches surpass those on the Adriatic (eastern) coast, whether in the resort of Viareggio or in the wilder Maremma; **Sicily** combines the beach with ancient sites and volcanic scenery. But wherever you are, savour the Italian lifestyle by calling into any local bar or, at dusk, watch the town's evening parade, known as the *passeggiata*, when posing and flirting are paramount.

Italy

ESSENTIALS

Population 57m **Capital** Rome (Roma) **Time Zone** Winter GMT+1, summer GMT+2.

CLIMATE

Very hot in July and Aug; May, June, Sept best for sightseeing. Holiday season ends mid-Sept or Oct. Rome crowded at Easter.

CURRENCY

Euro (€). I Euro = 100 cents = £0.89 = $1.46.

EMBASSIES AND CONSULATES IN ROME

Aus: V. Antonio Bosio 5, ☎ (06) 852 721. **Can**: Via Zara 30, ☎ (06) 8544 42911. **NZ**: Via Clitunno 44, ☎ (06) 853 7501. **SA**: Via Tanaro 14, ☎ (06) 852 5410. **UK**: V. XX Settembre 80A, ☎ (06) 4220 2603. **USA**: V. Vittorio Veneto 119A, ☎ (06) 852 541.

LANGUAGE

Italian; standard Italian is spoken across the country though there are marked regional pronunciation differences. Some dialects in more remote areas. Many speak English in cities and tourist areas. In the south and Sicily, with older people, French can be more useful than English.

OPENING HOURS

Banks: Mon–Fri 0830–1330, 1430–1630. **Shops**: (usually) Mon–Sat 0830/0900–1230, 1530/1600–1900/1930; closed Mon am/Sat pm July/Aug. **Museums/sites**: usually Tues–Sun 0930–1900; last Sun of month free; most refuse entry within an hour of closing. Churches often close lunchtime.

POST OFFICES

Generally, Mon–Fri 0830–1400, Sat 0830–1230. Some counters (registered mail and telegrams) may differ; in main cities some open in the afternoon. *Posta prioritaria* (priority mail) is now the main postal service in Italy. Stamps (*francobolli*) available from tobacconists (*tabacchi*). Poste restante (*Fermo posta*) at most post offices. Internet cafés in all significant towns but remember to bring your passport as new anti-terrorism measures require a photocopy of this to be made.

PUBLIC HOLIDAYS

All over the country: 1, 6 Jan; Easter Sun and Mon; 25 Apr; 1 May; 2 June; 15 Aug (virtually nothing opens); 1 Nov; 8, 25, 26 Dec. Regional saints' days: 25 Apr in Venice; 24 June in Florence, Genoa and Turin; 29 June in Rome; 11 July in Palermo; 19 Sept in Naples; 4 Oct in Bologna; 6 Dec in Bari; 7 Dec in Milan.

PUBLIC TRANSPORT

Buses often crowded, but regular; serve many areas inaccessible by rail. Services drastically reduced at weekends; not always shown on timetables. Taxis: metered, can be expensive; steer clear of unofficial ones.

RAIL PASSES

EP, IR Pass valid (see pp27–34). Some city passes (e.g. Rome) include local rail services.

RAIL TRAVEL

Website (and online bookings): www.trenitalia.com. National rail information ☎892021 (from within Italy only) or ☎+39 06 6847 5475 (from outside Italy). National rail company: Trenitalia, a division of Ferrovie dello Stato (FS). High-speed express services advisable between major cities. Services are classfied Eurostar Italia/Eurostar Italia Fast (ES), Alta Velocità/Alta Velocità Fast (AV) (Frecciarossa), Eurostar City, Intercity/Intercity Notte, Espresso (1st-/2nd-class long-distance domestic trains; stop only at main stations) and Regionale (stops at most stations). Services reasonably punctual. In summer 2009, Trenitalia introduced compulsory reservations on all types of services (except Regionale). Higher fares are payable on AV, ES, Eurostar City, Intercity and Intercity Notte. Some long-distance trains do not carry passengers short distances. Sleepers: single or double berths in 1st class, three (occasionally doubles) in 2nd. Couchettes: four berths in 1st class, six in 2nd, although there are an increasing number of four-berth 2nd-class couchettes. Refreshments on most long-distance trains. Queues at stations often long; buy tickets and make reservations at travel agencies (look for FS symbol or book online).

TELEPHONES

Public phones take coins or phonecards (*carte/schede telefoniche*); good for international calls. *Scatti* (metered) phones common in bars; pay the operator after use. The area code must be included even within the code area; for instance you must dial 06 (code for Rome) even when calling within Rome. Dial in: ☎+39, include first 0 in area code. Outgoing: ☎00 + country code. For international calls through an operator dial ☎170. Police: ☎113. Fire: ☎115. Ambulance: ☎118.

TIPPING

In restaurants you need to look at the menu to see if service charge is included. If not, a tip of 10% is fine depending on how generous you feel like being. The same percentage applies to taxi drivers. A helpful porter can expect up to €2.50.

TOURIST INFORMATION

Websites: www.enit.it, www.italiantourism.com. All regions and most towns have Tourist Boards and Tourist Offices, usually now called APT or IAT but, confusingly, the name depends on the area. Many have websites, but the smaller ones are often just in Italian.

VISAS

Visas not needed by EU or Commonwealth citizens or citizens of the USA.

Italy

Agriturismo, Agriturist,
Corso V Emanuele 101,
00186 Rome,
☎ (06) 685 2337,
www.agriturismo.it,
www.agriturist.it,
has information about
staying in rural cottages
and farmhouses.

Mountain Huts

Club Alpino Italiano,
Via Silvio Pellico 6,
20121 Milan,
☎ (02) 8646 3516,
www.caimilano.eu,
can supply details of
mountain refuge huts.
National website:
www.cai.it

Accommodation

Hotels: The Italian hotel rating system should only be treated as a rough guide, though one- and two-star hotels are budget. The law states that maximum rates should be displayed in each room, and any extras (e.g. breakfast) listed. Prices are often per room rather than per person, with Venice and Capri particularly pricey. Most establishments term themselves *hotel* or *albergo*, but some are still called *locande* (one-star).

Bed & Breakfast: B&Bs are booming, with lists available from Tourist Offices and B&B networks, booked via the internet. B&Bs are the perfect option for older travellers who wish to avoid student hostels, but check prices carefully.

Hostelling: HI youth hostels are plentiful, with around 90 members; prices include sheets and breakfast. The youth hostel headquarters is the Associazione Italiana Alberghi per la Gioventù (AIG) (www.ostellionline.org). If travelling and sharing with a friend, it may be just as cheap and more convenient to stay at a one-star hotel. Confusingly, a hostel can be used to mean any student or budget accommodation. Some hostels are glorified guesthouses, small, family-run, lacking a reception area. They also tend to have restricted check-in times so it is crucial to give accurate arrival times. In short, hostelling in Italy can be un-standardised and informal, much like the Italians themselves. On the plus side, the 'hostels' can be incredibly varied, ranging from convents and monasteries to romantic villas, forts, grain stores and castles. Many hostels have no website and prefer you to book through an agency such as www.hostelworld.com or www.hostels.com, with costs of around €25 per person in a dorm.

Camping: This is popular, but sites are often tricky to reach without a car. Most tend to be upmarket camping villages with bars, restaurants and pools with accommodation also in cabins, bungalows or caravans (bed-linen provided). **Touring Club Italiano** (TCI), (www.touringclub.it) publishes an annual guide,

Campeggi in Italia, or get a free list from Federcampeggio (www.federcampeggio.it), who can also make bookings.

Farm stays and Mountain huts: Farm stays and B&B in cottages and estates is well-established. *Agriturismo* (www.agriturismo.it) is a good first port of call. Mountain huts (*Rifugi*) are an option for hardy types but check access carefully. The best are in the Trentino Dolomites (book on www.visittrentino.it) but others are in Lombardy and affiliated to CAI, the Italian Alpine Club (info@caimilano.it).

FOOD AND DRINK

In Italy, meals are an important social occasion, but food is far more varied than the pasta and pizza stereotypes. A full meal may consist of *antipasti* (cold cuts, grilled vegetables, bruschetta), followed by pasta, a main course, then fruit, cheese or a *semi-freddo* (cold desserts, like tiramisu) or superb ice cream (*gelato*). Much of the pleasure of eating in Italy is derived from the sheer freshness and quality of the ingredients. *Trattorie* are simple establishments and are cheaper than *ristoranti* while *osterie* vary from simple and unpretentious to pricey gentrified-rustic restaurants. For drinking, try an *enoteca*, a wine bar, which may do light meals. *Alimentari* stores often prepare good picnic rolls while *rosticcerie* sell meaty take-aways, and *tavole calde* opt for cheap self-service. Smaller restaurants seldom have menus: just ask for the dish of the day. Regional cuisine means dishes vary enormously: in Trentino Alto Adige, up in the Alps, Austrian-style fare includes dumplings, smoked hams, sausages and apple strudel; Venice favours risotto and fish dishes, while Emilia Romagna (Bologna area) excels at pasta. Tuscany does superb soups, steaks and vegetables while, on the coast, or in the south, fish and shellfish predominate.

> Look for **cover charges** (*coperto*) and **service** (*servizio*), both of which will be added to your bill. Prices on **Menu Turistico** include taxes and service charges.

Coffee (*caffè*) takes many forms, from espresso to liqueur. It tends to come in small shots of espresso; if you want a larger cup of white coffee ask for cappuccino or caffè-latte. There are many fine Italian wines, though Italian beer tends to be bottled. Bars are good places to get a snack, such as a roll or toasted sandwich, as well as to sample the local 'fire waters' such as grappa.

If you're gathering picnic items, be aware that food shops close for a lengthy lunch break.

In restaurants, be aware of cover charges (*coperto*) and service (*servizio*), both of which will be added to your bill. Places serving a *menu turistico* include taxes and service charges but are best avoided – a sign the place caters to tourists and is of a lower standard, and not necessarily cheaper. You would do better off in a pizzeria or tiny trattoria.

CITIES: FLORENCE (FIRENZE)

One of the greatest of Italy's old city-states, Florence has one of the richest legacies of art and architecture in Europe. It is so popular that, from Easter till autumn, its narrow streets are tightly crammed and major sights get extremely crowded during this period. Be prepared to wait in line to enter the **Galleria Uffizi** – Italy's premier art gallery – or to see Michelangelo's *David* in the **Galleria dell'Accademia**. Nevertheless, few would omit Florence from a tour of Tuscany, and it's supremely rewarding providing you don't overdo the sightseeing, remember to take an afternoon siesta, and keep an eye on your valuables.

There are plenty of other galleries of world status if you don't feel able to cope with the Uffizi crowds. Try the **Museo dell'Opera del Duomo**, the **Palazzo Pitti** museums or the **Bargello**. Enjoy the city by walking around: take in the **Ponte Vecchio**, the **Duomo**, the banks of the **Arno** or the huge **Piazza Santo Spirito**.

You pay an entrance fee for every building you visit in Florence – even some of the churches have instituted small admission fees for tourist visits. **Combined entrance tickets** are available for some museums, and queues can be avoided at the state museums (for €3–4) by reserving visiting times in advance through **Firenze Musei**, ☎ (055) 294 883 (Mon–Fri 0830–1830 and Sat 0830–1230, www.firenzemusei.it). Most museums close on Mon, and some are closed Sun as well. The **Uffizi** is quietest an hour or so before it closes at 1850.

ARRIVAL AND DEPARTURE

[RAIL] **Santa Maria Novella (SMN)** is Florence's main rail hub. It is a short walk from the city centre; facilities include left luggage, currency exchange and an accommodation service. The Milan/Florence/Rome high-speed trains call at Santa Maria Novella.

[✈] **Amerigo Vespucci Airport**, 7 km northwest of the city, ☎ (055) 306 1300 (www.aeroporto.firenze.it) handles mainly domestic and some European services. The airport bus is operated by **SITA/ATAF**, ATAF ☎ (055) 56501 (www.ataf.net). SITA ☎ (055) 47821 (www.sitabus.it). Pisa's **Galileo Galilei Airport** (84 km) is the main regional hub for international flights, ☎ (050) 849 111 (www.pisa-airport.com). There are 3–5 trains daily between the airport and Florence's **Santa Maria Novella** rail station (1 hr 20 mins, ETT table 613). Many more journeys are possible by changing trains at Pisa Centrale station.

INFORMATION

MONEY Credit cards are useful only in the more expensive shops and restaurants. Banks that change money display the sign *Cambio* (Exchange). There are exchange kiosks at **SMN** station and at numerous locations. ATMs accept most major credit and debit cards, and have user instructions in English.

TOURIST OFFICES

The **Agenzia per il turismo di Firenze (APT)** has its head office at Via Manzoni 16, 50121 Firenze, ☎(055) 23 320 (www.firenzeturismo.it). The **City of Florence** has Tourist Information Offices at Borgo Santa Croce 29R, ☎(055) 234 0444, at Pza Stazione 4, just across the street from the train station, ☎(055) 212 245 (www.comune.fi.it), and the airport, ☎(055) 315 874 (www.firenzeturismo.it) and a combined City and Province of Florence office at Via Cavour 1r, ☎(055) 290 833 (infoturismo@provincia.fi.it). For tourist info, see also www.aboutflorence.com.

Bus tickets last for one hour from the time the machine stamps them, and you may change buses on the same ticket. A 24-hr pass costs less than the price of five single tickets, while multi-day passes are worthwhile if you take more than three trips a day.

POST AND PHONES The main **post office** is at Via Pellicceria 3, open Mon–Fri 0815–1900, Sat 0815–1330. To phone **Florence from abroad**: ☎00 (international) +39 (Italy) 055 (Florence) + number; to phone **Florence from elsewhere in Italy**: ☎055 (Florence) + number.

INTERNET Internet cafés are plentiful and mostly offer student discounts. **Internet Train**, a chain of internet points, sells credit on magnetic cards that can be used at outlets throughout Italy (www.internettrain.it). There are branches at Via Guelfa 54/56; Via dell'Oriuolo 40r (near the cathedral); Borgo San Jacopo 30r (near Ponte Vecchio); Via Porta Rossa 38 (near Mercato del Porcellino); Via de' Benci 36r (near Santa Croce church).

PUBLIC TRANSPORT

Most sights are in the compact central zone and the best way to see them all is on foot. You can cover much of the city in two days. You can also rent bicycles from the municipal rental location at Pza della Stazione, next to the SMN station, and at several other outlets around the city. Town maps are available from Tourist Offices and from ATAF (see below).

BUSES Florence's buses **Azienda Trasporti Autolinee Fiorentine (ATAF)** run from 0515–0100. There is an **ATAF information office** opposite the main entrance of SMN rail station, ☎800 424 500. Buy tickets for one, two or four trips (*biglietto per una/due/quattro corse*) from the ATAF office at the station, from ticket machines at the main stops, or from newsstands, tobacconists, or bars displaying the ATAF logo. Validate them in the machine immediately upon boarding. People caught with non-validated tickets are fined more than 50 times the value of the ticket. Tickets may also be purchased at machines near parking metres – these do not require validating and are valid for 80 minutes instead of the usual 70 minutes. There are also 24-hour (€5) and 3-day (€12) tickets available.

TAXIS Licensed taxis are white, but you will almost never find one cruising or even at the city's rare signposted taxi ranks, except at the train station. Furthermore, fares are high (starting at about six times the cost of a bus ticket) and taxis do not respond to independent calls, so you must get your hostel or restaurant to call one for you.

Italy

ACCOMMODATION

Florence is Europe's busiest tourism city as well as a major venue for trade fairs and for business travel, and has some magnificent luxury properties, such as the exquisite **Villa Cora**, Viale Machiavelli 18, ☎(055) 229 8451 (www.villacora.it), €€€. At the other end of the scale, hotel and hostel pickings are slim so book well ahead. Near the station is the family-run **Hotel Nuova Italia**, Via Faenza 26, ☎(055) 268 430 (www.hotel-nuovaitalia.com). **Hotel Abatjour**, Viale Cadorna 12, ☎(055) 485 688 (www.abatjour-florence.it), is a central bed and breakfast in an Art Nouveau building while **Hotel Bretagna**, Lungarno Corsini 6, ☎(055) 289 618 (www.hotelbretagna.net), is an ex-pension near the Ponte Vecchio. The **Tourist House Liberty**, Via XXVII Aprile 9, ☎(055) 471 759 (www.touristhouseliberty.it), is about a 10-min walk from the station. The cheapest beds are near the SMN station, but others are south of the Arno. The **Informazioni Turistiche Alberghiere (ITA)** booth at the SMN station, ☎(055) 212 245, may be able to find you a room if you arrive without a booking (small commission charged); open Mon–Sat 0830–1900, Sun 0830–1400, prepare to queue. In the case of hostels, advance booking is recommended: **Gallo d'Oro**, Via Cavour 104, ☎(055) 552 2964 (www.ostellogallodoro.com) is a central, efficient, friendly and highly popular hostel with library, Wi-Fi, bar and restaurant so book in good time (via www.hostelworld.com). **Ciao Hostel**, Via Guido Monaco 34, ☎(055) 321 018, occupies a large, central building with living room, kitchens, laundry, plus free Wi-Fi. **Ostello di Firenze (HI)**, Viale A Righi 2/4, ☎(055) 601 451 (www.ostellofirenze.it); **Ostello Santa Monaca (non HI)**, Via Santa Monaca 6, ☎(055) 268 338 (www.ostello.it); and **Archi Rossi (non HI)**, Via Faenza 94r, ☎(055) 290 804 (www.hostelarchirossi.com). There are **campsites** at **Camping Michelangelo**, Viale Michelangelo 80, ☎(055) 681 1977 (open all year), and **Camping Villa Camerata**, in the grounds of at the Ostello di Firenze (see above, open year round). A list of campsites in and around Florence is available from **Federcampeggio** (see p389).

FOOD AND DRINK

Thanks to its large student population, Florence has a fair range of reasonably priced eating places, found down small alleys, or close to the station, including in Via Spada, southeast of Pza Santa Maria Novella. Even better is the **Oltrarno**, just across the river, where the Santo Spirito district is vibrant, bohemian and student-orientated, while adjoining **San Frediano** district is where (hungry!) Florentine craftsmen are based. Although you can opt for fixed-price (*prezzo fisso*) meals, you will do better in price, atmosphere and quality in a small trattoria. An even cheaper option is the *tavola calda*, an uninspired but acceptable buffet-style self-service restaurant where you can choose a single dish or a full meal. These are found all over town, and cover and service charges are included in the price displayed for each dish. As in other Italian towns, drinks taken standing or sitting at the bar are a great deal cheaper than those consumed at a table, and restaurants outside the main sightseeing semicircle are usually cheaper than those close to the main sights. For picnic ingredients try an *alimentari* (shambolic-looking grocery shops) – but remember that they shut for lunch – or the huge **Mercato Centrale** (Central Market), near San Lorenzo.

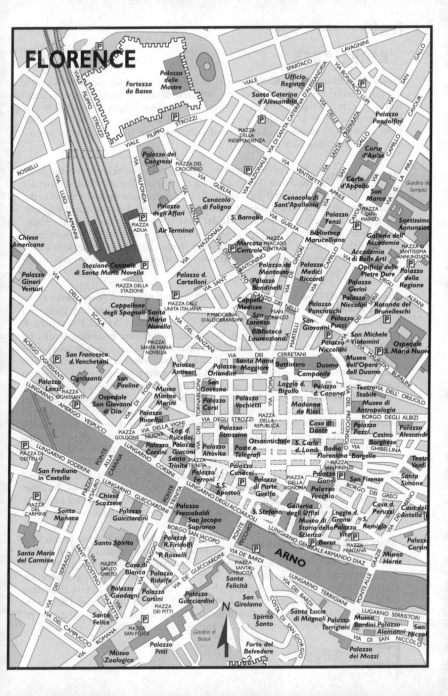

Italy

The city is divided by the **River Arno**, with most of its glorious medieval heart on the north bank. South of the river, the **Oltrarno** district is packed with artisans' workshops; this is the traditional working-class Florence, largely untouched by the major tourist sights at its heart across the river. Five bridges cross the Arno. The most central, the **Ponte Vecchio**, is lined with jewellers' shops, and is Florence's oldest bridge, dating back to 1345.

NORTH OF THE ARNO Most of the important sights lie in a semicircle north of the Arno, within a 2-km radius of the **Uffizi**. These include Florence's 'musts'. The **Galleria Uffizi** itself, Pzle degli Uffizi 6, contains works by many of the Renaissance greats, such as Giotto, Cimabue, Botticelli, Michelangelo and Raphael. The **Duomo** (Cathedral) of **Santa Maria del Fiore** is topped by Brunelleschi's dome. At the base of the **Campanile** (Bell Tower), designed by Giotto in 1334, are sculpted relief panels by Andrea Pisano. The **Baptistery** (Battistero di San Giovanni) is famed for its 14th–15th-century bronze door panels, the originals of which are now in the Museo dell'Opera del Duomo.

The **Museo dell'Opera del Duomo**, Pza del Duomo 9, houses other works taken from the **Duomo** for safe-keeping. Highlights are Michelangelo's *Pietà* and sculptures by Donatello and Della Robbia. The **Bargello**, Via del Proconsolo 4, possesses Italy's finest collection of Renaissance sculpture, including works by Michelangelo, Donatello and Cellini. **Piazza della Signoria** has a wonderful array of statuary and is dominated by the crenellated **Palazzo Vecchio**, which provides an insight into the life of the city's rulers, and is one of the few museums to go down the (successful) multi-media route in terms of presentation. Michelangelo designed the New Sacristy – and the Medici Tombs housed there – in Pza Madonna degli Aldobrandini, next to the church of San Lorenzo. He also designed the Laurentian Library and its magnificent staircase, entered from Pza San Lorenzo. **Santa Maria Novella**, on Pza di Santa Maria Novella, contains Renaissance treasures, including a fresco of the Trinity by Masaccio and frescos in the chancel by Ghirlandaio.

Outside the semicircle, 3 km northeast of the centre, the **Galleria dell'Accademia** (Via Ricasoli 60) contains Michelangelo's *David* and other masterpieces by the artist. There's more world-famous art at the **Museo di San Marco** (Pza di San Marco 1), notably Fra Angelico's luminous frescos, including the *Annunciation*.

SOUTH OF THE ARNO: THE OLTRARNO Cross the **Arno** by the Ponte Vecchio to reach the grandiose 15th-century **Palazzo Pitti**, Pza Pitti, housing the wealth of the Medici, a gallery of modern art, which takes up where the Uffizi leaves off, and the array of art from the Renaissance and the baroque in the Palatine Gallery. The home of Elizabeth Barrett Browning and Robert Browning, **Casa Guidi**, is on Pza San Felice 8. Further south, behind the Palazzo Pitti, lie the city's landscaped gardens, the **Giardino di Boboli**, laid out for the Medici in the 16th century, and a tempting retreat for a snooze after you've overdosed on art.

SHOPPING

Florence offers some of the finest quality products in leatherwork (particularly shoes and accessories), linen and jewellery, as well as more affordable hand-tooled paper. For window-shopping and people-watching, follow the wealthy fashionistas on **Via della Vigna Nuova** and **Via Tornabuoni**, where you can call into the Ferragamo shoe museum to be amused by Florentine fashion history. Then visit the Pza dei Ciompi flea market (open daily, go early), the **Mercato Nuovo** on Via Calimala, the daily market in the Pza San Lorenzo and around the **Mercato Centrale** (for cheap clothing, food, leather, silks and paper goods), or the sprawling Tuesday-morning market in the **Cascine** park for affordable buys. Hand-made perfumes and soaps can be had from the pricey but magical **Farmacia di Santa Maria Novella**, Via della Scala 16R (time to think of your neglected mother!). In general, olive oil, vinegars, cheese and dried mushrooms are good buys, all plentiful in the Mercato Centrale.

NIGHT-TIME AND EVENTS

Florence offers plenty to do and see, especially on the street. On summer evenings, street performers take over the Pza della Signoria, the Pza del Duomo and the Via Calzaiuoli. Opera is also popular, though it is an expensive way to spend an evening. The English-language listings guide *Florence: Concierge Information* can be picked up at upmarket hotel desks. *Firenze Spettacolo* (www.firenzespettacolo.it) the monthly listings guide available at newspaper stands and bookshops, has a section in English. A lively youth culture boosted by a floating summer population ensures that there are plenty of clubs and discos. Admission prices are high, however, and drinks are expensive. The scene changes in the summer when many locales move outdoors to the city squares, which become venues for music, dance and cinema. Admission is free, though consumption of at least one drink is expected. The historic centre also has quite a few pubs and cocktail bars, such as **Girasol** (www.girasol.it) and **Lo Stregatto** (www.lostregatto.it).

There are numerous theatres, the most important of which is the **Teatro Comunale**, and a big music and opera festival in May–July. **Cinema Odeon**, Via Sassetti 1, ☎(055) 214 068, shows English-language films every Mon, Tues and Thur.

FIESOLE

Fiesole, I8 km northeast, makes a handy escape from the summertime heat of Florence (🚌 7 from city centre) and provides excellent views of its larger neighbour. Its main sights are the **Roman Theatre** and its attendant museum, and the **Monastery of San Francesco**.

VIEWS OF FLORENCE

Despite the crowds, the view of the old city straddling the banks of the **Arno** from the **Ponte Vecchio** is still much as the Florentines' ancestors knew it, while from the top of the cathedral dome there's a magnificent view across the city's rooftops. A wider view of the city can be had from **San Miniato al Monte**, an art-filled church overlooking the city from behind the Boboli Gardens.

CITIES: NAPLES (NAPOLI)

There's nowhere quite like **Naples** – the city is a glorious assault on your senses: you need to bite the bullet but avoid the bullet in this unruly, raucous, run-down capital of the South. It might have a notorious reputation as a city of crime, but its ebullience, history, cuisine and range of treasures make it a compelling stop on a southern Italian journey. The old central axis, known as **Spaccanapoli**, is a sense-numbing immersion into the Neapolitan maelstrom, so break yourself in with a pizza and a peaceful gallery visit first.

Apart from the anarchic mood of the city itself, the main attraction is the **National Archaeological Museum**, whose glories include its Greek sculptures, mosaics and artefacts. For many, however, their abiding memory will be of dark, crumbling, medieval alleys, with washing lines strung above and assorted cooking smells emanating from within, where housewives haul up bucketfuls of shopping by ropes linked to high tenement windows. Out on the streets, you can wander for hours in the city's various districts, such as the **Sanità**, and be entertained by the ebullience of daily life. Behind the Pza del Plebiscito is the ironically named Via Solitaria, a long, busy, local street.

Originally the Greek colony of Neapolis, Naples became a desirable winter resort for wealthy Romans. Of the many families that later ruled Naples, the Anjou and Aragon dynasties of the 13th–16th centuries were among the most influential, and many remains from that era dot the city.

Naples is somewhat upstaged by its surroundings, notably the Neapolitan Riviera – including the ultra-scenic resorts of **Sorrento**, **Positano** and **Amalfi**, and the island of **Capri**, just a short boat ride away – as well as the astonishing Roman remains of **Herculaneum** and **Pompeii**. All can be reached in a day trip from Naples, though you might prefer to base yourself on the Riviera for exploring the area fully.

ARRIVAL AND DEPARTURE

[RAIL] Most long-distance trains use **Stazione Centrale**. Some use **Stazione Pza Garibaldi** which is also the Metro station directly beneath **Centrale**. **Mergellina** and **Campi Flegrei**, also terminals for some trains, are further west. The Metro links all three stations. **Stazione Circumvesuviana** handles trains to **Pompeii** (see p401) and **Sorrento**; it is adjacent to and also beneath **Centrale**.

[+] **Capodichino** (www.gesac.it) is 7 kms north of the centre. There are taxis and a daily bus service to **Stazione Centrale**, approximately every 20–30 mins. For **airport information**, [☎](081) 789 6259. Buses to the airport depart from Pza Garibaldi.

INFORMATION

Pick up a town map at the city Tourist Office and a copy of the monthly listing *Qui Napoli*. **Ente Provinciale per il Turismo (EPT)** provides information about hotels; its **main office** is at Pza dei Martiri 58, ☎(081) 410 7211. (www.eptnapoli.info), and it maintains a spartan but helpful office in the **Stazione Centrale**, and in the **Stazione di Mergellina**. See also www.inaples.it for useful tourist information. **Youth information (CTS)**: Via Scarlatti 198 (Vomero area), ☎(081) 558 6597; Via S. Freud 86/88, ☎(081) 545 2686.

PUBLIC TRANSPORT

The Line 2 Metro departing from Pza Garibaldi station goes to **Pozzuoli** and **Solfatara**; get off at Pozzuoli station, Solfatara is nearby. For train times see www.trenitalia.it. Trains can be infrequent and stations quiet out of peak hours. Naples' shiny new underground line from Piazza Dante to Vomero is an attraction in itself, with seven stations studded with contemporary artworks. **Buses** and **trams** are more frequent and more extensive. Frequent **hydrofoils** and **ferries** ply across the bay and out to Sicily, Capri and Ischia. Most leave from **Molo Beverello** (by **Castel Nuovo**) but some go from Mergellina. Three funicular railways (**Funicolare Montesanto, Centrale** and **Chiaia**) link the old city with the cooler **Vomero Hill** – take the funicular from Via Toledo to Vomero to admire the views. The city centre is best to explore by foot, taking care in the exciting but edgy Spaccanapoli area, which should be visited regardless.

TICKETS ☎800 56 88 66. Buy **train** tickets at kiosks and validate them in the machines near each platform. Buy **bus** tickets from news kiosks, tobacconists and bars. Day passes and cheaper weekend passes are available. A local **transit ticket** is valid for 90 mins and for three trips on any Metro, tram or bus (or one funicular ride and two other trips).

ACCOMMODATION

Wonderful though the city is, Naples is one of the few places in Italy where you need to be on guard from the word go, especially on arrival with luggage. Avoid hanging around near the station: the more lost-tourist you look, the easier a target you appear for dodgy youths whizzing past on mopeds. The Tourist Office can help with accommodation but confirm prices with the hotel before committing yourself. **La Concordia**, Piazzetta Concordia 5, ☎(081) 412 349 (www.laconcordia.it), is a friendly, good-value B&B. Cheap hotels cluster in and around the noisy, unsalubrious Pza Garibaldi. **Hotel San Pietro**, Via San Pietro ad Aram 18, ☎(081) 286 040 (www.sanpietrohotel.it), €€, is a large block just west of Pza Garibaldi (with the station behind you, take Corso Umberto leading diagonally left; the hotel is signed off to the right). Good value, with a big street market close by (so can be noisy). Also west of Pza Garibaldi is **Pensione Mancini**, Via Pasquale Stanislao Mancini 33, ☎(081) 553 6731 (www.hostelpensionemancini.com), €, a fair budget option which also has dorm facilities. For other B&Bs, see www.bed-breakfast-napoli.com, a comprehensive website featuring several B&Bs in both Naples and surrounding areas.

Italy

The **HI youth hostel**, **Ostello Mergellina**, 23 Salita della Grotta, ☎(081) 761 2346 (www.ostellonapoli.com), is behind the Stazione Mergellina. **Non-HI**: **Fabric**, Via Bellucci Sessa 22, Portici, ☎(081) 776 5874 (www.fabrichostel.com), is a sought-after hostel set in a former fabric factory; it has a bar, restaurant, internet and regular events. Equally popular is the central and friendly **6 Small Rooms**, Via Diodato Lioy 18, ☎(081) 790 1378 (www.6smallrooms.com). **Hostel of the Sun**, Via Melisurgo 15, ☎(081) 420 6393 (www.hostelnapoli.com), is central and clean, a 20-min walk or ☐ 2 from main station; get off at Via Depretis near Hotel Mercure. **Campsites** are mainly in Pozzuoli (on the Metro), west of Naples. **Camping Internazionale Vulcano Solfatara**, Via Solfatara 161, ☎(081) 526 2341 (www.solfatara.it), is the nearest.

FOOD AND DRINK

Naples is the birthplace of the pizza, the city's main contribution to the culinary world – authentically served with a fresh tomato sauce. The city's food is among Italy's best and cheapest. Pasta is the staple ingredient, as are deep-fried vegetables and seafood. There are plenty of inexpensive places to eat – try the area just to the west of Via Toledo or the many open-air food stalls around the station and Pza Mercato. As important as the sights is the pizza: the most famous pizzeria is **Da Michele** (Via Sersale 1, www.damichele.net) near the station – select either margherita or marinara – that's it for choice. Only eat pizza at places that display the '*vera pizza*' (true pizza) sign. Bars are the places to get to know the Neapolitans, who are notoriously voluble, as well as being friendly, superstitious and supreme fixers.

HIGHLIGHTS

Modern Naples is hectic, crowded and noisy. Petty crime is rife, notably pick-pocketing and bag-snatching, so be very careful, especially after dark.

Set in an imposing 18th-century Royal Palace and huge shady park, the **Museo di Capodimonte**, Via Miano 2 (take a bus from Pza Cavour or Pza Garibaldi to Porta Grande or Porta Piccola) also houses one of Italy's largest and richest collections of art – including important works by Italian masters such as Titian and Botticelli, art from Naples from the 13th to the 19th centuries, and modern paintings.

Do not miss the world-class **Museo Archeologico Nazionale** (National Archaeological Museum), Pza Museo Nazionale 19 (Metro: Cavour or Museo; free for under 18s and over 65s – EU citizens only; closed Tues), which contains an unparalleled collection from Pompeii and Herculaneum: sculptures, mosaics, and, most interesting of all, mundane everyday objects.

South of the museum is the heart of medieval Naples, Spaccanapoli, centred around Via Benedetto Croce and Pza Gesù Nuovo, where you'll find the **Gesù Nuovo**, a 16th-century church whose façade, originally part of a palace, is studded with peculiar basalt diamond-shaped extrusions. Within, it is one of the extreme expressions of the ebullient Neapolitan baroque style.

Not far away, **Santa Chiara**, Via Benedetto Croce, dates from the 14th century. In it are some exceptionally fine medieval tombs. Attached to it and bright with blooms, the gently decaying **Cloister of the Clarisse** is notable for its walks, which are lined with decorative 18th-century majolica tiles. Further east, the cavernous **Duomo** (Cathedral), Via Duomo, is dedicated to Naples' patron saint, San Gennaro. Housed here is a phial of his blood, which allegedly liquefies miraculously twice every year.

The massive **Castel Nuovo** (or Maschio Angioino) guards the port. The castle, begun in 1279, is chiefly recognisable for its massive round towers. The nearby **Palazzo Reale** was the seat of the Neapolitan royalty. Vast and handsome, within it are acres of 18th- and 19th-century rooms. The adjacent **Teatro di San Carlo**, begun in 1737, ranks second only to **La Scala**, in Milan, in the Italian opera league.

Santa Lucia, the waterfront district to the south, is where **Castel dell'Ovo**, built by Frederick II, sticks out into the bay. The third major castle in Naples, **Castel Sant'-Elmo**, occupies a peak high above the city – alongside the **Certosa di San Martino**. Inside the latter, whose courtyard is one of the masterpieces of the local baroque style, is **Museo Nazionale di San Martino**, which contains an important collection of Neapolitan paintings and Christmas cribs, the *presepi*. The **Museo Principe di Aragona Pignatelli**, Riviera di Chiaia, contains salons decorated entirely in local ceramics. This gallery houses one of the greatest of European art collections. Chiaia is the cool district for bars and chilling out.

SIDE TRIPS FROM NAPLES

In some ways, the surroundings of Naples offer more than the city itself. Your first impressions are likely to be mixed: it's a strange blend of mess and physical majesty, with the still-active Mount Vesuvius rising massively over the bay itself and a vast industrial zone sprawling along the shores.

Exploring the area is easily done by train, bus and ferry. The **Circumvesuviana** (www.vesuviana.it) is a private railway (half-hourly service, ETT table 623) linking Naples, Sorrento, Pompeii and Herculaneum, and there are regular trains and buses to Salerno (see p446), from where you can take a bus to Paestum or a bus or ferry to Amalfi.

THE SORRENTO PENINSULA This is an unbeatable area if you like beaches, ancient sites, boat trips and stunning coastal scenery. Not many places have all these right on the doorstep. The best approach is by ferry – from Salerno to Amalfi, or from Naples to Sorrento and on to Capri, for instance: here you will see villages and towns perched beneath towering limestone cliffs that will have you wondering how anyone ever managed to build on them. Virtually every accessible patch is either built on or cultivated with olives or lemons. The settlements are linked by a myriad network of tiny stepped paths, making it outstanding terrain for walking. If you want to try the walks in this region, purchase Julian Tippett's excellent *Landscapes of Sorrento and the Amalfi Coast* (published in English by Sunflower, and available locally).

Scenically, Amalfi has the edge over Sorrento. Because of the tortuous nature of the roads, driving or cycling here is not recommended; fortunately the bus network is excellent and cheap, and ferries (see www.caremar.it for schedules) are even better.

Sorrento (Tourist Office: Via Luigi de Maio 35, ☎(081) 807 4033, www.sorrento tourism.com) is the biggest resort on the Neapolitan Riviera, a limestone peninsula, easily reached by frequent trains from Naples on the Circumvesuviana (ETT table 623; check first, not all trains stop here). Curiously, it has no beach, but is perched on cliffs, with a concentration of upmarket hotels in the centre (there's less pricey accommodation up the hill on the west side; **Hotel Elios**, Via Capo 33, ☎(081) 878 1812 (www. hotelelios.it), €€, is quiet, with some sea views). Sorrento is served by ferry routes to Naples, Capri and Amalfi. Ferries are slow but atmospheric, while jetfoils are fast but bumpy, and confine you indoors. Internet point at **Sorrento Info**, a tourist information office located in Via T. Tasso 19 (www.sorrentoinfo.com).

A superb base is **Amalfi** (Tourist Office: Via delle Repubbliche Marinare, ☎(089) 871 107, www.amalfitouristoffice.it) – also reached by bus or ferry from Salerno – which has considerably more charm than Sorrento. It's squeezed at the mouth of a beautiful limestone gorge, with lemon groves spread over the surrounding slopes. Beaches are small and grey-sanded, but the water in summer is clean and warm. Just east of Amalfi, **Atrani** is remarkably unspoilt, and less busy than neighbouring Amalfi; on its sole, tiny square is the hostel/hotel **A Scalinatella**, Piazza Umberto I 5/6, ☎(089) 871 492 (www.hostel scalinatella.com), excellent value and right by the beach, with cheap dorm beds.

There are some great walks here, along stepped paths and tiny lanes. Take the frequent bus from Amalfi up to **Ravello** and return by one of several very attractive paths. This delicious hilltop village has stupendous views and extraordinarily numerous semi-feral cats. The Villa Cimbrone has an incomparably romantic terraced garden (open to the public, www.villacimbrone.com) overlooking the sea. Wagner set part of his opera *Parsifal* here, and classical music is still very much the thing in Ravello, with a long summer music festival based at the Villa Rufolo.

CAPRI Lying just off the Sorrento Peninsula, the island of Capri is renowned for its wonderful setting, with bougainvillea, cacti and jasmine growing everywhere around the Greek-looking dome-roofed white houses. Don't be too put off by the cruise-ship crowds that descend on the main town (itself reached by the entertaining funicular from the ferry). The town is crammed full of expensive boutiques but, unless you love window-shopping and people-watching, head away from the designer quarter. Instead, explore the quiet lanes and cliff-top paths that run eastwards towards Villa Jovis, the villa of Emperor Tiberius, who used to get his less-favoured guests drunk and then have them hurled off the cliffs.

Capri is light on formal sights, but stop at the Villa San Michele. This is the idiosyncratic former home of the Swedish doctor and author Axel Munthe. The Blue Grotto is a rip-off boat trip – the water colour is incredible but you get only a few minutes in the cave; longer cruises round the island may be well worthwhile, however.

ISCHIA The fertile island of **Ischia**, less well known than Capri, also has a remarkable setting, with spa resorts offering cures in radioactive waters, and some excellent beaches for lingering. There are about nine sailings daily from Naples to Capri and Ischia departing from Molo Beverello (40 mins to Capri, 80 mins to Ischia). Hydrofoils depart hourly from Mergellina (journey time 40 mins for both islands). There are several shipping operators serving the island.

HERCULANEUM (ERCOLANO) AND VESUVIUS The Museo Archeologico Nazionale (National Archaeological Museum) in Naples (see p398) has many of the finds from this famous Roman site. For background, see www.pompeiisites.org.

Herculaneum (Station: Ercolano; 10-min walk downhill to the site) was a wealthy Roman suburb that was buried in AD 79 by the eruption of Mount Vesuvius, though it was engulfed by mud rather than ash. Excavations have revealed an astonishing time capsule, with many house façades virtually intact. Unlike Pompeii, some upper storeys are in evidence; you can see half-timbered buildings and even the balconies, and some remarkable bathhouses, still roofed and with benches in position.

You enter the site through a tunnel piercing the mud that engulfed the town; originally this was the shore, and you get a further idea of the sheer scale of the disaster at the edge of the excavated town, where classical columns disappear upwards; the modern town lies on top, concealing much more. On your way back to the station, keep to the left of the main street for the fascinating (easily missed) medieval town – strikingly decayed and atmospheric, with a food market and crowded alleys. Several buses a day zigzag up from the station (most leave in the morning, so it's best done before you visit Herculaneum) to within a 30-min walk of the summit of **Vesuvius**, where you can peer into the crater; there's no smoke or molten lava to be seen, but the volcano is still active.

POMPEII (POMPEI) Also on the Circumvesuviana railway and a short ride from Naples, **Pompeii** (Station: Pompei, adjacent to the site) is much the larger and more touristy site, its ruins mesmeric and eerie, though things aren't quite as well preserved here and packs of stray dogs roam the streets. This substantial Roman town, excavated from the volcanic ash that buried it, gives a real feel for life at the time: you can see original graffiti on the walls and chariot ruts in the road, wander into houses and courtyards, identify shop counters and even lose the crowds in some of the more remote areas. Indeed the scale of the place is almost daunting. Highlights include the Forum, the Forum Baths, the Villa of the Mysteries, the outdoor and indoor theatres, the House of I Caius Secundus and the house of the Vettii (both with marvellous wall paintings), and the Lupanare, the restored main

Italy

brothel, complete with erotic frescos. On arrival at the site you can join guided tours, which can be worthwhile as nothing's explained once you're inside. As with Herculaneum, many of the best sculptures, mosaics and paintings have ended up in the National Archaeological Museum in Naples (see p398). **Camping Villaggio Spartacus**, Via Plinio 117, ☎(081) 862 4078 (www.campingspartacus.it).

PAESTUM There are a few trains every day from Naples' Central staton to Paestum station, a 10-min walk from the ruins. Otherwise get one of the frequent trains or buses from Naples to Salerno, where there are buses to **Paestum** (annoyingly the buses are operated by more than one company and tickets aren't interchangeable; the easiest ticket booth to find is by the rail station). However you decide to get there, it's definitely worth the effort, as Paestum (or Poseidonia as it was known originally) is quite different from Pompeii and Herculaneum and far less overrun. It was founded by Greeks from Sybaris in the 6th century BC and later colonised by the Romans. What remains are three magnificent Greek Doric temples, a good deal better preserved than most ruins in Greece itself. Most notable is the Temple of Neptune, dating from about 450 BC, standing to its original height. The outline of the surrounding ancient town is still in evidence, with the weed-grown foundations of buildings and the original main street, and the museum has finds from the site, including a famous tomb fresco of a diving swimmer.

WHERE NEXT FROM NAPLES?

You can take the train via **Foggia** to **Brindisi**; journey time 5 hrs by daytime service (direct route via Bari); ETT tables 626 and 631. An alternative (and extremely attractive) route goes via **Battipaglia** to **Taranto** (table 638). Despite the heavy industry when approaching **Taranto**, there is an archaeological museum, **Museo Nazionale**, which is beginning to rival that in Naples with its excellent collection of ancient Greek artefacts. From **Taranto**, continue to **Bari** or **Brindisi** (table 631). From **Brindisi** you can take ferries to **Corfu**, **Patras** and **Igoumenitsa**. There is also a nightly ship from **Naples** to **Palermo** (table 2625).

CITIES: ROME (ROMA)

The Romans have an inbuilt resistance to schedules and short lunch breaks. Life is too Latin for a Protestant work ethic. Indeed, they have no qualms about playing the tourist in their own city, from eating ice creams on **Piazza Navona** to tossing a coin in the **Trevi Fountain**, visiting the **Vatican** museums on a Vespa, lolling around the Villa **Borghese Gardens**, or peeking into the **Pantheon** while on a café crawl. In Italy's most bewildering but beguiling city, it has somehow never made more sense to 'do as the Romans do'.

The 'Eternal City', dominated by its seven hills (Aventine, Capitoline, Celian, Esquiline, Palatine, Quirinal and Viminal), is cut by the fast-flowing **River Tiber**. Don't expect Rome's legendary 'seven hills' to stand out as landmarks: they are too gentle, and merge into one another. Instead, treat the **Colosseum** and **Forum** as the city centre, set on the right bank of the Tiber, with the Pantheon just north, and the chic **Spanish Steps** beyond. On the left bank of the Tiber lies bohemian Trastevere, a great restaurant and nightlife centre, with the mausoleum-fortress of Castel Sant'Angelo further north, and the Vatican City to the west. If this sounds exhausting (and it is), Villa Borghese is Rome's green heart, but with baroque fountains and galleries attached – you'll find there's no escape from several millennia of art and architecture in a city that spawned a civilisation.

ARRIVAL AND DEPARTURE

🚈 There are four main railway stations. **Termini**, Pza dei Cinquecento, is Rome's largest, handling all the main national and international lines; bureaux de change, tourist and hotel information; well served by taxis, buses and night buses, and at the hub of the Metro system. **Tiburtina** serves some long-distance north–south trains. Services to Bracciano (1 hr 5 mins) and Viterbo (1 hr 50 mins) depart from **Ostiense**. **Porta San Paolo** serves the seaside resort of Lido di Ostia (45 mins). There are ATMs in the stations.

✈ **Leonardo da Vinci (Fiumicino)** is 36 km southwest of Rome, ☎(06) 65 951 (www.adr.it). **Taxis** into the centre are hassle-free, but expensive. Much cheaper is the 45-min train service, every 15 mins (every 30 mins late evenings, Sundays and holidays), to **Tiburtina** and **Ostiense** stations. There's an express rail link (30 mins) to **Termini** (0636–2336), €11, run by Trenitalia, ☎(06) 6847 5475. **Aeroporto Ciampino**, ☎(06) 65 951 (www.adr.it), is closer to town, 16 km to the southeast. There is a frequent rail service between Termini and Ciampino. **Airport Connection Services**, ☎(06) 338 3221 (www.airportconnection.it), has private taxis serving both airports.

Italy

Tourist Information

Main Tourist Office, APT
(Rome provincial Tourist Board): Via XX Settembre 26, ☎ (06) 421 381, (www.aptprovroma.it), Metro: Repubblica. See also www.turismoroma.it, www.060608.it. They are all superb websites with info on accommodation, itineraries and other services. Other branches: P.I.T. (Punti Informativi Turistici) also at Ciampino and Fiumicino airports, as well as a few others in the city. See also **Enjoy Rome**, Via Marghera 8a, ☎ (06) 445 1843 (www.enjoyrome.com), located near Termini station.

INFORMATION

TICKETS AND OPENING TIMES Most museums are closed on Mon (the Vatican mostly closes on Sun). Most places charge an entrance fee with admission free for under 18s and over 65s (EU citizens only); and reduced for 18–25s, teachers and students. The Roma Pass (www.romapass.it) is valid for three days and includes free admission to two museums plus discounts on others, theatre events and exhibitions, and free transport on city buses, Metro lines and some trains. Also, there are other combo ticket types, such as the 'Archaeologia Card' (€23 for nine sites and valid for seven days), or the two-day combined ticket that gives access to the Colosseo, Palatino and Foro Romano.

INTERNET ACCESS Internet café: **Internet Train**, Via dei Pastini 21, open Mon–Fri 1000–2300, Sat 1000–2000, Sun 1200–2000.

PUBLIC TRANSPORT

The Metro doesn't go where you want to go; the buses are crowded and confusing. Luckily, the *centro storico* (historic centre) is fairly compact, traffic-free and easy to see on foot. However, many of the most important sights lie outside this area. The main arteries are well served by buses, but stick to those and you miss Rome's ebullient streetlife, medieval alleys and baroque squares. Most hotels supply a basic street map. For more details, and bus and Metro maps, ask at newsstands, tobacconists and Tourist Offices. Romans are very willing with directions.

METRO, BUSES AND TRAMS are valid for all forms of transport (bus, Metro and tram) in Rome. Individual combined bus/Metro tickets, called BIT (*biglietto integrato a tempo*, €1), are valid for 75 mins. Tickets can be bought at newsstands and tobacconists or at railway and underground stations and bus termini. Validate (time stamp) the ticket in the machine as you enter the bus (or risk a fine). The BIG

To save time and money, buy a 1-day pass, called a **BIG ticket** (€4), a 3-day BTI pass (€11) or a 1-week CIS pass (€16). These

TRAINING FOR ITALIAN TRAINS
Aisle (*il corridoio*); arrival (*arrivo*); carriage (*la carrozza*); departure (*la partenza*); entrance (*l'entrata*); exit (*l'uscita*); express (but it isn't = *espresso*); fast (*rapido, veloce*); pendolino or IC (genuinely fast train services); first class (*prima classe*); luggage (*i bagagli*); lavatory (*il bagno, la toiletta, WC*); reserved (*riservato*); seat (*il posto*); station (*la stazione*); platform (*il binario*); train (*il treno*); window (*il finestrino*); late (*in ritardo*); as in 'the train is running late' (*il treno e' in ritardo*); the train for Rome is leaving from platform 14 (*il treno per Roma parte dal binario 14*).

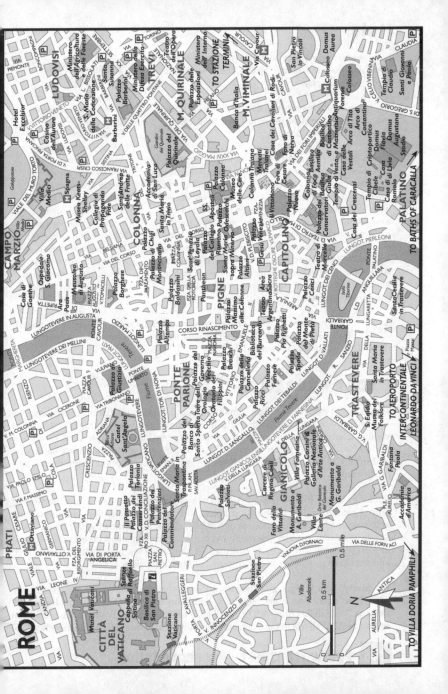

ticket needs to be validated once only. The 1-week pass just needs your name and the starting date. The 1-month pass needs your name only.

The Metropolitana has only two lines – A (red) and B (blue) – and is not much use in the centre. It is open 0530–2330 Mon–Fri and 0530–0030 Sat.

Rome's confusing but useful bus service is centred on Pza dei Cinquecento, with major stops *(fermate)* in Pza Venezia, Largo Argentina and Pza del Risorgimento. Buses are orange, the number is at the front and they generally stop without your having to flag them down. Only three (🚍 116, 117 and 119, small electric buses) are able to enter the narrow streets of the *centro storico* and do a useful round trip of most of the major sights in the centre, Mon–Sat only. **Night buses** run from 0030–0530. Buy tickets from the conductor on board. **Archeobus**: use this good bus service to explore the Via Appia Antica Park and all the ancient sites around there (see parcoappiaantica.it).

ROMANS AND RED LIGHTS

Italians don't always stop at red lights, considering them advisory rather than mandatory mechanisms. The red-light mentality explains volumes about the Romans. Journalist Beppe Severgnini says: 'We think it's an insult to our intelligence to comply with a regulation. Obedience is boring. We want to think about it. We want to decide whether a particular law applies to our specific case. In that place, at that time.'

TAXIS There are plenty of white metered taxis, available from ranks or by phone: **Radiotaxi**, 🖀(06) 3570; **Capitale**, 🖀(06) 4994. There are surcharges for luggage, at night (2200–0700) and on Sun and holidays.

ACCOMMODATION

Hotels range from the opulent – mainly located close to the Spanish Steps and the Via Veneto – to the basic, largely clustered around the Via Nazionale and Termini station. Central, reasonably-priced hotels get booked quickly so reserve ahead. For budget hotels, expect to pay around €70 per night, even without a private bathroom, and from €35 per person in a B&B, which can be a nicer option. Some do not take credit cards.

Booking: Rome Tourist Office (APT) has a superb website (www.turismoroma.it) with a search facility for booking hotels, B&Bs and hostels. Best online booking agencies: for hotels, guesthouses and B&Bs, check www.romeby.com (from 2-star hotels upwards). Also try www.italyby.com with places booked in real time, without any extra charge. For B&Bs, two of the best sites are www.bbitalia.it and www.bed-and-breakfast.it, with clear descriptions, ratings and prices.

For hostels and budget guesthouses, try www.hostelworld.com. Enjoy Rome (see p404) also make free hotel bookings. **Youth hostel (HI)**: **Ostello Foro Italico AF Pessina**, Viale delle Olimpiadi 61, 🖀(06) 323 6267 (www.ostellodiroma.it; 6 km from station, 🚍 32/280/628 to Lungotevere. Centrally located (non-HI) hostels near Stazione

Termini Ovest are **Marello**, Via Urbana 50, ☎(06) 482 5361 (€25–28 bed and breakfast), and the larger **YWCA** (40 rooms, 64 beds), Via Cesare Balbo 4, ☎(06) 488 0460 (www.ywca-ucdg.it; foyer.roma@ywca-ucdg.it), €33–50 for bed and breakfast. East of the centre is **Youth Station Hostel**, Via Livorno 5, ☎(06) 4429 2471 (www.youthstation .it), dorms €19.50–25. Further out to the south, and more of a cheap hotel, is **San Bernardo**, Via Laurentina 289, ☎(06) 540 7651, with bed and breakfast around €130.

FOOD AND DRINK

Italian **cafés and bars** often have hefty seating charges, so most Romans eat their breakfast, and often lunch, standing up at the bar. You generally pay first and take your receipt to the counter. Picnics can be fixed at delicatessens or grocery stores (*alimentari*) while takeaway pizza is readily available. **Restaurants** are more expensive than *trattorie*, which offer robust Roman-style food, washed down with local wine. Some have no name, their purpose defined only by cooking smells, loud chatter and paper tablecloths. *Pizzerie* are a cheap alternative, while you can combine wine-tasting with delicious snacks at an *enoteca*. **Vegetarian** restaurants are rare but most Italian menus are adaptable.

DOUGH ON THE GO

Fans of *pizza bianca* swear by this crispy 'white' focaccia snack rolled in oil, salt and herbs. Buy some at Antico Forno Roscioli pizza shop on Via de Chiavari 34, near Campo dei Fiori. Munch your snack sitting on a stone bench in peaceful Piazza Farnese, gazing at Palazzo Farnese, a palace designed by Michelangelo.

The Campo dei Fiori area is best for alfresco dining, while the streets off the nearby Pza Farnese have stylish but reasonably cheap venues. **Trastevere** has boisterous, crowded eateries, at once atmospheric yet touristy. Other popular places are around Pza Navona and the **Pantheon**, while the **Ghetto** and the hip, ex-slaughterhouse district of **Testaccio** offer a mixture of rough-and-ready places and traditional Roman cooking.

EXPLORING THE VATICAN

The **Vatican City**, a State within a State and home of the Pope and the Catholic Church, houses numerous treasures. The **Basilica di San Pietro** (St Peter's), worked on by, amongst others, Bramante, Michelangelo and Bernini (whose immense colonnade precedes it), dominates the Vatican (shorts and bare arms not permitted). The vast and elaborate **Vatican Museum**, Viale Vaticano, and the **Sistine Chapel** (enter from the museum), with Michelangelo's *Last Judgement*, considered his masterpiece, and his ceiling frescos depicting scenes from the Old Testament, draw in the crowds. Nearby is the **Castel Sant' Angelo**, built as a Roman tomb, converted into a fortress, used as a palace, and now a museum, set on Lungotevere Castello.

HIGHLIGHTS

Your wish-list may include the **Colosseum**, **Forum**, **St Peter's Basilica**, **the Vatican's Sistine Chapel**, **Piazza Navona**, **the Pantheon**, **Trevi Fountain** and the **Spanish Steps**. However, do spare time

Italy

for contemporary Rome and for watching the world go by from a café terrace: Rome is world-weary, but there's no reason why you should be.

Most museums are closed on Mon (the Vatican closes on Sun, except for the last Sun of each month unless it falls at Easter and Christmas). Most places charge an entrance fee with admission free for under 18s and over 65s and reduced for 18–25s, teachers and students (EU citizens only).

The **Capitoline** hill is occupied by Michelangelo's Pza del Campidoglio, which is dominated by Rome's town hall, the **Palazzo Senatorio**. On either side of this, the magnificent Capitoline Museums in **Palazzo Nuovo** and, opposite it, **Palazzo dei Conservatori**, both house important collections of classical sculpture. In addition, the Palazzo dei Conservatori also contains the **Pinacoteca Capitolina**, a rewarding art gallery featuring paintings by, among others, Rubens, Caravaggio and Titian.

The great basilica of Santa Maria Maggiore, **Pza di Santa Maria Maggiore**, dominates the Esquiline hill. Nearby, **San Pietro in Vincoli**, Pza San Pietro in Vincoli, houses the chains with which St Peter was imprisoned, and Michelangelo's superb statue of Moses. Beyond it, **Trajan's Market** (the world's first shopping mall; Via 4 Novembre) and **Trajan's Column** face the Forum, site of the temples and basilicas of Imperial Rome.

The **Celian** hill is quiet, covered mainly by the gardens of the **Villa Celimontana**, Pza della Navicella. In front of it, the formal **Farnese Gardens** on the **Palatine** are filled with the ruins of Imperial palaces. Below lies Rome's most famous landmark, the **Colosseum**, Pza del Colosseo, built by Emperor Vespasian in 72 AD. It held over 55,000 spectators and was the scene of the Roman games and gladiatorial combats.

At the base of the **Quirinal** hill is the **Trevi Fountain**, Pza Fontana di Trevi – into which, to ensure your return, you must throw a coin – while on its summit sits the president of Italy's residence, the **Palazzo del Quirinale**. Also on the Quirinal is the revamped **Palazzo Barberini**, Via delle Quattro Fontane 13, which contains Renaissance and baroque art.

The **Campo dei Fiori**'s vegetable market adds colour to the district near **Palazzo Farnese**, Pza Farnese, and **Santa Andrea della Valle**, Corso Vittorio Emanuele. The **Palazzo Spada**, Via Capo di Ferro 13, includes paintings by Titian and Rubens.

DAY TRIPS FROM ROME

The **EUR** complex (monumental architecture of the Fascist era, but also a funfair and a good Museum of Roman Civilisation) is on Metro line B, as is **Ostia Antica** (24 km southwest) with the sizeable remains of the ancient Roman port and a lovely rural atmosphere.

Trains from **Termini** run southeast to the **Castelli Romani** (Alban Hills), which include the wine areas of **Frascati** and **Castelli Romani**, and the papal residence of **Castel Gandolfo**. **Tivoli** is a charming spot, with the magnificent Imperial Roman Hadrian's Villa **Hadrian's Villa** (*Villa Adriano*) and the charmingly eccentric **Villa d'Este**, its garden flowing with fountains.

The old Jewish **Ghetto** is one of Rome's quaintest neighbourhoods. It faces Trastevere,
on the far side of the Tiber. On the **Janiculum**, the hill that dominates bohemian
Trastevere, **San Pietro in Montorio**, Pza San Pietro in Montorio, is adjacent to
Bramante's Tempietto – one of the greatest buildings of the High Renaissance. Below
it is the riverside **Villa Farnesina**, Via della Lungara 230, which was decorated in part
by Raphael.

To get under the skin of the city, indulge in café life in several iconic spots. The
first **Pantheon** was built by Marcus Agrippa but even though Emperor Hadrian's
later version in 117 AD was an improvement, he gave credit to his predecessor. Be
tempted by ice cream at Cremeria Monteforte, Via della Rotonda 22, or a *gran caffè*
at Caffè San Eustachio, Pza di Sant'Eustachio 81, which is supposed to serve the best
coffee in town. For a more rough-and-ready spot, join the crowds for a light lunch
at the lively **Campo dei Fiori** fruit and flower market before heading for the **Spanish
Steps** in elegant, bourgeois Rome. **Pza di Spagna** leads to the Pincio hill and the
Villa Borghese gardens. Here, the **Galleria Borghese** is as relaxing as the Vatican
Museum is overwhelming, and displays Bernini's *Rape of Persephone* as well as
masterpieces by Titian, Rubens, Raphael and Caravaggio (booking essential, www.
galleriaborghese.it).

If you came to Rome expecting only ancient art and architecture, think again. There
are new museums of contemporary and modern art, but, in the case of the Altar of
Peace, ancient Rome has been encased in a cutting-edge design. The **Ara Pacis
Museum** (www.arapacis.it) is a controversial white marble 'box' designed to house a
2000-year-old Altar of Peace that, ironically, was used for sacrifices. Less
controversial is Renzo Piano's futuristic **Parco della Musica** (www.auditorium.com),
a gorgeous musical extravaganza that shows that the Eternal City can still teach the
rest of us a few tricks.

Italy

SHOPPING

Best buys are from the **delicatessens** and **grocery stores** – olive oil, fragrant vinegars, dried *funghi* (mushrooms), packets of dried herbs – in and around Via della Croce and the Campo dei Fiori. In Via del Corso you can buy more mainstream fashion rather than the designer brands on offer in the elegant Via dei Condotti area. The sprawling Porta Portese flea market is an entertaining experience.

Rome has a strong artisan goldsmith and silversmith tradition (**Ghetto**, Via dei Coronari, Via dell'Orso), and is fairly well served by antiques shops (Via dei Coronari, Via Giulia, Via del Babuino). Take-home items might include terracotta from southern Italy, kitchen equipment made by Alessi, chunks of parmesan or pecorino cheese, ex-reliquaries from the flea market or bottles of heart-stopping grappa from a liquor store.

NIGHT-TIME AND EVENTS

Events: As a venue, the futuristic **Parco della Musica** has revolutionised Rome's music scene, and is the largest concert-hall complex in Europe. Rome stages exhibitions and festivals all year round, with summer wonderful for outdoor events, best checked out on the detailed 'news' section on the Tourist Board website (www.turismoroma.it).

August is an anomaly in that the city empties as the Romans escape the heat for the beach – but those who remain have a ball at the **Estate Romana** (July/Aug), which celebrates music and dance in parks, amid Roman ruins or in the grand Parco della Musica. Instead, on a lakeside stage, **Villa Ada** holds Rome Encounters the World, an eclectic festival of music from around the world (www.villaada.org). Grander (and pricier) are the open-air opera and ballet events in the Roman ruins of **Terme di Caracalla**, the Caracalla Baths. Even watching the sun go down in this setting justifies the price (www.operaroma.it).

Nightlife: Rome offers romantic restaurants, vibrant bars and cool clubs (jazz, salsa, African, Latin), as well as arts festivals, opera, and choral concerts in churches. The question is: do you want it, given that Rome itself is the most spectacular backdrop for any night on the town? For romance, begin in the baroque stage-set of **Piazza Navona** before strolling to the **Pantheon** for an ice cream beside the best-preserved Roman temple. From here, amble east to the **Trevi Fountain**, the symbol of *la dolce vita*. If Rome's illuminations have inspired you, move to the edge of the **Campidoglio** to view the Colosseum and Forum by night. Otherwise, head for lively Piazza di Spagna for a nightcap. On another evening, visit medieval **Trastevere**, moving seamlessly from trattoria to music club, or slipping away to funkier **Testaccio** for a more cutting-edge scene.

The city's most famous club, **Piper**, Via Tagliamento 9, ☎(06) 855 5398, is still going strong, and is far from being a mere monument to the 'swinging Rome' scene that brought about its birth in the 1960s. Everything about the joint is heterogeneous, from the clientele that it attracts to the entertainment it provides, but you can always bank on bonhomie and banging tunes. Another big venue that manages to create intimacy is **Qube**, Via di Portonaccio 212, ☎(06) 438 5445. The musical menu changes every night of the week, but if you're in town on a Friday, it's well worth checking out the 'Muccassassina' ('Homicidal Cow'), which is a fantastic transvestite night that you'll love whether you're gay, straight or just slightly curved. **Gilda**, Via Mario de' Fiori 97, ☎(06) 6784 838, is a famous disco with an ajoining restaurant (Le Cru). It is very popular among actors, writers and artists, and during the summer the venue moves to the nearby seaside resort of Fregene. **Alibi**, Via di Monte Testaccio 44, ☎(06) 574 3448 (www.lalibi.it), is a grand gay disco from Thursday to Sunday.

The handsomest – and also the most exuberant – bar in Rome is **Bar del Fico**, Piazza del Fico 24, ☎(06) 687 5568, another place that's simultaneously mega-cool and super friendly. If you enjoy looking at beautiful people and can't get to the mirror in the toilets, there'll be plenty of alternative admirables at the bar.

You can't beat a bit of live-and-direct, of course, and there are great gigs at **Radio Londra**, Via di Monte Testaccio 65b, which plays host to some exciting local outfits as well as big-brand bands who usually play stadiums. **Big Mama**, Vicolo San Francesco a Ripa 18, ☎(06) 581 2551 (www.bigmama.it), is one of the best live blues and jazz clubs in Europe. Gigs here have gone down in history.

WHERE NEXT FROM ROME?

*Join the **Rome–Palermo** route (p445) or head north on the **Bologna–Rome** route (p437), branching off if desired at **Orte** to pick up the **Pisa–Orvieto** route (p423). You can also head northwards to **Pisa** to take the **Ventimiglia–Pisa** route (p419) in reverse to the French border, from where you can head on through the French Riviera (see **Marseille–Menton**, p123).*

CITIES: VENICE (VENEZIA)

Venice can play cultural one-upmanship better than most cities. Even the cafés of **St Mark's Square** are awash with famous ghosts, and tourism is almost as ancient as the city itself. Built on 118 tiny islands, this former maritime republic once held sway over an empire stretching from northern Italy to Cyprus.

Today, Venice faces grave environmental threats, including rising waters, which regularly flood the St Mark's area and send Venetians scurrying for their Wellington boots, with everyone else teetering around on duckboards. Mose, a controversial new flood barrier, is being erected to save the city from exceptionally high waters. But if Venice is not to be doomed to a watery grave, the precarious lagoon world must be protected, both from the elements and from polluting human interference. The sight of oil tankers bearing down on the **Doge's Palace** may be just a bad memory, but cruise ships are not. Tourism also plays a part: Venice now has 15 million visitors a year, to a city with only 61,000 inhabitants, the same as it had after the Black Death in 1347. Around 1000 residents leave each year, driven out by exorbitant rents. Ironically, the city numbers around 450 souvenir shops but fewer than ten plumbers – for a city built on water.

Thankfully, Venice is still there for us for some time yet. Most day-trippers fail to stray far from St Mark's Square, which is a huge mistake. Beyond the crowds at the major sights, especially around St Mark's and the **Rialto Bridge**, Venice exudes a village-like calm. Even 15 minutes' walk from the main drag can deposit you alone in a Gothic square, with just pigeons for company. Surprisingly for a city built on water, walking is the best way to explore. Prepare yourself for serious walking as there are 400 bridges and around 180 canals. Expect to get lost, especially at night, which is part and parcel of the charm of this mysterious lagoon world. However, you're never far from the **Grand Canal**, which snakes through the centre, and Venice is perfectly safe. The best way to feel the spirit of city is simply to wander the narrow streets (*calli*), popping into churches as you pass and pausing to sit at a waterside café whenever the whim takes you.

ARRIVAL AND DEPARTURE

To get to Venice itself, take a train to **Santa Lucia** station (some terminate 10 mins earlier at **Mestre** on the mainland). A local service operates between **Mestre** and **Santa Lucia**, which has its own *vaporetto* (waterbus) stop, at the northwest end of the Grand Canal.

Marco Polo International Airport is 13 km northeast of Venice; **flight information**, (041) 260 9260 (www.veniceairport.it). Buses: ACTV 5 and blue ATVO operate half-hourly (hourly in winter/Sundays and holidays) between the airport and Piazzale Roma. To continue into Venice, transfer onto a **waterbus**. The regular motorboat service of **Alilaguna** operates from the airport (year-round, www.alilaguna.com) via the Lido to the Pza San Marco in the heart of

CITIES: VENICE (VENEZIA)

Venice. **Venice Treviso Airport** (www.trevisoairport.it) has buses to Piazzale Roma connecting with Ryanair flights (journey time 70 mins).

INFORMATION

Tourist Offices: Main Office: Pza San Marco 71 (overwhelmed); or Venice Pavilion, the most helpful office, on the waterfront, by the Giardini Ex-Reali; also at Santa Lucia station. Contact: ☎(041) 529 8711 (www.turismovenezia.it). Pick up the free *A Guest in Venice* guide from upmarket hotels, www.aguestinvenice.com. Another useful website for information on transport and visiting the city and its islands, is www.hellovenezia.com. A Mappa Sconti (discount map) is given together with the Rolling Venice Card for youths aged 14 to 29 (must present ID when purchasing the card). Price is €4. A three-day transport pass (city buses and vaporetti) can be bought with the Rolling Venice Card and costs €18. Buy the card at APT (Tourist Office) points (for a list, see www.turismovenezia.it). For details of card, see www.veniceconnected.com. The Chorus Pass is a combined ticket to some of the best churches (www.chorusvenezia.org).

INTERNET ACCESS **Venetian Navigator** (www.venetiannavigator.com) has a convenient branch in Calle Stagneri, between the Rialto Bridge and Campo Fava; another in Calle Caselleria, near St Mark's.

PUBLIC TRANSPORT

VAPORETTO (WATERBUS) Other cities have the bus, train, tram or Metro, but Venice has the *vaporetto*. These sturdy waterbuses, operated by the ACTV transport authority (www.actv.it), run at 10–20-min intervals in daytime and approximately hourly from midnight to 0600. Lines 1 (slow) and 82 (faster) run the length of the **Grand Canal**, connecting **Santa Lucia** station to Pza San Marco. Piers bear the line numbers – but make sure you go in the right direction. Lines 41 and 42 are round-the-islands services taking in **Murano**. The youth hostel on the Isola del Giudecca has its own stop on line 82. Lines that run at night are identified with a moon symbol.

There are quite a few travelcards available for tourists including 12-/36-/48-/72-hr, or 7-day options, and the popular 24hr pass for €18. With these tourists can travel on city buses and all *vaporetto* routes run by ACTV (including outlying islands such as Torcello, Burano and Murano). They can be purchased at Hellovenezia offices (www.hellovenezia.com) or pre-booked online at www.veniceconnected.com, which offers discounted rates depending on the season (high, mid or low).

WATER TAXIS These are sleek but expensive. They can be found at major strategic positions such as outside the train station or the airport, St Mark's Square and the Lido.

RADIO TAXIS ☎(041) 595 2080.

GONDOLAS The city's 400 gondolas, which can take up to six passengers each, provide a costly, conceivably romantic, means of getting around. Rates are fixed. If you decide to treat yourself, go in the evening when the canals are at their most magical. There are 'stands'

on several canals. Instead, try the short gondola ride on the *traghetto* (gondola ferry), which crosses the Grand Canal at eight points (signposted Traghetto) for only 50 cents.

ACCOMMODATION

Booking: check the Venice Tourism website (www.turismovenezia.it) for all accommodation (including B&B). Also try www.sleepitaly.com. For hostels, check www.hostelworld.com. For hotels, contact AVA (Venetian Hoteliers' Association), ☎199 173 309 (within Italy), ☎(041) 522 2264 (www.veneziasi.it), which has a free booking service (0800–2300) and reservation desks at Santa Lucia station (0800–2100); and at Marco Polo International Airport (1000–2200). B&Bs and guesthouses are now common, and dotted around, while budget places tend to be near the station. If Venice is full, do not stay in grim Mestre; opt for Padua or Treviso, 30 mins by train. B&B: **Da Zorzi**, Fondamenta San Giacomo, Giudecca 197, ☎(041) 528 6380 (book via www.sleepitaly.com). Apartment and rooms in a family-run B&B with garden on un-touristy island of Giudecca. Budget: **Collegio Armeno Moorat**, Raphael, Dorsoduro 2596, ☎(041) 522 8770 (www.collegioarmeno.com), is a grand baroque palace with very un-grand (budget) rooms in a quiet part of Venice. The HI youth hostel is **Ostello Venezia**, Fondamenta Zitelle 86, Isola della Giudecca, ☎(041) 523 8211 (Vaporetto line 82: Zitelle stop). One of the best-located hostels in Italy, set in an ancient granary on the lively (and 'real') island of Giudecca, a quick crossing to St Mark's. Ten minutes from the railway station is **Santa Fosca Hostel** (non-HI), Cannaregio 2372, ☎ (041) 715 775 (www.santafosca.com). Splashing out: **Locanda Leon Bianco**, Corte Leon Bianco, ☎(041) 523 3572 (www.leonbianco.it), is a romantic reasonably-priced (from €110) hotel overlooking the Grand Canal.

FOOD AND DRINK

Venice takes pride in its seafood-based cuisine. Restaurants around St Mark's over-charge, but stroll a bridge or two away to find more affordable *trattorie* and *pizzerie*. Venetian food tends to be overpriced and under-achieving, with the difficulty of transporting fresh produce adding 20% to prices. But seafood lovers will be satisfied with lagoon crabs, red mullet and pasta pungent with cuttlefish ink. The secrets of eating well on a budget include avoiding grim 'tourist menus', and lunching in rough-and-ready *bacari* (Venetian wine bars). These are mostly around the Rialto but close early in the evening. Also choose simple 'gondoliers' inns': if you see a gondolier going in, follow him immediately! *Pizzerie* are also a good budget option. Wherever you eat in central Venice, be ready to sacrifice either the food or the view: to have both at once is tricky. The city's most atmospheric café is **Florian** on Pza San Marco; pricey, but you are paying for the location. Famous **Harry's Bar** is at San Marco 1323 (www.cipriani.com).

For picnic food, head to the Rialto market – and also fill your mineral water bottle with wine for around €2 per litre at the basic bottle stores at Calle de la Bissa, near

Italy

the Rialto Bridge, on Campo Santa Margherita. Budget restaurants: **All'Aciugheta**, 4357 Castello, for cheap tapas at the bar or proper meals sitting down. **Osteria alle Botteghe**, Calle delle Botteghe, off Campo Santo Stefano, is similar. **Cavatappi**, Campo della Guerra, near San Marco, is a wine bar serving cold dishes including excellent cheese plates. **Cantina Do Mori**, Calle dei Do Mori, is a *bacaro* (tapas bar) near the Rialto.

HIGHLIGHTS

OUT ON THE WATER This great waterway sweeps through the six city districts (*sestieri*), with its switchback shape providing changing vistas of palaces and warehouses, markets and merchant clubs, courts, prisons and even the city casino. **The Grand Canal** was virtually the register of the Venetian nobility, with the palaces symbolising their owners' status and success. Yet the sea is a great leveller, with low tide revealing the slimy underpinnings of the noblest palace. A vaporetto ride along the Grand Canal – sit at the front – is one of the world's greatest voyages. Choose the slower Line 1 route and take a return trip to appreciate both banks (40 minutes each way). As well as presenting a pageant on the water, the canal offers a slice of local life. Dodging gondolas, water taxis and delivery boats, the ferry slides past a succession of palaces, churches and bridges. Look out for the fourth bridge (Ponte di Calatrava) over the Grand Canal, only added in 2007, and the only one to be illuminated at night. Later, join the locals on a short traghetto hop (by gondola ferry) across the Grand Canal (50 cents). As only four bridges cross this 4-km-long canal, this saves walking and is fun: tradition dictates you have to stand up.

PIAZZA SAN MARCO (ST MARK'S SQUARE) St Mark's Square is the city's 'drawing room,' home to **St Mark's Basilica**, the **Bell Tower**, the **Doge's Palace**, elegant cafés – and a maelstrom of visitors. Ideally see St Mark's early in the morning, before the queue is too long. The Basilica, crowned by bulbous domes, and encrusted with mosaics, was consecrated in 1094 to house the relics of St Mark the Evangelist. Above the church is a panoramic loggia and a gallery displaying the gilded Horses of St Mark. These gilded bronzes, dating from the 2nd century, were stolen from Byzantium by the Venetians in 1204. Just along the waterfront stands the **Palazzo Ducale** (Doge's Palace), the other unmissable sight, and an insight into the lifestyles of the Doges, former rulers of Venice and its maritime republic. Stairs from it lead down to the **Ponte dei Sospiri** (Bridge of Sighs), which crosses a narrow canal to the Palazzo delle Prigioni, the former prison for petty offenders. Prisoners were led across the bridge – hence the name. Back on the waterfront, make the short hop to **Isola di San Giorgio**, for a stunning view from the monastic lift over the lagoon. This is more atmospheric and less crowded than the view from the **Campanile di San Marco**, the Bell Tower on St Mark's Square.

The grandiose church of **La Salute** surveys the entrance to the Grand Canal, marking the beginning to the world's most princely waterway. The nearby **Guggenheim Collection**, in Palazzo Venier dei Leoni, is an outstanding collection of cubist,

Above: Lake Lucerne, Switzerland (muehle/Fotolia)

Below: Salzburg, Austria (Gregory Mitchell/BigStockPhoto)

Above: Trevi Fountain, Rome, Italy (Alison Rayner)
Below left: Orvieto, Italy (John Henshall/Alamy)

Right: Venice, Italy (Alexey Popov/BigStockPhoto)
Below right: The Leaning Tower, Pisa, Italy (Sarita P/SXC.hu)

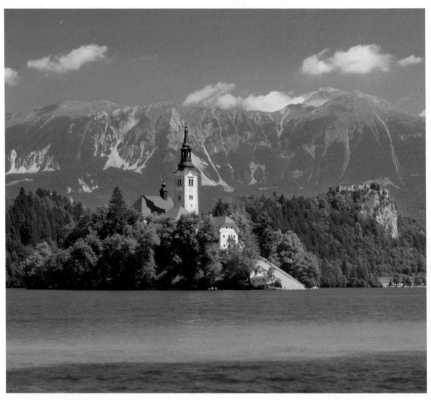

Above: Lake Bled, Slovenia (Simon Krzic/BigStockPhoto)

Below: Dubrovnik, Croatia (Croatian National Tourist Board)

abstract and Surrealist art. Further along, on the other side of the Grand Canal, is the **Galleria dell'Accademia**, Venice's greatest art gallery (expect queues) showcasing Venetian art up to the 18th century, including masters such as Bellini, Canaletto, Carpaccio, Guardi, Titian, Tintoretto and Veronese. Highlights include Tintoretto's *Transport of the Body of St Mark*, Titian's *Pietà*, Veronese's *Christ in the House of Levi* and Carpaccio's *Life of St Ursula* cycle of frescos.

The Grand Canal is home to two of the city's most gorgeous palaces, the Gothic **Ca' D'Oro** and the baroque **Ca' Rezzonico**. Both contain superb art collections, but together also offer a crash course in aristocratic Venetian architecture, unlike the Accademia. Away from the waterfront, other highlights include **I Frari** (Santa Maria Gloriosa dei Frari), a treasury of art, displaying masterpieces by Titian and Bellini. The **Scuola di San Rocco**, a confraternity house, with its interior painted by Tintoretto, is another great treasure. As the city is studded with delightful churches, drop into any you pass.

But Venice is also about the living, breathing, eating city. For a taste of Venice, in all senses of the word, explore the area around the **Rialto Bridge**, from the markets to the waterfront cafés and the tiny, traditional tapas bars (*bacari*) hidden in the alleys behind. To escape the crowds by day, head into the Castello district, and the Arsenale, the great Venetian shipyards, or walk the length of the Zattere, the city's waterfront stroll, and Venice's loveliest walk. By night, explore the mysterious, even murky, canals in the **Cannaregio** district, before finishing the evening in lively **Campo Santa Margherita**.

As for the outlying islands, **Torcello** is where the original Venice began, while **Burano** is a vividly painted 'fishermen's island'. **Murano** is only recommended if you have an interest in Murano glassware. Under the Venetian republic, so prized were the glassmakers that they were virtual prisoners, and left Venice on pain of death.

THE ISLANDS

Organised sightseeing tours depart to the outlying **Murano** island and its neighbours, **Burano** and **Torcello**. Murano has glass factories and a fine church, Santissimi Maria e Donato, with Byzantine paving and 13th-century mosaics, while Burano is generally more pleasant, with a lively little fishing community and brightly coloured houses. You can visit these and other islands just as easily – and much more cheaply – on an ordinary *vaporetto*, No. 12. The **Lido** is a glamorous (though, it must be admitted, overrated) bathing and sunbathing haunt, made famous during the *belle époque*.

PIGEON WARS

The city's pigeons are being driven out of Venice. Mayor Massimo Cacciari has vowed to dispose of the pigeons' last refuge on St Mark's Square and close down the stalls selling pigeon food. Although describing them as 'flying rats', so far he has shied away from imposing London's radical solution: bringing in the hawks to kill them.

SHOPPING

The Venetians' aptitude for commerce has been sharpened by eleven centuries of trade. Carnival

Italy

masks and Murano glass are the best buys in an expensive city, but choose the authentic versions, such as masks in the **San Polo** district, where mask-makers sell from their studios. Glass is best bought from Murano glassworks, after a glassmaking display. The glassworks are generally free to visit, but expect a hard sell afterwards.

NIGHT-TIME AND EVENTS

The city is busiest in autumn, with events such as the annual ten-day Venice Film Festival (in Sept), the oldest film festival in the world, and the highpoint of the city's social calendar. The Biennale is held in the **Giardini** (Gardens) and the **Arsenale** from June–Oct on even-numbered years. The biggest traditional event is Carnival, ten days of Lenten masked balls and street celebrations. **La Vogalonga** ('The Long Row') on Ascension Sunday is a marathon regatta around the Lagoon. The historic **Regata Storica** (first Sun in Sept) begins with a magnificent procession of traditional boats rowed by costumed crews along the Grand Canal. The opera venue is **La Fenice**, recently rebuilt after destruction by fire in 1996 (tours available). Concerts are held in the city's churches and confraternity halls. The **Palazzo del Cinema** on the Lido hosts the film festival while **Palazzo Grassi** is the venue for blockbuster art exhibitions.

Venetian nightlife may be distinctly tame, yet it is far from dead, and improving all the time. It is no longer a case of a cosy meal out followed by a gondola ride echoing to the strains of Celine Dion's greatest hits. Not that the simple watery Venetian pleasures should be mocked. Nothing beats the furtive feeling of slipping down the Grand Canal at night on a No. 1 vaporetto and watching strangers mingling inside a glittering palazzo. Or even the innocent pleasure of eating an ice cream while sauntering down the breezy **Zattere**, looking at illuminated water-craft going full tilt. For students, the liveliest spots are the bars on **Campo Santa Margherita** in Dorsoduro and, at weekends, the funky **Fondamenta della Misericordia** in Cannaregio, the place for live music, cheap bars, ethnic eateries and vino-filled Venetian students out on the town.

WHERE NEXT FROM VENICE?

Venice is on the *Milan–Trieste* route (p429). Ferries to *Patras* via *Corfu* take 30–31 hrs (ETT table 2875). A scenic route over the Alps into Austria via *Villach* (table 88) joins the *Innsbruck–Vienna* route (p377) at *Linz*, or you can change at *Villach* and join the same route further west at *Schwarzach-St Veit* (table 970).

ROUTE DETAIL

Ventimiglia–Sanremo ETT tables 580, 581

Type	Frequency	Typical journey time
Train	1–2 per hr	15 mins

Sanremo–Genoa ETT table 580

Type	Frequency	Typical journey time
Train	1–2 per hr	1 hr 50 mins – 3 hrs

Genoa–Rapallo ETT table 610

Type	Frequency	Typical journey time
Train	Up to 2 per hr	30 mins

Rapallo–Pisa ETT table 610

Type	Frequency	Typical journey time
Train	Every 1–2 hrs	1 hr 45 mins

KEY JOURNEYS

Nice–Genoa ETT tables 360, 361, 580

Type	Frequency	Typical journey time
Train	1–2 per hr	3 hrs – 4 hrs 10 mins

Nice–Pisa ETT tables 360, 580, 610

Type	Frequency	Typical journey time
Train	Every 1–2 hrs	7 hrs

Notes

For the key journey Nice–Genoa, change at Ventimiglia. There are a few through trains. For the key journey Nice–Pisa, change at Ventimiglia and Genoa.

Italy

From the French border (you can join this journey on to the **Marseille–Menton** route, p123), the line along the **Italian Riviera** has a wonderful sequence of coastal views. Against mountain backdrops, the vineyards, olive trees and palms flourish in the mild climes that attracted English visitors to the **Liguria** region in the 19th century. **Genoa** is gritty but engrossing, and **Pisa** (see p424) is a fine introduction to **Tuscany**.

VENTIMIGLIA

The railway line runs between the town and the pebble beach, which is situated right on the French/Italian border. It's a scruffy frontier town that the French invade on Friday, for the famous market. Despite a crumbling, steeply built Old Town, and a thriving cut flower and olive oil industry, there is little to detain visitors beyond the superb market, the place to stock up on bags, clothes, Parmesan cheese, oil and picnic lunches.

▨ In the town.

ℹ️ **Tourist Office:** Via Cavour 61, ☎/fax (0184) 351 183 (www.turismoinliguria.it).

SANREMO

The prime resort on the Italian Riviera stretches around an 8-km bay. It has a pleasant old town, with its narrow streets, steep steps and arches. The **Nobel Villa**, C. Cavalotti 112, was the house of the Swedish inventor Alfred Nobel, who established the series of international prizes named after him; it is open to the public. In early March each year, the town is filled with singers and musicians for Italy's masively popular yearly musical event: the **Festival di Sanremo**.

▨ In the town.

ℹ️ **Tourist Office:** Largo Nuvoloni 1, ☎(0184) 59059 (www.visitrivieradeifiori.it).
Internet Point Sanremo, Pza C. Colombo 42.

🛏 Modest rooms can be found at **hotels** like the **Villa Maria**, Corso Nuvoloni 30, ☎(0184) 531 422 (www.villamariahotel.it), and the central **Alexander**, Corso Garibaldi 123, ☎(0184) 504 591 (www.hotelalexandersanremo.com), which is an Art Nouveau affair in gardens. Campsite **Villaggio dei Fiori**, Via Tiro a Volo 3, ☎(0184) 660635 (www.villaggiodeifiori.it), offers tent space as well as bungalow accommodation (open all year).

GENOA (GENOVA)

Sandwiched between the mountains and the sea, **Genoa** is a concertina of a city, with slate-topped palaces and squat churches bearing down on the old port. 'La Superba' is Italy's foremost seaport and was once, like Venice, a proud maritime republic ruled by a Doge, or elected ruler. The city gained a huge facelift as European Capital of Culture in 2004 and is now gritty but gorgeous. As one of the most densely packed historical centres in Europe, Genoa is unfathomable. Renzo Piano, the renowned architect, sees his home town as a 'secret, inward-looking kasbah city'.

After the restoration of the waterfront, Genoa now has a port worthy of a maritime republic. Clustered around the **Porto Antico** are a traditional Genoese galleon, the **Museum of the Sea** and the superb **Aquarium**, designed to resemble a ship setting sail. Further along is the **Lanterna** (1544), the nation's oldest lighthouse. Porto Antico, the redesigned waterfront, functions as a new city piazza, with bars tucked into medieval arcades along the landward side. Much of the centre is pedestrianised, set among a maze of medieval alleys. The most patrician street is **Via Garibaldi**, lined with Renaissance palaces, including **Palazzo Bianco** (No. 11) and **Palazzo Rosso** (No. 18), both galleries bursting with Flemish and Italian masterpieces. The **Cattedrale di San Lorenzo**, which survived bombing by the British, is one of the most engaging churches. **Pza Banchi** was the heart of the old city and is now a lively pocket of old Genoa, with cheap cafés nearby, places to try typical pasta and pesto dishes. The **Palazzo Ducale**, on Pza Matteotti, was once the seat of the Doge, but now houses chic cafés and an exhibition centre. A funicular from Pza del Portello whisks you to **Sant'Anna**, high on the hill.

Expect a city ringed by ridge-top forts, with alleys burrowing under medieval palaces, funiculars reaching dizzying heights, and tunnels emerging from nowhere. Focus upwards as you walk: virtually every alleyway has striking architectural details, from friezes to frescos. Before developing a crick in your neck, abandon architecture for a fish grill, pasta and pesto, washed down by Ligurian white wine.

Nervi, a few stops along the line from Brignole station, is a delightful escape, with its dramatic coastline, beautiful promenade, and several revamped art museums. If you fancy a swim, there are a few *bagni*, private beaches with facilities such as showers, in Corso Italia (Albaro area), like **Bagni Lido** at No. 13.

There are two main stations. **Principe**; take 🚌 41 from here to get to the city centre. **Stazione Brignole** is further east; take 🚌 40 to the centre. Trains to the north use both stations; use 🚌 37 to transfer between them.

✈ **Cristoforo Colombo Airport** (7 km), 12–14 buses daily to the two main rail stations and Piazza de Ferrari.

ℹ **Tourist Office**: Tourist Office Genova Turismo, Stazione Porta Principe, ☎ (010) 246 2633 (www.turismoinliguria.it). **Internet**: 1pc4you, Pza Durazzo 12/N (near Stazione Porta Principe).

🛏 Cheap accommodation is easy to find, but can be tacky. Try the outskirts of the Old Town, near Brignole. **Youth hostel (HI)**: **Ostello di Genova**, Via Costanzi 120n, ☎ (010) 242 2457 (www.ostellogenova.it), 🚌 35/40 from Piazza Principe. Convenient for the waterfront is **B&B Acquarium**, Vico Palla 1, ☎ (010) 860 4214 (www.geocities.com/bb_acquarium).

Italy

🔲 The cheapest places for lunch are in the dock area, but most close in the evening. Street stalls all over the city sell fried seafood and chickpea pancakes. For Saturday night fever, head for the student-filled Via di San Bernardo and Stradina Sant'Agostino, or stroll down pedestrianised Via di San Lorenzo.

SIDE TRIP TO PAVIA Pavia, north of Genoa on the line to Milan, is reached by train in about 1 hr 15 mins (hourly; ETT table 610; station a 10-min walk from centre, or take 🚌 3/6). It's a quietly attractive old town, known for its medieval towers, churches and peaceful squares. The highlight of the area and one of the great buildings of Italy is the **Certosa di Pavia**, a Carthusian monastery, 8 km north. It has an incredible façade, of Carrara marble. Cistercian monks now live there and maintain a vow of silence. The monastery can only be seen by joining a guided tour. Buses from Pavia are frequent (from Pza Piave), then there's a 1.5-km walk to the entrance. **Tourist Office**: IAT Pavia, Piazza Petrarca 4, ☎(0382) 597 001 (www.pavese .pv.it), located a 10-min walk from station. To stay overnight, try the **Hotel Aurora**, Via Vittorio Emanuele II 25, ☎(0382) 23 664, €€, or the nearby **Camping Ticino** (2.5 km from Pavia) open during the summer (www.campingticino.it).

PISA

See p424.

RAPALLO

Icing-coloured *belle époque* hotels overlook the palm-shaded promenade that defines Rapallo's long seafront. Anchoring the far end of this classic Riviera scene is a picture-perfect stone **castle** almost surrounded by water. Admire the view from the cafés that overlook the beach below. The only must-see is **Museo del Merletto** (Tues–Sat), whose examples of hand-made lace includes high-fashion clothing, set among the rare plants and trees of **Parco Casale**.

WHERE NEXT FROM PISA?

Either venture into **Tuscany** *on the* **Pisa–Orvieto** *route or carry on along the coast to* **Rome** *– see ETT table 610. On the way to Rome you can visit the island of* **Elba**; *change at* **Campiglia** *for* **Piombino** *(table 609), then take the 1-hr ferry crossing to* **Elba** *(table 2699).* **Elba** *has clear waters, fine beaches and a ragged coastline of capes and bays, though in summer it gets impossibly tourist-ridden; there are paths and attractive villages to explore, plus Napoleon's villa and a cable car up to a 1019-m summit.* **Buses** *serve the island's villages and resorts.* **Accommodation** *is plentiful (with lots of campsites), but it gets heavily booked in July and Aug; contact the* **Tourist Office** *at Calata Italia 26, Portoferraio (in the dilapidated ten-storey block near the ferry port),* ☎*(0565) 914 671 (www.aptelba.it).*

Footpaths and a **funicular** (from Pzle Solari) climb to the **Santuario Basilica di Montallegro**, a shrine with expansive views over the Gulf of Paradise.

🚉 Near the promenade.

ℹ️ **Tourist Office**: Lungomare V. Veneto 7, ☎(0185) 230 346.

ROUTE DETAIL

Pisa–Lucca   ETT table 614

Type	Frequency	Typical journey time
Train	12–20 daily	25 mins

Lucca–Florence   ETT table 614

Type	Frequency	Typical journey time
Train	Every hr	1 hr 20 mins

Florence–Siena   ETT table 613

Type	Frequency	Typical journey time
Train	9–10 daily	1 hr 30 mins

Siena–Orvieto   ETT tables 609, 615

Type	Frequency	Typical journey time
Train	7–12 daily	2 hrs 5 mins

KEY JOURNEYS

Pisa–Florence
(via Empoli)   ETT table 613

Type	Frequency	Typical journey time
Train	1–2 per hr	1 hr 20 mins

Pisa–Florence
(via Lucca; change at Lucca)   ETT table 614

Type	Frequency	Typical journey time
Train	12–14 daily	2 hrs

Florence–Rome
(by Alta Velocità)   ETT table 642

Type	Frequency	Typical journey time
Train	1–2 per hr	1 hr 40 mins

Notes

Pisa to Orvieto: change at Florence.
Siena to Orvieto: change at Chiusi.

Italy

This trip winds around the heart of Tuscany, one of the culturally richest and least spoilt parts of Italy, with its green hills striped with olive groves and vineyards, as well as historic towns and cities overflowing with Renaissance art and architecture. (Check Tuscan sights on: www.turismointoscana.it; www.intoscana.it; and, for lovely Siena province, www.terresiena.it.)

PISA

The **Leaning Tower of Pisa** rates among the world's most familiar landmarks, part of a magnificent triumvirate of buildings around the **Campo dei Miracoli** (Field of Miracles), by the Cathedral and Baptistry. Some of Italy's finest medieval sculptures are here, many by Nicola and Giovanni Pisano (father and son) and other Pisanos (unrelated). The unusual architecture, characterised by distinctive stripes of marble and blind arcades, is thought to emanate from the Pisans' contact with the Moslems of North Africa and Spain.

The 11th-century, four-tiered **Duomo**, one of Italy's finest cathedrals, was the first Tuscan building to use marble in horizontal stripes (a Moorish idea). The original bronze entrance, **Portale di San Ranieri**, was cast around 1180 and is by Bonanno, one of the designers of the Leaning Tower itself. A fire destroyed much of the interior in the 16th century, but some of Cosmati's lovely floor survived, as did the 14th-century mosaic of Christ Pantocrator by Cimabue, in the apse, and a magnificent sculpted pulpit by Giovanni Pisano (c1300).

SAVING PISA'S LEANING TOWER

The famous tower, which reached a lean of 5 m, was closed to visitors in 1990 while the architects argued over how to stop it collapsing. A British engineer provided the solution − excavating soil from below the foundations to reduce the tilt by about 40 cm. Work was completed in 2001 and visitors can again climb the tower for a hefty entrance fee.

Construction of the circular **Baptistry** stopped when money ran out. The three lower storeys consist of Romanesque arcades. The top half, in Gothic style, with pinnacles and a dome, was added later (again by the prolific Pisanos, in the 1260s). It has a pulpit superbly carved by Nicola Pisano, whose design produced a whole series of similar pulpits during this period.

The **Leaning Tower** (Torre Pendente) began life in 1173, as a campanile for the Duomo. When it was 10-m-high it began to tilt and the architect fled. Construction continued, however, with successive architects trying unsuccessfully to restore the balance.

A special one-week ticket covers entry to the major museums and monuments in Pisa.

[RAIL] **Centrale**, south of the River Arno and a 20-min walk from the Leaning Tower, or **CPT** [bus] 1/3.

✈ Pisa's **Galileo Galilei Airport** is the main regional hub for international flights, ☎(050) 849 111 (www.pisa-airport.com). Frequent buses run to the city centre and rail station, which has a much-improved rail service (one–two trains per hour).

ℹ **Tourist Offices**: Piazza Vittorio Emanuele II 16, ☎(050) 42291 (www.pisaturismo.it); Piazza Arcivescovado 8, and at the airport, ☎(050) 502 518. **Internet**: Koinè, Via dei Mille 3/5.

🏨 There are several good budget hotels around Campo dei Miracoli, but they are popular and in term time students fill the best. **Hostel (non HI)**: **Centro Turistico Madonna dell'Acqua**, Via Pietrasantina 15, ☎(050) 890 622, 🚌 3.
Campsite: **Campeggio Torre Pendente**, Viale Cascine 86, ☎(050) 561 704 (www.camping torrependente.com), 1 km west of the Leaning Tower, signposted from Pza Manin (open summer only). **Budget hotels**: try **Pensione Rinascente**, Via del Castelletto 28, ☎(050) 580 460 (www.rinascentehotel.com), near Borgo Stretto, or **Hotel Roseto**, Via Pietro Mascagni 24, ☎(050) 42087 or 42596 (www.hotelroseto.it), just a few steps from the station.

DAY TRIP FROM PISA

Certosa di Pisa, 12 km to the east and served by regular CPT buses, is an enormous 14th-century Carthusian monastery with a frescoed church where all 11 chapels are painted in pastel colours. Each three-room cell has its own little patch of garden.

LUCCA

Despite its considerable beauty, **Lucca** never feels overrun, and has a leisurely, provincial feel, with bicycles used by the locals. The city comes alive in summer, when major rock concerts take place in key squares. Outside summer, Lucca is tranquil, with streets that are dotted with palaces, towers and handsome early churches, most of them dating from the city's heyday (11th–14th centuries). Start with a stroll around part of the 4 km of 16th–17th century walls – the most complete in Italy – that enclose the Old City and are themselves encircled by a green belt, a buffer between the medieval and modern towns. Some bastions have been restored and you can get a good idea of the town's original layout. The **Pza Anfiteatro** is an oval of medieval tenements clustered round the site of a **Roman amphitheatre**. Parts of the original arches and columns are visible in the buildings themselves, and the shape of the oval is effectively a fossilisation of the theatre.

The Romanesque **Duomo di San Martino**, in the south of the centre, has individually designed columns and loggias: look out for an exquisite early 15th-century **Tomb of Ilaria del Carretto** (by Jacopo della Quercia) and Tintoretto's *Last Supper*. Nearby **Casa Puccini** was the boyhood home of the opera composer Puccini, and is open to the public. The central **Church of San Michele** is in Foro, on the site of the ancient Roman forum, has a dazzling Pisan Romanesque façade, studded with mosaics, and surmounted by a huge bronze of Archangel Michael. Near the western city wall is the **Pinacoteca Nazionale**, housed in **Palazzo Mansi**, Via Galli Tassi 43. The 17th-century palace is of rather more interest than the pictures it displays, and the overdecorated interior includes a particularly spectacular gilded bridal suite.

Italy

Further southeast is **Palazzo Guinigi**, Via Sant' Andrea, a rambling complex of inter-connected medieval buildings. A climb of 230 steps leads up a turreted tower with an oak sprouting from the top, giving a fascinating view over the city's rooftops. The main museum, **Museo Nazionale Guinigi**, east of the centre on Via della Quarquonia, contains a huge and varied collection of local Romanesque and Renaissance art.

🚆 Just outside the city walls, an easy walk to the centre. There are frequent trains from **Pisa** (20 mins), **Viareggio** (20 mins) and **Florence** (1 hr 20 mins).

ℹ️ **Tourist Office**: Piazza S. Maria 35, ☎(0583) 91 991 (www.luccaturismo.it). It also has an internet point.

🏨 Finding space is always a problem, so book ahead. The local Tourist Office (APT) can help you find last-minute accommodation. **Youth hostel (HI)**: **San Frediano**, Via della Cavallerizza 12, ☎(0583) 469 957 (www.ostellolucca.it). **B&Bs: B&B Ai Cipressi**, Via di Tiglio 126, ☎(0583) 496 571 (www.aicipressi.it). There are several B&Bs so check the Lucca Tourist Office website. **Hotels: Hotel Moderno**, Via Vincenzo Civitali 38, ☎(0583) 55840 (www.albergomoderno.com); and **Hotel Diana**, Via del Molinetto, ☎(0583) 492 202 (www.albergodiana.com).

FLORENCE (FIRENZE)

See p390.

SIENA

Spread over low hills and filled with robust terracotta-coloured buildings, **Siena** has changed little since medieval times. Indeed, this most beautiful of Tuscan cities has contracted inside its walls in places – look out from just behind the **Campo**, the main square, and there's a vista down a green, rural valley, as pretty as a wine label. The city was Florence's tireless enemy for much of the Middle Ages, competing with it for supremacy politically, economically and artistically. Now it's a delightful place to visit, for its artistic treasures as well as just for the pleasures of discovering its myriad sloping alleys. The fan-shaped Campo dates from 1347 and is regarded as the focus of the city's life. The arcaded and turreted **Palazzo Pubblico**, on the south side, still performs its traditional role as the town hall, and its bell tower, the 102-m **Torre del Mangia**, soars above the town, with dizzying views. Part of the **Palazzo Pubblico** houses the **Museo Civico**, whose Sala della Pace and Sala del Mappamondo contain treasures of Lorenzetti and Martini among others. To the west stands the **Duomo**, the cathedral, with its striped marble façade studded with Renaissance sculpture. Inside, the floor comprises 56 separate sections, on which over 40 artists worked for nearly two centuries; other highlights are the elaborate pulpit by Nicola Pisano and a Donatello bronze. The **Museo dell'Opera del Duomo** contains masterpieces of painting and sculpture.

SAN GIMIGNANO

San Gimignano (32 km northwest, half-hourly buses from **Siena**, via Poggibonsi) is a perfect medieval hill town, although overrun with tourists. As a medieval Manhattan in miniature, it originally sported 70 towers. The towers, of which 14 survive, were partly defensive and partly status symbols. Pza del Duomo has some of the finest medieval buildings, while the frescos by Gozzoli in the **Church of Sant'Agostino** and the four fresco cycles in the **Collegiata** (cathedral) also stand out. The **Tourist Office** is on the main square while an internet café (Internet Train) is on Pza delle Erbe.

Terzo di Città (southwest of the Campo) has some of the city's finest private palaces, such as the **Palazzo Chigi-Saracini**, Via di Città 89. In the past, the city was divided into 60 *contrade* (wards named after animals), of which 17 remain, each with its own church, museum and central square with a fountain featuring the relevant animal. Rivalry between wards is strong, reaching a head in the famous twice-yearly **Palio**, a no-holds-barred horse race around the Campo (which is regarded as neutral territory) on 2 July and 16 Aug. Only ten horses can participate, so lots are drawn to decide which wards will be represented; the whole event is regarded as a matter of honour by the locals, with rehearsals for days beforehand and excitement mounting to fever pitch. Races last only 90 seconds or so, but are preceded by a two-hour procession and a lifetime of passion. Get there early if you want to watch – standing in the centre is free, if crowded.

� 2 km northeast (in valley below town). It is a tedious 45-min walk uphill to the centre, but there are regular shuttle buses (tickets from machine by entrance).

🚌 **Long-distance buses** (covering all Tuscany), run by **Sena**, **Lazzi** and **Train**, leave from Pza Gramsci bus station.

ℹ️ **Tourist Office**: Pza del Campo 56, ☎ (0577) 280 551 (www.terresiena.it; www.sienaonline.it). This office has good maps and information. There are also booths in the train and bus stations. **Internet**: there are various points in Via di Pantaneto, like Net Runner, ☎ (0577) 449 46.

🏨 **Private rooms** are best value, but you often have to stay at least a week and they can be full of students in term time. **Hotels:** budget hotels are often full. For the **Palio** (early July and mid-Aug), either book well ahead or stay up all night (many do). At other times, if the Tourist Office can't help, try the **Cooperativa Siena Hotels** promotion booth Piazza Madre Teresa di Calcutta 5, ☎ (0577) 288 084 (www.hotelsiena.com). One of the cheapest hotels is **Tre Donzelle**, Via delle Donzelle 5, ☎ (0577) 280 358 (www.tredonzelle.com), €. **Youth hostel (HI)**: Ostello **Guidoriccio**, Via Fiorentina 89, ☎ (0577) 52212 (www.ostelloguidoriccio.com), 2 km northwest of the centre (🚌 7/10/15). **Campsite**: **Campeggio Colleverde**, Strada di Scacciapensieri 47, ☎ (0577) 332 545 (www.campingcolleverde.com), 2 km north (🚌 3/8, both from Piazzade/Sale). For rural accommodation in the superb surrounds of Siena check out www.agriturismo.it.

ORVIETO

Orvieto, like Lucca, is less beset by the tourist hordes. Set in a valley of vineyards, this striking cliffside town is perched above a raised tufa-stone plateau. Dominating the town is the vividly striped **Duomo**, Pza Duomo, built in honour of a 13th-century miracle. With its triple-gabled exterior of gilded mosaics, bronze doors and bas-reliefs by Lorenzo Maitani, as well as its outstanding interior frescos by Luca Signorelli depicting the *Last Judgement* (in the **Cappella di San Brizio** in the right transept), it is one of the great churches of Umbria. Several grand buildings near the Duomo now contain museums.

The **Pozzo di San Patrizio**, Viale San Gallo, near the funicular terminal, is an astonishing cylindrical well with a diameter of 13 m and a depth of 62 m. A double-helix mule-ramp runs around the interior. The well was completed in 1537 to provide an emergency water supply for the city.

COMBINED ENTRY TICKETS IN ORVIETO

A combined ticket, the **Carta Orvieto Unica** (www.cartaunica.it), allows access to nine major sites in the town, including the Cathedral, the Pozzo di San Patrizio and the Cappella di San Brizio. The card also allows free use of the local electric minibus service (Lines A and B).

⊞RAIL By the bus station and connected by funicular 'Bracci' to Pza Cahen in the Old Town (takes 2 mins; every 10 mins weekdays 0720–2030, Sun and public holidays 0800–2030), from where you can then walk or take any of the frequent buses (Line A or B) to the centre. From the railway station you can reach the centre of Orvieto by the public funicular-plus-minibus route.

i **Tourist Office**: Pza Duomo 20, ☎(0763) 341 772 (www.orvietoonline.com). Local bus tickets and the combined sightseeing ticket, **Orvieto Unica**, can be purchased here. Pick up the current version of *Welcome to Orvieto* for useful listings. **Internet**: Caffè Montanucci in Corso Cavour 21, near the Cathedral.

⊞ If you want to experience the atmosphere of Orvieto at night, the best located central hotels (both inexpensive) are **Virgilio**, Piazza del Duomo 5, ☎(0763) 341 882 (only a few rooms have views), or **Duomo**, Via Maurizio 7, ☎(0763) 341 887 (www.orvietohotelduomo.com). The **Maitani**, Via Maitani 5, ☎(0763) 342 011, is worth splashing out on. **Hostels: Ostello Porziuncola**, Loc. Cappuccini 8, ☎(0763) 341 387.

TO Orvieto is famous for its wines: best known are the crisp fruity whites made from Trebbiano grapes, but reds and sweet wines are also produced. *Orvieto Classico* wines are fermented and stored in the underground passages and caves that honeycomb the soft local tufa, and are often sold under the Cardeto label (the largest Umbrian wine cooperative). Taste before you buy in local bars and *enoteche* (wine bars) such as the atmospheric **La Bottega del Buon Vino**, Via della Cava 24–26, which is also a restaurant. Orvieto is full of good eating places, though prices are high. There are picnic facilities in the **Parco delle Grotte** near the Pza Duomo; the public gardens of the **Rocca**, near the funicular terminal, can be enjoyed free, and have fine views over the **Paglia Valley**.

WHERE NEXT FROM ORVIETO?

Carry on to **Rome** *(p403); this route goes via* **Orte**, *where you can change for trains to* **Spoleto**. *See ETT tables 615 and 625.*

ROUTE DETAIL

Milano (Centrale)–Verona ETT table 600

Type	Frequency	Typical journey time
Train	1–2 per hr	1 hr 22 mins

Verona–Vicenza ETT table 600

Type	Frequency	Typical journey time
Train	1–2 per hr	27 mins

Vicenza–Padua ETT table 600

Type	Frequency	Typical journey time
Train	1–2 per hr	16 mins

Padua–Venice (Sta Lucia) ETT table 600

Type	Frequency	Typical journey time
Train	1–2 per hr	30 mins

Venice (Sta Lucia)–Trieste ETT table 605

Type	Frequency	Typical journey time
Train	Every hr	2 hrs 5 mins

Note

A change of train may be required at Venezia Mestre.

KEY JOURNEYS

Milan–Venice ETT table 600

Type	Frequency	Typical journey time
Train	1–2 per hr	2 hrs 35 mins

Venice–Ljubljana ETT table 89

Type	Frequency	Typical journey time
Train	1 night train	4 hrs 30 mins

Venice–Zagreb ETT table 89b

Type	Frequency	Typical journey time
Train	1 night train	7 hrs 52 mins

Italy

The places rather than the views are of primary interest on this trip from **Lombardy**, Italy's busiest and most prosperous region, to **Trieste** in the east, with the foothills of the **Alps** to the north. **Verona** and **Venice** are among Europe's most romantic cities.

MILAN

Italy's second largest city is Italy's economic powerhouse, its commercial, banking, fashion and design centre. After suffering bomb damage in 1943, Milan is less aesthetically appealing than Florence or Rome. Even so, it is Italy's most cosmopolitan city, and boasts Romanesque churches, grand galleries, a superb museum of Northern Italian art (the Brera) and one of the boldest cathedrals in Christendom. Milan's signature building is the **Duomo**, on Pza Duomo. This extravagant Gothic cathedral, overflowing with belfries, statues and pinnacles, has stairs leading to rooftop views. Leading off the square is the **Galleria Vittorio Emanuele II**, an iconic 19th-century iron and glass shopping arcade lined with chic cafés and boutiques. Beyond lies **Pza Scala**, home of La Scala, the world's most celebrated opera house (www.teatroallascala.org).

The **Pinacoteca di Brera**, Via Brera 28 (Metro: Lanza), is Milan's finest art gallery, featuring Italian artists of the 14th–19th centuries, including masterpieces by Mantegna, Raphael and Caravaggio. In addition, the **Pinacoteca Ambrosiana**, Pza Pio XI 2 (Metro: Duomo or Cordusio), presents works by Caravaggio, Raphael and Leonardo da Vinci. Milan's most celebrated work of art is Leonardo's *Last Supper* (1495–97), occupying a wall of a Dominican monastery refectory next to **Santa Maria Delle Grazie**. The 'Da Vinci Code' phenomenon ensures that the crowds continue to flock here, trying to unravel the 'mystery' through Leonardo links. (Tickets must be booked ahead: ☎(02) 9280 0360 (www.cenacolovinciano.net).)

Before leaving Milan, escape the urban chaos by visiting two peaceful spots. Milan's most beloved church is not the Cathedral but the largely Romanesque **Sant'Ambrogio**, a basilica begun in the late 4th century by St Ambrose, Milan's patron saint and former bishop. So smooth in speech was St Ambrose that honey liqueur was named after him. The other urban retreat is the castle and grounds of **Castello Sforzesco**, on Pza Castello, a fortress housing eclectic galleries and museums, displaying everything from arms and musical instruments to Egyptian art and works by Michelangelo. (Note that museums – including the Brera – are closed on Mon.)

For a rich *aperitivo* and a stroll in the evening go to **Navigli**, a lively area around the Milanese canals (Metro: Porta Genova). If you want to dance the night away, try **Alcatraz**, Via Valtellina 21 (www.alcatrazmilano.com; Metro: Maciachini), which hosts both concerts and disco nights.

⊹ There are three airports (www.sea-aeroportimilano.it) serving Milan: **Malpensa**, about 50 km northwest, **Linate**, 7 km from the city, and **Bergamo** (www.orioaeroporto.it), 45 km northeast. Intercontinental flights land at Malpensa; the other airports share international, charter and domestic air travel. The Malpensa Express train is a shuttle service to Malpensa Terminal 1 from Stazione Nord (Cadorna) and back (Metro: Cadorna); every 30 mins (takes 40 mins). Travellers flying Alitalia travel free. Malpensa Shuttle 🖼(0331) 258 411 (www.malpensashuttle.it) operates a service to Malpensa airport from Stazione Centrale. Buses leave for Malpensa every 20 mins. The shuttle also runs between Malpensa and Linate every 30 mins. Starfly 🖼(02) 5858 7237, at Linate airport operate a service to and from Stazione Centrale every 30 mins. 🚌 73 leaves from Corso Europa (S. Babila) for Linate every 10 mins. Regular shuttle buses connect Bergamo airport with both Bergamo (journey time 15 minutes) and Milan (journey time 1 hr) central railway stations.

🛈 Main IAT Milano – Tourist Office: Pza Duomo 19/A, 🖼(02) 7740 4343 (www.visitamilano.it, www.ciaomilano.it). Branch: Stazione Centrale. **Internet access:** Some **Mondadori** bookshops have internet points; there is one in Piazza del Duomo (open daily).

🏨 Lodging in Milan is expensive, but there are places to stay around Stazione Centrale, even if the area is rather seedy, despite the revamped station itself. **Hotel Virgilio**, Via P L da Palestrina 30, 🖼(02) 669 1337 (www.virgiliohotel.it), €€, and **Hotel Rallye**, Via Benedetto Marcello 59, 🖼(02) 2940 4568 (www.hotelrallye.net), €€, are both family-run hotels near Centrale. **Hotel Gelsomina**, Via Piero della Francesca 4/7, 🖼(02) 349 1742 (www.hotelgelsomina.it), €€, has en suite doubles and is clean and friendly; reached by tram, 3 km from the city centre. To splash out, choose the lovely inn known as the **Antica Locanda Solferino**, Via Castelfidardo 2, 🖼(02) 657 0129 (www.anticalocandasolferino.it). The Tourist Office will provide a full list of accommodation. **Hostel: Ostello Piero Rotta**, Via Salmoraghi angolo Via Calliano, 🖼(02) 3926 7095 (www.ostellomilano.it), Metro line 1 to QT8 station). **Camping: Campeggio Città di Milano**, Via G Airaghi 61, 🖼(02) 4820 7017, 🚌 72 from Metro station De Angeli.

SIDE TRIP TO TURIN (TORINO) West of Milan (ETT table 585) lies one of Italy's most elegant – and overlooked – cities, the capital of the Dukes of Savoy, who made it a showplace of broad avenues, baroque architecture and spacious squares. Always a well-kept and prosperous city, Turin has been undergoing a renaissance since its successful makeover for the 2006 Olympic Winter Games. The celebrations of the 150th anniversary of the Unity of Italy will take place in the city in 2011 (Turin was the first capital city before Rome) with many extra cultural events. Turin is far more patrician than Milan, but its arcaded streets invite strolling, while its *belle époque* cafés invite lingering, ideally over a hot chocolate or a Martini, two drinks the city has perfected. As for sights, the city itself is the main attraction, with its elegant arcades, grand squares and cosy cafés. The **Sacra Sindone**, the Holy Shroud (www.sindone.org) is displayed only rarely (the next is scheduled for April–May 2010) in the cathedral. The most memorable sights are the magnificently revamped **Egyptian Museum**, second only to the one in Cairo, and the **Cinema Museum**, one of Italy's most enthralling experiences. This is set in the Mole Antonelliana, the symbol of the city, and Turin's most bizarre building, which started out as a synagogue, before becoming the cinema museum and acquiring a surreal glass elevator, which speeds visitors to the top for views stretching towards the Alps.

Accommodation: Casa della Mobilità Giovanile, Corso Venezia 11, 🖼(011) 250 535 (www.openzero11.it); and **Ostello Torino**, Via Alby 1, 🖼(011) 660 2939 (www.ostellotorino.it). **B&B: B&B La Piazzetta**, Largo Saluzzo 36, 🖼(011) 650 3490. **Hotel:**

Italy

Hotel Bologna, Corso Vittorio Emanuele II 60, Loc. Porta Nuova, ☎(011) 562 0191, (www.hotelbolognasrl.it). **Budget Hotel**: **Albergo Alba**, Via Maria Vittoria 34, ☎(011) 812 0208 (www.albergoalba.it).

VERONA

Placed on an S-bend of the River **Adige** and best explored on foot, this beautiful city of pastel-pink marble thrives on the story of *Romeo and Juliet* (see below), but the real attractions are its elegant medieval squares, fine Gothic churches and massive Roman amphitheatre, the **Arena**, which comes alive during the annual opera festival in July and August (ticket office ☎(045) 800 5151, www.arena.it; the cheapest seats are unreserved, so arrive early). Dominating the large Pza Bra, it has 44 pink marble tiers that can accommodate 20,000 people – incredibly, the singers and orchestra are perfectly audible. By day, explore the Arena to savour the feeling the gladiators must have had while waiting for combat.

Via Mazzini, which leads off Pza Bra, is one of Italy's smartest shopping streets. This leads to Pza delle Erbe, which is surrounded by faded Renaissance palaces. Originally the Roman forum, the square is now a daily market. An archway leads to a serener square, Pza dei Signori, the centre of medieval civic life, and framed by the 15th-century **Loggia del Consiglio** and the crenellated **Palazzo del Capitano**.

Via Cappello was the supposed home of Juliet Capulet (of *Romeo and Juliet* fame), though the famous balcony immortalised in the play was added in 1935. Her statue, an even more modern addition, stands in the courtyard near the balcony. Although now a romantic shrine, this spot owes less to history than to legend (and Verona's astute sense of marketing). Nearby, the ornate Gothic tombs of the Scaligeri family are in the grounds of the small Romanesque **Church of Santa Maria Antica**. The Scaligeri ruled Verona in its 13th-century heyday and commissioned many of its finest buildings. An equestrian statue that once topped one of them stands inside their castle beside the river, now the **Castelvecchio Museum**, which displays Fine Gothic art as well as weapons and jewellery. Beyond it, **San Zeno Maggiore**, the most elaborate Romanesque church in Northern Italy, boasts a Madonna altarpiece by Mantegna and magnificent 11th–12th-century bronze doors. On **Piazza Duomo**, Verona's striped red and white marble Cathedral blends Romanesque and Gothic, forming a lovely backdrop to Titian's *Assumption*.

Apart from the amphitheatre, the city has numerous other Roman remains, including **Porta Leona** and the carved **Porta Borsari**, each a short walk from **Piazza delle Erbe**. Go across the river, over the partly Roman **Ponte Pietra**, Verona's best-known bridge. On the opposite bank are the remains of the **Roman theatre** (where plays were performed, as opposed to the amphitheatre, which held coarser public entertainments); although smaller than the amphitheatre, there's rather more to see, as entrance includes admission to the **Archaeological Museum**, housed in an old convent above the theatre, and there are great views of the city as well as collections of Roman statuary and bronze figurines, adjoining a palm-shaded cloister.

▣ **Stazione Porta Nuova**, a 15–20-min walk south of the centre (🚌 11/12/13/14 from stop A). Bike hire available.

✈ There are two airports: the main one is **Valerio Catullo**, www.aeroportoverona.it (buses every 20 mins, €4.50); Ryanair flights go to the more remote **Brescia** airport (buses connect with flights).

ℹ **Tourist Offices**: Via Degli Alpini 9; ☎ (045) 806 8680, fax (045) 800 3638 (www.tourism.verona.it). Also at the station. The **Verona Card** (€10/15) is a 1- or 3-day combined sightseeing/travel card valid for public transport and entry to the major sights. **Internet**: **Veron@Web**, Via Roma 17.

🏨 **Hotels**: There is plenty of budget accommodation but booking is essential for the opera season, July–Aug. One of the central, best-value budget options is **Locanda Catullo**, Via Valerio Catullo 1, ☎ (045) 800 2786 (locandacatullo @tiscalinet.it), €–€€, graciously old-fashioned but friendly. Also central are the 2-star **Sanmicheli**, Via Valverde 2, ☎ (045) 800 3749 (www.sanmicheli.com), €€ (on the way to the station), and (further east) **Best Western Hotel Armando**, Via Dietro Pallone 1, ☎ (045) 800 0206, €€. **Hostel (HI)**: **Villa Francescatti**, Salita Fontana del Ferro 15, ☎ (045) 590 360, 3 km from the station, 🚌 73 (🚌 90 on Sun) to Pza Isolo, from which the hostel is a short walk; camping in the grounds. **Campsite**: Castel San Pietro 2, ☎ (045) 592 037 (www.campingcastelsanpietro.com), open 1 May–mid-Oct, walkable from the centre (🚌 41).

🍽 For reasonably priced **restaurants**, look along Corso Porta Borsari, in the streets around Pza delle Erbe or the Veronetta district on the east bank of the Adige. The Pza delle Erbe's **food market** is also useful.

WHERE NEXT FROM VERONA?

Venture north into the Dolomites from Bolzano, or head via Innsbruck to Munich; see **Munich–Verona** *(p332). Services (ETT table 595; 1 hr 45 mins) to Bologna link with the* **Bologna–Rome** *route (p437) via Florence, where you can join the* **Pisa–Orvieto** *route (p423).*

VICENZA

This prosperous city was largely rebuilt in the 16th century to designs by Andrea di Pietro della Gondola, better known as Palladio, who moved here from Padua at the age of 16 to become an apprentice stonemason. He gave his name to the Palladian style of architecture, which applied elegant Romanesque concepts to classical forms. His first public commission was the imposing **Basilica**, on Pza dei Signori, hub of the city. This medieval palace was in danger of collapsing until he shored it up brilliantly with Ionic and Doric columns. Corso Palladio, the long, straight, main street, is lined with palaces. The **Teatro Olimpico** at the eastern end was Palladio's last work. Based on the design of ancient Roman theatres and opened in 1585, it is the oldest indoor theatre in Europe and still in use from May to early July, and from Sept to early Oct.

Italy

The acoustics are superb. **Palazzo Chiericati**, Pza Matteotti, houses the well-stocked **Museo Civico**, which contains paintings by such masters as Tintoretto and Memling.

Palladio's most famous villa, **La Rotonda**, is on a hillside about 1.5 km southeast of the centre (🚌 8/13). It has a round interior under a dome set in a cube of classical porticoes, a design often copied. Nearby is the **Villa Valmarana**, an 18th-century country house notable for its Tiepolo frescos and dwarfs on the garden wall.

🚆 A 10-min walk south of the centre (🚌 1/7).

ℹ️ **Tourist Office**: Pza Matteotti 12, ☎ (0444) 320 854 (www.vicenzae.org); branch at Pza dei Signori 8. The **Vicenza Card** (available from Teatro Olimpico's ticket office) gives free admission to six city monuments and museums and is valid for three days.

🏨 The cheapest **hotels** are away from the centre or in noisy locations, so it's worth considering 2-star places like **Hotel Vicenza**, Strada dei Nodari 5–7, ☎ (0444) 321 512. Book ahead for summer and autumn. **Youth hostel (HI)**: **Olimpico**, Via Giuriolo 9, ☎ (0444) 540 222 (www.ostellovicenza.com), 🚌 1/2/4/5/7 (stop nearby). **Campsite**: **Campeggio Vicenza**, Strada Pelosa 241, ☎ (0444) 582 311 (20 mins by 🚌 1 to Torri di Quartesolo from the station).

🍴 For eating out, look around Pza dei Signori.

PADUA (PADOVA)

The dignified old town has attractive arcaded streets and traffic-free squares. **Prato della Valle**, Italy's largest square, hosts a Saturday market. In the **University**, founded in 1222, you can see the wooden desk used by Galileo, who taught physics there, and visit the old anatomical theatre. Giotto's glorious depiction of the lives of Mary and Jesus in the **Cappella degli Scrovegni** (Scrovegni Chapel) in Corso Garibaldi alone justifies a visit to Padua (booking via www.cappelladegliscrovegni.it). The other major attraction is 'Il Santo' – the **Basilica di Sant' Antonio**, which is visited by some five million pilgrims each year, and has bronze sculptures by Donatello on the high altar and marble reliefs by Lombardo.

🚆 At the northern edge of town, 15-min walk to centre or 🚌 3/8/12/18.

ℹ️ **Tourist Office**: IAT point: Stazione Ferroviaria (in the station), ☎ (049) 875 2077 (www.turismopadova.it). Branches in Galleria Pedrocchi and Piazza del Santo. Padova Card, valid for two or three days, allows admission to 12 city sites and free local transport (www.padovacard.it).

🏨 There is a wide choice of places to stay (try around Pza del Santo), though booking is advisable. **Youth hostel**: **Città di Padova**, Via A. Aleardi 30, ☎ (049) 875 2219 (www.ostellopadova.it); 🚌 3/8/12/18. **Campsite**: **Campsite Sporting Center**, Via Roma 123–125, Montegrotto Terme, ☎ (049) 793 400, (www.sportingcenter.it), open Mar–mid-Nov, has a 2-star hotel on the premises. They also offer thermal treatments in the wonderful hot springs.

TO You should find a reasonably priced *trattoria* around Pza del Santo, where the local specialities include *piperata* (mutton in wine sauce). Don't miss **Caffè Pedrocchi**, Via VIII Febbraio, one of Italy's most famous cafés, where writers and artists used to meet during the 19th century.

VENICE (VENEZIA)

See p412.

TRIESTE

Italy's atmospheric easternmost city looks more Austrian than Italian, a reminder of its former role as the chief port of the Austro-Hungarian Empire (up to 1918). Rebuilt in the 19th century in a grand gridiron plan, it relishes its role as a crossroads between east and west. It's stately rather than intimate, with six-storey palazzi and Art Nouveau and classical façades. It's set on a beautifully curving bay, with the rugged limestone heights of the Carso – which saw one of the bloodiest battles of World War I – rising abruptly immediately inland.

Trieste is a major coffee port, and café life is part of its lifeblood. Perhaps the most evocative place is **Caffè San Marco**, Via Cesare Battisti 18 – with its high-ceilinged Art Nouveau interior. One of Trieste's oldest cafés, the **Caffè degli Specchi** (1839), occupies the majestic central square, Pza dell'Unita d'Italia, presided over by the vast Palazzo del Comune del Governo, aglow with its mosaic ornamentation. City sights include more than a dozen museums, including the **Museo di Storia ed Arte** (with a wide range of art and archaeology relating to Trieste), and the **Civico Museum Sartorio**, an opulent former family residence filled with objets d'art. A pleasant area for strolling is the **Capitoline Hill**, the heart of Roman and medieval Trieste. On top, beside the remains of the Roman forum, stands the 11th-century **Cathedral of San Giusto**, founded in the 5th century on the site of a Roman temple and containing early medieval mosaics and frescos. Narrow alleys drop down to V. Teatro Romano, named after the restored ruins of a **Roman theatre**. One of the best aspects of Trieste is its scope for **excursions**. Cycling around town is feasible (bicycle hire at the station and on the quay at Stazione Maritima). For a taster of the Carso, take the wonderfully old-fashioned **Villa Opicina tram** from Pza Oberdan (ultra cheap; tickets sold at booth). For a walk with intermittent views of the city far below, get off at the tall obelisk at the top, and walk along the track by the map board. Otherwise take ⊟ 42 (from Villa Opicina or Pza Oberdan) to **Grotta Gigante**, the world's largest show cave (closed Mon; absolutely must see: it's big enough to accommodate St Peter's, Rome). A short bus ride (⊟ 36 towards Grignano) west leads to **Castle Miramare**, a white marble pile in a stunning coastal location. Built 1856–60 for Maximilian of Habsburg as a love nest for him and Charlotte of Belgium, it reveals astonishingly ornate marquetry interiors designed to remind Maximilian of life in a ship's cabin. There's free entry to the surrounding park, which slopes down from the main road (get off the bus after going through two tunnels; retrace through one tunnel to reach the park gates): this is laced with trails and has many rare Mediterranean broad-leaf trees, as well as a pond and a grotto.

Piran (reached by ferry from Trieste in summer, also served by buses from Trieste, roughly every 2 hrs, plus buses every 20 mins if you change in Koper) is a marvellously well-preserved old port that once belonged to Venice but is now in Slovenia. It's a huddle of tiny lanes and stepped alleys full of washing lines and prowling cats. The centrally located HI youth hostel makes a great place to stay: **Hostel Val & Garni Hotel**, Gregorciceva 38a, ☎(+386) 05 673 2555 (www.hostel-val.com). Another recommended side trip is westwards to **Aquileia** (train to Cervignano, then change for a bus, direction Grado; also direct buses, direction Grado, from Trieste Airport/Ronchi dei Legionari). Sited on a fertile wine-growing coastal plain, Aquileia has striking remains of a Roman town, notably in the form of a huge mosaic floor in the basilica (the largest early Christian monument in western Europe, surpassing anything even in Rome), a burial ground, remains of a port and houses, and a very extensive museum of finds that include some remarkably life-like sculpted heads. The friendly **HI youth hostel** is in the centre of town at Via Roma 25, ☎(0431) 91024 (www.ostelloaquileia.it); it may be closed Nov–Mar, so check beforehand; internet, bike hire.

🚉 **Stazione Centrale**, Pza della Libertà 8. Adjacent to **bus station**.

✈ **Trieste Airport** (www.aeroporto.fvg.it), 33 km west, 30 mins by air bus (pay on board) or cheaper 🚌 51 (buy ticket in bar upstairs in airport) to Trieste bus station. Also buses to Monfalcone rail station for trains to Venice.

ℹ **Tourist Office**: Pza Unità d'Italia 4b, ☎(040) 347 8312 (www.turismofvg.it). **Internet**: **Bar Unità**, near Piazza dell'Unità d'Italia.

🏨 A quiet, comfortable mid-priced hotel in a side street near the station is **Hotel Italia**, Via della Geppa 15, ☎(040) 369 900 (www.hotel-italia.it); singles €65, doubles from €85 including an excellent breakfast. There are cheaper 1-star options (around €55 double, €40 single) such as the **Nuovo Albergo Centro**, Via Roma 13, ☎(040) 347 8790 (www.hotelcentrotrieste.it), a centrally located family-run ex-pension. There are also **B&Bs** (full list from Tourist Office) from around €30: **B&B Aachen**, Via Cesare Battisti 24, ☎(0338) 228 7085 (www.triestebedand breakfast.it). The **HI youth hostel** is 5 km out of town on the coast near Miramare Castle and has dorms only; Tergeste, Viale Miramare 331, ☎(040) 224 102 (ostellotrieste@ hotmail.com), 🚌 36 (from rail station, turn left, across road, then left again 50 m to bus stop).

WHERE NEXT FROM TRIESTE?

*Continue over the border to **Ljubljana**; see the* *Ljubljana–Dubrovnik route (p458).*

ROUTE DÉTAIL

Bologna–Florence
(by Eurostar Italia & Alta Velocità) ETT tables 620/642

Type	Frequency	Typical journey time
Train	1–3 per hr	58 mins

Florence–Arezzo
ETT tables 615, 620

Type	Frequency	Typical journey time
Train	1–2 per hr	1 hr

Arezzo–Perugia
ETT table 615

Type	Frequency	Typical journey time
Train	Every 2 hrs	1 hr 10 mins

Perugia–Assisi
ETT table 615, 625

Type	Frequency	Typical journey time
Train	Every hr	20 mins

Assisi–Spoleto
ETT table 625

Type	Frequency	Typical journey time
Train	5–8 daily	38 mins

Spoleto–Rome
ETT table 625

Type	Frequency	Typical journey time
Train	Up to 15 daily	1 hr 40 mins

KEY JOURNEYS

Florence–Rome
ETT tables 620/642
(by Eurostar Italia & Alta Velocità, direct route)

Type	Frequency	Typical journey time
Train	2–3 per hr	1 hr 37 mins

Notes

The Bologna–Florence high-speed line opened in December 2009, and non-stop journeys between these points now take only 35 minutes.

Italy

From the graceful old university town of **Bologna**, venture into verdant **Umbria**, with its mystical atmosphere and medieval hilltop towns – the garden of Eden to Dante. Art and history are intermingled in such places as the great pilgrimage city of **Assisi**, the Umbrian capital of **Perugia**, and the Roman town of **Spoleto**. **Florence** and **Rome** demand at least a few days each.

BOLOGNA

Bologna is the capital of Emilia Romagna, the most civilised region in Italy. The city mastered the art of living in medieval times, when a pink-bricked city grew up around Europe's oldest university, founded in 1088. In terms of tourism, the only reason that Bologna has languished is because Florence is a looming presence over the hills. Bologna is also the gastro-erotic heart of Italy, a place where tortellini, plump nuggets of pasta, were inspired by Venus' navel. The streetscape has real dignity in its arcades, red- and ochre-coloured buildings, stucco façades, greatly varied porticos, church spires, palaces and medieval towers, the latter built as status symbols by the city's wealthy nobles. The university's first permanent home is today in **Palazzo Poggi**, Via Zamboni. The two adjoining 13th-century squares, Pza Maggiore and Pza Nettuno, make the obvious central starting point. Around them lie the **Palazzo Comunale** (the town hall, which now houses Bologna's modern art collection), the 15th-century **Palazzo del Podestà**, the **Palazzo dei Banchi** and the **Basilica of San Petronio**. The Fountain of Neptune (1564) spouts in the northwest corner. At Pza San Stefano, the churches of **San Stefano** (**Crocifisso**, **Santo Sepolcro**, **Trinità**, **San Vitale** and **Sant'Agricola**) make up a complex of many churches, complete with cloisters and courtyards, that has retained its ancient atmosphere.

The two most distinctive towers still standing are the 98-m **Asinelli** (with a dizzying panorama from the top) and its crazily tilting partner, the **Garisenda**, by Pza di Porta Ravegnana. A row of 666 arcaded porticoes ascends a hillside to the 18th-century **Basilica di San Luca**, a 35-min walk from **Meloncello** (reached by 🚌 20 from Pza Maggiore), for a splendid vista of the city and the Apennines that adjoin it. Another great place for views is the Parco di Villa Ghigi, an area of Apennine foothills given to the city by a former rector of the university. Walk up from the Pza Maggiore and step out from city centre to a wild, open expanse with vineyards and cattle. Bologna, famous for its tortellini, has a gastronomic reputation in Italy second to none, especially for pasta, velvety sauces, meat, charcuterie

TICKETS

Central **Bologna** can be seen on foot. The bus system covers the suburbs (route maps from the Tourist Office). **Tickets**, sold at tobacconists' kiosks, are good for 1 hr once validated on board. You can get an 8-trip pass (Citypass) or an 11-trip pass (Ecodays) – both passes may be used by more than one person simultaneously. Day tickets are valid 24 hours. At the time of writing, admission to several Bologna museums is free of charge, except for temporary exhibitions. See Tourist Office website http://iat.comune.bologna. it for a full list.

and cheese. For cheaper eateries (*trattorie* and *pizzerie*) try the small streets around Pza Verdi, the hub of student life.

🚉 **Stazione Centrale**, 1 km north of Pza Maggiore; walk along Via dell'Indipendenza (🚌 25/30). A memorial to casualties of the 1980 station bombing stands by the renovated station entrance.

✈ **Gugliemo Marconi Airport**, ☎(051) 647 9615 (www.bologna-airport.it), 8 km. Aerobus (www.atc.bo.it) every 30 mins (0600–0015) to Centrale rail station, with a journey time of 20 mins.

i **Tourist Offices**: at the railway station, ☎(051) 239 660 (http://iat.comune.bologna.it); the airport and Pza Maggiore 1. **Internet: Everest Telecom**, Via della Zecca 3.

🛏 The Tourist Office has a wide-ranging list of **hotels** and **pensioni** in all categories. **Youth hostels (HI)**: Via Viadagola 5, ☎(051) 501 810 (www.ostellodibologna.com, 6 km from the centre), 🚌 21B/93/301 to San Sisto (100 m); and almost next door at Via Viadagola 14 (same phone number and website). HI hostel **Centro Europa Uno**, Via Emilia 297, San Lazzaro di Savena, ☎(050) 625 7007 or 625 8352 (www.centroeuropauno.it), is located about 5km outside the city (call in advance). **Camping**: **Centro Turistico Città di Bologna**, ☎(051) 325 016 (www.hotelcamping.com), open all year.

SIDE TRIPS FROM BOLOGNA   **Bologna** is on the line from **Naples** to **Venice**, via **Florence**; see ETT tables 620, 640, 642. **Ravenna** (1 hr 20 mins; ETT table 621) was the centre of Byzantine rule in Italy during the 6th and 7th centuries AD. The most impressive reminders of these periods are Ravenna's famed **mosaics** (the major sights cluster in the northwest corner of the Old Town). The 6th-century octagonal **Basilica of San Vitale** features depictions of the Byzantine Emperor Justinian and Empress Theodora. In the grounds are the **Mausoleum of Galla Placidia**, decorated with richly coloured mosaics, and the **National Museum**. **Sant'Apollinare Nuovo** dates from the same period; its walls are lined with green and gold mosaics showing processions of saints and virgins. The station is about 500 m east of town. **Tourist Office**: Via Salara 8, ☎(0544) 35755 (www.turismo.ravenna.it); in the centre of town. **Youth hostel (HI): Dante**, Via Nicolodi 12, ☎(0544) 421 164 (www.hostelravenna.com), 🚌 1/10/11/70 or 10-min walk southeast from rail station.

You can also take the line along the Adriatic coast to **Brindisi** (ETT table 631), though this trip isn't Italy at its best. On the way you could pause at **Rimini**, a somewhat charmless resort but with an excellent beach, fine Roman bridge and lively nightlife; it's a 40-min bus trip (ETT table 630) from the tiny independent republic of **San Marino** (just 60 sq km of it), memorably perched on the slopes of **Monte Titano**. Other worthwhile detours include **Peschici**, east of **San Severo** on the **Gargano massif** (a rugged limestone coast), and the area around **Monópoli** (notable for its *trulli* – curious drystone, white-domed structures of feudal origins). **Brindisi**, the port near the 'heel' of Italy, has a useful ferry to **Patras** in Greece (ETT table 2775).

The **Bologna–Milan** service (ETT tables 619, 620, 630; 2 hrs 5 mins) runs via **Modena** (a quietly attractive old town with a Romanesque cathedral and with a fine

Italy

collection of art and illuminated manuscripts within the Palazzo dei Musei) and **Parma** (a household name for its ham and cheese, worth a stop for the frescoed Baptistry, the sensuous Correggio frescos in Camera di San Paolo and the art in the Galleria Nazionale in Palazzo della Pilotta). The Alta Velocità high-speed train service (ETT table 642) does not run through Modena.

FLORENCE (FIRENZE)

See p390.

AREZZO

Arezzo was a major settlement in Etruscan, Roman and medieval times. Always a wealthy city, today its economy rests on jewellers, goldsmiths and antiques. Much of the centre is modern, but there are still attractive winding streets in the hilltop Old Town, with its Renaissance houses and the handsome Pza Grande.

One of the masterpieces of Italian Renaissance painting and the city's major attraction is Piero della Francesca's brilliant fresco cycle of the *Legend of the True Cross* (1452–66), on display in the 14th-century **Church of San Francesco**, Via della Madonna del Prato, in the centre of the old town.

The spacious **cathedral**, begun in 1278 and lit by 16th-century stained glass, is adorned by Piero della Francesca's fresco of Mary Magdalene, near the organ. The **Galleria e Museo Medievale e Moderno**, Via di San Lorentino 8, contains an exceptional collection of majolica as well as sculpture dating from the 10th–17th centuries. **Santa Maria delle Grazie**, Via di Santa Maria, is a particularly fine 15th-century church that contains a high altar by Andrea della Robbia.

> **AREZZO'S ANTIQUES FAIR**
> Don't expect to find a bargain by attending the **Fiera Antiquaria** (Antiques Fair), in Pza Grande on the first Sun of every month. Hugely popular with an ever more international clientele, it's the place to buy serious antique furniture, terracotta, linen and, of course, jewellery. Accommodation gets very heavily booked up.

There's less to detain you in the lower town, though you may like to pause at the **Museo Archeologico**, Via Margaritone 10, in an old monastery not far to the east of the station; it has a collection of Roman Aretine ware (50 BC to AD 60–70 terracotta with a shiny red glaze and adorned with bas-reliefs), Etruscan bronzes and 1st-century BC vases. Nearby is a ruined Roman amphitheatre, the **Anfiteatro Romano**.

🚆 In the modern sector, west of the centre: walk up the hill to the Old Town.

ⓘ **Tourist Office**: Piazza della Repubblica 28 (by the station), ☎(0575) 377 678 (www.apt.arezzo.it). Information Centre at Via Ricasoli. **Internet**: Informagiovani office, Pza Guido Monaco 2 (Mon–Sat).

🛏 Rooms are difficult to find over the first weekend of every month, but otherwise generally fine. There are several budget options near the station. **Hotel: Hotel Cecco**, Corso Italia 215, 📞(0575) 209 86 or 356 730 (www.hotelcecco.com). **Foresteria Arezzo I Pratacci**, Via Edison 25, Zona Pratacci (2 km from city centre), 📞(0575) 383 338 (www.foresteriaarezzo.it), offers budget accommodation and use of the kitchen. **B&B I Due Gigli**, Via Cavour 170, 📞(338) 8661934 (www.iduegigli.it), is in the heart of town.

PERUGIA

Warlike and belligerent, the splendid capital of Umbria was smitten by strife almost until the 19th century and has a host of monuments bearing an undeniably martial face. Ignore the unattractive modern suburbs and head straight for the almost intact medieval centre, by bus or escalator. From Pza Italia the pedestrianised Corso Vannucci, lined with fortified palaces, cafés and shops – the centre of activities for a cosmopolitan crowd almost around the clock – runs north to the city's heart in Pza IV Novembre, where the **Duomo** (cathedral) is located. All the other major sights are within easy walking distance of here.

The **Duomo** is a large, plain, medieval building, supposedly home to the Virgin Mary's wedding ring. In the centre of the square is the 13th-century Fontana Maggiore, a fountain that's a triumph of decoration by Nicola and Giovanni Pisano. Facing the fountain, the somewhat forbidding **Palazzo dei Priori**, Corso Vannucci, Perugia's civic head-quarters since 1297, has a great Gothic portal and long rows of windows. Fan-like steps lead up to the Sala dei Notari, covered with an entertaining array of frescos. The **Galleria Nazionale dell'Umbria**, on the fourth floor, contains works notably by Pinturicchio and Perugino, and is Italy's most important repository of Umbrian art; it also has a few Tuscan masterpieces, including Piero della Francesca's *Madonna and Saints with Child* and a triptych by Fra Angelico. See also **Collegio della Mercanzia**, with its magnificent 15th-century carvings, while the restored frescos of the **Collegio del Cambio** (the Bankers' Guild) are considered to be Perugino's finest works.

San Domenico, Pza G Bruno, is an enormous church with several outstanding works of art. Authorship of the 14th-century **Tomb of Pope Benedict XI** is unknown, but it's clearly the work of a master sculptor. Here, too, is a magnificent 15th-century, stained-glass window. The **Museo Archeologico Nazionale dell'Umbria**, in the monastery alongside San Domenico, includes Etruscan and Roman artefacts.

GUBBIO

Gubbio (ten buses a day run from Perugia's Pza dei Partigiani, by the FCU station) is a typical Umbrian hill town, largely medieval, with steep narrow streets, grey and tiered. The huge Pza Grande della Signoria, home of the turreted **Palazzo de Consoli**, provides superb views, while the **Museo Civico** contains the most complete extant record of the ancient Umbrian language, in seven bronze tablets – the **Tavole Eugubine** (300–100 BC). A funicular climbs to the pink-brick **Basilica of Sant'Ubaldo** from Porta Romana, wherein lies St Ubaldo, Gubbio's bishop saint. **Tourist Office**: Via della Repubblica 15, 📞(075) 922 0693 (www.regioneumbria.eu).

Italy

And don't miss the 10th-century **Church of San Pietro**, southeast of the centre (Borgo XX Giugno). The decorations, dating from the Renaissance, are unbelievably rich, with scarcely an unadorned patch. The paintings were executed by a host of artists, including Perugino. A highlight is the magnificently carved choir.

FS (State Railway), 4 km southwest of the centre (an uphill walk) or 15 mins by bus (6/7/8/9/11/15/130/135) to Pza Italia. Tickets from a forecourt booth or machine by the entrance. The private **FCU** (Ferrovia Centrale Umbria) railway terminal is **Stazione Sant'Anna**, from which you can get a *scala mobile* (escalator) to Pza Italia.

---

i **Tourist Office**: Pza Matteotti 18, (075) 573 6458 (www.regioneumbria.eu). **Internet** in Via Ulisse Rocchi 30, near the cathedral.

There is plenty of cheap, central accommodation, but book ahead if you're coming during the Umbria Jazz international jazz festival (ten days every July). **Youth hostels (non-HI)**: 2 mins from the Duomo: **Centro Internazionale per la Gioventù**, Via Bontempi 13, (075) 572 2880 (www.ostello.perugia.it, closed mid-Dec–mid-Jan). **Youth hostels (HI)**: **Mario Spagnoli**, Via Cortonese 4, (075) 501 1366 (www.perugiahostel.com), 9/10/11 to Via Cortonese and **Ostello Villa Giardino Ponte Felcino**, Via Maniconi 97, (075) 591 3991 (www. ostellopontefelcino.com), 500 m from Ponte Felcino station. **Campsite**: **Il Rocolo**, Str Fontana Trinità 1/N, Colle della Trinità, (075) 517 8550 (www.ilrocolo.it), open mid-April–mid-Oct, or you can rough camp by **Lago Trasimeno**, reached by bus and train.

St Francis and the Basilica di San Francesco

San Francesco (St Francis) expressed the wish to be buried simply, but the news of his death (in 1226) brought a flood of donations from all over Europe and construction of the **Basilica di San Francesco**, at the western end of the Old Town, began in 1228. It has a choice collection of masterpieces, making it something of an art gallery in itself; several great artists were employed, inspiring each other into innovative forms of painting that departed from the rigid Byzantine conventions. The basilica consists of two churches: the **lower church**, designed for peaceful meditation by the saint's tomb, and the soaring **upper church**, intended to mollify the faction who wanted a glorious monument. The upper church suffered severe damage during the 1997 earthquake, but has been completely restored.

ASSISI

One name is irrevocably linked with **Assisi** – St Francis. Born here in 1182, he practised what he preached: poverty, chastity and obedience, leading to a love of God and an appreciation of all living things. He founded the Franciscan order, and his home town became (and remains) a major pilgrimage centre, concentrated around the **Basilica di San Francesco**, erected in his memory and adorned with some of the most magnificent frescos in Italy (see panel).

St Francis's life initiated a wealth of art and architecture in Assisi. Still largely medieval, and clinging to a side of **Monte Subasio** high above the green Umbrian countryside, the town is instantly familiar from the landscapes in the frescos of the Umbrian painters.

The Pza del Comune, in the centre of the Old Town, is dominated by the 1st century AD **Tempio di Minerva** – a Roman temple partly incorporated into what is now the Church of Santa Maria. To the east of the centre, below the cathedral, is the **Basilica di Santa Chiara**. Santa Chiara (St Clare) was an early friend of St Francis and, with his guidance, established the Order of the Poor Clares, the female equivalent of the Franciscans. The old fortress, known as **Rocca Maggiore**, towers dramatically above the northern edge of the city, providing panoramic views of the town and surrounding countryside.

The **Basilica di Santa Maria degli Angeli**, near the station, surrounds a chapel used by St Francis and the spot where he died. Much more evocative, if you fancy a 4-km forest walk to the northeast, is **Eremo delle Carceri**, on the slopes of Monte Subasio. It was here, in caves, that the original Franciscans lived. You can see the cell used by St Francis and the altar from where he addressed the birds.

DAY TRIP FROM ASSISI

Spello (10 mins by train; ETT table 615) is the epitome of an Umbrian hill town, with tiers of pink houses, cobbled alleys and churches, and Roman gateways. The 13th-century **Church of Santa Maria Maggiore** contains a chapel full of brilliantly restored frescos by Pinturicchio and a 15th-century ceramic floor. Spello is far from overrun with tourists and is generally much quieter than Assisi. From the station it's a short walk up to the Old Town.

🚆 This is not in Assisi proper, but in **Santa Maria degli Angeli**, about 5 km southwest and uphill all the way. Buses run to the centre every 30 mins.

ⓘ **Tourist Office**: Pza del Comune, 📞(075) 813 8680 (www.regioneumbria.eu). It provides a map in English and has information about accommodation, including pilgrim hostels.

🏠 There is plenty of accommodation of every grade, but booking is advisable – essential for Easter, the **Feast of St Francis** (3–4 Oct) and **Calendimaggio** (a medieval celebration of spring held in early May). **Hotel: Albergo Ancajani**, Via Ancajani 16, 📞(075) 815 128, is a reasonable budget option. **Youth hostel (HI): Ostello della Pace**, Via di Valecchie 177, 📞(075) 816 767 (www.assisihostel.com), 10-min walk from Pza San Pietro; open only to groups from Nov–Feb (except New Year period). **Campsite: Fontemaggio**, 📞(075) 813 636 or 812 317 (www.fontemaggio.it), has a hotel and budget accommodation rooms as well as camping facilities. It is located 4 km east of town and uphill; take a taxi or follow the signs from **Porta Cappuccini**. **Internet Café**: **Bar Bibiano**, Vle Marconi 1.

SPOLETO

Founded by Umbrians in the 6th century BC, **Spoleto** has an interesting mix of Roman and medieval sights, the most spectacular being the cathedral, adorned on its entrance façade with eight rose windows of differing sizes. Its campanile, propped up by a flying buttress, was constructed from various bits of Roman masonry and other un-medieval elements – and yet still manages to present itself as a perfect blend of Romanesque and Renaissance styles. Within, a baroque makeover rather ruined the effect, though Fra Filippo Lippi's magnificent frescos depicting the life of the Virgin are timeless. Also of interest is **Cappella Eroli**, with a *Madonna and Child* by Pinturicchio, and the Cosmati marble floor. After several centuries of power the town fell into obscurity until being chosen (in 1958) to host Italy's leading performing arts festival in June/July, the **Spoleto Festival** (www.festivaldispoleto.com), which transforms the tranquil town into an unrecognisably invigorated place; prices, inevitably, soar.

Part of the small **Roman Amphitheatre**, Pza Libertà, at the southern end of the old centre, has been carefully restored and is now used for festival performances. Another section is occupied by the **Convent of Sant'Agata**, which houses a small collection of Roman artefacts. A walk through the **Arco di Druso** (AD 23), 100 m north, leads to Pza del Mercato, which was the Roman forum and is still a marketplace and the hub of Spoleto's social life. Nearby, the small **Pinacoteca Comunale** is housed in the **Palazzo del Municipio**, a visit to which requires a guide. The décor is magnificent and some of the paintings are outstanding, especially in the Umbrian section. The **Rocca**, a huge 14th-century castle to the southeast of town, guards one of the finest engineering achievements of medieval times, the **Ponte delle Torri**: a 240-m-long bridge, supported by ten arches 80 m high. From it there are magnificent views of the gorge below and there's a pleasant 2-km walk (turn right) leading to **San Pietro**, with a façade adorned by some of the region's finest Romanesque sculpture.

🚉 In the lower town, with a long uphill walk south to the medieval town (or orange bus to Pza Libertà – tickets from the station bar). Free city map from the station newsstand.

ℹ️ **Tourist Office**: Pza della Libertà 7, ☎(0743) 238 921 or 238 920 (www.regioneumbria.eu). **Internet**: **Spider Service**, Via di Porta Fuga 11.

🏠 Book well ahead during the **summer arts festival**. At that time accommodation can be very pricey. At other times, look in the lower town. Alternatively, try **Foligno**, 26 km northeast and linked by trains that run until late; it has a **youth hostel** (**HI**): **Ostello Palazzo Pierantoni**, Via Pierantoni 23, ☎(0742) 342 566 (www.ostellofoligno.it). There is also a hostel and B&B at **Villa Redenta,** Via di Villa Redenta 1, ☎(0743) 224 936 (www.villaredenta.com). **Campsites**: **Camping Monteluco,** ☎(0743) 220 358 (www.campeggiomonteluco.com), 15-min walk south from Pza Libertà, is very small and opens only Apr–Sept.

ROME (ROMA)

See p403.

ROUTE DETAIL

Rome–Naples
by Eurostar Italia & Alta Velocità   ETT tables 640/642

Type	Frequency	Typical journey time
Train	1–3 per hr	1 hr 45 mins (ES)
		1 hr 21 mins (AV)

Naples–Herculaneum   ETT table 623

Type	Frequency	Typical journey time
Train	3–4 per hr	20 mins

Herculaneum–Pompeii   ETT table 623

Type	Frequency	Typical journey time
Train	1–2 per hr	35 mins

Pompeii–Salerno   ETT table 640

Type	Frequency	Typical journey time
Train	Every hr	22 mins

Salerno–Messina   ETT tables 640/641

Type	Frequency	Typical journey time
Train	5–8 daily	5 hrs

Messina–Cefalù   ETT table 641

Type	Frequency	Typical journey time
Train	up to 15 daily	2 hrs 30 mins

Cefalù–Palermo   ETT table 641

Type	Frequency	Typical journey time
Train	up to 15 daily	50 mins

KEY JOURNEYS

Rome–Palermo   ETT tables 640/641

Type	Frequency	Typical journey time
Train	5–6 daily	11 hrs

Naples–Salerno   ETT table 640

Type	Frequency	Typical journey time
Train	Every hr	37 mins

Naples–Messina   ETT tables 640/641

Type	Frequency	Typical journey time
Train	5–6 daily	6 hrs

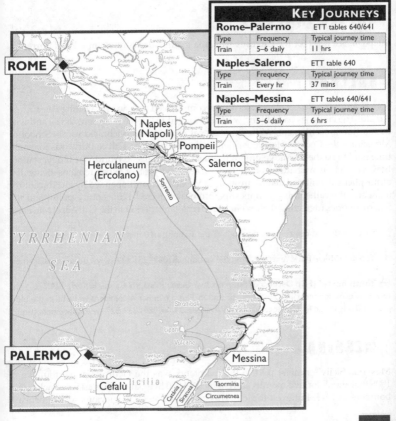

Italy

This coastal tour of southern Italy really gets going at **Naples**, a rewarding stop in its own right, beyond which are **Herculaneum** and **Pompeii**, two of the greatest sites in the ancient world. At the 'toe' of mainland Italy, you board a train ferry from **Villa San Giovanni** to **Messina**, on the island of Sicily. Successive invasions of Romans, Arabs, Normans, French and Spanish have shaped the Sicilian character; the land is a strange mixture of fertile plains, volcanic lava fields and virtual desert, while **Mount Etna**, the great volcano, is omnipresent, smoking in the background.

ROME (ROMA)

See p403.

NAPLES (NAPOLI)

See p396. See p399 for the **Circumvesuviana** to **Herculaneum**, **Pompeii** and **Sorrento**.

SALERNO

Spread around a crescent bay, Salerno is recommended as a stop for visiting Paestum or Amalfi. The city goes back a long way; it belonged to Greece in ancient times, and was then a Roman settlement, while in medieval times it was celebrated for its School of Medicine – the Code of Health, written here in verse in the 12th century, was for some time held to be the definitive pronouncement on the subject. World War II devastation, however, left it a shadow of its former self, the best of what remains being the atmospherically dilapidated centre around Via dei Mercanti, spanned by an 8th-century arch, and the cathedral – with its superb mosaic-covered 12th-century pulpit and the Salerno ivories (depicting Bible scenes) from the same period in the Cathedral Museum.

[RAIL] South of the old centre (turn right out of the station); a 10-min walk.

[i] **Tourist Office**: Pza V. Veneto 1 (near the station), ☎(089) 231 432 (www.turismoinsalerno.it).

[□] **Youth hostel (HI)**: Ostello di Salerno, Ave Gratia Plena, Via Canali, ☎(089) 234 776 (www.ostellodisalerno.it); 500 m from rail station. Plus a number of inexpensive B&Bs in the old part of town, including **Cometa**, Via Mario Avallone 34, ☎(089) 337 527 (www.bbcometa.com).

MESSINA

Messina, Sicily's nearest port to the mainland, was the victim of an earthquake in 1908 that shook for two months and claimed 84,000 lives, and of a massive attack by US bombers in 1943. But even those events can't take away its glorious setting beneath the mountains. Much has been rebuilt in a stable, squat style. The well-reconstructed **cathedral**, Pza del Duomo, has an ornate Gothic central entrance portal and mosaics in the three apses: try to catch the moving figurines on the clock tower as it chimes at midday, and climb the tower for the view.

🚈 Trains from the mainland arrive on **FS** ferries at **Stazione Marittima**, and continue to **Stazione Centrale** – departure point for city and long-distance buses.

ℹ️ **Tourist Office**: Via Calabria 301(near the station) and Pza Cairoli 45, ☎(090) 293 5292 (www.messina-sicilia.it, www.comune.messina.it).

🛏️ There's limited budget accommodation. The nearest **campsite** is **Nuovo Camping dello Stretto**, Via Circuito, Torre Faro, (090) 322 3051 (www.campingdellostretto.it), open June–Sept. Also, **Camping Il Peloritano**, (090) 348 496 (www.peloritanocamping.it), in Rodia, is about 20 km from Messina but reachable by bus, open Mar–Oct.

SIDE TRIPS FROM MESSINA   To the south, trains serve two of Sicily's most interesting places: **Taormina** and **Siracusa** (ETT table 641; 40 mins to Taormina, 2 hrs 45 mins to Siracusa), with the chance to ride around the base of Mount Etna. **Taormina** (Tourist Office: Largo Santa Caterina, ☎(0942) 23243, plus at Taormina Giardini station; www.gate2taormina.com) is a touristy but engaging resort, perched high over the Ionian Sea, with the looming presence of Mount Etna. The locals joke that this is the safest place in Sicily as it's supposedly where the Mafia like to go on holiday.

Of chief interest is the **Teatro Greco**, the Greek Theatre (3rd century BC, rebuilt 1st century AD, so it's essentially Roman in spite of its name), wonderfully positioned with a view over the sea and Mount Etna; operas, ballets and concerts are staged here in summer. Escape the endless parade mooching along the Corso Umberto by disappearing into the little lanes off to the side; or really escape the crowds by climbing up to the next village, Castelmola. There are a few other lesser (free) ancient sites dotted around Taormina, notably a Roman theatre abutting a church, the Naumachie (a Roman cistern, now a tiny public garden) and the remains of the Roman baths (just behind the police station). And don't miss the wonderful Giardino Pubblico/Villa Comunale, a little-visited public park with some entertaining follies, feral cats and yet more panoramas.

Tour buses from Taormina take you to the spectacular gorge of **Gola dell'Alcantara**, where you can hire boots and salopettes necessary for wading through the river. A bus runs up frequently from Taormina Giardini station (a period gem in itself) and to the adjacent seaside resort of **Giardini Naxos** (www.giardini-naxos.com), which has plenty of far less pricey accommodation than in Taormina. There's also a cable car from Taormina down to a reasonable, if hardly vintage-quality, beach.

For budget places to stay (€) in Taormina: **Taormina's Odyssey**, Traversa A N.2 di via G Martino, ☎(0942) 24533 (www.taorminaodyssey.com), which also has a cheap guesthouse in the town centre (see website for details), and **Locanda Diana**, Via Di Giovanni 6, ☎(0942) 23898, small and central, with basic rooms.

Catania (Tourist Offices: at central rail station, ☎(095) 730 6255, and in Via V. Vittorio Emanuele 172, ☎(095) 742 5573 (www.apt.catania.it, www.cataniainfo.it)), is not for everyone, despite its recently regenerated 18th-century historic centre, which has twice been destroyed by earthquakes. Built out of dark lava stone, the city can seem oppressive; however, it does have a lively young nightlife scene (find more details on www.vivicatania.net) and enough sights to while away a day or two, from the **Castello Ursino** to the church-lined **Via Crociferi** and vibrant **Via Etnea**.

Catania also makes a convenient stepping stone to the rest of Sicily, with good rail and bus links (rail and bus stations are close together; buses tend to be faster, more frequent and more reliable than trains, and get you from here to Palermo and Agrigento in under 3 hrs). The airport is served by buses from/to the city centre (stops include Corso Sicilia, Piazza del Duomo and Piazza Stesicoro). There are also bus connections to/from Enna, Palermo and Agrigento. The Roman theatre, Teatro Romano, is in Via Vittorio Emanuele, while the remains of the lava-built Anfiteatro Romano, the 3rd century AD Roman amphitheatre, are in Pza Stesícoro.Budget accommodation is not that plentiful; try the **non-HI hostels** – **Agorà Hostel**, Pza Currò 6, ☎(095) 723 3010 (www.agorahostel.com), which has a wine bar and DJ set lounge and internet facilities, or **Holland International**, Via Vittorio Emanuele II 8, ☎(095) 533 605 (www.hollandintrooms.it), 3-min walk from the rail station.

The chief scenic interest of this stretch of coast is **Mount Etna** (www.etnatura.it or www.etnaguide.com), Sicily's smokestack, the 3323-m volcano that is still very active. For a superb scenic route around the mountain, take the **Ferrovia Circumetnea** (Circumetnea Railway; private line, passes not valid, but the fares are cheap anyway), either from Giarre-Riposto on the Taormina–Catania line or Catania Borgo station (reached by Metro from Catania Centrale). Some trains run through to Riposto, but the chances are that you'll have to change on the way at **Randazzo** – an interesting medieval town that easily fills an hour or two; it's just over 2 hrs to Randazzo, then a further 1 hr 10 mins to Riposto (no service Sun or holidays: see ETT table 644).

To get up Mount Etna itself you can join any of a number of excursion buses from Catania, Giardini-Naxos or Taormina to the mountain (either to one of several lower vantage points, or, in summer only, up to within striking distance of the summit – although you're not allowed to stand at the very top of the crater for safety reasons). Alternatively there is a daily bus at 0815 from Piazza Giovanni XXIII by the Stazione Centrale to the **Rifugio Sapienza** (☎(095) 915 321, www.rifugiosapienza.com, a high-altitude refuge and a useful budget place to stay if you want to try one of several superlative walks on the mountain), returning in late afternoon. It's an amazing trip up for views and close-ups of the lava flows in recent years.

South of Catania, the coast is industrial sprawl virtually until **Siracusa** (Syracuse; Tourist Office: Via Maestranza 33, ☎(0931) 464 255 (www.aatsr.it), the power base in

Sicily from the 5th century BC up to 878. Siracusa is littered with classical sites, notably **Neapolis** with its supremely preserved Greek and Roman theatres, man-made grotto called the Ear of Dionysius (shaped like an upside-down ear lobe), 3rd-century BC sacrificial altar (Hieron's Altar) and quarries that were used as outdoor prisons during the war with Athens in 413 BC.

Below Neapolis, the skyline is dominated by the vast and quite bizarre shuttlecock-like modern church, the Santuario della Madonnina delle Lácrime, a useful landmark if nothing else to help you locate the nearby early Christian **catacombs** by the church of San Giovanni (in tunnels created by the Greeks for carrying fresh water around town, but used for burial by the Romans), a fascinating guided tour that also visits an altar from where St John preached. Close by, the **Museo Archeológico Paolo Orsi** (closed Mon) is a stupendous treasure house of Sicilian antiquities.

Beyond here, venture further south across a bridge into **Ortygia** (www.ortigia.it), the infinitely more charming cultural heart of Siracusa. This island is a languid, lovely place to stay, with its labyrinthine alleys, and corners lined with baroque palaces or strewn with ruined temples. **Piazza Archimede** and **Piazza del Duomo** form a stage set for Siracusan social life. On Piazza del Duomo, a Temple to Athena masquerades as a Christian church: this baroque **cathedral** was built onto the carcass of a Grecian Doric temple so ancient classical columns bulge through the external walls. One of the most charming spots is the freshwater spring known as **Fonte Arethusa**, on the southwest side of the island. Nearby is a tiny beach and a bracing walk or short **boat trip** around the headland. Ortygia has undergone a makeover, with the renovation of waterfront palaces and an influx of young couples opening B&Bs and laid-back inns in once dilapidated mansions. The side streets contain numerous inexpensive restaurants, some with waterfront views.

From Siracusa, you can carry on by train to **Noto** and **Ragusa**, two inland cities that were devastated by an earthquake in 1693 and were rebuilt in gorgeous honey-coloured stone. **Noto** is a simple grid of baroque streets; the cathedral is under long-term restoration, and until the work is finished is somewhat upstaged by **Ragusa**, within its fascinating crooked streetscape of its lower town (Ragusa Ibla). Tourist Office: ☎(0932) 221 529 or 244 473 (www.ragusaturismo.it). For accommodation, try the seaside a few kilometres from Ragusa: **Agricampeggio Capo Scalambri**, Punta Secca di Santa Croce Camerina, Via Cagliari 40, Marina di Ragusa, ☎(0932) 616 263 (www.caposcalambri.com), offers a campsite and unit accommodation.

CEFALÙ

Crammed between a rocky promontory and the sea, this idyllic fishing port and beach resort is a great place to rest, with plenty of restaurants, walks and views, and charming corners, particularly in Corso Ruggero. The Arab-Norman **cathedral**, a twin-towered, fortified medieval structure, dominates the town from its position just beneath the **Rocca**, the rock that protects it. It contains some of Sicily's best-

Italy

preserved – and earliest (1148) – mosaics. Dating from the time of the Norman kings, these are the work of Byzantine craftsmen. See the *Christ Pantocrator* in the main apse: it's one of the great works of medieval Sicilian Art.

The **Museo Mandralisca**, Via Mandralisca 13, contains, along with a variety of artefacts including some Greek ceramics, an important painting by Antonello da Messina, *Portrait of an Unknown Man* (c1460). Above the town, on the Rocca – ascend from Pza Garibaldi – a ruined medieval fortification provides magnificent views out over **Cefalù** and the coast. The attractive beach offers shallow bathing.

🚃 Via Moro, a 10-min walk from Corso Ruggero.

i **Tourist Office**: Corso Ruggero 77, 📞(0921) 421 050 (www.cefaluonline.com).
Internet: **Kefaonline**, Pza S. Francesco 1.

🏠 There is a wide range of accommodation, though in August things get very heavily booked. A budget option is **Locanda Cangelosi**, Via Umberto 1 26, 📞(0921) 421 591, (www.locanda cangelosi.it), near Piazza Garibaldi. **B&B Casa al Duomo**, Via Lo Duca 27, 📞(091) 344 887 or (0368) 786 8771 (www.cefalumare.it), located in the town centre, and **B&B Ale Robi Cefalu'**, Via Porpora 17, 📞(0921) 424 020 (www.alerobi.it), are other options. **Campsites: Costa Ponente Internazionale**, 📞(0921) 420 085 (Apr–Oct) and, beside it, **Sanfilippo**, 📞(0921) 420 184 (www.campingsanfilippo.com) – both 3 km west of town at Contrada Ogliastrillo (heading for La Spisa).

PALERMO

With huge **Monte Pellegrino** to the north and an arc of mountains behind the city, Palermo is a melting pot of styles, cultures and civilisations. The city, and western Sicily in general, is steeped in Arab-Norman architectural values rather than in Greek or Roman culture. Parts of the city are dilapidated, the legacy of wartime bombing and criminal neglect, but a renaissance has been under way for a decade – albeit a Sicilian renaissance, so one with as many false starts as fearless leaps. Palermo has a seductive atmosphere, with its ancient labyrinth of alleys, ornate churches and timeless souk-like markets. More North African than Italian, the **Vucciria** in Via Maccheronai, or vibrant **Ballarò** in Pza Ballaro (near the station), signal Palermo's status as a meeting of two continents.

> ### GETTING AROUND PALERMO
>
> Walking is the best way of getting around, but you might want to consider the buses. You can buy a **Palermo City Pass** lasting either for an hour or a day.

Palermo's unmissable sights include the **Palazzo Reale**, the Royal Palace, home to Cappella Palatina, created in 1132, an east-meets-west chapel of Moorish splendour, with its coffered ceilings equalled by shimmering Byzantine mosaics. Nearby, on Via dei Benedettini, is **San Giovanni degli Eremiti**, a Benedictine abbey, which incorporates a Byzantine basilica, a mosque, Norman cloisters and an Arab 'garden of delights.' The **Duomo**, on Corso V Emanuele, is yet another hybrid, part-Christian, part-Moorish.

The rich legacy of the ancient Greeks can be studied in one of southern Italy's best museums, the **Museo Archeologico Regionale**, at Pza Olivella; highlights include the panels of relief sculpture from temples at **Selinunte**. Deep inside the **Palazzo dei Normanni** are the lavishly ornamental mosaics by Arab and Byzantine craftsmen (1150). Its ceiling is the finest surviving example of Fatimid architecture anywhere. Other mosaics in the city can be seen in the **Martorana** in Pza Bellini (12th century).

The other great milestone of Sicilian style is the baroque: the local Palermitan baroque is ornate and ebullient. The richest examples of it can be seen in the interiors of the little oratories of **Rosario di San Domenico** at Via Bambinai 2, and of **Santa Zita**, behind the **Church of Santa Zita** at Via Valverde 3. In both, the stucco artist Giacomo Serpotta (1656–1732) unleashed the full throttle of his exuberance. His remarkably realistic stucco figures run riot around the walls.

One intriguing area stretches north from the main rail station to the **Teatro Massimo** (www.teatromassimo.it), the huge opera house (well worth taking the guided tour, Tues–Sun except during rehearsals, or during the opera season out of summer get a dirt-cheap ticket to a production; if it looks familiar it's because it featured in the film *The Godfather III*) in Piazza Verdi. For a peaceful oasis from the city's din, head to the **Orto Botanico** (Via Lincoln, entrance fee), a luscious botanic garden full of exotic species such as the *Ficus mangolioides* with its bizarre aerial roots. Another peaceful spot is **Piazza Marina**, just off the waterfront. Lined with restored palaces and restaurants, and overlooking tranquil gardens, this is the loveliest square in the historic centre. The neighbouring waterside is being restored but even the picturesquely decaying port has huge charm.

DAY TRIPS FROM PALERMO

Mondello (about 10 km) is Palermo's upmarket but engaging beach resort, while at **Segesta** (about 65 km), to the northwest, a near-complete Greek temple survives. In **Bagheria** (about 14 km), in the southeast, the quirky baroque **Villa Palagonia** is an oddity in an area once renowned for the holiday homes of the 17th- and 18th-century nobility. All of these places are accessible by bus.

Agrigento, on the south coast (2 hrs by train or bus), is one of Sicily's archaeological gems: the so-called Valley of Temples, built by the Greeks in the 6th–5th centuries BC (🚌 1/2/3 from rail station), the most complete of which is the Temple of Concord, in the eastern zone. For the western zone there's an admission charge, which also covers the archaeological museum. It takes at least half a day to see it all; if staying over, there are plenty of reasonably priced hotels in the unremarkable main town, which has a pleasant enough old centre; budget ones include **Belvedere**, Via San Vito 20, ☎(0922) 20051, €.

City buses run on a 2-hr time limit no matter how often you transfer (buy tickets from booths near bus stops, and stamp your ticket as soon as you board), making it cheap to get to outlying places. On the west side of town the **Convento dei Cappuccini** (Pza

Cappuccini) is a 1-km walk from Pza dell'Indipendenza: the Capuchin friars here have created extraordinary catacombs, with embalmed corpses dressed up and displayed according to their station (soldier, monk, lawyer, etc) – definitely a sight for the strong of stomach.

Some 8 km west, and a shortish ride on 🚌 389 from Pza dell'Indipendenza, **Monreale** is a hill town just perched above the suburbs: the cathedral, austere outside, reveals nothing of its glories – but inside it's absolutely covered with Byzantine mosaics executed during Norman times in the 12th century and of the highest standard of craftsmanship: if you see no other church in Sicily, see this one. The cloister has some quirky carved capitals, and the climb to the tower takes in some hair-raising rooftop views.

🚆 **Stazione Centrale**, in Pza Giulio Cesare, is at the southern end of the city. Located in the same square, and in the streets around it, are some of the termini of local, provincial and long-distance bus services. **Stazione Marittima**, Via Francesco Crispi, in the east, by the port, is the focus of ferry services (mostly Grimaldi and Tirrenia lines) from **Naples**, **Cagliari** (Sardinia), **Genoa**, **Livorno**, **Salerno**, **Ustica** and occasional hydrofoil connections to the Aeolian Islands. There is an ATM in the station.

ℹ️ **Tourist Office:** Pza Castelnuovo 34, ☎(091) 605 8351 (www.palermotourism.com). Another tourist information point is at the Falcone Borsellino airport.

🏨 Cheap accommodation is easy to find, though much of it is tacky. **Hotel Verdi**, Via Maqueda 417, ☎(091) 584 928 (www.albergoverdi.it), is on an atmospheric, if busy, street in the city centre. The mid-range is well catered for. **Hotel Regina**, Cso Vittorio Emanuele 316, ☎(091) 611 4216 (www.hotelreginapalermo.it). Away from the city, at **Sferracavallo** (🚌 101) near the sea, are two **campsites: Camping Trinacria**, Via Barcarello 25, ☎(091) 530 590 (www.campingtrinacria.it), and **Camping degli Ulivi**, Via Pegaso 25, ☎(091) 533 021 (www.campingdegliulivi.com). **Youth hostel (HI): Baia del Corallo**, Via Plauto 27, ☎(091) 679 7807 (www.ostellopalermo.it); 1 km from station.

WHERE NEXT FROM PALERMO?

*Ferries (ETT table 2675; once a week; 13 hrs 30 mins) depart to **Cagliari** (see p143), capital of Sardinia, and to **Naples** (table 2625; daily; 8–10 hrs), **Palermo–Salerno** (table 2661; two per week, 9 hours) and **Genoa** (table 2547; daily; 19 hrs).*

*Served by the ferry from **Palermo** and **Naples** as well as shorter 50-min hydrofoil crossings from **Milazzo** (west of Messina, ETT table 2570), the **Aeolian Islands** (also known as the **Eolian Islands** or the **Lipari Islands**) rise dramatically from warm, azure waters north of Sicily. Thought by the ancients to be the home of Aeolus, the God of the Winds, the volcanic archipelago has wonderful scenery and rich marine life including turtles, hammer fish and flying fish. **Lipari**, the main island, has an old walled town, while the isles **Vulcano** and **Stromboli** are extremely active volcanos. These are Sicily's loveliest islands.*

Croatia and Slovenia

Croatia and **Slovenia** emerged as independent countries following the break-up of Yugoslavia in 1991. Tiny Slovenia developed rapidly into an efficient and prosperous nation and joined the European Union in 2004. Croatia was more traumatised by the war that ensued, but since 2000 things have been looking up and the country is once again welcoming tourists in increasing numbers.

CROATIA

Croatia boasts a vast stretch of the Adriatic Coast with a total of 1185 islands dotted along its sinewy southern littoral. The area north and west of the capital, Zagreb, is mountainous, while to the east are the vast Slavonian plains, the area worst hit by the 1990s war. Travelling southwards the landscape becomes increasingly dramatic, culminating in Dalmatia with the spectacular rugged mountains of Gorski Kotar and Velebit, sea and islands. Coastal towns such as Split, and the islands Hvar and Korčula, spent several centuries under Venetian rule: traces remain in local architecture, dialects and cuisine. Inland Croatia is more Central European. The rather austere buildings, food and manners of the capital, Zagreb, remind one of the other grand cities that passed under Austro-Hungary.

YOUTH HOSTELS

Croatian Youth Hostel Association:
☎(385) (1) 484 7474 (www.hfhs.hr).

ACCOMMODATION

Massive amounts of money have gone towards revitalising Croatian tourism and offering curious travellers something different for their money. However, prices are not as cheerfully cheap compared to other former Eastern Bloc countries. **Private accommodation** (*sobe*) is generally the best-value option and can be arranged through local Tourist Offices. Owners usually live on the ground floor and let rooms or apartments upstairs. Prices vary depending on location and season: expect to pay between Kn75 and Kn170 per person per night. For stays of less than three nights you may have to pay a 30% surcharge, especially in high season. There are excellent **HI youth hostels** in Dubrovnik and Pula, and even Zagreb is now as good as several private hostels have recently opened. For the adventurous, there are barns, tepees and eco-farms.

FOOD AND DRINK

Along the Dalmatian coast, fish and other seafood predominate. Specialities include *lignje* (squid), *dagnje* (mussels), *crni rižot* (rice in cuttlefish ink) and *škampi* (scampi). Inland, meat in all its guises and dairy produce rule and the truffles of the inland Istria region are increasingly rated by gastronomes as some of the world's best. Look out for roadside restaurants serving *janjetina* (lamb) roast whole on a spit. Another traditional method of preparing meat is in a *peka*, a large iron pot with a dome shaped lid, buried to cook under glowing embers. Or you can live off sandwiches made from a quarter loaf of bread (*frtalj kruha*) and various salamis with fresh tomatoes.

ESSENTIALS [CROATIA]

Population 4.8m **Capital** Zagreb **Time Zone** Winter GMT+1, summer GMT+2.

CLIMATE

Continental inland and Mediterranean on the Adriatic coast, with very warm summers.

CURRENCY

Kuna (Kn); 1 Kuna = 100 Lipa. £1 = Kn8.35; $1 = Kn7.31; €1 = Kn5.01.
Credit cards, Euros and US dollars widely accepted.

EMBASSIES IN ZAGREB

Aus: Kaptol Centar, 3rd Floor, Nova Ves 11, ☎(01) 489 1200. **Can**: Prilaz
Gjure Deželića 4, ☎(01) 488 1211. **SA**: Trg D. Petrovića 3, ☎(01) 489 4111.
UK: Ivana Lučića 4, ☎(01) 600 9100. **USA**: Thomasa Jeffersona 2, ☎(01) 661 2200.

LANGUAGE

Croatian. English, German and Italian spoken in tourist areas.

OPENING HOURS

Banks: Mon–Fri 0700–1900, Sat 0700–1300, but may vary, some banks may
open Sun in larger cities. Most **shops**: Mon–Fri 0800–2000, Sat 0800–1400/1500;
many shops also open Sun, especially in summer. Some shops close 1200–1600.
Most open-air **markets** daily, mornings only. **Museums**: vary, some have limited
opening hours on the weekends.

POST OFFICES

Usual hours: Mon–Fri 0700–1900 (some post offices in larger cities open until 2200),
Sat 0700–1300. Stamps (markice) sold at newsstands (kiosk) or tobacconists (trafika).
Post boxes are yellow.

PUBLIC HOLIDAYS

1 Jan; 6 Jan; Good Friday; Easter Mon; 1 May; Corpus Christi; 22 Jun; 25 June; 5 Aug;
15 Aug; 8 Oct; 1 Nov; 25–26 Dec. Many local saints' holidays.

PUBLIC TRANSPORT

Jadrolinija maintains most domestic ferry lines; main office in Rijeka,
☎(051) 666 111; cheap and efficient. Buses and trams are cheap, regular
and efficient. Avoid overpriced taxis.

RAIL PASSES

IR and EP valid (see pp27–34). Domestic fares are cheap.

RAIL TRAVEL

National railway company: Hrvatske Željeznice (HŽ) (www.hznet.hr). Zagreb is a
major hub for international trains. Efficient services but there is a limited network
and services can be infrequent. Daytime trains on the Zagreb–Split line are
operated by modern tilting diesel trains.

TELEPHONES

Make international calls from booths in post offices (HPT) – pay the clerk after
the call; or from public telephone booths (only accept phonecards) – phonecards
sold at post offices, newsstands and tobacconists. Dial in: ☎+385 (omit initial
0 from area code). Outgoing: ☎00 + country code. Police: ☎92. Fire: ☎93.
Ambulance: ☎94. All-emergency number: ☎112.

TIPPING

Leave 10% for good service in a restaurant. It's not necessary to tip in bars.

TOURIST INFORMATION

Website: www.croatia.hr. Croatian National Tourist Board, Iblerov trg 10/4,
10000 Zagreb, ☎(01) 469 9333, fax (01) 455 7827.

VISAS

South African citizens need a 3-month tourist visa. For UK, Irish, US, Canadian,
Australian and New Zealand citizens no visa required for stays of up to 90 days.

Croatia and Slovenia

Top-of-the-range wines are pricey but can be excellent – the robust red, Dingač, from Dalmatia is particularly good. The cheapest solution is to buy wine 'on tap': look for the sign '*točeno vino*' and bring an empty bottle with you. Mix with still water and enjoy *bevanda* – a less headache-inducing method of enjoying rich red wine under the Adriatic sun. White wine can have similar treatment with sparkling water to make refreshing *gemišt*. Coffee (*kava*) is often served as espresso or cappuccino in bars, though some families prepare it Turkish-style at home. Tea (*čaj*) is normally either black or made from rosehip (*šipak*) and served with sugar and lemon; add rum for a winter warmer.

SLOVENIA

Slovenia, a pocket-sized land of beautiful Alpine mountains and lakes, undulating farmland and vineyards, blends Mediterranean charm with Austrian efficiency. Many Slovenes love hiking and skiing, and Triglav National Park offers ideal conditions for both. Slovenia became a member of the European Union in 2004 and joined the Eurozone in January 2007.

ACCOMMODATION

Bookings for all types of accommodation can be made through Tourist Offices. However, refurbished hotels and high standards make for prices comparable to those of other EU countries. Tourist Offices have lists of private rooms for rent; a 30% surcharge is sometimes made for stays of less than three nights. There is a shortage of youth hostels, but in **Ljubljana** and **Maribor** it is possible to stay in **university halls of residence** during the summer break (details from Tourist Offices). There are numerous small but well-equipped **campsites**. The **HI youth hostels** charge around €15–30 and are mostly in the Alpine northern part of the country; the official hostel website is www.youth-hostel.si.

FOOD AND DRINK

Places to eat go by many different names in Slovenia. A restaurant where you are served by a waitress is a *restauracija*, while a *gostilna* is an inn, which typically serves national dishes in a rustic setting. Both sometimes have a set menu (*dnevno kosilo*) at lunch, which is usually the least expensive option. There are also a variety of self-service places (*samopostrežna restauracija*) where you can eat standing up. Slovenian cuisine reflects historic ties with Vienna. Meat and dairy products predominate: *Wiener schnitzel* (veal in breadcrumbs) is a speciality, as is *pohana piska* (breaded fried chicken), and French fries are served with almost everything. Coffee shops offer a wide range of pastries, cakes and ice creams. A *zavitek* is a light pastry filled with cream cheese, either sweet or savoury.

ESSENTIALS (SLOVENIA)

Population 2m **Capital** Ljubljana **Time Zone** Winter GMT+1, summer GMT+2.

CLIMATE
Warm summers, cold winters; Mediterranean climate along coast; snow in the mountains in winter.

CURRENCY
1 Euro (€) = 100 cents = £0.89 = $1.46.

EMBASSIES IN LJUBLJANA
Aus (Consulate): Trg Republike 3, 12th floor, ☎(01) 425 4252. **Can**: Dunajska 22, ☎(01) 435 3570. **SA**: Prazakova 4 ☎(01) 200 6300. **UK**: Trg Republike 3, ☎(01) 200 3910. **USA**: Prešernova 31, ☎(01) 200 5500.

LANGUAGE
Slovenian. English, German and Italian often spoken in tourist areas.

OPENING HOURS
Banks: vary, but mostly Mon–Fri 0830–1230 and 1400–1630, Sat 0830–1200. **Shops**: mostly Mon–Fri 0800–1900, Sat 0830–1200. **Museums**: larger ones 1000–1800, many smaller ones 1000–1400; some close Mon.

POST OFFICES
Mon–Fri 0800–1800, Sat 0800–1200. Main post offices in larger centres may open evenings and on Sun. Ljubljana's main post office, Trg Osvobodilne Fronte 5, by station, open 24 hrs. Efficient postal service.

PUBLIC HOLIDAYS
1–2 Jan; 8 Feb; Easter Mon; 27 Apr; 1–2 May; 25 June; 15 Aug; 31 Oct; 1 Nov; 25–26 Dec.

PUBLIC TRANSPORT
Long-distance bus services frequent and inexpensive; usually buy ticket on boarding. Information: Trg Osvobodilne Fronte 5, next to Ljubljana station, ☎(01) 234 4606. City buses have standard fare, paid with correct change into box by driver; cheaper to buy tokens from newsstands/post offices. Daily or weekly bus passes in main cities.

RAIL PASSES
IR and EP valid (see pp27–34).

RAIL TRAVEL
Website: www.slo-zeleznice.si. National rail company: Slovenske Železnice (SŽ). Information: ☎(01) 291 3332. Tickets from stations or travel agents.

TELEPHONES
International calls best made in post offices (pay afterwards). Phone booths: buy phonecards from post offices or tokens from post offices/newsstands. Dial in: ☎+386 (omit inital 0 from area code). Outgoing: ☎00 + country code. Police: ☎113. Fire/ambulance: ☎112.

TIPPING
No need to tip bar staff or taxi drivers, although you can round sums up as you wish. In restaurants add 10%.

TOURIST INFORMATION
Website: www.slovenia.info. Slovenian Tourist Board, Dunajska 156, SI-1000 Ljubljana, ☎(01) 589 1858.

VISAS
Not generally necessary, but South Africans need a three-month tourist visa and return ticket.

LJUBLJANA

SLOVENIA

Postojna

Lesce-Bled

Zagreb

CROATIA

BOSNIA-HERZEGOVINA

Split

Brač

Korčula

DUBROVNIK

ROUTE DETAIL

Ljubljana–Zagreb   ETT table 1300

Type	Frequency	Typical journey time
Train	7 daily	2 hrs 15 mins

Zagreb–Split   ETT table 1330

Type	Frequency	Typical journey time
Train	3–6 daily	5 hrs 30 mins day, 8 hrs night train

Split–Dubrovnik   ETT table 2855

Type	Frequency	Typical journey time
Ship	2 per week	9 hrs 15 mins

KEY JOURNEYS

Ljubljana–Vienna   ETT table 91

Type	Frequency	Typical journey time
Train	1–2 daily	6 hrs 5 mins

Zagreb–Budapest   ETT table 89

Type	Frequency	Typical journey time
Train	3 daily	6 hrs 15 mins

Zagreb–Vienna   ETT tables 91/92

Type	Frequency	Typical journey time
Train	2 daily	6 hrs 40 mins

This route combines trains and ferries through two countries. From **Ljubljana**, at the heart of Slovenia, a scenic rail route follows the Sava River towards the Croatian capital, **Zagreb**. The journey from Zagreb down to the country's second city, **Split**, takes in mountainous terrain and skirts the borders with Slovenia to the west and Bosnia to the east. Split itself is at once a bustling and relaxed city with a Roman palace, and is a good base for ferry excursions to the **islands**; from here take the bus or the ferry to the wonderfully preserved town of **Dubrovnik**, one of the jewels of the Adriatic. Alternative starting points leading to Ljubljana include Venice (see Milan–Trieste, p429, ETT tables 605/606/1305); or Vienna via Graz and the old university town of Maribor (ETT table 1315); or from Villach via Bled, an attractive lake resort in the Slovenian Alps (ETT table 1300).

LJUBLJANA, SLOVENIA

The capital of Slovenia, Ljubljana, is a lively university town dominated by a hilltop fortress. The River Ljubljanica divides the city into two parts, joined in the city centre by an attractive and unique triple bridge, the **Tromostovje**. This links the city's old heart, **Stari Trg**, on the right bank, built below the hilltop castle, to **Novi Trg** on the left bank. The old town, on the **right bank**, is an inviting maze of cobbled streets with historic buildings. Recent years have witnessed a renaissance with the opening of numerous shops, restaurants and bars, many with river views and generally reasonably priced. It is a gentle stroll up to the **castle**, which gives a good view of the city below. Baroque **St Nikolas's Cathedral**, Ćiril-Metodov Trg, abuts the Bishop's Palace. Beyond, on Vodnikov Trg, lies the **central food market** (Mon–Sat 0600–1800), good for picnic shopping.

On the river's **left bank**, the 17th-century Franciscan **church** dominates **Prešernov Trg**. Within, the high altar is the work of Italian architect and sculptor Francesco Robba. The left bank of the city serves a generous portion of museums, including the **National Museum** and the **Museum of Modern Art**. If suffering from an overdose of Middle European culture, chill out on the green expanse of **Tivoli Park** (good for picnics). Check out the nearby **Museum of Contemporary History**, offering a lively portrayal of Slovenia through the 20th century, complete with the sound of gunfire and a video presentation. Antiques enthusiasts should visit the **flea market** at Cankarjevo Nabrežje, Sun 0800–1400.

The annual **International Summer Festival** takes place at various venues throughout the town, attracting well-known performers from all over the world (mid-June–Aug).

☒ Trg Osvobodline Fronte 6 (Trg OF), a 15-min walk from the main street, Slovenska Cesta.

✈ **Ljubljana Brnik Airport** (served by easyJet), 26 km, 45 mins by bus (hourly Mon–Fri, 0500–2000; every 2 hrs Sat and Sun 1000–2000; www.lju-airport.si).

ℹ **Tourist Offices**: Stritarjeva Ulica 2, ☎(01) 306 1215, (www.ljubljana-tourism.si); branch in station, ☎(01) 433 9475. Guided tours of the city meet at the Magistrat, Mestni Trg 1, every day 1000 (Apr–Sept), Fri–Sun 1100 (Oct–Mar).

☒ **Private rooms** are available for rent through the Tourist Office, but may be in short supply during the summer. You can stay in university halls of residence during the summer break; for details enquire, in advance, at the Tourist Office. There are seven **HI youth hostels** (www.youth-hostel.si), including: **Alibi M14**, Miklošičeva 14, ☎(01) 232 2770 (www.alibi.si).

☒ The riverside zone between Stari Trg and Novi Trg is the centre for friendly bars and reasonably priced eating places.

SIDE TRIPS FROM LJUBLJANA   **Kranj** (25 mins, ETT table 1300). The city of Kranj is home to a charming old town which lies on the banks of the Sava River. Highlights include the Prešern House, Church of Saint Cantianus and the Gorenjska Folk Museum. The compact historic streets can be covered in a day, but there is plenty more here, as well as hiking in the nearby Kamnik-Savinja Alps, to keep visitors occupied for at least a few days. **Tourist Information**: Koroška Cesta 29, ☎(04) 236 3030 (andrej.40@siol.net). The main accommodation around the Old Town are private rooms (*sobes*); contact the tourist information for details.

Smarna Gora (🚌 15 from Slovenska Cesta, 25 mins). Just a short bus ride north of town is this impressive summit, well worth visiting it you do not have time to delve deeper into Slovenia's Alps. The higher of the two peaks is comparatively low at 669 metres, but it's a popular haunt of paragliders and hang gliders. The rolling terrain is also perfect for walking. Less energetic souls may want to wander around Smlednik Castle or idle around nearby Zbilje Lake.

ZAGREB, CROATIA

Zagreb has a distinctly Austro-Hungarian flavour, both in architecture and, on first impression, the restrained manners of its citizens. Its oldest and most beautiful quarter is **Gornji grad** (Upper Town), with the cathedral-dominated Kaptol area. To reach it, begin from Trg Bana Jelačića, the main square, and follow Ilica, to reach Tomićeva, where you can take the funicular up to Strossmayer promenade for one of the best views over the city. A cannon is fired daily at 1200 from Lotrščak Tower. Next take Ćirilometodska to **St Mark's Church**, noted for its extraordinary 'coat of arms' red, white and blue tiled roof, and follow Kamenita to pass through an archway, housing a shrine complete with altar, flowers and flickering candles. Turn left up Radićeva, and take one of the series of steep wooden stairways to your right, which link the upper town to Kaptol. In the cathedral look for the inscription of the Ten Commandments on the northern wall, written in 12th-century Glagolitic characters unique to the old Slavic language. Zagreb's fine art collection is in the **Mimara Museum**, Rooseveltov Trg 4 (closed Mon). A less touristy gem is **Mirogoj Cemetery** with its glorious ivy-shrouded arcades (frequent bus service from Kaptol in front of the cathedral). The city is served by an excellent tram network. Far from its straight-laced image, Zagreb is the hub of all; both trendy and alternative. The early summer street festival Cest is D'Best is great, free and literally everywhere. The cult alternative venue **Mochvara** (www.mochvara.hr) on the banks of the Sava River is unlike any other, and for a distinctly urban local experience of cheap drinks and good music, find your way to **Krivi put** (The Wrong Way), at the bottom of Runjaninova (next to the Botanic Gardens), or sample the clandestine atmosphere of **Sedmica** (ex-residential flat at Kačićeva 7A).

🚃 In the centre of town. Left luggage and exchange offices. Bar and newspaper kiosks.

✈ **Zagreb Airport** (served by Wizzair and Germanwings) (www.zagreb-airport.hr) is 15km south of Zagreb, in Pleso. A scheduled bus runs 0700–2000 from the main bus station, journey time 25 mins, tickets Kn30 one way. Outside these hours buses run to connect with flights.

i **Tourist Offices**: Trg Bana Jelačića 11, ☎0800 53 53 (www.zagreb-touristinfo.hr), in the main town square. Alternatively, take tram 6/13, which follow the same route. Pick up a copy of *Zagreb Info A–Z*, *Zagreb in Your Pocket* and *Events and Performances*, all free and published in English. **Internet access**: Tkalčićeva 13 and 18, Teslina 12, Trg Petra Preradovića and Masarykova 5 (courtyard entrance), a friendly health-food café, gives patrons 30 minutes of free internet access.

🛏 Generally expensive (around Kn180 for a single); private rooms can be booked through the Tourist Office or various agencies. A small but wonderfully central private youth hostel, **Fulir Hostel**, Radićeva 3, ☎(01) 483 0882, is just off the main square (www.fulir-hostel.com). Besides **HI Hostel**, Petrinjska 77, ☎(01) 484 1261 (zagreb@hfhs.hr) there is also **Buzz Backpackers**, Đorđićeva 24, just 10-min walk from the station (no sign at the door so keep an eye out), plus **student halls of residence** doubling up as a hostel during summer months at Palmotićeva 59.

🍽 The central and certainly most obvious destination for coffee by day and beer by night is popular Tkalča, a lively Tkalčićeva street leading from Trg Bana Jelačića up to Gornji grad. The **farmers' market** at **Dolac**, overlooking Trg Bana Jelačića, is the best and most colourful place to shop for mostly organic veggies, as well as souvenirs. For an evening of food and drink in a typical central European beer hall, visit **Pivnica Medvedgrad**, Božidara Adžije 16. Try *rezano*, a half-dark and half-light beer on tap.

SPLIT, CROATIA

Split is much more than just a transit point for ferries. Its old core is uniquely built around the remnants of **Diocletian's Palace**, constructed 2000 years ago for the Roman emperor's retirement. The waterfront **Riva** buzzes all day with a string of pavement cafés as those waylaid for a few days survey the new arrivals sweeping off the ferries that constantly plough to and from the nearby islands. The traffic-free old town consists of narrow paved alleys, opening out onto ancient piazzas. From here the Tourist Office's self-guided walk leads through town; a series of information boards highlight Split's Roman roots, the **Cathedral of St Duje**, and the various buildings dating back to periods of Venetian and Austro-Hungarian domination. Climb the cathedral bell tower for fine views. Continue through the area of **Varoš**, where steep winding steps take you to the wooded Marjan peninsula. Split's best museums are the **Museum of Croatian Archaeological Monuments** and the **Meštrović Gallery**, both in Šetalište Ivana Meštrovića. Ivan Meštrović was a Split-born sculptor whose work can be seen all over the country and overseas, with one of the most striking examples the hulking statue of Grgur of Nin on the northern edge of Diocletian's Palace. There's a festival of music, opera and theatre, mid-July–mid-Aug.

🚉 The train station, bus station and ferry port are all next to each other, overlooking Gradska Luka, the town harbour. Left luggage; supermarket. The historic centre is just 100 m away.

✈ Split Airport, ☎(021) 203 5555 (www.split-airport.hr), 25 km from Split, 6 km from Trogir. Buses to and from Split every 20 mins.

Croatia and Slovenia

i **Tourist Office**: Peristyle (in Diocletian's Palace),
☎(021) 345 606 (www.visitsplit.com; tic-split@st.t-com.hr),
☎(021) 342 142. Situated on the seafront (or Riva).

🏨 Accommodation is scarce, especially in Aug. Try the Tourist Office for private rooms. Expect to pay Kn200 single, Kn320 double. Private rooms are cheaper but standards vary dramatically.

🍴 Simple eating places offer a fixed menu at budget prices. For typical Dalmatian food join the locals at **Kod Jose**, Sredmanuska 4, behind the market, or **Kod Fife**, Trumbićeva obala 11. For a cheap stand-up lunch with locals try *ribice*, tiny fishes deep fried and served with a glass of red wine, in a canteen-style establishment opposite the fish market (**Ribarnica**), Kraj Sv. Marije 8. Get ultra-fresh fruit and veg and local smoked cheeses on **Pazar**, the colourful open-air market held just outside the main walls, Mon–Sat 0800–1400, Sun 0800–1100. Just across the road from here the **all-night bakery** provides for midnight munchies. Split is a city where outdoor café life is an intrinsic part of the culture. The waterfront Riva is the most popular spot during the day with the action moving into the natural amphitheatre of the Peristyle at night.

DUBROVNIK, CROATIA

Dubrovnik is one of the most impressive medieval fortified cities on the Mediterranean. The best way to get a feel of the place and its glory is to walk the full 2 km circuit of the walls (open summer 0900–1930, winter 1000–1500), but do avoid the hottest hours, especially if you've sampled Dubrovnik's atmosphere to the full the night before. For centuries Dubrovnik was a refined and prosperous trading port, which managed to keep its independence by paying off various would-be conquerors. Fine buildings such as the Rector's Palace, the Sponza Palace and Jesuit Church still bear witness to this glorious past. There's a major festival, mid-July–mid-Aug, with outdoor theatre, opera, jazz and classical music.

🚌 Put Republike 19, 24-hr left luggage.

✈ Dubrovnik Airport is 20 km south of Dubrovnik and 5 km from Cavtat, 30 mins by bus.

⚓ Gruž Port, Gruška obala, the Jadrolinija coastal service ☎(020) 418 0000, runs Split–Dubrovnik, twice per week, journey time 7–10 hrs depending on stops, Kn115.

i **Tourist Office**: Cvijete Zuzorić 1, ☎(020) 323 887 (www.tzdubrovnik.hr). **Internet access**: Black Jack in Stari Grad and Dubrovnik internet centre, Pile (next to Tourist Office).

SIDE TRIPS FROM SPLIT

Trogir: The UNESCO World Heritage-listed city of Trogir lies a short bus ride to the north from Split. Wander around the narrow cobbled streets, stopping off at the cathedral and the Kamerlengo Fortress. The waterfront fills at night with pavement cafés and seafood restaurants in summer and there are regular boat excursions to the nearby islands. **Tourist Office**: Trg Ivana Pavla II 1, ☎(021) 881 412 (www.trogir.org).

Salona: 🚌 1 heads out to the ruins of the Roman town of Salona, where Diocletian originally lived before heading to his modest retirement pad in Split. Today the massive site offers a chance to delve through the centuries; highlights include the ruins of 5th-century basilicas, a 2nd-century amphitheatre and medieval walls.

🏠 **Youth hostel (HI)**, Vinka Sagrestana 3, ☎(020) 423 241 (dubrovnik@hfhs.hr); 100 m from the coach station and 300 m from the city walls. Clean and friendly. Open Apr–Oct.

🍴 Try along Prijeko, parallel to the central street, Placa, is the main area for eating out within the city walls. **Lokanda Peskarija**, Na Ponti (next to town harbour fish market) offers simple but finger-licking seafood fare at surprisingly moderate prices. For the cheapest beer in summer months contact the friendly lads with a fridge under Porporela lighthouse, on Old Town pier.

THE ISLANDS OF CROATIA

Between Split and Dubrovnik are some of the most impressive Croatian islands, reached by ferry from Split (Jadrolinija: www.jadrolinija.hr), before continuing south towards Dubrovnik. In summer frequent services allow easy island hopping.

BRAČ Less than an hour from Split by ferry. The ferry port of **Supetar** in the north is pleasant and never gets too busy. **Bol** (where fast passenger ferries arrive from Split) has the Zlatni Rat, a famously idyllic and hugely popular beach. **Vidova Gora**, the mountain that rears up behind Bol, allows visitors to escape the crowds and cool off in high season. **Local buses** connect most of the small towns and villages of the island. **Tourist Offices**: Porat 1, Supetar, ☎(021) 630 551; Porat Bolskih Pomoraca, Bol, ☎(021) 635 638. **Internet access: Internet Café**, Bol (town centre by the post office).

HVAR Hvar is renowned as the sunniest place in Croatia. This long verdant island is awash with lavender, other wild herbs and flowers with the highlight the impressive Venetian settlement of **Hvar Town**. The waterfront buzzes all summer long with holidaying Italians, outdoor concerts and clubs. A few ferries from Split service the waterfront in Hvar Town directly, but most of the larger Jadrolinija boats now come into **Stari Grad**, where buses transfer passengers over to Hvar Town. Hvar is also serviced by Krilo Jet (foot passengers only), a speedy catamaran departing daily from Split harbour at 1700 and docking at **Hvar**, **Prigradica** and **Korčula**. **Tourist Office**: Arsenal, Trg Sveti Stjepana, ☎(021) 741 059. **Internet access:** T-Mobile (Croatia) hotspots for Wi-Fi: ACI Vrboska, ACI Palmižana.

VIS The last inhabited Croatian island before Italy is a rugged, mountainous wildscape of lofty peaks and sheer rock walls. Ferries from Split and Hvar arrive in Vis Town, which boasts a Franciscan monastery and an archaeological museum, as well as the **Kut** district, a graceful old quarter where the grand old stone waterfront houses are a legacy of the wealthy Venetian merchants who once breezed through town. Across the mountainous interior lies **Komiža**, a quiet port that offers boat access to the islet of **Biševo**. Regular Jadrolinija **ferries** serve the waterfront in Vis Town. In summer Blue Line (www.blueline-ferries.com) ferries also come into Vis Town from Italy. Frequent buses connect Vis Town with Komiža, but public transport around the rest of the island is practically non-existent. **Tourist Office**: Šetalište Stare Isse 2, Vis Town, ☎(021) 717 017 (www.tz-vis.hr). **Internet access: Internet Café Nautic Apartments**, Kut. No hostels, but a variety of private rooms (*sobe*) are available. Call the Tourist Office in advance in summer.

ROUTE DETAIL

Salzburg–Lesce-Bled
ETT table 1300

Type	Frequency	Typical journey time
Train	3 daily	3 hrs 40 mins

Lesce-Bled Ljubljana
ETT table 1300

Type	Frequency	Typical journey time
Train	12–18 daily	45–70 mins

Ljubljana–Rijeka
ETT table 1305

Type	Frequency	Typical journey time
Train	2 daily	2 hrs 40 mins

Rijeka–Zagreb
ETT table 1310

Type	Frequency	Typical journey time
Train	4–5 daily	3 hrs 50 mins

Zagreb–Osijek
ETT table 1340

Type	Frequency	Typical journey time
Train	4 daily	4 hrs 30 mins

KEY JOURNEYS

Salzburg–Ljubljana
ETT table 1300

Type	Frequency	Typical journey time
Train	3 daily	4 hrs 18 mins

Ljubljana–Zagreb
ETT table 1300

Type	Frequency	Typical journey time
Train	7 daily	2 hrs 20 mins

This route, which overlaps the previous chapter at Ljubljana and Zagreb, traverses the **Julian Alps** of Slovenia, touches on the Adriatic Sea in Croatia and then stretches out across the vast **plains of Slavonia**. It begins in Salzburg in Austria, and runs through the Austrian Alps into Slovenia. From the mountain resort of **Bled** it continues on to Ljubljana, though there is an alternative rail line south through the mountains in the west of the country (see Side Trips from Lake Bled below), which rejoins the main route in southern Croatia at the port city of **Rijeka**. From Rijeka you can head off to the Croatian islands and Split and Dubrovnik by ferry, or continue on the main rail route to Zagreb and then out across the flat expanse of the Slavonian plains, a region that bore the brunt of the 1990s war and whose towns and cities provide an illuminating insight into those tumultuous events.

SALZBURG, AUSTRIA

See p380.

BLED, SLOVENIA

Though very touristy, **Lake Bled** in the Julian Alps and on the edge of the Triglav National Park is one of the most stunning stretches of water in Europe. A path around the lake's edge takes around 1 hr 30 mins (ask at the Tourist Office for maps showing more ambitious hikes), and there's excellent scope for hiring a rowing boat or lazing on the beaches; in winter you can skate on the lake and there's plenty of skiing. On the shore is a **16th-century castle** with great views and period furniture.

▣ Main station Lesce-Bled, 4 km southeast of the town of Bled.

ℹ️ **Tourist Office**: Cesta Svobode 15, ☎(04) 574 1122 (www.bled.si; bledec@mlino.si).

🏠 There is an excellent **HI youth hostel**, Grajska Cesta 17, ☎(04) 574 5250 (www.youth-hostel.si; bledec@siol.net) just a 5-min walk from the lake. Many of Bled's **hotels** fill with tourists in summer and prices inflate.

🍽 There are a variety of restaurants in Bled centre, including a number of cheap and cheerful pizza places. Food is also available in summer on the outdoor terraces of local pubs.

SIDE TRIPS FROM LAKE BLED   **Lake Bohinj** (from Bled Jezero station you can head on to Lake Bohinj, Bohinjska Bistrica, ETT table 1302). Lake Bohinj may not have a picturesque castle or island, but it is every bit as impressive as Lake Bled. One advantage of staying at this larger lake is that mass tourism is less dominant and there is the chance to get away from it all.

Croatia and Slovenia

Bled Jezero–Nova Gorica (1 hr 40 mins, ETT table 1302). Arguably Slovenia's most scenic mountain rail route. The line cuts away from Bled Jezero, Bled's less-used rail station, and visits Lake Bohinj and the town of Most na Soči on its way to the modern city of Nova Gorica. With half a dozen trains in each direction Mon–Fri (less at weekends), day trips are possible on this dramatic route past the craggy peaks, lakes and gorges of the **Julian Alps**. You can continue on through Nova Gorica (a town straddling the Italian border), via Sežana, to Rijeka and join the main route again at the Adriatic.

LJUBLJANA

See p459.

RIJEKA, CROATIA

This major transit point for ferries (to the nearby islands of the Kvarner Gulf, Split and Dubrovnik) and trains is something of an industrial eyesore, but it does have an impressive Austro-Hungarian era core, complete with grand 19th-century architecture and pavement cafés. **Trsat castle** offers sweeping views of the city and the Adriatic stretching out below. The heart of the city is along the **Korzo**, with its shops, restaurants and cafés. Down by the waterfront a sprinkling of bars buzz on late into the night. Rijeka also offers lots of art and culture exhibitions.

🚉 The main railway station is west of the centre.

✈ **Rijeka Airport** (served by easyJet) is 30 mins by city bus every two and a half hours before flight departure.

ℹ **Tourist Office**: Korzo 33, ☎(051) 335 882 (www.tz-rijeka.hr). **Internet access**: Free Wi-Fi access along Korzo. Also, **Bluenet N-2**, Franje Čandeka bb (Shopping Centre Andrea), closed 1300–1700 and Sun.

🏠 **PJ Boarding House** is a privately run hostel served by bus routes 4 and 5, Prvog Maja 34/1. Hostel Rijeka, Šetalište XIII. divizije 23, ☎(051) 406 420 (rijeka@hfhs.hr).

🍽 The cafés on the Korzo serve snacks and salads, while there are pizzerias and fast food outlets along its length.

SIDE TRIPS FROM RIJEKA   **Pula** (2 hrs south by bus). Pula is a port city with a remarkable Roman amphitheatre that dominates the waterfront. Although there are no beaches in the city centre you do not have to travel far south to find somewhere to lay out a towel. In summer tour boats also leave from the waterfront, some taking day trippers out to the **Brijuni Islands National Park**, a former playground of Yugoslavian strongman Marshal Tito. **Tourist information**: Forum 3, ☎(052) 219 197 or (052) 212 987 (www.pulainfo.hr).

Postojna (1 hr 30 mins, ETT table 1305, on the line between Rijeka and Ljubljana). A 2-km walk from the station brings you to the spectacular **Postojna Cave**, one of the largest cave systems in the world, with 23 km of underground passages adorned with stalactites and stalagmites. A miniature railway guides visitors through the chambers, where temperatures average 8°C the year through (woollen cloaks are available for hire at the entrance). Don't miss the 'human fish', a family of eyeless and colourless amphibians unique to the caves. Tours leave half hourly in summer, hourly the rest of the year. The Postojna Blues Festival (www.postojna-blues.si) takes place at the entrance during spring months. **Tourist information**: Postojnska Jama Turizem, Janska Cesta 30, ☎(05) 700 0100, fax (05) 700 0130 (www.postojnska-jama.si).

KARLOVAC, CROATIA

Trains run frequently through Karlovac and yet few travellers get out here. This often overlooked city is tucked in the dividing line between the mountains to the south and the Zagreb plains to the north and has good road and rail connections to the capital. Karlovac, the town on four rivers, was a pivotal stronghold for the Austro-Hungarians in their battles with the Ottoman Empire and the sturdy fortress that makes up the old town is a legacy of those days. In the 1990s the hastily assembled Croatian forces managed to halt heavily armed Serb forces from advancing on to Zagreb, but war damage at the heart of Karlovac has now largely been repaired.

🚂 Vilima Reinera 3, a 15-min walk from the city centre, or 24 hour information: ☎(060) 333 444.

ℹ️ **Tourist Office**: Petra Zrinskog 3, ☎(047) 615 115 (www.karlovac-touristinfo.hr). **Internet access**: VIP centre shop, Gundulićeva 8, and Knjižnica za mlade (Youth library), Banjačićeva 8.

🛏️ Private rooms (*sobe*) are available through the Tourist Office.

🍽️ There are several good riverside eateries, especially on Camp Korana.

SIDE TRIP FROM KARLOVAC **Turanj** (15-min bus ride south). This small town was the scene of the dramatic resistance of Croatian defence forces during the Homeland War in the 1990s. Today an **open-air war museum**, the only one of its kind in the country, is dedicated to the events of 1991–95. On show are a motley collection of military hardware including a poignant bullet-riddled old tractor that was converted into an armoured vehicle in those desperate days. Across the road from the museum a simple marble memorial remembers the dead.

ZAGREB

See p460.

Croatia and Slovenia

OSIJEK, CROATIA

Until the 1990s the largest city in the region of Slavonia, Osijek, was a thriving, cosmopolitan hub but by 1991 it was a city under siege, holding out against the Yugoslav Army and Serbian volunteers. Today, peace has returned and Osijek is recovering some of its lustre with cafés and bars along the Drava River buzzing again and many of the damaged buildings repaired. Osijek's centre is dominated by the river, the voluminous spires of the **Church of St Peter and St Paul** and the ornate *fin de siècle* buildings that line the grand **Europska Avenija**. Continue along this thoroughfare to **Tvrđa**, an 18th-century fortress built by the Austro-Hungarians to keep out the Ottoman threat.

🚆 Bartul Kašića.

✈ **Osijek Airport** is 20 km from central Osijek, by bus from Kino Urania Osijek bus station, 90 mins before flight departure, ☎(031) 215 651.

ℹ️ **Tourist Office**: Turistička Zajednica, Županijska 2, ☎(031) 203 755 (www.tzosijek.hr). **Internet access**: VIP internet café, L. Jeagera 24, ☎(031) 212 313.

🛏 Very limited budget options; best bet are private rooms (*sobe*), booked through the Tourist Office. Mid-Range hotel **Central**, Trg Ante Starčevića 4, ☎(031) 281 399 while not quite lush, is very central indeed. Singles from €48.

🍴 Down by the Drava River is the pinnacle of summer action with a floating pizzeria and a string of bars. For a traditional fill don't miss local speciality *fiš paprikas* (a spicy fish stew), or a *meze* of smoked meats that includes the renowned Slavonian spicy smoked salami, *kulen*.

SIDE TRIPS FROM OSIJEK   In 1991 **Vukovar** (40 mins by bus) was a charming baroque town with a mixed Serb and Croat population. Then came the most brutal siege of the war when the Yugoslav Army and Serb volunteers subjected Vukovar to months of shelling and infantry attacks that cost the life of up to 2000 citizens and defending forces, with around the same number of people still listed as 'missing'. Today the town, its **war cemetery** and the **massacre site** on Vukovar's outskirts provide a painfully vivid picture of what happened, and is an essential stop for anyone with more than a passing interest in the most savage conflict in Europe since World War II. For **tourist information** ask at the Hotel Dunav on the waterfront.

Ilok (1 hr southeast by bus). Right on the edge of the Republic of Serbia and Montenegro, Ilok was badly hit during the war, but is now a testament to human determination as its destroyed vineyards are restored and the locals get on with their lives. Wines are once again being produced here and it is a fascinating place to visit, sipping the local produce while overlooking the **castle** and the Danube with Serbia just across the river.

Scandinavia

Denmark, Finland, Norway and Sweden

The Scandinavian countries have a great deal in common. Their histories are dominated by Viking exploits and political upheavals. Denmark and Sweden, for example, sought to impose their authority over the Baltic, and national boundaries between all the countries have changed many times. Communication is easy as English is widely spoken and Scandinavians are, on the whole, very friendly. All these countries are expensive by European standards, with the highest prices found in Norway, and Scandinavian towns and buildings often exhibit a neat, tidy look. When waiting in line for services (i.e. train reservations or post offices), collect a number on entry (make sure it's the right machine, otherwise you may have to queue up again) and then wait your turn. In the summer, the main train routes in Scandinavia might be busy and advance reservation is advised for best possible prices and seating.

Food and Drink

While each country has its own specialities, the Scandinavians share a love of fish – herring, sole and dried cod in particular. Meat can include reindeer or elk, and the Danish open sandwich *smørrebrød*, topped with meat, fish or cheese, can be a meal in itself. There are good supermarkets where you can buy cheaper sandwiches and pastries. Coffee, tea and hot chocolate are widely available: a second cup of coffee is often free or half price. Alcohol is expensive, and you have to be over 18 or in some cases over 20 to buy it. Each country has its own specialities, covered later in this chapter, as well as the daily special menu (called some variation of '*Dagens Ret*'), which is always good value.

DENMARK

Protruding between the Baltic and the North Sea, **Denmark** incorporates some 400 islands, 78 of which are inhabited, as well as the peninsula of **Jutland**. It's low-lying and undramatic terrain, where you sense you're never far from the sea. With its 7000 km of coast, it has a long maritime tradition stretching back to long before the Viking period. Along the coast you'll also find quaint centuries-old fishing communities. **Copenhagen** is the brightest, liveliest spot in the nation, accounting for more than a quarter of the country's 5.5 million population. The island of **Fyn** (Funen) has some of the most attractive of Danish landscapes, and its main city, **Odense**, is celebrated as the birthplace of Hans Christian Andersen. Some of the nearby islands, such as **Ærø**, are winsome and fairy-tale, and tailor-made for

Essentials (Denmark)

Population 5.5m **Capital** Copenhagen (København) **Time Zone** Winter GMT+1, summer GMT+2.

CLIMATE	Maritime climate. July–Aug is warmest, May–June often very pleasant, but rainier; Oct–Mar is the wettest, with periods of frost.
CURRENCY	**Danish kroner** or **crown**, (DKK, DKr.). £1 = DKr.8.53; $1 = DKr.5.11; €1 = DKr.7.45
EMBASSIES AND CONSULATES IN COPENHAGEN	**Aus**: Dampfaegevej 26, 2nd floor, ☎70 26 36 76. **Can**: Kristen Bernikowsgade 1, ☎33 48 32 00. **Ire**: Østbanegade 21, ☎35 42 32 33. **SA**: Gammel Vartovvej 8, ☎39 18 01 55. **UK**: Kastelsvej 36–40, ☎77 34 86 51. **USA**: Dag Hammarskjölds Allé 24, ☎33 41 71 00. A list of all Embassies and Consulates can be found in *Copenhagen This Week* and *Playtime* magazine.
LANGUAGE	**Danish**. English is almost universally spoken.
OPENING HOURS	**Banks** (Copenhagen): Mon–Fri 0930–1600 (most until 1800 on Thur). Vary elsewhere. **Shops**: (mostly) Mon–Thur 1000–1800, Fri 1000–1900/2000, Sat 0900–1300/1400, though many in Copenhagen open until 1700 and may also open Sun. **Museums**: (mostly) daily 1000/1100–1600/1700. In winter, hours are shorter and museums usually close Mon.
POST OFFICES	Mostly Mon–Fri 1000–1700/1800, Sat 1000–1200 (but opening times vary greatly). Stamps also sold at newsagents.
PUBLIC HOLIDAYS	1 Jan; Maundy Thursday–Easter Monday; Common Prayer Day (4th Fri after Easter); Ascension Day (May); Whit Mon; 5 June; 24–26, 31 Dec.
PUBLIC TRANSPORT	Long-distance travel easiest by train. Excellent regional and city bus services, many dovetailing with trains; modern Metro in Copenhagen. Ferries or bridges link all the big islands. Taxis: green '*taxa*' sign when available; metered and most accept major credit cards. Many cycle paths and bike hire shops. Free use of City Bikes in Copenhagen.
RAIL PASSES	IR, EP valid (see pp27–34). Fares based on national zonal system. Copenhagen 24-hr klippekort: (DKr.120) valid in the greater Copenhagen area on buses, Metro and DSB trains. Also tickets available for 2/3/4/5/6/7/8 zones and an all-zone ticket (Dkr.405).
RAIL TRAVEL	Website: www.dsb.dk. Danish State Railways: Danske Statsbaner (DSB); some private operators e.g. ArrivaTog. IC trains reach up to 200 km/h. Re (*regionaltog*) trains frequent, but slower. Refreshment trolleys on most IC trains. Reservations recommended (not compulsory) on IC trains: DKr. 20 in standard class, reservation included in business class. Nationwide reservations ☎70 13 14 15. Baggage lockers at most stations, usually DKr.20 per 24 hrs. Usually free trolleys, but you may need a (returnable) coin.
TELEPHONES	Most operators speak English. Phonecards (DKr.30–100) available from DSB and some kiosks, post offices and newsstands. Dial in: ☎+45 + eight-digit number (no area code). Outgoing: ☎00 + country code. Directory enquiries: ☎118. International operator/directory: ☎113. Emergency services: ☎112.
TIPPING	Usually not expected, and often included in the bill in restaurants, but appreciated. Elsewhere (taxis, cafès, bars, hotels, etc) tipping is not expected.
TOURIST INFORMATION	Website: www.visitdenmark.com. Nearly every decent-sized town in Denmark has a Tourist Office (*turistbureau*), normally found in the town hall or central square; they distribute maps, information and advice. Some also book accommodation for a small fee, and change money.

TYPICAL COSTS Hostel accommodation around DKr. 100–120 for a dormitory, DKr.150–200 for a twin room; cheaper hotels generally around DKr.450, but most are DKr.550 and above; bed and breakfasts are from DKr.150; campsites around DKr.50 per person, per night. Eating and drinking out is expensive; café menu dish: Dkr.65 and above, restaurant menu dish: DKr.120 and above; coffee, tea and soft drinks in a café around DKr.25; 0.5 litre beer in a bar around DKr.45; 0.25 litre and bottled beer around DKr.27. Internet access is free in all libraries; internet cafés are few and far between and many cafés and most hotels have Wi-Fi areas.

VISAS   A list of the countries which require a visa can be found at www.newtodenmark.dk.

exploring on foot or by cycle. **Århus**, in Jutland, is the most vibrant city outside Copenhagen.

ACCOMMODATION

Local Tourist Offices have brochures and booklets (mostly free) listing all types of accommodation, and they can make same-day bookings if you turn up in person. Rooms in private homes are usually without breakfast.

HOTELS   Branches of the **Danish Tourist Board** have the free annual *Denmark Accommodation Guide*. This covers **hotels**, **holiday centres**, **holiday apartments** and **inns**, together with details of various discount schemes. Elsewhere expect to pay from DKr.350. In rural areas the old inns, known as *kros*, are charming places to stay and often have good restaurants serving traditional food. To find these and other quirky places to stay, visit www.tourist-in-denmark.dk. Hotels affiliated to **Horesta** (www.horesta.dk), the Danish hoteliers' association, are classified by one to five stars.

BED & BREAKFAST   Dansk Bed & Breakfast publish a brochure of around 300 bed & breakfast establishments throughout Denmark; it can also make bookings. **Dansk Bed & Breakfast**, ☎ (45) 39 61 04 05 (www.bbdk.dk).

HOSTELS   There are around 100 official (HI) **hostels** (*vandrerhjem*), graded one to five stars, and the general standard is excellent; most have private rooms (sleeping two–six) as well as dormitories (sleeping bags usually not allowed). International hostel cards can be bought on the spot for DKr.160. A Danish hostel card costs DKr.70. Hostelling headquarters: **Danhostel**, Vesterbrogade 39, ☎ (45) 33 31 36 12, (www.danhostel.dk).

CAMPING   The Camping Pass, available from any campsite, costs DKr.100 and is valid in Denmark, Sweden, Norway and Finland. Camping/caravan sites are graded from one to five stars. Many camps also have attractive self-catering cabins, costing DKr.2000 a week for four people. Rough camping is permitted in designated areas only (details from Tourist Offices). **Campingrådet**, ☎ (45) 39 27 88 44, (www.campingraadet.dk).

FOOD AND DRINK

Danish cuisine is simple, based on excellent local produce; standards are pretty high. Look for **Dagen's Ret** (today's special), which is noticeably cheaper than à la carte. Food is quite expensive, but usually of good quality, attractively presented and with large portions. Some **hotel breakfasts** consist of help-yourself buffets, which can keep you going for most of the day.

Fish features a lot – typically herring served in a sauce, or the likes of freshly caught sole, flounder or halibut steamed or lightly fried and served with Danish potatoes.

Smørrebrød are elaborately topped open sandwiches of meat, fish or cheese with accompaniments, served on *rugbrød* (rye bread) or *frankskbrød* (wheat bread). You can also try filling up on the ubiquitous *frikadeller* (pork meatballs). Standard café fare includes *wienerbrød* (real, flaky Danish pastries – a refreshing change from items sold as such in other countries).

There are many local **lagers** in addition to the internationally known **Carlsberg** and **Tuborg**, although the differences between brews are not easily discerned. The local spirit, schnapps, is known as *akvavit* – potato-based and consumed in a single gulp, preferably following herring. All alcohol is expensive, although less so than in the rest of Scandinavia.

FINLAND

Tucked up into Scandinavia's northeastern corner and stretching well into the Arctic, **Finland** is a relatively new country, having gained independence in 1917, and is the least-known and least-understood Scandinavian nation. It formerly belonged to its neighbours, first Sweden in the Middle Ages, then after 1808 it became an autonomous Grand Duchy of tsarist Russia. There are cultural overtones to be felt from both these countries, but theses days Finland also has a strong identity of its own. The southwestern corner is the most populous region by far and includes **Turku**, the country's long-standing spiritual and cultural hub, as well as the rewarding industrial city of **Tampere**. The capital, **Helsinki**, is especially striking for its 19th- and 20th-century architecture. Glaciers gouged out huge trenches that became thousands of lakes, making up the **Finnish Lake District** that, together with the vast forests, covers much of southern Finland. Comfortable trains link the major towns, which, like the lines themselves, are virtually all confined to the south. For scenic rail routes, head for the lake regions, notably from **Helsinki** to **Oulu**, and from **Pieksämäki** to **Tampere**. Travellers over 60 receive a 50% discount on all fares and there are 'family carriages' for those with children. Like the rest of Scandinavia, Finland is an easy place to meet people and the Finns are friendly and receptive to foreigners.

ACCOMMODATION

Some Tourist Offices **book accommodation** for a small fee.

HOTELS Hotels tend to be quite luxurious and expensive. Better for budget travellers are **kesähotelli** or **sommarhotellen** (summer hotels, open June–Aug, in

> You can mitigate the cost by buying vouchers (valid daily June–Sept, Fri–Sun rest of year) on the **Finncheque** (www.finncheque.fi) hotel discount scheme from local travel agencies or specialist Finland tour operators in your own country.

ESSENTIALS (FINLAND)

Population 5.2m **Capital** Helsinki (Helsingfors) **Time Zone** Winter GMT+2, summer GMT+3.

CLIMATE	Extremely long summer days; spring and autumn curtailed further north; continuous daylight for 70 days north of 70th parallel. Late June–mid-Aug best for far north, mid-May–Sept for south. Ski season: mid-Jan–mid-Apr.
CURRENCY	**Euro** (€). 1 Euro = 100 cents = £0.89 = $1.46.
EMBASSIES AND CONSULATES IN HELSINKI	**Aus**: C/-Tradimex Oy Museokatu 25B 00100, ☎(09) 4777 6640. **Can**: Pohjoisesplanadi 25B, ☎(09) 228 530. **Ire**: Erottajankatu 7A, ☎(09) 646 006. **SA**: Rahapajankatu 1A, ☎(09) 6860 3100. **UK**: Itäinen Puistotie 17, ☎(09) 2286 5100. **USA**: Itäinen Puistotie 14B, ☎(09) 616 250.
LANGUAGE	Finnish, and, in the north, **Lapp/Sami**. Swedish, the second language, often appears on signs after the Finnish. English is widely spoken, especially in Helsinki. German is reasonably widespread.
OPENING HOURS	**Banks**: Mon–Fri 1000–1630, with regional variations. **Shops**: Mon–Fri 0900–2000, Sat 0900–1500, though many shops open Mon–Fri 0700–2100, Sat 0900–1800; many shops also open Sun, June–Aug and Dec. **Stores/food shops**: Mon–Sat 0900–1800/2000/2100, small food shops also open Sun 1200–2100. **Museums**: usually close Mon, hours vary. Many close in winter.
POST OFFICES	Most *posti* open at least Mon–Fri 0900–1700. Stamps also sold at shops, hotels and bus and train stations. Orange postboxes.
PUBLIC HOLIDAYS	1, 6 Jan; Good Fri; Easter Sun–Mon; 1 May; Ascension Day (40th day after Easter); Whit Sun; Midsummer's Day (Sat falling 20–26 June); All Saints Day (Sat falling 31 Oct–6 Nov); 6 Dec; 25–26 Dec.
PUBLIC TRANSPORT	Timetables for trains, buses and boats dovetail conveniently. *Aikataulut* (in Finnish and Swedish; €31) covers all in detail, available at bus and rail stations. Buses: stops are usually a black bus on a yellow background for local services; white bus on a blue background for longer distances. Cheaper to buy tickets from stations or agents than on board. Bus stations usually have good facilities. Taxis: for hire when the yellow *taksi* sign is lit; hailing them in the street is acceptable; metered.
RAIL PASSES	IR, EP valid (see pp27–34). Finnrailpass: unlimited 2nd-class travel on Finnish Railways for any 3, 5 or 10 days (2nd class: €131/175/237; 1st class: €195/260/353 respectively). Helsinki Tourist Ticket available for 1/3/5 days; Helsinki Card includes museums (24/48/72 hrs).
RAIL TRAVEL	Website: www.vr.fi. National rail company: VR; Pendolinos (up to 220 km/h) run on major lines. Fares depend upon train type – those for S220 (Pendolino), IC (InterCity) and P (express) trains include a seat reservation. Sleeping cars: two or three berths per compartment (2nd class), single compartment (1st class). Sleeping accommodation generally costs less Mon–Thur (winter). Station: '*Rautatieasema*' or *Järnvägsstation*; virtually all have baggage lockers.
TELEPHONES	Almost all Finns have a mobile phone and public telephones no longer exist. Prepaid mobile phone services sold e.g. at R-kiosks. Dial in: ☎+358 + area code (minus initial 0). Outgoing: ☎00 + country code. Emergency services: ☎112.
TIPPING	Service charge included in hotel and restaurant bills, but leave coins for good service. Hotel and restaurant porters and sauna attendants expect a Euro or two. Taxi drivers and hairdressers do not expect a tip.
TOURIST INFORMATION	Website: www.visitfinland.com. Every Finnish town has a Tourist Office (*Matkailutoimisto*) where staff speak English. English literature, mostly free.
VISAS	National identity cards or passports issued by EU countries, Iceland, Norway and Switzerland sufficient. Visas not required by citizens of those countries, nor of Australia, Canada, New Zealand or the USA. South Africans need visas.

student accommodation) and **matkustajakoti** (the relatively cheap tourist hotels). Ask at Tourist Offices for the free brochures *Hotels in Finland* (not graded, but standards are high) or *Camping and Hostels*. If you visit in the autumn, 5-star hotels often offer 2-star prices. As is traditional in Scandinavia, **saunas** are pretty universal, even on ferries and in hostels; **M** is for men, **N** for women.

HOSTELS   The 80 **hostels** (*retkeilymajat*; pronounced 'ret-kay-loo-mayat') are well spread across the country and over half are open year-round. They're graded from two to four stars, all with dormitories sleeping five+ as well as singles, doubles and rooms for three–four; usually less than €20 per night (€2.50 discount for HI members). It's advisable to book ahead in July and Aug, and to warn if you will be arriving after 1800; booking is mandatory in winter. Many hostels have activity programmes, plus canoes, skis, boats and cycles. The Finnish hostelling association headquarters is **Suomen Retkeilymajajärjestö (SRM)**, (www.hostellit.fi).

CAMPING   Campsites are widespread too (about 350; around 200 belong to the **Finnish Campingsite Association** (www.camping.fi). Sites are classified from one to five stars; five-star sites typically have **camping cottages** sleeping up to five and are sometimes very well appointed (maybe including a sauna). Rough camping is generally allowed providing you keep 150 m from residents and remove any trace of your stay – www.environment.fi/everymansright explains what you can and can't do outdoors in Finland.

FOOD AND DRINK   Fixed-price menus in a *ravintola* (upmarket restaurant) are the best value, or you may want to try a *grilli* (fast-food stand), *kahvila* (self-service cafeteria) or a *baari* (snack bar). For self-caterers, try **Alepa**, **Siwa**, **K-market** or **Valintatalo** supermarkets. Some specials are *muikunmäti* (a freshwater fish roe served with onions and cream and accompanied by toast or pancakes) and for dessert *kiisseli* (berry fool). **ALKO** is the state-owned outlet that sells alcohol.

NORWAY

Stretching 1800 km, far above the Arctic Circle, **Norway** is one of Europe's great natural wonderlands. Its majestic fjords – massive watery corridors created by glacial action – make up one of the finest coastlines in the world, among a wild mountainous terrain that includes **Jostedalsbreen**, mainland Europe's largest glacier. **Bergen** makes the ideal access point for taking a cruise or a ferry to see the fjords at close range. The majestic scenery continues far north beyond the Arctic Circle. The downside of visiting Norway is the cost: prices are higher than most of the rest of Europe, and even by camping or hostelling and living frugally, you'll inevitably notice the difference. Be sure to stock up on the essentials before you go.

Scandinavia

ESSENTIALS (NORWAY)

Population 4.8m **Capital** Oslo **Time Zone** Winter GMT+1, summer GMT+2.

CLIMATE

Surprisingly mild considering it's so far north; can be very warm in summer, particularly inland; the coast is appreciably cooler. May and June are driest months, but quite cool; summer gets warmer and wetter as it progresses, and the western fjords have high rainfall year-round. Days are very long in summer: the sun never sets in high summer in the far north. July and Aug is the busiest period; Sept can be delightful. Winter is the time to see the Northern Lights (*Aurora Borealis*). Excellent snow for skiing Dec–Apr.

CURRENCY

Norwegian kroner (NKr./NOK); 1 krone = 100 øre. On slot machines, *femkrone* means a NKr.5 coin and *tikrone* a NKr.10 coin. £1 = NKr.9.87; $1 = NKr.5.97; €1 = NKr.8.69.

EMBASSIES AND CONSULATES IN OSLO

Aus: Strandvn 20, 1324 Lysaker, ☎67 58 48 48. **Can**: Wergelandvn 7, ☎22 99 53 00. **SA**: Drammensvn 88C, ☎23 27 32 20. **UK**: Thomas Heftyesgt 8, ☎23 13 27 00. **USA**: Henrik Ibsens Gate 48, ☎21 30 85 40.

LANGUAGE

Bokmål and **Nynorsk** are both variants of Norwegian. Almost everyone speaks English; if not, try German. Norwegian has three additional vowels: æ, ø and å, which are ordered alphabetically after z.

OPENING HOURS

Banks: Mon–Wed and Fri normally 0900–1500 (1530 in winter), Thurs 0900–1700. In the country some open and close earlier. Many have minibank machines that accept VISA, MasterCard (Eurocard) and Cirrus. **Shops**: Mon–Wed and Fri 0900–1700/2000 (malls), Thur 0900–1900, Sat 0900–1500/1800 (malls). **Museums**: usually Tues–Sun 1000–1700/1800. Some open Mon, longer in summer and close or shorter opening hours in winter.

POST OFFICES

Usually Mon–Fri 0900–1700, Sat 1000–1400, sometimes later if in connection with a shop. Postboxes: red posthorn and crown on yellow boxes for local mail; reversed colours for elsewhere.

PUBLIC HOLIDAYS

1 Jan; Maundy Thur–Good Fri; Easter Sun–Mon; 1 May; Ascension Day (40th day after Easter); Pentecost; 17 May (National Day); Whit Sun–Mon; 25–26 Dec.

PUBLIC TRANSPORT

Train, boat and bus schedules linked to provide good connections. Often worth using buses or boats to connect two dead-end lines (e.g. Bergen and Stavanger), rather than retracing your route. Rail passes sometimes offer good discounts, even free travel, on linking services. NorWay Bussekspress, Bussterminalen, Avgangshallen, Schweigaardsgt 8-10, N 0185 Oslo, ☎81 54 44 44 (premium rate), (www.nor-way.no), has the largest bus network, routes going as far north as Alta. Long-distance buses: comfortable, with reclining seats, ample leg room. Tickets: buy on board or reserve, ☎81 54 44 44 (premium rate). Another long-distance bus company is Lavprisekspressen, which has routes between the largest cities, and also to Copenhagen through Sweden, ☎67 98 04 80 (www.lavprisekspressen.no). Taxis: metered, can be picked up at ranks or by phoning; treat independent taxis with caution.

RAIL PASSES

IR, EP valid (see pp27–34). Eurail Norway Pass: (for non-Europeans), 3–8 days 2nd-class travel within one month; €192 for 3 days, add from €16 per extra day. Youth (under 26) get discount; seat reservations extra; 30% discount on ordinary single ticket on the Flåm Railway; not valid on Oslo airport trains; available from major NSB stations.

RAIL TRAVEL

Website: www.nsb.no. National rail company: Norges Statsbaner (NSB). All trains have 2nd-class seating. Most medium- and long-distance trains also have *NSB Komfort* accommodation. Sleeping cars have two-berth compartments, price is NKr.850 in addition to a normal ticket. Long-distance trains carry refreshments. Reservation possible on all long-distance trains, ☎81 50 08 88, then dial 9 for an English-speaking operator. Reserved seats not marked, but your confirmation specifies carriage and seat/berth numbers. Carriage numbers are shown by the doors at the ends, berth numbers outside compartments, seat numbers on seat-backs or luggage racks.

Stations: most have baggage lockers, larger stations have baggage trolleys. Narvesen chain (at most stations; open long hours) sells English-language publications and good range of snacks.

TELEPHONES

Telekort (phonecards) available from Narvesen, newsstands and post offices. Card phones spreading fast, some accept credit cards. Coin and card boxes usually together, green marking the ones for cards. Overseas calls cheapest 2200–0800 and weekends. Dial in: ☎+47. Outgoing: ☎00 + country code. Directory enquiries: ☎1880 or 1881. Operators speak English. These are all premium-rate calls. Emergencies: Police: ☎112. Fire: ☎110. Ambulance: ☎113.

TIPPING

Tip 10% in restaurants (but not bars/cafés) if you are satisfied with the food, service etc. Not necessary for taxis.

TOURIST INFORMATION

Website: www.visitnorway.com. Tourist Offices: *Turistinformasjon;* tourist boards: *Reiselivslag.* To be found in virtually all towns; free maps, brochures etc available.

TYPICAL COSTS

Norway is generally expensive to travel in. Hostel accommodation is around NKr.250 for a dormitory, NKr.580 for a twin; cheaper hotels are generally around NKr420–500 for a room; in larger cities like Oslo and Bergen this can be even higher. You can get an okay 'meal of the day' from approximately NKr90, but prices in restaurants and cafés are generally high; coffee in a café is around NKr20; a beer in a bar is around NKr50, in cheaper pubs and cafés you can get a beer for about NKr30. Internet cafés charge from NKr30–60 per hour, but keep in mind that most libraries offer internet access for free.

VISAS

National identity cards issued by EU countries, Iceland and Switzerland are sufficient. Visas not needed by citizens of Australia, Canada, New Zealand and the USA. South Africans need Schengen visas.

ACCOMMODATION

HOSTELS

Because Norway is so expensive, the **youth hostel** network is indispensable if you don't want to break the bank. There are some 75 hostels (*vandrerhjem*), many of which unfortunately open only mid-June–mid-Aug. The standard of hostel accommodation is very high, with singles, doubles and dormitories, and there's a good geographical spread. Booking ahead is highly recommended, especially in summer. The charge is NKr.400 for a single per night, excluding linen (HI members get a 15% discount). Hostelling headquarters is **Norske Vandrerhjem**, ☎(47) 23 13 45 10 (www.hihostels.no). **Private houses** can be quite good value, and in some cases almost the same price as hostels. More upscale are **guesthouses** and **pensions**.

HOTELS

Generally very pricey, but many cut rates at weekends and in summer. Advance booking is important, especially in **Oslo**, **Bergen** and **Stavanger**, which are popular towns for conferences as well as tourists. Local Tourist Offices provide lists of all types of accommodation; most will make bookings for a small fee.

CAMPING

Many of the more than 1200 official **campsites** (several with 5-star classification) have pre-bookable **log cabins** for two or four people. Campsites nearly always have cabins (*hytter*), sleeping two–four people and equipped with kitchen and maybe a bathroom. Rough camping is permitted as long as you don't intrude on residents (you must be 150 m from them) or leave any trace of your stay. Never light fires in summer.

Scandinavia

FOOD AND DRINK

Eating out is very pricey and you will save a lot by self-catering. Stock up at supermarkets and at *konditori* (bakeries), which often serve sandwiches and pastries cheaply. Restaurants sometimes have *dagens rett* (daily specials), relatively inexpensive full meals. Self-service cafeterias are also generally reasonable. Bigger towns have the usual array of fast food, plus hot dog and baked potato stalls on the street; you may find *smørbrød*, the ubiquitous and diverse open sandwich, more appetising. Refill cups of coffee often come free or half price, while tea with lemon is the norm – ask spedificially if you want it with milk (*te med melk*). The range of vegetarian food is generally pretty limited.

Breakfast served in hotels and hostels is buffet-style, with a wide choice: a good chance to fill up for free on the likes of porridge, herring, cheese, meats and bread and jam. Lunch is normally 1200–1500, and sometimes features all-you-can-eat *koldtbord* at fixed price, for a lot less than the equivalent evening meal. Dinner is traditionally 1600–1900, but habits are changing and 1800–2200 is now common in towns.

Fresh fish is in abundant supply, with numerous dishes based on salmon and trout; *klippfisk* (dried cod), *gravetlaks* (marinated salmon cured in dill) and *fiskesuppe* (a satisfying fish and vegetable soup) are among numerous specialities. Meat is generally costlier, and includes *elg* (elk) and *reinsdyr* (reindeer), as well as hearty stews, sausages and *kjøttkaker* (meatballs with potatoes). Beware that the heads of fish and other creatures are regarded as edible: in Voss you may encounter *smalahovud* (sheep's head), for instance.

Alcohol can raise the cost of living from expensive to exorbitant and is served only to people over 18/20, depending on strength (highly taxed wines and spirits are bought from state-owned shops known as Vinmonopol; lager from supermarkets is inexpensive). Many bars, especially in the capital, are voluntarily restricting the drinking age to 21, and rigorously checking ID. Nevertheless in winter you might like to warm up on *gløgg* (mulled wine).

SWEDEN

Scandinavia's largest country includes huge tracts of forest and thousands of lakes, with mildly rolling, fertile terrain to the south, and excitingly rugged uplands spilling over the Norwegian border and beyond the Arctic Circle into **Lapland**. The sheer amount of space is positively exhilarating, and it's the northern stretches that are easily the least populated. The beaches (including naturist ones) compare with the finest in Europe, and in summer the climate of the south is much like that of Central Europe, except with longer days. Mosquitoes can be a problem in the North, so take a strong repellent. Sweden has a conspicuously comfortable standard of living: owing to its tax and social welfare system you won't see much poverty – conversely, few are ostentatiously rich either; equality is the buzz word. For all their sophistication, Swedes are very aware of their country origins, and walking, nature and village life are close to their hearts. National costume is accepted as formal wear, and there's a thriving

Scandinavia

ESSENTIALS (SWEDEN)

Population 9m **Capital** Stockholm **Time Zone** Winter GMT+1, summer GMT+2.

CLIMATE

Often warm (especially in summer; continuous daylight in far north). Huge range between north and south; it can be mild in Skåne (far south) in Feb, but spring comes late May in the north. Winter generally very cold everywhere.

CURRENCY

Krona or crowns. (SEK) 1 krona = 100 öre (smallest denomination = 50 öre coin). *Växlare* machines give change. The best exchange rate is obtained from Forex, which has branches at many stations. Keep receipts so that you can re-convert at no extra cost. SEK1 = £0.08 = $0.15 = €0.10.

EMBASSIES AND CONSULATES IN STOCKHOLM

Aus: Sergels Torg 12, 11th floor, ☎(08) 613 29 00. **Can:** Tegelbacken 4, ☎(08) 453 30 00. **SA:** Fleminggatan 20, ☎(08) 24 39 50. **UK:** Skarpögatan 6–8, ☎(08) 671 30 00. **USA:** Dag Hammarskjolds Vag 31 ☎(08) 783 53 00.

LANGUAGE

Swedish. English is widely spoken.

OPENING HOURS

Banks: Mon–Fri 1000–1500/1600 (Mon–Thur in some larger cities, until 1730). Some, especially at transport terminals, have longer hours. **Shops:** mostly Mon–Fri 1000–1800/1900, Sat 0930/1000–1430/1600. In larger towns department stores open until 1900/2000; also some on Sun 1200–1600. **Museums:** vary widely; some closed Mon. In winter, many outdoor attractions close altogether.

POST OFFICES

Generally Mon–Fri 0900–1800, Sat 1000–1300, but there are local variations. Stamps also sold at newsagents and tobacconists. Post boxes: national and overseas mail are yellow; blue are local.

PUBLIC HOLIDAYS

1, 6 Jan; Good Friday; Easter Sun–Mon; Labour Day (1 May); Ascension Day (40th day after Easter); Whit Sun–Mon; 6 June; Midsummer's Eve–Day; All Saints Day; 24–26 Dec. Many places close early the previous day, or Fri if it's a long weekend.

PUBLIC TRANSPORT

Transport system is highly efficient; ferries covered (in whole or part) by rail passes and city transport cards. Biggest operator of long-distance buses is Swebus Express ☎(0) 771 21 82 18 (www.swebusexpress.se). Advance booking is required on some routes and always advisable in summer; bus terminals usually adjoin train stations.

RAIL PASSES

IR, EP valid (see pp27–34).

RAIL TRAVEL

Website: www.sj.se. National rail company: Statens Järnvägar (SJ); some local lines run by regional authorities, or private companies and some services in the far north are operated by Veolia. Central information line, ☎(0) 771 75 75 75. Supplement required on X2000 train. Sleeping cars: one or two berths in 2nd-class; couchettes: six berths; female-only compartment available. 1st-class sleeping cars (en suite shower and WC) on many overnight services; 2nd-class have washbasins, shower and WC and are at end of carriage. Long-distance trains have refreshment service. Many trains have family car, with a playroom, and facilities for the disabled. Seat reservations compulsory on X2000 and night trains. X2000 services operate between Sweden and Copenhagen via the Öresund bridge and tunnel, but it is better to use the frequent local trains for short journeys. A big town's main station shows 'C' (for Central) on platform boards. Stations: *Biljetter* indicates the rail ticket office or ticket machines. Large, detailed timetables are displayed for long-distance trains: yellow for departures, white for arrivals. Pressbyrån (at stations) sell English-language publications and snacks.

TELEPHONES

Coin-operated phones are no longer in use; phones accept credit cards and *Telia* phonecards (*telefonkorten,* from most newsagents, tobacconists, Pressbyrån kiosks). Dial in: ☎+46 (omit inital 0 of area code). Outgoing: ☎00 + country code. Emergency services (police, fire, ambulance): ☎112.

Scandinavia

TIPPING	Restaurants include a service charge but a tip of 10–15% is appreciated. Taxis 10%. Tip hotel staff, porters, cloakroom attendants at your discretion.
TOURIST INFORMATION	Website: www.visit-sweden.com. Swedish Travel & Tourism Council. Tourist offices are called *Turistbyrå*. Often a numerical waiting system in public places.
VISAS	Visas not required by citizens of Australia, Canada, EU, New Zealand and the USA. South Africans need visas.

tradition of handicrafts, particularly woodcrafts as well as Sámi (Lapp) items.

ACCOMMODATION

You can sleep in fair comfort at a reasonable price in Sweden. Tourist Offices have listings of most places to stay and charge a small booking fee. The official tourist board **Visit Sweden** (www.visitsweden.com) have listings of accommodation all over Sweden. Local Tourist Offices have listings for their area, including farmhouse accommodation. **Bed and Breakfast Service Stockholm** can provide rooms and flats in the capital.

HOTELS Hotel standards are high and the cost usually includes breakfast (prices from SEK450–700 for a single/SEK750–1000 for a double).

HOSTELS There are more than 300 HI hostels (*vandrarhem*), about half of which open only in summer (most do not allow sleeping bags); some are extremely characterful places and include castles and boats. Family rooms are available. Most hostels are shut 1000–1700, and charges are about SEK100–280 (additional SEK40 for non-HI members). Hostels are run by **Svenska Turistföreningen (STF)**. There are also more than 190 independent hostels operated by **Sveriges Vandrarhem i Förening (SVIF)**. Room-only accommodation in **private houses** is a good budget alternative (contact local Tourist Offices).

CAMPING **Sveriges Campingvärdars Riksförbund (SCR)**, Swedish Camping Site Owners' Association lists more than 600 campsites. You can rough camp for one night if you keep more than 150 m from the nearest house and leave no litter.

FOOD AND DRINK

Hearty buffet breakfasts are a good start to the day. Cafés and fast-food outlets are budget options for later on. *Pytt i panna* is a hefty fry-up; other traditional dishes are pea soup served with pancakes, and *Jansson's temptation* (potatoes, onions and anchovies). **Systembolaget** is the state-owned outlet for alcohol – shoppers must be over 20, but you can buy alcoholic beverages in some restaurants, pubs and bars at 18.

Bed and Breakfast Service Stockholm, Sidenvägen 17-178 37 Ekerö, ☎(46) (8) 660 55 65 (www.bedbreakfast.se).

Svenska Turistföreningen (STF), Box 25, 101 20 Stockholm, ☎(46) (8) 463 22 80 (www.stfturist.se).

Sveriges Campingvärdars Riksförbund (SCR), ☎(46) (031) 355 60 00 (www.camping.se).

Sveriges Vandrarhem i Förening (SVIF), Box 9, SE-450 43 Smögen, ☎(46) (0413) 55 34 50 (www.svif.se).

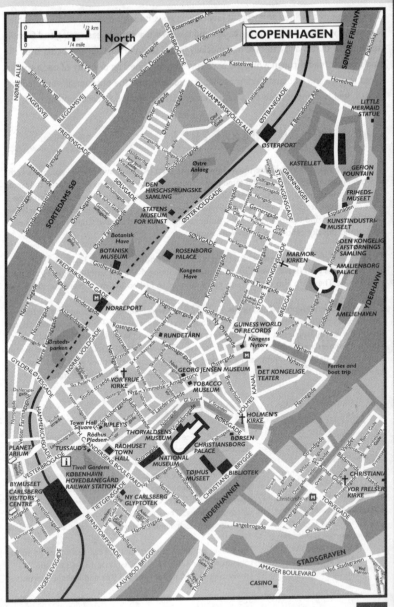

Denmark

Copenhagen is a refined and vibrant city of gorgeous Renaissance architecture, cobbled pedestrian walks and meandering canals and lakes, with a distinct, easy-going and friendly atmosphere that is a joy to take in, especially in the summertime. Cruise boats tour the canals that thread through a historic core revealing an appealing diversity of open spaces, spires, towers and statuary. Cycling is encouraged here, and the outdoor, almost Mediterranean, feel is compounded by an effervescent street life and excellent nightspots.

ARRIVAL AND DEPARTURE

The main rail station is **København Hovedbanegård (København H)** (www.dsb.dk), with an S-train (local train) station of the same name. There are dozens of shops and cafés in the large, bright concourse, including a supermarket, an internet café, a post office, a **bureau de change** and a newsagent stocking English-language newspapers. There is a left-luggage office (*bagagebokse*, DKr.40 per day) and toilets and showers. Buses to districts in and around Copenhagen stop right outside and the city centre is a 5-min walk away.

Take the train to **Helsingør** and catch the 20-min **Scandlines** ferry, ☎ 33 15 15 15; www.scandlines.com (leaves every 20 mins; less often during the night) to **Helsingborg** on the Swedish side. There are also direct trains every 20 mins to Malmö (much quicker than the ferry).

Copenhagen Airport Kastrup, ☎ 32 31 32 31 (www.cph.dk), is 8 km southeast of town. There is a tourist information desk, car hire desk, train ticket office, bank and hotel reservations desk in the arrival hall. Trains to København H every 8–12 mins (☎ 04 45 01 45) taking 12 mins, and the Metro every 3–5 mins (0500–2400 daily; every 15 mins 0000–0500 Thur–Sun and every 20 mins 2400–0500 Mon–Wed), taking 14 mins to Nørreport; you must buy your ticket before boarding the train. 🚌 250S/5A run every 10 mins to the city centre and take 40 mins.

THE LITTLE MERMAID

Combine a visit to this little statue (of Hans Christian Andersen fame) with other sights. From Kongens Nytorv walk along Bredgade to the **Marble Church** (Marmor Kirken), the **Gefion** fountain, the **Fortress** (Kastellet) and the **Little Mermaid** (Den Lille Havfrue).

INFORMATION

The Tourist Office has information covering all Denmark. Get the *Copenhagen Map* and a copy of *Copenhagen This Week* (published monthly; also at www.ctw.dk), both of which are free and incorporate masses of useful information. Also try to get hold of *The Copenhagen Post* (www.cphpost.dk), a weekly newspaper (out Fri) in English, for recent news and more up-to-date listings. The free magazine *Playtime* is an excellent guide updated each summer, great for those on a tight budget.

For budget travellers, the first port of call should be the youth tourism service **USE IT**, Rådhusstræde 13, ☎ 33 73 06 20 (www.useit.dk). All its services are free and include internet

Cities: Copenhagen (København)

TOURIST OFFICE

WONDERFUL COPENHAGEN

Postal address: Gammel
Kongevej 1, DK-1610,
København V, ☎ 70 22 24 42
(Mon–Fri 1000–1600),
(www.visitcopenhagen.dk).
Personal visits:
Vesterbrogade 4A, opposite
the station, by Tivoli's main
entrance (closed Sun,
except July–Aug).

access, short-term left luggage, poste restante, a share-a-car noticeboard and free condoms. They can book you a room in a private home or ring around hostels to check availability.

INTERNET ACCESS All public libraries have free internet access. The most central is 10-15 mins walk from the central station by the harbour: **Den Sorte Diamant**, Søren Kirkegaards Plads 1, ☎ 33 47 47 47 (see www.kb.dk). Some hotels and hostels have free wireless, as do many cafés. Internet cafés are few and far between, but there is one in the station (København H) and a large 24-hour net café near Tivoli's Vesterbrogade entrance, **Boomtown**, Axeltorv 1, ☎ 33 32 10 32 (www.boomtown.net).

PUBLIC TRANSPORT

Buses and trains (0500–0030 and night buses) all form part of an integrated system in the Copenhagen area and tickets are valid on both. Night bus fares are double. Most attractions are central, so for a single journey you will probably only need the cheapest ticket, DKr.21, which covers travel in two zones for 1 hr. Alternatively, buy either an all-zone 24-hr transport pass (DKr.120), or a **klippekort** ten-ride ticket covering 2/3/4/5/6/7/8 zones (DKr.130/170/220/265/305/360/390) and saving you about 40% or an all-zones ticket (DKr.405). These tickets must be validated in the machines on board buses and on S-train platforms. Bus tickets can be purchased on board, but train tickets must be purchased at one of the automated machines at the station. Bus route maps available at HT info bureau on Rådhuspladsen: ☎ 36 13 14 15; www.movia.dk. The **CPHCARD Card** gives unlimited use of public transport, free admission to more than 60 museums and attractions and discounts on many attractions in Greater Copenhagen for one or three days (DKr.225/450). It is on sale at the airport, DSB stations, HT ticket offices, hotels, hostels, campsites, travel agents, Tourist Offices or at www.copenhagencard.com (must be bought ten days in advance when purchasing online). The modern driverless 'mini metro', consists of three lines, with stations marked with a large letter M; red and white S signs mark rail stations. Tickets are valid for Metro, bus and train, with free transfers between these modes of transport. From the airport, there is a rail and Metro link to the city (DKr.28.50).

ACCOMMODATION

Booking ahead is advisable although some hostels may not take advance bookings. The Tourist Office (see above) has a same-day and advance booking service for most types of accommodation, but you must turn up in person. You will pay a DKr.100 fee but they can often get you a discount. For a DKr.30 fee you can book accommodation on the Tourist Office's own computers. See also **USE IT**, on the opposite page.

Denmark

An area in which the downmarket hotels tend to cluster is the central **Istedgade** (to the side of the train station, away from the centre). In the summer months, when demand is high, Copenhagen offers a good choice of **hostel accommodation**, but you must arrive early if you have not booked.

There are four HI **Danhostels**, one central: **Copenhagen City**, H C Andersens Boulevard 50, ☎33 11 85 85 (www.danhostel.dk), a gorgeous 'design hostel' with sleek interiors and minimalist furniture – it's also the largest city hostel in Europe with 1020 beds, 10-min walk from København H and a few mins from Tivoli; **Copenhagen Amager**, Vejlandsallé 200, ☎32 52 29 08 (www.copenhagenyouthhostel.dk), is 4 km southeast of the centre (Metro: Sundby or Bella Center, both 1 km away) but right beside the stops for ▪ 30/4A; **Copenhagen Bellahøj**, Herbergvejen 8, ☎38 28 97 15 (www.youth-hostel.dk), is 4 km northwest of the centre in the opposite direction – 20 mins on ▪ 2A, or night bus 82N; and **Ishøj Strand**, Ishøj Strandvej 13, ☎43 53 50 15 (www.ishojhostel.dk), is furthest out and has spacious rooms and beach access (Metro: Ishøj, then ▪ 300S). **Sleep in Heaven** in Nørrebro, Struensegade 7, ☎35 35 46 48 (www.sleepinheaven.com), has free internet access, free lockers and showers, and a chill-out room. Take ▪ 5A direction Husum to Blågårdsgade, or walk 15 mins from Nørreport Station. **Sleep-in Green** is a small, ecologically sound hostel open in summer only in Nørrebro, maximum stay 7 nights. Ravnsborggade 18, ☎35 37 77 77 (www.sleep-in-green.dk), take ▪ 66 direction Emdrup Torv to Griffenfeldsgade. The **City Public Hostel**, Vesterbo Ungdomsgård, Absalonsgade 8, ☎33 55 00 81 (www.city-public-hostel.dk), is open early May–mid-Aug. The most central **campsite** is **Bellahøj Camping**, Hvidkildevej 66, ☎38 10 11 50, (www.bellahoj-camping.dk), open June–Aug (▪ 2A or night buses 81N/82N).

FOOD AND DRINK

Copenhagen This Week and *Playtime* have many listings for restaurants and cafés; the latter is full of tips for eating on a budget. Brunch is a popular weekend ritual, and you can get a large brunch platter at many places from DKr.50–100. **Nyhavn** with its outdoor tables is pretty at night, but expensive. Traditional Danish fare is not cheap, but it's worth visiting one of the cellar restaurants (off Strøget) to sample the mainly Danish specialities. There are many good cafés and takeaways in the smaller streets around **Vor Frue Kirke** including Turkish, Greek and Italian restaurants offering good-value buffet menus. **Vesterbro** and **Nørrebro** (Skt Hans Torv and Blågårdsgade) are good areas for lively, cheapish eateries and bars buzzing with students and young professionals. The best foodies' shopping street, Vaernedamsvej, has all manner of exotic groceries, delis, bakers and cheesemongers. There are also plenty of **Netto** and **Fakta** discount supermarkets dotted around the city.

HIGHLIGHTS

Punctuated with pretty squares and invariably full of shoppers and strollers, **Strøget**

Cities: Copenhagen (København)

is the pedestrian-only zone at the heart of the city, and a great place to take in the capital's relaxed ethos. On the far side of Gothersgade, the green-roofed Dutch Renaissance-style **Rosenborg Slot** (Rosenborg Palace) peers out majestically over the **Rosenborg Have** (Rosenborg Garden), a tempting spot for sunbathing and picnics. The palace, no longer home to the royals, is now a museum (closed Mon, Nov–Apr) of lavish palace

furnishings and portraits of Danish royalty. The Crown Jewels are displayed in the basement along with the elaborate riding gear of Christian IV, who built the palace. From here, beaver-capped soldiers march east for the **Changing of the Guard** (daily at 1200) at the current royal domicile, **Amalienborg** (accompanied by a band when the Queen is in residence). This complex of palaces consists of a quartet of rococo estates near the quay, framing a courtyard overlooked by an equestrian statue of Frederick V. Nearby is the especially photogenic 300-year-old **Nyhavn** (New Harbour), bordered by picturesque 18th-century townhouses, cafés and masts of restored sailing vessels.

By contrast, in southeast Copenhagen lies **Christiania** – a self-governing, carefree, alternative society founded in the '70s when political activists and homeless took over a series of disused naval warehouses. It's great for an afternoon stroll: a maze of graffiti-painted alternative housing, cafés, bars and workshops. Cannabis is sold openly in 'Pusher Street', but be aware that it is officially illegal in Denmark. There are several lively bars and cheap places to eat – the vegetarian restaurant is well worth a visit; 20-min walk, or 🚌 66 (direction Opera; alight Prinsessegade) or Metro to Christianshavns Torv. Much debate within the Danish government means the future of this tax-free municipality is currently uncertain, so be sure to visit while you still can.

Other uniquely Danish attractions include **Kunstindustrimuseet** (Museum of Decorative Art), with a vast collection of applied art from all over the world, including some of the best examples of Danish design (closed Mon); the **Carlsberg Visitors' Centre** at the brewery at Gamle Carlsbergvej 11 (closed Mon) – yes, there's free beer at the end of the tour; the **Black Diamond**, Søren Kierkegaards Plads 1 (closed Sun; free entry), an immense granite and glass extension – concerts are held inside – to the Royal Library that reflects spectacularly from its waterfront site; and the **Rundetårn** (Round Tower) in Købmagergade, built as an observatory and offering great views of the city.

Some museums and galleries are closed on Monday, such as the **Statens Museum for Kunst** (National Gallery; Danish and international paintings, sculptures and installations). An exception is **Den Hirschprungske Samling** (The Hirschprung Collection;

closed Tues, free on Wed), a small gallery near the Botanic Gardens, showing Danish 19th- and early 20th-century paintings including works by the famous Skagen school painters. The **Nationalmuseet** (closed Mon; with Viking treasures, ancient and Renaissance collections) has free entry and the **Ny Carlsberg Glyptotek** (closed Mon); is free on Sun; probably the best gallery in Copenhagen. Don't miss Rodin's sculptures, the Roman collection and the French Impressionist paintings. Devotees of the philosopher Søren Kierkegaard and the fairy-tale writer Hans Christian Andersen might wish to visit their graves in **Assistens Cemetery** in Nørrebro (also a beautiful spot for a picnic!).

For clean, sandy **beaches** take the S-train, line C from København H to Charlottenlund, where you'll find the small **Charlottenlund** beach; further along the same line is **Bellevue beach**, and **Bakken amusement park** opened in 1583. By Metro from Nørreport Station you can reach the more modern beach at **Amager Strandpark**, where you can cycle, walk, sunbathe, kayak or do many other water sports, or indulge in a cocktail or two in the evenings (alight at Lergravsparken, Øresund, Amager Strand or Femøren).

LIGHTING UP THE TIVOLI

Best seen at night, when 100,000 fairy lights are switched on, Tivoli amusement park (founded 1843) is Copenhagen's playground, with everything from fairground rides to ballet – and dozens of eateries. Tivoli (www.tivoli.dk) is open mid-Apr–late Sept and mid-Nov–late Dec for the Christmas Fair. Every Saturday, fireworks are let off just before midnight. Entrance is DKr.85/45 (sometimes includes a concert).

SHOPPING

Prices are quite a bit higher than in other western European capitals, but the quality of almost everything you buy is bound to be superior. Design plays an important part in Danish everyday life and many ordinary household objects are worth buying on account of their look alone. Streets around **Vesterbro**, **Nørrebro** and **Studiestrœde** have many trendy boutiques, as well as shops selling second-hand books, CDs and so forth. **Ravnsborggade** and **Ryesgade** are two streets that make up the city's antiques quarter. Keep a look out for posters/signs for rummage sales and flea markets (*loppemarked*), usually held at weekends.

NIGHT-TIME AND EVENTS

There are comprehensive listings in *Copenhagen This Week* (www.ctw.dk), *Playtime* and *The Copenhagen Post*. Copenhagen's night scene is lively, and dress is almost always informal. There is no shortage of cafés and bars with live music. Clubs get lively around midnight and stay open until 0500 (the bakeries open at around 0600). The admission charge is usually reasonable but drinks, especially cocktails, generally come at a price.

Cities: Copenhagen [København]

In addition, the city has a long theatrical tradition, although most performances are in Danish. Among some 160 stages, **Det Kongelige Teater** (Royal Theatre), Kongens Nytorv, reigns supreme. See *Copenhagen This Week* for listings. Films are almost invariably shown in the original language and subtitled. Film buffs should visit the **Danish Film Institute** on Gothersgade.

One of the city's top venues is **VEGA**, Enghavevej, which, with its two concert halls and a dance bar, is the place to go for a massive weekend rave up. Another fabulous venue is **Rust**, Guldbergsgade 8. If you can't have fun here, with its dim lights, cheap drinks and wall-to-wall model clientele, you need specialist help. Thirsts can be quenched at both **Zum Biergarten**, Axeltorv 12, and **Heidi's Beer Bar**, Vestergade 18A, where vast selections of beers can lead to some epic nights (and horrific mornings). Of course, you can have a blast without drinking – no, you can – and if you're on the wagon, trundle to **Manefiskeren**, Badsmandsstraede 43, a no-booze zone whose DJs intoxicate you with their tunes. Those who crave a slab of Viking kerrang should park their longship outside **The Rock**, Skindergade 45, Copenhagen's high-BPM live metal HQ. Rock and alternative bands also deliver some great gigs at **Markbar**, Vesterbrogade 106. Rocksteady Eddies will find Stengade 30, Stengade 18, particularly irie, especially on Thursdays' 'Rub A Dub Dub' nights. A blues venue with international and local acts is **Mojo's Blues Bar**, Løngangstræde 21C. **The Copenhagen Jazzhouse**, Niels Hemmingsensgade 10, pumps out real northern soul (and funk), while indie freaks and goths hang around pallor-Valhalla, **Floss**, Larsbjornsstraede 10. If you're new in town, the most inclusive gay club for men and women is **Blender CPH**, Hausergrade 34, though the oldest gay club, **Centralhjørnet**, Kattesundet 18, still out-camps all pretenders to its burlesque throne on the city's well-developed scene. All sorts of good times are on offer at **Pussy Galore's Flying Circus**, Sankt Hans Torv 30, and probably the best bet for pleasing everybody is **Studenterhuset**, Kobmagergade 52, a student café where there's a musical theme night every night of the week, along with quizzes and theatrical events.

Annual events include the Fashion Design Festival in May, the Copenhagen International Jazz Festival in July and Copenhagen Pride (gay festival) in August. Out of town, the late June/early July **Roskilde Festival** features many international stars – Roskilde is 22 miles west of Copenhagen, about 30 mins by train.

WHERE NEXT FROM COPENHAGEN?

*Southwards to **Hamburg** (p277) via the train ferry between Rødby and Puttgarten (four to six per day; 4 hrs 30 mins journey time; ETT tables 50 and 720). Trains to **Malmö** and beyond in Sweden cross on the Øresund Fixed Link (ETT tables 703, 730, 735 and 737). Reservations are compulsory on long-distance services.*

FINLAND: HELSINKI (HELSINGFORS)

TOURIST OFFICE

Pohjoisesplanadi 19,
☎(09) 3101 3300,
(www.visithelsinki.fi);
five blocks from the station,
south on Keskuskatu,
left on Pohjoisesplanadi.
Most leaflets are free and
include a street map.
Get the free booklet
Helsinki – Visitors Guide.

Built on a series of peninsulas and distinctly a city of the sea, Helsinki (Helsingfors in Swedish) may seem something of an acquired taste, with a gritty, North-meets-East flavour spread across its relatively small geographic area, but in recent years this modern city has become one of the most culturally pulsating capitals in Europe. It became the capital of Finland in 1812 while under Russian influence and was rebuilt in a grand grid in the 19th century. With its public buildings proudly built upon great granite steps, the architecture has a distinctively Russian air – the city itself was originally modelled on St Petersburg. The wide boulevards are lined with cobbles and tram rail lines, and exude a unique sense of space, while visible from many streets is the onion dome of the Russian Orthodox cathedral. Many buildings have sunny yellow façades, which brighten up the place on days when the sun goes into hiding.

ARRIVAL AND DEPARTURE

[RAIL] **Helsinki Central Railway Station**, open 0630–2200. This amazingly innovative Art Nouveau structure of 1916 by Eliel Saarinen is a destination in itself, with allusions to the Art Deco style that was to emerge later; as a station it is central and reasonably well-equipped. English newspapers are available at R-kioski, the **VR** (Finnish Railways; ☎0600 41900 premium rate line; www.vr.fi) information office is open 0600–2200 daily, and there are several eateries and food kiosks. Lockers and a lost-property office are in the wing near platform 11 (open 0630–2200). The station is linked to the labyrinthine Metro stop at **Rautatientori** (Railway Square) and is the terminal for some local buses, while a number of trams have stops in front of the station.

Tourist tickets (from Tourist Office, HKL offices and vending machines) give unlimited city travel on buses, trams, Metro and local trains for one day, three days or five days (€6.80/13.60/20.40).

🚢 There are many **cruises**, both within Scandinavia and to **Tallinn (Estonia)** and **Germany**: check whether a visa is needed for your destination. The big companies are: **Silja Line**, ☎0600 157 00 (www.tallinksilja.fi) and **Viking Line**, ☎(09) 123 51 (www.vikingline.fi), both of which run several trips daily to Stockholm. **Tallink** (part of the same company as Silja Line), ☎0600 157 00 (www.tallinksilja.fi), has the cheapest ferries and catamarans to Tallinn. Buses to the city centre go from the ferry terminal (which has only limited currency exchange facilities, so come prepared with plenty of euros).

🚌 **Long-distance buses**: ☎0200 4000 (premium rate) (www.matkahuolto.fi). The main terminal is in the city centre at Simonkatu, under the Kamppi shopping centre. **Tickets** can be purchased at the terminal or on board. **Trams:** tickets cost less at kiosks than on board trams.

✈ **Helsinki–Vantaa**, ☎0200 14636 (premium rate) (www.helsinki-vantaa.fi), 20 km north, has an exchange bureau. **Finnair buses**, Elielinaukio (www.finavia.fi), depart from the railway station (platform 30). The journey takes about 30 mins and costs €5.90, or take the local 🚌 615, which costs €4.00. Other local 🚌 415/451 also go to the airport, but take twice as long.

INFORMATION

Budget travellers should drop in at **Youth Information Centre Kompassi**, Malminkatu 28, ☎(09) 3108 0080 (www.kompassi.info); Mon–Fri 1100–1600. Get *Helsinki Guide* and *Helsinki This Week*, for every conceivable listing and event. 'Helsinki Helps' (students wearing green and carrying green bags with an 'i') wander round the centre 0900–2000 (June–Aug), to provide general guidance in perfect English. They know more about goings-on for younger travellers than the Tourist Officers.

The **Helsinki Card** (www.helsinkiexpert.fi/helsinkicard) is available from the Tourist Office, the airport, passenger ferry terminals, the main rail station and hotels, and provides free public transport (including some ferry trips), a city sightseeing tour, free admission to more than

Finland

60 museums and sights and many other discounts (including restaurants, concerts and car rental): 24/48/72 hrs (€33/45/55). **The Helsinki Expert Tour Shop**, in the City Tourist Office, 📞(09) 2288 1500 (www.helsinkiexpert.fi) sells boat, bus, train and sightseeing-tour tickets and handles hotel reservations and car rentals.

INTERNET ACCESS   While Helsinki is one of the most wired and internet-savvy cities in the world, it doesn't have loads of public internet terminals. The most convenient are **mbar**, Mannerheimintie 22–24 (at the Lasipalatsi); **Café Aalto**, in the Stockmanns bookstore (Akateeminen kirjakauppa); and **Netcup**, Alexsanterinkatu 52.

PUBLIC TRANSPORT

Many of the sights are in the area between the station and Kauppatori, and trams are a quick way of reaching most of the others.

METRO   The Metro was designed primarily for commuters, though it can be used to reach a few tourist sights as well. The only line serves the north and east, but it is currently being extended. It operates 0530–2330 Mon–Sat, 0630–2330 Sun, and tickets are obtained from vending machines. Single tickets (€2.50) for city centre travel are sold on the tram or bus but are cheaper if bought from HKL offices and R-kiosks (the same applies for tram tickets), where you can also purchase ten-trip tickets. Tickets are valid for one hour.

PUBLIC TRANSPORT   A good network of **buses** and **trams** runs approximately 0600–2300 (a few continue until 0130). The public transport company is **HKL** (www.hkl.fi), with offices in Rautatientori Metro station, open Mon–Thur 0730–1900 (1800 summer), Fri 0730–1700 (1600 summer), Sat 1000–1500. The best way to get around is by tram. Tram 3B/3T is frequent, 0600–0130, and runs along a figure-of-eight route of the city, going to, or near, most of the main attractions. Many tram numbers are followed by a letter that denotes the direction; tram tickets can be bought on board, and are valid for unlimited transfers within one hour. For taxis try **Helsinki Taxi Center**, 📞0100 0700 (premium rate). Most local **cruises and ferries** leave from **Kauppatori**.

ACCOMMODATION

Helsinki Expert Hotel Booking Centre, 📞(09) 2288 1400 (www.helsinkiexpert.fi), is at the railway station (central hall), open 9000–1800 Mon–Fri, 1000–1700 Sat, 1 Jan–31 May and 1 Sept–31 Dec; 9000–1800 Mon–Fri, 1000–1800 Sat & Sun, 1 Jun–31 Aug. They also book motels, inns, youth hostels and apartments. **Good value** are **Hotel Anna**, Annankatu 1, 📞(09) 616 621 (www.hotelanna.com), €€, and **Omenahotelli Helsinki Eerikinkatu**, Eerikinkatu 24, near the Kamppi shopping centre. Book online at www.omenahotels.com or call 📞0600 18018 (premium rate).

Hostels: HI hostels are **Eurohostel**, Linnankatu 9, 📞(09) 622 0470 (www.euro hostel.fi); 2 km east of the station (tram 4 goes within 100 m). **Erottajanpuisto**,

Cities: Helsinki [Helsingfors]

Uudenmaankatu 9, ☎(09) 642 169 (www.erottajanpuisto.com). **Stadion Hostel**, Pohjoinen Stadiontie 4, ☎(09) 477 8480 (www.stadionhostel.com); trams 3t and 7a stop 500 m away. **Hostel Academica**, Hietaniemenkatu 14, ☎(09) 1311 4334 (www.hostel academica.fi), 800 m from station; open June–Aug. **Private hostels (non-HI): Hostel Satakuntatalo**, Lapinrinne 1A, near the Kamppi shopping centre, ☎(09) 6958 5232 (www.sodexo.fi/hostelsatakuntatalo), open June–Aug, and **Hostel Suomenlinna**, Suomenlinna, ☎(09) 684 7471, on a pristine, peaceful island only a 15-minute ferry ride from the centre of town. **Camping: Rastila Camping**, Karavaanikatu 4, ☎(09) 3107 8517 (www.hel.fi/rastila), opens all year and also has cottages for two to six people. It's 14 km east.

FOOD AND DRINK

Helsinki This Week gives a listing of eating places. Students can take advantage of the exceptionally low-priced student restaurants: **University restaurant**, Fabianinkatu 33, and **Porthania**, Hallituskatu 11–13. Many restaurants have lunchtime specials, which include prix-fixe menus and salad bar buffets. Fried fish is available in abundance around the port and at the **Kauppahalli**, where you can find cheap smoked salmon and reindeer sandwiches. For fast food try the Mannerheimintie area.

HIGHLIGHTS

Finland's many renowned 20th-century architects have graced the city with some of the most elegant modern architecture you could find anywhere. The **harbour** is a good place to start, with pleasant views and a market selling trinkets. To the east is the Byzantine **Uspenski Cathedral**, Kanavakatu 1, a magnificent reminder of Finland's Russian past, which still serves the Orthodox community. To the west, **Esplanadi** is a boulevard busy with street musicians and outdoor cafés in summer and a huge handicraft market in December. To the north, grand-scale **Senaatintori** (Senate Square) is dominated by **Tuomiokirkko**, the domed Lutheran Cathedral designed by Carl Engel. Under the plain, elegant interior is the church's crypt, holding a café that's great shelter from the hot summer sun. Flanking the square are the **Government Palace**, **Helsinki University** and the **University Library**: an impressive group. The **City Museum**, just south of Senate Square, is a high-tech survey of Helsinki's growth from seaside village to national capital (free entry Thur).

Valtion taidemuseo (Finnish National Gallery), Kaivokatu 2–4, incorporates the **Ateneum** (Museum of Finnish Art), Finland's largest collection of paintings, sculptures and drawings, which ranges from the 18th century to the 1960s (1700–2000, closed Mon, free on the first Wed of the month), with **Kiasma** (Museum of Contemporary Art) next to the post office at Mannerheimaukio 2 (www.kiasma.fi; Tue 1000–1700, Wed–Fri 1000–2030, Sat–Sun 1000–1800, closed Mon, free on the first Wed of the month) and **Sinebrychoff Art Museum** (Museum of Classic European Art), Bulevardi 40 (www.sinebrychoffintaidemuseo.fi; Tue, Fri 1000–1800, Wed–Thur 1000–2000, Sat–Sun

Finland

1100–1700, closed Mon, free on the first Wed of the month). In Mannerheimintie is the 1970s-era **Finlandia Hall**, designed by Finland's most famous architect, Alvar Aalto, who filled the interior with flowing, asymmetrical forms ('Aalto' means 'wave' in Finnish). Further north is the **Olympic Stadium**, worth the traipse out, if only to take in the view from the stadium tower (closed during competitions).Other attractions include the Sibelius monument in **Sibeliuksen puisto** (Sibelius Park), 🚊 18, and the cavernous **Temppeliaunkiokirkko** (Church in the Rock), Lutherinkatu 3, blasted out of solid rock. The rewarding **Design Museo** (Design Museum), Korkeavuorenkatu 23, shows off the latest concept in design by Finland's best known and up-and-coming designers (closed Mon, Sept–May).

Four main islands hug the Helsinki peninsula, linked to Helsinki, and each other, by ferries and/or bridges. The closest and most popular is **Suomenlinna** (15-min ferry trip from the South Harbour), sporting a fine fortress and a World War II U-boat, *Vesikko*. The island of **Korkeasaari** (🚊 16/11 to Kulosaari or Metro to Kulosaari station, then 🚊 11 – weekends only) is home to **Helsinki Zoo**, which specialises in species from the Arctic. **Seurasaari** (5 km from city centre; 🚊 24 from Erottaja) is the site of Finland's largest and oldest **open-air museum** (closed mid-Sept–mid-May), with 80 historic buildings, including peasant huts and Sámi (Lapp) tents. **Pihlajasaari** is a recreation centre, popular with walkers.

SHOPPING

Mannerheimintie, Helsinki's main thoroughfare, holds numerous shops and boutiques, including the vast **Stockmann** department store (great selection of English-language books and magazines). **Kauppatori** (Market Square), next to the port, has colourful stalls with freshly caught fish and is where you can find some of the city's best food buys.

NIGHT-TIME AND EVENTS

The Tourist Office has free entertainment guides and some hotels dispense copies. *Helsinki This Week* contains monthly listings May–Aug and two months' listings Sept– Apr. Reservations for all events are handled by **Lippup alvelu**, e.g. Stockmann department store, Mannerheimintie 1, ☎0600 10 800 (premium rate), (www.lippupalvelu.fi). **Finlandia Hall**, Mannerheimintie 13, ☎(09) 40241 is the main centre for classical music. It's next door to the **Opera House**.

Evenings are lively; options range from discos to sophisticated nightclubs. Most have a minimum age of 20 or 24. The best areas for bars are around the station, or further south around Uudenmankatu. In summer, there's a tram carriage converted into a pub which travels around town: you can hop on, have a beer and hop off again after a pleasant tour.

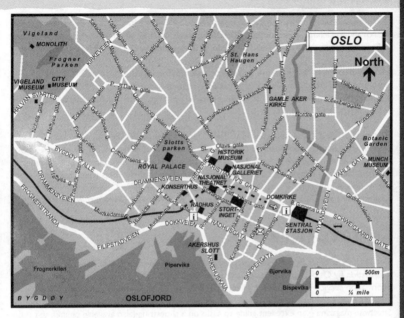

Hemmed in by water, forests and rolling hillsides, this former Viking capital is now a pleasant and laid-back modern-looking city. It is not a big place – nor is it as architecturally captivating as the other Scandinavian capitals – but is definitely worth a stop before venturing out to experience Norway's great outdoors. The city has a number of outstanding art museums – including one holding Edvard Munch's *The Scream* – as well as great harbour views from the Akershus fortress and a lively nightlife in the central districts of Grünerløkka and Grønland.

ARRIVAL AND DEPARTURE

RAIL The main rail station is the very central **Oslo Sentral-stasjon** (known as **Oslo S**). All long-distance trains stop here, as well as some local services. This modern construction feels more like an airport than a train station, and it is crammed with facilities of every kind. The **NSB** (Norwegian State Railways; ☎81 50 08 88; www.nsb.no) ticket office opens daily 0700–2300. The T-bane (Metro) is to the right as you leave the station.

TOURIST OFFICE

Fridtjof Nansens Plass 5 (by City Hall), ☎81 53 05 55 (www.visitoslo.com). Branch at Jernbanetorget 1 (by Sentralstasjon/ Central Station).

Norway

📻 There are usually daily sailings to Germany (**Kiel**) by **Color Line**, 📞81 00 08 11 (www.color line.no) and to Denmark (**Hirtshals**) by **DFDS Seaways**, 📞21 62 13 40 (www.dfdsseaways.no) or to **Frederikshavn**, six times a week from **Oslo**, by **Stena Line**, 📞23 17 91 00 (www.stenaline.no).

🚌 Long-distance buses: these use **Bussterminalen**, Schweigaardsgate 10, 📞23 00 24 00, which is easily reached from Oslo S by an enclosed walkway. Information about Norway bussekspress is given on www.nor-way.no, 📞81 54 44 44, or www.lavprisekspressen.no; for general information and bookings, 📞67 98 04 80.

✈️ **Gardermoen** (50 km north; www.osl.no). This is a stunning example of sleek Scandinavian modern architecture. Airport express trains take 20 mins to Oslo, 📞81 50 07 77 (www.flytoget.no); buses take 45 mins but are cheaper. You can also travel north from here direct to Lillehammer and Trondheim (ETT tables 783 and 785). Ryanair flights go to **Oslo Torp**, which has bus connections with Ryanair flights (booking not necessary); buses leave Oslo bus terminal (Galleri Oslo) around 3 hrs before flight departure, 📞67 98 04 80 (www.torpekspressen.no).

INFORMATION

Get *The Official Guide for the Oslo Region*, *Oslo What's On* and a map, all free. There is a tourist information by Oslo S station, inside Trafikanten Service Center, open daily. The youth tourism information service **USE IT** is at Møllergata 3; 📞24 14 98 20 (www.use-it.no); they offer free internet access and free luggage storage in summer (under 27). Make sure you get their (free) *Streetwise* magazine – an excellent guide to Oslo on a shoestring (also available online), and probably the most up-to-date guide you'll find. Hikers should visit **DNT**, Storgate 3 📞22 82 28 00, which hand out hiking route maps and has information on inexpensive mountain cabins. The widely available **Oslo Pass**, valid for 24/48/72 hrs, provides free city transport, free admission to most attractions and various discounts. The **Oslo Package** provides hotel room and breakfast and the Oslo Pass – including up to two children under 16 staying free in their parents' room.

INTERNET ACCESS   Oslo has a handful of internet cafés spread out along the main thoroughfares. There are also spots at Oslo Central Station, the bus station and at **QBA-café/bar/internet**, Olaf Ryes Plass 4, 📞92 03 22 28 (www.qba.no), open Mon–Fri 0800–0100, Sat–Sun 1000–0100. Many cafés have free wireless connection.

PUBLIC TRANSPORT

Oslo's centre is relatively small and outlying attractions are easily reachable on the excellent public transport system. **Trafikanten** (the tower-like building outside Oslo S), Jernbanetorget, 📞177 or 815 00 176 (open Mon–Fri 0700–2000, Sat–Sun 0800–1800, open until 2000 every day in the summer; www.trafikanten.no), handles transport queries, timetables and tickets. Get the (free) public transport map, *Sporveiskart Oslo*. Single tickets are valid for 1 hr. Multi-ride tickets include day cards (*Dagskort*) and 7-day cards (*Ukekort*).

🚇 **Metro**: T-lines converge at Stortinget. There are maps on the platforms and trains have a destination board. Most trams converge at Oslo S and most city buses at Oslo M (on Vaterland, by Oslo S). Most westbound buses and trams (including those to **Bygdøy** and **Vigelandsparken**) stop at the south side of Nasjonalteatret. **Taxis:** 02323, 02202 or 08000, or use the strategically positioned ranks. If you use an unregistered 'pirate taxi', agree a price beforehand and don't go alone.

Ferries to **Bygdøy** as well as sightseeing boats leave (Apr–Sept) from quay 3 on the Rådhusbrygge (No. 91), near the Tourist Office. Ferries to **Hovedøya**, **Langøyene** and other islands in the Oslofjord leave from Vippetangen (92/93/94).

ACCOMMODATION

The Tourist Offices by the City Hall and at Oslo S can book hotel accommodation and rooms in private houses. They also hand out lists of cheap accommodation in pensions and hostels, though they do not book this type of lodging. USE IT (see p494) books rooms in private homes for around Nkr.150–500 per person, for which you should book in advance in high season (May–Sept).

Hotels start at around NKr.650 for a single and NKr.850 for a twin room. There are also some bed and breakfast operations, charging typically around Nkr.400 for a single and NKr.600 for a double. **Oslo Budget Hotel**, 22 41 36 10 (www.budgethotel.no), is a moderate, low-budget hotel only 200m away from Oslo S. **Thon Hotel Astoria**, Dronningengate 21, 24 14 55 50 (www.thonhotels.no), is classier, with modern rooms at similar prices.

Youth hostels (HI): Haraldsheim, Haraldsheimvn 4, Grefsen, 22 22 29 65 (www.haraldsheim.no), is 4 km from Oslo S: Metro 4/6 Sinsen, tram 17 Sinsenkrysset, or 31/32 to Sinsenkrysset; **Holtekilen**, Micheletsvei 55, Stabekk, 67 51 80 40 (oslo.holtekilen@hihostels.no); open beginning May–end Sept, 8 km from Oslo S (15 mins by train). The other HI hostel is **Vandrerhjem Rønningen**, Myrerskogveien 54, 21 02 36 00 (www.oslo hostel.com); open late May–mid Aug), on the northern side of the city, by hiking trails, 25 mins by tram to the centre. All hostels have private rooms and dorms.

Private hostels (non-HI): Sentrum Pensjonat, Tollbugata 8, 22 33 55 80, is located in the centre, close to the theatre, cinema, restaurants and bars. **Perminalen Hotel**, Øvre Slottsgate 2, 23 09 30 81 (www.perminalen .com), is only two mins from Karl Johans gate.

DAY TRIP FROM OSLO

Tusenfryd, Amusement Park at Vinterbro (30 mins south by shuttle bus from the centre). With the Thunder Coaster – one of the world's largest wooden rollercoasters.

FOR FREE

Botanisk Hage (botanic gardens), **Nasjonalgalleriet** (National Gallery, closed Mon), **Domkirke** (cathedral), **Sculpture Park** in Vigelands-parken, park around **Akershus**, **Vigelands-parken** (Vigeland Park).

Norway

Campsites: **Bogstad Camping**, Ankerveien 117, Holmenkollen, ☎22 51 08 00 (www.
bogstadcamping.no), open all year (🚍 32 from Oslo S, 32 mins). **Ekeberg Camping**,
Ekebergveien 65, ☎22 19 85 68 (www.ekebergcamping.no), is closer (about 3 km:
10 mins on 🚍 34: Ekeberg Camping), but open only June–Aug. You can camp in the
forest north of town if you avoid public areas (head into the woods for about 1 km).
Oslo Fjordcamping, Ljansbrukveien 1, ☎22 75 20 55 (www.oslofjordcamping.no),
is close to the fjord and a nice beach, and is open mid-May–Sept (about 8 km from
Oslo S; 🚍 83 from Thon Hotel Opera, Fiskevollen).

FOOD AND DRINK

Eating out in Oslo is very expensive. For restaurant listings, see *The Official Guide for
the Oslo Region*. There are a number of pricey options for good Norwegian food, but
eating on a budget is possible if you stock up on hotel buffet breakfasts, scour
bakeries after hours and shop at a supermarket (e.g. **Kiwi**, Storgaten 32, open
Mon–Fri 0800–2000, Sat 1000–1800) or cheap delis on the east side of town, and
picnic in one of the parks. Try fresh (boiled) prawns from the harbour, on a roll, with
a dash of mayonnaise – it's as Scandinavian as any meal you'll eat here.

A great option for cheap eating is at BIT, which does sandwiches in Oslo City and
Universitetsgata 20. Also Dattera til Hagen, a colourful café at Grønland 10
(www.dattera.no) offers budget prices on tapas, sandwiches and salads.

HIGHLIGHTS

The **Bygdøy** peninsula, accessible via a short boat trip across the bay, is a great place
to visit some of the best maritime-related museums in Norway. Bygdøy also has
sandy beaches and pleasant picnic spots. Ferries leave from Rådhusebrygge 3 (pier
3, by the city hall) every 30 mins (every 20 mins at peak times in summer); they take
10 mins.

The first group of museums is at the first quay you reach upon arrival, dominated
by the glass tent of the **Frammuseet** (Fram Museum), which houses, in its entirety,
Fram, the Arctic exploration ship built in 1892 and used by Roald Amundsen and
two other explorers.

The **Kon-Tiki Museum** displays the late Thor Heyerdahl's raft *Kon-Tiki*, a replica of
vessels that he believed ancient civilisations used to migrate across the Atlantic from
South America to Polynesia; Heyerdahl made the voyage himself to give credence
to his theory (although DNA evidence has since called some of his ideas into
question). There are also several Easter Island statues and film screenings about his
expedition. From here, walk up the hill bearing right to the second, more impressive
group of museums.

The breathtaking **Vikingskiphuset** (Viking Ship Museum) houses three ninth-century ships, once completely interred underground for the voyage to Valhalla in the afterlife, and now gloriously resurrected and reassembled. The museum holds a number of striking iron, wood and leather artefacts. Some 150 Nordic buildings, including an ancient stave church, have been collected to form the nearby **Norsk Folkemuseum** (Norwegian Folk Museum), worth setting aside at least part of a day to see.

Back at Oslo harbour, the fortress-palace complex of **Akershus** looms to the east; you enter from Akersgt or over a drawbridge from Kirkegt. The extensive grounds hold several museums, notably **Norges Hjemmefront museum**, a fascinating place devoted to the history of the Norwegian Resistance. The huge **Forsvarsmuseet** (Defence Museum; open Mon–Fri 1000–1600 Sat–Sun 1100–1600, later in summer) dates as far back as the Vikings.

The site of **Domkirke** (cathedral), Stortorget 1, dates from 1697, but only the baroque carved altarpiece and pulpit survive from the original cathedral. It's worth a peek in for the vast painted ceiling and the elaborate stained-glass windows, designed by Gustav Vigeland's brother Emanuel.

Nasjonalgalleriet (National Gallery), Universitetsgata 13 (Metro: Nasjonalteatret), houses a huge collection of Norwegian art and has a room dedicated to Edvard Munch, displaying some of his most famous paintings, including a version of *The Scream*.

The sculpture-filled **Vigelandsparken/Frognerparken**, in northwest Oslo (main entrance from Kirkevn) – 🚌 20; tram 12: Vigelandsparken – is one of Oslo's most impressive and popular sights. Over 200 larger-than-life statues are sprinkled about the landscape of the huge park. The display culminates in a phallic 15-m column of bodies in rapture, which form the monolith of life. Edvard Munch gave much of his art to the city, most of it housed in the **Munchmuseet** (Munch Museum), Tøyengt 53 (Metro: Tøyen; closed Mon, Sept–May, free entry Oct–Mar), east of the centre; the most famous version of *The Scream* was stolen from here in 2004 and returned in 2006. The museum adjoins the extensive **Botanisk Hage** (botanic gardens). **Tryvannstårnet** TV/observation tower, 20-min walk north (or Metro: Voksenkollen), is a prominent landmark and offers captivating views of the countryside around Oslo.

SHOPPING

The best souvenirs to pick up on a trip to Norway are Norwegian handicraft items, including crystal, leather, silver and knitwear. The items are of the highest quality – a Norwegian sweater will last a lifetime – but few such items come cheap.

Karl Johans Gate is the city's main street, part of which is pedestrian and the majority of which is loaded with shops, restaurants and street performers. **Basarhallene**

(behind the cathedral) is an art and handicraft boutique centre, while the **Aker Brygge** complex is a good place to browse. Other major shopping complexes are **Paléet**, Karl Johansgt 37–43, and **Oslo City**, across from the station.

NIGHT-TIME AND EVENTS

See *Streetwise, The Official Guide for the Oslo Region* and *Oslo What's On* for listings. Oslo has a well-developed café culture, but also has a number of newer student-style bars and clubs.

Many cafés can be found along the stretch between the station and the palace and in the capital's trendy area of **Grünerløkka** to the northeast; hip, atmospheric, lively and doing its best to avoid gentrification. **Thorvald Meyers gata** here has about a dozen happening bars that get lively after 2300 or so.

Grønland is a grungy area east of the train station with the cheapest beer in town. The Aker Brygge, by the harbour, has waterfront bars, but is a bit more touristy and expensive.

Drinking anywhere in Oslo is expensive; alcohol is cheaper from supermarkets, but they can't sell it after 2000 (Sat 1800) and you can only get wine and spirits from special Vinmonopolet shops, e.g. Oslo Sentralstasjon, Jernbaentorget 1; (www.vinmonopolet.no). The drinking age is 18 (20 for spirits), and some bars only serve 21+, and ID is rigorously checked. Most places stay open until 0200.

Well-known operas are performed at the new opera house, **Den Norske Opera & Ballett**, Kirsten Flagstads pl 1, while the **Oslo Konserthus**, Munkedamsvn 14, stages folklore events in midsummer. Most movies are shown in their original language.

Spread over 14 islands with countless inlets, Stockholm has a stunning waterfront that rivals those of San Francisco and Sydney, and most visitors would probably rate it the most rewarding of the Scandinavian capitals. At its heart is the impressively intact original part of the city, **Gamla Stan**, with an enticing blend of dignified old buildings, cafés, and craft and designer shops; in contrast, the **Djurgården** is a huge natural park where the city comes to swim, canoe, fly kites, visit the zoo and the superb outdoor museum Skansen, or just admire the views.

Stockholm is airy and very much a harbour capital, a lovely place to be outdoors in summer (winter is perfectly romantic, if a bit austere), whether listening to an outdoor concert or taking a cruise, but there are plenty of superb indoor attractions, such as the **Nationalmuseum** and the historic *Vasa* warship. It's also a clean, safe and friendly place, and you get the sense that everything runs like clockwork.

ARRIVAL AND DEPARTURE

The labyrinthine and confusing **Centralstationen** (0400–2400) has showers (on the lower level), a bus information/ticket office and currency exchange and good food stalls. Anything you

Sweden

TOURIST OFFICE

Stockholm Tourist Centre: Sverigehuset (Sweden House), Hamngatan 27, Kungsträdgården, ☎(08) 508 28 508 (www.stockholmtown.com). From Centralstationen, walk up Klarabergsg. to Sergels Torg (marked by an oddly-shaped pillar), then right on Hamngatan for the Tourist Office. Also the **digital guide** in the main hall of Centralstationen (tourist info and hotel bookings).

need should be in (or adjoining) the main hall. If not, try the nearby Cityterminalen (see Buses, below). For train information, ☎0771 75 75 75 (www.sj.se).

🚌 **Cityterminalen** (long-distance bus station), **Klarabergsviadukten**: across the road from Centralstationen, but linked by tunnels, ☎(08) 762 59 97 (www.cityterminalen.com). **Swebus Express** is the largest domestic company, ☎0771 21 82 18 (www.swebusexpress.se).

⛴ Ferries to Helsinki: the overnight ships to Finland (see feature, p505) are run by **Silja Line**, with offices at Sveavägen 14, ☎(08) 440 59 90 and at Cityterminalen, ☎(08) 440 59 90 (www.tallinksilja.com), and **Viking Line**, office at Cityterminalen, ☎(08) 452 40 00 (www.vikingline.se).

✈ **Stockholm Arlanda**, ☎(08) 797 60 00, www.arlanda.se, is 45 km north of Stockholm. The **Arlanda Express** (airport rail link to Centralstationen), ☎0771 72 02 00 (www.arlanda express.com), takes 20 mins (every 15 mins, daily, 0505–2305, then every 30 mins until 0105). The **Flygbussarna** (airport bus), ☎(08) 588 228 28 (www.flygbussarna.se), takes about 40 mins from **Cityterminalen** and runs every 10 or 15 mins 0400–2345 plus through the night in connection with flights. Ryanair flies to **Skavsta** (80 mins by bus) and **Västerås** (1 hr 15 mins by bus) airports; bus timetables are tailored to flight times.

INTERNET ACCESS   Stockholm is fairly well wired when it comes to internet cafés. Internet cafés are common. Try the **Sidewalk Express Internet Points** that can be found on levels 1 and 2 at Centralstationen or in **7-eleven** stores.

INFORMATION

Small city maps are freely available, but a larger-scale one might come in handy. A wealth of free English-language literature includes *What's On Stockholm* (free bi-monthly tourist and events guide), *Hotels and Hostels Stockholm* (free hotel and youth hostel guide) and the official guide to Stockholm.

The **Stockholm Card** (**Stockholmskortet**, SEK375 for 24 hrs, SEK495 for 48 hrs or SEK595 for 72 hrs; www.stockholmtown.com/stockholmcard) from Tourist Offices, stations, the Silja Line terminal and most hotels, youth hostels and campsites, provides free public transport, free boat tour (Apr–Dec), free entrance to 75 museums and attractions as well as other discounts. The **SL Pass**, SEK100 for 24 hours, SEK200 for 72 hours and SEK260 for 7 days, is valid on all buses, trams, Metro and local trains, plus some ferries.

500 **Arrival and Departure – Information**

DAY TRIPS FROM STOCKHOLM

Björkö (an island in Lake Mälaren) is the site of the **Birka Vikingastaden** (Birka Viking Town; open May–Sept; www.raa.se), Sweden's oldest city, and an important Viking merchant centre.

PUBLIC TRANSPORT

Storstockholms Lokaltrafik (SL) runs the excellent bus and Metro network. Main office: lower level of Sergels Torg; ☎(08) 600 10 00 (www.sl.se). There's a branch in Central-stationen. Buy tickets for buses and the T-bana at SL Centers or ticket agents located in most ticket halls and visibly displayed with the SL logo. The **one-hour ticket** allows unlimited travel during that time in one zone (SEK40), two zones (SEK60), or three zones (SEK80). Stamp ticket with a validation as you enter the T-bana or bus. To bypass all the machines, you can buy a **pass for free transit**: 24 hours (SEK100), 72 hours (SEK200), or seven days (SEK260).

The Metro, **Tunnelbana (T-bana)**, has three lines (red, green and blue). Trains are fast and frequent, 0500–0100. Metro stations display a blue 'T' on a white circle. The décor along some lines is some of the most imaginative in Europe: walls are moulded to look like caves, are painted strident colours and hold original murals.

🚌 City buses are frequent, 0500–2400, and there's a night service (*nattbus*). 🚌 47 (to Gröna Lund, Skansen and Vasa Museet) and 69 (to Kaknästornet) are most useful.

The larger taxi companies, **Taxi Stockholm**, ☎(08) 15 00 00, **Taxi Kurir**, ☎(08) 30 00 00, and **Taxi 020**, ☎(020) 20 20 20, are usually cheapest and rarely cost more than SEK220 for journeys within city limits and SEK475 to/from Arlanda Airport. If you take an independent taxi, make sure you agree the fare before setting out.

⛴ The main operator is **Waxholmsbolaget**, Strömkajen; ☎(08) 614 64 65 (www.waxholmsbolaget.se). A **Boat Hiker's Card** allows five days of travel (SEK 420 from Waxholmsbolaget offices). Singles (SEK60–130) can be bought on board. See also Tours, p503.

ACCOMMODATION

Hotellcentralen (Hotel Central), the official accommodation booking service, is in the main hall of Centralstationen; ☎(08) 508 28 500 (www.stockholmtown.com/hotels). Advance bookings are free, but there's a fee for same-day bookings. Pick up a (free) copy of *Hotels and Hostels Stockholm* or download it from www.stockholmtown.se. A useful booking service for private rooms is **Bed and Breakfast Agency Sweden (BBA)**, Mariatorget 8, ☎(08) 643 80 28 (www.bba.nu).

Youth hostels (HI): AF Chapman & Skeppsholmen, Flaggmansvägen 8, Skeppsholmen, ☎(08) 463 22 66 (www.stfchapman.com), 🚌 65, a tall ship moored in the harbour; **Långholmen**, Kronohäktet, Långholmsmuren 20, ☎(08) 720 85 10 (www.lang holmen.com), once a prison (nearest Metro: Hornstull); **City Backpackers**, Upplandsgatan 2A, ☎(08) 20 69 20 (www.citybackpackers.org; Metro: T-Centralen);

Sweden

and **Vandrarhem Zinkensdamm**, Zinkens väg 20, ☎(08) 616 8100 (www.zinkens damm.com; Metro: Zinkensdamm).

The most central **campsite** is **Östermalms Citycamping**, Fiskartorpsvägen 2, Östermalm, ☎(08) 10 29 03 (www.camping.se), 1.5 km from city centre at Östermalm sports ground, 🚌 55 (late June–late Aug). **Bredäng Camping**, Stora Sällskapets väg 51, Skärholmen, ☎(08) 97 70 71 (www.camping.se), 10 km southwest of the city (Metro: Bredäng), open mid-Apr–mid-Oct; there's a **youth hostel** here too (open all year).

FOOD AND DRINK

Stockholm has a good range of cuisine, with restaurants that have done well to incorporate a fusion of international foods. By eating a main meal at lunchtime you can take advantage of good offers even on the more expensive restaurants. Small, inexpensive places like cafés and lunch restaurants can be found all over the city.

HIGHLIGHTS

Many museums are closed on Mon; most are open 1100–1600, with longer hours in summer. See *What's On Stockholm* or the Stockholm guide for details. On limited time or cash, head for the pleasant and atmospheric Gamla Stan, then take the ferry from there to Djurgården.

GAMLA STAN   Joined to the mainland by bridges, **Gamla Stan** is the city's immaculately preserved old quarter, with age-old merchants' houses, boutiques and craft shops to browse in and a very distinctive atmosphere all around. Seek out the main square, **Stortorget**, with its colourful façades, gabled roofs and rococo **Börsen** (Stock Exchange), and the timewarp street of **Prästgatan**. Conspicuous both for its size and its splendour is **Kungliga Slottet** (Metro: Gamla Stan), the royal palace (rebuilt 1760), whose apartments, treasury, armoury and palace museum can be visited (separate entrance for each), and where the royal palace guard changes at noon each day. Next to it, the **Storkyrkan** (cathedral) hosts royal marriages and has extensive baroque interiors as well as a fine 15th-century wooden sculpture of St George and the Dragon. The royal burial place is the 13th-century former monastery of **Riddarholmskyrkan**, which is adorned with ornate sarcophagi and coats of arms.

DAY TRIPS FROM STOCKHOLM

For suggestions and details, visit the tourist office on Hamngatan 27 in central Stockholm. One of the most impressive destinations is **Drottningholms Slott** (Drottningholm Palace), home of the royal family and sometimes called 'the Versailles of Sweden'. It is 11 km west of the city, and best reached by boat from Stadshuskajen, taking an hour, or Metro: Brommaplan, then 🚌 301/323. Several rooms are on view and there are tours of the 18th-century theatre. **Kina Slott** (the Chinese pavilion, a World Heritage Site), at the far end of the gardens, used to be a summer cottage.

TOURS

Strömma Kanalbolaget,
Nybroplan,
☎(08) 120 040 00
(www.stromma.se),
operate boat excursions
in the archipelago
and on Lake Mälaren.
Cinderellabåtarna
(Cinderella Boats),
Nybroplan,
☎(08) 120 040 00
(www.cinderellabatarna.com),
offer boat excursions to
Stockholm's verdant
outer archipelago.

FOR FREE

Tours of **Riksdagshuset**
(Swedish parliament);
Changing the Guard
at **Kungliga Slottet**
(Royal Palace); **Storkyrkan**
(Stockholm Cathedral);
Kulturhuset and
Bergianska Trädgården
(Bergius Botanic Garden).

In the 1970s, the remains of the Old Town wall were discovered and incorporated into **Stockholms Medeltidsmuseet** (Museum of Medieval Stockholm; Metro: Gamla Stan, ⬚ 43/62; free, currently relocated to Kulturhuset and reopens in early 2010). In front of the museum stands the **Riksdagshuset**, where the Swedish parliament meets; there are free guided tours from the rear of the building late June–early Sept (Mon–Fri, each hour from 1130–1530 in Swedish, 1200 and 1500 in English).

North of the centre (Metro: Universitetet), the **Bergianska Trädgården** (Bergius Botanic Garden; free) includes **Victoriahuset**, home of the world's largest water lily, while at **Fjärilshuset** (Butterfly House), Hagaparken, you can witness tropical butterflies and birds in a natural environment.

NORRMALM AND BLASIEHOLMEN

Norrmalm is the bland centre of modern Stockholm, where 1960s office blocks converge with shopping malls near the main rail station. At the centre of it all is the glass obelisk of **Sergels Torg** (where the **Kulturhuset**, Cultural Centre, Metro: Centralen, is home to changing exhibitions of Swedish contemporary arts and crafts). Things get even more interesting around the leafy park of **Kungsträdgården**, the foremost meeting place in the city, lined with cafés and full of street life.

Close by, **Medelhavsmuseet** (Museum of Mediterranean and Near Eastern Antiquities, admission charge), Fredsg. 2 (Metro: Kungsträdgården), is a wonderful treasure house of the ancient world, with a particularly striking Egyptian section. On **Kungsholmen** (immediately west of Centralstationen), the 1920s **Stadshuset** (City Hall), Hantverkargatan 1 (Metro: Centralen/Rådhuset), hosts the annual Nobel Banquet (Dec 10); daily guided tours. Of particular note are the striking mosaics in the Golden Room and royal murals in the Prince's Gallery.

The peninsula of **Blasieholmen**, to the east, is home to the superb **Nationalmuseum** (National Swedish Museum of Fine Arts; admission charge), Blasieholmshamnen (Metro: Kungsträdgården), with a choice collection of Swedish applied art and furniture, as well as international pieces, notably Russian Orthodox art. Linked to Blasieholmen by bridge, Skeppsholmen has a host of museums, including an outstanding gallery of modern art (**Moderna Museet**; admission charge). Further east from Norrmalm, **Östermalm** is a residential area with supremely elegant streets such as Strandvägen by the waterfront.

Sweden

Historiska Museet (Museum of National Antiquities; admission charge), Narvavägen 13–17 (Metro: Karlaplan/Östermalmstorg), is famous for the Guldrummet (Golden Room), an underground chamber that contains one of Europe's richest collections of prehistoric and medieval gold and silver jewellery.

DJURGÅRDEN   🚌 44/47 stop near each of the main attractions in the city's island park and gardens. There are ferries, operator **Waxholmsbolaget** (see p501), from Nybroplan (in Gamla Stan) in summer, and from Skeppsbron (east of Kungsträdgården) year-round, as well as a private vintage tram (No. 7) from Norrmalmstorg.

The eastern section of this large island, together with **Ladugårdsgärdet** (to the north), forms **Ekoparken**, a 56-sq-km nature reserve. Along the western side are various attractions. Don't miss **Vasamuseet** (Vasa Museum), built to house *Vasa*, a 17th-century warship that was discovered well preserved in mud and dredged up in 1961 from the harbour where she sank on her maiden voyage.

The **Nordiska Museet** (Nordic Museum; admission charge) gives a good overview of Swedish life and culture, with exhibits including Sami (Lapp) artefacts. The **Thielska Galleriet** (Thiel Gallery) is a turn-of-the-century mansion, of some architectural interest, which houses a tremendous collection of Scandinavian art, including works by Munch and the Swedish artist Carl Larsson, who produced renowned tableaux of childhood.

Aquaria Vattenmuseum (Aquaria Water Museum) is a high-tech complex that enables you to experience 24 hours in a rainforest and get close to marine creatures (entrance fees help to save endangered rainforest).

For something more frivolous, **Gröna Lund Tivoli** offers live entertainments and rides.

Skansen, Stockholm's most popular attraction, is an unmissable open-air museum consisting primarily of over 150 historical buildings – including houses, period shops, farms and workshops – and a large zoo specialising in Nordic fauna such as bears and wolves. Its highest point, Solliden, gives an impressive view over the city. You could easily pass an entire day here. Another excellent viewpoint is the immense TV tower known as **Kaknästornet**. It is Scandinavia's second tallest building, after southern city Malmö's Turning Torso skyscraper, with a viewing platform at 128 m (headphones give a commentary on what you can see).

SHOPPING

The main areas are Hamngatan, Drottninggatan, Birger Jarlsgatan, Sergels Torg, Gamla Stan and Götgatan. **NK**, Hamng. 18–20, and **Åhléns City**, Klarabergsg. 50, are well-stocked department stores. Specialities include Swedish crystal, glassware, handmade paper, textiles and ceramics. **Stockhome**, Kungsgatan 25, is a fun gift shop with a trendy twist, or check out traditional Swedish line **Västerlånggatan** in Gamla Stan. The most popular markets, a mixture of stalls and indoor food halls, are **Östermalmstorg**, **Hötorget** and **Söderhallarna**.

NIGHT-TIME AND EVENTS

What's On Stockholm carries listings, but you can also consult the Thursday supplement *DN På Stan* in the *Dagens Nyheter* daily newspaper or the Friday entertainment supplements in the Aftonbladet and Expressen dailies (listings are in Swedish, but easy to interpret). There are around 70 theatres and concert halls and, in summer, you can enjoy free concerts in the parks. All films are shown in the original language. **Cosmonova** (in Naturhistoriska Riksmuseet) offers highly advanced planetarium performances and IMAX films.

EVENTS

The biggest summer fest is at midsummer, celebrated all over the country, and particularly at Skansen, where it lasts three days. Other regular events include the **Stockholm Marathon** in early June, the **National Day** (6 June), **Stockholm Pride** (Aug), the **Cultural Festival of Stockholm** (Aug), and the **Stockholm International Film Festival** in November. **Regattas** are held frequently in the summer.

Södermalm, south of the water, is the best area for pubs (open till at least 0100), and is more bohemian and cheaper than the glitzy north side – though both are good for a people-watching wander in the evenings. Clubs are centred around **Stureplan** and **Norrmalm**; some stay open till 0500, but a few don't admit under 25s.

WHERE NEXT? FERRIES TO HELSINKI

Departing from Stockholm, the immense Viking Line and Silja Line ferries (ETT table 2465; see p489) that make the journey across the Baltic are a popular institution with the locals. There's a great view of the archipelagos at the Swedish end, and the food and drink are tax-free, a difference you are certain to notice in Scandinavia. Each has pubs and clubs that are very busy until 0500, especially at weekends. This journey is surprisingly cheap, especially if you don't take a cabin, though even seats still need to be booked; cheaper cabins have four beds and en-suite toilets/showers. Generally, late bookings are more expensive and mid-week is cheaper than weekends. Book a sitting for the all-you-can-eat buffet as soon as you get on board. The boats take about 16 hrs, leaving Stockholm about 1700, arriving in Helsinki 0930–1000, and you can sleep off your night's entertainment for a while after you arrive. Travellers have been known to spend all their nights on the boat, touring Helsinki and Stockholm on alternate days.

ROUTE DETAIL

Copenhagen–Roskilde
ETT table 700

Type	Frequency	Typical journey time
Local train	Frequent	20 mins

Roskilde–Odense
ETT table 700

Type	Frequency	Typical journey time
Train	Every 30 mins	1 hr 7 mins

Odense–Århus
ETT table 700

Type	Frequency	Typical journey time
Train	1–2 per hr	1 hr 40 mins

Århus–Aalborg
ETT table 701

Type	Frequency	Typical journey time
Train	1–2 per hr	1 hr 35 mins

Aarlborg–Frederikshavn
ETT table 701

Type	Frequency	Typical journey time
Train	Every hr	1 hr 8 mins

Frederikshavn–Gothenburg
ETT table 2320

Type	Frequency	Typical journey time
Ferry	4–6 daily	3 hrs 30 mins

Notes

There are also up to three HSS Fast Ferry services daily in summer between Frederikshavn and Gothenburg, taking 2 hrs.

KEY JOURNEYS

Copenhagen–Gothenburg
(via Malmö) Stopping train only ETT table 735

Type	Frequency	Typical journey time
Train	6–12 daily	4 hrs

This journey takes in the dramatic 18-km **Storebælt** (Great Belt) tunnel and bridge combination linking Denmark's two largest islands – **Zealand** and **Funen** – and also provides the chance to visit some of northern Denmark's lesser-known yet highly attractive towns. **Odense** makes a particularly useful base for exploring the area.

COPENHAGEN (KØBENHAVN)

See p481.

ROSKILDE

Roskilde was Denmark's first capital, and it is rich in history, with a cathedral that is the traditional burial place of Danish royalty. The Viking Ship Museum exhibits the intact remains of five original ships and shows a film about their excavation in the 1960s. Just next door is the museum harbour where, in the summer months, visitors are allowed in to the workshops to try their hand at maritime crafts and even venture out onto the fjord in a reconstructed Viking longship. The famous open-air Roskilde Festival (music) is held in June/July (www.roskilde-festival.dk) and features some of the biggest international rock groups as well as lesser-known Scandinavian bands.

ℹ️ **Tourist Office**: Gullandsstraede 15, ☎ 46 31 65 65 (www.visitroskilde.com).

🏠 **Youth hostel (HI):** Vineboder 7, ☎ 46 35 21 84 (www.rova.dk), just west of the Viking Ship Museum by the sea.

ODENSE

Odense, a busy manufacturing city, is the largest settlement on the island of **Fyn** (*Funen*) and the third largest in the country. Throughout Denmark it's known as the birthplace of Hans Christian Andersen, who turned to writing fairy-tales after failing in his ambitions to be an actor and novelist. Andersen's childhood home, **Barndomshjem**, Munkemølle-stræde 3–5, has a couple of period-era rooms crammed with his belongings (closed Mon mid-Aug–mid-June), but there's far more material in the extensive **H C Andersen Hus**, Hans Jensens Stræde 37–45, the site where he was born in 1805, including manuscripts, paper cuttings and his celebrated top hat (closed Mon mid-Aug–mid-June).

Two excellent art museums are **Fyns Kunstmuseum** (Funen Art Museum; closed Mon), Jernbanegade 13, a superb collection of Danish art, and the **Brandts Klædefabrik**, a large, open gallery space comprising photography, printing and fine arts museums with both permanent and temporary exhibits. Carl Nielsen, Denmark's greatest composer, was born near Odense in 1865, and is commemorated by the **Carl Nielsen Museet** at Claus Bergs Gade 11 (by the concert hall; opening times vary).

Scandinavia (Denmark and Sweden)

🚆 The railway forms the northern boundary of the city centre.

ℹ️ **Tourist Office**: Rådhuset, Vestergade 2, ☎63 75 75 20 (www.visitodense.com).

🏠 **Youth hostels (HI):** Next to the train station is **Danhostel Odense City**, Østre Stationvej 31, ☎63 11 04 25, fax 63 11 35 20 (www.cityhostel.dk); closed mid-Dec–early Jan. Several km south of the city centre is **Danhostel Odense Kragsbjerggaard**, Kragsbjergvej 121, ☎66 13 04 25 (www.dagkurser.com; open Mar–Nov). Take bus 61/62.

ÅRHUS

Denmark's second largest city is an active port and commercial and cultural centre, but even so most sights are within easy walking distance. Old Århus holds the monopoly on nightspots as well as a few museums, including three on one site – the **Kvindemuseet** (Women's Museum, closed Mon Sept–May), examining the role of women through history, the **Besættelsesmuseet** (open weekends only, plus Tues and Thurs June–Aug), paying homage to the Danish Resistance in World War II, and the free **Vikingemuseet** (Viking Museum; closed Sat–Sun). The imposing **Domkirke** (cathedral) has pre-Reformation frescos and is the longest church in Denmark.

Next to the botanic gardens to the west of the centre, the city's major attraction is **Den Gamle By**, an open-air ethnographic museum featuring close to a hundred traditional half-timbered Danish homes. Located 5 km south of the city the superb **Moesgård Museum** (closed Mon Oct–Mar) is home to the 2000-year-old preserved Grauballe man, discovered in a nearby peat bog in 1952; 🚌 6 passes by. In the town centre, you can use any of the 250 city bikes at 30 special bike stands around town, free of charge, any time of day (DKr. 20 deposit required). Return to a stand after use.

An hour's journey away in **Billund** is the **Legoland** park, a showpiece of this Danish invention: ☎75 33 13 33 (www.legoland.dk); open mid-Mar–Oct; closed Wed and Thur mid-Sept–mid-Oct).

🚆 The station is just south of the centre.

✈️ **Århus Lufthavn**, Kolind, ☎87 75 70 00 (www.aar.dk), (40 km), served by Ryanair; bus takes 40 mins.

ℹ️ **Tourist Office**: Banegårdspladsen 20, ☎87 31 50 10 (www.visitaarhus.com). **Århus Passet** (The Århus Pass), available for one or two days (DKr.119/149), gives free public transport, entry to all attractions and sightseeing trips.

🏠 **Youth hostel (HI): Danhostel Århus Vandrerhjem**, Marienlundsvej 10, Risskov, ☎86 21 21 20 (www.aarhus-danhostel.dk); closed late Dec–mid-Jan. **City Sleep-In (non HI)**, Havnegade 20, ☎86 19 20 55 (www.citysleep-in.dk).

AALBORG

Herring brought prosperity to this North Jutland town in the 17th century, and the legacy of that boom is the handsome old quarter, with finely preserved merchants' houses, such as the spectacularly ornate **Jens Bangs Stenhus**. **Nordjyllands Kunstmuseum** (North Jutland Museum of Modern Art, closed Mon) is home to one of the nation's foremost collections of 20th-century art – and has a sculpture garden too. The Zoo at Mølleparkvej 63 contains a wide collection of caged and free-roaming animals as well as an 'African village', with warthogs, zebras and giraffes. After the sun goes down, **Jomfru Ane Gade** is the street to hit for restaurants, music and bars (be sure to sample the local spirit, Akvavit). The Aalborg Carnival takes place in late May every year and throughout the summer open-air rock concerts are held in Mølle Park and in Skovdalen.

▢ A short walk south down Boulevarden from the town centre.

ℹ️ **Tourist Office**: Østerågade 8, ☎ 99 31 75 00 (www.visitaalborg.com).

▢ **Youth hostel (HI)**: **Aalborg Vandrerhjem**, Skydebanevej 50, ☎ 98 11 60 44, (www.dan hostelaalborg.dk), 3 km from Aalborg centre, close to the marina. Accommodation in four-bed rooms or in one of 30 cabins on an island sleeping five–seven.

GOTHENBURG (GÖTEBORG), SWEDEN

The huge cranes and shipyards that greet visitors arriving at Scandinavia's prime port mask the fact that this is Sweden's most attractive old city (and second largest, with a population of around half a million), created by Dutch merchants in the early 17th century. Boat tours take in the best of the waterside views from the old canals, while elsewhere there are atmospheric squares and numerous leafy parks that have earned Gothenburg the nickname of the Garden City. Much of the centre is traffic-free and easily managed on foot, though the trams that clatter around the streets add to its charm and are worth a ride. To get your bearings, go up **Skanska- skrapan** (Skanska Skyscraper), a striking red and white skyscraper, 86 m, which has a lookout (**GötheborgsUtkiken**; opening hours

*In summer there are English- language tours on **Ringlinien** (www.ringlinien.org), a vintage open-air tram (Saturdays during Christmas, spring and autumn, daily July) from Centralstation to Liseberg (see panel on next page). **Paddan sightseeing boats**, ☎(031) 60 96 70 (www.paddan.com), depart from Kungsportsbron (early Apr–early Oct; first departure 1030 June–Aug, 1130 Sept–Oct), first departure 1000, then up to four times per hour, lasting 50 mins: their harbour cruise is recommended, but be prepared to duck low under one or two of the bridges. Paddan also run dry-land tours on a 'convertible bus'. Several summer cruises are also available, around the harbour and further afield. Ask the Tourist Office for details.*

*The popular **Liseberg Amusement Park**, Örgrytevägen 5 (www.liseberg.se; tram 4/5/6/ 8/13), Scandinavia's largest amusement park, is dominated by the 150-m-high **Spaceport**, which offers panoramic views. Among the 30 or so gut-wrenching rides is one of Europe's longest rollercoasters. Open all year round.*

vary) with a small café (June–Aug only) near the top, giving superb harbour views. It's situated in **Lilla Bommen**, itself a charming area, with shops and craft workshops. Dominating the whole scene here, however, is the spectacular modern waterside **Göteborgs Operan** (Gothenburg Opera House) with performances of opera, ballet and concerts; guided tours 📷 (031) 10 80 00.

Kungsportsavenyn, usually known simply as 'Avenyn' (The Avenue), is the hub of the city, a 50-m wide boulevard lined with lime trees, shops and eateries, further enlivened by buskers and ad hoc street stalls. It leads up to **Götaplatsen**, the city's cultural centre, fronted by the fountain of **Poseidon** by the Swedish sculptor Carl Milles. Just off Avenyn is **Trädgårdsföreningen**, Nya Allén, a fragrant park full of flora and birdsong, speckled with works of art and other attractions.

The city's oldest secular building (1643) is **Kronhuset** (Crown Arsenal; closed Sun), Postgatan 6–8. Around it is **Kronhusbodarna**, a courtyard bounded by handicraft boutiques in 18th-century artisans' dwellings. Other good places for browsing are the **Antikhallarna** antique market in Västra Hamngatan, and **Haga Nygata**, a renovated historical area of cobbled streets, lined with craft, second-hand, antique and design shops, as well as cafés and restaurants. Opposite, the **Feskekôrka** resembles a 19th-century church, but is actually a thriving fish market, open Tues–Sat, also Mon in summer, and has a good seafood restaurant.

Some city museums close on Mondays but open daily in summer. Details, including those of special exhibitions, are given in the multilingual leaflet, *Göteborgs Museer*, which you find in Tourist Offices. Of particular interest are the **Göteborgs Maritima Upplevelsecentrum** (Gothenburg Maritime Centre), Packhuskajen (open Mar–Nov), the **Konstmuseet** (Art Museum; closed Mon), Götaplatsen and the **Universeum** (the National Science Discovery Centre; open daily), Södra vägen 50. In the large nature park of **Slottsskogen** (outside the city: tram 1/2: Linnéplatsen) are an observatory, a children's zoo and the **Naturhistoriska Museet** (Natural History Museum; closed Mon, Sept–Apr).

🚉 **Göteborg Centralstation**, at the northeast edge of the centre, is compact and has many amenities. Facilities include **Forex** foreign exchange (open daily), **Pressbyrån** (a chain selling papers, snacks, etc), lockers, showers and reasonably priced eateries. Most buses stop at Nils Ericsonsplatsen, next to the station. **Nordstan** is a huge shopping mall opposite the station, to which it's linked by a foot tunnel.

✈ **Landvetter Airport** (25 km), 📷 (031) 94 10 00 (www.landvetter.com); buses every 20 mins Mon–Fri and every 20–30 mins Sat and Sun to the central rail station.

Rail Tour: Copenhagen – Odense – Gothenburg

ENTERTAINMENT AND EVENTS

There is a wide selection of lively bars and clubs, centred around Avenyn; things get going around midnight, and places stay packed until 0500. At the **Göteborgskalaset** (Gothenburg Festival) in early Aug the town cuts loose and there is all-night partying in the streets.

🚢 **Stena Line**, ☎(031) 704 00 00 (www.stenaline.se), to/from Germany (**Kiel**), **Denmark** and Poland (**Gdansk**) sail from Majnabbehamnen, 15 mins west of town; Stena ships to/from Denmark (**Frederikshavn**) sail from Masthuggskajen, at the west end of the centre.

ℹ️ **Tourist Offices**: Kungsportsplatsen 2; ☎(031) 61 25 00 (www.goteborg.com). There is a **branch** at Nordstadstorget, in Nordstan. Pick up the free *Göteborg Guide*, a booklet containing listings and tips, and with a good town map. Also get a copy of *What's On Gothenburg*, a monthly guide to culture and events.

ℹ️ The centre's attractions are quite close together, but there's an excellent **tram** network if you don't feel like walking. Lines are colour-coded, and trams and bus stops show the numbers and destinations of lines using them, so it's easy to spot the stop and vehicle you need. Tickets must be bought in advance at **Pressbyrån**, **7-eleven**, or in the coin machines found on the trams. You can save by buying a multi-ride card (must be purchased in advance at Pressbyrån), giving you free rides during one or three 24-hour period on trams, buses and city boats. Not all vehicles have card-readers, so always have your receipt with you. **TidPunkten** supply information about routes, times and fares; ☎0771 41 43 00 (www.vasttrafik.se). **Main office**: Nils Ericssonterminalen (bus station). Others: Drottningtorget and Brunnsparken.

🏠 The Tourist Offices will book private rooms, as well as hotels, for a small fee. **Hotel Lorensberg**, Berzeliig 15, ☎(031) 81 06 00 (www.hotel-lorensberg.se), €€€. There are three reliable **HI youth hostels** (and many others). **Torrekulla Turiststation**, Kållered, ☎(031) 795 14 95; **Slottsskogens Vandrarhem**, Vegagatan 21, ☎(031) 42 65 20 (www.slottsskogenvh.se); and **Stigbergsliden**, Stigbergsliden 10, ☎(031) 24 16 20 (www.hostel-gothenburg.com). A **SVIF hostel** is **Liseberg Vandrarhem Kärralund**, Olbersgatan 9, ☎(031) 84 02 00 (www.liseberg.se), tram 5. This last hostel is near the closest **campsite** to town: **Lisebergs Camping & Stugbyar Kårralunds Timmerbyn**, Olbersgatan 1 (same ☎ and website), which has **cottages** as well as camping and is open all year.

🍴 The **seafood** is excellent, most restaurants clustering along the waterfront. For other types of cuisine, try around Avenyn or in Linnéstaden. The **Nordstan** complex offers a lot of eateries, including familiar fast-food outlets and a good supermarket, **Hemköp**, which has a deli section in the basement of the big store known as **Åhléns City**. For picnic items, the indoor **Stora Saluhallen market**, Kungstorget, has a tempting range of goodies.

WHERE NEXT?

The **Copenhagen–Oslo** (next page) route passes through Gothenburg. Services run northeast to **Stockholm**; for a longer route to the Swedish capital via the southern shore of Lake Vänern use the **Herrljunga–Hallsberg** service via **Mariestad** (ETT table 736).

Notes

A change of train is necessary at Gothenburg and/or Malmö. All long-distance trains in Sweden and Norway tend to be reservation-only. Supplements apply on the high-speed X2000 trains in Sweden.

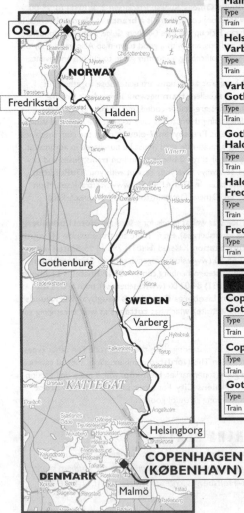

ROUTE DETAIL

Copenhagen–Malmö
ETT table 703

Type	Frequency	Typical journey time
Train	Every 8–12 mins	35 mins

Malmö–Helsingborg
ETT tables 735, 737

Type	Frequency	Typical journey time
Train	2–4 per hr	42 mins

Helsingborg–Varberg
ETT table 735

Type	Frequency	Typical journey time
Train	Every 1–2 hrs	1 hr 40 mins

Varberg–Gothenburg
ETT table 735

Type	Frequency	Typical journey time
Train	1–2 per hr	43 mins

Gothenburg–Halden
ETT table 770

Type	Frequency	Typical journey time
Train	2–3 daily	2 hrs 4 mins

Halden–Fredrikstad
ETT table 770

Type	Frequency	Typical journey time
Train	Every 1–2 hrs	35 mins

Fredrikstad–Oslo
ETT table 770

Type	Frequency	Typical journey time
Train	Every 1–2 hrs	1 hr 8 mins

KEY JOURNEYS

Copenhagen–Gothenburg (via Malmö) ETT table 735

Type	Frequency	Typical journey time
Train	6–12 daily	4 hrs

Copenhagen–Oslo ETT tables 735, 770

Type	Frequency	Typical journey time
Train	2–3 daily	8 hrs 30 mins

Gothenburg–Oslo ETT table 770

Type	Frequency	Typical journey time
Train	2–3 daily	4 hrs

NB

There is also a direct Malmö–Oslo overnight train six days per week (summer only).

From the Danish capital, the route crosses over to **Malmö** in Sweden via a huge tunnel and bridge link (opened in 2000), then heads along the coast to the Swedish port of **Helsingborg** – in the Middle Ages this region was in Danish hands, and the Sound was vigilantly guarded, with passage tolls demanded from every ship that made its way in and out of the Baltic. Another option for border crossing is heading from Copenhagen to **Helsingør**, then crossing by ferry to **Helsingborg**. Sweden's western seaboard has superb sandy beaches much of the way up to the impressive historic city of **Gothenburg**. Continuing further on the same route, you cross over into Norway just before **Halden**.

COPENHAGEN (KØBENHAVN), DENMARK

See p481.

MALMÖ, SWEDEN

See p529.

HELSINGBORG

During much of the Middle Ages, Helsingborg was Danish and functioned as an important garrison town; the massive fortified keep, the **Kärnan**, still dominates the place. The bustling port is a pleasant enough base, with an old quarter to explore, but you should also pay a visit to the rewarding 15th-century **Church of St Maria** and the entertainingly eclectic **Stadsmuseet** (town museum). On the east side of town **Fredriksdal** is an open-air museum of reconstructed buildings.

RAIL Next to the ferry terminal.

i **Tourist Office**: Rådhuset, Stortorget, ☎(042) 10 43 50 (www.helsingborg.se).

Youth hostels (HI): KFUM Nyckelbo, Scoutstigen 4, ☎(042) 92005 (www.nyckelbo.se); **Miatorp**, Planteringsvägen 71, ☎(042) 13 11 30 (www.miatorp.nu).

WHERE NEXT?

*Continue southwards for **Lund**, joining with the **Copenhagen–Stockholm** route (p528). You can also take the ferry across to Denmark to Helsingør (itself served by frequent trains for Copenhagen, taking 47 mins; ETT table 703), best known for Kronberg Slot, the Elsinore of Shakespeare's Hamlet.*

Scandinavia (Denmark, Sweden and Norway)

VARBERG

Varberg was discovered in the late 19th century as a **bathing station**, and has some appealing period survivals, notably the **wooden pavilion** (Societetshuset) in the **park**, and the rectangular bathing section of 1903, with changing rooms and sun-loungers ranged around a tamed expanse of sea water. The dominant feature of this spa-like port is the moated 13th-century **castle**, which doubles as a youth hostel (**Fästningens Vandrarhem** non-HI, ☎(0340) 868 28) with plenty of idyllic beaches (including nudist ones) within close range. Within walking distance is **Apelviken Bay**, popular with surfers.

ℹ️ **Tourist Office**: Brunnsparken, ☎(0340) 868 00 (www.visitvarberg.se).

🏠 **Youth hostel (HI): Vare**, Vare, ☎(0340) 411 73, 7 km south of the centre.

GOTHENBURG

See p509.

HALDEN, NORWAY

Halden is another old border post, on the attractive **Iddefjord** and overlooked by the star-shaped **Fredriksten Fort**, a huge 17th-century castle east of the town. Other highlights include the **Frederikshalds Theater**, with its fully restored baroque stage, and **Rød Herregard**, a furnished 18th-century manor house with an enviable collection of art.

🚉 On the south bank of the river.

ℹ️ **Tourist Office**: Torget 2, ☎69 19 09 80 (www.visithalden.com).

🏠 **Youth hostel (HI): Halden Vandrehjem**, Flintveien, ☎69 21 69 68 (halden.hostel@vandrerhjem.no), 2 km from station, open late June–early Aug.

FREDRIKSTAD

With three sides of its edges still protected with fortified walls, Fredrikstad guarded the southern approaches to Oslo and has survived as one of the best-preserved fortress towns in Scandinavia. It's conducive for wandering, particularly around the walls and along the cobbled alleys of **Gamlebyen** (the Old Town) over on the east bank. **Fort Kongsten** is a pleasant 15–20-min stroll.

OSLO

See p493.

🚉 A 5-min walk southeast of the centre.

ℹ️ **Tourist Office**: Tøyhusgaten 41, ☎69 30 46 00 (www.fredrikstad-hvaler.no).

WHERE NEXT?

*Follow the routes to **Malmö** or **Stockholm**, or the **Oslo–Bergen–Oslo** circuit.*

ROUTE DETAIL

Oslo–Voss — ETT table 780

Type	Frequency	Typical journey time
Train	3–5 daily	5 hrs 30 mins

Voss–Bergen — ETT table 781

Type	Frequency	Typical journey time
Train	14 Mon–Fri, 9 Sat, Sun	1 hr 15 mins

Bergen–Stavanger — ETT table 2240

Type	Frequency	Typical journey time
Ship	2 Mon–Fri; 1 Sat; 2 Sun	4 hrs 10 mins

Stavanger–Kristiansand — ETT table 775

Type	Frequency	Typical journey time
Train	3–6 daily	3 hrs

Kristiansand–Kongsberg — ETT table 775

Type	Frequency	Typical journey time
Train	3–5 daily	3 hrs 25 mins

Kongsberg–Oslo — ETT table 775

Type	Frequency	Typical journey time
Train	1–2 per hr	1 hr 25 mins

Notes

Seat reservation is compulsory on most Norwegian long-distance trains.

Scandinavia (Norway)

Undoubtedly one of Europe's most spectacular train journeys, this circuit encounters some of the most stunning of Norwegian landscapes. The trip incorporates two lines, connected by a catamaran voyage between Bergen and Stavanger. From Oslo the route steadily climbs, past the year-round resorts of **Gol** and **Geilo**, and up to the holiday centre of Ustaoset (990 m), followed by a bleak but magnificent mountainscape of icy lakes and rocky, snow-capped ridges. Shortly after leaving Finse, the train enters a 10-km tunnel to emerge near Hallingskeid. The next stop is **Myrdal**, where you can divert to the hugely popular loop via train, boat and bus to the north via **Flåm** dubbed *Norway in a Nutshell* and offering a glimpse of a superb fjord. The main line then descends to the lakeside town of **Voss**. Thereafter, the scenery's a little less wild, although still impressive.

After you've had a look around the quaint harbour city of Bergen, the catamaran to Stavanger is fast and enjoyable. Even the last leg back to Oslo passes consistently pleasant countryside, lakes and forest, and gives access to the cities of **Kristiansand** and **Kongsberg**.

If the Oslo–Bergen train is booked up, make Bergen–Oslo reservations and do the circuit in reverse, which has the advantage of saving the really dramatic stuff for later on.

OSLO

See p493.

VOSS

Mountains rise straight out of the lakeside resort, itself just 56 m above sea level. Sights are pretty much limited to the 13th-century baroque-embellished **church**, as most of the town is modern and geared towards winter sports; its après-ski atmosphere is distinctly lively. A cable car, **Hangursbanen**, runs up to 600 m, covering a height difference of about 570 m in 4 mins. For water sports, contact the Voss Rafting Senter, ☎56 51 05 25 (open all year, for rafting May-Oct).

[RAIL] 5-min walk from town centre.

i **Tourist Office**: Uttrågata 9, ☎56 52 08 00 (www.visitvoss.no), a 3-min walk from the railway station, has plenty on hiking.

🏠 **Youth hostel (HI)**: Evangerveien 68, ☎56 51 20 17 (www.vosshostel.com); closed mid-Dec–mid-Jan, call ahead in autumn. By the lake, 1 km from the town centre.

WALKING TRIPS

You can get almost everywhere on foot in Bergen, but take the **Fløibanen** (funicular) from the centre up Mt Fløyen (320 m), for a panoramic view. At the top there's scope for pleasant picnics and walks in the woods.

BERGEN

An old Hanseatic port, Norway's extremely appealing second city is the gateway to some of the country's most magnificent fjords. Placed on a peninsula and surrounded by mountains, Bergen has meandering cobbled streets lined with gabled weatherboard houses and dignified old warehouses.

The city centres on the waterfront **Fisketorget** open Mon–Sun 0700–1900 June–Aug; Mon–Sat 0700–1600 Sept–May, a working fish (and various other things) market. At the centre of the old quarter, **Bryggen** contains a fine row of medieval houses designated a UNESCO World Heritage Site.

Tiny **Theta Museum**, Enhjørningsgården Bryggen, was the clandestine one-room centre for Resistance operations in World War II, until it was discovered by the Nazis in 1942. When the **Bryggens Museum** was being constructed, the remains of the original city of 1050–1500 were found and incorporated. Other museums in town are the art museums and those housed in the university (Christiesgt.), which also runs the botanic garden.

GRIEG'S HOME

Classical music lovers may like to visit **Troldhaugen**, home of Edvard Grieg, Norway's greatest composer. Crammed with memorabilia, it is little altered since his death in 1907. Open daily in summer, and weekdays all year except Easter and Dec; there's a museum and concert hall. Buses from the main bus station to Hopsbroen, from where it's a walk of 15–20 mins.

Gamle Bergen (Old Bergen), at **Sandviken**, is an open-air museum of some three dozen 18th- and 19th-century wooden houses and shops, many furnished in period style, located on cobbled paths and streets. You can wander round for nothing, but have to join a tour if you want to see the interiors. Yellow buses 🚌 20/23/24, take 10 mins from the Tourist Office.

🚉 **Strømgaten**; 10-min walk east of the centre; walk straight ahead down Marken and keep going.

🚢 Most ferries and local boats leave from Strandkaiterminalen and Skoltegrunnskaien. Hurtigruten leaves from Nøstet. International sailings also use Skoltegrunnskaien, on the north side, including Smyril Line with ferries to Scotland, Shetland and the Faroe Islands (🚌 20/24/26/80/90 from bus station to Bontelabo). **Flaggruten** catamarans to **Stavanger** leave from Strandkaien, on the east side. Their office is in Strandkaiterminalen, ☎ 55 23 87 00 (www.tide.no). Pick up a boarding-pass 30 mins before departure; be certain to book ahead in July.

ℹ️ **Tourist Office**: (the best outside Oslo) Vågsalmenningen 1, ☎ 55 55 20 00 (www.visitbergen.com). The **Bergen Card** (valid for 24 or 48 hrs, from Tourist Offices, station, hotels and campsites) offers free local transport, free or discounted admission to most of the attractions, and 'a surprise on

Scandinavia (Norway)

the menu' at selected restaurants. If you want to wander further afield on foot, or even on skis, **Bergen Turlag** (Bergen Touring Association), in DNT office, Tverrgt 4–6, ☎ 55 33 58 10 (www.bergen-turlag.no) can provide walking maps for the surrounding mountains.

🛏 Advance booking recommended – Bergen is often chock full of tourists and conference-goers. **Youth hostels (HI)**: **Montana**, Johan Blyttsvei 30, ☎ 55 20 80 70 (www.montana.no) at the foot of Mt Ulriken (🚌 31), and the **YMCA**, Nedre Korskirkealmenningen 4, ☎ 55 60 60 55 (www.bergenhostel.com), is conveniently located, within sight of the Tourist Office.

🍴 There's a **supermarket** next to the YMCA on Nedre Korskirkealmenningen. Buy fruit and cheap (but delicious) smoked salmon or prawn sandwiches from the **fish market**. The large red and white building on Zachariasbryggen contains several mid-market restaurants.

Bergen has plenty of nightlife. **Ole Bulls Plass**, southeast of the quay, is good for bars, as is the area behind Torget. There are more student-frequented bars and cafés up towards the university. Look out for events at the **Kulturehuset**, on an old wharf to the south.

DAY TRIPS TO THE FJORDS Three fjords near Bergen are among the deepest and most popular in the country: the **Hardangerfjord** (south of Bergen) is a major target for tourists, alternating verdant lowlands and precipitous cliffs scattered with waterfalls; **Nordfjord** (north of Bergen) twists over 100 km to the foot of the **Briksdal glacier**; the **Sognefjord** (north of Bergen) is the longest (205 km) and deepest (1300 m) in Norway; in some places the shoreline is gentle, in others it soars straight up to 1000 m. Two of its most spectacular arms are the **Nærøyfjord** and **Aurlandsfjord** (see *Norway in a Nutshell*, p519). Several boat tours, including day trips, depart from Bergen.

STAVANGER

The centre is small and easily walkable, with an excellent pedestrianised cobbled shopping area, and there's a good bus network to reach outlying attractions. **Gamle Stavanger** (the Old Town) is the area on the west side of the harbour. It's lovely for a stroll, with cobbled walkways and rows of early 18th-century wooden houses at crazy angles. The impressive stone **Domkirke** (St Svithun's) was established in 1125 and is the only church in Norway to have kept its original medieval atmosphere. You can also peek inside **Ledål**, a mansion of 1800 still used by the royal family when visiting the town, and **Breidablikk**, an 1880s ship owner's house. **Valbergtårnet**, a 19th-century watchtower perched on top of a hill in the centre, provides an excellent view of the harbour.

Stavanger is well-placed for day trips to the **Ryfylke fjords**: head for Pulpit Rock (Preikestolen), which has a sheer drop of 600 m (ferry to Tau, then bus to the base of the rock; or via sightseeing boats into the steep-walled Lysefjord). Some 5 km west of town, at Ullandhaug, the **Jernadergarden** is an Iron Age farm (c350–550 AD), excavated and reconstructed: 🚌 6/7/x60 from the Sparkassen, opposite the cathedral.

🚉 Jernbanevej, 10 mins from the harbour and Tourist Office; round the left side of the lake and straight on.

⛴ **Flaggruten**, 📞55 23 87 00 (www.tide.no), catamarans for Bergen leave from Hurtigbåtterminalen. **Fjord Line**, 📞81 53 35 00 (fjordline.com) sail for Hirtshals (Denmark). There are no longer any direct sailings between Norway and England.

ℹ️ **Tourist Office**: Domkirkeplassen 3; 📞51 85 92 00 (www.regionstavanger.com). Exchange, cash machine next door.

🏠 Essential to reserve in advance – Stavanger is often booked out for conferences and is short on cheap hotels. The only **youth hostel (HI)** is **Stavanger Vandrerhjem**, Henrik Ibsensgt. 19, 📞51 54 36 36 (www.hihostels.no/stavanger; open early June–mid-Aug), south of the centre. Otherwise, try the **Stavanger Lille Hotel**, Madlaveien 7, 📞51 53 43 27 (www.slh.no), €, or **Havly Hotell**, Valberggt. 1, 📞51 93 90 00 (www.havly-hotell.no), €€.

NORWAY IN A NUTSHELL   This hugely popular circuit from **Myrdal** via **Flåm** and the **Sognefjord** uses the main rail line to Myrdal and rejoins it at Voss (or vice versa), combining a train, bus and ferry to link them (ETT tables 781 and 781a). You can do it as a day excursion from Bergen, or en route to or from Oslo; the mainline trains must be booked in advance. It's not an escorted tour: you simply buy a ticket and follow the relevant timetable. Rail passes are not valid between Myrdal and Flåm, but rail-pass holders do receive a 30% discount. At **Myrdal**, you board a local train for a breathtaking journey down the branch to **Flåm**, taking about an hour. The descent covers 866 m in 20 km (at a gradient of up to 1:18), with superb views of towering cliffs, chasms and cascades. There are 16 tunnels on the route, including one 'turn around', in which the line makes a 360° turn completely within the mountain. The train stops at the particularly spectacular **Kjosfossen waterfall** for photographers to descend.

The railway ends at **Flåm**, a tiny village at the head of the **Aurlandsfjord**, accessible by rail on the **Sognefjord**. There are at least a couple of hours to relax, lunch and shop before boarding a ferry (refreshments available) for a 2-hr journey along the Aurlandsfjord and **Nærøyfjord**. After you disembark at **Gudvangen** (accommodation available here also), the bus back to Voss follows an incredibly steep and breathtakingly dramatic road out of the fjord.

KRISTIANSAND

Ferries from Newcastle in England and Hirtshals in Denmark serve this bustling port and resort at the southern tip of Norway. In summer, the town's pleasant beaches are busy. Much of the town was laid out in the 17th century by Christian IV, after whom it is named. His plan included the **Christiansholm Festning**, Strandpromenaden, built to guard the eastern approach to the harbour; the circular fortress is now the major sight (open mid-May–mid-Sept) with views to match. Forming the northeastern part of the old quarter, **Posebyen** has many carefully preserved little wooden houses, while the neo-Gothic **Domkirke** (cathedral), Kirkegt, of 1885 asserts a massive presence. The **fish market** on the quay is a good place to pick up some smoked salmon or prawns for a picnic lunch.

DYREPARKEN

(20 mins from the centre of Kristiansand by 🚌 O1/M1) is a virtually cageless zoo and Norway's most visited attraction. There is also an amusement park with a special children's area (Cardamom Town).

🚉 On the west side of the centre, a few blocks from the Tourist Office, along Vestre Strandgate.

ℹ️ **Tourist Office**: Rådhusgt 6, ☎38 12 13 14 (www.sorlandet.com). Also information kiosk at Torvet (Lower Market Square) mid-June–early Aug.

🏨 No HI-Hostels in Kristiansand, but for fairly cheap accommodation you could try **Centrum Budget Hotel**, Vestre Strandgate 49, ☎38 70 15 65 (www.motell.no), which is only 150 m from the railway station.

KONGSBERG

Silver put the town on the map following the discovery of silver deposits of unique purity in the early 17th century in the nearby mountains. Kongsberg also established Norway's National Mint. Mining remained the town's *raison d'être* for three centuries: most of the mines (*sølvgruvene*) closed early in the 19th century, but the last one survived up to 1957. Just out of town are the disused **silver mines** at **Saggrenda** (8 km west, 🚌 410); tours (daily mid-May–Aug; Sat, Sun in Sept; Sun in Oct) take you by train into the mountain to 560 m below sea level. In the town centre a striking legacy of the silver-boom heyday is the **Kongsbergkirke**, a sumptuous triumph of baroque church architecture on the grand scale. Close to Nybrufoss waterfall is the **Norsk Bergverksmuseum** (Norwegian Mining Museum), housed in an old smelting works. **Den Kongelige Mynts Museum** (Mint Museum) is an offshoot of the industry: coin production moved to Kongsberg in 1686 (the National Mint is still here). The 32 buildings that form the **Lågdalsmuseet** (folk museum, 10-min walk south of the centre) date mainly from the 18th and 19th centuries and include Norway's only remaining turret-barn.

🚉 On the west side of the river, next to the Tourist Office.

ℹ️ **Tourist Office**: Schwabesgate 2, ☎32 29 90 50 (www.visitkongsberg.no).

🏨 **Youth hostel (HI)**: Vinjesgate 1, ☎32 73 20 24 (www.hihostels.no/kongsberg). Just southwest of the town centre.

ROUTE DETAIL

Oslo–Hamar — ETT tables 783, 785

Type	Frequency	Typical journey time
Train	every 1–2 hrs	1 hr 22 mins

Hamar–Lillehammer — ETT tables 783, 785

Type	Frequency	Typical journey time
Train	every 1–2 hrs	45 mins

Lillehammer–Dombås — ETT table 785

Type	Frequency	Typical journey time
Train	2–5 daily	1 hr 50 mins

Dombås–Trondheim — ETT table 785

Type	Frequency	Typical journey time
Train	3–4 daily	2 hrs 37 mins

Trondheim–Bodø — ETT table 787

Type	Frequency	Typical journey time
Train	2 daily	9 hrs 45 mins

Bodø–Narvik — ETT table 787

Type	Frequency	Typical journey time
Bus	2 daily	6 hrs 30 mins

Narvik–Gällivare — ETT table 761

Type	Frequency	Typical journey time
Train	2 daily	4 hrs 20 mins

Gällivare–Boden — ETT table 761

Type	Frequency	Typical journey time
Train	3 daily	2 hrs

KEY JOURNEYS

Oslo–Boden (via Stockholm) — ETT tables 750, 760, 761

Type	Frequency	Typical journey time
Train	1 daily	23 hrs

Boden–Stockholm — ETT tables 760, 761

Type	Frequency	Typical journey time
Train	2 daily	13 hrs

Boden–Helsinki (via Luleå and Kemi; by bus Luleå–Kemi) — ETT tables 761, 769, 794

Type	Frequency	Typical journey time
Train	1–3 daily	Up to 23 hrs

Notes

The direct route between Oslo and Boden includes a change of train in Stockholm. Travellers from Trondheim to Narvik not wanting to visit Bodø can connect onto the Bodø to Narvik bus at Fauske (55 km east of Bodø).

Scandinavia (Norway and Sweden)

The real attraction of this extremely popular route into the **Arctic Circle** is the scenery itself, providing the unique experience of the Midnight Sun in summer. The scene gradually evolves from gentle and bucolic in the area north of **Oslo** to breathtakingly dramatic in the northernmost reaches, which are inhabited by reindeer and by the **Sami** (the more common term Lapp is considered somewhat derogatory) – the Nordic region's original, traditional inhabitants. Distances here are serious: Norway is an extremely long country – 1752 km from tip to tip – and sections of the route take as long as 10 hours. In particular, the recommended side trip from **Dombås** to **Åndalsnes** is an epic one, plunging through tunnels, across bridges and past cascading waterfalls and the highest vertical canyon in Europe. From **Narvik**, you can continue on the scenic Ofoten line over to **Boden** in Sweden, or change at **Gällivare** and take the equally picturesque Inlandsbanan to **Mora**, and then on to **Stockholm**.

An equally thrilling and somewhat less touristy trip is the four-hour ferry (not covered by rail passes, but inexpensive) from Bodø to Moskenes in the stunning **Lofoten Islands**, where jagged peaks and homely fishing villages beckon. You can opt to do the Bodø to Narvik section by boat, via Svolvær in the Lofoten Islands.

OSLO

See p493.

HAMAR

This tiny town, set on Lake Mjøsa, is worth a stop for the **Hedmarksmuseet** (www.domkirkeodden.no), a regional open-air museum, a 2-km walk north of the centre, with some 65 historic buildings and the ruins of a medieval cathedral, which had been under cover for a decade to protect it from pollution. On the same site is a herb garden emulating a medieval monastery garden and an art centre where you can observe traditional artisanry.

RAIL On the southern edge of the centre.

i **Tourist Office:** Vikingskipet, Åkersvikveien 1, ☎ 62 51 75 03 (www.hamar-regionen.no). In the Vikingskipet (Viking Ship) of the Hamar Olympiske Anlegg (Hamar Olympic Arena).

Youth hostel (HI): Vikingskipet Motell og Vandrerhjem, Åkersvikveien 24, ☎ 62 52 60 60 (www.815mjosa.no/hamar).

LILLEHAMMER

Lillehammer is both a major skiing centre and an appealing lakeside town, typified by winsome wooden houses that cling to the hillside. It hosted the 1994 Winter Olympics and many of the facilities can now be visited – and in some cases used (see Day Trips). In winter, the downhill and cross-country ski trails and skating rinks are some of the best maintained in the country. Many are open during the summer too – including chairlifts, summer ski-jumping and an Alpine bobsled track, and the surrounding area is laced with paths ideal for hiking.

DAY TRIPS FROM LILLEHAMMER At **Hunderfossen**, 15 km north (10 mins by train), you can try out the 1994 Olympic luge and bobsleigh tracks (up to 60 mph; on wheels in summer), or 'play, learn and experience' at the **Hunderfossen Family Park** (open summer; www.hunderfossen.no). Worth it if only to get a photo next to the 12-m model trolls. Several operators run rafting and canoeing trips in the **Gundbrandsdal Valley**, ranging from a half-day taster to an epic two-day voyage down the Sjoa River. Ask for details at Tourist Offices in **Lillehammer** or **Dombås**. Sjusjøen, reached by regular buses from Lillehammer, is a lakeside sports town set high up on a plateau where the snow stays till late in the year. A couple of ski rental shops can kit you out for cross-country skiing and sell you a map of the vast network of groomed tracks (*løype*). In summer, it's a good place for water sports. **Youth hostel (HI)**: Fjellheimen, Sjusjøen, ☎62 34 76 80 (www.sjusjoen-hotel.no), is a large complex by a lake, perfect for nature exploration.

🚊 West of the centre.

ℹ️ **Tourist Offices**: Jernbanetorget 2, ☎61 28 98 00 (www.lillehammer.com). *Lillehammer This Month* lists events and opening times.

🏨 **Gjestebu Overnatting**, Gamleveien 110, ☎61 25 43 21 (www.gjestebu.no), is central and comfortable. **Øvergaard**, Jernbanegaten 24, ☎61 25 99 99 (home.c2i/overgaard), charge NKr.245 per person for a double, including linen. **Youth hostel (HI)**: **Lillehammer Vandrerhjem Stasjonen**, Jernbanetorget 2, ☎61 26 00 24 (www.stasjonen.no). Next to the railway station.

DOMBÅS

The branch line to **Åndalsnes** (ETT table 785) diverges at this popular centre for winter sports. The journey out to Åndalsnes is reason enough for a visit, but it'll also get you to the **Geirangerfjord**, arguably the most stunning of all the fjords. The green-blue water wends its way for 16 km between cliffs (of up to 1500 m) and past tumbling waterfalls. Get a bus from Åndalsnes to **Hellesylt** or **Geiranger** (at opposite ends of the fjord) and take the ferry between them (70 mins), then bus back to Åndalsnes – or on towards **Ålesund**, a coastal town with a superb mix of architectural styles.

Scandinavia (Norway and Sweden)

RAIL **Station:** a few mins walk from the centre.

i **Tourist Office:** Frichgården, ☎61 24 14 44 (www.dovrenett.no).

⌂ **Youth hostel (HI):** Trolltun Gjestegård, ☎61 24 09 60 (www.trolltun.no), 2 km from rail station.

TRONDHEIM

Norway's first capital was founded in 997 by the Viking king Olav Tryggvason, whose statue adorns a column in the market square. Trondheim still has strong royal connections – monarchs are crowned in the cathedral and it has been the seat of the monarchy since the 12th century – and is now Norway's third city and a major university town, with more than 20,000 students who give it some of the best nightlife in Norway. The narrow streets of the compact old centre make a pleasant strolling ground, but after dark, prepare to find out how Norwegians party.

The **Nidaros Domkirke** (cathedral), Bispegata, is cavernously Gothic in design, and well worth seeing for its decorative stonework and elegant stained-glass windows. Northwards from the cathedral lies **Torvet**, the main square, while further on at the water's edge is **Ravnkloa**, home to a fish market. From here run hourly boats usually mid-May–mid-Sept to the island of **Munkholmen**, a monastery–cum–fortress-cum-prison; it's now a popular place for swimming.

Trondhjems Kunstforening (Trondheim Art Gallery; closed Mon), Bispegata 9A, exhibits some of Norway's greatest art, including a few works by Munch, while the **Nordenfjeldske Kunstindustrimuseum** (National Museum of Decorative Art), Munkegata 5, has a collection of contemporary arts and crafts (closed Mon, late Aug–late May). Other sights include the **Gamle Bybro** (Old Town Bridge), with views of the wharf and its 18th-century warehouse buildings.

RAIL North of the centre; also the bus station, 15-min walk to the Tourist Office (cross the bridge, after three blocks turn right on to Olav Tryggvasonsgata and left up Munkegata).

i **Tourist Office:** Munkegata 19, ☎73 80 76 60 (www.visit-trondheim.com); entrance from Torvet – market square.

⌂ **Trondheim InterRail Centre**, Elgesetergate 1, ☎73 89 95 38 (www.tirc.no; open late-June–mid-Aug), is an excellent dorm-style choice, not just because it is centrally located, but because you meet other travellers. **Pensjonat Jarlen**, Kongensgt. 40, ☎73 51 32 18 (www.jarlen.no), is the cheapest in town. **Youth hostel (HI)**: **Trondheim Vandrerhjem**, Weidemannsvei 41, ☎73 87 44 50 (www.trondheim-vandrerhjem.no), 2 km east (🚌 63 Singsaker; infrequent Sat–Sun).

DAY TRIPS FROM TRONDHEIM Don't miss **Ringve Museum**, Lade Allé 60, 3 km east of town: 🚌 3/4: Fagerheim (from Munkegata towards Lade). This national music museum holds an astounding collection of antique musical instruments (free, Nov–Mar). The assortment of buildings at **Trøndelag Folkemuseum**, Sverresborg, includes turf huts and a small stave church from 1170 (buses from Dronningensgate (D1): 🚌 8 towards Stavset; 10 mins).

BODØ

Mostly levelled by bombing during World War II, Bodø has little to detain you, but is the departure point for ferries to the Lofoten Islands. The **Domkirke** (cathedral), is notable for its unusual detached spire, while the **Norsk Luftfartsmuseum** (Norwegian Aviation Museum), Olav V gata, has a good collection of airliners from various eras.

🚉 300 m east of the Tourist Office.

i **Tourist Office**: Sjøgt. 3, 📞 75 54 80 00 – called Bodø Turistinformasjon (www.visitbodo.com).

⛴ **Ferries**: Hurtigruten cruises and ferries to the islands leave from quays on the road near the station.

🚌 Long-distance bus station is 300 m further along Sjøgata from the tourist office.

🏨 For central budget accommodation, try **Opsahl Gjestegaard**, Prinsens gate 131, 📞 75 52 07 04 (www.opsahlgjestegaard.no), €. **Camping**: **Bodøsjøen Camping**, Båtstøveien 1, 📞 75 56 36 80 (www.nafcamp.com), 3 km southeast of town.

THE LOFOTEN ISLANDS   Bodø is the best place to catch a ferry to the spectacular **Lofoten Islands** (www.lofoten-tourist.no), a chain of improbably jagged glacier-carved mountains sheltering fishing villages, farms, sheep and thousands of birds (including puffins). This is the Norwegian scenery at its best – mild climate, comparatively uncrowded and the sense that you are with nature at its purest. It's excellent terrain for walking, horseriding and cycling (it is possible to hire bicycles), and there are some great boat trips – including to the beautiful cliffside bird colonies of **Værøy** and to **Trollfjord**. **Røst** and **Værøy** support colonies of puffins; both also have very inexpensive accommodation. Tailor-made seakayak trips and courses can be booked at Sandvika Camping, west of Kabelvåg.

The islands' main town is **Svolvær** (pop. 4500), on **Austvågøy**. **Tourist Office**: Svolvær Torg, 📞 76 06 98 00 (www.lofoten.info), open until 2200 Mon–Fri and 2000 Sat–Sun (June–Aug). (Arriving from the south, Svolvær is easily reached from Skutvik, which is midway between Narvik and Bodø.) Ferries link Svolvær with Skutvik, Fiskebøl with Melbu, Moskenes with Bodø, and with Værøy and Røst. There are also flights from Bodø. The main islands are linked by bridges and tunnels. There's a picturesque fishing village with the modest name of **Å**, 5 km south of Moskenes, with cottages, an HI hostel (Å Vandrerhjem, 📞 76 09 11 21; www.lofoten-rorbu.com) and a campsite. Fishing, caving and hiking trips can all be arranged here. There is also an express boat service from Svolvær to Narvik, taking 3 hrs 30 mins.

NARVIK

Endowed with fine ocean views, this small modern port was invaded in 1940 by the Germans in a bid to control shipments of iron ore; within days the British destroyed the German fleet and the Allies recaptured the town. The first section of the **Nordland Røde Kors Krigsminnemuseum** (Red Cross War Museum) commemorates the town's important role in World War II as well as the work of the Resistance. Narvik's prosperity owes virtually everything to the Ofoten railway line, which transports iron ore from Sweden, then ships it out to sea from town; the **Ofoten Museum** provides a thorough overview of the industry and its history. For panoramic views towards the Lofoten Islands, take the *Fjellheisen* (cable car) up **Fagernesfjellet**, at the top of which is a restaurant, lookout station and a host of walking trails; allow 2 hrs to hike up without the lift.

🚆 900 m from the Tourist Office.

🚌 **Bus station**: in the city centre.

ℹ️ **Tourist Office**: ☎76 96 56 00 (www.destinationnarvik.com).

🏨 **Breidablikk Gjestehus,** Tore Hundsgate 41, ☎76 94 14 18 (www.breidablikk.no), €, up the hill from the main road, is a moderately priced pension. **Spor 1 Gjestegård**, Brugata 2a, ☎76 94 60 20 (www.spor1.no), €, is just as cheap and has very friendly owners. **Youth hostel (HI)**: Dronningensgate 58, ☎76 96 22 00 (www.narvikvandrerhjem.no).

GÄLLIVARE, SWEDEN

Iron and copper ore mining dominates the scene, and tours (contact Tourist Office for details) enter the open-cast copper mine and the underground iron mine. In Malmberget (the site of the mines north of town) are the museum village, **Kåkstan**, and the **Mining Museum**. Gällivare is also a good place to immerse yourself in the Sami (Lapp) culture, whose heritage is reflected in the (current) name of its mid-18th-century church, **Lapp-kyrkan**. About 2 km from the centre of town, up the road to Dundret, **Vägvisaren** is a small family business specialised in adventures based on Sami culture.

The top of Dundret, the 820-m hill that looms to the south of the town, is a **nature reserve** with panoramic views. It's 7 km to the top and you should allow at

INLANDSBANAN

Gällivare is the northern end of the superbly scenic Inlandsbanan, which runs 1067 km through central Sweden from **Mora** (summer-only service; overnight stop required at Östersund; ETT table 753). For a 100 km sample, ride from Gällivare to Jokkmokk (2 hrs). There's only one train a day in each direction, giving you rather longer than you might need there; alternatively, daily buses from Gällivare allow you a 5-hr stay. **Jokkmokk** grew from a Sami mission into a sizeable town and its prime role today is to keep the Sami culture alive. **Tourist Office**: Stortorget 4, ☎(0971) 222 50, (www.jokkmokk.se).

least 3 hrs to come down (it can take twice that), but you can get great views from 4 km. When the **Midnight Sun** is visible there are bus tours to the top.

🚉 On the western edge of town.

ℹ️ **Tourist Office**: Storgatan 16, ☎(0970) 166 60 (www.gellivare.se).

🏨 **Hotell Dundret**, Tingshusgatan 3, ☎(0970) 162 005 50 40 (www.hotelldundret.se) €. **Vandrarhemmet Rallarrosen STF (HI)**: Barnhemsvägen 2A, ☎(0970) 143 80 (info@www.explorelapland.com).

BODEN

See p535.

The **Aurora Borealis**, or **Northern Lights**, is a stunning natural spectacle of glowing light in the sky, an atmospheric phenomenon caused by collisions between air molecules and charged particles from the sun that explode upon entering the earth's atmosphere. It occurs sporadically in winter throughout northern Scandinavia. Visitors have the best chance to catch the Midnight Sun in the far north during summer.

ROUTE DETAIL

Copenhagen–Malmö
ETT table 703

Type	Frequency	Typical journey time
Train	Every 8–12 mins	35 mins

Malmö–Lund
ETT tables 730, 735, 737, 745

Type	Frequency	Typical journey time
Train	2–4 every hr	15 mins

Lund–Linköping
ETT table 730

Type	Frequency	Typical journey time
Train	Every hr	2 hrs 30 mins

Linköping–Norrköping
ETT table 730

Type	Frequency	Typical journey time
Train	Up to 3 per hr	22 mins

Norrköping–Stockholm
ETT table 730

Type	Frequency	Typical journey time
Train	1–2 per hr	1 hr 15 mins

KEY JOURNEYS

Copenhagen–Stockholm
ETT table 730

Type	Frequency	Typical journey time
Train	4–6 daily	5 hrs 20 mins

Stockholm–Oslo
ETT table 750

Type	Frequency	Typical journey time
Train	1–2 daily	6 hrs 5 mins
	1 night train (not daily)	9 hrs 5 mins

Stockholm–Helsinki
ETT table 2465

Type	Frequency	Typical journey time
Ferry	2 daily	16 hrs

Notes
During the reconstruction of Malmö C. station, some trains are diverted to serve suburban stations instead. Please check before travel.

RAIL TOUR: COPENHAGEN – MALMÖ – STOCKHOLM

This route is an excellent introduction to Southern Sweden's beautiful landscape, and also allows visits to three historically wealthy Swedish cities. The journey also passes by countless picturesque forests and lakes.

COPENHAGEN (KØBENHAVN), DENMARK

See p481.

MALMÖ, SWEDEN

Sweden's fast-growing third city (pop. 260,000) is a lively place, with plenty of good bars, clubs and coffee houses, and an excellent festival in August. Capital of the Skåne province, Malmö was part of Denmark for much of the Middle Ages and came under Swedish sovereignty in 1658: even today the Skåne accent has something of a Danish tinge. Most recently, many young Danes have moved here to avoid strict Danish marriage laws. Enclosed by a canal that loops round through a park and doubles as the castle moat, the city's well-groomed historic centre dates back to Danish times and features a pair of fine cobbled squares. Leaving the station southwards along Hamngatan, you soon reach the large central square, **Stortorget**, presided over by the statue of Carl Gustav, who won Skåne back from Denmark. The square is flanked on the east by the 1546 **Rådhuset** (town hall), itself on the line of Södergatan, the main pedestrianised street. Just behind stands **St Petri Kyrka** (St Peter's church) – Sweden's second-largest church – its whitewashed Gothic interior complementing its baroque altar and medieval frescos. Off Stortorget's southwestern corner lies **Lilla Torg**, a smaller and slightly more charming square with medieval brick and timber façades, outdoor cafés and restaurants; live music sparks up the atmosphere on summer evenings. From here walk a few minutes west to the formidable 15th-century fortress, **Malmöhus Slott**, open daily 1200–1600, whose circular towers and assorted buildings hold a set of captivating museums covering a range of themes – including city history, military exhibits, art and natural history.

If the weather permits, kick back in one of the three great parks, **Kungsparken**, **Slottsparken** and **Pildammsparken**; or head down to the 3 km-long **Ribersborg beach**, within walking distance. You can pick up provisions for a picnic at the excellent **Saluhallen** covered market in **Lilla Torg**.

Consider getting the **Malmökortet** (Malmö Card), valid for 1/2/3 days for one adult and two children (under 16) for free local buses, free parking, free admission to the castle, all of Malmö's museums and a bus tour, plus savings on sightseeing trips, shopping, entertainment and eating out (SEK130/160/190) Available from the Tourist Office and Forex Offices.

RAIL **Malmö C**, just north of the Old Town.

Scandinavia (Denmark and Sweden)

ℹ️ **Tourist Office**: **Centralstation**, ☎(040) 34 12 00
(www.malmo.se). Get the useful free *Malmö This Month*
two-monthly guide for events and listings. For information
on the Malmö Festival in August see the website
(www.malmofestivalen.se).

🏠 The Tourist Office (see above) make free hotel bookings.
Bed and Breakfast Centre, ☎(0) 8730 0003, supply lists of
private rooms. **Youth hostel (HI)**: **STF Vandrarhem Malmö City**, Rönngatan 1,
☎(040) 611 62 20 (www.stfturist.se/malmocity), is very central; **Vandrarhem Malmö
Eriksfält** Backavägen 18, ☎(040) 822 20 (www.stfturist.se/malmoeriksfalt), 3 km south
of the city centre, 🚌 2; (non-HI) **Villa Hilleröd**, Ängdalavägen 38, ☎(040) 26 56 26
(www.villahillerod.se), is just west of the centre. Campsite: **Malmö Camping & Feriecenter**,
Strandgatan 101, ☎(040) 15 51 65 (www.camping.se); open all year.

WHERE NEXT?

*Malmö to Gothenburg X2000 trains taking 2 hrs 45 mins – supplement payable – slower
trains taking 3 hrs 10 mins run from Malmö to Gothenburg, see Copenhagen–Gothenburg (p506).*

LUND

The handsome ancient university town is one of the most rewarding spots to visit in
southern Sweden. A religious centre in the 12th century, much of medieval Lund is still
visible. There's a decent range of accommodation and plenty of student eating and
drinking haunts.

🚉 A 5-min walk west of the centre.

ℹ️ **Tourist Office**: Kyrkogatan 11, ☎(046) 35 50 40 (www.lund.se).

🏠 **Youth hostel (HI)**: **Vandrarhem 'Tåget' Lund**, Vävaregatan 22, ☎(046) 14 28 20
(www.trainhostel.com), 300 m from the station – known as 'The Train', it's possibly the only
hostel in the world made up of railway carriages.

LINKÖPING

The town's prime attraction is **Gamla Linköping**, Malmslättsvägen (5 mins on
🚌 203/205/207, or 20-min walk), an ambitious living museum that seeks to recreate
19th century Linköping, much of which was painstakingly relocated piece by piece
and rebuilt here – it includes a small chocolate factory, as well as working craft shops,
houses, street lamps and old signs. Try to visit when the buildings are open; otherwise you may have to content yourself with viewing them from the outside.

Linköping's **Domkyrkan** is one of Sweden's oldest cathedrals, with a 107-m green spire visible from far outside the town, and containing fine stone carvings along the south doorway. The north doorway is a survival of the original Romanesque building that was later added to with Gothic stylings. The fascinating crypt is full of ancient carved tombstones, and an intricate astronomical clock that strikes twice daily (1200 and 1500; Sun and holidays 1300 and 1500), and there's also an entire miniature theatre filled with moving figurines.

Flygvapenmuseum (Airforce Museum), next to Malmen military airfield, 6 km west of Linköping (🚌 213 from Resecentrum, the central train/bus station, www.sfhm.se), is an assemblage of some 60 military aircraft dating from 1912 – several of the cockpits are open to sit in and try your hands at the controls (closed for development until summer 2010).

🚉 A 5-min walk east of the centre.

ℹ️ **Tourist Office**: Storgatan 15, ☎(013) 190 00 70 (www.linkoping.se).

🏠 **Youth hostel (HI)**: **Linköpings Vandrarhem & Hotell**, Klostergatan 52A, ☎(013) 35 90 00 (www.lvh.se), also has apartments; central.

NORRKÖPING

Norrköping is a prosperous textile centre, with a museum celebrating the town's industrial legacy. For most visitors, however, the main reason for a stop is **Kolmårdens Djur och Naturpark** (Kolmården Zoo and Safari Park; www.kolmarden.com), open early May–early Oct. The zoo is the largest in Europe and consists of two separate sections: the main zoo (with a dolphin show) and the safari park. The cable car is great for views of the landscape. It's 30 km northeast of town: 🚌 432 (roughly hourly) takes about 50 mins; 🚌 481 runs 10 km to **Löfstad Slott** (Löfstad Castle), a lavish 17th-/18th-century mansion on vast manicured grounds that remains unchanged since the last owner died some 60 years ago (www.lofstad.nu).

🚉 Norrköping C, a 5-min walk north of the centre.

ℹ️ **Tourist Office**: Dalsgatan 9, ☎(011) 15 50 00 (www.destination.norrkoping.se).

🏠 **Youth hostel (HI)**: **Turistgården**, Ingelstagatan 31, ☎(011) 10 11 60 (www.turistgarden.se).

Rock carvings depicting wild beasts, human figures and sailing ships – and dating from 1500 to 500 BC – can be seen at **Himmelstalund**, 2 km west of Norrköping.

STOCKHOLM

See p499.

ROUTE DETAIL

Stockholm–Uppsala ETT tables 760, 765

Type	Frequency	Typical journey time
Train	1–2 per hr	40 mins

Uppsala–Sundsvall ETT table 760

Type	Frequency	Typical journey time
Train	5–8 daily	2 hrs 42 mins

Sundsvall–Umeå ETT table 768

Type	Frequency	Typical journey time
Bus	6 daily	4 hrs 5 mins

Umeå–Luleå ETT tables 761, 768

Type	Frequency	Typical journey time
Bus	7–8 daily	4 hrs 10 mins
Train	1 daily	5 hrs

Luleå–Kemi ETT table 769

Type	Frequency	Typical journey time
Bus	4–6 daily	3 hrs 30 mins

Kemi–Oulu ETT table 794

Type	Frequency	Typical journey time
Train	6 daily	1 hr 9 mins

Oulu–Tampere ETT table 794

Type	Frequency	Typical journey time
Train	10 daily	5 hrs 8 mins

Tampere–Turku ETT table 795

Type	Frequency	Typical journey time
Train	7–9 daily	1 hr 44 mins

Turku–Helsinki ETT table 791

Type	Frequency	Typical journey time
Train	13–17 daily	1 hr 57 mins

Notes

There are direct buses from Umeå to Luleå;
from Luleå to Kemi, change at Haparanda.
Although there is once again a direct service
between Haparanda and Kemi (Mon–Fri only),
some buses do not cross the border, so
passengers must walk approx. 800m from
Haparanda to the Finnish bus station in Tornio.
Trains from Umeå to Luleå go via Boden.

The coastal Swedish towns north of Stockholm offer a variety of attractions, from the lively university town of **Uppsala** to the clean refinement of **Gävle** (pronounced 'Yevle'). A long but enjoyable bus ride connects **Sundsvall** with **Umeå** (no rail pass discounts). The northern stretch of the route runs above the Arctic Circle, where reindeer roam and local Sami peoples retain their traditional-meets-modern ways of life. Later, you cross over into the wild territory of northern Finland, then head south past the characterful cities of **Tampere** and **Turku**.

STOCKHOLM

See p499.

UPPSALA

No visitor to Sweden should miss out on the country's former capital, home of its oldest university as well as its religious centre. The 16th-century **Uppsala Slott** (Red Castle), overlooking the town, was built by King Gustaf Vasa, who broke ties with the Vatican and pointed his cannons directly at the archbishop's palace. Beneath the castle is what's left of the old city: Ingmar Bergman's film *Fanny and Alexander* was filmed here (Bergman himself was also born here). The central sights are easily walkable if you don't want to wait around for a bus. Furthest from the station are two gardens (the **Botanic Garden** and **Linnaeus' Garden**; see below) in different directions: 30 mins at a slow pace. On summer weekends, the Lennakatten vintage railway runs on a narrow-gauge line from Östra station (behind Uppsala C).

Dominating the skyline are the twin towers of Scandinavia's largest church, the French-Gothic **Domkyrkan**. Completed in 1435, it took 175 years to build and was heavily restored in the 18th and 19th centuries. Virtually every inch of the church's side chapels is covered with tapestries or wall and ceiling paintings; the most impressive chapels include those of St Erik, Gustaf Vasa and the botanist Linnaeus (see below).

Founded in 1477, the **old university building** (**Gustavianum**) features an anatomical chamber where the public dissection of executed convicts was a 17th-century tourist attraction, and is open to visitors (closed Mon). Books, manuscripts and maps are on display in **Carolina Rediviva Universitetsbiblioteket** (library), Dag Hammarskjölds väg 1. Most notable here is one half of a 6th-century Silver Bible – a rare example of the extinct Gothic language, penned on purple vellum parchment – and the original manuscript of Mozart's *Die Zauberflöte* (*The Magic Flute*).

The great 18th-century professor of botany, Linnaeus (Carl von Linné), developed the definitive system of plant and animal classification. His former residence is now a museum,

Scandinavia (Sweden and Finland)

Linnémuseet, in the small **Linnéträdgården** (Linnaeus' Garden), Svartbäcksg. 27. Also worth a visit is the larger **Botaniska Trädgården** (Botanic Garden), Villavägen 8.

Gamla Uppsala (Old Uppsala), 5 km north, was the cradle of Swedish civilisation and thought to be the centre of a pre-Christian pagan cult. Hundreds of tombs are dominated by huge grassy mounds, resting places of three 6th-century kings. Alongside them are the **Uppsala Kyrka** (church) and a small museum village.

[RAIL] **Uppsala C**. East of the centre, a 5-min stroll to the Tourist Office: walk straight up Bangårdsgatan to the river, turn right and cross the second bridge – the Tourist Office is halfway along the block.

[i] **Tourist Office**: Fyristorg 8, [☎](018) 727 48 00 (www.uppsala.to).

[🏠] **Uppsala Room Agency**: [☎](018) 10 95 33 (rumsformedling@swipnet.se), (Mon–Fri 0900–1700), can book private rooms. **Samariterhemmets Gästhem**, Samaritergränd 2, [☎](018) 56 40 00 (www.svenskakyrkan.se/samariterhemmet/shgasthm.html), €€, run by the Church of Sweden, is probably the cheapest hotel. **Hotel Uppsala**, Kungsg. 27, [☎](018) 480 50 00 (www.profilhotels.se), €€, is a comfortable business hotel. **Grand Hotell Hörnan**, Bangårdsg. 1, [☎](018) 13 93 80 (www.grandhotellhornan.se), €€€, is old-style classy and more expensive. **Youth hostel (HI)**: **Sunnersta Manor**, Sunnerstavägen 24, [☎](018) 32 42 20 (www.sunnerstaherrgard.se), 5 km south (🚌 20 to Herrgårdsvägen). **(Non-HI)**: **Uppsala City Hostel**, St Persgatan 16, [☎](018) 10 00 08 (www.uppsalacityhostel.se), right in the city centre. **Camping: Fyrishov Stugby**, Idrottsg. 2, [☎](018) 727 49 60 (www.fyrishov.se), by the river, 2 km north (🚌 1/111/13). Open all year.

SUNDSVALL

Spread over the mainland and onto the island of Alnö, the town is primarily a timber port, though it does maintain a charming centre dominated by grand, late 19th-century limestone and brick structures built after a disastrous fire in 1888 destroyed most of Sundsvall's wooden buildings. The **Kulturmagasinet** is an interesting complex of restored warehouse buildings, now housing a small local museum, a gallery, a café and a library. For a look at a unique modern church interior, have a peek inside the red-brick **Gustav Adolfs Kyrka**. Otherwise, head out of the centre to the medieval **Alnö gamla kyrka** (🚌 1 to Alnö), a church with several well-preserved 16th-century frescos; or to **Norra Bergets Hantverks- och Friluftsmuseum**, an open-air museum with an eclectic mix of panoramic views, reached by a 3-km climb up the hostel Gaffelbyn.

[RAIL] A 10-min walk from the main square.

[i] **Tourist Office**: Stora Torget, [☎](060) 658 58 00 (www.sundsvallturism.com).

[🏠] **Lilla Hotellet**, Rådhusgatan 15, [☎](060) 61 35 87 (www.lilla-hotellet.se), €€, an old sweet factory, and now a lovely, homely and inexpensive hotel in the centre. **Youth hostel (HI): Vandrarhem Sundsvall**, Norra Stadsberget, [☎](060) 61 21 19 (www.gaffelbyn.se), next to Norra Berget outdoor museum, 20-min walk from centre, or 🚌 Plus Bus (PlusTrafik, ☎(060) 744 90 10, one hour in advance).

UMEÅ

Umeå is a rapidly growing university town with a youthful population and northern Sweden's largest town. A popular activity is shooting the nearby rapids in rubber rafts (mid-May–mid-Sept). One place really worth lingering is **Gammlia**, a complex of seven museums, including a Ski Museum and an excellent open-air museum with buildings from all over the region; most sections open only in summer. For students and young people, nightlife revolves around the university campus – especially the **Universum**, the student union.

🚆 A 5-min walk north of the centre. Luggage lockers.

ℹ️ **Tourist Office**: Renmarkstorget 15, ☎(090) 16 16 16 (www.visitumea.se). Free hotel reservation service.

🏨 Inexpensive options are **Tegs Hotell**, Verkstadsgatan 5, ☎(090) 12 27 00 (www.tegshotell.se), €, or **Pensionat Pendlaren**, Pendelgatan 5, ☎(090) 12 98 55 (www.pendlaren.com), €. **Youth hostel (HI):** Västra Esplanaden 10, ☎(090) 77 16 50, (www.umeavandrarhem.com).

BODEN

Primarily a rail junction and once Sweden's largest garrison town, Boden is a pleasant enough place to wait between trains. Fearing attack by Russia after the 1809 invasion of Finland, the Swedes erected a mighty complex of fortresses, among them the **Rödbergsfortet**, whose ramparts date from the early 1900s. The **Garnisonsmuseet** (Garrison Museum), on the southwestern edge of town, is chock-full of militaria.

🚆 **Boden C.** A 20-min walk northwest of centre.

ℹ️ **Tourist Office**: Kungsgatan 40, ☎(0921) 624 10 (www.upplevboden.nu). Pick up a copy of the mostly Swedish-language *Bodenturist*.

🏨 **Youth hostel (HI):** **Bodens Vandrarhem**, Fabriksgatan 6, ☎(0921) 133 35 (www.bodensvandrarhem.com), is 2 mins from the station.

WHERE NEXT FROM BODEN?

*For those with a real taste for epic journeys, carry on far into **Lapland** and the Arctic Circle by taking the **Oslo–Boden** route in reverse (p521), or by returning to **Stockholm** via Gällivare and taking the Inlandsbanan (p526; ETT table 753). Between Boden and Kemi are **Haparanda** and **Tornio** – effectively one town but in two time zones, linked by bridges.*

KEMI, FINLAND

This tiny, laid-back town has a few draws: the **Jalokivigalleria** (Gemstone Gallery), at the end of Kauppakatu (open during the snow castle season and in the summer 0900–1700, rest of the year Mon–Fri 1000–1600; also home to the Tourist Office) has excellent displays of many gemstones as well as copies of some famous diamonds and royal regalia and the genuine – but never worn – Finnish royal crown. Every year the elaborate **Kemi SnowCastle** (www.snowcastle.net) is open to the public Feb–mid-Apr for exhibitions and events, even restaurants and accommodation. Ask for details at the Tourist Office. For a once-in-a-lifetime experience, hop on an **Arctic icebreaker** (www.sampotours.com) and throw yourself off the prow in an orange drysuit to bob about among the ice floes.

[RAIL] A 5-min walk east of the centre: straight along Kauppakatu.

[BUS] **Asemakatu**, ☎ 0200 4000. Walk around the Medivire office building in front of the rail station and it's on the far side. It's better equipped than the rail station. **Information Office**; when it's closed, get tickets on board – you don't need them if you have a valid rail pass. Booking is not necessary.

[i] **Tourist Office**: Kemin Kaupungin Matkailutoimisto, Kauppakatu 29, ☎ 040 568 2069 (www.kemi.fi/matkailu), in the Gemstone Gallery (open during the SnowCastle season and in the summer 0900–1700, rest of the year Mon–Fri 1000–1600).

[HOTEL] **Hotelli Merihovi**, Keskuspuistokatu 6–8, ☎ (016) 4580 100 (www.merihovi.fi) is smart and comfortable; **Hotel Palomestari** (Finlandia), Valtakatu 12, ☎ (016) 257 117 (www.hotellipalomestari.com), €€, is more chain-like but similar in price.

SIDE TRIP TO ROVANIEMI   Helsinki-bound trains from Kemi descend from Rovaniemi, giving you the option of a 1 hr 30 mins' northward trip to see Rovaniemi itself, the capital of the Finnish province of Lapland. Thoroughly destroyed in 1944 and subsequently redesigned and rebuilt by Alvar Aalto, it feels quite distant from its Sami roots, but it has the impressive **Arktikum** (Science Centre and Museum of the Arctic Regions) at Pohjoisranta 4 (www.arktikum.fi). You can take a 10-min bus ride to the Arctic Circle from Rovaniemi too. **Tourist Office**: Lordi's Square, Maakuntakatu 29–31, ☎ (016) 346 270 (www.rovaniemi.fi). **Accommodation**: **Guesthouse Borealis**, Asemieskatu 1, ☎ (016) 3420 130 (www.guesthouseborealis.com), is a favourite with young travellers, €; **youth hostel (HI): Hostel Rudolf**, Koskikatu 41–43, ☎ (016) 321 321 (www.rudolf.fi); check in/out at **Clarion Hotel Santa Claus**, Korkalonkatu 29.

OULU

The mostly modern town (pop. 140,000) of **Oulu** is one of Finland's high-tech industry hubs. A few of the centre's older buildings such as the city hall recall the

19th-century tar boom – in which Oulu was also a world leader – and a short walk away is the **Science Centre Tietomaa**, Nahkatehtaankatu 6 (www.tietomaa.fi), an interactive science and technology museum that's entertaining even for non-kids (open Mon–Fri 1000–1600, Sat–Sun 1000–1800). There's an assemblage of Sami artefacts and other local miscellanea at the nearby **Pohjois–Pohjanmaan Museo** (Northern Ostrobothnia Museum), Ainola Park (closed Mon, free Fri). The town's harbourside market square looks out to a number of wooded islands, linked to the town by bridge.

WHERE NEXT?

*An alternative, but longer, way to Helsinki is by taking the **Helsinki–Oulu** journey (p540) in reverse.*

Rautatienkatu, east of centre. From Kemi there are about six–eight trains daily, taking around I hr 5 mins.

i **Tourist Office: Oulun Kaupungin Matkailuneuvonta**, Torikatu 10, ☎044 703 1330 (www.oulutourism.fi). Walk six blocks along Asemakatu, then left on Torikatu. Get *Oulu This Week* and *Look at Oulu* (plus free map).

Hotelli Turisti, Rautatienkatu 9, ☎(08) 5636 100 (www.hotellituristi.fi), €€: small family-run hotel opposite the railway station. **Youth hostel (non HI): Kesähotelli Oppimestari**, Nahkatehtaankatu 3, ☎040 319 3106, open mid June–early Aug. **Nallikari Camping**, Leiritie 10, ☎(08) 558 61350 (www.nallikari.fi), open year-round.

TAMPERE (TAMMERFORS)

Finland's second city was once the nation's industrial fulcrum, but the atmospheric red-brick factory buildings and warehouses have since been converted into museums, galleries and shopping centres, and **Tampere** today stands as a surprisingly attractive place, flanked by lakes and graced with abundant green spaces. Exit the station and head a few streets to the right to reach the granite **Tuomiokirkko** (cathedral), Tuomiokirkonkatu, built in 1907 with resplendent frescos and stained glass. From the station, Hämeenkatu leads across the **Tammerkoski**, a series of rapids that connect the city's two largest lakes and provide it with hydroelectric energy.

To the north you'll see the former **Finlayson factory**, now a centre for crafts and artisan works. More on the life of the factory's workers can be found at **Amurin työläismuseokortteli** (Amuri Museum of Workers' Housing; open mid-May–mid-Sept; closed Mon), Satakunnankatu 49, where 32 houses and shops from the workers' district are preserved with a genuinely lived-in feeling. Close by, the city library in Hämeenpuisto, is a curvaceous masterpiece of Modernism by Reima and Raili Pietilä, built in 1986. There's also a **Lenin Museum** in Hämeenpuisto, near the end of Hämeenkatu. This marks the spot where Lenin met Stalin in the early 1900s – Lenin lived in Tampere after the 1905 revolution.

Scandinavia (Sweden and Finland)

Two of Tampere's galleries give an excellent survey of Finnish art: the **Hiekka Art Museum**, Pirkankatu 6 (closed Mon, Fri–Sat), contains earlier works amassed by goldsmith Kustaa Hiekka, including some of his jewellery, while the lakeside **Sara Hildén Art Museum** (20-min walk or 🚌 16 northwest of the centre; closed Mon Sept–May) displays some of the nation's finest modern art through changing exhibitions. The latter is located next to **Särkänniemi**, an amusement park encompassing a children's zoo, an aquarium, a dolphinarium, a planetarium and the Näsinneula tower – at 168 m, the country's tallest structure and one that allows for some great views all around.

Towards the surreal end of the scale is **Moominvalley**, Hämeenpuisto 20 (Tampere City Library, separate entrance), an interactive museum dedicated to the Moomins, the characters of Tove Jansson's wonderfully innovative children's books (www.tampere.fi/moomin; closed Mon Sept–May).

The **Spy Museum**, Satakunnankatu 18 (www.vakoilumuseo.fi), in the Finlayson area in the centre of Tampere, is the world's first espionage museum opened in 1998. The museum tells the story of the characters and bizarre methods of espionage. There is also a spy test to see if you would be suited for the job.

🚆 A 5-min walk east of the centre; left-luggage office.

ℹ️ **Tourist Office**: Rautatienkatu 25A, at the train station, 📞 (03) 5656 6800 (www.tampere.fi/tourism). Walk up Hämeenkatu and turn left just before the bridge: it's on the riverside. *Tampere* is a free comprehensive listing that includes a map; there's also a self-guided walking tour.

🏨 There is just one HI hostel but some hotels have reasonably priced rooms as well: **Hostel Sofia**, Tuomiokirkonatu 12A, 📞 (03) 254 4020 (www.hostelsofia.fi). Another affordable option is **Omenahotelli Tampere**, Hämeenkatu 28, 📞 0600 18018 (premium rate) (www.omenahotels.com), comfortable and right in the centre of the city.

Camping: **Camping Härmälä**, Leirintäkatu, 📞 (09) 6138 3210 (www.fontana.fi/harmala), 5 km south of the centre (🚌 1 to within 200 m). Open mid-May–late Aug.

TURKU (ÅBO)

Finland's oldest city and its capital until 1812, Turku is home to the country's oldest university and is a vibrant commercial and cultural centre, with a pulsating nightlife. Its cathedral is very much the nation's spiritual heart.

Turku's much-rebuilt but nonetheless impressive **Tuomiokirkko** (cathedral) is easily spotted by the tower's distinctive face, the result of several fires over the centuries; look out for some intriguing tombs, including that of **Karin Månsdotter**, a local flower girl who became Queen of Sweden in 1568. **Turku Castle**, Linnankatu 80, 3 km from the centre near the ferry terminal, is unappealing from the outside, but the interior is a wondrous maze of passageways (closed Mon). These fortifications were the seat of Finland's government for over 500 years.

Towards town and across the river by footbridge, the **Sibelius Museo** (Sibelius Museum), Piispankatu 17, displays over 350 musical instruments, as well as memorabilia of the great composer revered throughout Finland (although he had no connection with Turku itself); concerts are sometimes given here (closed Mon).

WHERE NEXT?

*Turku is served by ferries to **Stockholm** (10 hrs 30 mins, ETT table 2480), some of which stop at **Mariehamn** or **Långnäs** in the **Åland Islands**, an archipelago of 6000 low-lying, forested isles belonging to Finland.*

South of the cathedral, **Luostarinmäki**, near Vartiovuori Hill, is an 18th-century area of town that has been turned into an open-air museum, busy with artisans' workshops. A recent addition to the city's museums is **Aboa Vetus** (Old Turku) and **Ars Nova** (New Art), Itäinen Rantakatu 4–6 (closed Mon, mid-Sept–Apr). In 1992, excavations for Ars Nova revealed medieval city remains. They were left in situ and now form the basis of 'Aboa Vetus', leaving history and contemporary art to rub shoulders. **Apteekki-museo** (Pharmacy Museum), Läntinen Rantakatu 13, consists of a restored 18th-century home and an old pharmacy that looks ready to re-open for business. At **Forum Marinum**, Linnankatu 72 (www.forum-marinum.fi; closed Mon, Oct–Apr), four historic ships are on display; in summer take Pikkuföri ferry (open mid-June–late Aug), which gives river tours of the town.

▣ **Turku** is northwest of the centre, a 15-min walk from the Tourist Office. One or two trains continue to **Satama** (*Hamnen*; the harbour). **Kupittaa** is also fairly central, but not as well equipped as Turku.

▣ **Ferries**: At the southwest end of town. ▣ 1 (to the main square) is more frequent than the trains, and also goes to the airport.

ⓘ **Tourist Office**: Aurakatu 4, ▣ (02) 262 7444 (www.turkutouring.fi).

▣ **Hotelli Artukaisten Paviljonki**, Messukentänkatu 11, ▣ (02) 284 4000 (www.artukaistenpaviljonki.fi), is good value. **Youth hostel (HI): Hostel Turku** near the Radisson at Linnankatu 39, ▣ (02) 262 7680 (www.turku.fi/hostelturku). **Linnasmäki**, Lustokatu 7, ▣ (02) 412 3500 (www.linnasmaki.fi). open mid-May–mid-Sept (4 km from centre). **Bed and breakfast**: **Hotel Harriet**, Käsityöläiskatu 11, ▣ 040 910 3333 (www.hotellikultainenturisti.com).

HELSINKI

See p488.

ROUTE DETAIL

Helsinki–Parikkala ETT table 797

Type	Frequency	Typical journey time
Train	4–5 daily	3 hrs 30 mins

Parikkala–Retretti ETT table 797

Type	Frequency	Typical journey time
Train	5–6 daily	30 mins

Retretti–Savonlinna ETT table 797

Type	Frequency	Typical journey time
Train	5–6 daily	26 mins

Parikkala–Joensuu ETT table 797

Type	Frequency	Typical journey time
Train	4–5 daily	1 hr 15 mins

Joensuu–Kuopio* ETT tables 799, 798

Type	Frequency	Typical journey time
Train	2–4 daily	3 hrs 15 mins*

Kuopio–Oulu ETT table 798

Type	Frequency	Typical journey time
Train	3–4 daily	4 hrs 8 mins

Notes

Helsinki to Oulu: direct 7–8 day trains and 2–4 night trains (all via Kokkola).
Parikkala to Retretti to Savonlinna: additional buses run throughout the day.
*Joensuu to Kuopio: change trains at Pieksämäki. There are also direct buses from Joensuu to Kuopio that only take around 2 hours.

KEY JOURNEYS

Helsinki–Stockholm ETT table 2465

Type	Frequency	Typical journey time
Ship	2 daily	16 hrs

Helsinki–Oulu ETT table 794

Type	Frequency	Typical journey time
Train	7–8 daily	6 hrs 29 mins (day)
	2–4 nightly	9 hrs 3 mins (night)

Helsinki–Tallinn ETT table 2410

Type	Frequency	Typical journey time
Ship & high-speed craft	Up to 15 daily	1 hr 30 mins – 3 hrs 30 mins

This satisfying trip takes in all that is quintessential about Finland, from the rolling farmlands of the south to the untamed swathes of forest and thousands of lakes in the country's heartland, with **Kuopio** one of the main highlights. The branch line from **Parikkala** to **Savonlinna**, an especially rewarding route that follows the natural causeway of the Punkaharju ridge along the Russian border, is included as part of the main route.

HELSINKI

See p488.

PARIKKALA

Change here for trains to **Retretti** and **Savonlinna**.

RETRETTI

The **Retretti Arts Centre**, 33 km from Parikkala (option of a cruise in summer), is a spectacular visual and performing arts complex (**Taidekeskus**; www.retretti.fi) housed partly in man-made caverns in the **Punkaharju esker**, a 7-km-long ridge of pine-crowned rocks, but it also spreads into the surrounding woodlands. There are concerts held underground with superb acoustics.

SAVONLINNA

Sited among several lake islands linked by walking bridges, this small town was hugely fashionable with the tsars in the mid-19th century. The must-see is **Olavinlinna**, the best-preserved medieval castle in the Nordic countries, built originally in 1475, still largely intact and full of character. The courtyard is the venue for the town's other major draw, the annual international **Opera Festival** (July–Aug: tickets go on sale the previous Nov, ☎(015) 476 750, www.operafestival.fi); the Tourist Office may have last-minute tickets.

🚆 **Savonlinna–Kauppatori** station is the first stop and more central than the main one. five–six trains daily make the 50-minute trip from **Parikkala**, serving **Retretti** en route.

ℹ️ **Tourist Office**: Puistokatu 1, ☎(015) 517 510 (www.savonlinnatravel.com).

🏠 **Youth hostels (HI):** Most central is **Vuorilinna**, Kylpylaitoksentie, ☎(015) 739 5 430 (www.spahotelcasino.fi), June–Aug only, *SS Heinävesi*, is a boat moored in the harbour with a number of rooms available in the summertime; enquire at the Tourist Office to book, while 6 km away is **SKO Hostel**, Opistokatu 1, ☎(015) 572 910 (www.sko.fi), open all year.

JOENSUU

Worthy of a few hours' stop, Joensuu is the capital of Finnish Karelia (what is left of it after the eastern half was ceded to the Soviets in 1944), and although much expanded, a fair number of its 19th-century wooden buildings survive. It also has the worthwhile **North Karelian Museum**, an Art Nouveau **town hall**, Lutheran and Orthodox **churches** and the university's **botanic gardens**, with an engaging butterfly and insect collection.

i **Tourist Office**: Koskikatu 5, ☎0400 239 549 (www.jns.fi).

🖃 There are three **HI hostels**; the nearest to the station, and the only one open all year, is **Finnhostel Joensuu** in the Eastern Finland Sport Institute, Kalevankatu 8, ☎(013) 267 5076 (www.islo.fi). Slightly cheaper and 1 km north of the centre is **Partiotalo**, Vanamokatu 25, ☎(013) 123 381 (www.youthhostel-joensuu.net), June–Aug only.

KUOPIO

The main reason to stop here is the outstanding **Suomen Ortodoksinen Kirkkomuseo** (Finnish Orthodox Church Museum), Karjalankatu 1, about 1 km northwest of the centre (🚌 7). The Russian Orthodox religion once flourished in this area and precious 18th-century icons and other sacred objects were safeguarded here from the Nazis. The result is an eclectic and fascinating collection. Other central sights include a pretty Lutheran cathedral, **Old Kuopio Museum** (an open-air ethnographic museum; closed Mon), and a harbour with summer lake cruises when the Midnight Sun reigns. In mid-June, the **Kuopio Dance Festival** (www.kuopiodancefestival.fi) takes over the town with dozens of lively performances of folk, ballet and modern dance.

i **Tourist Office**: Haapaniemenkatu 17 (by the market square), ☎(017) 182 584 (www.kuopioinfo.fi).

🖃 **Hostelli Hermanni**, Hermanninaukio 3A, ☎040 910 9083 (www.hostellihermanni.fi), €, is a 10-min walk south of the centre and has both cheap rooms and dorm beds. **Youth hostel (HI)**: **Puijon Maja**, Puijontornintie, ☎(017) 255 5250 (www.puijo.com), 2 km from the centre.

SIDE TRIP FROM KUOPIO TO LAKE LADOGA

The **Valamon Luostari** (Valamo Monastery, ☎(017) 570 111, www.valamo.fi, daily) at Heinävesi, is the centre for the Russian Orthodox religion in Finland (guided tours in summer). Monks migrated here during World War II from the 800-year-old monastery of the same name in Russia. You can stay at the monastery's hotel or guesthouse, but wearing shorts is not acceptable and photographs of the monks are generally discouraged. The Orthodox **Lintulan Luostari** (Lintula Convent), ☎(017) 563 106 (www.ort.fi), 20 km away in Palokki (open daily 0900–1800 June–Aug, and on request in May and Sept), offers more modest accommodation. A full-day excursion is the easiest way to visit both briefly.

OULU

See p536. The Stockholm–Helsinki trip passes through here.

Seinäjoki

Jyväskylä

F I N L A N D

Kristiinankaupunki

Parkano

Jämsä

Mikkeli

*Lake
Ladoga*

Pori

Tampere

Lahti

Vyborg

St Petersburg

Turku

Porvoo

Espoo

Helsinki

Novgorod

Hanko

Narva

Tallinn

B A L T I C   S E A

E S T O N I A

Tartu

R U S S I A

Pärnu

Kuressaare

Roja

Ventspils

Riga

Jūrmala

L A T V I A

Liepāja

Daugavpils

L I T H U A N I A

N

Klaipėda

Ukmerge

Kaunas

Vilnius

R U S S I A

Kaliningrad

Minsk

Gdańsk

| 0 | 100 km |
| 0 | 50 miles |

POLAND

BELARUS

Baltic States

The landscape of the Baltic states (**Estonia**, **Latvia** and **Lithuania**) belongs to the northern European plain, which, though unspectacular, has its distinctive charms. Forests of birch give way to low, rolling hills, scattered woods, lakes, great lazy rivers and rocky outcrops.

Ruined castles and 18th-century estates, largely unknown to outsiders, dot the territory. The Estonian coast is studded with islands.

Estonia and Latvia are both Germanic in character, the dominant religion and architecture being Protestant. Lithuania was, for several centuries, a commonwealth with Poland, and differs strongly in its Catholic mood. All three countries have developed at a breakneck pace, joining the EU and NATO in 2004. Unfortunately, the rush to build and modernise and an influx of cash from foreign banks created a property bubble that burst in late 2008. Housing prices plummeted, unemployment soared and Latvia, the worst hit by far, even had to accept a humiliating €7.5bn loan from the IMF. On the bright side, local hotels and restaurants have slashed their prices, so there are plenty of deals to be had here if you're not afraid to haggle. For general information on the Baltic States, check out the websites www.baltictimes.com and www.inyourpocket.com.

ESTONIA

ACCOMMODATION

There should be no problem with accommodation in Estonia, which has a variety of hostels and inexpensive hotels. **Home stays** offer accommodation in farmhouses, summer cottages, homes and small boarding houses. While English is extensively spoken in towns, it's much less common in the countryside. The Estonian Youth Hostel Association (www.balticbookings.com/eyha) can make reservations at 40 hostels throughout the country from 150EEK.

FOOD AND DRINK

As elsewhere in the Baltic States, starters are varied and plentiful and are eaten in quantity, while the main course may be more modest. The most popular drink is beer (*õlu*), and Estonian beers (both dark and light) have a growing reputation – try the many varieties of **Saku** and **A. Le Coq**. In winter, try mulled wine or the excellent Estonian liqueur, **Vana Tallinn** (great in tea or in cocktails).

Essentials (Estonia)

Population 1.3m **Capital** Tallinn **Time Zone** Winter GMT+2, summer GMT+3.

CLIMATE	Warm summers, cold, snowy winters; rain possible all year.
CURRENCY	**Kroon** or **crown** (EEK); 1 Kroon = 100 Sents. Banks give much better exchange rates than the many exchange bureaux scattered around Tallinn and other big cities. £1 = 17.42EEK; $1 = 10.65EEK; €1 = 15.65EEK. The Kroon is tied to the Euro at this rate but there are no immediate plans to adopt the Euro.
EMBASSIES AND CONSULATES IN TALLINN	**Aus**: There is no Australian embassy, only an honorary consul. The British Embassy can help in an emergency. **Can**: Toomkooli 13, ☎627 3311. **UK**: Wismari 6, ☎667 4700. **USA**: Kentmanni 20, ☎668 8100.
LANGUAGE	**Estonian**. English is widely spoken.
OPENING HOURS	**Banks**: Mon–Fri 0900–1700. **Shops**: Mon–Fri 0900/1000–1800/1900, Sat 0900/1000–1500/1700; many also open Sun. **Museums**: days vary (usually closed Mon and/or Tues); hours commonly 1100–1700.
POST OFFICES	Stamps sold at shops, post offices, newsstands and Tourist Offices.
PUBLIC HOLIDAYS	1 Jan; 24 Feb; Good Fri; 1 May; 23 June (Victory Day), 24 June; 20 Aug; 25, 26 Dec.
PUBLIC TRANSPORT	Bus services often quicker, cleaner and more efficient than rail but getting pricier. Book international services in advance from bus stations or online at www.eurolines.ee. Pay the driver at rural stops or small towns.
RAIL PASSES	IR, EP not valid, but rail fares are cheap.
RAIL TRAVEL	Regional train services are operated by Edelaraudtee (www.edel.ee), local services around Tallinn by Elektriraudtee (www.elektriraudtee.ee) and an international sleeper train to Moscow by GoRail (www.gorail.ee).
TELEPHONES	Dial in: ☎+372. Outgoing: ☎00 + country code. Local calls: ☎dial number as it is (there are no area codes in Estonia). Pay phones take phonecards (from post offices and newsstands). Police: ☎110. Fire and Ambulance: ☎112.
TIPPING	Not necessary to tip service at the bar or counter, but tip 10% if served at your table. Round up taxi fares to a maximum of 10%.
TOURIST INFORMATION	Website: www.visitestonia.com. **Turismiamet (Estonian Tourist Board)** shares an office with the Tallinn Tourist Board on the corner of Kullassepa and Niguliste, ☎645 7777 (tourism@eas.ee), but try their excellent website first, with links to other useful Baltic websites. There is also a Tourist Information Office in Viru shopping centre, Viru väljak 4, ☎610 1557. **Ekspress Hotline**, ☎1182, is an English-speaking information service covering all Estonian towns.
VISAS	Visas not needed by EU citizens or those of Australia, Canada, Japan, New Zealand and USA. Since January 2008 Schengen visas have covered the Baltic states.

Baltic States

LATVIA

ACCOMMODATION The best selection of hotels in Latvia is available in Riga, the nearby seaside resort of Jūrmala and the bohemian city of Liepāja on the west coast of Latvia. Most camping facilities are located near the nation's 495km of coastline, but cheap country lodging and homestays can be arranged online via **Lauku ceļotājs** (www.celotajs.lv). The Latvian capital offers dozens of good hostels.

FOOD AND DRINK Many Latvian dishes are accompanied by a richly seasoned gravy, and are usually eaten with superb rye bread. Latvian beer (*alus*) is good and strong – try **Bauskas**, **Tērvetes** or **Užavas**. The bitter Riga **balsam** is famous throughout the former Soviet Union and is considered very good for health. Add it to coffee, champagne and cocktails, or just drink it on its own, whether you're ailing or not.

ESSENTIALS (LATVIA)

Population 2.3m **Capital** Riga **Time Zone** Winter GMT+2, summer GMT+3.

CLIMATE	Similar to Estonia.
CURRENCY	**Lat.** 1 Lat = 100 Santīmi. £1 = 0.80Lat; $1 = 0.51Lat; €1 = 0.70Lat. The Lat is tied to the Euro but there are no immediate plans to adopt the Euro.
EMBASSIES AND CONSULATES IN RIGA	**Can**: 6th Floor, 20/22 Baznīcas Iela, ☎6781 3945. **UK**: Alunāna Iela 5, ☎6777 4700. **USA**: Raiņa Bulv. 7, ☎6703 6200.
LANGUAGE	**Latvian**, spoken by two thirds of the population. English and Russian are understood all over Latvia.
OPENING HOURS	**Banks**: mainly Mon–Fri 0900–1600, some Sat 0900–1230. **Shops**: Mon–Fri 0900/1000–1800/1900 and Sat–Sun 0900/1000–1700. **Museums**: days vary, but usually open Tues/Wed–Sun 1100–1700. They often close on national holidays.
POST OFFICES	Mon–Fri 0900–1800, Sat 0900–1700. In Riga, Brīvības Bulv. 32, Mon–Fri 0730–2000, Sat 0800–1800, Sun 1000–1600.
PUBLIC HOLIDAYS	1 Jan; Good Fri; Easter Sun/Mon; 1 May; 4 May (Independence Day); 23–24 June (Midsummer celebrations); 18 Nov; 25, 26, 31 Dec.
PUBLIC TRANSPORT	Cheap for Westerners. Bus/tram fare in Riga is 0.60 Lat. Taxis are best avoided by foreigners who do not know both Russian and the city layout. The long-distance train network has improved, but buses provide a more extensive service.
RAIL PASSES	IR, EP not valid, but rail fares are cheap.

RAIL TRAVEL	Website: www.ldz.lv. Comfortable overnight trains operate to St Petersburg and Moscow; best to take berth in 2nd-class coupé (compartment of four berths). They also have 1st-class deluxe compartments with two berths. Reservations compulsory for all sleepers; Russian-bound trains will require proof of entry visa when booking. Very little, if any, English is spoken on either domestic or international trains.
TELEPHONES	Phonecards for 2, 3 or 5 Lati sold at post offices, shops and kiosks. Dial in: ☎ +371 followed by local 8-digit number. Outgoing: ☎ 00 + country code. Police: ☎ 110. Fire and Ambulance: ☎ 112.
TIPPING	Not necessary to tip service at the bar or counter, but tip 10% if served at your table. Round up taxi fares to a maximum of 10%.
TOURIST INFORMATION	Website: www.latviatourism.lv. **Riga Tourist Information Centre**, Rātslaukums 6, ☎ 6703 7900 (www.rigatourism.com).
VISAS	Visas not needed by Australian, Canadian, EU, Japanese, New Zealand or US passport holders. Since January 2008 Schengen visas have covered the Baltic states.

LITHUANIA

ACCOMMODATION

If you have no luck with the agencies listed on this page, Lithuania has an extensive system of Tourist Information Offices that cover all the main towns (for Vilnius see p555) and can help you find accommodation.

FOOD AND DRINK

Local specialities include: *cepelinai* (the national dish – meatballs in potato), *blynai* (mini pancakes) and *kotletas* (pork cutlets). Fish and dairy products are common in all dishes. Lithuanians eat their **evening meal** early and in smaller restaurants you should aim to order by 2000; service is leisurely, so relax and make an evening of it. Vodka (the best is **Kvietine**) and very sweet liqueurs are the main spirits. Lithuanian beer (**Utenos**, **Svyturys** and other brands) is easily available. Wine is becoming increasingly popular as closer links are established with western and central Europe.

INFORMATION

Lithuanian Hotels Reservation Centre Service
(www.lithuanianhotels.com).

Bed & Breakfast: **Litinterp**
(www.litinterp.lt) can arrange accommodation with local families.

Lithuanian Youth Hostels Association
Filaretai Youth Hostel, (www.lithuanianhostels.org).

ESSENTIALS (LITHUANIA)

Population 3.4m **Capital** Vilnius **Time Zone** Winter GMT+2, summer GMT+3.

CLIMATE

Similar to Estonia.

CURRENCY

Litas (Lt); I Litas = 100 Centų (singular: Centas) (ct). Credit cards widely accepted. £1 = Lt3.81; $1 = Lt2.34; €1 = Lt3.45.

CUSTOMS ALLOWANCES

Standard EU regulations apply (see pp40–1).

EMBASSIES AND CONSULATES IN VILNIUS

Aus: 23 Vilnius St, ☎521 23369. **Can**: Jogailos 4, ☎524 90950. **UK**: Antakalnio 2, ☎524 62900. **USA**: Akmenu 6, ☎526 65500.

LANGUAGE

Lithuanian. English is widely spoken, as is German on the coast.

OPENING HOURS

Banks: mostly Mon–Fri 0900–1800. **Shops**: Department stores and smaller shops of interest to tourists in the Old Town usually open every day from 1000–1900. Supermarkets stay open until 2200. Specialist shops all close on Sunday and around 1700 on Saturday. **Museums**: Opening hours are highly erratic. Check www.lnm.lt for updates.

POST OFFICES

All towns have post offices with an international telephone service.

PUBLIC HOLIDAYS

1 Jan; 16 Feb; 11 Mar; Easter Sun and Mon; 1 May; the first Sun in May (Mothers' Day); 6 July; 15 Aug; 1 Nov; 25, 26 Dec.

PUBLIC TRANSPORT

Similar to Latvia (see p546).

RAIL PASSES

IR, EP not valid, but rail fares are cheap.

RAIL TRAVEL

Website: www.litrail.lt. Major domestic routes are to Kaunas and Klaipeda, while international services run to St Petersburg, Moscow and Kaliningrad (Russia), to Minsk (Belarus) and to Berlin (Germany). All sleeper trains have 2nd class (four-berth compartments); those to St Petersburg also have 1st class (two-berth compartments). There are no longer through trains to Warsaw; change at border or take overnight bus.

TELEPHONES

Phonecards sold at newsstands. Dial in: ☎370. Outgoing: ☎00 + country code. Prefix domestic long-distance calls with 8. Police, Fire, Ambulance: ☎112.

TIPPING

Not necessary to tip service at the bar or counter, but tip 10% if served at your table. Round up taxi fares to a maximum of 10%.

TOURIST INFORMATION

Website: www.tourism.lt. **Lithuanian State Department of Tourism**: Svitrigailos g. 11M, LT-03228 Vilnius, ☎52 10 87 96 (vtd@tourism.lt).

VISAS

Not needed by Australian, Canadian, EU, Japanese, New Zealand and US passport holders. Since January 2008 Schengen visas have covered the Baltic states.

We have included Russia's second city in this chapter on the Baltic States as it's very much dominated by the Baltic itself and is a tremendously atmosphere-laden city. You'll need to obtain a Russian visa well in advance; the journey from Berlin or Warsaw involves transit through Belarus, and a separate transit visa is required for this. There are direct services from St Petersburg to Moscow, 650 km away (most are overnight trains, but new daytime high-speed trains cover the distance in just 3 hrs 45 mins; ETT table 1900). St Petersburg (formerly Leningrad), capital of Russia 1712–1918, was the brainchild of the westernising Tsar, Peter the Great. Almost every other building, lining broad avenues and vast expanses of water, seems to be a palace or architectural monument of some kind. There are more than 8000 listed buildings here. Despite crumbling façades and peeling paintwork, St Petersburg is blindingly beautiful in summer or winter.

ARRIVAL AND DEPARTURE

🚉 **Moscow Station** (Moskovskiy vokzal; Metro: Mayakovskaya or Ploshchad Vosstaniya) for trains to Moscow and onwards to the south. **Vitebsk Station** (Vitebskiy vokzal; Metro: Pushkinskaya) for trains to **Belarus**, **Ukraine**, **Poland** and the **Baltic States**.

Russia

Ladoga Station (Ladozhskiy vokzal; Metro: Ladozhskaya) for trains to **Helsinki**. Tickets can be bought most cheaply at the Central Railway Booking Office (**Tsentralnye Zhelezno-dorozhnye Kassy**), Naberezhnaya kanala Griboedova 24, at windows 100–104, 2nd floor. Metro: Nevskiy Prospekt. Hotels and travels agencies will add a service charge for bookings.

🚢 Sea Terminal, **Morskoy Vokzal**, Morskoy Slavy ploshchad 1, 📠 (812) 322 6052 (numerous buses, trolleybuses and commercial minibuses). Boats from Moscow arrive at the River Passenger Terminal, Obukhovskoy oborony 195 (Metro: Proletarskaya), 📠 (812) 262 0239.

✈ **Pulkovo**, 📠 (812) 704 3444. St Petersburg's international airport is located 17 km south of the city centre. The currency exchange office has limited opening hours and is generally unreliable. Route Taxis (minibuses) link both terminals (domestic flights: Pulkovo 1; international flights: Pulkovo 2) to Moskovskaya Metro station 0700–2200, taking 10–15 mins.

Tickets for all local surface transport (buses, trams, trolleybuses and commercial minibuses) are sold on board by conductors or the driver. There are ticket inspectors (not in uniform), so make sure you buy your ticket immediately. A *yediniy bilet* covers all state transport for a calendar month and is good value if you are staying a long time. For the Metro, **tokens** (*jetony*) must be dropped into the turnstiles, but most people buy magnetic cards, valid for a set number of journeys.

INFORMATION

TOURIST INFORMATION

City Information Office at 14/52 Sadovaya ul, Metro: Gostinyy Dvor, Neviskiy Prospekt, 📠 (812) 310 2231. The useful *St Petersburg in your pocket* is available online (www.inyourpocket.com).

Events listings are available weekly in the *St Petersburg Times* (www.sptimes.ru), the English weekly entertainment newspaper *Where St Petersburg* and www.timeout.ru (in Russian).

MONEY

Hard currency is not an option in many shops, so always have plenty of roubles for small services, although larger retailers and hotels now all accept credit cards. ATMs are fairly common in Nevskiy Prospekt, in hotels and the Metro, but some offer only extremely limited sums. The best deal is offered by **exchange offices**. The centre of St Petersburg is quite safe to wander around in the evening but petty crime is a serious problem, so keep an eye on personal belongings.

PUBLIC TRANSPORT

Public transport is comprehensive and startlingly cheap. It runs 0530–0100, but is infrequent after 2300. Official transport maps abound, and are available in English (try Dom Knigi at Nevskiy Prospekt 28).

METRO

The Metro is cheap and reliable, although not comprehensive. All four lines are colour coded, but you'll need basic knowledge of the Cyrillic alphabet. Two intersecting stations on different lines will have different names. Stations are indicated by a sign bearing a large blue letter 'M'.

BUSES Look out for the signs: Red T for trams, A on yellow for buses, Blue T for trolleybuses. Still incredibly cheap and much less crowded are the commercial buses and minibuses that cover all main routes and some more unusual areas.

TAXIS Official cabs are mostly yellow and have an orange light on top. If you order a cab from a hotel the cost will be extortionate, but will at least be fixed in advance. Flagging a cab down on the street is risky for non-Russian speakers.

RIVER TOURS

It would be a sin to visit St Petersburg and not take a canal or river tour. Or take a hydrofoil (*raketa*) service (0900–1830 in summer, 30 mins) to the 18th-century palace and gardens at Peterhof, departing outside the Hermitage Museum.

ACCOMMODATION

BRIDGES

From 0125–0530 May–Nov St Petersburg's bridges are raised to let ships pass up and down the river. Take care: many visitors spend at least one night on the *wrong* bank of the river.

Unlike in Moscow, there is a broadening range of medium-price and budget hotels. Websites offering accommodation include www.hostelbookers.com/st-petersburg and www.russianhostels.ru.

A number of highly select, tiny apartment-cum-hotels offer cosy intimacy and independence at very central locations. www.cityrealityrussia.com has a good range. At the cost of some minor inconvenience, go for the **Oktyabrskaya Hotel**, Ligovsky Prospekt 10, ☎(812) 578 1144, US toll free 1-800-755-3080 (www.oktober-hotel.spb.ru), Metro: Ploshchad Vosstaniya, just across the road from the Moscow Station. Insist on the upgraded rooms (nice bathrooms). The ever popular **Hotel Russ**, Artileriiskaya ul.1, ☎(812) 273 4683 (www.hotelruss.spb.ru), Metro: Mayakovskaya, has 143 rooms and slightly Soviet-style interiors.

The **St Petersburg Youth Hostel (HI)**, 3-ya Sovetskaya ulitsa 28, ☎(812) 329 8018, (www.ryh.ru), Metro: Ploshchad Vosstaniya, is surely one of the most successful ventures of its kind in Russia. It provides excellent back up in all situations, and has an attached student/youth travel agency, Sindbad, which can book onward journeys. If that's booked up, try **Hostel All Seasons**, 4th Floor, Yakovlevskiy pereulok 11, ☎(812) 327 1070 (info@hostel.sbp.ru), Metro: Elektrosila or Park Pobedy. Another **HI** hostel is the **Puppet Theatre Hostel**, Nekrasova ulica 12, ☎(812) 272 5401 (www.hostel-puppet.ru), Metro: Mayakovskaya or Chernyshevskaya; ▤ trolleybus 3/8/15.

For **bed and breakfast**, go for the long-established **HOFA** (Host Families' Guest Association), ☎275 1992 (www.hofa.ru). They can do visas and find a room with ordinary families in St Petersburg and other cities of the former Soviet Union.

Russia

FOOD AND DRINK

There's no need to spend the earth on dining in St Petersburg. Most places offer excellent food, although on Nevskiy Prospekt itself cafés are thin on the ground. Take a hop and a skip off the main road, however, and if you're paying more than €8 a head without drink you're not really on a budget. Do not drink unboiled tap water.

HIGHLIGHTS

Whether seen under a sheen of snow, or in the summer sun, St Petersburg is a seductive place with countless beautiful grand old buildings set on seemingly endless French-style boulevards, or lining intricate canalways, and museums galore. For the best view, get out and walk; winter, summer, rain or shine, it's what the locals do. St Petersburg's elegant main avenue, **Nevskiy Prospekt**, extends 5 km eastwards from Dvortsoviy Ploshchad to the Alexander Monastery. Shops, clubs and museums are clustered in the near reaches of this avenue, and it has some striking palaces and bridges to keep bringing you back to it. The **State Hermitage** is not only one of the world's largest and most magnificent museums, but it incorporates the **Winter Palace**, former residence of the Russian imperial family. Take a tour of the incredibly rich state apartments, and don't forget to go upstairs to see works by Matisse, or down to the gold collection – everything from Greek gold to Chinese, Indian and Iranian treasures. Check the website (www.hermitage.ru) for current opening hours and admission charges. Although 19th-century novelist **Fyodor Dostoevsky** is most closely associated with the Haymarket, the setting for *Crime and Punishment*, it is his last home in the city that has been refurbished as a **museum** (Kuznechniy pereulok 5/2; www.md.spb.ru). You should also visit the **apartment** of Russia's greatest poet, **Alexander Pushkin** (Naberezhnaya reki Moyki 12). If you want to go to the **Mariinsky Theatre** (known as the **Kirov** abroad), but cannot afford the price, check out the ticket touts out front, or get a Russian to buy a ticket for local prices and dress up when you go in; only foreigners dress shabbily here.

WHERE NEXT?

*Ferries serve **Tallinn** (see p560). Trains to **Moscow** (see p563) take around 5–8 hours, with some travelling through the night (ETT table 1900).*

ROUTE DETAIL

Vilnius–St Petersburg
ETT table 1820

Type	Frequency	Typical journey time
Train	1 daily	13 hrs

Vilnius–Riga
ETT table 1800

Type	Frequency	Typical journey time
Bus	5 daily	4 hrs 40 mins

Riga–Tartu
ETT table 1800

Type	Frequency	Typical journey time
Bus	2 daily	4 hrs 5 mins

Tartu–Tallinn
ETT table 1880

Type	Frequency	Typical journey time
Train	3–6 daily	3 hrs 10 mins

Tallinn–St Petersburg
ETT table 1870

Type	Frequency	Typical journey time
Bus	5 daily	7 hrs 30 mins

Notes
The direct train Vilnius–St Petersburg runs via Daugavpils (Latvia) and Pskov (Russia). Warsaw to Vilnius: change at Šeštokai. Polish railways also operate an overnight direct bus (journey time: 9 hours), ETT table 93.

KEY JOURNEYS

Warsaw–Vilnius
ETT table 1040

Type	Frequency	Typical journey time
Train	1 daily	9 hrs 20 mins

Riga–Tallinn
ETT table 1800

Type	Frequency	Typical journey time
Bus	8 daily	4 hrs 50 mins

Tallinn–Helsinki
ETT table 2410

Type	Frequency	Typical journey time
Ship & high-speed craft	Up to 15 daily	1 hr 30 mins – 3 hrs 30 mins

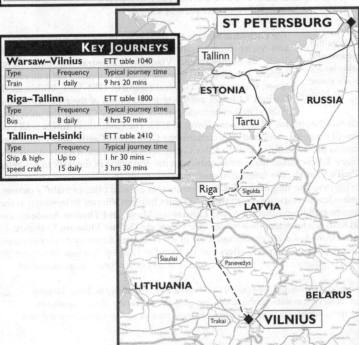

Baltic States

This intriguing route crosses the frontiers of the three independent Baltic Republics of **Lithuania**, **Latvia** and **Estonia**, and of Russia. The through journey can be taken by bus or a combination of bus and rail, with ample time to absorb a landscape of dense forest of pine and silver birch, gently undulating verdant uplands and isolated farmsteads. Extend the journey by beginning from **Warsaw** (p567), or omit **St Petersburg** and take the ferry from **Tallinn** across the **Gulf of Finland** to **Helsinki** (p488). There are more buses if you skip Tartu and go directly from Riga to Tallinn.

VILNIUS, LITHUANIA

Lithuania and its capital Vilnius are less colourful, less visited and less tourist-friendly than their Baltic rivals, Latvia and Estonia. Nevertheless, the cobbled winding streets of the old part of the town are attractive and Vilnius' appeal can partly be said to rest in its comparative obscurity. The main street that bisects the town, Gedimino, could be a useful place to start and return to as it connects the old and new parts of Vilnius.

> Avoid the districts of **Uzupio** and **Kalvariju** late at night.

> Note that **museums and galleries** are usually closed on Mon.

The **Cathedral Square**, the focal point of the city, witnessed mass anti-Soviet demonstrations in the run-up to independence in 1991. **Sts Stanislav and Vladislav Cathedral** was built on an ancient site dedicated to the god of thunder. Rebuilt eleven times, it received its classical façade in 1783–1801. Within its **St Casimir's Chapel** are the splendid tombs of the members of the Polish-Lithuanian royal dynasty. **Sts Johns' Church**, the university church, has the striking Observatory Tower of 1753. The **Gediminas Tower** is all that remains of the royal castle and now contains the **Gediminas Castle Tower Museum**. Adjacent to the Sts Stanislav and Vladislav Cathedral is **Kalnu Park**, a shady streamside sanctuary. T Kosciuskos leads eastwards from the north side of the park to **Sts Peter and Paul's Church**, the finest baroque church interior in Vilnius, with over 2000 stucco figures. The **Tuskulenai Estate** opposite was a burial place of Stalin's victims. Gedimino leads westwards from the square into modern Vilnius, terminating at the Parliament building. Adjacent to the **Lithuanian Music and Theatre Academy** are the old KGB headquarters, now home to the **Genocide Victims' Museum**, Gedimino 40 (entrance from Auku 2A; conducted tours of the cells, sometimes by former inmates, Wed–Sun). **Vilnius Picture Gallery** can be found at Didzioji 4, where tickets for all the branch galleries can be purchased (student and other concessions available).

🚆 The railway station is at Gelezinkelio 16. There is a 24-hr currency exchange close by. Luggage lockers are available at the station, but given the complexity of coins needed to operate them, it is easiest to use the proper baggage store at the bus station over the road.

🚌 **Buses**: Sodu 22, information ☎1661. Left-luggage office. Most international buses do not pass through Vilnius and you need to pick them up at Kaunas. Eurolines Baltic International (☎215 13 77), however, run to most cities in Europe.

ℹ️ **Tourist Offices**: Vilniaus 22, ☎52 62 96 60. They will book accommodation and arrange guides. Buy *Vilnius in Your Pocket*, an objective guide to the sights, hotels, restaurants and bars. Go for the local **website**: www.vilnius-tourism.lt, which covers local history and all the sights, complete with plentiful colour images to help you choose your route.
Medical care: Baltic-American Clinic in Vilnius University Hospital at Nemencines 54A, ☎234 20 20.
Money: Plentiful cash machines around town. Gedimino 12 and Traku 3/1.
Post and phones: The **Central Post Office**, Gedimino 7, ☎52 62 54 68. Buy phonecards from post offices or Spauda kiosks. The **Vilnius area code** is 370 5.
Internet access: Not many cybercafés in Vilnius, but try Collegium, Pilies 22, ☎52 61 83 34.
Shopping: Markets (haggling permitted!) may be found at Pilies 23 (souvenirs) and Gedimino (general). Gift shops selling handicrafts and amber proliferate in the Old Town.

🚌 **Public transport**: The most attractive part of the city, the Old Town, is best explored on foot (easy walking distance from bus and train stations). Public transport runs 0500–2300. Buy tickets at kiosks (cheaper) or from the driver.

🏨 The **Filaretai Hostel**, Filaretu 17, ☎52 15 46 27 (info@filaretaihostel.lt) can book accommodation for the whole of the Baltics (🚌 34 from the station). **Litinterp Agency**, Bernardinu 7–2, ☎52 12 38 50 (www.litinterp.lt), books bed and breakfast accommodation and has its own hostel at this address.

🍴 The cheapest food is from supermarkets or the colourful food market at **Hales Turgaviete** on the corner of Pylimo and Bazilijonu.

SIDE TRIPS FROM VILNIUS
Trakai, the old medieval capital (Tourist Office: Vytauto 69, ☎2 85 19 34), has an impressive (restored) castle, dating from the 14th century, on a picturesque lake (open daily). Frequent buses and trains; just under 1 hr.

Don't miss **Grutas Park**, the sculpture graveyard for the Lenins, Stalins and their local acolytes who used to dominate every town and village square in Lithuania. Also a large museum dedicated to the Soviet period. Take any bus to Druskininkai and say 'Grutas' to the driver so that he puts you off at the right stop, about 90 mins after leaving Vilnius.

Kaunas (Tourist Office: Laisves aleja 36, ☎37 32 34 36, www.kaunastic.lt) was the pre-war capital, and retains an air of elegance as Lithuania's second city. Laisves, the city's pride and joy, is a pedestrianised, tree-lined boulevard, bordered with shops and cafés that reflect increasing prosperity. Near the **Vytautas the Great War Museum** at Donelaičio 64, the **MK Ciurlionis State Art Museum** (www.ciurlionis.lt) houses a vast collection of modern Lithuanian and folk art. The famous **Devil's Museum** is a

Baltic States

collection of over 2000 depictions of devils from all over the world, including Hitler and Stalin dancing upon Lithuania. A walk eastwards, along **Putvinskio**, leads to the funicular, which ascends the 'green hill' for a fine view over the city; you can pay using a trolleybus ticket. **Perkunas House** is the finest example of late Gothic architecture in the town, and houses handicraft displays at weekends. **Litinterp Guesthouse-Agency**, Gedimino 28–7, ☎22 87 18 (kaunas@litinterp.lt), will find you somewhere for bed and breakfast.

Klaipeda, once the German port of Memel, is the gateway to the Curonian Spit, a tongue of land covered in sand dunes and pine trees that leads to Kaliningrad. The Old Town has been rebuilt; make a point of seeing the Clock Museum and the Post Office there. Trains and buses take 3-4 hrs from Vilnius. Buses to Kaliningrad travel the whole length of the Curonian Spit, and this journey is a sightseeing tour in itself.

RIGA, LATVIA

Of the Baltic Republics, Latvia has the strongest remaining links with Russia, and roughly 30% of its inhabitants are Russian speakers. You'll hear Russian all the time on the streets of Riga. Nevertheless, the country and its capital have asserted their independence from Russia, and Riga has witnessed a growth in tourism. Riga has four cities – a 17th-century Hanseatic town preserved as the historic core, a large monumentally Parisian-style quarter of boulevards, parks and Art Nouveau architecture and the odd Stalinist building beyond the fortifications, a Soviet industrial and urban wasteland and finally a new financial centre of glass skyscrapers. There is no need to stray from the northern shore unless you want to cross the bridge to look at the Old Town's church spires from a distance. You can walk the Old Town but you might need public transport for the Parisian-feeling area.

The nightlife is active with many bars and nightclubs. Only order from a printed menu and pay as you go to avoid being cheated; always check the bill and your change. In summer, there are numerous live bands playing in the centre of town with packed outdoor cafés selling local beers.

Riga's Old Town is a mass of winding streets, attractive old buildings and a great number of worthwhile churches. Don't miss the **cathedral** and the other large churches of the Old Town, the **Central Market** or **Riga Castle**. Adjacent to the rail and bus stations is the eye-opening **Central Market** on Nēģu Iela. Housed in five huge former Zeppelin hangars, it's a mixture of meat, varieties of bread, dairy products, vegetables and anything else edible. The approaches often consist of lines of women selling things like outdated lingerie to make a bit of money.

Cross the road by the tunnel and proceed up Aspazijas Bulv. On the right is the beautifully restored National Opera, and the old moat, set in a linear park on the site of the old fortifications. The wide expanse of **Brīvības Bulv.** on the right, leads to the **Freedom Monument**. A guard is mounted (and changed) every hour by the new

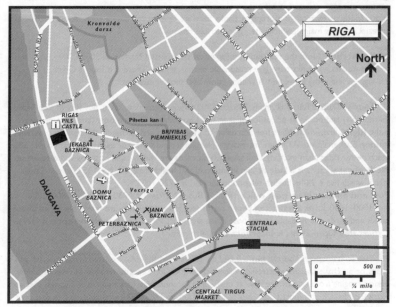

Latvian Army. Turn left down Torņa Iela. The **Pulvertonis** (Powder Tower) on the left now houses the **Latvian War Museum**. The road continues past the surviving (but much restored) section of the Old Town wall, dating from the 13th century. It ends with the picturesque **Swedish Gate**, built in 1698, ironically just 12 years before Riga fell to Peter the Great.

Riga Castle dates from 1330 and contains the official residence of the President of Latvia and **museums of Latvian history**, **foreign art** and **Latvian culture**. On the cobbled cathedral square, the **cathedral** is the largest place of worship in the Baltics, and is renowned for its organ. In Mazā Pils Iela, **The Three Brothers** are the most famous of Riga's old houses, dating from the 15th century. For an excellent view of the city, ascend the tower of **St Peter's Church**. **Town Hall Square** still hosts a large monument to the Latvian Red Riflemen who were Lenin's bodyguard and fought with the Bolsheviks, but its highlight is the restored **House of the Blackheads**, a lay order of bachelor merchants. It was blown up by the Soviets in 1948 to clear the Square of any German links but was rebuilt in the 1990s. The **Occupation Museum** (free) displays the sufferings of the Latvian people under the Nazi and Soviet regimes.

International trains are booked at windows 1–6, immediate departure tickets for local services from windows 7–12. Bear in mind that the station is now Riga's largest shopping centre, in which trains are largely an irrelevance. Most people come here to buy designer clothes, try exotic foods or to arrange mortgages. Banks here are open seven days a week. Avoid exchange bureaux (Valūtas maiņa), which often give terrible rates.

🚌 **Bus station**: Near the rail station, adjacent to the Central Market, ☎9000 0009 (www.autoosta.lv). Banks here give reasonable exchange rates. There is a Tourist Office, left-luggage and a day hotel with a waiting room and shower facilities.

ℹ️ **Tourist Office**: Rātslaukums 6, ☎6703 7900 (www.rigatourism.com); buy *Riga in Your Pocket* (bi-monthly) and books at prices lower than most bookshops. On sale here (and in some hotels) is the **Riga Card**, which offers free admission to major sights and unlimited city transport journeys.
Money: Cash machines/ATMs are increasingly plentiful around town. For exchanging cash, banks offer much better rates than exchange bureaux. Credit cards are widely used in shops and restaurants.
Medical care: Latvia is a little behind in international health care, but try ARS Clinic at Skolas Iela 5, which has a 24-hr English telephone service, ☎6720 1007.
Post and phones: **Main post office**: Brīvības Bulv. 32, Mon–Fri 0730–2000, Sat 0800–1800, Sun 1000–1600. It has a number of phone cabins (pay after call). There are numerous digital phone boxes and cards are available at any post office and most shops. The **telephone code** is (371).
Cybercafés: Open 24 hrs is **Interneta bārs**, Arhitektu 1.

🚌 **Public transport**: You can buy a 0.60 Lats ticket from the driver of trams, trolleybuses and buses, or purchase cheaper electronic *e-talons* tickets good for a specific number of rides or a time period ranging from one to five days at newsstands around Riga. Large pieces of luggage cost an extra 0.80 Lats. If you must take a cab, call **Lady Taxi**, ☎2780 9000, a reliable service that only employs women drivers.

🏨 **Riga Hostel**, Mārstaļu Iela 12, ☎6722 4520, is right in the Old Town, as is the **Naughty Squirrel**, Kalēju Iela 50, ☎6722 0073, which is run by an Australian expat. For an excellent budget hotel beyond the Central Market, try **Dodo Hotel**, Jersikas Iela 1, ☎6724 0220. **Jakob Lenz Guesthouse**, Lenču Iela 2, ☎6733 3343, is a good central option.

🍴 As Riga has grown in popularity, the streets of the Old Town have seen a rapid increase in the number and variety of bars and restaurants. There are eating places to suit all pockets from Russian fast-food joints (serving *pelmeni*, a Russian-style ravioli) to local specialities and branches of familiar Western chains. The LIDO chain of Latvian self-service buffets offers hearty local fare for very reasonable prices. The national drink is Riga Black Balsam, a potent herbal liquor with a bitter taste, which is often drunk with coffee or blackcurrant juice. It can be bought at any bar or supermarket. Don't forget to try the local rye and sourdough breads known as *rupjmaize* and *saldskābmaize*.

SIDE TRIPS FROM RIGA
Jūrmala is a 30-km-long string of seaside resorts, west of Riga, a popular holiday destination since the 19th century. It's a continuous length of beach, sand dunes and fragrant pines between the Baltic and the Lielupe River. The best place to visit is **Majori** and its vicinity. The **Tourist Office** at Lienes Iela 5, ☎6714 7900 (www.jurmala.lv), has English-speaking staff, and will organise accommodation. **Frequent trains** from Riga take 30 mins to Majori station. **Kuldīga** is probably the most perfectly preserved Latvian town; four to six buses a day, taking 3 hrs.

Rail Tour: Vilnius – Tallinn – St Petersburg

A visit to 'Livonian Switzerland' is an excellent day out. Take a train to Sigulda and head straight for the ruins of **Sigulda Castle**, which dates from 1207, and includes an auditorium for cultural events. The **New Castle** is a 19th-century structure, and contains a moderately priced restaurant. Continue to the cable-car station and cross the beautiful **Gauja River Valley** which offers views of Turaida Castle in the distance. Bungee jumpers launch themselves from here at weekends.

From the far side of the valley, find the path to the right to the ruins of **Krimulda Castle**, where it veers left; then look for the path on the right, signposted for **Gutman's Cave**, dropping steeply via steps to the valley floor, where the path veers to the left (with the river on the right) to reach the celebrated cave. Gutman was a Latvian Robin Hood and his sandstone cave has graffiti dating back to the 17th century. Where the path ends at a roadside picnic area, carry on along the road, looking for a path on the right that ascends steeply up the opposite side of the valley and to **Turaida Castle**, one of the most attractive in Latvia; there's a great view from the tower. Here you can hire horses, take a carriage ride or use the bobsleigh track at Šveices 13, ☎2924 4948, in summer, try a wheeled sledge.

Tourist Offices: **Sigulda Tourist Information Centre**, Valdemāra Iela 1a, ☎6797 1335 (www.sigulda.lv). **Gauja National Park Information Centre**, Baznicas Iela 3 (www.gnp.gov.lv).

TARTU, ESTONIA

Tartu is Estonia's university town, built into a wooded hill, with picturesque views. Avoid it on Mondays and Tuesdays when most museums are closed. The concrete river bridge replaces the original stone bridge of 1784, which symbolised Tartu and which was bombed by the Russians in 1944. It is hoped that the original may be rebuilt in due course. The **Tartu Citizens' Museum**, Jaani 16, is an 1830s town house. **St John's Church** has been totally restored, including its terracotta statues. The **University** was founded by King Gustav Adolphus of Sweden in 1632 (whose statue is behind it) but the classical university building dates from 1809.

The **Town Hall Square** is probably the most photographed spot in Tartu. At one end is the bridge and at the other, the fine neoclassical **Town Hall**, built in 1778–84. Notice the leaning house (No. 18) – one wall is built on the foundation of the town wall, the other isn't. Take time out to explore **Toomemägi**, the hill behind the Town Hall. You can cross the 'sighing bridge' to ascend 'kissing hill'. There's a sacrificial stone upon which Tartu students burn their notes at the end of final exams. The excellent **Estonian National Museum**, Kuperjanovi 9, covers everything a museum should, but look out for the collections of gloves and beer tankards. It has also opened the grounds of Raadi Manor house, to the east of Tartu, to the general public.

🚉 Tartu no longer has a station as the building is being redeveloped. The platform is accessible from the south end and tickets are bought on the train. The simplest way into the town centre

Baltic States

Around Tallinn

Kadriorg Palace of 1718 (tram 1 or 3 to the **Kadriorg** terminus) was created for Peter the Great and is in itself well worth a visit, as much for the gardens as for the interior. It also houses the **Foreign Art Museum** (closed Mon) and the living quarters of Konstantin Päts, Estonia's president in the 1930s. The nearby **Peter the Great House Museum** is where the ruler stayed while his palace was being built. It is now overshadowed by **KUMU**, Estonia's first purpose-built art gallery, which opened in 2006. Its five storeys finally do justice to a collection of 200 years of Estonian art, which had previously been scattered around the town. Take tram 1 back to Põhja, just before the railway station, and walk to the **Patarei Harbour**, famous for the abandoned prison, which only closed in 2004, and which visitors are free to explore. The harbour is the final home of the *Lembit* submarine, built in Britain in 1937 for the Estonian navy, and of *Suur Tõll*, an ice-breaker that first saw service in 1914. The open-air **Ethnographical Museum** is by the sea at Vabaõhu-muuseumi tee 12, ☎ 654 9100 (www.evm.ee), about 6 km southwest of the town. There's a host of reconstructed buildings from all over Estonia, and folk performances at weekends in summer (🚌 21 from the rail station).

is right along Vaksali, and then left along Riia, or by local bus.

🚌 **Bus station**: Soola 2, junction of Riia and Turu. No banks or tourist information, but the Town Hall Square is only a 10-min walk.

ℹ️ **Tourist Office**: Raekoda (Town Hall), ☎ (372) 744 2111 (www.visittartu.com).

🏨 **Vaksali 4**, Vaksali 4, ☎ (372) 510 4698 (www.hostel4.ee), is beside the old railway station so a short bus ride into town or a 20-min walk. **Hotel Tartu**, Soola 3, by the bus station ☎ (372) 731 4300 (www.tartuhotell.ee), has a number of basic rooms as well as the normal ones, but the communal areas are certainly those of a hotel and not a hostel.

TALLINN

Over the past few years, Tallinn has become something of a tourist mecca both for Finns on boozecruises and Western Europeans exploring further afield. Said by some to be the Prague of the Baltic States, the old parts of the town are compact, manageable and a delight to explore on foot both in the day and at night. Nightlife in Tallinn goes on into the small hours particularly on the long summer nights (the summer season is very short so the locals and visitors need to take advantage of it while it is there). Live music is common and there is a vibrant atmosphere on the streets.

The increase in tourist traffic has led to a sharp rise in the number of shops with top-quality local goods (linen, leather, suede and woollen products) and a wide variety of craft stalls and stores selling local specialities. The old part of Tallinn is thick with attractive cobbled streets, picturesque painted houses, medieval churches and fortifications. Against a stretch of the medieval wall surrounding the Old City, which can be entered through a number of gates, there is a **craft market**, specialising in traditionally patterned fishermen's knitwear and multi-bobbled hats. Katariina käik is a medieval alley tenanted by craftswomen and is lined with ancient gravestones. **Tallinn City Museum**, Vene 17,

Above: Reine, Lofoten Islands, Norway (Sonia Marotta)

Below: Stockholm, Sweden (Mikael Damkier/BigStockPhoto)

Above: St Petersburg, Russia (Sarah Balog/SXC.hu)

Below: Tallinn, Estonia (Stefan Shopov/BigStockPhoto)

Above: Prague, Czech Republic (Chris Hart/BigStockPhoto)
Below left: Riga, Latvia (Stillman Rogers)

Below right: Warsaw, Poland
(Dariusz Kopestynski/BigStockPhoto)

Above: Athens, Greece (Alison Rayner)

Below: Istanbul, Turkey (Baloncici/Fotolia)

has a section on modern history, with videos bringing to life the drama of 1989–1991. From here it's a short walk through the **Vana Turg** (Old Market) into the **Raekoja plats** (Town Hall Square), with its outdoor cafés on the cobbles, and watched over by the Gothic town hall of 1404 (sporting **Vana Toomas**, or Old Thomas, the city guardian, on its tower – which can be climbed).

St Nicholas Church houses medieval art, including a striking 15th-century *Dance of Death*, while the **Orthodox Cathedral of Alexander Nevsky** of 1900 is worth a look if you've never seen the interior of a Russian church. No hint of Estonia here. Behind the church is a stretch of wall with the **Virgins Tower** and museum of fortification. Across Lossi plats is **Toompea Castle**, the seat of government: walk around its 18th-century façade (hiding the medieval structure) and see **Tall Herman**, the tower from which the Estonian flag, banned in the Soviet era, now proudly flies.

From here Toomkooli leads to the cathedral (called the Dome Church or Toomkirik), Tallinn's oldest church, founded by the Danes and much rebuilt. It contains fine gravestones and crests of Swedish and German noblemen, plus a memorial to one of many Scottish Jacobite naval officers who left Britain and joined the Russian service (closed Mon). Nearby **Toompea Hill** has two good viewpoints, one over the Old Town and the other looking towards the harbour.

Returning to the **Orthodox Cathedral**, Pikk Jalg (long leg) drops between the walls

Baltic States

of **Toompea** and **Tallinn** proper (the two communities didn't get on). The charming gate leads to Pikk. On the corner is the **Church of the Holy Ghost**, with a memorial to British sailors who helped in the fight for Estonian independence in 1918–20, while at Pikk 17 is the **Estonian History Museum**, housed in the **Great Guild Hall** (1407–10) and with captions in English. Its shop behind the Museum in Börsikäik is the best source for tasteful and sensibly priced local souvenirs.

🚆 Toompuiestee 37. For many years rail was the most old-fashioned and backward of all means of transport in Estonia, although the station has been recently renovated, within an upmarket restaurant and day spa. Services are now being brought up to scratch too. Tickets for domestic trains are bought on board. First class to Tartu is well worth the extra EEK 50 (about £2/$4) for the additional space, computer connections and free coffee. The booking hall only sells tickets on the trains to Russia if you show them your visa, unless you are getting off in Estonia.

Bus station: Lastekodu 46, 📞 125 50, some distance from the centre (take a tram). To be sure of a seat, buy tickets before travel. Some bus journeys can now be booked online; see www.bussireisid.ee. Fares can vary considerably between bus companies, and also depend on times of travel. The bus station has offices for Eurolines, Ecolines and Hansabuss, which all run international services. There's no Tourist Office and the money exchange offers some of the worst rates in Tallinn.

ℹ️ **Tourist Office**: Niguliste 2/Kullassepa 4, 📞 645 77 77 (www.tourism.tallinn.ee), good for timetables for buses, trains and ferries to Finland, and for current information on museum opening hours and concerts. Poor for guidebooks and cards, which are best bought over the road at **Raamatukoi** bookshop. The Tourist Office sells the **Tallinn Card**: includes admission to major sights, unlimited city transport journeys, a boat trip in **Pirita Harbour**, a city tour and discounts in some restaurants. Good value for longer stays.

Medical care: Medicover, Pärnu mnt 102C, 📞 605 15 00 (www.medicover.com), recognises insurance policies.

Money: Plenty of cash machines and banks. Avoid exchange bureaux. Some tourist shops accept Euros but will give change in EEK.

Cybercafé: **Metro Kohvik** (www.metro24.ee) in the bus station under Viru Centre, open daily 0700–2300.

🚌 **Public transport**: Trams connect harbour, rail and bus stations with Viru väljak (Viru Square); also buses and trolleybuses. Tickets can be bought from the driver but are half the price if bought in booklets of ten from kiosks; 24- and 48-hour tickets offer further savings.

🛏️ **Hostels Academic**, Akadeemia 11, 📞 6620 22 75, **Citybike**, Uus 33, 📞 511 18 19 (also at Nunne 31); **Hostel Vana Tom**, Väike-Karja 1, 📞 631 32 52; **Eurohostel**, Nunne 2, 📞 644 77 88.

🍴 A plethora of bars, liquor shops, nightclubs, coffee shops and restaurants have opened in the wake of the tourist invasion. There are prices to suit all budgets and many branches of familiar American fast-food outlets as well as countless pizzerias, which offer filling fare.

Rail Tour: Vilnius – Tallinn – St Petersburg

SIDE TRIPS FROM TALLINN   Pärnu (ETT table 1890; 2 hrs 45 mins; take bus from station to town centre) is a 19th-century resort town built around mud baths beside what had been a major harbour. It's a good stop for a few hours if you're making the journey from **Riga** to **Tallinn** by bus, although deserves longer if you have the time. **Tourist Office**: ☎447 30 00 (www.visitparnu.ee). In the Old Town you can explore the fortifications overlooking the former moat and see churches dating from Swedish and Tsarist occupations. A walk along the beach reveals two Art Deco gems – the functionalist **Rannahotell** and the neoclassicist **Mud Bath**. Supeluse (Bathing street) starts at the Mud Bath, and runs through attractive parkland back to town. Don't miss the **Chaplin Centre**, an arts centre where you may still be welcomed by the headless Lenin statue parked outside.

Haapsalu is Estonia's second resort (**Tourist Office** at Posti 37, ☎473 32 48, www.haapsalu.ee). Look for the remains of the **Bishops' Castle and Church**. The resort area has been restored, and the modern beach is to the west of the town. Estonians regard the islands of **Hiiumaa** and **Saaremaa** as the country's true heartland. Kuressaare is the capital of Saaremaa, the largest island (**Tourist Office** at Tallinna 2, ☎453 31 20, www.saaremaa.ee). Accommodation should be booked in advance. The castle at Kuressaare is the best preserved in Estonia, and the rest of the island boasts historic churches, windmills and a meteorite crater. Buses from **Tallinn** take about 4 hrs; flying is also an option.

ST PETERSBURG

See p549. Visas are required by all non-CIS nationals.

MOSCOW

If you want to venture further into Russia from St Petersburg (and already have your visa sorted out) Moscow is the obvious next stop. The noisy, bustling, thrusting hub of Russia, it has finally emerged from the shadow of its Communist past. Many of the older buildings have been restored to their former pastel shades of yellow, blue and pink; some have sadly been torn down. However, most striking for visitors are the large buildings of all styles that dominate the Moscow skyline, from the many glittering onion-shaped cathedral domes within the Kremlin to the overpowering Stalinist-Gothic towers. As in Soviet times, the attractions are the **Kremlin** complex of museums and churches, **Red Square** and **St Basil's Cathedral**, the restored **GUM department store**, the **Bolshoi Theatre**, several excellent art galleries and the ornate, often beautiful **Metro stations**.
The infamous headquarters of the KGB, the **Lubyanka**, is still standing. While central Moscow is relatively safe to walk around (not the case further out), you should be extra careful with valuables. It is not a cheap city. Accommodation can be very pricey and restaurants range from reasonable to extortionate.

POLAND

In the space of just a few years, **Poland** has established itself as one of Europe's prime travel destinations. Look for amazing Old Town squares (for example in **Kraków, Poznań, Toruń, Chełm** and **Zamość**), some dazzling Baltic beaches, stunning lakes (especially in Mazuria), memorably beautiful mountains (in the south of the country), tremendous nightlife and enough shrines to keep a shine on your rosary. Young Poles are justifiably proud of their country and many speak excellent English. Among the older population, you may find some German or Russian speakers, but don't expect a lot of English. Polish railway staff are famously monolingual!

ACCOMMODATION

Expect huge variations in prices. A Kraków hotel in high season might charge several times more than a comparable place in a grim industrial city. Agencies like www.polhotels.com offer online booking options, often with a small discount on rack rates. There is a growing range of pensions (*pensjonaty*), which can be great value, but note that breakfast is often charged as an extra. Rooms in private houses (*kwatera prywatna*), often touted to young travellers at main railway stations, are a bit hit and miss. Check you won't be staying out in some distant estate before committing. Youth hostels are often lacklustre and spartan, but there are a growing number of independent backpackers' hostels. For modestly priced hotel rooms, look for names like Dom Turysty, Dom Sportowy and Hotel PTTK. The latter is a major Polish countryside agency, which, apart from nationwide hotels, also oversees mountain huts in the Tatras (www.pttk.pl).

Youth Hostels
The hostelling organisation is **Polskie Towarzystwo Schronisk Młodzieżowych (PTSM)**, (www.ptsm.org.pl).

FOOD AND DRINK

Kiosks and cafés serve the ubiquitous pizzas, chips and dodgy-looking burgers. A common Polish fast-food is *zapiekanka* (cheese and mushrooms on toast). The wholesome local food is often excellent value. Look particularly for *pierogi* (tiny dumplings often filled with vegetables or meat), fried or grilled pork, and a great range of soups. *Barszcz* is one of the classics. Beer and vodka are very cheap, the latter coming in a thousand varieties. Try vodka flavoured with honey, juniper or lemon. Cheap mineral water is available everywhere.

Poland

ESSENTIALS

Population 38.2m **Capital** Warsaw (Warszawa) **Time Zone** Winter GMT+1, summer GMT+2.

CLIMATE

Temperate, with warm summers and cold winters; rain falls throughout year.

CURRENCY

Złoty (Zł.), divided into 100 Groszy. British pounds, American dollars and Euros are useful. Kantor exchange offices usually give better rates than banks and opening hours are longer. Credit cards increasingly accepted but not universal. £1 = 4.59Zł; $1 = 2.81Zł, €1 = 4.16Zł.

EMBASSIES AND CONSULATES IN WARSAW

Aus: ul. Nowogrodzka 11, ☎22 521 34 44. **Can:** ul. Jana Matejki 1/5, ☎022 584 31 00. **Ire:** ul. Mysia 5, ☎22 849 66 55. **NZ:** Al. Ujazdowskie 51, ☎22 521 05 00. **UK:** ul. Kawalerii 12, ☎22 311 00 00. **USA:** Al. Ujazdowskie 29/31, ☎22 504 20 00.

LANGUAGE

Polish; many older Poles speak German; younger Poles (particularly students) often understand English. Russian is widely understood, but speaking Russian is not always a way to endear yourself to Poles.

OPENING HOURS

Banks: Mon–Fri 0800/0900–1600/1800, Sat 1000–1300. **Shops**: Mon–Fri 0700–1900, Sat 0900–1300. **Food shops**: Mon–Fri 0600–1900, Sat 0600–1600. Many stores are now open daily or round the clock in major cities. **Museums**: usually Tues–Sun 1000–1600; often closed public holidays and following day.

POST OFFICES

Known as *Poczta*: Mon–Fri 0700/0800–1800/2000, Sat 0800–1400 (main offices). City post offices are numbered (main office is always 1); number should be included in the poste restante address. Post boxes: green (local mail), red (long-distance).

PUBLIC HOLIDAYS

1 Jan; Easter Sun–Mon; 1, 3 May; Corpus Christi; 15 Aug; 1, 11 Nov; 25–26 Dec.

PUBLIC TRANSPORT

PKS buses: cheap and often more practical than trains. Tickets normally include seat reservations (seat number is on back), bookable from bus station. In rural areas, bus drivers often halt between official stops if you wave them down.

RAIL PASSES

IR, European East valid (see pp27–34). **Bilet weekendowy**: unlimited travel on IC/EX/TLK trains (except Warsaw–Berlin) 1900 Fri to 0600 Mon, 119Zł 2nd class, 199Zł 1st class. **Bilet turystyczny** (tourist ticket): unlimited travel on PKP local trains 1900 Fri to 0600 Mon and on public holidays, 60Zł (1st class 80Zł).

RAIL TRAVEL

Website: www.pkp.pl. Cheap and punctual, run by Polskie Koleje Państwowe (PKP). At stations, departures (*odjazdy*) are on yellow paper, arrivals (*przyjazdy*) on white. IC, express (*ekspres* – prefixed Ex) and semi-express trains (*pospieszny*) are printed in red (all bookable). Black *osobowy* trains are the slowest. About 50% more for 1st class, but still cheap by Western standards and probably worth it. Overnight trains usually have 1st-/2nd-class sleepers, plus 2nd-class couchettes and seats. TLK are low cost, long-distance trains. Most long-distance trains have refreshments. Left luggage and refreshments in major stations. Few ticket clerks speak English.

TELEPHONES

Public telephones that accept cash are very rare. Most take phonecards available from post offices, kiosks and tobacconists (ask for 'Karta Telefoniczna'). Yellow phone booths allow you to write SMSs and emails. Dial in: ☎+48. Outgoing: ☎901. General emergency number from mobile or landline: ☎112.

TIPPING

Tipping is normal and expected. Ten per cent is standard in bars, cafés and restaurants, and also for hairdressers and tour guides.

TOURIST INFORMATION

Websites: www.poland-tourism.pl. IT Tourist Information Office can usually help with accommodation. Also Orbis offices, for tourist information, excursions and accommodation www.hotelsinpoland.com has info/bargains).

VISAS

No visas are needed for stays of up to 90 days for citizens of Australia, Canada, Ireland, New Zealand, UK and USA (but passports must be valid for at least six months after planned departure date from Poland). Citizens of South Africa need visas.

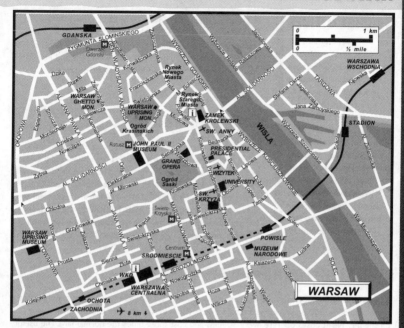

The Polish capital is sometimes overlooked by the tourist crowds heading for Kraków. But Warsaw absolutely deserves a visit. True, it has its fair share of post-war concrete blocks, but the very heart of the city (north of the main railway line and entirely on the west bank of the River Wisła) is packed with sights. A wander through the Old Town square and **Stare Miasto**, around the **Royal Castle**, gives a superb introduction to Poland. The tourist heart of the city thus has a real buzz, with many good-value student cafés.

ARRIVAL AND DEPARTURE

Warszawa Centralna is the principal rail station at Al. Jerozolimskie 54, ☎ (+48) 22 19436 (www.intercity.pl); it's not a pleasant spot, and best avoided at night. At any time of day, keep a close eye on your luggage. Some 30-min walk to the Old Town (with Hotel Marriott in front of you), turn left along Al. Jerozolimskie, then walk or take any tram two stops to the bottom of Nowy Świat, for numerous buses to the Old Town. Left luggage (24 hours, lockers 24 hours for a maximum of 72 hours); tourist information (May–Sept 0800–2000, Oct–April 0800–1800), rail information (24 hours), post office, bus information, currency exchange (24 hrs) and ticket office (0130–2330). Other large stations in the city are: **Warszawa Wschodnia** on the east bank of the Wisła (Vistula) River, and the western suburban station, **Warszawa Zachodnia**, 3 km west of **Centralna**, opposite the PKS bus station.

Poland

TOURIST OFFICES

☎(+48) 22 9431
(note: numbers like this one with four numbers are available from mobile phones or without prefix from regular phones in a given city). Offices with English-speaking staff, which will help with accommodation: **Warsaw airport Frederic Chopin** (open until 2000); **Warszawa Centralna** (central rail station), main hall upstairs; **Krakowskie Przedmieście 39**.

✛ **Warsaw airport Frederic Chopin**, ul. Żwirki i Wigury 1, ☎(+48) 22 650 42 20, lies 10 km south of the city, with two terminals (arrivals and departures). **Airport City Bus** no. 175 (611 at night) every 20 mins (30 mins weekends and holidays), stopping at major hotels and **Warszawa Centralna** rail station.

INFORMATION

The monthly *Warsaw Insider* magazine, is an expat publication full of useful tips. *Warsaw in Your Pocket* is another useful guide, available on the net at www.inyourpocket.com/poland/warsaw. Monthly magazines available in the pricier hotels, like *Welcome to Warsaw* and *Warszawa: What, Where, When* are less useful as they are aimed at business tourists, but have handy maps. *The Warsaw Voice*, an English-language newspaper, has good features and local news items (www.um.warszawa.pl; www.e-warsaw.pl).

PUBLIC TRANSPORT

Trams and buses operate on a frequent network, ☎(+48) 22 9484 (www.ztm.waw.pl). Buses run from 0500–2300 on weekdays. Prepaid tickets (from kiosks, etc) are cheaper than paying on the bus. Night buses operate every 30 mins and cost three times the normal fare. The useful PPWK-published Warsaw map shows bus routes. The single underground line (Metro) runs north to south through the centre of the city (red 'M' on yellow background denotes a Metro station); trains run every six minutes, 0430–2330. Covering all public transport, 24-hr tickets are excellent value. You can pick up taxis easily, but the reliable ones have a number on the roof. Alternatively ring for one – e.g. ☎9191 9633 or 9644.

ACCOMMODATION

Hotels: Check www.hotelsinpoland.com for reduced rates, which can make even the normally pricey hotels affordable, especially at weekends. Some good moderate options are: **Harenda**, Ul. Krakowskie Przedmieście 4/6, ☎22 826 00 71, €–€€: good central location with a 'ranch' underneath that's a favourite with drinkers, and **Hetman**, ul. Kłpotowskiego 36, ☎22 818 57 80, €: clean, cheap, friendly and a 5-min walk from the Praski in the Praga district.

Budget options: For a selection of **private rooms** (about 60–90Zł. per night) contact the Syrena office at ul. Kruczna 17 (Mon–Fri 0900–1900, Sat 1100–1900, Sun 1400–1900, ☎22 628 75 40, office@syrena-pl.com), next to the Lokomotyva pub near the Central Station. **Student halls** are available during summer vacations (late June–mid-Sept) and can be booked through Almatur Student Travel at ul. Kopernika 23, ☎22 826 26 39.

They are the same cost as youth hostels without the hassle of lockouts and curfews. Non-HI hostels include **Nathan's Villa**, ul. Piekna 24/26, ☎22 622 29 46 (www.nathansvilla.com; free internet access, 15 mins from Centralna station) and **Oki Doki**, Plac Dabrowskiego 3, ☎22 826 51 12 (www.okidoki.pl; dorms from 34zł, breakfast not included; 10 mins from Centralna).The **HI youth hostels** are at ul. Smolna 30, ☎22 827 89 52 (www.hotel smolna30.pl), **Dizzy Daisy**, ul. Tamka 30, ☎22 826 30 95 (www.dizzydaisy.eu), central **Agrykola**, ul. Myśliwiecka 9, ☎22 622 91 10 (www.agrykola-noclegi.pl); **TO-TU Hostel**, ul. Krasiczyńska 8, ☎22 811 29 96 (www.puhit.pl), and **PTSM**, ul. Karolkowa 53A, ☎22 632 88 29 (www.hi hostels.com), tram 13/20/23/24/26/27 to al Solidarności. **Campsites**: The campsite **Majawa** at ul. Bitwy Warszawskiej 15–17, ☎22 822 91 21, offers bungalows as well as tent space, or try **Rapsodia**, ul. Fort Wola 22, ☎22 634 41 64 (www.rapsodia.com.pl).

PUBLIC TRANSPORT IN POLAND

Bus tickets are sold at RUCH kiosks or any corner shop with Bilety MZK on it (or from the driver at slightly higher cost, but don't expect change); punch tickets once on board and when changing vehicles. Always buy an extra ticket for large luggage items such as rucksacks or suitcases (over 60 x 40 x 20 cm).

FOOD AND DRINK

Eating out in Warsaw a few years back was often a dour affair. But nowadays you'll find huge choice, from Polish classics to Mediterranean and Asian fare. Snacks and fast food can easily be found, with plenty of alfresco cafés, particularly in the Old Town.

HIGHLIGHTS

RYNEK STAREGO MIASTA (OLD TOWN MARKET SQUARE) AND AREA Very much a focal point, this square is lined with painstaking reconstructions of the original burghers' houses. At Nos. 28-42 is the **Muzeum Historyczne Warszawy** (Warsaw Historical Museum, Tues–Sun; Sun free), www.mhw.pl, which chronicles the city's turbulent history. A short film, *Warsaw Will Remember*, shows the city before, during and after WWII (screenings in English Tues–Sat at 1200).

Continue along Świętojańska to pl. Zamkowy, dominated by **Zamek Królewski** (Royal Castle). Restored after the war, the castle's mixed architecture and stylised interiors are a showcase for furniture, tapestries, paintings and more. Tickets (free Sun) in the castle's courtyard.

NORTHWARDS AROUND THE BARBAKAN AND KRASIŃSKI PARK The 16th-century **Barbakan** (Barbican) was once part of the city walls, but is now a haunt of artists out to make a quick złoty or two. From here ul. Freta (note No. 16 with its museum dedicated to Marie Curie (Maria Skłodowska), the woman who discovered radioactivity), leads to 18th-century Rynek Nowego Miasta

Poland

(New Market Square), less flamboyant than its Old Town counterpart, with the **Church of the Blessed Sacrament**, founded in 1692 by Queen Maria in memory of her husband (King Jan III Sobieski), who defeated the Turks at Vienna. From Rynek Nowego Miasta, ul. Długa leads to pl. Krasińskich, site of a monument and museum to the 63-day-long Warsaw Uprising, and **Krasiński Palace** (now a library), fronting the **Krasiński Park**.

MUSEUMS   Pride of place among the many museums (closed Mon unless mentioned) goes to **Muzeum Narodowe** (National Museum), www.mnwart.pl, al. Jerozolimskie 3 (Sat free), which has an impressive collection of paintings, successfully hidden during the war. The **Ethnographic Museum**, ul. Kredytowa 1 (Sat free), has a collection of Polish folk art and world-wide tribal art. The **Pope John Paul II Collection Museum**, pl. Bankowy 1 (free first Sun of the month, closed Mon), has a huge collection of art including works by Titian, Breughel, Rembrandt and Rodin. The **Frederic Chopin Museum**, ul. Okólnik 1, has an interesting but select collection of the great Polish composer's memorabilia.

PALACES   Surrounded by water, the late-18th-century **Łazienki Palace**, ul. Agrykola 1, was the classical summer residence of Stanislaus Augustus Poniatowski, Poland's last king. Its park contains the **Chopin monument**, plus smaller palaces, pavilions, a moated amphitheatre, an Egyptian temple, an orangery and the Biały Dom (White House), with its chinoiserie interiors.

Some 10 km from the centre of town stands the extravagantly baroque **Wilanów Palace**, ul. Stanisława Kostki-Potockiego 10–16 (closed Tues; free Sun), the former residence of King Jan III Sobieski; the grounds include a baroque chapel, an orangery and a museum of modern poster art; park open daily until dusk; ▣ 116/130/522.

THE ROYAL ROUTE

The city's main thoroughfare is the **Royal Route**, which starts at Krakowskie Przedmieście by the **Stare Miasto** (Old Town) and heads south, along Nowy Świat and Al. Ujazdowskie, 10 km to Wilanów, the royal summer palace, taking in 15th-century **Kościół Św. Anny** (St Anne's Church), the **Adam Mickiewicz Monument** and finally the **Presidential Palace** (or Namiestnikowski Palace), where the Warsaw Pact was signed in May 1955. Just off Krakowskie Przedmieście, in the **Ogród Saski** (Saxon Gardens), the Tomb of the Unknown Soldier is guarded around the clock. Dominating Pl. Piłsudskiego is the neoclassical **National Theatre** (1825–33). Returning to Krakowskie Przedmieście, Chopin played the organ in the **Kościół Wizytek** (Wizytki Church), while **Kościół Św. Krzyża** (Holy Cross Church) is a masterpiece of baroque, and also the resting place of Chopin's heart (in an urn on the left column by the nave).

Cities: Warsaw (Warszawa)

JEWISH WARSAW Before World War II, Warsaw had one of Europe's largest Jewish communities. During the Nazi occupation, the population fell from 380,000 to just 300. There are two great monuments: to the **Heroes of the Warsaw Ghetto**, ul. Zamenhofa, and the white marble **Monument to Concentration Camp Victims**, at the point where hundreds of thousands of Jews were herded onto trains bound for the concentration camps. The 'Our Roots' agency at ul. Twarda 6 next to the restored Nożyk Synagogue organises tours of Jewish Warsaw, ☎22 620 05 56.

SHOPPING

Local specialities include silver, leather, crystal and amber, with Cepelia stores having the best selection of folk art. Desa is a chain of antique shops (there are restrictions on what can be exported). Some of the best shopping is in the Old Town. Krakowskie Przedmieście (for books), ul. Nowy Świat, ul. Chmielna and the streets off Plac Trzech Krzyży are spotted with boutiques and one-off shops. Try Wola antique market, Koło Bazar, corner of ul. Obozowa and ul. Ciołka, for clothes, furniture and books (Sat 1900–Sun 1300; 🚌 129/159/167 or tram 5/24/28). Warsaw has many shops open non-stop or at least every day until well into the evening (e.g. the Empik retail entertainment chain). For late or weekend shopping try Galeria Centrum, Marszalkowska opposite the Palace of Culture, or Złote Tarasy, next to the main train station. There are also plenty of shopping malls throughout the city, open every day, generally from 0900–2100.

NIGHT-TIME AND EVENTS

TOURS

For a more leisurely view of Warsaw, tour the city by boat on the River Vistula: **WARS** ferries sail every weekend in summer from River Café, Old Town to Łazienkowski Bridge and back.

The city has countless ultra trendy bars and clubs with local and international DJs spinning mainly dance music but at the right venue you'll find everything from hip-hop and R'n'B to disco and soul. These clubs make Warsaw the Polish city for all-night parties and rubbing shoulders with beautiful people. However, be aware of strict bouncers upholding impossible dress codes (your Converse and Levis will usually be a no-go). **Dekada** (ul. Grójecka 19/25; Wed–Sat), a colourful place for all sorts with a different theme each night, including Ladies' Wednesdays and Disco Fever (women free admission), and the place to dance your trainlag away. Get in for as little as 10zł some nights, and attack one of the better bars in town before whirling it up to chart tunes or winding down at a table in the 1950s tram. If not content with the night's events by 0400, **Luzztro** (al. Jerozolimskie 6) parties hard till well past sunrise and sometimes into the afternoon!

EsSence (ul. Krucza 16/22), allegedly has the best cocktails in town, and is a good place to start off the night. The Swedish barman's special drink mixes include rhubarb

Poland

and homemade chilli syrup, among others. But if that doesn't take you, there are numerous other clubs and bars in the vicinity. In addition to a thriving club culture Warsaw's Old Town and Praga districts also offer chilled-out bars for a quieter drink. One to get you started is the quirky boho joint **W Oparach Absurdu** (ul. Zabkowska 6) where you'll get a welcome break from British stag and hen parties.

For live music check out the listings in free magazines in shops or hit the web (www.inyourpocket.com). Warsaw's rock, indie, alternative and jazz scene has picked up over the years. Try the legendary **Tygmont** (ul. Mazowiecka 6/8) for live jazz, or the three-level **Stodoła** (ul. Batorego 10), which tends to host international charts stars. **Fabryka Trzciny** (ul. Otwocka 14) or **Café Kulturalna** (ground floor, Palace of Culture) are perfect if you need something less mainstream.

For other diversions, try the cinemas in the PKIN tower, which often have original language or English-subtitled screenings. Or take in a performance at the **Buffo Theatre**, ul. Konopnickiej 6, ☎22 625 47 09, which has gained cult status with young Poles.

WHERE NEXT FROM WARSAW?

*Warsaw is on the **Poznań–Zakopane** route (p573); if you just want to see one Polish city take this to **Kraków**. Alternatively head northeast to **Vilnius** to join the **Vilnius–St Petersburg** route (p553).*

ROUTE DETAIL

Poznań–Toruń
ETT table 1020

Type	Frequency	Typical journey time
Train	4 daily	2 hrs 15 mins

Toruń–Warsaw
ETT table 1020

Type	Frequency	Typical journey time
Train	8–10 daily	3 hrs

Warsaw–Kraków
ETT table 1065

Type	Frequency	Typical journey time
Train	Every 1-2 hrs	3 hrs 10 mins

Kraków–Zakopane
ETT table 1066

Type	Frequency	Typical journey time
Train	5–10 daily	3–4 hrs

KEY JOURNEYS

Berlin–Poznań
ETT table 1001

Type	Frequency	Typical journey time
Train	3 daily	3 hrs

Poznań–Kraków
(via Wrocław)
ETT table 1075

Type	Frequency	Typical journey time
Train	7 daily	7 hrs 45 mins

Poland

This succinct exploration of the best of Poland encounters its two finer cities – **Kraków** and **Toruń** – as well as the Polish capital, and ends up at the foot of the majestic **Tatra Mountains**. The earlier parts of the journey are low-lying and unspectacular, but the cultural highlights more than compensate. **Poznań** can be reached by train from **Berlin**, and from **Kraków** you can venture out to **Auschwitz** – a grim reminder of the atrocities of the Third Reich – or see the extraordinary **Royal Wieliczka Salt Mine**; it's also feasible to extend the journey into **Slovakia**.

POZNAŃ

The capital of **Wielkopolska** is one of Poland's most engaging and oldest cities. It was the seat of Poland's first bishop in the 10th century. A long-held status as a great trade centre (it's still an important place for trade fairs) has contributed to the architectural heritage of its Old Town.

> Almost all museums are closed Mon and some are free on Fri or Sat.

The city's focal point is Stary Rynek, a spacious square with gabled burghers' houses and a spectacular multicoloured 16th-century Renaissance **Town Hall**, where at midday two mechanical goats emerge from above the clock to lock horns. Inside is the **Chamber of the Renaissance** with its beautifully painted, coffered ceiling (1555) and the **Historical Museum of the City of Poznań**. In the partly reconstructed **Royal Castle** on Przemysław Hill is the **Museum of Applied Arts**, with a wide-ranging collection through the ages, and a cellar full of poster art.

Several churches form an outer ring around the market square. One of the finest can be found on ul. Gołębia, south of the square, the baroque **Poznań Parish Church** (Kościół Farny) dedicated to St Mary Magdalene. The **Jesuit College** next door, once Napoleon's residence, now hosts Chopin concerts. A short walk to the east is **Ostrów Tumski**, the original part of the city, an island in the middle of the **River Warta**; here stands the **cathedral**, heavily restored after World War II.

Poznań has two zoos and a vast palm house (in the botanic garden). Fifteen km south of the city is the 75-sq-km **Wielkopolski Park Narodowy** (a national park), easily accessible by train.

🚆 **Poznań Główny**, 24-hr rail information office, tourist information, cash machines, currency exchange, left luggage and shops; a 10-min walk to centre or take trams 5/8 to the centre from Most Dworcowy station. Buy tickets from one of the kiosks at the western exit. All international and domestic trains call here (www.poznan.pl).

ℹ️ **Tourist Offices**: The most central is at Stary Rynek 59/60, ☎ (061) 852 6156. **Glob-Tour** office at the station (24 hrs). **City information centre**, Arkadia shopping centre, ul. Ratajczaka 44, ☎ (061) 851 9645 (www.cim.poznan.pl). Get the map of Poznań, plus *Welcome to Poznań*

& *Wielkopolska* bi-monthly magazine (information in English). The PPWK-published map of Poznań is useful for travel outside the centre (shows bus routes).

🏨 Poznań has a number of trade fairs (the main one being in June) during which hotel prices double: at such a time ask at Tourist Information Offices such as Glob-Tour (at the Central Station) about renting private rooms or staying in university accommodation. The central **Fusion Hostel**, ul. Św. Marcin 66/72, ☎61 852 12 30, is fashionably designed, but caters to small budgets, offering rooms and dorms for as little as 55Zł. **Tourist Guest House**, Stary Rynek 91, ☎61 852 88 93, €, has rooms and dormitories. A non-HI hostel option is the centrally located **Frolic Goats Hostel**, ul. Wrocławska 16/6, ☎61 852 44 11 (www.frolicgoatshostel.com; from the main station take tram 5 to ul. Wrocławska; dorms from 50Zł). There are a number of **budget hotels** on the edge of the city which also offer cheap accommodation, such as **Gold**, ul. Bukowska 127A, ☎61 842 07 74, or **Strzeszynek**, at ul. Koszalińska 15, ☎61 848 31 29, € (also runs a nearby campsite next to a lakeside recreation centre; buses). The most central **campsite** is **Lake Malta**, Krańcowa 98, ☎61 876 61 55. **HI youth hostels** at ul. Berwińskiego 2/3, ☎61 866 40 40; Głuszyna 127, ☎61 878 89 07; ul. Drzymały 3, ☎61 848 58 36; and ul. Biskupińska 27, ☎61 840 71 28.

TORUŃ

Pomerania's capital is an almost perfectly intact medieval city on the **River Wisła** (Vistula), second only to Kraków in terms of Polish architectural heritage. **Toruń** has two diverse claims to fame: one is its gingerbread (which comes in dozens of varieties), the other the great astronomer Nicolaus Copernicus (1473–1543), who broke new ground in arguing that the Sun, and not the Earth, is the centre of the solar system. The obvious starting point is the Rynek Staromiejski (Market Square). Its main building, the 14th century **Ratusz** (Town Hall), houses the **Muzeum Okręgowe** (Regional Museum) and has panoramic views. Copernicus's house and alleged birthplace at ul. Kopernika 15–17 is now the **Nicolaus Copernicus Museum**, its interior recreated as it was in his day.

Toruń hosts many annual international festivals, including **Probaltica** (music festival) early May; **Kontakt** (theatre festival) first week in May; the **Gingerbread Festival** in June, a **street theatre festival** (July–Aug) and the **Organ Music Festival** all through summer.

🚉 **Main station: Toruń Główny**, left luggage (main hall, window 7), restaurant; 🚌 22/27 to Old Town. Toruń Miasto, on a branch line, is more convenient for the city centre.

ℹ️ **Tourist Office**: Rynek Staromiejski 25, ☎56 621 09 31 (www.it.torun.pl).

🏨 The inexpensive **Orange Hostel** is centrally located in the Old Town, 19 Prosta Street, ☎56 652 00 33 (www.hostelorange.pl; free internet access and use of kitchen). **Youth hostel (HI)**: **Dom Turysty PTTK**, ul. Legionów 24, ☎56 622 38 55 (a 10-min walk from the Old Town); **Fort IV**, Schronisko Turystyczne, ul. Chrobrego 86, ☎56 655 82 36 (18 bedrooms in an old fort for as little as 21Zł a bed; 🚌 14 from train station). **Campsite: Tramp**, ul. Kujawska 14, near the train station, ☎56 654 71 87, open May–mid-Sept, huts and small hotel open year round, mini-golf. Student dorms available (€) in summer: ask at tourist information.

Poland

WARSAW (WARSZAWA)

See p567.

KRAKÓW

Kraków is by far the most popular tourist destination in Poland, and justifiably so. The city's main square rivals St Mark's in Venice as one of the finest piazzas in Europe. Kraków was once Poland's capital, and, though it lost that status in 1596, so much of Polish history has been forged in Kraków. After Poland was partitioned, Kraków was briefly an independent city-state, and then became part of the Austro-Hungarian province of Galicia. During the 20th century, Kraków was Poland's pre-eminent city of ideas. Be it in the arts, politics, commerce or in church affairs, Kraków has always punched above its weight. But Kraków is also an important centre of industry. It is home to the huge steel works at Nowa Huta, just northeast of the city. As a tourist attraction, Nowa Huta district provides a completely different experience from its romantic counterparts, but this fascinating, carefully designed socialist suburb is more than just concrete blocks and just a tram-ride away from the beaten path.

The city's main sights are concentrated on the north bank of the River Wisła. Focal points are the Old Town square (Rynek Główny), Wawel Hill with the castle and cathedral, and the old Jewish quarter, Kazimierz. All are within walking distance of each other.

RYNEK GŁÓWNY The Old Town Square is a gem, but to experience it at its best you will have to see it at dead of night or at dawn on a sunny spring morning. No other space in Poland is so utterly dedicated to tourists, and the impact of the square's magnificent architecture is often lessened by the sheer number of visitors. The centrepiece is the medieval cloth hall (Sukiennice), a fine covered market in 16th-century Renaissance style. The distinctive colonades were added much later. Nowadays the Sukiennice houses stalls that trade in jewellery, amber and pricey souvenirs, while on the upper floor there is a gallery of 19th-century Polish art (www.muzeum.krakow.pl; under renovation until mid-2010).

All that remains of the Gothic town hall is the **Ratusz** (City Hall Tower), Rynek Główny 1, which has a fine view from the top and houses one of the stages of the Ludowy Theatre. In the opposite corner of the square, **St Adalbert's**, built in Romanesque style but since partially redecorated in baroque fashion, is the oldest and smallest church in Kraków. Within the vaults is an exhibit dedicated to the history of the Old Town Square.

Further north, **Bazylika Mariacka** (St Mary's Basilica) has a wooden Gothic altar, 13-m-high and adorned by 200 figures, created by Wit Stwosz, the 15th-century master carver of Nuremberg. Legend has it that a watchman was shot down from the church tower by Tartar invaders. The *hejnał*, the melody he trumpeted to sound the alarm, is repeated hourly. For military architecture explore the **Floriańska Gate** and barbican.

THE UNIVERSITY DISTRICT Central Europe's second oldest university was founded in 1364. Distinguished students include the Polish astronomer Nicolaus Copernicus and Pope John Paul II. **Collegium Maius**, ul. Jagiellońska 15, is the oldest college, a magnificent example of Gothic architecture in which 35 globes are on display, one dating from 1510 and featuring the earliest illustration of America, marked 'a newly discovered land'. Tours (1000–1420 Mon–Fri, 1000–1320 Sat, closed Sun) take in the alchemy rooms (supposedly Dr Faustus's laboratory), lecture rooms, the assembly hall and professors' apartments.

WAWEL Kraków's most important sites are the dramatic **cathedral** and fortified **Royal Castle** (both built by King Casimir the Great), high on **Wawel Hill** and bordered by the **Wisła** (Vistula) River. The Gothic cathedral of 1320–64 replaced an 11th-century church, whose relics are displayed in the castle's west wing. The most striking of the 19 side chapels is the gold-tiled, domed Renaissance **Zygmuntowska** (Sigismund's Chapel), built 1519–31. Climb the tower for a great view plus the 2.5-m diameter **Zygmunt Bell**, rung on church or national holidays. The Royal Castle, chiefly a Renaissance structure of 1502–36, has a superb courtyard with three-storey arcades. Displayed in the Royal Chambers you can see 142 exquisite **Arras tapestries**, commissioned in the mid-16th century.

KAZIMIERZ An easy 20-min walk due south from the Old Town Square will bring you to Kazimierz, once a separate community outside the walls of Kraków, and later the city's Jewish quarter. Steven Spielberg's film *Schindler's List* captured something of Jewish life in Kraków, while recent years have seen something of a Jewish revival in Kazimierz. There are several synagogues and a number of restaurants that proclaim their Jewish credentials (some not as kosher as they may seem). Check out the **Synagoga Stara** (Old Synagogue) at ul. Szeroka 24 (open till 1700 Tue–Sun, till 1400 Mon), the Jewish centres at ul. Skawińska 2, ul. Miodowa 24, ul. Rabina Meiselsa 17 and ul. Szeroka 2 (exhibition, bookshop, a restaurant with Jewish food and music; organises guides to Auschwitz). Kazimierz is also home to one of the world's greatest and most important Jewish Culture Festivals, held in the summer.

🚂 **Kraków Główny** (main station) is a short walk from the centre. Currency exchange, accommodation information, left luggage (0500–2300), luggage lockers (24hrs), showers, restaurant. Head left from station, turn right down Basztowa, enter the large underpass and head for *Planty/Basztowa* exit to right. **Główny** has services to **Oświęcim** (for Auschwitz museum), **Zakopane** and **Wieliczka**, as well as long-distance trains.

ℹ️ **Tourist Office**: Main offices: ul. Szpitalna 25, 📞 12 432 01 10; Jordan ul. Pawia 8, 📞 12 422 60 91 (www.krakow.pl/en/turystyka; www.explore-krakow.com; www.jordan.pl), near **Główny** station. Regional: Rynek Główny 1/3 (Sukiennice) and ul. Floriańska 40. Full information, tickets and a monthly listings magazine (English supplement) can be obtained from **Centrum Informacji Miejskiej** (Cultural Information Centre), ul. Św Jana 2, 📞 12 421 77 87.

Poland

🖳 If you've travelled round Poland and become used to good value accommodation, prepare for a shock if you arrive in Kraków in high season. Market rules apply, and prices rocket. See www.hotelsinpoland.com for bargains and www.jordan.pl for specific details of accommodation and Tourist Offices in the city. It's common to be approached by individuals at the station – check location and price; pay only when you've seen the place. A centrally located option is the **Hotel Saski**, ul. Sławkowska 3, 🖀 12 421 42 22 (www.hotelsaski.com.pl), €€, (note the antique lift); **Ascot Hotel**, ul. Radziwiłłowska 3, 🖀 12 384 06 06, a mid-range hotel with free web access just outside the Old Town walls. Bargains at pricier hotels can often be netted via the web or Tourist Offices in the city. There are also some comfortable and reasonably priced apartments: **Redbrick**, ul. Kurniki 3, 🖀 12 628 66 00 (www.redbrick.pl), is minutes away from Kraków Główny station and the Old Town, and has fully-equipped apartments for up to six people and a reception ready to assist guests 24hrs.

There are plenty of student rooms available during the summer. Try **Bydgoska**, ul. Bydgoska 19, 🖀 12 636 80 00 (www.bydgoska.bratniak.krakow.pl), or **Żaczek**, al. 3 Maja 5 (www.zaczek. bratniak.krakow.pl), or ask at Tourist Offices. Non HI-hostels include **Nathan's Villa**, ul. Św. Agnieszki 1, 🖀 12 422 35 45 (www.nathansvilla.com; free internet), just 2 mins from the Castle, and **Deco Hostel**, equally central at ul. Mazowiecka 3A, 🖀 12 631 07 45 (www.hosteldeco.pl; free internet, breakfast included). **Youth hostels (HI):** ul. Grochowa 21, 🖀 12 653 24 32; **Hostel Atlantis**, ul. Dietla 58, 🖀 12 421 08 61 (www.atlantishostel.pl), one of the top hostels in town. The **Smok** campsite, ul. Kamedulska 18, 🖀 12 429 83 00 (www.smok.krakow.pl), is open all year, and rooms are also available.

🍽 **Rynek Główny** and the surrounding streets are packed with restaurants. For premium locations on the Old Town Square, expect to pay premium prices. Make for the small streets around the university to find the best deals.

NIGHT-TIME AND EVENTS

Many young travellers are drawn to Kraków by the city's amazing nightlife. Kraków's sheer number of bars, the best of which are often hidden, subterranean joints down back alleys, and its large student population make it a great city for drinking and dancing the night away. The Old Town boasts a large percentage of the city's watering holes and can be the place to head for a relaxing drink in a chillout atmosphere or to warm up for the night ahead. For the former, try **Budda Drink & Garden** (Rynek Główny 6; daily 1200–0100) if just for the funky décor, or **Nic Nowego**, ul. Św. Krzyża 15, Irish-owned and packed with ex-pats.

One-day Kraków bus ticket: 11Zł; **single journey**: 2.50Zł. **Taxis** are quite cheap: 🖀 12 9191 or 9661.

For livelier surroundings close to Rynek Główny, **Cień** (ul. Jana 15; www.cienklub.com) and **Wielopole 15** (named after its address), a complex housing four clubs that are enough to keep you busy well into the wee hours. Cień has urban music nights but its dance floor is usually raving to house or techno. A selective door policy means groups of guys may have trouble getting in at Cień, whereas Wielopole 15 offers more leniency as well as musical variety.

Jazz plays a key role in Kraków's musical make-up and it's worth visiting one of the city's many jazz clubs. Wednesday nights at **Piec'Art** (ul. Szewska 12) is one of the best nights for live jazz and **Harris Piano Jazz Bar** (Rynek Główny 28) hosts Polish and international jazz and blues musicians most nights of the week.

Finally, for a break from the tourists, walk southeast to Kazimierz, the Jewish quarter that has become an arty suburb brimming with retro bars and a few clubs centred around Plac Nowy. **Alchemia** (ul. Estery 5) is a one-of-a-kind pub that has exhibitions, cinema nights and frequent live music – a great spot for an afternoon drink and some food though come nightfall don't be surprised if your table becomes a dancefloor! Just as hip is the bar **Le Scandale** (Plac Nowy 9) where you can relax outside with a cocktail in the early evening then throw some shapes till the early hours.

DAY TRIPS FROM KRAKÓW   **Auschwitz** (now **Oświęcim**), synonymous with the atrocities of the Holocaust, was the largest Nazi concentration camp. Between 1.5 and 2 million, mainly Jewish, men, women and children were transported here in cattle trucks from across Europe to meet brutality and death. Piles of glasses frames, shoe-polish tins, baby clothes and monogrammed suitcases confiscated from the victims are displayed. Screenings of liberators' films are regularly shown in several languages. Nearby Birkenau (free bus from the main museum) was an even more 'efficient' Nazi death factory. National Museum of Auschwitz–Birkenau, ul. Więniów Oświęcimia 20, ☎33 844 81 00, 33 844 80 99, www.auschwitz.org.pl (daily, Aug–Sept with guided tours only, free admission). Frequent buses from PKS station (around 20 daily, take 1 hr 40 mins; much easier than going by train). Tours are organised by tourist information centres and many hotels. Accommodation: International Youth Meeting House and Education Centre, ul. Legionów 11, Oświęcim, ☎033 843 21 07, (www.mdsm.pl).

The **Royal Wieliczka Salt Mine**, Daniłowicza 10, ☎12 278 73 02 (www.kopalnia.pl). Mined for over 700 years, it has 560 km of tunnelling. It's a dazzling spectacle, with 40 chapels carved entirely from salt, larger-than-life salt statues and an underground lake. Guided tours in English; allow at least 2 hrs. Entry is pricey. Hop on 🚌 304, departing from ul. Kurniki near Galeria Krakowska.

WHERE NEXT FROM KRAKÓW?

Join the eastern end of the **Prague–Poprad Tatry** *route by travelling to* **Poprad Tatry** *and changing at* **Plaveč** *(two services daily, summer only, taking 6–7 hrs; ETT tables 1078 and 1182). There is also a daily train from Kraków to* **Žilina** *with a connection for Poprad Tatry (journey time 8 hours, ETT tables 1077 and 1180).*

Poland

ZAKOPANE

Every Pole knows Zakopane, a resort town in the **Tatra Mountains**, three hours south of Kraków by train. It's the place to which the Kraków intelligentsia came (and still come) to rest and play. With beautiful late 19th-century villas, wooden churches, leafy avenues and easy access to Poland's highest mountains, Zakopane is a year-round resort: excellent winter sports, rock climbing and summer hiking. For information on access to wilderness areas, ask at the PTTK office (ul. Krupówki 12), Tourist Information (ul. Kościuszki 17, www.zakopane.pl) or the less-central Tatra National Park Information Centre (ul. Chalubinskiego 44). If you're hiking into the mountains, book mountain huts well ahead (or risk ending up sleeping outside), and take your own food. The high season, when the trails and huts are very busy, runs from late June to late August. May, early June and September usually offer good hiking conditions without the crowds, but be aware that winter snow may linger well into spring at higher elevations, especially on north-facing slopes. As for day hikes from Zakopane, one of the best is to the summit of **Giewont** (7 hrs round walk); there's also a cable car up to **Kasprowy Wierch** (1985 m), from where there's a ridge path that hugs the Slovakian border. Keep an eye open for approaching bad weather, and don't venture out into the High Tatras without a good map and equipment. The less energetic may like to take the modern funicular railway from the centre of town to Gubałowka (1120 m) for excellent views south to the main Tatra range; there are cafés at the top.

From Zakopane you can also venture to the **Pieniński National Park**, with its time-warp villages and castles. A great favourite is to go rafting in the Dunajec River Gorge here (see www.flisacy.com.pl). The office at ul. Jagiellónska 107b, Krościenko/Dunajcem (www.pieninypn.pl) organises rafting trips and excursions by bus to places of interest such as the spa town of **Szczawnica**, which makes a good base and has accommodation.

▦ Left luggage, currency exchange. It's a15-min walk to the town centre. Buses from Kraków arrive very close by.

ℹ️ **Tourist Office**: ul. Kościuszki 17, ☎(018) 201 2211 (www.zakopane.pl); arranges accommodation and has useful maps.

▤ Book ahead. **Dom Turysty PTTK**, ul. Zaruskiego 5, ☎18 206 32 81 (www.domturysty.z-ne.pl), €. **Youth hostel (HI)**: **Szartka Schronisko PTSM**, ul. Nowotarska 45, ☎12 206 62 03 (www.schroniskomlodziezowe.zakopane.org.pl), one of the largest hostels in Poland. **Sabala**, ul. Krupówki 11, ☎(018) 201 5092 (www.sabala.zakopane.pl), €€.

POLAND: OTHER HINTS

Poland is a large country, and does not lend itself to being covered in a single rail route. Its beach resorts are popular in summer, even with young Poles. Hel, an old-style resort at the end of a remarkable peninsula (and served by direct train from Gdańsk, around 150 mins, ETT table 1099), oozes Baltic style and offers regular seaside attractions by day and decent nightlife. There are several campsites, but you might also try one of the pensions such as Hotel VHM, ul. Lena 9F, ☎ (058) 675 1244 (www.vhm.pozdrowie.pl). If travelling to and from Hel by train, stop off at Puck, an attractive small town with a picture-perfect Gothic church and fishing harbour.

An alternative route to Hel in the summer season is by boat. Żegluga Gdańska (www.zegluga.pl) has several services daily from end of June to end of August to Hel from Gdańsk, Gdynia and Sopot (inter-rail not accepted, one-way fares from 40Zł) and also operates a network of other services in the Bay of Gdańsk and Vistula Lagoon, including day trips to Kaliningrad (visa required).

If making for any of these north coast resorts, Gdańsk is definitely worth a look. It has superb Baltic Gothic architecture, a rich Hanseatic history and took centre stage as Solidarność (Solidarity) developed a powerful resistance to the authorities in Warsaw. The cranes of the former Lenin shipyard, where Lech Wałęsa shot to international fame, still dominate the skyline. Hostel accommodation is available at Pepperland Hostel, ul. Długa 23/28, ☎ 793 376 667, and at Lucky Hostel, ul. Księdza Robaka 3, ☎ 58 776 22 40 (www.lucky-hostel.com).

The Mazurian Lakes are relatively undiscovered by foreigners (apart from elderly Germans digging out old family connections). They are very well served by train, with a network of routes running east from Malbork, which, with its massive fortress (closed Mon), is the natural gateway to the region. Malbork also benefits from a direct night train from Berlin (ETT table 51). Mikołajki serves as a fine centre for watersports, hiking and fishing. Moving east from the lakes towards Belarus, you find yourself in a peculiarly foreign part of Poland, with a substantial Orthodox population, little pockets of Russian-speaking old Believers living deep in the forests (especially around Suwałki) and even some Tatar communities who still retain their Islamic faith. A daily train service runs north from Suwałki (just after midday), giving an easy route north into Lithuania (ETT table 1040).

Just as remote are the Bieszczady Mountains in the southeast corner of the country. Bears, wolves and great birds of prey still hold sway in these upland forests. Sanok is the best gateway for exploring the Bieszczady region; a twice daily train trundles east through the hills to Ustrzyki Dolne, from where regular buses penetrate even the remotest valleys. Look for unspoilt small towns and villages with wooden churches (e.g. at Ulucz) and abandoned synagogues (e.g. at Lesko). With the opening up of the old military airfield at Rzeszów to civilian flights (direct flights from London, Bristol, Dublin, Birmingham, Liverpool, and East Midlands with Ryanair) and opportunities for travelling on into Ukraine (now visa-free for EU citizens), Bieszczady looks set to become a prime spot for travellers. Heading south from Bieszczady into Slovakia, there is a stunning cross-border rail link south from Nowy Łupków to Medzilaborce in Slovakia, an oddball town noted for its connections with Andy Warhol (twice daily, Fri, Sat and Sun only from late June to late August, ETT table 1079).

CZECH REPUBLIC AND SLOVAKIA

Bang in the middle of Europe, **Slovakia** and the **Czech Republic** have much in common. Indeed, from 1919 to 1993 the two republics were united as Czechoslovakia. A double dose of totalitarianism, inflicted first by the Nazis followed by some heavy-duty pressure from Moscow under the Communists, kept both the Czechs and Slovaks in their place. In 1968, they rebelled against Soviet influence, but the so-called Prague Spring was short-lived. Second time around in 1989 they defiantly despatched communism in the Velvet Revolution. Just four years later, the two countries split and went their separate ways – often dubbed the Velvet Divorce.

The move to a market economy hasn't always been easy. An urban élite in **Prague** has undoubtedly made good, but in more rural areas (and especially in Slovakia) the supposed benefits of capitalism are not so evident. Yet both countries are wonderful places for travelling on the cheap. Prices in cities are creeping up, though, as they consolidate their positions as players on the European tourism circuit.

Of course you'll find some decaying industry. **Kladno**, the steel town just outside Prague, is not called Black Kladno for nothing. But you'll also run across stunning areas of mountains and forests, towns with delightful squares, sleepy villages and imposing castles. For real highlights, look to the **High Tatras** in Slovakia for fabulous Alpine scenery and **Carpatho-Ruthenia** for picture-perfect wooden churches and the remarkable Rusyn culture. In the Czech Republic close to the German border you'll find a trio of intriguing spa towns. All that, plus two engaging capitals: **Prague** and **Bratislava**.

Czech Republic and Slovakia

ACCOMMODATION

There is a wide choice of one- to five-star **hotels**, **private rooms** and **pensions**, and, at a much more basic level, old-style **tourist hotels**, **hostels** and **inns** with a few spartan rooms, plus *chaty* (simple chalets) and *chalupy* (traditional cottages) in the countryside. However, quality (once outside the top range) can sometimes leave a lot to be desired, despite relatively high prices, so if you are on a budget, it can still make more sense to look at private rooms rather than cheap hotels. Credit cards are accepted in bigger hotels, though some places insist on payment in cash. The Czech Republic is the most popular of the former Eastern bloc countries and the deluge of tourists has resulted in a real shortage of beds, so always book ahead (directly or through Tourist Offices). There are plenty of **campsites** (usually May–Oct only), most of which cater for caravans as well. Rough camping is forbidden.

On arriving at a station, you're often greeted by locals offering rooms. This can be a good way to find somewhere to stay, but be sure to ask the price first. Note that **youth hostels** are not very common in Slovakia, only in bigger towns, although student dormitories are available in larger towns and cities in both countries in June–Sept, during the summer break.

YOUTH HOSTELS

Browse the websites of the official HI youth hostels associations:
www.czechhostels.com (Czech Republic) and www.ckm.sk (Slovakia).

FOOD AND DRINK

Czech cuisine is hearty, and features lashings of meat with cream-based sauces, but vegetarian options include fried cheese (*smažený sýr*), risotto and salads. Pork with cabbage and dumplings (*vepřové–knedlíky-zelí*) is on virtually every menu, as is *guláš*, a bland beef stew. Try goose (*husa*) and potato soup (*bramborová polévka*). Slovak food has a lot in common with Hungarian; a typical dish is *bryndzové halušky*, gnocchi with grated *Bryndza*, a ewes' milk cheese that's only produced in Slovakia and Romania.

The cost of eating and drinking is reasonable, especially in a self-service *bufet* (where you stand while eating, though these appear to be a dying breed). *Kavárny* and *cukrány* serve coffee and very sweet pastries. Pubs (*pivnice*) and wine bars (*vinárny*) are good places to eat. Czech and Slovak beers are excellent, and Moravian wine and the sweet *Tokaj* from South Slovakia are worth a try. Beers include **Pilsner**, **Budvar**, the famous **Zlatý Bažant** and black beer (*černé pivo*); spirits include herb-based **Becherovka** or **Fernet**.

ESSENTIALS (CZECH REPUBLIC)

Population 10.4m **Capital** Prague (Praha) **Time Zone** Winter GMT+1, summer GMT+2.

CLIMATE

Mild summers and very cold winters.

CURRENCY

Czech Korunas or Crowns (Kč); I Koruna = 100 haleru. No restrictions on foreign currencies. Credit cards widely accepted. £1 = 29Kč; $1 = 17.7Kč; €1 = 25.4Kč.

EMBASSIES AND CONSULATES IN PRAGUE

Aus: 6th Floor, Solitaire Building, Klimentska ul. 10, Praha 1, ☎296 578 350. **Can**: Muchova 6, 160 00 Praha 6, ☎272 101 800. **Ire**: Tržíště 13, ☎257 530 061 (www.irishembassy.cz). **NZ**: Dykova 19, ☎222 514 672. **SA**: Ruská 65, 100 00 Praha 10, ☎267 311 114. **UK**: Thunovská 14, Praha 1, ☎257 402 111 (www.britain.cz). **USA**: Tržíště 15, 118 01 Praha 1, ☎257 320 663 (www.usembassy.cz).

LANGUAGE

Czech and **Slovak**. The two languages are closely related Slavic tongues. English is widely spoken among young people, especially in the cities. German and Russian are also encountered, particularly among older folk.

OPENING HOURS

Banks: Mon–Fri 0800–1800. **Shops**: Mon–Fri 0900–1800, Sat 0900–1200 (often longer in Prague on Sat and also open Sun). **Food shops**: usually open earlier plus on Sun. **Museums**: (usually) Tues–Sun 1000–1800. Most castles close Nov–Mar.

POST OFFICES

Usual opening hours are 0800–1900. Stamps also available from newsagents and tobacconists. Erratic postal services. Post boxes: orange and blue.

PUBLIC HOLIDAYS

1 Jan; Easter Mon; 1, 8 May; 5, 6 July; 28 Sept; 28 Oct; 17 Nov; 24–26 Dec.

PUBLIC TRANSPORT

Good long-distance bus network, run by ČSAD or private companies. You can buy tickets from the driver; priority to those with reservations.

RAIL PASSES

IR, EP European East (see pp27–34). Net ticket valid 1 day, 2nd class 450Kč (900Kč for a group of 2–5 people); extra charge for SC trains. SONE+ gives 1 day's unlimited travel on Sat or Sun for up to 5 people (max. 2 adults). Regional tickets also available, valid only on purely local trains. Kilometrická banka 2000 (KMB); 2000 km of 2nd-class travel within six months, 2000Kč; some restrictions apply. Rapid Integro-Doprava travelcard, valid for all public transport up to 50 km from Prague 100Kč, 72 hrs 330Kč, 5 days 500Kč.

RAIL TRAVEL

Website: www.cd.cz. National rail company is České Dráhy (ČD). Network cheap and extensive, often crowded. Main line trains are IC/EC (supplement payable), Ex and R. Fastest Praha-Ostrava trains are SC (SuperCity) tilting trains with special fares. A handful of branch lines have been privatised. Other trains: spešný (semi-fast), osobný (very slow). Some dining cars; sleepers and couchettes; seats for express trains may be reserved at least 1 hr before departure at counter marked R at stations.

TELEPHONES

Dial in: ☎+420; all numbers are 9 digits, the first two digits determine the geographical area. Outgoing: ☎00 + country code. Police: ☎158. Fire: ☎150. Ambulance: ☎155.

TIPPING

You should tip at pubs and restaurants, in hotels and taxis and hairdressers. In general, round up the nearest 10Kč unless you are somewhere upmarket, when you should tip 10%.

TOURIST INFORMATION

Website: www.czechtourism.com, www.travelguide.cz. Information: Vinohradska 46, PO Box 32, 120 41 Praha 2–Vinohrady, ☎221 580 611, fax 221 580 636.

VISAS

Visas not needed for EU citizens; or for citizens of Australia, Canada, New Zealand or the USA for stays of less than 90 days. Citizens of South Africa need a visa.

ESSENTIALS (SLOVAKIA)

Population 5.4m **Capital** Bratislava **Time Zone** Winter GMT+1, summer GMT+2.

CLIMATE

Similar to Czech Republic.

CURRENCY

Euro (€). 1 Euro = 100 cents = £0.89 = $1.46.

EMBASSIES IN BRATISLAVA

Aus: represented by embassy in Vienna. **Can**: represented by embassy in Prague. **Ire**: Carlton Savoy Building, Mostova 2, ☎(02) 5930 9611 **UK:** Panska 16, ☎(02) 5998 2000. **USA**: Hviezdoslavovo Namestie 4, ☎(02) 5443 3338.

LANGUAGE

Slovak, a Slavic tongue closely related to Czech. Some Russian (unpopular), German, Hungarian (especially in the south), plus English and French. You will find entire villages speaking other languages, e.g. Rusyn or Hungarian.

OPENING HOURS

Banks: Mon–Fri 0800–1800. **Shops**: Mon–Fri 0900–1800, Sat 0800–1200. **Food shops** usually open 0800 and Sun. **Museums**: (usually) Tues–Sun 1000–1700. Most **castles** close national holidays and Nov–Mar.

POST OFFICES

Usually post office hours: 0800–1900. Stamps also available from newsagents and tobacconists. Post boxes are orange.

PUBLIC HOLIDAYS

1, 6 Jan; Good Fri; Easter Mon; 1, 8 May; 5 July; 29 Aug; 1, 15 Sept; 1, 17 Nov; 24–26 Dec.

PUBLIC TRANSPORT

Comprehensive long-distance bus network, often more direct than rail in upland areas. Buy tickets from driver; priority given to those with bookings.

RAIL PASSES

European East, IR valid (see pp27–34). Bratislava tram/bus tickets are available for 24/48 hrs, also for 3 or 7 days.

RAIL TRAVEL

National rail company: ŽSSK (www.slovakrail.sk), running on the network of ŽSR. Trains cheap, but often crowded. Apart from a small number of EC and IC trains, fastest trains are *expresný* (Ex). *Rýchlik* (R) trains cost as much as express; cheaper are *zrýchlený* (semi-fast) and *osobný* (very slow). At stations, departures (*odchody*) are on yellow posters, arrivals (*príchody*) on white. Sleeping cars/couchettes (reserve at all main stations, well in advance in summer) on most overnight trains. Seat reservations recommended (at station counters marked R) for express trains. Reservation agency: MTA, Páričkova 29, Bratislava, ☎(02) 5596 9343 (www.mta.sk).

TELEPHONES

Slowly improving phone connections. Dial in: ☎+421, omit initial 0 from area code. Outgoing: ☎00. Bratislava code: ☎02. Information: ☎12 111 (national), ☎12 149 (international). Police: ☎158. Fire: ☎150. Ambulance: ☎155. General number for emergencies ☎112.

TIPPING

Tipping is expected at hotels, hairdressers, in eateries and taxis. In general, round up to the nearest €0.10, unless you are somewhere very upmarket, where you should tip 10%.

TOURIST INFORMATION

Website: www.slovakia.travel.sk. Slovak Tourist Board (SACR), Namastie L Stura, PO Box 35, 974 05 Banska Bystrica, ☎(048) 413 61 46. SACR in Bratislava: Dr. V. Clementisa 10, 821 01 Bratislava, ☎507 00 801 (www.sacr.sk).

VISAS

Visas not needed for EU citizens; or for citizens of Australia, Canada, New Zealand or the USA for stays of less than 90 days. Citizens of South Africa need a visa.

Even in the '70s and early '80s, a steady stream of travellers of all ages were making for **Prague** from the West. Before the Iron Curtain wavered in 1989, Prague was for many Westerners the only glimpse they'd had of life in 'the other Europe'. Two decades later and the stream of travellers has become a flood. During the spring and summer months, Prague is packed. Yet, for all the crowds, the Czech capital has a very special appeal. You'll find architectural styles galore, everything from Gothic to Cubist, on both sides of the **Vltava River**, which languidly loops through town. Plenty of parks, a pulsing nightlife and a galaxy of classical music offerings all add to Prague's heady mix. Prague locals have bittersweet feelings about the tourist crowds. Rowdy and inebriated Brits have done nothing to smooth ruffled feathers. And watch your pockets. Robbery in some parts of the city centre is all too common. That said, Prague, be it in spring sunshine or in the bitter cold of snowy winter, remains one of Europe's most engaging capital cities.

ARRIVAL AND DEPARTURE

RAIL TICKETS can only be purchased in Czech currency at ticket office windows. Credit card and cheque purchases can be made at **Czech Railways** travel agencies at Holešovice and Hlavní railway stations or online at http://eshop.cd.cz.

🚆 **Praha Hlavní Nádraží** (Prague Main Station), Wilsonova 8, ☎ 221 111 122 (www.cd.cz), rail reservations 0800–1800; often long queues; English spoken. To reach the centre of town, either hop one stop (direction Háje) on the Metro, which you will find clearly signed at basement level within the station concourse, to Muzeum or turn left out of the main station entrance, passing through the park. Both routes will take you to the top of Wenceslas Square in about five minutes although the park route is unsafe outside daylight hours. Some long-distance and international services also use **Nádraží Praha-Holešovice**, Partyzanska, in Prague 7 (a little way out). From here take the Metro, a few metres from the railway station, for four stops to Muzeum (direction Háje) – this is far quicker than travelling by any of the trams from across the station car park and buses from here are normally destined for the suburbs. Both stations are on Metro line C and have exchange bureaux, left luggage and accommodation services. **Rail information service**, ☎ 840 112 113 (24 hrs). Avoid **taxis** (extortionate fares). **Masarykovo** (Hybernská, Prague 1) and **Smíchov** (Nádražní, Prague 5) stations cover many local trains.

🚌 **Central Bus Station** (long-distance services): Křižíkova 6, ☎ 900 144 444 (24 hrs), Metro: Florenc. Take Metro line C two stops to Muzeum (direction Háje) or Metro line B two stops to Můstek (direction Zličín) to reach the centre of town.

✈ **Ruzyně Airport**, 20 km northwest of the city centre (flight enquiries, ☎ 220 113 321; www.prg.aero). Accommodation desks and 24-hr currency exchange. 🚌 119 (every 8 mins; 26Kč including Metro fare) from Dejvická Metro; **Airport Express**, every 30 mins (0535–2205) from Praha Hlavní Nádraží railway station (50Kč). **Cedaz's** excellent minibus service (☎ 221 111 111, www.cedaz.cz) runs every 30 mins (0730–1900) and to Náměstí Republiky, but costs more

Czech Republic

Prague Information Service (PIS) (www.pis.cz): in the **Old Town Hall** (Staroměstská radnice), Staroměstské náměstí 1 at the **Praha Hlavní Nádraží** rail station; at Rytířská 31; and, from Apr to Sept, in the Malostranská mostecká věž; (Lesser-Town Bridge Tower), and at Ruzyně Airport.

Free brochures, accommodation services, information about cultural events, tickets, tours, trips, transport and travel cards. **For information:** 📱124 44 or 📱221 714 444.

A **Prague Card** from Prague Information Service gives admission to some 40 sights over four days, with the option to include city transport.

(120Kč to centre); they also provide a door-to-door service with zonal fares. Fixed price taxis should charge 550Kč to the centre, but often demand far more. Or order a taxi from **Taxi AAA** (English spoken), 📱222 333 222, or pick up from Terminal 1 – Exit D and Terminal 2 – Exit E.

INFORMATION

INTERNET ACCESS The Bohemia Bagel chain of coffee shops is not just great for bagels. Two of their five branches around town (in Malá Strana at Lázeňská 19, open 0730–1900, and in Staré Město at Mazná 1, open 0800–2300) offer internet access (more details on www.bohemiabagel.cz). For bagel-free net access try Grial (www.grial.cz) with branches at Belgická 31 (open till 2300 daily) and Myslíková 12 (open to 2200 daily). Grial also offers good facilities for scanning, copying and CD/DVD burning.

PUBLIC TRANSPORT

METRO, TRAMS AND BUSES All public transport runs from about 0500 to 2400; there are also night services, at approximately 40-min intervals. Efficient Metro (3 lines; red, yellow and green) plus good tram network (buses mostly serve suburbs and are little use for visitors); beware pickpockets on popular tourist routes (especially No. 22). Night trams all stop at Lazarská, just off Vodičková. A funicular runs up Petřín Hill between 0900 and 2330 (2320 Nov–Mar); trams 12/22/23.

TAXIS Avoid if possible – over-charging of foreigners is endemic. Always agree a fare before getting in. Calling a taxi is always cheaper than hailing on the street. Reputable services include **AAA**, 📱222 333 222 (English-speaking), **Profi**, 📱844 700 800, and **Taxi Praha**, 📱222 111 000. They should, theoretically, charge a flat rate within Prague.

TICKETS

A **26Kč transfer ticket** (*přestupní jízdenky*) allows 75 mins on all forms of public transport; a **18Kč non-transfer ticket** gives up to 20 mins or 5 stops on the Metro, no transfers. If you are doing a lot of travelling around, there are **1**, **3** or **5-day** (100Kč, 330Kč, or 500Kč) **tourist tickets** (*denní jízdenka*), valid on all forms of public transport. Tickets from Tabák or Trafika tobacconists/newsagents or from Metro stations; also available from the Čedok desk at the airport. Punch your ticket in the yellow machines at the Metro station entrances or inside trams and buses. Plain-clothes inspectors often flash their badge and ID – fines are hefty. Children aged up to 5 travel free; those aged 6–15 half price.

Czech Republic

ACCOMMODATION

Hotels are often pricey. In July, Aug and Sept, **CKM** also lets cheap rooms in student hostels. Accommodation hawkers offering private apartments/rooms wait for visitors arriving by train – agree a price first. There are several **campsites** within the city boundary (camping rough is forbidden). **TravelGuide.CZ** ☎545 113 943, (www.travelguide.cz) provides detailed information about over 3000 hotels and hostels and 140 campsites in the Czech Republic – and can also book these for you.

Hostels: There are four **HI** youth hostels: **Hotel Extol Inn** (actually a comfortable modern hotel with reductions for HI members: singles 790Kč, doubles 1350Kč with breakfast), Přístavní 2, ☎220 876 541 (www.extolinn.cz; Metro: Vltavská); **Hostel Advantage**, Sokolská 11, ☎220 805 684 (www.advantagehostel.cz; Metro: IP Pavlova; a 5-min walk from Wenceslas Sq.; dorms 350Kč, doubles/singles with shared bathroom 500/600Kč per person); **Pension BETA**, Jaromírova 46, ☎222 564 385 (www.pension beta.cz; Metro: Vyšehrad), and **Travellers' Hostel**, Dlouhá 33, ☎224 826 662 (www. travellers.cz), a 3-min walk from the Old Town Square; laundry, bar, kitchen, internet and email service, luggage room, parking, plus super-trendy nightclub, Roxy. **Hostel Junior (non-HI)**, Senovážné nám. 21, ☎233 353 742 (www.junior.prague-hostels.cz), cheap, cheerful, buffet breakfast included, 5-min walk from Wenceslas Square. Numerous other private hostels include **A&O Hostel**, U Vystaviste 1/262, ☎220 870 252 (www.aohostels.com), close to Holešovice station and the lively **Clown & Bard Hostel**, Borivojova 102, ☎222 716 453 (www.clownandbard.com); pay on arrival – cash only; mixed dorms in high season from 300Kč, doubles from 500Kč, per person; take tram 5/9/26 from the main railway station to Husinecká.

Campsite: **Camp Sokol Troja**, Trojska 171A, Praha 7, ☎233 542 908 (www.camp-sokol-troja.cz), 5 km from the city centre.

FOOD AND DRINK

There are three main categories of eating house: *restaurace* (restaurant), *vinárna* (wine bar/restaurant) and *pivnice* (pub). **The Old Town**, **Malá Strana** and **Castle District** are all groaning with places to eat of all shapes and sizes, but bear in mind that, the nearer the major sights, the higher the price, but not necessarily the quality. It is well worth wandering fractionally off the beaten track to find cheaper grub in more plentiful portions, washed down with a range of beers and spirits – restaurants with menus only in Czech are normally a safe bet. **Prague 3 Žižkov** district, for example, is blessed with the city's largest collection of authentic pubs. In addition to Czech and international dishes, Italian cuisine is becoming popular here and almost every street in the centre boasts its pizzeria. **Wenceslas Square** is the home of fast-food joints, both home-grown and household-name, as well as booths offering grilled sausage, roast chicken and clammy sandwiches. To find out more about the latest and best local eateries, try the listings in the weekly English-language broadsheet, *The Prague Post* (www.praguepost.com).

HIGHLIGHTS

Old Prague divides easily into five main areas: **Staré Město** (Old Town), **Nové Město** (New Town) and **Josefov** (the Jewish Quarter), all on the east bank, and **Malá Strana** (Lesser Quarter) and **Hradčany** (Castle District) to the west of the **River Vltava**.

STARÉ MĚSTO, NOVÉ MĚSTO AND JOSEFOV At the heart of **Staré Město** is the picturesque **Staroměstské náměstí** (Old Town Square; Metro: Staroměstská, line A). Here, visit the **Staroměstská radnice** (Old Town Hall), with its astronomical clock and fabulous views over the Old Town, the baroque **Kostel Sv. Mikuláše** (Church of St Nicholas), the baroque **Kinský Palace** and the Romanesque **Dům U kamenného zvonu** (House of the Stone Bell), which hosts art exhibitions and classical concerts. The dramatic 1915 monument to Jan Hus in the middle of the square is a traditional rallying point for Czechs.

The old Jewish ghetto of **Josefov** (Metro: A/tram 17: Staroměstská) was cleared in 1893, leaving behind the only functioning medieval synagogue in Central Europe (the Old-New Synagogue) and a haunting **Old Jewish Cemetery**. The surrounding buildings (which include the **Pinkas Synagogue**, with a Holocaust memorial, among others) constitute the **Jewish Museum** (☎222 317 191, www.jewishmuseum.cz, Sun–Fri 0900–1800), actually set up as such by the Nazis as a museum to what they thought would be a vanished race. You can get one ticket to cover all six sites; it's open daily except Sat and Jewish holidays.

Nové Město is a sprawling area with fewer sights, but all visitors spend time in the lively **Václavské náměstí** (Wenceslas Square) (Metro: Můstek or Muzeum), which witnessed the climax of the 'Velvet Revolution' in 1989. At the top end is a shrine to **Jan Palach**, who burned himself to death on 16 Jan 1969 in protest at the Warsaw Pact invasion. Just off Na Příkopě is the excellent **Mucha Museum** (Panská 7) featuring works by the famous Art Nouveau artist and illustrator.

MALÁ STRANA This area is a picturesque town of narrow cobbled streets of orange/yellow-rendered houses, with diminutive squares squeezed between the river and the wedge-shaped plateau of Hradčany. Here, **Malostranské náměstí** (Lesser Quarter Square) is particularly worth visiting (tram 12/22/23: Malostranské náměstí), dominated by the **Kostel Sv. Mikuláše** (Church of St Nicholas) – Prague's finest church – and ringed with baroque palaces. The **Wallenstein Gardens** on Letenská, northeast of the square, contain exquisite grounds. Not far away are the even more delightful **Velkopřevorské náměstí** (Grand Prior's Square) and the adjoining **Maltézské náměstí** (Square of the Knights of Malta), which contain churches, embassies and palaces, together with the celebrated John Lennon Wall, a pop-art folly (tram 12/22/23: Hellichova). Visit the **Church of our Lady Victorious** (Panna Marie Vítězná) at Karmelitská 9, to see the wax effigy of Baby Jesus, still an object of pilgrimage. Further east, off Valdštejnské náměstí, the baroque Ledeburské gardens zigzag up the terraces below the castle.

Czech Republic

HRADČANY The huge hilltop Castle District is the focal point of Prague (tram 22/23: Pohorelec Pražsky hrad; Metro: Hradčanská, line A). Dominating the whole complex is the magnificent **Katedrála Svatého Víta** (St Vitus Cathedral), the core of which was commenced in 1344, but completed in 1929. Highlights include the St Wenceslas Chapel, the late Gothic Royal Oratory, the fabulous baroque tomb of St John Nepomuk and the oak-panel relief in the ambulatory.

> The beautiful sandstone **Charles Bridge** (Karluv most), commissioned by Charles IV in 1357, is a Prague icon. At each end are high towers, and the parapet is lined by 31 statues (mainly 1683–1714, with a few copies and later works) – some cleaned up, others stained black with pollution.

The castle area is open daily 0500–2400, castle gardens daily 0900–1800, castle buildings open daily, Changing of the Guard at castle gates, on the hour. For further information on the castle district, ☎224 371 111 (www.hrad.cz), obtainable at the information centre in the second courtyard.

> Most museums are open Tues–Sun 1000–1800.

Nearby, much of the **Starý královský palác** (Old Royal Palace) was built for King Vladislav Jagello in the 15th century. Don't miss the magnificent late Gothic **Vladislav Hall**, the so-called **Riders' Stairs**, the **Spanish Hall** (built by Rudolf II) and the **Bohemian Chancellery**, where the most famous of Prague's four defenestrations occurred, when Protestant nobles threw Frederick II's ambassadors from the window in 1618. The castle is now the seat of the President of the Republic.

Beyond the Castle area lies an imposing district, beginning with **Hradčanské náměstí** (Hradčany Square). If you walk up Loretánská, you come to the **Černín Palace** (not open to the public), from whose window Foreign Minister Jan Masaryk plunged to his death in 1948. A short stroll away is the Strahov Monastery, Strahovské nadv. 1, the star attraction of which is the historic library with ancient tomes, frescoed walls and an eccentric collection of paraphernalia (tram 22: Pohořelec). The **Belvedere** (Royal Summer Palace), Prague's finest Renaissance building (tram 22: Belvedere), houses exhibitions – don't miss the 'singing fountain' in the gardens. South of the castle, wander through **Petřínské sady** (Petřín Hill), a traditional lovers' spot with its lush woods, orchards, 1891 model of the Eiffel Tower, a minor maze and funicular to Malá Strana.

The absorbing National Gallery collection (www.ngprague.cz; Tues–Sun 1000–1800) is scattered round five main venues: **Šternberg Palace**, Hradčanské náměstí 15, ☎233 090 570, contains a collection of European art; **St George's Convent**, Jiřské náměstí 33, ☎257 531 644, houses old Bohemian art; **St Agnes' Convent**, U Milosrdných 17, ☎224 810 628 (tram 17; Metro B: Nám. Republiky), is devoted to 19th-century artists of the Czech national revival; the **Veletržní palác**, Dukelskych hrdinu 47, ☎224 301 122 (tram 12/14/17), houses the collection of contemporary and 19th- and 20th-century art; and **Zámek Zbraslav** (Zbraslav Castle), Bartoňova 2, ☎257 921 638 (🚌 129/241/243/314; Metro C), has a remarkable display of 19th- and 20th-century Czech sculpture.

At **Vyšehrad** (Metro C: Vyšehrad), south of Nové Město, is the ancient citadel where the Slavs first settled. Sights include the Slavín Pantheon with 600 leading Czechs buried in the cemetery next to the Church of St Peter and St Paul, plus St Martin's rotunda, pleasant gardens and breathtaking views over the Vltava from the bastions.

SHOPPING

In the narrow streets and *pasáže* (covered arcades) of Malá Strana, Nové Město and Staré Město are small souvenir shops, selling glass (often fiendishly expensive), ceramics, wooden toys and puppets; try **Czech Tradition** at Melantrichová 17, for local handicrafts, or the museum shops at Prague Castle, the Jewish Museum and the Decorative Arts Museum. The three main department stores and supermarkets are: **Kotva**, Náměstí republiky 8 (Mon–Fri 0900–2000, Sat 1000–1900, Sun 1000–1800); **Bílá Labuť**, Václavské nám. 59 (Mon–Fri 0900–2000, Sat 0900–1800, Sun 1000–1800) and **Tesco**, Národní 26 (Mon–Sat 0800–2100, Sun 0900–2000).

NIGHT-TIME AND EVENTS

As capital of a country famed for beer and absinthe production, Prague boasts an incredible number of drinking holes. The centre of town hosts a range of more upmarket bars and pubs, aimed fair and square at tourists. For a more authentic, youthful vibe head to Žižkov. For breweries try the Nové Město.

The city has a thriving live music scene. The English-language weekly *Prague Post* and www.prague.tv have details of all the goings on. The city's two main live music venues, Palác Akropolis (Kubelíkova 27, Žižkov; www.palacakropolis.cz) and Roxy (Dlouhá 33, Staré Město; www.roxy.cz) also host club nights playing a varied mix of hip-hop, techno, drum'n'bass and house in funky surroundings and come highly recommended. Roxy also has a theatre and gallery.

ADVANCE TICKETS

Prague offers an extraordinary number of concerts, festivals, exhibitions and other events, year-round. Either contact **Ticketpro** at PIS, Staroměstské náměsti, ☎296 333 333 (www.ticketpro.cz), or try www.prague-info.cz (☎221 714 444, Mon–Fri 0900–1800) for details and tickets to the latest events.

Karlovy Lázně (Novotného lávka, Staré Město, Smetanovo nábřeží 198, ☎222 220 502, www.karlovylazne.cz) offers four floors of mainstream dance and overpriced drinks in a central location at the eastern end of the Charles Bridge. Don't expect to meet many Czechs here though.

If you can't stand the pace, look for a dazzling range of classical music, opera and theatre. Puppet and mime shows are also popular. The monthly listings in *Kultura v Praze* (www.heartofeurope.cz) are a good source of information.

ROUTE DETAIL

Praha–Brno
ETT table 1150

Type	Frequency	Typical journey time
Train	Every hr	2 hrs 45 mins

Brno–Bratislava
ETT table 1150

Type	Frequency	Typical journey time
Train	8 daily	1 hr 30 mins

Bratislava–Trnava
ETT table 1180

Type	Frequency	Typical journey time
Train	Every 1–2 hrs	35 mins

Trnava–Piešťany
ETT table 1180

Type	Frequency	Typical journey time
Train	Every 1–2 hrs	28 mins

Piešťany–Trenčín
ETT table 1180

Type	Frequency	Typical journey time
Train	Every 1–2 hrs	32 mins

Trenčín–Žilina
ETT table 1180

Type	Frequency	Typical journey time
Train	Every 1–2 hrs	1 hr 10 mins

Žilina–Poprad-Tatry
ETT table 1180

Type	Frequency	Typical journey time
Train	Every 1–2 hrs	2 hrs

KEY JOURNEYS

Prague–Munich
ETT table 57

Type	Frequency	Journey time
Train	3 daily	6 hrs 20 mins

Prague–Vienna
ETT table 53

Type	Frequency	Journey time
Train	7 daily	4 hrs 30 mins

Prague–Berlin
ETT table 60

Type	Frequency	Journey time
Train	6 daily	5 hrs

Prague–Hamburg
ETT table 60

Type	Frequency	Journey time
Train	3 daily	7 hrs

From the Czech capital, the train heads past Kolín (the connection for Kutná Hora, with its old medieval town huddled around a superb Gothic church), through the Bohemian–Moravian uplands to **Brno**, in the centre of South Moravia, a land of rolling hills, dotted with elegant châteaux and medieval castles where many Czech and foreign films are set, peaceful nature reserves and areas with karst limestone scenery and underground caves. It's also the main Czech wine-growing region (with attractively painted wine cellars dotting the hills) and features a range of folk festivals and charming village traditions.

Bratislava, also served by direct trains to Vienna and Budapest, certainly deserves a day or two. It is more than just a minor version of Prague. Beyond, lies the finest part of the route, skirting the lovely Fatra Hills, and then getting a first glimpse of the **High Tatras**. Bear in mind that it can take far longer than expected to explore the mountainous regions. Trains and buses can both be very slow as you move east in Slovakia. Slovakia, although less explored by tourists, nonetheless has more than its fair share of attractions. These include spas (including cave therapy, fresh air and mud cures and potent waters), Renaissance towns almost untouched by time, deeply rural areas with folk architecture and striped fields, breathtaking national parks and craggy castles that used to guard the trade routes between Poland and Hungary. Beyond **Poprad Tatry**, it's feasible to continue into Poland by bus.

DAY TRIPS FROM BRNO

The **Moravský kras** (*Moravian Karst*) limestone caves form a series of dramatic underground rivers, stalagmites and stalactites in the middle of a forest, ☎516 413 575 (www.caves.cz, all caves closed Mon). There are several trains a day to nearby **Blansko** (35 mins). Take the frequent bus from **Zvonařska** central bus station to explore **Mikulov**, a lovely hill-top town with a castle (rebuilt in the 1950s, but it still looks impressive from afar), charming old houses and noted wine-cellars, overlooking the Austrian border (40 mins).

PRAGUE (PRAHA)

See p587.

BRNO

High-rise blocks and an unmistakably industrial look might tempt you to skip Brno, which expanded in the 19th century as a textile making centre, but it does have

En route to Brno is the stunning town of **Kutná Hora** with an ancient silver mine, the lovely Gothic church of **Sv. Barbara**, endless Renaissance and medieval architecture and also an extraordinary 'bone church' 2 km from the centre in Sedlec (just by the train station) richly and gruesomely decorated with the bones of long-expired nobles.

Czech Republic and Slovakia

a scattering of good sights (most close Mon, and are either cheap or free) within 1 km of the station in the largely traffic-free centre. The neo-Gothic **Chrám sv. Petra a Pavla**, (Cathedral of Sts Peter and Paul), crowns Petrov Hill, while the 13th-century **Spilberk Castle** was the most notorious prison in the Austro-Hungarian empire – you can visit the horrifying prison cells (closed Mon). A little way southwest is the **Augustinian Monastery**, where in 1865 the monk Mendel studied genetics, breeding pea plants in the garden. Garden and plants remain, and there's also a small museum, the **Mendelianum**, Mendlovo náměstí 1 (closed Sat and Sun).

The **Old Town Hall**, Radnická 8, is Gothic-, Renaissance- and baroque-style and displays a 'dragon', a stuffed crocodile from 1608. Brno's most bizarre sight is the crypt of the **Kapucínský klášter** (Capuchin Monastery), containing 150 mummified bodies, air-dried since 1650 (closed Mon).

🚉 Exchange facilities, left-luggage. For the town centre, head across the road in front of the station and up Masarykova street.

ℹ️ **Tourist Office: TIC**, Old Town Hall, Radnická 8, ☎ 542 427 150 (www.brno.cz).

🏨 Reserve well in advance as Brno is a trade fair city and its hundreds of hotels and pensions tend to book up months ahead. **Penzion na Starém Brně**, Mendlovo nám. 1A, ☎ 543 247 872 (www.penzion-brno.com); **Pension Venia**, Riegrova 27, ☎ 549 240 915. The **Travellers' Hostel**, Jánská 22, ☎ 545 212 263 (www.travellers.cz), is centrally located but only open July–Aug; free internet access. The helpful staff at the Tourist Office can provide you with comprehensive accommodation info, and are happy to arrange this for you.

DAY TRIP FROM BRATISLAVA

Towering above the Danube and Morava rivers, **Devín Castle** (www.castles.sk), open Apr–Nov, closed Mon, is a picturesque ruined fortress at the edge of the Little Carpathian mountains. There are frequent buses (🚌 28/29) and boats (from Fajnorovo nábrežie, ☎ (02) 529 32 224, cheap). **Pezinok** (25 mins by bus, ten daily) is a pretty vintners' town in the wine-growing region, boasting a Renaissance castle and centre. Don't miss the **wine festivals** at the end of Aug and early Sept.

BRATISLAVA, SLOVAKIA

Bratislava often gets short shrift. Overshadowed by Prague, it has sometimes been hard for the Slovak capital to make its mark. But the city is superbly placed midway between Prague and Budapest, and less than an hour by train east of Vienna. Bratislava fans always argue that the city has all the merits of Prague without the crowds. There will not be a lot to detain you in the dreary suburbs, but the **Old Town** (**Staré Mesto**) is a gem. The main sights cluster within the old city walls on the east side of **Staromestská**. West of that is a prominent hill topped by the rather austere castle (Bratislavský hrad). The Danube riverfront is dominated by the hideous bridge (Most SNP) that leads over to the huge Petržalka estate.

The Old Town is full of atmospheric lanes. In and around Ventúrska, Michalská and Panská you'll find excellent baroque palaces. Look out for the **Mozartov dom** (which has only the most tenuous of links with the composer), the Rococo **Mirbach Palace** and the **Pálffyho Palace**. Noteworthy Gothic structures include the Franciscan church and the striking tower of **St Klara's Convent** (today not a convent at all but a library). Climb St Michael's Tower at Michalska 22 (closed Mon) for a great panoramic view. At the west side of the Old Town stands **St Martin's Cathedral**, nowadays rather hemmed in by **Staromestská**. Immediately on the west side of Staromestská, under the shadow of the castle, is Bratislava's old Jewish Quarter. The castle itself houses extensive museums (all closed Mon).

Bratislava's Old Town is full of bars, cafés and restaurants that spill out onto the streets on sunny evenings, with the highest concentration on **Ventúrska**. Once darkness falls the city's nightlife is a bit limited. But if you're determined to stay out until the wee hours it pays to wander to the outskirts of the Old Town where there are some options. **Nu Spirit Bar** (Medená, 6; www.nuspirit.sk; closed Mon) has live jazz, as well as soulful house and funk DJs. **Radosť** (Obchodná 48; www.mojaradost.sk) is an underground chill-out bar and club, with DJs playing electro and house. **Cirkus Barok** (Rázusovo Nábrežie; www.cirkusbarok.sk) is a very popular dance club on a ship, moored on the north bank of the Danube between the new bridge and the hydrofoil terminal. It has several floors, playing mainly pop and R'n'B seven nights a week.

The English-language listings magazine *What's On* (monthly) covers all that's happening in Bratislava and Slovakia as a whole.

🚆 Bratislava has two main train stations. The chief one, **Hlavná stanica**, is served by virtually all services to other Slovak destinations. It is 1.5 km north of the Old Town and trams 2/3/8/13 provide reliable links. The station has exchange facilities, cafés and left luggage. A second station at **Petržalka** (3 km south of the city centre on the south side of the Danube) has fewer facilities, but it is the terminus for fast trains to and from Vienna via Kittsee. An alternative link with Vienna (via Marchegg) is slightly slower but uses the much more convenient Hlavná stanica. For all Slovak train information, see www.slovakrail.sk.

ℹ️ **Tourist Office: BIS**, Primaciálne nám. 1, ☎(02) 5935 6111, 5441 4393 (www.bratislava.sk). BIS also arranges all categories of accommodation, but only if you present yourself at the office.

🏠 Budget accommodation is hard to find here. Student accommodation is only possible during July and Aug – try **Belojanis**, Wilsonova 6, ☎(02) 5249 7735, (very basic). More upmarket is the **Hotel Spirit**, Vančurova 1, ☎(02) 5477 7561 (www.hotelspirit.sk), which is very near the rail station. Take tram 13 from the main railway station to Vysoka to get to the **Patio Hostel**, Špitálska 35, ☎(02) 5292 5797 (www.patiohostel .com; dorms in high season are from 630SKK). Book early for the **Gremium Pension**, Gorkého 11, ☎(02) 2070 4874, (www. penziongremium.sk). **Downtown Backpackers**, Panenská 31, ☎(02) 5464 1191 (www.backpackers.sk), 🚋 61/81/93/208. www. hotelsearch.sk provides a database of pensions, hotels and hostels.

WHERE NEXT FROM BRATISLAVA?

It's just over 1 hr to **Vienna** *(ETT tables 996/7), and just over 2 hrs 30 mins to* **Budapest** *(table 1175).*

Czech Republic and Slovakia

📷 Head for the old heart of town to find decent places to eat – Michalská and Hlavné námestie are lined with lively cafés, pubs and bars serving snacks, wine, coffee and sticky cakes. Panská and the charming streets and squares close by boast some good restaurants, pizzerias and gallery cafés. Check out the latest eateries in *The Slovak Spectator* (www.spectator.sk), the weekly English-language newspaper, or browse www.gurmania.sk.

TRNAVA

Dubbed somewhat ludicrously the 'Slovak Rome', Trnava is a picturesque walled university town boasting 12 churches and unspoiled, cobbled lanes. It's an easy day trip from Bratislava. While you're there don't miss Trojičné námestie, with its fine houses and public buildings and plague column. The huge Rococo **Univerzitný kostol**, on Hollého, is one of Trnava's most interesting and elegant churches, but it's just as rewarding to wander the town's sleepy, leafy alleyways and squares.

🚆 The centre is a 10-min walk up Hospodárska st., then right down Bernolákova brana st.

ℹ️ **Tourist Office: TINS**, Trojičné námestie 1, ☎033 323 6440 (www.trnava.sk).

🏨 Cheap accommodation is thin on the ground: if you are travelling in a group, try **Hotel Inka**, Ul. Vladimíra Clementisa, ☎(0805) 590 5111 (www.hotelinka.sk), €€–€€€, or try the similarly priced **Hotel Nukleon**, J. Bottu 2, ☎033 55 21 0956 (hotelnukleon@hotelysk.sk), €.

PIEŠŤANY

Slovakia's Piešťany offers cures, elegant cafés and peaceful, riverside parks, and is just over an hour's train ride from the capital. Recently renovated, its smartest spa hotels (€€€) are now largely populated with holidaying well-heeled Russians. Take a leisurely swim in the **Eva** pool, sample the granny-filled cafés on Winterová and explore the tranquil parks on **Kúpeľný island**, so relaxing it's almost comatose.

🚆 A 15-min walk west of the centre (signposted).

ℹ️ **Tourist Office: Tourist Information Centre**, Pribinova 2, ☎033 771 96 21 (www.pic.piestany.sk). **Informačné stredisko Piešťany** (in the Hotel Eden), Winterová 60, ☎(0838) 16186 (www.piestany.sk.) The Tourist Office at Hotel Eden also arranges all categories of accommodation and has some reasonably priced rooms of its own, €€–€€€.

TRENČÍN

Trenčín, dwarfed by a towering castle on a crag, is a charming old town on the river Váh. The massive reconstructed castle is open daily for guided tours and provides spectacular views particularly at night. Mierové námestie (the main square), lined with

Rail Tour: Prague – Bratislava – Poprad-Tatry

DAY TRIP FROM ŽILINA

Five trains per day make the short run through from Žilina to Martin, taking 30 mins (ETT table 1185). Plenty more journeys are possible by changing at **Vrútky**. Martin is an outstanding base for walking or skiing in the Malá and Veľká Fatra mountains, and for visiting the **Slovak Village Museum** (at Jahodnické háje), 3 km away.

trees and pastel-coloured houses, includes some cafés, pubs and a pizzeria. Trenčín also makes a good base for hiking in the **Považský Inovec woods**. There is a branch line from Trenčianska Teplá (8 km from Trenčín) to **Trenčianske Teplice spa** (with pseudo-Turkish baths) on the narrow-gauge railway. Try the Hammam baths (men only) and the Zelená žaba spring-water baths, the marked walks up to Krájovec and, if you're in town in the summer, the international art, film and music festivals.

🚃 A 10-min walk east through the park for the centre.

ℹ️ **Tourist Office: Kultúrno-informačné centrum mesta Trenčín**, Sládkovičova ulica, ☎(032) 650 4294 (www.trencin.sk).

🏠 The best source of accommodation is via the helpful Tourist Office – booking ahead is strongly recommended. Cheap accommodation includes student digs at the **Domov Mládeže**, Staničná 6, ☎(032) 652 2380 (dmtn@centrum.sk), by the railway station, €, open July–Aug, or the **Autocamp** in Ostrov, ☎(032) 743 4013 (www.web.viapvt.sk/autocamping.tn), €, 10–15-min walk from the railway station, open May–mid-Sept.

ŽILINA

Although the town isn't much to write home about, the rail route to Žilina alone justifies the journey. And Žilina has something of the Slovak soul, for the town is intimately associated with the development of Slovak national consciousness in the late 19th century. A pilgrimage here is mandatory for every Slovak schoolchild. Budatín chateau (incorporating the regional museum) is almost on the doorstep; Orava Castle is further afield. The onward train journey to both Banská Štiavnica and Kremnica, former mining towns with exquisite architecture, is spectacular. Žilina is an ideal base for exploring the Malá Fatra mountain ranges and the **Kysuce Nature Reserve**. As a well-known Slovak holiday area, the region is criss-crossed with well-marked paths of varying lengths and difficulty. The **Vrátna dolina valley** is one of the most renowned beauty spots – take the chairlift to Snilovské Sedlo for stunning views. Stop-offs on the way to Poprad-Tatry include **Liptovský Mikuláš**, for its beautiful lake. Part of the Slovak karst system, **Demänovská Dolina** boasts some astonishing underground stalactite and stalagmite caves (hourly bus from Liptovský Mikuláš).

🚃 Northeast of the centre, on Národná ulica.

ℹ️ **Tourist Office: Tourist Information Centre**, Republiky 1, ☎(041) 723 31 86 (www.tikzilina.sk). **Selinan CK Travel Agency**, ☎(041) 562 0789 (www.zilina.sk).

Czech Republic and Slovakia

📷 **Camping** is one possibility in Žilina, if you have your own tent – try the Tourist Office for details. Or, you can stay cheaply at **Penzión Majovey**, Jána Milca 3, ☎ (041) 562 4152 (www.slovanet/majovey), €€.

POPRAD-TATRY

Poprad, sandwiched between the High and Low Tatra Mountains, is undistinguished, but **Spišská Sobota** (3 km east of the station) has gorgeous carvings.

🚊 I km north of the town centre. Catch the frequent TEZ train for the mountains – it departs from the upper north-facing station concourse at regular intervals (ETT table 1182).

ℹ️ Tourist Office: **City Information Centre**, Štefánikova 72, ☎ (052) 16186. **Popradská informačná agentúra**, Námestie. sv. Egídia 2950/114, ☎ (052) 772 1700 (www.poprad.sk).

📷 **Tatranská informačná kancelária**, ☎ (052) 442 3440, can arrange accommodation, and the **Popradská informačná agentúra**, has information about chalets, pensions and hotel accommodation. The High Tatras are very busy in the summer and ski seasons, so book ahead.

📷 Eating out well is something of a challenge as the spas and hotels are almost dead to the world at night – try some of the larger hotel restaurants or the occasional pub.

SIDE TRIPS FROM POPRAD-TATRY   From Poprad and Štrba, the TEZ railway (ETT table 1182) climbs into the stunning alpine **High Tatra Mountains**, stopping at **Starý Smokovec**, **Štrbské Pleso** and **Tatranská Lomnica** for spas, hiking and skiing. Although the Alpine range is only 25 km long, paths of varying difficulty provide a wealth of choice for walkers and skiers.

Buses also cover the **Spiš** region – Renaissance villages among rolling hills, striped fields and tiny white churches: the town of **Levoča** and **Spišský hrad (Spiš Castle)** are unmissable UNESCO World Heritage Sites. **Stará Ľubovňa** (reached by train) is home to a fascinating regional **open-air museum**. The bus from here takes you to the **Pieniny National Park** and the chance to float down the River Dunajec at Červený kláštor, also the site of a 14th-century monastery (open Tues–Sun) and a camping and caravan site on the river banks.

WHERE NEXT FROM POPRAD-TATRY?

It's feasible to continue into Poland by heading on east to **Plaveč** then north to **Kraków**, joining the **Poznań–Zakopane** route (p573); (ETT tables 1182 and 1078). However, this connection only works in high summer, so you may have to reach Poland by changing at **Žilina** (ETT tables 1180 and 1077). There is also an infrequent bus service between Poprad-Tatry and Zakopane.

WHERE ELSE IN SLOVAKIA AND THE CZECH REPUBLIC?

If you visit **Prague** and follow our tour from Prague via **Bratislava** to the **Slovakian Tatra Mountains**, you'll catch the flavour of urban and rural landscapes in both countries. Yet there is much more besides. If you have extra time, there are two easy excursions, one in each country, that are both rewarding.

THE SPA TOWNS OF BOHEMIA

In the northwest corner of the Czech Republic, close to the German border, are three towns that are truly outstanding examples of **European spa culture**. All have their origins in the Austro-Hungarian spa tradition, and all were once favoured holiday destinations for Europe's royalty. The three are, from the smallest to the largest, and with their old German-language names in brackets: **Františkovy Lázně** (Franzensbad), **Mariánské Lázně** (Marienbad) and **Karlovy Vary** (Karlsbad). Each has its own distinctive charm. Františkovy Lázně is a tiny picture-perfect community with the air of an outdoor sanatorium and a nice line in erotic sculptures. Fertility treatments are one of the town's medical specialisations.

Mariánské Lázně is three times as big and has a feast of *belle époque* decadence, a lovely Russian Orthodox church and some beautiful parks and woodland. In Karlovy Vary, very much larger than the other two, the real world intrudes on the pursuit of health and recuperation, and there's a bustle about the town, especially during the annual film festival (in July each year).

All three spa towns offer good value hotels, more geared to long-stay clients nursing their ailments than passing trade, but if space is available casual guests are accepted. Plan for leisurely days taking the waters, going for healthy walks, and enjoy afternoon tea and waltzes aplenty! If you really want to catch the spa atmosphere, head for one of the two smaller towns.

If you're uncertain whether you can cope with such unalloyed commitment to healthy living, **Karlovy Vary** makes for a good compromise. At least there you can sup on something stronger than the spa waters. Try the **Jan Becher Museum** (T G Masaryka 57; open daily 0900–1700), which provides an interesting history of the locally produced Becherovka spirit, as well as ample opportunity to sample the product itself. And once you've tired of tea dances, make for the **Rotes Berlin bar** (Jaltská 7, ☎353 233 792, www.rotesberlin.cz) where local DJs entertain a young crowd every evening with a varied but reliable mix of indie, techno and house.

For direct trains from Prague to Františkovy Lázně (4 hrs) via Mariánské Lázně (ML) (3 hrs 15 mins) see ETT table 1120. From ML, a very beautiful minor railway runs through the Bohemian hills to Karlovy Vary, taking around 80 mins for the journey (see ETT table 1118). There are also direct trains from Prague to Karlovy Vary (3 hrs 20 mins, see ETT table 1110). To escape from this trio of spa towns, FL also has a useful **direct train north into Germany** every two hours, over yet another exceptionally scenic route (ETT table 1122). It runs to Zwickau, from where there are good onward connections to Dresden and Berlin.

THE HILL COUNTRY OF NORTHEAST SLOVAKIA

The Tatra Mountains are hard to leave, but if you have a day or two free, head yet further east for a glimpse of a real outpost of Europe. A network of small railway lines (not all shown in the ETT) penetrate the deep valleys of **Carpatho-Ruthenia**, home to one of Europe's hidden minorities, the **Rusyns** or Ruthenes. **Bardejov** (ETT table 1196) is a pristine medieval town that looks as though it was built last week. It is a fine example of a township founded by migrants from Germany who settled through this mountainous region in the 13th century.

Still further east, you'll start running across the wooden churches and folk architecture of the Rusyns, particularly around **Humenné** (ETT table 1194). The town itself isn't remarkable, but there is an excellent outdoor museum (ask for the skanzen, closed Mon) with fine examples of Rusyn-style cottages and a Uniate church, an unusual variant of Christianity common in Rusyn areas. It bridges the gap between Roman Catholicism and Orthodox Christianity.

From Humenné, you can head north (still ETT 1194) to **Medzilaborce**, a place in the very back of beyond that has a memorably bizarre museum devoted to the life and work of Andy Warhol (closes early afternoon and always closed Mon). From here it is possible on Fri, Sat and Sun, only from late June to late August, to continue north by twice daily train (ETT table 1079) over the Carpathian Mountains into southeast Poland.

Southeast Europe

Of the countries covered in this section, **Greece**, **Turkey** and **Hungary** are the most accessible to travellers, more cosmopolitan and with a better tourism infrastructure, yet less spontaneously welcoming. **Bulgaria** and **Romania** present more difficulties, but also more opportunities to really get to know the people. Hungary's traditions and architecture are central European, with many reminders of the heady days of the Austro-Hungarian Empire. The others share a history of being subject states of the Ottoman Empire (Turkey), their architectural and cultural high points coming with liberation, and their most revered buildings, monasteries and towns being those that maintained the national spirit during the long centuries of subjugation.

Nowadays, the young in all these countries have a social life to rival that of their counterparts in western Europe. Cafés are lively and stimulating meeting places. Head for **Hungary** for its elegant capital and fine towns; to **Greece** for its vibrant light and relaxing beach life, with archaeological treasures always within reach; to **Romania** for a country with rural beauty but dilapidated cities and a capital trying to recapture its role as the Paris of the East; to **Bulgaria** for magnificent scenery and wildlife, inexpensive skiing, quality wine at bargain prices, some fine cities and great beaches; and to **Istanbul**, at the very edge of Europe, for a taste of Asia beyond, as well as to see countless historical sites, buildings and monuments, even if most aren't well preserved.

BULGARIA

This little-known country on the eastern side of the Balkan Peninsula has beautiful mountain scenery, rich in wild flowers and birds. There are cities like **Plovdiv** and **Veliko Tarnovo** (both accessible by train), with picturesque old quarters built during the 19th-century National Revival. Monasteries like Rila, UNESCO's World Heritage Site, and Bachkovo have stunning frescos and impressive buildings. They can be reached by bus from **Sofia** and **Plovdiv** respectively. The large resorts on the Black Sea coast are now very popular and attract increasing numbers of tourists annually. There are some pretty villages as well as the more cosmopolitan charms of Varna, the largest port. Folk traditions are still part of rural life, and hospitality to visitors is warm. Bulgaria became a member of the EU in 2007.

ESSENTIALS (BULGARIA)

Population 7.9m **Capital** Sofia (Sofiya) **Time Zone** Winter GMT+2, summer GMT+3.

CLIMATE
Hot summers; wet spring and autumn; snow in winter (skiing popular).

CURRENCY
Leva (Lv.); 1 Lev = 100 stotinki (st), obtainable only in Bulgaria; re-exchanged for hard currency before leaving. Credit cards increasingly accepted. £1 = 2.25Lv.; $1 = 1.36Lv.; €1 = 1.96Lv.

EMBASSIES
Aus: ulitsa Trakiya 37, ☎ (02) 946 1334. **Ire**: ulitsa Bacho Kiro 26–28, ☎ (02) 985 3425. **SA**: ulitsa Bacho Kiro 26, ☎ (02) 981 6682. **UK**: ulitsa Moskovska 9, ☎ (02) 933 9222. **USA**: ulitsa Kozyak 16, ☎ (02) 937 5100. Citizens of Canada and New Zealand: use UK Embassy.

LANGUAGE
Bulgarian (Cyrillic alphabet); English, German, Russian and French in tourist areas. Nodding the head indicates 'no' (ne): shaking it means 'yes' (da).

OPENING HOURS
Banks: Mon–Fri 0900–1700. Some exchange offices open longer hours and weekends. **Shops**: Mon–Fri 0800–2000, closed 1200–1400 outside major towns, Sat open 1000–1800. **Museums**: vary widely, but often 0800–1200, 1400–1830. Many close Mon or Tues.

POST OFFICES
Stamps (marki) sold only at post offices (poshta), usually open Mon–Sat 0800–1800. Some close 1200–1400. Caution: postal services are not very reliable.

PUBLIC HOLIDAYS
1 Jan; 3 Mar; Orthodox Easter Sunday and Monday, dates variable; 1, 6, 24 May; 6, 22 Sept; 1 Nov; 25, 26 Dec.

PUBLIC TRANSPORT
Buses (good network) slightly more expensive than trains; both very cheap for hard currency travellers. Sofia: buses and trams use same ticket but different tickets for the subway; punch it at machines inside, get new ticket if you change. Daily/weekly cards available.

RAIL PASSES
IR, Balkan Flexipass valid (see pp27–34). Domestic rail fares are cheap.

RAIL TRAVEL
Website: www.bdz.bg. Bulgarian State Railways (BDŽ) run express, fast and slow trains. Quickest on electrified lines between major cities. Often crowded; reservations recommended (obligatory for express). Most medium- and long-distance trains have 1st and 2nd class, plus limited buffet service. Overnight trains between Sofia and Black Sea resorts have 1st- and 2nd-class sleeping cars and 2nd-class couchettes. One platform may serve two tracks, platforms and tracks both numbered. Signs at stations are mostly in Cyrillic.

TELEPHONES
Use central telephone offices in major towns for long-distance calls. Dial in: ☎ +359 and omit the initial 0 of the area code. Outgoing: ☎ 00 + country code. Main emergency number: ☎ 112. Police: ☎ 166. Fire: ☎ 160. Ambulance: ☎ 150.

TIPPING
Waiters and taxi drivers expect a tip of about 10%.

TOURIST INFORMATION
Website: www.bulgariatravel.org. Main Tourist Office: 1 Sveta Nedelya Sq., Sofia 1000, ☎ (02) 933 5826, closed Sat and Sun.

VISAS
Not required by citizens of the EU, Australia, Canada, New Zealand or the USA. Citizens of South Africa must obtain visas before travelling.

Southeast Europe

ACCOMMODATION

In **Sofia** (particularly at the airport, railway station and in the city centre) various agencies offer accommodation booking and information. Small private hotels and B&B-type accommodation are increasingly available and good value. The main hotels also have information desks, often useful for maps and a monthly free city information guide in English. Youth travel and accommodation: www.usitcolours.bg.

FOOD AND DRINK

Bulgaria produces a wide variety of excellent fruits and vegetables. Soups are popular all the year round, with yoghurt-based cold ones on offer in summer. Meat is generally pork or lamb, either cooked slowly with vegetables or grilled. Desserts include seasonal fruit, ice cream, gateaux and sweet pastries. Vegetarians can go for the varied and generally excellent salads, and dishes such as stuffed peppers or aubergine dishes like *kyopolou*.

Tea is often herbal or Chinese and served without milk. Coffee is normally espresso. Bottled fruit juices are readily available, as are imported soft drinks. Local beers are lager-style and good value. **Grozdova**, **slivova** and **mastika** are strong, served in large measures, traditionally with cold starters. Tap water is safe and there are many local mineral waters. Bulgarian wine is often of high quality, and very good value.

GREECE

Inexpensive, friendly and beautiful, with a wonderful array of archaeological sites, Greece offers a seductive mix of culture and relaxation, with plenty of opportunity to linger in tavernas or laze on a beach as well as visiting ancient ruins. Wild flowers make a colourful spectacle in spring – an ideal time for travelling – while in summer it's often too hot to do more than flop in the shade, and by autumn the landscape is parched but still excellent for sightseeing.

Most visitors will probably at least pass through **Athens**, and spare more than a fleeting glance at the famous classical remains. From Athens' port, Piraeus, you can escape the noise and pollution of the capital by taking a ferry to the islands of the Aegean Sea. Close by are the **Saronic Gulf Islands**, farther east are the **Cyclades**, while farther east still, towards Turkey, lie the **Dodecanese**. Within these archipelagos the islands are strongly contrasting, some ruggedly mountainous such as **Náxos**, **Santorini** and **Kárpathos**, some good for nightlife and beaches such as **Íos** and **Mykonos**, others peaceful and uncrowded such as **Iraklia**. Further afield are the major resorts of **Corfu** (one of the Ionian Islands, and therefore reached by ferry from Patras rather than Piraeus), **Rhodes** and **Crete** (the most southerly and largest of all the islands, with superb ancient remains and astonishing scenery). The islands are covered in great detail in *Greek Island Hopping* by Frewin Poffley (Thomas Cook Publishing).

Essentials (Greece)

Population 10.7m **Capital** Athens (Athína) **Time Zone** Winter GMT+2, summer GMT+3.

Climate	Uncomfortably hot in June–Aug; often better to travel in spring or autumn.
Currency	Euro (€). 1 Euro = 100 cents = £0.89 = $1.46.
Embassies and Consulates in Athens	**Aus**: Level 6, Thon Building, Cnr Kifisias and Alexandras Ave, Ambelokipi, ☎ 210 870 4000. **Can**: Ioannou Gennadiou 4, ☎ 210 727 3400. **Ire**: 7 Vas. Konstantinou Ave, ☎ 210 723 2771/2. **SA**: 60 Kifissias Ave, Marousi, ☎ 210 610 6645/6. **UK**: Ploutarchou 1, ☎ 210 727 2600. **USA**: Vassilissis Sofias Blvd 91, ☎ 210 721 2951.
Language	**Greek**; English widely spoken in Athens and tourist areas (some German, French or Italian), less so in remote mainland areas.
Opening Hours	**Banks**: (usually) Mon–Thur 0800–1400, Fri 0830–1330, longer hours in peak holiday season. **Shops**: vary; in summer most close midday and reopen in the evening (Tue, Thur, Fri) 1700–2000. **Sites and museums**: mostly 0830–1500; Athens sites and other major archaeological sites open until 1900 or open until sunset in summer.
Post Offices	Normally Mon–Fri 0800–1300, Sat 0800–1200; money exchange, traveller's cheques, Eurocheques. Stamps sold from vending machines outside post offices, street kiosks.
Public Holidays	1, 6 Jan; Shrove Mon; 25 Mar; Easter; 1 May; Whit Mon; 15 Aug; 28 Oct; 25, 26 Dec. Everything closes for Easter; Greeks use the Orthodox calendar and dates may differ from Western Easter.
Public Transport	KTEL buses (www.ktel.org): fast, punctual, fairly comfortable long-distance services; well-organised stations in most towns (tickets available from bus terminals). Islands connected by ferries and hydrofoils; see Thomas Cook Publishing guide *Greek Island Hopping*. City transport: bus or (in Athens) trolleybus, Metro and electric rail; services are crowded. Outside Athens, taxis are plentiful and good value.
Rail Passes	IR, EP, Balkan Flexipass valid (see pp27–34). A pass for Greece is available as part of the Eurail range for those resident outside Europe; 1st class adult or 1st class youth passes are valid for 3–10 days within 1 month. See www.eurail.com. A multiple-journey card may still be available for 10, 20 or 30 days in 2nd class, but this is unconfirmed.
Rail Travel	Website: www.ose.gr. Trains run by Hellenic Railways (Organismós Sidiródromon tis Éllados; OSE), ☎ 1110 (within Greece), limited rail network, especially north of Athens. Reservations essential on most express trains. IC trains (supplement payable) are fast and fairly punctual, higher supplement applies on ICityE trains. Stations: often no left luggage or English-speaking staff, but many have bars.
Telephones	Dial in: ☎ +30. Outgoing: ☎ 00. You must now include the area code (such as 210 for Athens) even if you're phoning from inside that area. General emergency/ police/operator: ☎ 100. Fire: ☎ 199. Ambulance: ☎ 166. Tourist police (24 hrs; English): ☎ 171.
Tipping	Not necessary for restaurants or taxis.
Tourist Information	Website: www.gnto.gr. **Greek National Tourism Organisation**; see p616.
Visas	Not needed for EU citizens; or for citizens of the USA, Canada, Australia and New Zealand. Citizens of South Africa must obtain visas before travelling.

Southeast Europe

A particularly idyllic area for exploring is the Peloponnese peninsula, with the seaside town of Nafplion and some impressive classical sites and scenic treats. The rail network is sparse, and many services are erratic, but buses are generally efficient and plentiful.

ACCOMMODATION

Greece is over-supplied with accommodation, from de luxe hotels to pensions, village rooms and self-catering apartments, plus a limited number of youth hostels. You should have no problem finding a bed in **Athens**, **Patras** or **Thessaloniki (Salonika)** even in high summer (though the very cheapest Athens dorms and pensions are often very crowded in July and Aug).

Rooms are hardest to find over the Greek Easter period (note this date is different from Easter elsewhere, as it's based on the Orthodox calendar), so try to book ahead. Outside the Easter and July–Sept peaks, accommodation costs up to 30% less. You should also get a 10% discount if staying three or more nights. Cheaper places will keep your passport overnight unless you pay in advance.

Youth hostels aren't especially cheap and are being phased out by the government. **Campsites** at major sights (including **Delphi**, **Mistra** and **Olympia**) can be good value, with laundries, hot showers, cafés and even swimming pools. You can get a list of sites from the National Tourist Office, the Greek National Tourism Organisation (see p616), or visit www.panhellenic-camping-union.gr.

FOOD AND DRINK

Greeks rarely eat breakfast (many start the day with coffee and a cigarette), but cafés in tourist areas advertise 'English breakfast'. Traditional Greek meals are unstructured, with lots of dishes brought at once or in no particular order. Lunch is any time between 1200 and 1500, after which most restaurants close until around 1930. Greeks dine late, and you will find plenty of restaurants open until well after midnight.

The best Greek food is fresh, seasonal and simply prepared. Seafood dishes are usually the most expensive. Pork, chicken and squid are relatively cheap, and traditional salad – olives, tomatoes, cucumber, onions, peppers and feta cheese drowned in oil, served with bread – is a meal in itself (though Greeks eat it as a side dish). The majority of restaurants in touristy areas have a bilingual Greek and English menu. In smaller places, visit the kitchen to choose what you want.

Coffee is easier to find than tea; iced coffee (**frappé**), made from Nescafé and drunk with a straw, is now more popular than the tiny, strong cups of old-fashioned Greek coffee. Aniseed-flavoured **ouzo** is a favourite aperitif. **Retsina** (resinated wine) is an acquired taste. Greek brandy, **Metaxa**, is on the sweet side. Draught lager is not widely available and is neither as good nor as cheap as bottled beer: Amstel, Heineken and Mythos, brewed in Greece and sold in half-litre bottles. Tap water is safe but heavily chlorinated. Bottled mineral water is available in all the main towns.

HUNGARY

The **Great Plain**, Alföld, extends across more than half this landlocked country, with the most appreciable hills rising in the far north. Hungary's most scenic moments occur along **Lake Balaton** (much developed with resorts, one of the most pleasant being **Keszthely**) and the **Danube Bend** (or Dunakanyar), north of Budapest, with a trio of fine towns – **Szentendre** (with its ceramics museum), **Visegrád** (with its ruined palace) and **Esztergom** (dominated by a huge basilica). **Budapest** is the obvious highlight, exuding the grace of an old central European city, memorably placed on the Danube.

ACCOMMODATION

There is a wide range of accommodation, with some superb **hotels** of international standing in the capital. Some castles are being turned into hotels of varying standards. For the medium to lower price bracket, **private rooms** are very good value, as is the small pension. Steer clear of the old Soviet-style tourist hotels and youth hostels as they are very basic with limited facilities. **Spas** offer good weekend packages. **Campsites** are, on the whole, very good and can be found near the main resorts. Many have cabins to rent, but contact the authorities first in order to book. Camping rough is not permitted and could net a hefty fine. Information on accommodation addresses, phone numbers and services: **Tourinform:** ☎(36) (1) 438 8080 (www.hungary.com). HI youth hostels website: www.miszsz.hu.

FOOD AND DRINK

Cuisine has been much influenced by Austria, Germany and Turkey. Portions are generous and most restaurants offer a cheap fixed-price menu. Lunch is the main meal of the day, and a bowl of *gulyás* (goulash) laced with potatoes and spiced with paprika is a 'must'. Try smoked sausages, soups (sour cherry soup is superb) and paprika noodles or pike-perch. Dinner is early and you should aim to begin eating well before 2100. In order to avoid the pitfalls of ordering in another language, try eating in an **Önkiszolgáló** or **ételbár** (inexpensive self-service snack bars). **Csárda** are folk restaurants usually with traditional music, but menus can be limited and slightly more expensive. Still in the moderate range are the **Vendéglő**, where home cooking often features. **Étterem** are larger restaurants with a more varied menu. Leave a tip, generally equivalent to 10% of the total. Hungary has some very decent wines, such as **Tokaji** and **Egri Bikavér** (Bull's Blood), while **pálinka** is a fiery schnapps.

ESSENTIALS [HUNGARY]

Population 10.8m **Capital** Budapest **Time Zone** Winter GMT+1, summer GMT+2.

CLIMATE   Continental, with bitterly cold winters and hot summers (May–Aug); spring and early autumn can be pleasant times to visit. Wettest in May, July, Oct and Nov.

CURRENCY   Forints (Ft). You can buy your currency at banks and official bureaux. Credit cards/ Eurocheques/small denomination traveller's cheques widely accepted; Euros more useful than dollars or sterling. £1 = 310Ft; $1 = 184Ft; €1 = 255Ft.

Southeast Europe

EMBASSIES AND CONSULATES IN BUDAPEST	**Aus**: Királyhágó tér 8–9, ☎457 9777. **Can**: Ganz u. 12–14, ☎392 3360. **Ire**: Szabadság tér 7–9, ☎301 4960. **NZ**: Nagymező utca 47, ☎302 2484. **SA**: Szépvölgyi út 35–37, ☎436 9500. **UK**: Harmincad u. 6, ☎266 2888. **USA**: Szabadság tér 12, ☎475 4400 and 475 4703.
LANGUAGE	**Hungarian** (Magyar). Both English and German are widely understood.
OPENING HOURS	**Banks**: commercial banks Mon–Thur 0800–1500, Fri 0800–1300. **Food shops**: Mon–Fri 0700–1900, others: 1000–1800 (Thur until 1900); shops close for lunch and half-day on Sat (1300). **Food/tourist shops, markets, malls** open Sun. **Museums**: usually Tues–Sun 1000–1800, free one day a week, closed public holidays.
POST OFFICES	Mostly 0800–1800 Mon–Fri, 0800–1200 Sat. Stamps also sold at tobacconists. Major post offices cash Eurocheques and change Western currency; all give cash for VISA Eurocard/MasterCard, VISA Electron and Maestro cards.
PUBLIC HOLIDAYS	1 Jan; 15 Mar; Easter Mon; 1 May; Whit Mon; 20 Aug; 23 Oct; 25, 26 Dec.
PUBLIC TRANSPORT	Long-distance buses (*Volánbusz*, www.volanbusz.hu); slow ferries along Danube.
RAIL PASSES	IR, EP, European East valid (see pp27–34). Tickets for 7 and 10 days are available covering the whole MÁV network. A day ticket for the Balaton area is also available. Budapest Card: 2 or 3 days' unlimited travel on public transport, free/reduced entry to sights. Website information: www.budapestinfo.hu.
RAIL TRAVEL	Website: www.mav.hu. Comprehensive rail system; most towns on the Hungarian State Railways (MÁV) network. Express services connect Budapest with major towns and Lake Balaton: IC services require reservation and supplement. InterPici (IP) trains are fast railcars connecting with IC trains (reservation also compulsory). Most EC trains require supplement but not compulsory reservation. Other trains include *gyorsvonat* (fast trains) and *sebesvonat* (semi-fast). Local trains (*személyvonat*) are very slow. Book sleepers well in advance. (Traineurope can book for you, see p30.)
TELEPHONES	Phonecards on sale at newsstands, tobacconists, post offices, supermarkets. Payphones take 10, 20, 50 and 100 forint coins. Dial in: ☎+36. Outgoing: ☎00. Domestic long distance calls: ☎06. Directory Enquiries: ☎198. International Directory Enquiries: ☎199. Police: ☎107. Fire: ☎105. Ambulance: ☎104.
TIPPING	Round up by 5–15% for restaurants and taxis. People do not generally leave coins on the table; instead the usual practice is to make it clear that you are rounding up the sum. Service is included in some upmarket Budapest restaurants.
TOURIST INFORMATION	Websites: www.hungary.com; www.gotohungary.com; www.tourinform.hu. **Hungarian National Tourist Office**, Bartók Béla út 105–113, H-1115 Budapest, ☎(1) 488 8700. **Tourinform** branches throughout Hungary.
TYPICAL COSTS	Hostel accommodation 2500–3500Ft for a dormitory bed, 6000–8000Ft for a bed in a twin room; cheaper hotels generally 15,000–20,000Ft for a double room. You can eat well on tourist menus for 1200–1500Ft; coffee in café 250–350Ft, for a cappuccino 300–400Ft; 0.5 litre beer in a bar 350–500Ft (draught beer is cheapest). Internet cafés charge 200–500Ft per hour. Entry to the Széchenyi Baths 3000Ft.
VISAS	Not required by citizens of the EU, Australia, Canada, New Zealand or the USA. Citizens of South Africa must obtain visas before travelling.

ROMANIA

The lofty **Carpathian Mountains** snake through the heart of the country, rising to over 2500 m in the region of **Transylvania**, the terrain of the original Count Dracula. Much of the countryside is rugged and remote, and travel can be a real adventure, though be warned that standards for tourism are not on a par with those of Western countries. The brutal dictator Ceauçescu, before his execution in 1989, destroyed many villages and rehoused large communities in hastily erected apartment blocks; **Bucharest** has many legacies of his era and is not the most appealing of European capitals, and many other towns suffered a similar fate. If you really want to get off the beaten track by rail, venture into **Maramures** in the country's northwestern corner, or go to the **Republic of Moldova**, or explore the churches and monasteries of **Bucovina** in the northeast. Prices are low and you'll still find places where tourists are rare, and the reception from locals is almost universally warm despite the obvious poverty of the inhabitants. Romania became a member of the EU in 2007.

ACCOMMODATION

Hotels vary a great deal in quality, even within each category (one to five stars). At the bottom end they can be basic and inexpensive, while some match the highest international standards and prices. **Private rooms** may be booked at Tourist Offices in some towns, and in a few tourist areas touts will meet trains at the station to offer their rooms – which may be centrally located in attractive old houses, or far out in grim suburban tower blocks, so make sure you know what you're agreeing to. **Campsites** should generally be avoided, as standards of cleanliness and hygiene can be appalling. Book in advance for hotels on the **Black Sea coast** in summer and in **mountain ski resorts** at winter weekends. It's well worth using an **accommodation agency** to book – try www.captaingo.ro for hotels all over Romania, while the website of Romania's rural tourism agency, **Antrec** (www.antrec.ro) is a great resource for pensions and homestays in the countryside. There are a few decent hostels: see www.hostelworld.com/romania.

FOOD AND DRINK

There are many restaurants in the main cities, offering a variety of foods, in principle. In practice you often end up with pork, potato and vegetables. Chicken, beef, veal and lamb are also available, and fish can be delicious, especially Danube carp (termed, unfortunately, *crap*). The traditional accompaniment is *mămăligă*, a polenta-like purée of maize flour. Unsmoked frankfurters (*pariser*) and light liver sausages (*cremwurst*) are tasty. Other local specialities are *sarmale*, stuffed cabbage leaves (sometimes without meat), *ciorba*, a sour soup, and *mititei*, herby meatballs grilled outdoors in summer. There's plenty of takeaway stalls and pizzerias.

Cafés serve excellent cakes (*prăjitură*), soft drinks, beer and coffee; *turceasca* is Turkish-style ground coffee, while *Ness* is instant coffee. Wines are superb and very cheap. Try the plum brandy known as *ţuică* (pronounced 'tswica'), or its double-distilled version *palinca*. Tap water is safe to drink.

ESSENTIALS (ROMANIA)

Population 21.7m **Capital** Bucharest (Bucureşti) **Time Zone** Winter GMT+2, summer GMT+3.

CLIMATE

Hot inland in summer, coast cooled by breezes; milder in winter, snow inland, especially in the mountains.

CURRENCY

New Leu (plural: Lei) I new leu = 100 bani. Carry pounds, dollars or, ideally, euros in small denominations: new notes are preferable. Traveller's cheques are tough and expensive to change; only ever change cash inside a bank: most exchange offices are simply not to be trusted. Credit and debit cards are accepted in most hotels, restaurants and shops, though not bars. Credit cards are not necessarily needed for car rental: most firms accept a cash deposit. Bancomats (automatic cash dispensers) are ubiquitous: even the smallest village usually has one. £1 = 4.80 Lei, $1 = 2.95 Lei; €1 = 4.25 Lei.

EMBASSIES AND CONSULATES IN BUCHAREST

Aus: See Budapest, Hungary. **Can**: Str. Tuberozelor 1–3, ☎ (021) 307 50 00. **Ire**: (Consulate): Str. Buzesti 50–52, ☎ (021) 310 21 61. **SA**: See Budapest, Hungary. **UK**: Str. Jules Michelet 24, ☎ (021) 201 73 00. **USA**: Str. Tudor Arghezi 7–9, ☎ (021) 200 33 00.

LANGUAGE

Romanian; English understood by younger people, plus some German, and Hungarian throughout Transylvania.

OPENING HOURS

Banks: Mon–Fri 0900–1700, plus Sat 0900–1300 city centre branches; private exchange counters open longer. **Shops**: usually 0800/0900–1800/2000, closed Sun; shopping malls open until 2200, including Sun. Local food shops and kiosks often 0600–late. **Museums**: usually 0900/1000–1700/1800; open weekends, almost all closed Mon (and maybe Tues).

POST OFFICES

Mail usually takes five days to reach Western Europe and up to two weeks to reach North America. Post offices in every town, open Mon–Fri, plus Sat morning.

PUBLIC HOLIDAYS

1–2 Jan; Easter Mon (Romanian Orthodox); Pentecost (50 days after Easter Sunday); I May; I Dec (National Unity Day); 25–26 Dec.

PUBLIC TRANSPORT

Buy bus/tram/Metro (*metrou*) tickets in advance from kiosks (as a rule) and cancel on entry. Taxis inexpensive; if meter not in use agree a price first and always pay in lei, not foreign currency. Trains are best for long-distance travel, although bus routes are expanding and connect important towns and cities.

RAIL PASSES

IR, ED, Balkan Flexipass valid (see pp27–34).

RAIL TRAVEL

Website: www.cfr.ro. Rail company: Compania Naţională de Căi Ferate (CFR). Network links major towns; main lines mostly electrified and quite fast, but branch lines very slow. Service fairly punctual and very inexpensive. Buy tickets in advance From Agentia de Voiaj CFR, or at the station. Wasteels has offices in Bucharest and Brasov stations. Except local trains, reserve and pay a speed supplement in advance (tickets issued abroad include supplement): cheapest are *tren de persoane* (very slow), then *accelerat* (still cheap), *rapid* and finally IC trains (prices approaching Western levels). Food usually only available on IC and some *rapids*; drinks sold on other trains. Couchettes (*cuşeta*) are inexpensive but a little grim; sleepers (*vagon de dormit*) are expensive. Note that an increasing number of services/branch lines are being taken over by private operators – tickets are not interchangeable.

TELEPHONES

Buy telephone cards from post offices and newsstands for use in public phones all over the country. Calls from hotel rooms are expensive. Dial in: ☎ +40 (omit initial 0 from area code). Outgoing: ☎ 00 + country code. Police: ☎ 112. Fire: ☎ 112. Ambulance: ☎ 112. Emergency service dispatchers speak English.

TIPPING	Small tips are appreciated for good service at restaurants, hotels and in taxis. Only tip 10% at top-notch restaurants.
TOURIST INFORMATION	Website: www.romaniatourism.com. **Romanian National Tourism Authority**, Dinicu Golescu Blvd, 010873, Bucharest 1, ☎ (021) 314 9957. Local Tourist Offices are not particularly helpful; most of the time you are better off asking at a travel agency.
TYPICAL COSTS	Hostel (HI) accommodation 50–75 Lei; cheaper hotels generally 70–100 Lei for a double room; to stay as a guest in someone's home 30–80 Lei per night (often includes two meals). You can eat well on tourist menus for around 35 Lei; fast-food outlet around 10 Lei; coffee in café around 3.50 Lei; 0.5 litre beer in a bar 3–7.50 Lei (draught beer is cheapest). Loaf of bread around 1.20 Lei; pair of jeans around 100 Lei. Internet cafés charge around 4.50 Lei per hour.
VISAS	Not required by citizens of the EU, Australia, Canada, New Zealand or the USA. Citizens of South Africa must obtain visas before travelling.

TURKEY

Turkey is where Europe meets Asia and traces of many ancient cultures, which followed this route or settled down in these lands can be seen everywhere. Most of the country is in Asia and, apart from **Istanbul**, is not covered by this book (though it is covered by Euro Domino and InterRail passes; see 'Rail Passes', p27 for more information). It's an intoxicating blend of Western and exotic influences, with much to recommend a visit: cheap prices, outstanding ancient sites, great diversity in its landscapes, and a hospitable welcome from its people. There are plenty of activities too, including water sports, mountain trekking and nightlife. For getting around, the bus network is good and inexpensive and travels around the coast: it is generally more useful than rail, though there are reasonable train services to the interior as well as Istanbul and **Izmir**. Be aware that road traffic, including the roads to the airports, often can be a mess in Istanbul, so it would be advisable to plan accordingly.

The coast of the Mediterranean and Aegean is partly developed with large resorts, but some areas are idyllically unspoilt, and there is plenty of scope for visiting historic sites nearby: good seaside towns to head for include **Marmaris** (not the busy town centre, but the surrounding numerous attractions), **Bodrum** (good for nightlife), **Antalya** (busy, but a good base) and **Dalyan** (relatively unspoiled and peaceful beach resort), **Alaçatı**, **Cunda** (a well-preserved old Greek town), **Kekova** (with an eerie ancient submerged city), **Safranbolu** (a well-preserved, peaceful old city and one of the nine World Heritage Sites in Turkey), **Kalkan** (a typical Mediterranean fishing village), while the haunting remains of **Ephesus** and **Termessos** head a long list of spectacular classical sites. Other breathtaking classical sites not to be missed are **Phaselis**, **Aphrodisias**, **Aspendos**, **Myra** (the tomb of St Nicholas (the inspiration for Santa Claus) is nearby), **Sardis** and **Nemrut** mountain (which has an artificial hill with enormous ancient statue heads and a temple built for a Roman client king).

ESSENTIALS (TURKEY)

Population 73.4m **Capital** Ankara **Time Zone** Winter GMT+2, summer GMT+3.

CLIMATE

Very hot summers, more manageable in spring or autumn. Cool Nov–Mar, colder in central and eastern regions.

CURRENCY

Turkish New Lira (TL). Credit cards widely accepted. £1 = TL2.47; $1 = TL1.50; €1 = TL2.18. These values tend to change, since a floating exchange rate is used.

CONSULATES IN ISTANBUL

Aus: 2nd Floor, Suzer Plaza, Askerocagi Caddesi No. 15, Elmadag, ☎(212) 243 1333. **Can**: Istiklal Cad. 373, Beyoğlu, ☎(212) 251 9838. **UK**: Mesrutiyet Caddesi 34, Beyoğlu, ☎(212) 334 6400. **USA**: Istinye Mahallesi, Kaplıcalar Mevkii No. 2, Istinye ☎(212) 335 9000.

LANGUAGE

Turkish, written in Latin alphabet. English and German often understood.

OPENING HOURS

Banks: 0830–1200, 1300–1700, Mon–Fri (some private banks are open at lunchtime). **Shops**: 0930–1900; until around 2400 in tourist areas. **Government offices**: 0830–1230, 1300–1700 (closed Sat and Sun). In Aegean and Mediterranean regions, many establishments stay open very late in summer. **Museums**: many close on Mon.

POST OFFICES

Post offices have PTT signs. Major offices: Airport, Beyoğlu and Sirkeci open 24 hrs all week (limited services at night). Small offices: 0830–1700 (some close 1230–1300).

PUBLIC HOLIDAYS

1 Jan; 23 Apr; 19 May; 30 Aug; 29 Oct.

PUBLIC TRANSPORT

Excellent long-distance bus system (generally quicker than rail), run by competing companies (the best are Varan and Ulusoy). Shorter rides via *dolmuş* (shared taxis) that pick up passengers like a taxi, but only along a set route and much cheaper. IDO runs the ferries. Ankara and Istanbul have a modern Metro line, Istanbul also has a light-rail and tram route.

RAIL PASSES

IR, Balkan Flexipass valid (see pp27–34).

RAIL TRAVEL

Website: www.tcdd.gov.tr. Routes are tortuous and slow, but a high-speed line now runs between Istanbul and Ankara. Operated by TCDD (Turkish State Railways). Beyond Istanbul, consult the *Thomas Cook Overseas Timetable* for Asian Turkey.

TELEPHONES

Telephone offices have Türk Telekom signs. Telephone cards (available in 30, 50, 60 and 100 units) are the best way to make calls. Dial in: ☎+90. Outgoing: ☎00+ country code. Emergency: ☎112; Police: ☎155; Fire: ☎110.

TIPPING

A 10% tip is usual in restaurants, unless service is included. Do not tip barmen directly. 10–20% is customary at hair salons. Do not tip taxi drivers.

TOURIST INFORMATION

Websites: www.tourismturkey.org, www.gototurkey.co.uk.

VISAS

Required by citizens of Australia, Canada, Ireland, Italy, Spain, UK and the USA. Obtainable at the border (fee).

Inland you get a real sense of adventure as you head into some rugged terrain, although the towns tend to be drab in appearance. **Cappadocia**, another World Heritage Site, is a surreal volcanic landscape, where rocks have been eroded into strange cones and columns, many adapted into cave dwellings. There are several underground cities, some going down to eight levels, connected by a complex network of tunnels – these cities were present when the Hittites came to Anatolia about 1800 BC and were used as a refuge by the early Christians, to escape persecution.

Single women wishing to escape harassment would do well to wear a wedding ring.

ACCOMMODATION

Turkey's accommodation spectrum is as varied and colourful as the country itself. You can hang your hat in converted Ottoman palaces (known as 'Special Licence Hotels') that aren't as expensive as you might think and almost define the word 'atmospheric', choose a usual-suspect, international McHotel that will deliver neither nice surprises nor hideous shocks, or go for a hostel. In fact, the Turkish hostel scene is particularly well developed and organised, and two great sites to check out are www.youthhostelturkey.com and www.eurohostels.co.uk. Perhaps surprisingly, the Turkish Touring and Automobile Association (TTAA) is the best organisation to consult for all-round accommodation options, and the 'Touristic Facilities' page on their website (www.turing.org.tr/eng) changes daily, to show the TTAA's current best-hotel selections.

FOOD AND DRINK

Turkish cuisine has many fans, and generally the fare is more varied than in Greece. Try vegetable stews, shish (lamb) kebabs, pizza and spicy meat dishes, or for a real blow-out the all-encompassing *meze*, with a bit of everything. Tea is the national drink, but there are good-value wines and beers, and *raki* is the highly distinctive aniseed-flavoured brandy.

EXPLORING TURKEY

Turkey is covered by InterRail (but not Eurail) passes. The railways are quite efficient, with modern trains and air-conditioning, and the network spreads across the whole country, taking in some little-visited parts of the vast interior, with its mountainous terrain and remote steppes. The network doesn't include the western and central Mediterranean areas, though these are the parts most sun-seeking tourists tend to visit, so there you have the option of local buses or car rental if you want to venture to resorts such as Marmaris or Fethiye on the gorgeous though hardly undiscovered Aegean coast between Izmir and Antalya. For tips on itineraries, see www.turkeytravelplanner.com; or www.seat61.com and click on 'Turkey'. For rail times, consult the *Thomas Cook Overseas Timetable*.

GREECE: ATHENS (ATHÍNA)

Modern Athens is a noisy, bustling, exhilarating but exhausting city of over 4 million people. Revamped for the 2004 Olympic Games, it is now less polluted and more pedestrian friendly, and with its countless trendy bars and restaurants (notably in the areas of Psirri and Gazi) offers one of the best nightlife scenes in Europe. Yet many Athenians live a laid-back, village-style life amid the concrete apartment blocks, and hardly a corner is without a tiny café or taverna. Street crime rates are remarkably low and it's a conspicuously friendly place. Its enduring appeal lies in the great sights of the ancient city where the seeds of Western democracy, philosophy, medicine and art were planted. You can visit most of the sights on foot as it is quite compact and best seen early in the morning to avoid the worst of the heat and crowds.

TOURIST INFORMATION

Greek National Tourism Organisation (GNTO), Tsoha 24, 115 21 Athens, ☎(00 30) 210 870 7000 (www.gnto.gr); sightseeing information leaflets, fact sheets, local and regional transport schedules and up-to-date opening times of sights. There are also **GNTO offices** in the city centre at Amalias 26 (near Syntagma Square) and at **Eleftherios Venizelos Airport**. The **tourist police** in Athens, ☎171, can help with lists of licensed accommodation. **International Student and Youth Travel Services**, Filellinon 4, Syntagma, ☎210 321 2084

ARRIVAL AND DEPARTURE

🚆 All trains now use **Larissa Station** (*Stathmos Larisis*), Theodorou Diligiani, ☎210 529 7777. It is about 2 km northwest of **Syntagma** (Metro: Stathmos Larisis). **International rail tickets** can be bought at Larissa Station or **OSE offices** in Athens: 1–3 Karolou St, ☎210 524 0996; 6 Sina St, ☎Call centre 1110.

⛴ The **Piraeus Port Authority** serves the Greek islands, (www.greekferries.gr) or visit a local travel agency for ferry timetables. The port itself, 8 km southwest of Athens, is served by the **Metro** (green line). If you are island hopping, Thomas Cook's guidebook *Greek Island Hopping* combines a guide to every Greek island with ferry timetable information.

✈ The new **Eleftherios Venizelos Airport** is 27 km northeast of the city centre and served by both Olympic Airways and international airlines. For international flight information, ☎(00 30) 210 353 0000. There is a rail service from the airport to Larissa Station, though a change of trains may be necessary. Metro (line 3) runs to Syntagma every 30 mins, 🚌 E95 runs to Syntagma, 🚌 94 to Ethniki Amyna Metro station and 🚌 E96 to Piraeus every 15 mins 0600–2300 and then at 30-min intervals during the night (apart from the E94). Tickets valid for 24 hrs can be used on the Metro, bus or trams. **Olympic Airlines reservations:** ☎210 966 6666.

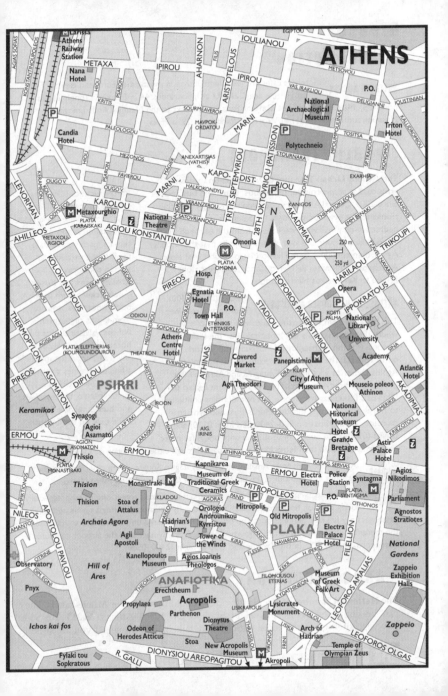

Greece

INFORMATION

INTERNET ACCESS Internet cafés are less plentiful than in most other European capitals. The most reliable are **Café4U** at Ippokratous 44 in Exarcheia (open 24 hrs non-stop), **Museum Internet Café** at Patission 46 next to the National Archaeological Museum, and **Plaka Internet World** at Pandrosou 29 in Plaka.

PUBLIC TRANSPORT

The **Athens Urban Transport Organisation**'s website, www.oasa.gr, shows **metro, trolleybus, tram** and **bus routes**. Since 2004, Central Athens has become increasingly walkable thanks to the new 'Archaeological Promenade', a 4-km long pedestrian-only walkway, which leads from the Akropoli Metro station, skirts around the foot of the Acropolis, past the Ancient Agora, then continues from Thissio Metro station, east along Andrianou to Monastiraki Metro station, and west along Ermou to Kerameikos Metro station.

METRO, TROLLEYBUSES AND BUSES
Metro (0500–2400): There are three lines. The **M1** runs from **Piraeus** north to the centre of town, where there are stations at Monastiraki (for the Plaka), Omonia (for the Archaeological Museum) and Victoria then on to **Kifissia**. The **M2** operates from Aghios Antonios to Aghios Dimitrios via Omonia, Syntagma and Akropoli (for the Plaka and the Acropolis). The **M3** runs from Egaleo to Doukissis Plakentias (with some but not all trains continuing to the airport), passing through Monastiraki and Syntagma en route. **Trolleybuses** (0500–2400, Sun from 0530) and **buses** (0500–2330, Sun from 0530): the network is far more comprehensive than the Metro. Most routes pass through either Syntagma or Omonia.

Metro tickets (Covering 1 zone, 2 zones or all lines, valid 90 mins) are available from station kiosks or self-service machines; validate them in the machines at station entrances. **Trolleybuses** and **buses** – buy **tickets** from blue booths near bus stops or from kiosks throughout Athens. Validate tickets on board. Failure to validate any transport ticket incurs a fine of 60 times the ticket cost. The **24-hr ticket** is valid for the **Metro, trolleybuses** and **buses**; validate ticket once only, on the first use.

TRAMS A tram line runs from Amalias, close to Syntagma Square, in the city centre to the seafront at Paleo Faliro, the beach suburb of Glyfada and Neo Faliro Metro.

TAXIS Yellow taxis swarm the city centre, but it can be difficult to get one to stop, especially during the rush hour, around lunch time and early afternoon. Sharing a taxi is normal; all passengers pay full fare. Some airport taxi drivers will overcharge unwary visitors so make sure the meter is switched on when your journey begins. From Syntagma to the airport it should cost approximately €25 in the daytime and €30 at night (2400–0500).

ACCOMMODATION

The **Hellenic Chamber of Hotels** provides a booking service for Athens hotels. They can be contacted before arrival at Stadiou 24, 10564 Athens, ☎213 216 9900 (www.grhotels.gr). The Tourist Office has details of 1-star hotels if you are seeking cheaper options. Athens has many private hostels for budget travellers. Standards vary widely.

Hostels cluster in the **Plaka** area, noisy but ideally located for the main sights, or between **Victoria** and the stations (where the tackiest accommodation is found). Some of the cheapest 'hostel' accommodation near the station is extremely overcrowded in high season with tight-budget travellers. However, except in the height of summer, you should have plenty of options. **Camping** is not a good idea; campsites are far from the centre, dirty and poorly serviced, and not dramatically cheaper than hostels.

Among the best budget choices in the Plaka area are the **Student and Travellers Inn**, Kidathineon 16, ☎210 324 4808 (www.studenttravellersinn.com), and **Athens Backpackers**, Makri 12, ☎210 922 4044 (www.backpackers.gr). Alternatively, try **Athenstyle Hostel**, 10 Agias Theklas, ☎210 322 5010 (www.athenstyle.com), in the lively nightlife district of Psirri.

FOOD AND DRINK

On a tight budget, eat on the move: *giros*, a kind of *souvlaki* (kebab), slices of pork with onions, tomatoes, *tzatziki* (yoghurt, cucumber and garlic) and fries wrapped in flat bread, is a meal in itself and there are lots of other street snacks to choose from. Try *spanakopita* (spinach pie) and *frappé* coffee. **Plaka** restaurants tend to be touristy, but those at Plateia Filomousou, off Kidathineon on the edge of the Plaka, are a little less so. Around Exarcheia Square (behind the National Archaeological Museum), there are many down-to-earth tavernas and *souvlaki* places, popular with local students.

HIGHLIGHTS

THE ACROPOLIS Occupied since neolithic times (5000 BC), the 'Sacred Rock' was Athens's stronghold until it was converted into a religious shrine. What you see today dates from the 5th century BC. It's on a steep hill and can only be reached on foot: smog occasionally limits the otherwise spectacular views. The Tourist Office has fact sheets on the major sites – highlights are the **Parthenon**, the **Temple of Athena Nike**, the great gateway to the Acropolis, and **Propylaea**.

Pericles built the **Parthenon** (Home of the Virgin), between 447 and 432 BC. Designed by Iktinus and Phidias, it is the finest example of Doric architecture still in existence. Detailed examination of the temple reveals irregularities: columns are closer together at the corners, where light can shine between them; columns are of differing widths and bulge one third of the way up; the roof line is curved. But it was designed to be seen from afar, giving an impression of perfect symmetry – one of the finest optical illusions ever devised. Most of the friezes (known as the **Elgin Marbles**) that adorned the Parthenon's exterior are in London's British Museum. The **New Acropolis Museum** (Makrigianni 2–4; ☎210 924 1043; www.newacropolismuseum.gr), next to the Akropoli Metro station, is an ultra-modern all-glass building. It displays ancient sculptures from the Acropolis and affords impressive views up to the hilltop site.

The **Erechtheum**, northwest of the Parthenon, is most notable for its six caryatids – graceful sculptures of women. Due to the effects of air pollution, the originals have been removed and replaced by replicas. Four of the originals are on display in the **Acropolis Museum**, and will be transferred to the New Acropolis Museum. The **Temple of Athena Nike** (Victory), with its eight small columns, stands on the southwest corner of the Acropolis. Built around 420 BC, during a pause in the Peloponnesian War, the temple was once the only place looking out to sea over the defensive walls. It is considered one of the finest Ionic buildings left in Greece.

The bulky **Propylaea**, the great gateway to the Acropolis, takes up most of the western end of the hill and welcomes thousands of visitors. Arrive early for uninterrupted photo opportunities. There's a fantastic view of the Acropolis and all of Attica from the **Monument of Filopapou**, located on the pine-covered slopes of Filopapou Hill, where Athenians traditionally gather to fly kites on the first day of Lent.

BEYOND THE ACROPOLIS Most of the city suburbs are anonymous concrete swathes distinguished only by dark green awnings, but close to the Acropolis you can pick out many other ancient ruins. Just below the Acropolis hill, on the south side, are two ancient theatres. Now scant ruins, the **Theatre of Dionysius**, built in the 4th century BC, is the earliest such structure in the Western world. The **Roman Odeon of Herodes Atticus** has been reconstructed and hosts impressive, open-air performances at the annual Athens Festival (June–Sept).

The remains of the **Temple of Olympian Zeus** are also clearly visible east of the Acropolis. There are only 16 surviving columns (of the original 104), but you can still absorb the grandeur of what was the largest temple in Greece. Next to it is **Hadrian's Arch**, constructed by the enthusiastic Roman emperor-builder to mark where the ancient Greek city ended and his new city began.

Athens' top venue for contemporary culture is **Technopolis** at 100 Pireos in Gazi. Based in the old city gasworks, this vast arts complex hosts art and photography exhibitions, concerts and festivals.

MUSEUMS AND CHURCHES Many of Athens' museums were modernised for the 2004 Olympic Games. For an incomparable collection of relics from Athens and many other Greek sites, head to the **National Archaeological Museum**, 44 Patission: allow a full day. Exhibits range through Minoan frescos, Mycenaean gold, a collection of over 300,000 sculptures, and much more.

Plenty of other museums offer insights into ancient and modern Greek life. These include the **Museum of Cycladic and Ancient Greek Art**, 4 Neofitou Douka (www.cycladic.gr); the **Benaki Museum**, Koumpari and Vasilissis Sofias; and the **Byzantine and Christian Museum**, Vasilissis Sofias 22, which houses icons from this later glory of Greek culture.

Cities: Athens (Athína)

The website http://odysseus.culture.gr has information on state-run museums in Greece. From **Lycabettus Hill**, Athens' highest at 278 m, the view surpasses even that from the Acropolis. There's a whitewashed church and an expensive café-restaurant at the summit. Take the **funicular railway** up and the path down for the best round trip.

SHOPPING

For jewellery, ceramics, leather goods and fashion with a Greek slant – lots of linen and cotton in bright colours – try **Pandrossou Street**, between Monastiraki and Mitropoleos. For antiques, bric-a-brac and vintage clothing, the flea market on Ifestou, on the opposite side of Monastiraki, is a better bet. Streets such as Adrianou and Pandrossou in the **Plaka** quarter have plenty of tourist-oriented shops and stalls, with clothes, leather, pottery and marble on offer.

NIGHT-TIME AND EVENTS

Plaka is where most of the nightlife happens. Most **cinemas** show the latest English-language movies with the original soundtrack; see the English-language weekly *Athens News* for listings. There's traditional music and dance at the **Dora Stratou Garden Theatre**, ☎210 921 4650 (www.grdance.org). For clubs and bars, head for the buzzing night-time districts of Psirri and Gazi, popular with young Athenians. During the **Athens Festival** (June–Sept), **ancient Greek drama**, **classical music** and **ballet** are staged in the Odeon of Herodes Atticus, Megazon, and Lycabettus Hill Theatre. For information, ☎210 928 2900 (www.greekfestival.gr). Each July, the three-day **Rockwave Festival** (www.rockwavefestival.gr) is held at the Terra Vibe stadium, north of Athens city centre.

WHERE NEXT FROM ATHENS?

*Athens is well placed for beginning a trip to the **Kiklades** (Cyclades) archipelago and other islands. For full descriptions consult **Greek Island Hopping** by Frewin Poffley, published annually by Thomas Cook.*

*The other main area to head for is the **Peloponnese** (southwest of Athens; ETT tables 1440, 1450, 1452 and 1455), a largely unspoilt peninsula ringed by railways, and with limestone peaks, sandy bays and a stunning heritage of ancient and medieval sites. **Korinthos** (Corinth) is the first place across the gorge-like Corinthian Canal; Old Corinth (7 km away) features the columns of the 6th-century BC **Temple of Apollo** – a huge central forum flanked by the odd row of crumbling ancient shop buildings, plus the Fountain of Peirene – and the fortress of Akrokorinth on a crag high above the old city. From Athens, excursion buses visit **Epidavros** (Epidauros), site of the most famous of all ancient Greek amphitheatres – its acoustics as perfect as ever. **Mycenae** (Mikines) is the other must-see, the 3000-year-old royal residence of the kingdom of Agamemnon.*

HUNGARY: BUDAPEST

Budapest always was the most westernised of the Warsaw Pact capitals, and with the fall of the Iron Curtain it rapidly demolished many of its communist monuments (though the Liberation Monument survives and others have been assembled in a Statue Park) and embraced capitalism. It's a place to indulge yourself in spas, Hungarian cuisine and thriving cultural life. The grey-green Danube splits the city into **Buda**, on the west bank, and **Pest** on the east. Buda is the photogenic, hilly old town, with its pastel-coloured baroque residences, gas-lit cobblestone streets and hilltop palace, while Pest is the thriving, mostly 19th-century commercial centre, with the imposing riverside State Parliament building, its wide boulevards and **Vörösmarty tér**, the busy main square. Between Buda and Pest, Margaret Bridge gives access to **Margaret Island** (**Margit-sziget**), a green oasis and venue for alfresco opera and drama in summer.

ARRIVAL AND DEPARTURE

[RAIL] There are three major stations: **Nyugati pályaudvar** (Western Station), designed in 1877 by the Eiffel firm from Paris (Tourist Office; accommodation; exchange; left luggage); **Keleti pályaudvar** (Eastern Station; accommodation; exchange; K&H Bank Mon–Sat; left luggage 24 hrs); and **Déli pályaudvar** (Southern Station; post office; accommodation; exchange; left luggage). All three are fairly central, close to hotels and on the Metro: Keleti and Déli on line 2, Nyugati on line 3, trams 4 and 6. Enquiries and bookings: ☎+36 (1) 371 9449 (international) or ☎06 (40) 49 49 49 (domestic); www.mav-start.hu. Rail tickets can also be bought from **Wasteels**, at Platform 9 in Keleti station (Mon–Fri 0800–2000, Sat 0800–1800; www.wasteels.hu) or at **Vista Travel Center**, Andrássy út 1. (Mon–Fri 0930–1800, Sat 1000–1430; ☎(1) 429 9999), and from **MÁV** personal customer service desks at the main stations (Keleti Station: 0400–2330, Déli Station: 0600–2000, Nyugati Station: Mon–Fri business hours).

✈ **Ferihegy Airport** ☎(1) 296 9696, flight information ☎(1) 296 7000 (www.bud.hu), 16 km east from the centre, has two terminals. There's a rail service 2–3 times an hour from the airport station, near Terminal 1, to Budapest Nyugati station, taking 25 mins, with shuttle buses to Terminal 2. Otherwise there is 🚌 200E, which connects passengers from both terminals (also 🚌 93 from Terminal 1 only) with Kőbánya-Kispest, the terminus of the Metro line 3 (pre-purchased ticket is slightly cheaper than a ticket from the bus driver). In addition there's an airport minibus service taking visitors directly to their destination, ☎(1) 296 8555. Some hotels have collection services, plus taxis are available.

INFORMATION

INTERNET ACCESS   For the fastest public internet access in Budapest, the central **Private Link Hungary**, József körút 52, ☎334 2057, offers discounts for IYH members and students (24 hrs). One of the few actual internet cafés is **Kávészünet**, Garibaldi u. 5, ☎06 30 670 6415, with good music, cakes and sandwiches. The code for Budapest is ☎1. Outside Budapest, dial ☎06 1 within Hungary.

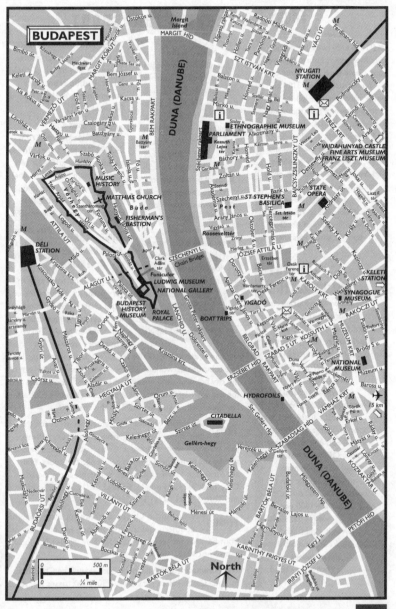

Hungary

TOURS

Legenda, Vigadó tér, 📱 (1) 266 4190 (www.legenda.hu), offer river cruises. Mahart Passnave boats leave Budapest (Vigadó tér boat station), 📱 (1) 318 1223 (www.mahartpassnave.hu), for the charming town of Szentendre and follow the Danube bend to Visegrád (both daily May–Sept, weekends Apr and Oct) and Esztergom (daily June–Aug, Fri–Sun May and Sept). They also run trips from the International Landing Stage, 📱 (1) 484 4000, and hydrofoils to Vienna and Bratislava (daily mid-Apr–late Oct). Book at least 3 days ahead.

TOURIST INFORMATION

The nationwide Tourinform tourist bureaux are an excellent source of information. **Tourinform**, 1052 Deák tér (Sütő utca. 2), 📱 (1) 438 8080 (open 0800–2000), are helpful, with multilingual staff (www.tourinform.hu). Their hotline (from abroad) is 📱 (+36) 30 30 30 600 or (in Hungary, toll free) 📱 06 80 630 800. **Budapest Tourist Office**: branches at Ferihegy Airport Terminals 1 and 2 and Liszt Ferenc tér 11; open 0800–2000 Apr–Oct, 0900–1800 winter, 📱 (1) 322 4098 (www.budapestinfo.hu). **Ibusz** books accommodation and organises tours, Vörösmarty tér 6.

PUBLIC TRANSPORT

Metró tickets are available from kiosks in stations or from machines that require coins. All tickets must be stamped in the machines at the station entrance. A single is 300Ft; the ticket (*vonaljegy*) is valid for all kinds of public transport. Transfer ticket for two rides (*átszállójegy*) 470Ft: validate on both vehicles. One-day and seven-day travel passes (1550Ft, 4600Ft), valid for all kinds of public transport, are available. You can also save a small amount by buying tickets in blocks of 10 or 20.

Night lines run 2300–0500 on the most popular routes. There are also 82 km of **cycle lanes. Public transport information**, 📱 (1) 461 6500 (www.bkv.hu).

METRO Fast and inexpensive; runs 0430–2310; just **three lines**, all intersecting at **Deák tér.** These include M1 (yellow line), M2 (red line) and M3 (blue line). Line M1 was the first continental metro, built in 1896.

BUSES, TRAMS AND SUBURBAN TRAINS For areas not on the metro, the bus, trolleybus and tram system is very useful as it covers the city extensively. A similar method for ticket stamping exists, with machines on board. Ticket inspectors wearing red armbands can fine 12,000Ft (6000Ft if paid on the spot). The suburban network of HÉV trains travel several km out of the city boundary, and embrace the ruins of **Aquincum** and the old town of **Óbuda**. Local tickets and passes (but not European rail passes) are valid to the city limit.

TAXIS Abundant at all times. Remember to check that the meter is running, have the address of where you are going written down and negotiate the fare before setting off. It may be easier to use public transport. Taxis are forbidden in the castle area. Reputable firms include: **City Taxi**, 📱 (1) 211 1111, **Főtaxi**, 📱 (1) 222 222 and **Tele 5 Taxi**, 📱 (1) 555 5555.

FERRIES From Apr to Oct, boat services operate from the southern end to the northern end of Budapest, from Boráros tér to Pünkösdfürdö, daily 0900–1715; local passes not valid.

The **Funicular (Sikló)** from the Buda side of the Chain Bridge to Buda Castle Palace runs daily 0730–2200; passes not valid.

The **Budapest Card**, available at hotels, Tourist Offices, travel agencies, airport and main underground stations, allows free travel by public transport, ample discounts in restaurants, and reductions on more than 60 sights throughout Budapest (valid for 48 or 72 hours – cost includes one adult accompanied by a child up to 14).

You can explore the Buda Hills around the city on three different forms of transport: **Cogwheel Railway (Fogaskerekű)** from Városmajor (two stops from Moszkva tér on trams 18 or 56) to Széchenyi Hill, local tickets, passes are valid. **Chairlift (Libegő)** from Zugliget (🚌 158 from Moszkva tér) to the lookout on János Hill (Budapest's highest point at 526 m), local tickets, passes not valid, special fare, operates daily except every 2nd Mon. **Children's Railway (Gyermekvasút)**, with children on duty, from Hűvösvölgy (tram 56 from Moszkva tér) to Széchenyi Hill. The narrow-gauge railway travels at 20 km/h for roughly 12 km through the Buda forests (taking 40 mins, not Mon, Sept–Apr). Special pedal-operated vehicles for 2–6 persons (called *bringó–hintó*) are for hire at Margit-sziget (Margaret Island) and Városliget (City Park).

ACCOMMODATION

The city offers a wide choice of one- to five-star hotels, pensions and hostels (in summer heat air-conditioned rooms are advisable). **Advance booking** is strongly recommended, particularly in early Aug during the Hungarian Grand Prix. Spa hotels generally offer competitive weekend packages.

Private rooms are less expensive than hotels. Rooms are usually a few stops from the centre of town. These, as well as hotel and pension accommodation, are bookable at **Tourinform** and **Ibusz** (see 'Tourist Information'). Outside the main offices and at railway stations, you may well find people offering private accommodation; make sure you know the price and location – usually the rooms they offer will be safe and clean. Ibusz can also book apartments. Booking websites include: www.hotelshungary.com, www.budapestinfo.hu and www.budapesthotels.com.

Hotel Benczúr, Benczúr utca 35, 📞(1) 479 5650 (www.hotelbenczur.hu), lies parallel to the elegant Andrássy út, offering a central location. **Hotel Carlton** is ideally located below Castle Hill, Apor Péter utca 3, 📞(1) 224 0999 (www.carltonhotel.hu) €€€. The **Hotel Citadella**, Citadella sétány, 📞(1) 466 5794, has wonderful views. **City Hotel Pilvax**, Pilvax köz 1–3, 📞(1) 266 7660 (www.taverna.hu), €€, is very centrally located by the river. Basic and well located near the Opera House by Andrássy út is **Medosz Hotel**, Jókai tér 9, 📞(1) 374 3000 (www.medoszhotel.hu), €€.

Youth hostel and **student accommodation** is plentiful. There are 11 **HI hostels** (www.miszsz.hu). **Domino Hostel**, Váci utca 77 (entrance Havas utca 6), 📞(1) 235 0492 (www.dominohostel.com) is right in the centre of the town. Hostel organisations advertise widely at the stations and often offer free transport to hostels. **Camping** places at the Rómaifürdő stop of the HÉV and at the Zugliget libegő (🚌 158 from Moszkva tér).

Hungary

FOOD AND DRINK

Rich, spicy and meat- or fish-based, Hungarian cuisine is delicious. Cold fruit soups make wonderful starters, followed by game, goose, pike, perch, pork, goulash soup or paprika chicken, washed down with sour cherry juice, *pálinka* spirit or **Tokaji aszú** wine. Budapest's elegant coffeehouses offer irresistible cakes, pastries and marzipans. Check local listings and websites for the latest recommendations. However, you can be sure of finding a lively café, bar or restaurant on or near Liszt Ferenc tér and Ráday utca, all of which compare very favourably with Western prices. There are plenty of eateries in the Castle district too, although this can get a bit more pricey. Finally, ask your hotel staff for their recommendations – they will also make reservations for you.

HIGHLIGHTS

BUDA The Buda hills offer marvellous views of the city and the Danube. To the west lie woods and paths, circumnavigated by a cogwheel railway from **Városmajor** to **Széchenyi Hill**. On **Gellért-hegy** (Gellért Hill) is the gigantic **Liberation Monument**, which commemorates the Soviet liberation of Budapest (🚌 27 from Móricz Zs. körtér, Villányi út to Búsuló Juhász, and then 400 m walk up). **Várhegy** (Castle Hill) was first built in the 13th century and is the prime historic feature in Budapest; its streets have retained their medieval form. **Budavári Palota** (Buda Palace), a vast neo-baroque edifice, was originally built as part of the fortifications of the city during the Middle Ages and remained a royal residence for 700 years, but was virtually destroyed during World War II and then rebuilt. There are three museums in the palace: **Budapest History Museum**, **Museum of Contemporary History** and **Hungarian National Gallery** (all closed Mon). Walk up the hill from Déli or Moszkva pu. tér Metró stations, or catch the **Budavári sikló** funicular (daily 0730–2200) from Clark Ádám tér at the foot of the Chain Bridge or take 🚌 16A/116 from Moszkva tér to Dísz tér or 🚌 16 from Deák ferenc tér to Dísz tér. It's possible to visit the **Castle caverns** at the corner of Dárda and Országház utca.

Look out for **Halászbástya** (Fisherman's Bastion), with its seven conical turrets connected by a walkway, built mainly for decoration and presenting a perfect river panorama, and the nearby square (Szentháromság tér), always filled with tourists, street entertainers and market stalls.

SPAS

Budapest boasts ten spas, offering mixed and segregated bathing, endless treatments and often stunning architecture at affordable prices. **Széchenyi Fürdő** (Széchényi Baths) is one of the most famous baths. Located in the City Park, its neo-baroque building houses several indoor and outdoor pools. Just south of Buda Palace, the Art Nouveau **Gellért** has a much-photographed 'champagne' bath (Kelenhegyi út 2–4), and nearby the **Rudas fürdö** **(Rudas Baths)** (Döbrentei tér) are an amazing time warp (men only). Further north the **Király fürdö** **(Király Baths)** (Fő utca 84) were built in the 16th century – their green cupolas are a reminder of the Turkish occupation. For further details ask **Tourinform**, or see the booklet *Budapest Baths* (Hungarian National Tourist Office).

The **statue of St Stephen** (Szent István), legendary king of Hungary, is overlooked by the neo-Gothic **Mátyás templom** (Matthias Church), the coronation church of Hungarian kings, and resplendent with its multicoloured roof tiles. The surrounding streets are cobbled, below fine baroque and Gothic buildings and façades. It's worth wandering down Táncsics Mihály utca, Tárnok utca, Tóth Árpád sétány and Úri utca to explore.

Do visit the picturesque **Margaret Island** (Margit-sziget). Vehicles are allowed only as far as the Thermal and Grand hotels: the walks along the river are delightful, as are the Japanese garden, open-air theatre, cinema and two 13th-century ruins (trams 4/6 or 🚊 26).

One thousand years of Hungarian existence in the Carpathian basin are commemorated by statues of rulers and princes in the **Millennium Monument** in Hősök tere (Heroes' Square), built in the 19th century. This opens onto leafy **Városliget** (City Park), with its zoo, **Közlekedési Múzeum** (Transport Museum; free for InterRailers), boating lake-cum-ice rink and the romantic **Vajdahunyad vár** (Vajdahunyad Castle), replicating sites from pre-Trianon Hungary and built around the 1890s. Don't miss Andrássy út, Budapest's most famous avenue, home of the **Opera House** (Metro M1 Opera). Close by is the **Liszt Museum**, Vörösmarty utca 35 (closed Sun), where the composer lived. There are also museums to the Hungarian composers Bartók and Kodály.

PEST This is the city's busy commercial sector, built in two semicircular avenues with broad tree-lined boulevards radiating from it, and home to the elegant shopping street Váci utca and the street cafés of Vörösmarty tér. The imposing **Parliament**, Kossuth Lajos tér, has a richly ornate interior and was built in 1904 in Gothic style (highly reminiscent of London's Palace of Westminster), and can be visited by pre-arranged guided tour (book through Tourinform). **Dohány Street Synagogue** (Dohány utcai Zsinagóga), the second largest synagogue in the world, is built in Moorish style. It has a museum, a cemetery and memorial park with a symbolic weeping willow. **St Stephen's Basilica** (Szent István Bazilika) houses the mummified fist of St Stephen; the view from the top (access via the lift or stairs) is definitely worth it.

SHOPPING

The main shopping streets are Váci utca, including **folk art** and **black ceramics** at Váci utca 14, Petőfi Sándor utca and Andrássy út. Best buys include Zsolnay and Herend **porcelain**, **glass**, **antiques**, **wine**, **salami** and **leather**. Try the **Budapest Wine Society**, Batthyány utca 59, and the **Vino Veritas**, Dohány utca 58–62. **Markets** abound, some open-air, others flea markets (the best is **Ecseri Piac**, Nagykőrösi út 156; Mon–Sat, until 1500, 🚊 54 from Boráros tér to Fiume utca). The huge **Arena Plaza** (www.arena plaza.hu) on the right side of the Keleti (Eastern) Railway Station is the largest mall. Do not miss the spectacular building of the **Central Market Hall** (Nagycsarnok), on the Pest side of Liberty Bridge, where you can buy food, wine and spices downstairs, with textiles and crafts upstairs.

NIGHT-TIME AND EVENTS

There is always plenty for all tastes in Budapest. Check monthly listings guides and English-language newspapers such as *Time Out Budapest*, *Budapest Funzine* (www.funzine.hu) or *Where Budapest*, a free monthly information guide.

Music has always been popular in Hungary. Opera, recitals and cinema shows can be checked in *Time Out Budapest* or *Budapest Times* (www.budapesttimes.hu). The stunning neo-Renaissance **Opera House**, Andrássy út. 22, ☎(1) 353 0170 (www.opera.hu), which was completed in 1884, was the first modern theatre in the world (guided tours daily 1500 and 1600). Operetta, too, has its place, and the less ornate building at Nagymező utca 17, ☎(1) 312 4866 (www.operettszinhaz.hu) is usually packed for patriotic programmes of light music. Organ recitals are often given at **Matthias Church** (Mátyás templom), Várhegy and at **St Stephen's Basilica** (Szent István Bazilika). The **Palace of Arts** (Művészetek Palotája) is a popular concert venue and cultural institution with live music, theatres and dance performances – check www.mupa.hu for programmes. Festivals include the **Budapest Spring Festival** (www.btf.hu) and the **Budapest Autumn Festival** (www.bof.hu), both with orchestral concerts, opera, dance and theatre, and the **Sziget Festival** (www.sziget.hu), one of the biggest music festivals in Europe, held on a Danube island.

Many cinemas show English-language movies. Bars are to be found all over the city; the nightclubs in the red-light area in district VIII are only for the extremely broad-minded.

EASY DAY TRIPS FROM BUDAPEST

Don't let the opportunity to explore outside the capital pass you by. Take the slow riverboat to **Szentendre** (1 hr 30 mins by boat, 40 mins by HÉV suburban train from Batthyány tér M2 Metro station running every 10–30 mins, or 30 mins by the yellow Volánbusz bus from Árpád híd bus station at the Árpád híd M3 Metro station, running every 20–60 mins), a touristy but enticing town with exquisite architecture, street cafés and a marzipan museum; or drift up the Danube towards **Esztergom**'s massive Catholic basilica, palace ruins and museums (5 hrs by boat, 1 hr 40 mins by train). Halfway between Esztergom and Szentendre in the Danube bend (Dunakanyar) is **Visegrád**'s lofty citadel and ruined palace.

Vác is another captivating medium-sized town with a baroque main square; it's less touristy than Szentendre and lies on the other bank of the Danube; you can easily manage both in one day by visiting Szentendre first and then take the hourly bus from Szentendre bus station at the HÉV terminus to Váci Rév, where a ferry takes you to the centre of Vác. Vác has frequent trains to Budapest Nyugati station until 2330.

Wine lovers should head for **Tokaj**'s vineyards and wine cellars (3 hrs by train), home to golden Tokaji wine, known as the 'wine of kings and the king of wines'. If you are pushed for time, check out details of guided tours operated by Tourinform, among other agencies (see p624), for organised trips to the Hungarian plains.

Istanbul is unique in being a city on two continents, with the Bosphorus dividing Europe from Asia, and the European side itself (shown on the map) split by the Golden Horn. Istanbul is a fascinating, complex melting pot in which a multitude of different cultures co-exist.

To the ancient Greeks it was Byzantium. The Emperor Constantine christened it Constantinople, relocating his capital here from Rome in AD 330. Constantinople it remained until renamed by Kemal Atatürk, father of modern Turkey, in 1923. In 1453 it fell to the Ottoman Sultan Mehmet II, and became the glittering, cosmopolitan capital of an even greater empire stretching from the Danube to the Red Sea – the city was as much Greek, Armenian and Balkan as Turkish.

The Asian side is usually called **Anadolu Yakasi**. The European side is itself split by the Golden Horn (Haliç), an estuary off the Bosphorus. Most of the historic tourist sights are in **Sultanahmet**, south of the Golden Horn. Places not to be missed include **Topkapi Palace**, **Aya Sofya Museum** and the **Covered Bazaar**; also try to visit one of the mosques (such as the **Suleimaniye** and the **Blue Mosque**) and to take a boat trip on the Bosphorus. Nationals of Australia, Canada, Ireland, Italy, Spain, the UK and the USA need visas for Turkey; these can be obtained on entry.

Turkey

ARRIVAL AND DEPARTURE

TOURIST OFFICES

Branches: **Atatürk Airport**; **Karakoy Maritime Station**; **Hilton Hotel**, Cumhuriyet Cad., Harbiye; **Sultanahmet Meydani**; **Taksim Meydani Maksem**; and **Sirkeci Station**. ☎(0212) 518 8754.

Tourist police ☎(0212) 527 4503.

🚆 There are two rail terminals. **Sirkeci Station**, ☎(0212) 520 6575, near the waterfront at Eminönü (express tram or 10-min walk beside tram line to Sultanahmet) serves trains to **Europe** via **Greece** or **Bulgaria**. The bureau de change in the station will exchange only cash, but there are others immediately outside and automatic cash dispensers in the forecourt. Rail services to **Asian Turkey** and beyond use **Haydarpaşa Station**, ☎(0216) 336 4470, across the Bosphorus (by ferry). Note that in **Greek rail timetables**, Istanbul is still referred to (in Greek script) as **Constantinopolis**.

✈ **Atatürk Airport**, ☎(0212) 465 3000, is in **Yeşilköy**, 25 km west of Istanbul. The Havas bus service, ☎(0212) 444 0487, to the airport departs from Taksim, in front of the THY Sales Office (Cumhuriyet Avenue, No. 14), every half hour from 0400–0100. Trams run from 0500–0000. **Havaş buses** to **Taksim** depart from the airport every half hour from 0400–2100, and every 10 minutes from 2100–0100. X**ESabiha Gökçen Airport**, ☎(0216) 585 5000, is in **Pendik/Kurtköy**, on the Anatolian side of Istanbul, 40 km to Kadıköy and 50 km to Taksim. **Havaş buses** to the airport depart from Taksim (and vice versa) every hour from 0400–0100.

INFORMATION

INTERNET ACCESS

There are internet cafés nearly everywhere in Istanbul, including Sultanahmet, Beyoğlu and Kadıköy. The local municipality provides free wi-fi access in the main avenue in Beyoğlu, İstiklal Cad. One of the best internet cafés in Beyoğlu, where you can also find good music and food is **Omayra Café**, near the Galatasaray High School, Istiklal Cad. Aznavur Pasajı, Kat:3, ☎(0212) 244 3002 (www.omayracafe.com). Another internet café in Kadıköy is **Barcan Café**, Serasker Cad. No. 91 D.4 Caferağa, ☎(0216) 346 9668 (www.barcan.net).

PUBLIC TRANSPORT

TRAMS

There is one express tram line, running from Kabataş (one connection of the ferry/seabus lines), passing through **Sirkeci station** west along Divan Yolu and Millet Cad, out to the **old city walls**. At the Yusufpaşa tram station, near Aksaray, after a 5-min walk, you can pass to the Metro line, which goes all the way to the Atatürk Airport. Buy tickets from kiosks by the stops: place them in the metal containers at the entrance to the platforms. Istanbul's oldest trams and tramline, dating from the turn of last century, have been reprieved and refurbished, and run down the 1.2-km length of Istiklal Cad., the Beyoğlu district's fashionable pedestrianised shopping street. They connect with the *Tünel*, a short, steep, underground railway built in 1875 to connect the hilltop avenue – then the main thoroughfare of the smart European quarter called Pera – with the warehouses and docks of the Golden Horn waterfront.

BUSES Large fleets of buses cover most of Istanbul, but routes can be confusing and there is no bus map, so ask for details at major stops or Tourist Offices. The major departure points are Taksim, Eminönü (near the Galata Bridge) and Beyazit.

TAXIS The yellow taxis offer a simpler alternative to the buses. Fares are not expensive, but ensure that the driver starts the meter when you get in.

FERRIES These run regularly across the Bosphorus, between **Karaköy** on the European side and **Haydarpaşa** and **Kadiköy**; and between **Eminönü** on the European side and **Üsküdar**. Schedules can be confusing and piers chaotic, so ask for details at the Tourist Office, or consult Thomas Cook Publishing's *Greek Island Hopping*.

Akbil are magnetic travel counters sold for a small deposit at Eminönü and Taksim. They can be used on all forms of public transport, can be refilled, and each unit costs less than a full-price fare.

Bus tickets are sold from kiosks or from street vendors and are surrendered into machines on board.

FAST FERRIES AND SEABUSES These faster ships also run on the traditional ferry lines, but they have separate piers, and their timetables are different. Schedules can be found on www.ido.com.tr/en

ACCOMMODATION

Most **budget accommodation** lies in the Sultanahmet district (the area behind Aya Sofya), in the back streets between Sultanahmet Square and the water and especially in Yerebatan Cad. **New Backpackers Hostel**, Akbıyık Cad. 14/1, ☎(0212) 638 5586 (www.newbackpackers.com). There is also a collection of similarly priced **private hostels**. Although basic and often crowded, these are cheap and marvellously placed for Istanbul's main sights, only a 2-min walk to the Blue Mosque. There are often a few people hawking rooms to arriving rail passengers, but they are usually touting for establishments far from the centre. Make sure you know where they are and how to get there before accepting. It is best to ask the Tourist Office. Another hostel in **Kadıköy**, on the other side of the Bosphorus, and near lively nightspots, is only a short walk from the Harem Bus terminal and the Haydarpaşa Railway Station: **Hush Hostel**, Caferağa Mah. Miralay Nazım Sok. No. 20, ☎(0216) 330 9188 (www.hushhostelistanbul.com).

Most of Istanbul's **top-range hotels** congregate north of the Golden Horn around Taksim and Harbiye, areas of less historical interest and a considerable distance from the main sights. There are, however, plenty of hotels south of the Golden Horn, so it is possible to stay in this more atmospheric part of the city without having to slum it, with a particular concentration of hotels of all categories in Sultanahmet, including good three-star hotels to youth hostels. A cheap option is **Hotel Antique**, Küçük Ayasofya Cad., Oğul Sok 17, ☎(0212) 516 4936/516 0997 (www.hotelantique.com), €€. For those who prefer to be nearer to Taksim and Beyoğlu, try **World House Hostel**, Galipdede Cad. No. 85, ☎(0212) 293 5520 (www.worldhouseistanbul.com).

There are **campsites** around Istanbul, all a long way from the centre. They include

Turkey

Şile, Ağva, Kıyıköy, Kerpe, Kefken, most with beautiful beaches. A useful website for budget and mid-priced hotels is www.istanbul.hotelguide.net.

FOOD AND DRINK

Istanbul's eating options are as varied and colourful as the city itself. Some of the restaurants and cafés in Sultanahmet are conveniently priced. In the daytime, you can also head for the **Grand Bazaar**, where there are lots of indoor and outdoor cafés, or **Istiklal Caddesi** and the streets off it.

Located near two seas, Istanbul is naturally a great place for **seafood**, though it is relatively expensive. It's also good for vegetarians, with plenty of meat-free dishes and wonderful fresh fruit. The best place to eat is in **Çiçek Pasaji** (Flower Passage), off pedestrianised Istiklal Cad., where a covered arcade and the alleys around it are packed with restaurant tables. The cheapest places are in the lane behind the arcade, called **Nevizade**. Some small restaurants off the streets above İstiklal Caddesi, like Kallavi Street, offer delicious home food at reasonable prices. If you like street food, you can try the new and more hygienic street-carts offering various cheap eats. The *simit*, a roll with a hole; fish sandwiches at the Eminönü and Kadıköy waterfronts; *nohutlu pilav*, rice with chickpeas; *kokoreç*, skewers of grilled lamb tripe; the familiar *döner kebab*, a roll of lamb on a vertical skewer, and *gözleme*, Turkish crêpe.

HIGHLIGHTS

Memorable landmarks surround **Sultanahmet**, where the **Aya Sofya Museum** and the **Blue Mosque** sit squarely opposite one another, with the **Topkapi Palace** nearby. These, with many others, create a memorable skyline, best seen from the Bosphorus at dawn, or from the top of the **Galata Tower**, north of the Golden Horn (daily 0900–2000), built in 1348 by the Genoese.

TOPKAPI This is a sightseeing 'must', spectacular both outside and in, with glowing displays of jewels and cloth. If you see nothing else in Istanbul, see the amazing contents of **Topkapi Palace** (0900–1800; closed Tues), seat of the Ottoman Sultans from the 15th to the 19th centuries. The complex, at the tip of the old city peninsula, has now been converted into an all-embracing collection of the Imperial treasures, stretching through three courtyards. Allow at least half a day to take in the cream of the exhibits, which include Islamic armour, imperial robes, jewellery and precious objects, porcelain and miniatures. One of the most fascinating parts of the Topkapi is the extensive **Harem** area, which housed the wives, concubines and children of the sultans, with their attendant eunuchs. You can only visit the harem on scheduled tours. Book as soon as you get to Topkapi.

AYA SOFYA Aya Sofya (0900–1800; closed Mon) was the largest domed structure in the world until St Peter's in Rome was built. The current building was originally constructed as a church nearly 1500 years ago on the orders of the Byzantine Emperor Justinian, and was the religious focal point of the Eastern Orthodox Church for nearly one thousand years. Inside, massive marble pillars support a vaulted dome 31 m in diameter and 55 m high, and around the gallery (up the sloped flagstone walkway) are some outstanding mosaics. The interior is an uneasy mixture of Christian and Islamic influences, and the décor that remains is an intriguing harmony of religions.

MOSQUES AND MUSEUMS Undoubtedly the most beautiful of Istanbul's many mosques is the **Suleimaniye**, built between 1550 and 1557 for Sultan Suleiman the Magnificent by his court architect Mimar Sinan. Seen from the banks of the Golden Horn, the complex of domes and spires is the most striking sight in the old city.

DAY TRIPS FROM ISTANBUL

Take a ferry or catamaran from Kabataş to the **Princes' Islands**, an archipelago of nine islands, where princes and princesses were sent into exile in the Byzantine period. The only transport is by horse carriage.

For a day on the beach, try **Kilyos** on the European side of the Black Sea coast.

Opposite Aya Sofya, the **Blue Mosque** or Sultanahmet Mosque was built in 1609–16, its exterior almost mesmeric with its sequence of nested half-domes. Thousands of turquoise Iznik tiles pick up the gentle light that filters in through the windows. The interior is open outside prayer times and contrary to what the many touts and hustlers say, you don't have to pay admission, join an expensive tour or to have your shoes looked after (carry your own footwear in).

West of the Blue Mosque are the remains of the **Hippodrome**, with three columns dating from the early centuries of the Byzantine era: the 4th-century Column of Constantine, the 6th-century Obelisk of Theodosius, and the bronze Serpentine Column. A few fragments of the Hippodrome wall can be seen nearby. Across from the Hippodrome, the **Ibrahim Pasa Palace** houses the **Museum of Turkish and Islamic Art** (0900–1830; closed Mon), including some priceless ancient Persian carpets.

The **Yeni Mosque** (meaning 'new', although built between 1597 and 1633) is unmissable to those arriving at Eminönü or crossing the **Galata Bridge**. There are a miserly two minarets here.

All mosques are open daily except during prayer times. Take your shoes off when you enter, and dress modestly. If you're female, cover your head, shoulders, and preferably arms (a shawl is useful).

A new museum pass (Müze kart) enables its holder to enter more than 300 museums and ancient sites all around Turkey free of charge for one year and costs only TL20. These passes are sold at museum entrances.

Some distance west of Sultanahmet, the **old city walls**, now partially restored, stretch across the landward end of the peninsula from the Sea of Marmara to the Golden Horn. Built at the command of the 5th-century Emperor Theodosius, they protected all the land approaches to the ancient city. The **Istanbul Archaeology Museum** (0900–1900; closed Mon), one of the biggest archaeology museums in the world, is between Sultanahmet and Eminönü, and has fascinating finds from various civilisations of the Middle East.

The **Bosphorus Strait**, leading north from the Sea of Marmara to the Black Sea, is sprinkled with impressive imperial palaces and pavilions built by a succession of sultans. The best way to see them is by boat; popular excursion trips run up to Rumeli Kavaği and Anadolu Kavaği from Eminönü, pier 3. Two boats run each way. The most prominent palace en route – and the one not to miss – is the **Dolmabahçe** (0900–1600; closed Mon, Thur), which has a 600 m water frontage. Built in the 19th century, this served as the final seat of the Ottoman sultans – a compromise between what the sultans thought of as modern European style and their age-old love of lavish adornment. Atatürk died here in 1938.

Turkey's first modern art gallery, **Istanbul Modern** (1000–1800; closed Mon) in Karaköy, hosts an excellent collection of modern Turkish masterpieces. Free on Thursdays, but watch out for the prices at the café.

SHOPPING

The most famous of the markets is the **Kapali Carşı** (Covered Bazaar), Beyazıt: go along Divan Yolu from Sultanahmet, with 5 km of lanes, streets and alleys. Keep moving, because you'll be pressured to buy if you pause to browse. There are thousands of stalls here, roughly grouped according to merchandise, with whole alleys selling gold, silver, brass or leather. In Istanbul, bargaining is a sport in itself.

NIGHT-TIME AND EVENTS

Istanbul's thriving nightlife is to be found on the north side of the Golden Horn in the side streets off Istiklal, in the **Beyoğlu** area, and in **Ortaköy**, which has a huge number of bars and restaurants, with the benefit of a Bosphorus view. If you prefer to have a leisurely stroll, try a Bosphorus walk along from Bebek to Rumeli Hisari or the ancient city walls. On the other side of the Bosphorus, in Kadıköy, you can visit **Kadife Sokak**, also known as Barlar Sokağı for good music and live performances. This is a smaller and calmer area compared to Beyoğlu, but quite cosmopolitan and frequented by young people. Many bars in this street hold art performances, including **Karga Bar**, Kadife Sokak No. 16, ☎ (0216) 449 1725-26 (www.kargabar.org).

From April to October the city has a number of international festivals (see www.istfest.org). In April the **International Film Festival** features films from around the world; June's **Istanbul International Music Festival** (featuring classical music: at the Cemal Resit Rey Hall, Harbiye and the Atatürk Cultural Centre, Taksim) is followed in July–August by the **International Jazz Festival**, held over two weeks.

BRATISLAVA

SLOVAKIA

Budapest

HUNGARY

Sighişoara

ROMANIA

Braşov

Bucharest
(Bucureşti)

Snagov

SERBIA

Veliko Târnovo

BULGARIA

TURKEY

GREECE **ISTANBUL**

ROUTE DETAIL

Bratislava–Budapest ETT table 1175

Type	Frequency	Typical journey time
Train	5 daily	2 hrs 30 mins

Budapest–Sighişoara ETT table 1600

Type	Frequency	Typical journey time
Train	3 daily	9 hrs 45 mins

Sighişoara–Braşov ETT table 1600

Type	Frequency	Typical journey time
Train	10 daily	1 hr 50 mins

Braşov–Bucharest ETT table 1600

Type	Frequency	Typical journey time
Train	Every 1–2 hrs	3 hrs

Bucharest–Veliko Târnovo ETT tables 1500, 1525

Type	Frequency	Typical journey time
Train	1 daily	5 hrs 50 mins

Veliko Târnovo–Istanbul ETT tables 1525, 1550

Type	Frequency	Typical journey time
Train	1 daily	14 hrs 20 mins

KEY JOURNEYS

Vienna–Budapest ETT table 1250

Type	Frequency	Typical journey time
Train	7 daily	2 hrs 40 mins

Budapest–Bucharest ETT table 60

Type	Frequency	Typical journey time
Train	6 daily	13 hrs 30 mins

Budapest–Istanbul ETT table 60

Type	Frequency	Typical journey time
Train	1 daily	36 hrs 12 mins

BRATISLAVA – BUCHAREST – ISTANBUL

Southeast Europe

This winding route through Slovakia, Hungary, Bulgaria, Romania, easternmost Greece and ending in the western tip of Turkey gives a fascinating insight into parts of Eastern Europe still unfamiliar to most Westerners.

In Romania the route includes the capital, Bucharest, another rapidly changing city, beautiful old towns and stunning mountain scenery, particularly in Transylvania, one of the most colourful and multi-ethnic areas in Europe – the rural land of Dracula (real and legendary), with Bran Castle the must-visit sight near **Brașov**. Sit on the west side of the train (the right side, heading south) for spectacular mountain views between Brașov and the Romanian capital, **Bucharest**, itself somewhat blighted by petty crime and dominated by a charmless Communist palace, although it boasts some splendid, if decaying, architecture and a lively social scene. Beyond the Danube, you're into the wine-growing country of Bulgaria. The fortified town of **Veliko Tarnovo** is worth leaving the train for; the bus from Gorna Orjahovitza can be more convenient than the through train (🚌 10 leaving every 20 mins or so).

BRATISLAVA, SLOVAKIA

See p596.

BUDAPEST, HUNGARY

See p622.

SIGHIȘOARA, ROMANIA

Sighișoara (or Segesvár) is a wonderful Transylvanian town with winding streets, covered stairways and breathtaking architecture, set in spectacular medieval fortifications. It was one of the strongholds of the Saxon community, and also has large populations of Hungarians and gypsies. From the commercial centre, you enter the old town by the 14th-century **Clock Tower**, now a history museum (closed Mon). Beyond this is an ancient house where Vlad the Impaler (Dracula) was reputedly born about 1431, and to the right, the 15th-century church of the **Dominican Monastery**, Piața Muzeului 8, is famous for its bronze baptismal fonts dating back to 1440. At the highest point of the citadel and reached by a roofed wooden stairway is the **Biserica din Deal** (Church on the Hill), Str. Scolii 7, built in Gothic style 1345–1525, adorned with some remarkable frescos.

🚉 1 km north of the centre. Tickets: **SNCFR Agency**, Str. 1 Decembrie 1918, 18, 📞(0265) 771 246 (Mon–Fri 0830–1500).

ℹ️ **Tourist Office**: Octavian Goga 8, 📞(0265) 770 415 (office@sighisoara-infotourism.com).

🏨 **Casa Wagner**, Piața Cetății 7, 📞(0265) 506 014 (www.casa-wagner.com), up in the medieval city, is the most popular place in town: reserve well in advance. A cheaper pension, **Casa Saseasca**, Piața Cetății 12, 📞(0265) 772 400, on the other side of the square, is just as good. Cheaper still are pensions in the lower town: the **Hera**, Str. Eminescu 62, 📞(0265) 778 850 has both 2- and

I-star rooms. **Hostels: Nathan's Villa Hostel**, Str. Libertatii 8, ☎(0265) 772 546 (www.nathansvilla.com), is 250 m west of the station and slightly better than the **Burg Hostel (HI)**, Strada Bastionului 4–6, ☎(0265) 778 489, in the medieval city.

BRAŞOV

Baroque buildings dominate much of the beautiful centre of Romania's second city, also in Transylvania, while imposing gates guard the road into the Schei quarter to the southwest. In central Piaţa Sfatului (Council Square) stands the **Old Town Hall**, now the local **History Museum** (closed Mon); from its tower trumpeters sounded the warning of impending attack, by Tatars or Turks, for many centuries. Nearby, the **Biserica Neagra** (Black Church, closed Sun) overshadows the same square with its Gothic pinnacles. Dating from the 14th century, this is one of the greatest monuments of Transylvania's Saxon (German) community, and displays historic prints and fine carpets brought by merchants from Turkey. You can get great views of the city and surrounding mountains from the summit of **Mt Tâmpa**, reached by a cable car or by footpaths; the base of the hill is fortified with a wall and bastions.

🚉 Blvd Gării 5, about 2 km northeast of the old town. 🚋 4 runs from the station to Piaţa Livada Poştei on the edge of the old town. **Wasteels**, Blvd Gării 5, ☎(0268) 424 313, Mon–Fri 0800–1900, Sat 0800–1400.

i **Tourist Information: Centrul de Informare Turistica Brasov**, Piaţa Sfatului 30 (inside History Museum), ☎(0268) 419 078 (www.brasovtravelguide.ro).

🏨 The cheapest sleep in central Braşov is the I-star **Aro Sport**, Str. Muresenilor 12, ☎(0268) 477 664, while the **Postavarul**, Str. Politehnicii 2, ☎(02680) 477 448 is better located but a little more expensive; enter through the grander Coroana. The best hostel is the **Kismet Dao**, Str. Democratiei 2, ☎(0268) 514 296 (🚌 50 from Piaţa Livada Poştei to the end of the line). **Hostel Mara Brasov (HI)**, Piaţa Sfatului 11, ☎(0746) 968 216 (www.mara.inbrasov.ro), is right on the central square.

DAY TRIPS FROM BRAŞOV   The ski resort of **Poiana Brasov** is a 20-minute bus ride from Brasov (🚌 20 from Livada Poştei). Two more ski resorts, **Sinaia** and **Predeal** lie on the main rail line from Bucharest to Braşov, and most trains call here, making it easy for you to break your journey (ETT table 1600). The inexpensive 2-star **Hotel Caraiman**, Blvd. Carol I 4, ☎(0244) 312 067 is at the top of the staircase outside the station; there are plenty of other places to stay but prices in Sinaia and Predeal are higher than elsewhere in Romania. **Bran Castle** has been associated by the tourist industry with **Count Dracula** and is visited by every coach tour to the area. Although there's no factual connection with Vlad the Impaler, the castle looks the part, bristling with medievalism (though it's largely renewed inside). It's 26 km from **Braşov**, with regular buses and minibuses from Autogara No. 2, on Str. Lunga, as well as tours laid on by the Tourist Office. There is a wealth of excellent private accommodation in homes and cheap pensions in Bran, easily found once you're there.

BUCHAREST (BUCUREŞTI)

Bucharest was once known as 'The Paris of Eastern Europe', for its decadent lifestyle and for the elegant mansions lining its 19th-century boulevards. However, the city has been vandalised over the years, above all by communist planners. Perversely for many people, the city's main sight is the so-called **People's Palace**, now officially known as the Palace of Parliament, a huge edifice whose construction required the demolition of a quarter of the city's historic centre. B-dul Unirii, lined with fountains and trees, leads from Piaţa Unirii (hub of the Metro system), which offers the major vista of the Palace. Tours of the interior start from the south door (daily 1000–1600); these pass through a succession of grandiose public halls with chandeliers, marble and mirrors. Its construction costs almost bankrupted the country. One wing contains Bucharest's newest museum, the National Museum of Contemporary Art, or **MNAC**, displaying works by Romania's contemporary artists (closed Mon–Tues). Most other sights are along Calea Victoriei, the historic north–south axis, which is also lined with the smartest shopping street. Near its mid-point is Piaţa Revoluţiei, scene of the most dramatic events of Ceauçescu's overthrow during Christmas 1989; here the **Atheneum** concert hall faces the former Royal Palace, now the **National Art Museum** (closed Mon–Tues). To the south along Calea Victoriei is the **National History Museum** (closed Mon–Tues), which houses Romania's finest archaeological collection and National Treasury. To the north of Piaţa Revoluţiei are the **Peasant Museum** (closed

Mon) which has the city's best souvenir shop, the **Art Collection Museum** (closed Mon–Tues) and the **George Enescu Museum** (closed Mon), all in former palaces.

The **Bucharest History and Art Museum** (closed Mon), housed in the 19th-century Sutu Palace on Piaţa Universitatii, forges some links with the legend of Dracula, in fact the local prince **Vlad Tepeş** (Vlad the Impaler). Angry protests in June 1990 against the hijacking of the 1989 revolution by the functionaries of the communist regime were centred on Piaţa Universitatii. You can still see political graffiti here, as well as memorials to those killed in both revolution and the aftermath. To the west of the city in a pleasant leafy suburb is **Cotroceni Palace**, home of the president of Romania. There is a medieval art collection here (closed Mon). Bucharest has a large number of pleasant parks: to the north in the largest, Herăstrău Park, is the open-air **Village Museum**, Sos. Kiseleff 28–30, open daily. This fascinating collection of re-erected buildings brought from all over the country includes churches, houses, watermills and windmills. Elsewhere, the quintessential Bucharest experience is to be had walking through the **Lipscani** district north of Piata Unirii, visiting the tiny 15th- and 16th-century Romanian Orthodox churches.

⊞ Virtually all trains use the **Gară de Nord**, 5 km northwest of the city centre on Calea Griviţei (☎ 9521 for **general information**). This is chaotic and crowded, and it's teeming with pickpockets. It is served by the **Metro** (**Metrou**), although you'll have to change trains to reach the city centre. Other stations are mostly for local or seasonal trains. The **Gară de Nord** has a computerised ticket office, allowing you to join any queue and buy any ticket virtually until departure time. **Tickets and reservations** can also be purchased up to 24 hrs in advance at **Agenţia de Voiaj SNCFR** (in Bucharest at: 10–14 Domnita Anastasia Str., ☎ (021) 313 2644; and Calea Griviţei 139, ☎ (021) 311 0857).

✛ **Henri Coanda Airport** (formerly known as Otopeni Airport), ☎ (021) 204 1000, 19 km north of the centre, handles almost all international flights. There is a good **bus service** (⊟ 783) to the city centre (Piaţa Unirii) every 15 mins (30 mins at weekends), costing about US$1. For taxis, try to agree a fare of US$12 (paid only in lei) – you should pay no more than US$20 from the centre to the airport. **Baneasa Airport**, 6 km north of the centre, handles Bucharest's budget airline traffic. There is a good **bus service** (⊟ 131), which runs every ten minutes to Piata Romana. A standard Bucharest transport ticket is all you need. Avoid taxis at Baneasa: most are not to be trusted.

ℹ There is a Tourist Information Office at the **Gară de Nord**, but it offers little beyond very simple maps and promotional flyers. There are car hire desks at both airports and at all the big hotels, such as the InterContinental, Hilton, Radisson and Howard Johnson. **Cultural Travel & Tours**, ☎ (021) 336 3163 (www.cttours.ro), can arrange tours of Bucharest and southern Romania.

Internet access: There is free Wi-Fi – no password required – in and around Piata Universitatii. Most cafés, bars, fast food outlets and restaurants have free Wi-Fi. Internet cafés are few and far between: **Best Café Internet**, Blvd Kogalniceanu, ☎ (021) 312 4816, opposite the Opera House is closest to the city centre. Bucharest's hostels usually have an internet terminal available free.

⊟ The **Metro** (0500–2330) is efficient and fast, linking central Bucharest to the **Gară de Nord** and the **suburbs**. There are three main lines and most city maps carry a Metro plan. **Magnetic**

tickets (for a minimum of two trips) must be bought as you enter a station and passed through a turnstile; there are also better-value 10-trip and day-tickets.

Buses, trams and **trolleybuses** run throughout the city, although it can be hard to work out their routes, as maps are rare. They are rundown and crowded, but very cheap. Buy any number of tickets before boarding from the **grey aluminium kiosks** by most stops. **Express buses**, including those to the airports, require special magnetic tickets.

Taxis are plentiful and inexpensive. Just make sure you get in one displaying its tariffs on the driver's door (fares from 1.39–1.99 lei/km are standard; beware any taxi charging more than 2 lei/km). Always make sure the meter is running. Never take a taxi outside the station or a hotel. Good, trusted companies include **Meridian**, ☎(021) 9444, **Cristaxi**, ☎(021) 9641, **Cobalcescu**, ☎(021) 9541 and **Leone**, ☎(021) 9425.

🛏 **Accommodation**: There is no central reservation agency so try and book accommodation before you arrive in Bucharest. Try www.bucharest.inyourpocket.com for details of hotels, hostels and short-stay apartments in all price ranges in Bucharest. Good agencies include www.roczare.ro, www.unid.ro and www.cert-accommodation.ro. You may be offered space in a hostel and a free lift by a tout at the Gară de Nord: always ignore them. No hostels send personnel to the station. Budget hotel options in Bucharest have all but disappeared and are now limited to the excellent, cheap 2-star **Hello Hotel**, Calea Grivitei 143, ☎(037) 271 6464, €, next to the slightly more expensive **Ibis**, €€, across the road from the station. Also close to the station is **Coco's**, Str. Dinicu Golescu 29, ☎(021) 311 0535, €. Hostels are a growing business in Bucharest and there are three city centre places to choose from. **La Historia**, Str. Dumitru 3, ☎(072) 174 7418, is right in the heart of the Lipscani district just north of Piata Unirii, and above a lively bar. The **Midland Youth Hostel**, Str. Biserica Amzei 22, ☎(021) 314 5323, is next to the city's central market, Piata Amzei. The oldest in the city is the **Youth Hostel Villa Helga** (**HI**), Str. Busolei 7, ☎(021) 212 08028. Take 🚌 86 from the station to the Piata Gemeni stop. If you want to stay by the station, try **Villa 11**, Str. Institutul Medico Militar 11, ☎(072) 249 5900. There are no campsites anywhere near Bucharest.

🍴 Eating well is not expensive in Bucharest, or you can opt for pizzas/hamburgers, or patisseries/cafés. **Panipat** is a chain of good if pricey takeaway bun shops (pizzas and pastries). The area around Piaţa Universităţii has several cafés frequented by students and young people.

NIGHTLIFE Check out *Bucharest In Your Pocket* – available in hotels, hostels and on newsstands – for bar and club listings. The Lipscani area is the centre of Bucharest nightlife. Great places include **Bordello's**, Str. Selari 9–11, ☎(021) 317 9099, an Irish pub with a twist serving food and drink. Inside the same courtyard is **Oktoberfest**: a big beer hall serving cheap beer. Str. Smardan is home to a string of clubs: try **Arcade**, Str. Smardan 30, with a DJ most nights, and **El Comandante**, Str. Stavropoleos 8, a cellar club featuring live acts. **Club A**, Str. Blanari 14, remains a student favourite and still serves the cheapest drinks in the city. For big-name foreign DJs head to **Studio Martin**, Blvd Iancu de Hunedoara 61 (Metro to Stefan cel Mare), on Friday and Saturday nights.

Films are shown in Romania in their original language with subtitles. There is a multi-screen **cinema** at the Bucuresti Mall, five minutes on 🚌 123 from Piata Unirii.

Green Hours 22 Jazz Café, Calea Victoriei 120, has live jazz at the weekend and an eclectic mix of theatre/comedy during the week.

SIDE TRIP TO SNAGOV   Only 40 km from the city, **Snagov** is the playground of Bucharest. Imposing villas surround the attractive lake, and on an island is a 15th-century monastery where Vlad the Impaler is thought to be buried. There is only one train a day, but buses and tours operate at other times. There are plenty of places to stay and eat on the lake. Try the Complex Astoria, bookings through **Snagov Tur**, ☎ (021) 323 9905 (www.snagov.ro). The same people can also arrange fishing trips, boat hire and transport to and from Bucharest.

WHERE NEXT FROM BUCHAREST?

*About 225 km east of Bucharest (2 hrs 30 mins by train, ETT table 1680; book ahead in summer; delays likely due to reconstruction of the line), **Constanţa** on the Black Sea coast is a long-standing port dating from the 6th century BC (an excellent collection of Roman statues and mosaics, plus a display on the exiled poet Ovid in its archaeology museum), with a pleasant waterfront graced by 19th-century buildings, an aquarium and dolphinarium, an elegant promenade and a rococo-style casino. There is ready access to sandy beaches and a choice of resorts. Costinesti and Neptun are the favoured beaches for young Romanians, and these have the liveliest discos and nightlife as does the Tomis Boulevard.*

VELIKO TARNOVO, BULGARIA

Former capital 1185–1396, this spectacularly situated town perches on steep hills separated by the River Yantra. **Tsarevets Hill** (sometimes floodlit at night) has the restored ruins of the medieval citadel. Nearby are Byzantine churches and the **Samovodska Charshiya** (Bazaar), a photogenic area of restored workshops interspersed with modern jewellers, souvenir shops and cafés.

🚆 Neither the bus nor the rail station is central. 🚌 5/13 run from the train station to the centre. Trolleybuses 1/2 and 🚌 12 go from the bus terminal to the centre. Trains from Sofia to Varna stop at Gorna Oryahovitsa just 7 km north of Veliko Tarnovo (eight local trains per day connect to the town), or take the shuttle bus to Gorna Oryahovitsa bus station from which 🚌 10 goes into town every 20 mins.

🏨 Often booked up as the town is popular with Bulgarìans. Possibilities include **Hotel Etar**, ul. Ivailo 2, ☎ (062) 621 838, €, or **Hotel Lucky**, ul. Nikola Pikolo 3, ☎ (062) 651 224, €.

ISTANBUL, TURKEY

See p629.

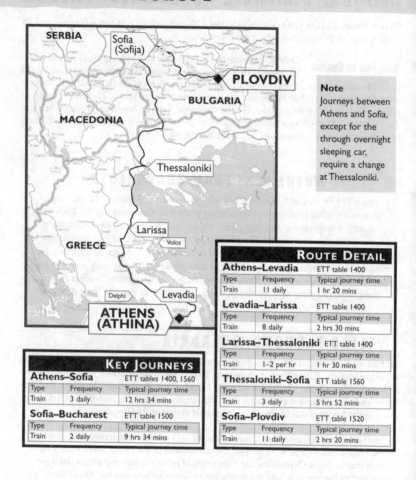

Note

Journeys between Athens and Sofia, except for the through overnight sleeping car, require a change at Thessaloniki.

ROUTE DETAIL

Athens–Levadia — ETT table 1400

Type	Frequency	Typical journey time
Train	11 daily	1 hr 20 mins

Levadia–Larissa — ETT table 1400

Type	Frequency	Typical journey time
Train	8 daily	2 hrs 30 mins

Larissa–Thessaloniki — ETT table 1400

Type	Frequency	Typical journey time
Train	1–2 per hr	1 hr 30 mins

Thessaloniki–Sofia — ETT table 1560

Type	Frequency	Typical journey time
Train	3 daily	5 hrs 52 mins

Sofia–Plovdiv — ETT table 1520

Type	Frequency	Typical journey time
Train	11 daily	2 hrs 20 mins

KEY JOURNEYS

Athens–Sofia — ETT tables 1400, 1560

Type	Frequency	Typical journey time
Train	3 daily	12 hrs 34 mins

Sofia–Bucharest — ETT table 1500

Type	Frequency	Typical journey time
Train	2 daily	9 hrs 34 mins

RAIL TOUR: ATHENS – THESSALONIKI – PLOVDIV

It's worth allocating time to take some of the diversions from the main route. North of **Athens**, the towns on the railway tend to be modern and unprepossessing, but nearby are some of the most wonderful ancient sites in Greece, including **Delphi**, near **Levadia** (itself a town in the cornfields of the Thessalian plain) and the extraordinary **Meteora** monasteries perched on crags beneath mountains a couple of hours west of **Larissa**. Near **Litohoro** rises **Mt Olympus**, marking the border between **Thessaly** and **Macedonia**, and its lofty summit, a demanding two-day hike. Beyond **Thessaloniki** (worth a stop for its archaeological museum), the route enters Bulgaria, passing through its fast-changing capital, **Sofia**, and ending at **Plovdiv**, its more appealing second city. From **Plovdiv**, you can head east to join the **Bratislava–Istanbul** route (p635).

ATHENS (ATHÍNA)

See p616.

LEVADIA

Overlooked by a 14th-century sandstone castle tower, the modern town is a common stopping point for travellers en route to Delphi, 56 km west. In ancient times those heading to the Oracle at Delphi could stop at Levadia's Oracle of Zeus Trofonios on top of **Profitis Ilias**, one of the two hills overlooking the town, on which the **castle** now stands.

🚉 3 km from the centre, but **taxis** are available.

SIDE TRIP TO DELPHI Delphi (buses from Levadia and Athens) is synonymous with its Oracle, the greatest spiritual power in ancient Greece, said to be situated over the centre of the world (amusingly also referred to as the 'belly button of the world'). This belief was strengthened by leaking volcanic gases, which induced lightheadedness and trance-like stupors. People came from far and wide to seek wisdom; prophecies were given so ambiguously that they could never be proved wrong. The most dramatic aspect of the **Temple of Apollo** (the Oracle), however, is its location, perched on the slopes of **Mt Parnassus** and reached by the paved, zigzagging **Sacred Way**. Delphi is one of the largest remaining ancient sites in Greece, with a host of other ruins, notably a **Stadium** and an **Amphitheatre**. The famous bronze of a charioteer is among many beautiful artefacts in the outstanding **Delphi Museum**.

Thousands of visitors make for Delphi, so come early (or out of season). **Accommodation** is a problem: in high season hotels and pensions are often full, while many of them are closed off season. The **Sibylla Hotel**, ☎22650 82 335 (www.sibylla-hotel.gr), €€€, is a friendly, low-cost, family-run hotel, just up from the Tourist Office, and has great views. **Tourist Office**: Municipality of Delphi, ☎22650 82 900. Alternatively, stay in the pretty village of Arahova (11 km east of Delphi), which is a popular winter ski resort where prices actually drop during summer (which is regarded as 'low-season').

Southeast Europe

LARISSA

Larissa is the starting point for some outstanding day trips.

[RAIL] I km from the centre of the town.

[i] Tourist Office: GNTO, Ipeirou 58, **☎**24106 18 189 (www.gnto.gr).

DAY TRIPS FROM LARISSA **Volos**: Apart from the waterfront **Archaeological Museum** there's little of note in this ugly industrial port (where Jason set sail in the *Argo* in search of the Golden Fleece), but it's the main base from which to explore the lush forests and charming old villages of the mountainous **Pilion peninsula** to the east (best done by car, or take either of two bus routes from Volos); or you can take a ferry to the **Sporades Islands** (of which **Skiathos** is the most beautiful and most touristy). Six **trains** a day run from Larissa to Volos, taking about 1 hr (ETT table 1425). **Bus station info**, **☎**24210 25 527. **GNTO Office**: Platia Riga Fereou, **☎**24210 36 233 (www.gnto.gr). **Tourist Police**: 179 Olekobriou 28, **☎**24210 39 065.

Kalampaka and the **Meteora monasteries**: The major tourist attraction in central Greece, the hilltop monasteries of the **Meteora**, are reached on foot from Kalampaka, to which there are two direct **trains** a day from Larissa; additional journeys are possible by changing at **Paleofarsalos** (ETT table 1408). The journey takes about 1 hr 20 mins–2 hrs. Paleofarsalos is on the main rail route between **Athens** and **Salonika**, if you want to visit Meteora without going to Larissa.

LITOHORO

Litohoro is the access point for **Mt Olympus** (2917 m), home of the ancient gods: it actually has nine peaks. You don't need special equipment (other than suitable footwear) for the full ascent, but it does demand real fitness and takes two days – treat it with respect, as more people die here than on any other Greek mountain. Book a bunk in one of the mountain refuge dormitories (hot meals available) through the EOS office. Getting to the top involves taking a taxi or hitching a lift to the car park 6 km from Litohoro, at the 1000 m level, then hiking through ravines to the refuge at around 2000 m. It is best to spend the night here before making the demanding trek to the summits. The final stretch to **Mitikas**, the highest peak, requires strong nerves.

[RAIL] Near the coast, 5 km east of town. Buses link the station to town.

[i] Tourist Office: Odos Ag. Nicolaou 15, **☎**23523 50 103 (www.litohoro.gr), mid-May–end Aug. Out of season, visitors can try Town Hall next door at Odos Ag. Nicolaou 17, **☎**23523 50 100.

[⌂] Papanikolau Pension, Nikolau Episkopou Kitrous 1, **☎**23520 81 236, €€, has cosy furnished studios for 2–3 people.

DAY TRIP FROM LITOHORO

Dion: This is a comparatively uncrowded archaeological site, not as spectacular as the likes of Delphi but still impressive. There are several **buses** daily from Litohoro village and station to Dion village, 8 km north of Litohoro and 2 km west of the site. Highlights are the **marble** and **mosaic floors**, the **Sanctuary of Isis**, the extensive **public bath complex**, and a length of the **paved road** that led to Olympus. The **museum**, in the centre of the village, has a fine collection of finds from the site.

THESSALONIKI (SALONIKA)

The second largest city in Greece was founded in 315 BC; many of the interesting sights are within a 10/15-min walk of the Plateia Aristotelous, an elegant pedestrian-only square giving onto the sea and rimmed by popular open-air cafés. The old town was destroyed by fire in 1917 and suffered a severe earthquake in 1978. Thessaloniki today is a modern, busy city, laid out along a crescent bay – yet it's a worthwhile place to stop over, with some elegant corners and a lively night scene (thanks primarily to the large number of young people who study here). A good area to eat and go out at night is **Ladadika**, a short taxi ride west of the centre, where former warehouses have been refurbished to house countless bars, tavernas and small clubs. Alternatively, try the bustling tavernas that line the narrow alleys of Athinos, just off Plateia Aristotelous in the centre.

Buses cover the city comprehensively. Buy bus tickets from the conductor, who sits at the rear, or from a kiosk.

Thessaloniki (Salonika) became strategically vital to the Romans, straddling the Via Egnatia, their highway between Constantinople and the Adriatic, and later to the Byzantines and their Turkish conquerors. It was one of the greatest cities of the Ottoman Empire, rejoining Greece only in 1913.

On the seafront promenade, The White Tower, the most prominent surviving bastion of the Byzantine-Turkish city walls, is regarded by locals as the symbol of the city, and stages an exhibition tracing the city's history. A 5-min walk northeast from here, the vast **Archaeological Museum** (www.amth.gr) houses archaeological treasures from different parts of Macedonia. Next door, the highly regarded **Museum of Byzantine Culture** (www.mbp.gr) displays religious icons depicting sultry-eyed saints. The city's Roman heritage includes remains of the **Forum**, Odos Filipou, the **Palace of Galerius**, Plateia Navarinou, the **Baths**, the 4th-century Rotonda, and the **Arch of Galerius**, beside Odos Egnatia, near Plateia Sintrivaniou. The city also has a fine collection of Byzantine churches (giving Thessaloniki status as a UNESCO World Heritage Site) the most notable of which are the restored 4th-century **Agios Dimitrios**, and the 8th-century **Agia Sofia**, decorated with stunning golden mosaics. Those who enjoy food shopping should also check out the colourful **Modhiano covered market**.

RAIL I km west of town centre. ☐ 3 from the station to the centre, via Plateia Aristotelous.

i **Tourist Office**, Tsimiski 138, ☎ 2310 221 1000. **Information desk** at the station.

Southeast Europe

Tourist Police: Odos Dodekanissou, near Plateia Dimokratias, ☎2310 554 871.
Main post office: 26 Aristotelous. **Phone office**: 27 Karolou (Ermou).
Internet access: Perhaps the best internet café in the city is the 24-hour **Cyberia**, Str. Stefan Karadja 18b, ☎(02) 986 2791, while the central **Internet Club**, Str. Sveti Naum 4A, ☎(02) 963 3750, offers expert help over a cup of tea or coffee.

🛏 **Accommodation**: The cheaper hotels mostly cluster along Egnatia – the continuation of Monastiriou, east of the station. **Youth hostel**: 44 Al. Svolou, ☎2310 225 946 or **Backpacker's Refuge** (www.backpackers-refuge.biz.ly).

SOFIA (SOFIYA), BULGARIA

When Bulgaria was liberated from the Turks in 1878, Sofia became its capital, and imposing public buildings, squares and parks were created. Though Sofia is one of the oldest cities in Europe, it is still one of its least-known capitals. Traces of Thracians, Romans, Byzantines, Slavs and Ottoman Turks can all be seen here. The city takes its name from the restored 6th-century basilica of St Sofia, which stands in a central square. The main sights are easily covered on foot. Sofia nowadays is a lively, changing city with many new cafés, bars, restaurants and small family-run hotels. Its excellent museums, art galleries and concerts and **Mt Vitosha** (about 30 mins from the centre by public transport), all deserve a visit.

The **Alexander Nevski Memorial Church**, with its neo-Byzantine golden domes dominating the skyline, is the most photographed image of Sofia: don't miss the superb collection of Bulgarian icons in its crypt. Nearby, the tiny **Russian Church** is an exuberant, vividly decorated gem, its gold domes contrasting with its emerald-green spires. The 4th-century **St George's Rotunda** lies hidden in a courtyard behind the Sheraton Hotel. If you only have time for one museum, visit the **National History Museum** (fixed route taxi 21 from the National Palace of Culture), which has the fabulous Thracian gold treasures. In the foothills of Mount Vitosha, **Boyana Church**, with its sophisticated 13th-century frescos, is also on UNESCO's World Heritage list.

Central Station, Bul. Mariya Luiza, 1.5 km north of the centre. **Buses, taxis, tourist information, currency exchange**. Be extra cautious here, as petty crime is common.

Sofia Airport, 11 km east from the centre; ☎(02) 937 2211-3.

i **National Tourist Information Centre**, Pl. Sveta Nedelya 1, ☎(02) 933 5826, is a useful first stop for information. **Alma Tour**, ul. Serdika 12, ☎(02) 805 6800, offers all kind of tourist services. For information on hiking and a variety of alternative holidays, try **Zig Zag Holidays**, Bul. Aleksandar Stamboliyski 20V, ☎(02) 980 5102. **Train and bus tickets** are sold by the **Transport Service Centre**, underneath the **National Palace of Culture**, Pl. Bulgariya, ☎(02) 932 4280.
Internet access: The best internet cafés in Sofia are the 24-hour **Garibaldi**, ul. Graf Ignatiev 6, ☎(02) 989 4285, and **Site**, Bul. Vitosha 45, ☎(02) 986 0896. All hostels have internet terminals. There are also several free Wi-Fi zones like Oborishte Park, Central Bus Station, and many bars.
Post and phones: **Central Post Office**: ul. Gurko 6, opposite the **Rila** agency. **International phone calls** can be dialled directly from the **Central Telephone Office**, ul. Gurko 4, next to the post office.
Money: Some bureaux de change open 24 hrs on Bul. Vitosha, and there are plenty of exchange facilities in the Central Station. Bureaux may give a better deal than banks (but check rates/commission). ATMs available. Changing money on the street is risky and should be avoided.

Central Bus Station, Bul. Mariya Luiza 100, 200 m east of the Central railway station. Significantly cleaner, 24-hr left-luggage, ATMs, cafés and fast-food outlets. Central Sofia is compact with a good network of **trams, trolleybuses** and **buses**; buy tickets (single trip) from drivers, kiosks or street vendors. A **one-day pass** is good value if you're planning more than three rides, but single tickets are extremely cheap. **Trams 1/7** run from the station along Bul. Mariya Luiza and Bul. Vitosha through the town centre.

Private rooms are good value (30–45Lv for a twin room), as are the small **hotels** in the foothills of **Mount Vitosha** at **Simeonovo** and **Dragalevtsi**. Many hostels in the city centre offer clean and tidy dorms at very reasonable prices (15–25Lv per bed).

WHERE NEXT FROM SOFIA?

Join the **Bratislava–Istanbul** route by taking the train east to **Tulovo** (ETT table 1520).

Southeast Europe

▣ Sofia's restaurants have increased in number and quality, but prices (for foreign visitors) remain low. Side streets off Bul. Vitosha, particularly to the east, have a mixture of Western fast-food outlets and **international** cuisine. In the foothills of **Mount Vitosha** several traditional **taverns** serve **local specialities**. The more popular restaurants need to be booked ahead. **Street kiosks** have excellent coffee and very cheap fast food. Recommended **nightspots** include **Chervilo**, Bul. Tsar Osvoboditel; **Swingin' Hall**, Bul. Dragan Tsankov 8; and the biggest folk venue **Help**, Bul. Hristo Botev 61. Sofia boasts plenty of restaurants and bars open 24 hours. The most popular are **Happy**, Pl. Sveta Nedelya 4; **Ugo**, bul. Vitosha 45; and **Victoria**, Bul. Tsar Osvoboditel 7.

PLOVDIV

> **ETHNOGRAPHIC MUSEUM**
> Don't miss the Ethnographic Museum, Arghir Kuyumdzhiouglu House, with its wonderful wooden ceilings and interior; it also has many exhibits of traditional craftwork.

Plovdiv was described by the Greek writer Lucian in the 2nd century AD as 'the largest and most beautiful of all cities in Thrace'. The unification of Bulgaria was announced here in 1885: Sofia became capital of the unified state and Plovdiv's influence dwindled. As the second city, Plovdiv has uninspiring suburbs of industrial buildings and tower blocks, but the characterful **Old Town** is a different world, with coarsely cobbled streets full of National Revival period houses and a charm that Sofia lacks.

Buses and trolleybuses run throughout Plovdiv, but much of the hilly **Old Town** is only accessible on foot. It's a 10–15-min walk northeast along tree-lined Ivan Vazov, diagonally across from the station, to the central square. Here you will find **Hotel Trimontium** and the main **post office** and telephone building. Archaeological finds date Plovdiv to around 4000 BC, and the city was occupied by Thracians and Philip II of Macedon before the Romans took over in 72 BC. Remains include the partially restored 2nd-century marble **Roman Theatre**, one of Bulgaria's best archaeological sites, recently accommodating various festivals, concerts and other cultural events. The remains of the **Roman Forum**, including marble floors, can be seen in the central square near Hotel Trimontium. The city's most important contribution to recent Bulgarian culture is the National Revival period houses, scattered around the Old Town: the **Balabanov House** now hosts recitals and exhibits works by contemporary Bulgarian painters.

▣ I km southwest of the centre on Bul. Hristo Botev.

ⓘ **Plovdiv Tourist Information Centre**, Pl. Tsentralen I, ☎(032) 620 229, offers maps, booklets, and arranges accommodation. **Arkan Tours**, ul. Lerin 7A, ☎(032) 640 205, offers equestrian and adventure tours.

▣ Plovdiv has a few modern hotels and numerous guesthouses to choose from at very affordable prices.

> ## WHERE NEXT FROM PLOVDIV?
> *Join the **Bratislava–Istanbul** route by taking the train east to **Tulovo** (ETT table 1525).*

DISTANCES (approx. conversions)
I kilometre (km) = 1000 metres (m) I metre = 100 centimetres (cm)

Metric	Imperial/US	Metric	Imperial/US	Metric	Imperial/US
I cm	3/8 in	10 m	33 ft (11 yd)	3 km	2 miles
50 cm	20 in	20 m	66 ft (22 yd)	4 km	2½ miles
I m	3 ft 3 in	50 m	164 ft (54 yd)	5 km	3 miles
2 m	6 ft 6 in	100 m	330 ft (110 yd)	10 km	6 miles
3 m	10 ft	200 m	660 ft (220 yd)	20 km	12½ miles
4 m	13 ft	250 m	820 ft (275 yd)	25 km	15½ miles
5 m	16 ft 6 in	300 m	984 ft (330 yd)	30 km	18½ miles
6 m	19 ft 6 in	500 m	1640 ft (550 yd)	40 km	25 miles
7 m	23 ft	750 m	1/2 mile	50 km	31 miles
8 m	26 ft	I km	5/8 mile	75 km	46 miles
9 m	29 ft (10 yd)	2 km	1½ miles	100 km	62 miles

24-HOUR CLOCK
(examples)

0000 = Midnight	1200 = Noon	1800 = 6 pm
0600 = 6 am	1300 = 1 pm	2000 = 8 pm
0715 = 7.15 am	1415 = 2.15 pm	2110 = 9.10 pm
0930 = 9.30 am	1645 = 4.45 pm	2345 = 11.45 pm

TEMPERATURE
Conversion Formula: $°C \times 9 \div 5 + 32 = °F$

°C	°F	°C	°F	°C	°F	°C	°F
-20	-4	-5	23	10	50	25	77
-15	5	0	32	15	59	30	86
-10	14	5	41	20	68	35	95

WEIGHT
I kg = 1000g 100 g = 3½ oz

Kg	Lbs	Kg	Lbs	Kg	Lbs
1	2¼	5	11	25	55
2	4½	10	22	50	110
3	6½	15	33	75	165
4	9	20	45	100	220

FLUID MEASURES
I ltr. (l) = 0.88 Imp. quarts = 1.06 US quarts

Ltrs.	Imp. gal.	US gal.	Ltrs.	Imp. gal.	US gal.
5	1.1	1.3	30	6.6	7.8
10	2.2	2.6	35	7.7	9.1
15	3.3	3.9	40	8.8	10.4
20	4.4	5.2	45	9.9	11.7
25	5.5	6.5	50	11.0	13.0

MEN'S SHIRTS

UK	Europe	US
14	36	14
15	38	15
15½	39	15½
16	41	16
16½	42	16½
17	43	17

MEN'S SHOES

UK	Europe	US
6	40	7
7	41	8
8	42	9
9	43	10
10	44	11
11	45	12

LADIES' CLOTHES

UK	France	Italy	Rest of Europe	US
10	36	38	34	8
12	38	40	36	10
14	40	42	38	12
16	42	44	40	14
18	44	46	42	16
20	46	48	44	18

MEN'S CLOTHES

UK	Europe	US
36	46	36
38	48	38
40	50	40
42	52	42
44	54	44
46	56	46

LADIES' SHOES

UK	Europe	US
3	36	4½
4	37	5½
5	38	6½
6	39	7½
7	40	8½
8	41	9½

AREAS

I hectare = 2.471 acres

I hectare = 10,000 sq metres

I acre = 0.4 hectares

Index

Index

Europe by Rail

Feedback Form

Please help us improve future editions by taking part in our reader survey. Just take a few minutes to complete and return this form to us, or even better, e-mail your feedback to *books@thomascook.com* or visit *www.thomascookpublishing.com*.

We'd also be glad to hear of your comments, updates or recommendations on places we cover or you think that we ought to cover.

1. Why is this your preferred choice of budget travel guide?
   (Please tick as many as appropriate)

   a) the price ☐

   b) the cover ☐

   c) the content ☐

   d) other _____

2. What do you think of:

   a) the cover design? _____

   b) the design and layout styles within the book? _____

   _____

   c) the content? _____

   _____

   d) the maps? _____

3. Please tell us about any features that in your opinion could be changed, improved or added in future editions of the book, or any other comments you would like to make concerning this book _____

   _____

   _____

   _____

   _____

cut along the dotted line

4. What is the single most useful/helpful aspect of this book?_____

_____

_____

_____

Your age category: ☐ under 21 ☐ 21–30 ☐ 31–40 ☐ 41–50 ☐ 51+

Mr/Mrs/Miss/Ms/Other

Surname_____ Initials _____

Full address: (Please include postal or zip code) _____

_____

_____

Daytime telephone number: _____

E-mail address: _____

Please detach this page and send it to: The Series Editor,
Europe By Rail, Thomas Cook Publishing, The Thomas Cook Business Park,
Coningsby Road, Peterborough PE3 8SB, United Kingdom.

Alternatively, you can e-mail us at: *books@thomascook.com*